THE NEW INTERNATIONAL COMMENTARY ON THE OLD TESTAMENT

R. K. HARRISON, *General Editor*

The Book of
ISAIAH
Chapters 1 – 39

by
JOHN N. OSWALT

GRAND RAPIDS, MICHIGAN
WILLIAM B. EERDMANS PUBLISHING COMPANY

Copyright © 1986 by Wm. B. Eerdmans Publishing Co.
255 Jefferson Ave. SE, Grand Rapids, Mich. 49503

Library of Congress Cataloging-in-Publication Data

Oswalt, John.
The Book of Isaiah, chapters 1–39.

(The New international commentary on the Old Testament)
Bibliography: p. 65.
Includes indexes.
1. Bible. O.T. Isaiah I-XXXIX—Commentaries.
I. Bible. O.T. Isaiah I-XXXIX. English. New
International. 1986. II. Title. III. Series.
BS1515.3.O84 1986   224'.1077   86-8892

ISBN 0-8028-2368-8

CONTENTS

v

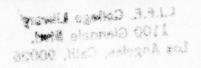

AUTHOR'S PREFACE

The completion of the first of two volumes on the book of Isaiah is a time for gratitude to God for his faithfulness in enabling this much of the work to be finished. It is also a time to express gratitude to many others whose help has been of inestimable value along the way. Pride of place must go to my wife, Karen, whose interest, support, and loyalty have made the work possible and worth doing. At an early stage, when the task seemed overwhelming, Mr. and Mrs. Joseph P. Luce extended substantial financial help. That encouragement meant so much then and all along the way. The administration of Asbury Theological Seminary generously granted sabbatical leaves on two different occasions for research and writing. Two research assistants, Mr. Steven Miller and Mrs. Sandra Patterson, did much to relieve me of the tedium of bibliographical research and to enable me to discover the most profitable studies quickly. Many persons have assisted in the typing and retyping of the manuscript. Among these have been Miss Deborah Jones, Mrs. Carole Piscatelli, Mrs. Harriet Norris, Miss Helen Pielemeier, and Mrs. Ina Guetschow. To each one I owe a debt of gratitude. During the whole process, Professor R. K. Harrison and the editors at Eerdmans Publishing Company have been unfailingly kind and encouraging. All of the above persons have meant much to the work. I trust that its value to the people of God and to all who study his Word will be such as to justify their faith and their efforts. To God be the glory.

JOHN N. OSWALT

PRINCIPAL ABBREVIATIONS

AB	Anchor Bible
AfO	*Archiv für Orientforschung*
AJSL	*American Journal of Semitic Languages and Literatures*
Akk.	Akkadian
AnBib	Analecta biblica
ANEP	J. B. Pritchard, ed., *Ancient Near East in Pictures*. 2nd ed. Princeton: Princeton University, 1969.
ANET	J. B. Pritchard, ed., *Ancient Near Eastern Texts*. 3rd ed. Princeton: Princeton University, 1969.
AnOr	Analecta orientalia
ANVAO	Avhandlinger i norske videnskapsakademi i Oslo
ARAB	D. D. Luckenbill, ed., *Ancient Records of Assyria and Babylonia*. 2 vols. Chicago: University of Chicago, 1926–1927.
Aram.	Aramaic
ASTI	*Annual of the Swedish Theological Institute*
AUSS	*Andrews University Seminary Studies*
AV	Authorized Version (King James)
BASOR	*Bulletin of the American Schools of Oriental Research*
BAT	Botschaft des Alten Testaments
BDB	F. Brown, S. R. Driver, C. Briggs, *Hebrew and English Lexicon of the Old Testament*. Repr. Oxford: Clarendon, 1959.
BHK	R. Kittel, ed., *Biblia Hebraica*. Stuttgart: Württembergische Bibelanstalt, 1937.
BHS	K. Elliger and W. Rudolph, eds., *Biblia Hebraica Stuttgartensia*. Stuttgart: Deutsche Bibelstiftung, 1967–1977.
Bib	*Biblica*
Bib Leb	*Bibel und Leben*
BibOr	Biblica et Orientalia

BJRL	*Bulletin of the John Rylands Library*
BKAT	Biblischer Kommentar: Altes Testament
BO	Bibliotheca orientalis
BR	*Biblical Research*
BSac	*Bibliotheca Sacra*
BSO(A)S	*Bulletin of the School of Oriental (and African) Studies*
BT	*The Bible Translator*
BTB	*Biblical Theology Bulletin*
BZ	*Biblische Zeitschrift*
BZAW	Beihefte zur *Zeitschrift für die alttestamentliche Wissenschaft*
CBAT	The Complete Bible: An American Translation
CBQ	*Catholic Biblical Quarterly*
CBQMS	Catholic Biblical Quarterly Monograph Series
CIS	*Corpus inscriptionum semiticarum*
ConBOT	Coniectanea biblica, Old Testament
CTA	A. Herdner, ed., *Corpus des Tablettes en Cunéiformes Alphabétiques Découvertes à Ras Shamra-Ugarit de 1929 à 1939.* 2 vols. Paris: Imprimerie Nationale, 1963.
CTM	*Concordia Theological Monthly*
DBSup	*Dictionnaire de la Bible, Supplément*
EeT	*Eglise et Theologie;* Ottowa
EHAT	Exegetisches Handbuch zum Alten Testament
EncJud	*Encyclopedia Judaica*
EvQ	*Evangelical Quarterly*
EvT	*Evangelisches Theologie*
ExpTim	*Expository Times*
FB	*Forschung zur Bibel*
FRLANT	Forschungen zur Religion und Literatur des Alten und Neuen Testaments
GKC	*Gesenius' Hebrew Grammar.* Ed. E. Kautzsch. Tr. A. E. Cowley. 2nd ed. Oxford: Clarendon, 1910.
GTJ	*Grace Theological Journal*
HSAT	Die Heilige Schrift des Alten Testaments
HSM	Harvard Semitic Monographs
HTR	*Harvard Theological Review*
HUCA	*Hebrew Union College Annual*
IB	G. A. Buttrick, et al., eds., *The Interpreter's Bible.* 12 vols. Nashville: Abingdon, 1952–1957.
IDB(S)	G. A. Buttrick, et al., eds., *The Interpreter's Dictionary of the Bible.* 4 vols. Nashville: Abingdon, 1962. *Supplementary Volume.* Ed. K. Crim, et al., 1976.
IEJ	*Israel Exploration Journal*

Int	*Interpretation*
ISBE	G. W. Bromiley, et al., eds., *The International Standard Bible Encyclopedia*. 4 vols. Rev. ed. Grand Rapids: Eerdmans, 1979–.
ITQ	*Irish Theological Quarterly*
JA	*Journal of Archaeology*
JAOS	*Journal of the American Oriental Society*
JB	Jerusalem Bible
JBL	*Journal of Biblical Literature*
JBR	*Journal of Bible and Religion*
JCS	*Journal of Cuneiform Studies*
JETS	*Journal of the Evangelical Theological Society*
JNES	*Journal of Near Eastern Studies*
JNSL	*Journal of Northwest Semitic Linguistics*
JOTS	*Journal of Old Testament Studies*
JPSV	Jewish Publication Society Version
JQR	*Jewish Quarterly Review*
JRT	*Journal of Religious Thought*
JSOTSup	*Journal of the Society of Old Testament* —Supplement Series
JSS	*Journal of Semitic Studies*
JTS	*Journal of Theological Studies*
KAI	H. Donner and W. Röllig, eds., *Kanaanäische und aramäische Inschriften*. 3 vols. Wiesbaden: Harrassowitz, 1962–1971.
KAT	Kommentar zum Alten Testament
KB	L. Koehler and W. Baumgartner, *Lexicon in veteris testamenti libros*. Leiden: Brill, 1958.
KHCAT	Kurzer Hand-Commentar zum Alten Testament
Lat.	Latin
lit.	literally
LQ	*Literary Quarterly*
LXX	Septuagint (Greek version of the OT)
mss.	manuscripts
MT	Masoretic text
NASB	New American Standard Bible
NCBC	New Century Bible Commentary
NEB	New English Bible
NIV	New International Version
NorTT	*Norsk Teologisk Tidsskrift*
NTS	*New Testament Studies*
OBL	*Orientalia et biblica Lovaniensia*

OTL	Old Testament Library
OTS	*Oudtestamentische Studiën*
par.	parallel
Past Bon	*Pastor Bonus*
PEQ	*Palestine Exploration Quarterly*
PJ	*Palästinajahrbuch*
RB	*Revue Biblique*
RevExp	*Review and Expositor*
RHPR	*Revue d'Histoire et de Philosophie Religieuses*
RSP	*Ras Shamra Parallels.* 3 vols. Vols. I–II ed. L. Fisher; vol. III ed. S. Rummel. Rome: Pontifical Biblical Institute, 1968–1979.
RSV	Revised Standard Version
SAWW	Sitzungsberichte der österreichischen Akademie der Wissenschaften in Wien
SBLDS	Society of Biblical Literature Dissertation Series
SBT	Studies in Biblical Theology
SHVL	Skrifter utgivna av Kungliga Humanistiska Vetenskapssamfundet i Lund
SJT	*Scottish Journal of Theology*
SKZ	*Schweizerische Kirchenzeitung*
SNVAO	Skrifter utgitt av Det Norske Videnskops-Akademi i Oslo
ST	*Studia theologica*
STU	*Schweizerische theologische Umschau*
Sym.	Symmachus (Greek version)
Syr.	Syriac (version)
Targ.	Aramaic Targums
TB	*Theologische Beiträge*
TDNT	G. Kittel and G. Friedrich, eds., *Theological Dictionary of the New Testament.* 10 vols. Tr. and ed. G. W. Bromiley. Grand Rapids: Eerdmans, 1964–1976.
TDOT	G. Botterweck and H. Ringgren, eds., *Theological Dictionary of the Old Testament.* Vols. I–. Tr. J. Willis, et al. Grand Rapids: Eerdmans, 1974–.
TEV	Today's English Version
TGA	*Theologie der Gegenwart in Auswahl*
THAT	E. Jenni and C. Westermann, eds., *Theologisches Handwörterbuch das Altes Testament.* 2 vols. Munich: Chr. Kaiser; Zurich: Theologischer Verlag, 1971–1976.
TLZ	*Theologisches Literaturzeitung*
TS	*Theological Studies*

TTS	*Trierer theologische Studien*
TWOT	R. L. Harris, et al., eds., *Theological Wordbook of the Old Testament*. 2 vols. Chicago: Moody, 1980.
TynBul	*Tyndale Bulletin*
TZ	*Theologisches Zeitschrift*
Ugar.	Ugaritic
UH	C. H. Gordon, *Ugaritic Handbook*. Rome: Pontifical Biblical Institute, 1947.
UT	C. H. Gordon, *Ugaritic Textbook*. AnOr 38. Rome: Pontifical Biblical Institute, 1965.
UUA	Uppsala universitets årsskrift
VT	*Vetus Testamentum*
VTSup	*Supplement to Vetus Testamentum*
Vulg.	Vulgate
WMANT	Wissenschaftliche Monographien zum Alten und Neuen Testament
WTJ	*Westminster Theological Journal*
ZAW	*Zeitschrift für die alttestamentliche Wissenschaft*
ZBK	Zürcher Bibelkommentar
ZDMG	*Zeitschrift der Deutsche Morgenlandischen*
ZDPV	*Zeitschrift des Deutschen Palastina-Verein Gesellschaft*
ZPEB	M. Tenney, et al., eds., *Zondervan Pictorial Encyclopedia of the Bible*. 5 vols. Grand Rapids: Zondervan, 1975.
ZTK	*Zeitschrift für Theologie und Kirche*

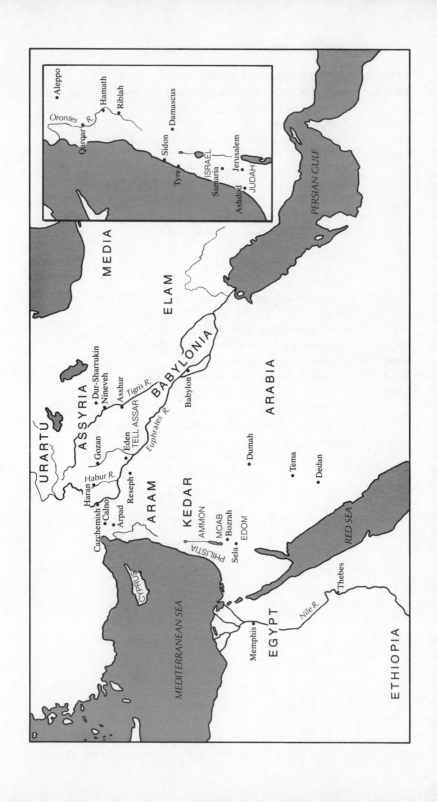

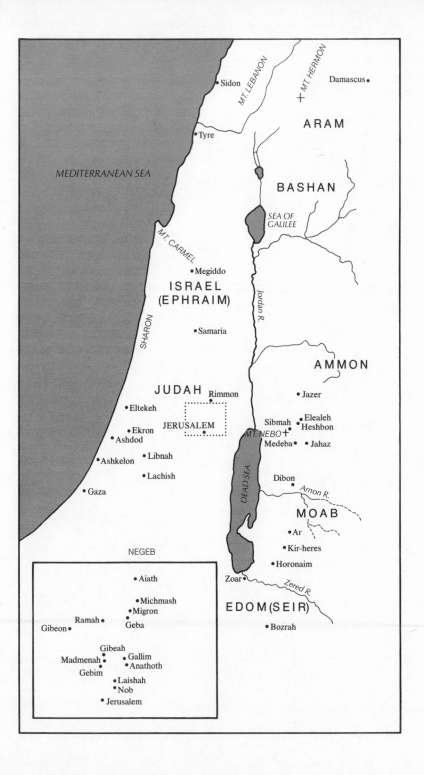

The Book of
ISAIAH
Chapters 1–39

INTRODUCTION

Of all the books in the OT, Isaiah is perhaps the richest. Its literary grandeur is unequaled. Its scope is unparalleled. The breadth of its view of God is unmatched. In so many ways it is a book of superlatives. Thus it is no wonder that Isaiah is the most quoted prophet in the NT, and along with Psalms and Deuteronomy, one of the most frequently cited of all OT books. Study of it is an opportunity for unending inspiration and challenge.

Were the book of Isaiah merely a monument to Hebrew religion, it would be a most impressive monument indeed. In fact, it comes to us as a word from God, a revelation of the inevitable conflict between divine glory and human pride, of the self-destruction which that pride must bring, and of the grace of God in restoring that destroyed humanity to himself. To read the book with the open eyes of the spirit is to see oneself, at times all too clearly, but also to see a God whose holiness is made irresistible by his love.

I. TITLE

The title, "The Book of Isaiah," is dictated by the opening words (1:1), "The vision of Isaiah the son of Amoz." That the time span given for the "vision" covers at least twenty-five years (and potentially as much as fifty years)[1] makes it plain that the entire compilation of Isaiah's prophecies is subsumed under that heading and not simply one vision or another. (See

---

1. Uzziah died in 739 B.C., while Hezekiah took the throne not later than 716 B.C. With that date of accession Hezekiah reigned until 686 B.C. If Isaiah was active during the entire reign, his ministry would have spanned 55 years. For further discussion of these chronological matters, see J. N. Oswalt, "Chronology of the OT," *ISBE*, I:673–685.

3

the commentary below on 1:1 for a further discussion of the import of "vision.")

No other author is mentioned in the book, and indeed, Isaiah is specifically named again in 2:1; 7:3; 13:1; 20:2; 37:2, 6, 21; 38:1, 4, 21; 39:3, 5, 8. That Isaiah is not mentioned as the author of chs. 40–66, along with other factors which will be discussed further in sections II and III below, has caused many scholars to question whether these chapters should be included in "the book of Isaiah." That the identity of these supposed other authors has been so assiduously suppressed (if in fact there were other authors) and that no form of the book other than the present one is known,[2] however, make it clear that the original transmitters of the book intended it to be understood as a unit whose meaning was to be found solely by reference to the life and teachings of the prophet Isaiah.

II. BACKGROUND

As with most of the OT books, a knowledge of the historical background of the book of Isaiah is essential to understand its message.[1] This is so because God's revelation is always incarnational. That is, it is mediated through a specific setting in time and space. While this initially causes problems for us as we try to understand the particular characteristics of that setting, it is ultimately a great blessing to us, for we are best able to grasp truth when it is put into the concrete forms of daily life.

One of the unique features of Isaiah's book, and one which has led to the theory of multiple authorship that will be discussed below, is its address to three different historical settings. The first of these is during Isaiah's lifetime, from 739 to 701 B.C. This time span is covered in chs. 1–39. The second and third periods are long after Isaiah's death. They are the periods of exile (605–539 B.C.), chs. 40–55, and of the return (the total period is 539–400 B.C., but probably here restricted to 539–500 B.C.), chs. 56–66.

2. The earliest edition of the book now known is that found in the caves at Qumran on the shores of the Dead Sea in 1947. It is referred to as 1QIs[a] (the first of several portions of Isaiah found in Cave 1 at Qumran). It is dated to ca. 125–100 B.C. (F. M. Cross, et al., eds., Scrolls from Qumran Cave I [Jerusalem: Albright Institute of Archaeological Research and the Shrine of the Book, 1972], p. 3).

1. For further information see such a standard history of Israel as J. Bright, A History of Israel, 3rd ed. (Philadelphia: Westminster, 1981).

A. 739–701 B.C.

This span of time saw the emergence of Assyria's last period of greatness, a period which would not end until Assyria's final destruction by the Medo-Babylonian coalition in 609 B.C.[2] The Assyrian homeland was located in what is now northern Iraq along the Tigris River. Two great cities, Asshur and Nineveh, were at the heart of the Assyrian empire. Like the preceding and following great empires, Assyria expanded primarily southeastward down the Mesopotamian valley toward Babylon and the Persian Gulf and westward toward the Mediterranean. The mountains to the east and north of the valley and the desert south of it prevented much movement in those directions.

The great period of expansion mentioned above came at the end of a hiatus of some seventy-five years (823–745 B.C.). During that time Assyria had been governed by a succession of weak rulers who were unable to hold the conquests of earlier emperors. This weakness had given Assyria's neighbors, especially the more distant ones, a period of relief from the pressures of Assyrian expansionism. Judah and Israel were no different from the rest. From roughly 810 until 750 B.C. the two kingdoms had enjoyed a peace and prosperity they had not known since the time of Solomon. The northern kingdom, Israel, was ruled during this time by a man named Jeroboam, the second Israelite king to bear that name (2 K. 14:23–29). The southern kingdom, Judah, also had a single monarch for much of this time, King Azariah or Uzziah (2 K. 15:1–7; 2 Chr. 26:1–23). These long and comparatively stable reigns gave both kingdoms, but especially Israel, a false sense of complacency. God was surely pleased with them, they felt, otherwise they would not be experiencing such blessings. The prophets Amos and Hosea were commissioned to disabuse the Israelites of this wrong notion, but without much apparent success. Israel continued on an apostate road, which could lead only to destruction.

Judah is depicted in the Bible as being somewhat less corrupted by apostasy. Apart from Uzziah's one attempt to act as high priest (2 Chr. 26:16–21), he is represented as being a faithful king. This situation too can only have increased the Judeans' spiritual complacency as they compared themselves to their "godless" relatives in Israel.

A word must be said here about the nature of the apostasy into which Israel, and later Judah, fell. This is pungently defined in Hosea

---

2. Cf. such histories of Assyria as A. T. Olmstead, *A History of Assyria* (Chicago: University of Chicago, repr. 1975); R. W. Rogers, *A History of Babylonia and Assyria*, 2 vols., 6th ed. (New York: Abingdon, 1915); H. W. F. Saggs, *The Greatness That Was Babylon* (London: Sidgwick and Jackson, 1962), pp. 105–153.

(chs. 1–3) and Ezekiel (chs. 16 and 23) as prostitution, the debasing of oneself with unworthy lovers for gain.[3] For the Hebrew people this meant "forgetting God" (Deut. 8:11), that is, forsaking their sole allegiance and obedience to him and serving other gods, particularly those representing power and fertility. Such a denial must also carry with it the abuse of those weaker than oneself, because the primary goal has now become satisfying one's own needs through manipulation of the environment. Thus, for the prophets, idolatry, adultery, and oppression are always indissolubly linked.

The complacency of the Hebrews came to a crashing end shortly after the accession of the Assyrian king Tiglath-pileser III in 745. For it became obvious very quickly that the period of Assyrian weakness was over. In short order Pul (probably his personal name, 2 K. 15:19) had established his personal ascendancy over the former Assyrian territories and had made it plain that he expected to extend his dominion as far as possible.

First Israel and then Judah lay directly in the path of that expansion, and Menahem, the king of Israel between 752 and 741 B.C., was in a position of having to pay tribute to Assyria almost at once (2 K. 15:19–20). But that tribute was only an appetizer for the Assyrian lion. Some time prior to 731 he returned, this time to swallow up the whole region of Galilee north of the Jezreel Valley (2 K. 15:29).

As Judah saw the increasing pressure upon Israel to the north, her court was called upon to make a difficult strategic decision. Should Judah be pro-Assyrian or anti-Assyrian? Neither option was pleasant, but the former one had some attractions. Ever since the division of Solomon's kingdom after his death, Judah had been inferior to Israel in area, wealth, military power, and influence. There had been almost constant tension between the two countries, sometimes exploding into open warfare, with Judah almost invariably humiliated. Now if Assyria were to cut Israel down to size or to destroy it completely, Judah would emerge the winner. Furthermore, if Judah joined Assyria soon enough, not merely when she had to, Assyria might leave Judah alone as a faithful ally.

Thus it appears that with the accession of Ahaz to the throne of Judah in 735 B.C. a new pro-Assyrian foreign policy was adopted.[4] This would explain why Pekah king of Israel and Rezin king of Damascus

3. See J. Oswalt, "Prostitution," *ZPEB*, IV:910–12.
4. This may be indicated even more certainly if, as E. R. Thiele maintains, Ahaz was a co-regent with a still living Jotham (until 731) (*The Mysterious Numbers of the Hebrew Kings*, rev. ed. [Grand Rapids: Eerdmans, 1965], pp. 127–28, 131). This suggests that the pro-Assyrian party forced Ahaz upon his father.

mounted an attack upon Judah in 735 (2 K. 16:5; 2 Chr. 28:5–15). It is also possible that this attack was coordinated with another from the south, since it is also reported that the Edomites and the Philistines made inroads into Judean territory at this time (2 K. 16:6; 2 Chr. 28:16–18). Perhaps it is more likely that the two neighbors, knowing that all the Judean troops were concentrated in the north to deal with the threat there, merely took advantage of the situation.

In any case, Ahaz and his court were terrified by the Syro-Israelite threat (Isa. 7:2) and sent to Tiglath-pileser for help (2 K. 16:7–9). These events provided the catalyst for the first great public phase of Isaiah's ministry. From his point of view Judah should be neither anti-Assyrian nor pro-Assyrian but pro-God! He saw Judah turning away from trusting God and becoming caught up in the trappings of human pomp, politics, and power (Isa. 1:21–23; 2:12–17). All of that could only lead to the same apostasy which was now enmeshing Israel (2 K. 16:3–4). Furthermore, Isaiah saw with prophetic clarity that Assyria was no friend of Judah's. The conquerors would take all that Judah would give voluntarily and then take the rest by force (Isa. 8:5–8). The prospect of Judah's asking Assyria for help against Israel, indeed, *paying* for help, was all too much like one mouse asking a cat for help against another mouse. Only the cat could be the winner in such an arrangement.

Nevertheless, Ahaz would not veer from his chosen course, and eventually, when Tilgath-pileser had deposed Pekah and destroyed Damascus (732 B.C.), Ahaz was summoned to appear before him in the ruined city, there to enter into an even more binding treaty which required a recognition of the Assyrian gods (2 K. 16:10–16; cf. also 2 Chr. 28:20–21).[5] According to Isaiah (7:14–16), the irony of this situation is that the respite which Ahaz gained by this treaty would have been his in any event.

Tiglath-pileser III died in 727, undoubtedly to the universal rejoicing of the subject nations, fired by the hope that with his death they could throw off their chains (cf. Isa. 14). A number of insurrections broke out promptly, among them one led by the former Assyrian vassal, the Israelite king Hoshea. Unfortunately for Hoshea and for what remained of Israel, their hopes were doomed. Although Shalmaneser was not to be the king that Tiglath-pileser had been, he still prosecuted the matters of state with

---

5. It is not clear whether the Galilean territory mentioned above was taken at this time or earlier. Most authorities believe it was at this time; cf. Bright, *History*, p. 274; Y. Aharoni, *The Macmillan Bible Atlas* (New York: Macmillan, 1968), pp. 147–48, etc.

dispatch. By 724 B.C. he had secured his empire in the east well enough to turn once more to the west, where he laid siege to Samaria. Over the next three years the inhabitants of that city experienced all the horrors of siege warfare that are depicted so graphically in 2 K. 6:24–29. Sometimes a city could hope to outlast its besiegers, trusting that a turn of events elsewhere in the world might force the siege troops to be withdrawn. Such was not to be the case for Samaria, whose sin was too deep. The forecasts of Amos (3:9–11) and Hosea (8:5–6; 14:1 [Eng. 13:16]) some fifty years earlier came true with a vengeance in 721 B.C.

Either shortly before or shortly after the fall of Samaria, Shalmaneser died and was succeeded by a man named Sargon.[6] Trouble broke out again all over the empire. A major trouble spot was Babylon, where a man from Chaldea, the extreme southern part of Mesopotamia, was asserting himself. This man's name was Marduk-apal-iddina (the Bible's Merodach-baladan, 2 K. 20:12; Isa. 39:1). But Sargon was unable to deal with this problem in a decisive way because of even more severe troubles in the north from the region around Lake Van that the Assyrians called Urartu.[7] Apart from a very effective punitive raid extending from Hamath in Syria down the Mediterranean to Gaza in 721, Sargon was engaged in Urartu for some seven or eight years.

During this time both Babylon and the small countries just north of Egypt gained a breathing spell. In Judah, the king, either in his own right or as co-regent, was Hezekiah.[8] As with Ahaz his father, Hezekiah's coming to the throne appears to reflect a change in Judah's foreign policy. Whereas Ahaz had been firmly pro-Assyrian, Hezekiah was firmly anti-Assyrian. The precise reason for this shift is unclear; however, it seems likely that the failure of Ahaz's policies was a major factor. Exactly as

6. The Bible indicates that Shalmaneser took the city (2 K. 17:3–7 names Shalmaneser at the beginning, but only says "the king of Assyria" took the city; so also 2 K. 18:9–10). However, Sargon claims to have conquered it (*ARAB*, II:51). Some now believe that Sargon may have been the general in charge of the siege (H. W. F. Saggs, *The Greatness That Was Babylon*, p. 111), or that the actual fall of the city came so shortly before his accession that Sargon claimed it himself (H. Tadmor, *JCS* 12 [1958] 37–39).

7. It is significant that a major source of the trouble in Urartu was the Medes. For this reason S. Erlandsson, *The Burden of Babylon*, ConBOT 4 (Lund: Gleerup, 1970), pp. 160–66, concludes that Isaiah (or a later editor) was not speaking in ch. 13 about the fall of Babylon in 539, but about Assyria in his own day, using Babylon as a cover (just as the author of Revelation was to use it for Rome in a later day). See the commentary on ch. 13. In any case it is significant that the destructive power of the Medes was not unknown to Isaiah.

8. See the commentary on 38:1 and the notes there.

Isaiah had foretold, Assyria clearly did not intend to halt her conquests at Bethel, the northern border of her Judean "ally." Thus it must have seemed as if Judah's only chance was to stand and fight. Egypt, feeling the hot breath of the conqueror, was no doubt only too eager to encourage the Judeans and their neighbors in such a course.

Thus Judah shifted from dependence upon Assyria toward dependence upon Egypt. As one can imagine, Isaiah scorned the latter course just as he had the former, but, if anything, with even more vehemence (chs. 29–31). At least Assyria had been strong; Egypt did not even have strength—she offered help which she could not supply (31:1–3) and hope which she would betray (ch. 20). It is not clear that Hezekiah was the instigator of this policy; Isaiah never condemns him as such. However, he was at least the prisoner of it.

The Bible depicts Hezekiah as a good king, one who sought to purge the land of idolatry and the temple of paganized worship. He also reportedly sought to reestablish the Mosaic law (2 K. 18:1–6; 2 Chr. 29:1–36) and was an energetic ruler who extended the borders of his kingdom (2 K. 18:8). One of his more interesting efforts was the attempt to draw people from Israel (now an Assyrian territory) back into the orbit of Jerusalem by inviting them to a Passover whose date had been moved to correspond to the dating which had been used in the north (2 Chr. 30:1–5, 10–11). Evidently this was not successful, but it gives some indication of Hezekiah's vision.

It is not clear to what extent Hezekiah was a participant in the confederation formed against the Assyrians from 715 to 713 B.C. by the Philistines and others of the south Syrian area (Isa. 14:28–31; 17:14; 20:1–6). That no punitive action was taken against him by the Assyrians may indicate that he was not involved. In any case the attempt was ill-fated from the outset. Sargon had achieved a decisive victory over Urartu in 714 and was going from strength to strength. He himself may not have led the army (Isa. 20:1), despite his claims in his annals.[9] In any case, Ashdod, the Philistine city which was the leader of the confederacy, was taken and destroyed, and her leader, who had fled to Egypt for asylum, was given up to Assyria. So much for Egyptian dependability!

Sargon was now in a position to pluck the thorn that was Babylon from his side. All his other perennial enemies were either defeated or dormant, and his own power was increasing. So in 710 he mounted an overwhelming campaign against Merodach-baladan and defeated him decisively. As a result Sargon achieved a pinnacle of world dominance that

9. *ARAB*, II:62, 63; *ANET*, pp. 286–87.

none of his predecessors had known. In every direction his enemies lay broken at his feet. Thus it is not surprising that in the lavish inscriptions of the new city which he founded in honor of himself (Dur-Sharrukin, "mountain of Sargon") he styles himself as lord of the universe.[10] Others had claimed this title before him, but none with as much reason. More than any other, his pride fits the description in Isa. 14.

But Sargon also fits that chapter in another way. For less than a year after the palace in Dur-Sharrukin had been dedicated in 706, Sargon suffered a fate unknown among Assyrian monarchs—he was killed on the battlefield. Mystery surrounds the event, but it is plain that it was viewed as the ultimate disgrace.[11] Dur-Sharrukin was soon abandoned and all Sargon's glory was forgotten. How are the mighty fallen!

The hearts of those oppressed by Assyria leapt up and revolts broke out anew. Sargon was dead; perhaps his successor would be a weakling. In Babylon the perennial war-horse, Merodach-baladan, once again emerged. It is unclear whether it was at this time or at some time prior to 710 that his envoys had visited Hezekiah (Isa. 39:1). At either time their purpose would have been the same: encouraging a fellow opponent of the Assyrian machine.

For whatever reason Hezekiah rose to the bait on this occasion. He became the moving force in a new coalition composed of Philistia, Judah, Edom, and Moab. The Philistines were evidently reluctant to join, so following the very same policy Israel and Syria had tried on Judah thirty years earlier, Hezekiah attacked them, deposed their king, and installed a man who would take his orders. Behind this policy one discerns the hand of Egypt, promising help and support. Isaiah was bitterly opposed to the entire proceeding: Egypt was worse than useless and Assyria could be left to God. The secret politicking and conniving were a bold-faced affront to God that could only bring disaster (cf. 22:5–14; 29:15–16; 30:1–18).

Isaiah was only too correct. Sennacherib was at least as effective a leader as Sargon and he was building upon the extensive conquests of the previous fifteen years. Thus in the campaigns of his first three years Sennacherib soundly defeated Babylon, resecured his eastern border, and stood at the gates of Jerusalem. The fate Isaiah had predicted in 735 had come to pass; the Assyrian flood had reached Judah's neck.

10. *ARAB*, II:53.

11. Note that, in contrast to most other Assyrian monarchs, Sennacherib does not identify his father (e.g., *ARAB*, II:115–16, 203). Saggs does not agree (*Greatness*, p. 118).

The events of Sennacherib's third campaign are fairly clear.[12] The Assyrian army advanced down the Mediterranean coast to Tyre. The city was captured after its king had fled to Cyprus, and a new Assyrian vassal was put on the throne. The destruction was severe enough that Tyre was never again able to achieve its former supremacy (cf. Isa. 23). With Tyre captured, many of the surrounding nations capitulated, and the way stood open for Sennacherib to attack the Philistine cities of Ekron and Ashkelon. Ekron may have been an unwilling partner in the confederacy, since its king, Padi, was being held in custody in Jerusalem. Nevertheless, both Ekron and Ashkelon felt the destructive power of Assyria and soon fell. Then Sennacherib apparently began to move inland and to destroy systematically the frontier fortresses of Judah that were situated in the rolling hill country (the Shephelah) between the Philistine plain and the central ridge (2 K. 18:13). Chief among these was the great city of Lachish, which various conquerors of Canaan had used as a stronghold for centuries. Interestingly enough, Sennacherib did not report the attack on Lachish in his annals, but he did cause a group of monumental reliefs celebrating the fall of that famed city to be made for his palace in Nineveh.[13]

It is not clear when Hezekiah's Egyptian allies mounted their stand against the Assyrians at Eltekeh.[14] Sennacherib reports that it took place before the attacks upon Ekron and Ashkelon. As Bright points out,[15] however, the speech of the Rabshaqeh outside Jerusalem (Isa. 36:1–20) that occurred during the siege of Lachish seems to presuppose that the Judeans were still depending upon Egyptian help. Such dependence is inexplicable if the Egyptians had already suffered defeat. Moreover, Isa. 37:9 reports that Sennacherib was concerned about a possible Egyptian attack and so wrote a letter to follow up the Rabshaqeh's visit. Thus the battle must have come subsequent to the Rabshaqeh's visit and the fall of Lachish.[16]

12. *ANET*, pp. 287–88.

13. *ANEP*, nos. 371–74.

14. Located on the coastal plain some 40 miles northwest of Jerusalem and about 10 miles northwest of Ekron.

15. Bright, *History*, p. 304.

16. This is by no means the only alternative. Another is, of course, that the biblical account is not a reliable historical document, being either entirely fictional or so garbled as to be useless for historical reconstruction. However, the reference to the siege of Lachish, which was reported only by the Bible until the discovery of Sennacherib's reliefs, calls this point of view into question (cf. Bright, *History*, pp. 300–311). A third alternative is that the Egyptians had not suffered nearly as decisive a defeat at Eltekeh as Sennacherib would like his readers to believe and had, in fact, regrouped for another attack. While this theory is not impossible, it is unreported in any literature and it assumes a tenaciousness which

Scholars disagree considerably about what happened next. All agree that Hezekiah paid Sennacherib a very large tribute and that the Assyrian emperor returned home, boasting that he had penned up Hezekiah "like a bird in a cage." Apart from the significant burden of the tribute, however, he left what appears to have been the chief city of the confederacy intact and one of the main instigators of the rebellion still secure on his throne. This behavior is not at all consistent with Assyrian policy or with Sennacherib's behavior on this campaign. If any city should have been destroyed and any king deposed, they should have been Jerusalem and Hezekiah. A rather lame suggestion, an argument from silence, is that something happened elsewhere in the empire that required Sennacherib to leave before the job was finished. The biblical explanation is at least as plausible, however: a plague decimated the Assyrian army and forced its general's hasty departure. That Sennacherib should not mention such a disaster is entirely characteristic of the adulatory tone of the Assyrian annals in general. Furthermore, the veracity of the theology of the book of Isaiah (see below) is, to a large extent, dependent upon the veracity of this account. It is indeed the culminating proof of the wisdom of trusting in God.

In view of the above, the following may be the way in which the events took place: When it became plain that Lachish was going to fall, and since Egyptian help was still delayed, Hezekiah sent tribute to Sennacherib, seeking to buy him off. Nonetheless, the Assyrian officer appeared outside the gates and demanded full capitulation with consequent deportation (Isa. 36:16–18). Acting on encouragement from Isaiah, Hezekiah refused to do so. When the Rabshaqeh and his security force with-

---

is quite uncharacteristic of Egypt at this time. Still another alternative is put forward most cogently by Bright, who argues that the Bible has combined accounts of two attacks on Judah by Sennacherib, one in 701 B.C. and another not long before his assassination (cf. Isa. 37:37–38) in 686 B.C. One of Bright's reasons for advancing this thesis is that the Tirhaqah mentioned in Isa. 37:9 does not seem to have become king until sometime after 690. Scholars have not been much troubled by this, however; those on the left dismiss it as one more evidence of biblical unreliablity, while those on the right have pointed out that Tirhaqah was brother of the reigning monarch in 701 and would have been a likely candidate to lead the army. At any rate, the two-attack theory has, perhaps unfortunately, not received much currency among scholars. For further discussion of this matter and related ones, see B. Childs, *Isaiah and the Assyrian Crisis*, SBT 2/3 (London: SCM; Naperville: Allenson, 1967); R. E. Clements, *Isaiah and the Deliverance of Jerusalem*, JSOTSup 13 (Sheffield: JSOT, 1980); J. Bright, *History*, pp. 298–309; J. A. Wilson, "Tirhaqah," *IDB*, IV:652; L. Wood, *A Survey of Israel's History* (Grand Rapids: Baker, 1970), p. 360, n. 73.

drew to Libnah, where Sennacherib was preparing for the Egyptian threat, there must have been general rejoicing in Jerusalem (Isa. 22:1–14?). But the rejoicing was short-lived, for even before he dispatched the Egyptians, Sennacherib sent a letter to Hezekiah restating his demands.[17] The impact upon Hezekiah was predictable: he was in despair. But in the extremity of his need he turned to God and received word that he had nothing to fear. An Egyptian tradition reported by Herodotus (ii.141) seems to indicate that Isaiah's words proved true. The Assyrian army never got to Jerusalem to mount a siege. Instead, it met its fate while pursuing the Egyptian army somewhere within the northern border of Egypt. Interestingly enough, although Sennacherib lived for another nineteen years, he never mounted another major campaign to the west.

B. 605 – 539 B.C.

As will be noted further below, chs. 40–66 are not at all tied to specific historic events, as are particularly chs. 6–39. Several explanations for this are possible, but it suffices here simply to note the phenomenon. However, it is possible to speculate with some degree of confidence on the general time frame which these chapters seem to be addressing. Chs. 40–55 seem to be offering hope to a people yet in exile, while chs. 56–66 appear to speak to a returned people who face both old and new problems.

Many dramatic changes occurred during the seventh century in the Near East—not only the flowering of the Assyrian empire under Esarhaddon and Ashurbanipal but also that empire's swift and final destruction within twenty years of Ashurbanipal's death. Babylon was sacked and looted in what Sennacherib hoped would be a "final solution" to the persistent troubles there, but Babylon also succeeded Nineveh as ruling city of the world empire by 605 B.C. This century also saw the clear beginning of the shift of influence away from the center of the Near East and toward the south and east, where it would remain for some three hundred years.

For our purposes here, it is enough to say that a coalition of Babylonia and Medo-Persia (the Medes being a more northern group, and the Persians a more southern group, from the mountainous regions east of Mesopotamia) combined to topple the Assyrian empire, or its remains, in 609. At first the Babylonians were the dominant figures in the alliance.

17. For a discussion of the theory that chs. 36 and 37 are merely two different versions of the same event, see the introduction to those chapters in the commentary.

Thus they took the richer, southern parts of the Assyrian corpse, while the Medes took the sparser, northern parts.

But in some ways the Neo-Babylonian empire (650–539 B.C.) was but a brief, brilliant interlude in a much larger movement, the Medo-Persian one. For it is evident that these people never intended to be satisfied with the outer edges of the Assyrian spoils, nor did they intend to have a larger portion—they intended to have it all. Thus they only bided their time through the reigns of the strong Babylonian monarch Nebuchadrezzar and his progressively weaker successors until they were ready to move. In 539 B.C. they ushered in what is known as the Persian empire.

But the Judean exile was confined to that brief, bright interlude of Babylon's political ascendancy. Undoubtedly, however, the Jews did not find it bright. Since the people had been so convinced that they were the darlings of the divine Sovereign, the prophets had despaired of ever getting them to face their peril (note Ezek. 1–30). Thus the final blow, the destruction of Jerusalem in 586, had fallen with shattering force. Beyond that, Babylon continued the Assyrian policy of deportation, in which the leadership of a conquered nation was exiled to some distant land where they would be less inclined to foment rebellion out of nationalistic fervor. In their place people of a more docile, assimilated stance would be brought in, people who would have no interest in the freedom of this new place in which they happened to live. Such a deportation for the Judeans occurred at least once prior to 586, in 598 (2 K. 24:8–17). Then with the destruction of Jerusalem it was carried out again with more severity (2 K. 25:8–21).

As a result of these disasters, many came to the conclusion that their faith had been a farce, while others, still convinced that God was real enough, concluded that he had abandoned them. Thus they were in danger of succumbing to the attractive Babylonian religions and losing their existence as a people, no longer to be the vehicle through which God's self-revelation could come to the world.

Chapters 40–55 of Isaiah directly address this situation, telling the people that God has not only not abandoned them but has especially chosen through them to demonstrate his superiority over the Babylonian deities. This superiority will be seen in his ability to destroy those idols, to redeem his people from their sins, and to bring those people back to their homeland. In other words, just as God could and should be trusted in the Assyrian crisis, so also he may be trusted in a new age with new problems.

As it turned out, this promise, like the earlier ones, proved entirely trustworthy. Although no nation had ever returned from exile, another overwhelming change occurred, brought about by a man whom the com-

pilers of the book would have us believe was named in advance by predictive prophecy. That man was the first Persian emperor, Cyrus. Finally,
in 539 the time had come for the Medo-Persians to complete the conquest
they had started seventy-five years earlier. Then they had needed Babylon's
help. Now they needed that help no longer, and in the dramatic events
pictured in Dan. 5, they swept into Babylon and ended the Neo-Babylonian
empire.

Cyrus brought in a new foreign policy. The Persians reasoned that
people are at least as likely to obey a conqueror they like as one they hate.
Thus he completely reversed the previous policy, granting exiles the right
to return home and offering imperial funds for the rebuilding of national
shrines (Ezra 1:1-4; *ANET,* p. 316). In this respect he lent considerable
impetus to the syncretistic trends which were already at work in the religions of the Near East and would only gain speed in centuries to come.
Some might call the great god Marduk, some Ashur, some Bel, some
Amon-Re, some Yahweh, but surely all were manifestations of the One.
To this Isaiah's book answered with a resounding no! Note Isa. 45:4-5,
"I have surnamed you, though you knew me not. I am the Lord, and there
is no other; beside me there is no God. I will gird you, though you knew
me not, that men may know from the east and from the west, that beside
me there is none."

C. 539-400 B.C.

The formal period of the Exile ended sometime not long after Cyrus's
decree in 539 B.C. when a group of zealous Jews, led by a descendant of
the royal line named Zerubbabel and the high priest Jeshua (Ezra 2:1-2;
3:1), started the long trek back to Judah and Jerusalem. According to Ezra
2:64-65, about 50,000 people were involved in the return. It is likely that
many of these were fired by an idealistic vision of "the promised land"
and an intention to purge their religion of those errors which had landed
them in exile in the first place. Without such visions, it is hard to imagine
why they would have left homes and businesses in Babylon and set out on
such an arduous journey.

Unfortunately, the realities were such that all visions were rather
quickly dashed. The returnees were not welcomed with open arms by the
descendants of those who had been left behind. Rather, they were treated
with hostility and suspicion. The work on the second temple, begun with
a flurry of trumpets, was shortly abandoned as workers lost interest and
settled down to the mere task of survival. It was only some twenty years
later that the prophets Haggai and Zechariah were able to muster enough

concern, faith, and guilt to get the work going again. Finally, in 516 B.C., the building was finished. But it was no match for Solomon's temple and it never captured the Hebrew people's imagination as the former had done. Furthermore, the efforts of Haggai and Zechariah seem not to have been very effective beyond getting the temple finished, for when Ezra and Nehemiah came on the scene some seventy-five years later, they found both the religious and the civil life at a very low ebb. Under the leadership of Ezra and Nehemiah, however, the people regained a sense of national identity as the people of God. As a result the Jews, who had been teetering on the brink of being absorbed into the surrounding culture, were able to find the energy and the direction to sustain themselves as a distinct people.[18]

During this period both the religious and civil history are somewhat scanty. We know, of course, that Judah was a dependent political unit of the Persian empire functioning as a part of the Fifth Satrapy, which was called "Beyond the River." The river in this case was the Euphrates, and the region appears to have included all of the eastern coast of the Mediterranean that would today be called Syro-Palestine. It is not entirely clear where the capital city of this satrapy was located. Most likely it was Damascus. Under the satrap were local governors, as indicated by Ezra 4:17, where the governor is in Samaria, and Neh. 5:15, where Nehemiah is appointed governor of Judah.

Using the biblical books which come to us from this time (Haggai, Zechariah, Ezra, Nehemiah, Malachi), one may construct some picture of the religious life of Judah during this period. In general three groups may be identified: those who were deeply concerned about God and the relationship of Judah to him; those who were concerned about religion; and those who cared little for either. In this last group were those who saw no necessity for maintaining any distinction between themselves and their neighbors. Thus intermarriage and the relaxation of the ceremonial law were serious problems (Ezra 9; Neh. 13; Mal. 1-2), especially since this third group seems to have been the largest.[19]

18. Some helpful books on the restoration and return (second temple period) are: E. Bickerman, *From Ezra to the Last of the Maccabees* (New York, 1962); D. Gowan, *Bridge Between the Testaments: A Reappraisal of Judaism from the Exile to the Birth of Christianity,* Pittsburgh Theological Monograph Series 14 (Pittsburgh: Pickwick, 1976); L. Rost, *Judaism Outside the Hebrew Canon,* tr. D. E. Green (Nashville: Abingdon, 1976); D. S. Russell, *Between the Testaments,* rev. ed. (London: SCM; Philadelphia: Fortress, 1965).

19. Paul Hanson has put forward the theory that the religious life of the restoration period was dominated by a struggle between the "visionary" followers of "II Isaiah" and the "establishment" followers of Ezekiel. In that light Hanson

In a general way Isa. 56–66 corresponds to the above picture. The chapters censured the religiously complacent, asserting that a foreigner or a eunuch who serves God faithfully from the heart is a better Jew than one whose bloodlines are perfect but whose relationship to God is perfunctory at best. Another theme which, like the previous one, plays up a contrast is the inability of human beings to bring about the promised salvation but the complete ability of God through his Spirit to do so. Thus, if chs. 40–55 speak of hope to a people who fear themselves cast off, chs. 56–66 call for a realized righteousness from a people who have lapsed into a careless dependence upon position.

III. UNITY OF COMPOSITION

Along with what is known as the JEDP theory of the origins of the Pentateuch, the belief in the multiple authorship of the book of Isaiah is one of the most generally accepted dogmas of biblical higher criticism today.[1] This theory is based very heavily upon what is considered to be lack of unity in the composition. That the three main sections of the book differ significantly cannot be gainsaid. A novice Bible student with some skills in observation can feel the change in tone and focus at ch. 40, and it takes only slightly more perspicuity to detect a similar change at ch. 56. Further studies reveal that certain vocabulary is used in one section but not in the others. Similarly, some theological concepts are restricted to one or another of the sections.[2]

Thus as early as J. C. Döderlein (1775) and J. G. Eichhorn (1780–83) the theory began to emerge that these differences reflected different authors, whose works had been combined. As this position gained more and more influence in Europe and then in America, scholars became less and less interested in seeing any unity among the parts of the book.

has reorganized the contents of Isa. 56–66 to reflect what he believes was their order of origin. The organizing principle he uses is the supposed development of the conflict. Ultimately the "establishment" won and the "visionaries," shut out of real influence in the official life of the nation, resorted to writings which Hanson calls proto-apocalyptic. See *Dawn of Apocalyptic* (Philadelphia: Fortress, 1975). See the next section for a fuller discussion.

1. For a brief, unemotional presentation of the history of the question, see B. S. Childs, *Introduction to the Old Testament as Scripture* (Philadelphia: Fortress, 1979), pp. 316–18.

2. For a handy statement of these diversities, see S. R. Driver, *Introduction to the Literature of the Old Testament,* 9th ed. (London: 1913), pp. 238–240.

A clear indication of this trend is that most commentaries since 1900 treat chs. 1–39 in one volume by one author and chs. 40–66 in another volume by another author, as though they were separate books.[3]

But despite this broad agreement on literary grounds, it must still be said that there is no concrete evidence that any part of the book ever existed without the other parts. To be sure, this is an argument from silence. Nonetheless, every edition of Isaiah back to that found at Qumran and dated to at least the first century B.C. presents chs. 1–66 as a physical unit. The nearest thing to objective proof of a lack of unity in the composition appears in Y. Radday's impressive investigation, *The Unity of Isaiah in the Light of Statistical Linguistics*. Radday did a computerized study of numerous linguistic features of the book of Isaiah and compared these in the various sections of the book. As a control he studied other pieces of literature, both biblical and extrabiblical, which were reputed to have come from one author. As a result of these researches he concluded that the linguistic variations were so severe that one author could not have produced the whole book of Isaiah.

As might be expected, these conclusions were greeted with approbation by critical scholars who saw their position as being vindicated. But in fact Radday's conclusions call into question some scholarly views. For instance, chs. 49–66 are seen as a linguistic unit as opposed to chs. 40–48.[4] If this were to prove true it would radically alter much of the theology of "II Isaiah" that has assumed the unitary nature of chs. 40–55. Beyond this, Radday concluded that while chs. 23–35 may not have come from the pen of "I Isaiah," they definitely belong to the first part of the book, a position which many critical scholars would deny, since they date significant portions of these chapters to 539 B.C. and much later. Thus his findings do not fully satisfy anybody in one sense, neither those who see the book as a unit nor those who see the disunity along certain lines.

A number of questions may be raised concerning Radday's methodology. The very infancy of the field of statistical linguistics raises some questions. Do we yet know enough to speak with confidence about the possible limits of variation in a given person's usage?[5] More seriously, is

---

3. Since the publication of B. Duhm's commentary in 1892, chs. 56–66 have often been treated as "III Isaiah."

4. Radday, *Unity*, pp. 274–77.

5. Note that another sort of computerized study of the book's characteristics led to the conclusion that it is a unitary composition: L. L. Adams and A. C. Rincher, "The Popular Critical View of the Isaiah Problem in the Light of Statistical Style Analysis," *Computer Studies* 4 (1973) 149–157; while yet another,

the analysis of the language in predetermined sections of the book (the language of chs. 1–12 as opposed to the language of chs. 40–48) able to do justice to variations in similar segments, such as paragraphs and sentences? Does not the "averaging" involved in treating the book in sections tend to level off some variations which might otherwise appear? None of this is to question the integrity with which Radday's study was undertaken and performed, but it is to point out that the evidence is still not as objective as a manuscript in which only chs. 1–39 (or some such) would appear.[6]

As just noted, the most striking argument for the unity of the composition of Isaiah is the present form of the book. If in fact the present composition is the work of at least three major authors and a large number of editors or redactors, it becomes very hard to explain how the book came to exist in its present form at all. The degree of unity which is to be found in the book (e.g., the use of "the Holy One of Israel" 13 times in chs. 1–39 and 16 times in chs. 40–66 and only 7 times elsewhere in the Bible) becomes a problem. Thus it becomes necessary to posit a "school" of students of "I Isaiah" who steeped themselves in the style and thought of the "master." It would be out of such a group that "II Isaiah" sprang during the Exile and from which, later still, came the writings which now constitute chs. 56–66. Aside from the fact that there is no other evidence for the existence of this "school,"[7] it is hard to imagine how it ever would have come into existence for Isaiah (and not the other prophets) in the first place.[8]

A. Kasher, "The Book of Isaiah: Characterization of Authors by Morphological Data Processing," *Revue de l'Organizations Internationales pour l'Etude des Langues anci par Ordinateur* 3 (1972) 1–62, concluded that the composition is not a unity, but his results pointed to different divisions of the book than did Radday's. For a review of the difficulties inherent in the statistical approach, cf. R. Posner, "The Use and Abuse of Stylistic Statistics," *Archivum Linguisticum* 15 (1963) 111–139.

6. It is ironic that those who lauded the reliability of Radday's methodology as it applied to Isaiah were much less convinced of its reliability when he recently reported that the same methodology established the unity of the book of Genesis. Cf. Y. Radday, et al., "Genesis, Wellhausen and the Computer," *ZAW* 94 (1982) 467–481.

7. Cf. P. Ackroyd, "Isaiah I–XII: Presentation of a Prophet," *VTSup* 29 (1978) 29, for a comment on this lack of evidence. See also R. E. Clements, "The Prophecies of Isaiah and the Fall of Jerusalem," *VT* 30 (1980) 434–35; and W. R. Watters, *Formula Criticism and the Poetry of the Old Testament*, BZAW 138 (Berlin: de Gruyter, 1976), pp. 67–68.

8. 8:16, "Bind up the testimony, seal the teaching among my disciples," is frequently referred to as the impetus for the founding of a school. But this is hardly reason enough. In fact, the context makes it plain that the reference is to Isaiah's predictions concerning the outcome of the Syro-Ephraimite War.

This improbability is increased in view of recent scholarship's tendency to reduce the original Isaianic statements to a smaller and smaller corpus. It is now argued that what is truly Isaianic is not of much more extent than the material of Amos or Hosea. Yet we are asked to believe that of all the prophets, only Isaiah sparked a movement which would continue for some five centuries and eventually produce a book in the "founder's" name that would be some five to six times the volume of the original input. That such a superstructure of thought must be created to reconcile the conclusion of compositional disunity with the present form of the book suggests that the conclusion is at least questionable.[9] Furthermore, it must be pointed out that there is an amazing lack of unity among scholars as to the extent and origins of the supposed compositional units in the book. The supposition gained from popular writings that there is broad scholarly agreement upon the nature and extent of I, II, and III Isaiah vanishes almost at once when research is undertaken into the scholarly writings. In fact, it is not far off the mark to observe that the only genuine agreement is the negative one which began the process: the book of Isaiah is not a unity.[10]

Given the complexity of the theory which must be contrived to explain the book's present form if it is not a compositional unit, and given the inability of that theory to produce agreement as to the compositional structure of the book, one is driven to reconsider the historic position of the Church, namely, that the book is a compositional (if not stylistic) unit.[11] Upon examination several reasons emerge in support of this ar-

9. For what is perhaps the most comprehensive attempt to explain the present form of the book while assuming it is not a compositional unit, cf. W. L. Holladay, *Isaiah: Scroll of a Prophetic Heritage* (Grand Rapids: Eerdmans, 1978). Holladay reflects the contemporary understanding that the "school theory" does not go far enough to explain how the supposedly many diverse materials and points of view could have been so well brought together in the present text. Rather, as he illustrates, it is necessary to assume a more or less continuous process of editing previous writings, adding new ones, and re-editing from 700 B.C. down to the time of the Maccabees (165 B.C.). Holladay presents this theory about as well as could be expected, given its highly complex and theoretical nature; however, it is so massive and intricate as to strain the credulity of all but the most arcane readers.

10. For a handy review of the various compositional theories see S. Erlandsson, *The Burden of Babylon*.

11. For some of the argumentation in favor of compositional unity see the following: O. T. Allis, *The Unity of Isaiah* (Philadelphia: Presbyterian and Reformed, 1950); J. J. Lias, "The Unity of Isaiah," *BSac* 72 (1915) 560–591; 75 (1918) 267–274; R. Margalioth (Margulies), *The Indivisible Isaiah* (New York: Yeshiva University, 1964); E. J. Young, *Who Wrote Isaiah?* (Grand Rapids: Eerdmans, 1958).

gument. Not the least among these is Margalioth's observation of the numerous phrases which appear in both parts of the book but only rarely elsewhere in Scripture. Furthermore, the appearance of similar concepts in various parts of the book (e.g., in chs. 1–5 and 60–66, or in chs. 7–12 and 36–39) also suggests a kind of unity which none of the theories quite succeeds in explaining.[12] But perhaps the most compelling argument for the compositional unity of the book is based on its thought structure. The unity of thought which runs through the book has been largely ignored in recent years, because of the attempt to isolate the supposed component parts. Each part has been exegeted by itself without reference to its larger literary context. But unless one assumes that the process of the formation of Isaiah was completely random or was controlled by societal reasons unrelated to the actual statements of the book, this is an unreasonable way to proceed. Without automatically assuming that one writer sat down and started writing at 1:1 and worked straight through to 66:24, one may still logically expect that there were reasons for putting one set of ideas in conjunction with another that were more significant than mere word association (to which some scholars resort to explain why one statement followed another). In fact, whoever assembled the book and however it was assembled, there is an observable structure about its thought that explains the power of the book and without which the book becomes little more than a collection of sayings put together for no apparent reason.

While the following suggestions are not the only way to understand the thought of the book, they have not been imposed from the outside but emerge from an inductive study. As such they reflect a unity of thought that argues against the book's having been composed out of diverse materials which were then exposed to a complex redactional process extending over hundreds of years (esp. since there is no external evidence that such a process ever existed).

Since the structure of the book will be discussed in detail later in the Introduction, it will suffice here merely to sketch the outlines in order to convey the sense of the point being made. The central theme of the book relates to the nature and destiny of the people of God. While this people is, on the one hand, destroyed and corrupted (ch. 1), it is called to be a manifestation of the glory of the only God in the world (2:1–5). This calling may be summed up in the word *servanthood*. The book then seeks to answer the question: How can a sinful, corrupt people become the servants of God? This theme is developed in the following way: Chs.

12. Cf. also Young, *Who Wrote Isaiah?*, pp. 58–60, for examples of similar concepts.

1–6 set forth the problem (chs. 1–5, sinful yet called) and the solution (ch. 6, a vision of the Holy One). The rest of the book works out the ramifications and the implications of this introduction. Chs. 7–39 are unified by their recurring emphasis upon trust.[13] They demonstrate that Israel's problems stem from her tendency to trust the nations instead of God. Furthermore, they show that God alone is trustworthy, and that Israel can only become God's servant, a light to the nations, if she comes to that place of radical trust.[14] But is it not enough for God to be shown trustworthy. True enough, that trust is the essential basis for a person or a nation to lay aside pretensions to self-sufficiency and accept the servant's role. But what will actually motivate that person or nation to do so? For example, in Judah's case, although God had demonstrated his supreme trustworthiness in delivering Jerusalem from Sennacherib, Judah would still not relinquish her trust in the nations and their idols. The result was that God would not and could not defend her from Babylon.

The Judeans had encountered the truth of chs. 7–39, but they had not acted upon it in a long-term way. Why not? The problem was motivation. What could motivate the Judeans to trust God? The answer is found in chs. 40–48 and in the kind of vision of God given to Isaiah in ch. 6. When the nation as a whole, repining in exile in Babylon, can sense not only God's inestimable greatness but also his boundless love in continuing to choose them as his own despite their sin, then they will be motivated to trust him and join Isaiah in answering "Here am I."

But before that "Here am I," between motivating vision and willing response, must come another step. Can sinful Israel become servant Israel merely by choosing to do so? No, and neither could Isaiah of the unclean

13. On the basis of a gap which appears between chs. 33 and 34 in the Qumran scroll A of Isaiah (1QIs[a]), W. Brownlee has suggested that the final redaction of the book consisted of two duplicate structures of 33 chapters each (*The Meaning of the Qumran Scrolls for the Bible* [New York: Oxford, 1964], pp. 247–259). R. K. Harrison (*Introduction to the Old Testament* [Grand Rapids: Eerdmans, 1969], pp. 787–89) finds evidence for a similar structure, but believes that it supports the single authorship of the book. My studies have brought me to the conclusion that chs. 34–39 are an intrinsic part of the thoughts of chs. 7–33. See section X below for further discussion of this point.

14. Throughout this section there are intimations, esp. of a predictive sort, which require the entire book to be included in the interpretation of any part. For example, the references to the Messiah in chs. 9 and 11 require those in chs. 42–53 in order to be understood. Likewise the references to Babylon in chs. 13 and 14 point beyond ch. 39. Even if one assumes the book to be a compositional disunity it still becomes necessary to say that the unknown editors intended it to be interpreted as a unit. See, for instance, R. Lack, *La Symbolique du Livre d'Isaïe*, AnBib 59 (Rome: Pontifical Biblical Institute, 1973).

lips become Isaiah the messenger through mere choice. Put another way, the question is, by what means shall Israel's servanthood be achieved? The answer, as revealed in chs. 49–55, is the Servant. Here comes the rounding out of the vision of the Messiah as initially given in chs. 9 and 11. By means of his self-giving and by means of his ideal servanthood, Israel's sins may be forgiven and the hopes of chs. 40–52 are able to give way to the realization and celebration of chs. 54–55.

Despite the joy of the realization that God has not only chosen *and* redeemed, however, there remains the outworking of that servanthood. Here, as was revealed to Isaiah at the close of his vision, all is not gladness and light. Rather, the realities of human inability and divine ability must find a concrete meeting point. These realities are dealt with in chs. 56–66, coming to their climax with the revelation of God's glory through his people in ch. 66.

Whatever this unity of thought in the book may say about authorship, it does speak to the need for a rebirth of attempts to interpret the book as a whole. I hope that these volumes will make some small contribution to that rebirth. Continuation of recent trends to interpret small sections of the book without reference to their larger context must inevitably be self-destructive. It is only in its wholeness that the grandeur of the book's message can be seen. Without that wholeness, scholarly study of the book will of necessity become only the interest of antiquarians.

IV. DATE AND AUTHORSHIP

As the previous sections have already suggested, these are vexed questions. The historic position of the Church was derived from the apparent claims of the book beginning at 1:1. That verse seems to say that everything which follows is a report of the visionary experiences of Isaiah the son of Amoz. Furthermore, in 2:1; 7:3; 13:1; 20:2; 37:6, 21; and 38:1 words are attributed directly to Isaiah. While Isaiah is not named as the source of any of the materials in chs. 40–66, it is evident that the burden of proof is upon those who propose other sources, for no other sources are named.

As mentioned above, there are at least two reasons for questioning Isaiah's authorship of chs. 40–66. One of these is the radical change of style in these chapters from that found in chs. 1–39; chs. 40–66 are much more lyrical and exalted. Of more substance is the observation that the other prophets, while predicting the future, do not seem to address their words to people in the future as seems to be the case with chs. 40–55 (550 B.C., some 150 years later than Isaiah) and chs. 56–66 (500 B.C.?

23

some 200 years later than Isaiah). Yet a third objection is not often stated explicitly, but it is almost always implied: no specific prediction of the future is possible, and whenever such appears to occur (e.g., with the exile to Babylon [39:5-6] or the deliverance by Cyrus [45:1]) these are always either contemporary with, or after, the fact. Other objections are given, but these are the major ones.

The difficulty with these concerns is that they cannot be confined to discrete sections of the book. Thus the references to Babylon in chs. 1-39 are the work of "II Isaiah," as are chs. 34 and 35, which are stylistically similar to chs. 40-55. Furthermore, chs. 24-27 are said to be of an apocalyptic style that is to be dated to 500 B.C. if not later. So that which is genuinely the work of Isaiah, the supposed genius who set the whole process in motion, erodes to a smaller and smaller corpus.

When these criteria are turned upon chs. 40-66, the same kind of atomization occurs there. As Duhm observed as early as 1895, the style and concerns of chs. 56-66 are not those of chs. 40-55, thus requiring yet a third "author."[1] However, studies since Duhm's time have failed to come to any consensus about this third author. Some, like C. C. Torrey, have maintained that Duhm was mistaken and that the variations in style and concerns between chs. 40-55 and 56-66 are within acceptable limits for one writer.[2] But the prevailing opinion has come to be that represented by Paul Hanson,[3] and more recently by Elizabeth Achtemeier,[4] namely, that these chapters are a composite which stems ultimately from several parts of the postexilic community, and not any one author.

The end result of these inquiries into the authorship of the book is at least twofold. First, it is very difficult to obtain agreement among scholars as to the date and authorship of any but a few chapters of the total book. The titles "I, II, and III Isaiah" are retained for convenience, but in fact are very misleading as to matters of date and authorship.

Second, the results of these inquiries have devalued the religious message of the book. Since it is agreed that the prophet can speak only to his immediate historical context and even then not in specific prediction, much of the religious argument of the book is reduced to rhetoric, and

1. B. Duhm, *Das Buch Jesaja,* HKAT (Göttingen: Vandenhoeck & Ruprecht, 1892), p. 19.
2. C. C. Torrey, *The Second Isaiah: A New Interpretation* (New York: Scribner's, 1928), pp. 20, 21.
3. P. Hanson, *The Dawn of Apocalyptic* (Philadelphia: Fortress, 1975).
4. E. Achtemeier, *The Community and Message of Isaiah 56-66: A Theological Commentary* (Minneapolis: Augsburg, 1982), esp. pp. 11-16.

faulty rhetoric at that.[5] Thus the argument that God is to be preferred to the idols because he has foretold the Exile is false (41:21–24). Likewise, the promises of a great messianic deliverance (which, by definition, cannot be far in the future) did not come true. Perhaps even more telling, the claims that God controls history and can be trusted were in fact only manipulations of the record after the fact.

This is not to say that multiple authorship must be rejected because of its necessarily deleterious effects on the book's theological value, but it does raise the question as to whether the admitted influence of the book for at least twenty-five centuries does not weigh against some of these theories.

This is not the place to launch into a lengthy critique of these positions, but it is necessary to elucidate the position from which this commentary is written and to explain some of the reasons why the prevailing critical views are not accepted. For this commentary the theological and ideological unity of the book is a primary datum. Other data, especially those relating to date and authorship, must be considered in the light of this datum. For instance, it must be asked whether the hypothesis of a complex redactional process functioning over several hundred years can satisfactorily account for that unity, especially since there is no evidence that such a group process existed. Furthermore, it is questionable whether a group process ever produces literature of power. Note that both Holladay and Achtemeier[6] refer to "Third Isaiah" as an entity while agreeing that no such individual existed. They are reflecting the conviction that literature produced by committee does not display such unity.

In this light, it is my conviction that the essential content of the book has come to us through one human author, Isaiah the son of Amoz. It is he who received the revelations from God and who directed the shaping of the book. This is not to deny one of the most helpful assertions of form criticism, namely, that verbal messages tended to be self-contained units which could be grouped together with other such units in various ways. In fact, as Harrison points out, had earlier critics recognized this characteristic of ancient Near Eastern literature, they would have been less inclined to dissect the biblical books on the basis of modern canons of literary unity.[7] What we have in the book, then, comes nearest to what we

---

5. For a good example of one who boldly embraces this conclusion, see R. P. Carroll, *When Prophecy Failed* (New York: Seabury, 1979), pp. 130–156. Far from seeing "II Isaiah" as the greatest prophet of the OT, Carroll sees him as being the most mistaken.

6. Holladay, *Scroll,* p. 163, n. 1; Achtemeier, *Community,* p. 16.

7. Harrison, *Introduction,* pp. 777, 780.

call an anthology, a collection of sermons, sayings, thoughts, and writings of Isaiah, all arranged according to the theological scheme outlined in the previous section. Thus it is not at all necessary to assume that all the materials in the book are in the chronological order in which they were first delivered. Nor is it necessary to deny that during the collection of the materials into book form brief editorial or transitional materials were added, either by Isaiah himself or those working with him.[8]

But what about the problems of stylistic differences and differences of historical context of chs. 40–66 from chs. 1–39? How are these to be explained if all of the essential content of the book is to be derived from Isaiah between approximately 740 and 690 B.C.? First of all, it must be maintained that, computer studies notwithstanding, attribution of authorship on the basis of style is not a precise science. It is a matter of observation that different subject matters, as well as different periods in a person's life, produce different styles. Thus, it is not at all beyond the realm of possibility that some years after the completion of what are now chs. 1–39, new visions of God's greatness, particularly as it related to a future era, provoked in Isaiah a new style consistent with the broadened vistas he was now seeing. A similar case in point seems to be the gospel of John and the book of Revelation, if tradition is correct that the two books should be attributed to the same person. Quite different styles are evoked by different subject matters and a different period of life.[9]

The matter of historical context is the most serious objection in attribution of the materials in chs. 40–66 to Isaiah. It is certainly not typical for the prophets to address themselves at length to times other than their own. However, this phenomenon is not as rare as is depicted by some who would like to limit the work of the prophets to ethical comments on social issues of their own day. In fact, this kind of thing occurs in Ezekiel (chs. 37–48), Daniel (chs. 7–11), and Zechariah (chs. 8–13), not to mention shorter portions in several of the other prophetic books.

At the same time, it must be admitted that the material in Isaiah is unusually extensive and unusually suited to the specific historical context

8. If this understanding of the prophetic books as anthologies is accepted, students are much less troubled by the lack of tight structural connections between various segments of the book (as between Isa. 31 and 32).

9. Should further studies point more conclusively to a different hand (or hands) at work in the latter part of the book, I would be driven to conclude that Isaiah used amanuenses to assist him in putting his final thoughts together. I cannot conceive of the present unity being arrived at without the guiding hand of a single master. Furthermore, as soon as the compilation of the book is moved beyond the lifetime of Isaiah, it becomes well nigh impossible to avoid the conclusion that the book's great theological assertions are based upon falsehoods. See below in section VIII for further discussion of this point.

in the future. Why should this have come to Isaiah rather than to Jeremiah or Ezekiel, who were closer to exilic times?[10] While it is impossible to give a definite answer, some suggestions may be offered. Given the theme of the first part of the book—trust in human power, as exemplified in the nations, is foolish, whereas trusting in God, the Lord of the nations, is wise—and given that God's triumph over Assyria is the culminating proof of that power, how should one treat the upcoming defeat at the hands of Babylon that Isaiah has foreseen? If God "loses" to Babylon, does this not mean that the whole argument of chs. 7–39 is invalid? Thus questions are raised in the first part of the book that require the issue of the Exile to be addressed in advance. Likewise, the vision of the Messiah that is depicted so well against the backdrop of the Judean kingship in chs. 9 and 11 would require the kind of reinterpretation which is seen in chs. 40–55 in order to be valid for that coming postmonarchical day. But even more, the vision which Isaiah has for his people as servants of God is incomplete without that picture of the motivating and delivering hand of God. By inspiration Isaiah knows that the kind of trust he is calling for will not be realized until the fires of the Exile have purged the idolatrous Israelite heart. Thus his message, to be complete, must take that era into account.

In the same way, his vision of servanthood would have been incomplete had it failed to demonstrate an awareness of the genuine difficulties to be found in the implementation of that vision as the postexilic community would experience it. The visionaries who would return from the Exile full of the awareness of their chosenness and of God's power to redeem needed also to be aware of the complete necessity for dependence upon God and his ability. Only in this way would God's light rise to shine upon the world.

What has just been said is that the very nature of the message found in chs. 1–39 of Isaiah demands that the materials found in chs. 40–66 be included both for the sake of completeness and for the validity of Isaiah's message.[11] Thus there is a logical necessity for the address to the future communities. It may also be observed that one probable reason for the

10. By the same token, of course, if one denies unitary authorship, one is hard put to explain why the materials were appended to Isaiah's book rather than to Jeremiah's or Ezekiel's. The answer given, of course, is that Isaiah had a continuous school of followers (which the others did not).

11. Interestingly enough, contemporary scholars generally delete from "I Isaiah's" authorship the very elements of hope or of future relevance which we have here pointed to as requiring further development. But if this is done it also removes any impetus for the kind of school which they posit growing up to expand on the "master." According to their view the "master" left nothing that required expansion. As an example see S. H. Blank, "The Current Misinterpretation of Isaiah's *She'ar Yashub,*" *JBL* 67 (1948) 211–16.

survival of the Judean exiles as a community may well have been the existence of Isa. 40–66 in advance of the Exile, both predicting that event and pointing beyond it to a return.

Another factor here that must not be overlooked, however, is the remarkable absence of concrete historical references in chs. 40–66. Accepting the theory of multiple authorship, B. S. Childs says that the later community expunged these references in order to make the total work appear to be that of "I Isaiah."[12] But surely another alternative presents itself. Perhaps these references are lacking not because they were expunged but because the materials *do* stem from Isaiah, who was speaking predictively.[13] In any case, there appears to be no middle ground. There is no good reason why a "II Isaiah," addressing his own contemporaries, would have avoided explicit references to his own times. Either those references have been removed, which raises serious interpretative problems, or they were never there because the material was given many years in advance. This commentary opts for the latter.[14]

V. OCCASION

The occasion for the book of Isaiah was the Assyrian crisis, which would bring about the destruction of Northern Israel and threaten the existence of Southern Judah. Above everything else this was a theological crisis, and it was one of the first magnitude. Among the questions raised were: Is God truly the Sovereign of history if the godless nations are stronger than God's nation? Does might make right? What is the role of God's people in the world? Does divine judgment mean divine rejection? What is the nature of trust? What is the future of the Davidic monarchy? Are not the idols stronger than God and therefore superior to him? Surely it is not far from the mark to say that Judah survived Ahaz's apostasy because of Isaiah's ministry and that Hezekiah was faithful as he was and could

---

12. Childs, *Introduction*, pp. 325–27.

13. A good case can be made for the eighth-century B.C. context of the writing of these chapters. See esp. J. B. Payne, "Eighth Century Background of Isaiah 40–66," *WTJ* 29 (1967) 179–190; 30 (1967) 50–58; but also Young, *Who Wrote Isaiah?*, pp. 61–68.

14. It may be asked whether one *must* opt for single "authorship" in order to see the book as a whole. B. Childs seems to indicate not and one wishes the very best for his endeavors. However, the assumptions which have given rise to the various theories of multiple authorship are generally inhospitable to the principles necessary to understanding the book as a whole.

exercise trust at the critical moment for Jerusalem's survival on account of that ministry.

Because of the far-reaching nature of the theological questions raised by these events, it was not possible that the book could close without reference to the future. As noted in the previous section, it was only by reference to the Exile and to the postexilic period (and indeed far beyond that to the messianic era) that these questions could be examined and answered in their fullest implications.

VI. CANONICITY

The importance of the book of Isaiah in the canon of Hebrew literature is clear. As early as 190 B.C. the book of Sirach (Ecclesiasticus) makes reference to the writings of Isaiah that "comforted Zion" (Sir. 48:24; cf. Isa. 40:1; 61:1, 2) and foretold the future. Shortly thereafter, it was being copied profusely by the scribes at Qumran as illustrated by the numerous fragments of various copies found there as well as by the great Isaiah scroll (1QIs[a]), which must be dated to at least 100 B.C. That the text form of that scroll as well as the fragmentary 1QIs[b] is essentially identical to that of the normative MT of A.D. 950 indicates that as early as 100 B.C. the book was considered of such authority that its final form was already well established. A further evidence of the reverence in which this book was held is that it is quoted by the NT writers (most of whom were Jews) more times than all the other prophets together (21 direct quotations and numerous allusions).

VII. HEBREW TEXT

By and large, the original Hebrew text of Isaiah has been well preserved. While there are a number of instances where obscure statements suggest the possibility of textual corruptions, these are remarkably few in proportion to the whole. The major witnesses to the text are the LXX, the Targum, and the scrolls from Qumran (1QIs[a], 1QIs[b]). The variations from the MT are relatively few, ranging from almost none in 1QIs[b] to the expected periphrastic expansions of the Targ., which still usually gives witness to an MT-like original behind it.[1]

1. See J. F. Stenning, ed., *The Targum of Isaiah* (Oxford: Clarendon, 1949), for text and translation.

The most significant textual variations occur in the LXX and in 1QIs[a]. Those in the LXX are frequently suspect because they appear most often to be attempts to smooth out or to interpret difficult passages in the MT. Since most of the MT readings are not simply impossible (and not therefore themselves suspect as corruptions), one must reject most of these LXX variants as secondary.[2]

The variants in 1QIs[a] are most controversial in nature, with opinions about them ranging from almost complete rejection by H. Orlinsky to very frequent acceptance by R. Clements.[3] The truth is probably somewhere between these two extremes. While a number of 1QIs[a]'s readings can be explained as being the results of tendentiousness or as copyists' errors, others have all the marks of being more original than the MT readings.[4] Some of these, interestingly enough, support conjectures which scholars had previously put forward for correcting the MT. For example, at 14:4 the MT has *maḏhēḇâ*, which is unintelligible but which ancient commentators suggested might mean "place [or city] of gold" (cf. AV). On the basis of the ancient versions (LXX "oppressor," Targ. "transgressor"), however, several scholars suggested that the original must have been *marhēḇâ*, "fury," and that *d*, which is very similar to *r* in the block Hebrew script, must have been written mistakenly. 1QIs[a] now supports this conjecture. A similar example appears in 33:8, where the MT has *ʿārîm*, "cities," as a parallel to "covenants." Changing the *r* to *d* would yield the better *ʿēḏîm*, "witnesses." 1QIs[a] also supports this suggestion.

A more substantial variant appears at 21:8, where the AV, following

2. For the best edition of the Septuagint of Isaiah, cf. J. Ziegler, ed., *Isaias*, Septuaginta, Vetus Testamentum Graecum xiv (Göttingen: Vandenhoeck & Ruprecht, 1967). While it was formerly thought that these variants (where secondary) were the work of the LXX translators themselves, the evidence from Qumran now suggests that these translators were merely following closely a Hebrew original of a somewhat different text type from the MT, designated Alexandrian by F. M. Cross. Cf. his "Evolution of a Theory of Local Texts," in *Qumran and the History of the Biblical Text*, ed. F. M. Cross and S. Talmon (Cambridge, Mass.: Harvard University, 1975), pp. 306–320.

3. See esp. Orlinsky, "Studies in the St. Mark's Isaiah Scroll I," *JBL* 69 (1950) 149–166; "II," *JNES* 11 (1952) 153–56; "III," *JJS* 2 (1951) 151–54; "IV," *JQR* 43 (1952) 329–340; "V," *IEJ* 4 (1954) 5–8; "VI," *HUCA* 25 (1954) 85–92. Cf. Clements, *Isaiah 1–39*, NCBC.

4. Note that the RSV incorporated 1QIs[a] readings at Isa. 3:24; 7:1; 14:4, 30; 15:9; 21:8; 23:2; 33:8; 45:2, 8; 49:17, 24; 51:19; 56:12; 60:19. Such modern versions as NEB, JPSV, and NIV are more cautious. The only Qumran readings of these which all three accept are at 14:4 and 45:2. JPSV rejects all the rest except 45:8 and 60:19. NIV rejects all the rest except 21:8; 33:8; 45:8; 49:24; and 51:19. NEB rejects 3:24; 7:1; 15:9; 45:8; and 56:12 and accepts the rest.

the MT, has the very strange "and he cried, A lion: My Lord, I stand continually. . . ." While it is not impossible to wring meaning from these words,[5] it is still very difficult and the text appears to be corrupt. This impression is strengthened by the difficulties which both the LXX and the Targum have in integrating "lion," which they both have, into their translations. 1QIs[a] seems to provide the solution when it reads *hārō'eh,* "the seer," instead of *'aryēh,* "lion." The error could well have occurred during copying by dictation since the two words sound so much alike.

Apart from a few cases such as the examples just cited, however, the text of Isaiah has been well preserved over the years. The reverence in which the book has been held has undoubtedly contributed to this preservation. The rise of the present "continuous redaction" theory offers a serious threat to the text's integrity, however. The easy confidence with which some scholars profess to be able to distinguish between various "strata" in a verse or passage is amazing, particularly when textual evidence is altogether absent. All too easily they separate "secondary" and "tertiary" from "primary" materials, deleting as glosses elements which might be embarrassing to their reconstruction of the book and its contents.[6] These tendencies must be steadfastly resisted. Our mandate is to interpret the text as it is before us unless there is manuscript evidence to correct that text. To do anything else is to build our interpretations upon air.[7]

VIII. THEOLOGY

Unless the book of Isaiah is a great theological document, it is nothing. Whatever may be its strengths as a piece of literature, they pale by comparison to the breadth and the sweep of the book's theological insights.[1]

5. JPSV has "And like a lion he called out. . . ."

6. O. Kaiser is particularly guilty of this in his commentary on chs. 13–39 (OTL). But he is certainly not the first to embark upon such a course. For an example of an unwarranted deletion as a gloss, see 8:7, where all the witnesses support the originality of "the king of Assyria and all his glory" but which the scholars delete (cf. *BHS*).

7. Cf. M. Goshen-Gottstein, "The Textual Criticism of the Old Testament: Rise, Decline, Rebirth," *JBL* 102 (1983) 365–399, for the most recent review of this topic.

1. It is my conviction that whatever may be the conclusions to which one comes on the issues of authorship and composition, failure to interpret the book as a whole is to fracture a theological unity which depends upon every part of the whole for its full vitality. It is as though one could interpret a great painting by studying its parts in isolation. Cf. R. Clements, "The Unity of the Book of Isaiah," *Int* 36 (1982) 117–129.

While it is not possible to explore these in any detail here, it is necessary that we sketch an outline of the leading ideas in the book to serve as a guide to those who wish to explore those ideas further. The thought of Isaiah can be organized under four heads: God, Humanity and the World, Sin, Redemption. Of necessity these topics overlap somewhat, but wherever possible this overlap will be minimized. Before looking at these individual headings it would be well to make one general comment: Isaiah is a book of contrasts. Again and again polar opposites are played off against each other, as is apparent from even cursory study of the first six chapters. Some of the contrasts are: divine glory versus human degradation; judgment versus redemption; height versus depth; God's wisdom versus the idols' stupidity; fecundity and abundance versus barrenness and desolation; arrogance versus humility. Other examples of this feature could be cited, but these are enough to illustrate the book's use of the device. There is no reason to conclude that the author is merely enamored with a literary device. Rather, as is clear from ch. 6, his whole pattern of thought has been affected by the tremendous contrast between the greatness of God and the corruption of humanity. But caught up with this contrast is the amazing paradox that if humanity will lay aside its pretensions to deity, the true God will raise us to fellowship with himself (57:15). These two thoughts form the heart of the book's theology.

A. GOD

Perhaps in no other biblical book are the wonder and grandeur of the biblical God so ably displayed. This should not be surprising when we think of the vision which was vouchsafed to Isaiah at the opening of his ministry. Certainly throughout this book which bears his name God is "high and lifted up" (6:1). He is the "Holy One," and "the whole earth is full of his glory" (6:3). This awareness of divine majesty shapes every presentation of God. He it is with whom the people must contend (8:12–15); he it is in whose hand Assyria is only a tool (10:5) and for whom mighty Cyrus is an errand boy (45:1–5). The nations of the earth, great and small, are but tinder in his hand, a drop in a bucket (14:22–23; 40:15, 21–23; 47:1–4). He is the "I am" before whom idols fade to nothingness (2:6–22; 43:8–13). But his greatness is not merely in his power; it is also in his ability to stoop. Conquerors cannot bend down to the lowly; the God of eternity is mighty enough to do so (9:5 [Eng. 6]; 11:1–9; 40:10–11; 57:14–15). Isaiah seems to be saying that if humanity could ever glimpse the true picture of God's greatness and glory, our problem would be on its way to being solved.

But God is not merely great and majestic; he is also holy. It cannot be an accident that Isaiah's favorite appellation for God is "the Holy One of Israel."[2] Above everything else the realization which struck the prophet in his call experience (ch. 6) was the realization of the terrifying "otherness" of God. He was not merely a superhuman, as were the pagan gods, nor was he a great "grandfather in the sky." He was of a completely different order from his creatures. This idea is expressed through terms for height and removal (6:1; 8:12–13; 37:23; 40:25; 45:15; 55:8–9; 60:9). Because God is other than his world, its Maker, he is the One who has the right to be called Holy; no other has this right (6:3; 17:7; 40:25; 43:3, 15; 45:11; 54:5).

But it was not merely God's ontological otherness which captured Isaiah's thinking. In fact, the primary characteristic that set this God apart from humanity, made him holy, was his moral and ethical perfection.[3] Thus Isaiah's response to his vision of God was "I am unclean" (6:5). This uncleanness was not merely ceremonial, as the words "unclean lips" testify. Before the presence of this moral and ethical perfection the prophet knew that the whole issue of his life and that of his people were defiled and corrupt. Their problem was not that they were finite before the Infinite or mortal before the Immortal or partial before the Complete. Their problem was that they were morally filthy before the Morally Pure. This is nowhere clearer than in 5:16: "The Lord of Hosts is exalted in justice, and the Holy God is sanctified in righteousness." The primary mark of God's holiness is his moral and ethical purity.

This aspect of God's character reveals itself in several ways in the book, especially through the contrast with the people's character. Their lying, stealing, oppression, and murder are a direct affront to his nature (1:4, 21–23; 5:20; 9:16 [Eng. 17]–10:4; 30:12; etc.), as is mere cultic obedience (28:5–10; 58:1–5; 65:2–5). When they are exalted the result is arrogance and faithlessness (3:11–15; 22:15–25; 32:5–7; 59:5–8), but God's exaltation is seen in his faithfulness (10:20; 12:6; 29:23; 30:18; 31:4–5; 49:7), especially toward the lowly (29:19; 57:15). Because of his

2. 1:4; 5:19, 24; 10:20; 12:6; 17:7; 29:19, 23; 30:11, 12, 15; 31:1; 37:23; 40:25; 41:14, 16, 20; 43:3, 14, 15; 45:11; 47:4; 48:17; 49:7 (2 times); 54:5; 55:5; 60:9, 14. Cf. H. Ringgren, *The Prophetical Conception of Holiness* (Uppsala: Uppsala University, 1948); see also J. Oswalt, "Holiness and the Character of God," *Asbury Seminarian* 31 (1976) 12–21.

3. Rudolph Otto's well-known book *The Idea of the Holy*, tr. J. W. Harvey (London: Oxford, 1928), explores the "otherness" in an excellent way. But if the book has one weakness, it is its failure to do justice to the dimension of moral perfection which is an inescapable element of the biblical idea.

faithfulness, because he alone is the Maker, and because he will do what is right, he may be trusted to redeem (41:14; 43:3, 14–15; 47:4; 48:17; etc.); and his willingness to redeem against all the odds will be the vindication of his holiness as well as the expression of it (10:20; 12:6; 29:19, 23; 41:16; 60:9, 14). Refusal to trust in him is in fact a denial of his holiness (8:13; 30:11–12; 31:1). Finally, it is God's purpose that his people should share his character (35:8; 48:2; 60:14; 62:12).

Because God alone is great, and because he alone is holy, the worship of other gods is sheerest folly. Above everything else, it is stupid. Nowhere else in Scripture is the stupidity of idolatry subjected to such exquisite sarcasm as in the book of Isaiah. Who would be so blind as to bow down to a piece of wood the other half of which had just been used to cook supper (44:9–20; see also 41:6–7; 2:8, 20; 17:7, 8; 30:22; 31:7; 57:12–13)?[4] Nor is Isaiah content to limit his attack to the making of idols. These other gods whom the idols represent are merely reflections of humanity with all the limitations of humanity. They are attempts to glorify human beings, but in fact they only magnify the essential helplessness of our species (2:6–22). They are unable to explain the past or to predict the future (41:22–23; 43:8–9; 44:6–8; 45:20–23); they cannot affect the present in any material way (41:23; 45:16, 20; 47:12–15), because the gods do not transcend this world. They are continuous with it and expressions of it. Therefore they did not make it and cannot control its destiny. They are helpless participants in the system. Isaiah represents this by saying that the gods know neither how the world began nor how it will end. God is not so; he is other than this system. As such he is qualified to be its Maker, Sustainer, Director, and Judge. Thus he is able to explain the past and to foretell the future (41:26–29; 42:24–26; 44:7–8; 45:21; 46:10; 48:3–6, 12–16; etc.). The gods, being contingent, cannot do a new thing, such as delivering from exile, but God can. They are

---

4. It is the opinion of Y. Kaufmann, *The Religion of Israel*, tr. and abridged M. Greenberg (Chicago: University of Chicago, 1961), pp. 16–17, that this sarcasm betrays the complete ignorance on Israel's part of the ruling principle of paganism: continuity. In other words, Israel was so far from being pagan as not even to understand it. This is a laudable point of view and much nearer to the truth than that which says that Israelite religion was merely an extension of paganism. However, this sort of attack does not prove Kaufmann's point. Suppose Isaiah understood fully the pagan principle, as I think he did, that the wooden idol Baal partakes of the power of the storm Baal which in turn reflects the power of the deity Baal. Knowing all this, would he not attack this theory at its weakest point—the insanity of worshiping the creature, especially one's own creature? I think he would. For further discussion see J. Oswalt, "The Myth of the Dragon and Old Testament Faith," *EvQ* 49 (1977) 163–172.

doomed to mere repetition of the natural cycles, but God is free to do anything, even something brand new, to serve his sovereign, faithful purposes (42:8–9, 16–17; 43:18–19; 46:11; 48:6–8).[5]

A further implication to be drawn from the sovereign and holy lordship of God is his rule of history. Whatever others before him may have understood, Isaiah realized that God, unlike the idols, had plans and purposes for human experience (14:24–27; 19:12; 23:8–9; 25:1; 37:26; 45:9–11, 18; 46:10–11). Moreover, these plans were part of a comprehensive whole. Isaiah expected that history would find its climax as the nations of the world flowed to a redeemed and glorified Zion, there to share in the divine character itself (2:1–5; 11:9; 25:7–8; 60:1–22).

But the historical events which were to confront Israel and Judah during Isaiah's lifetime and in the two centuries following could not be easily integrated with that picture. Nations that worshiped idols would destroy first Israel and then Judah, and though Judah survived she would be but an administrative unit in a vast pagan empire. Is this divine control of history?

What Isaiah was able to do was to demonstrate that God's purpose was much larger than short-term victory or defeat and that his control of human destiny extended even to those who would not acknowledge him. How can it be that violently pagan Assyria should destroy Samaria, the city of God's people, no matter how sinful? Is Assyria stronger than God? Oh no, Assyria is but a tool in the hand of God (10:15). In a world that perceived battles between warring nations as a contest between their respective gods, this was a daring and, indeed, astonishing insight. Yet, on the other hand, it is not astonishing if a person adopts Isaiah's premises. If God is indeed the *only* God (26:13; 44:8; 45:14, 22; etc.), if he is indeed the transcendent One who is other than the psycho-socio-physical system of this world (2:10, 19, 21; 6:1–3; 24:21–22; 31:3; 40:25–26; etc.), if he is the One who directs all things (8:12–13; 14:26–27; 19:12; 26:21; etc.), if he is faithful to his promises and righteous in his ways (1:16–20; 2:1–4,

---

5. A cursory glance at the references cited in the text will make it apparent that the bulk of the polemic against the pagan deities is to be found in chs. 40–49. This may give rise to the question whether it is justifiable to say that a major feature of the theology of the *book* is its attack upon the idols. I would maintain that it is justifiable on the ground that chs. 1–39 prepare for chs. 40–49 just as ch. 41 prepares for chs. 42–49. That is, general statements are made about the absolute sovereignty of God. In an idolatrous world such as the ancient Near East was, such statements must assume unfavorable comparison with the other gods. That this is so is supported by the several brief statements which are scattered throughout chs. 1–39 (2:8, 18, 20; 17:7–8; 27:9; 30:22; 31:7; 37:19). It only remains for the implications to be made explicit, as they are in chs. 41–49.

11–12; 11:1–16; etc.), it only takes a rigorous commitment to logic to conclude that the events of history are not a contest between God and the gods, but are in fact the outworking of the interaction between the single divine purpose and human obedience and rebellion.[6] Thus, just as the Assyrians were to be instruments of punishment, Cyrus was to be the instrument of redemption (45:1–7). Furthermore, the nations of humanity, before whose glory the Judeans were tempted to prostrate themselves, were all accountable to the righteous God and under his judgment (chs. 13–23). Never again after Isaiah could Judah conceive of herself as the only place where God worked. Zion might be his throne, but the earth was his stage.

B. HUMANITY AND THE WORLD

Nowhere is Isaiah's love of paradox more evident than in the area of humanity and the world. By his use of paradox he avoids the pitfalls that have dogged so much thought upon this topic. Apart from revelation, two extremes seem to prevail. On the one hand, humanity is seen as being ultimate, the measure of all things, the logical center for all thought and contemplation. On the other hand, humanity is nothing, one more blob of protoplasm made more contemptible by its ability to cloak its rapaciousness with murmurings about "value" and "destiny." The world is seen in similar ways. On the one hand, it is made god itself; all life springs from it; it must be nourished and cherished as Mother. On the other hand, the universe is at heart nothing more than a complex of forces operating at random with but an appearance of regularity. Out of these forces life has been belched, on at least one chunk of matter, with no more purpose than that of a bubble of gas erupting from the molten lava in a volcano's center.

For Isaiah, these seemingly contradictory positions are in fact directly related. To assume that the physical universe and the humanity which has emerged from it are ultimate is to bring oneself inexorably to the opposite conclusion (2:6–22; 14:4–21; 47:5–15). For the universe contains no justification for itself in itself. The growth and change that seem so much a part of it are really only an ongoing process of decay. The humanity that seems to stand at the pinnacle of it all is continually mocked by its own transitoriness and death. The values that it touts most highly—

6. It can be asserted that the very concept of "history" rests upon this idea of interaction between divine purpose and human response. Without such an idea, existence is but a series of unrelated events grouped somewhat on the recurring cycle of nature. Cf. R. G. Collingwood, *The Idea of History* (Oxford, 1946), pp. 46–52; cf. also G. von Rad, *Old Testament Theology,* tr. D. M. G. Stalker (London: SCM; New York: Harper & Row, 1965), II:99–115.

unselfish love, justice, equity, and peace—are precisely those it most regularly denies in practice.[7] If the world and human life are thought to be of ultimate significance, then it must be admitted that nothing is of ultimate significance, for these are surely not.

Again and again Isaiah makes his point that human pretensions to significance and the actions that arise to support these pretensions must always reduce us to nothing. The harder we try to make ourselves something, the more like nothing we become.[8] Isaiah notes frequently that it is God who smashes these pretensions (so, e.g., 2:12–17). And so it is. If our formula assumes that x equals significance when in fact it is y, the formula will always fail because it does not take into account the presence of y. So it was for the Judeans. Though they tried to exclude the Holy One from their computations, he was too real to be so excluded (30:8–18).

On the other hand, just as pretensions to significance must lead to insignificance for creation, so will the giving of true significance to God result in glory for humanity and the world. It should never be said that Isaiah is a world-despiser or one who believes that human beings are mere worms. To be sure, these are a result of denying God his true place, but they are not an accurate description of the real nature of things. It is hard to find a greater valuation put upon humanity and the world than that in Isaiah.[9]

When God, the personal Creator, is exalted as Holy Lord, the purposeful Maker, then the universe is a place of value and significance. Likewise, human beings are important because God chooses to make them reflections of his glory and to share his holy character with them. Are the failures and atrocities of humanity signs of its fundamental worthlessness? No, they are the results of refusals to let God be Lord. If we will allow him his rightful place, then redemption, exaltation, and glory are ours.

A similar paradox is found in human accomplishment and failure. When human beings believe they can accomplish anything, their works are fundamentally destructive (e.g., 1:2–8; 5:20–25; 30:1–5, 15–17;

7. Thus, according to a philosopher such as Nietzsche we ought to drop our pretensions and admit what we practice, that power is all. Cf. *The Antichrist* in W. Kaufmann, ed., *The Portable Nietzsche* (New York, 1954), pp. 565–656.

8. See 1:29–31; 2:11, 17, 22; 3:1–5; 5:15; 8:19–22; 9:12–16 [Eng. 13–17]; 10:12–19; 13:11; 14:12–16; 15:6–7; 17:4; 19:11–15; 22:15–25; 23:6–9; 24:1–23; 26:4–6; 28:1–4, 14–15; 30:15–17; 37:23–29; 41:21–29; 45:9–13; 46:1–2, 5–7; 47:7–11; 57:3–13.

9. See 2:2–4; 11:1–16; 19:16–24; 25:6–9; 27:2–6; 32:1–8, 15–20; 33:17–22; 35:1–10; 40:1–5; 41:17–20; 43:1–7; 44:1–5; 45:12–13, 18–19; 49:19–21; 52:13–53:12; 54:1–55:13; 60:1–22; 61:3–4; 65:17–25.

59:4–15). On the other hand, to admit that we are essentially helpless before God's omnipotence is to discover him enabling us for great things (e.g., 6:5–8; 7:9; 8:9–10; 10:20–27; 12:1–6; 26:1–9; 37:14–20, 30–38; 40:27–31). Thus, to pretend to be king in any absolute sense is to be truly powerless, as Ahaz learned and Hezekiah knew. Titles mean nothing if the territory which we supposedly control is worthless (3:6–8). In any event, the worth of a territory is not determined by size. Whether it be a heap of rubble or a mighty empire, it has no ultimate worth in itself (10:12–19; 47:1–9). On the other hand, to be a servant of the Most High is ultimately to have more authority and capacity than any of earth's sovereigns in their own right (30:29–33; 52:13; 65:13–16; 66:12–24).

C. SIN

Above everything else, sin is rebellion for Isaiah. This is illustrated graphically by the fact that the book begins and ends on this note (1:2; 66:24).[10] But this conclusion is drawn from more than a merely formal matter; it reflects the whole tenor of the book. God is the only Lord, the only Holy One. He has made all things for his sovereign purposes; he is directing history to its final conclusion of universal health and peace. How incredible, then, that a human being, the work of his hands, should stand up against him and say no! (10:15; 29:15–16; 64:8). Yet we have done so, and all the evil in the world springs from that refusal to accept God's fundamental lordship.

For Isaiah this rebellion is an expression of human pride.[11] We refuse to accept our creatureliness; we refuse to admit that we are dependent. We will be high and mighty and we will revere those who make the pretense of being high and mighty. We will make ourselves the sole source of our identity. From such a root, says Isaiah, springs a vicious plant. Initially there is alienation from God and from others, as each self refuses to be dependent upon others and instead seeks to use others for its own ends (5:8–25). From alienation springs unfaithfulness: we cannot afford to be true to others because it might decrease our independence (28:1–10). From unfaithfulness springs oppression as one self seeks in increasingly

10. *pāša'*, "to rebel," also occurs in 24:20; 27:4; 10 times in chs. 40–55; 6 times in 56–59. Its presence in the opening and closing words of the book suggests a conscious placement on the part of the final editor(s).

11. Derivatives of *gā'â*, "to rise up," appear 23 times in the book. Most frequent of these is *gā'ôn*, "exaltation" (12 times). The occurrences are about equally divided between references to God's rightful height and humanity's foolish pretension to such. Cf. *TWOT*, I:143–44.

overt ways to force other selves to do its bidding (58:1–59:15). Finally, the fruit of alienation, unfaithfulness, and oppression is destruction—the rampant self seeks to destroy everything it cannot control (10:7–14). This is sin, a pattern of behavior that has its source in a proud refusal to admit dependency. (See esp. ch. 1.)

To Isaiah the most astonishing thing about this rebellion is its stupidity (1:2–3). To him, any clearheaded examination of the facts of life ought to make it plain that humanity is not ultimate. Which of us can escape death, the grinning mocker of all our pretensions to greatness (ch. 14)? Which earthly nations can forever conquer their fellows and remain in perpetual dominance (chs. 13–23)? Which human leaders enshrined in their own pomp and power can be depended upon never to fail their people (chs. 7, 21, 28–30)? Yet we persist in our folly because the alternative is too distasteful. To become the servant of God is seen as being so bad that we will deny the facts of existence to avoid it (47:7–15).

D. JUDGMENT AND REDEMPTION

God's response to sin is judgment or redemption, depending upon the response of humanity to God's actions. If we will turn from our own attempts to care for ourselves and turn to dependence upon God (30:15), then he will do everything necessary to clear the record and restore us to fellowship (30:18; 53:12; 63:1–6). Moreover, the whole tenor of the book makes it plain that while mere wishful thinking cannot avert judgment, God is not content for judgment to be the last word. Thus in the larger structure of the book chs. 1–39, which tend to emphasize judgment, are followed by chs. 40–66, which tend to emphasize redemption; but it is also true within segments, as in chs. 1–6 and 7–12, as well as chs. 30 and 31, and especially chs. 56–59 and 60–66.[12] Furthermore, while judgment may indeed be final (22:14; 25:10–12; 66:24), it is also possible that judgment may become the vehicle for redemption (cf. 4:2–6). Thus, again, in the book as a whole, the heavy hand of God through the Assyrians and the Babylonians becomes the stimulus for the people to turn to God's outstretched hand of blessing. But judgment also recurs frequently throughout the parts (10:20–27; 26:21; 30:16–22; 37:1–7; 42:18–43:7; 50:1–3; 51:17–23; etc.).

12. If it were true that the "original Isaiah" said nothing of redemption but only preached judgment (so, e.g., Kaiser, but also others), it becomes very difficult to explain where the supposed later writers and editors got the idea for redesigning the final product along its present lines.

1. Judgment

Judgment takes many forms for Isaiah. It may come as natural disaster (24:4–5), military defeat (5:26–30), or disease (1:5–6), but all these are from the hand of God (43:27–28). The prophet does not know of a world where the Lord is merely an observer. All things emanate from him and have their meaning in relation to his will. Thus to live in contradiction to the Creator's purposes is to run headlong into the very structure of his universe. This is nowhere clearer than in the opening chapter of the book. There are natural and inevitable results of rebellion against the Creator, and they cannot be averted or altered except by a change in one's relationship to him (cf. also 59:1–15).

At the same time it should not be suggested that judgment is merely the outworking of the natural and impersonal consequences of our sin. For Isaiah, judgment is also the outworking of the personal outrage of an offended Deity. God is not a force to Isaiah; he is overwhelmingly Person. Thus he reacts to his people with passion. His love is passionate, and thus his hatred for all which corrupts his people is passionate as well (9:11, 16, 20 [Eng. 12, 17, 21]; 10:4). Nor can there be a neat separation between sin and sinner. People feel the results of his anger upon themselves (5:24–25; 65:6–7). But the point of difference is this: the sinner may repent and God will no longer be angry with him (10:25; 12:1; 26:20, 21; 30:18; 40:1–2, 27–31; 51:20–23; 54:7–8; 60:15; etc.). God does not hold his anger in some arbitrary pique but longs to extend his compassion to his people if they will but turn to him.

2. Redemption

According to Isaiah, the basis of redemption lies precisely in the faithfulness of a God who is willing to let his anger go and is unwilling that his people should be estranged from him. Far from exulting in their destruction, he longs that they might move through that abasement which their pride has brought upon them to cleansing and new life (1:16–19; 6:5–7; 27:1–9; 29:22–24; 33:5–6, 17–22; 43:25–44:3; 49:14–23; 57:16–19).

Furthermore, particularly (but not solely) as elucidated in the second part of the book, redemption has its basis in God's creatorhood. Because God is independent of his world as its creator, he is able to break into the apparently endless chain of cause and effect and deliver his people from the seemingly inevitable consequences of their sin (11:15, 16; 14:24–27; 17:7; 42:5–9; 43:1–2, 10–13; 48:13–18).

Thus it is plain that the means of salvation can only be through God's activity. Humanity is helpless to redeem itself in God's sight or even to change its behavior. If there is to be a restoration of the relationship and a substantive change of behavior it must be because the Creator becomes the Redeemer. This emphasis upon the necessity of God's defeating the enemies without and within by himself is distinctly Isaianic (4:4; 6:6–7; 12:5; 25:1, 6–9; 28:16–17; 32:15–20; 33:2, 10–12; 37:6–7; 41:25–29; 42:14–17; 44:22; 46:13; 50:2; 52:10; 59:15–20; 63:1–6). In this respect the nations of the earth are just as much God's tool for redemption as they were for judgment. Why is it that Cyrus the Persian will declare all exiles of the former Babylonian empire free to return? Because it pleases God so to direct him (44:21–45:7).

But it is evident that God cannot merely abrogate the justice upon which the cosmos is founded and declare that the effects of human sin will be suspended. Sin and transgression must be covered, atoned for. The train of effects of which sin is the initial cause must somehow be diverted. Nowhere in Scripture is this principle more clearly stated than in 52:13–53:12. Many will be accounted righteous *because* he bore their iniquities. It is this substitutionary atonement which ultimately makes possible God's announcement of pardon and redemption. In this sense the blood of God's enemies that stains the hem of his garment as he labors alone to bring deliverance is his own (63:1–6). He has become the enemy in order that even the enemy might know redemption if he chooses.

Who is this atoning One through whom redemption comes? It is the ideal king, the promised anointed one (Messiah). This picture of the one who suffers with his people (7:14–17), redeems his people (9:1–6 [Eng. 2–7]), rules over his people (11:1–5), and suffers for his people (42:1–9; 49:5–6; 50:4–9; 52:13–53:12) gives a total view of the means whereby God expects to deliver his people from both the causes and the effects of sin. Central to the book's attitude about arrogance and pride is the picture of One who will establish his rule through the moral force of his own humility and self-giving rather than through brute force. Moreover, it is clear that this individual is in some sense identified with God himself, not only by the statement in 9:5 (Eng. 6; "mighty God") but also by the application to him of "high and lifted up" (52:13; elsewhere used only of God, 6:1 and 57:15) and by the implied question, What human being can atone for the sins of others?

The conditions for redemption are everywhere the same in the book: a renunciation of one's own pride and a corresponding acknowledgment of God's sole rulership, an acceptance of God's provision for deliverance, and a willingness to function as God's servant. These are seen in recurring appeals throughout the book, but nowhere clearer than in the opening chapter, especially vv. 18–20. So long as persons insist upon their own exaltation, there is no hope of their entering into a redeeming relationship with God (2:11, 17; 5:15). On the other hand, to abandon trust in oneself and to commit one's way to God is to discover all the resources of the Most High at one's own command (12:2; 26:2–6; 30:15; 55:6–9; 57:15). Ultimately the entire book is an appeal to abandon the folly of human pride, to accept God's lordship, and to experience the wonder of life as it was meant to be (11:1–16; 65:17–25).

In Isaiah's view, chief among the many conditions resulting from redemption would be restoration of God's holy image in his people, restoration to the land, reestablishment of social justice, and fulfillment of the servant role by God's people. One of the book's recurring points is that God will make his people like himself. Redemption is not merely people's deliverance from the guilt of past sins, but also the sharing of his holy character. This is clear in the prophet's call experience but also in many other places (4:3–4; 11:9; 32:15–18; 35:8–10; 60:21). Even more than in individual passages, the whole shape of the book points in this direction. Yes, salvation is by divine initiative alone; human beings can do nothing to bring it about (chs. 40–55). However, the outworking of that salvation is in lives of justice, righteousness, and purity, which are achieved not by human work but by divine provision (chs. 56–66).

As sin and pride resulted in the destruction of the land and the people's being cast out from it (10:20–23; 24:1–23; 34:1–17; 39:5–7), so redemption would bring about the re-creation of the land and the resettlement of the people in their land (11:10–16; 25:6–9; 27:6; 30:23–26; 35:1–10; 41:17–20; 43:4–7, 19–21; 49:8–13). The two elements here are significant. Sin produces destruction of the natural order. This is not mere apocalyptic imagery. Whenever human beings live as though they were gods and creation was theirs to do with as they wish, creation suffers. Not only are the divinely ordained principles violated, but the creation becomes merely a means with no value of its own.[13] The result is the desolation that Isaiah depicts.

But the Hebrew prophets knew that the earth is the Lord's (6:3). It is not god itself, nor is it a possession of ours to violate. It is the possession of our Father lent to us in trust. So long as we cherish it out of a sense of responsibility to its true owner, it will bless us. But if we abuse it, it will not have any bounty to give us. In fact, in its desolation it will curse us. And God, the Owner, will not tolerate such destruction

---

13. On the other hand, the solution to this problem is not to deify nature, making it an end in itself. This must inevitably issue in a determinism and a fatalism whereby human values are of no significance.

of his property. Ultimately then, God's people may dwell in his land only if they are in a relationship of obedience and submission to him. If they are, then the land is theirs to enjoy forever.[14]

Not only is the cosmos violated by those who refuse to submit to God, but so are other people. The factors are the same in each case. Proud human beings refuse to relate to each other according to the Creator's principles, and they insist upon seeing other human beings as insignificant except as possible means to their own ends. This is the foundation of the social injustice that Isaiah and all the other prophets condemned with such vehemence. Because God values people for themselves, we must also. We dare not view them as means and try to use them as such (cf. 58:3–9). Nor may we simply ignore them as unimportant to our goals. The redemption of God must change that. To admit his Lordship over us is to begin to allow him to make us see others as he sees them and to value them as he values them. Any attempt to please God with mere cultic righteousness flies in the face of what his righteousness is about (chs. 56–58; 66:1–4; 1:10–17).

As sin results in the degradation and devaluation of the sinner, so redemption results in a renewed significance and worth. This is expressed by Isaiah as the impartation of God's glory or reality. Divine glory, imparted to those in obedient submission to him, has an enduring quality that can never be taken away. The two parts of the book express these antitheses (sin produces degradation, but submission produces glory) very clearly, with the latter appearing climactically in chs. 55–66 (55:5; 58:8; 60:7, 9, 13, 19; 61:3; 63:14; 66:18, 19). In many ways this theme is the summation of Isaiah's theology: God alone is truly glorious (real); to seek significance (glory) anywhere else is to invite destruction. But God does not want us to destroy ourselves; rather, he wishes to impart his glory to all who will abandon their trust in themselves, accept his free grace, and commit themselves to righteous living. It is the servants of the Holy who find true glory.

To be redeemed, in Isaiah's view, is to have gladly accepted the role of servant. To refuse to do so is to fly in the face of reality. Human beings who seek to find significance in their own "kingship," refusing to entrust their Creator with their own destiny, find dissolution (23:9; 30:12–14). But those who accept their Maker's humiliatingly free grace and adopt the role of servant will find a power that defies all human wisdom

14. In this sense the Jewish people are the paradigm for the entire world. The land of Israel represents the world and the Jews represent the entire human race.

(42:1–4). In that servanthood is a significance and an abundance that the former independence could never secure (43:10–15; 65:12–16).

IX. PROBLEMS IN INTERPRETATION

In a book as large as this a host of significant interpretative problems could be identified. The task here is to identify only those that are judged to be of the greatest significance for understanding the message and import of the book. In that light four have been chosen for discussion. They are closely interrelated but can be treated separately for clarity's sake. They are the unity of the book, the significance of prediction, the identity of the Servant of the Lord, and the function of the book in the total canon.

A. THE UNITY OF THE BOOK

This question has already been discussed above as a higher-critical issue; however, it also has important interpretative ramifications. A study of recent commentaries on Isaiah will make it abundantly clear that whatever may be said about ongoing redactional processes imparting a certain over-all unity to the book has little impact upon matters of interpretation. Pericopes, paragraphs, even verses adjudged to have come from historical settings differing from that of the context in which they appear are regularly interpreted without reference to that context. The only corrective to this atomization of the text is an infrequent comment at the end of a discussion referring to the "secondary" interpretations that may be derived from the material's being inserted into the present text. The resulting fragmentary approach to interpretation is all too plain, with the further result that much of the power which the book as a whole has exerted upon its readers for the past twenty-five centuries is vitiated.[1] If the book is to remain a significant document of, and for, the human race, it must be seen as a whole.

How may this interpretation of the book as a whole be recovered? Is the only recourse to accept the older position of single authorship? This is certainly a viable alternative in my mind. Nor does it require the surrender of many of the insights of modern literary studies. It is entirely possible to assume that the book is an anthology of many different materials coming from a variety of settings in the prophet's life, but that they

---

1. Cf. O. T. Allis, *The Unity of Isaiah: A Study in Prophecy* (Philadelphia: Presbyterian and Reformed, 1950), pp. 43–48.

have been assembled together according to an overall literary and theological grid, either by the prophet himself or by his immediate followers.

But is this way of seeing the book—a way which is all but impossible for many honest scholars—the only means of recovering the book's unity? I think not. Another way has been proposed by Brevard Childs in his "canonical interpretation."[2] Fundamental to this understanding is the claim that whatever the history of the formation of the Scriptures, it is their canonical form which the community of faith has identified as being authoritative. According to Childs it is this form of the text that "alone bears witness to the full history of revelation."[3] Furthermore, it is the final form of the text that offers us the community's mature judgment upon the meaning of any prior components which have been incorporated into the final document.[4] In Childs's view, to remove these from their setting and to argue that their "original" meaning is of greater interpretative value than their final one is to pay too little attention to the process of revelation.

This approach has much to commend it, and if it could be generally accepted it would go far toward countering the fragmentation that is increasingly characteristic of the interpretation of Isaiah. Especially meritorious is the idea that the final form of the book offers the community's best judgment upon the meaning and significance of the materials included in the book. However, the common dictum that origins determine outcomes, a dictum applied from psychiatry to earth sciences, seems to rule in biblical studies as well. The result has been that Childs's point of view has received little more welcome from the establishment of biblical studies than it has from conservatives, who are generally unwilling to grant a diverse set of origins for a given book.[5]

But even those who accept neither conservatives' views on the book's origin nor the suggestions of Childs as to the final form of the book being the fullest form of the revelation ought, in my view, to give more credence to the axiom "the whole is more than the sum of its parts." To analyze the physical components of a human being is not to understand humanity. Nor can the message of Isaiah be understood by means of such analysis. By whatever means, the book's unity is a present historical fact. Analysis of separate parts without sufficient attention to the whole is not

2. Childs, *Introduction*, pp. 69–83.
3. Ibid., p. 76.
4. Ibid., p. 77.
5. Cf. the May, 1980, issue of *JSOT* (no. 16), which was devoted entirely to responses to Childs's views.

an adequate practice of historical-critical exegesis.[6] If a scholar does indeed believe that Isaiah reached its final form only in the late postexilic period, it is incumbent upon him or her to interpret the book holistically in that light.[7] To fail to do so, apart from any judgments about theological value, is to pay insufficient attention to the data. In terms of theological values, why should it be assumed, apart from some preconceived theory, that the supposedly "original" elements are of greater significance than the supposedly "later"? At the least it is incumbent upon the interpreter to give as much attention to the whole as he or she has given to the parts.[8]

In summary, whatever one's theory about the origins of the book, it is necessary for the interpreter to consider each part of the book in the light of the whole for pronouncements concerning that part's meaning to have genuine validity.

B. THE SIGNIFICANCE OF PREDICTION

Perhaps no issue has divided recent interpreters of prophecy more than this one. The chief question revolves about the function of the prophetic literature: Does it exist to foretell the future or does it exist to call a particular people to faith in God? Is it universal or particular? During most of its history, and the more so during times of despair, the Church has inclined toward the former, tending to find itself and its own times in the pages of the prophets. In the last couple of centuries a rather violent reaction has set in wherein the predictive element has been almost wholly stripped from the prophets. They are seen as moralistic preachers who

---

6. It is, of course, the canons of historical-critical exegesis coupled with the denial of the biblical claims as to historic provenance that have brought us to this impasse. The Reformers, accepting the biblical claims at face value, insisted, rightly I think, that each book must be understood in its historic setting. So long as books were understood as wholes, this presented no particular problem. But when books began to be dissected and various parts assigned to vastly different provenances, *and* scholars continued to insist that the original historical context of each part gave the ruling interpretation of that part, then came the problem. It is interesting that ancient Near Eastern literature, for which there is much clearer evidence of redaction than there is for biblical literature, is not, by and large, subjected to the kind of fragmentary interpretation which biblical literature is. Cf. K. A. Kitchen, *Ancient Orient and Old Testament* (London: Tyndale, 1966), p. 23.

7. Cf. R. A. Traina, *Methodical Bible Study* (New York: Biblical Seminary, 1952), p. 226.

8. Among recent critical commentaries Wildberger's comes the closest to achieving this balance of treatment, but it still falls considerably short of the ideal. The presupposition of literary- and form-criticism that "earlier is better" still exerts tremendous force.

called their Israelite and Judean compatriots to repentance and reform. Their only relationship to later times is by analogy: to the degree that our situation is like theirs, to that degree the message has relevance to us.[9] This position would not deny that the prophets spoke of the future, and this point has even been recovered to a certain extent in recent years.[10] However, this prediction is always held to be of the most general sort that would be consistent with an enlightened conscience, an awareness of Scripture, and a feel for the course of events. Unless God's people respond to his word, dire things will happen to them. If they respond, good things will happen.

Today, the majority of interpreters would resolutely deny to the prophets any more specific predictions. Whenever such predictions appear in the prophetic literature scholars invariably ascribe them to a secondary author unless the original author is judged to have lived long enough to have written the material after the fact. This last statement succinctly sets out the normal interpretative principle as applied to all that would appear to be specific predictions: they must be written after the fact. It is not hard to imagine why a thoroughgoing naturalist would take such a position. There is no "outside" by means of which these predictions could come. But it is much more difficult to imagine why modern theologians and commentators, most of whom consider themselves at least theists, if not supernaturalists, would hold such a view. Surely if there is such a deity, and if he is able to make special knowledge about himself available to his messengers, it is no great feat to make special knowledge about the future available to these messengers.

It is even more difficult to understand why it is insisted that the prophets wrote their predictions after the fact, when so frequently they rest the claims for the validity of their theology upon the proof of their predictions. In other words, if a hearer said, "How do I know your pronouncements about God are correct?", the prophet replied, "Look at my predictions." To insist that the predictions were written after the fact is to assert that the great exponents of ethical righteousness in human history falsified their evidence. Is there any way around this impasse? It is possible to say that the original Hebrew prophets made no predictions, but that their followers, in an excess of zeal to prove their masters correct, doctored the evidence. But this does not help us very much. Once more we are back

9. A. Kuenen, *The Prophets and Prophecy in Israel*, tr. A. Milroy (London: 1877), pp. 332–364, 574–585; J. Lindblom, *Prophecy in Ancient Israel* (Oxford: Blackwell; Philadelphia: Fortress, 1962), p. 199.

10. G. von Rad, *Theology*, II:112–125; O. Kaiser, *Introduction to the Old Testament*, tr. J. Sturdy (Minneapolis: Augsburg, 1975), p. 215.

to a subjective fragmentation of the text according to a priori reasonings about what could or could not have happened. Furthermore, in this day when it is so fashionable to point out the interconnections between biblical and nonbiblical prophecy, it seems strange that the very element most characteristic of nonbiblical prophecy, namely, foretelling the future, should be denied to biblical prophets.

Thus it must be argued that while prediction of the future is not the primary function of biblical prophecy, it is a legitimate element whereby the ethical pronouncements are validated and whereby God's ability to shape history according to his purposes and human responses is demonstrated. If specific predictions are always suspect then the whole prophetic message, as far as it is supposed to convey eternal verities, is suspect.

This point is nowhere more true than in Isaiah. Too much of the whole fragmentation of the book rests upon the assumption that it is not possible for a prophet of the eighth century B.C. to foretell accurately and to speak to the events of the sixth and fifth centuries B.C. While this assumption is by no means the whole of the argument against the single authorship of the book, it still forms altogether too much of the basis for that argument. Once one grants that Isaiah of Jerusalem *could* have written such material, the arguments from style, vocabulary, themes, etc. become very nebulous.

Furthermore, much of the book's teaching is directly related to prediction. The prophet claims that reliance upon Assyria for protection from Syria and Israel is misguided not merely because it is a repudiation of trust in God but because the prophet knows the future and knows that such reliance is unnecessary (7:8–9). He goes on to predict that reliance on Assyria will result in an Assyrian onslaught (8:4–8).[11] While it might be argued that no special revelation was necessary in order to recognize that likelihood, it certainly did take special revelation to predict that the Lord would bring about Assyria's downfall (10:16–19, 33–34).

But of much deeper import here are the predictions relating to the messianic child. The whole validity of Isaiah's calls to trust God depends upon the validity of his predictions concerning that child. If those predictions are only literary window dressing, then trust in the God that Isaiah proclaims is quite foolish. If those predictions either have not been realized or are not in some definite sense realizable, the prophet's appeal to his own people and to all his later readers is foolish.

By the same token the oracles against the nations are so structured

---

11. Note that even here commentators are unwilling to allow the least specificity, many insisting that the reference to Assyria in 8:7 is a gloss.

as to be specific claims that Zion's God does know and does exercise control over the future (14:26–27). Shall we say that Babylon (chs. 13–14) is put first in the series only by later zealots who sought to prove in a tangible way that Isaiah knew what he was talking about, or shall we grant that he himself knew the evidence? To take the former tack is to grant that Isaiah had no evidence to give and that these later followers have completely altered the thrust of his preaching.

So it goes throughout the book. Isaiah denounces trust in Egypt because he knows Egypt will not help her clients; he counsels defiance against Sennacherib because he knows God will honor Hezekiah's repentance; he excoriates Hezekiah's courting of Babylon because he knows Babylon is the ultimate enemy; etc. But even more in the second half of the book the whole message is made to appear to be tied to prediction. God's superiority over the idols is not merely that he alone is the Creator (43:1; 44:1, 24, 45:18–19) but that he has foretold the Exile in Babylon (41:22; 42:9; 43:9; 44:7). If it is in fact not true, then once more the argument falls to the ground and the lofty theology becomes highly dubious.[12] Furthermore, it is the prediction of deliverance through the Lord's servant Cyrus that is made the proof of Israel's chosenness. If this is an after-the-fact realization, what purpose is served by attempting to make it appear a prediction? Beyond this, it hardly needs to be said that ch. 53 is couched as a prediction of the means whereby Israel's sin may be covered and Israel may indeed become the servant of God.

Numerous other examples of this characteristic of the book could be cited. However, these are enough to illustrate the point that at least in Isaiah theology and prediction are inextricably intertwined. If specific prediction is denied to the prophet (or prophets), then their theology is groundless.

C. THE SERVANT OF THE LORD

It is well known that "the Servant of the Lord" is a dominant, recurring theme in chs. 40–55. In one way or another this concept appears some twenty times in these chapters.[13] It has been of special interest because of

12. Whatever one may think of R. P. Carroll's *When Prophecy Failed,* one cannot avoid a certain admiration for his consistency. He is unwilling to praise the theology of Isaiah while dismissing the validity of its predictive elements. In a forthright manner he dismisses both, making the book's teaching primarily an exercise in continuous reinterpretation of failed predictions (pp. 36–37, 130–156).

13. See 41:8, 9; 42:1, 19; 43:10; 44:1, 2, 21, 26; 45:4; 48:20; 49:5, 6; 50:10; 52:13; 53:11; 54:17.

the Christian Church's identification of Jesus as this Servant in ch. 53 (a tradition as old as Philip's exposition to the Ethiopian eunuch as recorded in Acts 8:30–35).[14] This has created a problem for some Christian interpreters because most of the references specifically identify the Servant as Israel or Jacob. An earlier method of handling such statements was to say that the intended referent was the "new" Israel, that is, the Church, the Bride of Christ.[15] This is certainly not indicated in the text, however, and sober commentators at least as far back as Calvin have dismissed the idea.[16] Concurrent with the rise of higher criticism the pendulum began to swing in the other direction with an argument that in fact the Servant was merely a personification of the nation, as "Church" is a personification of the totality of Christians.[17] This view attained prominence in the latter half of the nineteenth century and has regained some currency at the present time. Along the way some have accepted the individual references but argued that it was a historical figure, perhaps even II Isaiah himself, who regarded himself as the "Suffering Servant."[18]

As Christopher North notes in what is still perhaps the most useful study of the problem, the positions can be resolved into four groups: the historical individual, the mythological, the messianic, and the collective.[19] As North shows, and as H. H. Rowley agrees,[20] the first two positions have fatal flaws. The first fails for a number of reasons but chiefly because the data are too ambiguous to identify who the individual was, whether the prophet or someone else. The great number of suggestions that scholars have put forward, most of which have only their original proponent in support, attest to this ambiguity.

The mythological interpretation fails simply because, despite some-

14. The Gospels indicate that this tradition had its origin with Christ himself. In a cautious yet unambiguous way, J. Jeremias agrees with this point of view in *The Servant of God* (with W. Zimmerli), rev. ed., SBT 1/20 (London: SCM; Naperville: Allenson, 1965), pp. 99–106.

15. Cf. Augustine, *Sermons on the Liturgical Seasons,* tr. M. S. Muldowney, The Fathers of the Church, 38 (New York, 1959), pp. 80–81.

16. See Alexander on these passages for a straightforward exposition of the plain meaning of the text.

17. O. Eissfeldt, "The Ebed-Jahwe in Isaiah x1–1v," *EvT* 44 (1932–1933) 261–68.

18. Duhm perhaps began this process when he isolated the "Servant Songs" and related them to the fate of an unknown prophet.

19. C. R. North, *The Suffering Servant in Deutero-Isaiah: An Historical and Critical Study,* 2nd ed. (London: Oxford, 1956), pp. 192–219.

20. H. H. Rowley, *The Servant of the Lord and Other Essays on the Old Testament* (London: Lutterworth, 1952), pp. 49–53.

times strenuous efforts to the contrary, it still remains plain that the OT writers never made use of ancient Near Eastern myth as their neighbors did. They would use it as a foil for their own theology or they would make allusions to it, but they never used it in the thoroughgoing way which the creation of a mythological "Servant figure" would presuppose.

For North only the messianic interpretation remains, because he restricts his study to the so-called Servant Songs (42:1–4; 49:1–6; 50:4–9; 52:13–53:12), where the nation Israel is not identified as the Servant and where the Servant is in fact said to have a mission of redeeming his people (49:5–6; 53:5, 11). To be sure, North is unwilling to recognize a specific prediction of Jesus of Nazareth, but he is willing to grant that the prophet sees by revelation the outlines of a figure whom we now know was Jesus.

Certainly the data seem to bear out this position. While it is not impossible to conceive of the nation as a whole suffering because of, and for the sake of, the world, it *is* impossible to think of it suffering to redeem itself. Yet, it is precisely said that this Servant will restore Jacob (49:5) and will suffer for the transgressions of "my people" (53:8). Furthermore, the whole thrust of chs. 49–52 is in increasing anticipation of the salvation of Israel. Then chs. 54 and 55 ring with the triumph of salvation realized. What has come between? Ch. 53. Are we to believe that the nation has suffered for its own redemption? Hardly. The whole thrust of that chapter is that the Servant has suffered for others and not for himself. Thus North's position seems to be eminently reasonable.

H. H. Rowley professes himself to agree with the main lines of this argument as well. He too believes that the Servant passages point ultimately to an individual who was yet in the future from the prophet's perspective.[21] He does not like North's term "messianic" for such a view because he does not believe that the prophet identified his Suffering Servant with the Davidic Messiah of the earlier parts of the book of Isaiah (chs. 9, 11, 32, 33, etc.).[22] However, he sees no essential conflict between himself and North.

But Rowley does make an additional observation that is not without significance. Where North sees something of a straight-line progression from the collective to the individual in Isaiah's total treatment of servant-hood,[23] Rowley sees a great fluidity in moving back and forth between the

21. Rowley, *Servant,* p. 53.
22. Ibid., pp. 61–88, esp. p. 88.
23. Somewhat along the lines of Delitzsch's pyramid from people as a whole, level one, to a faithful remnant within the people, level two, to the individual Servant, apex, a concept which North cites favorably, *Suffering Servant,* p. 216.

collective and the individual. This perspective seems to accord best with the data. The straight-line point of view would seem to suggest that the prophet slowly abandoned the idea that the people could ever become God's servants and replaced this with the idea of an individual servant who would be what the people would not or could not be. But careful study of chs. 40–55 indicates that this is not the case. Instead of abandoning the idea of the people's becoming true servants, he rather asks, and answers, the question of *how* they can become such servants. How can the broken, sinful Israel ever be the servants of God as he has promised? The answer is "the Servant." Because he will be what they could not, and indeed will be that for all people, they can become what God has promised: his servants who can reveal his redeeming light. Thus chs. 54 and 55 depict a nation which, through the ministry of the Servant, have become the servants of God (54:17), redeemed and clean (54:8), a witness to God's glory and a light to the nations (55:4–5).[24] Thus perhaps a better figure for the total Servant-concept in Isaiah is that of a circle where the movement is from the circumference to the center and back again. God continues to call his people to be his servants in order that the world may know him as he is. But that is only possible because the Servant has redeemed us and thereby made us the evidence of God's true nature. Thus the answer to the question of the Servant's identity is a resounding "both-and." On the one hand, the Servant is the people of God. But on the other hand, the Servant is the One who incarnates servanthood and Godhood, who *shows* us the nature of servanthood and in so doing *enables* us to become that servant.

D. FUNCTION IN THE CANON

Without doubt the book of Isaiah is the most holistic of the biblical books. In its present form it encompasses the sweep of biblical theology better than any other single book in the canon. As we have noted, it is a matter of disagreement as to why it does so. The prevailing critical opinion is that the book is the result of a long process of development that covered the critical period of the growth of biblical thought from the destruction of Samaria through the appearance of normative Judaism in the intertestamental period.

Others, with whom I identify, would argue that such a long period

---

24. Strangely enough Delitzsch seems not to recognize this connection, for on 54:17 he denies any developmental relationship between the Servants mentioned there and the development of the Servant motif in chs. 41–53.

of development cannot explain the book's unity, but that its holistic view is the result of divine revelation given at a critical turning point in Israelite history, which revelation shaped Israelite religion over the succeeding centuries rather than merely reflecting that religion as it unfolded.

But whatever one's view on these issues, the fact remains that the book does indeed encompass both "OT" religion and "NT" religion. Thus it depicts a God of majesty and power whose decrees are absolute and whose judgments are inescapable. At the same time it shows us that this glorious God delivers his people out of free grace alone. Nor are these separate Gods; he is One in his judgments and in his grace. One of the disservices that the modern theory of multiple authorship has done for the Church is to make it possible to divide off the "judgmental" I Isaiah from the "gracious" II Isaiah. Whatever one's opinion of this theory, to do this is a rejection of the whole meaning of the present form of the book. Even if it is the work of multiple authors, it is clear that those authors intended their works to be read as one. They, if they existed, did not mean to separate the God to whom all the world is accountable—the Great and the Terrible—from the God who carried every living being written on his hands—the Slow to Anger and the Infinitely Compassionate. To bifurcate these two in Isaiah is to destroy the book's function in the canon.

That function is to be the bridge between the Already and the Not Yet. It prepared God's people to understand that the Messiah who would come was not a contradiction of the Law and the Prophets, but was indeed the fulfillment of them. He did not destroy the Law; rather he was the means offered by God himself for the realization of that Law. Like the rest of the OT, the earlier chapters of Isaiah have sprinkled through them glimpses of God's grace, and, like the NT, the later chapters do not let us forget that God's grace does not supersede his justice but exists to fulfill it. So too, the book's Messiah is both glorious and gentle, destroyer and deliverer.

Thus only a holistic interpretation of Isaiah will permit it to have its correct function in the canon. Clearly its author or authors felt that the various parts were not in contradiction to each other. In fact, the multiple-authorship theory must hold that editors have consciously taken portions of later material and have inserted them in the midst of earlier portions (e.g., chs. 24–27). Why else would they do this except to try to make the readers consider the theology as one? Of course, if all this points to a single author, the case for the holism of the book is only strengthened.

Surely this is why the NT, especially Jesus, makes such extensive use of Isaiah. Here was the bridge between the particular truths committed to that era and those of another era. Isaiah provided the means for Christ and his followers to demonstrate that what God was saying to them was not a denial of what had come before but was indeed only the logical extension and development of that precursor. Isaiah showed that Christianity was not a Jewish heresy but was in fact part and parcel of biblical religion. If the book is read in its wholeness today it will continue to unite the two Testaments as no other book can.

X. ANALYSIS OF CONTENTS

In general there is not much disagreement about the main sections of the book of Isaiah. They are: chs. 1–5(6), 7–12, 13–23, 24–27, 28–35, 36–39, 40–48, 49–55, 56–59, 60–66. While there is some difference of opinion about these, the distinctions tend to be clear enough to make the conclusions obvious. However, it is not merely the extent of the sections that is before us here, but more importantly the relationships among those sections. It is especially incumbent upon us to show these relationships in view of the foregoing pleas for a holistic interpretation.

It is my conviction that the overarching theme of the book of Isaiah is servanthood. Of course this point of view is explicit in chs. 40–55, but I am convinced that it is implicit in all the others and forms the thread which binds the book together. God has called all people, but particularly his own people, to lay down their self-exaltation and be dependent upon him, to become evidence of his character and deliverance in order that the whole world might know him as he is and thus be delivered from their own destruction.

In this light chs. 1–5 form an introduction to the book as a whole. The inclusiveness of the themes in these chapters suggests that they were very consciously written as an introduction. Here we see the problem: proud, arrogant, sinful Israel is anything but the servant of God. Nevertheless, Israel is declared as the means through whom God's light and blessing will come to the world. In the words of chs. 40–48, Israel is to be his witness. But this poses a nearly unanswerable question: How can *this* Israel become *that* Israel? The rest of the book functions as an answer to that question. In short, the answer is God, God who has the power (chs. 7–39) and the grace (chs. 40–66) to make the impossible possible.[1]

---

1. This way of understanding the book is helpful for comprehending the differing, but complementary, views of the Messiah in the two parts of the book. Seen from the point of view of God's majesty, the Messiah is as he appears in chs. 9 and 11. But seen in the light of God's grace, he is as he appears in chs. 49–53.

The perceptive reader will no doubt have noticed that ch. 6 is missing from the above statement. In a real (though brief) way this chapter answers the question posed by chs. 1–5, while the rest of the book answers it in a more involved way. How can *this* Israel become *that* Israel? When they, like Isaiah, have recognized not only their complete helplessness to do anything about that condition, when they have received his grace as a wholly unmerited act, then they will be in a position to hear his call to bear his message, then they will be able to respond with an obedience which will leave the outcome in his hands. In many ways the rest of the book is a fleshing out of the themes of ch. 6. Chs. 7–39 express the majesty of God and yet the people's sinfulness (cf. 6:1–5). Chs. 40–55 tell of God's willingness and ability to deliver his people (cf. 6:6–8). Chs. 56–66 deal with the realities, sometimes harsh, of trying to be God's light in an unreceptive environment (cf. 6:9–13).[2]

A more detailed analysis of chs. 7–39 shows a recurrence of the theme of trust. In the unfolding of that theme a dominant relationship is one of contrast. Shall Israel/Judah trust the great nations of humanity or shall they trust in God? This issue is especially apparent in the two historical segments that begin and end the division (chs. 7–12 and chs. 36–39). Chs. 36–39 are frequently seen as a somewhat unfortunate addendum to chs. 1–35 that have been copied out of Kings by someone who thought that the book of Isaiah ought to contain these stories of Isaiah. However, a more holistic study demonstrates that chs. 36–39 are remarkably similar to chs. 7–12 (two Judean kings facing terrible odds, the challenge coming at the same spot: the conduit of the upper pool on the highway to the Fuller's Field, 7:3 and 36:2; the one trusting human might and power, the other trusting God, although not completely).

In fact, then, this section examines the basic prerequisite for the stance of servanthood: an abandoning of oneself to complete trust in God. Ahaz believed that God was not trustworthy. He believed that Assyria was more able to help him against Israel and Syria than God was. Isaiah responded that this stance would bring Assyria upon Judah as destroyer. Nonetheless, God would prove his trustworthiness by delivering Judah and

2. I am aware of the simplicity of this type of analysis. Not everything in the three segments will fit neatly into these categories. Nor am I suggesting that an author sat down and wrote a whole section with the ruling thought which I have identified at the forefront of his mind. I do believe, however, that these themes fairly describe the bulk of the materials in each section and that this analysis suggests a much more considered collection and editing process than current theory allows.

by giving a king who would rule over the nation not in arrogance but in compassion.

After chs. 7–12, chs. 13–35 function to substantiate the claims made there. Is God trustworthy? Can he deliver his people from the nations? Is his glory greater than that of any human nation? Is it foolish to look to the nations for help when God is near at hand? The answer to all these is a resounding yes. Chs. 13–23 are a series of pronouncements against the nations. Chs. 11 and 12 spoke in a general way about God's sovereignty. Now the nations are taken one by one, from Babylon in the east (chs. 13, 14) to Tyre in the west (ch. 23), and each one is shown to be under God's judgment.

Chapters 24–27 turn away from the previous particularity to a more general statement that God is not merely a reactor on the stage of history, as chs. 13–23 might suggest, but is indeed the sovereign actor. Upon him one's mind may be fixed and one can dwell in security (26:3–6). He *will* deliver his people (27:12–13).

Not only have the Judeans succumbed to trusting the nations (instead of trusting God and becoming a light to the nations), but they have also looked to human leadership to save them from their troubles. Chs. 28–33 in particular address this problem, showing the folly into which these human leaders have led them (including the trusting of one more of the nations—Egypt, 30:1–7; 31:1–5). Instead of these foolish leaders, the promise is held out once more of a king who will rule in righteousness and peace (32:1–8; 33:17–22).

The teachings of chs. 13–33 are summed up and brought to a powerful conclusion in chs. 34 and 35. In a striking contrast the results of misplaced and correctly placed trust are detailed. To trust in this world is to reduce oneself and the world to desolation (ch. 34). On the other hand, to trust God is to place oneself in a garden of abundance, blessing, and holiness (ch. 35). Looking back over chs. 7–35 one gets the impression of looking at a programmed learning experience. Ahaz was given a test (a pre-test, if we keep the analogy intact). His choice was whether to trust God or Assyria. Unfortunately, he chose the wrong answer. Chs. 13–35 function as the didactic material giving instruction in support of the correct answer—God is to be trusted.

Chapters 36–39, then, are the post-test. Once again a Judean king is put in a position where he must trust God. Has he learned the lessons? Or will he too follow in his father's footsteps? The answer is that he will trust. As he does God demonstrates in a decisive way that he can be trusted. Indeed, there is a solid basis for Israel's accepting the position of servanthood: God is trustworthy.

Although the segment answers some questions, it raises others. Is not Hezekiah the promised Messiah, the "Child" of chs. 7–9? Furthermore, what if trust is only for a single occasion and not a pattern of life, as it was not for the Judeans? The answer to the former question is an obvious no. Not only is Hezekiah most certainly mortal (despite God's grace of added years, ch. 38), but he is also very fallible and parades his wealth before the Babylonians rather than giving praise to the God who has extended his life (ch. 39). Thus Hezekiah is clearly not the Messiah. We will have to look beyond this segment for a further elucidation of that person's identity.

The second question is more complex, for it raises again the issue of servanthood. In order for Israel to become God's servant is it enough to know that God is sovereign and can be a source of blessing to his people? Clearly not, for Hezekiah and his people have not become God's servants, a light to the nations, simply because they have seen God's power and his faithfulness. In fact, they are still prone to sell themselves to the highest bidder among the nations. Evidently, realization of servanthood demands something more than merely a one-time recognition of God's power. A glance back to ch. 6 helps at this point. There we see that neither a realization of God's glory nor even an experience of deliverance is an end in itself. Rather, we realize these in order that we may allow him to cleanse us and make us a light to the nations.

Thus chs. 36–39 effectively answer the first question of the potential servant—yes, God is great enough and faithful enough to be trusted— but they then move us forward to the next question: What about my sinfulness and my fallibility? Am I worth anything as a servant; would God even care to use me? Or am I, like Isaiah, simply undone by the uncrossable gap between the tinsel of human glory and the terrifying blaze of God's glory? Thus the chapters form a pivotal point between the revelation of God's glory and the revelation of his grace, both its need and its availability. Of course, they also form a historical pivot. Up to this point the Judeans had been assuming that the Assyrians were the great threat to their existence as a nation. Here, by inspiration, the prophet shows that the real threat, not only as a nation but also as the representative of a way of life, is Babylon.

The latter part of the book of Isaiah answers three remaining questions of servanthood: What will motivate us to serve God (chs. 40–48)? What means will make it possible for us to serve, even if we wish to (chs. 49–55)? What are the marks of the servant's life in an imperfect world (chs. 56–66)? As noted above, the shift in emphasis is possible not merely because of a change in historical provenance (a time when the Judeans are in captivity and then when they have been restored—some 140 and 200 years in the future from Isaiah's perspective), but also because of the theological development of the book. The grace of God must follow the glory and the justice of God if the grand theological design revealed to Isaiah at his call was to be unfolded to the world.

Chapters 40–55 put a whole new face on things. The Judah once reveling in her special hold on God has now been decimated by the victorious Babylonian armies; the temple of God has been destroyed, and the cream of Judah's civilization has been carried off into exile in southern Mesopotamia. Yes, God may have shown himself victor over Assyria, but what now? Has he not been defeated? Defeated by the Babylonian gods, but perhaps even more by our sin? Has the vision of servanthood, of being a light to the nations instead of a lackey to the nations, disappeared? Isaiah's answer is that the new circumstances will not have made the "old truth uncouth."[3] They will in fact only bear out what has been said before. What a comfort it must have been to Judeans in the captivity to realize that words which they may have read many times before without understanding were in fact written for *their* time and were written to prove that God would not be defeated either by sin or by Babylon.

Chapters 40–49 emphasize two points: (1) there is no contest between the Lord and the idols; (2) no matter what may have happened Israel is chosen and precious in God's sight. Ultimately, in fact, Israel will be the evidence of God's superiority over the Babylonian gods. What a tremendous motivation to service. Not only has God not cast them off, but he plans to make special use of them. He *will* deliver them; he will use them; they are, and will be, his servants. That sense of chosenness, of having a special place, is what is necessary to bring God's people to the place of wanting to trust him. Yes, they had known God was trustworthy, had known it for centuries. But not until they are in total desolation (as Isaiah had been—6:5) and then discover that God has not given up on them but intends to redeem them (6:6–7) will they be moved to offer themselves to him (6:8).[4]

3. This is perhaps another reason for Isaiah's being inspired to speak of the Babylonian captivity. Otherwise, it would have been possible that the teachings of 739–701 were indeed invalid in the light of new circumstances which the old prophet never envisioned. By not only speaking to his own day but also to that day far in the future, he can make it plain that the God who defeated the Assyrians was *not* defeated by the Babylonians. Indeed, he can point out, as noted above, that the Babylonian captivity was not only not a surprise to God but that it had been foretold in some detail well in advance.

4. It is interesting to note that in this first section (chs. 40–48) the ideal Servant appears only once (49:1–7), whereas the rest of the references to servanthood apply to Israel. God is here assuring the nation that *they* are and will be

Chapters 40–48 fall into three natural divisions. Ch. 40 is an introduction which primarily focuses upon God's will and his ability to deliver. Chs. 41–45 particularize these emphases by applying them specifically to Babylon and predicting Babylon's fall at God's hand through his unwitting servant Cyrus. Another way to see the relationship here is to see Babylon's fall as the logical effect of God's greatness and his election of Israel.

Once again, however, a question is raised: Is the destruction of Babylon all that is necessary to establish Israel's servanthood? Or does a deeper captivity prevent Israel from serving God whether she is in Babylon or her own land? In short, who will deliver Israel, or indeed, anyone who wishes to serve God, from bondage to sin? By what means may our chosenness be realized? Once more, as deliverance from physical bondage demanded the servant Cyrus, so deliverance from spiritual bondage calls for the Servant, One who will be what Israel is not, so that she may have the possibility of becoming what she is to be. Thus chs. 49–53 speak of the means of servanthood, the means whereby Israel, and the world, can experience God's choosing of them. As noted above, the major emphasis here is upon the ideal Servant (49:1–6; 50:4–10; 52:13–53:12) while the minor emphasis is upon the nation as servant (54:17). There is also a clear change of focus after 53:12. Until 52:13 the language is plainly anticipatory, with the people crying out to God to do something that they cannot do (e.g., 51:9–11), and God responding that he will act on their behalf (e.g., 51:12–16). After 53:12 the language is that of gratitude for deliverance accomplished and the call to take advantage of what is ours for the taking. Thus it is very difficult to avoid the conclusion that however the prophet or the editors may have viewed the Suffering Servant, they did at least see him and his suffering as somehow instrumental in the completion of what deliverance means for God.

In some ways chs. 56–66 are a puzzle. Ch. 55 ends on a high note of exultation over God's deliverance from both captivity and sin. We have talked of the basis, the motive, and the means of servanthood. What more is left? Is not this segment just something tacked onto previous writings and tacked on in a rather loose way? Hardly. Once again ch. 6 gives us the clue. Why is Isaiah delivered from his uncleanness? So that he can revel in his deliverance? No, so that he can speak for God; so that he can, in fact, be God's servant in considerably less than ideal circumstances. So

his servants. This accords well with the motivating purpose of the segment. In the next segment (chs. 49–55) the ideal Servant is more prominent, for there the question is asked, "How can sinful people become servants?" The answer is, of course, "through the ministry of the Servant."

it is for Israel. It is one thing to be delivered from Babylon and to recognize, however dimly, that God has in store a means of delivering from sin more effectual than bulls and goats. It is another thing altogether to live this out in the presence of the nations on the stage of history. Yet that living out, that becoming a pure vessel through whom God's light could shine, was what deliverance was all about. This theme is what chs. 56–66 address. Particularly they stress the contrasting themes of human inability and divine ability. Chs. 56–59 place most stress upon the former while chs. 60–66 emphasize the latter more heavily. In the first segment mere legalistic righteousness is shown not to be what God has in mind for his servants (56:1–8; 58:1–14). Rather, God's character must infuse every part of the life, manifesting itself in devotion and justice. Ultimately, as in deliverance, this is only possible through God's power as manifested through his Spirit (57:14–21; 59:16–21).

The final segment, and the climactic one of the book, continues these thoughts but presents them with reversed emphasis. Here God's ability to glorify his people in the presence of the world is stressed. Those who once had sought their own glory (9:8–9 [Eng. 9–10], etc.), or those who had been seduced by the glory of the nations (30:1–5, etc.), may look to that day when God, the only true source of glory, will share his with human beings (60:7, 9, 13, 19; 62:2; 66:19). God will vindicate his servants in the sight of their oppressors (65:8–16). He will bring all things to fulfillment (65:17–25). Nonetheless, it is God who will do this; human might and righteousness are not sufficient (63:1–65:7). We are his servants not because we grow slowly nearer perfection; we are his servants as we make a radical renunciation of our selfish efforts and allow him greater and greater room to work through us.

Perhaps better than any other single biblical book, this one reveals the name and the nature of the God who invites us to be his servants. He is holy, he is just, he is steadfast love. He is glorious, he is terrible, he dwells with the lowly and contrite. He is faithful, he is forgiving, he demands perfection. He is passionate, both in loving right and hating evil. He calls us to lay aside our independence and trust in him, for he has chosen us and redeemed us in Christ and will empower us to be like himself.

Outline

I. Introduction to the Prophecy: The Present and Future of God's People (1:1–5:30)

ANALYSIS OF CONTENTS

A. God's Denunciation, Appeal, and Promise (1:1–31)
1. Superscription (1:1)
2. Israel's Condition (1:2–9)
3. God's Desire: Justice, Not Hypocritical Worship (1:10–20)
a. The folly of empty cult (1:10–17)
b. The wisdom of obedience (1:18–20)
4. God's Response to Present Realities (1:21–31)
a. The announcement of judgment (1:21–26)
b. The fate of the wicked (1:27–31)
B. The Problem: What Israel Is versus What She Will Be (2:1–4:6)
1. The Destiny of the House of Jacob (2:1–5)
2. The House of Jacob Forsaken (2:6–4:1)
a. Trusting in mankind (2:6–22)
(1) Full, but empty (2:6–11)
(2) High, but low (2:12–17)
(3) Reduced to the caves (2:18–22)
b. The folly of human dependence (3:1–4:1)
(1) Boys for men (3:1–7)
(2) Rapine for leadership (3:8–15)
(3) Shame for beauty (3:16–4:1)
3. Israel Restored (4:2–6)
C. A Harvest of Wild Grapes (5:1–30)
1. The Song of the Vineyard (5:1–7)
2. Woe to the Wild Grapes (5:8–25)
a. Greed and indulgence (5:8–17)
b. Cynicism and perversion (5:18–25)
3. Coming Destruction (5:26–30)

II. A Call to Servanthood (6:1–13)
A. The Vision (6:1–8)
B. The Commission (6:9–13)

III. Whom Shall We Trust? Basis for Servanthood (7:1–39:8)
A. God or Assyria? No Trust (7:1–12:6)
1. Children, Signs of God's Presence (7:1–9:6 [Eng. 9:7])
a. Will you believe (Shear-jashub)? (7:1–9)
b. God is with us (7:10–8:10)
(1) The sign of Immanuel (7:10–17)
(2) The razor of Assyria (7:18–25)
(3) The sign of Maher-shalal-hash-baz (8:1–4)
(4) Assyria at the flood, yet God is with us (8:5–10)
c. Our way—darkness; his way—light (8:11–9:6 [Eng. 9:7])
(1) Pay attention to God (8:11–8:23 [Eng. 9:1])
(2) Unto us a child is born (9:1–6 [Eng. 2–7])
2. Measured by God's Standards (9:7 [Eng. 8]–10:4)
a. Ephraim's pride (9:7–11 [Eng. 8–12])
b. Leaders who mislead (9:12–16 [Eng. 13–17])
c. Loss of brotherhood (9:17–20 [Eng. 18–21])
d. Oppression of the helpless (10:1–4)

61

3. Hope Despite Destruction (10:5–11:16)
    a. The destroyer destroyed (10:5–34)
        (1) Assyria, God's tool (10:5–11)
        (2) Assyria under judgment (10:12–19)
        (3) Restoration promised (10:20–27)
        (4) Assyria leashed (10:28–34)
    b. The Shoot from Jesse (11:1–16)
        (1) The Prince of Peace (11:1–9)
        (2) The promised return (11:10–16)
4. The Song of Trust (12:1–6)
B. God: Master of the Nations (13:1–35:10)
  1. God's Judgment on the Nations (13:1–23:18)
    a. Judgment on the Mesopotamian powers (13:1–14:27)
        (1) Introduction: God's destruction of human pride (13:1–18)
           (a) Mustering God's army (13:1–5)
           (b) The day of the Lord against the proud (13:6–18)
        (2) The destruction of Babylon (13:19–22)
        (3) Downfall of the king of Babylon (14:1–23)
           (a) Promised deliverance (14:1–4a)
           (b) The song (14:4b–21)
               (i)   Peace on earth and turmoil in Sheol (14:4b–11)
               (ii) Fallen from heaven, cast out on earth (14:12–21)
           (c) The Lord's promise (14:22–23)
        (4) The Lord's plan for Assyria (14:24–27)
    b. Judgment upon Judah's neighbors (14:28–17:11)
        (1) The Philistines (14:28–32)
        (2) The Moabites (15:1–16:14)
           (a) Lament (15:1–9)
           (b) Response (16:1–14)
               (i)   Plea for mercy (16:1–5)
               (ii) The fall of Moab's proud vines (16:6–12)
               (iii) Within three years (16:13–14)
        (3) Syria and Ephraim (17:1–11)
           (a) Desolate ruins (17:1–6)
           (b) They have forgotten God (17:7–11)
    c. Judgment on all nations (17:12–18:7)
        (1) Roaring, but chaff (17:12–14)
        (2) God's message (18:1–7)
    d. Judgment on Egypt (19:1–20:6)
        (1) Egypt has nothing to offer (19:1–24)
           (a) Egypt's might confounded (19:1–15)
           (b) Egypt will come to Judah (19:16–25)
        (2) The folly of trusting Egypt (20:1–6)
    e. Judgment on Babylon and her allies (21:1–22:25)
        (1) Babylon (21:1–10)
        (2) Dumah (21:11–12)
        (3) Arabia (21:13–17)
        (4) Jerusalem (22:1–25)
           (a) The valley of vision (22:1–14)

XI. SELECT BIBLIOGRAPHY

P. Ackroyd, "Isaiah I–XII: Presentation of a Prophet," *VTSup* 29 (1978) 16–48.
————, "Interpretation of the Babylonian Exile: A Study of 2 Kings 20, Isaiah 38–39," *SJT* 27 (1974) 329–352.
L. L. Adams and A. C. Pencher, "The Popular Critical View of the Isaiah Problem in Light of Statistical Style Analysis," *Computer Studies* 4 (1973) 149–157.
B. Albrektson, *History and the Gods*. ConBOT 1. Lund: Gleerup, 1967.
W. F. Albright, *Archeology and the Religion of Israel*. 5th ed. Garden City: Doubleday, 1968.
————, "The Chronology of the Divided Monarchy of Israel," *BASOR* 100 (Dec. 1945) 16–22.
————, "The High Place in Ancient Palestine," *VTSup* 4 (1957) 242–258.
————, "The Son of Tabeel (Isaiah 7:6)," *BASOR* 140 (Dec. 1955) 34–35.
J. A. Alexander, *Commentary on the Prophecies of Isaiah*. New York: Scribner's, 1846.
O. T. Allis, *The Unity of Isaiah: A Study in Prophecy*. Philadelphia: Presbyterian and Reformed, 1950.
A. Alt, *Kleine Schriften zur Geschichte des Volkes Israel*, II. Munich: Beck'sche, 1953.
S. Amsler and O. Mury, "Yahweh et la sagesse du paysan. Quelques remarques sur Esaie 28, 23–29," *RHPR* 53 (1973) 1–5.
B. W. Anderson and W. Harrelson, eds., *Israel's Prophetic Heritage: Essays in Honor of James Muilenburg*. New York: Harper & Row, 1962.
G. W. Anderson, "Isaiah 24–27 Reconsidered," *VTSup* 9 (1963) 118–126.
R. T. Anderson, "Was Isaiah a Scribe?" *JBL* 79 (1950) 57–58.
N. Avigad, "The Epitaph of a Royal Steward from Siloam Village," *IEJ* 3 (1953) 137–152.
A. Barnes, *Notes on Isaiah*. 2 vols. Repr. Grand Rapids: Baker, 1980.
H. Barth, *Die Jesaja-Worte in der Josiazeit*. WMANT 48. Neukirchen-Vluyn: Neukirchener, 1977.
J. Begrich, *Der Psalm des Hiskia*. Göttingen: Vandenhoeck & Ruprecht, 1926.
A. Bentzen, *Jesaja, I, Jes. 1–39*. Copenhagen: Gad, 1944.
————, *King and Messiah*. London: Lutterworth, 1955.
G. R. Berry, "Messianic Predictions," *JBL* 45 (1926) 232–37.

S. H. Blank, *Prophetic Faith in Isaiah*. New York: Harper & Row; London: Adam & Charles Black, 1958.

————, "The Current Misinterpretation of Isaiah's *She'ar Yashub*," *JBL* 67 (1948) 211–15.

G. J. Botterweck and H. Ringgren, eds., *Theological Dictionary of the Old Testament*, I–. Tr. D. E. Green, et al. Grand Rapids: Eerdmans, 1974–.

C. Boutflower, *The Book of Isaiah, Chapters I–XXXIX in the Light of the Monuments*. London: SPCK, 1930.

C. A. Briggs, *Messianic Prophecy*. New York: Scribner's, 1886.

J. Bright, *A History of Israel*. 3rd ed. Philadelphia: Westminster, 1981.

C. Brockelmann, *Hebräische Syntax*. Neukirchen: Verlag der Buchhandlung des Erziehungsvereins, 1956.

G. W. Bromiley, et al., eds., *The International Standard Bible Encyclopedia*. 4 vols. Rev. ed. Grand Rapids: Eerdmans, 1979–.

F. Brown, S. R. Driver, and C. A. Briggs, *A Hebrew and English Lexicon of the Old Testament*. Repr. Oxford: Clarendon, 1959.

W. Brownlee, *The Meaning of the Qumrân Scrolls for the Bible*. New York: Oxford, 1964.

D. A. Bruno, *Jesaja, eine rhythmische und textkritische Untersuchung*. Stockholm: Almquist och Wiksell, 1953.

J. Buda, *De origine Isaiae 36–39*. Bansha Bystrica: Machold, 1937.

K. Budde, "Jesaja 13," in *Abhundlungen zur semitischen Religionskunde und Sprachwissenschaft*. Festschrift F. F. Graf von Baudissin. Ed. W. Frankenberg and F. Küchler. BZAW 33. Berlin: Töpelmann, 1918. Pp. 55–70.

M. Burrows, J. Trever, and W. H. Brownlee, *The Dead Sea Scrolls of St. Mark's Monastery, I: The Isaiah Manuscript and the Habakkuk Commentary*. New Haven: American Schools of Oriental Research, 1950.

M. Burrows, "Variant Readings in the Isaiah Manuscript," *BASOR* 111 (Oct. 1948) 16–24; 113 (Apr. 1949) 24–32.

G. A. Buttrick, et al., eds., *The Interpreter's Bible*. 12 vols. Nashville: Abingdon, 1952–1957.

G. A. Buttrick, et al., eds., *The Interpreter's Dictionary of the Bible*. 4 vols. Nashville: Abingdon, 1962. *Supplementary Volume*, ed. K. Crim, et al., 1976.

J. Calvin, *Commentary on the Book of the Prophet Isaiah*. 4 vols. Tr. W. Pringle. Repr. Grand Rapids: Eerdmans, 1948.

R. A. Carlson, "The Anti-Assyrian Character of the Oracle in Is. ix 1–6," *VT* 24 (1974) 130–35.

R. P. Carroll, *When Prophecy Failed: Cognitive Dissonance in the Prophetic Traditions of the Old Testament*. New York: Seabury, 1979.

————, "Inner Tradition Shifts in Meaning in Isaiah 1–11," *ExpTim* 89 (1978) 301–304.

C. P. Caspari, *Jesajanische Studien*. Leipzig: 1843.

W. Caspari, "Jesaja 34 and 35," *ZAW* 49 (1931) 67–86.

T. K. Cheyne, *The Prophecies of Isaiah*. 3rd ed. 2 vols. New York: Whittaker, 1895.

B. S. Childs, *Introduction to the Old Testament as Scripture*. Philadelphia: Fortress, 1979.

————, *Isaiah and the Assyrian Crisis*. SBT 2/3. London: SCM; Naperville: Allenson, 1967.

————, *Myth and Reality in the Old Testament.* SBT 1/27. London: SCM; Naperville: Allenson, 1960.

P. Churgin, *Targum Jonathan to the Prophets.* Yale Oriental Series 14. New Haven: Yale, 1927. Repr. with L. Smolar and M. Aberbach, *Studies in Targum Jonathan to the Prophets.* New York: KTAV, 1983. Pp. 229–380.

R. E. Clements, *Isaiah 1–39.* NCBC. London: Marshall, Morgan & Scott; Grand Rapids: Eerdmans, 1980.

————, *Isaiah and the Deliverance of Jerusalem: A Study in the Interpretation of Prophecy in the Old Testament.* JSOTSup 13. Sheffield: JSOT, 1980.

————, "The Prophecies of Isaiah and the Fall of Jerusalem in 587 B.C.," *VT* 30 (1980) 421–36.

A. Condamin, *Le Livre d'Isaïe: Traduction critique avec notes et commentaire.* Etudes Bibliques. Paris: Lecoffre, 1905.

J. Coppens, *La Prophétie de la 'Almah.* Analecta lovaniensia biblica et orientalia, II/35. Louvain: 1952.

M. G. Cordero, "El Santo de Israel," *Mélanges Bibliques rédigés en l'honneur de André Robert.* Paris: Bloud et Gay, 1957.

P. C. Craigie, "Helel, Athtar and Phaethon (Jes 14:12–15)," *ZAW* 85 (1973) 223–25.

M. Dahood, *Proverbs and Northwest Semitic Philology.* Rome: Pontifical Biblical Institute, 1963.

————, "Some Ambiguous Texts in Isaias (30, 15; 52, 2; 33, 2; 40, 5; 45, 1)," *CBQ* 20 (1958) 41–49.

————, "Textual Problems in Isaia," *CBQ* 22 (1960) 400–409.

————, *Ugaritic-Hebrew Philology.* BibOr 17. Rome: Pontifical Biblical Institute, 1965.

G. Dalman, *Jerusalem und seine Gelände.* Gütersloh: Mohn, 1930.

J. D. Davis, "The Child Whose Name is Wonderful," *Biblical and Theological Studies.* Princeton Centenary Volume. New York: Scribner's, 1912.

————, "Medeba or the Waters of Rabbah," *PTR* 20 (1922) 305–310.

L. Delekat, "Die Peschitta zu Jesaja zwischen Targum und Septuaginta," *Bib* 38 (1957) 185–199.

F. Delitzsch, *Commentary on the Old Testament, VII: Isaiah.* Tr. J. Martin. Repr. Grand Rapids: Eerdmans, 1973.

R. R. Deutsch, *Die Hiskiaerzahlungen: Eine Formgeschichtliche Untersuchung der Texte Jes. 36–39 und 2 Reg. 18–20.* Basel: Basileia Verlag, 1969.

A. Dillmann, *Der Prophet Jesaia.* KHAT. Leipzig: 1890.

J. C. Döderlein, *Esaias.* Altsofi: 1825.

M. Drechsler, *Der Prophet Jesaja.* Stuttgart: 1849.

G. R. Driver, *Canaanite Myths and Legends.* Edinburgh: T. & T. Clark, 1956.

————, "Isaiah 1–39: Textual and Linguistic Problems," *JSS* 13 (1968) 36–57.

————, "Linguistic and Textual Problems, Isaiah 1–39," *JTS* 38 (1937) 36–50.

————, "Notes on Isaiah," in *Von Ugarit nach Qumran: Beiträge zur alttestamentlichen und altorientalischen Forschung.* BZAW 77. Festschrift O. Eissfeldt. Ed. J. Hempel and L. Rost. Berlin: Töpelmann, 1961. Pp. 42–48.

S. R. Driver, *Isaiah: His Life and Times.* 2nd ed. London: 1897.

————, *A Treatise on the Use of Tenses in Hebrew.* 3rd ed. Oxford: Clarendon, 1892.

B. Duhm, *Das Buch Jesaja.* HKAT. Göttingen: Vandenhoeck & Ruprecht, 1892.

67

J. Eaton, "The Origin of the Book of Isaiah," *VT* 9 (1959) 138–157.

W. Eichrodt, *Der Heilige in Israel. Jesaja 1–12.* BAT. Stuttgart: Calwer, 1960.

————, *Der Herr der Geschichte. Jesaja 13–23 und 28–39.* BAT. Stuttgart: Calwer, 1967.

O. Eissfeldt, *The Old Testament: An Introduction.* Tr. P. Ackroyd. New York: Harper & Row, 1965.

I. Eitan, "A Contribution to Isaiah Exegesis," *HUCA* 12–13 (1937–1938) 55–88.

K. Elliger and W. Rudolph, eds., *Biblia Hebraica Stuttgartensia.* Stuttgart: Deutsche Bibelstiftung, 1967–1977.

I. Engnell, *The Call of Isaiah: An Exegetical and Comparative Study.* UUA 4. Uppsala: Lundequistska, 1949.

————, *Studies in Divine Kingship in the Ancient Near East.* Uppsala: Uppsala University, 1943.

S. Erlandsson, *The Burden of Babylon: A Study of Isaiah 13:2–14:23.* ConBOT 4. Lund: Gleerup, 1970.

G. H. A. von Ewald, *Prophets of the Old Testament.* 5 vols. Tr. J. F. Smith. London: Williams and Norgate, 1875–1881.

F. Feldmann, *Das Buch Isaias übersetz und erklärt.* 2 vols. EHAT. Münster: Aschendorf, 1926.

L. Finkelstein, *The Commentary of David Kimchi on Isaiah.* New York: Columbia University, 1926.

J. Fischer, *Das Buch Isaias übersetzt und erklärt.* 2 vols. HSAT. Bonn: Hanstein, 1937–1939.

L. R. Fisher, ed., *Ras Shamra Parallels.* 2 vols. Rome: Pontifical Biblical Institute, 1968–1973.

J. A. Fitzmyer, *The Aramaic Inscriptions of Sefire.* BibOr 19. Rome: Pontifical Biblical Institute, 1967.

W. B. Fleming, *The History of Tyre.* New York: AMS, 1915.

G. Fohrer, *Das Buch Jesaja.* ZBK. 2 vols. Zürich/Stuttgart: Zwingli, 1960–1967.

————, "Der aufbau der Apokalypse des Jesajabuchs," *CBQ* 25 (1963) 34–45.

————, "The Origin, Composition and Tradition of Isaiah 1–39," *ALUOS* 3 (1963) 3–38.

H. Frankfort, *Kingship and the Gods.* Chicago: University of Chicago, 1948.

A. Friedrichsen, *Hagios-Qadosh.* Oslo: 1916.

S. B. Frost, *Old Testament Apocalyptic.* London: Epworth, 1952.

K. Fullerton, "Isaiah 14:28–32," *AJSL* 42 (1925–1926) 86–109.

————, "The Problem of Isaiah, Chapter 10," *AJSL* 34 (1917–1918) 170–184.

C. J. Gadd, *Ideas of the Divine Rule in the Ancient East.* London: Oxford, 1948.

O. H. Gates, "Notes on Isaiah 1:18b and 7:14b–16," *AJSL* 17 (1900–1901) 16–21.

E. Gerstenberger, "The Woe-Oracles of the Prophets," *JBL* 81 (1962) 249–263.

W. Gesenius, *Commentar über der Prophet Jesaia.* Leipzig: 1821.

————, *Gesenius' Hebrew Grammar.* Tr. E. Kautzsch. Ed. A. Cowley. 2nd ed. Oxford: Clarendon, 1910.

S. Gevirtz, "West-Semitic curses and the problem of the origins of Hebrew law," *VT* 11 (1961) 137–158.

H. L. Ginsberg, "Reflexes of Sargon in Isaiah after 715 BCE," *JAOS* 88 (1968) 47–53.

————, "Some Emendations in Isaiah," *JBL* 69 (1950) 51–60.

BIBLIOGRAPHY

————, "Introduction," in *The Book of Isaiah*. Philadelphia: Jewish Publication Society, 1972. Pp. 9–24.

C. H. Gordon, " *'Almah'* in Isaiah 7:14," *JBR* 21 (1953) 106.

————, "Belt Wrestling in the Bible World," *HUCA* 23 (1950–1951) 131–36.

————, "Homer and the Bible," *HUCA* 26 (1955) 43–108.

————, *The World of the Old Testament*. Garden City: Doubleday, 1958.

————, *Ugaritic Literature*. Rome: Pontifical Biblical Institute, 1949.

————, *Ugaritic Textbook*. 3 vols. AnOr 38. Rome: Pontifical Biblical Institute, 1965.

N. W. Gottwald, "Immanuel as the Prophet's Son," *VT* 8 (1958) 36–47.

D. Gowan, *When Man Becomes God. Humanism and Hubris in the Old Testament*. Pittsburgh: Pickwick, 1975.

G. B. Gray, *A Critical and Exegetical Commentary on the Book of Isaiah I–XXVII*. ICC. Edinburgh: T. & T. Clark, 1912.

J. Gray, "Canaanite Kingship in Theory and Practice," *VT* 11 (1961) 193–220.

M. Greenberg, "The Stabilization of the Text of the Hebrew Bible," *JAOS* 76 (1956) 157–167.

H. Gressmann, *Altorientalische Texte zum Alten Testament*. Berlin: de Gruyter, 1909.

A. Guillaume, "Some Readings in The Dead Sea Scroll of Isaiah," *JBL* 76 (1956) 40–43.

H. Gunkel, "Einleitungen," in *Die Schriften des Alten Testaments*. Göttingen: 1921.

————, "Jesaja 32 eine prophetische Liturgie," *ZAW* 42 (1924) 177–208.

H. Guthe and O. Eissfeldt, *Jesaja*. HSAT. Bonn: Hanstein, 1922.

E. Hammerschaimb, "The Immanuel Sign," *ST* 3 (1949–1951) 321–339.

J. Hanel, *Die Religion der Heiligkeit*. Gütersloh: Bertelsmann, 1931.

P. Hanson, *The Dawn of Apocalyptic*. Philadelphia: Fortress, 1975.

R. Harris, et al., eds., *Theological Wordbook of the Old Testament*. 2 vols. Chicago: Moody, 1980.

R. K. Harrison, *Introduction to the Old Testament*. Grand Rapids: Eerdmans, 1969.

G. Hasel, *The Remnant. The History and Theology of the Remnant Idea from Genesis to Isaiah*. 2nd ed. Andrews University Monographs 5. Berrien Springs, Mich.: Andrews University, 1975.

J. H. Hayes, "The Usage of Oracles Against Foreign Nations in Ancient Israel," *JBL* 87 (1968) 81–92.

W. A. Heidel, *The Day of Jahweh*. 1929.

E. Henderson, *The Book of the Prophet Isaiah*. London: Hamilton, Adams, 1840.

V. Herntrich, *Der Prophet Jesaja*. Göttingen: Vandenhoeck & Ruprecht, 1957.

H. W. Hertzberg, *Der erste Jesaja*. Kassel: Oncken, 1952.

A. J. Heschel, *The Prophets*. New York: Harper & Row, 1962.

D. R. Hillers, *Covenant: The History of a Biblical Idea*. Baltimore: Johns Hopkins, 1969.

————, *Treaty-Curses and the Old Testament Prophets*. BibOr 16. Rome: Pontifical Biblical Institute, 1964.

P. K. Hitti, *History of Syria*. New York: Macmillan, 1951.

F. Hitzig, *Der Prophet Jesaja, übersetzt und ausgelegt*. Heidelberg: 1833.

W. L. Holladay, *Isaiah: Scroll of a Prophetic Heritage*. Grand Rapids: Eerdmans, 1978.

V. Holmgren, *Bird Walk Through the Bible*. New York: Seabury, 1972.

G. Hölscher, *Die Profeten*. Leipzig: Hinrichs, 1914.

————, *Die Ursprunge der judischen Eschatologie*. Giessen: Töpelmann, 1925.

L. Honor, *Sennacherib's Invasion of Palestine*. New York: Columbia University, 1926.

A. Van Hoonacker, *Het Boek Isaias*. Brugge: Sinte Katharina Druk, 1932.

H. B. Huffmon, "The Covenant Lawsuit in the Prophets," *JBL* 78 (1959) 285–295.

H. D. Hummel, "Enclitic *Mem* in Early Northwest Semitic, Especially Hebrew," *JBL* 76 (1957) 85–107.

H. Hvidberg, "The Masseba and the Holy Seed," in *Interpretationes ad Vetus Testamentum Pertinentes*. Festschrift S. Mowinckel. Ed. A. Kapelrud. Oslo: Land og Kirche, 1955. Pp. 97–99 (*=NorTT* 56).

J. P. Hyatt, *Prophetic Religion*. New York: Abingdon, 1947.

W. A. Irwin, "The Attitude of Isaiah in the Crisis of 701," *JR* 16 (1936) 406–418.

W. H. Irwin, *Isaiah 28–33: Translation with Philological Notes*. BibOr 30. Rome: Pontifical Biblical Institute, 1977.

————, "Syntax and Style in Isaiah 26," *CBQ* 41 (1979) 240–261.

S. Iwry, "*Maṣṣēbā* and *Bāmāh* in IQ Isaiah^A 6, 13," *JBL* 76 (1957) 225–232.

E. Jacob, *Theology of the Old Testament*. Tr. A. W. Heathcote and P. J. Allcock. New York: Harper & Row, 1958.

E. Jenni, "Jesajas Berufung in der neuern Forschung," *TZ* 15 (1959) 321–339.

F. C. Jennings, *Studies in Isaiah*. Neptune, N.J.: Loizeaux, 1935.

J. Jensen, *The Use of tôrâ by Isaiah: His Debate with the Wisdom Tradition*. CBQMS 3. Washington, D.C.: Catholic Biblical Association, 1973.

A. R. Johnson, *Sacral Kingship in Ancient Israel*. Cardiff: University of Wales, 1955.

D. R. Jones, "Exposition of Isaiah Chapter One verses Eighteen to Twenty," *SJT* 19 (1966) 318–327.

O. Kaiser, *Introduction to the Old Testament*. Tr. J. Sturdy. Minneapolis: Augsburg, 1975.

————, *Isaiah 1–12: A Commentary*. OTL. 2nd ed. Tr. J. Bowden. Philadelphia: Westminster, 1983.

————, *Isaiah 13–39: A Commentary*. OTL. Tr. J. Bowden, Philadelphia: Westminster, 1974.

————, "Die Verkündigung des Propheten Jesaja im Jahre 701," *ZAW* 81 (1969) 304–315.

M. M. Kaplan, "Isaiah 6:1–11," *JBL* 45 (1926) 251–59.

Y. Kaufmann, "Biblical and Mythological Polytheism," *JBL* 70 (1951) 179–197.

————, *The Religion of Israel*. Tr. and abridged by M. Greenberg. Chicago: University of Chicago, 1960.

C. Keil and F. Delitzsch, *Commentary on the Old Testament*. 10 vols. Tr. J. Martin, et al. Repr. Grand Rapids: Eerdmans, 1973–.

P. K. Keizer, *De profeet Jesaja*. Kampen: Kok, 1947.

E. J. Kissane, *The Book of Isaiah*. Dublin: Bowne and Nolan, 1926.

G. Kittel and G. Friedrich, eds., *Theological Dictionary of the New Testament*. 10 vols. Tr. and ed. G. W. Bromiley. Grand Rapids: Eerdmans, 1964–1976.

R. Kittel, ed., *Biblia Hebraica*. 3rd ed. Stuttgart: Württembergische Bibelanstalt, 1937.

M. Kline, *Treaty of the Great King*. Grand Rapids: Eerdmans, 1963.

R. Knierim, "The Vocation of Isaiah," *VT* 18 (1968) 47–68.

A. W. Knobel, *Der Prophet Jesaja*. 4th ed. Leipzig: S. Hertzel, 1898.

BIBLIOGRAPHY

L. Koehler and W. Baumgartner, *Lexicon in veteris testamenti libros*. Leiden: Brill, 1958.

E. König, *Das Buch Jesaja eingeleitet, übersetzt und erklärt*. Gütersloh: Bertelsmann, 1926.

H. Kosmala, "Form and Structure in Ancient Hebrew Poetry," *VT* 16 (1966) 152–180.

E. G. Kraeling, "The Immanuel Prophecy," *JBL* 50 (1931) 277–297.

J. Kroeker, *Jesaia der ältere (Cap. 1–35)*. Berlin: Acker-Verlag, 1934.

R. Lack, *La Symbolique du Livre d'Isaïe: Essai sur l'image littéraire comme élément de structuralisme*. AnBib 59. Rome: Pontifical Biblical Institute, 1973.

G. E. Ladd, "Apocalyptic, Apocalypse," *Baker's Dictionary of Theology*. Ed. E. F. Harrison, et al. Grand Rapids: Baker, 1960. Pp. 50–54.

M. J. Lagrange, "Apocalypse d'Isaie (xxiv–xxvii)," *RB* 3 (1894) 200–231.

R. Lapointe, "Divine Monologue as a Channel of Revelation," *CBQ* 32 (1970) 161–181.

T. Lescow, "Das Geburtsmotive in den messianischen Weissagungen bei Jesaja und Micha," *ZAW* 79 (1967) 172–207.

H. Leupold, *Exposition of Isaiah*. 2 vols. Grand Rapids: Baker, 1963–1971.

E. Liebmann, "Der Text zu Jesaja 24–27," *ZAW* 22 (1902) 1–56, 285–304; 23 (1903) 209–286; 24 (1904) 51–104; 25 (1905) 145–171.

L. J. Liebreich, "The Position of Chapter Six in the Book of Isaiah," *HUCA* 25 (1954) 37–40.

J. Lindblom, "Der Ausspruch über Tyrus in Jes 23," *ASTI* 4 (1975) 56–73.

———, *Prophecy in Ancient Israel*. Oxford: Blackwell; Philadelphia: Fortress, 1962.

———, *A Study on the Immanuel Section in Isaiah, Isa 7, 1–9, 6*. Lund: Gleerup, 1958.

R. Lowth, *Isaia*. 1779. *Isaiah: A New Translation*. 2 vols. London: T. Caldell, 1824. 10th ed. 1834.

D. Luckenbill, ed., *Ancient Records of Assyria and Babylonia*. 2 vols. Chicago: University of Chicago, 1926–1927.

M. Luther, *Lectures on Isaiah: Chapters 1–39*. Vol. 16 of *Luther's Works*. Ed. J. Pelikan, et al. St. Louis: Concordia, 1969.

S. D. Luzzatto, *Il Profeta Isaia volgarizzate e commentato ad uso degl' Israeliti*. Padua: 1855.

J. G. Machen, *The Virgin Birth of Christ*. 2nd ed. London: Clarke & Co., 1930.

A. A. Macintosh, *Isaiah XXI: A Palimpsest*. Cambridge: Cambridge University, 1980.

J. W. McKay, "Helel and the Dawn-goddess: A Re-examination of the Myth in Isaiah 14:12–15," *VT* 20 (1970) 451–464.

R. Margalioth (Margulies), *The Indivisible Isaiah: Evidence for the Single Authorship of the Prophetic Book*. New York: Yeshiva University, 1964.

K. Marti, *Das Buch Jesaja erklärt*. KHCAT 10. Tübingen: Mohr, 1900.

R. Martin-Achard, "L'oracle contre Shebnâ et le pouvoir des clefs, Es 15 22, 15–25," *TZ* 24 (1968) 241–254.

J. Mauchline, *Isaiah 1–39: Introduction and Commentary*. Torch. London: SCM, 1962.

E. Meyer, *Der Prophet Jesaja erklärt*. Pforzheim: 1850.

J. H. Michaelis, *Hebrew Bible with annotations*. 1720.

D. Michel, "Studien zu den sogenannten Thronbesteigungpsalmen," *VT* 6 (1956) 40–68.

W. Millar, *Isaiah 24–27 and the Origin of Apocalyptic.* HSM 11. Missoula: Scholars, 1976.

M. S. and J. L. Miller, *Harper's Encyclopedia of Bible Life.* 3rd ed. San Francisco: Harper & Row, 1978.

W. Möller, *Die messianische Erwartung der vorexilischen Propheten.* Gütersloh: Bertelsmann, 1906.

S. Mowinckel, *He That Cometh.* Tr. G. W. Anderson. Nashville: Abingdon, 1954.

————, *Jesaja Disciplinen.* Oslo: Ascheboog, 1926.

————, *The Old Testament as Word of God.* Tr. R. B. Bjornard. New York: Abingdon, 1959.

————, *Psalmenstudien, II. Das Thronbesteigungsfest Jahwäs und der Ursprung der Eschatologie.* Kristiana: Dybwad, 1922.

————, *The Psalms in Israel's Worship.* 2 vols. Tr. D. R. Ap-Thomas. Nashville: Abingdon, 1962.

J. Muilenburg, "The Literary Character of Isaiah 34," *JBL* 59 (1940) 339–365.

P. A. Munch, *The Expression bajjôm hāhū. Is it an Eschatological Terminus Technicus?* ANVAO. Oslo: 1936.

C. W. E. Nägelsbach, *The Prophet Isaiah.* Tr. S. T. Lowrie and D. Moore. Edinburgh: T. & T. Clark, 1878.

C. R. North, *The Suffering Servant in Deutero-Isaiah: An Historical and Critical Study.* Oxford: Oxford University, 1948.

M. Noth, *History of Israel.* Tr. P. R. Ackroyd. New York: Harper & Row, 1958.

F. Nötscher, "Entbehrliche Hapaxlegomena in Jesaia," *VT* 1 (1951) 299–302.

H. S. Nyberg, "Hiskias Danklied Jes 38, 9–20," *ASTI* 9 (1973) 85–97.

A. T. Olmstead, *History of Assyria.* Chicago: University of Chicago, 1923.

C. von Orelli, *The Prophecies of Isaiah.* Tr. J. S. Banks. Edinburgh: T. & T. Clark, 1889.

H. M. Orlinsky, "Studies in the St. Mark's Isaiah Scroll I," *JBL* 69 (1950) 149–166.

————, "Studies in the St. Mark's Isaiah Scroll II: Massoretic Yiswahu in 42.11," *JNES* 2 (1952) 153–56.

————, "Studies in the St. Mark's Isaiah Scroll, III," *JJS* 2 (1951) 151–54.

————, "Studies in the St. Mark's Isaiah Scroll, IV," *JQR* 43 (1952) 329–340.

————, "Studies in the St. Mark's Isaiah Scroll V," *IEJ* 4 (1954) 5–8.

————, "Studies in the St. Mark's Isaiah Scroll VI," *HUCA* 25 (1954) 85–92.

————, "The Treatment of Anthropomorphisms and Anthropopathisms in the Septuagint of Isaiah," *HUCA* 27 (1956) 193–200.

A. E. Osborn, "Divine Destiny and Human Failure, Isaiah 2," *Biblical Review* 17 (1932) 244–48.

J. N. Oswalt, "The Golden Calves and the Egyptian Concept of Deity," *EvQ* 45 (1973) 13–20.

————, "The Myth of the Dragon and Old Testament Faith," *EvQ* 49 (1977) 163–172.

————, "Recent Studies in Old Testament Eschatology and Apocalyptic," *JETS* 24 (1981) 289–301.

R. R. Ottley, *The Book of Isaiah According to the Septuagint.* 2 vols. London: Clay and Sons, 1904–1906.

S. A. Pallis, *The Babylonian 'akitu' Festival*. Copenhagen: Bianco Lunos Bogtrykkeri, 1926.

J. B. Payne, "The Unity of Isaiah: Evidence from Chapters 36–39," *Bulletin of the Evangelical Theological Society* 6/2 (1963) 50–56.

J. Pedersen, *Israel: Its Life and Culture*. 4 vols. repr. in 2. Copenhagen: Branner og Korch; London: Oxford University, 1963–1964.

A. Penna, *Isaia*. La Sacra Biblia. Torino: Marietta, 1958.

O. Pfeifer, "Entwöhnung und Entwöhnungsfest im AT: der Schüssel zu Jes 28, 7–13," *ZAW* 84 (1972) 341–47.

R. H. Pfeiffer, *Introduction to the Old Testament*. New York: Harper & Brothers, 1948.

O. Plöger, *Theocracy and Eschatology*. Tr. S. Rudman. Richmond: John Knox, 1968.

M. Pope, "Isaiah 34 in Relation to Isaiah 35 and 40–66," *JBL* 71 (1952) 234–243.

E. Power, "The Prophecy of Isaias against Moab (Is. 15.1–16.5)," *Bib* 13 (1932) 435–451.

J. B. Pritchard, ed., *Ancient Near Eastern Texts*. 3rd ed. Princeton: Princeton University, 1969.

J. B. Pritchard, ed., *The Ancient Near East in Pictures*. 2nd ed. Princeton: Princeton University, 1969.

O. Procksch, *Jesaja I–XXXIX*. KAT. Leipzig: Deichert, 1930.

Y. T. Radday, "Genesis, Wellhausen and the Computer," *ZAW* 94 (1982) 467–481.

————, *An Analytical Linguistic Concordance to the Book of Isaiah*. The Computer Bible. Ed. J. A. Baird and D. N. Freedman. Wooster, Ohio: Biblical Research Associates, 1971.

————, *The Unity of Isaiah in the Light of Statistical Linguistics*. Hildesheim: H. A. Gerstenberg, 1973.

A. Rahlfs, *Septuaginta, II*. Stuttgart: Württembergische Bibelanstalt, 1935.

H. G. Reventlow, "Das Amt des Mazkir," *TZ* (1959) 161–175.

J. Ridderbos, *Het Godswoord der Profeten, 2:Jesaja*. Kampen: Kok, 1932.

————, "Jahwah malak," *VT* 4 (1954) 87–89.

L. G. Rignell, "Isaiah, Chapter I," *ST* 11 (1957) 140–158.

————, "Das Immanuelszeichen; Einige Gesichtspunkte zu Jes. 7," *ST* 11 (1957) 99–119.

————, "Some Observations on Style and Structure in the Isaiah Apocalypse Is 24–27," *ASTI* 9 (1973) 107–115.

H. Ringgren, *The Messiah in the Old Testament*. SBT 1/18. London: SCM; Naperville: Allenson, 1956.

————, *The Prophetical Conception of Holiness*. Uppsala: Uppsala University, 1948.

J. R. Rosenbloom, *The Dead Sea Isaiah Scroll: A Literary Analysis*. Grand Rapids: Eerdmans, 1970.

J. M. Rosenthal, "Biblical Exegesis of 4QpIs," *JQR* 60 (1969) 27–36.

E. R. Rowland, "The Targum and the Peshitta Version of the Book of Isaiah," *VT* 9 (1959) 178–191.

H. H. Rowley, *The Relevance of Apocalyptic: A Study of Jewish and Christian Apocalypses from Daniel to Revelation*. Rev. ed. New York: Harper & Brothers, 1946.

————, *The Servant of the Lord and Other Essays on the Old Testament*. London: Lutterworth, 1952.

_____ , *The Zadokite Fragments and the Dead Sea Scrolls*. New York: Macmillan, 1952.

_____ , *The Faith of Israel*. Philadelphia: Westminster, 1956.

_____ , ed., *Studies in Old Testament Prophecy*. Festschrift T. H. Robinson. Edinburgh: T. & T. Clark, 1957.

W. Rudolph, "Jesaja 23, 1–14," *Festschrift Friedrich Baumgärtel*. Ed. J. Herrmann. Erlanger Forschungen 10. Erlangen: Universitätsbund, 1959.

_____ , "Jesaja 24–27," in *Beiträge zur Wissenschaft vom Alten und Neuen Testament*. Stuttgart: Kohlhammer, 1908.

S. Rummel, ed., *Ras Shamra Parallels*, III. Rome: Pontifical Biblical Institute, 1979.

H. W. F. Saggs, *The Encounter with the Divine in Mesopotamia and Israel*. London: Athlone, 1978.

_____ , *The Greatness That Was Babylon*. London: Sidgwick and Jackson, 1962.

_____ , "The Nimrud Letters," *Iraq* 21 (1959) 158–179.

S. P. Schilling, *Isaiah Speaks*. New York: Crowell, 1959.

W. H. Schmidt, "Wo hat die Aussage: Jahwe der Heilige ihren Ursprung?" *ZAW* 74 (1962) 62–66.

M. Scott, "Isaiah 7, 8," *ExpTim* 38 (1926–1927) 525–26.

R. B. Y. Scott, "Introduction and Exegesis of the Book of Isaiah, Chapters 1–39," *The Interpreter's Bible*, V. Ed. G. Buttrick, et al. Nashville: Abingdon, 1956. Pp. 156–381.

_____ , "Isaiah xxi:1–10; The Inside of a Prophet's Mind," *VT* 2 (1952) 278–282.

_____ , "The Literary Structure of Isaiah's Oracles," in *Studies in Old Testament Prophecy*. Festschrift T. H. Robinson. Ed. H. H. Rowley. Edinburgh: T. & T. Clark, 1950. Pp. 175–186.

_____ , "The Relation of Isaiah, Chapter 35, to Deutero-Isaiah," *AJSL* 52 (1935–1936) 178–191.

J. J. Scullion, "An Approach to the Understanding of Isaiah 7:10–17," *JBL* 87 (1968) 288–300.

I. L. Seeligmann, *The Septuagint Version of Isaiah: A Discussion of Its Problems*. Leiden: Brill, 1948.

E. Sellin, *Israelitische-judische Religionsgeschichte*. Leipzig: Quellen & Meyer, 1933.

P. Skehan, "Some Textual Problems in Isaiah," *CBQ* 22 (1960) 47–55.

J. Skinner, *The Book of the Prophet Isaiah*. Cambridge Bible. Cambridge: Cambridge University, 1925.

R. Smend, "Anmerkungen zu Jes. 24–27," *ZAW* 4 (1884) 161–224.

G. A. Smith, *The Book of Isaiah*. 2 vols. Rev. ed. Expositor's Bible. London: Hodder and Stoughton, 1927.

N. H. Snaith, "The Interpretation of El Gibbor in Isaiah 9:5 (EVV, 6)," *ExpTim* 52 (1940) 36–37.

_____ , *The Jewish New Year Festival*. London: SPCK, 1947.

O. H. Steck, "Beiträge zum Verständis von Jes 7. 10–17 and 8. 1–4," *TZ* 29 (1973) 161–178.

_____ , "Bemerkungen zu Jes 6," *BZ* 16 (1972) 188–206.

_____ , "Rettung und Verstockung: Exegetische Bemerkungen zu Jes 7. 3–9," *EvT* 33 (1973) 77–90.

J. Steinmann, *La Prophète Isaïe*. Paris: Cerf, 1950.

J. F. Stenning, *The Targum of Isaiah*. Oxford: Clarendon, 1949.

H. Tadmor, "The Campaigns of Sargon of Assur," *JCS* 12 (1958) 77–100.

S. Talmon, "DSIsa as a Witness to Ancient Exegesis of Isaiah," *ASTI* 1 (1962) 62–72 (repr. in *Qumran and the History of the Biblical Text*, ed. F. M. Cross and S. Talmon [Cambridge, MA: Harvard University, 1975], pp. 116–126).

E. F. Thiele, *The Mysterious Numbers of the Hebrew Kings*. Rev. ed. Grand Rapids: Eerdmans, 1965.

D. W. Thomas, ed., *Documents from Old Testament Times*. New York: Harper & Row, 1958.

C. C. Torrey, *The Second Isaiah: A New Interpretation*. New York: Scribner's, 1928.

R. Traina, *Methodical Bible Study*. New York: Biblical Seminary, 1952.

F. W. C. Umbreit, *Praktische Kommentaar op Jesaja*. Utrecht: Kemirk en Zoon, 1856.

J. C. Van Dorssen, *De Derivata van de stam 'mn in het Hebreeuwsch van het Oude Testament*. Amsterdam: 1951.

A. H. Van Zyl, "Isaiah 24–27; Their Date of Origin," *New Light on Some Old Testament Problems. Papers read at 5th meeting of Die Ou-Testamentiese Werkgemeenskap in Suid-Afrika*. Potchefstroom: Pro Rege, 1962.

R. de Vaux, *Ancient Israel*. Tr. J. McHugh. New York: McGraw-Hill, 1961.

————, "Jerusalem and the Prophets," in *Interpreting the Prophetic Tradition*. Cincinnati: Hebrew Union College; New York; KTAV, 1969. Pp. 275–300.

————, "Titres et Fonctionnaires Egyptiens à la cour de David et de Salomon," *RB* 48 (1939) 394–405.

B. Vawter, "The Ugaritic Use of GLMT," *CBQ* 14 (1952) 319–322.

P. Verhoef, *Die Dag van die Here*. Exegetica 2/3. The Hague: Uitgeverij van Keulen, 1956. Pp. 12–28.

J. Vermeylen, *Du prophète Isaïe a l'apocalyptique: Isaïe, i–xxxv, Miroir d'un demi-millenaire d'experience religieuse en Israel*. Paris: Lecoffre, 1977.

L.-H. Vincent and A.-M. Steve, *Jerusalem de L'Ancien Testament*. 2 vols. Paris: Gabalda, 1954–1956.

W. Vischer, *Die Immanuel-Botschaft im Rahmen des königlichen Zionsfestes*. Theologischen Studien 45. Zurich: Evangelischer Verlag, 1955.

W. Vogels, "L'Egypte Mon Peuple—L'Universalisme d'Is 19, 16–25," *Bib* 57 (1976) 494–514.

G. von Rad, *Old Testament Theology*. 2 vols. Tr. D. M. G. Stalker. Edinburgh: Oliver and Boyd; New York: Harper & Row, 1962–1965.

————, "The Origin of the Concept of the Day of Yahweh," *JSS* 4 (1959) 97–108.

T. C. Vriezen, *An Outline of Old Testament Theology*. Tr. S. Neuijen. Oxford: Blackwell, 1958.

H. M. Weil, "Exégèse d'Isaie III, 1–15," *RB* 49 (1940) 76–85.

M. Weippert, "Zum Text von Ps. 195 und Jes 22⁵," *ZAW* 73 (1961) 97–99.

A. Weiser, *The Old Testament: Its Formation and Development*. Tr. D. Barton. New York: Association Press, 1961.

M. Weiss, "The Pattern of the 'Execration Texts' in the Prophetic Literature," *IEJ* 19 (1969) 150–57.

A. Welch, *Kings and Prophets of Israel*. London: Lutterworth, 1952.

S. Wernberg-Møller, "Studies in the Defective Spellings in the Isaiah Scroll of St. Mark's Monastery," *JSS* 3 (1952) 244–264.

C. Westermann, *Basic Forms of Prophetic Speech*. Tr. H. C. White. Philadelphia: Westminster, 1967.

J. C. Whitcomb, *Darius the Mede*. Grand Rapids: Eerdmans, 1959.

C. F. Whitley, "The Language and Exegesis of Isaiah 8:16–23," *ZAW* 90 (1978) 28–43.

H. Wildberger, *Jesaja*. BKAT. 3 vols. Neukirchen-Vluyn: Neukirchener, 1965–1982.

R. J. Williams, *Hebrew Syntax: An Outline*. 2nd ed. Toronto: University of Toronto, 1976.

R. D. Wilson, "The Meaning of 'Alma' (A.V. Virgin) in Isa. vii:14," *PTR* 24 (1926) 308–316.

—————, *A Scientific Investigation of the Old Testament*. Philadelphia: Sunday School Times, 1926.

D. J. Wiseman, *Chronicles of the Chaldaean Kings [626–556 B.C.]*. London: British Museum, 1956.

—————, ed., *Peoples of Old Testament Times*. Oxford: Clarendon, 1973.

—————, "Secular Records in Confirmation of the Scriptures," *Journal of the Transactions of the Victoria Institute* 87 (1955) 25–36.

H. M. Wolf, "A Solution to the Immanuel Prophecy in Isaiah 7:14–8:22," *JBL* 91 (1972) 449–456.

G. E. Wright, *Biblical Archaeology*. Rev. ed. Philadelphia: Westminster, 1962.

—————, *The Book of Isaiah*. The Layman's Bible Commentary. Richmond: John Knox, 1964.

Y. Yadin, *The Art of Warfare in Biblical Lands*. 2 vols. New York: McGraw-Hill, 1964.

E. J. Young, *The Book of Isaiah*. 3 vols. Grand Rapids: Eerdmans, 1964–1972.

—————, *Introduction to the Old Testament*. Grand Rapids: Eerdmans, 1958.

—————, *My Servants the Prophets*. Grand Rapids: Eerdmans, 1954.

—————, *Studies in Isaiah*. London: Tyndale; Grand Rapids: Eerdmans, 1954.

—————, *Who Wrote Isaiah?* Grand Rapids: Eerdmans, 1958.

—————, "Isaiah 34 and Its Position in the Prophecy," *WTJ* 27 (1965) 94–96.

J. Ziegler, *Isaias*. Septuaginta Vetus Testamentum Graecum. 2nd ed. Göttingen: Vandenhoeck & Ruprecht, 1967.

W. Zimmerli and J. Jeremias, *The Servant of God*. Rev. ed. SBT 1/20. London: SCM; Naperville: Allenson, 1965.

E. Zolli, "Jes. 5, 30," *TZ* (1950) 231–32.

Text
and
Commentary

I. INTRODUCTION TO THE PROPHECY: THE PRESENT AND FUTURE OF GOD'S PEOPLE (1:1 – 5:30)

A. GOD'S DENUNCIATION, APPEAL, AND PROMISE (1:1 – 31)

1. SUPERSCRIPTION (1:1)

1 *The vision of Isaiah son of Amoz, which he saw concerning Judah and Jerusalem in the days of Uzziah, Jotham, Ahaz, and Hezekiah, kings of Judah.*

When we look at the canonical shape of the early part of the book of Isaiah, the location and the function of ch. 6 are of paramount importance. If that chapter does indeed mark the beginning of the prophet's ministry, as many commentators have maintained, then the reason for placing it after chs. 1–5 is open to question.[1] Other commentators have argued that the present order of the materials generally corresponds to the chronological order in which they were experienced.[2] But if that is so, the significance of ch. 6 becomes questionable. Was it in fact only introductory to a segment of the prophet's ministry? The whole quality and impact of the experience seem to demand greater importance than that.

Among several possible explanations which might be put forward, two alternatives seem to offer the best solution to the problems. These relate to the possibilities that events described in ch. 6 did or did not occur prior to the delivery of the messages in chs. 1–5. The one alternative is that the call did occur prior to the prophecies of chs. 1–5, but that those

1. E.g., Gray.
2. E.g., Alexander.

who edited the book into its present form, Isaiah or his followers, have consciously placed it after those prophecies. What possible reason might they have for doing so? Might it not be that ch. 6 was felt to be an appropriate solution, if applied on a national scale, to the problems outlined in chs. 1–5? Furthermore, ch. 6 is intimately connected with the materials of chs. 7–9. Had the book begun with the present ch. 6, the insertion of the present chs. 1–5 between it and chs. 7–12 would have been very disruptive.

On the other hand, it may be that chs. 1–5 were preached before the experience recorded in ch. 6.[3] That Isaiah is said to have preached during the reign of Uzziah may support this contention. Thus Isaiah would have been a devout and perceptive young man who recognized the terrible plight of his people and sought to draw them back to God before he had accurately seen himself before God. This has certainly been the experience of many a young minister.

Further consideration of these alternatives will be made during the discussion of ch. 6 itself. But enough has been said here to give some explanation of why the prophet's call might be placed six chapters into the book.

At any rate, it is clear that chs. 1–5 are a powerful, though general, statement of the hopes and realities of Judah's situation.[4] As such, they introduce the content of the book in a remarkably fine way. This perhaps reinforces the suggestion that ch. 6 is where it is for literary and logical reasons rather than historical ones. The folly of Israel's present choices (1:2–17, 21–23; 2:6–4:1; 5:1–30) is placed against the shining backdrop of what she might, nay, will, be (1:18–20; 2:1–5; 4:2–6). A striking feature of the section is this interchange between judgment and hope. The prophet moves back and forth between these two themes and although he concludes the section on a note of impending doom, it is still clear that doom is not to be the final outcome.

This message corresponds very closely to the theme of the book as a whole, as noted in the Introduction. Chs. 1–39 may speak forcefully, although by no means univocally, of inevitable judgment, but chs. 40–66 speak of equally inevitable restoration and return. In fact, if one were driven by the data to conclude that multiple authors wrote the book, it seems to me one would have to believe that chs. 1–5 were written as a

3. For the arguments in favor, see J. Milgrom, "Did Isaiah Prophesy During the Reign of Uzziah?" *VT* 14 (1964) 164–182.

4. K. Budde, "Zu Jesaja 1–5," *ZAW* 49 (1931) 16–40, 181–211; 50 (1932) 38–72.

conscious effort to provide an introduction to the whole, inclusive of both parts.

While chs. 1–5 may be justly said to introduce the book as a whole, it may also be said that ch. 1 introduces the introduction.[5] In a very succinct way this chapter details Judah's situation in God's sight and calls them to return to him. It constitutes what Ewald called "The Grand Arraignment." While we may question whether the chapter is set up in every detail as a lawsuit (cf. G. A. Smith), we can agree that many of the elements are present.[6] In any case, the chapter sets the stage for what follows, declaring the inevitably destructive results of leaving God, the foolishness of rote religion, the necessity of justice, the corruption of the leadership, and in it all the possibility of redemption and restoration. These are the great themes of the book and they are stated in a grippingly concise way here.

1 The superscription is typical of the prophetic books in general, in that it identifies the prophet at the outset. Furthermore, it follows the pattern of all but Ezekiel, Jonah, Haggai, and Zechariah in the structure of the rubric, i.e., "The word of the Lord/oracle/vision which came to the prophet/the prophet saw at such and such a time."[7] While the four prophetic books just mentioned vary from this literary pattern to some extent, they too identify the prophet, the material, and the time in the opening sentences of the book.[8]

This concern for the identification of the prophetic source at the outset and the lack of any other attribution later in the book provide strong prima facie evidence of the ancient community's understanding of the single authorship of the book.[9] While it must be granted that this does not constitute proof, it must at least indicate that the Hebrew people made every effort to make it appear to have come from a single prophet.[10] Why they should make such an attempt, if indeed they did, has not been given enough attention.

5. G. Fohrer, "Jes. 1 als zusammenfassung der Verkundigung Jesajas," *ZAW* 74 (1962) 251–268.

6. R. J. Marshall, "The Structure of Isaiah 1–12," *BR* 7 (1962) 19–32; H. B. Huffmon, "The Covenant Lawsuit in the Prophets," *JBL* 78 (1959) 288–295.

7. Kaiser's denial that the prophet would give such information about himself is unfounded; cf. Jer. 1–3.

8. G. Tucker, "Prophetic Superscriptions and the Growth of a Canon," in *Canon and Authority,* ed. G. Coats and B. Long (Philadelphia: Fortress, 1977), pp. 56–70.

9. So Young.

10. B. S. Childs, *Introduction to the Old Testament as Scripture* (Philadelphia: Fortress, 1979), pp. 325–26.

The vision. Titling the book as a vision is rare among the prophets. Obadiah is the only other prophet to use it at the opening of a book. Ezekiel employs it in two places to describe the work of a prophet. More typically the prophetic announcements are titled "The word [or words] of the Lord."[11] The root *ḥzh,* when it denotes physical sight, suggests intensity (e.g., 33:20; 57:8). More frequently, it denotes something like insight or perception. Thus it is sometimes used in theophanic settings (Exod. 24:11; Job 19:26, 27; Ps. 11:7; 17:15; etc.) and indicates the prophet's awareness of the true meaning of things.

of Isaiah. The genitive of possession indicates who had this vision and by whom it is reported. While it is not here specified that the vision is from God (as do the other prophets with "the word of the Lord"), there is no doubt in the light of the rest of the book that Isaiah would never have claimed himself as ultimate source of the vision. He was but the mediating source for "the high and lifted up" (cf. ch. 6).

The meaning of Isaiah is "Yahweh saves" (cf. Delitzsch—"Yahweh has wrought Salvation"). One could hardly imagine a more appropriate name in the light of the overall message of the book. For while it is true that Yahweh judges and destroys, these are not the final expressions of his will. Ultimately he intends to save.

son of Amoz. Since the names are spelled differently, there is no reason to equate Isaiah's father with the prophet Amos. Jewish tradition suggests that Amoz was the brother of King Amaziah, the father of Uzziah, thus making Isaiah of royal blood.[12] Isaiah's access to the kings and the forthright way in which he addressed them might be taken as evidence for this contention, but other prophets such as Elijah and Elisha spoke equally freely with kings, and there is no likelihood of royalty in their lineage. So it must be said that the claim for Isaiah's royalty is without any objective evidence.

Of perhaps greater significance is the appearance of the name Amoz on a seal, where he is identified as a scribe.[13] Again, in view of the obvious literary qualities of the book, it is tempting to see Isaiah as a member of a scribal guild. Once again, however, no objective evidence links Amoz the scribe with Amoz the father of Isaiah.

which he saw concerning Judah and Jerusalem. This geographical identification is used by some (cf. Kaiser, Scott, Smith, et al.) as evidence

11. So Young.

12 *Pesiqta de Rab Kahana* 117b; T.B. *Megilla* 10b; cf. T.B. *Sota* 10b.

13. Cf. D. Diringer, *Le iscrizioni Antico-Ebraiche Palestinesi* (Florence: 1934), p. 235; J. C. L. Gibson, *Textbook of Syrian Semitic Inscriptions, I: Hebrew and Moabite Inscriptions* (repr. Oxford: Clarendon, 1973), p. 62.

that the superscription was not originally intended to refer to the book as a whole. For, it is argued, there are clearly prophecies relating to Israel (8:23 [Eng. 9:1]; 28:1–8; etc.) as well as to other nations (chs. 13ff.) in the book. But this observation is surely beside the point. Isaiah sees all of the covenant people Israel as being typified in Judah and Jerusalem.[14] Thus, as in ch. 2, Jacob is addressed by references to Zion and Jerusalem. Even more important, however, is the recognition that, whatever Isaiah may say about Israel or the other nations is adduced in support of his basic message to Judah and Jerusalem. The Ephraim which is addressed (28:1) is the Ephraim which has threatened the Holy City (7:1–2). The Babylon to whom Isaiah speaks is typical of that vaunting human pride from which God has promised to deliver his own (11:12). Thus it is entirely possible that this phrase was created to introduce the whole book, especially if the superscription was written after the fall of Samaria in 721 B.C.

in the days of Uzziah . . . Judah. See the Introduction for a discussion of the historical situation during this period.

2. ISRAEL'S CONDITION (1:2–9)

2 *Hear O heavens! Give ear,*[1] *O earth!*
    For the Lord has spoken:
"Children I have raised and brought up;
    but they have rebelled against me.
3 *The ox knows its owner;*
    the donkey its master's trough;
Israel does not know,[2]
    my people does not understand."
4 *Woe! Sinning nation,*
    guilt-laden people,
evil generation,
    corrupt children.
They have forsaken the Lord;
    they have turned away from the Holy One of Israel;
        they have turned back.

14. Delitzsch says that the one thing we can be sure of is that Isaiah was a native of Jerusalem.
1. Lit. "ear me." See J. Stampfer, "On Translating Biblical Poetry; Isaiah Chapter 1 and 2:1–4," *Judaism* 14 (1965) 501–510.
2. The Vulg. has "know *me*" and LXX has "know *me* . . . understand *me*," supplying pronouns which the MT lacks. However, the pronoun is not necessary in the context.

5 *Why be beaten anymore?*
Why continue to rebel?
The whole[3] head is sick,
the whole heart chronically ill.
6 *From the sole of the foot*
to the top of the head,
there is no sound spot[4]—
only wound and bruise and running sore,[5]
not cleaned or bandaged or softened with oil.
7 *Your land is desolate;*
your cities burned with fire.
Your soil? Foreigners are devouring it right in front of you—
a heap, like a ruin of strangers.
8 *The daughter of Zion is left*
like a hut in a vineyard,
like a shack in a cucumber patch,
like a city besieged.
9 *Unless the Lord of Hosts had left us a little remnant,*
we would have been like Sodom,
we would have been compared to Gomorrah.

This opening section of the chapter gives the charge against Israel: She has forsaken the Lord and is, as a result, broken and desolate. Two subsections may be identified. In the first (vv. 2–3) God himself opens the proceedings and makes the charge. In the second (vv. 4–9), the prophet amplifies the charge and substantiates it on the basis of Israel's condition.

In the light of vv. 7–9, which seem to draw upon some serious military invasion of Judah, commentators have proposed various dates for the passage. These occasions include the invasion of Israel and Syria in 735 (e.g., Delitzsch), that of Sennacherib in 701 (e.g., Kaiser, Cheyne), and that of Nebuchadrezzar in 586 (Kissane). Few take the last position today. While it is entirely plausible that the prophet may have written the introduction to his book toward the end of his life and after the contest with the Assyrians in 701, it must also be said that he may have written

3. While the absence of the article on the word being modified by *kol* normally calls for the translation "every" instead of "all," poetry frequently omits the article (cf., e.g., Isa. 9:10 [Eng. 11]; Ps. 111:1), making it possible to translate "all" here, better fitting the metaphorical sense.

4. For the suggestion that the rare *me̱tōm* (v. 6) is actually the more common *tām* to which a preceding enclitic *mem* has become attached, see H. D. Hummel, *JBL* 76 (1957) 105.

5. Lit. "the wound is not squeezed together." It is unclear whether this means the wound is not closed, or that infection has not been squeezed from it.

it earlier in his life when the end results of the Assyrian expansion under Tiglath-pileser III (see the Introduction) were already becoming manifest. As a prophet, he was quite capable of seeing Judah's desolation before she saw it herself.

2–3 In the opening words, the heavens and earth are called to listen in on what amounts to a divine monologue.[6] God is meditating on the strange situation that has developed. The tone makes it clear that what follows will be not so much a legal presentation as a personal one. While the covenant is clearly in view here, it is in the background and remains there. Israel's offense is against common decency and common sense. Even animals know better.

The opening appeal is strongly reminiscent of Deut. 32:1 and 30:19, where Moses called upon the heavens and the earth to witness the covenant of blessing or curse. It seems likely that Isaiah consciously reverts to the Deuteronomic language here.[7] The covenant has been broken and its curses fall upon the people. Likewise, the use of the term *Israel* in v. 3 probably points up Isaiah's consciousness of the covenant,[8] as does the use of *know* in the same verse.

Isaiah's references to the covenant are not nearly as explicit as those of Jeremiah. In fact, Isaiah does not use the word *bᵉrît*, "covenant." Yet it cannot be denied that Isaiah knows of the covenant. It appears to be the ground of all his thinking, but not a source for legal appeal. Rather, it is a pattern for living, without which life cannot be sustained.[9]

Thus the appeal to the heavens and the earth is not merely a matter of legality; it is a matter of the whole order of life. What God's people are doing is an offense against nature. Sin, pride, and oppression are contrary to creation as God envisioned it. An ox or an ass is intelligent enough to know to whom it belongs and upon whom it can depend. But God's children are not so. Thus the stars and the earth following obediently in their courses are called to see the spectacle of thinking, feeling human beings living in ways which are contrary to their own natures.

According to Smith, this mode or method of appeal in Isaiah ad-

---

6. R. Lapointe, "Divine Monologue as a Channel of Revelation," *CBQ* 32 (1970) 161–181.

7. L. G. Rignell, "Isaiah Chapter 1: Some exegetical remarks with special reference to the relationship between the text and the book of Deuteronomy," *ST* 11 (1957) 140–158.

8. W. Eichrodt, "Prophet and Covenant: Observations on the Exegesis of Isaiah," in *Proclamation and Presence: Old Testament Essays in Honor of G. H. Davies*, ed. J. I. Durham and J. R. Porter (London: SCM, 1970), pp. 170–71.

9. Ibid., pp. 172–74.

dresses the conscience. It is a direct appeal to persons, making use of every avenue but always striking at the roots of action. The prophet wishes to change their ways of thinking, of feeling, and especially of acting.

In line with this approach, the relationship between Israel and God is described in terms of child and parent. This relationship has even greater immediacy than that of Covenant God and Covenant People. God is our Father and we have rebelled against him. Unlike the pagan religions, in which the god's fatherhood was primarily seen in terms of begetting, the Hebrews saw God in the role of nurturing and rearing Father (cf. Hos. 11:1; Ezek. 16:1ff.). This view made rebellion against him all the more unnatural. To refuse to submit to the one who engendered you is bad enough; to refuse to submit to the one who has cared for you is incomprehensible.

Isaiah fortifies his depiction of the unnatural character of sin by reference to the animals. Neither the ox nor the ass was considered very intelligent in the ancient Near East yet even these animals knew who cared for them.[10] Israel could surely do better then they. But no, Israel does not know that much.

As mentioned above, *know* is a covenant word. Israel's knowledge of God came directly out of experience with him in Egypt and at Sinai. Because he had revealed himself in and through the covenant relationship, Israel could know him (Exod. 6:7). This knowledge is not primarily intellectual. Both *yāḍaʿ*, "know," and *bîn*, "understand" (v. 3), came directly out of experience. Thus Israel was doubly culpable. One's experience of the natural world ought by itself to lead to submission to the Creator. How much more should experience of God's election-love lead to submission to the Deliverer?

The biblical writers make much of the relationship between submission and knowledge. Whereas submission will bring a right understanding (Prov. 1:7), refusal to submit can only result in foolishness (Rom. 1:18–32). W. F. Albright referred to this way of thinking as being "empirico-logical" and argued that the Hebrews possessed a unique capacity to apply the logic of experience to religious thought, whereas her neighbors applied such logic only to mundane affairs.[11] Be that as it may, Isaiah believed that the Hebrews ought to be able to reflect on life as deeply as an ox or an ass could.

---

10. E. Neilsen, "Ass and Ox in the Old Testament," *Studia Orientalia Ioanni Pedersen,* ed. F. Hvidberg (Copenhagen: Munksgaard, 1953), pp. 263–274.

11. W. F. Albright, *History, Archaeology and Christian Humanism* (New York: McGraw, 1964), p. 71; cf. also pp. 92–100.

4–9 Kaiser refers to this as a taunt-song, but Westermann's suggestion that it is a lament seems more apropos.[12] While there is certainly anger here, there is none of the glee which is apparent in such a song as that celebrating Babylon's overthrow in chs. 13 and 14. Rather, the tone is of sadness and grief. The prophet sees the condition of his people and knows it to be the logical outcome of their behavior, but he is not happy about it.

4 This verse is a powerful piece of poetry that describes Israel's condition in terse, hard-hitting terms. It begins with the cry of desolation that occurs frequently in the first part of Isaiah (e.g., 5:8; 6:5; 28:1; etc.). *Woe!* is a cry of grief and doom, of sorrow and death. While it can introduce a sort of grimly glad pronouncement of judgment (so Marti, Drechsler, Barnes), it can also express a grief-stricken sense of loss (above all 6:5) as it seems to do here. For this reason the NIV and JPSV translate "Ah." But that word does not capture the full meaning of the Hebrew; the now archaic "Alas!" comes closer.

Having compared his people unfavorably to the natural world, which demonstrates wisdom and orderly obedience, the prophet now turns to a direct description of their condition. They are sinful and corrupt, having forsaken the Lord. The poetic form is instructive (see the Introduction) in that the two parts of the verse seem to be synonymous.[13] Thus, to be sinful is to spurn the Lord and vice versa. What this points up is the intimate connection between the moral life and one's relationship to God. Morality without submission to the One from whom morality stems may be merely another form of human pride. On the other hand, sin and evil, guilt and corruption, cannot be avoided when the vital link with the personal Lord is removed.

Within each half of the line there is also poetic development. The first half is divided into four parts with a two- or three-word thought in each. These form two couplets, each having two parts. The two parts within each couplet are synonymous and the two couplets are synonymous. The effect is like a series of karate chops—short, sudden, devastating: *Woe! Sinning nation, guilt-laden people; evil generation, corrupt children.*[14] In the first couplet, *nation* and *people* are synonymous, as are *sinning* and *guilt.* In the second, *generation* is matched with *children* and *evil* with *corrupt.*

---

12. C. Westermann, *Basic Forms of Prophetic Speech,* tr. H. White (Philadelphia: Westminster, 1967), p. 203.
13. See Young's comment on Marti.
14. *mašḥiṯîm,* lit. "corrupt ones."

This twofold understanding of Israel appears throughout the Bible. On the one hand, they are a people with a political and national identity. But on the other hand, they are a family, children[15] not merely of Abraham and Jacob but of God. And their sinfulness meets them on both levels of their existence. As a people they habitually miss the way (*ḥōṭēʾ*, participle). They struggle under the weight of the perverted character (*ʿāwōn*) that may be both cause and result (both "iniquity" and "guilt" are appropriate translations) of their straying.

As a family, they demonstrate the opposite of what family life is about. The descendants ought to be better than their parents, but these are worse. The children ought to be a source of life and regeneration, but these are sources of destruction and degeneration. Thus, as people and family Israel has lost her way. What has happened?

The prophet answers the question when he says that they *have forsaken* (*ʿāzaḇ*, the word used of divorce) *the Lord*. Righteousness is found only in the Lord and in those related to him. It is not the independent possession of anyone. The first appearance of *the Holy One of Israel* is significant in this context. (For a full discussion of the phrase see the Introduction.) This understanding of God makes the rejection of him all the more reprehensible. Their God is *the* Holy One. There is no other God for them.[16] He is the only one who is truly Other and thus deserving of their worship. But his otherness is not merely a matter of essence; it is also a matter of character. The otherness of this God is distinctively moral. Thus to act immorally is a particular affront to him, and to forsake him is to be doomed to act immorally. But he is not merely the Holy One; he is the Holy One of Israel. This altogether good One, the only almighty One, has committed himself to Israel, and Israel's response has been an almost casual rejection of him.

It is probable that part of the rejection Isaiah has in mind relates to idolatry. The language used here is very similar to that of Deuteronomy when it speaks of idolatry (28:20; 29:25, 26; 31:16).[17] The final phrase, whose meaning is disputed, probably has this connotation of leaving the Lord for idols (cf. Ezek. 14:5).[18] This understanding explains the motivation behind what Isaiah saw as rejection of the Lord. Central to idola-

---

15. *zeraʿ*, "seed," of Abraham; cf. 14:8; Jer. 33:26; John 8:33.

16. Whether they were philosophical monotheists by this time is debatable; cf. Y. Kaufmann, *The Religion of Israel*, tr. and abridged by M. Greenberg (Chicago: University of Chicago, 1960), pp. 295–300.

17. Rignell, op. cit.

18. G. R. Driver, "Linguistic and Textual Problems, Isaiah I–XXXIX," *JTS* 38 (1937) 36–37; A. Guillaume, "Isaiah 1,4; 6,13," *PEQ* 79 (1947) 40–42.

trous worship is the achievement of security through manipulation of personalized forces (see the Introduction for a fuller discussion of idolatry). But central to Israelite faith was the surrender of manipulative control and the acceptance of God's grace, such acceptance being evidenced by a life like his, marked by ethical purity. This distinction between these two ways always posed a dilemma for the Israelites. To attempt to control one's own destiny implied denial of God, but acceptance of God's way meant a frightening relinquishment of power. Typically, they tried to keep both God and the gods, with unhappy results. For the most part, they did not consciously abandon God, but their attempt to keep both amounted to abandonment and was, in the eyes of the prophets, rebellion.

5, 6 One of the recurring themes of Deut. 27–30 is the destructive results of forsaking God. To live in covenant with him is to experience blessing, but to break the covenant is to experience curse. In vv. 5–8 Isaiah delineates the ways in which Israel was now experiencing the results of her sin. First (vv. 5–6), he uses the metaphor of health, which fits in with his appeal to the natural order. Health is the natural and normal state of the body, all other things being equal. On the other hand, if there are wounds, open sores, and sickness, we know that something is wrong (cf. Hos. 5:13 for a similar use of sickness in a theological sense). If this is the case, measures need to be taken to combat an unnatural situation. The same is true of rebellion (vv. 7–8), says Isaiah. Just as naturally as disease produces certain symptoms, so does rebellion. And those symptoms were present for everyone to see. The nation is desolate, stripped, and forsaken. Surely this should be a sign that a cure is needed.

But Israel's ill health is not merely a matter of disease. She has been beaten and smitten. The words occurring in v. 6 describe injuries received in battle: slash wounds *(peṣaʿ)*, lacerations *(ḥabbûrâ)*, and bleeding wounds *(makkâ ṭᵉrîyâ)*. The results of rebellion do not merely come in some sort of automatic, impersonal way, but they come as a result of a confrontation with an offended Almighty. However, the passive force of *be beaten* in v. 5 is significant here. Whether the Lord's sword falls upon his people is a matter of their choice. God has not decided, in some arbitrary way, to punish Israel. Rather, the political and social catastrophes they were experiencing were the natural results of living in ways contrary to those God designed for them.

EXCURSUS

Isaiah's emphasis upon rebellion as an offense against nature speaks to the meaning of the *wrath of God*. Two extremes need to be opposed here. The one is the picture of God as a raging, red-faced tyrant who dares anyone to oppose his arbitrary decrees. But God's decrees in the matters of the spirit are not more arbitrary than those in the realm of the physical. If I choose to smash my car into a brick wall while traveling at 100 miles per hour, I will most certainly experience the wrath of God—the natural results of my unnatural act. As someone has said, I will not have broken any natural laws, only demonstrated them. The same is true in the spiritual realm. If I live in ways contrary to my nature, I will experience the destructive results of my behavior. In this sense, the *wrath of God* is a metaphor, as is the *love of God*.

But this understanding can lead to an opposite error, namely, that God is without personality, a benign but unfeeling unmoved Mover. The whole import of Scripture is opposed to such a view. If God is anything, he is a Person, intimately and passionately involved with his creatures. His emotions are neither fickle nor arbitrary; they are real and deep. His hatred of sin is as intense as his approval of righteousness is profound.

Thus a genuinely biblical view of God's response to sin must always hold these two extremes in tension. On the one hand, he does not respond out of arbitrary rage, but on the other hand, he does respond personally and directly.

But how can Israel bear the sufferings which have come upon her because of her rebellion? Must they not finally crush her and destroy her? This question must have become particularly real to Isaiah as he recognized more and more how difficult repentance was for his people. In this light, the language of Isa. 53 suddenly stands out. What are the sickness and pains which the Servant bears?[19] They are those which have been occasioned by the rebellion of his people. Ch. 53 shows a clear conceptual unity with ch. 1, even to the use of the same metaphors.[20]

7–9 In these verses, the prophet changes the imagery. First, he moves from the picture of a sick and injured body to that of the desolation of a conquered land. While this image is much more realistic (so much so that many commentators do not consider it to be an image), it still should be considered as an image. For whether the countryside, the cities, or even the soil of Israel is an actual waste at the time of the writing is beside the point. It is already spiritually so. Spiritually and, to a greater

19. See G. R. Driver, "Isaiah I–XXXIX: Textual and Linguistic Problems," *JSS* 13 (1968) 36, for the suggestion that the reference is to pustules.
20. It is not possible to say whether this unity is conscious or unconscious. But in either case, any reconstruction of the supposed history of the book which does not do full justice to this conceptual unity is failing to do justice to the data.

or lesser extent, physically Israel is a wasteland. The essentially figurative nature of the passage is further supported by the shift to agricultural imagery in v. 8.

Again, while Isaiah does not make specific reference to the old covenant traditions, his fundamental reliance upon them is obvious in the light of almost word-for-word similarities between v. 7 and the curse formulas found in Lev. 26 and Deut. 28, 29. He is at one with those passages in believing that it is impossible to enjoy the fruits of nature without being in submission to nature's Lord.[21] In fact, these curses, like the Edenic curse, ought to be grounds for gratitude. If it were possible for us to find happiness and satisfaction in the creation, and if that happiness prevented us from realizing that ultimate happiness is to be found in God alone, that would not be a good thing. We would not call a blessing that which gave short-term pleasure while depriving us of an eternal relation with our Maker. On the contrary, when our attempts to find ultimate joy in the temporal continue to meet with disaster and frustration, and when that disaster and frustration drive us to the ultimate Source of joy, the curse is not an evil but a good one.

The phrase *a heap, like a ruin of strangers* (v. 7) is ambiguous in its use of the genitive. Most commentators agree with Young in calling it a subjective genitive, meaning that the strangers are responsible for the ruin. The parallelism seems to support this understanding in that strangers are the actors in the first bicolon. At the same time, Delitzsch's argument for the objective genitive ought not to be dismissed too easily. As he points out, the word is used exclusively of the overthrow of Sodom and Gomorrah (e.g., Deut. 29:23). Thus he concludes that the prophet is pointing to an overthrow of God's people like that which happens to those who are strangers to him.[22]

As mentioned above, the prophet shifts the figure again in v. 8. He uses the images of harvest shelters to connote the kinds of desolation, helplessness, and transiency which he sees resulting in Israel because of her rebellion. Since the farmers customarily lived in villages and walked out to their fields, and since time was too precious during harvest to waste walking back and forth, the families built little lean-tos in the fields and camped there until harvest was over. What a forlorn picture those little shacks were after the harvest was over. Useless, deteriorating, they were

21. Cf. C. S. Lewis, *The Problem of Pain* (New York: Macmillan, 1943), pp. 65–71.

22. "Strangers," *zārîm,* is distributed throughout the book (25:2, 5; 43:12; 61:5), indicating that Bewer's attempt to derive it as here from Akk. *zāru,* "to hate," is unnecessary (*AJSL* 17 [1900/1901] 168).

the very opposite of what God promised his people they would be. Some have argued that since the "harvest" had not yet come for Jerusalem, Isaiah was thinking of the shelters as they looked prior to harvest. But this argument rationalizes the figure of speech too much. Surely the prophet's sole point is to convey as vividly as possible the true condition of God's people.

Isaiah here refers to *the daughter of Zion.* Exactly what is meant by this phrase is difficult to determine. Young suggests it is "the Daughter which is Zion," Stampfer "Zion's beloved," and JPSV "Fair Zion." Once again, it seems likely that the prophet is attempting to convey an impression rather than a precise denotation. He is evoking all that is fresh and fair, desirable and hopeful about Zion, and then deliberately replacing that image with its opposite. The same kind of rhetorical device seems to be in use in 3:17 and 4:4, although the plurals in these texts possibly suggest a more literal usage (see also 10:32; 16:1; 62:11).[23]

9 Although Zion is little more than a shack in a vineyard, she is at least that. There is hope for her; she is not completely destroyed. That this is so, the prophet makes plain, is God's doing. The clear implication is that God could have made his people like Sodom and Gomorrah—extinct. But he has chosen not to. This is not an act of weakness, for it is *the Lord of Hosts* who has done this. This appellation is a favorite phrase among the prophets, occurring in all but Ezekiel, Joel, Obadiah, and Jonah as an indication of God's power in human affairs. He is the God who has numberless hosts to do his bidding in any affair at any moment (2 K. 6:15–18). This is the One who has spared a remnant for Israel. In an excess of form-critical zeal, some have concluded that there could have been no possibility of repentance or of restoration contained in the first part of Isaiah's preaching (or "I Isaiah").[24] They reach this conclusion on the basis of the commission given to Isaiah in ch. 6. To be sure, Isaiah is not commissioned to bring his people to repentance, but nowhere is he forbidden to preach repentance and promise restoration. It is only said that such preaching will further harden the people. This was directly lived out in Ahaz's life when promises of hope brought nothing but further commitment to self-reliance on the Judean king's part.

A more balanced appraisal is that of Kissane, who, when citing the several references to the remnant in the first part of the book (1:27;

23. The interchange of Israel (vv. 3, 4) with Zion here points out the high degree to which Isaiah understood the part (Jerusalem) to represent the whole (Judah).

24. So, e.g., R. Clements, *Isaiah and the Deliverance of Jerusalem,* JSOT-Sup 13 (Sheffield: JSOT, 1980), p. 75.

2:2–4; 7:3; 10:18, 21, 22; etc.), calls the remnant Isaiah's most characteristic idea. This may be somewhat excessive, but it is much nearer the
mark than the previously cited position. Isaiah believes there is hope for
his people even if he himself does not live to see it, and he dares to believe
that even out of a hut in a cucumber patch God is able to do great things.[25]

3. GOD'S DESIRE: JUSTICE, NOT HYPOCRITICAL WORSHIP (1:10–20)

a. THE FOLLY OF EMPTY CULT (1:10–17)

10 *Hear the word of the Lord, governors of Sodom;*
  give ear to the teaching of our God, people of Gomorrah.
11 *"What is the abundance of your sacrifices to me?" says the Lord;*
  "I am glutted with burnt offerings of rams and fat of fatlings;
  for the blood of bulls and lambs and goats I have no desire.
12 *When you come to appear before me,*
  who requested this from your hands—trampling my courts?[1]
13 *Do not bring vain offerings anymore.*
  Incense—it is an abomination to me.
New moons, sabbaths, calling of assemblies—
  I cannot bear iniquity and solemnity.
14 *Your new moons and seasonal festivals, my very being*[2] *hates.*
  They have become a weight upon me;
  I am weary of carrying them.
15 *When you spread out your hands,*
  I will turn my eyes from you.
Even though you multiply your prayers,
  I am not listening.
It is blood that fills your hands.
16 *Wash, to be clean!*[3]
  Take away the evil of your deeds from before my eyes.
Stop doing evil;

25. Calvin, "Judge not by largeness of number unless you prefer chaff to
wheat."
    1. Verse 12 betrays a certain roughness in style. *BHS* recommends altering
"when you come to appear before me" to "come to see my face" with the Syr.,
while NEB and JPSV read with LXX "Trample my courts no more."
    2. Heb. *napšî*, "my soul," means "my inmost being, my truest nature."
    3. MT points *hizzakkû* as a Hithpael, "make yourself clean." However, the
versions seem to take it as a Niphal, "be clean," the only difference being the
accent. Cf. A. Honeyman, "Isaiah 1:18, *hizzakkû*," *VT* 1 (1951) 63–65.

17 *learn to do good.*
Seek justice;
straighten out the ruthless.[4]
Do justice for the orphan;
contend for the widow."

In this section the prophet lays out two alternative means of relating to God. One way is through religious ceremonies—cult—performed in manipulative ways (vv. 10–15), the other is through a life of ethical purity (vv. 16, 17). He closes with a challenge to choose between these ways (vv. 18–20).[5]

According to Westermann, vv. 10–17 constitute a variant of the prophetic judgment speech that he calls "the prophetic torah."[6] It contains a summons to hear (v. 10), a reproof (vv. 11–15), and instruction (vv. 16–17). The announcement of judgment is "intimated" in v. 15. While this may be so, the variation from other prophetic judgment speeches seems so great as almost to demand the creation of a new form.

At any rate, the language, like that of vv. 4–9, is intensely bitter. Isaiah's contempt for hypocritical cult is boundless. Like the other prophetic announcements on the subject (Hos. 6:4–6; Amos 4:4–5; 5:21–25; Mic. 6:6–8; Jer. 7:4, 21ff.; Ps. 50:8–15), his words are laden with sarcasm. In the days when a rampant higher criticism tended to deny any complex cult to Israel prior to late preexilic times, these harsh prophetic statements were taken as evidence in support of that position.[7] It was argued that the prophets opposed cultic ceremony because they saw it as something new, a priestly imposition upon the older, more ethical faith. It is now recognized that such a position was simplistic.[8] There is every reason to believe, as the Scripture claims, that Israel had a complex cult

4. For the MT "correct oppression," the versions have "deliver the oppressed," apparently taking *ḥāmôṣ* as a passive participle. However, this also necessitates some change in the meaning of *'aššᵉrû*. Bewer, *AJSL* 17 (1900/1901) 168, suggests Akk. *'šr,* "to take care of," while Driver, *JTS* 38 (1937) 37, points to Aram. *'šr,* "to strengthen."

5. Because of the possibility that the chapter is composed of chronologically diverse materials, it is not possible to be dogmatic about structural divisions. Some commentators would include vv. 21–23 with vv. 10–20 and begin a new division with v. 24. In that case, vv. 21–23 would be pointing out which alternative God's people have in fact chosen.

6. C. Westermann, *Basic Forms of Prophet Speech,* pp. 203–205.

7. J. Wellhausen, *Prolegomena to the History of Ancient Israel,* tr. J. S. Black (New York: World, 1957), p. 59.

8. H. Schungel-Straumen, *Gottesbild und Kultkritik vorexilischen Propheten* (Stuttgart, 1972); R. E. Clements, *Prophecy and Covenant,* SBT 1/43 (London: SCM; Naperville: Allenson, 1965), pp. 86–102.

long before the age of the prophets and that what the prophets opposed was not the existence of cult but rather the attempt to use cult in magical, manipulative ways without reference to the character and attitude of the worshiper.[9] As several commentators have pointed out (Delitzsch, Bentzen, Kaiser, etc.), if the prophetic word is taken to be an attack on the existence of cult, then v. 15, by the same token, would be evidence against the prior existence of prayer, a position which hardly needs refutation.[10]

The relationship of this segment to the foregoing one may be explained in one of at least two ways. One possibility would be that Isaiah is addressing an unrecorded response to his previous statement. According to this hypothesis, the response would have been something like, "We are *not* rebellious! How dare you call us sick and desolate? Look at the temple [cf. Jer. 7:2–11]. Look at how faithful we are in worship." To those statements, then, Isaiah responds with his biting denunciation of their hypocrisy. How dismayed they must have been when their defense became in his hand only further evidence of their apostasy.[11]

While the previous suggestion has much to commend it, there is another possible relationship. It may be that the prophet, having described his people's condition, now moves to possible remedies for that condition. His method is to demolish any false hopes (viz., we can be cured if we will become more careful about worship procedures), in order to identify the true hope, namely, repentance and reproduction of God's ways. This latter suggestion has in its favor that it does not depend upon a hypothetical link between the two paragraphs. However, both alternatives seem to offer valid possibilities.[12]

10 One of the marks of the Isaianic style is its facility with transitions. This appears especially in vv. 9 and 10. In particular v. 9 seems to be the transitional one. It bridges the gap between the desolation of the hut and the sinfulness of Sodom and Gomorrah. On the one hand, in terms of physical destruction (v. 8) Israel is almost like Sodom and Gomorrah.

9. Cf. D. R. Jones, "Exposition of Isaiah Chapter 1 verses Ten to Seventeen," *SJT* 18 (1965) 457–471.

10. See also J. P. Hyatt, "The Prophetic Criticism of Israelite Worship," in *Interpreting the Prophetic Traditions* (Cincinnati: Hebrew Union College; New York: KTAV, 1969), p. 208. D. E. Gowan, "Prophets, Deuteronomy, and the Syncretistic Cult in Israel," in *Transitions in Biblical Scholarship* (Chicago, 1968), pp. 93–112, contains very helpful bibliographical information.

11. Kaiser, Delitzsch, and Cheyne.

12. Some would see no intentional relationship between the paragraphs. Rather, they are joined because both have reference to Sodom and Gomorrah. Cf. W. L. Holladay, *Isaiah: Scroll of a Prophetic Heritage* (Grand Rapids: Eerdmans, 1978), pp. 6–7.

But that is casual similarity. On the deeper and more important level, that of spiritual condition, Israel *is* Sodom and Gomorrah (v. 10).[13] The bitter tone of the oracle is thus set from the beginning. In respect to the word and the teaching of not merely God, but their own God, they are no different from Sodom and Gomorrah.[14]

teaching here is probably ironic, for the word being translated is *tôrâ* or "law." It is probable that already in some circles the word was coming to have the exclusively priestly and cultic cast that it eventually received as "law" (cf. Calvin). Isaiah is saying that the instruction which God gave Moses did not have chiefly to do with cultic prescription and legalistic righteousness. Rather, God's *tôrâ* has to do with character and attitudes and relationships, all of which may be symbolized in the ceremonies but which are not to be replaced by the ceremonies. This *tôrâ* has been called the prophetic torah,[15] but recently it has been argued that this understanding stems originally from the wisdom traditions with their emphasis upon practical character.[16]

11–15 The tendency of the Hebrew people is easily understood. Throughout the history of religion the trend has always been to maximize the physical while minimizing the spiritual. The physical aspects of religion are observable and, to some extent, measurable, whereas the spiritual aspects are very difficult to measure. How can you be sure you are being loving toward your neighbor? Yet you can count the number of times you have gone to church, and you can record the amount of money you have given.

But the Israelites' problem was further compounded by the prevailing view of cult during their time. Rooted in the concept of continuity (cf. the Introduction), the understanding was that a representative and the person or thing being represented could become identical if proper procedures were followed. Thus the sacrificial animal could *become* the sinner, and in the animal's death the sinner died. No repentance, no change of behavior was necessary. What was necessary was that the procedure be followed exactly.

While overtones of this can be found in the Scriptures (notably in the ritual of the scapegoat in Lev. 16), the essential understanding of the

---

13. Cf. Jer. 23:14 for a similar expression. Note also Rev. 11:8, where Jerusalem is the spiritual Sodom, apparently an allusion to this verse.

14. Verse 10 is a good example of parallelism. It indicates that no distinction is to be made between "rulers" and "people"—they are as one.

15. S. Mowinckel, *Psalmenstudien II* (Kristiana: Dybwad, 1922), pp. 118–19. Cf. Westermann, *Basic Forms*, pp. 203ff.

16. Jensen, *Use of tôrâ*, pp. 83, 120.

cult is markedly different. The ceremonial activities are but symbolic of free and responsible attitudinal changes on the part of both God and worshiper (cf. Ps. 51:17, 18 [Eng. 16, 17]; 66:18; Amos 5:22–24; Mic. 6:6–8; note esp. 1 K. 8:23–53, where Solomon's prayer of dedication of the temple emphasizes repentance and faith). This capacity to make a distinction between the symbol and that which is symbolized is of critical importance for the understanding of Hebrew religion. Nevertheless, when surrounded by religions that promised automatic propitiation and blessing without commitment or ethical change, it was very easy for the Israelites to slip back into the mode where precision of ritual and careful attention to type and numbers of sacrifices made it possible for people to feel, think, and do whatever they wished.

This was the kind of religion to which Isaiah and the other prophets objected. Of what use to God were sacrifices and festivals, sabbaths and blood, if they were not accompanied by the kind of devotion that manifested itself in lives lived according to his holiness? Such sacrifices were not pleasing to God; they were an abomination (v. 13). He was not happy they had come into his courts; he wished they would leave (v. 12). He did not find their endless worship services a pleasure; rather, they were a terrible burden (v. 14). The repetition of terms throughout the passage contributes to the general atmosphere. The reader (or listener) gets the impression of an endless round of activities all repeated continuously to no effect. The weariness of God becomes palpable.

13 The rationale for Isaiah's attack becomes clear in this verse. He opposes the offerings because they are vain, not because they are cultic activity. The same point is made in the final phrase, *I cannot bear iniquity and solemnity,*[17] which may contain a hendiadys (cf. NIV "evil assemblies"). Here the ironic tone surfaces again. What God cannot bear is "religious sin." The fundamental contradiction between the two terms is obvious, the more so because of the way Isaiah has juxtaposed them. It is religion which leaves iniquity unchallenged and unchanged that the prophet and, more importantly, God detest. This religion is in fact a support for the continuation of iniquity. God hates it.

15 In the same way, prayer which lifts bloody hands to God is revolting to him. He will not look at such a worshiper or listen to what he says. It is not because prayer is displeasing in itself. What is displeasing

17. NEB "sacred seasons and ceremonies"; AT "fasting and festival"; LXX "fasting and idleness." Gray considers MT to be milder and therefore less likely to be the original.

is the attitude of the one praying. He wants to separate his religion from his life—in fact, to have God confirm him in his sin. But God will not do so.[18]

Commentators have debated the meaning of *blood* in this context. The plural *dāmîm* is normally reserved for bloody acts, like murder (Ps. 51:16 [Eng. 14]), but some have argued that the people were not actually murderers and that, therefore, the references must be to the blood of the vain sacrifices (Calvin, Alexander, Herntrich, Duhm, etc.). But others (Delitzsch, Drechsler) have argued that violence must be intended, especially in the light of the stress upon justice in vv. 16 and 17. Probably the solution is to see the charge as hyperbolic. Whatever the worshipers' personal involvement in violence and injustice, they are certainly implicated in the excesses of their society.[19]

16, 17 Now the prophet, having shown what God does not want, turns to show what he does desire. In a series of terse imperatives that stand in sharp contrast to the lengthy and repetitive statements of the previous verses, God's demands are set out. The evident simplicity, in comparison to complex ceremonial codes, is strongly reminiscent of Deut. 10:12, 13 and Mic. 6:8, which make the same point; namely, that at heart God's expectations are simplicity itself. The eight statements include three which are negative and five which are positive, the negative relating to the past and the positive to the future.

Wash, to be clean is probably another hendiadys giving a meaning like "wash so that you are clean." The reference is, of course, to repentance, that change of attitude which the NT calls "the baptism of repentance" (Acts 13:24, etc.; cf. also Acts 2:38) or "the washing of regeneration" (Tit. 3:5). Young was concerned that no Pelagian tone enter in here with its suggestion that a people can make *themselves* clean in God's sight. But surely the prophet's point is to stress the responsibility the people do have. Of course, apart from God's free grace in forgiveness, repentance and changing the course of one's life are valueless. But Isaiah's point is to say that unless the people accept their own responsibility, God's grace cannot be applied to them. What concerns him is the tendency of cultically oriented people everywhere to see religion as something done for them and to them, rather than as a way of thinking, acting, and living that a person elects in response to God's grace.

The contrast between evil (v. 16) and good (v. 17) is a significant

18. Westermann, *Basic Forms*, pp. 203–204, holds that "your hands are full of blood" is a specific accusation standing between the reproof (vv. 11–15a) and the instruction (vv. 16ff.).

19. The absence of *kî*, "because," before "your hands are full of blood" only adds force to the charge.

one in that good expresses that which is in keeping with the plan of creation (Gen. 1:4, 10, 12, 18, 21, 25, 31; 2:18), while evil expresses what is not in keeping with that plan (Gen. 6:5–7). Thus, injustice and oppression are wrong because they are in defiance of the nature of creation. Similarly, to do good is to learn to value persons as the Creator does. While Isaiah's vision of obedience to God is on a more national scale at certain points in his prophecy,[20] it cannot be said that he disregards obedience as it applies to persons. This passage alone gives the lie to such a position.

In the light of Isaiah's numerous attacks upon the leadership of Judah and also Israel,[21] it may be that this passage has special reference to the kings. Perhaps Isaiah is saying that it is the kings in particular who have forsaken justice for manipulative cult. In the ancient Near East, the concerns for justice, oppression, and the helpless were the special province of the king.[22] The unique aspect of the biblical treatment, however, is in the motive supplied for such behavior. In the other nations the attitude seems to be pro-forma—it is the thing to do. But among the Hebrews this activity is expected because it is an expression of the character of God as he has revealed himself to them. He cared for them when they were strangers, outcast, and helpless, because this is what he is like. And if they are to be his people, they must be like this, too. A similar situation is seen in the law, where many individual laws are similar to those in other parts of the ancient Near East. But the motive for keeping the laws is quite different.

This concern that manipulative cult, whether practiced in external accord with the Torah (as here) or in a more idolatrous mode (ch. 2), cuts the nerve of practical obedience to God recurs again and again in the book. It can hardly be accidental that the final chapter (66:1–4, 17) contains the same sort of denunciations with much the same scathing sarcasm as is found in this first chapter. As J. P. Hyatt has said, because religious ceremony tends to put God in the past, to become magical, to be man-centered and man-pleasing, to make God familiar, and to blur his moral demands, it is a positive threat to the kind of relationship with God that Isaiah and the other prophets knew was possible.[23] On the other hand, when there exists a trusting and obedient relationship to a present, moral Sovereign, then the

20. Cf. Delitzsch on this passage.
21. Cf. F. C. Fensham, "Widow, Orphan, and the Poor in Ancient Near Eastern Legal and Wisdom Literature," *JNES* 21 (1962) 129–139.
22. Cf., e.g., KRT C vi:33–37; Aqht 11:5, 7 (*ANET*, pp. 149, 153). Cf. also Isa. 1:23, 26; 3:14; 7:4–9; 22:8–11; 28:1, 3, 14; 29:15; 32:7; etc.
23. Hyatt, "Prophetic Criticism," pp. 211–17.

ceremonies can be very helpful in symbolizing that relationship (58:13, 14; 66:18–23;[24] cf. also Ps. 51:18–21 [Eng. 16–19];[25] Mal. 3:1–4).[26]

b. THE WISDOM OF OBEDIENCE (1:18–20)

18 *"Come now, let us argue it out together," says the Lord.*
"Even if your sins were like scarlet,[1]
  they could become white like snow.
Even if they were red like crimson,
  they could be like wool.
19 *If you are willing and listen,*
you will eat the best from the land.
20 *But if you refuse and rebel,*
  the sword will devour you."[2]
For the mouth of the Lord has spoken.

This passage provides a conclusion to the contrast between cult and ethical behavior that is drawn in vv. 10–17. But it is not limited to that connection. It also reflects upon the whole charge that began in v. 2. It suggests that in the light of Israel's condition there is only one intelligent course of action—obedience and submission. Most commentators believe it to have been an independent oracle because of the abrupt shift from v. 17 and

24. I am aware that many scholars date chs. 56–66 as postexilic, and that they would see these passages as thus supporting a later, more acceptive attitude toward cult. However, 66:1–4 and 17 are just as violent as anything in so-called I Isaiah.

25. Many commentators on the Psalms would insist that Ps. 51:21 (Eng. 19) is not original but is the work of a later writer who wished to blunt the apparently total rejection of sacrifice in the previous verse. But the point is that this approach is consistent with Scripture: until the heart is right, sacrifice is a mockery; but for the willing heart sacrifice can help the process along, and, as such, becomes pleasing to God.

26. G. A. Ahlstrom, "Some Remarks on Prophets and Cults," in *Transitions in Biblical Scholarship*, ed. J. C. Rylaarsdam (Chicago, 1968), p. 118.

1. 1QIs^a and the versions have *kšny*, "like scarlet," as opposed to the anomolous MT *kešānîm*. See J. R. Rosenbloom, *The Dead Sea Isaiah Scroll* (Grand Rapids: Eerdmans, 1970), p. 5.

2. The phrase "be devoured by the sword" is not clear. The LXX has "the sword will devour you," and some commentators would read "you will eat the sword," in keeping with an Arabic idiom for dying. Yet, the verb is clearly a passive in the MT (now pointed as a Pual and so explained by GKC, p. 388 n. 2, but probably originally a Qal passive; cf. C. H. Gordon, *UT*, pp. 73–74), and if *hereḇ* is construed as an adverbial accusative (so Delitzsch), the present rendering is correct. There is a significant wordplay in vv. 19 and 20 in that *'ākal*, "to eat," appears in both verses. Thus the people will either eat the best of the land or be eaten by the sword.

because of the somewhat self-contained nature of the message.[3]

18 The exact connotation of *Come now, let us argue it out together* has occasioned a number of scholarly differences. Some have suggested that it represents the final stage in the lawsuit where charges and counter-charges are presented. But in fact that is not what takes place. The charges have already been stated. Others have proposed that this is the Lord's final summation before the jury, but that proposal seems to overlook the recip-rocal and cohortative nature of *niwwāḵᵉḥâ*. Cheyne proposed (but later withdrew) the translation "let us bring our disputing to an end." The problem is resolved if it can be seen that what God is asking the people to debate with him is the wisdom of the two alternatives that are left them. Should they continue as they are and be destroyed, or should they obey God and be blessed? There may also still remain some doubt in the hearers' minds whether these consequences will necessarily follow, and that issue could also enter into the interchange. But if it can be agreed that it is not the past which is being discussed but the future, then the difficulties are removed.

A further matter for controversy in this verse is over the precise intent of the conditional statements: *Even if your sins were like scarlet, they could become white like snow; even if they were red like crimson, they could be like wool.* Marti and Duhm argued that unconditional forgiveness was out of place with the whole tenor of the context. Thus they argued that the intent was sarcastic: *If your sins are as scarlet, shall they be white as snow?!* etc. The prophet would be mocking the people's belief that cultic behavior, by itself, could nullify their sinfulness.[4] Although several modern commentators have followed this line of thought (e.g., Gray, Scott), others (e.g., Kaiser, Skinner) have argued against it. Early on, Delitzsch pointed out that the Hebrew and Greek texts lack evidence of interrogation. But also from the theological point of view there is no reason to fault the common interpretation. The context makes it plain that forgiveness will be given as a result of a changed attitude. In fact, the prophet may be making just that point: although forgiveness is not obtainable through cultic manipulation, it is available in concert with changed attitudes and behav-iors. As Calvin says, God does not contend with us as though he wished to pursue our sins to the utmost. There is hope, but in God's way, not ours.[5]

3. Cf., e.g., Westermann, *Basic Forms,* p. 79.
4. So O. H. Gates, "Notes on Isaiah 1:18b and 7:14b–16," *AJSL* 17 (1900/1901) 16–21. Another alternative which avoids unconditional forgiveness would be, "If your sins are . . . then let them be . . ." (cf. Kissane).
5. Cf. D. R. Jones, "Exposition of Isaiah Chapter 1 Verses Eighteen to Twenty," *SJT* 19 (1966) 318–327, for a similar statement.

There is a delicate balance to be maintained here between human freedom and divine sovereignty. On the one hand, it ought not to be said that obedience produces forgiveness. God forgives and cleanses not because he must, but because he wishes to and has made a way for that to be done through the death and resurrection of Christ.[6] But, on the other hand, it is also plain that God does not proclaim forgiveness to those who are unwilling to obey. All the rhetorical language of the prophets, urging people to obey, is in opposition to any position that God's forgiveness can ever be experienced apart from a disposition to obey him.[7]

19, 20 The verb tenses in the conditional sentences suggest disposition and act. In each case the first verb of the pair is in the imperfect, suggesting ongoing, not-yet-completed activity, whereas the second verb is, in both cases, in the perfect tense, suggesting momentary, completed action. Thus the sense is something like "If you are disposed to be willing and so obey[8] . . . if you are disposed to refuse and so rebel. . . ." The primary emphasis in Scripture is upon act. It is not how one feels but what one does that is of primary importance (note Jesus' parable expressing this point of view, Matt. 21:28–32). But, at the same time, unless the disposition is fundamentally changed, the spring of action will always be unsteady and insecure. This seems to be what these verses embrace, and it is because of such statements that John Wesley came to the conviction that God intends to purify not only our behaviors but also our dispositions.[9]

4. GOD'S RESPONSE TO PRESENT REALITIES (1:21–31)

a. THE ANNOUNCEMENT OF JUDGMENT (1:21–26)

21 *Oh, it has become a prostitute,*
   the faithful city, full of justice.
Once righteousness lived there,
   but now murderers.[1]
22 *Your silver has become dross;*
   your wine cut with water.[2]

6. For this reason I prefer the present translation to that of Gates and Kissane. See above, n. 1.

7. Cf. Westermann, *Basic Forms,* on the announcement of salvation.

8. Lit. "hear." Hebrew does not recognize a distinction between hearing and doing. If you do not obey a command you did not truly hear it.

9. Wesley, "Christian Perfection," *Wesley's Standard Sermons,* ed. E. H. Snyder, 5th ed. (London, 1961), II:147-177.

1. On the hypothesis that "murderers" is too concrete for the rest of the verse, see the comment above on 1:15. "Murderers" itself is probably an image (cf. Jer. 2:34 and 1 John 3:15).

2. Cut wine—mutilated, castrated (Lat. *castrare vinum*), mixed drinks.

23 *Your rulers are rebels,*
   friends of thieves.
Every one loves bribes,
   and runs after gifts.
The orphan they deprive of justice,
   and the case of the widow never reaches them.
24 *Therefore the Sovereign, the Lord of Hosts,*
   the Mighty One of Israel, announced,
"Woe! I will get satisfaction from my foes;
   I will be avenged on my enemies.[3]
25 *I will bring back my hand*[4] *upon you,*
   and I will burn away your dross completely.[5]
I will take away all your impurities.
26 *I will restore your judges as at the first,*
   and your counselors as in the beginning.
After this your name will be,
   City of Righteousness, Faithful City."

In this final section of his opening statement, Isaiah turns to discuss the present condition of the nation and what God's response will be. He seems to be saying, "Yes, in theory, Israel could know forgiveness and healing (vv. 18–20); but, as a matter of fact, Israel's condition is so far gone that destruction cannot be averted." But, as throughout the book (2:1–4, 6; 8:23ff. [Eng. 9:1ff.]; 10:33–11:1; 33:10–22; 61:1–11; etc.), God's final purpose is not destruction. His final purpose is blessing achieved through purification. Yes, he will avenge himself upon his enemies (v. 24) and it is true that those enemies are his own people, but it is all in order that Zion might be redeemed (v. 27). At the same time, it cannot be gainsaid that while his purpose for the community is ultimately beneficial, those individuals who insist upon rebellion (v. 28) and arrogance will know only destruction (v. 31).

The structure of the segment has occasioned a great variety of analyses. Some, like Kissane, argue that it was composed as a unit. The majority, however, noting the considerable variety in vocabulary and poetic form, see it as a composite structure. But there is little unanimity as to the extent and date of components. If there is any agreement it is that there are three elements: vv. 21–26, 27–28, and 29–31 (cf. NIV). These are usually grouped together into two units, some opting for vv. 21–28,

---

3. The Hebrew verbs *'ennāḥēm*, "I will get satisfaction from," and *'innāqᵉmâ*, "I will be avenged upon," are probably examples of wordplay.

4. Note that LXX retains "hand" here as in 36 out of 38 other times in the book, in spite of its supposed anti-anthropomorphic bias.

5. *kabbōr*, lit. "as lye," thus, "thoroughly."

29–31 (Wildberger, Duhm, Gray, Skinner), while others (Scott, Kaiser, RSV) prefer vv. 21–26, 27–31. This commentary takes the latter position, in part because vv. 21–26 seems to fit the form of a classical judgment speech,[6] thus making the segment complete in itself, but also because the *kî,* "for," which begins v. 29 (untranslated in most modern versions, but cf. RSV and AV) seems to require a link with something preceding. Furthermore, the sense of such a structure is good in that vv. 27 and 28, while agreeing with the closing thoughts of v. 26, reintroduce the contrast between the fates of the righteous and sinners, the latter fate being amplified in vv. 29–31. Thus, vv. 27 and 28 provide another careful transition (see above on 1:9). It is this very care which makes it difficult to assign the two verses to the preceding or the following segment.[7]

As previously noted, vv. 21–26 seem to take the form of a prophetic judgment against the nation. Thus vv. 21–23 constitute the reason for the judgment,[8] while v. 24a expresses the messenger formula. Verses 24b–26 close the formation with the announcement of judgment, which comes through the intervention of God (vv. 24b–25), and the results of that intervention. The two phases of the announcement highlight God's beneficial purposes. From the strong language in which the intervention is stated (esp. v. 24b, "I will get satisfaction from my foes; I will be avenged on my enemies"), one might logically expect the result to be annihilation. But, in fact, the intended result is purification and reinstatement. The unexpectedness of the result makes it even more significant.[9]

21 The opening word *'êkâ* and the 3/2 meter of the first half of the verse (see the Introduction) indicate that what follows is in the character of a lament.[10] At the same time, it must be pointed out (as most commentators do not) that the remaining verses of the unit go to a balanced meter and do not retain the "limping" 3/2. This means that a too-facile labeling of the whole unit as a lament is to be avoided. The shift in the metric style also means that there is no justifiable reason for dropping phrases *metri causa* (for metrical reasons) as some are wont to do (cf. Kaiser). The meter is too unpredictable, and we still understand too little

6. Westermann, *Basic Forms,* p. 117; cf. Jones.
7. Those who do assign it to the previous segment generally do not consider it an integral part of vv. 21–26.
8. Note the twofold aspect (Westermann, *Basic Forms,* p. 171) of accusation (vv. 21, 22) and development of the accusation (v. 23).
9. Note that this understanding coincides with that expressed in ch. 6. There will be healing of the nation, but only *after* destruction.
10. Young points to the prominence of the final *s* sound throughout as also contributing to the lament quality.

of the principles of Hebrew meter to justify such emendation without corroborating manuscript evidence.

Jerusalem becomes here, more so than before, a representative of the nation as a whole. As Jerusalem is, so are the people; as the people are, so is Jerusalem.[11] And whatever might be the case, whatever Jerusalem might be if she would repent, this city, the center of Israel's religious ideals, had become the center of oppression and greed. The cause for the prophet's lament is obvious. If Hebron or Lachish or Gezer were to be a center of rebellion and wickedness that would be bad. But for Jerusalem to become such a place indicated that the rot was not merely superficial and regrettable; it was central and catastrophic.

Jerusalem's, and Israel's, condition is represented here as prostitution.[12] Although Isaiah does not explicitly say so, many authors believe he means to say that Israel has deserted the Lord, her husband, and has prostituted herself with other lovers, the gods (cf. Hos. 2:2; 3:1; Ezek. 16; 23). The references to keeping faith (vv. 21, 26) probably support this. This prophetic usage (cf. Jer. 2:20–25; 3:1–16) of the images of marriage and prostitution speaks again of the natural consequences of obedience and disobedience. To prostitute oneself is to divert one's gifts and abilities to base purposes—not to find oneself but to lose oneself.[13] On the other hand, to commit oneself to God in love and faithfulness *is* to find oneself. *Ṣedeq*, "righteousness," denotes "the principle of right action, whereas *mišpaṭ*, 'justice,' is the embodiment of that principle" (Skinner). Those who keep faith with God manifest these, are indeed full of them,[14] because of their relation to the One who is righteousness and justice.

22, 23 As Alexander notes, the figure changes here from adultery to adulteration. The theme remains the same: sorrow over what once was. The pure has become impure, the precious, base. Verse 23 begins to explain the meaning of this figure. The ruling class, society's silver and fine liquor (Delitzsch), has become so perverted that they who are to promote order and obedience are themselves rebels,[15] while they who are

11. Cf. B. S. Childs, *Isaiah and the Assyrian Crisis,* SBT 2/3 (London: SCM; Naperville: Allenson, 1967), esp. pp. 11–19; R. E. Clements, *Isaiah and the Deliverance of Jerusalem,* JSOTSup 13 (Sheffield: JSOT, 1980); R. de Vaux, "Jerusalem and the Prophets," in *Interpreting the Prophetic Tradition* (Cincinnati: Hebrew Union College; New York: KTAV, 1969), pp. 275–300.

12. Cf. J. Oswalt, "Prostitution," *ZPEB,* IV:910–12.

13. Note the word order: "How she has become a prostitute—the faithful city—." Sad irony.

14. *mᵉlēʾᵃtî*; cf. GKC, § 90l.

15. Paronomasia is conveyed in several ways. For instance, judges do not pursue peace, *šālôm,* but payments, *šalmōnîm.*

entrusted with responsibility for justice are through their own greed actively promoting injustice. The nation has prostituted itself with other gods and the leadership has become trash. Little wonder that Isaiah sees no hope for them.

Isaiah here for the first time makes a connection which ought not to be overlooked—the connection between idolatry and social justice. He will revert to it (29:17–21; 46:5–13; 48:17, 18; 56:9–57:12), and the other prophets mention it frequently (Jer. 23:13, 14; Ezek. 16:47–52; Hos. 4:1–14; Amos 2:6–8; Mal. 3:5). What they are saying is that social injustice is ultimately the result of refusal to entrust oneself to a fair and loving God. Whenever persons begin to believe that the cosmic order is basically uninterested in human welfare and that those who succeed are those who know best how to capture the cosmic forces for their own purposes (the underlying attitudes of idolatry), the relatively more helpless and vulnerable begin to be crushed. The more helpless the individual, the more devastating the crushing. As noted above on 1:17, the rest of the ancient Near East protected the helpless in theory, but they lacked any understanding of life to undergird that theory. The tragedy of Israel is that they had the necessary understanding, but found it very hard, as do all the children of Adam and Eve, to make the necessary surrender of their own self-sufficiency.

24 The horror of the perversion which has taken place in Judah is emphasized in the messenger formula by means of a mounting up of divine titles that occurs nowhere else in the book. It is as though a wave looms higher and higher over a sodden, drifting hulk. The listener waits for the inevitable crash in which the boat will be smashed to oblivion. The term *ʾāḏôn, Sovereign* (or Lord), as applied to God, is almost peculiar to Isaiah (only elsewhere in Exod. 23:17 [par. 34:23]; Mal. 3:1).[16] In Isaiah it occurs exclusively in threats (3:1; 10:16, 33; 19:4) in conjunction with the following phrase, *Lord of Hosts* (see above on 1:9). The combined effect of the two phrases is one of complete mastery, of total dominance. Who would be so foolish as to defy the Lord, Yahweh of Hosts? The effect is only heightened by the addition of *the Mighty One of Israel,*[17] a phrase which elsewhere (Gen. 49:24; Isa. 49:26; 60:16; Ps. 132:2, 5) has positive connotations. But he who is mighty to save can also be mighty to destroy, all the more so because the enemy is his own, Israel (cf. 1 Pet. 4:17).

16. Cf. also Ugar. *ʾadn* in KRT C (*UT,* 125) 44, 57, 60; *ANET,* p. 147, "sire."

17. Note that the LXX omits this title and instead has "Mighty Ones of Jacob" after "Woe!"

The announcement oracle[18] begins with *Woe!*, which is normally more characteristic of reproach than threat, but the threat is unmistakable. It is not the enemies of Israel who will feel the heat of God's wrath, but it is Israel, who has become his enemy, that will do so (Gray). Again, the prophet's use of irony and sarcasm is telling. Did Israel feel they were under a special dispensation from God as his particular children? Isaiah stands up to say that God's children are those who do his will, whoever they may be (cf. 56:1–8), while those who rebel against him are his enemies, though they be Israel (cf. ch. 57).

25, 26 Both these verses begin with the identical verb *'āšîḇâ*, a Hiphil causative of *šûḇ*, "to return," but the English translations tend to blur the duplication. In v. 25 the Lord will cause his hand to return, whereas in v. 26 it is their judges he will cause to return. Most of the translations give the idea that the Lord will turn his hand against Israel. This is a possibility, but it is also possible that the idea of "return" is as significant in v. 25 as it is in v. 26. In this case the idea might be that after a time of abandonment the Lord will put his hand upon them again for purification (Exod. 4:7; 1 Sam. 14:7; 2 Sam. 8:3; Jer. 6:9; cf. NEB). Here the hopeful note begins to emerge. God's hand will not be upon them to destroy but rather to restore. The slag and the tin will be removed; the rulers will be as they once were, and the city name, *City of Righteousness, Faithful City,* will reflect the return to the old values (v. 21). It is not clear whether an ideal past or an actual one is in view here. Does the prophet have in mind the halcyon days during David's reign and the early part of Solomon's,[19] or is he merely saying in general terms that Israel's moral state has declined across the years and that her vision of what she is called to be needs to be restored? In the absence of specific information the latter position seems to have more to commend it, although it is not possible to be dogmatic.[20] In any case, the prophet looks forward to a time when God's people, having passed through the fires, will relate to him, and thus to one another, as they ought.

The absence of a messianic ruler is interesting. Again the reference seems to be more general than specific, with specific details following

---

18. Heb. *nᵉ'ûm*.

19. The mention of judges and counselors can hardly be used to say that Isaiah considers the premonarchical age to have been ideal. The traditions of that age are too unanimous (even if one grants a reworking/rewording during the monarchy) in their condemnation to support such an idea.

20. Cf. Gowan, op. cit., for the argument that the official Yahwism had been syncretistic from the conquest on and that what the prophets hark back to is more ancient than the conquest.

later (cf. Young). However, the mention of judges and counselors does introduce one of the themes of the book, that of a just, impartial rulership which will govern out of a sense of responsibility for the people rather than out of greed. The very corruption of the rulers fueled the fires of longing for a king who would one day rule in righteousness and peace.

b. THE FATE OF THE WICKED (1:27–31)

27 *Zion with justice will be redeemed;*
    her repentant ones with righteousness.
28 *But rebels and sinners will be crushed[1] together,*
    and those who forsake God will perish.
29 *For[2] they[3] shall be ashamed[4] of the oaks in which you delighted,*
    and you will be disgraced by the gardens which you chose.
30 *For you will be like an oak with falling leaves;*
    like a garden in which there is no water.
31 *Then the mighty one[5] will become tow,*
    and his work[6] a spark.
    Both of them will burn up together,
    with no one to quench the fire.

This segment concludes the brief introduction to the book. It sounds a similar note to that which concludes the longer introduction (5:24–30) and to the concluding verse of the book as a whole (66:24). That note is that the reality of hope which stems from God's good intentions toward us cannot blot out another, grimmer reality: continued arrogant rebellion

---

1. Lit. "a crushing of rebels and sinners together."
2. Kaiser believes that a taunt song preceded the *kî*, "For," which opens v. 29.
3. MT and 1QIs[a], "they"; Targ., 3 mss., and all modern translations, "you"; LXX has 3rd person throughout.
4. Cf. *TWOT*, I:97–98, for a discussion of *bôš*. See also *TDOT*, II:50-60.
5. There is little agreement over the exact translation of v. 31. One problem revolves about *ḥāsōn*. Is it strength (wealth) (LXX, JPSV) or the strong (wealthy) one (AV, RSV; NEB "strongest tree"; cf. also Procksch, Duhm, and Gray)?
6. A second problem in this verse concerns *pāʿŏlô*. The most straightforward rendering of the form is "his (its) worker" (AV, JPSV). But all the versions agree that it is "his word." 1QIs[a] seems to have "your [plural] wealth" and "your work." All of this suggests that the exact meaning of the verse has been ambiguous for a long time and will not be settled easily. The general meaning is clear enough. For a discussion of the issues see M. Tsevat, "Isaiah I 31," *VT* 19 (1969) 261–63; S. E. Lowenstamm, "Isaiah I 31," *VT* 22 (1972) 246–48.

against God will result in destruction. The prophet seems to be attempting to avoid any possible misunderstanding of his message. Let no one presume upon God's grace, he seems to say. At the same time there is a note of hope even in these searing words. That note is for those who have been under the jackboot of the mighty. The mighty will perish; their judgment is sure (10:15–19; 13:1–14:27; 40:6–8; 47:1–15).

27, 28 As noted above, these verses seem to fill a transitional function. They lead from the promise of purification for the repentant of Zion (vv. 25, 26) to the destruction of the rebellious (vv. 29–31). *Zion* is a favorite term of Isaiah's, occurring forty-seven times in the book with twenty-nine of the occurrences in chs. 1–39. Micah shows a similar frequency with nine occurrences in four chapters. The only other book where Zion occurs so often is the Psalms, where it appears twenty-eight times. These occurrences in the Psalms (as well as the 15 in the book of Lamentations) indicate that the term is a poetic and hymnic one which draws from the Jerusalem imagery to create a larger picture of the chosenness, hope, and beauty which belong to those who are in God (2:3; 4:3; 8:18; etc.). This imagery is doubly effective when Zion is said to be desolated and destroyed (1:8; 3:16, 17, etc.; see also Lam. 1:6; etc.). Here the focus is upon the positive aspects of the term. Zion will be redeemed. She will not be cast off. Her chosenness and her beauty are not passing; they are constant as a gift from God. It is the desolation and destruction which are passing.[7] Scott argues that the contrast between the righteous and the sinner goes at least as far back as Abraham's praying over Sodom.

Skinner doubts that *be redeemed* (Niphal of *pāḏâ*) is an expression of "I Isaiah"; he argues that it occurs only in "suspect" passages (29:22; 35:1; 50:2; 51:11).[8] One need not claim that the main point of chs. 1–39 is redemption in order to insist that a simplistic removal of all redemption passages is out of order. As far as typical words go, the term for redemption in the second part of the book is *gā'al,* which does not occur at all prior to ch. 43 but occurs twenty-two times after that. If v. 27 was the work of a supposed later writer, it is probable that *gā'al* would have been used. Thus there is hardly reason to deny that *pāḏâ* is authentic to the

---

7. For a brief but helpful discussion of Zion theology see *ZPEB,* V:1063–66. Note also von Rad's discussion of Zion in "Deutero-Isaiah" (*Old Testament Theology,* tr. D. M. G. Stalker [Edinburgh: Oliver and Boyd; New York: Harper & Row, 1965], II:292–97).

8. One may be pardoned for wondering if the appearance of the concept of redemption—a supposedly "II Isaianic" concept—was part of the reason why earlier scholars had "suspected" the passages.

earlier prophecy of Isaiah, whether one accepts the multiple authorship theory or not. At any rate, the presence of the concept of redemption here supports the suggestion that the chapter consciously introduces the entire book and not merely chs. 1–39, for the concept, while present in the earlier chapters, is much more prominent in chs. 40–66.

The understanding of the function of *justice* and *righteousness* here has tended to follow the lines of theological constructs. On the one hand, Calvin and Young have insisted that it is God's justice and righteousness alone by which Zion will be redeemed. On the other hand, Kissane argued that it is through the just and righteous behavior of Zion that she will be delivered, a concept which Gray felt was foreign to the Isaiah who wrote the bulk of chs. 1–39. From the passage itself it must be apparent that there is no basis for dogmatism in either direction. There is no indication as to whose justice and righteousness will be the means of salvation. From the larger context, however, the correct answer seems to be "both-and." Those who will not dispose themselves toward justice and righteousness cannot be redeemed; those who will, can (1:19, 20; cf. also 33:14–16). At the same time it is only through God's gracious gift that a person can be righteous in his sight. He is the source of all righteousness and justice (1:25, 26; cf. also 33:5; 51:4, 5; 53:11).[9] Perhaps the best expression of this dual aspect occurs in 56:1: "Maintain justice and do what is right, for my salvation is close at hand and my righteousness will soon be revealed." It is as humanity chooses to do what God makes possible that restoration and redemption occur. By the same token, those who refuse what God makes possible—rebels who transgress his laws, and sinners who miss the true targets of life—can only find disintegration and destruction.

29, 30 These verses make it plain that it was the worship of idols to which "rebellion" and "forsaking God" (v. 28) referred (for the same equation in other prophets, cf. Jer. 1:16; 9:13, 14; Ezek. 20:8; Hos. 4:10). What this means is that it is not possible to forsake the Lord and turn to nothing else. One leaves a commitment to him only for a commitment to other gods. The suggestion that one can abandon God and thus be free is as much a lie today as it was in Eden.

The LXX translation of "idols" for *ʾêlîm*, "oaks,"[10] gives further evidence that the trees and gardens referred to were a part of idol worship. The reference may be to the sacred groves which were a part of the fertility

9. Note that the second part of the book is as strong on God as the source of justice and righteousness as is the first part (contra Gray).

10. The terebinth *(pistaci Palestina)* is a fairly large, impressive tree which drops its leaves in the winter.

cult of Baal and Ashtoreth,[11] although the prophet may have in mind merely the worship of spirits assumed to inhabit trees.[12] At any rate, to leave the God who made the trees in order to worship the trees is the height of folly. To put one's trust in the creation is to have that trust betrayed, to be *ashamed, bôš,* and *disgraced, ḥāpar.* This is the regular meaning of "to be ashamed" in Scripture. A person has put his or her trust in something or someone; that trust has been betrayed and the result is disgrace. The biblical writers are convinced that only in God can one trust without fear of one day being put to shame (e.g., Ps. 34:6 [Eng. 5]; 119:6; Isa. 29:3; 45:7). How foolish then when God has chosen Judah, that Judah should choose a tree (see Young; cf. 65:11–12). Morever, what a person worships so that person will become. The creation is not the source of life; the gods have no creative power in themselves. Thus those who depend upon the creation are doomed to wither and dry up. Choose the garden and there is no water (Ps. 1:4; Isa. 32:12–14; 34:8–12; 64:10, 11; Jer. 17:6), but choose the One who made the garden and there are streams of living water (Ps. 1:3; Isa. 30:23–25; 35:6, 7; 41:18; 44:3; 48:21; 55:1; 66:12; Ezek. 47:1–12; John 7:38).

The use of trees here is a testimony to Isaiah's gift of imagery and to the multiple allusions his images can sustain. Not only can the oak be used to conjure up the whole range of idolatry and the finally destructive results of idolatry, but it also can stand for those who are proud, dominating, and apparently self-sufficient, like a great tree.

31 But in fact, the prophet says, the mighty of the earth will one day be stripped bare. Then it will be seen that they are not mighty at all. They are merely *tow,* the chaff from flax, good for nothing but burning. In making themselves apparently self-sufficient, they have cut themselves off from the only source of life (Ps. 1:4, 5). This use of tree imagery for the apparent power of the mighty is a frequent one in Isaiah (2:13; 6:13; 10:33, 34; 32:19; 33:9; cf. also Zech. 11:1–3). Thus it is interesting that God promises that his own people will be as glorious as Lebanon and Carmel (35:2; 60:13, 21; 61:3; 65:22). The Lord does not destroy the forest of human pride to leave us a field of stumps (6:13). Rather, the destruction is in order that the true glory of humanity, that which it derives from its Lord, may appear (66:9, 13, 21, 22).

11. Cf. Deut. 7:5; 16:21; Judg. 3:7; 1 K. 15:13; 2 K. 17:10; Isa. 17:8; 27:9; 57:5; 65:3; 66:17; Jer. 17:2.
12. There is considerable argument about the date of the passage in the light of assumptions about the type of worship. Marti and Guthe make it postexilic, while Duhm places it prior to 722.

B. THE PROBLEM: WHAT ISRAEL IS VERSUS WHAT SHE WILL BE (2:1–4:6)

1. THE DESTINY OF THE HOUSE OF JACOB (2:1–5)

1 *The word[1] which Isaiah the son of Amoz saw*
concerning Judah and Jerusalem.
2 *And it will happen in future days,*
that the mountain of the house of the Lord
will be established as the highest of mountains,
and lifted up above the hills,[2]
and all the nations will stream[3] to it.
3 *Many peoples will come and say,*
"Come, let us go up unto the mountain of the Lord,
unto the house[4] of the God of Jacob,
that he may teach us from[5] his ways,
and that we might walk in his paths.[6]
For it is from Zion that instruction goes forth,
and the word of the Lord from Jerusalem.
4 *Then he will judge between the nations,*
and decide for many peoples.

1. On *dābār* see *TWOT*, I:178–181; *TDOT*, III:84–125.
2. The poetic structure of this phrase is difficult, so that J. Kselman, "Note on Isa. 2:2," *VT* 25 (1975) 225–27, has suggested that *rûm*, "to be high," ought to be restored after "mountains": "Over the mountains it will be lifted, raised above the hills." This suggestion is attractive in view of the frequent paralleling of *rûm* and *nāśâ*, "to lift" (3 times in ch. 2: vv. 13, 14, 15), but with no textual support it is very precarious.
3. *nāhᵃrû* is a denominative verb from *nāhār*, "river." The nations will not merely come; they will pour out in a river toward Zion.
4. Note that the emphasis upon the temple as the source of truth contradicts any suggestion that Isaiah rejected everything related to cult.
5. Skinner holds this to be a *min* partitive, "some of his ways." This yields a rather strange meaning. More likely it is "source" (R. J. Williams, *Hebrew Syntax: An Outline*, 2nd ed. [Toronto: University of Toronto, 1976], § 322), "out of his ways," or "explicative" (Williams, *Syntax*, § 326): " . . . teach us, that is, his ways."
6. Jensen, *The Use of tôrâ by Isaiah* (Washington, D.C.: Catholic Biblical Association, 1973), points out that the use of *dereḵ*, "way," and *'ōrāḥ*, "path," in parallel is almost exclusively a wisdom phenomenon and concludes that this passage comes from a wisdom context. At any rate, it expresses the conviction that the true function of the priesthood (temple) is instruction in right living (cf. Hos. 4:6; Mal. 2:6, 7).

And they will beat their swords into plowshares,[7]
and their spears into pruning hooks.
Nation will not lift up the sword against nation,[8]
and they will not learn war anymore.[9]
5 *O House of Jacob, Come, let us walk in the light of the Lord.*

Chapters 2–4 form the second major unit in the introductory section, chs. 1–5. As such, they depict in the starkest terms the contrast between what Israel is destined to be and what she is in fact. To be sure, this is Israel as typified in Judah and Jerusalem (2:1a), but the references to Jacob (2:3, 5, 6) and Israel (4:2) indicate that it is not merely the political state of Judah/Israel that Isaiah's vision encompasses.[10] The unit runs in a full circle from the ideal to the real and back to the ideal again. G. A. Smith sees a dialectic in operation wherein the utopian visions of a young, somewhat naive prophet (2:2–5) are refined through the sobering conflict with reality (2:6–4:1) into a somewhat more realistic hope which incorporates a remnant and has little to say about delivering the world (4:2–6). Smith's observation of the details of the segments seems accurate enough, but his explanation of them is highly speculative. It seems equally likely that the import of the section is that the Israel of 2:6–4:1 can only fulfill the destiny given her in 2:2–4 by experiencing the judgment expressed throughout 2:6–4:1 and the purification described in 4:2–6. This schema would correspond well with the thought of ch. 1 and indeed the whole book: proud, self-sufficient Israel can become the witness to the greatness of God only when she has been reduced to helplessness by his just judgment and then restored to life by his unmerited grace.

1 The appearance of another superscription here so shortly after the opening one and in the absence of another in the rest of the book has occasioned a great deal of scholarly comment. It is generally agreed today that the superscription once introduced an independent prophetic saying

7. Thus LXX (cf. AV, RSV); Targ. "spades"; NEB "mattocks"; cf. 2 K. 6:5, "axe."

8. 1QIs[a] and about 50 Hebrew mss. begin this sentence with a *waw*, "and" or "then."

9. Why what is now Mic. 4:4 should not be included here, if it was original, is not clear. Duhm's remark that it was left out because of the awful prospect before Isaiah seems insupportable in view of 9:1–6 (Eng. 2–7) and 11:1–9.

10. R. Davidson (*VT* 16 [1966] 1–7) argues that this oracle must have been originally addressed to Israel. But the present context suggests it was addressed to Judah finally. "Israel" is perhaps used consciously because of the general nature of this chapter. Note that chs. 40–66 also use the term "Israel" when there is no possible reference to Northern Israel.

or collection of sayings. Thus its presence here is testimony to the composite nature of the book (see the Introduction). But the reason for its retention here, when the superscriptions of other sayings or collections have been dropped, is not clear. Most scholars accept some form of the idea that it signals the beginning of specific prophecies after the introductory chapter.

A further question relates to the extent of the materials that this superscription introduces. Basically, there are three possibilities: (1) it introduces chs. 2–12;[11] (2) it introduces a collection of materials extending at least through 4:6 and maybe other portions as far as 10:11; (3) it introduces 2:2–4.[12] The second alternative is probably most widely held today, but of course it leaves room for a great deal of variety from the minimum of chs. 2–4 (e.g., Mauchline) to the maximum of almost everything except 6:1–9:5 (Eng. 6) and chs. 11 and 12 (e.g., Kaiser). The latter position assumes that the original collection bore little resemblance to the present order and thus represents an extreme of form criticism. While it is apparent that diverse materials have been collected in the book to serve the central theological construct, atomization of the text is unwarranted. Thus it seems most appropriate to see the superscription as applying to chs. 2–4 and possibly to ch. 5 with the understanding that a new group of sayings begins at ch. 6.

The word which Isaiah . . . saw is an uncommon construction. Much more common is "the word of the Lord came to . . ." (e.g., Jer. 14:1; Ezek. 13:1; Hos. 1:1; Joel 1:1; Jon. 1:1; Mic. 1:1; Zeph. 1:1). Only Amos shows a somewhat similar phrase with "The words of Amos . . . which he saw . . ." (1:1). Here *word (dābār)* apparently has its broader meaning of "event, thing, matter." But it still retains the idea of an announcement. Thus Isaiah is saying that he has perceived (in a visionary mode, *ḥāzâ*) some things about Judah and Jerusalem and here expresses them in an oracular and binding way.

2–4 The abruptness of the shift in mood from ch. 1 is very striking. There repentance was viewed as a hypothetical possibility and restoration as an end product of destruction. The main focus of attention was upon Israel's rebellion, hypocrisy, and injustice. Suddenly here, with no transition at all, the focus is upon Israel's glorious destiny as a lighthouse

---

11. A variation of this analysis had wide currency among earlier commentators (Lagarde, Stade, Cheyne, Marti), namely, that 2:2–4 had originally formed the conclusion to ch. 1, with the superscription coming before 2:6.

12. According to P. R. Ackroyd, "Isaiah I–XII: Presentation of a Prophet," *VTSup* 29 (1978) 16–48, it is a later editor's way of expressing his belief in the Isaianic authorship of the segment.

to the nations for truth and peace. One is tempted to ask, "What happened?" Will God merely forget Israel's sin? How can *this* Israel become *that* Israel?

That this passage appears with almost word for word similarity at Mic. 4:1–3 raises the question of ultimate authorship. The suggestions can be grouped into three categories: (1) Micah borrowed from Isaiah; (2) Isaiah borrowed from Micah; (3) both borrowed from some common source. The possibility of literary dependence need not cause concern among those who take a high view of inspiration since the Synoptic Gospels have evident dependencies. Such a strained position as that the two prophets were inspired independently is unnecessary. It is enough to believe that inspiration can involve guidance in the utilization of existing materials. Study of the Micah passage indicates that it fits more naturally there than it does in Isaiah. The opening conjunction in the first verse (Isa. 2:2; Mic. 4:1) makes no sense in Isaiah but perfectly good sense in Micah. Furthermore, there is an additional verse in the Micah passage that seems to round out the poetic form (Marti, Gray). These considerations do not settle the question, however, for the supposed original final verse (Mic. 4:4) contains at least two phrases which have an Isaianic ring to them: "none shall make them afraid" (Isa. 17:2) and "The mouth of the Lord has spoken" (except for Mic. 4:4, this expression is unique to Isaiah: 1:20; 40:5; 58:14). Thus Scott believes that the original (including the present Mic. 4:4) was spoken by Isaiah, written down by Micah, and later incorporated in Isaiah's book in truncated form. The majority of recent scholars, in the light of what is now believed about oral tradition and literary formation, doubt if either author copied from the other. It is more likely that the saying, certainly one of remarkable beauty and force (cf. Wright), had become a common possession of the several priestly and prophetic communities within the nation and that one or both of these prophets drew it from that common heritage.

The date assigned to the passage has ranged from early (Ewald, Hitzig, Cheyne, Skinner, Wright) to late (postexilic; Marti, Gray, Mauchline, Scott), with several alternatives between. A good part of the basis for a postexilic date has been the assumption that as eschatology it could not have been written prior to the Exile. As Kaiser points out, however, this need not be the case (see comment on v. 2). On balance, there seems no reason to deny this passage to the late eighth century B.C. and to the prophetic inspiration of either Micah or Isaiah. (That a passage of this beauty and power came from an unknown is akin to believing an unknown could have written the "Moonlight" sonata—and have remained unknown.)

That there is a question about the ultimate authorship of the passage

115

ought not to obscure the more important question of the function of the passage in its present context. If indeed, as seems likely, Isaiah is here using an oracle from some other source, the question is only made more striking. He evidently chose to put it in this place and with this abruptness and after this heading. Why? Young proposes that the prophet leaves the opening abrupt in order to make plain that what follows is a quotation. That may be so, but it does not answer the larger theological questions. In its present context the passage seems to fulfill two functions. First, it emphasizes the certainty of Israel's destiny. Whatever the present may be, however grim the immediate future may be, the distant future beckons the Judeans to live in its certain light. The heading supports this conviction. The words that follow so abruptly are not merely a lovely poem taken from Israel's heritage. They are here constituted as a prophetic word with all the force which that setting can convey. The second function has already been alluded to. It is motivational. What can convince the present Judeans to live lives of faithfulness and righteousness? Not so much the threat of punishment as the promise of greatness. And what can convince coming generations that the destructive lash under which they bow is, indeed, not to their final dissolution but to their restoration? It is the conviction that they exist not merely as another nation but in order that the nations might be redeemed.[13]

2 *in future days* translates a phrase which literally means "in the afterward of these days." The Hebrews did not face the future as we do. Rather, they faced the past and backed into the future. So the past was before them and the future behind them. Thus this phrase is not a technical one in the OT referring to a millennial age or even a period beyond that.[14] Evidence of its meaning can be found in the usages of Gen. 49:1; Num. 24:14; Deut. 31:29; Jer. 23:20; 30:24, where the events referred to are within time and not at the end of time or beyond time. However, this is not to deny that the phrase can be used in a more technical way (cf. Jer. 48:47; 49:39; Ezek. 38:16; Dan. 10:14; Hos. 3:5) to indicate the consummation of history. What is important is to evaluate the context to see how the phrase is being used. On that basis it cannot be said that this passage can only refer to the millennial age. In a more proximate sense it can relate to the Church age when the nations stream to Zion to learn the ways of her God through his incarnation in Christ. To be sure, we await Christ's

---

13. See H. Junker, "*Sancta Civitas, Jerusalem Nova:* Eine formkritische und überlieferungsgeschichtliche Studie zu Is 2," *TTS* 15 (1962) 17–33.

14. Cf. Akk. *ahirat ūmī;* G. W. Buchanan, *JNES* 20 (1961) 188.

second coming for the complete fulfillment of this promise, but the partial fulfillment began at Pentecost.

It is in this light that one must view the promise of the eminency of the temple mount. It may be that the cataclysms signaling the end of time will thrust the temple mountain higher than those surrounding it, but that is not necessary to the meaning of the passage (see Calvin). Many of the ancient religions saw their gods as dwelling on a high mountain (Olympus for the Greeks or Cassius for the Phoenicians). What Isaiah was asserting was that one day it would become clear that the religion of Israel was *the* religion; that her God was *the* God. To say that his mountain would become the highest of all was a way of making that assertion in a figure which would be intelligible to people of that time.

3   The nations encourage one another over the good thing that has been revealed to them. Calvin remarks that this is the evidence of genuine faith: seeking to draw in as many others as possible. Centuries after Isaiah, Malachi commented that if the Jews would not appreciate what they had in God, the Gentiles certainly would (Mal. 1:11, 14),[15] a prediction which came true in the Christian era and one which Isaiah seems to allude to here (cf. also 56:1–8).

that he may teach us . . . and that we might walk. . . . The presence of the conjunctions at the beginning of each of these clauses suggests a connection not only between the clauses but with the preceding cohortative *let us go.* It appears that this connection is one of purpose.[16] Thus the going is for the purpose of being taught, and the being taught is for the purpose of walking. There is a profound truth here. Those who will not leave their own self-sufficiency and come to God cannot learn his (and their own) ways. But the learning is for the purpose of living. It is not an end in itself (2 Tim. 3:7). Here is one more way in which the scriptural picture of the interlocked partnership of divine and human is displayed. Unless God teaches we cannot walk, but unless we come he cannot teach. There is also the important implication that cultic, or positional, righteousness is worthless unless it is accompanied by realized, actual righteousness.

it is from Zion that instruction goes forth. The emphatic position of *Zion* here stresses the fact that there are not many ways to heaven. There is one way: by means of truth which has been mediated through the his-

---

15. Mauchline's attempt to make the distinction between "all nations" (v. 2) and "many peoples" (v. 3) support the idea that not everyone will believe seems strained in a poetic passage.

16. GKC, § 165a; Williams, *Syntax,* §§ 187, 518.

torical experience of the people whose life has come to be centered upon Jerusalem. One does not need to give the actual city some sort of semi-eternal status to recognize the point of the saying. Jerusalem has become a symbol of God's self-revelation through history, and there is no life apart from him who has revealed himself supremely in that context.

4 This verse probes the causes and cures for conflict. What is it which accounts for wars and all those lesser hatreds which lead up to war? It is unbridled self-aggrandizement. When a person, or a nation, decides that he must supply his own needs and that he is the final judge both of what his legitimate needs are and how those needs may be met, the weaker are trampled and violence results.[17] This was the picture painted in ch. 1. The warfare (vv. 7–9), the manipulative cult (vv. 10–15), the injustice (vv. 16, 17, 21–23), the posturings of the mighty (vv. 23, 29–31) were all the result of refusal to submit one's desires to God. From whence comes peace? From the recognition that God is the source of all good, that our needs and our destiny can be submitted to his judgment, and from the knowledge that he does all things well. Persons who have learned such truths and are walking in them (v. 3) can know *šālôm,* or "well-being," and when two persons are walking in this way they can know such *šālôm* together because both can know that their interests are being cared for by God, and both know that the other will submit his or her needs to God rather than attempt to satisfy them by force (John 14:27). When these principles are extended to the nations, world peace can result. However, the thought of producing peace on any other ground is folly (Jer. 6:14; 8:11). Until persons and nations have come to God to learn his ways and walk in them, peace is an illusion. This does not mean that the Church merely waits for the second coming to look for peace. But neither does it mean that the Church should promote peace talks before it seeks to bring the parties to a point where they will submit their needs to God.

5 Many commentators see this verse as the work of a later editor (Marti, Gray, etc.) supplying a transition to the following passage. Transitional it may be, but its very fitness for the passage argues in favor of its originality, unless one assumes that Isaiah himself had no hand in the present order. The verse clearly harks back to the statement of the Gentiles in v. 3, *Come, let us go up . . . that he may teach . . . and that we might walk.* As Delitzsch commented, the prophet is attempting to use the example of the Gentiles to provoke God's people to a holy jealousy. The

---

17. As when a modern Germany decides that it has a greater right to Polish territory than do the Poles or if a modern America should decide it had a right to take by force the oil of the Middle East.

emphatic position of *House of Jacob* and its correlation with *God of Jacob* in v. 3 supports this contention. Surely, he seems to be saying, if the Gentiles will come seeking the truth we have (see also 9:17–24 [Eng. 18–25]; 24:14–16; 42:10, 12; 66:18–21], if they will come to the light we hold (9:1 [Eng. 2]; 60:1–3, 19), then we ought to walk in that light. Thus, as noted above, the passage is intended to function in a motivational way, to encourage both present and future generations to leave their foolish rebellion and to embrace their calling in God. This truth is no less applicable to the Church today than it was to Israel then. The Church's future is secure. The only question is whether we choose to be a part of that future through present obedience to the Lord of the Church.

2. THE HOUSE OF JACOB FORSAKEN (2:6–4:1)

a. TRUSTING IN MANKIND (2:6–22)

(1) Full, but empty (2:6–11)

6 *For you have forsaken*[1] *your people, the house of Jacob.*[2]
   For they are full[3] *from the east;*[4]
and divinations[5] *like the Philistines.*
   With the children of foreigners they clap hands.
7 *Their*[6] *land is filled with silver and gold;*
   there is no end to their treasures.
Their land is filled with horses;
   there is no end to their chariots.
8 *Their land is filled with idols.*
   To the work of their hands they prostrate themselves;
      to that which their fingers have made.
9 *Mankind is humbled,*

1. The forsaking here, *nāṭaš,* is not in any sense absolute, but refers to their present condition (Wildberger; cf. 32:14, 15).
2. JPSV reads "you have forsaken [the ways of] your people, O House of Jacob," an attractive suggestion.
3. Most commentators suggest that something has fallen out here, possibly *qᵉšāmîm,* "divinations" (cf. LXX, RSV). See comment below.
4. Note that *qeḏem* means "ancient" as well as "eastern." Cf. Calvin: "they are filled with the East."
5. But cf. Driver, *JSS* 13 (1968) 37, who argues that the meaning "divination" is insupportable here and proposes that it merely means "to speak bad Hebrew." Gray wishes to add *k* and make it "traders." However, Delitzsch's proposal, "diviners of the clouds," still seems plausible.
6. Heb. "his," probably in reference to Jacob.

> *and man[7] is brought down.*
> *Do not forgive them.*
> 10 *Enter into the rocks;*
> *hide yourselves in the dust*
> *from before the terror of the Lord*
> *and from the splendor of his might.*
> 11 *The arrogant eyes of man will be downcast,*
> *and the haughtiness of men will be brought low.*
> *The Lord alone will be exalted in that day.*

As mentioned above, 2:6–4:1, sandwiched between two segments whose tones are hopeful (2:1–5; 4:2–6), is in stark contrast with them—the tone here is hopelessness. In contrast with the dignity of humanity under God as represented in those passages, here Isaiah depicts the foolishness of humanity attempting to exalt itself. 2:6–22 speaks in more general terms about this folly and its results, while 3:1–4:1 speaks more specifically. This segment shows a Judah which has exalted and adulated human leadership, experiencing the complete destruction of that human greatness to the point that she is led by children and incompetents. The section seems to say that true human greatness cannot appear until God's greatness is permitted to shine over all. Until that takes place, humanity's potential is zero.

While there is little disagreement concerning the general teaching of 2:6–22, there is great disagreement over its structure and form. Most scholars have accepted Duhm's judgment that it is, formally speaking, the most corrupted material in the book. This judgment is based upon the difficulty of finding metric or strophic unity, upon certain difficult verses where a word or words seem to be missing (as in v. 6), upon the inexact repetition of refrains (vv. 9, 11, 17; 10, 19, 21), upon the abrupt opening, and upon the appearance of passages said to be editorial (vv. 18, 20–21, 22). Even those commentators who see the chapter as a unity feel obligated to do a good deal of emendation.[8]

Those who deny the unity are even less inhibited.[9] But even if it could be demonstrated that one or other of these reconstructions was cor-

7. The distinction (LXX, AV) between the translation of *'ādām*, "mean man," and *'îš*, "great man," is not warranted by Hebrew usage. The terms are synonymous (cf. 31:8). See also on 5:15, n. 8.
8. E.g., Kissane; B. D. Napier, "Isaiah and the Isaian," *VTSup* 15 (1966) 240–251.
9. So Scott: vv. 6–11, 18–21, 12–17; Duhm: vv. 11–17, 6–10, 18–21; Gray: vv. 19, 6–9 (11), 10–17 (18, 20–21, 22). Skinner denies that it is possible to reconstruct the originals (cf. also Kaiser).

rect (which it cannot in the absence of any textual evidence), it is the present text which commands our attention. What is the significance of the present structure for our faith? The implication that the text has been handled carelessly or cavilierly is insupportable.[10] If indeed there has been a rearrangement of materials, a hypothesis not to be rejected out of hand, there is every reason to believe that this was done with care and under the inspiration of God. Thus, dissolution of the present structure in search of some elusive original does not bring us nearer to what God intended his people to hear;[11] it takes us farther away. To be sure, there are errors both of intention and of accident, and these must be ferreted out. But editing and restructuring are not in the category of error.

In fact, the structure of the passage is quite intelligible as it stands. Verses 6–11 depict the cause of the problem (human pride and self-sufficiency) and state briefly the effect (humiliation). Verses 12–17 continue the statement in a figurative way with greater force. Verses 18–22 state the effect even more strongly and close with the devastating v. 22, the final word on human glory. The use of the recurring refrains and the interweaving of verbally different but thematically similar refrains only serve to heighten the effect.[12] If this be evidence of the material being "worked up" (*entwickeln,* Wildberger), then so be it, but it has been worked up to a very good result.

The recurrence of *the day of the Lord,* or *that day* (vv. 11, 12, 17, 20), and the shift from second to third person in reference to God has suggested to Kaiser that the occasion of the passage was a feast day when the prophet had intended to petition God on behalf of his people, but was so overcome by their sin that what began as a petition became a denouncement. This is an attractive suggestion but rather speculative (cf. Hos. 9:5, 6).

6 The abruptness of the shift from 2:5 has caused many commentators to assume that the original beginning has been lost, or that originally the people were accused of forsaking the Lord (as does the Targ.). Once again, the chief question must deal not so much with origins as it does with the significance of the present text. Why the abruptness? It may be that the opening *kî,* "for," helps to explain the relationship to the preceding. Why is it imperative that the people of Israel learn to walk in the light? Because God has forsaken them in their present condition and

10. On the value of the MT, cf. H. M. Orlinsky, "Studies in the St. Mark's Isaiah Scroll I," *JBL* 69 (1950) 149–166.

11. B. S. Childs, *Introduction to the Old Testament as Scripture* (Philadelphia: Fortress, 1979), pp. 336–38.

12. Napier, op. cit.

no future hope can obscure that fact. The very abruptness of the shift serves to underscore this truth. They cannot, in the expectation of some ideal future, continue to live in their sin. Rather, that expectation ought to motivate them to deal with the realities of the present. If they will not change their ways (as in fact they did not), then restoration can only come to them through humiliation and the destruction of their false hopes.

What is the cause of their trouble? It is the exaltation of mankind, such as was exemplified in the religions of Israel's neighbors. The contrast between v. 3 and v. 6 is noteworthy. There the nations have come to Jerusalem to learn God's ways. Here Jacob is full of the Gentiles' ways. There God is exalted and peace holds sway. Here mankind is exalted and terror holds sway.

The exact sense of *they are full from the east* is unclear. It may be that the prophet is merely making a general statement that Israel has borrowed the ways of Assyria and Babylonia, the great ancient civilizations. If the translation *divination* is correct in the following stich, however, then it appears that some parallel term for "divination" is needed here. It has been proposed (cf. *BHS*) that *miqsām*, "divinations," has dropped out by accident because of its similarity with *miqqeḏem*, "from the east." The line would thus read, "They are full of divinations from the East and soothsayings like the Philistines" (cf. RSV; note also LXX and Targ.). In any case, the prophet is saying that Israel has borrowed the pagan ways from east to west.

The final phrase of v. 6 is also difficult. The variety of translations in the versions underscores that difficulty. As the text stands, *with the children of foreigners they clap hands* seems to refer to the making of alliances with foreigners that involved at least tacit recognition of the foreign gods. That meaning is not attested elsewhere, however, and thus some have suggested a confusion of homophones here, with *śāpaḵ*, "to abound," being the correct word. This suggestion would entail either understanding *children* as metaphorical for practices ("in the practices of foreigners they abound") or radical emendation.[13]

The use of divination and magic was strictly forbidden to Israel (Lev. 19:26; Deut. 18:9–14), for by these practices the pagans sought to gain control of their own destinies and to manipulate the gods. As has always been the case with the human race, they saw achievement of national and personal security as the paramount aim, and believed that manipulation of the gods through magic was the way to achieve that aim. But

13. On the former cf. JPSV, Targ.; on the latter see D. W. Thomas, *ZAW* 75 (1963) 88–90; cf. also Driver, *JSS* 13 (1968) 37.

God called the Hebrews to commit their security to him in trust and to give their attention to justice and righteousness. This was the dilemma Israel faced throughout her history. Listen to God or listen to the nations? At this point, the prophet says, they have listened to the nations.

7, 8 Having made the general charge that Judah and Jerusalem are full of pagan ways, Isaiah now proceeds to detail those ways. The charge is that they are full of wealth (v. 7a), armaments (v. 7b), and idols (v. 8a). This is very reminiscent of Deuteronomy (esp. 17:16–17), where the accumulation of military power and wealth is forbidden to the king on the grounds that they will turn the king away from God. This is exactly what happened in the case of Solomon (1 K. 10:26–11:8). The desire for this world's security led to assimilation of this world's gods.

Everything that could make Judah great, physically speaking, she had. Uzziah's long reign during the Assyrian lull prior to Tiglath-pileser III's accession (745 B.C.) had given an opportunity unlike any since Solomon's time to amass wealth and power (2 Chr. 26:6–15). But unless that wealth and power were understood to be God's gift alone and not the work of human hands through idols, it would finally prove to be a curse. For idolatry is ultimately the creation of God in man's image for the purpose of achieving human ends. It is thus the utmost exaltation of mankind.

But idolatry is finally foolishness, and Isaiah represents this through the word he uses here. It is *ʾĕlîlîm*, "worthless ones" (cf. Zech. 11:17, "worthless shepherd," and Job 13:4, "worthless physicians"). There is probably a wordplay intended, for "god" is *ʾel*. But these are not gods, they are no-gods (40:18–20; 41:6, 7, 28, 29; 44:9–20; 45:16–20; 46:1, 2, 5–7). How foolish to call divine what human hands have made.[14] If deity is in any way the image or product of humanity, then the world is without sense or purpose.

9–11 Isaiah has said that Israel is full of the world's best wisdom: it is through wealth, power, and control of one's destiny that human beings become great. But in fact that will not be so. They will be humbled and brought low (v. 9). Their eyes will be cast down in shame, their former eminence will be nothing (v. 11). They will hide in the rocks and crannies (v. 10; cf. vv. 19–21; Rev. 6:15–17). Why will this be so? Certainly because the true source of greatness will appear. The God from whom

---

14. Y. Kaufmann's argument that the Israelites did not understand the nature of idolatry (the gods were more than mere images) because of statements like Isaiah's does not stand up. Isaiah is attacking the philosophy at its weakest point. For while the idol was not all there was to the god, it was certainly continuous with the god. Yet it had been made by a human being. See the Introduction for further discussion.

their self-worship has alienated them will appear, and there will be no more cause to glory in human greatness than there would be to praise a flashlight in broad daylight. But the exaltation of mankind devalues humanity in another way, a way that has appeared in modern existentialist philosophy. If man is indeed the measure of things then life is without meaning or value, for each of us knows that we do not contain the meaning of life within ourselves. Having striven to become sovereigns of the universe we have become meaningless victims of a vast cosmic bad joke: able to conceive of meaning when there is none. Thus, even before the appearance of God, our quest for total self-sufficiency has reduced us to nothing. How much more will that be true when we see him in *the splendor of his might*. The Assyrian kings were fond of using such phrases to boast of the impact of their appearance outside the walls of some little city (cf. Sennacherib, *ANET*, p. 287), but it will be true terror to meet the Holy God having lived our lives for ourselves.

9 *Do not forgive them* has occasioned a good deal of scholarly discussion, in part, one would suppose, because of the theological difficulty it creates, but also because of the abruptness of the phrase. Skinner suggests it was transferred into the text from the margin of an already corrupt version of the original. He is forced to this suggestion because the versions all attest the phrase. Other suggestions range from emendation of *tiśśāʿ*, "you shall (not) forgive," to *śēʾṭ*, "lifting up" (thus "How can there be lifting up for them?"[15]), to a wholesale redivision of the consonants (Scott).[16]

Assuming the traditional rendering to be correct, how does one understand the phrase? It seems to express the prophet's deep despair over his people's condition. He seems almost afraid that God might relent and, in violation of his own justice, forget their heinous sins. As such, this phrase exposes the problem of sin. It cannot be simply forgotten, it must be punished; otherwise, the whole chain of cause and effect upon which the world is built would be broken. But the punishment for playing god can be no less than banishment from God, a denial of God's purpose in creating human beings—fellowship with himself. What might the solution be? Chs. 1–39 never really answer the question. Only in the second part

---

15. Driver, *JSS* 13 (1968) 37.

16. NIV "Do not raise them up" is based on a possible rendering of *tiśśāʿ*, but "forgive" would be more common for this construction with the preposition *l* attached to the following word (cf. BDB, p. 671), unless *l* were taken to be the sign of the direct object as in Aramaic (F. Rosenthal, *A Grammar of Biblical Aramaic* [Wiesbaden: Harrassowitz, 1963], p. 56). LXX seems to support the traditional interpretation: "I will not free [pardon?] them."

of the book does the answer come (43:1–7; 44:21–22; 52:7; 53:12; 59:15–21; 53:1–6). But whatever the answer, it is not to be found in acting as if the sin had not been committed.

(2) High, but low (2:12–17)

12 *For the Lord of Hosts has a day*
    against all that is proud and high,
    against all that is lifted up—it will be brought down—[1]
13 *against all the cedars of Lebanon, high and lifted up,*
    and against all the oaks of Bashan,
14 *against all the high mountains,*
    and against all the lofty hills,
15 *against every high tower,*
    and against every fortified wall,
16 *against every ship of Tarshish,*
    and against every lovely vessel.[2]
17 *The loftiness of man is bowed down,*
    and the height of mankind will be brought low.[3]
    The Lord alone will be exalted in that day.

This strophe expands on the theme of vv. 9–11 in a poetic way. It leaves no doubt that God alone is high and lifted up (vv. 11, 17; 6:1; 52:13; 57:15). Nothing else is high except by his permission. The contrast with vv. 1–4 is very striking. There as an act of grace God promises to lift Jerusalem to the highest place from which Israel will teach the nations God's ways. Here, having learned the ways of the nations and having tried to use those means (wealth, power, and idolatry) to exalt themselves, the Hebrews, along with everything else which exalts itself, are hammered to

---

1. The last phrase seems to break the parallel structure, and some modern translations replace it with a parallel to "lifted up" (so RSV, NEB, CBAT, but cf. JB, AV, NASB, NIV). The LXX seems to support this with an apparent conflate reading "against everyone that is high and lofty and they shall be humbled."
2. A hapax legomenon which has been traditionally taken to be from *śākâ* and having something to do with appearance or display (AV "pleasant pictures"). But the parallelism clearly demands something to do with ships (LXX "every display of fine ships"; conflation?). *BHS* suggests emending to *sᵉpînôṭ*, "ships." Scott emends to *kᵉsîyôṭ*, "canopy, awning" (with reference to ships; cf. Ezek. 27:7). Perhaps it is simplest to see it as an Egyptian loanword, *sk.ty*, a kind of ship (Kaiser, *BHS*), which may be a cognate of Ugar. *ṭkt* (see H. R. Cohen, *Biblical Hapax Legomena in the Light of Akkadian and Ugaritic*, SBLDS 37 (Missoula: Scholars, 1978), pp. 41–42.
3. *šāpēl*, "to be bowed down," occurs exclusively with this meaning in Isaiah (2:9, 11, 12, 17; 5:15 [2 times]; 10:33; 29:4; 32:19; 40:4; 57:15 [2 times]).

the ground. When we exalt God we, too, are lifted up (57:15). When we exalt ourselves we inevitably humiliate ourselves, leaving God alone exalted.

The day of the Lord is a prominent theme in the prophets (13:6; Amos 5:18, 20; Joel 1:15; 2:1, 11, 31; Zeph. 1:7, 14; Zech. 14:1; Mal. 3:23 [Eng. 4:5]).[4] It appears that the phrase must have been used popularly to denote a time when God would vindicate his people and bless their endeavors. But the prophets' word was that the day of the Lord would be a time of destruction and terror, and only after that time could blessing come (Amos 8:11; Isa. 11:10; 12:1; Zech. 14:1; Mal. 3:23 [Eng. 4:5]). They needed to disabuse the Israelites of the idea that merely because they were called by God's name they deserved his favor. Surely blessing did result from election but only if that election was confirmed in humble and righteous living.

It seems extraordinary that many commentators have difficulty seeing anything but a literal reference here (so Cheyne, Skinner, Gray). It is hard to understand why God should be against anything in nature merely because it is strong or tall. The various attempts to explain this view are all strained and all verge upon the figurative (cedars of Lebanon used to build great buildings, nature under punishment for mankind's sin; cf. Delitzsch, Cheyne). Clearly, what God opposes is human arrogance and pride. It is these which the prophet is attacking (vv. 9, 11, 17, 19–22; cf. Mauchline). Moreover, Isaiah regularly uses nature, and particularly trees, in a symbolic way (1:30; 6:13; 9:9 [Eng. 10]; 10:33–11:1; 44:14; 60:16; cf. also Ezek. 31:1–18 for an extended figure). There is thus every reason to see the passage as figurative (although not allegorical, where each element must represent one specific thing). The prophet has chosen a number of items that visually represent the spiritual condition of Israel. Kaiser has suggested that he has visualized a windstorm, accompanied by an earthquake, sweeping down from the north (God's home, 14:13; cf. UT, 51:iv:19–20; ANET, p. 133), and reaching all the way to the southernmost anchorage at Elat.[5] All that is great and impressive is knocked down. So

4. On the "day of the Lord" cf. G. von Rad, "Origin of the Concept of the Day of the Lord," *JSS* 4 (1959) 97–108; A. Lefèvre, "L'expression 'en ce jour-là' dans le Livre d'Is," in *Mélanges Bibliques rédigés en l'honneur de André Robert* (Paris: Bloud et Gay, 1957), pp. 174–79; P. A. Munch, *The Expression Bajjôm Hahu': Is It an Eschatological Terminus Technicus?* (Oslo: 1936); P. Verhoef, *Die Dag van die Here,* Exegetica 2/3 (The Hague: Uitgeverij van Keulen, 1956), pp. 12–28; R. Klein, "The Day of the Lord," *CTM* 39 (1968) 517–525.

5. Cf. 2 Chr. 20:36, 37. "Tarshish" was long believed to be a reference to Tartessus in Spain and thus figured for the end of the world (Jon. 1:3), but it may be a reference to one of a number of places for refining metal. Ezion-geber seems a strange place from which to embark for Spain. At any rate, these would be large, ocean-going ships.

it will be with human pride on the day when the Lord acts. As surely as the wind uproots the trees and knocks down the ship, as surely as the earthquake moves the mountains and cracks the walls, so will the terror of the Lord remove all human pomp and pretension.

(3) Reduced to the caves (2:18–22)

18 The idols will pass away[1] completely.
19 They will go into caves in the rocks,
    holes in the dust,
from before the terror of the Lord,
    and from the splendor of his might,
when he arises to strike terror upon the earth.
20 In that day men will cast away
    their idols of silver and idols of gold,
which they made for themselves to worship,
    to moles[2] and bats
21 in order to go into the caverns of the rocks,
    and into the cracks of the cliffs,
from before the terror of the Lord,
    and from the splendor of his might,
when he arises to strike terror upon the earth.
22 Be done with man,
    in whose nostrils is breath.
Why take any account of him?

As mentioned in the introduction to 2:6–22, this final strophe states in the most forceful way the effect of human attempts at self-aggrandizement. Although the author still expresses himself in figures, these figures are even more explicit than those of vv. 12–17. The more prosaic style has caused scholars to pronounce it the work of an annotator amplifying vv. 9–11 (Duhm, Marti). But there is no reason to believe that the prophet himself could not have amplified and interwoven his thought in this way. The idols by means of which they sought to deify themselves will be cast aside and their precious metals left to the bats and the moles, the unclean to the unclean. Human beings who sought to sit on the throne of God will scurry for shelter in the crannies and crevices of the rocks when God, the only God, appears. Before him who could believe that human beings were of any account at all?

1. MT has lost the plural ending on this verb through haplography; cf. 1QIs^a (Rosenbloom, *The Dead Sea Isaiah Scroll*, p. 7; cf. also *BHS*).
2. MT *laḥpōr pērôṯ;* Theodotion *parparot;* 1QIs^a *lhprprym.* MT seems to have mistakenly divided a noun which is formed on a reduplicated pattern.

18 This verse seems transitional in force. Thus some scholars see it as the conclusion to vv. 12–17 in that it states the final effect of the theophany. Others put it, as we do, with vv. 19–22 because it seems to speak of more direct results, as those verses do. In any case, the point is plain. When God appears all the attempts to deify parts of creation are seen for what they are—foolishness.

19–21 The ultimate in humiliation is depicted here. Human beings become troglodytes. Their ravenous ambition to be God has robbed them even of the dignity which could have been rightfully theirs. Had they submitted to God in recognition of his greatness and his right to rule in their lives (the fear, *yir'â,* of the Lord), then they would have been his friends (Ps. 25:14), little less than God himself in dominion over creation (Ps. 8:6–9 [Eng. 5–8]). But having refused the fear of the Lord, they now know terror of him *(paḥaḏ),*[3] for he now comes as their enemy and they have no defense (1:24). Here is the paradox of faith: to attempt to exalt myself is to become nothing, adrift in a meaningless universe, in dread over nameless horrors which threaten me; to submit to the exalted Lord is to know myself picked up, declared his child, and made vice-regent of the universe, my Father's home.

20 This verse demonstrates again the prophet's skill in irony and sarcasm, for in the structure of the verse *idols of silver and idols of gold* (using *'ĕlîlîm* "worthless ones"), comes at the end of the first stich, whereas *moles* and *bats* come at the end of the second.[4] Thus the effect is to juxtapose the supposed preciousness of the idols with the squeamishness felt toward the small, unclean rodents. Mighty gods? Hardly. The same people who made the idols *for themselves to worship* (a telling phrase) now fling them away to their true domain. The God who alone is worthy of worship has appeared.

22 This verse makes it plain that the passage has not been talking chiefly about idolatry. It does not say "be done with idols." Rather, it says *Be done with man.* Idolatry is a result, not a cause. It is the exaltation of man that results in idolatry. The tendency of human beings to make ourselves the center of all things and to explain all things in terms of ourselves is the problem. From the heights of vv. 6 and 7 we have plunged to this depth. Is there any cause to glory in humanity? None whatever. For we

---

3. "To strike terror upon the earth" (lit. "to cause the earth to tremble in awe") is another of Isaiah's paronomasias, *la'ărōṣ hā'āreṣ.*

4. Cf. S. Libermann, *"laḥpōr pērôṭ wᵉlā'ᵃṭallēpîm* (Is. 2:20)" [To the moles and the bats], *Leshonenu* 29 (1965) 132–35; N. H. Tur-Sinai, *"laḥpōr pērôṭ wᵉlā'ᵃṭallēpîm* (Is. 2:20)" [To the moles and the bats], *Leshonenu* 26 (1961) 77–92.

are mortal, as transitory as a sigh, as impermanent as a breath (Ps. 90:3–8). Although most modern commentators, beginning with Duhm, have discounted this verse's originality (it is lacking in the LXX, though present in the other versions), and some have even called it "meaningless, or at least unsuitable" (Scott), its fitness for this context is striking (cf. Delitzsch and Kissane). In a biting and abrupt way (similar to v. 9c in its imperative mood),[5] it sums up the import of all that has been said. That mortal human beings should attempt to exalt themselves over God is ludicrous; such actions are the perfect evidence that those who do them are not worthy of being taken into account. If Israel's glorious destiny is to be achieved, it will not be through dependency upon man (cf. Ps. 8:6 [Eng. 5]; 56:5, 12 [Eng. 4, 11] for similar reflections upon man's intrinsic worth). That thought leads directly into the next segment, ch. 3, where the folly of dependence upon human leaders is explored more specifically. Thus v. 22, in a very effective way, sums up the general statement of 2:6–21 and moves into the specific and concrete statement of 3:1–4:1.

b. THE FOLLY OF HUMAN DEPENDENCE (3:1–4:1)

(1) Boys for men (3:1–7)

1 *For behold, the Sovereign, the Lord of Hosts,*
   is about to remove[1] *from Jerusalem and from Judah*
both stay and staff:
   every stay of bread and every stay of water:
2 *mighty man and warrior,*
   judge and prophet, diviner and elder,
3 *captain of fifty and man of rank,*
   counselor, skilled craftsman, and one who knows charms.[2]
4 *I will make boys their captains,*
   and tyrants[3] *will rule over them.*
5 *The people will oppress each other,*
   each man against another,

5. One almost wonders if God is being addressed here (as in v. 9), since the prophet says that man is not worthy of God's consideration.

1. With *hinnēh*, the active participle has an inceptive function. Thus, "is *about to* remove."

2. It is virtually certain that the AV "eloquent orators" is incorrect. Lit. "one who knows whispering" refers to an enchanter (3:20; Jer. 8:17; Eccl. 10:11).

3. "tyrants" (AV and RSV "babes"), *ta'ălûlîm*, is either an abstract noun meaning "caprice, wantonness" or a literal plural, meaning "wantons." *'ālal* in the Hithpael means "to act without consideration" (Num. 22:29; Exod. 10:2; 1 Sam. 6:6; Judg. 19:25). NEB "Who shall govern as fancy takes them" is an attempt to represent this meaning in English.

> *each man against his neighbor.*
> *Boys will insult elders,*
> *and the worthless the honorable.*
> 6 *When a man seizes one of his brothers,*
> *of his father's house [saying],*
> *"You have a cloak; you shall be our leader,*
> *and this ruin will be under your hand,"*
> 7 *in that day, he will lift up [his voice],*[4] *saying,*
> *"I am not a healer.*[5]
> *In my house there is no bread and there is no cloak.*
> *You shall not make me a leader of people."*

The segment 3:1–4:1 follows upon 2:6–22 by giving particulars of the general statements given there. It continues the contrast between the high and the lowly by depicting in concrete and graphic language the foolishness of depending upon human leadership and human glory. Such dependence must ultimately have disastrous effects. In place of the "great" men which the nation had adulated, expecting them to do miracles on its behalf, it will be ruled by incompetents and wastrels. In place of all their glory, there will be shame and loss. Thus, although not necessarily written or spoken as a unit, the materials in 2:6–4:1 support a single point: dependence upon humanity will not lead to a realization of the destiny depicted in 2:1–5. In fact, it leads in a diametrically opposite direction: to dissolution.

The structure of the materials in the chapter is a matter of considerable disagreement. While it is generally recognized that there are two larger groupings (3:1–15 and 3:16–4:1), there is no unanimity concerning the relationship between the two groupings and even less agreement over the internal arrangement of 3:1–15 (see below). As to the relation of 3:16–4:1 to 3:1–15, there seems to be every reason to understand it as a final particularization of the fate and folly of human glory. Through the use of imagery Isaiah makes the nature of human pride and the results of that pride vivid and palpable as no abstract argument could. Other examples of the use of imagery to cap or reinforce an argument appear in

4. Note that 1QIs[a] affixes a *waw* to *yiśśā'*, "he will lift up," in an apparent attempt to express the "then" idea even though the *waw* confuses the tenses. Cf. Rubenstein, *VT* 6 (1952) 70. "To lift up the voice" is a common Ugaritic idiom (cf. *UT*, 129:15; 127:40; 1 Aqht 117, 136). For the same ellipsis, where the subject of the verb is left unexpressed, cf. 42:2.

5. *ḥōḇēš*, "healer," LXX translates as *archēgós*, "leader" (NEB "master"), Targ. as "head." However, the metaphorical usage of "healer" is entirely in keeping with Isaiah's understanding of the deeper needs of the community of 1:5, 6; 5:7. He may be saying that a refugee will perceive the true needs better than do the present lovers of glory.

1:30, 31; 5:1–7; 14:9–20, 34, 35; 44:12–20; 47; 55:12, 13; 63:1–6. In this light, there is no reason to separate the two parts of the chapter from each other.

3:1–15 is an oracle of judgment upon Judah and Jerusalem. The result of their misplaced dependence will be to be ruled by those who are, figuratively speaking, children. To make great men the source of a nation's greatness is always to end up with a dearth of great men. Unless the greatness comes from within the community itself, a condition which is ultimately the result of trust in God, no great leaders will rise from it. Instead, the leaders will merely reflect the spiritual poverty of the community. This was happening in Israel during the early years of Isaiah's ministry; one weak leader followed upon another as the nation seemed bent upon devouring itself before Assyria could reach it. Isaiah is here warning Judah that she is in no position to be smug. Her present glorification of humanity was destining her for the same fate.

As mentioned above, the structure of this segment is occasion for debate. Most modern commentators have adopted some form of Duhm's division (vv. 1–12, 13–15) but with considerable variety.[6] Much of the weight of this argument must rest upon the assertion that vv. 13–15 are a separate poem by virtue of their court setting. However, the content of vv. 13–15 follows logically on from vv. 8–12 (cf. Kissane) and argues well for the essential unity of the material. On the other hand, after v. 7 there is a shift from the future to the present and from the concrete back to a somewhat more abstract style.[7] All of this seems to argue in favor of Procksch's division of vv. 1–7 and 8–15.[8]

1 *For behold, the Sovereign, the Lord of Hosts.* This phrase sets the stage for the announcement of judgment. The *kî,* "for," either links the following statement to v. 22 (Young citing Dillmann), giving the reason why one should no longer trust in man, or more probably (cf. Marti) it connects with the entire argument in 2:6–22, stating in particular terms God's response to the exaltation of humanity (cf. 2:9, 11, 12–21). The repetition of titles for God, as noted in 1:24 (see also 10:16, 33), contrib-

---

6. See Gray and Skinner with Duhm; Procksch, vv. 1–7, 8–15; Kaiser, vv. 1–9 (11), 12–15; Kissane, vv. 1–4, 5–7, 8–11, 12–15; Wildberger and Eichrodt, vv. 1–11, 12, 13–15; Scott, vv. 1–7, 8–12, 13–15.

7. Kaiser argues that vv. 8 and 9 supply the reason in the threat formula. But to do this he must jettison v. 10 and attach v. 12 to vv. 13–15, neither of which is justified merely in order to create a recognizable form.

8. For a general treatment, cf. Schedl, "Rufer des Heils in heilloser Zeit," *TGA* 16 (1972) 92–98; H. M. Weil, "Exégèse d'Isaie 3,1–15," *RB* 49 (1940) 76–85.

utes to the atmosphere of judgment. It is the sovereign, the Lord of Hosts, whom the Judeans face. Sovereign God, not sovereign man, holds their fate. All of this is capped through the use of *behold, hinnēh,* which in prophetic speech typically introduces a threat.[9] While *hinnēh* usually occurs with the third person, as here, Isaiah seems to prefer the first in several other places (cf. 8:7; 10:33; 28:2).

stay (mašʿēn) and *staff (mašʿēnâ)* are closely related in Hebrew, the first being in the masculine gender and the second in the feminine. That the masculine form appears only here with this vocalization while the feminine form is a variant of the normal form of this word *(mišʿenet)* suggests that the prophet was engaging in a conscious wordplay to stress the totality of the removal (Skinner compares the English "bag and baggage"). The specification of bread and water seems out of place to many commentators in that all the succeeding references are to support derived from leaders.[10] However, the judgment which Israel was then experiencing and which Judah would one day experience did involve physical deprivation as well as political destruction, so there is no reason to exclude this statement merely for the sake of unity.[11] Beyond this consideration there is a distinct possibility that the phrases are being used figuratively, and thus for impact: God will remove our bread and water, namely, our adored leaders.

2, 3 The Lord will take away the great men, including the military leaders *(mighty man, warrior, captain of fifty*[12]*)*, political leaders *(judge, elder, man of rank, counselor),* religious leaders *(prophet, diviner, one who knows charms*[13]*),* and *skilled craftsman.*[14] This is, of course, exactly what took place when Assyria, and later Babylon, conquered a city (2 K. 24:14).

9. See J. Blau, *VT* 9 (1959) 130–37.
10. See Hitzig, Knobel, Cheyne, Duhm, Skinner, Wildberger.
11. Also note Mauchline's point that it is easier to imagine someone removing such a passage than inserting it in the context. Delitzsch points out that a stich is missing from the line if it is removed.
12. "captain of fifty" may have been political as well. Cf. R. Knierim, *ZAW* 73 (1961) 159–160 (2 K. 1:9; Exod. 18:25).
13. Note Young's comment with reference to diviners and enchanters that they will be deprived of both legitimate and illegitimate means of support.
14. The recognition that the final functionary described in v. 3 is an enchanter has caused many to presume that the particular skill being described in the preceding words was with magic (e.g., Gesenius). However, *ḥᵃrāšîm* does not necessarily imply magical craft. Thus, esp. in view of 2 K. 24:14, which specifies craftsmen and smiths as among those carried off in the Exile, and since the poetry does not demand a rigid pairing here (judge, prophet, diviner, and elder are apparently chiastic), it is best to leave the skill unspecified.

Those leaders who could foment rebellion after the conquering army had passed on were deported and replaced by more docile peoples from some faraway region. Particularly prominent in Isaiah's list are persons who could give guidance, who could tell someone what to do. Because Judah and Jerusalem had relied on human discernment rather than divine, the day was coming when that support would be removed. Then, perhaps, they would be forced to rely on God's leadership again. The absence of any mention of the king is interesting. Delitzsch is probably correct when he says that in these times the real power had passed out of the king's hands and into the hands of the nobles and great men. It was certainly so by Jeremiah's time (Jer. 38:4–6, 25–27).

4, 5 When a people commit themselves into the hands of human leaders, the result is disaster. The prophet's sense of contrast is clear. Judah will go from mighty man to child. In some cases, after the Exile, that may have been literally true: teenagers may have had to take over leadership simply because there was no one else. But more probably Isaiah is speaking figuratively: Judah will be ruled by incompetents. In fact (v. 12), that is already so. The leaders may posture like great men but they are children. When a nation permits its rulers to believe that they rule in their own right and because of their own competence, that nation brings upon itself the official graft, self-serving, and irresponsibility which result. Then, when the government begins to collapse, all types of authority fall into contempt and the natural inclinations of fallen human beings are allowed to run free (v. 5). The result is not some sort of hierarchy but an anarchy where all devour each other alike.[15]

6, 7 Isaiah brings this prophecy of a time when Judah will be ruled by nobodies to a climax with a concrete example. He foresees a time when the land will be so deprived of leadership and so poverty-stricken that possession of a coat will constitute grounds for election to rule. Kaiser believes that the reference is to the kind of sleeveless, fringed mantle which ancient Near Eastern rulers wore.[16] As Young points out, however, *śimlâ* is the regular word for cloak or mantle and there is nothing in the context which automatically distinguishes this *śimlâ* from any other. It would be a time when possession of any kind of coat would set one above the common crowd.

Contrary to Gesenius and the versions, the opening *kî* almost certainly should not be translated "for." Rather, it introduces a

---

15. *niggaś*, "to oppress," a Niphal with a reflexive meaning.
16. Cf. pictures in G. E. Wright, *Biblical Archaeology*, rev. ed. (Philadelphia: Westminster, 1962), p. 199; *ANEP*, nos. 439, 441, 447.

temporal/conditional statement of which v. 7 is the apodosis, *When a man seizes . . . (then) he will lift up. . . .* Although the LXX and the Targum do not understand it, *this ruin will be under your hand* seems to be a fine example of the prophet's gift for irony (LXX "Let my meat be under you"; Targ. "Let this tribute be under your hand"). *Hand* is the expression of authority and power. But what is there left to rule? A ruin, nothing more. Yet even a heap of ruins is more than the chosen man cares to take on. Unlike those self-confident rulers of another day who thought in their arrogance that they could do anything, this man, chastened by disaster, fears he can do nothing. As a leader, he could neither feed nor clothe his people and he will not accept the responsibility. How are the mighty fallen, Isaiah seems to say. Judah will go from a time when no mantle of glory was too great to assume to a time when even a dump heap constitutes more responsibility than a person would want.

(2) Rapine for leadership (3:8–15)

8 *For Jerusalem has stumbled,*
   and Judah has fallen;
because their tongue and their works are toward[1] *the Lord,*
   to defy the eyes of his glory.
9 *The expression of their faces answers against them,*
   and their sin like Sodom they declare,[2] *they do not hide it.*
Alas for their own selves,
   for they have brought evil on themselves.
10 *Say of the righteous that it shall be well;*
   for the fruit of their works they shall eat.
11 *Alas for the wicked; it shall be evil;*
   for the thing which his own hands did will be done[3] *to him.*
12 *My people—its oppressors are children,*
   and women rule over it.
My people—your guides cause you to go astray,[4]
   and the way of your paths they confuse.

---

1. For *'el*, "to, toward," used in the sense of *'al*, "against," see BDB, p. 41. But in the light of the parallel phrase, English "against" may not capture the sense as well as a more periphrastic "in front of" or "directed toward."
2. Ginsberg, "Some Emendations in Isaiah," *JBL* 69 (1950) 53, suggested "their sins have told everything" for "their sin, like Sodom, they declare" (dropping *kiseḏōm* and repointing "sins" to become the subject).
3. 1QIs^a has *yāšûḇ*, "will return," for MT *yēʿāśeh*, "will be done." Wildberger insists that 1QIs^a must be the correct reading because *yēʿāśeh* is not otherwise used in this way. But surely *lectio difficilior* supports the MT.
4. The paronomasia reflected in some English translations, e.g., RSV "leaders mislead," does not represent the Hebrew.

13 *The Lord takes a stand to contend;*
    he stands up to judge the peoples.[5]
14 *The Lord will come in judgment*
    against the elders of his people and its princes:
"It is you who have burned up the vineyard;[6]
    the plunder of the poor is in your houses.
15 *Why is it*[7] *that you crush my people,*
    and grind the faces of the poor?"
        says the Lord, the Lord of Hosts.

As noted above on 3:1–15, vv. 1–15 are united by their perspective upon the present situation. It is this situation which will account for the destruction and humiliation forecast in vv. 1–7. Verses 8–11 speak more generally of the people while vv. 12–15 focus upon the leadership of the people. If it is true that a day will come when there will be no one of the stature to lead God's people, it will be so because the leadership in Isaiah's own day was craven and rapacious (vv. 14, 15), leading the nation to its own destruction (vv. 9, 12). How foolish of Judah to adulate those who were destroying them, while at the same time shaking off God's easy yoke (cf. Calvin).

8 The verse begins with *kî*, "for," which may provide a specific connection with the preceding verse, indicating why the elected leader will refuse his election (Young). In view of the general tone adopted, however, it seems better to relate the *kî* to the entire preceding section (3:1–7). In this view, the prophet would be saying that good government will disappear from the land because the land will have collapsed. Most commentators regard *has stumbled* and *has fallen* as prophetic perfects which are used to describe future events so certain that they are seen as having already occurred. This is very probable. At the same time, a case may be made for seeing them as describing the present, as vv. 8b–15 seem to do. In this view, Jerusalem was then fallen in a moral and spiritual way and the coming destruction would be the result of the fall. Such a view accords well with 1:2–9. *Their tongue* is the concrete equivalent of "words" and *their works* is a synecdoche which includes the entire expression of their lives. All this is lived out directly in front of God and in defiance of him.

5. "his people" (LXX, Targ., Syr., Vulg.) would fit the context better than "peoples" (*ʿammîm*) of the MT. Hummel, op. cit., p. 54, may be correct in suggesting that the original was "his people" (*ʿammô*) plus enclitic *mem*, which later translators misunderstood.
6. LXX has "my vineyard" but it is not supported by other versions.
7. *mallāḵem*, lit. "What is to you." Cf. NIV, RSV "What do you mean?"; NEB "It is nothing to you"; CBAT "What mean you?"

The phrase *the eyes of his glory* may be compared to 52:10, "in the arm of his holiness," i.e., "his holy arm." Unfortunately, "his glorious eyes" does not make good sense in English, but the idea is clear and some such paraphrase as "defying him to his face" captures it. In the face of the God whose glory is everywhere manifested, most of all in his own faithfulness, the people of Israel persist in rebellion.

9 The phrase here translated *the expression of their faces* may be interpreted in two ways. Against the interpretation here adopted are numerous commentators (e.g., Duhm, Marti, Cheyne, Gray) who follow the Targums and Syriac in translating "their partiality." This interpretation is in line with Deut. 1:17; 16:19; Prov. 24:23; 28:21, where *hikkîr pānîm*, "pay regard to faces," refers to a judge being unduly influenced by the person and status of the criminal. In favor of *the expression of their face* are Calvin, Gesenius, Dillmann, Delitzsch, Mauchline, and Young, all of whom argue that the reference here is to the whole people and not only to judges and that, furthermore, it is brazenness which is being discussed in the context, not a particular sin like partiality.[8] It may also be added that there seems to be an intended contrast in the figures in the two verses that supports the translation *expression*. As opposed to the glorious face of God (v. 8), there are the brazen faces of his people, stubbornly and flagrantly pursuing their rebellion.

Alas for their own selves. In Hebrew *nepeš* expresses the idea of a person's essential being.[9] Thus it is frequently used in reflexive statements to express one's own self (47:14; Num. 30:3; Job 9:21; Ezek. 14:14, 20). That seems to be the sense in this context. It is the people themselves who will suffer for their acts. In the words of the epigram, "They have no one to blame but themselves" (cf. Skinner).

10, 11 These verses carry on the theme of retributive justice opened in v. 9b.[10] In language reminiscent of the Wisdom literature, the

8. Note W. Ehrlich, *Randglossen zur Hebräischen Bibel* (Leipzig: 1912), p. 14, where he emends to simply "their mouths testify" (changing *p^enêhem* to *pîhem*).

9. AV "soul" conveys the trichotomous concept of the Greeks whereas the Hebrews had a more unitary concept of the person. (Cf. *TDNT,* IX:614–631.) So Gen. 2:7, "man became a living *being.*"

10. Virtually all recent commentators, fastening upon the idea that individual retribution is a late concept, have treated vv. 10–11 as a late interpolation (so Duhm, Marti, Procksch, Kaiser, Wildberger, Gray, Scott; see also Jensen, op. cit., p. 131 n. 35). Against this view is Herntrich's comment that the doctrine of the remnant presupposes the understanding of personal retribution. Kissane also notes that there is little difference between this statement and that of 1:19–20,

prophet asserts that those who do right will experience good while those who do wrong will experience evil. While we may wrestle, as did Job and the Preacher, with the short-term paradoxes which such a doctrine raises (cf. also Mal. 2:17; 3:13), its ultimate truth must be the cornerstone of the whole biblical message. God is consistent and his ways are consistent. To live according to those ways is to reap blessing in part now, but especially ultimately. To live in defiance of those ways is to reap evil, if not now, then certainly ultimately. This sentiment could have been expressed at this point as a source of encouragement to those saints who were going to be swept into the maelstrom created by their wicked compatriots. The prophet assures them that, whatever the short-term effects, they would have no reason to regret their choice in the long term.[11] (Note that a similar theme is expressed throughout the book of Revelation, e.g., 2:10, 11.)

12–15 In these verses Isaiah moves to an indictment of the leadership. They are acting irresponsibly and unjustly, destroying the very thing entrusted to them. This theme of foolish leadership, especially on the level of elders and princes, recurs throughout the book (7:1–17; 14:4–21; 22:15–25; 28; 29; 32:3–8), and it is against this backdrop that the longing for, and the promise of, one who will rule in justice and righteousness stands out.

12 If the MT is correct,[12] the prophet is saying that in one sense

which is not held to be late. But even more telling are the remarks of W. Holladay, "Isa III 10–11: An Archaic Wisdom Passage," *VT* 18 (1968) 481–87, who insists that the language of the passage is very old, which accounts for the difficulties in translating it (and the diversities among the versions). He demonstrates that the various emendations proposed (*'ašrê,* "happy," for *'imrû,* "say," and "it will be well with him" for "it is well") are in fact not supported by Hebrew usage.

11. See Calvin; cf. also Kissane, who sees vv. 9b–12 as a soliloquy on this theme.

12. The versions disagree with the sense derived from the MT (cf. AV) on the correct reading of the first half of this verse. LXX "My people, your exactors glean you and extortioners shall lord it over you"; Targ. "As for my people, whose officers plunder it like the gleaners of the vineyard and like creditors do they rule over it"; Vulg. "My people, exactors spoil you and women are dominating you." Cf. G. Low, "Den historika bakgrunden til Jes. 3:12a," *Svensk Exegetisk Arsbok* 9 (1944) 49–53; Y. Yalon, "Readings in Isaiah," *Beth Maacah* 12/30 (1967) 3–5. The crux of the problem relates to *me'ôlēl,* "children," a hapax legomenon. The LXX, Targ., and Vulg. seem to treat it like a denominative verb from the noun *'ôlēlôt,* "gleaning" (17:6; 24:13; Mic. 1:7; Jer. 49:9; all figurative for remnant). However, *'ôlēl,* "child," is fairly common (Isa. 13:16; Jer. 6:11; 19:20; etc.), and if the prefixed *mem* were actually an old enclitic *mem* originally attached to the preceding word and now displaced, as Hummel suggests, the AV rendering "children" may be correct. Once the reading "glean" was adopted,

Judah is already ruled by those incompetent to do so (vv. 4, 5). Their incompetence is seen in their inability to lead aright. The very persons who should show them the right way are causing them to go off the path. Some commentators believe that there is a reference to Ahaz's youth and perhaps some undue influence of the queen mother here. But the context gives no reason to make this specific application. It is much more likely that a general figure is being used here to express Isaiah's contempt for men who are not leading.[13]

13–15 God will not allow the practices of the leadership to go unchallenged. He calls them to account and testifies against them. Their sin is that they have abused the trust given them (v. 14). This understanding of the function of the rulers is very important for an understanding of Israel's kingship. The king is not absolute; he is not God incarnate, able to make his own laws. Thus kingship was not privilege but responsibility, the responsibility of building up God's people. This concept was powerful enough that even a king like Ahab, of whom the Bible has little good to say, felt bound by the laws of God with relation to Naboth. Jezebel, coming from Phoenicia, was very impatient with such an idea (1 K. 21:1–16). Zechariah shows a similar understanding of rulership when he accuses leaders of his own time of being shepherds who devoured the flock (Zech. 11:1–17).

The solemnity of the Lord's judgment is underlined by the emphasis of the MT: literally, "Taking his stand for judgment is the Lord, standing to judge his people." The Lord stands in his awesome power and righteousness over against those who devour his people. Sooner or later, they must run headlong into him (Ps. 82:1–8). He leaves no doubt as to the responsibility for the condition of the land: *It is you who have burned up the vineyard* (cf. 5:1–7; Luke 20:9–18). When government becomes corrupt it is usually those who are helpless who are hurt first and most often, especially if the leaders think of the people as their own preserve which they can use to their own advantage. But God says that the people, es-

---

nāšîm, "women," could have been misread as *nôšîm*, "creditors," to correspond with the sense of the first stich. Or, if "glean" were correct and "youths" the mistake, then *nôšîm* would have been read as *nāšîm* to correspond with "youths." At this remove dogmatic conclusions are not possible. The reading of the MT, corresponding as it does with vv. 4, 5, may be somewhat easier and therefore less likely, but the fact that it expresses the same thought as an Arabic proverb gives it a certain authenticity.

13. The reference to women reflects the prevailing attitude of the day. It may also express something of the unhappy memory of Queen Athaliah (2 K. 11:1–20).

pecially the helpless, are his and asks with the burning eyes of v. 8 how the rulers dare to treat his heritage as they do. Not only are the poor plundered, but they are devastated, broken into pieces, and then ground to powder.[14]

(3) Shame for beauty (3:16–4:1)

16 *The Lord says,*
"Because the daughters of Zion are haughty,
and walk with outstretched neck,
and glancing eyes,
going along with mincing steps,[1]
jingling the ornaments on the feet,
17 *the Sovereign will put a scab on*
the heads of the daughters of Zion,
and the Lord will lay bare their foreheads.[2]
18 *In that day the Sovereign will take away the beauty of the ornaments*
and the sunbands and the crescent necklaces,
19 *the pendants and the bracelets and the veils,*
20 *the headdresses and the ankle chains and the scarves and the perfume*
bottles and the amulets,
21 *the signet rings and the nose rings,*
22 *the fine robes and the capes and the cloaks and the purses*
23 *and the mirrors and the linen garments and the turbans and the*
shawls.
24 *So instead of fragrance there will be a stench;*
instead of a waistband, a rope.
Instead of ornately dressed hair,[3] baldness;

14. Schrieber, "Bemerkungen zu Jesaja (3:15; 21:12)," *VT* 11 (1961) 455, argues that "grind the face" is a wordplay designed to evoke the ironic thought in the hearer that the leaders were enjoined from partiality ("lifting up faces"). Alexander suggests that the figure is of the prone poor being walked on until their faces are ground into the roadway.

1. *ṭāpap,* "mincing steps," is related to the noun "child" and probably reflects short, childlike steps. It is also probably onomatopoeic like the English "tap."

2. AV "secret parts" is a conjectural translation of *pōṯ,* which occurs only once elsewhere (1 K. 7:50) with the apparent meaning of "sockets." But Driver, *JTS* 38 (1937) 38, has pointed out the Akk. *pūtu,* "forehead," which fits the parallelism much better.

3. *maʿᵃśeh miqšeh* would normally refer to metal work (cf. Exod. 25:18, 31, 36; 37:7, 17, 22; Num. 8:4; 10:2). The phrase may have come to denote merely artistry and thus be applicable to hair-dressing as here. Note Young's comment that *qšh* can also mean "turn around" and thus the phrase might mean braiding.

> *instead of a fine garment, a girding of sackcloth;*
> *instead of beauty, shame.*[4]
> 25 *Your men by the sword will fall,*
> *your mighty men in battle.*
> 26 *Her gates will lament and mourn;*
> *she will be empty; on the ground she will sit.*
> 4:1 *Seven women will seize one man in that day,*
> *saying, "We will eat our own food and wear our own clothes;*
> *only let us be called by your name.*
> *Take away our reproach!"*

In 3:16–4:1 the prophet continues the contrast which has been central to his thought from 2:6 onward: the contrast between glory contrived by human means and the shame which results from that contrivance. In an extremely powerful figure Isaiah makes the whole argument very concrete: wealthy women, secure in their luxury and their allure, are reduced to scabrous hags begging to belong to someone. Almost all the commentators see the primary function of the passage to be an indictment of the women of Jerusalem in Isaiah's day like those of Amos 4:1–3 and Jer. 44:15–30. In this sense, it would parallel the indictments of male pride found earlier in this section.[5]

Seen in its overall context, however, the figurative usage just mentioned could be more important than the literal one. Figuratively speaking, it is not merely women who love ostentation and luxury, it is all humanity. Nor is it merely women who through an abundance of possessions (vv. 18–23) attempt to enhance themselves. It is all humanity which with haughty looks (2:11; 3:9) parades its self-sufficiency across the stage of the world. Surely, there must have been proud, ostentatious women in Jerusalem or the figure would have had no basis, but to limit the statement to those women is to lose its considerable impact as a closing to the whole argument from 2:6 onward. The use of *daughters of Zion* (cf. 1:8) reinforces the likelihood of a figurative aspect,[6] as does the personification of Zion as a woman in vv. 25 and 26.

4. MT appears to read "for instead of beauty," with the final word missing. Interpreters have suggested that *kî* is not a preposition here but a noun from the root *kwh*, "to burn." If so, this is the only occurrence of the noun in the OT. The text would then read "burning instead of beauty" (cf. AV). 1QIs[a] reads "for instead of beauty, shame" (so RSV). Except for the initial *kî*, this phrase corresponds in form to the preceding four contrasts, which the suggested MT reading does not. The 1QIs[a] reading is easier, but corruptions are almost always harder. Cf. Young.

5. Cf. Scott's comment.

6. The appearance of the plural "daughters" here as opposed to the singular elsewhere may be for the purpose of allowing a double reference: both to Zion and to the women of Zion.

16–17 *Because the daughters . . . the Sovereign will. . . .* As has been said from 2:6 onward, the effect of self-exaltation is a confrontation with the only truly self-sufficient Being in the universe, the only One whose glory is not derived. The result of that confrontation is a humiliation, a stripping away of all false supports. The direct cause of the humiliation is the attempt to exalt ourselves. So the woman who depended for her identity upon her elegant neck, her fluttering eyes, and her dainty walk (produced by the hobbling effect of ankle chains) finds herself with a shaven head, the worldwide sign of female disgrace.

18–23 The authenticity of this passage has been widely challenged on several grounds: (1) it is prose whereas what precedes and follows it is in poetic form; (2) the thought of v. 24 follows very naturally upon v. 17 if vv. 18–23 are removed; and (3) the amount of detail seems excessive. While these observations are accurate enough, the conclusion does not necessarily follow,[7] especially if the larger segment is in some sense figurative. Then the piling up of details only adds weight to the figure, making it more impressive and expressing the depth of the prophet's anger, not merely over feminine dress but also at the pretensions of human pride which these trappings symbolize.[8] Furthermore, while vv. 17 and 24 read well without vv. 18–23, they also read well with it, the list of details serving to substantiate the general statements of vv. 16 and 17. While many of the terms are now only generally understood, there is no reason to think them obscure in the prophet's own time.[9] Just as people from many different walks of life today are familiar with particular terms, dress, and clothing (e.g., a "French twist"), the same would have been true then. Our understanding is limited only because these terms occur so infrequently in the Bible that we lack sufficient contexts to define them.[10]

18 *sunbands.* In late Hebrew *šāḇîs* indicated a decorative band of net. However, Schroeder conjectured that the word was related to *šemeš,*

---

7. So Budde argued, as Wildberger says, "vehemently" (*ZAW* 50 [1932] 38–44).

8. As Young points out, it would be difficult to present such a list in other than prose form. But also the shift to prose adds a certain dry irony to the overall statement.

9. Contra Duhm, who thinks only a technician would have known them.

10. For detailed study of the terms, see N. W. Schroeder, *Commentarius philologico-criticus de vestitu mulierum Hebraearum ad Jesaie 3:16–24* (1745); A. F. Hartmann, *Die Hebraerin am Putztische und als Brant* (1809–1810); H. W. Hoenig, "Die Bekliedung des Hebraers," diss. (Zurich, 1957); E. Platt, "Jewelry of Biblical Times and the Catalog of Isa. 3:18–23," *AUSS* 17 (1979) 71–84, 189–201; *ISBE,* II:406–407.

"sun," in connection with the following word *crescents*, or "moons" (so *BHK*). Subsequent appearance of Ugar. *šapš* seems to confirm the reading without emendation of the *b* to *m*.[11]

crescents. Cf. Judg. 8:21, 26 (AV "ornaments," RSV "crescents").

19 *pendants*. *nṭp* means "to drop." Perhaps drop-shaped earring (Koenig; cf. NIV; Judg. 8:26, AV "collars").

veils. In Arabic *raʿl* designates a two-part veil, one part of which is thrown back over the head above the eyes with the other part covering the lower part of the face.

20 *headdresses*. The Targum has "crowns."[12] Cf. 61:3, 10 (AV "beauty," "ornaments"; RSV "garland"), where a wreath may be intended. A circlet of gold or silver may be meant here.

ankle chains (Targ.). Probably designed to give a short mincing step in connection with ankle bracelets (vv. 16, 18 *ʿaḵāsîm*) (cf. also Num. 31:50; 2 Sam. 1:10).

scarves. Targum "hairpins," LXX "braiding" (?), AV "headbands," RSV and NIV "sashes," NEB "necklaces." Adornment for a bride (Jer. 2:32).

perfume bottles. Literally "houses of breath" or "houses of the soul." Scott takes it to be a kind of amulet (NEB "lockets"; Targ. "earrings").

amulets. Cf. v. 3.

22 *fine robes*. Cf. Zech. 3:4; Targum "tunics."

purses. Driver argues that a bag large enough to hold a shekel of silver would have been too large for a lady's handbag and points to an Arabic word having the same consonants, *ḥarāṭatu*, meaning "flounced skirt."[13]

23 *mirrors* (RSV "garments of gauze" with LXX B). Targum and other LXX texts support "mirrors."

turbans. Cf. 62:3; Job 29:14; Zech. 3:5.

24 Isaiah here sets out the conditions which will result when God has stripped away all the accoutrements of human glory (note the opening *kî*, here translated *so*). He does so through five contrasting pairs, beginning in each case with the pretension and following with reality. The reality

---

11. Cf. Gordon, *UT*, p. 494.

12. While the Targ. follows the order of the MT closely and seems to translate, as far as can be told, rather literally, the LXX differs markedly both in order and translation through v. 22.

13. Driver, *JSS* 13 (1968) 37.

possibly refers to the conditions of exile: stench, rope, baldness, sackcloth, and shame. In any case, the picture is one of disgrace, the disgrace which results from abandoning God for trust in man (cf. Deut. 28:56, 57).

25, 26 As noted above, these verses personify Jerusalem as a destitute woman, lending support to the idea that the primary function of 3:16–4:1 is figurative.[14] Stripped of her warriors the city is emptied out with no more going in or out at the gates. All that she has depended upon is taken away and she is left helpless. Young refers to a coin from the time of Vespasian that depicts Jerusalem as a dejected woman sitting under a palm tree with a Roman soldier before her.

4:1 The prophet sums up the condition of the women and of Zion in one graphic verse. This verse makes even more concrete the picture drawn in 3:25, 26. Warfare has always meant destruction of the male population (Germany and France are said to have lost 1,000,000 men each and Britain 500,000 in World War I). So it would be in the Jerusalem that Isaiah foresaw. The situation would become so desperate that the ratio of men to women would be one to seven. No longer would there be any dependence upon flirtation and allure to "catch." Now the women would not even ask for support if they could only have some legal and social identity.[15] Here is the final end of our desire to avoid dependence. We will become dependent in the most degrading and disadvantageous ways. Instead of the exaltation and building-up which comes from glad submission to God and one another (60:1–62:12), our drive to be sufficient in ourselves brings only humiliation, despair, and bondage.

3. ISRAEL RESTORED (4:2–6)

2 *In that day*
the Branch of the Lord
will become beauty and glory,
the fruit of the land

14. Kaiser (cf. also Wildberger) treats 3:26–4:1 separately, calling it an elegy. However, the *qinah* (3/2) rhythm is not maintained throughout. Moreover, in its present setting its function cannot be separated from 3:16–24.

15. It is dubious whether a passage like this should be used to support male leadership of families (as Young does). That principle is better taught elsewhere (e.g., Eph. 5:22–33). This passage seems to be reflecting the social and legal situation of those times where a woman's identity was dependent upon identification with a male. That does not seem to be a biblical principle. Rather, both males and females are made for each other to find a mutual identity in each other (Gen. 2:18–24; Prov. 5:15–20; 31:10–31; 1 Cor. 7:3–5).

> *exaltation and honor*
> *for the survivors of Israel.*[1]
> 3 *It will come to pass that the remainder in Zion and the remnant in Jerusalem shall be called holy, every one written for life in Jerusalem,*
> 4 *when the Sovereign will have washed away the filth of the daughters of Zion, and the blood-guilt of Jerusalem he will have cleansed with a spirit of judgment and a spirit of burning.*
> 5 *Then the Lord will create over the whole establishment of Mount Zion and over its assemblies[2] a cloud during the day and smoke,[3] and brightness of flaming fire by night. For over all the glory will be a canopy.[4]*
> 6 *It will be a shelter[5] for shade from the heat of the day, for a cover and protection from pouring rain.*

With this segment the prophet brings to a close the subsection beginning at 2:1. He started with an announcement of Israel's destiny as the people of God, through whom God's law could be made known to an expectant world (2:1–5). But that vision stood in direct contrast to the present condition of Israel. In essence she was reduced to Judah and Jerusalem, and even Judah, instead of teaching the world, was being taught *by* the world. They were learning dependence on human greatness for their life. But Isaiah shows in a series of stunning contrasts how such dependence does not exalt but rather humiliates (2:6–4:1). The climactic contrast appears in 3:16–4:1 where Jerusalem is compared to haughty Judean ladies who will be reduced to abject misery by the coming exile. But does this predicted destruction mean that God will give up on Israel, that, in fact, her destiny will become unreachable? 4:2–6 answers this question in the negative. God will not give up on his people. In fact, the coming fires of the Exile will only serve to make his people more what God has always wanted

1. The meter of the following verses makes it difficult to take them as poetry without emendation (cf. Gray). Verse 2 does seem to be in poetic form (cf. Wildberger).

2. Commentators disagree over whether *miqrā'ehā* designates "those who assemble" or "places of assembly." The former is the most common meaning and there is no reason to deviate from it here.

3. "and smoke" would seem to go best with "and brightness of flaming fire" (cf. RSV), but the Masoretic punctuation clearly places it with "a cloud during the day." The writer is perhaps thinking of smoke as an indication of God's presence (6:4) rather than as a concomitant of fire.

4. The final phrase, "over all the glory will be a canopy," becomes less difficult to understand if it is seen to be a direct allusion to Exod. 40:34.

5. "shelter" (*sukkâ*, same as 1:8) stands in an emphatic position indicating a primary function of the canopy mentioned at the end of v. 5.

them to be (v. 4). The prophet reinforces his assertion of the redeemed Israel's essential unity with her past by the large number of allusions to the Exodus (vv. 5, 6). They will not lose their royal priesthood (Exod. 19:6) because of coming judgment. In truth, they will find it (cf. Mal. 3:3, 4).

The evidently eschatological flavor of this passage has caused many commentators to date all or part of it after the Exile. Duhm goes far as to assign it to the second century B.C. Although Kaiser and Wildberger are reluctant to go as far as Duhm, they still place it during the second temple period.[6] The evidence for such dating is rather tenuous, depending in large part upon the conclusion that eschatological and apocalyptic thinking were the result of the failed hopes of the postexilic period.[7] However, that conclusion is almost in the nature of an assumption, depending as it does upon an evolutionary view of religious development. There is little hard evidence which points to a late date. While it is true that the Book of Life (v. 3) is mentioned frequently in the later prophets (Dan. 12:1; Mal. 3:16; Rev. 3:5), it also appears in Exod. 32:32. Furthermore, the use of Exodus language does not support a late date unless Mic. 7:15–17 and Isa. 11:11–17 are also to be dated late. In favor of an early date is the verbal and thematic unity between 4:2–6 and the material preceding it, including the reference to the daughters of Zion (3:16; 4:4), the idea of destruction resulting in a remnant (3:6, 7; 3:25–4:1; 4:3, 4), filth and bloodshed (1:15; 3:24; 4:4). In the absence of more conclusive evidence for a later date of composition and given the appropriate ways in which this material fits at this point, there seems to be no reason to depart from the traditional understanding (cf. Skinner).

2 *In that day* provides a direct connection between this segment and what preceded it (2:12, 17; 3:7, 18; 4:1). But the relationship is one of contrast. In those references the coming day was one of retribution and judgment, when the false hopes and complacency of the Judeans would be swept away. Yet God's final purpose is not destruction. If it was true that God's coming day would not merely vindicate the people, neither would it annihilate them. Rather, God's coming day would only be complete when cleansing and restoration had taken place (cf. Zech. 12–14 for

6. Cf. E. Lipinski, "De la reforme d'Esdras au regne eschatologique de Dieu [4:3–5a]," *Bib* 51 (1970) 533–37, for yet another point of view.

7. Cf. more recently P. Hanson, *The Dawn of Apocalyptic* (Philadelphia: Fortress, 1975).

the same theme). Thus, this segment forms a necessary counterpoise and conclusion to the prophecies which preceded it.

Traditionally, beginning with the Targum, *the Branch of the Lord* has been interpreted as referring to the Messiah (as it does elsewhere: Jer. 23:5; 33:15; Zech. 3:8; 6:12). But almost all modern commentators dispute this interpretation here (Calvin also). Their main evidence is that the parallel phrase *the fruit of the land* has no obvious messianic connection. On the other hand, if "fruit" is taken in a more literal sense, "branch" can be paralleled to it without great difficulty (cf. NEB "the plant which the Lord has grown"). On this view, the Lord would be promising renewed fruitfulness for the land, either figurative or literal,[8] after the desolation of judgment.[9]

While such an interpretation is certainly consistent with the statements of Isaiah in other places, as well as with the other prophets, the question remains, as Mauchline notes, as to why Isaiah used this rather ambiguous word in what could have been otherwise a very simple statement. Nor can the witness of the Targum be too easily gainsaid. Although it is obviously influenced by Zechariah and possibly Jeremiah, it still constitutes a very early understanding.[10]

Those who accept the messianic interpretation of *Branch* have felt constrained to give *the fruit of the land* a messianic connection. Delitzsch, and more recently Young, have sought to make *the Branch of the Lord* reflect Christ's divine nature whereas *the fruit of the land* would reflect his human nature.[11] But this position rests too much on scholarly ingenuity, as Barnes has shown in detail. If the branch is the Messiah, then the point would seem to be that the real and lasting produce of Israel is God's gift, not the result of her own fruitfulness and power.[12] God will take away that honor *(tip'eret)* which she created for herself (3:18) and give her a new

8. See Kaiser for the figurative interpretation; see Cheyne for the literal.
9. For other expressions of such a thought see 30:23, 24; 32:14–20; 35:1–2, 6–7; 41:17–20; 43:16–21; 51:3; 55:12, 13; Jer. 31:12; Ezek. 34:26–29; 47:1–12; Amos 9:13–15; Zech. 9:16–10:1; Mal. 3:11.
10. Is it not also possible that the Zechariah passages constitute an interpretation of Isaiah?
11. Young gives the most detailed and complete defense of the messianic interpretation despite its flaws on this particular point.
12. Mauchline suggests that it is the remnant itself which is conceived of as the sprout and the fruit. This interpretation has much to commend it, esp. in view of the concept of the ideal servant in chs. 42–55. What actual Israel was called to be, but could not be, the Servant became for her sake. So, perhaps, the ideal Branch is what Israel was called to be.

source of honor and exaltation. Israel herself is not the sprout, but rather that which has come from her by God's grace. When God gives her glory, then she will know her true greatness, the greatness which eluded her when she sought to produce that glory herself. The thought that the Messiah is the mediator of God's glory is a prominent one in the NT (Luke 2:32; 9:26, 32; John 1:14; 2:11; 11:4; 17:5, 22, 24; 1 Cor. 2:8; 2 Cor. 4:6; Col. 1:27; Heb. 1:3).

3, 4 A nation which has become progressively more unlike God in his moral character will, in that day, become holy. This is the purpose of judgment and of redemption, that people should be like God. Indeed, this was the purpose of the Exodus and the giving of the law. God's desire is that we should be holy as he is holy (Lev. 19:2; 22:31–33). In part, that means to become his possession, for whatever belongs to him is sanctified by his presence. So the objects in the temple were holy and could not be put to common use (cf. Lev. 10:1–11). But to be holy means also the manifesting of a distinctive character. The so-called Holiness Code (Lev. 17–26) stresses that it is through the cultivation of certain kinds of ethical behavior that persons demonstrate the holiness of God. Israel had increasingly failed to cultivate such behavior. More than that, she seemed incapable of doing it. What should be done?

With the other prophets, Isaiah sees hope through the very punishment for sin. The fiery judgment would be a factor in the cleansing process. Although it would not be for many, still some would realize why the judgment had come upon them and would turn away from their sins which had brought the judgment (Ezek. 36:25–26; 39:23–26; Dan. 9:4–19). In this sense, the purgative fire is a gift from God (cf. 6:6, 7). This element of real ethical change dare not be overlooked in the interpretation of *every one written for life*. Several commentators treat this as being merely evidence of God's having predestined some to life.[13] But to do so overlooks the plain evidence of Mal. 3:16, which indicates that a person's name being entered into the book of life is also a response to choices which he or she has made. In no sense is human salvation the result of human initiative. Rather, we are saved because we have responded to divine initiative. But those who will not respond will not be saved.

But is the divine initiative merely to be seen as a purgative fire? Will the fire alone *wash away the filth* and *cleanse the blood-guilt* (note 1:15) of God's people? Can this fire atone for sin (6:7)? Here correlation with other Scriptures seems to support the messianic interpretation. Sin

13. Cf. Young in particular.

must be borne (Lev. 1:4, etc.; 16:20–22; Isa. 53:4, 5), and it cannot be borne apart from bloodshed (Lev. 16:11–19; 17:11; Isa. 53:12; Matt. 26:28). According to Zechariah, it is through the Branch that the guilt of Judah will be removed (3:8, 9) and a fountain opened for the cleansing of her sin and uncleanness (13:1).

The plural *daughters of Zion* has caused interpreters some concern because if it is taken literally it is too restrictive, seeming to leave the sins of the sons uncleansed. Thus the LXX inserted "sons." Gray (with Marti) chose to delete "daughters." Scott wished to make "daughters" singular. However, if "daughters" is taken in a figurative sense as representative of Jerusalem, as suggested above (3:16, 17), the problem is removed.[14] In fact, the evidently figurative use of the phrase in this passage offers the strongest support for the figurative interpretation of the phrase in 3:16, 17.

It is not possible to be dogmatic of the interpretation of "spirit" in the phrase *a spirit of judgment and a spirit of burning*. Many commentators understand it to refer to the Spirit of Yahweh.[15] Thus Calvin, arguing that the Spirit is known by what he does, suggests that the sense is of judgment and burning done by the Spirit. But others believe that a figurative use of "wind" is intended.[16] Here the allusion would be to the hot searing wind off the desert (Scott) or to the storm wind accompanying a theophany (Kaiser; cf. 11:15; 27:8). But it may be that neither of these is correct. Such usages as "a spirit of confusion" (19:14), "a spirit of justice" (28:6), "a spirit of deep sleep" (29:10), "a spirit in him, so that he shall hear a rumor" (37:7; perhaps also 11:2), all seem to suggest a kind of periphrastic construction in which "spirit" almost serves to introduce an abstract concept. If this interpretation is correct, it would be appropriate to translate "through the process of burning and judgment."

5, 6 Several images would be invoked in the hearers' minds by the allusions to the pillar of cloud and fire contained in these verses. First, they would help to establish a sense of continuity with the past and let the hearers know that the searing words recorded in 2:6–4:1 did not mean that God would abandon his ancient covenant (Exod. 13:20–22). Second, they would reaffirm that God's ultimate intention was to share his presence (the glory, Exod. 40:34–38) with them as intimately as possible (cf. Ezek. 10:3–5, 18–19; 11:22–25 vs. 43:1–5). Third, the cloud would speak to

14. Cf. GKC, pp. 396–401, on the uses of the plural for singular concepts.
15. See Gray, Delitzsch, Skinner, Mauchline, etc.
16. See Cheyne, Kaiser, Scott, Wildberger.

them of God's care for them expressed through the protection and guidance afforded by the pillar (Num. 9:15–23).

In this case, however, the cloud seems not to be merely a pillar over the temple, but a canopy which covers all of Mount Zion and those who assemble there. The glory which the canopy of cloud covers (Exod. 40:34) no longer resides merely within the temple precincts; now it is the possession of all who worship the God of Zion (Ezek. 39:25–29; John 17:10, 22, 24). The canopy of cloud and fire, so terrifying to God's enemies, will be a source of comfort to the remnant. The same fire which purged them is now their protection and hope. In language reminiscent of Ps. 91, the author asserts that neither blinding sunlight nor driving rain can hurt God's people. This reference is apparently an antinomy which, by expressing the opposites, includes everything between. Thus, the author is saying that there is nothing in the created universe which can harm those who belong to God. Some have felt this mention of the sun and the rain to be somewhat mundane and thus to offer a rather weak conclusion to the segment. However, when it is remembered that in a pagan worldview the natural forces are deities to be feared, this assertion gains considerable strength. Those who "abide in the shadow of the Almighty" (Ps. 91:1) have nothing to fear from the "principalities and powers" (Rom. 8:38; Eph. 1:21, 22; 6:12) of this world.

C. A HARVEST OF WILD GRAPES (5:1–30)

1. THE SONG OF THE VINEYARD (5:1–7)

1 *Let me sing for my beloved,*
the song of my beloved for his vineyard.
A vineyard belonged to my beloved,
on a fruitful hill.[1]
2 *He dug it up and removed its stones;*[2]

1. A number of assonances in the Hebrew of the song seem likely to have added to its beauty. In v. 1 the recurrence of long *a*s, *i*s, and *o*s is notable. There is also the recurrence of segholization in the latter half of the verse. This may account for the use of *qeren ben šāmen,* "fruitful hill" (lit. "a horn a son of oil"), because of the *qerem,* "vineyard." Arabic uses the term "horn" for "hill" fairly frequently, a usage which is preserved in the English name for the twin hills in lower Galilee where the Crusaders suffered defeat, the "Horns of Hattin."

2. Lit. "he stoned it," a Piel privative expressing removal; cf. Ps. 51:9 (Eng. 7), lit. "sin me with hyssop"; cf. also the modern English expression "she dusted the table."

he planted it[3] *with good vines.*
   He built a tower in its midst,
      And also a wine vat he hewed out in it.
   Then he waited [for it] to produce grapes;
      but it produced wild grapes.[4]
3 Now, inhabitant of Zion, man[5] of Judah,
      judge between me and my vineyard.
4 What more should be done for my vineyard,
      that I have not done for it?
   Why, when I waited for it to produce grapes,
      did it produce wild grapes?
5 Now, let me make known to you
      what I am about to do to my vineyard:
   taking away its hedge so that it will be destroyed,
      breaking down its wall so that it will be trampled.[6]
6 I will make it a ruin;[7]
      it will not be pruned,
      and it will not be hoed;
      thorns and thornbushes will grow up.
   Upon the clouds I will lay the charge
      not to rain any rain upon it.
7 For the vineyard of the Lord of Hosts
      is the house of Israel,
   and the men of Judah
      are a planting in which he delights.
   He waited for justice and, behold, oppression;
      for righteousness and, behold, a cry.

Chapter 5 brings the introductory oracles to a close. If ch. 1 introduced the reader to the book as a whole, and chs. 2–4 laid bare the enormous conflict between what Israel was called to be and what, in fact, she was,

3. All three verbs in the first half of the verse end in *-ēhû*, and the first two are vocalized identically.

4. Lit. "stinking things." Vulg. has *labruscas*, "wild grapes," which fits the context well (LXX "thorns").

5. LXX and 1QIs[a] have "inhabitants" for MT "inhabitant," but both LXX and 1QIs[a] agree with MT on "man." Thus MT may represent the easier reading.

6. The verbs here are infinitives abslute. Delitzsch calls them explicative while Young says they are used adverbially, modifying an understood verb (as in *môt tāmût*, "you will surely die," Gen. 2:17). However, they may merely stand in place of a finite verb, being governed in person, number, and "tense" by the main verb; cf. J. Huesman, "Finite Uses of the Infinitive Absolute," *Bib* 37 (1956) 271–295, esp. 286.

7. *bāṭâ*, "ruin," on the basis of Driver (*JTS* 38 [1937] 38), who cites the Akk. *batū*, "to reduce to ruins, raze utterly."

ch. 5 brings us back to the realities of Israel's condition at the moment of Isaiah's speaking. Whatever the future might hold, however redemption might occur, the plain fact was that somehow present sin must be faced and dealt with. No future hope, such as that contained in 4:2–6, could ever obscure or obviate present evil. This message is ever the same. Yes, there is hope, but that hope cannot annihilate the present, somehow removing us from its responsibility.

The parable of the vineyard (vv. 1–7) sets the stage for the rest of the chapter, which includes a discussion of six conditions (wild grapes) that exist in the people and are contrary to God's expectations for them (vv. 8–25), and an announcement of coming destruction (cf. vv. 5, 6) at the hand of Gentile armies. It is a word which is devoid of hope, but that note has already been sounded in ch. 4. Here the need is to face the present and its relation to what lies immediately ahead.

Verses 1–7, perhaps because their artistry is so widely acclaimed, have come in for intensive study.[8] That very intensity may account for some of the wide divergencies regarding the more technical aspects of the poem. For instance, there is little agreement concerning the poetic structure[9] or the exact nature of the genre.[10] But the general sense is very clear, as it must have been to its first hearers: Israel (as typified in Judah and Jerusalem, v. 3) is compared to a vineyard whose owner has lavished a great deal of care upon it only to discover that the vineyard does not produce good grapes. In a way similar to Nathan's, when he used a story to get King David to condemn his own actions (2 Sam. 12:1–7), so Isaiah sets his hearers up to judge themselves: God has cared for them like a

8. Significant articles dealing with the passage include: P. Haupt, "Isaiah's Parable of the Vineyard," *AJSL* 19 (1902/1903) 193–202; W. Graham, "Notes on the Interpretation of Isaiah 5:1–14," *AJSL* 45 (1928/1929) 167–178; H. Junker, "Die literärische Art von Is v. 1–7," *Bib* 40 (1959) 259–266; W. Schottroff, "Das Weinbergleid Jesajas 5:1–7, ein Beitrag zur Geschichte der Parabel," *ZAW* 82 (1970) 68–91; D. Lys, "La vigne et la double je: Exercise de style sur Esaie 5:1–7," *VTSup* 26 (1974) 1–16; J. Willis, "The Genre of Isa. 5:1–7," *JBL* 96 (1977) 337–362.

9. See, e.g., Duhm; Haupt, op. cit.; Gray; and H. Kosmala, "Form and Structure in Ancient Hebrew Poetry," *VT* 16 (1966) 167–68. All attempts to produce an exact metrical structure rest upon more or less extensive emendations and thus open themselves to serious question. For a convenient elucidation of one recent theory, syllabic meter, see D. Stuart, *Studies in Early Hebrew Meter*, HSM 13 (Missoula: Scholars, 1976). However, this approach does not seem to apply to the passage any more immediately than the others.

10. Cf. Willis, op. cit. He notes at least 12 different interpretations involving nearly as many different genres.

vineyard, yet the fruits of their lives are bitter and sour. Is not God more than justified if he decides to remove his protection from them?[11]

The passage can be divided into four segments, the first three containing two verses each (1–2, 3–4, 5–6) and the last segment one verse (7). Verses 1 and 2 explain the setting; vv. 3 and 4 ask the hearers for a verdict; vv. 5 and 6 announce the owner's decision; and v. 7 makes the specific application to Israel. There is a definite lengthening of the poetic line in vv. 5–7, a factor which could enhance the sense of doom inherent in the content of the verses. Although the song has sometimes been considered an allegory (see most notably the Targ. but also Luther, and, to a lesser degree, Calvin), the text offers little reason to do so. The final application, as well as vv. 2 and 4, emphasize merely the comparison of Israel's unrighteousness in view of God's care. This stress upon a single point more aptly fits the accepted definition of parable.[12]

1 The presence of $y^e\underline{d}î\underline{d}$ and $\underline{d}ô\underline{d}$, both meaning *beloved,* as well as the use of *vineyard,* which has sexual overtones in Canticles as well as in extrabiblical sources,[13] has led some to conjecture that this was actually a love song from the grape harvest, sung either by the lover or the lover's friend. This has been put forth as a solution to the supposedly over-familiar *beloved* in Isaiah's reference to God.[14] But even this solution is not applicable apart from emendation (note Wildberger's comment on Gray's suggestion), for it is not the vineyard which is called beloved, but the owner of the vineyard, and that by the singer. Furthermore, the song is more an accusation than a love ballad. If the poet started out in the love-song genre, he certainly did not adhere to the form. What is more likely is that certain key words and phrases have been incorporated in order to capture attention and set a mood.[15]

As for the likelihood of Isaiah calling God "his beloved," there is no reason to think that just because Isaiah recognized God's awesome holiness and power, he could not have been deeply enamored of him.

11. See also Ps. 80:9–19 (Eng. 8–18); Cant. 4:12–16; 8:11–13; Jer. 2:21. Cf. Luke 20:9–16.

12. Cf. A. T. Cadoux, *The Parables of Jesus: Their Art and Use* (London: James Clarke, 1930), p. 52.

13. Cf. "The Myth of Enki and Ninhursag," where the giving of fruit and habitation are linked (*ANET,* pp. 39–40). Cf. also *UT,* 130 (also called V AB, A), where wine and love are put together (*ANET,* pp. 135–36).

14. Cf. Gray and Scott.

15. Calvin considers Isaiah to be the friend of the Bridegroom who sings the Bridegroom's song for him (cf. Procksch, Scott, Kaiser). This may be, but it depends in part upon a severely weakened sense for $y^e\underline{d}î\underline{d}$ and $\underline{d}ô\underline{d}$.

Bernard of Clairvaux can hardly be accused of having a petty view of God, yet his treatises and hymns on passionate affection for God are the more lovely because the God they adore is so exalted. So it was with Isaiah. He is the "Prince of the Prophets" not merely because he saw God high and lifted up, but also because he learned that the high God lived in delight with the humble (30:18; 57:15). Such a God could be truly adored. In this light, that Israel could fail to respond to Isaiah's beloved would only make her defection more culpable in the prophet's eyes (cf. 2:9).

2 This verse describes the activities of the farmer preparing his vineyard. Having chosen an exposed hillside which gives every evidence of high fertility, he now digs up the ground and carries off the stones. Removing the stones is an essential task in a land where the limestone outcroppings help to produce the fertile *terra rosa* soil, but also produce untold numbers of surface rocks. These stones would be piled about the perimeter of the field as a wall to keep out marauding animals. Those left over from the wall could be used later to build a watchtower, if the owner possessed enough energy and interest.[16] Before building the tower, however, the vines would be planted. Although the exact meaning of *sōreq*, which is used to describe the vines, is not known, it is evident that they were more than ordinary ones.[17] Once the vines were planted, then there would be an interval of two years before grapes would be produced. During this time of waiting and anticipation, the wall could be strengthened, the watchtower built, and the facilities for pressing and gathering the juice completed. These facilities usually consisted of two vats hewn out of the hillside, one above the other, and connected by a shallow trough.[18] The upper one would be used for pressing the grapes and the lower one as a settling basin for the juice which had run down the trough from the press. What the prophet is emphasizing here is the farmer's prior commitment. He has done all this back-breaking work in the expectation (*qāwâ*, "wait expectantly, hope") of receiving a crop of good grapes. The result was bitter, both in fact and in spirit, for the grapes were worthless. All the hard work had been to no purpose; all the hope had been in vain.

3, 4 Now the prophet begins to draw his net. Undoubtedly he had captured the attention of his hearers. The occasion may have been at

16. For a photograph of vineyard walls and watchtower see *ZPEB*, V:883.

17. It may refer to a particularly rich color of red (cf. Arabic) or it may be a locality famous for good vines. The Sorek Valley, southwest of Jerusalem, is such a location.

18. The emphatic position of "wine vat" in the Hebrew may emphasize the difficulty of the work involved in hewing it out.

the end of the grape harvest (Kaiser), and that would have made the song doubly appealing. But it would have been of interest to Judean hearers at any time of the year because of the prominence of viticulture in that part of Israel. Everyone who heard Isaiah could empathize with the farmer's hard work and anxious expectation. Likewise, everyone of them could feel the shock and disgust over the bitter fruit. When the singer asked what more he could have done to ensure good grapes,[19] given the degree of audience participation common in that part of the world, it is likely that some shouted "nothing!" while others announced what they would do with such a disappointing investment.

5, 6 Whatever may have been his hearers' responses, Isaiah wants them to have no doubt as to what the owner will do.[20] He will not merely abandon his worthless vineyard, he will also assist in its destruction. He will take down the *hedge*, which probably refers to the thorns which have grown up on top of the wall; he will break the wall down and, as a result, leave the vines unprotected from animals, either grazing or wild ones. If the vineyard can produce only wild grapes, then there is no use cultivating it. It may as well return to a wild state. So intense is the husbandman's anger at the useless plot of ground that he even enjoins the clouds from raining upon it. Numerous commentators have expressed the opinion that the use of this particular thought would have revealed the identity of the owner since only God can prevent the rain. That is certainly true. But that does not stop angry individuals from trying to prevent it. In fact, some of the hearers may very well have laid the same kinds of injunctions on the clouds and this remark would only increase their sympathy for the frustrated owner.

7 It is possible, then, that some or most of Isaiah's audience had not yet understood the application of his parable to themselves. The prophet does not leave them in doubt.[21] In terse phrases made more telling by paronomasia,[22] he unveils and drives home the awful portent of his parable. The vineyard is Israel, the source of God's delight and the object of his desire (60:21; 61:3). Yet the fruit of God's labor is not the justice and righteousness he had worked for, but instead oppression and violence.

---

19. Note the shift in person. The prophet began the poem speaking for God. Now, as the intensity increases, he speaks *as* God.

20. ʿattâ ʾôḍîʿâ-nāʾ, "now let me make you know." The Hiphil cohortative with the ʿattâ expresses a good deal of intensity.

21. The opening kî, although not causal, serves to emphasize the connection with the foregoing (cf. R. J. Williams, *Hebrew Syntax*, pp. 72–73).

22. "He waited for mišpāṭ [justice], but behold, mišpāḥ [oppression], for ṣeḍāqâ [righteousness], but behold ṣeʿāqâ [outcry]."

Israel's destruction is left unmentioned. It does not need to be, for once the equation between Israel and the vineyard has been made, the coming of judgment is inexorable.

Skinner points out the number of ways in which this parable is apt for portraying the truths of biblical religion: (1) true religion is a divine culture in human history; (2) election is intended to produce righteousness; (3) divine husbandry may be thwarted by an inner degeneracy; (4) judgment, that is, withdrawal of God's protection and gracious influence, is the inevitable result of sin. To these Scott adds a fifth insight: sin is not merely failure to rise to the best, it is perversion of the good.

2. WOE TO THE WILD GRAPES (5:8–25)

a. GREED AND INDULGENCE (5:8–17)

8 Alas for those who join house to house,
　　and bring field together with field,
until the end of a place
　　and you are made to live alone[1] in the midst of the land.
9 In my ears, the Lord of Hosts,
　　"Surely many houses will become desolate;[2]
great ones and fair ones without an inhabitant.
10 For a ten-yoke vineyard will produce one bath,
　　and a homer of seed will produce an ephah.
11 Alas for those who rise up early in the morning
　　to pursue strong drink.
Late in the evening,
　　wine inflames them.[3]

1. Whether "live alone" is to be seen as a punishment or a desire is unclear. MT has hûšabtem, a Hophal perfect, meaning "you are caused to dwell." The versions all have "you will dwell." If the subject of the verb is God, then the idea of punishment might be more fitting.
2. Lit. "In my ears, the Lord of Hosts, if . . . shall not be desolate." A word may have dropped out at the beginning, such as "said" or "swore" or "uncovered" (cf. 22:14). The ellipsis is not impossible, however, and surely adds force to the pronouncement through its abruptness. 'im-lō' represents a shorthand version of a fuller oath form. The full form probably ran something like, "As the Lord lives, may something dreadful befall me if what I say does not happen" (cf. Num. 14:23; 2 K. 5:20).
3. Ginsberg, JBL 69 (1950) 52, would emend yadlîqēm, "it inflames them," to yidlōqûn, "they chase after." This reading would fit the parallelism, but the MT also fits the statement of insensitivity which follows in v. 12. For the connection of wine and music at feasts see Amos 6:5, 6.

12 *Lyre and harp,*
   timbrel and flute,
      and wine are their feasts.[4]
But the work of the Lord they do not perceive,
   and the work of his hands they have not seen.
13 *Therefore, my people go into exile—*
   from lack of knowledge.
Their glorious are men of famine;[5]
   their multitude are parched with thirst.
14 *Therefore Sheol opens wide its throat,*
   and stretches open its mouth immeasurably.
So her[6] *honored and her multitude go down;*
   her raucous and those who exult in her.[7]

4. The form of this line is unusual and has given rise to such alternates as the LXX "with lyre . . . they drink wine" (Targ. agrees with MT). Ginsberg (*JBL* 69 [1950] 52) would drop "wine" as being contrary to the meter and change *mišteh*, "feast," to some form of *š*ᵉ*y* having to do with "interests." Thus they would be interested in musical instruments and revelry but not in God's work. Although the suggestion makes sense, there is no manuscript evidence to support it. Delitzsch points out that Ezek. 38:5 shows a comparable syntax when it says "They all are shield and helmet," a forceful way of saying "they are armed."

5. MT "its honor, men of famine." LXX seems to understand *mty* (MT "men") as *mēṭê*, "dead ones," although it paraphrases the entire phrase to "there has been a multitude of dead bodies because of hunger and thirst." Ewald and Hitzig altered *mᵉṭê* to *mᵉzê* (Deut. 32:24), giving "wasted with famine," an attractive option.

6. This pronoun probably refers to Jerusalem. Both "people" and "Sheol" normally take masculine pronouns.

7. J. A. Emerton, "The Textual Problems of Isaiah v. 14," *VT* 17 (1967) 135–142, considers the verse at length. He joins with those who consider the 3rd fem. suffixes to refer to Jerusalem or Zion and proposes to emend ʿālēz bāh to ʿōz lēbāh, "the strength of her heart," i.e., stubbornness or courage. He is forced to admit that the versions do not support such a reading, but he still believes it preferable to the difficult "he who exults in her." Ginsberg (*JBL* 69 [1950] 53) argues that the verse is the ending of a lost denunciation of Jerusalem parallel to that found in Zeph. 3:11–13. Without accepting his thesis in its entirety, one can still point out that the presence of *ʿlz* in that passage (Zeph. 3:11) lends support to the authenticity of the word here. That the verse refers to Jerusalem need not be contested, esp. in the light of 22:2, which contains the same two roots (*š*ᵉ*h, ʿlz*) as does the last stich of this verse. However, it does not necessarily follow that something has been lost between vv. 13 and 14. It is at points like this that form-critical dogma can become a procrustean bed upon which the text is forced. The question is whether the verse functions well in this context. If it does, why should not the prophet have put it here rather than an editor? As to its function, that is evident. There is an easy flow of thought from v. 13 through v. 16, as has been noted. Those who have trampled upon justice and righteousness in their thirst

15 *So man is bowed down,*
   and mankind[8] falls,
      and the eyes of the haughty are downcast.
16 *The Lord of Hosts is exalted in justice,*
   and the Holy God is sanctified in righteousness.
17 *Lambs will feed as in their pasture,[9]*
   and the waste places of the fatlings,[10] kids[11] will devour.[12]

In this section Isaiah specifies the "wild grapes" which Israel has produced. They include greed (vv. 8–10), debauchery (vv. 11–12), arrogance (vv. 18, 19), perversion (vv. 20, 21), and injustice (vv. 22–23). All of these are introduced by the word *hôy,* conventionally translated "woe." As noted above (see on 1:4), the term introduces a lament as much as a threat. The prophet is not merely angry and denunciatory. He is also grief-stricken over the sins of his people. The laments are twice broken by a repeated

---

to exalt and please themselves have thrown open the door to death for the whole people, a death in which all will be equal. Why is this so? Because God's essential character includes justice and righteousness.

8. There is no reason to assert that *'āḏām* means "the mean man" while *'îš* means "the mighty man" (so AV) in this context. They are simply a synonymous pair (cf. Prov. 12:14; etc.) together expressing the ultimate collapse of all designs based upon human eminence. See also on 2:9, n. 7.

9. "as in their pasture" (AV "after their manner"; cf. Vulg., Sym.) is supported by Mic. 2:12.

10. *mēḥîm,* "fatlings," occurs only twice in Hebrew, here and in Ps. 66:15, where the reference is to a sacrificial animal. However, in view of the paucity of occurrences it cannot be proven that the reference must be to animals here (cf. AV "waste places of the fat ones"). Duhm and Ottley proposed *mᵉḥûyîm,* "wiped out ones" (cf. LXX "those taken away").

11. Reading *gdym* for MT *grym,* "strangers," which does not fit the context or the sense (strangers would hardly feed on ruins; furthermore, a word is needed to parallel "lambs"). If "fatlings" could be construed as a construct with "strangers," good sense would be achieved: "the fatlings of strangers will feed upon the ruins." This reading would require taking the final *mem* on *mēḥîm* as an enclitic; cf. H. Hummel, "Enclitic *mem* in Early Northwest Semitic, Especially Hebrew," *JBL* 76 (1957) 85–107. However, "kids" would make an excellent parallel with "lambs" and requires the least emendation of the text. LXX is often adduced in support of "kids" (cf. *BHK*), but the translation there is a paraphrase and gives no direct support to this rendering. Driver, *JTS* 38 (1937) 38, 39, adduces Akk. *gurū,* "young beasts."

12. Ginsberg (*JBL* 69 [1950] 53, 54) proposed a thorough reworking of the verse in which *kᵉḏōḇrām* was divided into *kr* (for *kd*), "pasture," and *brym,* "stout ones," while *hārᵉḇôṯ,* "waste places," was changed to *rᵉḥōḇôṯ,* "wide spaces." The resulting translation would be "The lambs shall graze in the pastures of the stout, the kids in the wide places of the fat." Although this is an attractive reading, it lacks any versional support.

therefore (*lāḵēn*, vv. 13, 14, 24; *'al-kēn*, v. 25). These "therefore" segments (vv. 13–17 and 24–25) serve to delineate the larger unit (vv. 8–25) as well as to subdivide it into two parts (vv. 8–17, 18–25; note the repeated connection of drunkenness and injustice in the two subdivisions, vv. 10–12, 22–23).[13]

The problem which Isaiah is addressing in vv. 8–17 is the emergence of a wealthy landed class which turned its attention more and more to pleasure and indulgence. The northern state of Israel had experienced the same trend earlier in the eighth century B.C. as witnessed by Amos (3:15–4:3; 6:1–8). Whether this was the result of a long-term development (as seems most likely) or because of some more immediate factor is unclear.[14] At any rate, what Smith calls the twin instincts of gathering and squandering have never been the sole possessions of Judah or Israel. Around the world people are driven by the desire to possess more and more and then to spend what they possess more and more lavishly, but only to please themselves. Isaiah's response to this can be summed up in the words of Another, "What shall it profit a man if he gain the whole world and lose his own soul?" (Matt. 16:26).

8 According to the Torah all the land belonged to God, and while he allowed families to possess parcels of that land, it was never theirs to dispose of as they wished. It had to be kept in the family. In the extreme event that keeping the land in the family was impossible, then it should be bought back as soon as possible. Failing that, it must automatically return to the heirs of the sellers in the Jubilee, or fiftieth year (Lev. 25:23–28; Ezek. 46:16–18).[15] It is evident, however, that these prescriptions had come to be revered only as ideals, with the result that those who possessed the means were dispossessing the poor and reducing them to servitude on their own land. While this may have been perfectly legal, that did not

---

13. Most commentators do not accept the doubling of the "therefores" as original. It is frequently argued that another "woe" oracle dropped out between vv. 13 and 14 and that v. 14 was the conclusion to that oracle (cf., e.g., Wildberger). As for v. 25, many see it as having become displaced from after 9:20 (Eng. 21; cf. Kaiser). As will be demonstrated in the commentary, however, the passage as it stands makes excellent theological sense, rendering the various attempts at restructuring largely academic tours de force.

14. Kaiser believes it to be the result of an influx of capital from Uzziah's commercial enterprises, while Mauchline suggests that the threatened invasion of Rezin and Pekah (ch. 7) created a panic atmosphere.

15. For a similar situation cf. Nuzi in eastern Assyria where selling land could only be accomplished through a legal fiction where the buyer was adopted by the seller and then gave the seller a "gift" in return for the "inheritance." See E. Chiera and E. A. Speiser, *JAOS* 47 (1927) 37–40; *ANET*, p. 219.

make it morally defensible. Isaiah accuses the landgrabbers of wanting to possess everything in sight until they could live by themselves in their own little world.[16] It is hardly accidental that the final commandment in the Decalog deals with covetousness, or that Paul sees covetousness as being at the heart of idolatry—the placing of ultimate value in this world (Col. 3:5; cf. also Isa. 57:17).

9–10   But covetousness is always self-defeating in the final analysis. To acquire is to lose, to give is to get. That is the paradox of biblical teaching (Matt. 16:25). So the great houses that were built after all the smaller ones had been bought and razed will be themselves abandoned and desolate. Nor does there need to be some historical or political upheaval to cause this. How many of the world's great castles and mansions have been lived in for any appreciable time? They are simply too pretentious to be borne. By their very immensity they reduce their owners to beetles scuttling about inside them. So they shortly become museums, monuments to human acquisitiveness, and thus under the ban of God (Jer. 22:13–17).

Not only will the great mansions be empty, but the land so assiduously acquired will be infertile. While this may look forward to the postexilic time when the long-abandoned land had become unproductive, it may also refer to those periodic droughts or blights which undercut all our human self-sufficiency. In all cases, it refers to that blight upon the spirit which covetousness produces.[17] "He gave them their request, but sent leanness into their soul" (Ps. 106:15). So the land which required ten yoke of oxen to plow it in a day would only produce about eight gallons of wine (a bath), while ten ephahs (a homer, about 6 bushels) of seed would only produce one ephah (about 3 pecks) of grain. The land belongs to God and to treat it as my own to do with it as I wish is inevitably to remove its capacity to bless me (cf. Lev. 26:14–20; Deut. 28:15–35; Mic. 6:12–16).

11–12   These verses introduce the second cause for Isaiah's lament. It seems likely that he is continuing to address the wealthy who, by virtue of their abundance, can spend the entire day, from early morning until latest night, pursuing their own pleasure, particularly in drinking.[18] It is important to notice the reason why the prophet opposes these practices.

---

16. Note C. S. Lewis's treatment of this theme in *The Great Divorce* (New York: Macmillan, 1946).

17. Targ. makes the unproductivity a punishment for not giving tithes, perhaps in response to 2 Chr. 36:21, which makes the Exile a punishment for refusing to give the land its sabbaths.

18. Delitzsch thinks drinking is mentioned here because of free association with the mention of wine in 5:10. However, the connection between the desire for superfluity of wealth and the desire for superfluity of pleasure is a direct one.

He does not oppose them because they are wrong in themselves, but because they have become all-absorbing to the point where spiritual sensitivity has become dimmed. The revelers no longer have any interest in or ability to recognize how God is at work in the world. When the passion for pleasure has become uppermost in a person's life, passion for God and his truth and his ways is squeezed out. Furthermore, the use of alcohol in the quest for pleasure can only heighten the degree to which one becomes insensitive to responsibilities and values. Calvin says that to become addicted to good food and drink is to bear reproach of becoming voluntarily like brute beasts, not directing the mind toward God, the author of life. As the prophet said in 1:3, however, Israel's insensitivity is worse than that of the animals, who at least have an instinct toward correct choices.

13–14 What will be the result of this arduous pursuit of property and pleasure? A sad irony: My people must leave my land.[19] The thought is reminiscent of Hos. 1:8. My people are in fact not my people. From the outset their particular destiny and privilege has been to know God (Exod. 6:7), but it is evident that they do not know him. If they did, violence and oppression would not have replaced justice and righteousness. This is the meaning of *lack of knowledge* in this context (cf. Hos. 4:1, 2). It is not that they do not know certain facts or certain prescriptions. In contrast to the Targum, which has "the law of the Lord they do not perceive" in v. 12 and "they knew not the law" here, there is every reason to think they did have some perception of the law (cf., e.g., 1:11–13). What they did not have was the experiential relationship with God that gave life to his commandments and meaning to what he was doing in the world (cf. Jer. 9:23–26; 22:15, 16).

Dillmann comments that God's work, which the people do not understand (vv. 12, 13), is the accomplishment of salvation through human history. Duhm disparages this view by saying that the Israelites could hardly be expected to be familiar with Protestant dogmatics. He believes that the reference is to nothing more than the coming judgment, and that the Israelites' debauchery has blinded them to that reality. The latter is certainly an Isaianic and prophetic teaching (22:1–25; 28:7, 8, 14–22; 32:9–14; 56:12; Mic. 2:6–11; Amos 6:1–8; Hos. 12:1–9; Jer. 5:12–17), and it is probably true that most people lacked any overarching view of God's purposes. But, at the same time, to limit the "work" of God here to coming judgment is to miss its coherence with one of the plain accents of Scripture as well as of the rest of the book (2:1–5; 4:2–6; 11:1–9; 35:8–10; 42:16; 43:18–21; 45:14–19). Surely what the prophet is saying

19. Note that *gālâ*, "go into exile," is in the perfect tense, indicating that for the prophet it is an already accomplished fact.

is that these drunken people simply do not perceive what God is about in his world, and what he is about includes the establishment of justice, righteousness, and love through divine *ḥeseḏ* as much as it does retribution upon recalcitrant human arrogance (vv. 15, 16).

As a result of their lack of perception, the honorable as well as the rabble will be deprived of the necessities for life, and death will swallow them all up together. There is no distinction of rank and no place for pomposity in the nether world (cf. ch. 14). All attempts to gain pride of place and power reach the same level in the grave.[20]

15, 16 The verbal similarity of these verses with some of the statements in 2:6–22 (vv. 9, 11, 17) has caused the majority of commentators to conclude that they do not belong in this context. They certainly do repeat those thoughts, but that is hardly reason to excise them from this context, where they fit so well (see n. 7 above). To assume that a person could never repeat himself by adapting an earlier thought to a new setting or by expanding the implication of an earlier thought into a fuller treatment is to demand a compartmentalized approach which flies in the face of human experience.[21]

As for the appropriateness of the content of vv. 15 and 16 to this passage, it can hardly be doubted that human self-exaltation is exactly what the passage is about. If one isolated vv. 10–13 from their context,

20. Sheol (see *IDB*, I:787–88) was a shadowy place where all alike went in death (Ps. 6:6 [Eng. 5]; 88:5–7 [Eng. 4–6]; 141:7). Some contend that the OT does teach a blissful afterlife for the righteous (see M. Dahood, *Psalms*, AB [Garden City: Doubleday, 1970], III:xli-lii) and that Sheol is used then merely as a metaphor for death. Ugaritic usage indicates that *nepeš* can mean not only breath but the place from which the breath emanates, the throat (cf. Akk. *napištu*). Thus it is here, in parallel with mouth, as Delitzsch already recognized (cf. Hab. 2:5). *UT*, 67:1:7 (also called I* AB) seems to contain a remarkable parallel to this passage in that it is referring to the throat of that god of death.

21. But do the two verses fit the context here? Duhm asserts that they break the connection between vv. 14 and 17 while Mauchline suggests that a condemnation of haughtiness is out of place here. In fact, there is no evident connection between vv. 14 and 17. Among commentators who see vv. 8–17 as being a combination from many originals, v. 17 is "logically" connected in three different places: after v. 10 (Ewald, Cheyne, Kissane), after v. 13 (Marti, Gray, Mauchline), after v. 14 (Skinner, Kaiser, Wildberger). This lack of unanimity suggests strongly that the connection (or lack thereof) between v. 17 and some earlier verse is largely the result of the commentators' predilections. Verse 17, insofar as it can be understood, functions as a graphic summary of the ultimate results of self-aggrandizement. As such, it stands somewhat independently and captures the meaning of all the verses which precede it, beginning with v. 9. But it cannot be tightly connected to vv. 10, 13, or 14 any more than it can to v. 16. One wonders whether Duhm was serious in his comment that v. 15 could not follow v. 14 since the dead could not have lifted their eyes in any event.

it might be possible to say that human pride has nothing to do with the quest for pleasure, but even v. 13 suggests that there is a supposed distinction between the noble and the multitudes, which distinction will be obliterated in the coming exile. And if, as is evidently the case, vv. 8, 9, and 14 are coupled with vv. 10–13, then it becomes impossible to maintain that pride is not at issue here. It is pride which drives a person to possess more, and it is pride which drives a person to seek more and more exotic entertainments which will set one off from the "madding crowd." The drinking feasts described in v. 12 are the diversions not of the poor but of the mighty. And because the mighty give themselves to these pursuits rather than to the knowledge of God, the whole nation will go down to the grave together.

16 This verse is of great theological importance, for it expresses the truth that what makes God truly God, what sets him off as divine, is neither his overwhelming power nor his mysterious numinousness. Rather, what marks him as God is his essential justice and righteousness.[22] These characteristics are what must eventually humiliate all human beings in his presence. Finally, it is not our limited intelligence, limited power, or limited life span that drags us down to humiliation before God. It is our inability to love justice and to do rightly that makes a mockery of all our pretensions to have ultimate meaning in ourselves (cf. 6:3–5). It is this which marks God as truly holy. *Holy* was originally a morally neutral word, merely designating that which pertained to deity.[23] But the Hebrews discovered, as here, that what was truly unique to the God who had revealed himself to them as the only God was his moral nature. Thus God's holiness is best attested to in the self-denying choice of a just and upright life (Mic. 6:6–8). (See the comments on ch. 6.)

17 The sense of the verse is generally clear,[24] but the textual problems are severe enough to render dogmatic interpretation impossible. The sense is that flocks will soon graze on the ruins of Judah, ruins which will of course include the fine houses and banquet halls upon which so much attention had been lavished (vv. 9, 12).There is possibly a subtle irony present. The frenetic energy spent in acquiring and enjoying, all at the expense of justice and righteousness, are replaced by the quiet cropping of the flocks. So it will always be. God's peace will prevail, either by design or default.

22. Note the verbal and logical connection with 5:7. Since God's character is constituted this way, so must his vineyard's character be.
23. See Fisher, *RSP*, I:27; von Rad, *Old Testament Theology*, I:205–206.
24. See n. 21 above.

b. CYNICISM AND PERVERSION (5:18–25)

18 *Alas for those who draw iniquity with cords of vanity,*[1]
and sin as though with cart ropes,
19 *who say, "Let his work hasten, let it speed*
that we may see it;
let the counsel of the Holy One of Israel draw near,
let it come that we may know it."
20 *Alas for those who say of evil good*
and of good evil,
setting darkness for light
and light for darkness,
setting bitterness for sweetness
and sweetness for bitterness.
21 *Alas for those who are wise in their own eyes,*
and discerning in their own sight.
22 *Alas for the mighty at drinking wine,*
and the valiant at mixing liquor;
23 *justifiers of the wicked for the sake of a bribe,*
yet taking from them the righteousness of the righteous.[2]
24 *Therefore, as a tongue of flame devours stubble*
and chaff sinks down in the flame,
their root will be like mold
and their flower, like dust, will fly away.
For they have rejected the law of the Lord of Hosts;
the word of the Holy One of Israel they have despised.
25 *Therefore, the Lord was angry with his people;*
he stretched out his hand and struck them.
The mountains trembled,
and their corpses were like dung in the streets.

1. "cords of vanity" ("emptiness," not really "falsehood," RSV) makes an odd parallel with "cart ropes." Targ. suggests a progressive bondage moving from light string to heavy ropes, but the form iniquity-cords ropes-sin does not support this idea. M. Dahood, "Ugaritic *t'at* and Isa. 5:18," *CBQ* 22 (1960) 73–75, followed by Driver, *JSS* 13 (1968) 38, suggests that *šāw'*, "vanity," is a misreading of *šû*, an otherwise unattested Hebrew word for sheep (cf. Akk. *šu'u*, "sheep," and Ugar. *t'ot*, "ewe"). When this interpretation is coupled with a re-pointing of *'ªgālâ*, "cart," to *'egel*, "calf" (the final *he* becoming the definite article on "sin"), excellent sense is achieved: "They draw iniquity with a ewe-rope, sin with a calf-halter."

2. *ṣaddîqîm*, "righteous ones," is followed by singular pronouns. While it is possible that the plural is understood as a distributive (cf. Young), it is also possible that the plural ending is a misreading of an original enclitic *mem;* cf. Ginsberg, op. cit.; Hummel, op. cit., p. 94.

For all this his anger does not turn back;
still his hand is stretched out.

In this segment, the bitterness of the wild grapes is revealed even more powerfully than in vv. 8–17, for here the prophet exposes the underlying cynicism which is responsible for the people's refusal to live in obedience to God's nature. They doubt that God really is active in the world and they imagine that they are better able to determine what is really right and wrong than he is. The result is a perversion where values are reversed: debauchery is more honorable than courage, drunkenness is preferable to sobriety, the wicked are pronounced innocent, while the righteous are condemned. For such a vineyard, destruction is the only open course, and in another double "therefore" (as in vv. 13–14), that destruction is promised.

18–19 These verses very possibly deal with the people's response to v. 12.[3] There Isaiah had charged them with being so intoxicated with the quest for pleasure that they had become insensitive to God's workings in the world. Far from being convicted by that charge, they call out in a mocking fashion for Isaiah's God to hurry up and get his work out where they can see it.[4] If the work referred to is the coming judgment, as some believe, then the effrontery is the more brazen. They are daring God to punish them. Their use of Isaiah's epithet *the Holy One of Israel,* as in 30:11, is hardly an acceptance of what the title means, but rather a way of taunting Isaiah and deriding what they considered his pietistic excess. To this Isaiah responds with a further "woe." They are sinning with a "high hand" and not out of mistake or ignorance. They are pulling the iniquity to themselves with ropes. They have not fallen into it. They are consciously choosing evil and exerting concerted effort to make that choice. This is the tragedy of sin: what was once done somewhat innocently, or at least naively, becomes something we must do, at whatever cost, even though in order to continue it we must explain away God and his moral law. Typical of such an attitude is the demand for God to act prior to the exercise of faith. But no act is sufficient to coerce faith (otherwise Satan would believe). Only when faith is offered freely are God's acts able to confirm that faith.

20, 21 Here Isaiah continues his denunciation of those who mock God's ways. In order to justify their own behavior, they must, in the most sophisticated reasonings possible, demonstrate that their evil behavior is

---

3. Cf. JPSV, p. 361 n. f.
4. Cf. J. Jensen, op. cit., p. 55. Isaiah claims a knowledge of Yahweh's counsel not derivable from empirical observation or the Wisdom tradition (v. 21), and the policymakers of Judah questioned the authenticity of such knowledge.

good, their darkness is light, and their bitterness sweet. This attitude is the end result of refusal to admit the absolute authority of a revealed Word (cf. v. 24). For sin is not content to live alongside righteousness anymore than disease will coexist with health. Sin can only be satisfied when righteousness is destroyed. If the ethical imperative is dependent upon human reason alone, that reason is no match for rampant self-interest. In fact, self-interest will press reason into service to justify its own behavior. Only a prior commitment to the revealed wisdom of God (Prov. 1:7; 3:7; 9:10) and a commitment to call good good, despite the reasonings of the wise of this world,[5] can make possible genuine long-lasting righteousness both in individuals and in society. The path of those who chart their own course leads inexorably from self-aggrandizement to the ultimate reversal of moral values.

22, 23   If it is correct to think of vv. 20 and 21 as expressing the attitudes which are the ultimate end of self-serving, what is the function of vv. 22 and 23? Are they not anticlimactic? They are not if they are understood to be a graphic summary of points made in vv. 8–21 (as 3:16–4:1 are of 2:6–3:15). Here are pictured the great men of the nation, who are only great behind a bar. The terms used refer to military heroes and champions, but these are only champion drink-mixers. When these national leaders are called upon to judge a case, they can be depended upon to free the guilty and convict the innocent—if the price is right. What is this but a picture of what the prophet has been condemning?[6] Courage, honor, and bravery mean nothing. What matters is how many beers a man can hold before going under the table. Innocent and guilty? Who can tell the difference? Who *cares* if there is a difference in a society where serving oneself is all that matters?[7] This is a vineyard gone completely wrong. The grapes are all bitter and human sophistry cannot make them sweet.

24, 25   As noted above, these verses conclude not only vv. 18–25, but also vv. 8–25.[8] Furthermore, v. 25 provides the transition to the final

5. The attack upon the wise in v. 21 is reminiscent of 30:1–7; 31:1–13, where the wisdom of dependence on Egypt is shown to be foolishness. The present text seems to refer to a more general condition of which that is only a specific example.

6. Cf. Young.

7. Gray cannot see a connection between vv. 22 and 23, but as Kaiser asserts, the connection is a direct one. When the great men of the nation have no higher goal than petty pleasure, justice cannot be maintained.

8. In view of the fact that most interpreters include v. 25 with vv. 26–30, some explanation of its inclusion with vv. 18–24 here is necessary. It must be granted at the outset that the verse is transitional. By referring to the past judgment of God and yet indicating that judgment is not complete, it sets the stage for the

segment of the chapter. There is nothing to be done with the vineyard except to destroy it. Gray sees little connection between v. 24 and vv. 22 and 23, and to be sure, if one limits v. 24 to being a response to those two verses, as Gray does, there is a problem. But if it is a response to vv. 18–23, as we take it here, then it is entirely apt, for as noted above, the whole issue is whether God's law and word will be obeyed in the face of our human desires for self-service.[9] If not, then the life drains out of the human enterprise and all our attainments become dust and ashes. We are reduced to stubble in the face of devouring flame, because we have abstracted ourselves from the only source of life, namely, God.

The prophet mixes his figures of speech as he tries to show the impermanence of those who reject God's law. Strict logic cannot be applied to the statement *a tongue of flame devours stubble . . . their roots will become like mold,* but the point is plain. No plant is ultimate in itself. Its life is derived and when the conditions for life are not present, destruction and decay are all that are left to it.[10]

25 Now the prophet moves from figure of speech to a more specific announcement. It is because Israel has rejected God's law and the word of her Holy One that God has already begun to act in judgment.[11] They have felt his outstretched hand already and that hand is still outstretched. The hedge is about to be taken away and the animals summoned to come in and trample the vines.

---

final verses with the picture of imminent military destruction. Furthermore, that v. 25 begins with ʿal-kēn, whereas vv. 13, 14, and 24 have lākēn, might be taken as evidence of its separation from vv. 8–24. However, the case for seeing it as a conclusion to vv. 8–24 is strong. That ʿal-kēn is different may indeed point to its function as a conclusion (for a similar sequence, see 16:7, 9). Furthermore, if v. 25 begins the next segment, the "therefore" hangs in the air without adequate grounding. When it is coupled with v. 24 (as RSV, NIV, CBAT, TEV, NEB [although transposed after 10:4], and JPSV) it shows that the coming judgment and the incomplete past judgment arise from the same cause, that described in vv. 8–23.

9. Calvin's comment is worth repeating: "If contempt for the law of God is the source, head and accumulation of all that is evil, there is nothing against which we ought more carefully to guard than that Satan should take away our reverence for it."

10. Cf. 14:29; 37:31; Amos 2:9; Hos. 9:16; Mal. 4:1 (Eng. 3:19). Cf. also the Eshmunazar sarcophagus (*CIS,* I, no. 3, pl. II; *ANET,* p. 505): "May they have no root down below and no fruit up on top."

11. It is possible that the perfect tenses are to be understood as "prophetic perfects" and that the judgment described, while complete in the prophet's mind, is yet in the future. However, the apparent reference to the earthquake during Uzziah's reign (Amos 1:1) and the apparent indication of incompleteness which the refrain gives seem to support the idea that the prophet is referring to judgment begun.

At this point many commentators begin to reconstruct the text on a more or less radical scheme. The chief spur to this reconstruction is the appearance of the same refrain in 9:11, 16, 20 (Eng. 12, 17, 21), and 10:4 as appears here in v. 25. On the basis of the assumption that the prophet could not have used the same refrain in two different contexts, attempts have been made to reconstruct the original text. The variety of these attempts calls into question the validity of the enterprise. Duhm and Wright interpose 5:25–30 between 9:6 and 7 (Eng. 7 and 8) to begin the section. Smith puts 5:25 between 9:6 and 7 (Eng. 7 and 8) and 5:26–30 between 10:4 and 5. Driver (NEB) does the same with vv. 24 and 25, but leaves vv. 26–30 in place. Ziegler leaves 5:8–30 where they are but transposes 10:1–4, putting it between 5:24 and 25. Kaiser and Wildberger interchange the two passages (!), resulting in 5:8–24; 10:1–4 and 9:7–20 (Eng. 8–21); 5:25–30. Holladay, noting the lack of agreement, merely proposes to make 5:8–30; 9:7 (Eng. 8)–10:4 a unit, with 6:1–9:6 (Eng. 7) having been inserted in the middle.[12] None of these proposals treats the present form of the text seriously, all seeming to assume that it is the result of a somewhat careless mistake or of a capricious scribe (who put vv. 25–30 after v. 24 because both begin with fire). But this will not do. It is the present text which holds authority over us, and except in cases where textual corruption has occurred (for which there is no evidence here), it is this text which we are called upon to interpret. If in fact the prophet or one of his disciples reorganized original materials into the present form (of which the diversity noted above is hardly convincing), then it was done for conscious theological purposes, and it is that theological intent to which the Church must give its attention.

3. COMING DESTRUCTION (5:26–30)

26 *He raises a signal flag*[1] *to a distant nation,*[2]
  and whistles to it from the ends of the earth,
 and behold, speedily, quickly, it comes.
27 *There is none faint,*
  and none stumbles in it.

---

12. Holladay, op. cit., pp. 10–11.
1. *nēs,* "signal flag," is a favorite term of Isaiah's. God will not only raise a flag to call the destroyers (13:2; 18:3; 31:9), he will also raise one to call his children home (11:10, 12; 49:22; 62:10).
2. Heb. *gôyim,* "nations," but succeeding pronouns are singular and Jer. 5:15 shows the same form as *gôy mimmerḥāq,* suggesting that the plural *m* on *gôyim* was displaced from the following word.

It is not drowsy,
> *and it is not sleepy.*
28 *Its arrows are sharp,*
> *and all its bows are strung.*
Its horses' hooves are thought of as flint,
> *and its wheels are like the whirlwind.*
29 *It has a growl like a lionness,*
> *and it roars[3] like the young lions.*
It growls and seizes its prey;
> *it carries it off [4] and there is none to deliver.*
30 *It will growl over it in that day like the sound of the sea,*
> *and if one looks to the land,*
>> *behold, the darkness of distress;*
>> *light darkened with its clouds.[5]*

As he has detailed the wild grapes (vv. 8–25), so Isaiah has alluded to the coming destruction of the vineyard (vv. 13–17, 24, 25). Now he makes that allusion explicit in a powerful piece of poetry. The wild animals are called and now come to trample the vineyard. They come quickly but also insistently. Those who mocked Isaiah asked for God to hurry his work. Isaiah now assures them that God's plan is coming to sudden fruition, more sudden than they can imagine. It is likely that he has Assyria in mind here, since Assyria was to ravish almost all of Judah before the eighth century was out, but the impact of the prediction is heightened by its figurative and poetic qualities.[6] For Isaiah at that point, it was not so important to specify who the destroyers would be as it was to indicate the imminent, irresistible, and wholly-to-be-expected nature of what lay ahead.

3. 1QIs[a] has *yšʾg*, "it roars," in accord with MT Qere (Ketib *wᵉšāʾag*).

4. *plṭ*, "to flee away," is given the meaning "to make secure" in the Hiphil (BDB, p. 812), but perhaps to be understood as "to cause to go away," thus "drag off."

5. Verse 30 is very difficult to interpret. The Hebrew is elliptical and open to several understandings. The opening phrase is "he/it will roar over him/it." The context would seem to indicate that the army roars over its prey, but it is possible that it is the Lord who roars over the army (cf. Duhm, JPSV). Furthermore, the Masoretic punctuation supports "behold darkness, sorrow and light; it is dark in the clouds," which is unintelligible. Finally, *ʿᵃrîpîm*, "clouds," occurs only here in Hebrew but is apparently cognate to Akk. *irpatu*. The combination of these difficulties has caused some scholars to suggest that a copyist incorporated here at the end of a section some miscellaneous marginal jottings. Cf. P. Skehan, "Some Textual Problems in Isaiah," *CBQ* 22 (1960) 47; E. Zolli, "Jes. 5:30," *TZ* 6 (1950) 23, 24.

6. Gray's comment on whether Assyria was at the end of the earth is telling: "Isaiah is a poet."

If this segment is excised from its present setting, as many wish to do (see above on 5:25), then ch. 5 and the whole introductory section merely taper off to an ineffectual stopping point. But with these verses in place, the chapter and the section rise to a crescendo of intensity and emphasis that effectively underlines Isaiah's understanding of Israel's great need.[7]

26 Isaiah here introduces the theme which will be amplified later (esp. 10:5–34): the nations are but an instrument in the Lord's hands. The great imperial armies sweeping the world in the ninth to the fifth centuries B.C. were not the shapers of the world's destiny but were themselves shaped by the One who holds all things (cf. 40:21–24; 45:1–9). It is upon his signal that they rise and move; at his whistle they come out of their hive like bees to do his bidding. (Cf. the remarks of Cyril and Theodoret on the beekeeper's use of a hiss or whistle; cf. also 7:18; Zech. 10:8.)

27–29 In these verses a succession of terse phrases, which actually begins with v. 26c, lends support to the picture of the rapid and remorseless onslaught of the enemy army. By not expressing the subject at any point, the cadence is shortened so that the feeling is one of quick march.[8] Verses 27 and 28 are chiastic, with v. 27 showing what is not the case, while v. 28 shows what is the case. There is no laggard, stumbling and sleepy. Neither is there anyone half-prepared, with broken sandal-thong or slack equipment belt. Instead, everyone is intent on the task, with arrows sharpened and bow already strung.[9] The horses' hooves are hard as flint, so they will not break down on the journey, and the chariot wheels are turning so fast that they blur like a whirlwind (66:15; Jer. 4:13). The sound of the onrushing horde is like the roar of a lion at the moment of its spring. Like the lion, once this army has seized its prey and begun to drag it off, there will be no one to deliver Israel from its mouth.[10]

7. If the present chs. 1–5 are introductory and were put into their present order for that reason (cf. comment on chs. 1–5) then it is possible that materials reminiscent of other, subsequent materials (such as 5:25 is reminiscent of 9:7 [Eng. 8]–10:4) were consciously included here for their introductory function. Cf. P. Ackroyd, "Isaiah I–XII: Presentation of a Prophet," *VTSup* 29 (1978) 43 n. 77: "We have to accept that elements, probably of a long poem, have been used deliberately to underline the judgment theme of 5:1–22 and must be interpreted in their present context."

8. Verse 28 begins with an ellipsis, lit. "which its arrows . . .," the subject of the relative being the army.

9. Bows were kept unstrung until just before the battle, at which time the bow was bent against the foot (Heb. *dārak*, "trodden") and thus strung. These warriors are ready for battle.

10. Cf. an Egyptian palette depicting a lion eating a man in *Views of the Biblical World*, ed. B. Mazar (Jerusalem: International Publishing, 1960), III:110. See also the Nimrud ivory, ibid., I:98.

30 The army's rumble is not only like the lion's roar, it is also like the steady crash of breakers. This sound would be especially ominous, for the sea was an element about which the Hebrews always felt uneasy (Judg. 5:17; 2 Chr. 20:35–37; Jon. 2:1–9; Rev. 20:13; 21:1). But neither would there be any hope in the land, where they felt more comfortable. There would be only darkness and distress, the light of day being obscured by the clouds of battle.

II. A CALL TO SERVANTHOOD
(6:1 – 13)

A. THE VISION (6:1 – 8)

1 *It was in the year of King Uzziah's death that I saw the Sovereign sitting on a throne, high and lifted up, and the skirt[1] of his robe was filling the temple.*

2 *Seraphim were standing about him, each one having six wings. With two he was covering his face, with two he was covering his feet, and with two he was flying.*

3 *And each one called to the other:*
> *"Holy, holy, holy is the Lord of Hosts;*
> *Filling all the earth is his glory."[2]*

4 *And the foundations of the thresholds[3] shook because of the voice of the caller, and the house was full of smoke.[4]*

1. There is no evidence that robes had trains in the ancient Near East. *šûlāyw* refers to the hem of the garment (Exod. 28:33, 34) or to the lower extremities covered by the skirt (Jer. 13:22; Nah. 3:5). Cf. G. R. Driver, "Isaiah 6:1: 'his train filled the temple,'" in *Near Eastern Studies in Honor of W. F. Albright*, ed. H. Goedicke (Baltimore: Johns Hopkins, 1971), pp. 87–90.

2. Lit. "filling all the earth his glory." LXX "all the earth is full of his glory."

3. *'ammôt hassippîm* is uncertain. The second term is relatively frequent as "threshold, sill," but the first is unknown except as "cubit" or "mother city" (2 Sam. 8:1). The common suggestion of "foundation" rests upon a supposed derivation from "mother," *'ēm*, while "doorposts" "assumes an emendation (*'m[n]t*). LXX apparently combines the two terms with its "lintels."

4. Targ. has "thick darkness," which seems to be in keeping with the tendency of that paraphrase here to remove some of the immediacy of the experience. So "I saw the glory of the Lord" (v. 1); "holy ministers," "ministered" rather than "flew" (v. 2); "glory of the shekinah" (v. 5); "in his mouth was a speech" for "in his hand was a coal" (v. 6).

5 *And I said, "Alas for me, for I am destroyed;[5] for a man of unclean lips I am and in the midst of a people of unclean lips I live, for the King, the Lord of Hosts, my eyes have seen."*

6 *Then one of the seraphim flew to me with a live coal[6] in his hand. He had taken it from the altar with tongs.[7]*

7 *He touched my mouth and said, "Behold, since[8] this has touched your lips, your iniquity[9] is taken away[10] and your sin is atoned for."*

8 *Then I heard the voice of the Sovereign, saying, "Whom shall I send, and who will go for us?" So I said, "Behold, me;[11] send me."*

The function of this chapter in its present context presents a serious problem. Suggested solutions are almost as numerous as the writers on the subject, and the number of writers is myriad. Older commentators, perhaps echoing Calvin, tended to treat the experience as occurring subsequent to

5. *niḏmēṯî* is a Niphal perfect 1st common singular of *dāmâ*, "to be cut off, ruined, destroyed." It thus expresses more strongly than something like "I will die" the prophet's conviction that he cannot continue to exist having seen what he has.

6. LXX has "stone," and thus has proven attractive to commentators in the light of the only other occurrence of *riṣpâ* in 1 K. 19:6, where it is thought to refer to the hot stones used for baking bread. However, bread is also baked in the coals in the Near East, so the reference is inconclusive. There is no indication of removable stones in the descriptions of the altars in Exodus, 1 Kings, or 2 Chronicles.

7. Everywhere else *melqāḥayim*, "tongs," is associated with the lampstand and is translated "snuffer" (Exod. 25:38; 37:23; Num. 4:9; 1 K. 7:49; 2 Chr. 4:21), but the root *lqḥ* means "to take," so "tongs" seems most appropriate. Thus the instrument could have been used to pick up not only hot lamps but also other objects.

8. Brockelmann (*Hebräische Syntax* [Neukirchen: Verlag der Buchhandlung der Erziehungsvereins, 1956], § 164a) indicates that the construction is a conditional one: "If this . . . then this." Since the thing has already taken place, the construction is best rendered: "Since . . . then. . . ."

9. *ʿāwōn* is frequently translated "guilt" (so virtually all modern translations here except NEB). While there is the element of responsibility or culpability inherent in the word, "guilt" conveys too much passivity. The word speaks of the willful perversion of God's ways and all that results from those choices (Lev. 26:39; Josh. 22:20; Isa. 5:18; etc.).

10. *sûr* has the meaning "to turn aside" when speaking of motion (Gen. 19:2), but when it speaks of a thing it means "to take away." It is frequently used of such things as idol altars (2 Chr. 14:2) and idols themselves (1 K. 15:12). It is also used with reference to the "stony heart" (Ezek. 36:26) and the "foreskin of the heart" (Jer. 4:4).

11. *hinnēnî*, lit. "behold me," is an invitation to scrutiny. As such, it is the response of one who has nothing to hide. See, e.g., Abraham (Gen. 22:1) and Moses (Exod. 3:4).

Isaiah's initial call. This view preserved a chronological explanation of the present order.[12] Yet the experience described in the chapter is of such power and immediacy that it is hard to imagine it as anything other than inaugural (cf. Skinner's comments). This is not to say that Isaiah may not have been preaching before, but only that he was not doing so because of a decisive experience. The view that the experience described in ch. 6 constituted Isaiah's call has tended to carry the day, but that still leaves unanswered the fundamental question: why does not the report of the call appear first in the book? As early as Marti the suggestion was made that the call narrative appeared at the beginning of a scroll including 7:1–9:5 (Eng. 6) and that the later compiler(s) did not wish to tear it (figuratively) from that context and put it before the materials which they had arranged (the present chs. 1–5) as introductory to the book. This view, in one form or other (the supposed scroll is now frequently limited to 6:1–8:18),[13] has come to prevail in most modern commentaries (e.g., Fohrer, Kaiser, Wildberger). With it has come the increasing conviction that the words of vv. 9–13 were not part of the original experience, but that they express Isaiah's reflection upon his call after some years of unsuccessful preaching, and in the light of the looming Syro-Ephraimite crisis.[14] This view is in part due to an overemphasis upon the connection of ch. 6 with chs. 7 and 8. For a fuller discussion, see below on vv. 9–13.

The weakness of the view that ch. 6 is where it is in the book because of its physical contiguity with the material of chs. 7 and 8 is that it tends to make the creation of the present book the fitting together of a patchwork of scrolls without much concern for overall order and coherence. On this view, the major concern of the compiler(s) would be for getting all the pieces into the whole at some place according to some approximate chronological scheme. Concern for a theological statement would have been secondary or tertiary, according to such a position. Such can have hardly been the case. The same modern scholars who say that ch. 6 is where it is simply because it was part of a scroll with the materials now comprising chs. 7 and 8 also say that the compiler(s) willfully disarranged the long poem on God's wrath (9:7–20 [Eng. 8–21]) so that four

12. H. L. Ginsberg, "Introduction," *The Book of Isaiah* (Philadelphia: Jewish Publication Society, 1972), pp. 16–18, tends to adhere to the idea of chronological order for the materials of chs. 1–12.
13. Cf. H.- P. Müller, "Glauben und blieben. Zur Denkschrift Jesajas Kapitel VI 1–VIII 18," *VTSup* 26 (1974) 25–54.
14. For an expression of this opinion see M. Kaplan, "Isaiah 6:1–11," *JBL* 45 (1926) 252–59. More recently see O. Steck, "Bemerkungen zu Jesaja 6," *BZ* 16 (1972) 188–206.

or five of its verses now appear in ch. 5 (vv. 26–29, 30?) while four verses from the lament of ch. 5 now appear between 9:20 (Eng. 21) and 10:4, 6. Surely persons who could shift paragraphs at will could also shift a chapter to make a theological point.

Several writers have sought to come to grips with the theological significance of the call narrative's present location.[15] Of these, Ackroyd's account is the most thoroughgoing and comprehensive. He proposes that chs. 1–12 form an intentional arrangement of Isaiah's twin messages of certain doom and certain salvation. That both were sooner or later fulfilled accounts for the magnetic attraction of Isaiah for other and later traditions, according to Ackroyd. In this view ch. 6 functions like a hinge, containing as it does words of utter doom and yet the example of the prophet's own cleansing and the concluding note of hope. Already in 1954 Leibreich had pointed the way to a similar conclusion: "from the point of view of the present order and arrangement of the chapters, chapter 6 is a suitable conclusion to the chapters before it and an equally suitable introduction to the chapters which follow."[16]

The recognition of the double function of ch. 6 is fundamental to an understanding of its position in the book. However, another issue must be considered before that thought can be pursued further—the question of chs. 1–12 as a whole. Is it true, as Ackroyd, Marshall, Ginsberg, and others have suggested, that chs. 1–12 form a unit? It is the position of this commentary that they do not. The generality of chs. 1–5 sets them off as introductory. They deal with broad issues, behaviors, and consequences. As such they do not have a more direct relationship with chs. 7–12 than they do with any other segment of the book. They set the stage for what follows. On the other hand, chs. 7–12 are predominantly specific. They deal with a particular historic occasion and the implication of that occasion in both the near and the distant perspectives. The recurrence of Assyria is a key to this understanding. Furthermore, the chapters deal with a very specific theological problem: why trust? To be sure, ch. 12 is a climax, but it is not a climax to chs. 1–11. It does not deal with the issues of pride, pretense, and the idolization of human potential. Nor does it

15. P. R. Ackroyd, op. cit., pp. 16–48; L. Brodie, "The Children and the Prince," *BTB* 9 (1979) 27–31; L. Liebreich, "The Position of Chapter Six in the Book of Isaiah," *HUCA* 25 (1954) 37–40; R. J. Marshall, "The Structure of Isaiah 1–12," *BR* 7 (1963) 19–32; O. Steck, "Bemerkungen zu Jesaja 6," *BZ* 16 (1972) 188–206.
16. Liebreich, op. cit., p. 40. Most scholars see the connection with chs. 7 and 8 (cf. Steck) or even chs. 7–11 (Brodie), but few recognize the connection with chs. 1–5.

bring to the fore the need for repentance, cleansing, and ethical obedience. Rather, the focus is upon God's trustworthiness and his capacity to save those who will trust him. Thus, the climactic movement only extends as far back as ch. 7. The connection of chs. 7–12 with chs. 13–39 is another issue which will be dealt with at the appropriate point. Let it merely be said here that there is a theological connection between a condemnation of trust in the nations, a promise of deliverance from the nations (as these two themes appear in chs. 7–12), and an announcement of doom upon the nations (chs. 13–23).

The literature on ch. 6 is immense, a testimony to its continuing fascination and appeal.[17] Comments upon its power, clarity, literary excellence, and importance as a religious document can be multiplied on every hand. As noted above, however, there is disagreement over the significance of the experience and its function in this context. While both Habel and Knierim consider the account to fit the standard form of a prophet's call, Ginsberg maintains it is not a call because prophets (like Moses and Jeremiah) were never given a choice, as Isaiah was.[18] The consensus seems to be emerging that two forms are involved here:[19] a call form and a judgment form. The call of Moses offers relevant parallels (Exod. 3:1–4:17), but so does Micaiah's announcement of judgment (1 K. 22:19–23).[20] Just as the account combines two kinds of experiences, so it functions in two ways in its context. On the one hand, chs. 1–5 have raised a serious problem. Sinful, arrogant Israel is going to be the holy people of God to whom the nations will come to learn of God (cf. 43:8–14; 49:5, 6; Ezek. 36:22–38). But how can this be? Ch. 6 provides the solution. Sinful Israel can become servant Israel when the experience of

17. For a full bibliography see Wildberger. Recent important works are I. Engnell, *The Call of Isaiah: An Exegetical and Comparative Study,* UUA 4 (Uppsala: Lundequistska, 1949); K. Gouders, "Die Berufung des Propheten Jesaja (Jes. 6:1–13)," *BibLeb* 13 (1972) 89–106, 172–184; E. Jenni, "Jesajas Berufung in der Neuern Forschung," *TZ* 15 (1959) 321–339; R. Knierim, "The Vocation of Isaiah," *VT* 18 (1968) 47–68; O. Steck, op. cit.; C. Whitley, "The Call and Mission of Isaiah," *JNES* 18 (1959) 38–48. Recent works dealing with the prophetic calling are K. Baltzer, "Considerations Regarding the Office and Calling of the Prophet," *HTR* 61 (1968) 567–581; N. Habel, "The Form and Significance of the Call Narratives," *ZAW* 77 (1965) 297–323; G. Meagher, "The Prophetic Call Narrative," *ITQ* 39 (1972) 164–177; I. Seierstad, *Die Offenbarungserlebnisse der Propheten Amos, Jesaja und Jeremia,* SNVAO (Oslo: 1946), II:2.

18. See Ginsberg, op. cit.

19. Knierim has pointed the way here (op. cit., p. 59).

20. Young dismisses the relevance of this passage far too easily. See further n. 40 below.

Isaiah becomes the experience of the nation. When the nation has seen itself against the backdrop of God's holiness and glory, when the nation has received God's gracious provision for sin, then she can speak for God to a hungry world. (Can it be coincidental that chs. 60–66 follow immediately upon the promise of 59:21?) To those who point out that ch. 6 speaks of cleansing for Isaiah but doom for the nation, it must be admitted that this is true, but it must also be pointed out that it is illogical to think that what is available to one member of the nation could never be available to the whole nation (note how carefully Isaiah's identity with the nation is established—both are unclean), especially when strong promises of the nation's eventual purging and utility have been made. No, whatever the immediate future might be, if ever there should come a time when Isaiah's experience should be duplicated on a national scale, then the promises of 1:16–19; 2:1–4; and 4:2–6 could be experienced. Without the lived-out truth which ch. 6 presents, chs. 1–5 present an irreconcilable contradiction. This could well be the reason, then, why an inaugural vision is placed six chapters into the book it inaugurates.

But ch. 6 is not merely the conclusion of chs. 1–5. As we have noted at other places (1:9; 2:5; 5:25), one of the marks of this book's style seems to be its smooth transitions, so smooth that it is frequently difficult to decide whether an element is the final one in the preceding segment or the initial one in the following. So it is in this case. For just as ch. 6 is the conclusion to chs. 1–5, it is also the introduction to chs. 7–12. This position is much more widely accepted than the previous one,[21] but it is usually argued on more formal grounds than theological ones. In particular, it is usually pointed out that chs. 6–8 have a common autobiographical thread. But the relationships among these chapters are more profound than that. In a real sense, chs. 7–12 are a fulfillment and an explication of the word given to Isaiah in his call. Immediately in ch. 7 is seen the hardening impact of the prophet's gracious invitation to trust. In a real sense the destruction which comes to Judah from Assyria's hand in the declining years of the eighth century B.C. is caused by Ahaz's refusal of Isaiah's invitation (8:6–8; 6:11, 12). Thus the nation is cut down like a field of stumps (10:33, 34; 6:13). Yet, in one of those stumps life remains so that the nation might learn that God can be trusted (11:1–12; 6:13).

So it is impossible to link ch. 6 solely to chs. 1–5 or solely to chs. 7–12. It functions with both sections, both showing the way of hope for the future (in chs. 1–5) and explaining the present situation (in chs. 7–12).

21. See Budde, Müller, etc.

175

In this sense it is a genuinely strategic chapter, shaping and defining the book as a whole.

The vision which 6:1–8 report was clearly fundamental to the entire course of Isaiah's ministry and to the shape of his book. The glory, the majesty, the holiness, and the righteousness of God became the ruling concepts of his ministry. Furthermore, it is this experience which explains Isaiah's contempt for, and horror of, any kind of national or individual life which did not pay adequate attention to the one God.

Attempts to determine the nature of the vision are bootless. Whether it was ecstatic or mystical or "actual" has no bearing upon the reality of the event for Isaiah's ministry.[22] How he saw the Sovereign is insignificant. What matters is that he saw him and saw him in such a way as to change the shape of the rest of his life. Similarly, attempts to prove that the vision took place in either the earthly temple or a heavenly one are generally of no consequence. They are frequently based upon overly literal interpretations of an imagery whose primary purpose is to convey theological truth.[23] Once again, the reality of the experience for Isaiah and the truths which it conveyed to him are of fundamental significance. Precisely how or where the experience occurred has little to do with those questions.

1 *In the year of King Uzziah's death.* It is apparent that for some reason Isaiah wished to locate this vision in time.[24] What that reason was is less apparent. Engnell and Ringgren have suggested that an enthronement ceremony may have been the occasion for the experience.[25] If so, the enthronement ceremony at the beginning of Jotham's reign might have been particularly moving. Another possibility is that Isaiah wanted to indicate the inaugural nature of his vision and so placed it in this way at the beginning of his ministry.[26] But an even more compelling reason is

22. Cf. Wildberger on the difficulty of distinguishing among these.

23. Such, for instance, is the argument that the earthly temple could not have been intended because no distinction is made between the holy place and the holy of holies (Cheyne).

24. The date of Uzziah's death cannot be fixed absolutely. Thiele's approach to the biblical data suggests a date of 739 B.C. See J. Oswalt, "Chronology of the OT," *ISBE,* I:673–685. Others propose a date as late as 735. It is not necessary that the vision occurred after Uzziah's death (which the text does not say) for the above explanation to be valid. Uzziah was an old man and the indications of his approaching death would have been apparent, giving the same occasion for the vision even before the actual event, but in the same year.

25. I. Engnell, *The Call of Isaiah;* H. Ringgren, *The Prophetical Conception of Holiness* (Uppsala: Uppsala University, 1948), p. 26.

26. Kaplan (*JBL* 45 [1926] 259) believes the vision only came after years of preaching for repentance and that the verse is to make the vision *seem* inaugural.

the theological one. Judah had known no king like Uzziah since the time of Solomon. He had been an efficient administrator and an able military leader. Under his leadership Judah had grown in every way (2 Chr. 26:1–15). He had been a true king. How easy it must have been to focus one's hopes and trust upon a king like that. What will happen, then, when such a king dies, and coupled with that death there comes the recognition that a resurgent Assyria is pushing nearer and nearer? In moments like that it is easy to see the futility of any hope but an ultimate one. No earthly king could help Judah in that hour. In the context of such a crisis, God can more easily make himself known to us than when times are good and we are self-confidently complacent. "In the year of King Uzziah's death . . . mine eyes have seen the king."

I saw the Sovereign. Although the Hebrews normally believed that to see God was to die (Gen. 32:30; Exod. 19:21; 20:19; 33:20; Deut. 18:16; Judg. 13:22), it was also true that various individuals were permitted to see him (frequently in context with the references just cited). These appearances served different purposes, but an element of encouragement and confirmation was frequently involved (Gen. 16:9–13; 28:13–15; Exod. 24:9–11; 34:5–10; Judg. 6:11–24). Because the person had seen God he was enabled to act in the way required. Cheyne says that the use of *ᵃḏōnāy*, "the Sovereign," here (and in vv. 8 and 11) is a Masoretic emendation. He argues that the Masoretes did not want to admit that a person could see Yahweh. Therefore they softened the assertion by changing the divine name to this title. However, that the name is used in v. 5 (lit. "Yahweh of Hosts") argues in favor of the originality of the term. On this view, the prophet is perhaps stressing that the deity he saw is the absolute overlord of the earth with whom all people have to do.

sitting on a throne. The whole quality of Isaiah's experience is one of awe, perhaps more so than any other recorded theophany. Part of this is due to the visual imagery which the prophet uses. The reader, visualizing the scene, is with Isaiah and feels the raw edge of terror at being where humanity dare not go. It is unimportant whether Isaiah was in the actual temple at the time of the event. In his vision he was there and the reader is with him. Evidently the veil had been removed and there, where the ark should be, is a great throne.[27] Here again the absolute sovereignty of God is being stressed. He alone is king. *hēḵāl*, the word here used for *temple*, contributes to the concept of God's kingship. It is a loanword

27. Many conceptions of the temple suggest that there were steps up to the holy of holies, the elevation making the space a cube (1 K. 6:2, 20; cf. *IDB*, IV:537).

whose ultimate origin is in the Sumerian language of the third millennium B.C.: E. GAL (lit. "big house"), a term used for the house of the god who was considered to be the king of the city-state. This origin shaped the meaning of the word as it was borrowed into successive Semitic languages. Its essential meaning was "palace," but whether the palace of the human king or the divine king depended strictly upon the context (cf. 1 K. 21:1 and Ps. 45:16 [Eng. 15]). So here the temple is God's palace. He is king, not Uzziah or Jotham or Ahaz.

high and lifted up. According to their position in the sentence these words should modify *throne.* This God sat on a high and towering throne. However, the Masoretic punctuation separates the two words from *throne,* making them modify *the Sovereign.* This is in accord with other usages of this combination in this book. In these other occurrences (52:13; 57:15) the phrase modifies persons rather than things. So here, as the passage is now punctuated, it is saying that God was lifted up, exalted, by means of the throne. The emphasis upon God's exaltation is entirely in keeping with the themes of the book. Human attempts at self-exaltation are the height of folly. Only God is exalted.

As in Exod. 24:10, where the pavement under God's feet is described, so here the description of God's appearance can rise no higher than the hem of his robe. It is as though words break down when one attempts to depict God himself. When we press the elders of Israel, they tell us how blue the pavement under God's feet was; when we press Isaiah, he tells us how immense God's robe was. Did the robe fill the temple? No, God did! The import is clear. There is a barrier beyond which the simply curious cannot penetrate. The experience is too personal, too awesome, too all-encompassing for mere reportage. Each one of us must aspire to our own experience of his presence.

2 As Isaiah stands, or more likely, lies prostrate, at the door of the temple, his whole consciousness riveted upon the immense Being whose presence dominates his house, he becomes aware of other beings about the throne. The Hebrew says they were "over" God, but that need not be taken literally. The servants were standing, as it were, while the king was seated. Thus they were literally above him, but still on the same plane as he (attending him, Gen. 45:1; Judg. 3:19; 2 Sam. 13:9). It is not possible to describe these attendants in any complete way. They are said to have hands, feet, faces, and wings, but nothing more is said of their appearance. Since they are called *seraphim* (Heb. *śᵉrāpîm*), a term elsewhere applied to serpents (Num. 21:6; Isa. 14:29; 30:6), some scholars believe that they were serpentine or dragonlike in appearance.[28] However, the chief meaning of the term may be "fiery" (so Num. 21:6), so that the name of the snake is merely derivative (referring to their bite), and the use of the term for the ministering beings would indicate they were "fiery ones."[29] There is no reason to dismiss automatically either of these possibilities. Composite figures are known from all over the ancient Near East, and while none is so far attested in Israel, it is possible that use was made of them.[30] Such mysterious, awesome beings would be quite appropriate in this sort of vision. On the other hand, fire is everywhere associated with God's holiness (Exod. 3:1–6; 13:21; 19:18; Lev. 10:1–2; Num. 11:1–2; 1 K. 18:24; Isa. 6:6–7) so that it would be entirely appropriate for those who declare that holiness (v. 3) to be "fiery" in their appearance.

In any case, the seraphim typify the appropriate response to God's holiness. As Smith said, they are all wings and voice, perfectly ready for praise and service. One pair of wings is used to cover[31] their faces, for even the most perfect of creatures dare not gaze brazenly into the face of the Creator. The sight would be too much. Another pair covers their feet. The precise meaning of this action is not clear. The Targum has "body" for "feet" and says the body was covered so that it might not be seen. "Feet" is sometimes used in ancient Near Eastern literature as a euphemism for genitalia, and it is possible that such a meaning is intended here (cf. also Ruth 3:4, 7, 8).[32] In any case, the sense is the same, with the part standing for the whole body. As the creature should not look upon the Creator, so the created should not be displayed in the sight of the Creator. But to be in the presence of the Creator is not primarily to be prostrated with awe. Rather, it is to be filled with praise. So, with the third

28. So Gray, but contradicted by Skinner. More recently K. Joines, "Winged Serpents in Isaiah's Inaugural Vision," *JBL* 86 (1967) 410–15, has maintained that they are similar to the protective uraeus-deities of Egypt.

29. Lacheman adopted this point of view, asserting that what Isaiah saw was the cherubim glinting in the sunlight ("The Seraphim of Isaiah 6," *JQR* 59 [1968] 7–8).

30. See *IDB*, I:131–32; *ISBE*, I:642–43. See also *ANEP*, p. 212. It is possible that the biblical injunctions against mingling human and animal mitigate against such compounds, however (Lev. 20:15–16).

31. The verb "cover" is in the imperfect, indicating a continuing durative action.

32. See J. Sasson, *Ruth: A New Translation with a Philological Commentary and a Formalist-Folklorist Interpretation* (Baltimore: Johns Hopkins, 1979), pp. 69–71.

pair of wings the seraphim were flying, all the while calling out their ecstatic song.

3 The statement that the seraphim were calling to each other is probably an indication that the singing was antiphonal, but it may also be a way of saying that they were delighting with one another in the glory of God (Ps. 145:11). The significance of the verbal element here ought not to be overlooked. The content of this experience is not merely numinous, emotive, and nonrational. Had God only wished to convey his otherness to Isaiah, that could have been done without words. But here the cognitive and rational element is introduced, providing one more indication that revelation does not come merely through raw experience, but also through divinely given cognitive interpretation of that experience (see also v. 7). Thus it is interesting that it is in response to the calling that the doorposts shook and the house filled with smoke.

It can hardly be doubted that this experience accounts for the common title for God in Isaiah, "the Holy One of Israel/Jacob," occurring twenty-six times here and only six times elsewhere (2 K. 19:22 [=Isa. 37:23]; Jer. 50:29; 51:5; Ps. 71:22; 78:41; 89:19 [Eng. 18]). Whatever else this experience did for Isaiah, it convinced him that God alone is holy. But what did *holy* mean for him? Ringgren demonstrates that the cognates are hardly definitive.[33] They all use the term as an adjective of deity, and they all use it to define that which pertains to the deity, but they do not define the term itself. It is evident, however, that what is holy is distinct from whatever does not pertain to deity. Thus, holiness is distinctness, the distinctness of the divine from all other things. There is no reason to believe that the term had any moral connotation about it at the outset. Rather, the character of a given deity determined the character of that which was dedicated to it. Thus, women who were devoted to Baal and Asherah prostituted themselves to the worshipers of these deities and were called holy women ($q^e d\bar{e}\check{s}\hat{o}t$, Hos. 4:14; Gen. 38:21). The remarkable thing about the OT conception of holiness is a function of the OT understanding of God's character. What was distinct about this deity was not so much his origin, his essence, or his numinous power. Rather, it was his attitude toward ethical behavior. Other nations had laws and they saw those laws as deriving from the deity (cf. the Code of Hammurapi and its forerunners, the codes of Eshnunna and Lipit-Ishtar), yet none of them saw those laws as being an essential expression of what made God to be God. But this is exactly what the OT says. The entire nation will be holy to God (Exod.

33. Ringgren, op. cit., pp. 5, 6. See also H.- P. Müller, "*qdš*," *THAT*, II:590–609.

19:6), and they will manifest that special relationship through a particular species of ethical behavior. This is the meaning of the so-called Holiness Code in Leviticus. "You shall be holy as I am holy" (Lev. 19:1) does not refer to ritual purity but rather to ethical behavior. Thus for the Hebrews, holiness came to have a very particular ethical cast. To oppress the helpless was to profane God's name (Jer. 34:16). To make use of a prostitute, regardless of the fact that she was called "holy," was to defile the holy name of God (Amos 2:7). To be holy was to behave ethically and to be unholy was, in an ultimate sense, not to be cultically impure, but to be ethically impure (Ezek. 36:22–32). So for Isaiah the announcement of God's holiness meant that he was in the presence of One distinct from—other than—himself. But for Isaiah as a Hebrew, it also meant that the terrifying otherness was not merely in essence but in character. Here was One ethically pure, absolutely upright, utterly true.

But was this statement merely about *a* god, or was it about *the* God? If this experience was the cause of Isaiah's emphasis upon God's holiness, may it not also be the cause of his emphasis upon God's uniqueness? Who is this sovereign who sits enthroned in a temple? He is the thrice holy, the holiest of all. He is *the* holy one. There is no other to whom that appellative can be justly given. This is the function of the threefold *holy,* the trisagion.[34] It is the strongest form of the superlative in Hebrew. Its use here indicates that Israel's God is the most "godly" of all the gods.

Indeed, he alone deserves to be called holy, for as the second half of the poetic phrase indicates, his glory fills the entire earth.[35] This statement indicates that God's presence (his glory, Exod. 40:34) is not restricted to a temple. But it is also a way of saying that the earth's abundance is merely a reflection of this God's being. As was said above, his being is profoundly ethical. Thus, where God's glory is manifested, there is judgment for sin, for the two cannot exist side by side (Ps. 29:1–9; 89:6–19 [Eng. 5–18]; Isa. 6:5; Josh. 7:19; Jer. 13:15–17; Amos 4:13; 5:8, 9; 9:5,

34. There is nothing in the context to cause us to take this as a reference to the Trinity as the church fathers did. As early as Calvin, the weaknesses of the argument were pointed out. 1QIs[a] has only two "holies," a probable haplography. For a discussion of the pros and cons, see B. Leiser, "Trisagion of Isaiah's Vision," *NTS* 6 (1960) 261–63; N. Walker, "Disagion versus Trisagion: A Copyist Defended," *NTS* 7 (1961) 170–71.

35. *kābôd,* "glory," comes from a root whose meaning is "to be solid, heavy" (thus "liver" is *kābēd,* the heavy organ). So the glory of God is not an ephemeral aurora, but an expression of his stunning importance and reality. The ultimate expression of God's glory is Christ (John 1:14), through whom God means to share his glory with us (Col. 1:27).

6).[36] Micah makes a similar statement when he says that the Lord will come out of his temple to tread the high places of the earth (Mic. 1:2–3).

4 As the seraphim fly back and forth about the throne singing to one another of God's incomparable glory, the sound of their voices causes the doorways to shake. Why the doorways should be singled out is unclear. Gray suggests it is because the seraphim were keepers of the doors, while Delitzsch believes that Isaiah was aware of this shaking because he was standing (or prostrated) in the doorway. On this supposition, the entire building was shaking, but Isaiah was particularly aware of it at the spot where he was. At any rate, the hymn was thunderous, rocking the great building to its foundations. All the while the sanctuary was filling with *smoke*. Probably this should be understood as the smoke of incense, in which case smell is added to sight and sound as the sensory elements of the experience. It is also reminiscent of the cloud said to accompany the presence of God (Exod. 13:21; 14:19; 40:34; 1 K. 8:10; cf. Isa. 4:5, which has "a cloud of smoke"). Some commentators believe that the smoke only arises at this point to close off the vision of God (so Kaiser and Scott). It is just as likely, however, that during the entire experience the smoke was billowing throughout the space,[37] adding to the immediacy and mystery of the experience. The holy God is not to be surveyed casually with unveiled eyes.

5 At this point, the prophet becomes aware of himself. He has been aware of the desperate need implicit in the political situation. He has been made aware of the awesome holiness of God with all that that means of his transcendence and yet his immanence, and now he is suddenly and brutally aware of himself. He who had been pronouncing woe upon others (if the assumption is granted that the experience came after he had begun to preach; cf. 5:8, 11, 18, 20, 21) now must pronounce woe upon himself. If the experience did come at the outset of his ministry, then its force here is that every member of the nation must come to recognize his or her condition before God. Prophetic announcement is not enough. Personal confrontation is necessary.

Such confrontation cannot help but produce despair. For the finite, the mortal, the incomplete, and the fallible to encounter the Infinite, the Eternal, the Self-consistent, and the Infallible is to know the futility and the hopelessness of one's existence. Modern existential angst is a species of such despair, for confronted with the apparent meaninglessness of our existence in this universe we wonder why we should go on living. Exis-

36. Cf. Knierim, op. cit., p. 56.
37. Note the imperfect verb "was filling."

tentialism presumes there *is* no meaning in the universe and that we are thus meaningless. Isaiah knows, more horribly, that there is Meaning, but that he has no part in it.

But it is not the recognition of his finitude which crushes Isaiah; it is his uncleanness. The primary element about God's holiness that distinguishes him from human beings is not his essence but his character. Nor is this uncleanness merely ritual, for it is an uncleanness of the lips, of the expression of their lives. Among the pagans, uncleanness was a positive element related to the demonic. Thus it was necessary to eliminate the unclean in order for the clean, or beneficial, gods to have their effect.[38] Among the Hebrews, uncleanness was merely a negative: the absence of God's presence, or the presence of that which was contrary to his will and character. Here, then, Isaiah recognizes with sickening force[39] that his character is not, any more than is his people's, in keeping with God's character. Their lips do not belong to God, else they would continually pour forth praise like the seraphim. Why, then, are the lips unclean? Because that of which they are an expression, the heart and the will, do not belong to God. That which God possesses is clean, for it is like him. Thus, it is not merely purification of the lips which is necessary. Nor is it mere ritual purification that is needed. In some way, sin and iniquity must be removed if Isaiah (and his people) are ever to serve God with clean lips.[40]

It cannot be mere coincidence that in the year of King Uzziah's death Isaiah saw the King. The prophet has recognized that the fate of the nation, as well as his own fate, does not finally rest in the hand of any human king, however competent and faithful that king may be. Rather, it is in the hands of the only One who is true Monarch of creation. As is often the case, it was only when the lesser king was removed that the greater King could be seen. Alt suggests that it may be because of this experience that Isaiah is ever after reluctant to accord the title of king to anyone but God.[41] The combination of *King* with *Lord of Hosts* is remi-

---

38. *ANET*, pp. 333–34.

39. Something of the force of the recognition is conveyed by the emphatic position of the predicate "a man unclean of lips."

40. On the basis of 1 K. 22:19–23, some scholars believe this event to be the search for a messenger to carry the word of the heavenly council's judgment. On this basis they explain the reference to the people's lips. Surely the uncleanness referred to is more than unfitness for bearing a message if it is an expression of the condition of the entire nation.

41. A. Alt, "Gedanken über das Konigtum Yahweh," *Kleine Schriften* (Munich: Beck'sche, 1953), I:376.

niscent of the combination of titles used in the judgments in 1:24 and 3:1, 15, and suggests again that what Isaiah pronounces upon his people has been made terrifyingly real in his own experience.

6 This verse speaks of the depths of God's grace. Isaiah does not plead for mercy, nor does he make great vows if God will but deliver him. All of the evidence makes it appear that he considers his case hopeless. Yet out of the smoke comes a seraph with a purifying coal. God does not reveal himself to destroy us, but rather to redeem us (so with Jacob in Gen. 32, and with the Israelites in Exod. 19–24).

The identification of the altar from which the coal was taken is uncertain. Gray believes it to have been the altar of sacrifice, while most other commentators assume it was the incense altar. There would be something entirely fitting about the coal having been a charred portion of the whole burnt offering, for as Young points out, in the Bible there is no atonement apart from bloodshed (Lev. 16:14–19; 17:11; Matt. 26:28; Heb. 9:22).[42] At the same time, incense taken from the altar which stood just in front of the holy of holies could also have an atoning and purifying effect (Lev. 16:12; Num. 16:46, 47), so it may be this effect which is intended.

In any case, the fire is of great significance here. As noted above (on v. 2) the title "seraph" may denote "fiery one," and here again fire enters in. The appropriateness of fire as an image of God's holiness is apparent. Fire can be a source of great blessing but it is never easily controllable. Fire can destroy but also cleanse. Fire is fascinating but also slightly terrifying. Fire translates mass into energy. So it is with the holiness of God. Without forcing the imagery to say more than it does, one cannot doubt that "our God is a consuming fire" (Deut. 4:24; Isa. 33:14; Heb. 12:29); yet that fire is a fire of righteousness, in the midst of which only unrighteousness is devoured (Ps. 50:3–23; Isa. 33:13–15; cf. also Ps. 24:3–6; Dan. 3). So it is by fire, the fire of God's own purity, that the repentant are made like himself (1:25).

7 The fiery coal from the hand of the fiery one touches the prophet's mouth. God has a provision for sin and iniquity whereby their effect is mitigated and their power is broken. Engnell compares this to the purification of the oracular priests in Mesopotamia.[43] Certainly the situations are similar in that both involve the declaration of a divine word concerning a particular situation. There is a significant difference, however. In the

---

42. Contra Smith's comment that this passage demonstrates that only confession is necessary for forgiveness.

43. Engnell, op. cit., pp. 40, 41; cf. also J. Lindblom, *Prophecy in Ancient Israel*, p. 186.

Mesopotamian case, the priest engages in the ritual in order to bear the message, whereas Isaiah gives no indication that he seeks purification for such a reason. In fact, he does not seek purification at all. It is given to him. Thus, in Mesopotamia the message is primary and the purification a means to that end. In Isaiah's case, the alienated condition and the cleansing from it are primary and the bearing of the message is secondary. Those who lay heavy stress upon the similarity with Mesopotamia (and Egypt) are forced to assume that an expression of judgment upon Israel had been made prior to v. 5, and that it was Isaiah's desire to carry this message which prompted his concern over his lips.[44] Such an assumption is unwarranted by anything in the biblical text at this point. As the text stands now, sin and iniquity are dealt with because they exist and because those in whom they reside cannot have fellowship with God, a condition contrary to God's desire (Hos. 11:8–11; 2 Pet. 3:9). There is, of course, nothing in the burning coal itself that can deal with a condition of the heart. Yet as Calvin points out, it is not possible to separate the signs from the truth. In the same way bread and wine do not take away sin. Yet there is a link between the image and the reality that may not be broken without losing an essential value. When God takes away the iniquity and sin in which we have lived for years, the experience is a wrenching, searing one. But more deeply, what causes sin and iniquity? It is that arrogant self-sufficiency which refuses to bow the knee. This is the ultimate uncleanness of which Isaiah had been accusing his people and now finds resident in himself. This spirit never gives up without a fight. Apart from the fires of self-surrender and divine surgery the clean heart is an impossibility.

8 Now, for the first time, God speaks. It is as if Isaiah was not ready to hear before this moment, as if the possibility of service could not be appreciated until this time. But for whatever reason, God makes it plain that while spiritual experience is never merely a means to an end, neither is it an end in itself. Unless that experience issues in some form of lived-out praise to God, it will turn upon itself and putrefy. It is very possible, in the light of 1 K. 22:19, that *who will go for us* is an address to the heavenly host, either visibly present or implied.[45] That Isaiah is neither directly addressed nor coerced is suggestive. Perhaps it is so because Isaiah does not need coercion, but rather needs an opportunity to volunteer.[46]

44. R. Knierim, op. cit., pp. 58, 59.

45. If "us" is a plural of majesty (with the older commentators) the singular in "whom shall I send" seems strange.

46. Westermann's assertion (*Basic Forms*, p. 115) that this circumlocution is necessary because a man can hardly be designated as a messenger of God seems to fly in the face of such prophetic calls as those of Moses, Gideon, and Jeremiah (cf. N. Habel, op. cit., pp. 299, 301, 308).

Having believed with certainty that he was about to be crushed into non-existence by the very holiness of God and having received an unsought for, and unmerited, complete cleansing, what else would he rather do than hurl himself into God's service?[47] Those who need to be coerced are perhaps too little aware of the immensity of God's grace toward them. So, unlike Adam and Eve, who sought to hide from the searching voice, Isaiah, permitted for a moment to eavesdrop on the councils of God, cannot keep silent. "Would I do?" Such a grateful offering of themselves is always the cry of those who have received God's grace after they have given up hope of ever being acceptable to God.

The sequential relationship of the elements ought not to be overlooked. Each element leads to the next. The king's death prepares the way for the vision of God; the vision of God leads to self-despair; self-despair opens the door to cleansing; cleansing makes it possible to recognize the possibility of service; the total experience then leads to an offering of oneself.

B. THE COMMISSION (6:9–13)

9 Then he said, "Go and say to this people,
  'Hear indeed, but do not understand.
  See[1] indeed, but do not know.'
10 Make the heart of this people fat;
  make its ears heavy and its eyes clouded,
  lest it should see with its eyes,
  and hear with its ears,
  and understand with its heart,
  and turn and be healed."
11 Then I said, "How long,[2] O Sovereign?"
And he said,
  "Until cities crash into ruins without an inhabitant,
  and houses are bereft of humankind,
  and the ground is ruined in desolation."

47. Cf. Ps. 51:13–17 (Eng. 11–15).
1. With 1QIs[a]; MT has "and see . . .," possibly a dittography. See J. Rosenbloom, *The Dead Sea Isaiah Scroll* (Grand Rapids: Eerdmans, 1970), p. 13.
2. Young points out the similarities with the uses of the Akk. *adi mati*. So, e.g., "How long, O my lady, shall the crippled and weak seek me out; How long, O my lady, wilt thou be angered so that thy face is turned away . . ." ("Prayer of Lamentation to Ishtar," *ANET*, pp. 384–85).

12 *The Lord will make mankind distant,*
   and multiply the forsaken in the midst of the land.
13 *If there is still a tenth in it,*
   it will be burned again.[3]
   Like the terebinth and the oak
      which leave a stump when they are cut down,
   the holy seed is its stump.[4]

Almost all sermons on Isa. 6 conclude with v. 8, probably because of the frankly disturbing character of the remainder of the chapter. It is especially disturbing to Christians whose whole upbringing has conditioned them toward an emphasis upon God's forgiving grace and will to deliver. Yet

---

3. However, note that the LXX and Sym. translate *b'r* with "for foraging" and "for a feeding," suggesting that "devour" (as in 3:14 and 5:5?) may be more appropos here (so Wildberger and Kaiser).

4. The question of the authenticity of the final phrase of v. 13 has evoked firm opinions on both sides. However, the paucity of evidence has led much of the argument to depend upon theological a prioris, namely, whether it is logical to think that a word as bleak as this would have included any ray of hope. Many have asserted emphatically that it did (Engnell and Lindblom), others that it did not (Blank and Wildberger). As regards the evidence, the LXX alone leaves out the phrase. The Targ., Peshitta, and Qumran all have it. Further, the LXX not only leaves it out but also reinterprets the preceding two words ("a stump is in them") so that the version reads "and still there is a tenth upon it and again it shall be for spoil, like a terebinth or an oak when it is torn from its place." This looks suspiciously like an easier reading. Moreover, if it is correct, it removes the occasion for the supposed gloss in the MT, because it contains no reference to "stump," which would provoke the gloss. 1QIs[a] has compounded the confusion by supplying *bāmâ*, "high place," for MT *bām*, "in them." This has led to a radical reinterpretation of the passage, adopted by NEB, "like an oak or a terebinth, a sacred pole thrown out from a hill shrine" (leaving out the final phrase, which 1QIs[a] retains). See W. F. Albright, "The High Place in Ancient Palestine," *VTSup* 4 (1957) 254-55; W. H. Brownlee, "The Text of Isaiah 6:13 in the Light of DSIa," *VT* 1 (1951) 296-98; G. R. Driver, *JSS* 13 (1968) 38; F. Hvidberg, "The Masseba and the Holy Seed," *Interpretationes ad Vetus Testamentum Pertinentes*, ed. A. S. Kapelrud; Festschrift S. Mowinckel (*NorTT* 56; 1955), pp. 97-99; S. Iwry, "Massebah and Bamah in IQ Isaiah[A] vi:13," *JBL* 76 (1957) 225-232. For a critique of this position, and an excellent defense of the MT reading, see U. Worsheck, "The Problem of Isa. 6:13," *AUSS* 12/2 (1974) 126-138. One must wonder whether the 1QIs[a] reading is not merely a conflate of *bām*, "in them" (MT), and *bāh*, "in it" (about 100 medieval mss.), for the accuracy of the Qumran copyist was not high. Furthermore, as Worsheck notes (p. 137), 1QIs[a] frequently adds an *h* after the 3rd plural pronominal suffix (34:7; 41:17, 27), and this may be but one more example of that tendency. On balance, the arguments against are not strong enough to justify altering the MT, which, in principle, must be allowed to stand until proven defective.

these verses depict God as preventing repentance so that total destruction may occur. The only glimmer of hope appears in the enigmatic final phrase, and the authenticity of that phrase is open to question since it does not appear in the LXX.[5] So difficult is it to believe that this could be the content of an inaugural vision that it has become rather common to assert that these are Isaiah's reflections upon his call after some years of preaching to a progressively more recalcitrant people.[6] However, such a view fails to take seriously enough the concept of the prophetic word as a causal factor. The proclamation in some sense produces the effect it predicts.[7] Thus there is no reason to doubt that from the outset Isaiah expected his preaching to have the effect it did. Indeed, as Fohrer and Lindblom have pointed out, the element of unavoidable doom was inherent in Isaiah's earliest preaching.[8] This is not to say, however, that these words sum up the content of Isaiah's preaching—he could still preach eventual healing and hope—but that the effect of his preaching would be hardening and destruction.[9]

9 *say to this people.* While the use of *this* may express divine displeasure (so Duhm, noting 8:6, 12; 9:15 [Eng. 16]; 28:11, 14; 29:13, 14), it does not necessarily do so. Several of the references just noted are equivocal, and Kaiser points to such instances as Exod. 3:21; 5:22; 17:4; 18:18; and Num. 11:14 where the demonstrative has no particular pejorative connotation. Certainly the statement lacks any element of warmth that "my people" might suggest.

hear indeed (lit. "hear a hearing"). The infinitive is functioning in

---

5. The authenticity of vv. 12 and 13 is also challenged on the basis of the changes in meter, content, and person. But these matters are ambiguous at best. For example, the content of v. 12 is identical with v. 11, while that of v. 13, so far as it is understandable, is not fundamentally different from v. 11 or v. 12. It seems to fit the pattern of a concluding figure of speech as noted above on 3:18–4:1. The change of person is not at all conclusive. See 3:16, 17, where the same change occurs in a context where there is no question about the connection between the two verses. As to meter, it is a notoriously unsatisfactory basis for critical judgment.

6. Apparently originated by Ewald and adopted by Gray. So also Hesse, *Das Verstockungsproblem im Alten Testament,* BZAW 74 (Berlin: de Gruyter, 1955), p. 84; R. P. Carroll, "Ancient Israelite Prophecy and Dissonance Theory," *Numen* 24 (1977) 144; A. Schoors, "Isaiah, Minister of Royal Anointment," *OTS* 20 (1977) 85–107; A. Key, "The Magical Background of Isa. 6:9–13," *JBL* 86 (1967) 198–201.

7. Von Rad, *Old Testament Theology,* II:89, 90, 152–54; J. M. Schmidt, "Gedanken zum Verstockungsauftrag Jesajas (Jes. 6)," *VT* 21 (1971) 68–90.

8. Fohrer, "Wandlungen Jesajas," in *Festschrift für Wilhelm Eilers,* ed. G. Wiessner (Wiesbaden: 1967), pp. 61–63; Lindblom, *Prophecy in Ancient Israel,* p. 187.

9. So Kaiser.

an adverbial way to strengthen the main verb (as in "you shall surely die," lit. "to die you will die," Gen. 2:17). It expresses for the Hebrew the strangeness of the contradiction, for to hear was normally synonymous with acknowledging and doing (Deut. 1:43; 6:3). Here the prophet is saying that the disease of pride and rebellion has gone so deeply that they will simply misperceive the truth of what they hear (cf. 2 Tim. 3:7).

10 Here is the heart of the difficult statement. Isaiah's preaching will not make it easier for the people to believe and repent. It will make it more difficult. The faculties of perception and response (eyes, ears, and heart)[10] will be dulled and apathetic. But why should God desire to harden people's hearts? Why should he wish them not to be healed?[11] The text itself gives no reason, but we may offer some general deductions. It is evident that something is more important than healing. What could that be? Surely it is a pure revelation of the character of God and of the human condition. As it happened, such a revelation could only harden Isaiah's generation in its rebellion (3:8, 9; 5:18, 19). For Isaiah to declare faithfully what he knew to be so would not result in an admission of guilt and a turning to God. Rather, it would bring about a more adamant refusal to recognize need.[12] What was the alternative? Perhaps if the prophet would alter the truth in certain ways the people might be more responsive and, after a fashion, be healed. Yet such a healing would be a mockery. For what can heal except God's truth? It is as though Isaiah should tell them that they did not need to see God as he did nor be cleansed as he was to be a servant of God as he was. The ultimate result would be deadly. It would confirm that generation in its syncretism and pervert the truth for all generations to come. It would sell the future for the apparent sake of the present. But if the truth could not save the present generation, if it would, in fact, destroy that generation, it could, faithfully recorded, save future generations.[13] This, then, was Isaiah's commission, as it is of all

---

10. Note the chiastic arrangement: heart, ears, eyes, ears, heart. A "fat heart" speaks of a slow, languid, self-oriented set of responses, incapable of decisive, self-sacrificial action.

11. The LXX, as quoted in the NT (Matt. 13:13–15; Acts 28:25–27), takes the responsibility from God and places it with the hearers, but the MT is the harder reading and thus more likely original.

12. It is a fallacy to suppose that voluntary, loving trust can be compelled. It is either given freely or not at all.

13. Von Rad makes the point that since the destruction is considered to be God's act then it is a part of a salvation-history whose ultimate end is not destructive but salvific (*Old Testament Theology,* II:155); note also the careful delineation of Isaiah as a part of a people. Whenever the people will respond as Isaiah did, they may experience cleansing as he did. God's ultimate purpose of reconciliation with all people remains the same.

servants of God, not to be successful in a merely human sense but to be faithful.[14]

11, 12 *How long, O Sovereign?* It is difficult to know the exact interpretation of this phrase. It is tempting to see in it a note of indignation or objection (Exod. 10:3, 7; Num. 14:27). Habel takes it in this way and couples it with the objections found in other prophetic calls.[15] However, this is not strictly an objection. The others whom Habel cites (Moses, Gideon, Jeremiah) are all speaking of their inability for the task given. Isaiah is not. At the most, he is expressing a sense of sorrow and an implied request for mercy upon God's people (2 Sam. 2:26; Ps. 6:4 [Eng. 3]; 94:3; Zech. 1:12). Fohrer believes that the prophet is asking when he can cease preaching judgment and turn to the preaching of salvation.[16] Young points out that it may be a simple request for information! But surely whatever else may be said, this is a cry of dismay.[17] This is not the sort of message the prophet wished to bear, nor does he wish to see his people destroyed. Yet it is not a refusal, nor an insistence that God justify himself. He is determined to obey, but he does so with a heavy heart.

The answer to Isaiah's cry is not comforting. There will be no reprieve for Judah. God's justice will be carried out to its full extent until the land is empty. So the prophecies of Deuteronomy would come to fulfillment (Deut. 28:21, 63; 29:28). The land was not theirs to possess as their own. Rather, they possessed it in trust from the true landowner, God. So long as they remained in God's favor, by living lives in keeping with his character, then the land was theirs to develop and to enjoy. But if they ceased to live in obedience to God, the land would vomit them out as it had the Canaanites before them (Lev. 18:25–27).

All of this would be done by the Lord. Judah's destruction would not be at the hand of nations whose gods were too strong for Yahweh. The other gods did not enter into the picture. The coming desolation had to do with Yahweh and his people, nothing more (Isa. 5:26; 17:18, 19; 10:5, 6).

13 As the verse now stands in the MT, it offers a faint, but sure, ray of hope. Yes, the desolation will be complete. Not even a tenth part will remain. The nation will be like a forest whose stumps are burned after the trees are cut down. Yet even from such blasted stumps a shoot

14. E. Jenni (*TZ* 15 [1959] 338) suggests that this prediction of short-term failure was given precisely in order to preserve the prophet and his followers from the consequences of that failure.

15. Habel, op. cit., p. 312.

16. Fohrer, op. cit., p. 61.

17. S. Blank, "Traces of Prophetic Agony in Isaiah," *HUCA* 27 (1956) 81–83.

can burst forth. So it will be for Judah (cf. 10:33; 11:1). Utter desolation is sure, but that desolation is not the end. There will be offspring holy to the Lord, for the Lord is not finished with Israel. God's promise to Abraham to bless the nations through his offspring is not to be forgotten (cf. 49:19, 32).

In this sense, the chapter is much like the book of Amos, which, while filled with judgment, nonetheless ends on a hopeful note.[18] This is not to deny or in any way to mitigate the force of the judgment, but it is to say that in God's overall purposes judgment is never his last word. This is consistent with the present structure of chs. 7–12 as well as with the book as a whole.

18. Cf. G. Hasel, *The Remnant. The History and Theology of the Remnant Idea from Genesis to Isaiah,* 2nd ed., Andrews University Monographs 5 (Berrien Springs: Andrews University, 1975), pp. 233–248.

III. WHOM SHALL WE TRUST? BASIS FOR SERVANTHOOD (7:1–39:8)

A. GOD OR ASSYRIA? NO TRUST (7:1–12:6)

1. CHILDREN, SIGNS OF GOD'S PRESENCE (7:1–9:6 [Eng. 9:7])

a. WILL YOU BELIEVE (SHEAR-JASHUB)? (7:1–9)

1 *And it came to pass in the days of Ahaz, the son of Jotham, the son of Uzziah, king of Judah, that Rezin, king of Aram, along with Pekah, son of Remaliah, king of Israel, went up against Jerusalem to make war against it, but he was unable to do so.*

2 *And it was told to the house of David, saying, "Aram has lodged¹ with Ephraim," and his heart shook and the heart of his people as the trees of the forest shake before the wind.*

3 *And the Lord said unto Isaiah, "Go out to meet Ahaz; you and Shear-jashub, your son, to the end of the watercourse of the upper pool, unto the highway of the Fuller's Field.*

4 *And you shall say to him, 'See that you keep calm and do not be afraid,² neither let your heart be weak because of these two tail ends of smoking firebrands, because of the hot anger of Rezin and Aram and the son of Remaliah,*

---

1. *nāḥû (nûaḥ)* means "to rest, settle down and remain" (BDB, p. 628); so the Hebrew says lit. "Aram has settled down upon Ephraim," a usage not paralleled elsewhere in the OT. But the sense is evidently of united action (LXX "made agreement"; cf. O. Eissfeldt, *STU* 20 [1950] 23–26). Possibly its use here is accounted for by the wordplay with *nûaʿ*, "to shake."

2. *hiššāmēr*, "be careful," may stand alone. But it may also form a single thought with "be calm," i.e., "keep calm." See Williams, *Syntax*, pp. 40–41.

5 *because Aram has taken evil counsel against you, Ephraim and the*
son of Remaliah, saying,
6 *"Let us go up against Judah and let us terrify it and break it open*[3]
for ourselves; let us crown a king in its midst: the son of Tabal.""[4]
7 *Thus says the Sovereign Yahweh,*
      "It will not arise,[5]
      and it will not be.
8 *For the head of Aram is Damascus,*
      and the head of Damascus is Rezin.
   Within sixty-five years
      Ephraim will be too shattered to be a people.
9 *The head of Ephraim is Samaria,*
      and the head of Samaria is the son of Remaliah.
   If you do not believe
      you will not be established."[6]

As noted in the Introduction (see above), chs. 7–39 are united around the
theme of trust. This theme is developed by contrast, the contrast between
trust in the nations and trust in God. Whereas trust in the nations will lead
to desolation (ch. 34), trust in God will lead to abundance (ch. 35). Chs.

   3. The verbs used here indicate the violent nature of the planned attack.
As Speier has shown (*JBL* 72 [1953] 74), *neqîṣennâ* as "tear apart, destroy," is
well paralleled by *nabqi'ennâ*, "to divide, cleave."
   4. The MT renders the name *ṭābe'al*, "good for nothing," but the LXX
appears to be translating an original *ṭābe'ēl*, "the goodness of God." That the name
appears Aramaic in this form suggests that the proposed new ruler was a Syrian.
Cf. W. F. Albright, "The Son of Tabe'el," *BASOR* 140 (1955) 34, 35; E. Vogt,
"Filius Tab'el," *Bib* 37 (1956) 263–64; but cf. also A. Vanel, "Ṭâbe'él en Is. VII 6
et le roi Tubail de Tyr," *VTSup* 26 (1974) 17–24.
   5. For a similar use of *qûm* as "to take place," see 1 Sam. 13:14; 24:21;
Amos 7:2; Nah. 1:6.
   6. The prophet uses a wordplay here, since "believe" is a Hiphil of *'mn*
and "be established" is a Niphal of the same root. The root idea is "to be firm,"
so the wordplay could be brought out by some such translation as "unless you hold
firm (in faith) you will not be made firm (in life)." Security is not found in alliances,
but in faith. Some commentators, e.g., Kaiser, Scott, and Skinner, make a point
that this concept of faith is a first here with Isaiah. but this is only so if one accepts
the hypothesis that OT faith did not develop as the Scripture suggests; for as early
as the Exodus the Bible has Moses challenging the people to believe in God, and
this same word, the Hiphil of *'mn*, is used of the Israelites' response to God after
the Red Sea crossing (Exod. 14:31). In fact, from the very beginning of God's
revelation, the issue had been: will human beings believe what God says? It was
not new with Isaiah.
   Note that the verbs are plural, indicating that the choice is not only that
of Ahaz, but also of the entire royal house and, to some extent, that of the nation
as a whole.

7–12 provide a historical introduction to the unit. Faced with the threats of Syria and Northern Israel, Ahaz had an opportunity to trust God for deliverance. Instead he trusted Assyria, his worst enemy. The result, as Isaiah predicted, was that Assyria herself overran the land. But that could not alter God's ultimate plan. Assyria was but a tool in his hand, and out of the destruction which she would precipitate would emerge a larger opportunity for God to demonstrate himself trustworthy: the restoration from captivity.

If ever Israel is to become the servant nation, through whom God chose to manifest himself to the world (2:2–5; 12:4–6; 43:8–21; 60:1–3), then the most basic truth she must learn is that God can be trusted, whereas the nations cannot. If she continues to refuse dependence upon God, while attempting to depend on the nations, then she has neither message nor hope. But if she has indeed encountered a God who is greater than all the nations combined and who can, in fact, be depended upon in every situation, then she has something to declare. This is the issue introduced in ch. 7 and carried on through ch. 39: Will Israel recognize that to depend upon the nations is to lose her distinct mission to them, whereas refusal to depend upon them is to become a blessing to them? Until a person or a nation is convinced of God's complete trustworthiness, they cannot lay aside the lust for their own security and become God's servant.

The subdivision 7:1–12:6 incorporates four segments: 7:1–9:6 (Eng. 7); 9:7 (Eng. 8)–10:4; 10:5–11:16; 12:1–6.[7] They are united by recurring attention to Assyria (7:17, 18, 20; 8:7; 10:5, 12, 24; 11:11, 16) and the implications of trust in her rather than in God. As noted above, those implications are at first negative: whatever we trust in place of God will eventually turn on us and destroy us (8:6–8). There are other implications, however, for Assyria is not her own master; rather, the Lord is (8:12–15; 10:5–19). If his people will learn that it is he with whom they must come to terms, not Assyria (9:7 [Eng. 8]–10:4; 10:20–27), then they will discover out of the disaster how truly trustworthy God is (11:1–12:6).

The decision over where to end the first segment (7:1–9:6 [Eng. 7]) is not an easy one. The thought begun in ch. 7 clearly continues on into ch. 8, as does the personal involvement of Isaiah in the events described. The question is whether to include 8:23–9:6 (Eng. 9:1–7) with chs. 7 and

---

7. Note that the MT versification differs from that of the English versions (which follow LXX): MT 8:23 = Eng. 9:1; MT 9:1 = Eng. 9:2; etc. This fact highlights the interrelationship of the materials.

8 or to conclude Isaiah's reminiscences with 8:16, 17, or 18.[8] Since 8:16–22 continue the thought of the foolishness of relying on some understanding of events that does not recognize God's sovereignty (8:12–15) and since 8:23 (Eng. 9:1) grows directly out of 8:22, there seems to be no option but to include 8:23–9:6 (Eng. 9:1–7) in the unit, although it is difficult to define the exact relation of those verses to chs. 7 and 8.[9]

One of the emphases which ties the segment together is the use of children, with Shear-jashub in 7:3; Immanuel in 7:14; 8:8, (10); Maher-shalal-hash-baz in 8:3; Isaiah's children in 8:18; and the royal child in 9:5 (Eng. 6). Over against the machinations of the nations stand a group of children, helpless and innocent. Yet in their innocence is a power which causes Isaiah to believe that right and justice are the great issues, not force and trickery. In this light the thought seems to move from the folly of not trusting (7:1–8:22) to the reason for trust (8:23–9:6 [Eng. 9:1–7]); strength is weakness; weakness is strength. The development of the thought is by continuation, that is, with each segment leading into the next. First is the occasion of the entire subdivision: the Syro-Ephraimite threat, with Ahaz's refusal to commit himself to God (vv. 1–9, 10–12). This results in Isaiah's diatribe against Ahaz and the announcement of a much greater threat— Assyria (7:13–25; 8:1–10). Both these segments use children as their centerpieces. The first uses the Immanuel motif and the second Maher-shalal-hash-baz. Immanuel is positive in that it points to the deliverance from Syria and Israel, but it is also negative in that it shows that what overwhelms Judah's enemies will overwhelm her as well. 8:1–10 develops the negative side of that thought: Judah has rejected the gentle brook; she will get a rushing river. Following 8:10 is what appears to be wider reflection on the whole incident and its causes. There has been too much attention to secondary causes—conspiracies, and not enough attention to the first cause—God (8:11–15). Until a change occurs, all the attempts to find guidance and deliverance will find only darkness and despair (vv. 16–22). But (as with 6:13) God is not content for darkness and despair to reign. If his people will change and will see his light, then they can be delivered from their enemies by a child (8:23–9:6 [Eng. 9:1–7]).

The basic information regarding the historical situation is given in 7:1–9. But coupled with it is God's word concerning that situation. In

8. For 8:16, see H.-P. Müller, "Glauben und Bleiben zur Denkschrift Jesaja Kapitel VI 1–VIII 6," *VTSup* 26 (1974) 25–54; for 8:18, see Duhm, pp. 17, 24; cf. also T. Lescow, "Jesaja's Denkschrift aus der zeit des syrisch-ephraimitischen Krieges," *ZAW* 85 (1973) 315–331.

9. This is not to address the question of what was "original," but to deal with the ideological and theological structure of the present text.

every circumstance there are two perspectives, the human and the divine, and, as here, the two are frequently in conflict. From Ahaz's point of view Syria and Ephraim constitute a major threat, but from God's point of view they are negligible and need not occupy the king's time. It is not always easy to gain the divine perspective. Yet, unless we seek it, we are always in danger of paying too much attention to the passing and paying too little attention to the significant. Furthermore, apart from a diligent search for God's perspective in every circumstance, we conclude too easily that God is concerned only about spiritual affairs and not about practical matters, a fallacy which leads eventually to the loss of God in all affairs.

1 This verse roots the following revelations squarely in history. Much as been said in recent years about the inadequacy of the "revelation as history" motif.[10] Undoubtedly it is simplistic to suggest that a historical event was in itself revelation. However, the critique has swung opinion too far in the opposite direction. For now it is said that Israel's understanding of history was identical to that of her neighbors.[11] So it has been said that Hebrew prophecy gives the lie to a connection between revelation and history in Israel.[12] But what is unique to Hebrew prophecy is that it is revelation in the specific context of history, as here. It is not mystical or metaphysical, for those are merely speculative. Instead, history becomes the vehicle for a revelation which may thus be experienced and confirmed. To be sure, the event is not the sum total of the revelation. But the revelation is rooted in and grows out of history. So much is this so that prophetic teaching is meaningless apart from an adequate understanding of its historical context.

These are not merely spiritual truths discovered by a religious genius in a vacuum. Rather, they are revelations from God authenticated by their connection with unique events in time and space that are the common possession of those who have experienced those events. Thus the truth of the events and the truth of the revelation are inseparably linked. It has been suggested that the verse is the work of a later editor because it contains the genealogy of Ahaz and because it tells of the failure of the attack too soon. Because of general similarities with 2 K. 16:5 it is widely

10. For the classic critique, see J. Barr, "Revelation Through History in the Old Testament and in Modern Theology," in *New Theology*, 1, ed. M. Marty and D. Peerman (New York: Macmillan, 1964) 60–74.
11. So, e.g., H. W. F. Saggs, *The Encounter with the Divine in Mesopotamia and Israel* (London: Athlone, 1978), pp. 64–92.
12. But see von Rad, *Old Testament Theology*, II:99–125.

assumed that that verse was the editor's source.[13] As Delitzsch pointed out, however, it is quite possible that any borrowing went in the opposite direction, especially since the singular *yāk̠ôl* is consistent with the singular main verb in Isaiah whereas the plurals *yāṣurû* and *yāk̠ᵉlû* of Kings are not consistent with the main verb there.[14]

In its present position the verse serves two important functions. First, the relating of Ahaz to Uzziah helps to link this material to ch. 6. It is very likely that the author is saying that what follows in ch. 7 and beyond is an outworking of that earlier event. Indeed it is, for here we see how the word of God's glory and grace at first produces a hardening which eventually leads to destruction and only then paves the way for restoration.[15] The second function of the verse is to let the hearer know from the outset the truth of Isaiah's pronouncement. The promised attack would not occur. Thus we know what Isaiah knew: Ahaz's anxiety and feverish preparations were unnecessary. This knowledge helps us to realize even more his folly in refusing to trust God with the outcome.

Although it is not mentioned here, something else lies in the background: Ahaz's decision to appeal to Assyria for help (2 K. 16:7–9). We do not know whether the decision had yet been acted upon when God sent Isaiah to confront the king, but it is sure that it was at least under consideration. The situation abounds with ironies: it was probably the encroachment of the Assyrian empire that prompted Syria and Israel to unite and to try to force Judah into a defensive coalition with them (see the Introduction); Assyria hardly needed to be urged and paid a great sum to do what she had been planning all along.

Furthermore, the real threat to Judah's independence was not Syria and Israel, but Assyria, whom Ahaz was inviting into the affairs of the region. Yet Ahaz could not see the long-range issues. He could only see the short range, and he was to pay the full price for his short-sightedness.

This decision to appeal to Assyria had spiritual implications as well as political ones, for Assyria's "help" could only be procured through a covenant with her. Such a covenant would involve the recognition of the

13. A part of this assumption relates to the thesis that 6:1–8:18 was originally a personal memoir of Isaiah. Since this verse does not fit that hypothesis well it is dismissed. But neither do the 3rd person pronouns referring to Isaiah throughout fit the hypothesis. As Scott points out, only a thoroughgoing reworking could turn the chapter into a personal memoir.

14. Cf. H. Orlinsky, "Studies in the St. Mark's Isaiah Scroll, IV," *JQR* 43 (1952) 329–340.

15. O. Steck, "Rettung und Verstockung. Exegetische Bemerkungen zu Jesaja 7, 3–9," *EvT* 33 (1973) 77–90.

Assyrian gods and an admission of their lordship. This is probably the significance of Ahaz's journey to Damascus and the redesign of the temple altar after a Syrian plan (2 K. 16:10–16; 2 Chr. 28:22–24). It is in this light that Isaiah's challenge to trust God becomes especially pointed for Ahaz. He must either commit himself to Assyria and, in effect, deny God, or he must commit himself to God and leave Assyria in divine hands. We know which he chose, and all because of an attack which was doomed before it began!

2 With this verse the actual account of the event begins. The phrase *house of David* is an expression for the king and his courtiers much like "the White House" is for the president of the United States and his staff. But there may also be a hint of irony in its use here (as in v. 13). It is *David's* house which is terrified. How are the mighty fallen! A part of the terror may relate to the events described in 2 Chr. 28. Apparently the attack described here and in 2 K. 16 occurs after a successful campaign against outlying parts of Judah. Ahaz had been defeated by both Syria and Israel, perhaps separately, and had suffered great loses (2 Chr. 28:5–8). Now, if not before, the two armies are acting in concert and moving against Jerusalem. The result is the almost total immobilization of the will depicted by the prophet in the figure of leaves shaken in the wind. Undoubtedly, the additional attacks of Edom and the Philistines only added to the terror (2 Chr. 28:17, 18). Yet another cause of concern for the "house of David" would be the announced intent of the enemy to bring the dynasty to an end by putting a tributary of theirs, a man named Tabeel, on the throne of Judah (v. 6).

The exact date of the attack is uncertain. but it must have taken place between Ahaz's accession in 736 and the beginning of the siege of Damascus in 734. For several years Tiglath-pileser III, the Assyrian monarch, had been occupied with matters in the north and east of his empire, but it would have been clear that he would soon return to follow up his earlier conquests in the direction of the eventual goal, namely, Egypt. Probably the hiatus and the certainty together provoked Pekah and Rezin into action.[16]

3 Ahaz was evidently investigating the city's water supply in preparation for the coming siege when Isaiah met him. Until Hezekiah's tunnel was completed, Jerusalem had no completely dependable source of water

16. Cf. E. Vogt, "Jesaja und die drohende Eroberung Palästinas durch Tiglath-Pilizer," *FB* 2 (1972) 249–255; H. Donner, "The Syro-Ephraimite War and the End of the Kingdom of Israel," in *Israelite and Judaean History,* ed. J. H. Hayes and J. M. Miller, OTL (Philadelphia: Westminster, 1977), pp. 421–434.

within its walls, so this would have been a matter of considerable concern. Without water a city could not hope to endure a siege for more than a few days. The location of this pool is unknown. It has been variously located on the north, west, and south where pools are known to have existed. Burrows places it at the confluence of the Kidron and Tyropoeon valleys.[17] This would accord well with what is known of the location of the Fuller's Field and would be appropriate for the Rabshaqeh (36:2), who had come up from Lachish in the south.

Shear-jashub, your son. Isaiah was commanded to take his son with him as he went out to meet Ahaz. The son's name means "a remnant will return." Evidently that name was to have significance for Ahaz, but it is never specified what that significance was. As a result, a great deal has been written about the possible interpretations. Chiefly, these revolve about whether the implications of the name are positive or negative.[18] Did Isaiah mean to emphasize that although there would be destruction, that destruction would not be total? Or did he mean to say that the coming destruction would be so devastating as to leave but a remnant? Kaiser has suggested that the meaning was neutral, depending upon Ahaz's choice for its ultimate implication. However, two factors militate against this. First, the child was named before this event, suggesting that already, probably out of his experience in the temple, Isaiah foresaw a destruction which would leave but a remnant.[19] Second, the emphatic position of "remnant" (Shear) in the name suggests that "only a remnant" is intended. Thus the essential message of the name is negative, but it is not unremittingly so. This ambiguity is precisely in keeping with Isaiah's overall message as it is contained in the present book. It is neither judgment only nor salvation only. Rather, it is impending doom which cannot obscure God's intention

17. M. Burrows, "The Conduit of the Upper Pool," *ZAW* 70 (1958) 221–27; cf. J. Gray, *I & II Kings,* OTL, rev. ed. (Philadelphia: Westminster, 1970), pp. 679–682; R. Amiran, "Water Supply at Ancient Jerusalem," in *Jerusalem Revealed,* ed. Y. Yadin (Jerusalem: 1975), pp. 75–78.

18. See S. Blank, "The Current Misinterpretation of Isaiah's She'ar Yashub," *JBL* 67 (1948) 211–15; A. Gunneweg, "Heils und Unheilsverkündigung in Jes. VII," *VT* 15 (1965) 27–34; G. Hasel, "Linguistic Considerations Regarding the Translation of Isaiah's Shear-Jashub. A Reassessment," *AUSS* 9 (1971) 36–46; L. Koehler, "Shear-Yashub und der nachte Relativsatz," *VT* 3 (1953) 84–85. The Targ. paraphrases, "the remnant that have not sinned and they that have turned from sin, your disciples."

19. This consideration points to the authenticity of 6:13 as well as to the fact that the message of hardening was an integral part of the call experience, not a result of the experiences during the Syro-Ephraimite war.

to bless.[20] But what would the name have suggested to Ahaz? If it is true that Ahaz had already suffered defeat at the hands of Syria and Israel, then it is entirely possible that he now dreaded total annihilation. To that fear Isaiah's son's name says, "No, there will be a remnant of Judah (and the house of David) preserved from destruction. You may believe that the promised threat is bootless" (cf. chs. 7–9).[21] This interpretation seems to fit the context best, whatever the name meant in its original setting.[22]

4–6 With a biting metaphor Isaiah shows Ahaz that he has nothing to fear from the kings of Israel and Syria. They are merely the smoking ends of sticks where a bonfire has been. The fire is gone and these are all that remain. It may have been that Tiglath-pileser was already on the march and they would soon be called home to their own defense. But in any case, their tenure as forces in the affairs of the region was to be of very short duration. The glory of Ephraim and Syria was already gone and what remained of them was but the smoking ends of what had once been.[23] But from a strictly human point of view Ahaz's concern was clearly merited. What the two kings contemplated was not merely a punitive raid to bring Ahaz into line. Rather, it was a war of annexation, the conclusion of which would see a puppet king ruling the territory. Nevertheless, Ahaz need not panic or take heroic measures for defense. The same kinds of words were addressed to Joshua when he faced the impossible task of succeeding Moses and leading the conquest of Canaan (Deut. 31:6, 7; Josh. 1:6–9). In that case as well as this one, the potential source of courage and confidence was in the awareness that whereas our understanding and strength are limited, the One who is with us is limitless both in understanding and power. Thus, the outcome is not in the enemies' hands; it is in the hands of God, whom we know and love. Such a realization, while not guaranteeing a favorable outcome, still takes the dread from it, with the result that we may be at our best.

20. This is seen in the use of the remnant in 10:21. R. P. Carroll (*ExpTim* 89 [1978] 301) asserts that a shift has taken place from negative in 7:3 to positive in 10:21, but both are implicit in the name itself.

21. It is also tempting to relate the name to the return of the captives reported in 2 Chr. 28:8–15.

22. It must also be held as a possibility that the son was sent because God (and possibly Isaiah) knew that Ahaz would not believe. Thus the son's name would merely be a prejudgment of Ahaz's unbelief. However, this would mean that the appeals of vv. 9 and 11 had no function except to make Ahaz's choice the more culpable, which, in fact, makes the appeals deceitful.

23. The continuing reference to Pekah as the son of Remaliah is probably a contemptuous way of pointing out Pekah's role as a usurper who had not descended from the royal line.

7–9 Some have concluded on form-critical grounds that these verses came from another occasion than that of vv. 3–6.[24] A good part of the argument seems to rest upon the fact that vv. 3–6 are prose while vv. 7–9 are poetry. However, the use of a poetic oracle to confirm a prose statement is not uncommon in Isaiah (8:3–10; 8:23–9:6 [Eng. 9:1–7]; 11:10–16). In this light it is unnecessary to assume a conflation here, particularly in the light of the fact that vv. 7–9, the saying of the Lord, are placed in contrast with the saying of Pekah and Rezin in v. 6. The two kings have arrogantly announced their plan; now the King, the Sovereign (v. 6; cf. 6:18), announces his plan (cf. Jas. 4:13–17). Again, the point is one of perspective. If there is no one who sits above the earth (Isa. 40:22), then we are at the mercy of the whims of men (40:27). But if there is such a One, then we need not fear what men can do to us (40:28–31; Ps. 56:5, 12 [Eng. 4, 11]). Rezin's scope of action is merely Ephraim. But God's scope is the world. If Ahaz can believe that, his whole perspective will be altered, and he and his house will be truly established.[25]

7 God announces that the coalition's violent plan will never occur. How Isaiah knew this is not particularly important. Some who wish to maintain a naturalistic worldview would argue that the prophet understood world events better than Ahaz and his court, but it is hardly likely that Isaiah's intelligence system, humanly speaking, was better than the king's. On the other hand, his intelligence of the character of the world's Lord was obviously superior to the king's, and that is what made the difference.

8 The second half of the verse is problematic for two reasons: first, because it seems out of order coming after the statement about Syria; and second, because it appears that Ephraim ceased to be a people in 722/21, which was only some twelve to thirteen years after this announcement, not sixty-five. One suggestion is that the statement was an addition which a later scribe made in the margin after Esarhaddon and Ashurbanipal had made final major deportations of the Israelites about 670/669 (cf. Ezra 4:2, 10). According to this supposition the marginal note was later put into the text at this point.[26] Apart from the negative presuppositions about Scripture and predictive prophecy that this suggestion betrays, it is

24. So, e.g., M. Saebø, "Formgeschichtliche Erwägungen zu Jes. 7:3–9," *ST* 14 (1960) 54–69.

25. R. de Vaux points out that Jerusalem's deliverance is not linked here to any concept of the city's inviolability but rather to the faithfulness of God ("Jerusalem and the Prophets," *HUCA* 40 [1969] 289–290; repr. in *Interpreting the Prophetic Tradition* [Cincinnati: Hebrew Union College; New York: KTAV, 1969], pp. 275–300).

26. So M. Scott, "Isaiah 7:8," *ExpTim* 38 (1926/1927) 525–26.

very difficult to explain how an intentional addition would have been placed where it now is rather than in the more logical place after the discussion of Ephraim. The present order looks more like a cryptic original than an intentional alteration. The statement that an event sixty-five years in the future would be of no consequence to Ahaz misses the point. Like all of us, Ahaz was required to exercise faith in the veracity of God's word at that moment, whether or not he lived to see the complete fulfillment of it. Christ's return is a fitting example for us in the present day.

9 The final statement in this verse sums up the whole issue. Unless Ahaz comes to the point where he can believe in God's sovereignty to the extent of entrusting himself and his nation to God, he is doomed to live in the shaky, panicky condition he now experiences (v. 2). He need not enter into the terribly risky covenant with Assyria, if he will but take firm hold of the covenant which God offers. Assyria will not offer the security Ahaz wishes. Only through trusting in the present and ultimate veracity of God is any real security possible.

b. GOD IS WITH US (7:10–8:10)

(1) The sign of Immanuel (7:10–17)

10 And the Lord spoke to Ahaz again, saying,

11 "Ask for yourself a sign from the Lord your God,
   as deep as Sheol or as high as the heights." [1]

12 But Ahaz said, "I will not ask, and I will not test the Lord."

13 Then he said, "Hear now, house of David. Is it too little for you to try the patience of men, that you must also try the patience of my God?

14 Therefore, the Sovereign, he will give you a sign. Behold, a maiden shall conceive and bear a son, and she[2] will call his name Immanuel.

---

1. The verbs ha'mēq and hagbēah may be imperatives or infinitives in the Hiphil stem. šeʾālâ may be an emphatic imperative "ask!" or more probably a locative of "Sheol" with the original long a preserved in pause. In that case, taking the verbs as infinitives, a literal rendering would be: "Ask . . . making deep to Sheol, making high to the heights." Cf. Job 11:7, 8 for a similar expression.

2. Most of the Greek versions and a number of medieval Hebrew mss. read "You [masc. sing.] shall . . ," but the MT has the harder reading and there is no reason to think it corrupt.

15 *Curds and honey he will eat before he knows*[3] *how to reject evil and choose good.*

16 *For before the lad knows how to reject evil and choose good, the territory whose two kings you dread will be desolate.*

17 *The Lord will bring upon you, and upon your people, and upon the house of your father days unlike any since the day Ephraim departed from Judah—the king of Assyria."*

In this paragraph the prophet puts Ahaz to the test. Although he invites Ahaz to test God, it is really the king himself who is being tested. Will he in fact respond to the words of v. 9b by believing God and becoming established, or will he instead reject such belief? Undoubtedly, as an Israelite king he had given lip service to the idea, but now he must act upon it or deny it. Isaiah challenges him to seek evidence that the exclusive trust he is recommending is indeed viable. But Ahaz does not want such evidence. Why? Apparently it is because his mind is already made up. He is going to trust his and his nation's fate to Assyria, and he does not want some (trumped-up?) evidence that such a drastic decision is unwarranted. Any sign provided by Isaiah could only be an embarrassment to him, so he attempts to avoid the dilemma by an appeal to piety. So it always is. Evidence cannot create faith; it can only confirm it. Where there is not faith, evidence is merely unwelcome, something which needs to be explained away.

But why should Ahaz hand himself over to the tender mercies of his ultimate enemy, a far worse threat than Syria or Ephraim? Once abandon a heartfelt conviction that God does truly care for us and is intimately involved with us, once abandon his perspective for our own, then suddenly decisions which are utterly foolish viewed from his perspective become intelligent and wise. When we cannot trust God, it suddenly makes good sense to trust our worst enemy. So John Wesley said, "If a man will not believe God, he will believe anything. Why he may believe a man could put himself into a quart bottle!" (*Letters*, VI:123).

Isaiah's message to the unbelieving house of David is that what they have rejected as foolish—reliance upon God's care and presence—is ultimate wisdom, while *their* wisdom—that Assyria can be trusted to look out for Judah's interests—is errant nonsense. "God is with us" means that

---

3. *l^{e}da^{c}tô* appears to an infinitive construct of *yd^c*, lit. "to his knowing"; LXX "before he knows." Infinitives construct typically introduce temporal clauses by having the inseparable preposition *b* attached to them. Here *l* seems to perform that function instead of its more normal purposive function; cf. GKC, § 114o.

God's word will be kept, Syria and Israel's attack will not succeed, but it also means that he must let Judah see for a certainty that no one else—most of all Assyria—is with them. For this reason the prophecy of Immanuel is both good and bad, joy and sorrow.

10 *And the Lord spoke to Ahaz again.* The *again* may indicate that this confrontation between Isaiah and Ahaz took place at another place and time than that recorded in vv. 1–9 (cf. Gen. 8:10; etc.). If so, the general context remains the same, for Isaiah is evidently continuing to challenge Ahaz to believe God in the Syro-Ephraimite crisis. However, *again* may merely indicate a second part of a single conversation, vv. 3–9 being the promise and vv. 10, 11 the challenge (cf. Gen. 18:29; etc.). There being no evidence of a change in time or location, it seems best to see the paragraph as a direct continuation of vv. 1–9.

The statement that *the Lord spoke* is a good example of the prophetic self-understanding. The prophet does not speak for himself and he does not merely speak as bidden. Rather, when he speaks, God speaks. Yet this is not a kind of possession where the prophet is a helpless tool in a divinely manipulative hand,[4] nor is there any evidence that it is the result of "capturing" God through a mechanical application of ritual or drugs.[5] Rather, it is the clear-eyed recognition that the Transcendent can relate to the finite in such a way that neither the Transcendent is contained nor the finite violated. Neither God nor Isaiah has become other than himself in the process, yet there has been such a community of thought and desire between the two personalities that Isaiah's words are God's.[6] This relation is the foundation of a doctrine of revelation. If Isaiah was deluded in his astonishing claim, why study his book at all? If he was correct, then the world dare not dismiss as easily as it is wont to Isaiah's, and Israel's, religion as merely one more of humanity's quests for the Divine. Isaiah did not claim to speak *about* God, he claimed to speak *for* God.

11 Ahaz is now challenged to give God a chance to prove his trustworthiness. Although our faith is not to be in the signs, nevertheless God has, throughout all the ages, given his people evidence by which their faith might be strengthened. To this extent "the leap of faith" concept, as popularly held, is incorrect, presuming as it does that God cannot, or will not, intersect the world of space/time/matter and that thus there is no

---

4. Cf. A. J. Heschel, *The Prophets* (New York: Harper & Row, 1962), pp. 307–366, for a thorough investigation of prophetic ecstasy. See esp. pp. 319 and 358.

5. See J. Lindblom, *Prophecy in Ancient Israel*, p. 106; cf. 1 Sam. 9, and note that this is different from the great prophets.

6. See Lindblom, op. cit., pp. 178–79.

evidence for faith external to our own psyches.[7] Rather, according to the Scriptures, God has always given such evidence, sometimes in greater or lesser abundance, but he never asks us to believe without rational foundation. True, the will to believe must come first, but when that will is exercised there is evidence freely offered (John 7:17). In fact, the hallmark of the Judeo-Christian faith is that God has acted in space/time/matter in unique ways. If we now deny that he can or has done so, the whole reason for being a Christian drops to the ground.

In the Bible, signs may be miraculous, as in the deliverance from Egypt (Deut. 6:22) or the feeding of the five thousand (John 6:14),[8] but they may also be a symbolic means whereby a prediction is made memorable. In this way they provide a benchmark for the fulfillment to be recognized (Num. 16:38; Ezek. 12:6; Isa. 8:3, 4, 18; cf. 1 Sam. 2:34 and Luke 2:12, where no symbolism is involved, but where the evidential aspect is). Delitzsch well says that "signs authenticate divine causality retrospectively or divine certainty prospectively."

It is commonly assumed among commentators that the references to the depths and the heights necessarily mean that Isaiah was calling on Ahaz to ask for a miraculous sign. But that does not necessarily follow. All the prophet is saying is that there is no limit on what Ahaz may ask. Such a sweeping statement confirms again Isaiah's sense of community with God. He is neither being presumptuous nor does he have any fear of being left hanging. He knows the mind of God.

But he is also putting every ounce of effort into the appeal. This is the significance of the reference to *your God*. This God who speaks through Isaiah, who offers to put himself at Ahaz's command, is not some strange unknown deity. He is the One who has bound himself to Israel, and even more particularly, to the house of David, in covenant love. He is not the possession of priests and prophets; rather, he is personally known to Ahaz, his own anointed. Why should Ahaz prevent his own God from demonstrating his love for him?

12 But it is all in vain. Ahaz's mind is made up, his options shut off. He has already concluded that his only hope is alliance with Assyria. He may even have persuaded himself that this was God's way out of the crisis. But at any rate, his problem was to avoid a blunt statement that nothing Isaiah could say or do would make him believe that God could

7. For a critique of this popular view of Kierkegaard's thought see V. Eller, *Kierkegaard and Radical Discipleship* (Princeton: Princeton University, 1968), pp. 119ff.

8. Note how the signs were not able to convince those who did not wish to believe (John 6:30 after 6:14).

deliver them from Syria and Ephraim without Assyria's help, but still prevent Isaiah from doing or saying something which would make his chosen course look like he did not believe God.

He made a choice which indicated his skill at diplomacy and quick thinking. To a casual onlooker he made it appear that he did not have a problem of too little faith, but rather was possessed of such deep faith that he did not want to ask for evidence. To do so, he alluded to Scripture, but like others before and after him, he took the scriptural statement out of its context. His allusion was to Deut. 6:16, where testing (or tempting, AV) the Lord was forbidden. However, the sense of that passage is of a demand for proof arising from doubt and rebellion. Such a testing is indeed repugnant to God (so also the NT: Matt. 16:4; Mark 8:12; Luke 11:29); but a testing of God which grows from faith and, out of faith, dares to rest its weight upon God, that testing God invites (so 2 K. 20:8–11; Mal. 3:10; cf. also Ps. 34:7 [Eng. 6] for a different expression of the same thought). It is obviously not belief which prompts Ahaz's statement. If it were, he would not have continued with the plans for an alliance with Assyria. Rather, it is unbelief which gives rise to his announcement, an unbelief profound enough that it will not even permit evidence that it is wrong.

13–17 Both Delitzsch and Smith see Ahaz's rejection in v. 12 as the turning point in the fortunes of the house of David. That resolute act of unfaith signaled an abandonment of God by the dynasty and opened the door for its eventual destruction. It is this which, in their view, provides the setting for the Immanuel prophecy. Although Ahaz, through his distrust of God, has brought the strictly human dynasty to an end, God is still with David and Judah, as finally evidenced in the divine-human Messiah, Immanuel.[9] This is an attractive solution to the problem of the cause of the Immanuel prophecy's appearance at this point. Otherwise, the reason for a messianic prophecy occurring here is obscure at best. It may well be that the reference to the house of David in v. 13 supports this view. The human house of David is finally without hope; it has tried God's patience too far. From this point on, however long it should take for that human dynasty to come to complete collapse, the only hope is in God's eventual miraculous provision. Against this view, it must be admitted that, apart from the appearance of the Immanuel prophecy, nothing in the immediate context requires the reader to see Ahaz's choice as the radical turning point in the dynasty's fortunes. At the same time, the apocalyptic flavor of the

---

9. Cf. S. Porubcan, "The Word '$\partial \underline{t}$ in Isaiah 7:14," *CBQ* 22 (1960) 144–159, for a more recent expression of a similar position.

wider context (8:23–9:6 [Eng. 9:1–7]; 11:1–16) does suggest that the consequences of this act are much more far-reaching than one would suppose from merely reading the bare facts of the event.

Largely because 7:14 is directly quoted (via the LXX) in Matt. 1:23 as support for our Lord's virgin birth, this passage has attracted immense interest.[10] Probably the greatest single focus of attention has been upon the translation of *ʿalmâ* with arguments for and against the LXX translation *parthénos,* "virgin."[11] But only slightly less absorbing has been the attempt to identify the child Immanuel. Since Duhm, the idea that the primary reference was to Christ has been largely discounted, except by conservatives, because of a refusal on the part of most scholars to accept a view of inspiration that would allow the possibility of genuinely predictive prophecy. But having rejected that identification, scholars have been unable to agree with one another. Some suggest he is a son of Ahaz, others the son of Isaiah.[12] Yet others suggest that no one in particular was in-

10. Some of the more important general treatments are: K. Budde, "Das Immanuelzeichen und die Ahaz-Begegnung, Jesaja 7," *JBL* 52 (1933) 22–54; E. Hammershaimb, "The Immanuel Sign," *ST* 3 (1949–1951) 124–142; L. Koehler, "Zum Verständnis von Jesaja 7, 14," *ZAW* 67 (1955) 48–50; T. Lescow, "Das Geburtsmotiv in den messianischen Weissagungen bei Jesaja und Micha," *ZAW* 79 (1967) 172–207; J. Lindblom, *A Study of the Immanuel Section in Isaiah. Isa. vii, 1–ix, 6* (Lund: Gleerup, 1958); W. McKane, "The Interpretation of Isaiah VII 14–25," *VT* 17 (1967) 208–219; J. Motyer, "Context and Content in the Interpretation of Isa. 7, 14," *TynBul* 21 (1970) 118–125; S. Mowinckel, "Immanuelprofetien: Jes. 7: Streiflys fra Ugarit," *NorTT* 42 (1941) 129–158; J. J. Stamm, "Die Immanuel-Perikope im Lichte neuerer Veröffentlichungen," *ZDMG* Supp. 1 (1969) 281–290; O. Steck, "Beiträge zum Verständnis von Jesaja 7, 10–17 und 8, 1–4," *TZ* 29 (1973) 161–178; W. Vischer, *Die Immanuel-Botschaft im Rahmen des Königlichen Zionsfestes,* Theologischen Studien 45 (Zurich: 1955).

11. See C. Feinberg, "The Virgin Birth in the OT and Isaiah 7:14," *BSac* 119 (1962) 251–58; C. Gordon, "Almah in Isaiah 7, 14," *JBR* 21 (1953) 106; K. Hartmann, "More About the RSV and Isaiah 7:14," *LQ* 7 (1955) 344–47; E. Lacheman, "Apropos Isaiah 7:14," *JBR* 22 (1954) 42; C. Lattey, "The Term *ʿalmah* in Isaiah 7:14," *CBQ* 9 (1947) 89–95; W. Müller, "A Virgin Shall Conceive," *EvQ* 32 (1960) 203–207; M. Rehm, "Das wort *ʿalmah* in Is. 7:14," *BZ* 8 (1964) 89–101; J. Steinmueller, "Etymology and Biblical Usage of *ʿAlmah,*" *CBQ* 2 (1940) 28–43; B. Vawter, "The Ugaritic Use of *glmt,*" *CBQ* 14 (1952) 318–322.

12. On the former, see Hammershaimb, op. cit.; J. Scullion, "An Approach to the Understanding of Isa. 7:16–17," *JBL* 87 (1968) 288–300. On the latter, see T. Bird, "Who Is the Boy in Isa. 7:16?" *CBQ* 6 (1944) 435–443; N. Gottwald, "Immanuel as the Prophet's Son," *VT* 8 (1958) 36–47; H. Wolf, "A Solution to the Immanuel Prophecy in Isaiah 7:14–8:22," *JBL* 91 (1972) 449–456.

tended. Instead, the prophet was saying that many children born within a few months of this encounter would be named Immanuel because of the coming withdrawal of Syria and Israel.[13] That none of these proposed solutions has attracted general approval indicates the unsatisfactory nature of each in some way.

But the traditional understanding is not without problems either, for it has tended to ignore the bearing of the sign upon Ahaz's own situation. Calvin typifies this difficulty by making the child of v. 16 another than the one mentioned in vv. 14 and 15. Yet there is no warrant for such a distinction. The text gives every reason to believe that a single child is intended in all these verses. Furthermore, to separate vv. 16 and 17 from vv. 14 and 15 destroys the contexts of both sets of statements. One solution is to suppose that the prophet understood himself to be speaking of the Messiah but expected him to be born in the near future.[14] The difficulty with this position is that it requires a candid admission that Isaiah's much-vaunted sign to Ahaz did not occur. No such child was born, even though the two enemy nations did withdraw. But the sign was surely twofold: the birth of the child was to point to and to accompany the withdrawal. If he was not born, the whole credibility of Isaiah, including his theology, is called into question. To avoid such an unacceptable result, many conservative commentators and scholars have opted for a "double-fulfillment" theory.[15] While still maintaining that the primary reference was to Christ, they have understood that the sign was fulfilled in a secondary way during Ahaz's lifetime.[16] The enigmatic nature of the prophecy argues against the idea that the primary fulfillment was intended to occur in Ahaz's time, then to be ingeniously applied later to Christ. But to suppose that the sign did not occur in any sense until 725 years after the fact flies in the face of the plain sense of the text.

A final problem raised by this passage is its ambiguous nature. Does it prophesy weal or woe? Those who say it foretells blessing (as

13. See Duhm; Eichhorn; Gray; H. Ginsberg, "Immanuel (Is. 7:14)," *EncJud* VIII:1293–95; McKane, op. cit., p. 214.

14. So Smith; see also R. P. Carroll, *When Prophecy Failed* (New York: Seabury, 1979), pp. 138–140.

15. Cf. esp. Barnes, and more recently C. Lattey, "The Emmanuel Prophecy: Is. 7:14," *CBQ* 8 (1946) 369–376; D. Moody, "The Miraculous Conception," *RevExp* 51 (1954) 495–521. Against such a theory see Young. For a survey of conservative attitudes on the question, see E. Hindson, "Development of the Interpretation of Isa. 7:14," *GTJ* 10/2 (1969) 19–25.

16. So also with Jesus' prophecy of the end times when the destruction of Jerusalem in A.D. 70 is evidently telescoped with events at the end of history (Matt. 24; Mark 13; Luke 21).

might be expected from the nature of the name Immanuel) are forced to
discard or reinterpret v. 17 along with vv. 18–25, which are assumed to
be an expansion of v. 17 in its present form.[17] On the other hand, those
who say it prophesies destruction frequently wish to delete or alter v. 16.[18]
But such artificial systematizing is not only without text-critical grounds,
it is also theologically suspect. The presence of a transcendent and holy
God with us may well mean weal and woe together. To the extent that we
are dependent upon him, his presence results in blessing; but to the extent
that we refuse to depend upon him, his presence is an embarrassment and
a curse. Both realities are implicit in his presence. So it was when Christ
walked the roads of Palestine. The same One whose presence was a blessing at the table of Zacchaeus (Luke 19:1–10) was a curse at the table of
Simon the Pharisee (Luke 7:36–50).

13 *try the patience of men.* The AV and RSV "weary" does not
fully express the thought here. Both men and God are worn out from
trying to get the Davidides to act in faith in this crisis. The Targum reads
"prophets" for "men" and most commentators take "men" to refer to the
prophet himself. That may be so, but it may also refer to that faithful
group of people in the land who were looking to their king for courageous,
spiritual leadership.

my God. The change from "your God" in v. 11 is ominous. Isaiah
seems to be saying that Ahaz has rejected the God who would have supported and established him. No longer can the prophet speak of "your
God," now it is only "my God," who is evidently foreign to Ahaz (see
1 Sam. 15:26–30 for a similar experience in Saul's life). Such an understanding lends support to the position mentioned above concerning the
long-term import of Ahaz's act. He has alienated himself and his house
from God. The whole verse seems pregnant with threat.

14 If Ahaz will not ask for a sign, God in his sovereignty will
give one in any case. It is impossible to ascertain whether this is the sign
God intended to give had Ahaz asked, or whether it is especially given in
view of Ahaz's refusal to ask. At any rate, it is the one he receives. As
noted above, it confirms Isaiah's earlier promise (vv. 4–9), but it also
confirms the foolishness of not trusting that promise. That the positive side
would have applied had Ahaz received the sign in faith lends some weight
to the idea that this was the intended sign. Had Ahaz received it in faith,
Immanuel would have appeared solely as the vindication of the house of

17. See McKane, op. cit.
18. See E. Kissane, "Butter and Honey Shall He Eat (Is. 7:15)," *OBL* I
(1957) 169–173.

David. As it was, he was to appear as a shame to the house of David: they had not believed, and so received the just result of that unbelief. Nevertheless, God, in faithfulness to his own promise, would raise up from the wreckage a true Son of David.

a maiden shall conceive. It is not possible to be dogmatic as to why Isaiah used the ambiguous *ʿalmâ* here instead of the unambiguous *beṯûlâ.*[19] Nor is it clear what meaning should be assigned to *ʿalmâ.* Typically, the meaning given is "a young woman of marriageable age,"[20] with the clear implication that the conception is a natural one. However, conservative scholars have frequently pointed out that the word is never used of a married woman in the OT.[21] So they have argued that the word denotes a sexually mature, but unmarried, young woman. It would be axiomatic in Hebrew society that such a woman would be a virgin. While the viginity would not be the main focus, as with *beṯûlâ,* nonetheless it would still follow. The English "maiden" comes very close to having the same denotations and connotations. Such an understanding has the significant virtue of explaining the origin of the LXX *parthénos,* "virgin," something those commentators opting for "a young woman of marriageable age" do not mention. Unless *ʿalmâ* had overtones of virginity about it, the LXX translation is inexplicable.

But if Isaiah wished to stress the virginity of the mother here, why did he not use *beṯûlâ?* Young, noting that *beṯûlâ* is frequently accompanied by some such statement as "she had not known a man," argues that *it* was the ambiguous term. However, this is manifestly not so, for *beṯûlâ* has no implication in addition to virginity, whereas *ʿalmâ* does.[22] The conclusion to which we are driven is that while the prophet did not want to stress the virginity, neither did he wish to leave it aside (as he could have done by using *ʾiššâ* or some other term for "woman"). In fact, he may have used this term precisely because of its richness and diversity. The Ugaritic cognate *(ǵlmt)* is used with reference to a goddess who was understood to

---

19. See n. 9 above for a selected bibliography.

20. KB, p. 709; see also A. Myers, "Use of *ʿalmah* in the OT," *LQ* 7 (1955) 137–140.

21. See Gen. 24:43; Exod. 2:8; 1 Chr. 15:20; Ps. 46:2 (Eng. 1); 68:26 (Eng. 25); Prov. 30:19; Cant. 1:3; 6:8. Note that the LXX translates *ʿalmâ* with *parthénos* in Gen. 24:43. In Prov. 30:19 it might be argued that the context suggests that the *ʿalmâ* (RSV "maiden") was sexually experienced. However, that does not necessarily obtain. In fact, the air of mystery in vv. 18–19 is enhanced if the girl is without sexual experience prior to the moment described there.

22. Cf. *TDOT,* II:338–343. Note that *parthénos* in its Greek usage denotes primarily a state of innocence with chastity assumed but not always explicit. Cf. *TDNT,* V:826–837.

be a perpetual virgin.[23] Without conceding that Isaiah has merely adapted a myth,[24] one may still think that he adapted well-known linguistic forms which would make it plain that whatever might occur along the way, the ultimate fulfillment of this prophecy would be no ordinary event.

Possibly, then, it is the dual focus of the oracle that explains the use of ʿalmâ here. In the short term, the virgin conception does not seem to have had primary importance. Rather, the significance is that a child conceived at that moment would still be immature when the two threatening nations would have been destroyed (vv. 16, 22).[25] Had Isaiah used beṯûlâ here, Ahaz would probably have been so caught up with that thought that he would have missed the specific linkage to his own time.

On the other hand, the very two-sidedness of the sign in Ahaz's time demanded something more. Yes, the disappearance of Syria and Ephraim could be seen as evidence that God was with them. But what of Assyria, foolishly trusted and soon to turn on its hapless client? Was God still with them in that? And suppose even greater powers than Assyria strode onto the world's stage, what then? If we can believe that the transcendent One is really immanent, and the immanent One truly transcendent, then there is reason to live courageously and unselfishly. But no child born to a young woman in Ahaz's day is proof of God's presence in all times. But if a virgin overshadowed by God's Spirit should conceive and give birth, it would not only be a sign of God's presence with us. Better than that, it would be the reality of that experience. So Ahaz's sign must be rooted in its own time to have significance for that time, but it also must extend beyond that time and into a much more universal mode if its radical truth is to be any more than a vain hope. For such a twofold task ʿalmâ is admirably suited.[26]

23. *UT,* 1:19; 51:VII:54:7; 77:7; 128:II:22; Krt 204. For this interpretation of *ǧlmt* cf. Gordon, op. cit.; Vawter, op. cit. Note also S. Rummel, *RSP,* III:297–98. On the idea of the "perpetual virginity" of goddesses who were both fecund and virgin at the same time, see W. F. Albright, *From the Stone Age to Christianity,* 2nd ed. (Garden City: Doubleday, 1957), pp. 233–34.

24. Contra Lacheman, op. cit.

25. The time reference of the verbs *hārâ* and *yōleḏeṯ* is not clear, since the latter is a fem. participle and the former either an anomalous fem. participle or, more likely, a verbal noun. (The normal fem. participle should be *hōrîâ*.) Ginsberg (op. cit., p. 1294) argues that *hārâ* must be "she will conceive" (cf. Judg. 13:3–5), or else the following verb would have to become a converted imperfect to convey futurity.

26. The presence of the article may indicate a definite woman known to Ahaz or to Isaiah or to both, or it may emphasize the general grouping of "woman" (as does capitalizing a noun in English).

she will call his name Immanuel. The custom of the mother's naming her child is not uncommon in the OT (cf. Gen. 4:1, 25; 29:31–30:13, 17–24; 35:18; Judg. 13:24; 1 Sam. 1:20; 4:21), especially if the mother has reason for a unique emotional investment in the child or if the father cannot perform the task. This emphasis upon the mother and the corresponding de-emphasis of the father's role cannot help but be suggestive in the shaping of the ultimate understanding of the sign. No man sired by a human father could be the embodiment of "God with us."

In contrast with Shear-jashub and Maher-shalal-hash-baz, both of whom are treated in a straightforward manner as Isaiah's sons, there is an aura of mystery about the Immanuel figure. This is so even without the NT quotation of 7:14. His father is not identified at all and his mother only generally. He is touched upon only briefly, but then appears again suddenly in 8:8 as possessor of the land and yet again in 8:10 by means of a wordplay. The enigmatic nature of the references makes it extremely difficult to identify the child of Ahaz's time. In the context of the house of David and being spoken of as owner of the land, it is tempting to think of a newly conceived crown prince. The recognition that *curds and honey* represent food of royalty in some Mesopotamian texts lends further credence to the idea, as does the thought that through Hezekiah God was able to demonstrate his faithful presence.[27] However, that Hezekiah was twenty-five years old at his accession in 516 (2 K. 18:2) means that he was born in 741, at least six years before these events. To hold that the child was "the crown prince, as yet unborn,"[28] raises again the question of Hezekiah. Are we to think Isaiah did not know that the crown prince was already born? Furthermore, if Ahaz was to father this child, it seems very odd that the fact should be ignored. Finally, v. 22 makes it very plain that curds and honey are not intended as symbols of royalty but of the generally depopulated nature of the region.

The suggestion that no particular child was intended is even less attractive, in the light of the particularity of Isaiah's children as well as of 8:8 and of the description here. The facts of *a* child's conception and birth are significant to the framework of the sign. The child will be born in a certain time frame, and its specific existence in that time frame is intrinsic to the function of the sign.[29] It would not be necessary that Ahaz know of the birth, only that at some point he become aware that the promised child had been born.

27. So Hammershaimb, op. cit.
28. So Scullion, op. cit., p. 298.
29. See E. Kraeling, "The Immanuel Prophecy," *JBL* 50 (1931) 282.

Perhaps the most attractive option is that Immanuel and Maher-shalal-hash-baz were one and the same.[30] If this were so, this passage would form a more poetic statement of the child's identity, pointing to the ultimate Immanuel, whereas 8:1–4 would constitute a more prosaic account and be limited merely to the person of Maher-shalal-hash-baz. The references to his conception and birth in 8:3 lend support to the connection, as does the reference to Immanuel in 8:10, shortly after the discussion of the birth of Isaiah's son.

15–17 The two-edged nature of the Immanuel sign comes to the fore in these verses.[31] Kaiser suggests a parallel structure in which vv. 14 and 16 portray the positive side, while vv. 15 (as explained by v. 22) and 17 present the negative side. This is possible, although it seems overly neat. The hope and the judgment are more tightly intertwined than that. As noted above, the reality of God's presence with his people can portend joy and sorrow at the same time, depending upon the people's character. So here, the same agency by which Syria and Ephraim will be depopulated, Assyria, will also depopulate Judah. In this sense, it is not necessary to separate v. 16 from v. 15; in fact, the opening *kî* of v. 16 can be taken as causal, indicating why the child will eat curds and honey: Judah will be delivered from her neighbors' threat.[32] (Verses 21 and 22 make it plain that the abundance of these foods is the result of depopulation—in this case, of the general region.) But if the significance of the sign had stopped merely with deliverance, Ahaz could have credited his own political maneuverings with the outcome rather than God. That was not to be the case, for v. 17 follows on the heels of v. 16 without so much as a conjunction. By depending on himself rather than God, Ahaz has unleashed a whirlwind which will not be content to devour his troublesome northern neighbors. Led by the God he has disdained, it will come sweeping over him and his nation as well.

15 *before he knows how to reject evil and choose good* has been interpreted in two ways. Some believe it refers to moral discrimination

30. See esp. Wolf, op. cit.

31. Many scholars have been unwilling to accept the two-sidedness and have tried to make the material all positive (Gray; McKane, op. cit.) while others wish to make it all negative (Blank, op. cit.; Kissane; Skinner; J. Stamm, "Die Immanuel Weissagung," *VT* 4 [1954] 20–33). But all of them must resort to textual emendation to make their case.

32. Various attempts have been made to make v. 16 refer to Judah in order to see the passage as threat. Kissane's solution is ingenious: he divides off the last phrase so that it then goes with v. 17. Thus "[v. 16] . . . good, the land will be abandoned. Whereas you are in fear of the two kings, [v. 17] the Lord will. . . ." But there is no mss. evidence to support this solution.

(as in Gen. 2:17; 3:5; Deut. 1:39; 1 K. 3:9; Isa. 5:20) and, in that light, suggest an elapsed time of twelve to twenty years. Others point to 8:4, where it is said that Isaiah's son will not be able to speak clearly before Damascus and Samaria are plundered, and argue that this is the correct interpretation of good and evil here: distinguishing between what is helpful and what is harmful. (2 Sam. 11:35 is appealed to here since it appears that Barzillai is not speaking of moral discernment, but of his capacity to appreciate pleasure; cf. RSV.) Either idea would fit here. Within three years Damascus had been destroyed and most of Samaria's holdings had been plundered. But it is also true that it was not until some twelve or thirteen years later that Samaria was destroyed and Israel ceased to exist. On balance, given the evident connection of the phrase with moral discernment at several points, and given a lack of clear evidence to the contrary, the best interpretation seems to be that by the time the child has reached an age of official accountability, both of the threatening powers will have ceased to exist.

17 Although *the king of Assyria* is widely regarded as a gloss, it is not necessarily so. Delitzsch points out that the syntax is quite correct in its use of *ʾeṭ* with a more definite object following a less definite one (e.g., Gen. 26:34). Furthermore, by holding this phrase back until the end of the line its impact is doubled. It is not at all difficult to see the prophet using a device such as this to give a final blow to Ahaz's self-sufficiency. Verses 14–16 had perhaps lulled him into complacency. Even if he had done the wrong thing, it was going to turn out all right. Good days would come. But with devastating suddenness Isaiah lets him know that good days will not come. What is coming upon Jerusalem is the awful thunder of war-chariots. Whatever a man trusts in place of God will one day turn to devour him.

(2) The razor of Assyria (7:18–25)

18 *It will come to pass in that day that the Lord will whistle for the fly which is at the end of the streams of Egypt and for the bee which is in the land of Assyria.*

19 *They will come and lodge, all of them, in the steep ravines, and the clefts of the crags, and in all the thornbushes and brambles.*[1]

---

1. The final word in this list of hiding places, *nahᵃlōlîm* (note the assonance with the preceding noun, *naʾᵃṣûṣîm*), occurs only here and its meaning is uncertain. The LXX has "trees," the Targ. "fine houses," and the Vulg. "holes." The AV "bushes" (and NEB "stinkwood"?) seem to be based upon the medieval commentator Saadya's statement that it denotes a small bush as opposed to the large bush denoted by the previous word. "Waterholes" (NIV, JPSV) and the extrapolation from it, "pastured" (RSV), is taken from the verbal root *nhl*, "to guide to water or refreshment" (BDB, pp. 625–26).

20 *In that day the Sovereign will shave with a razor hired[2] from beyond the River—the king of Assyria—the head and the hair of the legs.[3] It will also sweep away the beard.*

21 *It will come to pass in that day that a man will keep alive a heifer from the herd and two from the flock.*

22 *And it will come to pass from the abundance of milk produced, that he will eat curds,[4] for curds and honey are what everyone who is left in the midst of the land will eat.*

23 *And it will come to pass in that day that every place in which there were a thousand vines worth a thousand [shekels][5] of silver will be given over to briars and thornbushes.*

24 *With arrows and the bow one will go there because all the land will be in briars and thornbushes.*

25 *On all the hills which were once digged with a hoe, no one will go[6] for fear of briars and thornbushes. It will become a place for the wandering of cattle and the trampling of sheep.*

The recurrence of the phrase "in that day" (vv. 18, 20, 21, 23) causes many commentators to see this passage as a collection of short oracles which may or may not have been uttered at the same time as the Immanuel sign. The congruence of vv. 15 and 22 suggests that the two paragraphs were delivered at the same time. But in any case the function of these verses is to spell out in more detail the veiled threat of v. 17. This section answers the question "How will the coming days be unlike any since the division of the nation?" The answer is a grim one. The armies of their enemies will blanket the land like swarms of bees or flies. The Judeans will be disgraced in defeat. The countryside will be so depopulated that

2. Note that LXX has evidently confused *śkr*, "to hire," with *škr*, "to be drunken," for it reads "with a razor that is great and drunken."

3. "the hair of the legs" may with "head" express totality as in our "top to bottom," but it may also refer to the pubic hair, as "legs" can sometimes act as a euphemism for the genitalia (cf. Exod. 4:25).

4. The LXX lacks "he will eat curds," and Gray, Skinner, and Kaiser take LXX to be more original since they believe the phrase is the work of one wishing to lessen the negative impact. In view of the latter half of the verse, however, it is difficult to see how the insertion of this phrase would make the statement more positive. In fact, without that phrase the second half of the verse does not connect sensibly with the first half. The loss in LXX seems to be a sort of haplography.

5. MT lit. "a thousand silver," i.e., a thousand pieces of silver (so NEB), probably shekels (so Young, Kaiser, RSV); cf. AV "silverlings."

6. In form *tābô'* could be either 2nd masc. sing., "you will (not) come," or 3rd fem. sing., "she [i.e., the fear, a fem. noun] will (not) come." Delitzsch says the form should be *t^ebô'ēm* if "fear" were the subject, but does not explain or justify the assertions. Likewise GKC, § 118l, says "fear" is an accusative of cause, but without justification. Skinner points out that the shift to a 2nd person after successive 3rd person references would be rather strange.

there will be no one to eat the produce of the few remaining animals or to cultivate the once-fertile hills. The land will return to wilderness. Had Ahaz been able to believe that God is indeed present with his people, it need not have been so. But because he trusted something less than God, that object of trust now becomes the instrument of the very devastation he dreaded.

18–19 In 5:26 Isaiah depicted God as whistling for the nations to come and devastate his land. Now he specifies which nations those are. They are Assyria from the north and Egypt from the south. Throughout its history Israel has been caught between the civilizations of the Nile and Mesopotamian valleys, each of them desiring the Levantine region for its access to the other culture. But the prophet sees these great political and military movements not as the work of imperialistically minded powers, but as events which occur at the command of the one God who accomplishes his saving work in history. Assyria and Egypt are insects trained to swarm at their master's command. Now that command is issued and they come.

Although older commentators in particular sought to demonstrate that the bee was especially symbolic of Assyria, while the fly symbolized Egypt, no clear evidence supports this interpretation. The two insects and the two lands form a parallel pair by which Isaiah can depict the swarming, suffocating, inescapable aspects of the enemy armies.[7] They will be everywhere, even in the most inaccessible places where the inhabitants were wont to hide from their invaders. The nature of the land offers many such hiding places: caves in the sides of steep wadis, towering crags such as Masada on the shore of the Dead Sea, and wilderness such as the wilderness of Judea southeast of Jerusalem.[8] But none of these is of any use against an enemy as ubiquitous as bees or flies.

In 735 B.C. Egypt was not much of a threat to Judah and would not be for many years to come. Thus some students of Isaiah think that he was speaking predictively of the events of 609–605 when first Egypt defeated Judah and then a few years later the new Mesopotamian power, Babylon, conquered them (so Delitzsch). That it is not Assyria who attacks in that instance, however, makes it unlikely that these verses specifically predict those events. It is more likely that Isaiah is speaking generally, demonstrating Judah's vulnerability to powerful enemies on either hand apart from God's protection. In the next verse, he deals more specifically with the imminent threat which Assyria would pose.

7. Cf. the Targ., where flies are numerous and bees are strong.
8. Cf. Josephus for the story of Herod's rooting out rebels from the caves of Arbela (*Jewish Wars* xvi.2–4).

20   Isaiah stresses again that the coming attack by Assyria will not be at her own volition. She will be but an agent of the Sovereign, a tool in his hand. This concept was fundamental to Israel's survival as the people of God. If they should ever come to believe the prevailing view that the gods of the conquered people had been defeated by the gods of the victors, then their faith was lost. But if they could believe that in all things their God was Sovereign and that his ultimate purpose was good, then they could survive any shock that would come to them.

hired from beyond the River is probably an ironic comment upon Ahaz's alliance with Assyria. He had hired Assyria from beyond the Euphrates to attack his enemies. But that same razor, in God's hands, would turn upon him shortly. There is no need to say with many commentators that *the king of Assyria* is a gloss. While the phrase may be such an editorial insertion, it is also entirely possible that the very abruptness with which it comes, as in v. 17, is a device of the prophet to hammer home Ahaz's folly in relying on that king. Ahaz may well have sought to keep his covenant with Tiglath-pileser secret. If so, Isaiah here shocks Ahaz with his evident knowledge of the affair, for the reference to the *king of* Assyria would be unnecessary unless the agreement between the two kings were in the background.

to shave your head may be a reference to the way in which captives were treated, but more probably it is a figurative expression of the disgrace which comes to a defeated nation. The figure here is one of complete humiliation: *all* the hair on the body is shorn off, even to that badge of respect, the beard. Humanly speaking Judah will have no honor left.[9]

21–22   Although some commentators, following the lead of the Targum, have tried to make these verses speak of the blessedness of the remnant,[10] it is clear that the main theme of this utterance along with the following is of the depopulation of the land so that it reverts from a crop-growing to a herding region in which there will be so few people that a minimum of animals will produce more than enough food. The exact significance of a man's owning a heifer and two goats or sheep is debatable. Those favoring a positive view point out that many a poor man in the Near East today would feel rich with a heifer and two goats. In the light of the context, however, it seems more likely that it is being said that a man will

---

9. For a similar practice as applied to women, see the shaving of the heads of French women known to have consorted with Germans during World War II.

10. The Targ. has "good things" for MT "making milk" and "all the righteous who remain" for MT "everyone who remains."

be able to save only these from the debacle.[11] The use of the verb *keep alive* (or "preserve") also seems to support this view. Of greater significance is that the milk which a heifer, not a cow in her prime, and a couple of goats will produce will be enough so that it will have to be curdled to keep it. Because of the paucity of inhabitants, the same situation will hold true across the land. In the light of v. 15, it is evident that Isaiah is thinking of this condition as existing in the near future, as it certainly did in Northern Israel by 721, but also in Judah as a result of the various Assyrian campaigns between this time and 701.

Although I take the position that the primary reference of the oracle is negative, I see no need to deny the positive element in it. To be sure, curds and honey are not the bread and wine of a cultivated land, but they are still a desirable food. Although Ahaz, through his policies dictated by human wisdom, will have plunged the land to disaster, nonetheless God is still with his people, and the survivors of Ahaz's act, few though they be, will be provided for.

23–25 In continuing to deal with the effects of depopulation, Isaiah now turns to its impact upon tillable land. In fact, he says, it will revert to wilderness. Even the finest vineyard, stocked with the most costly plants,[12] will shortly become briars and thorns. The only thing it will be fit for will be hunting (v. 24). To go there without protection would be to fall prey to wild animals that would have reestablished themselves in its thickets.[13]

25 This verse may be a conscious allusion to the song of the vineyard in 5:1–7. The mention of the hillsides, the briars and thorns, and the trampling of the animals supports such a suggestion. The fertile hillsides, once carefully terraced and worked,[14] are now abandoned to the briars and thorns,[15] fit only for the pasturage of the animals.

11. Typically flocks and herds would have included many animals, not merely one or two.

12. The prophet may be speaking hyperbolically, since a shekel would be an exorbitant price for a single vine.

13. For those of us who wish to preserve wilderness and hold population down it is necessary to make a conscious shift in point of view to understand this Hebrew horror of wilderness and depopulation. Nature was viewed as being only barely under control, waiting for an opportunity to break out and destroy the hard work of civilization whenever the population of humanity dropped.

14. Note the use of the imperfect ("once digged with a hoe") to indicate continuing activity in the past.

15. The threefold mention of briars and thorns in the three verses caused Kaiser to comment that the oracle was probably not Isaianic (cf. also Scott).

for fear of briars and thornbushes is a difficult phrase, for it is unclear from the Hebrew whether "fear" is the subject or the object of the verb *tābô'*, "go, come." The AV (so also JPSV) follows both LXX and Targum in making "fear" the subject. Thus it renders "on all the hills that shall be digged with a mattock, there shall not come thither the fear. . . ." Whether or not this is linguistically possible, it manifestly flies in the face of the context. Whereas vv. 23 and 24 speak of desolation, this verse, using the same language, is made to speak of promise. Furthermore, the latter half of the verse does not make sense in this light. If the land is cultivated with no briars there, it is hardly the place where herds and flocks are allowed. On balance, in the light of the context (as well as 5:5 and 6) it seems clear that the present rendering is the correct one.[16]

(3) The sign of Maher-shalal-hash-baz (8:1–4)

1 *The Lord said to me, "Take for yourself a large tablet and write upon it with an ordinary[1] stylus: to Maher-shalal-hash-baz.*

2 *And call[2] to witness for me reliable witnesses: Uriah the priest and Zechariah son of Yeberekiah."*

3 *Then I drew near to the prophetess and she conceived and bore a son, and the Lord said unto me, "Call his name Maher-shalal-hash-baz.*

4 *For before the lad knows how to call 'my father' or 'my mother,' the riches of Damascus and the spoil of Samaria will be carried off before the king of Assyria."*

However, this points up the subjectivity of literary appreciation. Is it not also possible that the very repetition was chosen to highlight the coming desolation and as such is a mark of literary excellence?

16. JPSV, in its footnotes, makes the novel suggestion that the good land of v. 23 is intended to correspond to parts of the body where hair is the thickest while the hillsides correspond to those parts where hair is more scant. This suggestion is evidently made in the light of v. 20. But the text gives no reason to make such a connection.

1. H. Gressmann (*Der Messias*, FRLANT 43 [Göttingen: 1929], p. 239 n. 1) suggested *'ĕnôš*, "man," was an error for *'ānûš*, which he translated "hand." F. Talmage (*HTR* 60 [1967] 465–68) adopted the same emendation but related the word to Akk. *enēšu* with the meaning "broad and flexible," which he suggested referred to a stylus capable of making bold, easily readable strokes. Wildberger, noting that the common Hebrew meaning of *'ānûš* is "incurable" or "unfortunate," argues that Isaiah was to write with a pen of disaster, a figure suggestive of the phrase which was to be written. P. Humbert, *ZAW* 50 (1932) 90–92, and S. Morenz, *TLZ* 74 (1949), cols. 697–99, have pointed out the non-Hebraic character of the child's name and refer to Egyptian analogs; Humbert thinks the reference to writing means to write in Hebrew as opposed to Egyptian.

2. "Call," 1QIs[a], LXX, Targ., Syr.; MT has "I will call." See comment below.

Chapter 8 continues the developments of ch. 7 in the light of the Syro-Ephraimite crisis. There the sign and its explanation were primarily for Ahaz and the house of David. Here a very similar sign is put before the people as a whole. Here too the sign has a double implication. On the one hand it is a message of hope and confidence (vv. 3, 4), but on the other it is also one of impending doom (vv. 5–8). Nonetheless, and here the materials of ch. 8 go beyond those of ch. 7, the coming doom is within God's purposes, and he will not give the devouring nations permission to run amok indefinitely (vv. 9, 10). The concluding section of the chapter (vv. 11–22) consists of wider theological reflection upon the whole experience. It is the nation's general inability to believe that God could be involved in their daily affairs which has landed them where they are. If they had paid as much attention to God as to the supposed conspiracies of their neighbors, if they had sought God's will as earnestly as they had endeavored to divine the future through magical means, then they would not be sinking into the darkness as rapidly as they were. As throughout this segment, the question remains, "Is God really with us?" Isaiah knows it, but king and people alike have difficulty believing it.

The similarity of 8:1–4 to 7:10–17 is too close to be coincidental. The relation of the sign to the birth and naming of a child is the same, even to the use of the same language ("she shall conceive and bear a son," 7:14; "she conceived and bore a son," 8:3). Moreover, the significance of the signs is the same: before the child reaches a certain age, Samaria and Damascus will cease to be a threat to Judah. These similarities have prompted some writers to conclude that it is these events to which 7:10–17 (at least initially) refers.[3] This seems highly likely in that it satisfies the demand of those verses for some specific fulfillment of that prophecy during Ahaz's time. Furthermore, the occurrence of the name Immanuel in 8:8 and an allusion to it in 8:10 argue that 7:10–8:10 constitutes a unit dealing with the Immanuel theme. This is not to say that Maher-shalal-hash-baz in any way exhausts or completes the Immanuel motif. In fact, it is evident that he does not, for Assyria will destroy not only Damascus and Samaria, she will sweep on into Judah. Obviously, then, the unfolding of the actuality of God's presence waits some larger personage than the son of the prophet. Nevertheless, in the light of the fulfillment of the events that his name symbolized, Maher-shalal-hash-baz was a strong interim reminder that God's immanence is the one factor which ought to influence all our plans.[4]

---

3. See the articles of Gottwald and Wolf referred to above on 7:10–17.

4. O. H. Steck, "Beiträge zum Verständnis von Jesaja 7:10–17 und 8:1–4," *TZ* 29 (1973) 161–178, is of the opinion that the real value of the event was to

1   The prophet speaks now in the first person, as throughout the chapter. Isaiah himself is becoming a part of the process of signs that God is giving his people (v. 18). No longer is the encounter on a formal level between a king and a prophet. It is now on a personal level as Isaiah comes face to face with the hardness of his people. Even if he wished to do so, he cannot remain aloof.

Take for yourself a large tablet. Evidently God's intent here is that anyone should be able to read the oracle (cf. Hab. 2:2, "Make it plain on tablets, so he may run who reads it"). A *gillāyôn* is not a scroll or a stone tablet *(lûaḥ)*, but a flat piece of wood (Ezek. 37:16) or metal (Isa. 3:23), and thus appropriate for posting as a sort of placard.

It is not clear what is meant by *an ordinary stylus* (lit. "the stylus of a man"). The idea of an "ordinary stylus" is dependent upon the interpretation of Deut. 3:11, where the "cubit of a man" is understood to be an ordinary cubit. As Wildberger points out, however, a cubit is the length of a man's forearm, so the "ordinary" element may be read in unnecessarily there. If this idea is correct, it is still far from certain what it means. Many commentators assume it to be a figure of speech for a common style of script that could be easily read (cf. the English expression "he wrote a clear hand").

to Maher-shalal-hash-baz is made up of a *lamed* followed by two participles *(māhēr* and *ḥāš)* and two nouns which are apparently accusatives of direction *(šālāl* and *bāz),* resulting in the ominous meaning "speeding to the plunder, hurrying to the spoil." The function of the *lamed* depends to some degree on whether the phrase was already understood as a name. If not, then it may merely function as a marker of the accusative case. If it is already understood as a name, then the *lamed* is probably functioning as a preposition with the meaning of "referring to" or "belonging to." In view of the later birth and naming of the child, it seems likely that the placard is not only a prediction of the coming attack upon Syria and Israel, but also of the birth of the child. Functioning in this twofold way, the writing would have even greater impact: first when the child was born, then again when Tiglath-pileser began to sack their former enemies.

2   *call to witness.* The MT has a first person imperfect verb at this point, "I will call to witness" (so NIV). This makes God the subject, which seems rather strange under the circumstances. However, it is not a priori impossible if it were supported by the ancient versions. In fact, none

contribute to the hardening of the people as the king had been hardened through 7:10–17. There is doubtless an element of truth here; yet he seems to be forcing a single level of significance upon the entire passage (7:1–8:13) in the light of 6:9–13, when in fact there are many levels of significance coming into play.

of them support it. The Vulgate has a past tense (converted imperfect?, "I called," subject Isaiah), but it too stands alone, for the LXX, Targum, Syriac, and 1QIs[a] all have an imperative. In view of this textual support, the imperative seems the best reading.[5]

The purpose of having the writing witnessed is not clear. Wolf is of the opinion that the document is in fact a marriage document.[6] While this idea is very intriguing, it has only circumstantial evidence (v. 3) in its support. On the other hand, there is no other instance where a prophetic writing was witnessed, and thus it is certainly possible that the document was some sort of legal instrument.[7] Yet another possibility is that the act was done for the benefit of the witnesses. It is certainly suggestive that the high priest who modified the high altar to correspond with the one at Damascus (2 K. 16:10–16) was also named Uriah. It seems almost certain that this is the same man. Thus, just as Ahaz was forced to become party to the sign of Immanuel, so Ahaz's priest (and is Zechariah a royal prophet?) is made party to the sign of Maher-shalal-hash-baz. God will not allow them to slip into apostasy. They must do it deliberately. In any case, that the writing had been witnessed by men of public stature made it impossible to level a charge of "prophecy after the fact" against Isaiah in coming years.

3 That the conception and birth of the child seem to take place after the writing of the scroll troubles some commentators.[8] Yet it need not cause any difficulty. It only calls for an act of faith on Isaiah's part, and ours, similar to that which he was asking of his king and people. Only when faith is reduced to vague generalities does this kind of act become incomprehensible.

Noting that *drew near* is a euphemism used several times in the OT for the first intercourse between a man and his wife and that *'almâ* is frequently used of a woman about to be married, Wolf argues that Shear-jashub's mother had died and that Isaiah had initially referred in 7:14 to the prophetess who was to become his wife.[9]

the prophetess. While it is possible that Isaiah's wife is so titled

---

5. See Rosenbloom, *The Dead Sea Isaiah Scroll,* p. 16.
6. Wolf, op. cit., pp. 450–51.
7. Steck, op. cit., p. 178, takes it that the witnessing was to make the people's unbelief more indefensible.
8. Gray wishes to place v. 3 before v. 1, while Duhm and Kaiser wish to make the verbs pluperfect.
9. Wolf, op. cit., p. 454; so also Gesenius.

merely because she was the wife of a prophet,[10] it is also entirely possible that she was a prophetess in her own right (cf. Exod. 15:20; Judg. 4:4; 2 K. 22:14; Neh. 6:14).[11]

4 Here the initial meaning of the words first published at least nine months earlier (v. 1) becomes apparent. God's word is sure. Not only will Ephraim and Syria withdraw from Judah, they will be themselves plundered. Although the name seems ominous in the extreme it is precisely like Immanuel in its initial implications: Judah's enemies will be destroyed, and God can be trusted. Within a short time, these events will take place. Exactly when a child can say "my father" and "my mother" is not clear. If the first gurgled "pa-pa" or "ma-ma" is intended, then certainly the devastation of Damascus and the stripping away of Samaria's provinces that took place in 732 happened within a year of Maher-shalal-hash-baz's birth. If a more careful articulation is supposed then the birth may have taken place two or three years prior to 732. Possibly Isaiah did not intend to give an entirely precise indication, but only to say that the events were imminent. Again, as in 7:17 and 20, it is not merely Assyria as a nation, but the king of Assyria, the one with whom Ahaz has entered into alliance, whose rapacity is identified.

(4) Assyria at the flood, yet God is with us (8:5–10)

5 *The Lord spoke to me again, saying,*
6 *"Because this people has rejected the waters*
   of Shiloah which flow gently,
and rejoices over Rezin and the son of Remaliah,
7 *Therefore, behold, the Sovereign is about to*
   bring up¹ against them
the waters of the River, mighty and abundant—
   the king of Assyria and all his glory.²
He will go up over all his channels
   and go over all his banks.

10. In the Mishna the priest's wife is called a priestess (e.g., *Ketuboth* vii.1; cf. Cheyne, p. 52).

11. Cf. A. Jepsen, "Die Nebiah in Jes. 8, 3," *ZAW* 72 (1960) 267–68; C. B. Reynolds, "Isaiah's Wife," *JTS* 36 (1935) 182–85.

1. Note the use of the participle to indicate imminence. And the flood was much more imminent than anyone knew. It had taken 125 years (beginning with Shalmaneser's first great push ca. 860 B.C.) for Assyria to reach from the Euphrates to Galilee. Now within 60 years she would be in Egypt.

2. Young points out that the use of "glory" in such a context is particularly Isaianic (10:15; 16:14; 17:3, 4).

8 *He will pass over into Judah, overflowing mightily,*[3]
 reaching to the neck.
 And it will come to pass that his wings will be outstretched,
 filling the breadth of your land, O Immanuel."
9 *Break forth,*[4] *O peoples, and be shattered;*
 give ear, all the nations of the earth.
 Gird yourselves and be shattered;
 gird yourselves and be shattered.
10 *Take counsel, but it will be frustrated;*
 speak a word, but it shall not stand;
 for God is with us.

As with 7:18–25, the same sign which is a testimony to God's faithfulness is also a word of destruction to those who will not believe. God's presence does not mean automatic blessing to his people despite their unbelief. The fact of his presence may make them even more subject to the powers of judgment, because of all people, they should have known better. So a Judah, delighting over the spoliation of her enemies, learns to her horror that Maher-shalal-hash-baz applies to her as well as them.[5]

5, 6 It is impossible to determine how soon after the birth of Maher-shalal-hash-baz this oracle was given to Isaiah. But it is evident from the language that some time had elapsed. If *rejoice* is correct in v. 6, then it may be subsequent to 734 when Tiglath-pileser's campaign had forced Syria and Ephraim to withdraw from Jerusalem.

In the light of the references to Rezin and Pekah in v. 6b (on which see below), *this people* has been interpreted by some as being Ephraim and Syria.[6] Yet everywhere else where the identification can be ascertained

---

3. *šāṭap weʿārab,* "he overflowed and he passed over," expresses a single idea (R. J. Williams, *Hebrew Syntax,* §§ 223–24). *šāṭap* probably lacks *waw* conversive because the phrase modifies *weḥālap,* "and he will pass over."

4. The meaning of *rōʿû* is not certain. To take it from *rʿh* (AV "associate yourselves") would require a reflexive form, which this is not. But it could be from *rʿʿ,* "to do evil," or *rʿʿ,* "to break forth." *rwʾ,* "to make an uproar," usually occurs in the Hiphil. The LXX has "know," which would suggest an original *deʿû.* This reading is attractive since it offers a good parallel with "give ear" in the next line and since *d* and *r* are easily confused in the Hebrew script. However, the LXX is undeniably the easier reading and that suggests that since good sense can be made of the MT it should be retained. Note the assonance of *rōʿû . . . wāhōttû.* Cf. M. Saebø, "Zur Traditionsgeschichte von Jes. 8, 9–10," *ZAW* 76 (1964) 132–144.

5. Westermann, *Basic Forms,* p. 174, notes that 8:6–8 form a classic judgment speech.

6. See Cheyne; K. Fullerton, "The Interpretation of Isa. 8:5–10," *JBL* 43 (1924) 264 (unless v. 6b is emended); L. Rignell, "Das Orakel 'Maher-salal-Has-bas' Jesaja 8," *ST* 10 (1956) 42.

the phrase refers to Judah, the people immediately at hand (cf. 6:9; 8:12; 9:15 [Eng. 16]; 28:11, 14; 29:13), and there is every reason to believe the same is true here. The people cannot blame their fate upon their king. They have been as much terrified by the enemy (7:2) as he and as little willing to commit themselves to God.

the waters of Shiloah. With a lovely figure of speech Isaiah compares the help of God to an apparently ineffectual little stream, whereas the help of the mighty nations of the world seems like the Euphrates. What we do not realize is that the supposedly mighty river can sweep over us and swallow us up for its own devices. This paradox, that what is mightiest seems least so in appearance, is found throughout Scripture. Those who trust in God must look deeper than appearance.[7] It seems likely that the stream referred to came from the Gihon spring on the west side of the Kidron Valley and flowed around by conduits to pools at the lower end of the city where the Kidron and Tyropoeon valleys met. As best as can now be determined, the famous Siloam tunnel which brought the water directly under the city to the pool of Siloam did not exist at this time, having been dug during the reign of Hezekiah.

and rejoices over Rezin and the son of Remaliah presents a serious problem of interpretation. In what sense did the people of Judah rejoice over the two kings? In fact, the MT at its most literal seems to say they rejoiced *with* them. If there was a pro-Ephraimite and Syrian party in Judea, the Bible does not mention it. Far from rejoicing in them, the Judeans were terrified of them. This problem has caused some scholars to believe that *this people* refers to Ephraim, stating that she has rejected the God of Jerusalem and the house of David (so the Targ.), and has chosen the two kings as her leader.[8] Although such an interpretation is possible, both *this people* and the reference to Shiloah (Siloam)[9] seem to indicate that the focus is upon Judah. In this light, and noting 7:2, it was suggested, perhaps first by Hitzig, that *māśôś*, "rejoice," should be emended to *māsôs*, "melt" (in fear) (so Delitzsch, RSV). This fits the situation well and can be easily explained since the words are homophones. It may be correct, but the syntax is very difficult since *Rezin and the son of Remaliah*

7. See Gen. 16:4; 17:19; 50:20; Exod. 4:10–12; Judg. 7:4–8; 2 K. 5:8–14; Neh. 2:11–16; Isa. 52:13–53:12; Dan. 3; Zech. 4:6; Luke 1:36, 37; Luke 2:1–52; 1 Cor. 1:18–2:5. See G. A. Smith for an eloquent comparison of the poverty of Jerusalem with the glory of Nineveh and Asshur.

8. See above, n. 6.

9. As Wildberger points out, there was no time when Ephraim and Syria rejected Jerusalem (Shiloah) as a source of help. They never considered the possibility.

are either objects of the verb or objects of the preposition "with," neither of which makes very good sense with "melt."[10] As a result, many modern scholars discard the whole phrase as an ill-conceived gloss (so Gray, Skinner, Kaiser, Wildberger, etc.). If this is the case, however, it is so ill-conceived as to make its creation incomprehensible. On balance, it seems best to remain with the MT and understand that the rejoicing, as suggested above, is over the discomfiture of their enemies, either actual or as predicted by Isaiah. It may well be that the Judeans were congratulating themselves over Ahaz's diplomatic coup in allying himself with Assyria. It was not God who had delivered them, but their own wisdom (or God *through* the instrumentality of their wisdom). To all of this Isaiah says that the celebration is too early. The same River upon which they depended to engulf their enemies will shortly sweep over them.

Therefore, behold is the messenger formula introducing the announcement section of the judgment speech.[11] In the light of the nation's choices, God is about to act. As in other similar instances, Isaiah stresses that it is the Sovereign Lord who brings the judgment (cf. 7:7, 14, 17, 18, 20). Assyria does not inundate God's land in spite of God. No, if she comes, it is because God brings her.

The use of the Euphrates as the metaphor here is very satisfying for several reasons. Assyria came from across the Euphrates; it was a mighty river compared to anything the Israelites had seen in their home territory; its floods are swift and devastating. So was Assyria. Like Germany in 1939 and 1940, the Assyrians seemed almost superhuman. They could strike anywhere, it seemed, with speed and power. The majesty of their massive armies must have been stunning in itself. Like a mighty river rushing against a bank, they must have seemed inexorable. Ahaz had let loose the torrent, and did he think that it would meekly subside when it came to a national boundary? No, once out of its banks, the river would reach as far as it possibly could.

8 Yet the flood will not destroy Judah; it will stop short of total destruction. Just when the tide seems about to engulf the mouth and nose, cutting off the last breath, it halts. This seems to be the sense of *reaching to the neck*. Isaiah is not here offering much hope. Rather, he is telling what a near thing it will be. But he does imply that Assyria will not annihilate Judah.

The final phrase of the verse probably makes the same point, although its exact meaning is much debated. First of all, has Isaiah changed

10. See Gray for a discussion of the difficulties of the various options.
11. See Westermann, *Basic Forms,* p. 174.

metaphors? Has he moved from flood to bird? And is it bird of prey (Procksch) or bird of protection (Duhm)? Probably he has switched metaphors, but it is one suggested by the situation. An army fans out over the land like the fingers of a flood pouring through depressions and reaching up valleys.[12] This spreading out of army or flood suggests the spreading of wings, and that suggests a bird, in this case a bird of prey, extending its wings as it whistles down upon a victim. Gray, fastening on the closing, with its hopeful note, assumes the bird must be protective (as in Ps. 91:4), and that a radical change of thought has occurred. However, this is not necessary. The land over which the bird hovers is Immanuel's land. Nothing can change that. Thus, just as the flood may reach the neck but no further, so those hovering wings will not carry off the lamb. Why? Because Judah is so wise or powerful? No, because of Immanuel who is pictured as a helpless child. What can stop the flood? Only the trickling waters of Shiloah, which the Judeans had rejected as being of no use (cf. Num. 14:9; Ps. 46:7, 8 [Eng. 6, 7]).

O, Immanuel comes rather abruptly here, and the abruptness has caused a good deal of speculation over possible interpretations.[13] If it is correct that Maher-shalal-hash-baz was the initial fulfillment of the Immanuel prophecy, as seems very likely, then the inclusion of the name here becomes more understandable. This is especially true in the light of the similar structures of 7:13–25 and 8:1–10, which makes it appear that the points of the Immanuel and Maher-shalal-hash-baz signs are identical. However, that Judah is called Immanuel's land makes it abundantly clear that Maher-shalal-hash-baz, or someone else who may have constituted the initial fulfillment of the sign, was not the ultimate fulfillment. Ultimately, Immanuel is the owner of the land, the one against whom Assyria's threats are ultimately lodged, the one upon whom deliverance finally depends. That cannot be Isaiah's son, nor even some unknown son of Ahaz. It can only be the Messiah, in whom all hope resides. It is as if Isaiah, plunging deeper and deeper into the dark implications of his sign, is suddenly brought up short by the deepest implication: God *is* with us and, best of all, will be with us, not merely in the impersonal developments of history, but somehow as a person.

9, 10 In these verses the tone shifts dramatically. Isaiah is no

---

12. So the Targ. reads "the people of his army" for "his wings."

13. It comes so abruptly that Gray suggests it is incorrect. He believes the Hebrew consonantal text, now divided *'rṣk 'mn'l*, was originally *'rṣ k'mn 'l*, which would read " . . . land, for God is with us." Thus the phrase did not contain the name, in his view, but rather an affirmation similar to that at the end of v. 10. However, there is no textual evidence for such emendation.

longer envisioning a helpless Judah floundering in the overpowering Assyrian flood.[14] It appears that the memory that Judah is Immanuel's land
has changed his perspective. It is in that light that he brings the direct
treatment of the Immanuel signs to a close. Here he comes with that
penetrating vision which can see beyond near disaster and judgment to
ultimate victory and hope. Yes, Judah may now be the pawn of the great
nations, her sins may have plunged her into the midst of their plottings
and machinations. Yet, when all is said and done, all those plots and plans
must eventually come to nothing, except as they coincide with those of
the God who has chosen to be with us in the contingencies of our existence.

Break forth, O peoples begins a series of commands to the nations.
They are invited to do everything they can to make ready for war against
God's people. Nevertheless, after each imperative, as here, the prophet
announces with supreme confidence and heavy irony that the results of
their preparation will be their own destruction.

According to Young, *Gird yourselves* may refer to an ancient custom
of belt-wrestling. However, that seems too arcane in view of the numerous
references in Scripture to "girding on one's sword" (Deut. 1:41; 1 Sam.
17:38; 25:13; 2 Sam. 21:16; 1 K. 20:11; armor, Ps. 45:4 [Eng. 3]). Soldiers wore a wide belt (girdle) which carried the sword and a dagger,[15]
and in addition, the breastplate was fastened on with belting around the
back. In these ways a man preparing for war "girded" himself. There was
also another sense in which girding represented preparation for action.
This was "girding up the loins" (Exod. 12:11; 2 K. 4:29; 9:1; Job 38:3;
40:7; Prov. 31:17; Jer. 1:17; cf. also 1 Pet. 1:13). It evidently refers to
tucking the hem of one's robe into the belt in order to free the legs (cf.
Elijah running before Ahab, 1 K. 18:46).

it shall not stand is a fitting conclusion to the segment 7:1–8:10
because it reverts to the note upon which Isaiah began. He had said that
Ephraim's and Syria's boastful plans would not stand (7:7). Indeed, they
did not. Already enough time may have elapsed to demonstrate the truthfulness of that statement. But now larger figures have moved onto the
stage, at least one of them at God's specific command. What of them?
Isaiah gladly announces that the truth still holds. To the extent that the
plans of the nations are the result of their own rapacious arrogance, they

14. Marti's comment that the two verses cannot be Isaianic because an
exception would have to be made for Assyria is shortsighted at best. Isaiah is here
dealing with the ultimate victor, not any intermediate ones. He is expressing the
very faith, on a long-term basis, that he asked of Ahaz.

15. Cf. *ANEP*, no. 40; L. Grollenberg, *Atlas of the Bible*, tr. and ed.
J. M. H. Reid and H. H. Rowley (Camden: Nelson, 1956), p. 85, pl. 234.

will not stand, for God is with us. That does not mean magical deliverance without reference to the manifest sins of his people, but it does mean that their destiny is not in the hands of sinful human nations, and furthermore, it means that judgment and destruction are not the final *word*. Judgment is unto salvation when God is with us.

It is hard to overstress the philosophical significance of *God is with us*. The nonbiblical approach is for an individual to seek to be with God— in fact to be united with God. This inevitably results in varying forms of pantheism or panentheism. If humanity is to attain unity with God it is impossible that God should transcend the psycho-physical world, for that world is finally our only means of access to him. But the biblical view exactly reverses the process. Transcendence is the given; it is nonnegotiable and irreducible. God *is* distinct from his world. This means that it is impossible for humanity to attain union with God by its devices. Instead God makes fellowship between us and him possible by entering our realm. Far from our trying to escape our finitude and mortality by making God identical to this world, God, who is part of this world, has entered into our finitude and mortality through Christ and thus brings us to fellowship with himself (John 3:13; Rom. 10:6; 2 Cor. 4:6; Col. 1:15–20).

c. OUR WAY—DARKNESS; HIS WAY—LIGHT (8:11–9:6 [Eng. 7])

(1) Pay attention to God (8:11–23 [Eng. 9:1])

11 *For thus said the Lord unto me with a strong hand and admonished me from walking in the way of this people, saying,*

12 *"Do not say 'conspiracy' to all which this people says 'conspiracy,' and what it fears do not fear and do not tremble before it.*

13 *The Lord of Hosts, him you[1] shall sanctify; he shall be your fear and he shall be your cause of trembling.*

14 *For the Lord can be a sanctuary[2] and he can be a stone for tripping over and a rock for stumbling upon for the two houses of Israel;[3] a snare and a trap for the inhabitants of Jerusalem.*

1. Note that the pronouns are all 2nd plural, indicating that the words of God are not addressed to Isaiah alone but also to his faithful hearers.

2. The abrupt shift from "sanctuary" to "stumbling block" in v. 14 has led Duhm and others (esp. those who assume his emendation of vv. 12, 13) to conclude that the passage is wholly negative and that *miqdāš* is an error for *môqēš*, "snare." Although this reading is supported by the Targ., the MT is clearly the harder reading and makes excellent sense.

3. The reference to "the *two* houses of Israel" in parallel with "the inhabitants of Jerusalem" is somewhat enigmatic. It evidently refers to Northern Israel and Judah. For Judah treated separately from Jerusalem, see 2:1; 3:1, 8; etc.

229

15 *Many among them will stumble; they will fall and be crushed, become ensnared and taken captive."*

16 *Bind up the testimony, seal[4] the instruction among my disciples.[5]*

17 *I will wait for the Lord who hides his face from the house of Jacob; I will wait for him.*

18 *Behold, I and the children the Lord has given me are signs and symbols in Israel from the Lord of Hosts, who dwells on Mount Zion.*

19 *And when they say to you, "Inquire of the mediums[6] and the spiritists[7] who chirp and mutter' —should not a people inquire of its God?[8] On behalf of the living to the dead?*

20 *To the instruction and the testimony! If they will not speak according to this word, there is no dawn for them.[9]*

21 *They shall pass through it, distressed and hungry, and it will come to pass when they are hungry they will become angry. Then they will curse their king[10] and their god and look upward.[11]*

4. "Bind" and "seal" are infinitives absolute (according to the Qere), apparently used as emphatic imperatives (short form). Cf. GKC, § 113bb; Deut. 5:12.

5. Young's argument that the disciples are God's here flies in the face of the context which calls for a uniform interpretation of the 1st person pronouns in vv. 16–18. This is manifestly not possible on Young's supposition. In fact, he sees each of the three verses as referring to different personages. Whitley (op. cit., p. 29) emends to "bind the oracle from the learned" (cf. 29:11).

6. *ʾōḇōṯ*, "mediums," refers to those who traffic with the dead as well as to the spirit itself. The term appears in the OT in Lev. 19:31; 20:6, 27; and Deut. 18:11 where the practice is forbidden; 1 Sam. 28:3–19, in the witch of Endor story; 1 Chr. 10:13; 2 K. 21:6 (2 Chr. 33:6) where Manasseh, in a fulfillment of Isaiah's prophecy, established the practice; and in 2 K. 23:24 where Josiah abolishes it.

7. *yiddeʿōnîm*, "spiritists," if correctly ascribed to the root *ydʿ*, "to know," refers to those who know how to contact and communicate with a familiar spirit. It may also refer to those who are masters in occult knowledge.

8. 1QIsᵃ has the singular of "god," which it uses elsewhere of pagan gods and may thus indicate the Qumran understanding of the passage.

9. The Hebrew of this sentence presents numerous problems. Lit. "If they will not say as this word, which there is not to him it dawn." The present translation is justified in that pronoun disagreement (they-him) is not uncommon in the Hebrew prophets and that *ʾašer* can function as *kî* (cf. 2 Sam. 2:4; Young). But another possibility is to take the *ʾim lōʾ* as an asseverative (P. Skehan, "Some Textual Problems in Isaia," *CBQ* 22 [1960] 48), translating "Those for whom there is no dawn will surely speak thus (enticing to spiritism)." Cf. Delitzsch. This suggestion is very attractive, and while none of the versions supports it, neither do they agree among themselves how it should be translated.

10. Whitley points out (op. cit., pp. 31–33) that *ptkrʾ*, "false god," the word with which the Targ. translates *mlk*, is used in the same way in Amos 5:26

22 *They will look earthward, but behold, distress and darkness, anguished gloom,[12] and they will be cast into darkness.*

23 (9:1) *But there will be no gloom for her[13] who was in anguish. As he at first humbled the land of Zebulon and the land of Naphtali,[14] so afterward[15] he will glorify[16] the way of the sea, beyond Jordan, Galilee of the Gentiles.*

Verses 8:11–23 (Eng. 9:1) constitute a reflection upon all which has preceded from 7:1 onward. As such they prepare the way for the final annunciation of the child in 9:1–6 (Eng. 2–7). They make plain the central theme of the segment, as well as that of the entire division: in what, or in whom, shall we trust? One possibility, when faced with potential calamities or disasters, is to forget God's sovereignty and proceed accordingly (vv. 11, 12), but to do so is to invite calamity of a more profound nature, for God is the one fact we dare not overlook (vv. 13–15). It is sheer

---

and Zeph. 1:5 and argues that the original reference in all three places was to the god Molech. He also favors "curse by the name of" which the Targ. does not support.

11. The rather enigmatic "look upward" may apply in the sense that, having looked up to king and god, they have been frustrated (so NIV). It would thus be a postpositive circumstantial clause. However, this is not normal syntax for a circumstantial clause (cf. Williams, *Syntax*, § 494), and one cannot escape the impression that it is an opening phrase the conclusion of which is missing (cf. 5:30).

12. *me'ûp ṣûqâ,* "anguished darkness," is an attributive genitive expression which again conveys the spiritual nature of the condition in which the people find themselves. Driver, noting this as inappropriate to invasion, proposes an unknown verb with these radicals meaning "escape" (op. cit., p. 46). Ginsberg fastens upon the 1QIs[a] reading *m'yp* and posits a root *'yp,* "to shine," pointing this *mē'îp,* "from shining," and emending the final word to *minn'gōah,* "from brightening" (op. cit., p. 62).

13. The sudden appearance of the feminine "to *her* that was in anguish" may indicate that the land is the antecedent.

14. The apparent use of locative *he* on *'ereṣ* when it is in construct is problematic. That this may well be a sign of the accusative is already suggested by GKC, § 90f.

15. A major problem in this verse is the meaning of "the former" and "the latter." Since *'et,* "time," is almost always fem. there is a problem of agreement. Whitley (op. cit., pp. 35–36) may be correct when he suggests that the fem. *h* has fallen off in both cases by haplography with the following *h* beginning the Hiphil verbs. It is also true, however, that *'et* is construed as a masc. in certain cases (e.g., 13:22).

16. The Hiphil form of the verbs *hēqal,* "humiliate," and *hikbîḍ,* "glorify," is rare enough to cause speculation as to possible other meanings, but cf. Jer. 30:19 (with *ṣ'r* in place of *qll*) for a similar thought and usage. For a full discussion of these and other problems, cf. J. A. Emerton, "Some Linguistic and Historical Problems in Isaiah 8:23," *JSS* 14 (1969) 151–175.

foolishness, when he has made his way (which is also our way) clear (vv. 16–18, 20), to resort to some other means (v. 19) to find a path out of darkness. Such other means can only make the darkness, and our anguish, more intense, for they lead away from him who is light. Nevertheless, God will not be defeated. He will shed his light upon his people, and it is typical of his grace that the location of that light will be in the very part of the land which first felt the hand of his wrath, namely, Galilee.

It is not difficult to see how the phrase "the way of this people" supplies the unifying theme of the segment. Faced with the great political and military upheavals of their time, how easily the people focused upon the various human machinations (conspiracy!) as the source of their troubles and as that which needed their primary attention. Similarly, faced with a myriad of choices, none of them very good, how easily the people resorted to magical means of divination to learn the future and to find guidance. Isaiah's response is that given God's terrifying holiness, his written revelation, and his desires to give his people light, dependence upon anything other than him is sheer insanity. Scholars who see this segment as composed of unrelated bits and pieces, and almost all do, miss the importance of this thematic unity. Surely the language is abrupt and often elliptical, lacking the smooth transitions which we associate with a unified treatise. This may indicate that the material was not all composed at the same time. However, this abrupt and enigmatic speech may be precisely the result of such an intense spiritual experience as v. 11 seems to indicate. In any case, it is a mistake to miss the theological unity which characterizes the segment in its present form.[17]

11 The opening *for thus* (Heb. *kî kô*) suggests an intended linkage with the preceding segment. If this is correct, the connection may be in the sense that the following reflection undergirds what has been said in vv. 9 and 10. The reason why the plans of the nations will be thwarted is that they rest on all the wrong assumptions, which Isaiah's own people in fact share.

with a strong hand suggests that this experience of God's inspiration was especially intense and direct. Ezekiel uses a similar expression in 1:3 and 3:14 to describe the opening and closing of his famous vision.[18] It is not likely that Isaiah himself was in any danger of succumbing to the ways of his people, but his disciples (v. 16) may have been. In any case it was evidently very important that this divine analysis of the people's approach

---

17. Cf. H. Junker, "Die Messianische Verkundigung im Buch Isaias: Der erste und die letzte Zeit, Is. 8:11–9:6," *Past Bon* 49 (1938–1939) 338–346.
18. Cf. also 1 K. 18:46; 2 K. 3:15; Ezek. 3:22; 33:22.

to their problems be revealed at this point in their experience. In future days its correctness would be manifest.

12, 13   While the general sense of these verses is clear, namely, give attention first to God, not to human affairs, the precise sense has occasioned a good deal of controversy. This controversy has centered upon the meaning of *qešer*, "conspiracy," in v. 12 and its relation to *taqdîšû* in v. 13 and *miqdāš* in v. 14. If "conspiracy" is the correct rendering, to what does it refer?[19] Suggestions have included a fifth column of Judeans supporting the Syro-Ephraimite coalition (Kaiser), the coalition itself (Skinner), and even Isaiah and his disciples (as Jeremiah was later accused of conspiracy with the Babylonians) (Young). But it is not necessary that the reference is to a specific conspiracy. Rather, the prophet may be talking about a general approach to the explanation of events, especially unpleasant and trying events. How easy it is, when situations go against us, to become paranoid and react accordingly.[20] Isaiah challenges his people to reject paranoia and see God's hand in the events of their time. To refuse to do so is to become more and more fearful, more and more unstable, for it means that our lives are ultimately in the hands of unknown powers, too devious for us to know or control. This in turn leads us toward the occult in an effort to gain control over these unknown and devious powers.

him you shall sanctify seems out of touch with the previous thought; for what does sanctity have to do with conspiracy? That the verses form an antithetic parallelism is plain from the duplication of fear and dread: do not fear what they fear—he shall be your fear, etc. Duhm, noting this parallelism and seeing no connection between sanctity and conspiracy, argued that *taqdîšû* was an error for *taqšîrû* and that the meaning was: if you are looking for a conspirator to explain your problems, then look to God. This emendation is very neat and has been adopted by numerous commentators (e.g., Scott, Wildberger, and Kaiser [with modifications]). It raises a rather serious theological problem, however, for while God is sometimes seen as the ultimate source of tragedy and disaster (45:7), he is not depicted as doing so in a devious, conspiratorial manner. Noting this problem (and that v. 14 makes a play on *qdš* with *miqdāš*, "sanctuary"), Cheyne opted to emend in the opposite direction, changing *qešer*

19. G. R. Driver, "Two Misunderstood Passages of the O.T.," *JTS* 6 (1955) 82–87, argues for "difficulty" (so also Kaiser), but such references as 1 Sam. 22:8, 13; 2 Sam. 15:12, 31; 2 K. 11:14; Amos 7:10; Neh. 4:2 (Eng. 8) make it plain that something much more specific involving the plotting of a group is intended.

20. Amid the shocks of our own time, the "conspiracy theory" of history keeps emerging, as, for instance, in the Kennedy assassination.

in v. 12 to *qāḏôš*, "holy," in the sense of awesome and terrifying (so also Gray and Kissane). But the lack of any textual evidence for either emendation should drive us back to the text, which has less severe difficulties than might appear at first glance.[21] In order to understand the thought, it is necessary to understand what it means to sanctify God. That which is holy is distinct from the common or ordinary. Thus to sanctify God is to demonstrate that he is "high and lifted up" (6:1) in power and in character, as well as in his very essence. To fail to sanctify him is to make him appear helpless, indifferent, and unimportant (Lev. 22:32; Num. 20:12; Ezek. 36:20, 21; Amos 2:7). This is exactly what the Judeans did when they sought to solve the riddles of their times according to human explanations and means: they made God appear insignificant.[22] Rather, Isaiah calls upon them to make God the most significant fact of of their existence, demonstrating by their attitudes and behavior that God is indeed holy.

14, 15 The attitude we take toward God will determine what aspect of him we will experience. To those who sanctify him, who give him a place of importance in their lives, who seek to allow his character to be duplicated in them, he becomes a sanctuary, a place of refuge and peace.[23] But to those who will not give him such a place in their lives, he becomes a stone to trip over. He does not change; only our attitude determines how we experience him. Those who make a place for him discover that he has in fact made a place for them. They know that what happens to them comes from One who is both all-powerful and good. In that certainty they can accept and apply whatever comes to them with equanimity and confidence. Those who will not make a place for him will keep colliding with him and tripping over him, for he is there, whether they acknowledge him or not. Because he is a fact of which their hypothesis does not take account, their experiment will keep failing and he will be the cause of it, not because of some vindictive streak in him, but simply because he is and they are trying to live as if he were not. As the NT makes plain, it is in Jesus that the double-edged nature of God's self-revelation becomes most pointed: to those who accept him as God's suf-

21. Cf. N. Lohfink, "Is. 8:12–14 [e emendveris]," *BZ* 7 (1963) 98–104.

22. The "fear of the Lord" is the acknowledgment of the significance of God, putting him in his proper place of lordship over the world and one's life. It is not terror, but neither is it mere reverence (Ps. 25:12–14; 34:8, 12–15 [Eng. 7, 11–14]; Prov. 1:7; Matt. 10:28). Cf. *ISBE*, II:289–292.

23. As in English, the Hebrew word for sanctuary means both "holy place" and "refuge." Where the god was, one ought to be safe. So Jehu's slaughter of the priests of Baal (2 K. 10:18–27) and the removal of Athaliah from the temple (2 K. 11:15, 16) take on added significance (cf. also Isa. 4:5, 6; Ps. 27:5; 31:22 [Eng. 21]; Prov. 18:10; Ezek. 9:6; 1 Pet. 2:7).

ficient sacrifice, he is life and peace; to those who refuse to do so, he becomes a fact over which to stumble again and again (Matt. 21:44; Luke 2:34: Rom. 9:33).

As noted above, it is unnecessary to see vv. 16–23, as many do, as a radical break from vv. 11–15.[24] In fact, they constitute a further development of the thought contained in those verses. Those who choose to sanctify God will take refuge in his character as revealed in his Word and have reason for hope. Those who refuse to do so will be driven to magic and the occult and thus into deeper darkness and despair.

16 This verse is commonly interpreted to refer to a withdrawal of Isaiah from public ministry when he perceived that he had been unsuccessful in altering the course of the nation during the Syro-Ephraimite crisis. According to this position, his oracles were sealed up and committed to his disciples to be published at some later date when events would have vindicated him and them. Such an interpretation is possible, but it overlooks an equally possible alternative,[25] and one which accords better with the theological content of the segment. It is significant that the terms $t^e\hat{u}d\hat{a}$, "testimony," and $t\hat{o}r\hat{a}$, "instruction, law," are terms used elsewhere in conjunction with one another (as well as with "commandments" and "statutes") to denote the revelation of God (cf. Deut. 4:44, 45; 1 K. 2:3; Neh. 9:34; Ps. 19:8 [Eng. 7]; 78:5; and 119 throughout).[26] Is it not possible then that Isaiah is here referring to the revealed word of God (certainly so in v. 20), and that the binding and sealing is an act of affirmation and attestation?[27] He is evidently including his own oracles in the statement

24. There are numerous treatments of the complex linguistic and grammatical problems in this passage. Most complete are G. R. Driver, "Isaianic Problems," *Festschrift für Wilhelm Eilers* (Wiesbaden, 1967), pp. 43–49; H. L. Ginsberg, "An Unrecognized Allusion to Kings Pekah and Hoshea of Israel," *Eretz Israel* 5 (1958) 61–65; C. F. Whitley, "The Language and Exegesis of Isa. 8:16–23," *ZAW* 90 (1978) 28–42.

25. Cf. D. Jones, "Tradition of the Oracles of Isaiah of Jerusalem," *ZAW* 67 (1955) 226–246, but as P. Ackroyd notes (*VTSup* 29 [1978] 29), to use this as evidence of the "Isaianic school" is to stretch the evidence.

26. Elsewhere the word used of testimony is $^e\bar{e}d\hat{u}t$, a synonym of $t^e\hat{u}d\hat{a}$, both coming from the same verbal root. One cannot help but wonder if the easy dismissal of these terms as referring to more than Isaiah's writings is not in part due to the fact that the ideas are "Deuteronomic" and thus supposedly later than Isaiah.

27. This understanding would help to alleviate some of the uncertainty over "sealing in [b] my disciples." Delitzsch suggests it is to be sealed up in them spiritually, but this is not necessary if what is taking place is a ritual of affirmation and attestation by and among them. For binding and sealing in this sense, cf. Neh. 10:1, 2 (Eng. 9:38; 10:1); Jer. 32:10–12. The last reference could also be used to support the idea of hiding for a future date, however (vv. 13, 14).

(so v. 18), but the context demands that he not be limiting the ground of his hope merely to his own experience (v. 17). If this is a correct understanding, then Isaiah, in response to God's admonition of vv. 12–15, is reaffirming his dependence upon God as revealed in Scripture and challenging those who follow him to do the same (cf. Josh. 24:14, 15).

17 Here is Isaiah's affirmation of dependence upon God. Although God seemed to be hiding his face from Judah and Israel, Isaiah would not lose his faith in him nor turn to some other source for his own strength and courage. In words reminiscent of the great assertion of 40:31, he says that God's timing is best and that he will wait for his action, knowing that all other action in defiance of him is futile. This waiting upon God is often a prerequisite to receiving his blessing, for in the act of waiting we confess our own helplessness and our complete dependence upon him. Without these characteristics, God's work is both hindered and misappropriated (cf. Acts 1:8).

Two different words for *wait* are used here. The first is *ḥākâ* and the second *qāwâ*. The first expresses more the actual act of waiting (30:18), while the second expresses the attitude of expectant dependence (40:31); however, no sharp distinction should be drawn between them.[28]

18 Part of the ground of Isaiah's ability to depend upon God, even though God's immediate aspect was grim, was Isaiah's own experience. Whatever else might be the case, he could not gainsay that. While *the children* might refer to the disciples (so Calvin), the mention of *signs and symbols* makes it likely that he is thinking of Shear-jashub and Maher-shalal-hash-baz. Their very existence, as well as the strangely evocative names he had felt led to give them, was testimony of God's working among his people. Furthermore, they were evidence that although God's face might be hidden for a time, it was still true that his dwelling was upon Mount Zion (2:2). They were thus an indication that the coming upheaval and destruction was ultimately only temporary.[29]

19–23 (9:1) But for those who did not have the certainty Isaiah had, the temptation was strong to turn to spiritism. Having lost the only real source of confidence, belief in an all-wise and all-loving creator, they turned to more limited but supposedly less-demanding sources. Mauchline is undoubtedly correct when he points out that the revival of superstition is concomitant with the loss of faith. Our own age confirms this. We have proclaimed ourselves as being "of age" and thus no longer in need of the

28. See *TDOT,* IV:361–62.
29. Isaiah's own name, "The Lord saves," is perhaps to be understood as confirmation of this.

supernatural.[30] But in fact the cosmos cannot be explained on purely physical or natural terms. Thus if we will not have the Spirit who asks for our commitment to him, we must sooner or later have the spirits, who appear to ask for nothing, but in fact intend to make us slaves.

19 It is difficult to determine how much of this verse is intended to be the enticement of the spiritists and how much, if any, is intended as response. Traditionally (cf. AV) it has been understood that the latter half of the verse is response. If so, it is an exceedingly elliptical response. One would expect something like: "If they say . . . then you should. . . ." But the apodosis is not developed in that way. It is developed as the prophet's response to the very idea of such a suggestion. The final phrase is even more elliptical, saying merely *on behalf of the living to the dead*. To construe it as response one must supply missing words: "[Should they consult] the dead on behalf of the living?" These problems have caused most modern commentators to see the entire verse as part of the enticement, reading it "And when they say to you, 'Inquire of . . . ,' should not a people consult its gods, the dead on behalf of the living?" There is some difficulty in equating the dead with the gods, but the prophet, knowing of ancestor worship, may have intended to make the point that the dead were indeed this people's gods (cf. the witch of Endor, 1 Sam. 28:13). At the same time, there is in the traditional reading an irony implicit in the very ellipses that corresponds well with the Isaianic attitude toward idolatry. It is ridiculous to consult the dead on behalf of the living, yet how easily those who reject life turn to the dead to discover the meaning of life.

chirp and mutter. It was apparently a common belief in the ancient Near East that the dead spoke in birdlike, whispered voices,[31] and it is to this that Isaiah refers (cf. also 29:4). The LXX translation of *yiddeʿōnîm*, "mediums," as "ventriloquists" gives a good idea of a devout Jew's estimates of the real source of the chirping and muttering.

20 *to the instruction and the testimony.* The prophet bursts out against occult knowledge. One does not have to go to the occult to discover the meaning and destiny of one's life. It is not hidden to those who will look in the right place. God has been shouting it from the rooftops and recording it for all future generations (65:1–5; John 7:37–39). The way

30. The term is that of Dietrich Bonhoeffer, *Letters and Papers from Prison,* 3rd ed., tr. R. H. Fuller, ed. E. Bethge (New York: Macmillan, 1967), pp. 152–57.

31. So in the Akkadian "Descent of Ishtar" (obv. 10, *ANET,* p. 107) and the Gilgamesh Epic (VII, iv, 38, 39; *ANET,* p. 87), as well as the *Aeneid* vi.492.3; the *Iliad* xxiii.101; and Horace *Satires* I.i.viii.40.

of life is only hidden (Isa. 8:16) from those who refuse to hear what God has made plain (Rom. 1:18–32). In every age the Church needs to hear this word anew. For apart from the recorded Word of God any light Christianity has is but darkness. So this was a favorite phrase of John Wesley's as he sought to implement his dictum that every teaching must be tested by Scripture. This is still true. Unless the Christian Church can agree that the Bible, as it stands, is the very Word of God, it is without consensus, authority, or light.

If they will not speak . . . no dawn for them. The creation is unable to provide the reason and destiny of its own existence. Around the world attempts to explain life by proceeding from the given produce very similar and equally unsatisfying explanations whether in mythological or scientifically technical language.[32] This failure is not surprising. Only a Creator who transcended his creation could tell why the world was created and how we were meant to live (cf. 41:22–24; 43:9). If there is such a Word, then to refuse to live by it is to condemn oneself to a night from which there is no morning.

21, 22 These verses, along with v. 23 (Eng. 9:1), grow technically more and more difficult,[33] but the general sense is clear. Those who lack a truly transcendent perspective on their affairs, who succumb to the occult for their guidance, plunge themselves further and further into gloom, spiritual famine, and despair.[34]

They shall pass through it. The antecedent of *it* (fem.) is not given. The Targum supplies "land," which would be the correct gender (so RSV, NIV), while the LXX has "you," meaning that the disasters will come upon "you." Whitley suggested that it should be repointed to *bō'* with no consonantal change, the antecedent being *rā'ēb,* "hunger." Yet another

---

32. So both Sumerian myth and modern science suggest that chaotic matter has always existed. Cf. J. Campbell, *The Mythic Image* (Princeton: Princeton University, 1974), pp. 22, 40, 76–80, for some of the basic similarities in world religions.

33. So too the scholarly suggestions for resolution of the difficulties grow more ingenious. Kissane wishes to transpose 8:20–23b (Eng. 9:1b) after 5:30, while Skehan (op. cit., pp. 48–51) proposes to bring 14:24–27 to this place with vv. 21 and 22 inserted between 14:25a and b.

34. Some scholars, such as Driver and Skehan, justify interpretations of one sort or another on the ground that Isaiah is "obviously" referring to the Assyrian invasion here. I remain unconvinced. While this is certainly in the background of the entire section, he is here speaking more figuratively of a spiritual condition which is just as likely to exist long after the immediate crisis was past, indeed whenever the law and the testimony are ignored.

alternative is to take the implication from the previous verse. What they will pass through is a condition of "no dawn" (i.e., darkness), which in v. 22 is *ḥašēkâ*, a feminine noun. For translation purposes, however, the AV alternative is best: leave the text as it stands.

The specific cause of their distress is their emptiness.[35] Empty, sensing themselves in darkness, their natural response is anger, a diffused rage which vents itself on every object which crosses their path, but especially toward those who are deemed in some way able to relieve the problems but unwilling to do so, hence they curse their king and their god.

Having looked upward and found no help, they look downward and find the same. How can those who are in gloom and anguish like themselves help anyone else? Those who depend upon earth for solutions to the earth's problems only compound their darkness. Light for our darkness must come from outside ourselves if it is to come at all. Darkness can swallow up failing light, but it can never produce light.

23 (9:1) But the gloom is not final. God will not be satisfied that his people have experienced the just results of their rebellion. That experience is not an end in itself but a means, a means whereby God's goodness can be manifested in the salvation of a land now aware of the true source of its life. When every human attempt to bring light has failed, then God will bring light, not because he must, not because human craft has discovered the key to force him, but merely out of his own grace. It is part of that grace that the source of the light will be in the very part of the land which first felt the lash of Assyria—the area around the Sea of Galilee. So God never permits a humiliation for which there is not a corresponding exaltation planned.

Galilee of the Gentiles. The area between the Sea of Chinnereth and the Mediterranean north of the Jezreel Valley had always been something of a melting pot, with Hebrews, Canaanites, Arameans, Hittites, and Mesopotamians all contributing to the mix. It was in this region, through which the various inland powers reached westward and southward toward the seacoast, that Israel commonly encountered the rest of the world (hence the name). But the area was destined to see an even more intense mixing after 735, for this was the first part of Israel to be stripped away by Tiglath-pileser, with its inhabitants resettled in Mesopotamia and new settlers from that area brought in.[36] The humbling of Israel was begun. She had thought

---

35. Young suggests correctly that the conjunction on "hungry" is *waw specificum* (GKC, § 118n).

36. See 2 K. 15:29; cf. also the annals of Tiglath-pileser III (*ANET*, pp. 283–84).

the land was hers. Now she was to begin to see that she was only a tenant by the permission of the true landlord.[37]

Isaiah's concern over the fate of Northern Israel's most northern provinces and his prophecy concerning their future destiny are more indications that his outlook was not narrowly Judean or Jerusalemite in scope. All Israel was involved in rebellion against God (8:14) and all Israel would participate in the redemption and restoration, if only in remnant form.

(2) Unto us a child is born (9:1–6 [Eng. 2–7])

1 (2) *The people walking in darkness*
have seen a great light;
upon those who dwell in the land of death's shadow,[1]
a light has shone.
2 (3) *You have enlarged the nation,*
and increased its joy.[2]
They rejoice before you,
like the rejoicing at harvest,
and as they exult
when dividing booty.
3 (4) *For this burdensome yoke,*
the staff across his shoulders,
the rod his taskmaster,
you have broken as in the day of [3] *Midian.*

37. This interpretation is based upon the traditional reading of the text. However, it must be admitted that there are numerous problems in the verse which are not easily solved. See nn. 14–16 above.
1. Almost all modern commentators assume that the MT *ṣalmāweṭ*, "shadow of death," is a "popular etymology" (Kaiser) of what is actually a noun from the root *ṣlm* (cf. Akk. *ṣalāmu*, "to be black"). However, the appearance of *ẓl*, "shadow," in Ugaritic (*CTA*, 4.2.27 = *UT*, 51:II:27) parallel to *ngh* as here raises the possibility that MT is correct after all. Cf. M. Dahood in *RSP*, II:14; L. Grabbe, *Comparative Philology and the Text of Job*, SBLDS 34 (Missoula: Scholars, 1977), pp. 27–29.
2. Reading *lô*, "to it," with the Qere, rather than *lō'*, "not," with the Ketib (and AV). The MT (and AV) "You have increased the nation, you have not increased the joy" makes no sense in the context. Since "to it" and "not" are homophones, it is very likely that "not" is a copyist's error as indicated by the *Qere* and the versions. Another attractive possibility, but one which demands emendation for which there is no textual evidence, is to change *haggôy lō'*, "the nation not," to *haggîlâ*, "the rejoicing," giving "You have increased the rejoicing; you have enlarged the joy" (see *BHS*).
3. "in the day of" frequently refers to a defeat; cf. Ps. 137:7; Ezek. 30:9.

4 (5) *For every boot, stamping in rhythm,[4]*
and every cloak rolled in blood,
shall be for burning,
fuel for the fire.
5 (6) *For a child will be born to us;*
a son is given to us.
Authority will be upon his shoulder,
and his name will be called:
Wonderful Counselor, Mighty God,
Everlasting Father, Prince[5] of Peace.[6]
6 (7) *To the increase[7] of his dominion and to peace*
there shall be no end.
Upon the throne of David,
and upon his dominion,
to establish it and to support it
with justice and righteousness.
The zeal of the Lord of Hosts
will accomplish this.

In this segment Isaiah reaches the climax of the section begun at 7:1. In place of an unfaithful monarch whose shortsighted defensive policies will actually plunge the nation into more desperate straits, there is lifted up the ideal monarch who, though a child, will bring an end to all wars and establish an eternal kingdom based upon justice and righteousness. As a child, he is the culmination of Isaiah's use of children to indicate God's providential mastery of history. Here, however, the names no longer express some future event or situation as do Shear-jashub and Maher-shalal-hash-baz. Neither do they directly express the relation between God and his people, as does Immanuel. Rather, they express the remarkable nature of this individual and thus, indirectly, the saving character of his reign. In this respect, he is the ultimate expression of the truth that God is indeed with us (Immanuel), not for our destruction, but for our redemption.

As an expression of God's ultimate purpose, 9:1–6 (Eng. 2–7) forms the conclusion to the reflections which began at 8:11. The depen-

4. Lit. "boot, booting with shaking." Both verb and noun come from the same root *s'n*. Cf. Akk. *senu*, "sandal," although not strictly a boot, a foot covering worn by soldiers. The rendering of "shaking" as "noise" or "din" (cf. AV) is based upon a medieval emendation which has little to commend it.
5. Carlson (op. cit.) suggests that the use of *śar*, "prince," here instead of *melek*, "king," is a conscious reflection of the Assyrian word for king, *šarrum*.
6. "of peace" is probably an attributive genitive.
7. Jewish commentators made much of the presence of a "final" form of the initial *mem* in *marbê*, "increase." But this is evidently only a dittography, since the preceding word ends with -*îm* and this one begins with those same letters.

dence upon our own resources and perspectives for guidance can only lead further into the darkness. That had been the way of Ahaz, refusing the instructions and testimonies of God. But into the helplessness of that darkness, God would, through the coming King, yet shine the light of his own delivering power. The segment exhibits something of the form of a hymn of praise as it glorifies God (*kî*, "for") as the cause for the rejoicing. Verses 2 and 3 tell the people's new situation, which is a result of God's activity in freeing them and putting an end to war (vv. 4, 5). But that activity is itself a result, the result of the birth of the ideal king (v. 6). Verse 7 then is a description of that king's reign.

1 (2) Following the lead of the previous verse,[8] this verse explains why there will be no gloom where in fact the darkness had been absolute. With the suddenness of dawn (cf. 60:1) comes the announcement that light has appeared to these people. They did not produce it nor are they responsible for it. Where they had been groping in darkness, or sitting in the land of death's shadow, they suddenly find themselves blinking in the light. Throughout the Bible, God's presence is equated with light (42:16; 2 Sam. 22:29; Job 29:3; Ps. 139:11, 12; 1 John 1:5). So here, there is light for these people because their sin and rebellion are not enough to keep God from manifesting himself to them. True, they could not continue to choose their sin and have the light, but if they wished to be freed from their sin, nothing could prevent God's light from shining, as it, in fact, has in Jesus.

All these events are manifestly in the future from the prophet's point of view, yet the verbs are all in the perfect tense. Apparently these are prophetic perfects.[9] Isaiah has a point of view different from the

---

8. The skill with which transitions are handled in the book has been commented upon before (see on 1:10 and 2:22 above). Here it emerges again, so much so that there is no agreement whether 8:23 (Eng 9:1) should be the first verse of the following section, as in the Vulg. and the English versions, or the last verse of the previous section, as in the MT and most modern commentaries. A. Alt has most recently argued in favor of putting it with the following ("Jesaja 8:23–9:6: Befreuingsnacht und Krönungstag," *Kleine Schriften* [Munich: Beck'sche, 1953], II:206). The important point is that the verse is such an effective bridge between the two sections.

9. For the alternative point of view, which takes the verbs as genuine past tenses, see Scott, who regards vv. 1–6 (Eng. 2–7) as an ascension hymn and its language as metaphoric in the style of the Psalms, or R. H. Kennett, "The Prophecy in Isa. 9:1–7," *JTS* 32 (1906) 321–342, who seeks to date the passage to Maccabean times. (See also M. Treves, "Little Prince Pele-Joez [Is. 9:1–7]," *VT* 17 [1967] 464–477.) Neither of these positions does justice to the data, which demand that a real person put a real end to oppression and war, and neither does justice to the material in its context.

normal one. In the uncertainty of his own milieu he nonetheless can look at a future moment and describe its events with the certainty of completed actions. No medium or spiritist could do that. The spirits could not explain the origins of the earth, much less the end of it (cf. 41:21–24). But God could give that kind of insight to his prophet.

2 (3) As a result of God's revelation of himself through his Messiah, joy sweeps over the people, the joy of abundance. Instead of depopulation and dwindling away (7:20–23), the nation swells and grows (49:19–23); instead of the harvest's being meager (5:10), it is abundant (35:1, 2); instead of becoming spoil themselves (8:1), they will divide the spoil (33:23). What is dealt with here are all the elemental fears of people, and the prophet says that in place of fear there is joy. But it is important to see that the real source of joy is the Lord. It is before him that they rejoice (2 Sam. 6:16; Ps. 27:4, 6). And this is true, for apart from the presence of the Creator who gives meaning to life, all other joys are dust and ashes (Ps. 16:11).

3 (4) Now the immediate cause of the rejoicing is explained. They rejoice because the Lord has freed them. It is not necessary to look for some specific liberation which Isaiah has in mind. It is apparent from the whole context that it is final deliverance which is in view. This is what God holds out to his people and that for which they justly pray and believe. Two extremes are to be avoided here. One extreme is to take the way that the Christian Church has often taken, saying that true bondage is to personal sin from which Christ frees us, and thus turning a blind eye on actual physical oppression. The other extreme is the way of certain forms of liberation theology that seem to suggest that the only sin is the sin of political oppression, and that Christ's only purpose in coming was to give human beings political freedom.

Neither extreme is adequate in itself. To make God's promises primarily political is to overlook the profound insight of the NT (and the OT) that the chief reason for the absence of *šālôm* (harmonious relationships) among human beings is the absence of *šālôm* between God and human beings through sin. Without *šālôm* between persons, freedom cannot long exist. But to act as if the forgiveness of sin and the consequent personal relationship are all that matters is to succumb to a Platonic distinction of existence into a "real" spiritual world and an "unreal" physical world, a distinction which is thoroughly unbiblical. The Messiah lifts the yoke of sin in order to lift the yoke of oppression. The Church forgets either yoke at its peril.

this burdensome yoke. The Assyrian emperors delighted in telling how they imposed their heavy yokes upon captive peoples.[10] Here Isaiah looks off to a day when One mightier than the Assyrians of this world will break those yokes to pieces. He, too, will impose a yoke, but, paradoxically it will be easy (Matt. 11:29, 30). It will not be an expression of arrogance and cruelty[11] but of gentleness and kindness.

in the day of Midian. But is this prophetic dream of freedom just a dream? Or is there reason to believe that such a thing might be? With these few words Isaiah calls to mind historic events which would give credence to the eschatological hope. Gideon and his people, faced by an oppressive horde, discovered that in God weakness is strength, and they watched in amazement as God used them to bring deliverance (Judg. 6, 7). So the prophet alludes to those events as evidence that the picture he projects is entirely feasible, given the character and power of their God.

4 (5) How will the Lord put an end to oppression? By putting an end to the warfare upon which oppression rests. God will not supplant oppression with greater oppression, nor will he replace warfare with warfare. Instead, he will do away with wars (cf. Ps. 46:10, 11 [Eng. 9, 10]; 2 Cor. 10:4). If some Christians feel justified in taking up arms against oppression, that is as it may be, but "Christian" armies of conquest are surely an abomination. The figure Isaiah uses to depict the cessation of war is a powerful one. He uses the lesser to include the greater and in so doing insures inclusion of the total. If even the boots and cloaks are being burned, we may be sure the weapons are disposed of, and even more surely, those who wielded them. The boots whose tread shook the earth are now silent. The cloaks in whose fabric is mixed the blood of conqueror and conquered now feed the flames. Wars have ceased to the end of the earth (Ps. 46:11 [Eng. 10]). Speed the day.

5 (6) Here comes the third in the series of verses opening with *kî,* "for," clauses. There is joy *because* God has delivered from oppression, and he does that *because* he has brought an end to war. But how will he do *that*? This verse supplies the answer. It lies in the coming of a person, thus fitting biblical thought throughout. Ultimately, God's truth is not merely in the realm of ideas; ultimately, it is meant to be incarnated (cf. Mal. 2:17–3:1; Col. 1:15, 19, 20, 27). Who is this person through whom God intends to bring war to an end and establish true freedom upon the earth? Evidently, he is a royal person (note the references to a kingdom, government, and throne), yet he is never called king. Von Rad and Har-

---

10. Cf. *ANET,* pp. 287, 288.

11. Note that the "heavy yoke" which Solomon had imposed was a central issue in the split of Israel and Judah (1 K. 12:4–14). Cf. also Deut. 28:48.

relson conclude that this reference is an intentional slap at the Jerusalem monarchy.[12] If such as these are called "kings" then the title is too tainted for this one to bear. He will be in fact what they were in name only.[13]

But this person will also be a child, and it is inescapable that the childish aspect of the deliverer is important to Isaiah, for it appears again in 11:6, 8 (as it is, of course, implied in 7:3, 14; 8:1–4, 8, 18). Medieval Jewish commentators, combatting the prevailing messianic claims of Christians, argued that all this was simply in recognition of the birth of the crown prince, Hezekiah, and was only a simple royal birth hymn. However, this view flies in the face of the chronology of Hezekiah's birth,[14] and even more seriously, it is evident from the language that no merely human king is being spoken of.[15] This is clearly an eschatological figure, the Messiah.[16]

If a crown prince's birth is not in view, then what is the meaning of the emphasis upon this person as a child? Surely, it is for two reasons. First, it emphasized that (contra Rignell; cf. n. 15) the divine ruler will not merely be God, but although partaking of the divine attributes, will have the most human of all arrivals upon the earth, namely, birth. The expected perfect king will be human and divine.[17] But the language also makes another point. This point underlines the central paradox in Isaiah's conception of Yahweh's deliverance of his people. How will God deliver from arrogance, war, oppression, and coercion? By being more arrogant, more warlike, more oppressive, and more coercive? Surely, the book of Isaiah indicates frequently that God was powerful enough to destroy his enemies in an instant, yet again and again, when the prophet comes to the heart of the means of deliverance, a childlike face peers out at us. God is strong enough to overcome his enemies by becoming vulnerable, transparent, and humble—the only hope, in fact, for turning enmity into friendship.

12. Von Rad, *Old Testament Theology*, II:171–73; W. Harrelson, "Non-royal Motifs in the Royal Eschatology," in *Israel's Prophetic Heritage: Essays in Honor of James Muilenburg*, ed. B. W. Anderson and W. Harrelson (New York: Harper & Row, 1962), p. 151.

13. But the omission of the title may also suit a polemical purpose for the names. See on Carlson below.

14. Ignoring this objection, Mowinckel (*He That Cometh*, tr. G. W. Anderson [Nashville/New York: Abingdon, 1954], pp. 102–110) and Lindblom (SKHVL 4 [1957–1958] 36–38) continue to argue in favor of Hezekiah.

15. Cf. L. Rignell, "A Study of Isaiah 9:2–7," *LQ* 7 (1955) 31–35, who goes to the opposite extreme, arguing that the language can apply only to God.

16. The Targ. explicitly identifies the person as the Messiah.

17. Young's (and Calvin's) attempt to argue from "son" to "Son of God" seems misguided.

The titles underscore the ultimate deity of this child-deliverer.[18] Although some commentators have expended a great deal of energy attempting to make these titles appear normal, they are not. Perhaps the primary way in which this is attempted is by reference to the Egyptian throne-names (cf. Wildberger). It was customary to give five throne-names to an Egyptian king upon his coronation. These were related to the various gods and were understood to have magical effect. Such names as "Mighty Bull appearing in Thebes" and "Enduring in Kingship, like Re in Heaven" were typical. On this basis some suggest that the same practice was followed for the equally human kings of Israel. However, several factors tell against this equation. First, there are not five names here but four, and only emendation can produce a fifth.[19] Second, this is not a coronation hymn but a birth announcement. Third, the Egyptians believed their kings were gods and the names express that belief. But the Hebrews did not believe this. They denied that the king was anything more than the representative of God.[20] To be sure, throne-names were probably used in Israel (cf. 2 K. 23:34; 24:17), but there is no evidence that they were of the Egyptian sort. R. A. Carlson has argued that the titles are part of a polemic against the Assyrians, attacking the extravagant claims made by the Assyrian monarchs about their wisdom and power.[21] On this view, Isaiah's use of the titles means that wisdom and power really belonged to that king whom God would send to them. This view has much higher likelihood than the Egyptian one, but the point remains that such extravagant titling was not normal for Israelite kings. It is an expression of a belief that the one who would be born to rule over Israel in justice and righteousness would be possessed of divine attributes.[22] All of this points

18. The classic defense of this position is that of J. D. Davis, *The Child Whose Name is Wonderful* (New York: 1912). For a more recent defense, see J. Coppens, "Le roi ideal d'Is. 9, 5–6 et 11, 1–5, est it une figure messianique? (oui)," in *Memoir A. Gelin* (Le Puy, 1961), pp. 85–108.

19. The accentuation of the MT supports the combining of "Wonder" and "Counselor."

20. Cf. von Rad, *Old Testament Theology*, II:320. Despite strenuous attempts to find evidence of beliefs in divine kingship in Israel, the most that can be said is that there may have been a belief in adoption (Ps. 2:7; 2 Sam. 7:14). But even that view lacks unambiguous evidence.

21. Carlson, "The Anti-Assyrian Character of the Oracle in Is. ix, 1–6," *VT* 24 (1974) 130–35.

22. The Jewish interpretation recognizes the divine element when it attempts to make the first three titles be those of God, who is doing the naming. See S. D. Luzzato, *Il Propheta Isaia volgarizzate e commentato ad uso degl' Israeliti* (1855); cf. Skinner on this point.

to a remarkable congruence with the Immanuel prophecy.[23] Somehow a virgin-born child would demonstrate that God is with us (7:14). Now he says "to us a child is born" (Isaiah including himself with his people in their deliverance as he did in their sin [6:1]) and this child has those traits which manifest the presence of God in our midst. Surely this child (also described in 11:1–5) is presented to us as the ultimate fulfillment of the Immanuel sign.

Wonderful Counselor (lit. "wonder of a counselor"). Throughout the first part of the book especially, the folly of human wisdom is derided, for usually such counsel lacked any spiritual wisdom (1:26; 3:3; 5:21; 19:11–15; 28:7–10; 29:9–14; 30:1, 2; 31:1–3; 47:10–13). By contrast, the Coming One would give wondrous counsel, unfailing in the depth of its wisdom. For it is true wisdom which knows that in weakness is strength, in surrender is victory, and in death is life (42:1–4; 49:4, 21; 50:4–9; 52:13–53:12; 55:6–9; 57:15; 58:6–12; John 12:24–26). So this counselor is a wonder because his counsel goes beyond the merely human.

Many commentators dismiss *Mighty God* as a reference to deity on the basis of the fact that *gibbôr* can be a noun, "hero," as well as the adjective "mighty," or that *'ēl* (or *'ĕlōhîm*) may be used adjectivally to mean "great" (Jon. 3:3).[24] Thus, they read "great hero." Apart from the attempt to deny deity to the person in question, however, there is no reason to depart from the traditional rendering.[25] Wherever *'ēl gibbôr* occurs elsewhere in the Bible there is no doubt that the term refers to God (10:21; cf. also Deut. 10:17; Jer. 32:18). This king will have God's true might about him, power so great that it can absorb all the evil which can be hurled at it until none is left to hurl (53:2–10; 59:15–20; 63:1–9).

Everlasting Father. Again, some commentators dismiss the possibility of a divine element, insisting that fatherhood is the essential point whereas "everlasting" is only a modifier. But surely the phrase must be taken as a whole. Many kings claimed to be "father" to their people and even to their captives, yet their fatherhood was of a strictly temporal and self-tainted character. This person's fatherhood is claimed to be forever. Such a claim cannot be ignored. It is either the royal bombast typical of the ancient Near East, which is, in fact, atypical for Israel, or it is a serious statement of a sort of fatherhood which will endure forever. When one sees that God's fatherhood is such that it does not impose itself upon

23. Cf. Skinner.
24. "Hell" is used in the same way in profane English.
25. Supported by Targ., Syr., Vulg. The LXX lacks the titles in the oldest mss.

its children but rather sacrifices itself for them, it becomes plain that "everlasting fatherhood" must be of that sort (cf. Matt. 6:25, 26; 11:27–30; 18:12–14; 23:9–12; Luke 23:34; Rom. 8:15–17).

Prince of Peace. It is appropriate that this title should come as the last of the series, for it is the climactic one (cf. 32:17). What sort of king is this? He is a peaceful king, one who comes in peace and one who establishes peace, not by a brutal squashing of all defiance, but by means of a transparent vulnerability which makes defiance pointless. Somehow through him will come the reconciliation between God and man that will then make possible reconciliation between man and man (53:5; 57:19; 66:12; Luke 2:14; John 16:33; Rom. 5:1; Heb. 12:14).

6 (7) *. . . there will be no end.* Again, it becomes clear that Isaiah has an eschatological figure in mind. This person will not be a king among kings in Israel. Rather, he will be the final king, the king to end all kings. Thus the prophet envisions the ideal Davidic monarch. God has not rejected his ancient promise to David, but the existence of the promise does not legitimize everything that some descendant of David, such as Ahaz, might do. It does mean, as with Israel, that God will so work in history as to keep his promise and his integrity at the same time. There will be one who establishes the throne of David in a final way by basing it upon justice and righteousness instead of violence and coercion. In this way he will manifest the truth of "God with us," not merely in deliverance from the Syro-Ephraimite threat but in an endless rule of justice, righteousness, and peace.

The zeal of the Lord of Hosts will accomplish this. By this statement Isaiah acknowledges that the picture he has painted will not be realized in the ordinary course of affairs. It will only happen because of God's passionate involvement with his people. *Zeal* and jealousy are two sides of the same concept. Both bespeak a kind of concern for someone that desires an exclusive place in that person's affections. "Jealousy" as it is used today connotes a petty, self-centered, unreasoning interest. But its better connotation depicts a consuming concern for the other's best and an unwillingness that anything should hurt or destroy another (cf. Zech. 1:14; 8:2). Isaiah knew that God loved (desired) his people intensely. He could not adopt a blasé, disinterested attitude toward them. That being so, the prophet was confident that God would not react casually to the bondage which would be the result of their drift from one false lover to another. No, he would not rest until, in the power of his holiness (Josh. 24:19), he had restored them to himself and given them that kind of government which would allow them to find themselves in him.

248

2. MEASURED BY GOD'S STANDARDS (9:7 [Eng. 9:8] – 10:4)

a. EPHRAIM'S PRIDE (9:7–11 [Eng. 9:8–12])

7 (8) *The word which the Sovereign sent concerning Jacob,*
       which will fall upon Israel.
8 (9) *The whole people will[1] know.[2]*
       Ephraim and the inhabitants of Samaria,
       who say in pride and arrogance of heart,
9 (10) *"The bricks have fallen,*
        but we will rebuild with hewn stone;
       the sycamores have been cut down,
        but we will replace them with cedars."
10 (11) *But the Lord will lift up the adversaries of Rezin[3] against them,*
        and spur[4] on his enemies.
11 (12) *A ram from the east and Philistines[5] from the west.*
        And they will devour Israel with a wide open mouth.
        In all this, his anger does not turn back;
        his hand is still outstretched.

The segment 9:7 (Eng. 8)–10:4 answers a theological question posed by the previous one. On what basis will Ephraim's designs against Judah come

1. Reading a *waw* consecutive, not a conjunction (cf. *BHK*).
2. *weyādeʿû* seems strange at this point. In that the word connotes knowing by means of experience, the LXX "learn" seems to give the correct nuance. However, D. W. Thomas, "A Note on the Meaning of *ydʿ* in Hosea 9:7 and Isaiah 9:8," *JTS* 41 (1940) 43, 44, has proposed that a homophonic root (cf. Arabic) meaning "to be humiliated" is involved. This suggestion is very attractive and may prove correct. 1QIsᵃ has *yrʿ*, but this is apparently the easily committed confusion of *resh* and *dalet*.
3. Most commentators regard the present text as corrupt, either changing "adversaries," *ṣr*, to "princes," *śr* (cf. Cheyne), or omitting "Rezin" as a mistaken gloss (*ṣrryw* instead of *ṣry rṣn;* cf. LXX "adversaries of Mount Zion," apparently reading *ṣry hr ṣyn*). However, these alternatives may not be necessary if both Aram and Philistia in v. 11 (Eng. 12) are taken as figures signifying a surrounding by enemies rather than literal statements. If these mean generally east and west, then both problems are solved: the "adversaries of Rezin" can refer to Assyria as it logically should (in this the prophet would be saying that their very alliance had gotten them into difficulty), and the necessity of finding some historical attack by the two countries is removed. Young's suggestion that the Aram referred to is other than the Aram of which Rezin is king is interesting but lacks evidence.
4. If "lift up" is taken as a "prophetic perfect" (past in form, but not in import), then "spur" should probably be taken as a perfect, rather than an imperfect (unless this is an example of an original preterite without *waw* consecutive); cf. Williams, *Syntax*, pp. 32–33.
5. Attempts to discover a time when the Philistines attacked Northern Israel have not been successful. But see n. 3 above.

to nought? Is it not in fact because of Ahaz's alliance with Assyria and because of Assyria's superior might? Isaiah's answer is no. It is not Assyria with whom Ephraim, and later Judah, must come to terms; it is God. The world is judged by God's standards, standards which do not depend upon relative might but rather upon moral rectitude. If Ephraim goes under, it will not be because she was too weak militarily. It will be because she was measured according to the Sovereign's (9:7 [Eng. 8]) moral standards and found lacking. It is not Assyria's anger which Ephraim and Judah face but God's. Thus, while the passage is immediately addressed to the northern kingdom, its ultimate appeal is to all Israel.

This segment, then, seems to function in a kind of pivotal way for the remainder of the section, 10:5–12:6. Until this point Assyria has been presented as a mighty power, dependence upon which will issue in disaster. From this point onward it is made entirely clear that Assyria is but an instrument in God's hand, herself accountable to the same standard as everyone else. By that token, the God who delivered his people into Assyria's hand can deliver them from that hand. In fact, he will do so, by the power of that messianic figure already introduced in 8:23–9:6 (Eng. 9:1–7). While 7:1–9:6 (Eng. 7) and 10:5–11:16 each proceed by their own logic, they both proceed to the same point, namely, the Messiah. 9:7 (Eng. 8)–10:4 provides the link between the two. The relationship may be diagrammed in this way:

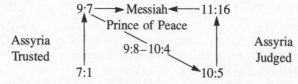

The issue of the historical reference of the segment has engaged commentators' attention a good deal. Is the author referring to events yet to occur, past events, or both? The apparent confusion in the verb tenses complicates the discussion. The "prophetic perfect," in which the tense of completed action is used to describe future events of whose occurrence the writer is absolutely convinced, is common in the book. But here perfects, perfects with *waw* consecutive, imperfects, and imperfects with *waw* consecutive all occur together in such a way that all versions are required to emend the text in some way in order to produce any consistency. The result is that one's assumptions tend to govern the direction of the emendations, and dogmatism about one's own view is not warranted. This commentary, agreeing with Westermann[6] that the first strophe (9:7–11

6. Westermann, *Basic Forms,* p. 171.

[Eng. 8–12]) takes the form of an announcement of judgment upon the nation, concludes that this strophe and the following three are predictive. A further point in favor of this conclusion is that it obviates the necessity of discovering, or of conjecturing, events which occurred in Israel (or Judah[7]) prior to Isaiah's time corresponding to these statements.

The poem gives evidence of careful structuring.[8] This structure is shown not only by the use of the refrain at the end of each strophe (vv. 11, 16, 20 [Eng. 12, 17, 21]); 10:4) and by the internal arrangement of the strophes (4 lines in each, except v. 14 [Eng. 15], on which see below), but also by the content, which moves from pride through false leadership and the loss of brotherly love to social injustice. These are the great themes of Isaiah's book (see on chs. 2, 3, 5; cf. also chs. 13, 14, 28–31), and it is completely in keeping with his reasoning that the root cause of human problems is arrogance, which then leads to the other problems, the end of which is oppression. Thus, in a brief but powerful way, the prophet reminds his hearers of that human behavior for which we stand condemned at the bar of God and as a result of which nations go down to destruction.

7–11 (8–12) As just mentioned, *the* sin for Isaiah, the source of all other sin, is the pride which exalts humanity above God, which makes God but a tool for the achievement of our plans and dreams. So it is this for which Ephraim and the inhabitants of Samaria are called to account. In a typically Isaianic touch, their attitude is described in a brief quotation (v. 9 [Eng. 10]) which gives the reader a better estimate of the Israelite's essential self-confidence than could twenty lines of exposition by the prophet. But their self-confidence is misplaced, for they are about to run headlong into the God they have ignored as he musters their ancient enemies against them. Since they would not turn to him, neither can he turn to them.

7 (8) The *word* of the Lord has been sent out against Jacob. Two extremes need to be guarded against in interpreting this statement. On the one hand, the *word* is not merely an element of speech in Hebrew as it is in English. This can be seen in the use of *dābār* (normally "word") for an event or happening (e.g., Gen. 34:14; Deut. 17:5; 1 Sam. 3:11; Isa. 38:7; 42:16; etc.). It is apparent that the Hebrew felt an essential unity among the oral or written symbol, the concept involved, and the event concep-

---

7. Kissane argues that the whole passage refers equally to both nations, something the text does not support.

8. See above on 5:25 for a discussion of prevailing views on the connection or lack thereof between 9:7–20 (Eng. 8–21) and 5:26–30. For a convenient statement of the opinion that they are connected, see K. Fullerton, "Isaiah's Earliest Prophecy Against Ephraim," *AJSL* 33 (1916/1917) 9–39.

tualized. Nor is this merely a Hebraic or Semitic characteristic. Cf. the Greek use of *lógos* in which the term and the thing portrayed are identified (John 1:1; cf. also 12:48). So, when God has made a pronouncement, in a real sense that event has come to pass (Isa. 55:10; see also Hos. 6:5; Ps. 107:20; 147:15, 18, 19; Heb. 4:12); as an event it will "fall" upon Israel.

But on the other hand, as Wildberger rightly maintains, the word of God is never something independent of the One who has spoken it. It does not somehow become a separate entity which will work its purpose regardless of its originator. Jonah knew this. He knew that his speaking a word of judgment upon Nineveh did not seal Nineveh's doom. For only God is sovereign, and should the circumstances warrant it, he could turn a word of disaster into a word of hope. So, too, this word is not final from God's point of view. It only becomes final when the stroke has fallen and Israel has not yet turned.

8 (9) Those who have thought they were independent will know the truth of God's word (Hos. 9:7; Ps. 14:4; Job 21:19), for through it they will come up against the unshakable fact that they are finite; there are limits to their abilities and potentials.

Isaiah stresses that the entire people will have this experience. None will escape the knowledge that their boasting was hollow. In a phrase which duplicates his favorite "Judah and Jerusalem," the prophet refers to *Ephraim and the inhabitants of Samaria*. This is an apt prelude to v. 9 (Eng. 10) because archeological investigations of the site of Samaria indicate that the Israelites had indeed built a city of great elegance and luxury in the short span of 150 years. Humanly speaking, their pride and self-confidence had some warrant. But we can never speak only humanly. To leave God out of our calculations is to invite disaster (Amos 5:11).

9 (10) As noted above, this quotation says a great deal in a short span about Ephraim's attitudes. Breezy and blasé, they refused to admit that they were limited. If someone knocked down the mud-brick wall, they would not merely rebuild it, they would rebuild it with finely dressed stone. If an invading army cut down the common sycamore fig trees, as invading armies were wont to do, then the Israelites would plant the much more valuable cedars in their place. In short, Israel could, by her own resilience and resourcefulness, turn disaster into accomplishment.

It is not necessary to assume that there had been any specific time when these words had actually been said in Israel. Rather, Isaiah uses them to convey the attitude which existed at that moment in the northern kingdom.[9] Could they have actually reacted this way to the hammer blows

---

9. Malachi's use (1:4) of similar words suggests that the expression may have been proverbial, although Malachi may be dependent upon Isaiah.

of Assyria? There is every reason to think so in the light of Hoshea's ill-fated revolt which brought his kingdom to an end. From this remove we may declare his action foolish, but if there is no one else upon whom to rely, then we must believe in ourselves even when such belief is an illusion.

10, 11 (11, 12) These verses present the second part of the judgment upon the nation, the first having been the accusation in vv. 8 and 9 (Eng. 9 and 10). The announcement of judgment is introduced by the statement of God's intervention, "But the Lord. . . ." How often "But the Lord . . ." has been written over against human arrogance and pomp. David thought he was all-powerful and could take any woman in the kingdom—"But the Lord . . ." (2 Sam. 11:27). Moses thought that power resided in his hand—"But the Lord . . ." (Num. 20:12). So, throughout history whenever humanity has forgotten that it is but a reflector of a glory not its own, when it has succeeded in lighting some guttering candle of its own making, then the Sun arises and all our glory is as nothing.

On every hand adversaries will arise, not in spite of the Lord, but at his bidding. From east and west they will come, before and behind, their mouths open to devour this hapless people which had been so confident in itself. Having taken themselves out from under the hand outstretched for blessing, they discover that the hand is still outstretched, but now lightnings flash from fingers which would have caressed them, and, indeed, would still if they would but return.

b. LEADERS WHO MISLEAD (9:12–16 [Eng. 13–17])

12 (13) *But the people did not turn to the one who smote them,*
and the Lord of Hosts they did not seek.
13 (14) *So the Lord will cut off from Israel head and tail,*
palm branch and bulrush, in¹ one day.
14 (15) *The elder and the noble man, he is the head,*
and the prophet teaching lies, he is the tail.²

1. MT lacks the preposition, which does appear in 1QIsᵃ. However, MT is the harder reading.
2. Most commentators accept the suggestion of Koppe (adopted by Gesenius) that v. 14 (Eng. 15) is a later gloss. In favor of this suggestion is the fact that the verse does adopt a glossatory style (noun phrase plus *hû'* plus noun; cf. M. Goshen-Gottstein, "Syntax and the Biblical Text," *Textus* 8 [1973] 100–106), and that at least the following strophes have four lines whereas this one has five. In opposition to the hypothesis is the possibility that the prophet provided his own interpretation of the figure, as in 5:7. This possibility is favored by the fact that v. 15 (Eng. 16), and even v. 16 (Eng. 17), makes little sense unless v. 14 (Eng. 15)

15 (16) *The guides of this people go astray,*
and the ones guided are swallowed up.
16 (17) *Therefore, the Lord will not rejoice³ over its chosen men,*
nor will he be tender toward its orphans and widows.
For it is defiled and corrupted in every part;
every mouth speaks foolishness.
In all this, his anger does not turn back;
his hand is still outstretched.

That pride and arrogance which exalts humanity issues in an adulation of the "great" men of a society. But that very adulation renders them less and less able to lead their people. For just leadership can only come from persons who know their own weaknesses and corruptibility. Furthermore, when such a person knows that he or she is ultimately responsible to God, the task is approached with awe and dedication. But the person who believes, consciously or otherwise, that humanity is ultimate can all too easily accept the glowing things that people say about him or her (meaning it about themselves), and the only goal is to keep them saying those things. "Government" disappears as the leaders pander more and more to the ever-changing whims of a fickle people. This is the situation Isaiah describes in 3:1–12 and again in 28:1–29 (there too of Ephraim). Those upon whom the nation ought to be able to depend to set its course and to lift up the standards by which it can measure itself are actually looking to the people to find out what course and standards will be most popular. The result can only be progressive contamination of all goals and values by the rot of self-service and self-adulation.

12, 13 (13, 14) Verse 12 (Eng. 13) provides a transition from the previous verse, but it also gives a general statement of the progress of judgment. A people who will not respond to the initial judgment which falls upon them (cf. 1:5; Hos. 6:5; Amos 4:6–11) and seek from God both the diagnosis and the cure (cf. 8:19; Hos. 5:15–6:3) will shortly find their foolish rulers leading them into a situation where they will have no leadership at all.

---

is in place, so that those who take it as a later gloss are forced to conclude that these verses are late also (cf. Gray and Skinner). Furthermore, v. 14 (Eng. 15) is very much in keeping with Isaianic thought (3:1–5, 12; 19:15; 28:1–29). The appearance of false prophets argues against lateness when prophecy was no longer common. Cf. the Targ., which has "scribes" instead of "false prophets."

3. 1QIs^a has *yhmwl* in place of MT *yśmh*. With the meaning "to spare," *yhmwl* makes a better parallel with "to have compassion" in the next line (cf. *BHS*, which notes an Arabic root *smh* also meaning "to spare"). However, the 1QIs^a reading is suspect because it is possible to see the MT reading giving rise to it but hardly vice versa (cf. 59:19).

head and tail, palm branch and bulrush. By means of this antinomy the prophet includes in the coming destruction the totality of the leadership, from the most honored, the waving palm, to the most humble, the bowing rush (58:5). 19:15 uses the same language for the foolish leadership of Egypt.

in one day. Abruptly, suddenly, the judgment will fall, without time for preparation or amelioration. The only preparation for judgment is to live each day as if this were the day (Matt. 24:36–44; 1 Thess. 5:4). Fortunately for humanity, the God who can destroy in a day is also the God who can and does redeem in a day (Zech. 3:9).

14, 15 (15, 16) Here the writer interprets the figure, and with wry humor defines his competitors, the false prophets, as the tail. Delitzsch suggested that this image was intended to compare these prophets' fawning flattery to a dog's wagging tail. Equally likely it merely conveys Isaiah's contempt for those who sold their integrity to the service of the rulers (1 K. 22:5–28; Jer. 28:1–17). Because of this self-serving attitude on the part of the leaders of the nation the people can receive no truly objective guidance. The leadership says and does only what is most likely to maintain itself in power. The result is seen in v. 15 (Eng. 16): since the guides are off the path, of course those guided are off as well. (Note Jesus' version of this truth in Matt. 15:14.)

16 (17) As a result of its foolish leadership the nation has come to the point of complete corruption so that God's aid is denied to both the strong, the choice young warrior, and to the weak, the orphans and widows. He does not take joy from the young men's prowess in battle, so they are defeated and there is no help for the defenseless at home. The reason for this situation is plain enough, for like rotten fruit, the decay has reached every level of society. The evidence of this decay is seen in the expression of their values: they speak foolishness (cf. 6:5). This is not harmless triviality but rather that perversion of truth which makes good evil and evil good (5:20; Ps. 14:1). To speak or act in error is one thing, but to speak or act foolishly represents a conscious denial of reality (cf. Gen. 34:7; Josh. 7:15; Judg. 19:24). Such an attitude is far from constituting a return to the Lord and his values. So the outstretched hand is still one of judgment.

c. LOSS OF BROTHERHOOD (9:17–20 [Eng. 18–21])

17 (18) *For wickedness burns like a fire;*
it devours thorns and thornbushes,
it kindles the thickets of the forest
and billows up in a mighty cloud.

18 (19) *By the outburst[1] of the Lord of Hosts,*
       the earth will be burned,[2]
and the people will be as fuel for the fire;
       a man will not spare his brother.[3]
19 (20) *They will cut on the right,*
       but be hungry;
devour on the left,
       but not be satisfied.
A man will eat the flesh of his own seed.[4]
20 (21) *Manasseh, Ephraim, and Ephraim, Manasseh,*
       and they together upon Judah.
For all this his anger does not turn back;
       his hand is outstretched still.

The initial spark of pride issued in a misplaced adulation of human leadership. Such leaders must inevitably lead their people astray and fail. When that happens the result is anarchy. It is the old cry of "Every man for himself." With the restraints removed, all the ugliness of self-serving appears. Usually blood relations may be depended upon, but not so when "self" becomes all important. Wickedness knows no bounds once it is unleashed. Nor is this solely an ancient phenomenon. Some of the scenes reported in Germany's last hours before the end of World War II are strongly reminiscent of Isaiah's pictures. Of course, as Mauchline and Delitzsch correctly point out, there are two fires described here, but they

---

1. The MT has "the overflow" of God, a graphic picture of God's anger against that which destroys creation.

2. *n°tm,* "burned, scorched," has been interpreted by W. Moran ("The Putative Root *°tm* in Isaiah 9:18," *CBQ* 12 [1950] 153) as coming from the root *nw°,* "to reel," with an enclitic *mem.* (Cf. the Vulg. *conturbata* and H. D. Hummel, *JBL* 76 [1957] 94.) Wildberger, however, argues convincingly for the classic understanding (Niphal of *°tm* as "scorched, burned") on the basis of the context.

3. Gray, among others, argues that the final phrase, "no one will spare his brother," is misplaced and ought to occur before the final phrase of v. 19 (Eng. 20). This argument is based primarily on context. But this is a risky basis for argument. It is just as likely that the phrase belongs where it is as an introduction to the specific manner in which the fire of sin will consume the land.

4. Reading *zer°ô* instead of MT *z°rô°ô,* "his arm." While such a figure might serve to convey very graphically the self-destructive tendencies of Israel, it does not fit the theme of fratricide very well. LXX Codex A has "brother" while the Targ. has "plunder goods of his neighbor," fostering the hypothesis that the original was *rē°ô* rather than *z°rô°ô* (see *BHS*). Both these readings look like explanations of the MT (esp. the Targ.), however, and are suspect on that ground. Of greater value is Honeyman's suggestion (*VT* 1 [1951] 221–23) that "seed," *zera°,* should be read and understood as a general term for family (cf. Wallenstein, *VT* 2 [1952] 179–180).

are intimately related. One is the consuming fire of sin. The other is the fire of God's wrath. But the two are aspects of one another. Because sin is contrary to God's purposes it has the seeds of its own destruction within it. It *is* a fire because it is outside of God's plan. In this sense, its own results are the judgment of God. So as sin both fuels a lust for greater lawlessness and, at the same time, devours its perpetrators, the last scraps of filial attachment are stripped away, leaving brother against brother.

17 (18)   Here Isaiah lays bare the true nature of sin. It is not a little misguided playfulness as it is so often depicted. It is a rebellion against God's order for life. As such, it can only be destructive, like a grass fire which works its way through the brush at the edge of the forest deceptively slowly but then increases speed until it bursts into the woods with a roar and an upward rush of smoke.[5] Because sin seeks gratification in denial of the created order, it can find such gratification only in increasingly flagrant denials. The sinful acts themselves cannot satisfy. Soon rebellion for its own sake, a raging fire, is all that is left.

18 (19)   As noted above, the very nature of sin is an aspect of God's judgment upon it, just as the results of breaking a natural law are an expression of that wrath. Looked at from one point of view, it is the sin itself which has scorched the land and pitted brother against brother. But on the other hand, sin issues in such results because God has decreed one way unto life and all other ways unto death.

19, 20 (20, 21)   The particularly devouring power of sin is seen in its capacity to destroy human relations. These connections, upon which humanity is most deeply dependent, cannot survive the fire of self-serving. It is sad when the environment is abused through sin; it is tragic when human relationships are destroyed. Yet, that had been the history of Israel up to and including Isaiah's own day. In the north, one bloody coup after another followed upon Jeroboam II's death in 752 until the final Assyrian victory thirty years later. The south had been spared a good deal of that kind of dynastic bloodshed because of the strength of the Davidic heritage, but the inter-tribal hostilities, which had begun even in the wilderness and had continued into the present with Ephraim's most recent attacks, were very real to them. It is this history which probably prompted Isaiah's reference to Ephraim and Manasseh and then Judah. *Ephraim* and *Manasseh* were the two largest northern tribes, and, both having sprung from Joseph, they symbolized well the fratricide that had characterized so much of Israel's, and especially Northern Israel's, existence. If the passage is

---

5. In typical fashion, the Targ. sees these figures as allegorical, the thickets being the remnant and the cloud, multitudes of armies.

understood in this way, it is not necessary to look for a specific historical instance, either before or after Isaiah, to correspond to this reference. By the same token, it is highly unlikely that the prophet was making a particular reference to the recent Syro-Ephraimite attack upon Judah. It is more likely that he was referring to the long history of hatred between the northern and southern parts of the nation, a condition which would continue until the Roman dispersion.[6]

d. OPPRESSION OF THE HELPLESS (10:1-4)

1 *Woe to those who decree iniquitous decrees,[1]*
    and write burdensome writings,[2]
2 *in order to turn aside the case of the poor,*
    and to deprive the oppressed of my people of justice,
so that the widow might become their spoil,
    and that they may plunder the orphans.
3 *But what will you do in the day of visitation,[3]*
    when devastation[4] comes from afar?
To whom will you flee for help;
    where will you leave your abundance?[5]
4 *Nothing will remain but to bow down beneath[6] the prisoner;*
    under the slain they shall fall.
For all this his anger does not turn back;
    his hand is stretched out still.

The final manifestation of human pride is in oppression (see also Mal. 3:5). It is one thing when competition or rank and favor pits brother against

---

6. This understanding obviates the need for emendation or historical reconstruction of the text to explain the lack of a reference to Syria.

1. *'āwen*, "iniquitous," carries with it the connotation of "troublesome, tiring, annoying," which is the very opposite of what *ḥôq*, "a statute," should be (Ps. 119:171). The meaning of *'āmāl* is very similar (cf. Ps. 94:20).

2. *mᵉkattᵉḇîm*, "writings," is probably a plural construct with an enclitic *mem* (originally *mᵉkattᵉḇê-mi*).

3. *pāqaḏ* has a broad range of meanings but all can be grouped together under the idea of an inspection by the commander. The results of such an inspection may be positive or negative depending solely on the conditions of the situation.

4. *šû'â*, "devastation," is parallel to "cloud" in Ezek. 38:9, suggesting some such meaning as "storm."

5. *kāḇôḏ*, lit. "glory, heaviness," conveys something of the same idea as "treasure" in English: not merely "money" but the glitter, the desirability, the significance, and the power of wealth.

6. *taḥaṯ* has the literal meaning "under," so some commentators believe the prophet is saying that these formerly high and mighty persons will be under the captives and the slain. It is hard to make any sense of that interpretation except as a figurative one. A more normal sense would be "in the same place as"; cf. Exod. 16:29; Lev. 13:23; Josh. 5:8; etc.

brother and region against region. It is another when persons begin consciously to deprive the helpless of their rights in order to oppress them. At this point, the lowest limits of cynicism and self-serving have been reached. The brutal nature of warfare and conquest can at least be masked with the trappings of destiny and courage. Oppression of the helpless has no such coverings. Its essential ugliness cannot be hidden. It was especially unjustified in a society where equal treatment before the law was understood to grow out of the very character of God (Exod. 23:6–9; Lev. 19:15; Deut. 10:17; 16:19; 24:17). Although some scholars see the passage as referring primarily to Judah (and make this further grounds for separating it from 9:7–20 [Eng. 8–21]), nothing in the passage demands this view.[7] The demand for justice was common to both parts of the nation and was prophetically supported in the north as well as in the south (cf. Amos 5:12).[8] Isaiah's point is that the fate of a people, his own and any other, is determined by their relation to the standards of God.

1, 2 Those responsible for maintaining the laws of the country are doing so in such a way as to enrich themselves at the expense of the helpless.[9] Scholars are not agreed whether v. 1 speaks of the promulgation of new and oppressive laws (cf. Kaiser and Skinner) or whether it refers only to unjust decisions based on existing law (cf. Gray and Delitzsch). Either is possible and probably both were practiced. Such partiality was a particular affront to God, who is in himself just but who also is concerned for those who lack the normal "leverage" to ensure that justice is done them.[10]

3, 4 But the Master has only entrusted his servants with their positions and will shortly come to survey *(pāqaḏ)* their stewardship (cf. Matt. 24:45–51). What will they do then? As Young notes, it is not for Isaiah a matter of "if" the Master will come but only "when." Human beings are not self-existent. They are under the hand of a Creator to whom

---

7. While it is frequently argued that these verses have been transposed from some other context (see above on 5:25–29; cf. also Gray for a statement of the pros and cons), any discussion of the function of the strophe in this context (which would explain the supposed transposition) is regularly omitted. In fact, as pointed out in the text, its function is integral with 9:6–19 (Eng. 7–20), as the repetition of the refrain suggests (contra, e.g., Skinner).

8. "My people" can refer to the entirety of Israel, as well as only to Judah (cf. 32:18; 51:4).

9. The three main clauses of the sentence are linked by infinitives (at the beginning and the middle of v. 2). These introduce purpose clauses: (1) Oppressive judgments are rendered; (2) so that the rights of the poor are denied; (3) so that they may be plundered.

10. Note the continuity of Jesus with the prophets in his charge against the Pharisees (Mark 12:40).

they must sooner or later give account. To act as if they were accountable only to themselves is to fly in the face of reality.

For these people, *the day of visitation* will be a day of disaster with neither help nor hiding place, for the only refuge is the very One who brings the disaster (see Gray). All the ill-gotten wealth will be lost as devastation sweeps in from far away.[11] The position and power which enabled them to walk on the backs of the poor will be meaningless before God's judgment.

4 The exact meaning of the verse is open to dispute because of uncertainties over the meaning of the first word, *biltî*.[12] However, the general sense is plain enough. These great men (and women) who have enriched themselves at the expense of the helpless will suffer the same fate as everyone else: huddling among the captives, lying in the heaps of the slain. Before the wrath of God, status, power, and wealth mean nothing.

So for all these offenses against God—pride, false leadership, devouring one's brothers, oppression of the poor—the divine hand is outstretched. It is not Assyria's overwhelming power which dictates the future of Ephraim and Judah; it is their failure to submit to God and to live in accordance with his principles. It is that failure which will destroy them. God *is* with us for good or ill. We will either live in the glory of that fact or die by smashing ourselves against it. The Assyrias of this world do not hold the balances: God does, and the Assyrias are weighed with the rest of us.

3. HOPE DESPITE DESTRUCTION (10:5 – 11:16)

a. The DESTROYER DESTROYED (10:5–34)

(1) Assyria, God's tool (10:5–11)

11. The coming from a great distance may refer to Assyria or it may also be a way of expressing God's sovereignty: he is not merely a local God.

12. The use of *biltî* here is not normal. At best it is elliptical; at worst it is a corruption. If it is correct, then the apparent meaning is "except" with the sense "There is nothing except to bow down. . . ." Usually, however, there is a preceding negative when this sense is intended. For other examples where the negative is omitted, cf. Gen. 43:3; Num. 11:6; Dan. 11:18; Amos 3:3, 4. Several emendations have been suggested. Kissane offered *kî tikrᵃʿû*, "when you bow. . . ." P. Lagarde found the Egyptian deities Bettis and Osiris in the verse! C. Labuschagne (*VT* 14 [1964] 97–99) proposed *blt ykrʿ*, giving *blt* the archaic meaning "no" (cf. Ugar. *bl*).

5 *Woe to Assyria, rod of my anger;*
  a staff is he in the hand of my wrath.[1]
6 *Against a profane nation I will send him,*
  and of my wrath I will command him:
 to gather spoil and to take plunder[2]
  and to make a trampling place like mud in the streets.[3]
7 *But he does not so consider;*
  nor does his heart so think.
 Rather, it is in his heart to annihilate,
 · *and to cut off nations, not a few.*
8 *For he says, "Are not my officers altogether kings?*
9 *Is not Calneh like Carchemish,*
  or Hamath like Arpad,
  or Samaria like Damascus?
10 *As my hand found the kingdoms of worthless idols,*
  whose images surpass those of Jerusalem and Samaria,
11 *shall I not do to Jerusalem and her idols*
  as I did to Samaria and her worthless things?

At this point in the discourse the tone changes radically. Assyria remains a key figure (10:5, 12, 24; 11:11, 16), but now the destroyer is the destroyed. It is true that what is trusted in place of God will destroy us (7:1–8:22), but that does not mean the destroyer is supreme, nor that he or it holds our destiny. No, whatever may happen to us, it is still God who is supreme, it is still he to whom we look. This is the theological issue which undergirds this segment of chs. 7–12. It is the necessary continuation of the truth that the Sovereign Lord is with us. To be sure, we ignore him at our peril, for he is with us. But by the same token, when we have brought destruction upon ourselves he is still with us, and his purposes are always for good. Yes, Assyria may come with all her engines of war, but she comes at God's command, and unless she bows to the same morally consistent law which is incumbent upon all God's creatures (9:7 [Eng. 8]–10:4), she will disappear at the same command (10:5–34). In

---

1. Verse 5b reads lit.: "A staff it is in their hand my anger." While not perhaps "absolutely refractory" (Skinner), it is very difficult, esp. since it seems to contradict the preceding phrase. There Assyria is the rod in God's hand. Here his anger is in their hand. Many emendations have been suggested, perhaps most commonly the dropping of "in their hand" (RSV). Procksch suggested "the staff of my anger is he in my hand." The discovery that Hebrew uses the enclitic *mem*, however, allows for the possibility that the final *mem* of *bydm* is not the 3rd plural pronoun (MT) but rather an enclitic following the noun (so Young; cf. also H. D. Hummel, *JBL* 76 [1957] 94); hence "in the hand of my wrath."
   2. Note the paronomasia in Hebrew; lit. "to spoil spoil, plunder plunder."
   3. On "mud in the streets" cf. Ps. 18:43 (Eng. 42).

her place will rise the kingdom of true power, of righteousness and peace (11:1–16). In that hour, the folly of trusting Assyria, the creature, and the wisdom of trusting God, the benevolent Creator, will be fully manifest.

It is difficult to determine when the passage was first spoken and whether it was spoken as a unit. The conjectures of scholars are manifold but none is easily provable. That Carchemish did not fall until 717 (10:8) suggests that the diatribe against Assyria was after that date. Sennacherib's attack in 701 provides the latest possible date. At any rate, it is not necessary to the significance of the present order that this material be of the same date as the previous chapters. The materials are arranged logically and not necessarily chronologically. (Though Kaiser considers vv. 10 and 11 to be contradictory, thus indicating that v. 10 is an interpolation, a careful reading shows that the contradiction is only apparent; for further comments on the unity see below on v. 12.)

In 10:5–34 the amazing doctrine is stated that the gods are not necessarily on the side of the victors and that defeat for us is not defeat for God. Although this understanding has been a part of the western philosophy of history for sixteen hundred years, it is still difficult for us to translate it into feelings. Like our ancient Near Eastern forebears we instinctively believe that the victor's gods are God indeed and that the defeated's god is unmasked as a charlatan. Against this, Isaiah envisions a God who is not the prisoner of history, who is not the alter ego of either victor or vanquished, but who guides all events to an outcome in keeping with his own joyous and beneficent plan. All are under his hand. He is neither the possession nor the manifestation of any of his creatures. This is the doctrine of transcendence, a truth of unparalleled importance for life and understanding. Isaiah was not the first to formulate it (contra the older evolutionary theory of Israelite religion), for it is implicit in the first three commandments of the Decalog, but it may be fair to say that he was the first to apply it to the historical process in a thoroughgoing way.

The section divides itself into three subsections: 10:5–19, which demonstrates that Assyria is but a tool in God's hand; 10:20–27, an address to the people of God assuring them that since God is sovereign and Assyria is not, a remnant will return from Assyria's captivity; 10:28–34, a picturesque statement of the reality of Assyria's threat, but also the certainty of her destruction.

In 10:5–19 Isaiah states dramatically the twofold truth that the people are about to feel the rod of Assyria, but that Assyria is only a rod, and as such is subject to the will and purpose of the One who swings it. Assyria's great sin is the one which Isaiah has inveighed against before, namely, the sin of pride, of acting as if there were no God, of exalting oneself to the place reserved only for the Creator (1:29–31; 2:6–22; cf. also 13:11; 14:13–15; 47:7–11). Assyria's power and glory do not make her immune from destruction, for she too is responsible to One whose power and glory are greater than hers. As the statement is now constituted it is divided into three parts. Verses 5–11 assert that Assyria is God's tool, though she has no thought of that; vv. 12–14 express the pride of Assyria for which judgment is promised; vv. 15–19 tell the nature and extent of the coming judgment.

5, 6 Although these two verses are dealing with Assyria's role as God's instrument to punish Israel, the opening *Woe* makes it plain that Assyria's judgment is already in view. Because she refuses to see herself as such an instrument, woe lies ahead for her. As mentioned above, the concept that the enemy, who did not even acknowledge God, could be a rod in his hand had a revolutionary flavor in Isaiah's time. It spoke of an overriding moral purpose in history that went beyond local or national gods and their self-serving natures.

There is probably an ironic note in v. 6. Undoubtedly the Hebrew people considered the Assyrians to be the most "godless" and "profane" people they knew. Yet, Isaiah has the audacity to say that the Assyrians are God's tool to punish them and that they are the godless and profane ones! How could this be? First, it is plain that the prophet considers all peoples to be instruments of the Sovereign. Even the vilest of persons is serving God's purposes, if only to illustrate the ultimate results of evil. This is not to say that God manipulates people in a cynical way. It is to say that God is present in and through the processes of history, bringing out of them that which will most effectively serve goodness and truth. But second, there is a relativity of accountability. Relatively speaking, Israel is more profane and godless than Assyria because she has had more light to reject. If her moral state is still higher than Assyria's, it is also true that she has fallen the farther distance. So Jesus' words, "To whom much is given, much is required" (Luke 12:48), apply to Israel and Assyria; they also apply to the modern West.

7 But it is not necessary to know oneself commanded in order to be commanded. Assyria did not see herself as the servant of Yahweh, but she was. Her purpose was not purgative or cathartic or judgmental. It was merely conquest and aggrandizement. Foolishly, the Assyrian emperors garnered to themselves the praise, believing that their personal and national eminence was due to their own achievements. They did not realize that they were where they were because of the larger purposes of God. Such a truth is hard on human pride. We want to believe that we have made our own way and that the credit is ours. In fact, none of us has anything that we did not receive. Assyria, failing to realize this truth, believed her superior wealth and power gave her the right to sack the world (cf. Rom. 1:19-21; 1 Cor. 4:7).

8-11 Isaiah now speaks for the Assyrian king and demonstrates how far he is from considering himself the servant of Jerusalem's God. Verse 8 was certainly an apt statement. The chieftain of every little city-state along the Mediterranean coast styled himself *mlk*, "king." The officers in Sargon's army had more authority and responsibility than most of these "kinglets." What was Hezekiah to the one who was "king of kings" (Ezek. 27:7) that he should be a functionary of Hezekiah's god? In a masterful survey of recent history, the prophet has the Assyrian list his conquests, beginning at the Euphrates and coming steadily southward until the wave crests upon Samaria just to the north.[4] "How were any of these cities different from another? They all fell before me." Servant? No, conqueror. So it is always to a conqueror. None of the conquests is viewed as having any individual worth or uniqueness. They were numbers to be checked off a list.

As for serving Yahweh, what is he but one more of the *worthless idols* (*'ĕlîl*, "good for nothing") of the nations? The Assyrians had subdued Marduk and Hadad, Baal and El. What could the god of some out-of-the-way place like Jerusalem have over those great gods? In any event, Yahweh had already been defeated at Samaria, so Jerusalem was as good as lost.[5] Plainly the Assyrians, if this is a correct representation of their thought, did not consider the God of Judah to be any different from the other gods. This attitude probably reflects an inability to grasp a religious system at odds with the one prevailing throughout the world. Yahweh had no image because he was not a part of the world and could not be manipulated or conquered through the world. To the Assyrians such a god would have

---

4. The conquests are listed not in chronological but in geographical order. The farthest north is Carchemish on the bend of the Euphrates about 350 miles from Jerusalem. (It fell in 717 B.C.) Calneh is probably Kullani (modern Kullanhou) about 50 miles south of Carchemish (it fell in 738 B.C.; cf. Amos 6:2; not Calneh in Mesopotamia, Gen. 10:10). Not far away is Arpad (fell in 740 B.C.). Hamath (fell in 738 and 720 B.C.) is situated on the Orontes about 100 miles south of Arpad and about the same distance north of Damascus (which fell in 732 B.C.). Another 100 miles southwest is Samaria (which fell in 721 B.C.). For a similar kind of listing see 36:19; 37:12, 13 (par. 2 K. 18:34; 19:12, 13).

5. Some argue that this passage constitutes an early form of teaching concerning the inviolability of Jerusalem (cf. K. Fullerton, "The Problem of Isaiah, Chapter 10," *AJSL* 34 [1917/1918] 170-184). However, it is plain that the city has no built-in inviolability (as per Jer. 7) but only such as comes from obedient dependence upon God (10:12, 20).

been incomprehensible. It was hard enough for the Israelites to grasp. But it is a truth foundational to all of life. Even Assyrias are subject to a God of that sort.

(2) Assyria under judgment (10:12–19)

12 *And it will come to pass when the sovereign will have brought to an*
end his deeds on Mount Zion and Jerusalem he[1] will visit judgment
upon the fruit of the greatness of the heart of the king of Assyria and
upon the beauty of the height of his eyes.
13 *For he has said, "With the strength of my hand I have done this*
      and with my wisdom, for I have understanding.
So I have removed the borders of the people
      and their preparations I have plundered.
I have brought down those who sit like a Mighty One.
14 *My hand has found the wealth of the nations,*
      as though in a nest.
Like gathering abandoned eggs,
      I have gathered all the earth,
and there was not a fluttering wing,
      or an opened mouth chirping."
15 *Will the axe glorify itself over the one who swings it,*
      or the saw exalt itself over the one who moves it?
As though a rod should move them who lift it,
      or a staff should raise him who is not wood!
16 *Therefore, the Sovereign, the Lord of Hosts,*
      will send leanness upon his fatness,
and instead of his glory,
      burning will burn like the burning of fire.
17 *The Light of Israel will become a fire,*
      and its Holy One a flame.
It will burn up and devour
      his thorns and thornbushes in a single day.
18 *The glory of his forest and of his garden,*
      both soul and body, it will destroy
      like the wasting away of a sick man.
19 *The remainder of the trees of the forest*
      will be few in number
so that a child can write them.

But what is so sinful about failing to realize that one's role in history is not conqueror but servant? Why should the "woe" fall upon us merely for ignorance? Isaiah makes it plain that Assyria was not merely ignorant.

1. Following LXX; MT has 1st person singular.

Rather, she was strutting, arrogant, and cruel in ways which earned her the cheerful hatred of peoples all over the Near East, most of whom had never heard of Yahweh. Yet, arrogance and cruelty are not wrong because people dislike them. People dislike them because they are wrong. They sense them to be contradictions of life as God has designed it. Thus, when the Sovereign has finished his work on Mount Zion (not Assyria accomplishing her rapacious intent), then Assyria herself will come under the judgment of God, a judgment which will make it plain that her boasting pride was unwarranted.[2]

Most commentators believe that at least v. 12 is an interpolation (Duhm would excise vv. 10 and 11 as well) on the basis that it is in prose and that it interrupts the flow of the poem. Against this view, Skinner sees vv. 8–12 as a unit to be followed by vv. 7, 13, and 14. In its present setting, v. 12 functions as a transitional element making it plain that what is done to Jerusalem and Samaria (and their idols) (vv. 8–11) is not done in spite of Yahweh but because of him, and that the coming punishment upon Assyria is fully justified by her rapacious and arrogant attitude (vv. 13, 14). Whether this transitional function makes the phrase more or less likely to be original depends rather heavily upon one's presuppositions.[3]

13 God is at work in his world, even when persons in whom he is at work do not know him. There is no sin in ignorance, but the sin comes in when those persons take the praise for their abilities and accomplishments to themselves when in their deepest heart they know that praise is due Someone else (Rom. 1:19–21). This is what the Assyrian monarchs have done. Nominally thanking Ashur, they in fact praised themselves for the strength and skills which made them rulers of the world.[4] Such an attitude must inevitably result in a devaluation of others. The superior person has the right to take from the inferior (so Nietzsche, and then Hitler). Such taking is not a matter for shame, then, but an entirely justified accomplishment. The superior race has a right to determine the boundaries of the conquered as it does to sack all that the inferiors have diligently stored up. The very possession of such superior skills and abilities is the justification for the rapacity. To take such a position is, in fact, to usurp the place of God (note that the Mighty One [v. 12] is an epithet of God in 1:24; 49:26; 60:16; and Gen. 49:24). But the fact that there are those

---

2. Note the similarity with 2:6–22, particularly in the proud heart and arrogant eyes which separate one from God and bring destruction.

3. Cf. P. Skehan, *CBQ* 14 (1952) 236, for an ingenious argument for the secondary nature of the verse.

4. For the validity of Isaiah's representation of the Assyrian monarch's attitudes, see the Assyrian Annals (*ANET*, pp. 275–301).

not as blessed as others, that pillaging them is possible (like picking abandoned eggs out of a nest when there are no parents who seek to protect them) does not make the pillage right. Superior skills and abilities are a gracious gift from God given for his purposes. They do not represent an innate superiority over other persons and are not grounds for devaluing and destroying those persons.

15–19 Because Assyria has arrogated to herself what was in fact a gift from God, because she did not see herself as the tool of a God as superior to Ashur as the sun is to a mirror, the word of judgment is announced. Two metaphors are mixed in this announcement: sickness and fire. Because of this mixing some commentators have believed that the text is corrupt.[5] However, the prohibition against mixing metaphors is not necessarily an ancient one, as 5:24; 8:8; and 28:18 show (Skinner). At issue is whether the two metaphors serve the same point, and they clearly do. All the health, vigor, and glory in which Assyria exulted will be eaten away by disease or by fire. All that will be left will be a wasted, burned-out hulk (a prophecy which came true with devastating suddenness between 629 and 605).

Again, as is common when Isaiah wishes to stress God's ultimate authority, he calls him *Sovereign* (v. 16). God is the ruler of the world, not Tiglath-pileser or Sargon or Sennacherib or any modern dictator. The hosts belong to Yahweh and they march at his call. For one who has seen the Lord high and lifted up, Assyria's vast army and suffocating glory meant little. Before the consuming reality of God, all human works are but tinder (v. 17). Although some are counted briars and thorns (cf. 5:6) while others are seen as towering forests,[6] the differences mean little to a raging fire. Ephraim and Assyria go up together (cf. 9:17 [Eng. 18]), for both are an offense against him.

5. Kaiser argues that the sickness is slow whereas the fire is swift. But surely the similarity is in the devouring nature of the two figures: as disease, particularly a lingering one such as *rāzôn* denotes seems to eat up the body, so fire eats up the pastures and woodlands. Gray's questioning of the authenticity is based upon the irregularity of the meter and is of somewhat greater moment. A syllable count shows the same kinds of irregularities: v. 16: 19, 14; v. 17: 9, 8, 10, 8; v. 18: 9, 10, 7; v. 19: 10, 6. But any attempt to "correct" the text on the basis of meter or syllable counts is decidedly premature. From another point of view the chiastic arrangement of the figures (sickness, fire, fire, sickness) may be an indication of good poetry.

6. Note the continuing use of forest imagery to convey glory, pride, self-sufficiency, and power (1:29–31; 2:13; 6:13; 9:17 [Eng. 18]). This imagery would have been of particular force to the people of Judah: the lack of great forests there would make them more awesome.

(3) Restoration promised (10:20–27)

20 *In that day the remnant of Israel,*
    the escaped of the house of Jacob,
will not again rest upon their smiter,
    but will rest upon the Lord, the Holy One of Israel in truth.
21 *A remnant will return,*[1]
    the remnant of Jacob,
        unto the mighty God.
22 *Even if your people, O Israel, are like the sand of the sea,*
    only a remnant will return.
Destruction is decreed;
    righteousness overflows.
23 *For an end, a decreed one, the Sovereign, the Lord of Hosts, is about*
to make in the midst of the earth.
24 *Therefore, thus says the Sovereign, the Lord of Hosts,*[2] *"Do not fear,*
my people, inhabitants of Zion, because of Assyria. With a rod he will
smite you and he will lift a staff over you in the manner of Egypt.
25 *But yet a little while and indignation*[3] *will be complete, and my anger*
toward their destruction."[4]
26 *Then the Lord of Hosts will brandish a whip over him like the smiting*
of Midian at the rock of Oreb, and when his staff was upon the sea
and he lifted it after the manner of the Egyptians.
27 *In that day he will take away his burden from upon your shoulders,*
    and his yoke from upon your neck.
The yoke will be broken from fat.[5]

The focus changes abruptly from Assyria to Israel with the promise that, since Assyria is under God's hands, the destruction which she brings will

---

1. The word *šûḇ*, "return," also has the connotation of "repent," so in the name Shear-jashub not only a physical return is prophesied but also a spiritual one. The Targ. makes this explicit in vv. 21 and 22 by adding "that have not sinned and they that have turned from sin" after "a remnant shall return."

2. LXX and Targ. omit "Sovereign." Targ. "God of Hosts" suggests that MT may be influenced by v. 23.

3. Syr. "*my* anger"; all other ancient versions, including Targ., "anger."

4. The last phrase is elliptical. Luzzato proposed to redivide *taḇlîṭām*, "their destruction," into *tbl ytm*, "the whole world." Driver (*JSS* 13 [1937] 39) proposed to alter Luzzato's reading to *tkl ytm*, giving "my wrath will be utterly completed."

5. LXX reads the final phrase "his yoke will be broken from off your shoulder"; Targ. "the nations will be destroyed from before the anointed one." Duhm proposed to read "broken" with the previous phrase and then to read *'l mpny šmn* as *'lh mpny-rmn*, "he came up from Penê Rimmon" (cf. RSV, NEB, etc.). Another possibility is to read *šmn* as *šmrn*, "Samaria" (cf. Kaiser, Wildberger). There is no ancient support for either of these emendations.

not be total but will be subject to God's larger purposes. Although the passage is unified by the recurring idea of deliverance, it is apparent that there are two parts to it, neither of which is necessarily dependent upon the other. The first, vv. 20–23, concentrates upon the remnant, a concept with both negative and positive aspects. The second part, vv. 24–27, offers the hope that, as the Egyptian oppression was ended by divine deliverance, so too will the Assyrian be. It is not necessary to argue that the two passages were spoken at the same time or even that they were originally spoken in direct connection with vv. 5–19. It is apparent, however, that their location here in the final edition of Isaiah's work was not accidental. Assyria's destruction by God necessarily means that there is hope for Israel; but that destruction is not arbitrary. It is an expression of a divine consistency which will result in Israel's deliverance.

If this is the case, however, why do vv. 28–34 revert to a presentation of the Assyrian threat? This seems to be the sort of Isaianic device seen previously (3:16–41; 5:26–30; cf. chs. 34, 35) where a theme which has been presented in cognitive terms is then restated in concrete, visual terms. Isaiah has said in vv. 5–19 that while Assyria's march toward glory has seemed nearly superhuman, her arrogance will not go unpunished, with the result (vv. 20–27) that a remnant will survive the onslaught. Verses 28–34 are a visual representation of that truth.

20 *In that day.* As noted above (3:18; 4:1, 2; 7:18, 20, 21, 23), this phrase identifies a moment when God's hand is particularly seen in human history. Customarily, this is a hand of judgment, but as here and in 4:2, that judgment is not to be considered in merely destructive terms, for there shall be a purified remnant which will emerge from the chaos of that day (Mal. 3:19–23 [Eng. 4:1–3]).

the remnant of Israel. The concept of a remnant seems to have been part of Isaiah's understanding from the beginning of his ministry, for it is already there in the call narrative (6:13). Likewise, it appears in the name of his son Shear-jashub, "a *remnant* will return." As noted above, there is a negative overtone to this name as it applies to Ahaz. It points to a destruction from which only a portion of Ahaz's people will return. Yet it has also a positive connotation in its promise that some *will* survive. In this sense, while the term "remnant" does not appear again after 17:3, it is still perhaps the most apt summary of the entire book, since it captures the interwoven themes of redemption and judgment that prevail from beginning to end.

As G. Hasel has shown, the remnant motif occurs frequently in Assyrian texts, where it was used in a wholly negative sense to describe the thoroughness of their conquest.[6] Isaiah takes the Assyrian term, agreeing with their estimate of the situation, but then shows that even a remnant, in God's hand, is more enduring than all Assyria's might (cf. v. 19 where it is Assyria which is but a remnant).

rest upon their smiter. It is a mistake to attempt to draw too close a connection between this phrase and the actual events, as Duhm and others have done. The issue is not which king rested and which king was smitten. The point of this section from 7:1 onward has been to show the foolishness of putting one's trust in Assyria, which has no concern for Judah's best interests. Isaiah's warning to Ahaz was that if Judah persisted in trusting Assyria, the day would come when Assyria would gobble up Judah. That the actual attack came in Hezekiah's day is of no significance to the overall meaning and appropriateness of this statement in this context. Isaiah is looking forward to a day when a restored Judah will have become wise enough to put her trust in God, who is her Holy One and whose intentions for her are pure, whose power is unique, and whose commitment to her is total.[7]

in truth. The root meaning is of dependability and consistency as in the English "be true to." So the idea here is of a loyal, enduring trust in God, not one which is fickle and wavering (cf. Wildberger).

21 *A remnant will return.* Here Isaiah makes direct use of the name of his son Shear-jashub, again indicating the connection of this passage with the overall section. Those who argue that this context's softening of the term's original harshness is a sign of a later tradition's reformulation of the original proclamation surely do not give adequate weight to the potential richness of a term within its original usage.[8] To say that the prophet could have used the name only in the narrow way that it originally appeared is to fail to take seriously enough human flexibility and creativity, without even mentioning divine insight.

remnant of Jacob seems to be a specific attempt to highlight the continuity within God's people. Though it will be but a remnant, nonetheless it will be an authentic representative of the ancient promises, the long

6. G. Hasel, *The Remnant,* Andrews University Monographs 5, 3rd ed. (Berrien Springs: Andrews University, 1980), pp. 96–98.

7. Virtually all commentators agree that the passage reflects intimate understanding of the theology and terminology of the immediate context (cf. v. 5 with v. 20). Why then date the passage late because it does not correspond precisely with the events? It corresponds perfectly with the main point of the section.

8. Cf. R. P. Carroll, "Inner Tradition Shifts in Meaning in Isaiah 1–11," *ExpTim* 89 (1978) 301.

history. Its significance will not be narrowly Judean, but rather the germ of the people as a whole will be present in it.[9]

The Mighty God. While it is not clear that a direct reference to 9:5 (Eng. 6) is intended, the broad connection is plain. There will come a day when God's government will be established and his might demonstrated in his Messiah. Did Isaiah understand that God's might would be demonstrated in condescension and submission? Without even referring to ch. 53, one can say that he did in the light of chs. 9 and 11. Furthermore, the prophet's general revulsion against the trappings of human imperial might suggest the same thing. The mighty God would come as a lamb and a remnant of his people would see the reality of the power of goodness.[10]

22, 23 Nevertheless, despite the ring of assurance that the people will not be annihilated, it is still true that the remnant will be but a fragment of the original. The promises to Abraham will not be abrogated; indeed, they will be fulfilled (Gen. 22:17; 32:12). But they cannot be used as a hedge to protect oneself from judgment (Luke 3:7–9), which is apparently what some were doing in Isaiah's day. They were evidently arguing that God's promises to multiply them would be kept to the extent that they would always be a numerous people. Isaiah responds that it does not matter how numerous they might be or become; righteousness cannot be abrogated because of position.[11] The one who is Sovereign has decreed their destruction because of their sin, and the number of their population will have nothing to do with the outcome.

24–27 There is no doubt that these verses do not follow vv. 20–23 closely. They do not pick up the remnant theme at all; instead, they focus very explicitly upon deliverance from the Assyrians' oppression. At the same time, however, the two passages do not contradict each other but are complementary. The decreed destruction and oppression (vv. 22, 23) will not be total. A remnant will survive it (vv. 20–22) as surely as Israel survived earlier oppressions (vv. 24, 26, 27). As already stated, it is not possible to determine whether the passages were spoken at the same time or at different times and later joined by the prophet himself or by later

9. Note that this is precisely the intent of the genealogies of Chronicles: to demonstrate that this is the people of the promise (1 Chr. 1–9).

10. See John 1:14; Rev. 5:9–14.

11. The apostle Paul makes this same point in Rom. 9–11 where this verse is quoted (9:28). While the promises are sure, they do not function as mechanical guarantees in the face of calculated unbelief. As Hasel notes (*Remnant,* p. 33), Young is certainly incorrect when he argues that the remnant will return after Israel has become as the sand of the sea.

editors. The reference to Zion (v. 24) makes it appear that Isaiah "of Jerusalem" is certainly the speaker.

If the previous verses were somewhat negative and somewhat positive, these are wholly positive, harking back to great deliverances of the past and asserting that ultimately Zion has nothing to fear from Assyrian power but only from divine anger, which will be soon gone, redirected against the Assyrians (vv. 25, 26). Delitzsch suggested that the function of the section is to make explicit what vv. 20–23 made implicit. Thus the coming destruction which cannot be averted is not a cause for despair. It becomes a reason to hope.

24 *Therefore, thus says the Sovereign, the Lord of Hosts.* The direct antecedent of *Therefore* is not clear. Skinner suggests that it refers to v. 19. Kissane and Alexander related it to v. 15. But there is also a sense in which it connects with vv. 20–23. Since a remnant will return, since the destruction has been decreed by God, there is reason for hope. If we can believe that the events of our lives are in the hands of and under the guidance of a providential Father, then even punishment may result in hope because his purposes are good and his power is unlimited.

will smite you . . . in the manner of Egypt. The people are reminded of their previous oppression under Egypt and of God's deliverance. Thus, historical analogy becomes reason for hope. This principle is the heart of the Judeo-Christian faith. However inscrutable God's ways may be at times, this much is clear: God has revealed himself within a course of history, and based upon that history, we may believe certain things about him (cf. John 20:30, 31). It is useless to speculate theology upon events which did not occur. The whole validity of the theology is lost (1 Cor. 15:16, 17). But what God has done once, he can and will do again.

25 *toward their destruction* is a difficult phrase which Luzzato's, but especially Driver's, emendations smooth out considerably (see n. 4 above). A point in favor of the emendation ("my wrath will be utterly completed") is that it makes the two phrases of the verse synonymous, a common feature of Hebrew poetry. At the same time the MT (cf. also AV, RSV) provides a transition to the following verse that is sorely missed when the emendation is made (cf. NEB). The present reading prepares the way for the redirection of God's wrath that is discussed in v. 26.

26 God's anger against Israel's enemies is illustrated not only by his handling of Egypt at the Red Sea, but also by that of Midian at the rock of Oreb (Judg. 7:25) during Gideon's deliverance. Again, the reason for hope is God's previous activity in history.

27 The *burden* and the *yoke* are ancient terms of servitude. Once again, God promises deliverance from the bondage which the Hebrews' own sin has brought upon them (9:3 [Eng. 4]; see also Jer. 30:8, 9). If the MT is correct (see n. 5 above), then the picture drawn is of an ox who has eaten so well and been worked so little that the very fat of its neck breaks the yoke away (Delitzsch citing Kimchi). An incongruous picture, but a decidedly graphic one, for God's promise to bless his people.

(4) Assyria leashed (10:28–34)

28 *He came upon Aiath;*
> *he passed over into Migron;*
>> *at Michmash he left his baggage.*

29 *They cross over the crossing;*
>> *at Geba they lodge for the night.*
> *Ramah trembled;*
>> *Gibeah of Saul has fled.*[1]

30 *Cry aloud, daughter of Gillim;*
>> *listen, O Laishah;*
>>> *answer her,*[2] *O Anathoth,*

31 *Madmenah retreated;*
>> *the inhabitants of Gebim have hid.*

32 *While it is still day, he will be standing in Nob,*
>> *shaking his fist*
> *at the mountain of the house of Zion,*
>> *the hill of Jerusalem.*

33 *Behold, the Sovereign, the Lord of Hosts,*
>> *is about to lop off the boughs with an awful crash.*
> *The heights of the high will be felled,*
>> *and the high ones be brought down.*

34 *He will slash away the thickets of the forest with iron,*
>> *and Lebanon will fall by a mighty one.*

Perhaps the major interpretative question in this passage relates to the last two verses. Are they addressed to Assyria as described in the previous verses or are they addressed to Judah as are the following verses beginning with 11:1? Commentators are divided, with good reason. The reference is not at all clear. Those who favor making Judah the subject (e.g., Calvin, Kissane, Kaiser) are impressed by the reference to the shoot coming up from the stump (11:1), a point which follows very naturally if Judah is the forest being cut down. A further support for this interpretation is that the

---

1. Driver (*JTS* 13 [1937] 39) proposes to read *nûs* as an Aramaism meaning "to tremble" (cf. NEB). The correction does not seem necessary in view of the variety of responses indicated in the following verses.
2. With Syr. *(ᵃnîhā); cf.* RSV, NEB. The MT has *ᵃnîyâ,* "poor."

general context of the section (chs. 7–12) to this point has been of judgment upon the arrogance of Judah.

But others (Delitzsch, Skinner, Cheyne, Wildberger) have pointed out that making this passage one of judgment upon Judah does not fit the immediate context, which depicts judgment upon Assyria. In this light, 10:28–34 may be another of Isaiah's graphic and concrete illustrations of a point.[3] The inevitability of the march is suddenly broken in upon and the oppressor swept away. For a similar application of the forest imagery to one of Israel's great neighbors, see Ezekiel's description of Egypt and her destruction (Ezek. 31). As for the connection with Isa. 11, two possibilities present themselves. The first may be merely free association. The tree imagery having been applied to Assyria, it may have then seemed appropriate to have the following passage about Judah's restoration also begin with that kind of imagery. Or there may have been a more causal connection in that the fall of the overshadowing might of Assyria makes it possible for the shoot from Jesse's stump to spring upward into the sunlight. On balance, the argument for relating the passage to its immediate context and making it a parable of Assyria's destruction seems strongest.

28–32 The discovery of Sennacherib's annals (as well as the report in 2 K. 19 and Isa. 36:2) makes it plain that this is neither a prophecy nor a report of Sennacherib's attack in 701 B.C. (contra Calvin). That attack came up from Lachish southwest of Jerusalem. Scott suggests it is actually Israel's approach to Judah during the Syro-Ephraimite War, but the lack of any connection with the present context makes that suggestion suspect. Skinner points out with some cogency that Sargon, after destroying Samaria, may have ordered a raid as far as the walls of Jerusalem for the purpose of terrorizing the Judeans. However, no literal attack is necessary for this account to serve its purpose in this setting. By means of short, hard-hitting phrases it depicts an army's relentless progress southward from a point some fifteen miles north of Jerusalem until it finally stands overlooking the Holy City.[4] That the route taken diverges from the main north/south road at about Bethel and traverses the edge of the Jordan

3. Gray (followed by Scott) is impressed by the change of meter in vv. 33 and 34 and so concludes that the verses are connected to neither the preceding nor the following. But the change of meter serves to underline the point that Assyria's power is limited by God's power. Still a third alternative is proposed by D. L. Christenson, "March of Conquest in Isaiah 10:27c–34," *VT* 26 (1976) 385–399. He proposes that the actor throughout is Yahweh. But that simply flies in the face of the thrust of ch. 10.

4. See Y. Yadin and M. Avi-Yonah, *The Macmillan Bible Atlas,* rev. ed. (New York: Macmillan, 1977), p. 99.

Rift gives authenticity to the story because this way, though more difficult in terrain, would have avoided the potential strong points at Gibeon, Ramah, and Gibeah.[5] The net effect is to picture an army, like Assyria's, which is all but unconquerable. Where one would have thought the deep Wadi Suwenit between Michmash and Geba (cf. 1 Sam. 14:6–15, esp. v. 13, "And Jonathan went upon his hands and feet," for a description of the terrain) would have stopped them long enough to mount a defense, they instead leave the baggage train behind in Michmash and leap across the wadi before nightfall. The news that the enemy is lodged in Geba (v. 29), with no significant barriers between them and Jerusalem, strikes terror into the hearts of the neighboring villages. Ramah and Gibeah are outflanked. Gallim, Laishah, Anathoth, Madmenah, and Gebim lie directly in the path of the juggernaut as it makes the final march to the outskirts of Jerusalem on the following day. Although Nob has not been positively identified, it was probably in the vicinity of Mount Scopus northeast of Jerusalem. In a climactic gesture, the victorious enemy stands astride that high point and hurls taunts at Jerusalem. Obviously, nothing can save the city from such overwhelming force.

33, 34 *Behold, the Sovereign* introduces a sudden and dramatic change. The short, terse phrases describing the army's progress are abruptly replaced by long, sedate cadences which tell of a great tree's swift end.[6] In this way the prophet whips away the screen upon which inevitable defeat was painted and shows another factor which lies behind the screen, namely, the sovereign God who judges all humanity equally. Assyria is not insuperable. She, too, is subject to God and her arrogance will not go unpunished (cf. 2:12, 13). Any calculation which leaves out God is doomed to failure (8:12–15; 47:8, 9). Although, as noted above, this passage is not direct prophecy of events in 701, its general truth was surely borne out at that time. The spectacle of the decimated Assyrian camp, so recently

5. Aiath is probably the biblical Ai near the modern village of Deir Dibwan. Migron is not definitely identified but may be Tell Miriam near Michmash, or it may refer to the entire district (cf. 1 Sam. 14:2). Michmash is the modern Mahmas about 7 miles from Jerusalem. Both Ramah (modern er-Ram) and Gibeah (modern Tell el-Ful) lie on the main road, 5 and 3 miles from Jerusalem respectively. Geba is modern Jeba. Gallim may be Khirbet Ka'kul, Laishah el-Isawiyeh, and Madmenah Shufat. None of these is certain. It is more likely that Anathoth is modern Ras el-Kharrubeh.

6. The argument that the passage must refer to Israel because Assyria would not be referred to as a cedar of Lebanon is without force. Note Ezek. 31:3 (MT; cf. JPSV, RSV mg.), which precisely identifies Assyria as a cedar of Lebanon.

so overwhelming, must have brought Isaiah's words back to the Judeans' minds with a great deal of satisfaction.[7]

b. THE SHOOT FROM JESSE (11:1–16)

(1) The Prince of Peace (11:1–9)

1 A shoot[1] will go forth from the stock of Jesse,
    and a branch will bear fruit[2] from his roots.
2 And the Spirit of the Lord will rest upon him:
    a spirit of wisdom and understanding,[3]
    a spirit of counsel and might,[4]
    a spirit of knowledge and the fear of the Lord.
3 His delight is in the fear of the Lord;[5]
    so it is not according to what his eyes see that he will judge,
    nor is it according to what his ears hear that he will decide.
4 But he will judge the poor with righteousness,
    and will decide with uprightness concerning the downcast of
    earth.

7. Note that the pesher on Isaiah from Qumran (4QpIs) refers this passage to the march of Gog and Magog against Jerusalem. Cf. J. M. Rosenthal, "Biblical Exegesis of 4QpIs," *JQR* 60 (1969) 27–36.

1. *ḥōṭer*, "shoot," is not a common term. It occurs only here and in Prov. 14:3. The parallel term *nēṣer* is slightly more frequent (14:19; 60:21; Dan. 11:7). Neither has a particularly messianic meaning; both refer simply to a child descendant.

2. The versions are unanimous in translating the final verb of the verse as "go up." This is strong testimony that the original reading was *yiprāḥ*, "go up," rather than the MT *yiprâ*, "bear fruit." If the MT reading is correct, the point may be to stress that the little branch will one day be much more than that (Delitzsch).

3. "wisdom," *ḥokmâ*, is the ability to perceive relationships among elements (cf. *TDOT*, IV:364–385); "understanding," *bînâ*, is the ability to divide a thing into its constituent parts (cf. *TDOT*, II:99–107).

4. Cf. 9:4 (Eng. 5), "mighty counselor." Unless a king had both the ability to gather data for decision making and the forcefulness to make decisions, he was doomed to be ineffective.

5. Most modern commentators (e.g., Duhm, Gray) regard the phrase as a dittograph of the last phrase of v. 2. The LXX seems to support this view: "A spirit of fear of God shall fill him." Subsequently, it is argued, *rûaḥ*, "spirit," became altered to *hᵃrîḥâ*, "his smelling," in the MT. The sense of "delighting to smell" (RSV) appears in Amos 5:21 but it is still in the context of sacrifice here. H. Ringgren, *The Messiah in the Old Testament*, SBT 1/18 (London: SCM; Naperville: Allenson, 1956), p. 31, suggests that the allusion may be to incense used at the coronation; this explanation probably puts the phrase in the best light. G. A. Smith makes a great deal of the phrase, suggesting that since it says that the fear of the Lord is the Messiah's very breath, it is a reference to the sinlessness of our Lord. This interpretation makes far too much of the statement even if the reading were unquestionable.

He will strike the earth with the rod of his mouth,
and with the breath of his lips shall slay the wicked.
5 *Righteousness shall be the waistcloth of his loins,*
and faithfulness the waistcloth of his hips.
6 *The wolf will sojourn with the lamb,*
and the leopard will stretch out with the kid,
the calf, the young lion, and the fatling together,[6]
and a little child shall lead them.
7 *The heifer will feed with the bear,*
and their young will stretch out together,
and the lion will eat straw like an ox.
8 *The suckling will play beside the hole of the cobra,*
and the newly weaned child will reach out his hand over the
den[7] *of the viper.*
9 *They shall not do evil*
and they shall not destroy in all my holy mountain.
For the earth will be full of the knowledge of the Lord
as the waters cover the sea.

In 11:1–16 the messianic hope which began to be expressed in 7:14 and which was amplified in 8:23–9:5 (Eng. 9:1–6) comes to full flower. The Messiah is not merely promised or announced but is depicted as ruling.[8] In place of the craven and petty house of David, or the arrogant and oppressive empire of Assyria, here is a king in whose hands the concerns of the weakest will be safe. He will usher in a reign of safety and security to which the weary exiles may come streaming in return. Structurally, the segment brings to a close the unit which begins at 10:5. The entire unit makes the point that although Israel's (and Judah's) lack of trust in the Lord will have meant nearly total destruction at the hand of Assyria, that destruction is not God's final word. Assyria, too, will come under judgment and out of that judgment a remnant of Jacob's descendants will return to

6. The absence of a verb in v. 6c, as well as the mention of three animals instead of two, has prompted several proposals for emending "fatling," *mᵉrîʾ*. Some take it as a corruption of a verb *yirʿû*, "they shall graze" (*BHK*, Gray, Skinner, etc.), or *yimrᵉʾû*, "they shall fatten" (*BHS* and KB, p. 563, on the basis of an Ugaritic root). Scott proposes "friends," *mᵉrāʿîm* (so NEB). Nevertheless, the MT is not impossible and in the absence of a more compelling reading need not be emended.

7. *mᵉʾûrâ*, lit. "place or thing of light." Thus some interpreters have taken it to refer to the snake's glittering eye (so Targ.). But the opening of the snake's den seems to fit the context better.

8. Cf. Delitzsch. G. A. Smith speaks of Immanuel as a sufferer with his people and the "Prince of Four Names" in 8:23–9:5 (Eng. 9:1–6) as redeemer of his people.

277

God's land. However, as 8:23–9:5 (Eng. 9:1–6) suggested, so 11:1–9 confirms that such a return will be under the aegis of an anointed descendant of David. In fact, the root of Jesse will himself be the banner which will signal safe return. Prominent in that return is the sovereign activity of God. So the subdivision which began with words of judgment by means of Assyria (7:18–25) has now been turned to deliverance from Assyria (11:16), all of it in expression of the sovereign grace of a just and faithful God.

This segment 11:1–9 is specifically related to the messianic promise. It emphasizes three aspects of this figure: (1) his divine endowment for ruling (vv. 2 and 3a); (2) the absolute justice of his rule (vv. 3b–5); and (3) the quality of safety which will characterize his rule (vv. 6–9). The movement is from qualifications to performance to results. There is no sense in which God's re-establishment of his people somehow envisions a return to the theocracy. What it does envision is a time when the ruler will no longer see himself as privileged but rather as responsible, when he will become one for whom his people's welfare is uppermost. In a word, the ruler will be the servant, not because he is too weak to dominate, but because he is strong enough not to need to crush. This picture cannot be applied to any merely human king. It is either an unattainable ideal or the figure envisioned is somehow superhuman. That it is the latter is supported by the vision of the return which is linked to the Messiah's reign (vv. 10–16). That return is not merely an ideal, nor is the Messiah. He is a reality but a superhuman one.

1 The prophet has just depicted Assyria's swift and sudden destruction. The forest of her pride is nothing but a field of stumps.[9] So, too, with God's people (6:11–13). Both Jacob and Assyria have fallen under the judgment of God. But there is a difference. When Assyria was finally cut down in 609 B.C. by the combined forces of Babylon, Media, and Persia, nothing ever arose from the stumps again. Not so with Israel. From one of her stumps, as we are told in the call narrative (6:13c), the smallest shoot would venture forth. From that helpless shoot (53:1, 2) would come the restoration of that nation and with it the end of the war (9:4 [Eng. 5]) and the establishment of that which the world has sought but never attained, namely, genuine security.

Commentators (cf. Calvin) are possibly correct when they suggest that the use of *Jesse* is an attempt to downplay the house of David (cf. 7:1,

---

9. Although many interpreters see the fact of the stumps' already being cut down as evidence of the postexilic date of the passage, there is no reason to take such a position. The prophet merely sees what he is predicting as accomplished fact, much in the same way that the perfect tense is used to describe future events.

13). Salvation would not come from the pomp and glory of the royal house. Rather, it would come from the promise of one who could create a royal house from a peasant family. Deliverance is God's gracious gift, an exercise of his faithfulness. Nevertheless, God's promise to David stands. It is not merely through any of Jesse's sons that deliverance will come, but specifically through a descendant of David. Both earlier (9:6 [Eng. 7]) and later exegesis (16:5; 55:4–5; Jer. 23:5; 33:15) make the connection explicit.[10] It is possible that this use of the term *branch* provides the ruling interpretation for its use in Zechariah (3:8 and 6:12) and Jeremiah (23:5 and 33:15) where it clearly refers to the Messiah (note also 4:2).

2 In the OT there was the growing sense that the unaided human spirit was incapable of saving itself.[11] The initial expressions of this conception related to feats of skill and strength, for instance, in the craftsmanship of Bezalel (Exod. 31:3) or the might of Samson (Judg. 14:6). But it soon came to be related to more abstract matters, such as the capacity for leadership. So Saul and David were endued with the divine Spirit for their tasks (1 Sam. 10:10; 16:13). Thus, to say that God's spirit was upon someone became almost a code phrase for saying that the person was acting out of a capacity which was more than merely human.[12] This phrase came to be applied supremely to capacity for ethical behavior (44:3; Ezek. 36:25–27). Yet, the Davidic kings had come to manifest a spirit which had little of God in it. Craven, cynical, pompous, they seemed to be spiritually bankrupt, so much so that Isaiah was led to testify that the palace was empty (32:14) and envisioned a day when the Spirit of God would be visited on the people as a whole (32:15) through their leaders.[13]

This verse fits the picture just drawn in a perfect manner. The promised shoot from the stump of Jesse will be characterized by the very breath of God about him. Everything about his leadership will testify to a supernatural endowment for his calling. It is this which is critical. Unless the Messiah is truly endued with the Spirit of God, the results of his rule will be no different from those of an Ahaz.

But Isaiah can look forward to such a Messiah who will be able to perceive things correctly and who will be able to carry out correct decisions

10. Cf. also Ezek. 34:23–25; Zech. 12:7–12; 13:1.

11. J. Oswalt, "John Wesley and the Old Testament Concept of the Holy Spirit," *Religion in Life* 48 (1979) 283–292.

12. For other references, cf. Gen. 41:38; Num. 11:17, 25; Judg. 6:34; 11:29; 13:25; Dan. 4:8; 5:11, 14.

13. Note that ch. 32 is about the manifestation of the King and that the results of the Spirit's outpouring will be judgment, righteousness, and security, as in ch. 11.

because of a correct motivation. The basis of this king's activity will be that kind of experiential acquaintance with God which will issue in the recognition that the supreme reality of life is our accountability to a just, faithful, holy God. It is this understanding which characterizes true religion for the Hebrew. Pious feelings and ecstatic experiences are as nothing unless they are underlain by that pervading consciousness of God's reality and of our accountability to him.[14] Because the Messiah will be characterized by this fear of the Lord, he can be depended upon to perceive correctly (John 2:24, 25; Mark 2:8) and to act with integrity (Luke 4:1–13). The person who knows God in a full-orbed way and is supremely concerned to please him can be depended upon not to allow self-serving to cloud the issue, to cause him to trample other people. If there should come One in whom God's Spirit could dwell completely and purely, that person could be the Savior of the world (61:1).[15] The testimony of the NT (Luke 4:14, 18; John 1:14) and of the Christian Church is that Jesus of Nazareth is that person.

3–5 This paragraph moves from the endowment of the Messiah to a description of the manner in which he carries out his rule. He will not govern on the basis of appearances, but rather will operate out of a fundamental righteousness and faithfulness that will give his pronouncements an unshakable moral force.

Considerable controversy surrounds the first phrase of v. 3. If the text is correct, the sense is that the Messiah will "smell" with delight the attitude of reverent concern for God's ways just as God delights in the smell of incense. However, the passage is strange enough to merit considerable caution over its authenticity.

it is not according to what his eyes see appears again to be a reference to a more than merely human character possessed by the Messiah. A human judge can do no more than to make the best use of his or her natural faculties in attempting to reach a fair ruling. Somehow this king will go deeper than that and will pierce beneath appearances to the underlying

14. G. A. Smith remarks that this passage had a governing influence upon medieval pneumatology and gave an excessively intellectual cast to their understanding of the Spirit's work. He goes on to say that our age needs to recapture some of that intellectual emphasis. The passing of a century has not altered the validity of Smith's concern. If anything, that recovery is even more necessary today.

15. This OT understanding of the Messiah to be filled with God's Spirit explains Jesus' desire for John's baptism. In undergoing this form, he testified to his own affirmation of that truth. In this sense, his baptism coincided with the anointing of the OT king. (Cf. Matt. 3:17 and Ps. 27, which was probably a coronation psalm.)

reality. This is a sweeping promise, for, as Young observes, absolute justice demands absolute knowledge. In this light, it must be obvious that the king for whom Isaiah looks is more than a new edition of the present monarchy. Rather, he looks for a radically different kind of kingship (cf. John 18:36–38).[16]

he will judge the poor is an expression of a royal role not only in Israel but across the ancient Near East. The king who did not accept this role, at least in principle, could not hope to survive.[17] The poor, the helpless, and the outcast were to be accorded the special protection of the crown. However, there was a great gulf between the ideal and the actual. For then, as now, the poor lacked political power. Thus, if one's kingship rested upon the favor and goodwill of the rich and the powerful, primary attention to the needs of the powerless would always remain an ideal. In order for that ideal to become a reality, the king's authority would have to rest upon something other than political power. In that case, right decisions could be rendered without concern for political ramifications. These decisions could hardly be made unless the kingship was of a more than human sort. This seems to be exactly what Isaiah hoped for.

He will strike the earth with the rod of his mouth expresses the moral force possessed by a leader who owes allegiance to no earthly pressure groups. He can say what needs to be said in a given circumstance and the force of the truth is undeniable (Mark 12:34). The word itself becomes his weapon (Heb. 4:12; 2 Thess. 2:8b; Rev. 1:16b; 19:15). The normal form of Hebrew poetry would suggest that *the earth* is somehow synonymous with *the wicked*,[18] and the book of Isaiah does use the word "earth" in this sense several times (13:11; 24:17–21; 26:9, 21; 28:22), although only in 13:11 is it directly paralleled with words for wickedness or evil. Another alternative is to propose a variant reading,[19] but neither alternative is required. Hebrew poetic form also permits a development in the two stichs. Thus, in the first stich, it is said that the Messiah will carry out God's function of judging the earth, while the second stich emphasizes that it is the wicked who will have cause to fear that judgment (2:4; 51:5, 6; Ps. 82:8; Rev. 6:15–17; 20:11, 12).

5 The general sense of the verse is clear. The Messiah will bring

16. Cf. M. Tate, "King and Messiah in Isaiah of Jerusalem," *RevExp* 65/4 (1968) 409–421.

17. Cf. Ps. 72:2; 2 Sam. 23:3, 4; 1 K. 10:9; Prov. 29:4, 14; Isa. 1:23; *UT,* 127:46.

18. Cf. Targ. "the guilty of the earth."

19. So Gray, *BHS,* and NEB suggest 'rṣ, "ruthless," for 'rṣ, "earth." But this reading is without manuscript support (e.g., LXX has "earth").

justice and equity upon the earth because fundamental to his own character will be two essential qualities: uprightness and dependability born of integrity or faithfulness. Fundamentally, these are two characteristics of God upon which the whole biblical understanding of life is built (Isa. 5:16; 65:16; Ps. 40:11 [Eng. 10]; 119:75, 142; Zech. 8:8). Because he is as he is, the whole universe can be understood in a coherent and consistent way. If in fact the first principle of existence operated on the basis of arbitrary chance, then nothing could be known and, even more, there would be nothing to which commitment could be reasonably given. The two concepts are intimately connected, so much so that they are at times synonymous (1:26; 48:1).[20] Although their meanings overlap, each contributes a distinctive element. *Righteousness* is that capacity for doing the right thing in all circumstances and frequently involves keeping one's promises, so that there are times when it may be translated by "deliverance" (51:8) or "vindication" (54:17).[21] *Faithfulness* comes from the root which means to be dependable or true.[22] So, fundamental to both words is the idea of an integrity or consistency which results in complete dependability. These were the characteristics that the Israelite people saw in their God and longed for in their king. What Isaiah was depicting in the Messiah was someone who would combine divine traits with a human presence.

While the overall sense of the passage is clear enough, the particular force of the imagery remains somewhat ambiguous. What exactly was a *waistcloth?*[23] Some have referred it to the belt which was used to gather up the outer robe and into which the bottom hem of the garment could be tucked in preparation for strenuous activity ("gird up your loins," Job 38:3; Isa. 8:9; cf. also 5:27).[24] However, the same term also applies to the "loincloth" normally worn under the other garments (Job 12:18; Jer. 13:11). It is impossible to determine which usage is in view here. If it is the former, then these are the characteristics which bring all the Messiah's other attributes together, giving them dignity and force. If the latter sense is correct, then righteousness and faithfulness are those qualities most basic

20. Normally the synonym of "righteousness" (*ṣdq*) is "justice" (*mšpṭ*), while the synonym for "faithfulness" (*ʾᵉmûnâ*, root *ʾmn*) is "steadfast love" (*ḥsd*).

21. Cf. von Rad, *Old Testament Theology,* I:370–76.

22. Cf. *TDOT,* I:316–320.

23. The use of the same word for "waistcloth," *ʾēzôr,* in both parts of the parallel structure is unusual but by no means unheard of (see 15:8; 16:7; 17:12, 13; 51:8; 54:13; 59:10). Thus there is no need for emendation, contra Driver, *JTS* 13 (1937) 39, 40.

24. Young relates this term to belt-wrestling, a test of champions now known from several sources in the ancient Near East. There is no clear evidence of this practice in Israel.

and fundamental to all the others. In either case, the essential nature of these attributes is underlined.

6–9 With a classic set of images the prophet portrays the kind of security and safety which will result in the rule of the Messiah.[25] The most helpless and innocent will be at ease with those who were formerly the most rapacious and violent. There are three ways of interpreting such statements. The first is literalistic, looking for a literal fulfillment of the words. While this interpretation is possible, the fact that the lion's carnivorousness is fundamental to what a lion is and that literal fulfillment of the prophecy would require a basic alternation of the lion's nature suggest that another interpretation is intended (cf. the way the OT's statements about the Messiah have been reinterpreted by the Church).

A second means of interpretation is spiritualistic. The animals represent various spiritual conditions and states within human beings (cf. Calvin). While this avoids the problems of literal fulfillment, it introduces a host of other problems, chief of which is the absence in the text of any controls upon the process. Thus, it depends solely upon the exegete's ingenuity to find the correspondences (contra 5:1–7, where the correspondence is clearly indicated).

The third way of interpreting this passage, and others like it, is the figurative. In this approach one concludes that an extended figure of speech is being used to make a single, overarching point, namely, that in the Messiah's reign the fears associated with insecurity, danger, and evil will be removed, not only for the individual but for the world as well (Rom. 8:19–21). Precisely how God may choose to do this in his infinite creativity is his to decide. But that he will do so we may confidently believe.

The wolf will sojourn with the lamb expresses the sense of these verses that the apparently strong become dependent upon the apparently weak. The word *sojourn* is the word used of a stranger whose survival in a foreign land is dependent upon the goodwill of the natives. Likewise, these wild animals are depicted as depending upon the leadership of a child, the one supposedly least able to control their voracious instincts. But this mention of the child fits one of the recurring themes of chs. 7–12: a child, not a strutting monarch, is the one whom God chooses to rule this

25. Cf. also 35:9; 65:25; Ezek. 34:25. Similar statements also appear in the Sibylline Oracles (3:766–68) and in Virgil's *Eclogues* (4:21, 24; 5:60). Mowinckel (*He That Cometh*, p. 182) and others contend that Isaiah is reflecting an ancient royal myth at this point. However, the existence of such myths of a return to paradise in the ancient Near East has very little evidence in its support. Cf. M. Eliade, *The Myth of the Eternal Return*, tr. W. R. Trask (New York: Pantheon, 1954).

world's great. In innocence, simplicity, and faith lie the salvation of a globe grown old in sophistication, cynicism, and violence.

The force of the imagery here illustrates why an author would choose this means of making his point. The contradiction of a child playing about the den of poisonous snakes can almost be felt physically. One wants to snatch the child away from the presence of sudden, arbitrary death. In what more effective way could a writer communicate his conviction that in the Messiah's day, death itself will be conquered. One thinks of the NT's appropriation of Hos. 13:14 in 1 Cor. 15:55, "Death, where is thy sting?"

9 Those who take a literal interpretation of the passage, as Delitzsch does, find themselves constrained to argue that *they* here continues to refer to the animals, whereas a more figurative understanding allows for a wider, more natural interpretation. In this view, the central point of vv. 6–8 is merely being expressed in a more discursive way here. But also, there is a causal nexus being identified here. There will be safety and removal of anxiety *because* of a relationally based understanding of God and his ways. This interpretation suggests that attempts to arrive at a just world peace based upon mutual self-interest must finally fail. Only mutual commitment to the Holy One who is righteous and faithful can produce an environment where human beings can commit themselves to one another in trust (34:14–18). (Note the emphasis upon knowing in chs. 40–49. The exiles had to relearn the character of God. See also 53:11 and Jer. 31:34.)

(2) The promised return (11:10–16)

10 *It shall be in that day that the root*[1] *of Jesse which will be standing*[2] *as an ensign for the nations, him will the nations seek and his resting place will be glorious.*

11 *And it shall be in that day the Sovereign will again, a second time, [extend]*[3] *his hand to acquire the remainder of his people which shall*

---

1. *šōreš*, "root," is the normal word for the literal root of a plant. But it is also a favorite term for descendants or for that elemental hope which remains for a person (Deut. 29:18; Job 14:8; 2 K. 19:30; Isa. 40:24; Dan. 4:15, 23, 26; 11:7). Eventually, like "branch," *šōreš* became a term for the Messiah (Isa. 53:2; Sir. 47:22; Rev. 5:5; 22:16).

2. The sense of the participle "standing" seems to be continuous action. The Targ. suggests imminent action: "about to arise." The inconspicuous root will grow up to a place where all the nations cannot help but see him (cf. Phil. 2:11). The Vulg. takes "resting place" to refer to the sepulchre, but there is no reason to do so. The point is that the root will attain a position of the highest honor.

3. The absence of the verb in the MT has prompted several suggestions for emendation of the text. Most of these revolve around the word "second," which

*remain from Assyria, from Cush, from Elam, from Shinar, from Ha-
math, and from the islands of the sea.*

12 *And he will raise up an ensign for the nations,*
and will gather the exiles[4] of Israel;
the scattered of Judah he will assemble
from the four[5] corners of the earth.

13 *The jealousy of Ephraim will go away,*
and the oppressors of Judah[6] will be cut off;
Ephraim will not be jealous of Judah,
and Judah will not oppress Ephraim.

14 *And they shall fly on the shoulder of the Philistines toward the sea;*
together they will plunder the sons of the East.
Edom and Moab shall be those for whom they stretch their hands,
the sons of Ammon their obedient band.

15 *The Lord will destroy[7] the tongue of the Sea of Egypt*
and wave his hand over the River with his scorching[8] wind.
He will smite it into seven stream beds
and cause one to cross with sandals.

16 *It will be a highway for the remainder of his people,*

---

is missing from the LXX (but present in 1QIs[a] and the Targ.). So, *BHK* suggests
changing *šēnît,* "second," to *śeʾēt,* "lifting up." However, as Hasel (*Remnant*, p. 340
n. 454) points out, it is very difficult to see how a scribal error could change the
rather simple reading *śeʾēt* into the difficult reading *šēnît.* (*BHS* drops this suggestion
and proposes yet another emendation.) It seems best to assume that the omission
of the verb was idiomatically permissible in situations such as this. Young cites
the Hittite Annals of Mursilis, II, col. III, line 58, for a similar construction.

4. Heb. *nidḥê;* Skinner says this is a postexilic form but it occurs 21 times
in Deuteronomy and Jeremiah.

5. 1QIs[a] lacks the number "four" (as do Job 37:3; 38:13). "Four" is
present in Ezek. 7:2, and it appears in the versions.

6. The parallelism of v. 13 would seem to indicate that both the genitives
in the first half of the verse are subjective (jealousy belonging to Ephraim; oppressors belonging to Judah). As Delitzsch points out, however, *ṣōrēr,* "oppressor,"
everywhere else takes an objective genitive (e.g., Amos 5:12). It may be that the
poet has consciously introduced variation here or that this is the one example of
a subjective genitive with *ṣōrēr.* Kaiser's suggestion that this reference is to the
Samaritan schism is very strange in view of the fact that the jealousy and oppression stem all the way from the united monarchy (2 Sam. 2:8–4:12; 19:40–20:2;
1 K. 4:7–19; 11:28; 12:1–20).

7. *ḥrm,* lit. "to put under a ban" (cf. Josh. 6:17, 18), but perhaps to be
read *ḥrb,* "to dry up"; cf. LXX "will make desolate."

8. *ʿayām,* "scorching," occurs only here. If it is correct, then it may come
from Arab. *ʿāma,* "to glow with internal heat," thus "scorching" or "searing." Cf.
Targ. "a stroke of his might . . . by the word of his prophets." Luzzato, Gesenius,
and Cheyne propose to read *ʿōṣem,* "mighty" (cf. *BHS*, which notes that the latter
is supported by Syr. and Vulg.).

those who remain from Assyria,
as there was for Israel
in the day of his coming from the land of Egypt.

Just as the folly of Ahaz was responsible for the defeat of Judah and her ultimate dispersion (8:6–8), so the coming of the Messiah will result in a great restoration of God's people. From every part of the earth they will come (11:11), in a return as dramatic as the Exodus itself. While the general sense of these verses is clear, the specifics are not so clear. Is the prophet speaking of the return from Babylon in 539? If so, the Messiah had not yet been revealed and could hardly be the ensign around which the people rallied. Is Isaiah in fact speaking of the New Israel, the Church, as the Reformers maintained (cf. Calvin)? Certainly, believers were gathered to the Messiah from every part of the world, and v. 10, in a fashion reminiscent of 2:2–4, seems to begin the section with a reference to the nations at large. Nevertheless, the primary focus of the passage seems to be upon the historical nation of Israel, so that one is led to believe it points to some great final ingathering of the Jewish people such as that referred to by Paul in Rom. 11. If that has begun in the Zionist movement, as many believe, we may look forward with anticipation to its ultimate completion in a turning to God in Christ by the Jewish nation.

The allegation that the passage is postexilic (Cheyne) or even later (Duhm, Kaiser) rests upon the assumption that Isaiah could not have conceived of a time when Jews would be scattered over the known world. This viewpoint overlooks the inspiration of God's Spirit, but it also overlooks the prophet's own understanding of the political realities of his world, which unless altered by God would issue in such a dispersion. In fact, this passage is the completion of the themes of the section whose development proceeds as follows: Ahaz trusts Assyria despite God's promised presence; Assyria decimates Judah; but Assyria is an arrogant tool and God is truly *with* his people. Therefore, God must destroy Assyria and redeem his people if his character is really righteousness and faithfulness. Furthermore, the omission of any reference to Babylon is unaccountable if the passage was written after 586 B.C.[9]

10, 11 These verses appear to be in prose and both begin with the formula: *It shall be in that day.* These features suggest that they may have been independent of each other and of the larger context, but were brought to this point to act together as a general introduction, a function

9. On Kaiser's argument that the references to Assyria betray a usage of the late 3rd or 2nd century B.C., see Y. Kaufmann, *The Religion of Israel*, p. 350 n. 2, who shows that the Bible does not confuse Syria with Assyria. For a full discussion see G. Hasel, *Remnant*, pp. 343–48. Cf. Mauchline also.

they fulfill admirably. They make it plain that the Messiah will be the banner around whom the remnant will gather in God's grace. Apart from the revelation of the Messiah any return will be but a temporal matter whose ultimate significance is always in doubt.

the root of Jesse which will be standing as an ensign is significant for several reasons. The contrast with 5:26 is one of these. There God raises an ensign to call the nations to the dismemberment of his people. Here he raises another ensign to call his people home. Once again, the prophet emphasizes God's dependability. Not only will he keep his promises to his people, he will also keep his promises to Jesse's son. Though the hand of God may destroy, it will ultimately be used to redeem. This truth is underlined when we look at the full revelation of the Messiah in Jesus Christ. The way in which he was lifted up (John 12:32) is a testimony to God's faithfulness both to punish sins and also to make redemption possible. So, the nations come streaming to the God who, in himself, has satisfied his love and his justice and has opened for us a way into his presence.

the Sovereign will again, a second time, [extend] his hand expresses the power of God in restoration. The kings of the earth may claim sovereignty as they destroy the peoples around them, but the Sovereign can pluck their prey out of their hands at will. Moreover, the true display of sovereignty is in redemption. Anyone can destroy, but who can give life again? This is God's work (cf. chs. 34 and 35; 48:14–22; 49:22–26; 62:10–63:9). Nor is faith in this redeeming work of God without precedent. Once before he has shown his capacity and will to save, namely, in the Exodus (cf. v. 15). Therefore, there is every reason to believe, in spite of overwhelming odds, humanly speaking, that he can do it again.

from Assyria . . . sea covers the known world in a complete way. Assyria and Egypt were the dominant world powers, the one to the northeast and the other to the southwest. Egypt was apparently subdivided into three regions: the Delta *(Egypt),* the Nile Valley *(Pathros),* and Nubia or Ethiopia in the far south *(Cush). Elam* and *Shinar* refer to extreme southern Mesopotamia and Persia, while *Hamath* is to the north in Syria and *the islands of the sea* lie in the west.[10] This completeness suggests that these names were not being used literally, although the Jews were ultimately dispersed very widely.[11] Rather, the purpose is more figurative, attempting to say that God is able to restore his people from *everywhere* (cf. v. 12).

10. Gray sees "islands of the sea" as a typically Deutero-Isaianic phrase. In fact, it appears only here and in 24:15. "Islands" by itself appears 3 times in chs. 1–39, 9 times in chs. 40–55, and 3 times in chs. 56–66.

11. Cf. the Elephantine Papyri (*ANET,* pp. 491–92), which indicate that a group of Jews were upon the island of Pathros on the border of Egypt and Nubia ca. 409 B.C.

12 This verse seems to say in poetic form what the preceding verses say in prose. Returnees will come from the entire earth. The paralleling of Israel and Judah is significant because it speaks to Isaiah's vision of the remnant. He does not subscribe to the idea of "the ten lost tribes" in the sense that Judah merely becomes a new Israel while the rest disappear. The remnant will be a restoration of the whole.[12]

13, 14 The prophet, having envisioned the return of the scattered population, now pictures a restoration in terms of the conditions under King David. The two parts of the country will be united: no longer will Judah lord it over Ephraim, nor will Ephraim be motivated by jealousy of Judah. Furthermore, the old Israelite hegemony over the surrounding territory will be reestablished. The Shephelah between the hill country and the coast (*the shoulder of the Philistines*) will be reconquered. The peoples of Moab, Ammon, and Edom will be subdued. No longer will Israel live in fear of her neighbors. G. A. Smith denigrated this picture of enforced submission as being unworthy of the great prophet of peace. However, one should not impose nineteenth-century A.D. ideas of a mutually-agreed-upon cessation of war on the eighth-century B.C. prophet. In fact, the idea of peace as a result of the mutual agreement of nations is not a biblical one. The biblical (and Isaianic) idea is of a peace which results from mutual submission to an overwhelming Sovereign (e.g., 9:3–6 [Eng. 4–7]; 63:1–6; Rev. 19:11–16). Only when God has defeated his enemies and they have submitted to him is the vision of peace in 11:6–9 a possibility. The difficulty which the Hebrews had was in admitting that they, too, were the enemies of God who needed to submit to him.[13] They, as we, wished to see themselves as the darlings of God, who could use God to accomplish their own political purposes. This is not the picture that Isaiah is projecting here; rather, he is saying once again that Israel's sin cannot destroy the promises of God to Israel.[14] In a figurative way he points to a coming time of internal and external safety and security similar to that which they knew under David but to be secured by One greater than David.

12. Cf. also chs. 40–65, where the common reference is to Israel and Jacob and not to Judah in isolation (references to Judah appear in 40:9; 44:26; 48:1; 65:9). Note the chiastic structure of the verse where the first and fourth phrases are parallel, as are the second and third.

13. See 6:9–13; 8:14, 15; 63:10; Lam. 2:4, 5; Hos. 13:4–8; Rom. 5:10; Col. 1:21; Jas. 4:4.

14. There is no emphasis upon repentance here and little upon purification (except v. 13). However, the need for those is made clearly enough elsewhere (1:18–20; 4:2–4; 31:6, 7; 35:8–10; etc.). The emphasis here is upon God's intention and ability to restore them. If he will not, or cannot, do this, then there is no hope for Israel.

15, 16   In concluding this promise of the return, Isaiah recalls the Exodus.[15] As he did once before, the Lord will strike[16] the *tongue* (any bay or gulf) of the Egyptian, or Red, Sea. But he will also strike the Euphrates, for this return will be from Assyria as well as from Egypt. He will send a searing wind over it dividing the river into seven wadis, or stream beds, which the people will be able to cross without even taking off their sandals. The result will be a way prepared for the people of God to return. Thus it is always. God will make a way where human power cannot avail. In this recognition of, and dependence upon, God's gracious power lies the hope of the world. What we cannot do, he will.

A final word must be said about such passages as this one. Unless there were genuinely predictive prophecies pointing to the salvation and restoration of the Jewish nation, it is hard to understand how that nation retained its identity and its traditions when others did not. If these "prophecies" were all written after the fact, it seems unlikely that there would have been any surviving nation to receive them. Rather, in the words of the late G. E. Wright, "It is because of the prophecies such as this that the Hebrews as a people survived the destruction of their nation and the annihilation of most of their brethren and remained a people of the Lord."[17] In short, because of the confidence engendered by the prophetic promises the very disasters which spelled the end of the ancient world brought a transformation in Israel's faith that was to make it no longer a national religion but a genuinely universal one.

4. THE SONG OF TRUST (12:1 – 6)

1 *You will say in that day,*
   "I will praise you, Lord,
      for though[1] you are angry[2] with me,

15. The book frequently refers to the Exodus: 4:5; 10:26–27; 35:8–10; 43:16–17; 50:2; 63:11, 12.
16. Cf. n. 7 above. Perhaps the meaning is "to dry up."
17. Wright, *The Book of Isaiah*, The Layman's Bible Commentary (Richmond: John Knox, 1964), p. 51.
1. *kî*, "for," normally has a causal function in this setting: a song of praise with the *kî* introducing the reason for praise. But the singer is not praising God because he was angry, which the simple "for" would suggest. Rather, the praise is for the entire process and its outcome: anger, anger removed, comfort instead. In English it is necessary to add "though" to make the point clear.
2. Skinner observes that this word for anger, *'ānap*, is nowhere else used in the Prophets. It is, however, used by the psalmists (2:11; 60:3 [Eng. 1]; 79:5; 85:6 [Eng. 5]) and is entirely fitting in this hymnic setting.

> your anger turned away[3]
> and you comforted me.
> 2 Behold, God[4] is my salvation;[5]
> I will trust and not fear.
> For my strength and my song[6] is Yah, the Lord,[7]
> and he has become my salvation."
> 3 You will draw water with rejoicing
> from the springs of salvation.
> 4 You will say in that day,
> "Praise the Lord,
> call on his name;
> make known among the peoples his deeds;
> call to remembrance that his name is exalted.
> 5 Sing to the Lord, because he has done high things;
> let this be known[8] in all the earth.
> 6 Shout and sing, O inhabitant of Zion,
> for great in your midst is the Holy One of Israel."

3. In form *yāšōḇ* is identical to the jussive, which would be translated "let it turn back." However, the shortened form is not exclusively used to convey the jussive. Especially in the Psalms the jussive has an indicative force (Ps. 11:6; 18:13 [Eng. 12]; 47:5 [Eng. 4]; 107:29; cf. GKC, § 109k).

4. 1QIs[a] has *'el*, "God," twice. Kaiser takes the first to be the preposition "to, unto, in," and reads "*in* God is my salvation." On the basis of Syr., *BHK* proposed *'al*, "upon." Other commentators suppose the reading in 1QIs[a] to be a dittograph.

5. Note that Isaiah's name probably means "Yahweh is salvation." This verse seems to expand upon the meaning of the name.

6. Recent commentators have pointed out that one would normally expect "strength" to be followed by a synonym like "might" instead of "song." On this basis, Kissane notes Arab. *zamara*, "protection," and Young Ugar. *zmr*, "strength." However, "song" fits the larger context very well (as it also does in Exod. 15:2, to which Isa. 12:2 seems to allude), and the versional support for "song" is strong.

7. Note the use of the divine names here. It appears that the prophet uses both in a conscious way. Not only is *'el*, the God of the patriarchs (Gen. 14:22; 17:1; cf. also Isa. 40:18; 45:14), the almighty One, the Savior, used, but so also is *Yah*, the Lawgiver, the self-revealing One (Exod. 15:2). This use is interesting in view of the documentary theory. The names are evidently understood to be synonyms and thus interchangeable. The MT has "Yah" plus "YHWH" ("the Lord"). LXX lacks "Yah" but has "the Lord"; Exod. 15:2 has "Yah" but lacks "the Lord"; Targ. has both if "the Terrible One" is a paraphrase for "Yah," as seems likely. Perhaps the LXX represents the original whereas the MT is a conflation of that original and Exod. 15:2.

8. "let this be known" is based on the Qere, which is pointed as a Hophal participle. The Ketib appears to be a Pual participle, which elsewhere means "acquaintance."

This brief paean of praise incorporating two shorter fragments (vv. 1b–2, 4–6)[9] brings chs. 7–12 (or 6–12) to a fitting close. However one evaluates the conclusion current since Ewald (1840) that the chapter must be dated no earlier than postexilic times, it must be obvious (cf. Gray) that the chapter was written as a conclusion to the preceding ones.[10] There are a number of reasons for such an assertion. Chief among them is God as Savior. Throughout chs. 7–11 there is the recurring appeal to the house of David and to Judah to put aside their fears of the nations around them and to focus their primary attention upon God, who is master of the nations and who is utterly trustworthy. That trustworthiness is underlined by the promise that although their refusal to trust will issue in defeat and despair, it will not result in complete destruction of Israel as a people. Although God is under no external obligation to do so, he will deliver them from the chains which their own hands have forged. Ch. 12 looks to a time when the people will have drawn the appropriate conclusions, the very ones Isaiah has been pressing, as a result of God's gracious activity. The truths are made the more powerful because they are put in the lyrical

---

9. Note that vv. 4–6 show something of a threefold chiasm. Verse 4a, b parallels v. 6a, b, while v. 4c parallels v. 5b and v. 4d parallels v. 5a.

10. Ewald reached his conclusion on the basis of stylistic matters (differing vocabulary) as well as the obvious treatment of the restoration as an accomplished fact. Gray and others proposed to date it even later than postexilic times because of its affinity with "late" Psalms. As Kaiser points out, however, the language factors are not enough to deny its authorship to Isaiah, esp. since the dating of the Psalms has been subject to a great deal of re-evaluation in the light of the Ugaritic literature (see M. Dahood, *Psalms*, 3 vols., AB [Garden City: Doubleday, 1965–1970]). Kaiser, instead, attributes the chapter to another hand than Isaiah's because he sees no appropriate setting for it in the preaching of Isaiah. However, there is a certain circularity in this kind of reasoning. To be sure, if all promises of a return from exile are denied to "Isaiah of Jerusalem" then there is no place for the prophet to burst into a song of joy over that prospect. On the other hand, if ch. 11 is authentic to Isaiah, then there is every reason for him to incorporate such materials as these in his proclamation. Furthermore, the overall content of the chapter is closely connected to the entire subsection, as is shown in the exposition. (Cf. Kissane in support of an Isaianic origin.) If this chapter was put together by an editor much later than Isaiah in a conscious effort to conclude and summarize the materials now comprising chs. 7–11, it is very strange that there is no overt reference to the Messiah, who plays so significant a role in those chapters. Surely a conscious attempt at summarization would not overlook him. On the other hand, if the materials all stem from about the same time and ch. 12 is considered merely a climax to what has been said but not a conscious summarization, the absence of mention of the Messiah is understandable.

language of worship rather than in mere discursive prose. In this way, the hearer and the reader are no longer spectators or objects of instruction. Now they are participants involved on the emotional and volitional levels as well as the cognitive one.

1, 2 Here, the frequently repeated phrase *in that day* takes on a diametrically opposite tone from the one found in such places as 2:20; 3:18; 4:1; 7:18, 20, 21, 23. There the coming day was one to be dreaded, but here, as in 4:2; 10:20; and 11:10, it is a day to be hoped for. Once again, the prophet has underlined that judgment is not God's last word. For all who will, promise lies beyond judgment.

The central focus of these verses, as well as the entire song, is upon God. This is what Isaiah has been appealing for (8:12–23 [Eng. 9:1]; so also 31:1, 2; 33:17–22; 40:12–31; etc.). Whenever Israel focuses primarily upon her needs she is in difficulty, for supply of those needs becomes the ultimate goal and all else, including the Sovereign of the universe, becomes but a means to that end. This attitude is a sure prescription for spiritual disaster.

Thus praise and thanks are essential to robust spiritual life, not because God needs them like some neurotic tyrant, but because we need to give them. It is only in this way that we can refocus our attention upon how much we have received from a loving Father and in that appreciation stop attempting to use him as our servant (idolatry). Thus, Kilpatrick *(IB)* says, "Any revival of religion which may yet come to the world will be marked by a new outburst of thanksgiving."

The source of the praise is the amazing discovery that God's anger has been removed and that he, the former enemy, has in fact become a source of encouragement and tender support. This change is not merely an arbitrary change of outlook on the part of One who can do as he wishes. 40:1 helps to underline this point. Since God's anger is based on a just cause, and is not the result of personal pique, the comfort of God comes only after sin and iniquity have been punished. Since our sin is an offense against the laws of the universe and against the loving Author of life and well-being, it cannot be dismissed and its results merely abrogated, any more than a person who in a fit of rage has kicked a table can expect his foot suddenly to stop hurting. The Jews understood this principle when they said, "It is the blood that makes atonement" (Lev. 17:11; cf. also Gen. 4:3–5). So did the early Christians, as seen in Heb. 9:22, "Without the shedding of blood, there is no forgiveness for sin." So thoughtful hearers of Isaiah's word would understand that some sort of atoning sacrifice had been made and that God's just anger had not merely disappeared but had in fact been re-directed to another victim. But who can stand in another person's stead? Micah asks every devout Jew's question: can sacred oil, fatted calves, one's own children take the sinner's place (Mic. 6:6, 7)? Ultimately, the answer to each of these is no. Nevertheless, the prophet makes bold to say that there is a person who can take the place of the entire people (53:10–12).[11] Thus, ch. 12 asks a question by implication. How can God's anger be turned to comfort? From whence will come the atoning sacrifice? The question is not answered until it is considered in detail in chs. 40–55. Yet its presentation here prepares the way for that eventual answer and forces the reader to begin to think about it.

Behold, God is my salvation expresses the truth that there is no salvation apart from God. It is not merely *that* he saves; he *is* salvation. To know him is to know deliverance and not to know him is to be deluded about deliverance. This is why the prophets in general, and Isaiah in particular, heap such scorn upon attempts to find deliverance in the might of this world (30:1–5; 31:1–3; Jer. 42:7–17; Ezek. 29:6–9; Hos. 5:13, 14; 7:8–12; 8:8–10). Liberation, whether political or personal, is found in God or it is not found at all. Isaiah has been urging this understanding upon his people. Now he foresees a day when they will finally grasp the truth.

I will trust and not fear is what Isaiah was attempting to get Ahaz to say in 7:2–9. In fact, Ahaz could not say it. Overcome by his fear of Ephraim and Syria, he could not believe that God was with him. As a result, he put his trust in an alliance with his ultimate enemy, Assyria. How can God get Judah to believe that he is really with them? For they can never forsake their pride and their manipulative understanding of religion and become servants until they are able to commit themselves to God. Ultimately, Isaiah sees that this change will be possible only when God in an act of free grace moves on their behalf. For the Jews, this act of grace was the return from exile in 539 B.C. However, there has been a much more climactic demonstration of God's free grace in his Son. Should we not trust a God who would, without any prior commitment on our part, give his Son for us (Rom. 5:8; 1 John 4:9, 10)? Only fear, fear that God will not keep his word, fear of giving up control, can keep us from trusting.

Those who can leap across the chasm of fear into trust will discover what they have in the Lord. He is their strength, he is their song, and he

11. Despite its valid emphasis upon the objective national aspects of salvation in the OT, liberation theology continues to manifest a shallow grasp of the meaning of atonement for, and the repentance of, the oppressed. This lack suggests that the sin is not merely on the side of the oppressors but also on the side of the oppressed, where bondage may be as much subjective as objective.

will become their salvation. When the believer is helpless, then God's power is manifest (Deut. 7:6, 7; 2 Cor. 12:9), and that is a cause for singing. It is not an accident that the deliverance at the Red Sea issued in a song or that the throng gathered about the throne of the Lamb will be singing. For song is the natural expression of the spirit which is free, and no spirit is so free as that one which has discovered that its destiny is not dependent upon its striving but rather upon the infinite power of the Almighty (cf. 26:1–15).

3–6 The prophet now expands the scope of the song. Whereas vv. 1 and 2 tended to be more inner-directed, these verses are directed outward. The world must know who God is (2:1–4). They must be enabled to draw the correct implication from the salvation of God's people. Once again this is a theme which is allowed to lie dormant until chs. 40–55, but it is introduced here as a way of showing in advance the logical conclusion of the prophet's teaching. Far from trusting in the nations for her own salvation, Israel is intended to be the vehicle whereby the nations can come to God. For whatever they may believe, there is only One who can lay claim to the title the Holy One, and he is the God of Israel. Thus there is only One in whom salvation rests.

Verse 3 is somewhat difficult to place. On the one hand, it would seem to go with vv. 1 and 2 with its emphasis upon joyous salvation. However, both pronouns in those verses are in the singular (2nd person in v. 1a, 1st person in vv. 1b–2), whereas the pronouns in vv. 3–6 are in the plural. Furthermore, it can be argued that to *draw . . . from the springs* means to manifest God's salvation to the world (Ps. 116:13), in the practical areas of one's own life, as indicated in vv. 4 and 5. The frequent use of water as an image for salvation is very understandable in land as dry as Israel. What water is to the parched earth, God's delivering presence is to the one oppressed by sin and bondage (8:6; 31:21; 35:6–7; 44:3; 55:1; Jer. 2:13; Ps. 42:2, 3 [Eng. 1, 2]; 46:5, 6 [Eng. 4, 5]; John 4:15; 7:37, 38; Rev. 7:17). It is also likely that the Exodus imagery alluded to in the passage is carried on here with the idea of God's provision of water in the wilderness (Exod. 17:1–7).

4, 5 Verse 4 has many parallels in the Psalms. Ps. 105:1 and 148:13 are almost identical, but the thought is also expressed in such places as 145:4–7. The emphasis upon the name of the Lord here is not to say that some magical power is to be associated with the particular letters or sounds of the divine name. Rather, it refers to God's reputation and character (cf. Matt. 6:9). So, to call upon the name of the Lord is to worship him on the basis of the faithful, delivering character revealed in his behavior (1 K. 18:24). Thus, when Abraham had been brought to the promised land, he "called upon the name of the Lord" (Gen. 12:8). So, here Isaiah predicts that the restored people will gain a new conviction of God's holy character, so much so that they will not only commit themselves to him but will also want all those around to know what he is like as well. The world needs to know that in contrast to all the heights of creation (Isa. 2:12–17; 13:3, 11, 19; 16:6), the Lord is the only One who is truly high. So long as the world seeks to exalt itself, it pursues a will-of-the-wisp that will eventually exhaust it. But if it will recognize his unique glory, it will find well-being and gracious exaltation streaming from him who alone can give them (60:13, 15).

6 It is hardly coincidence that the final verse of this section of the book closes with the phrase *the Holy One of Israel*,[12] for it is this concept which underlies everything said here. As said above, holiness is the sum total of the attributes of deity. Fundamentally, it denotes that which separates God from mere humanity. What Isaiah had discovered in an experiential way was what the whole faith of Israel was about, namely, that the *only* Holy One in the universe is Israel's God. But beyond that, his character, the content of his holiness, sets him apart. For that character is radically different from the idols. He is upright and clean, pure and true. In the light of all this, the greatest folly a people could commit would be to treat this God like an idol, one among many who could be manipulated by the worshiper in rites expressing nothing but the unclean, self-serving motives of the worshiper, an impersonal force which had little to do with day-to-day political realities. Such a course could lead only to disaster (6:3). But precisely because of the holy nature of this God—the only God—there is hope (6:7, 13). For his otherness means that where humanity is fickle and perverse, he is faithful and true. Thus, because of God's holiness, the prophet can believe in a day yet to be when a restored people will in hilarious celebration delight in their only asset—the Holy One. This belief in turn points to the meaning of God's self-revelation: that he, the Holy One, might dwell among his creatures (Exod. 40:34, 35; Isa. 57:15; 66:1, 2; John 1:14; 14:15, 17).

---

12. The phrase "The Holy One of Israel" occurs 29 times in the Bible. Of these, 26 are in Isaiah, 13 in chs. 1–39 and 13 in chs. 40–60. The remaining 3 occurrences are in the Psalms (71:22; 78:41; 89:19 [Eng. 18]). If Isaiah is dependent upon the hymnic literature for the title, he certainly made it his own. On the other hand, Isaiah may have given the term its currency, from whence it entered the poetic repertoire. Cf. W. H. Schmidt, "Wo hat die Aussage: Jahwe der Heilige ihren Ursprung?" *ZAW* 74 (1962) 62–66.

B. GOD: MASTER OF THE NATIONS (13:1–35:10)

1. GOD'S JUDGMENT ON THE NATIONS (13:1–23:18)

a. JUDGMENT ON THE MESOPOTAMIAN POWERS (13:1–14:27)

(1) Introduction: God's destruction of human pride (13:1–18)

(a) Mustering God's army (13:1–5)

> 1 The burden[1] of Babylon which Isaiah son of Amoz saw:
> 2 On a bare hill, raise up an ensign;
>> lift up a voice to them.
> Wave a hand,
>> and let them enter the gates of the nobles.
> 3 I have commanded my holy ones;
>> moreover, I have called my warriors for my wrath,
>> those who will exult[2] in my exaltation.
> 4 A sound of a multitude on the mountains,
>> like a great people.
> A sound of a roar of kingdoms,
>> nations assembled.
> The Lord of Hosts is mustering
>> a host for war.
> 5 They are coming from a distant land,
>> from the end of the heavens,
> the Lord and the instruments of his indignation
>> to destroy all the earth.

1. The precise meaning of *maśśā᾿*, "burden," is not clear. It has frequently been taken to mean literally a threat (cf. Scott; so also H. S. Gehman, "The Burden of the Prophets," *JQR* 31 [1940–1941] 107–121). But Cheyne points out that the term has no threatening overtones in Zech. 9:1; 12:1; Prov. 30:1; 31:1; Lam. 2:14; or Jer. 23:33. Thus others have suggested that the term connotes a lifting up of the voice, hence "oracle" (Skinner; cf. KB). The truth may be halfway between these. On the basis of Jer. 23:33, S. Erlandsson, *The Burden of Babylon*, ConBOT 4 (Lund: Gleerup, 1970), p. 65, suggests that the meaning "burden" is only a pun on a term which is merely a synonym for "word"; cf. Isa. 2:1 and 13:1, where *ḥāzâ* is used with *dābār*, "word," and *maśśā᾿*, respectively.

2. *῾allîz*, "to exult," appears only in Isaiah (22:2 and 24:8, both of which convey the idea of unbridled delight).

As noted in the Introduction, few modern studies of the book of Isaiah make any attempt to analyze the present form of the prophecy. This is so, because it has been concluded that this form is merely the result of historical accident, betraying the hands of numerous redactors, all working out differing purposes and visions of reality. As in the present case, however, the materials are much more coherent than is usually granted. Nor is it necessary to insist that the book was first written in its present order or at the same time in order to maintain this point of view. It is only necessary to permit that the final editing process (why not by the author?) was carried out with the intention of creating a vision no less inspired than that involved in the original speaking and writing.

The chapters under consideration here call for such an interpretation, for the relationships among them are too clear and too powerful to have been arrived at merely by chance. As noted above (see on 7:1–9), one central theme runs through chs. 7–39—the trustworthiness of God. It is frequently said that the major theme of "Isaiah of Jerusalem"[3] is the inviolability of Jerusalem.[4] But that is not true of chs. 1–39 in their present form. Jerusalem is only inviolate if she finds the correct place in which to repose her trust: the living God. If she places it anywhere else, especially in the nations of mankind, she will be destroyed. Both chs. 7–12 and chs. 36–39 make this same point. Ahaz trusts Assyria and the promised result is destruction. Hezekiah trusts God and Assyria is destroyed. Between these two segments come the chapters under consideration here. They are united by this common theme: the God of Israel is the Lord of the nations.[5] Their fate is in his hands (chs. 13–23); he is the sovereign actor on the stage of history, not they (chs. 24–27); trusting the nations instead of the King is foolishness (chs. 28–33); the ultimate results are: trust the nations, a desert; trust God, a garden (chs. 34, 35). This analysis means that chs. 36–38 are not a historical appendix to the previous materials. They are, in fact, the living out of the truths taught in chs. 13–35. Ahaz failed the test, but Hezekiah has learned the lessons and at least initially passes the test with high marks.

3. A term used to identify the supposed author of the "original" parts (those dating prior to 700).

4. R. de Vaux, "Jerusalem and the Prophets," in *Interpreting the Prophetic Tradition* (Cincinnati: Hebrew Union College; New York: KTAV, 1969), pp. 285–87; J. Hayes, "The Tradition of Zion's Inviolability," *JBL* 82 (1963) 419–426.

5. This relationship is one of "continuation," the development of a theme toward an ultimate conclusion or summation. Cf. R. A. Traina, *Methodical Bible Study* (New York: Biblical Seminary, 1952), pp. 50–51.

Thus, whatever may be said about the ultimate origin of the materials in these chapters, they do not come to us as a hodgepodge of ideas, thrown together at random. Rather, they are related in such a way as to form a coherent and compelling statement which demands our attention and response today as much as it did then. We must trust either in the nations or in God, and no book on earth will ever make the case for trusting God more forcefully.

Chapters 13–23 form one of the most easily recognized units in the book of Isaiah because of the recurrence of the word *maśśā'*, "burden" (RSV, NIV "oracle"), throughout.[6] Furthermore, on first glance at least, it appears that all the pronouncements are of doom upon Israel's enemies. However, closer examination makes it clear that the situation is more complex. 14:1–4a; 17:4–11; and 22:1–14 are all addressed to Judah, the last as an oracle. 17:12–14 and 18:1–7 begin with "woe" rather than "burden" and are not clearly addressed to a people (although Ethiopia does appear in 18:1). Furthermore, the "oracles" have no geographical ordering.[7] Thus it is all the more imperative to attempt to discover the function of this material in the present order of the text. Only this function can explain why these materials have been grouped as they have in this place.[8]

Delitzsch is undoubtedly correct when he sees these chapters as following naturally upon the vision of Immanuel as ruler of the kingdoms. Young is also correct when he observes that the thought is generally an expansion of 10:5–34 with its attack upon the pride of Assyria. But perhaps Erlandsson gives the most perceptive key when he comments that these oracles are not so much an announcement of doom upon the nations as they are an announcement of salvation to Israel if she would trust her Lord.[9] Without doubt the nations never heard these words or, if so, only second-hand, but Israel heard them first-hand. Thus, they are an answer

6. See 13:1; 14:28; 15:1; 17:1; 21:1, 11, 13; 22:1; 23:1.
7. Cf. M. Weiss, "The Pattern of the 'Execration Texts' in the Prophetic Literature," *IEJ* 19 (1969) 150–57, who convincingly shows that only great imagination can find the same geographic pattern here which exists in the Egyptian Execration Texts.
8. Even if the segments are of vastly different dates, a conclusion Erlandsson effectively questions on methodological grounds (*Burden*, pp. 86, 87), there must have been an organizing principle leading the compilers to group them in this way at this point in the book.
9. Erlandsson, *Burden*, pp. 65, 66. Wright, "The Nations in Hebrew Prophecy," *Encounter* 26 (1965) 225–237, suggests that there is a sense of grief in these announcements because of the failure of the nations to abide by God's universal laws as seen in the treaty forms. But this suggestion seems to put more into the mouths of the prophets than is really there. Cf. J. H. Hayes, "The Usage of Oracles Against Foreign Nations in Ancient Israel," *JBL* 87 (1968) 81–92.

to questions raised in chs. 7–11. Can God deliver Israel from the pomp
and power of the world? Will he be able to restore her as ch. 11 promises?
The answer is a resounding yes. Furthermore, these chapters demonstrate
the folly of trusting in nations whose doom is already sealed. God is the
master of the nations. It is at his command that the armies move out to
destroy one after another, both great and small. Thus, it is foolish for
Israel to trust in her own system of alliances, with the necessary commitments to foreign gods, to save her. Only God, who has promised to save
her, can save her.

Furthermore, the section continues the treatment of pride which
appears in the first chapters of the book. It is the arrogance of the nations
that will finally bring them down (13:11, 19; 14:11; 16:6; 23:9). Because
they have exalted themselves in the face of God, creating gods in their
image (2:6–22; 17:7–11), they will not endure. Permanence is only an
expression of a relationship with the one permanent Being in the universe.

Observation of the segment suggests that this element of pride
provides the key to the organization. Chs. 13 and 14, which open the unit,
are clearly an attack not so much upon the historical Babylon (cf. 21:10
for that) as they are upon that which Babylon has always represented:
human glory. In this sense, Babylon was a much better choice to represent
this motif than Nineveh, which was always seen as somewhat less cultured
than Babylon even by the Assyrians.[10] Similarly, the oracle against Tyre
that closes the unit is expressed in highly charged images which suggest
that much more than historical Tyre is being attacked. Instead, it is the
commercial conquest upon which human wealth and glory have always
rested that is condemned. It is interesting that the imagery applied to
Babylon in the book of Revelation is particularly drawn from the description of Tyre here (Rev. 17:1–6). The recognition that Babylon was at the
eastern end of the civilized word while Tyre was at the west, along with
the highly symbolic language applied to each, suggests a bracketing effect
which underlines the point of the unit: all human pride and accomplishment are under God's judgment. Thus an Israel trusting in these is without
hope (22:1–25), but an Israel trusting in God has nothing to fear from the
nations of mankind (14:1–4a).

The development of the unit seems to proceed as follows: judgment
upon pride symbolized by the eastern power (13:1–14:27);[11] judgment

10. See Erlandsson, *Burden*, p. 88.
11. Erlandsson, *Burden*, pp. 160–66, argues very convincingly that the
entire section relates to Assyria: the destruction wrought by her, the folly of opposing her, and the certainty of her destruction at God's hand. Thus he argues that

upon neighboring nations, who threaten Judah but with whom Judah sought to ally herself against the eastern power (14:28–17:6); a restatement of the need for dependence on God and of the results of the absence of such dependence (17:7–18:7); judgment upon Egypt in whom Judah was tempted to trust (19:1–20:6); judgment upon the Chaldeans and their allies who called for revolt against Assyria (21:1–17); judgment upon sightless Judah (22:1–25); judgment on pride symbolized by the western power, Tyre.

In 13:1–14:27, the opening segment of the judgments upon the nations, the focus is upon Babylon (13:1, 19; 14:4, 22), an emphasis which seems odd to the reader having just come from chs. 7–12, where all the attention is on Assyria. Furthermore, there is no oracle in the entire unit (chs. 13–23) against Assyria. The brief words in 14:24–27 seem to be a postscript to the Babylon oracle. These two factors—the sudden appearance of Babylon, which was not an empire in its own right until nearly a century after Isaiah, and the absence of a reference to Assyria— have led many scholars to believe that this segment at least must be dated no earlier than the exilic times when Babylon's downfall was imminent.[12]

This point of view is not necessary, however. There is every reason to believe that Babylon, the center of culture and trade in the world long before the rise of the Neo-Babylonian empire, is being used in the symbolic way mentioned above to introduce this unit which portrays God's overthrow of national pomp and pride. The whole tenor of the language favors the symbolic interpretation (13:5, "from the ends of the heaven"; 13:10, the heavenly bodies darkened; 13:11, the world punished for its arrogance; etc.).[13] The cultural dominance of Babylon is indicated by the degree of independence granted to it by Assyria until its final revolt was quelled in 689. Even Tiglath-pileser III felt it necessary to be crowned king of Bab-

---

the original reference of ch. 13 is to Assyria. It is not necessary to accept this last point (see below) to recognize the essential correctness of his overall position. Note also that with the exception of 17:1–18:7, there is a rough chronological sequence for the pronouncements from 14:28 to ch. 23; cf. H. L. Ginsberg, "Reflexes of Sargon in Isaiah after 715 B.C.E.," *JAOS* 88 (1968) 47.

12. Skinner gives four reasons for such a conclusion: (1) Babylon was not a world power in Isaiah's day; (2) 14:1–3 has Israel in exile in Babylon; (3) Isaiah expected the overthrow of Assyria to be followed by the setting up of the messianic kingdom; (4) the forceful, vindictive style is not Isaianic. Lindblom argues that all references to the conversion and/or destruction of the nations are a result of the teaching of the Exile and the preaching of "Deutero-Isaiah" (*Prophecy in Ancient Israel* [Oxford: Blackwell; Philadelphia: Fortress, 1962], pp. 282–83).

13. Note how little a part historic Babylon plays here as opposed to Jer. 50, 51.

ylon.[14] Furthermore, it was during this period, from 720 to 708 B.C., that Sargon II had lost control of Babylon and during which time Babylon would have been currying favor wherever possible (as was still the case in 701 [39:1]). So, again Isaiah would have been warning against dependence upon this false hope.

In the same way, the Medes are used to represent fierce, implacable destruction (13:17–18). Many years before the Medo-Persian army of Cyrus accepted the surrender of Babylon in 539 B.C., the Medes had been recognized as a scourge by the Assyrians.[15]

Since Babylon was being considered as a symbol for Mesopotamia's glory and pride, and since Assyria, the particular expression of that power, had been fully dealt with in the immediately preceding context, it was only necessary for the prophet briefly to remind his hearers in 14:24–27 of the current reality and in that way to connect the symbols with the reality. In effect, then, it was unnecessary to construct a full-blown oracle against Assyria because it had already been covered in an oracle against Babylon.[16]

There are four larger sections in the two chapters: 13:1–18, God's Destruction of Human Pride; 13:19–22, Destruction of Babylon; 14:1–23, Downfall of the King of Babylon; 14:24–27, The Lord's Plan for Assyria.

1 In an unmistakable way, this verse links the oracle, and those that follow, to Isaiah.[17] There are really only two alternatives for understanding this statement: either it is an authentic statement of historical fact or a later author attempted to make it appear so (Kaiser). If the latter is the case, it must be asked why someone would make such an attempt. Is it not because the editor wished to persuade the readers that an evidence of God's power and authority is his capacity to reveal the course of events to people before those events come to pass (14:24, 26, 27; 41:21–27; 44:7, 8; 45:20, 21; etc.)? But if, in fact, Isaiah did not speak these words, the editor has resorted to a falsehood to prove a truth, something patently contradictory in a religion which stressed truthfulness as much as the Hebrew religion did. Nor will it do to say (with Gray) that someone merely

14. See Erlandsson, *Burden*, pp. 87–92. Cf. 2 K. 15:19, where the Babylonian throne-name "Pul" is used. Cf. also C. Boutflower, *Book of Isaiah, Chapters I–XXXIX* (London: SPCK, 1930), pp. 93–103.

15. See Erlandsson, *Burden*, pp. 86–87. In fact, it was the Persians, who had defeated the Medes, who peacefully took over Babylon in 539. It is difficult to imagine a contemporary of those events not referring to the Persians instead of the Medes.

16. Furthermore, in the providence of God, the symbolic use of Babylon gave the oracles a currency and power long after Assyria was gone.

17. See above, n. 1, for a discussion of the possible meaning of *maśśāʾ*.

thought Isaiah must have written it and inserted the conjecture here. It would have been unnecessary to insert the conjecture at this particular point unless it was felt theologically important to assert Isaiah's authorship here. If the editor has used a falsehood consciously or unconsciously to prove a "truth," then our acceptance of the "truth" becomes a matter of sheer credulity.

On the other hand, there are good reasons to accept the veracity of the statement. The Bible records that Isaiah ben Amoz had perceived that Babylon was the ultimate threat to Judah (39:5–7). Furthermore, as noted above, it is not necessary to believe that Isaiah had a complete picture of Nebuchadrezzar's Neo-Babylonian empire in mind to make these statements. He needed only to recognize that Babylon's glory was the true symbol of enmity toward God and that dependence on that glory for help against Assyria must finally prove as deadly as the dependence upon Assyria against Ephraim and Syria had been. Such a recognition would not come to the unaided human mind, but neither would it demand a suspension and replacement of the human faculties as some commentators seem to assume was necessary for a predictive prophecy to occur.[18]

2–3 The oracle begins with a picture of a call to arms. In a figure which Isaiah returns to frequently, a signal flag is run up on a barren hilltop where it can be seen by all around (cf. 5:26; 11:10, 12; 18:3; 49:22; 66:10). The army is called to enter *the gates of the nobles*, or perhaps "the noble gates." In either case, the allusion is to the haughty and elegant. The function of this army will be to cast down the proud (Jas. 4:6; 1 Pet. 5:5; Prov. 3:34). But this is not just any army. It has been called and assembled by God.[19] So these are God's warriors, consecrated to him to carry out his judgments and to exult in his being lifted up (v. 3). While the consecration may refer to certain purification rites carried out by soldiers prior to battle (1 Sam. 21:5, 6), it is more likely that the reference is merely to those who are set apart for God's use, whether they intend so or not (10:6, 7; 45:4–6; Jer. 22:7; Joel 2:2, 11).

4–5 In a series of elliptical phrases, either having no verb at all or utilizing a participle of imminence, these verses convey the sense of swiftly gathering doom (cf. 5:26–30). The *mountains* referred to may be

18. While Cheyne can say that the diction and style of 13:2–14:23 are not that of Isaiah, matters of diction and style are notoriously difficult to control. Thus Erlandsson, *Burden*, pp. 238–253, has come to the conclusion that the diction is indistinguishable from any "genuinely" Isaianic passage. The likelihood that Jer. 50, 51 are derived from Isaiah also argues for the authenticity of the material to Isaiah.

19. Note the emphatic "I" in Hebrew. No other than God has called.

the Zagros chain which parallels the Tigris River and forms the eastern boundary of Mesopotamia. They create a natural barrier against the invaders from the east. It is equally likely, however, that no particular mountains are referred to, but that they are representative of all the natural barriers depended upon for security. But here the enemy has surmounted the barriers and masses for the final attack. Nor is this merely a local skirmish. This army has come from all over the earth, even as far as *the end of the heavens*, the place where the earth and sky meet at the horizon (cf. Deut. 28:49, "the end of the earth"). Once again, the stress is upon this army as God's instrument. Who is coming? The Lord and the "vessels" of his wrath. This is truly the Master of history. How foolish to put one's trust in a host rather than in the Lord of Hosts.

(b) The day of the Lord against the proud (13:6–18)

> 6 *Howl, for the day of the Lord is near;*
> > *as destruction from the Almighty it will come.*
> 7 *Therefore, all hands will fall,*[1]
> > *and every human heart will melt.*
> 8 *They will be confounded;*[2]
> > *pains and anguish will seize them,*
> > > *they will writhe like a woman in labor.*
> *They shall be astounded at each other;*
> > *their faces shall be faces of flame.*
> 9 *Behold the day of the Lord comes,*
> > *pitiless and overflowing with wrath,*
> *to devastate the earth to devastation,*
> > *that its sinners*[3] *might be exterminated from it.*

1. For similar uses of "falling hands" cf. 35:3; 2 Sam. 4:1; Job 4:3; Jer. 6:24; 50:43; Ezek. 7:17; 21:12; Zeph. 3:16. Cf. also *UT*, 127:44, 45, and Akk. *nadê ahum*, "to throw the hands."

2. As *BHS* frames it, and Gray opines, "They will be confounded" may be part of a stich the rest of which is lost. While the Targ. and Vulg. follow the MT, the LXX supplies the subject "the old men."

3. Kissane argues that the use of "sinners" is proof that Judah was the original focus of ch. 13 (cf. 1:28; 4:4; 33:14, 15). On the other hand, Scott suggests that the use of "sinners" here indicates a late date, after a doctrine of a last judgment has been formulated. In fact, most of the occurrences of *ht'*, "sin," in Isaiah refer to Judah or Israel. This is not surprising since most of the book refers to them. Nonetheless, the context here supports the idea of universal judgment (cf. v. 11; *tēbēl* always refers to the entire world). As to the date, surely Amos's announcement of judgment upon the "sins" of Damascus, etc. is not from a late date nor does it presuppose a doctrine of final judgment.

10 *Even the stars in the heavens and their constellations[4]*
   will not shed their light.
The sun will be dark when it rises,
   and the moon will not give its light.
11 *I will visit[5] evil upon the earth,*
   and their iniquity upon the wicked.
I will turn back the pride of the arrogant
   and bring down the exultation of the mighty.
12 *I will make humanity rarer than fine gold,*
   and humankind than the gold of Ophir.[6]
13 *Therefore I will shake the heavens,*
   and the earth will tremble from its place[7]
in the anger of the Lord of hosts,
   and in the day of his wrath.
14 *Like a fleeing gazelle,*
   like a flock without a shepherd,
each one will turn to his people;
   each one will flee to his own land.
15 *Everyone found there will be pierced through,*
   and everyone caught will fall by the sword.
16 *Their children will be dashed to pieces before their eyes;*
   their houses demolished and their wives violated.
17 *Behold, I am rousing against them the Medes,*
   who do not consider silver
   and take no delight in gold.
18 *Bows will dash young men to pieces;[8]*

4. The singular form of the word translated "constellations" is *kᵉsîl*, "Orion." Jewish tradition holds that Orion is a "fool" *(kᵉsîl)* who has arrogantly challenged God and has been chained in the heavens.

5. *pāqaḏ* is the activity of a commander making an inspection. Thus it can connote appointment, punishment, commandment, or merely appearance. Here the idea is to punish.

6. Recent opinion places Ophir in east Africa. Procuring the high-quality gold of this area was one reason for Solomon's fleets (1 K. 9:26–28). Note that the Targ., probably feeling that preciousness connotes worth, makes "the righteous" more rare than gold. But this is contrary to the thrust of the whole passage.

7. The shift from 1st person, "I will shake the heavens," to 3rd, "the earth will tremble from its place," is troublesome to some commentators, who wish to emend one or the other to bring the two into exact parallelism. However, it is equally possible that the slight variation was poetically pleasing. Cf. Ps. 94:15.

8. The opening phrase of v. 18 is difficult; lit. "And bows [fem.] boys they [fem.] will dash to pieces." The figure of bows dashing people to pieces seems strange at first glance. The LXX has "They will shatter the bows of the young men," while the Targ. has "Their bows will pierce the young men," both seeming to be attempts to smooth the MT. But upon further reflection, the sense fits per-

on the fruit of the womb they will take no compassion,
on children they will not look with pity.

This passage begins fittingly with the word "Howl," for the following verses describes a scene of terror—the Day of the Lord (vv. 6, 9; cf. also Joel 1:5, 13, 15). It is a day when human strength will be helpless, when creation itself will tremble, when the almost boundless capacity for human cruelty will be unleashed. Like other prophets, Isaiah suggests that the cause of it all is the confrontation between the supremacy of God and that thirst for supremacy which is lodged in the human heart (v. 11; Amos 5:18–6:8; Mic. 5:10–15; Zeph. 1:7–16; 3:11; Mal. 3:19–21 [Eng. 4:1–3]; Isa. 2:11, 12, 17). Nor is it that the tyrant God can brook no rival. The human grasp for supremacy flies in the face of the natural order and uncages all these results just as the breaking of a physical law produces pain and disorder.

6 *As destruction from the Almighty* is a wordplay on *šdd*, the root of both *destruction* and *Almighty* (see also Joel 1:15; Ezek. 1:24; 10:5; Ruth 1:21; Ps. 68:15 [Eng. 14]; Gen. 49:25; Num. 24:4). The blow will be such a one that only God could have delivered it.

7–8 The immediate result of God's attack will be complete helplessness and impotence. Before God's power all the vaunted human greatness will be as nothing. Their nerve will desert them, and the weapons will fall from their limp fingers. They will stare at each other in an agony of both indecision and recognition. The recognition will be that everything in which they had reposed their trust had deserted them and they are stripped defenseless before God's piercing gaze. Probably it is this shame of having trusted in the wrong resources that accounts for the flaming faces of v. 8 (cf. Ps. 25:1–3), in that terror alone would be expected to produce paleness (Joel 2:6). All of this should provoke the modern reader to ask, "In what am I trusting to defend me before the Almighty?" There can be no other answer than that of the hymn writer: "Dressed in his righteousness alone, faultless I stand before the throne."

9–13 These verses amplify the universal nature of the Lord's judgment. Once again, it is the pride of humanity which provokes this disaster (v. 11b), so that nature, too, is caught up in the catastrophic events. The attempt by human beings to be independent has created shock waves which ultimately reach to the farthest constellations. On the earth, the immediate result of the lust for pomp and power is a devastating

---

fectly with the context, and the personification of weapons is well known in the ancient world, not least of all in Assyria; cf. Young, who cites W. G. Lambert, *AfO* 18 (1957) 40.

depopulation. The terrible death toll of World War I, when virtually an entire generation of European men was wiped out, and the frightening prospect that a nuclear war could leave the entire northern hemisphere uninhabitable, must take the statements of vv. 9 and 12 out of the realm of hyperbole and put them in the realm of principle.

9 *sinners* is placed in an emphatic position. The word conveys the idea of an archer who misses the target. So it is with sin, whether conscious or unconscious. It is to miss the goal God has envisioned for us. The inevitable result is devastation and destruction.

10 One of the features of the day of the Lord will be darkness.[9] The heavenly bodies will cease to shine and the world will be plunged into a terrible darkness. There is something entirely fitting about this, for evil always flourishes in the night-time hours (John 3:19, 20). Thus, if evil prefers darkness, darkness it shall have. Moreover, God is light (1 John 1:5; Ps. 139:11, 12), and the heavenly bodies are but reflections of him. (In Gen. 1:14, 15, they are called "light-bearers.") Thus, when God has withdrawn his blessing from the world, it is appropriate that the "lights" go out (cf. Matt. 27:45, 46).

There is probably another implication of these statements about the heavenly bodies. As noted in the comments on ch. 2, the ultimate expression of human pride is idolatry, the sin of making deity in the human image. The central figures in the pantheons of the idolatrous cults were the heavenly bodies: sun, moon, and stars. These bodies were endowed with human traits but were vested with superhuman power which could be manipulated by human beings through magic. Thus, their worship was an attempt to project humanity upon the stars in order to make humanity master of its own destiny (24:21; 34:4, 5; Jer. 7:18; 8:2; 44:17, 18, 19; Ezek. 8:16–18). It is in that context that Isaiah announces the extinguishing of the heavenly lights in God's great day. There is no universal power in the stars that human beings can capture for themselves. The stars are the obedient reflectors of a Light which lies beyond them (40:26).

11, 12 In these verses, the sin of pride is directly identified as the cause of God's wrath. The human attempt to reach a peak of ultimate, independent status will be blunted and turned back. In fact, humanity will receive its own sins come back upon itself. The irony of human behavior is that we expect to take advantage of others without being taken advantage of by others. In fact, we must expect to receive what we have done (33:1). In God's day all books will be balanced. The results will be the opposite

9. Cf. Amos 5:18; Joel 2:2, 31; 3:15; Ezek. 32:7; Mic. 3:6. Cf. also Matt. 24:29; Luke 21:25; Rev. 8:12.

of what pride expected. Instead of the earth being full of the presence and glory of humankind, it will be emptied by humanity. This is always the result of that which is attempted in defiance of God: the opposite of what was intended. A case in point would be Hitler's thousand-year Reich which ended in complete destruction hardly more than ten years after he proclaimed it.

13 This verse summarizes the thought of the previous four verses, indicating again that God is the Sovereign of all things, including heaven and earth, and that human sin has cosmic implications.

14–18 In these verses, there is a turn toward more this-worldly imagery with a special emphasis upon the savagery with which the proud city will be thrust down. It is often difficult for Americans, who are far removed from incessant warfare, both in time and distance, to grasp that almost casual cruelty to which most of the world is rather apathetic. The outrage over the My Lai massacre was in part a refusal to believe that "we" could do such a thing. But, in fact, prolonged and frustrating war normally results in a decreasing concern for pain and horror, and the people of the Near East to whom the book of Isaiah was written understood (and understand) this all too well. This is not to say that God is happy about such a turn of events, or that he wishes it to be so (Gen. 6:5, 6, 11, 12). It is to say that the building of human pride must eventually pit individual against individual, nation against nation in such a way that the most terrible savagery is the ultimate result. God wills this only in the sense that he has made a world of cause and effect where the denial of him and his ways must lead us to destroy ourselves.

14 This verse describes the flight which occurs when an army moves to attack a great city. Its glory and offers of wealth attracted many people from the surrounding region. In the Near East they would have come from the many small states and numerous ethnic groups. But as the city disintegrates about them, they quickly realize that its offers were empty and their only real refuge is with their own people.

15–18 The refugees fill the road because they are all too well aware of what a marauding army can do to them. The looting (v. 16) is bad enough, but worse than that are the rapine and the casual thirst for blood. A soldier can carry only so much loot; thus it soon becomes impossible to buy off any violent instinct which may have been nourished in the campaign (v. 17).

17 The *Medes* were a people of what is now central Iran, east of Mesopotamia. They inhabited the Zagros Mountains and the high plateaus east of the mountain range. As early as 836 B.C. the Assyrians referred to them as adversaries.[10] Although the Assyrians boasted of overcoming the Medes, they never occupied the Median capital of Ecbatana, and it was the Medes, along with the Babylonians, who destroyed the last vestiges of Assyria in 609. Because it was the Medes and Persians who overthrew Babylon in 539, many scholars believe that this reference is to that event and must therefore have been written about that time. However, it is equally significant to note that Isaiah makes no mention of the Persians, who were the main factor in the defeat in 539.[11] It seems unaccountable that anyone writing in the sixth century could have made such a glaring omission. On the other hand, it is quite possible that Isaiah of Jerusalem, writing in the late 700s, knew something of the Medes' fearsome reputation and used them as a figure of the pitiless destruction characterizing the Day of the Lord, without intending any specific prediction.[12]

(2) The destruction of Babylon (13:19–22)

19 Babylon, the jewel of kingdoms,
    proud beauty of the Chaldeans,
will be like God's overthrow
    of Sodom and Gomorrah.
20 She will not live there forever;
    she will not dwell there for endless generations.
The Arab will not tent there,
    and shepherds will not stretch out there.
21 But howling beasts will stretch out there,
    and owls will fill their houses.
The daughters of the ostrich will dwell there,
    and wild goats will leap about there.
22 Jackals will dwell among its fortresses[1]
    and hyenas in its exquisite palaces.

10. D. Luckenbill, *ARAB*, I:206. Cf. also C. Boutflower, *The Book of Isaiah, Chapters 1–XXXIX* (London: SPCK, 1930), pp. 87, 88. He notes that the Assyrians called the Medes "mighty," a rare accolade for the Assyrians to bestow on an enemy; cf. 13:3.

11. Cf. Gray.

12. Kissane cites 2 K. 17:6; 18:11 in support of this possibility. Erlandsson, *Burden*, pp. 91, 164–65, and Boutflower, *Book of Isaiah*, pp. 89, 90, speculate that Isaiah had in mind Sennacherib's violent conquest of rebellious Babylon in 689 B.C., and Boutflower suggests the Medes may have been involved in this event. But the figurative understanding of the oracle obviates the need for such a suggestion.

1. MT *'almānôt*, "widows." Probably a wordplay on *'armānôt*, "fortresses," indicating that the fortresses are only dejected widows. But possibly only a dialectal matter (an *l/r* interchange); LXX "there"; Targ. "castles."

Her time is near,
*   and her days will not be prolonged.*

In this segment, Isaiah draws the powerful contrast (as in chs. 24 and 34) between the temporary results of human pride and the ultimate results. As has been argued above (see on 13:1), Babylon in the late 700s B.C. was the showcase of the ancient world. She had emerged as the cultural and economic superior to the Assyrian cities in the north and was bidding for political sovereignty as well. Thus Babylon was the ideal image for the prophet to utilize as he sought to demonstrate how futile the greatest of human glory is against the Holy One of Israel. Undoubtedly, the inspired recognition that Babylon was Judah's ultimate enemy also prompted him in this direction, but the chief function of Babylon is figurative at this point. This understanding is supported by the fact that neither in 689, when Sennacherib put down the Babylonian rebellion with a violence much like that described in the previous verses (vv. 14–18), nor in Cyrus's much more peaceful takeover in 539 B.C. was Babylon abandoned. It is certainly true that Babylon, the jewel of the nations, was eventually abandoned and is today. In this way, Isaiah's prophecy has been fulfilled with a vengeance, but the fulfillment is more that of a principle than in a specific event. For these truths apply to Nineveh and Asshur equally as much as to Babylon. That monument to human glory and achievement, the sprawling imperial city, has no permanence in itself, and the day will come when the very weight of its glory will crash back in upon it and leave it desolate.[2] Only when the glory is a gift of God will there be continuing fruitfulness and joy (35:1, 2; 60:1–22, esp. 1–3, 13, 19).

19 For Isaiah, Sodom and Gomorrah were the paradigm for what he perceived to be happening in the world. Like Sodom and Gomorrah in their pride and sophistication, the cultures of his day would also be like them in experiencing divinely sent destruction (1:9, 10; 3:9). The NT follows this lead especially in relation to the end time (Luke 17:28–29; Rom. 9:29; 2 Pet. 2:6–10; Jude 7; Rev. 11:8).

20 Like v. 12, this verse speaks of the lack of human population. The point would not be disproven if from time to time bedouin tents were set up within the confines of what was once Babylon. The point is that humanity cannot sustain itself by itself. It cannot expect in its own strength

---

2. Cf. Browning's poem, "Ozymandias," based on the inscription of one of the Egyptian pharaohs, Rameses II. So also, the arrogant claims to sovereignty over the whole world by the Assyrian monarchs (cf. the annals of Ashurnasirpal, e.g., in Luckenbill, *ARAB,* I:138–141) lay buried in the rubble of Nineveh for 25 centuries.

to produce more and more of everything until it fills the earth. There has come the day, again and again, in war, in famine, or in pestilence when a self-sufficient portion of humanity has been brought face to face with its insufficiency. Thus far, in his mercy, God has allowed the torch to be passed to other civilizations, but as we move more and more toward a global society, Babylon's burden becomes more and more the word addressed to the entire earth. *God's* glory will fill the earth, not humanity's. If we will not learn that voluntarily, we must learn it involuntarily.

21, 22 Although precise identification of many of the animals mentioned in these verses is difficult,[3] the general sense is clear enough. These are animals which inhabit dark and lonely settings. There is something vaguely ominous about many of them. The mighty city is silent except for the hoots and howls of the night-dwellers. The lovely palaces and mighty fortresses alike have become the home of the jackals and hyenas who can only feed on the carrion left behind when the lions have eaten their fill. How are the mighty fallen!

(3) Downfall of the king of Babylon (14:1–23)

(a) Promised deliverance (14:1–4a)

1 *For the Lord will have compassion on Jacob,*
  and will again choose Israel,
      and will cause them to rest[1] in their own land.[2]
The stranger will be joined to them;
  they will be gathered to the house of Israel.
2 *Peoples will take them and bring them to their own place,*
  and the house of Israel will possess[3] them in the land of the
      Lord for servants and maidservants.
They will take their captors captive,
  and have dominion over their oppressors.[4]

3. Note such a standard work as F. S. Bodenheimer, *Animals and Man in Bible Lands* (Leiden: Brill, 1960).
1. The Hiphil of *nûaḥ* means to "put down after having been gathered up." Cf. Josh. 6:23; Judg. 6:18, 20; 1 Sam. 6:18.
2. Kaiser suggests that *ᵃḏāmâ*, "soil, land," may have had some of the connotations of our word "home." Cf. Ezek. 37:14.
3. *hiṯnāḥal*, "to possess," is a technical legal term normally applied to the land (Num. 32:18), but here applied to the oppressors themselves. The Jews will own their enemies as an inheritance (Lev. 25:46; cf. 57:13).
4. While v. 1 is clearly poetry and vv. 3, 4a are clearly prose, the form of v. 2 is not clear. The last two lines exhibit poetic parallelism but the first two do not.

310

3 *In that day, when the Lord has given you rest from your pain and your*
trouble⁵ and from the hard service which was imposed on you,⁶
4a *you will take up this taunt⁷ against the king of Babylon⁸ and you will*
say:

In this second part of the burden of Babylon, the major element is the
taunt-song, vv. 4b–21, rejoicing over the downfall of the haughty monarch
of the city. As such it is a powerful particularization of the more general
statements of ch. 13. No particular person is named nor is it clear any is
intended (see below on v. 4a), but the poem makes the destruction of
human pride and arrogance much more graphic by personifying it in this
way. The song itself, however, is bracketed by opening and closing statements which put the song in its appropriate context. It is God who rises
up against Babylon (vv. 22, 23), and he does so not merely because the
creature cannot exalt itself against its Creator, but because in its arrogance
the world power holds captive the people whom God has promised to
redeem (11:11–16) and through whom he intends to bless the world (11:1–9;
Gen. 12:2, 3; 18:17, 18). Thus, God's wrath is not only negative as against
sin, but also positive as against that which blocks the path of blessing.

The vision presented in vv. 1–4a is one of hope. The result of
Babylon's overthrow will be the promised deliverance. Although Israel's
lack of trust in God will have placed her back in bondage, as before in
Egypt, yet God will not forsake her. Although the world's glory and Israel's

---

5. ʿṣb, "trouble," is trouble which torments, whereas ʿml is trouble which
bows down (cf. 10:1).

6. Lit. "which was worked [Pual participle] on you," an awkward phrase,
but a direct allusion to Exod. 1:14.

7. māšāl, "taunt," connoted originally a poetic comparison, which later
became a mocking comparison and ultimately a parable or a proverb (cf. Num.
23:7; Deut. 28:37; Prov. 1:1; Hab. 2:6). So a person or nation which comes to a
bad end is held up as an example to others.

8. The use of "king of Babylon" has been significant for the dating of the
poem. So long as the Church accepted the possibility of predictive prophecy, no
problem was perceived. But with the rise of skepticism in that direction, the title
was taken to be proof of a postexilic date (e.g., Duhm). More recently, however,
it has been proposed that while the phrase "king of Babylon" is "undoubtedly"
late, the poem itself best relates to the Assyrian monarchs and that "king of
Babylon" is a later editorial change (H. Barth, *Die Jesaja-Worte in Der Josiazeit,*
WMANT 48 [Neukirchen-Vluyn: Neukirchener, 1977], pp. 136–38). However, it
is not necessary to make the title a later addition, nor is it necessary to surrender
the predictive element. It would have been possible for Isaiah, under the inspiration
of the Spirit, to recognize the long-term threat of Babylon (as ch. 39 certainly
depicts him doing), and to use the Assyrian emperors as models for the kind of
pride which would be epitomized in Babylon.

311

sin be ranged against him, yet he will keep faith with her and restore her to him, not only because he loves her, but also for the sake of his own name in the world (Hos. 11:8–11; Mic. 7:8–10; Ezek. 36:32–36; Isa. 50:1–3). As Delitzsch comments, these few verses contain the message of chs. 40–66 in a nutshell.[9] They leap across the intervening ideas and events and remind the reader again (as in 2:1–4 and 4:2–6) of God's ultimate purpose of blessing.

1, 2 These verses form a sort of epilogue to ch. 13 as the opening *kî,* "for," shows. Babylon—the oppressor—will be destroyed because of the Lord's compassion for his people. The prophet's vision is not limited to Judah. God will remember his entire people, as the parallel use of *Jacob* and *Israel* indicates.[10] The analogy with the Exodus is very clear throughout these verses. As God chose Israel once before in Egypt, he will chose her again in Mesopotamia (Deut. 4:37; 7:6, 7; Ps. 135:4). This election does not speak so much of Israel's status before God as it does of the individual Israelite's experience of him. God's choice of Israel to be the bearers of the covenant was fixed in God's promise to Abraham. But any specific group or generation of that people had to receive the choosing for themselves (2 Pet. 1:10). Here the prophet reminds his hearers, both present and future, that whatever punishment may come, it need not mean abandonment. God will once again choose. So it is with the Church. God's purposes for it remain unchanging. But how the Church experiences God in any generation will depend on the character of that generation of Christians. This much is sure: whatever bondage the Church may fall into, God will choose her again.

The result of the choosing will be that Israel will be put down on

---

9. Because of these similarities to chs. 40–66 as well as to Zech. 1:17; 2:13–16 (Eng. 9–12), it has become customary to date these verses to postexilic, or later, times (cf. W. Eichrodt, *Der Herr der Geschichte. Jesaja 13–23 und 28–39,* BAT [Stuttgart: Calwer, 1967], who refers to the constricting effect of the late Jewish horizon). However, the evidence for this view is not strong. As Kissane points out, even if one accepts the Deutero-Isaianic theory, there is no reason why a paragraph such as this from the earlier Isaiah could not have provided the framework for the later writer's views. As to the evidence that the concept of proselytism was postexilic (Skinner, etc.), it may be pointed out that chs. 2 and 11 distinctly anticipate this idea, as do Josh. 6:25; Ruth; and 1 K. 8:41–43. From the positive side, as already noted, this passage contains the important theological link which shows how the judgment of human pride fits into God's larger historical purpose. Without this link both chs. 13 and 14 cease to have significance within Isaiah's overall preaching: trust the nations—destruction and captivity; trust God—deliverance and abundance.

10. This usage is esp. prominent in chs. 40–49, but cf. also 10:20; 27:6.

her own soil again. But there will be more than merely a restoration of
the status quo. Another factor will be added. Now instead of Israel being
joined to aliens, the aliens will be added to Israel. In fact, then, the tables
will be turned. Israel will not be dependent upon the nations; the nations
will be dependent upon Israel (2:3; 60:1–3; 61:5–7). The language in
which this reversal is stated has been troublesome to many Christian commentators. They have seen the idea of reducing Gentiles to slaves as being
an unworthy sentiment. Thus, older commentators (but also Young) have
tended to spiritualize the passage, saying that it referred to the Church and
its dominion over all the earth. More recent scholars generally dismiss it
as an unfortunate expression of late Jewish nationalism. But it is not
necessary to take either position. This language can be taken as a figurative
expression of the prophet's inspired conviction that the present relationship
between Israel and the nations would not always obtain. The nations' pride
was passing, but the glory of Israel's God was unending, and the day would
come when the temporal would bow to the eternal.[11] Surely this has happened. Marduk and Baal and Chemosh are dead, but Yahweh lives on. So
too, Assyria and Babylon have long since walked off the pages of history,
but the people of Israel live on.

3, 4 Here again the analogy with Egypt is carried out. The Lord
will give relief from the pain, the trouble, and the hard service, in short,
the slavery. In his grace, the tables will be turned so that the slaves,
formerly bowed down, will stand over the fallen king, once so mighty.
These verses continue the theme of God's care for the lowly and his opposition to those who have exalted themselves. His day is for the lowly
and against the mighty. In that day, he promises rest to his people in their
own land (28:12; 32:18; Deut. 12:9; 2 Sam. 7:1; 1 K. 8:56; Ps. 95:1; Mic.
2:10). It is an expression of that release from their enemies that they will
be able to taunt the very one who had vaunted himself over them. Kaiser
comments that such an attitude is contradictory to NT principles, yet it is
the very sort of thing which is said about Babylon in the book of Revelation
(18:1–24). While it is incumbent upon Christians to foster concern for
their enemies and to seek reconciliation with them, nothing in the Christian
faith says we ought to be sad when those who deny God and would destroy
his people are overthrown.

4a *the king of Babylon.* As noted above, the song seems to be a

11. To say that this is nothing more than late Jewish nationalism presupposes that the late interpolator was ignorant of the more generous expressions of
other parts of the book (2:3, 4; 24:14, 16; 56:6–8), whereas it is often remarked
that the interpolators were masters at blending the various segments of the book
into a whole.

313

particularization of the more general statements of ch. 13. This being the case, the attempt to identify a precise historical figure is probably futile. Isaiah is using a concrete representation to discuss the nature and end of human pride. Nonetheless, there has been no dearth of attempts at identification. All of them have tended to founder on the fact that no single personage can be found the events of whose life fully correspond to those of the individual in the song. None of the kings of the Neo-Babylonian empire (e.g., Nebuchadrezzar or Nabonidus) fits, nor do any of the Assyrian kings of Isaiah's day (Sargon II or Sennacherib), although the latter kings certainly aroused the same kinds of hatred among the people that this poem describes. That Tiglath-pileser as well as Sargon and Sennacherib styled themselves as "kings of Babylon"[12] would make it easier for Isaiah to have patterned his representative figure after these great tyrants, but there is no indication that he has one particular person in mind.

(b) The song (14:4b–21)

   (i) Peace on earth and turmoil in Sheol (14:4b–11)

4b *"How the oppressor has ceased;*
        how fury[1] has ended.
 5 *The Lord has shattered the staff of the wicked,*
        the rod of the rulers,
 6 *which slaughtered the people in wrath,*
        which struck down without ceasing,
    subduing the nations in anger,
        persecuting[2] without restraint.

12. So Erlandsson, *Burden,* p. 88, citing J. A. Brinkman, "Merodach-Baladan II," in *Studies Presented to A. Leo Oppenheim* (Chicago: University of Chicago, 1964), pp. 12, 20–22. Note, too, that Sargon II, the king who completed the destruction of Samaria and crushed the combined western forces at Raphia in 920 B.C., died on the battlefield, an unheard-of thing for an Assyrian monarch. See below on vv. 16–18.

1. The meaning of MT *maḏhēḇâ* is unknown. From its position in the sentence, it should have a meaning parallel to "oppressor." Solutions have followed three general courses: (1) Assume that the *d* is an error for an original *r* and that the word was *marhēḇâ,* "fury." 1QIs[a] supports this reading, and we adopt it here. (2) Draw the root from Aram. *dhb,* "gold," with the word here being a noun, "golden thing," perhaps "city" (so AV). (3) Seek a similar root, like *dʾb* or *dbʿ*, which would yield some such meaning as strength, etc. Cf. H. Orlinsky, "*Madhebah* in Isaiah 14:4," *VT* 7 (1957) 202–203; cf. also Delitzsch.

2. *murdāp,* "persecuting," is frequently emended to *mirdaṭ,* "kick" (from *rdh;* so KB, p. 564), to agree with *rōḏeh,* "tread down, subdue," the first word in the line. But as a Hophal type noun meaning pursuit or persecution *murdāp* is a fit parallel without emendation.

314

7 *All the earth rests*[3] *and is at peace,*
they break forth in singing.
8 *Even the pine trees rejoice over you,*
and the cedars of Lebanon,
'Since you have been laid low
no axeman comes up against us.'
9 *Sheol beneath is in turmoil for you*
to greet your arrival;
it rouses the shadowy ones for you,
all the leaders[4] *of the earth;*
rising from their thrones,
all the kings of the nations.
10 *All of them will answer,*
they will say to you,
'You too are weak like us,
you have become like us.
11 *Your pride has been brought down to Sheol,*
the sound[5] *of your harps.*
Under you maggots are spread out,
and your covering is worms.' "

There is general agreement that this is one of the finest of Hebrew poems. It manifests a balance of terms, a forcefulness, and a power of imagery that is typical of the best of Hebrew poetry. The total impact is unforgettable.[6] It is divided into four stanzas of almost equal length, each one describing a different scene. The first (vv. 4b–8) depicts the relief which pervades earth with the tyrant gone. The second (vv. 9–11) tells of the astonishment in Sheol when the dead discover that even this man is mortal. The third stanza (vv. 12–15) moves from Sheol to heaven, showing that

3. On *šāqaṭ*, "to rest from oppression," cf. also Judg. 3:30 and Job 3:26.
4. Lit. "rams," a term from nature frequently applied to human leaders as an expression of potency and authority (cf. Jer. 50:8; Zech. 10:3).
5. The word *hemyaṭ* is taken to be from *hmh*, "to murmur," thus "the *sound* of your harps." However, Sym. has "He will kill your corpse," which is possible if the word is repointed to *hāmîṭ* and the alternate meaning of *nbl* (not "harp," but "corpse") is taken. However, this reading does not yield a very satisfactory parallel to the first phrase and is not supported by LXX or Targ. Yet another repointing yields "the death *[hammôṭ]* of your corpse" (possibly supported by 1QIs[a]; cf. J. Carmignac, "Six passages d'Isaie éclairiés par Qumran," in *Bibel und Qumran*, ed. S. Wagner [Berlin: Evangelische Haupt-Bibelgesellschaft, 1968], pp. 37–46).
6. H. Kosmala's argument that the poem is "peculiarly composite" is hard to square with the forcefulness of the result. Great art is rarely a joint effort ("Form and Structure in Ancient Hebrew Poetry," *VT* 16 [1966] 152–180).

the tyrant's ignominy is the more devastating because he pretended to be so much. Finally, vv. 16–21 return to the earth and tell of the final disgrace to overbearing pride: the denial of a decent burial and the destruction of his descendants.

Part of the power of the poem lies in its careful mockery of the lament form. That form typically uses an unbalanced line called the *qinah,* or "limping" line. The first of the parallel members is typically one-third longer than the second member, giving the limping effect. Frequently the incomparability of the dead is extolled and is a source of grief. Certain terms such as "how" and "never more" are also typical of the lament, as is the mournful question (cf. 2 Sam. 1:19–27). Here all these elements are turned directly around with a pitiless delight. This song for the dead is a song of joy, not grief. How terrible this man was! How wonderful that he has been hurled out of heaven! Here in fact the singer welcomes death as a blessing. And so it is. What would earth be if death did not put a limitation upon human fallenness?[7]

At the same time, such intense pleasure over destruction of one's enemy raises questions for a Christian. Is there any sense in which we can participate in such rejoicing? (Cf. Matt. 5:43–48.) First, it must be said that an evil principle is involved here more than a specific person. It is true that the fall and destruction of any individual is no cause for joy. Even the death of a Hitler is a loss to God. At the same time, there is no sense in which Christians are called upon to stand quietly by when the forces of evil are dealt a telling blow by the hand of God (Rev. 19:1–8). Wherever evil is weakened and righteousness triumphs, there is cause for joy.

4b–8 In this stanza the inhabitants of the earth, animate and inanimate, burst forth into song at the news of the tyrant's death. Something about human pride demands destruction of all works but one's own, and the Near East has known a steady succession of proud emperors who have insisted on their way at all costs. What a day it will be for that region and for the whole earth when human pride is cast down once and for all.

4b–6 The picture here of unceasing and relentless oppression accords very well with the claims of the Assyrian kings. In their annals they report at great length the violence and the unwavering nature of their assaults upon their neighbors.[8] If we accept their word, they mastered the technique of ruling through terror. The blows which would come upon anyone who dared to dissent from Assyrian domination were so massive and

---

7. Cf. D. Gowan, *When Man Becomes God* (Pittsburgh: Pickwick, 1975), pp. 126, 127.

8. Luckenbill, *ARAB,* I:78–80; II:60–62; etc.

so total that nation after nation was cowed into submission. The thought of being delivered from such terror must have been almost too delightful to speak of. Nevertheless, Isaiah is able to believe in a God who is larger than the gigantic world monarchs, who is able to break their sceptres,[9] symbols of their power, like matchsticks. The audacity of such faith is still almost breathtaking.[10] Yet that is precisely the burden of Isaiah's preaching: the God of tiny Judah is God of all the universe and before his bar all human pretension must bow.

7   The idea of singing in view of deliverance is a special feature of the book of Isaiah.[11] Many commentators have pointed out the occurrences which appear in the second part of the book (44:23; 49:13; 54:1; 55:1), but the concept also appears in the first part, as here, and in chs. 24–26, where the fierce song of the drunken conquerors is replaced by the jubilant song of the redeemed (24:9, 14, 16; 25:5; 26:1, 19).[12] In place of the wailing of mourners for this death (2 Sam. 1:24), there is a spontaneous outburst of laughter and joy. Herod, fearful that people might rejoice at his death, had imprisoned all the elders of the Jews with orders that they should be killed at the hour of his death.[13] It is a testimony to the immensity of his pride that he did not realize that upon his death his capacity to command would cease. But cease it did and in the general jubilation at his death the elders were released.

8   In what appears to be a typically Isaianic way, the poet reinforces the point of the previous verse with imagery, and, as is often the case, with tree imagery. Not only humanity will share in the song of deliverance but all of nature as well, for the Near Eastern tyrants boasted of their dominion not only over humanity but over nature, too. In each case evidence of dominion was the capacity to destroy. So the kings boasted of how many lions they had killed or how they had laid waste the trees.[14]

---

9. Cf. 9:3 (Eng. 4); 10:15, 24; 14:29 for this same idea of God's total control of the Assyrian rod. The use of the plural in this place ("staff of the wicked, the rod of the rulers") is a further indication that no single individual is in the prophet's mind.

10. Cf. L. Rost, "Das Probleme der Weltmacht in der Propheties," *TLZ* 90 (1965) 241–250.

11. *pāṣaḥ rinnâ,* "to break into singing," occurs only in Isaiah: here and in 44:23 and 49:13.

12. Note also the songs of the book of Revelation for a similar response to redemption.

13. Josephus *Antiquities* xvii.6.5, 6 (§§ 168–181).

14. So Isa. 37:4 quoting the Assyrians. Cf. Luckenbill, *ARAB*, I:236, 247, 248, 558, 792, 794, 804; II:366; A. T. Olmstead, *History of Assyria* (Chicago: University of Chicago, 1923), pp. 272–74.

This kind of dominion, so different from that envisioned in the Bible (Gen. 2:15; Deut. 20:19), has resulted in the near total decimation of the great forests which once covered much of the Lebanon mountains and parts of northern Mesopotamia. So nature, no less than humanity, will breathe a sigh of relief upon the great king's death.

9–11 With a sure feel for contrast, the author moves the scene from the earth to the underworld, showing that the same event which brought peace and quiet to the world has brought agitation to the realm of the dead. The source of the agitation is the discovery on the part of the dead that the terrible king who had dispatched so many of them to death is in fact no different than they. Although his glory had made him seem almost immortal, he too must bow to corruption and decay.

9, 10 The departed kings are pictured as seated on their thrones in Sheol, the underworld.[15] When the mighty king appears they rise as though to do homage, which one might expect if this were a normal lament. But instead they mock him by reminding him that in the sight of death all human distinctions are meaningless.

11 This verse continues the mockery of the lament by contrasting two radically different pictures of a funeral. In the first we see the royal corpse being carried on its final journey with all the pomp and ceremony which can be mustered to show the power and importance of a person. Somber and elegant music is playing and the corpse is decked out with every kind of finery.[16] But suddenly that picture is replaced with another more terrible, but much more realistic, one. There is nothing but silence and a rotting corpse covered with worms. The picture is like something

---

15. It is evident that the Hebrews conceived of the realm of the dead as a dusty, shadowy place where a dim reflection of the person lived on in inactivity (Job 7:9; 17:16; 26:6; Ps. 6:6 [Eng. 5]; 31:18 [Eng. 17]; 88:12, 13 [Eng. 11, 12]; 115:17). (For a modern author's vision of such a place, see C. S. Lewis, *The Magician's Nephew,* which also contains a powerful picture of the ultimate destructiveness of human pride.) It was not a place at which arrival was anticipated. Those who went there had nothing to look forward to, so the dead are called $r^e p\bar{a}$'$\hat{\imath}m$, "the slack ones." This conception was not fully worked out, however, for the concept of an immortal and faithful God contrasted with it and prevented such a thorough working out (Job 14:13–15; 19:25–27; Ps. 23:6; etc.). One such evidence of this contradiction is that while Sheol is personified here, there is no god or goddess of the underworld, who would be a central figure if this poem were written outside the Israelite milieu (cf. "The Descent of Ishtar," *ANET,* pp. 107–109). Here the existence of only one God rules out such a possibility and makes the human figures the main actors. For an alternate view of Sheol as signifying merely the grave, cf. *TWOT,* II:892–93.

16. Cf. Josephus's description of Herod's bier (*Antiquities* xvii.8.3 [§§ 197–98]).

by Hieronymus Bosch where behind a lovely feminine face we glimpse a decaying, grinning skull. So, says Isaiah, human pride is but pretty trappings on a corpse. The worms bring all of us, mighty and helpless alike, to the same level.[17]

(ii) Fallen from heaven, cast out on earth (14:12–21)

12 *How you have fallen from heaven,*
Day Star, Son of the Morning.
You have been hewn down to the earth,
weak upon the nations.
13 *But you said in your heart,*
"I will ascend to the heavens;
Above the stars of El
I will exalt my throne;
I will sit on the mount of assembly,
on the heights[1] of the North.
14 *I will go up upon the high places of the clouds;*
I will be like the Most High."[2]
15 *Instead[3] you are put down into Sheol,*
into the depths[4] of the Pit.
16 *Those who see you will stare at you*
and consider you.
'Is this the man who shook the earth,
making the kingdoms quiver,
17 *who made the earth like a desert,*
overthrowing its[5] cities,
refusing to send his captives home?'[6]

17. So Gilgamesh, denying that his mighty friend Enkidu could have died, is forced to the realization by a worm crawling from the corpse's nostril (*ANET*, p. 90).

1. *yark^{e}tê*, "heights," refers to the two sides of an angle or the apex of that angle and thus may denote both heights and depths (cf. Delitzsch).

2. "The Most High" as a title for God appears in Gen. 14:19–20 and frequently in Daniel (4:24, 25, etc.), where it is especially used to indicate God's absolute sovereignty.

3. The opening word, *'ak*, expresses the contrast well. Whatever may have gone before, "nevertheless" this is now the case.

4. Note the wordplay involved in "depths of the pit": *yark^{e}tê*, "depths," is the same word translated "heights" in v. 13. So again the contrast is drawn between presumption and reality (cf. n. 1 above).

5. For the lack of agreement between the masc. suffix "its cities" and the fem. antecedent "earth," see GKC, § 135.

6. Note that NEB, "who never let his prisoners go free to their homes, the kings of every land?", is following an emendation proposed in *BHK*. However, the ancient versions uniformly support the MT.

319

18 *All the kings of the nations, all of them,*
   lie in honor in their own tombs.[7]
19 *But you have been thrown from your grave,*
   like an untimely birth;[8]
   you are clothed with the murdered,
      those pierced with the sword,
   those who go down to the stones of the pit
      like a trampled corpse.[9]
20 *You will not join them in the grave,*
   for you destroyed your land,
         murdered your people.
   May he not be named forever—
      wicked seed.
21 *Establish for his sons a slaughterhouse,*
   for the iniquity of their fathers.
   May they not arise to inherit the earth,
      nor fill the face of the ground with cities.[10]

In vv. 12–15 the scene shifts from the underworld to heaven and illumi-
nates the pretense of human pride. That pride refuses to brook any rival,
even God himself, insisting that all his prerogatives will be its own. Some
of the church fathers, linking this passage to Luke 10:18 and Rev. 12:8,
9, took it to refer to the fall of Satan described in those places. However,
the great expositors of the Reformation were unanimous in arguing that
the context here does not support such an interpretation. This passage is
discussing human pride, which, while monumental to be sure, is still
human and not angelic. In fact, it is this very characteristic which makes
this passage of special interest. Since the earliest discoveries of ancient
Near Eastern religious literature this portion of the poem and other sections
of the Bible have been compared to that literature. In this case, the vigor

7. Lit. "house." Cf. the funerary text of the Phoenician king Eshmunazar
in which he refers to his tomb as a house (*ANET*, p. 505, translated "casket").
8. Skinner has suggested that *nēṣer*, "branch," is a confusion for "corpse,"
peger, but it is very hard to explain how such a confusion could have arisen.
NEB reads "carrion," which presupposes *nēṣel* for *nēṣer*. This suggestion may also
explain the LXX "corpse." Cf. *BHK* and Wildberger.
9. MT ends the verse here. But it may be that "like a trampled corpse"
should begin the next verse. So NEB, NIV, etc.
10. It seems somewhat strange that the people would want to prevent the
king's sons from filling the land with cities. LXX has "wars" in place of "cities"
and Targ. has "enemies," but neither lends particular confidence that it reflects an
original reading. Further reflection suggests that "cities" may be entirely plausible.
The garrison cities of a great empire were its bastions of commercial, military,
and cultural dominance of the various regions (2 Sam. 8:6, 14; 1 K. 9:15–19).

of this comparison was only increased by the discovery of the numerous verbal similarities with Canaanite myths uncovered at Ugarit.[11] It is interesting that despite this vigorous investigation there is no single mythical story which can be said to be the prototype for Isa. 14:12–15. But it is of greater significance that among the numerous stories of a challenge to the high god, all the challenges are by another god. The remarkable thing about the Isaiah passage is that the challenge is by a human being.[12] The prophet seems to be saying that ultimately the battle is not among the various manifestations of deity. Ultimately, the battle is between Creator and creatures, and the issue is whether we will accord him the right due him as Creator and bow to him in glad service or will continue to insist that we are as he is and continue to have our arrogance mocked by the worm.[13] By alluding to the great literature of his day, drawing upon the rich connotations of those stories, Isaiah drives home the point that making God in our image is the great folly of humanity.[14]

12 *Day Star, Son of the Morning* reflects the likelihood that *hēlēl ben-šāḥar* refers to the planet Venus, which never reaches the zenith before the sun rises and apparently extinguishes it. *hēlēl* probably comes from the root meaning "bright" and thus logically applies to the brightest star. In Canaanite mythology the god Athtar, with whom the gods attempt to replace Baal at one point, may also be the morning star.[15] In that story, however, Athtar does not seek the position and, upon finding himself unsuited for it, voluntarily leaves it. Recent attempts to derive the Isaiah account from the Greek myth of Phaethon, in which the central figure loses

11. Some representative works on this passage and its mythic allusions: W. F. Albright, *Yahweh and the Gods of Canaan* (Garden City: Doubleday, 1968), p. 201; B. S. Childs, *Myth and Reality in the Old Testament*, SBT 1/27 (London: SCM; Naperville: Allenson, 1960), pp. 68–70; P. C. Craigie, "Helel, Athtar and Phaethon (Jes 14:12–15)," *ZAW* 85 (1973) 223–25; S. A. Hirsch, "Isaiah 14:12, Helel ben Shahar," *JQR* 11 (1920/1921) 197–99; S. H. Langdon, "The Star Helel, Jupiter? (Is. 14:12)," *ExpTim* 42 (1930/1931) 172–74; J. W. McKay, "Helel and the Dawn-Goddess: A Reexamination of the Myth in Isaiah 14:12–15," *VT* 20 (1970) 451–464; J. Morgenstern, "The Mythological Background of Psalm 82," *HUCA* 14 (1939) 108–114.

12. D. E. Gowan, *When Man Becomes God. Humanism and Hubris in the Old Testament* (Pittsburgh: Pickwick, 1975), pp. 66, 67.

13. As a creature Satan is an apt example of this creaturely pride. Thus, while it cannot be said that these verses refer to him, they do apply to him as they do to all creatures.

14. For a further discussion of the Bible's use of mythological language, see J. Oswalt, "The Myth of the Dragon and Old Testament Faith," *EvQ* 49 (1977) 163–172.

15. So Craigie, op. cit., pp. 223–24. Cf. *ANET*, p. 140 (I AB:1:52–65).

control of the chariot of the sun and is struck by a thunderbolt of Zeus in order to save the earth from the sun's fire, suffer from the evidence that the Greek myth is derived from the Near Eastern stories rather than being the precursor of them. Once again, the indications are that the prophet was not dependent upon any one story, but used a number of current motifs to fit his own point.

weak upon the nations is translated by AV and RSV as "who weakened the nations." But the normal meaning of the verb is intransitive, and the parallel "cast down on the earth, weak on the nations" yields a good sense when appropriately interpreted as in NEB, "sprawling across the nations."

13, 14 There are a number of verbal similarities between this verse and several Canaanite poems. The term used for God is not the usual form "Elohim" but rather the short form "El," which is the name of the high god of the Canaanite pantheon, the god of beneficence and justice under whom Baal and his consorts serve somewhat restively.[16] The reference to the throne is somewhat similar to the Athtar account, in which he finds Baal's throne too large for him, but there is no attempt to supplant El, for El had in fact chosen Athtar in Baal's absence.

the mount of assembly is here associated, as the parallel shows, with Mount Zaphon or Mount Cassius in north Syria, where the gods were reputed to meet as did the Greek gods on Mount Olympus.[17] Although Zaphon was particularly associated with Baal, the divine assembly was presided over by El.[18] Thus Isaiah makes the kings of Babylon aspire to the kingship of the gods.

the high places of the clouds may have a cultic connotation in that the OT frequently uses *bāmôt*, "high places," to refer to hilltops where sacrifices were made to the gods. The Ugaritic cognate means only "back," and in this poetic context that may be the correct reading here ("the backs of the clouds"). In either case, the speaker is boasting of his intent to reach heights unattainable by anyone but the Highest of all. By contrast, the Bible depicts God's power as manifested in his stepping on the high places of the earth (Amos 4:13; Mic. 1:3), which prerogative he gladly shares with those who love him (Deut. 32:13; 33:29; 2 Sam. 22:34; Ps.

16. See M. Pope, *El in the Ugaritic Texts*, VTSup 2 (Leiden: Brill, 1955), pp. 27–32. Cf. Gen. 14:19; 16:13; 17:1; 21:33; etc.

17. For a full discussion, see Fisher, *RSP*, II:318–324. This terminology is applied to Mount Zion in Ps. 48:2, 3 (Eng. 1, 2).

18. Cf. *UT*, 137:14, 20, 31; *ANET*, p. 130. Cf. also R. J. Clifford, *The Cosmic Mountain in Canaan and the Old Testament*, HSM 4 (Cambridge, MA: Harvard University, 1972), pp. 42–48.

18:33; Isa. 58:14; Hab. 3:19). The human problem is that we will not accept God's gifts within the limits imposed by him. *We* wish to be God dispensing the gifts.

15 Despite the high pretensions, or precisely because of them, the king is plunged into the underworld. Death mocks every person's claim to be God. This truth is entirely congruent with the teaching of Gen. 3. The forbidden fruit was proffered to Adam and Eve as being able to make them like God (3:5). Instead it brought them the ultimate proof of their finitude: death (3:22; cf. also Job 20:6, 7).

16–21 The final scene of the poem returns to earth where the cycle began. Here the king is portrayed in his ultimate disgrace, as an unburied corpse. There is a sense of wonder among the onlookers, almost of awe, that one so mighty could possibly come to so terrible a fate. For among Israel's neighbors it was believed that if the body was not properly interred, the soul was doomed to wander the earth looking for a home.[19] Whether the Hebrews held such an idea is unclear, but it is clear that they saw the lack of burial as a disgrace, at least, as shown by the risk which the people of Jabesh-gilead took in order to retrieve and bury the bodies of Saul and Jonathan (1 Sam. 31:11–13; 2 Sam. 2:4–7).

16–17 Those who pass by the body of the king stare at him and wonder at the complete reversal of his fortunes. He had not merely made the earth his home, he had made it his plaything. He had but to sneeze and the repercussions had reached the farthest kingdom; people lived in terror of his next move. What he had failed to realize was what Nebuchadnezzar learned to his sorrow: that the kingdoms of the world belong to God and that he gives them in trust to whom he will (Dan. 4:25).

The frightful nature of this kind of pride is seen in the fact that it would prefer the world to be a desert in its own hands than a garden in the hands of someone else.[20] In fact, the capacity to destroy and oppress becomes a source of pride (cf. 14:6). This is perversion at its plainest.

But again the poet has turned the boast back upon the boaster. He who had exiled hundreds of thousands from their homes and would not let them return now is himself homeless, and in a much more profound sense. This man is a spiritual exile. His pride has driven him from the home

19. Cf. Homer *Iliad* 17, 24. Note that the picture here fits a death on the battlefield such as that of Sargon II. Cf. H. Tadmor, "The Campaigns of Sargon II of Assur," *JCS* 12 (1958) 97, 98; A. T. Olmstead, *History of Assyria* (Chicago: University of Chicago, 1923), pp. 267, 283; H. L. Ginsberg, "Reflexes of Sargon in Isaiah After 715 B.C.E.," *JAOS* 88 (1968) 49–53.

20. Cf. C. S. Lewis, *The Magician's Nephew* (New York: Macmillan, 1955), pp. 53–54.

which the Father has given in trust to all his children. Because pride denies God it must deny us what God has given, ultimately life itself.

18–20a These verses drive home the fact that the fallen king will not have a tomb, like all the lesser kings he had himself killed. He who held prisoners captive, not letting them go home, now has no house to which he can go.

19 There are a number of difficulties in this verse, including both textual problems and unfamiliar idioms. First is the question of the king's being cast from his tomb when it appears that he was never in it. The possessive suffix *your* may be the result of dittography from the first letter of the following word, but if that were so, it does not materially ease the problem. It is simplest to regard *from* not as indicating source but rather as deprivation, yielding the sense "cast out, without a tomb."[21]

like an untimely birth is an interpretation of (lit.) "abominable branch" (so AV), which must be either a textual corruption or a figure for something else, since there is no reason to think that an actual branch would have been seen as abominable. Both Symmachus and the Targum contain the reading "untimely birth," which may involve a correction from *nēṣer*, "branch," to *nēpel*, "miscarriage." But given the association of "branch" with offspring no such correction is required.

clothed with the murdered yields a very incongruous picture, yet no better interpretation of the phrase has emerged. If the battlefield imagery is retained, then it is possible that "clothed" means "covered," i.e., with a pile of corpses. But there may also be some idea intended of the multitude of those he has himself slain weighing him down and providing his only shroud. In either case the *pit* here referred to is the grave and not the underworld.

20a The judgment contained in this verse is a surprising one because it is unexpected. The reader expects to find the king judged for what he has done to the foreign lands which he has oppressed (so LXX *"my* land . . . *my* people"), but instead it is his own land and his own people he has destroyed and for which he is judged. The truth of this becomes clear upon reflection. For the pride which has fueled every great tyrant's imperial designs has been as destructive to his own land and people as it was elsewhere. Yet whatever he has done to other people, it is his own people for whose shepherding he was responsible and whose exploi-

---

21. R. J. Williams, *Hebrew Syntax,* § 321. Note that this is precisely what was said of Sargon, who died on the battlefield (Tadmor, *JCS* 12 [1958] 98 n. 315; Olmstead, *History,* p. 283). For biblical references to the place of interment for the disgraced see 2 Chr. 21:20; 24:25; Jer. 22:19; Ezek. 29:5.

tation is thus most reprehensible. This principle is not restricted to tyrants. Each of us, whatever we have done to those outside our own circle, is first of all responsible for what our pride has done to those closest to us.

20b–21 The final judgment is aimed at the destruction of even the monarch's name. The hope is expressed that his personal name will be forgotten and his family name be destroyed with his heirs. This sort of thing took place in Egypt in the fourteenth century B.C. when the pharaoh Akhenaten (Ikhnaton) forced through a series of sweeping and evidently unpopular changes. Upon his death he was succeeded by a first and then a second son-in-law, both of whose reigns were brief and ended suspiciously. With the end of the dynasty thus accomplished, the next dynasty did everything in its power to erase the memory of the heretic king, even to the dismantling of his temples and shipping the stones to opposite ends of the kingdom.

So here the reversed lament reaches the final point of parody. Instead of wishing that the deceased's name will endure after him and that his children will bring honor to that name through their own long and productive lives, the singer wishes the opposite: may the earth quickly be delivered from even having to remember that this man was.

So ends pride. Having sought to leave its mark on the world by brute force, it now sees all its works, and even its memory, destroyed by death. In contrast, Isaiah argues that those who lay aside their pride and become chosen servants of God are those who will live forever in his memory (11:10–16; 25:6–8; 26:19; 27:13; 40:27–31; 54:7, 8).

(c) The Lord's promise (14:22–23)

> 22 *"I will arise against them,"*
>   *announces the Lord of Hosts.*
> *"I will cut off from Babylon name and remnant,*
>   *offspring and progeny," announces the Lord.*
> 23 *"I will make it into a possession of porcupines*[1]
>   *and into pools of water;*
> *I will sweep it with a broom of desolation,"*
>   *announces the Lord of Hosts.*

These two verses serve as a further indication that the taunt-song itself is to be taken as a figurative statement and not as directed at one individual. It is Babylon as a whole which stands over against God in pride, and it is Babylon as a whole which will be wiped out and whose works will be scattered across the desert. This is so because God will do it. Never far

1. BDB; KB "owls."

from Isaiah's consciousness is the direct involvement of God in history. Intermediate causes may abound, but ultimately, when Babylon comes down, it will be because God did it. This consciousness keeps a person from slipping into a "practical atheism" of thinking and living as though God did not exist. He is the Lord of Hosts, the Almighty, and to fail to take account of him is to destroy ourselves.

(4) The Lord's plan for Assyria (14:24–27)

24 *The Lord of Hosts has sworn, saying,*
   "Surely, as I have intended so it shall be;
      as I purposed it will arise.
25 *I will break Assyria in my land;*
   upon my mountains I will trample him.
His yoke will go away from him,
   and his burden will go from his shoulders."
26 *This is the purpose which is purposed for the whole earth;*
   this is the hand stretched out over all the nations.
27 *For the Lord of Hosts purposes and who can prevent it;*
   his hand is outstretched and who will make him draw it back?

The oracle against the Mesopotamian world power comes to its conclusion with this passage. The absence of the word "oracle" makes it plain that these verses are not to be taken as a separate prophecy against Assyria, but rather are presented as an intrinsic part of the preceding prophecy. In this light, the abrupt switch from Babylon to Assyria has been very perplexing to commentators. Some have argued that these four verses were originally part of 10:5–19 and have been somehow displaced here. Erlandsson argues that the original reference in chs. 13 and 14 was to Assyria throughout.[1] Others argue that the passage is postexilic and that "Assyria" here is used, as in postexilic times, of Mesopotamia in general (so Kaiser).[2]

But all these arguments presuppose some sort of redactional shifting of the ground between the two parts and offer no consistent explanation to explain that shifting. On the other hand, it is possible to explain the shift in names without resorting to redaction, if it is granted that the prophet has been using "Babylon" in a representative way (see comment

1. Erlandsson, *Burden*, pp. 104–105.
2. The debate over authorship is very hot here with scholars about equally divided over whether Isaiah could have written the prophecy. Cf. Clements and Kaiser on the one hand, Wildberger and Childs (*Isaiah and the Assyrian Crisis*, SBT 2/3 [London: SCM; Naperville: Allenson, 1967], pp. 38, 39) on the other. Lindblom (*Prophecy*, p. 283 n. 101) considers "Assyria" to be a code word for Babylon during exilic times.

on 13:1 above). Here then the writer is making a transition from the general and symbolic to the specific and literal. The Mesopotamian power, symbolized by Babylon, represents the power and glory of this world ranged against the God of Israel who has promised to redeem his people. The superiority of the Lord to that symbol has been shown. But what about the specific, current representative of that power? Do these truths apply to the actual as well as to the symbolic? The answer is a resounding yes!

Understood in this way these verses need not be seen as the result of a mistake or of a somewhat inept later redaction.[3] They fit into the overall scheme of the segment, allowing 13:1–14:27 to be a general and introductory statement to God's judgment upon the nations, with 14:24–27 providing the transition to the actual nations of Isaiah's own day.[4]

24 When read in sequence with vv. 22 and 23, *The Lord of Hosts has sworn* takes on a new impact, occurring as it does at the end of a string of three "announces the Lord (of Hosts)." The decisiveness of God's promises[5] to act become clear as well as his direct involvement conveyed through the immediacy of speech. For Isaiah, God is *here*, taking direct part in all that happens.

Surely, as I have intended introduces the oath which the Lord has taken. The literal translation is "if it is not as. . . ." This is the characteristically shortened form of the biblical oaths in which the fate which one calls on oneself if the word is broken is left out. Here, as always, God swears by himself, calling upon himself for punishment should the vow not be kept (cf. Heb. 6:13, 14). This is the believer's guarantee: the veracity of a God who commits himself without reservation to his people.

so it shall be expresses the certainty found in Isaiah's writings, as again in v. 26, that history is not out of control. This theme appears in the segment relating to Assyria in 10:5–19, but it is by no means restricted

---

3. On the one hand, the present book of Isaiah is called great literature, yet on the other it is suggested that it attained its present form by a series of mistakes, distortions, and poorly thought-out additions. Both judgments cannot be correct. Even if the present work is the result of redaction and revision, there must have been some kind of purposive and intentional approach to such work, and in that case we should be able to discern it in instances such as this.

4. Clements suggests that the passage is here as the redactor's conclusion to a segment on Assyria beginning at 5:25, but such a suggestion ignores the fact that 5:25–14:27 is not a literary unit in its present form, a form which Clements's redactor must have been responsible for. Young, seeing 14:24–27 as a conclusion to 13:1–14:23, points out similar structures in 16:13, 14; 21:16, 17.

5. "The Lord has sworn" appears twice elsewhere in the book, 45:23 and 62:8, both in connection with promises.

to that place. In fact, it conveys a fundamentally Isaianic conception which emerges in various ways throughout the book. It is probable that for many Judeans the disappearance of the Solomonic empire and the rise of the Mesopotamian powers raised very serious theological questions. Was God still Lord of history if his people did not dominate history? Isaiah, from a divine vantage point, was in a position to say that the problem, far from going away, was going to become worse, since Israel would lose her very nationhood. Yet he insists that it is the God of Israel alone who guides history in a purposive and ultimately beneficial way (5:19; 10:6, 15; 19:12, 17; 23:9; 25:1; 34:2; 41:2, 3, 21–29; 42:5–9; 43:8–21; 44:28; 46:10–11). The problem is no less real today, and the modern reader must decide, as the Judeans had to, whether Isaiah is right or wrong. Assyria is gone these 2500 years, but Isaiah's people and his faith live on. Isaiah was not wrong.

25 The reference to Assyria's destruction within God's land has led many to conclude that this passage stemmed originally from the destruction of Sennacherib's army in 701 B.C. However, others have pointed out Ezekiel's references to the destruction of Israel's enemies on the mountains (39:4, 17). This point, along with the broadly general function of this first oracle, suggests that these phrases are a stock literary device and do not refer to a particular destruction.

The removal of the yoke and the burden is reminiscent of 9:3 (Eng. 4) and 10:27 (see above on those verses), and its presence here attests to the thematic unity of the book. In this section (vv. 13–23), the author is exploring the ramifications of the earlier statements, showing that God can deliver his people from the effects of their distrust because all the nations are under his judgment.

26, 27 These verses form the ultimate conclusion of the segment beginning in 13:1.[6] As they indicate, Mesopotamia is the symbol of *the whole earth . . . all the nations,* which stand over against God in pride and arrogance and against whom God's hand is stretched out. Here is the final issue of biblical faith. If there is one almighty Creator of the universe, who is intimately and purposefully involved with his creation, then there is no power on earth, least of all human pride, which can successfully rise up against him (43:13; Ps. 33:6–11; Prov. 19:21). There is no middle way. This is no limited, or developing, deity. This is the Holy One. Either we accept Isaiah's vision of God and seek to live in glad obedience, or we are

---

6. B. Childs sees a distinct literary form here and entitles it "summary-appraisal" (*Crisis*, p. 39), but Eareckson, *VT* 20 (1970) 490–91, questions this, asserting that v. 27 is a later comment on v. 26, coming from a wisdom tradition.

obligated to say that Isaiah was mistaken and to admit that there is no right way of living.

b. JUDGMENT ON JUDAH'S NEIGHBORS (14:28–17:11)

(1) The Philistines (14:28–32)

28 *In the year of the death of King Ahaz this burden came:*
29 *Do not rejoice Philistia, all of you,*[1]
    because the staff which smote you is broken;
for from the root of the serpent an adder will go forth,
    its fruit will be a flying serpent.[2]
30 *The poorest of the poor*[3] *will feed;*
    the needy will stretch out in trust.
But your root I will kill with famine,
    and your remnant he[4] *will slay.*
31 *Howl, gate! Cry out, city!*
    Be melted, Philistia, all of you.
For from the north comes a cloud of smoke;
    there is no break in its ranks.[5]

1. "Philistia, all of you" is perhaps occasioned by the fact that the Philistine nation was composed of five city-states, each having a king over it.

2. The language throughout this verse shows a number of similarities to other parts of the book, but esp. chs. 9–11. So "staff," 9:2 (Eng. 3); "smote," 9:11 (Eng. 12); 10:20, 24; 30:31; "root," 11:1, 10; 37:31; "serpent" *(śārap),* 30:6. While the paralleling of "root" and "fruit" seems like a mixing of metaphors to us, they both express the same idea and are thus good candidates to form a poetic pair.

3. Lit. "firstborn of the poor." The absence of any indication of whose people these are and the relative rarity of the idiom "firstborn" used in this sense has caused some to emend *beķōrê,* "firstborn ones of," to *beķārāy,* "my meadows" (so NEB). But this reading has no support in any of the ancient versions. (LXX lacks "firstborn" but does not have anything approximating "meadow.")

4. The change in pronoun from 1st person to 3rd person in "I will kill . . . he will slay" is troublesome to some. However, that kind of shift is not unknown in prophetic speech. It indicates the fluidity of the prophet's consciousness as he speaks sometimes *for* God and other times *as* God. (Cf. Exod. 7:17, where Moses uses "I" for both himself and God in the same sentence, and Zech. 9:10, where the same change from "I" to "he" occurs.) LXX and Targ. have "he" in this verse, whereas 1QIs[a] has "I." Only an original like the MT, containing both pronouns, can explain these two readings; cf. H. M. Orlinsky, "Studies in the St. Mark's Isaiah Scroll, IV," *JQR* 43 (1952) 337–39.

5. "No break in its ranks" may refer to the cloud figure, indicating a solid cloud wall, or to the army, indicating a straggler. In either case, the sense is the same. (LXX "no means to continue"; Targ. "none that delays at his appointed times.")

32 *What will he answer the messengers of the nation?*
That the Lord has established Zion,
and in her the downtrodden of my people take refuge.[6]

With this oracle Isaiah begins the series of judgments against those neigh-boring nations in whom Judah might be tempted to trust for deliverance from the Mesopotamian power. But, as always, the prophet declares that those nations are under sentence as well and can do nothing for or against Judah. If she is to experience an ultimate deliverance, it must come from God, who alone is ultimate. Nevertheless, the tendency to trust in defen-sive alliances against Assyria was a strong one, dating at least as far back as 853 when Shalmaneser III reports his encounter at Qarqar in Syria with an army composed of contingents from almost every country of the Levant as far south as Ammon.[7] Although that battle did not succeed in stemming the Assyrian tide, coalitions continued to be a favored mode of addressing the threat, as seen in the attempt of Pekah and Rezin to recruit Judah against Assyria (7:1; 2 K. 16:5-9);[8] in the alliance of Moab, Edom, and the Philistines against Sargon in 714;[9] and in the one sponsored by Hez-ekiah himself in 705 (2 K. 18:7, 8).[10] To all of these, Isaiah's word was an unrelenting no. Judah's salvation was in God.

The precise date and occasion of this particular oracle has been the source of considerable debate. Furthermore, its structure and language have provoked a number of suggested emendations and alterations.[11] Nevertheless, its main import is clear: the Philistine expectation of freedom from their oppressors is a vain one and any alliance with them would be an alliance with destruction.

6. The language of v. 32 is very reminiscent of the Psalms (cf. Ps. 46:2, 5, 8 [Eng. 1, 4, 7]; 48:9 [Eng. 8]; 62:8, 9 [Eng. 7, 8]; 87:5; 91:2, 9; 142:5; etc.). This is clearly the language of hymns. To reflect upon the truth that God has established us on a rock and has become our refuge is to move even the most tone-deaf to song (12:1-6).

7. Luckenbill, *ARAB*, I:611.

8. It is likely that Pekah was put on the throne in protest against Mena-hem's appeasement of Assyria (2 K. 15:19, 20), and that Tiglath-pileser's attack on Galilee (2 K. 15:29) was in punishment for Pekah's anti-Assyrian policies. These data form the basis for the hypothesis that Israel, Syria, and Judah tried to form a coalition. Cf. J. Bright, *History*, pp. 272-73; Scott, *IB*, V:234-35. It is also possible that Pekah and Rezin did not have coalition with Judah in mind, but were attacking Ahaz because he had already allied himself with Assyria (2 K. 16:7).

9. Luckenbill, *ARAB*, II:62.

10. Ibid., II:309-312.

11. So, e.g., the interchange between K. Fullerton and W. A. Irwin (*AJSL* 42 [1925/1926] 86-109; and 44 [1927/1928] 73-87, respectively).

28 This oracle is one of only three which are precisely dated in the book (the others are ch. 6 and 20:1, 2), but "precisely" is a very relative term under the circumstances, for there is no agreement over the absolute dating of Ahaz's death. 2 K. 18:1, 9, 10 have Hezekiah's reign beginning in 727, yet v. 13 dates Sennacherib's attack of 701 in Hezekiah's fourteenth year, making his reign begin in 716/15.[12] If the latter is correct, then the time of this oracle coincides with the time of the preparations for the Philistine revolt against Assyria (Isa. 20:1–6).

29 The most obvious interpretation of the *broken staff* would be that it refers to Ahaz; thus his death, to which v. 28 refers, would be the cause of the Philistine rejoicing. However, the biblical accounts make it plain that the Philistines had not suffered at Ahaz's hand. In fact, 2 Chr. 28:18 indicates that the reverse was true, with Ahaz losing several cities to Philistine invaders. Furthermore, v. 31 says that Philistia's destruction will come from the north, the direction from which the Assyrian hordes would come after threading the pass at Megiddo. A Judean attack would come from the west. In this light, older commentators interpreted the staff as being a reference to the Jewish nation or the Davidic monarchy,[13] both of which were in considerable disarray by the time of Ahaz's death and both of which had caused the Philistines great grief. In this view Hezekiah is the adder and the Messiah is the flying serpent. While this interpretation has a venerable history, going back as far as the Targums,[14] it still lacks conviction primarily because of the reference to Ahaz's death. If this tradition is correct, that reference is almost superfluous, yet the rarity of such datings in the book makes such superfluity very unlikely. One is left then with the belief that some significant event in that year prompted these words.

More recent commentators have concluded that the staff refers to an Assyrian monarch who died in the same year as Ahaz.[15] The most tempting possibility is Tiglath-pileser III, who died in 727. If the figure in 2 K. 18:13 referred to above is an error and Ahaz did die in 727 at the beginning of Hezekiah's reign, then the dates do coincide.[16] Furthermore,

12. Cf. J. Oswalt, "Chronology of the OT," *ISBE,* I:684–85.

13. So Calvin, Delitzsch, but also Kissane and Young.

14. The Targ. reads "for from the sons of the son of Jesse shall the Messiah come forth and his deeds shall be among you as a deadly serpent" (Stenning, pp. 50–51).

15. See, e.g., J. Begrich, *Gesammelte Studien zum Alten Testament,* Theologische Bücherei (Munich: 1964), pp. 121–23.

16. See E. Thiele, *The Mysterious Numbers of the Hebrew Kings* (Grand Rapids: Eerdmans, 1965), pp. 148–154.

Tiglath-pileser did do considerable damage to the Philistines and his death could have prompted such rejoicing and plans to throw off the Assyrian yoke, although no such plan is reported elsewhere in the Bible or in extrabiblical literature. Though his dates do not fit so well, another possibility is Shalmaneser III, who died in 721. He is attractive because it is known that there was widespread revolt at the change of dynasty and that it took the successor Sargon II almost a decade to restore full control.

At the same time it seems strange that Ahaz's death would be mentioned if it is in fact the death of another monarch that is important. This, coupled with the facts that Ahaz may have died in 715 and that a known Philistine revolt was beginning about then, suggests that the broken staff is not in fact any dead monarch, but merely the general Assyrian weakness which was still prevailing at that time and which was being used at the time of Ahaz's death as an argument for Judah to join the Philistine scheme.[17]

On this supposition Isaiah is warning that the serpent (a free association from staff?) is not dead. In fact, its offspring will be considerably more dangerous than anything yet seen.[18] Of course, Isaiah was exactly correct. The Assyrian dragon was not dead; it was just coming to its full strength in Sargon, then Sennacherib and Esarhaddon, and any attempt to stand against it in merely human strength was futile.

30 In stark contrast to the ominous serpentine prediction of the previous verse, this one begins with a quiet picture of sheep in a pasture, some feeding and others stretched out in sleep. These are identified as the very poorest ("firstborn of the poor" is a way of expressing the superlative, cf. Job 18:13 and also Col. 1:15) and most needy of people. Presumably, in the light of v. 32, it is the poor of Judah who are intended, in contrast to the mighty ones of Philistia. For those mighty ones there is no hope. They will be exterminated so thoroughly that nothing will remain of them to spring up again. The language here suggests the characteristics of the ancient sieges where the attacking army sought to starve the inhabitants

17. This position is taken by Wright as well as J. Bright, *History*, p. 281 n. 34.

18. The idea of a dead serpent's offspring could be taken to suggest successors to a dead king, but as a figure of speech it need not apply so literally. Most commentators assume three generations are involved: (1) serpent, (2) adder, (3) flying serpent. However, the Hebrew poetic parallelism suggests that the second statement is only an expanded synonym of the first: "serpent" equals "its"; "adder" equals "flying serpent." Note D. Wiseman's question of any evidence for the concept of a "flying serpent" in the ancient Near East in "Flying Serpents," *TynBul* 23 (1972) 108–110. He adduces Akk. *appu*, "to prick," instead of Heb. *'ôp*, "to fly." Cf. NIV "darting, venomous serpent."

of a city to the point where they were too weak to defend themselves from being overcome and slaughtered. So God teaches again that the helpless who depend on him are stronger than the powerful who refuse such dependency.

31, 32 These two verses repeat the form of vv. 29 and 30, the first promising doom on the Philistines and the second contrasting Judah's security. These verses particularly support the idea of the Philistine rebellion in 715 as the context of this passage, for they make it plain that the enemy will come from the north, and it seems likely that the envoys mentioned in v. 32 are those from Philistia seeking Judean involvement in the alliance.

Howl, gate invokes again the imagery of the siege, for often the battle surged around the gateway, as the Assyrian engineers brought their battering rams into play outside and as suicide squads inside prepared to counterattack if the first or second set of doors gave way. Then the place where the elders had held court in better days became a welter of blood (Ruth 4:1–6; Isa. 22:7; 28:6; *ANEP*, p. 131).

For from the north comes a cloud of smoke may be a figurative reference to the Assyrian army itself as the cloud or it may be taken somewhat more literally as the cloud of cities put to the torch along the line of the Assyrian advance. In either case, the onslaught is inexorable, marked by the perfect order of which the Assyrians were so proud (5:27, 28).[19]

32 Given the fact that Assyria is not broken and that the Philistines are under the judgment of God through the Assyrian army, Isaiah sees only one answer for the Philistine envoys: God who brought Zion into existence is Zion's only security (28:16). How hard it was for the Judeans to learn that, and how hard it is for us to learn it. We deceive ourselves if we believe that arms or wealth or cunning can give us stability and certainty. Stability and certainty must either come from within or they do not exist. Unless the Lord blesses Jacob, he cannot save himself (Gen. 32), or in the words of Jesus, "Whoever would save his life will lose it" (Luke 9:24). But the person who knows from whence he has come and where he goes, who has "lost his life" in dependence upon God, that person is truly secure whatever may happen (1 Pet. 2:4–10).

(2) The Moabites (15:1–16:14)

(a) Lament (15:1–9)

1 *The burden of Moab:*

19. Luckenbill, *ARAB*, II:26.

Surely[1] in one night Ar is desolated;
 Moab is cut off.
Surely in one night Kir is desolated;
 Moab is cut off.[2]
2 He went up to the house,[3] Dibon,
 to the high places, to weep.
For Nebo and Medeba,
 Moab wails.
On all its heads, baldness;
 every beard is cut off.
3 In its streets they are girded with sackcloth.
 On its rooftops and squares they all wail,
 going down in tears.
4 Heshbon cries out and Elealeh;
 their voice is heard as far as Jahaz.
Therefore, the armed men of Moab raise a shout;
 his inmost self is shaken.[4]
5 My heart cries out for Moab,
 her fugitives as far as Zoar and Eglath-shelishiyah,[5]
for they go up the way to Luhith weeping;
 they go on the way to Horonaim raising a cry of destruction.

1. The *kî* which opens each phrase is probably best understood here as "surely" (Williams, *Syntax,* § 449), unless it be taken as a remnant of a lament the opening statement of which is now lost ("I will lament for Moab *because* in one . . .").

2. The verse reads " . . . is destroyed Ar Moab is cut off . . . is destroyed Kir Moab is cut off." The MT points the names as compounds; however, in other places the first elements are treated separately or in compound with other words (Ar, Num. 21:15; Deut. 2:18; Kir-hareseth, Isa. 16:7; Kir-heres, Isa. 16:11). This suggests that the city name goes with the first verb while "Moab" goes with the second.

3. A number of alternatives have been offered to the reading "house." One is that it is a shortening of a place name such as Beth-gamul (Jer. 48:23). The most common is that it is an error for *baṯ,* "daughter" (of Dibon), and means "inhabitant of Dibon" (RSV, NEB, etc.)

4. Verse 4b has constituted a major problem for interpreters, both because of rare words and because of the odd poetry. One would expect the two parts to contain parallel statements, which is only generally so in the MT. For this reason *ḥᵃluṣê,* "armed men," is frequently repointed to *ḥᵃlāṣāyw,* "loins," and the verb altered to some root for "shake"; so, e.g., Gray. The LXX supports "loins" and leaves the verb as "shout," which results in a very odd reading indeed. Guillaume (*JTS* 15 [1964] 293–95) proposes a new meaning for the final verb *(yrʿ)* as "be faint" (cf. NIV). This would make the second phrase parallel with the first.

5. MT has no verb in this clause. Virtually all English translations, including AV, supply some such verb as "shall flee."

6 *For the waters of Nimrim are devastated;*
   for the green grass is destroyed.
 The grass is gone;
   there is no vegetation.
7 *Therefore, the gains they*[6] *have made*
   and their provisions,
 they carry over the Wadi of the Poplars.[7]
8 *The cry of distress goes around the border of Edom.*
   As far as Eglaim her wail,
   to Beer-elim her wailing.
9 *Although the waters of Dimon*[8] *are full of blood,*
   yet I will bring upon Dimon still more:
 To the fugitive of Moab a lion,
   yes, to the remnant of Admah.

Chapters 15–16 are the second oracle against a neighboring nation, and, like the one to the Philistines, it too seems to be set in the time frame of 715–711. The postcript, 16:13, 14, suggests that the oracle may have been in existence prior to this time but has been applied to these particular circumstances by prophetic inspiration. The three-year span mentioned in v. 14 could perhaps be applied to the time between the beginning of the revolt and its final quashing by Sargon.[9] However, the references to the destruction within the oracle are vague and general enough that dogmatism about the setting is not warranted.

Moab was the term used to describe the region on the east side of the Dead Sea, extending from the Arnon River, which drains into the Dead Sea about twenty miles south of the sea's north shore, to the Zered River at the southern end of the sea where the territory of Edom began (Num. 21:10–13). On the east the border would have been less well defined, merely extending to the edge of the arable land. The total territory would have been about thirty miles long and thirty wide.

Israel's relations with Moab were always somewhat ambiguous (as compared with Edom, where the hostility was mutually unrelenting). That there was a close kinship between the two nations is not only argued by the genealogical statements (Gen. 19:37; Deut. 2:9) but also by the near-

6. Lit. "he." Driver, *JTS* 38 (1937) 40, would instead change the other plurals to agree with this singular.
7. It is tempting to make some identification of *ʿărābîm*, "poplars," with Iye-abarim, which Num. 21:11 locates at the southern border of Moab. For the possible interchange of consonants, see GKC, § 19n.
8. 1QIs[a] and LXX read *Dibon*. Orlinsky characteristically argues for the priority of *Dimon* (*IEJ* 4 [1954] 5–8).
9. *ARAB*, II:193–95; *ANET*, pp. 286, 287.

identity of language and script as shown in the well-known Mesha Inscription.[10] The relative ease of emigration and immigration described in Ruth also points to rather close and harmonious relations. This closeness may account for what seem to be genuine tones of grief that appear in these chapters.

On the other hand, that both nations laid claim to the lands north of the Arnon (the land of Ammon which was given to Reuben and Gad, Num. 32:1–5; 33–38)[11] was a continuing source of conflict between them (Num. 21:24–30; Judg. 3:12–30; 11:22–26; 1 Sam. 14:47; 2 K. 3:4–27) until there was ultimately a deep hostility (Zeph. 2:9, 10).[12]

The segment begins with a lament over a sudden disaster which will fall upon Moab and reduce the nation to refugees (15:1–9). The second section (16:1–5) is a plea on behalf of the refugees, perhaps for shelter in Judah. The third section (16:6–12) contrasts Moab's former pride with her fallen state, and the fourth (16:13, 14) is the postscript covering the application. The thrust of the oracle is to discourage any who would be tempted to join with proud Moab for purposes of mutual security. Moab will be reduced to the most abject circumstances and will herself be forced to rely on Judah's only hope: the Messiah (16:5).

The language and style of chs. 15 and 16 are often very obscure. This difficulty, coupled with the fact that Jer. 48 duplicates certain portions but in different order and structure, has led many scholars to posit a very complex literary history for the present chapters.[13] However, there is virtually no agreement from one scholar to the next, as Kaiser has shown. Thus, while Hitzig dates the initial ideas and forms to Jonah, Duhm attributed them to a second-century B.C. redactor. At the least, the similarity between the statements in Jeremiah and Isaiah and the fact that they are admittedly reused in Isaiah suggest there may have been a standard poetic treatment of Moab that had entered "the common domain" and was thus drawn upon by both prophets.

The first part of the prophecy, 15:1–9, tells of the devastating effect of the disaster which was to befall Moab. As noted above, the actual nature of the attack cannot be determined from the general account here.

---

10. A celebration of the successful Moabite revolt against Israelite dominion under Ahab; cf. *ANEP*, nos. 274, 286; *ANET*, pp. 320, 321; *ISBE*, III:396–98.

11. Note that the Bible habitually labels the territory from just north of the Dead Sea to the Arnon as "Moab" (Num. 26:63; Deut. 34:5; etc.).

12. For a more detailed treatment of what is known of the Moabites, cf. A. Van Zyl, *The Moabites* (Leiden: Brill, 1960).

13. For a detailed argument for Isaianic authorship, see E. Power, "The Prophecy of Isaias against Moab," *Bib* 13 (1932) 435–451.

The major emphasis is upon the effect, which will be that the Moabites will be so demoralized that their only response will be weeping and flight. Although the cities are mentioned from the general direction of south to north, that the flight is southward makes it likely that the attack was to come from the north. The difference in the tone from the words addressed to Babylon, Assyria, or the Philistines is apparent at once and carries through into ch. 16. There is a much greater sympathy for the fate of the Moabites, whereas a sort of grim delight greeted the downfall of the others.

1 This verse acts as an introduction, repeating the same words over the two chief cities of Moab proper, *Ar* on the Arnon and *Kir* farther south, the central fortress. While the verse may not mean that the nation literally fell in one night, it surely does mean to stress that the blow was sudden and swift upon a land which perhaps felt reasonably secure.[14] All the prophets had spiritual clarity to know what should be obvious to all: there is no security in this world (cf. Amos 6:1–3; Isa. 5:26–30).

2–4 These verses describe the lamentation which will take hold of the whole land. It will be as if a death has occurred, as indeed it has, with mourning taking place everywhere so that even the warriors are demoralized and shaken to the core.

2 *He went up to the house* is a rather cryptic phrase which, if correct, probably is in parallel with *high places* and refers to a temple. For a similar expression see the Sumerian "Lamentation over the Destruction of Ur."[15] *Dibon* is located about three miles north of the Arnon and thus in the land that Israel claimed. It was Mesha's native city, and a high place of the Moabite god Chemosh was located there. Obviously a part of the reason for the lament at the sanctuary was that the god had been unable to deliver his people (Jer. 48:35).

Nebo is the great mountain at the north end of the Dead Sea from which Moses saw the promised land (Deut. 34:1). Its height would have made it a defensive strongpoint (Mesha, line 14). *Medeba* is located about five miles southeast of Nebo.

Shaving the head and cutting off the beard, along with gashing oneself (Jer. 48:37) and wearing sackcloth, were typical signs of mourning and lament (22:12; 2 Sam. 3:31; Jer. 4:8; 41:5; Lam. 2:10).

4 *Heshbon* and *Elealeh* were the northernmost cities in the area

14. Mesha's claim to have captured the Israelite center of occupation, Ataroth, in one night gives rise to the speculation that the statement in Isaiah, or in Isaiah's original, is in response to Mesha's.

15. *ANET,* p. 457, lines 116–133.

disputed by Israel and Moab, situated within about two miles of each other. *Jahaz*, however, is back to the south again, some ten to twelve miles away from Heshbon (Mesha, lines 18–22). Figuratively, the wailing of one city can be heard in every other.[16]

The end result of the attitude of helplessness that will sweep the land will be that even the armed men (lit. "prepared ones") will let out a cry of despair and defeat. They will be shaken to the very core ("the life," *nepeš*).

5–9 In these verses flight is added to lament, and the speaker is moved at the thought of long lines of frightened, uprooted people, clutching a pitiful bit of their possessions, trying to reach some place of security. These images should also grip us of the twentieth century, which has seen perhaps more refugees than any other century yet. The picture of an old woman pushing a perambulator containing a lamp, a framed picture, and a party dress down a road somewhere in France in 1940 should remind us that nothing we possess is ours to keep. Abundance is only to be found within (Matt. 16:26; John 10:10).

5 *Zoar*, if correctly identified, is located at the southern end of the Dead Sea within the territory of Edom. Evidently the refugees were escaping the main area of conflict farther north.

Eglath-shelishiyah is translated "a heifer of three years" by AV (with LXX), and commentators have labored with some success to extract sense from that (cf. Young, who sees it as a reference to a young cow which must suffer the yoke for the first time), but it is probably a place name, as also in Jer. 48:34.[17]

Luhith and *Horonaim* are not known, but may be in the vicinity of Zoar.[18]

This verse begins a series of distichs opening with *kî*. Young suggests that they give reasons for Isaiah's sympathetic reaction. This may be so, but the causal connection seems somewhat overdone in that case.

6–8 *Nimrim* may possibly be the Wadi Numeira on the south-

---

16. Kaiser suggests that the attack must have proceeded from Ar and Kir toward Heshbon and Elealeh, but that need not be the case, since this is clearly a poetic piece whose main purpose is to depict total demoralization. A literal interpretation then demands another attack from the north toward Jahaz, and the whole structure becomes very shaky.

17. Clements takes the reference here to have been originally a marginal cross reference to Jer. 48:34.

18. Kaiser, citing W. Schottroff, "Horonaim, Nimrim, Luluth und der Westrand des 'Landes Ataroth'," *ZDPV* 82 (1966) 202.

eastern shore of the Dead Sea. The sense may be that the crowd of refugees is so great that the oasis cannot support them and their animals, with the result (v. 7, "therefore") that they must abandon the animals and continue on with what little they can carry themselves. More figuratively, the dried up waters and dead grass may refer to the general devastation of the land as a whole.

gains and *provisions* speak poignantly of our human attempt to care for ourselves and to stock up enough in advance so that we will never be in want. Unfortunately, those provisions are hard to keep for ourselves and they cannot satisfy the want we have (32:9–15; Matt. 6:25–33).

Wadi of the Poplars is possibly the Zered River (Wadi el-Hesa), which formed the border with Edom.

The cries of the fugitives fill the land from end to end and border to border. They reach from the Zered in the south to Eglaim near Kir and Beer-elim north of the Arnon.

9 This verse puts a capstone on the horror, indicating that although people may flee, they will not escape. Blood will be added to blood.

Dimon is unknown and it was suggested as early as Jerome that the labials *b* and *m* were both used in the name *Dibon* and that the *m* is used here as a wordplay on "blood," *dām*.[19] If Dibon was as important a political and religious center as Mesha indicates it was, it would be fitting to close this portion of the lament by using the part to represent the whole.

still more is strangely vague and has provoked suggestions that an additional word has dropped out. At the same time the very vagueness may harbor an intentionally ominous quality.

The reference to *a lion* has been looked upon by many as a textual corruption.[20] Yet it is very similar to the figure used by Amos when he talks of fleeing a lion and meeting a bear (5:19).[21] In this same vein, the prophet here could be saying that running may not give any more security than staying behind. To strike out across the wilderness may deliver you *from* an army but *unto* a ravening animal. There is no security in our own efforts.

19. See J. P. Migne, *Patrologia Cursus Completus, Series Latina*, 221 vols. (Paris: Venit Apud Editorem, 1844–1864), 24:170.
20. Cf. *BHS*. JPSV emends *'aryēh*, "lion," to *'arayyāwâ*, "I drench it," on the basis of 16:9.
21. Wildberger notes Jer. 4:7 and 50:17 where the Chaldeans (and the Assyrians) are compared to devouring lions.

(b) Response (16:1–14)

  (i) Plea for mercy (16:1–5)

1 *Send a landlord's lamb*[1]
  from the rock of the desert to the mountain of the daughter of
  Zion.
2 *So it is that, like a wandering bird*
    pushed from the nest
  are the daughters of Moab
    at the fords[2] *of the Arnon.*
3 *Bring forth counsel;*
    perform the office of judge.
  Make your shadow like night
    in the midst of noonday brightness.
4 *Let my fugitives sojourn among you;*
    Moab—become a hiding place for him from the oppressor.
  When[3] *the ruthless*[4] *has ceased,*
    the violent man come to an end,
    and the trampler be finished from the earth,
5 *then will a throne be established in mercy,*
    and he will sit upon it in faithfulness in the tent of David:
  a judge who seeks justice
    and is prompt in righteousness.

The response to the lament for Moab contains three parts. The first, vv. 1–5, seems to be plea to Judah from the Moabites (see below). The second, vv. 6–12, is not so much a response to that plea as it is a reaction to it. It contrasts the former pride and abundance of Moab with its fallen state, which, it may be supposed, would lead to such a plea being entered. The final section, vv. 13 and 14, calls to the reader's attention that all these events could be expected to happen within three years, suggesting a possible date of 715/714 for these final verses at least. The overall thrust of the response is to stress again the helplessness of Moab despite her proud

1. Lit. "a lamb of the lord of the land," an ambiguous phrase since the genitive could be objective or subjective. Thus either *"from* the lord of the land" or *"to* the lord of the land." The present interpretation assumes the latter. LXX apparently redivides the Hebrew consonants to arrive at "I will send as it were creeping things on the earth" (?).
2. Apparently the absence of the preposition on "fords" prompted LXX and Targ. to translate ʿᵃḇārîm in other unsuccessful ways: LXX "against you Arnon, yet further"; Targ. "carried over the Arnon." The word is probably an accusative of location (with Young). Cf. GKC, §§ 118d, g.
3. For the use of kî as "when" see Williams, *Syntax,* § 496.
4. Reading ḥāmôṣ with 1QIsᵃ (see KB, p. 312), for MT hammēṣ.

abundance and to emphasize to the Judeans that they should not put their trust in Moab. In fact, Moab will one day come to them and their Messiah.

Verses 1–5 continue to present severe textual and interpretational difficulties.[5] The ancient versions frequently give dramatically different readings from the MT but with little agreement among them, testifying to the fact that they too were struggling with a difficult passage and were attempting to make sense of it in diverse ways. Earlier interpreters took the passage as Zion addressing Moab, but some thought it might be the counsel of the Edomites to the Moabites. More recently it has been thought to be a message which the prophet puts in the mouth of some of the Moabites to their embassy to Jerusalem requesting asylum for themselves. This interpretation is not without problems, as noted below, but on the whole it seems the best proposal to date. The messianic flavor of v. 5 has made it suspect in the eyes of most modern commentators. However, if the statement is being put in the mouths of Moabites (it can be granted that the Moabites themselves would not have much acquaintance with the promises of the Hebrew Messiah), and if Isaiah is granted any messianic expectations, then it is not at all impossible for him to introduce such a statement in this context. In fact, the use of the statements fits the overall thrust of this segment of the book very well (see on v. 5 below).

1 *Send a landlord's lamb* suggests the sending of tribute to an overlord, such as Mesha did for Omri of Israel (2 K. 3:4), as an indication of submission. Moab was excellent sheep-grazing country (Num. 32:4), and so this would be a logical tribute for those seeking Judah's protection.

from the rock . . . to the mountain seems to be a play on words. However, *sela'* is also a place name in Edom (2 K. 14:7; also Judg. 1:36?) that has been associated with Petra, the capital of Nabatea. Thus it may be that the fugitives of ch. 15 are visualized as having escaped to Edom and are sending their embassy from there. At the same time, it is not necessary to assume a direct connection between 16:1–5 and ch. 15. The point may simply be that the Moabites have retreated to some wilderness stronghold and are sending their plea for help to the greater stronghold, Mount Zion.[6]

5. Gray is very pessimistic about the state of the text. The most recent consensus is much more favorable toward the authenticity of vv. 1, 3, and 4a, taking v. 2 to be transposed from ch. 15 and vv. 4b, 5 to be a later addition. Cf. Wildberger.

6. Delitzsch points out that the same shift which appears here, that is, from judgment to fear to attachment and love, also appears in 14:32; 18:7; 19:6; and 23:18. The same point is being made throughout: why trust them when their only hope is our God?

2 That this verse does not follow v. 1 closely but can be connected with 15:8, 9 has prompted the suggestion that it was the original conclusion of the lament and, as such, immediately preceded what is now 16:1. In some way, then, the two verses became transposed.[7] This is certainly not impossible, but there is no manuscript evidence in support of such a transposition, and it is difficult to imagine how or why it would have taken place given the difficult reading it has created.

On the other hand, it is possible that this verse constitutes the opening words of the plea for asylum that the messengers were to make to the Judeans. Since the inhabitants of Moab[8] are like birds pushed from the nest, they must seek refuge elsewhere.[9] Thus the verse supplies the rationale for the request. If the refugees were in Edom, the reference to the fords of the Arnon at the north edge of Edom seems a bit strange. However, this may be merely a stereotyped phrase which has been pressed into service here to express the agitated flight of the Moabites (see also *sela*ʿ, v. 1).

3, 4a The message here moves into its request for refuge. *counsel* here is not so much advice as it is a plan of action, as the parallel phrase shows (cf. also 14:24, 26). To *perform the office of judge* was not merely to give a neutral decision; it was to take positive action on behalf of those who had a justifiable need for deliverance.[10] So, then, the request for the Judeans to become a shelter from the noonday sun is a figurative way of asking them to take steps to become a refuge from the terrible blows which had so demoralized the Moabites. In the Near East, the shelter of some great rock at noon was a gift for which to be devoutly thankful.[11]

my fugitives . . . Moab was a major reason for some older commentators' belief that the passage was addressed to Moab.[12] This view assumes that the fugitives mentioned are from Judah. But this interpretation is very strange in the context of Moabite destruction. Modern commentators, adducing support from the versions, solve the problem by changing

7. So Gressmann. Duhm placed it between 15:8 and 9.
8. The "daughters of Moab" may refer to the actual women of Moab, but equally likely it speaks of the villages and towns of Moab, and thus its inhabitants (cf. 3:16, 17; Ezek. 16:55–57).
9. Cf. 10:14; 31:5.
10. *TWOT*, II:947, 948.
11. See 4:6; 30:2, 3; 32:3; 49:2; 51:6; Judg. 9:15; Ps. 91:1; 121:5; Hos. 14:7. The permanent visitor in the land (Heb. *gēr*) came under special protection (Deut. 5:14; 10:19; etc.).
12. Calvin took 16:1–5 as an ironic statement telling the Moabites what they should have done in earlier times before it was too late.

"my fugitives," *niddāḥay,* to "the fugitives of," *nidd°ḥê.*[13] The present reading understands the fugitives to refer to Moab, but without emending the text. Rather, it sees the speaker as a personification of Moab with the "my" then referring to the speaker.[14]

4b, 5 As noted above, the prophet here puts words in the Moabite messenger's mouth. He looks forward to the day when the oppression which has driven the Moabites into the Hebrews' arms will be brought to an end by that ideal ruler of the Davidic house. Because of his attachment to mercy, faithfulness, justice, and righteousness, oppression will not be able to coexist with him (cf. Ps. 89:2–5 [Eng. 1–4]). He will offer a kind of security that will be more permanent than any heretofore known. This vision is clearly messianic, as comparison with 9:1–6 (Eng. 2–7) and 11:1–9 must show. Isaiah recognizes that Moab's hope is identical with Judah's. Both wait for a King of Israel who will somehow embody those traits which are in fact of the character of God (Ps. 89:14–38 [Eng. 13–37]). Here then is another way of expressing the truth of 2:1–4: Moab is representative of the nations which will come to the mountain of God to learn his ways, ways which are incarnated in a person who is the true ruler[15] of Israel.

(ii) The fall of Moab's proud vines (16:6–12)

6 *We have heard of the pride of Moab,*
   his excessive pride and arrogance,
his pride and overbearing,
   but his empty talk[1] is not so.
7 *Therefore, Moab howls for Moab,*
   all of it howls.

13. Vulg. has "my"; LXX "the exiles, O Moab"; Targ. "O kingdom of Moab."

14. As Delitzsch points out, the Masoretic punctuation calls for this reading ("Moab" is separated from "my fugitives" and joined to "become a hiding place for him").

15. Note that the person is not called "king" *(meleḵ)* (as also in chs. 9 and 11). Could it be that one who has seen the King (6:5; 33:17; 44:6) is reluctant to apply that term to the seed of David? Of course, as the Messiah was ultimately revealed he had full claim to the title.

1. JPSV takes *baddāyw* as a preposition with 3rd masculine singular suffix and translates "and of the iniquity in him." C. Rabin, *JSS* 18 (1973) 57, 58, cites the Vulg. *fortitudo* as support for an Arabic etymology of *bdd* as "strength." D. Dimant, *JSS* 18 (1973) 56, believes the Targ. translates *bdd* with the word for "nobles" which appears at an earlier place in the Targ. rendering of the verse. Note that *bdd* is used of foolish or empty talk when it is applied to diviners or sorcerers (44:25).

For the raisin cakes[2] of Kir-hareseth
   they moan, utterly stricken.
8 *For the fields of Heshbon wither,*
   the vine of Sibmah.[3]
The lords of the nations have broken down the choice vines
   which reached as far as Jazer
   and trailed into the desert.
Its shoots spread abroad;
   they went over the sea.
9 *Therefore I weep with the weeping of Jazer,*
   O vine of Sibmah.
I drench you[4] with my tears,
   Heshbon and Elealeh.
Because over your ripe fruit and over your harvest,[5]
   the shout of joy[6] has fallen still.
10 *Joy and gladness have been gathered*
   from the orchard,
and in the vineyard
   no one sings, no one shouts.
The treader does not tread wine in the wine vats;
   I have made the happy shouts to cease.[7]
11 *Therefore my bowels moan like a harp for Moab,*
   my inward parts for Kir-hares.
12 *When Moab appears on the high place*
   he will become weary.[8]

2. The AV rendering of *'ašîšê* as "foundations" comes from the Syriac. While "foundations" seems more suitable in reference to a fortress like Kir, "raisin cakes" is more likely in the total context. Jer. 48:31 has "men of Kir," an apparent confusion of *'šyšy* with *'nšy*.

3. 1QIs[a] has an interesting example of homoioteleuton, leaving out everything between Sibmah in v. 8 and Sibmah in v. 9.

4. There is apparently a transposition of letters in *'arayyāwek*. Read *'arawwāyek*, "I will drench you"; cf. 1QIs[a]. See n. 20 on 15:1–9.

5. Note also the assonance of *qêṣēk*, "your ripe fruit," and *qᵉṣîrēk*, "your harvest" (Jer. 48:33, *bᵉṣîrēk*, "your vintage").

6. *hêḏāḏ*, "shout," can indicate both the shout of joy and the exultant cry of a conqueror (Jer. 25:30). Therefore it would have a double meaning here and in v. 10.

7. Both LXX and Targ. make "treading" the subject of "ceased" and do not indicate who causes the cessation. So *BHK hāšbāṯ*, "it has ceased."

8. Depending upon one's perspective, *kî nirʾâ kî nilʾâ*, "(It shall be) when he (Moab) appears that he will be weary," is either a poetic device making use of assonance or a textual error of dittography, a later scribe having changed the original *r* to an *l* in the dittograph to make some sense of it. The first gives better parallelism with "he is not able" in the second stich.

344

> *When he comes to his sanctuary to pray,*
> *he will not be able.*

Verses 6–12 contain an elegiac reflection on Moab's pride[9] and abundance and on the futility of it all.

6 These words have frequently been taken as a response to vv. 1–5 and their plea for refuge. As such they would contain a not-so-subtle mockery of the suppliants who are no longer proud and overbearing, but now come creeping with piteous cries for mercy. It is also possible that the words are not so much a direct response as they are the beginning of a larger reflection on the ephemeral nature of human pride and glory. This interpretation would take some of the sting of mockery away that seems somewhat inconsistent with the apparently genuine grief expressed in v. 9.

his empty talk, if correctly translated, speaks of the foolishness of human pride, a favorite theme of Isaiah's (cf. 2:5–22). All the wealth and abundance which formed the basis of Moab's, or any nation's, claims to superiority can be stripped away in a single night (15:1). (How much more is this true in the nuclear age!) All that we have of intelligence or diligence or conducive environment is a gift to be gratefully received and held in trust. It is not a matter for foolish boasts.

Verses 7–11 contain an extended metaphor in which Moab is compared to a luxurious grapevine which had spread out over the whole region but now is trampled down, so that the shouts of laughter and excitement which once attended the harvest have now been silenced and replaced with wails of grief.

7 *Therefore, Moab howls.* It is difficult to know whether the "therefore" is intended to express the result of the emptiness of Moab's boasts or the prior result of the cause stated in v. 8.[10] That v. 8 begins with *kî,* "for," suggests that the latter alternative is the correct one: "Howl, because the fertile fields are empty."

raisin cakes, apparently small blocks of pressed raisins, were considered a delicacy and were used in various feasts (2 Sam. 6:19; Cant. 2:5; Hos. 3:1). There is no particular reason to associate them with Kir-

---

9. On Moab's pride see 25:10, 11; Zeph. 2:8. Note that the parallel, Jer. 48:29, is not construed as a response, but is more in the nature of a reflection, as suggested here. For Gray and others, the difference in tone between vv. 6 and 9 means that v. 6 has no connection with the following verses. The piling up of the various forms of the word for "pride" *(ge'ôn, gē', ga'awâ)* lends dramatic emphasis to the claim.

10. R. Traina, *Methodical Bible Study* (New York: Biblical Seminary, 1952), p. 5, calls this relationship substantiation.

hareseth except that like Heshbon (vv. 8, 9), Kir was a major city of Moab.[11]

8 According to Jerome, Heshbon and Sibmah were neighboring cities, Sibmah (modern Sumia) being a suburb of larger Heshbon. The synonymous parallelism here lends support to that identification.

The lords of the nations have broken down is in agreement with the first statement of the verses, that the vines are withered and bare. But many commentators, including Delitzsch, have observed on the basis of 28:1 that the verb has a passive significance. Thus they translate, "The choice vines have struck down (in drunkenness) the lords of the nations." However, Kissane's comment that it is wine (28:1), not the vines, which overcomes people is appropriate and points toward the present reading.

The vine is depicted not as staked up[12] but creeping along the ground northward toward *Jazer,* the extreme northern border of the territory claimed by Moab, to the east to the edges of the desert, and westward, even across the Dead Sea, probably indicating the export of Moabite wines and raisins to Judah.

9 The prospect of the destruction of the rich land reduces the prophet to tears. Some have suggested that this show of emotion was only feigned, since he was after all announcing the destruction of, if not an enemy, at least a hostile party. But this need not be the case. One need only think of a Jeremiah weeping over the fate of those he was denouncing. Furthermore, the prospect of the destruction of so much effort and care on the part of so many people and the reducing of ordered, cultivated lands to wilderness is certainly cause for despair, no matter who the people may be.[13] This speaks too of the compassion of God, for the prophet usually identified himself with God. The hand which metes out judgment is not separated from the spirit which grieves over the necessity and effects of such judgment. So the God who has stilled the shouts of joy (v. 10) is also the God who weeps for and with those who now cry (Hos. 11:1–9).[14] The God of the OT is not a force, not even a personalized force. He is a full-orbed personality interacting in depth with persons.

11. See 2 K. 3:25. Probably this is the same as Kir in Isa. 15:1.

12. The practice of allowing vines to remain unstaked, allowing the "head" from which the tendrils sprout to rest on a large flat rock, is still carried on in the hill country of Judah today.

13. The author recalls the sense of despair and grief which he experienced when reading through the Assyrian Annals in a course in Akkadian. The record of burning, looting, and killing became almost intolerable to read.

14. Contra Gray, who asserts that the same person cannot be intended by all the 1st person references in vv. 9–11.

10 The harvest was normally concluded with the gathering of the grapes, when the whole population would move out from the villages and live in makeshift shelters in the vineyards (1:8; Lev. 23:33–43).[15] This occurred in late September or early October. Particularly if the rest of the harvest had been good this was a great time of relaxation and exuberance. They knew that the demon of famine had been kept from the door for another winter. There was also a slight release from relentless labor before the next cycle had to be started. To all of this, the new wine, only recently trodden out in the great stone vats which resided in the vineyards for that purpose, added its own measure of gaiety.

But none of this would be so in the Moab which Isaiah envisioned. The vine of Moab is broken down and withered. All that has been gathered in this year are the former joy and gladness. God has ended the shouting.

11 *my bowels moan* may sound at first almost ludicrous to a Westerner. Yet, we know what it is to feel our stomach churn over some shock or anxiety or grief. So it should not come as a surprise that people of the Near East should see the upper abdominal area (the pit of the stomach?) as the seat of emotions (63:15; Cant. 5:4; Jer. 31:20; Lam. 1:20; 2:11; Phil. 1:8; Col. 3:12; so also the liver, Lam. 2:11).[16]

12 Not only are Moab's pride and abundance futile, but so too is his religion. When he goes to the high place the only thing he gets is weariness. The rituals repeated again and again do not produce the desired result. Chemosh, the national god, is unable to help.[17] Moab is left with nothing upon which to rely. Is there any reason for Judah to entrust herself to Moab? No! Is God able to deliver his people from the nations? Yes!

(iii) Within three years (16:13–14)

13 *This is the word which the Lord spoke to Moab formerly.*

14 *But now the Lord has spoken, saying, "In three years like the years of a hireling, then the glory of Moab will be few and small, not much."*

15. M. S. and J. L. Miller, *Harper's Encyclopedia of Bible Life,* 3rd ed. (San Francisco: Harper & Row, 1978), p. 184.

16. As is well known, unresolved feelings will make themselves apparent through disorders of the digestive tract. It is interesting to note that the Targ. makes it Moab's bowels. Apparently by the time the Targ. was written, compassion for one's enemies had become inconceivable.

17. "he will not be able" may refer to the worshiper, i.e., he will not be able to get what he wants. Or it may refer, as here, to the god and his ability to perform the requests (44:9–20; 47:13; 1 K. 18:25–29; Mal. 1:12–13; Matt. 6:7). Jer. 48:7, 13 envision a time when disillusionment with Chemosh will be so great that the Moabites will turn to the Lord.

Verses 13–14 are the prediction concerning the fulfillment of the oracle.[1]
Formerly (mē'āz) can refer to a long time (44:8; Prov. 8:22) or a short time
(2 Sam. 15:34) in the past. Thus this material on Moab could have been
derived from sources considerably older than Isaiah and compiled by him
for this purpose, or they could be words spoken by him a few months or
years prior to this indication of their significance by the Spirit.

like the years of a hireling is certainly an indication of reckoning on
a very painstaking scale, as one who enters voluntary indenture is not
going to stay in that state a moment longer than the agreement requires.[2]
Unfortunately, we have no certain historical date by which to examine the
fulfillment, but we may have confidence that it was fulfilled in a satisfactory
manner or else the Jewish community would not have permitted its inclusion here.

the glory of Moab. Once again national glory and pride falls before
the One in whom alone glory is found. Only that glory which is derived
from God, freely shared, will last (John 17:1–5, 22). All others will vanish
like fading grass (Isa. 40:6–8).

(3) Syria and Ephraim (17:1–11)

(a) Desolate ruins (17:1–6)

> 1 The burden of Damascus:
> Behold, Damascus is removed[1] from being a city;
> it will become a ruin,[2] shambles.
> 2 The cities of Aroer[3] will be forsaken.
> They shall be for flocks;
> they shall lie down and no one will frighten them.

1. Kaiser, confident that numerological interest is wholly apocalyptic (a
misplaced confidence, I think), asserts that this passage is the work of an over-
eager apocalypticist who expected the consummation of all things in three years.
(For a nonapocalyptic use, see 2 Sam. 24:12, 13; see also Jer. 25:11, 12; 29:10,
which are also attributed by some to apocalyptic.)
2. Cf. 21:16; Job 7:1–3.
1. *hinnēh . . . mûsār* is a participial construction indicating imminent action, "Behold, Damascus is on the point of being removed."
2. Note the wordplay between "from a city," *mē'îr,* and "ruin," *me'î.*
3. "the cities of Aroer" constitutes a problem in that the Targ. lacks the
name and the LXX adds "forever," suggesting that "Aroer," *'arō'ēr,* is a mistake
for *'adê 'ad.* The *r* and *d* are easily mistaken in Hebrew script. This suggestion is
strengthened by the fact that the only Aroers known in the Bible are from considerably south of Damascus in Moab and Judah (Josh. 12:2; 13:9; 1 Sam. 30:28).
At the same time "the cities of Aroer" constitutes a very typical wordplay: *'ārê*
'arō'ēr, and there may well have been a city of that name in Syria of whose
existence the Bible does not otherwise tell us.

3 *The fortress will be cut off from Ephraim,*
and dominion from Damascus,
and the remnant of Aram⁴
will be like the glory of Israel, says the Lord of Hosts.⁵
4 *In that day the glory of Jacob will be low,*
and the fatness of his flesh will be lean.
5 *It will be as when a reaper⁶ harvests grain*
and his arm gathers the ears of grain;
as one gathers gleanings
in the Valley of Rephaim.⁷
6 *Gleanings will be left in it*
as when an olive tree is beaten:
Two or three berries at the very top,
four or five on its fruitful branches.

After dealing with Judah's two southern neighbors, Philistia and Moab, Isaiah now turns to address the two on the north. Although the oracle is addressed to Damascus, the main focus after v. 3 is upon Northern Israel. This combined treatment suggests that the prophecy is one of the earlier ones, having originated during the Syro-Ephraimite alliance in 735–732. It is not possible to say with absolute confidence why it was included at this point in the collection of oracles against the nations; however, the stress upon failure to trust God and the results of that failure (vv. 7–11) remind one strongly of the emphasis of chs. 7–12, as does the following treatment (17:12–18:7), on the certainty of God's triumph. Thus, whether or not it was intended to do so, the entire segment (17:1–18:7) serves as an excellent midpoint summary to hold before the reader again the central issues: refusal to depend upon God is foolishness which will result in destruction by the nations. Nevertheless, God is in control of the nations and he will not permit them to obliterate his people. Despite all the raging of the nations, he is their master.

4. MT punctuation includes "and the remnant of Aram" with "from Damascus." But this reading makes the first part of the sentence very long and the second part very short. The present reading offers a better balance. (Cf. *BHS* and RSV, NEB, NIV.)

5. The LXX removes "says the Lord of Hosts" from v. 3 and attaches it to the beginning of v. 4, but the rest of the versions support the MT. Cf. *BHS* for an ordering which would agree with LXX.

6. It is unnecessary to repoint *qāṣîr* to *qōṣēr* to arrive at the meaning "reaper" (contra, e.g., Clements). As Delitzsch pointed out, this is a normal noun form although not otherwise attested with this meaning (cf. *pārîṣ*, "violent one").

7. "Rephaim" can mean both "mighty men" and "the dead" (BDB, p. 952). This double meaning along with the fertility of the valley probably accounts for its usage here (cf. Josh. 15:8; 2 Sam. 5:18, 22). On gleaning see Lev. 19:9, 10; Ruth 2:2, 7, 15.

1, 2 *Damascus* was one of the most strategic cities of the ancient world, for it stood at the mouth of a natural funnel through which ran the only convenient land route between Mesopotamia and Egypt. North of the city stands Mount Hermon and south of it are a series of basalt plateaus. Both of these constitute barriers to caravan travel. As a result, Damascus exercised an influence far beyond other cities of comparable size. Yet Isaiah says that Damascus will be turned from a city into a ruin. By the time of the prophecies against Philistia and Moab, this prophecy had already come true in large part, as Shalmaneser had conquered it after a ruinous siege in 732. For every influential power, there is always a greater one which can reduce it to desolation. The only hope is in the greatest power of all.

3 Here the prophet begins to treat Ephraim and Syria together. As they have linked themselves in an alliance, so too their fates are linked. Neither will constitute a source of power or stability; as Israel will lose the capacity to defend herself *(the fortress)*, so Damascus will lose authority to rule over neighboring cities *(the dominion)*. While Syria will not be totally destroyed, it will, like Israel, be left as just a shadow of itself. Its glory will be like Israel's, a condition the prophet goes on to describe in the next three verses.

4–6 As noted above (see on 6:3), the concept of glory in Hebrew carries with it the connotations of permanence, abundance, significance, and reality. The *glory* of Jacob, as shared by Syria, will be none of these. God will expose to the world that the "glory" of Israel, which she has achieved through her own strength, is nothing but a fraud. The arrogant haughtiness will be replaced by a creeping self-abnegation. One cannot help but compare the erect, powerful Adolf Eichmann of the war years with the hunched little man who sat before his Israeli inquisitors. So the hollow shell of this world's glory is ripped open to expose the true nature of what dwells within (3:16–4:1).

The prophet uses three figures of speech to describe what will remain to Israel (and Syria). The first is physical and the second two are agricultural. All three stress the pitiful nature of what will be left. Folds of gray skin hang from the man who once was fat and shining. The lush fields of the Valley of Rephaim southwest of Jerusalem are cut over, and all that remains of the rich crop are a few stray stalks fallen from the reapers' arms and left for the poor to pick up. The olive trees have been beaten with sticks to shake off the ripe fruit and only a few odd olives are left to be picked off by the poor (Deut. 24:20). In each of these ways, then, the prophet says that only bits and pieces will be left to Damascus and

Ephraim when God has done his work (24:13; Amos 3:12). Judah need not fear her neighbors; it is God with whom she should come to terms.

(b) They have forgotten God (17:7–11)

> 7 *In that day a man will regard his Maker,*
>   *and his eyes will look to the Holy One of Israel.*
> 8 *He will no longer regard the altars which are the work of his hands;*
>   *that which his fingers made he will not look to,*
>   *neither Asherahs nor incense altars.*[1]
> 9 *In that day his strong cities will be like a forsaken place on the heights*
>   *and summits*[2] *which they abandoned before the sons of Israel. It will*
>   *be desolate.*
> 10 *Because you*[3] *have forgotten the God of your salvation*
>   *and have not remembered the Rock of your refuge,*
>   *therefore, you will plant pleasant plants*
>   *and set out strange shoots.*
> 11 *On the day you plant you will make it grow;*[4]
>   *on the morning you sow you will make it bud,*
>   *but the harvest will flee away*[5]
>   *in a day of grief and unrelieved pain.*

This coming to terms with God is exactly what the prophet foresees as issuing from the coming destruction. No longer able to rely on their own strength, the people of Israel will finally turn back to the God they had forgotten. This repentance will not halt the destruction, but it will show them the fallacy of the course upon which they had been walking.

Virtually all modern commentators have argued that vv. 7–8 are

1. Note that *BHS* deletes the references to altars, Asherahs, etc., apparently in the interests of shortening the line. The ancient versions do not support this deletion. Kissane and others understand *ḥammānîm*, "incense altars," as a reference to Baal-Hamman, the Syrian sun-deity (so Targ.), but the general Hebrew usage is "incense altar" (Ezek. 6:4, 6), which may or may not have a derivation from Baal-Hamman. The word is used exclusively of pagan worship.

2. An attractive emendation (*BHS*, supported by the LXX) would change *haḥōreš weʾhāʾāmîr*, "heights and summits," to *hāḥiwwî weʾhāʾĕmōrî*, "Hivites and Amorites." The general sense would be the same as that suggested above.

3. The person here is 2nd feminine, perhaps indicating that the prophet is addressing the "virgin Israel" (Amos 5:2).

4. The normal rendering of *teśagśēgî* would be "hedge about" (so AV), taking the root to be *śûg*. But the parallel seems to demand "make it grow," and a suitable root, though not normally taking a form like this, is *śāgāʾ*.

5. *nēḏ* is translated "heap" elsewhere in the OT, but it makes better sense in this passage to take it as an anomolous verb form of *ndd*, "to flee away." (Both LXX and Targ. vary widely from MT on this verse and also from each other.)

misplaced, not only because they seem to interrupt the flow of thought from v. 6 to v. 9, but also because the theology is of a postexilic variety in which the revulsion against idolatry has gained great impetus. (Gray also argues that "Maker" is a late concept in that it occurs in this book only in 51:13 and 54:5. But that same argument might be turned around by making those references dependent upon this one, especially since Maker appears in Hos. 8:14, which is hardly postexilic in date.) As noted above on vv. 4–6, there may not be as much of a breach in the chain of thought as first appears. The concept of coming to terms with God may be the most natural one in response to the vision of coming judgment. In that case the structure of vv. 1–11 is chiastic with vv. 7, 8, providing the second theme, return, between recurring statements of the main theme, judgment. This question of the function of a passage in its present context is too little dealt with in the discussion of authorship and composition. Too often no explanation is attempted for the placing of an "interpolation" in its present setting other than accident or *tendenz*. But in too many cases this "explanation" will not do. A better answer is called for as to why the supposed "interpolator" inserted his passage where he did. And if this answer has any structural validity, then it is equally possible for the original author or editor to have inserted it there with that purpose as for some later editor to have done so.

7, 8 In these verses the author contrasts the gods who are made with the God who has made. In a tone reminiscent of 2:6–22 and 44:9–18, he points out the folly of investing one's own handiwork with ultimate significance. What we have made cannot save us, it is not fundamentally different from us, that is, holy. Yet somehow when life is going well it is very easy to live as though that were so (Hos. 4:7). It is "When Life Tumbles In"[6] that we are forced to look for One who is other than we, One who is beyond us, who holds us in his hands rather than vice versa (Isa. 10:20; Ps. 100:3; Hos. 3:5; 6:1; Mic. 7:7).

8 *Asherahs*. Asherah was the consort of El, the Canaanite high god. As such, she was the mother-goddess, the Canaanite version of the Mesopotamian Ishtar and Egyptian Isis. In some of the myths she appears alongside Astarte, Baal's consort, but in others she *is* Baal's consort. In the fertility cult she was represented by the grove of trees, perhaps poplars, surrounding the Baal altars on the high places. At other times the grove seems to have been replaced merely by poles. It is widely assumed that these trees or poles had phallic significance. (Cf. 27:9; Exod. 34:13; Deut.

---

6. The title of A. J. Gossip's famous sermon written on the occasion of his wife's sudden death; *The Hero in Thy Soul* (New York, 1929), pp. 106–116.

16:21; Judg. 6:25, 28; 2 Chr. 34:4–7; Mic. 5:14.) Instead of trying to manipulate forces of life considered to be sexually based, the people would be turning to the One who *is* life, who made sexuality, but is himself asexual.

9 This verse continues to be addressed to the reader in that it treats Israel in the third person, whereas vv. 10 and 11 speak directly to her in the second person. It continues from vv. 7 and 8 in that it begins, as v. 7 does, with *in that day*. It brings the reader back to the fact that Israel's new awareness of God will come only in the destruction and thus will not prevent it. God had called to his people in so many ways, hoping to avert the disaster (Hos. 11:1, 2; Matt. 23:37), but they will not hear until the disaster rips all their false supports from them.

heights and summits is one possible reading of the MT. If it is correct it perhaps refers to the Canaanite worship centers which were located on the hilltops and which were forsaken for a time at least before the victorious iconoclastic religion of Yahweh (Judg. 6:28). The irony of the present situation was that Israel had been sucked back into that paganism, forsaking the God who had made her victorious with the result that she would be as desolate as her enemies once had been.

10, 11 In words reminiscent of Deuteronomy, the prophet speaks directly to Israel, reminding her that it is because she has forgotten God that all her attempts to supply her needs have come to nothing. Even when the results of human achievement seem most promising, these results are bitter, as the two wars of our century and the present nuclear arms race ought to teach us.

In the theology of Deuteronomy, remembering and forgetting form a fundamental concept (e.g., 8:11–20). What is in view there is not primarily a mental activity, although it does involve such activity. Rather, remembering is a mental activity which issues in certain kinds of behavior, and the absence of the behavior negates any claimed mental activity. God wants his people to recall his unique, never-to-be-repeated acts on their behalf with the result that their present actions will be in keeping with his character. If their present actions are not of such a nature, then they do not truly remember what God has done. If God has touched my life, yet my life is not different, then I have not perceived the implications of that touch, and it is in fact void of significance (1 Cor. 11:24–29; Gal. 3:1–5). Thus, the Israelites may well have continued to look to Yahweh as their national god. They probably continued to see themselves as orthodox even while assimilating idolatry and paganism into their faith. But in fact, the significance of God's acts on Israel's behalf was lost on them, as their manipulative attempts to make themselves secure demonstrated.

The description of the activity in vv. 10b and 11 is reminiscent of that attributed to the Adonis cult, where potted plants were force-bloomed and then allowed to die as symbolic of the fertility cycle of the world.[7] This cult was a Greek version of the Tammuz worship, which is mentioned in the Bible (Ezek. 8) and which was widely practiced in the ancient Near East. The worshipers believed that by reenacting the myth of the dying and rising vegetation-god they would secure a good crop for themselves.

Whether or not the particular practices of the Adonis cult are in view here (Kissane, with Skinner, cautions that the similarities are only general, not specific), it is clear that the people are seeking to supply their own needs through their own activity. Such an approach can only be the result of a prior abandoning of the God who had shown himself both willing and able to care for them.

strange shoots (lit. "shoots of strangeness") is interpreted by some as meaning "shoots of a strange (god)." They have then suggested that *pleasant plants* refers to the plants of (the god) Naaman (the sweet one = Adonis?).[8] However, *pleasant* is used elsewhere in the book without any overtones of the divine name (32:12), and the form of *strange* is adjectival, not nominal (*zār*), so that the present reading seems preferable. Probably the reference to these exotic and beautiful plants does symbolize the lush and opulent Canaanite religion, which promised such a beautiful harvest.[9]

11 *you will make it grow.* No matter how successful one's techniques for forcing the best out of one's life, the harvest will be a bitter disappointment if those techniques avoid dependence upon God. Life's rewards have a way of slipping through the fingers of those who have grasped at those rewards, or they suddenly lose significance when they have been seized (40:24). But in God, life is given back to those who have surrendered it for love of him (65:21, 22; Matt. 16:25).

c. JUDGMENT ON ALL NATIONS (17:12–18:7)

(1) The roaring of chaff (17:12–14)

12 *Woe! The uproar of many nations*[1]—
like the roar of the sea they roar;

---

7. See R. de Vaux, *The Bible and the Ancient Near East* (New York: Doubleday, 1971), pp. 210–14.

8. A. Jirku, "Jes. 17:10c," *VT* 7 (1957) 201–202.

9. Delitszch suggests that the strange shoots refer to Israel's alliance with "foreign" Damascus. Cf. also Jer. 2:21.

1. "many nations" may refer to the multiple groups involved in the Assyrian imperial army, but it is just as likely to be simply poetic imagery. The synonymous parallelism of this verse is a good example of the poet's craft.

the tumult of the peoples—
        like the thundering of the mighty waters they thunder.
13 *Surely the peoples thunder like the thunder of many waters,[2]*
        but he will rebuke him and he will flee far away.
    He will be pursued like chaff on the mountains before the wind,
        like a tumbleweed[3] before the storm.
14 *At sunset—behold, calamity;*
        before morning—he is not.
    This is the portion of those who plunder us,
        the lot of those who loot us.

The relationships among 17:1–11; 17:12–14; and 18:1–7 have provoked a great deal of controversy, but very little unanimity.[4] The range of possibilities extends from no relationship to seeing 17:1–18:7 as a single unit (Alexander). Between these two are two other alternatives: 17:12–14 goes with 17:1–11 (Delitzsch); 17:12–14 goes with 18:1–7 (Gesenius, Duhm, Kissane). As may be seen from the outline above, this study adopts the latter point of view. Alexander's position has merit, however, for although 17:1 begins with a reference to Damascus, one is almost immediately moved beyond that narrow focus to a more general scope which covers the basic theological issues raised in chs. 7–12: the sinfulness of Israel in turning from God, the resulting destruction by the nations, the saving of the remnant, and judgment of the nations by Israel's God. These themes appear throughout 17:1–11 and they are reiterated in 17:12–14 and 18:1–7. Thus Alexander seems justified in stating that the two chapters form one statement of the doom of Judah's enemies.

That statement may not be pushed too far, however, for the materials are not unified in logical development or literary treatment. It is only a thematic unity. It is this unity which causes difficulty for Delitzsch's hypothesis. To say that vv. 12–14 are connected to 17:1–11 against 18:1–7 misses the fact that the central emphasis in vv. 1–11 is upon Judah's two northern neighbors while the attention of vv. 12–14 (and 18:1–7) is upon the destroying nations. Thus if there is an interconnection between two of

2. The first line of v. 13 duplicates the last line of v. 12 with only the change of the less common *kabbîrîm*, "mighty," to the more common *rabbîm*, "many." For this reason many commentators regard v. 13a as an original marginal note which crept into the text. The only textual support for this supposition is in the Syr. and 8 medieval Hebrew mss. The present reading regards the repetition as intentional, being introduced with a *lamed* of assertion, thus highlighting the contrast with the following statement.

3. Probably a species of wild artichoke which breaks off at the ground and rolls before the wind; Heb. *galgal*, "roller" (cf. Ps. 83:14 [Eng. 13]).

4. See Clements, Kaiser, Wildberger.

the three segments, it is between these later two, as Gesenius first claimed. That both begin with "woe" is further support of this thesis.

Nonetheless, to affirm a thematic unity is not necessarily to affirm a compositional unity. As has been observed, both 17:12–14 and 18:1–7 bear the marks of being self-contained units. What is being suggested here is that these two segments make the same point and have been grouped together here because they do so. That point seems to follow naturally upon 17:1–11, and the three segments together then serve to remind the reader that the judgments announced in vv. 13–23 are part of the larger theological construct which was introduced in chs. 7–12. (For the argument against taking 18:1–7 as one more of the oracles, see the introduction to that segment.)

Like 10:5–34, 17:12–14 declare that although the sins of Israel will bring the nations upon her like a flood (8:6–8), that flood will not prevail in any final sense. Only Israel's God is ultimate, and he will not permit his promises to his people to fail. God's name and character are at stake (Ezek. 36:23); if he cannot keep his promises, he is not God.

Although most commentators accept the authenticity of these verses (v. 13 seems to point to 701), Kaiser sees them as being proto-apocalyptic and thus postexilic. He bases this judgment on the sweeping imagery, but that is not an adequate foundation for such a radical point of view. To exclude sweeping imagery from preexilic prophecy is a glaring example of a priori reasoning.

12 The coming hordes of the enemy make a noise like the roaring of the surf. Like the sound of the sea, their rumble seems implacable and unrelenting. What can Israel do against them? Is there any hope? *Woe* here seems to be used in a very general way to express the grim and apparently hopeless situation confronting God's people.

13 In language reminiscent of Pss. 46, 48, and 76,[5] Isaiah asserts that the inevitable onslaught of the mighty Assyrians is, in fact, an illusion. They are not crashing, devouring waves, but rather *chaff* flying on the wind from the hilltop threshing floors,[6] or a rootless *tumbleweed* rolling before the storm. Both of these are lifeless and both are compelled by a

5. The use of sea imagery in Pss. 46, 48, and 76 in connection with Zion has caused both Erlandsson (*Burden,* p. 76) and Childs (*Crisis,* p. 51) to suggest that Jerusalem is in focus here. This is very plausible in view of the suggestion that 17:1–18:7 functions to reiterate the themes of chs. 7–12.

6. When the husks have been separated from the grains of wheat or barley, the mixture is tossed into the air. The chaff is blown away while the heavier grain falls back to the ground. For this reason threshing floors were located in the most windy places, the hilltops; cf. 29:5.

force outside themselves. Moreover, both are without significance. Their coming and going are of no importance. So those who are enabled to see the events of the world from God's perspective need not be troubled by the mighty conquerors who tread the earth's stage. They are not nearly so significant as they appear. Who could have believed in the spring of 1942 that Germany and Japan, between them ruling almost half the globe, would be utterly gone in three years?

As Wildberger shows, the presence of *g ʿr,* "to rebuke," in several passages relating to God's conquest of the sea makes it likely that Isaiah is here drawing on the literary imagery embodied in the widespread ancient Near Eastern myth of the high god's victory over the chaos monster in the form of the sea (cf. also 27:1; 51:9).[7] Not that Isaiah was adopting that theology; he was simply taking over what would be powerful and emotive imagery to convey the distinctly biblical theology.[8]

14 This verse climaxes the contrast which was developed in vv. 12 and 13. In a series of terse statements he shows that it is not Israel's fate which is at stake. In fact, it is the attackers who will be destroyed between night and morning. The comparison with the events of Sennacherib's attack is very inviting (37:36–38). Whether or not Isaiah intended it, his statement was prophetic. One is reminded of the early colonial flag with the coiled rattlesnake and the words "Don't Tread on Me." To tread on God's people is to invite disaster on oneself.

(2) God's message (18:1–7)

1 *Woe, land of whirring wings*
   which is beyond the rivers of Cush,
2 *Which sends envoys by sea*
   and in papyrus vessels over the surface of the waters.
Go, swift messengers
   unto a nation tall and smooth,[1]
unto a people feared on all sides,[2]

---

7. Cf. Job 26:12; Ps. 18:17 (Eng. 16); 76:8 (Eng. 7); 104:7; 106:9; Nah. 1:4.

8. Cf. Oswalt, "The Myth of the Dragon and Old Testament Faith," *EvQ* 49 (1977) 163–172.

1. *mᵉmuššāḵ* means "drawn out," from which "tall" is only an implication. JPSV translates "far," AV "scattered." *mōrāṭ* can have the connotation of "stripped bare" as well as "smooth." LXX and Targ. take the reference to be to Judah, translating "tall and smooth," "crushed and torn" (LXX, v. 7), and "robbed and spoiled" (Targ.).

2. Lit. "from it and beyond," which may be either temporal (1 Sam. 18:9) or spatial (1 Sam. 10:3).

a nation of might³ and subjugation,
whose land the rivers divide.
3 *All the inhabitants of the globe,*
    and dwellers on the earth,
    when the banner⁴ is lifted on the mountain, look;
        when the trumpet is blown, listen.⁵
4 *For thus says the Lord to me,*
    "I will be quiet and I will look⁶ from⁷ my dwelling,
    like dazzling heat on account of sunshine,⁸
    like a cloud of mist in the heat of the harvest."
5 *For before the harvest,*
    when the bud is fully developed,
    when the grape is ripening from the blossom,
    the tendrils will be cut off with pruning knives,
    and the young shoots he will completely remove.⁹
6 *All together they will be forsaken*
    to the vulture of the mountains
    and to the beast of the earth.
The vulture will summer on him,
    and every beast of the earth will winter on him.
7 *In that time a gift will be delivered to the Lord of Hosts*
    [from]¹⁰ a people tall and smooth,

3. *qaw-qaw* is taken by several to represent not "might," a reduplicated form of an Arabic word (BDB), but an onomatopoeic word for (foreign) "gibberish" (so NIV, JPSV; G. R. Driver, *JSS* 13 [1968] 46; see also 28:10, 11).

4. For the flag which calls people to attention, see 5:26, 11:10; 13:2.

5. "look" and "listen" are imperfect forms, so that "you will see" and "you will hear" are also possible (NIV, NEB, etc.). The imperative rendering is also possible, however (GKC, § 107n), and seems preferable in the light of the sending forth of messengers (AV, RSV, CBAT, etc.).

6. *nbṭ*, "to look," contains the idea of "to regard, consider, pay attention to" (cf. 5:12, where the people do not consider God's work; 66:2, where God says that he will pay attention to the humble and contrite).

7. AV *"in* my dwelling," NIV *"from* my dwelling." The texts from Ugarit have shown that the preposition *b* can mean "from" as well as "in."

8. It is possible that "sunshine," *ṣāḥ*, was actually the name of one of the summer months. An ink inscription on a clay jar at Arad seems to refer to such a month name (*PEQ* 95 [1963] 3, 4).

9. "completely remove" is lit. "he took away, he struck off" *(hēsîr hēṭaz)*. The first verb functions in an adverbial way; cf. Williams, *Syntax,* pp. 40–41. Clements believes that the verse is a reference to Egypt, giving grounds for refusing the envoy's requests. This interpretation is possible, but the total context of chs. 17 and 18 seems to make Assyria preferable.

10. There is no "from" in the MT. Its presence in the next line suggests that it was originally here also but was dropped accidentally because of the plethora of *m*s in the two words *ʿam mᵉmuššāḵ* (LXX and Vulg. have "from").

from a people feared on all sides,
  a nation of might and subjugation
whose land the rivers divide,
  unto the place of the name of the Lord of Hosts—Mount Zion.

As noted above on 17:12–14, this study considers 18:1–7 to be combined with 17:12–14 because both segments say the same thing in different words. From one perspective, 18:1–7 could constitute a particularization of the general statement made in the preceding segment in that the message is now placed in the particular context of the messenger bearing the message to the ends of the world.

In any case, this segment is not another of the oracles against the nations, as is evident superficially from the absence of *maśśā'*, "burden, oracle," at the outset. Instead, the same word is used as appeared in 17:12–14: "woe." Here, as there, the word points up the fateful and potentially disastrous times in which the prophet and his contemporaries were living. It is not directed to the Ethiopians (see on v. 2 below); no word of judgment is pronounced upon them. Rather, they are to be the bearers of a message that God will not allow oppression to come to its full fruition. This is not in any sense a judgment oracle. To be sure, the references to Ethiopia provide a transition to the oracles against Egypt; but the poem is not part of chs. 19–20. It is the closing segment of the treatment which begins in 17:1. As such it is similar to ch. 11 with its statement that despite the Assyrian threat which Judah's response to Damascus and Israel helped to provoke, God is the master of the nations and is able to make Zion the place to which all peoples will come (cf. also 2:1–4).

1 *land of whirring wings* has evoked several interpretations. Three of these are most prominent. The first is that it is a reference to insects, and that it is an identification of Cush as a land notable for its insects. This view is supported by the fact that *ṣilṣal*, "whirring," is used of insects in Deut. 28:42. However, it seems odd that so particular a description should be used of a faraway land of which the hearers would know very little. A second interpretation springs from the idea that *ṣēl* means "shadow" and that lands near the equator have a double shadow—it is sometimes on the north side of the object and sometimes on the south (cf. AV and JPSV). Again, however, this seems a far too particular description to be of much help to the average hearer in identifying a distant land. The third interpretation rests upon the LXX and Targum, both of which identify this phrase as a figure referring to ships. The prophet may be intending to say that the ships of the Ethiopians whiz up and down the rivers like winged insects. This view accords well with the reference to rivers in the second

359

line of the verse and with the opening lines of v. 2. It also supports the picture of the Ethiopians as emissaries to the world. Finally, the references to sails as wings are almost universal among sailors.

Cush is historically the land along the Nile south of the fourth cataract. It is included in what is today Ethiopia. As such, it was used as a metaphor for the ends of the earth.[11] This seems to be the purpose of its usage here. If one wishes to convey a message to all the earth, then one should call messengers from the ends of the earth. At the same time, it is possible that historical events may have prompted Isaiah's use of this kind of reference. About 715 B.C. a new dynasty began to rule in Egypt (the 25th). This dynasty was Nubian, or Cushite. This ruling family may have sent envoys to Judah as well as to Philistia and Moab to incite them to the revolt which produced Sargon's punitive action against Philistia in 711. If so, then it may have been the presence of these Ethiopian envoys in Jerusalem that sparked Isaiah's usage of them in this way.

2 The first two lines of this verse support the point just made, with the picture of the envoys travelling up and down the waters in light, swift boats made of papyrus reeds.[12] Many commentators translate *sea* as "Nile," pointing out that the Egyptians called the Nile "sea" just as some modern Arabs do the Euphrates (so also 19:5; Nah. 3:8). Whether the Ethiopian envoys to Jerusalem, if there were such, would have ventured on the Mediterranean in papyrus vessels is unknown, but the picture of the swift messengers would be the same in any case.

Go . . . introduces the directive to the messengers. It seems unlikely that this was said to actual envoys in response to their offers of aid to revolt against Egypt, because the directive is so enigmatic. If the prophet was intending to give a message to the Ethiopian rulers of Egypt, it seems more likely he would have said, "Return." Also, it is not at all clear who the people are to whom he sends the message. *tall and smooth* are frequently said to be references to the tall, bronze-colored Ethiopians, but the translation of those two words is not at all certain, so they cannot bear much weight. The rest of the verse has an even less clear reference to the Ethiopians, who were not great conquerors and not universally feared. Those who believe that the prophet is sending word back to the Ethiopians are forced to say he is speaking in diplomatic hyperbole. But this suggestion seems very odd for one who has such bitter words to say about reliance

11. In Persian times "Hind," or India, was the other end of the world (Est. 1:1). Interestingly enough, the Targ. of this verse has "beyond the rivers of India."

12. See *ANEP*, no. 109.

upon foreign powers, especially Egypt (19:1–15; 20:4–6; 30:1–5; etc.). Furthermore, it is odd that no attempt is made to link the envoys to the people, if indeed they are the envoys' own people.

If Isaiah is not speaking of the Ethiopians, then whom? The two alternatives are that he is referring to some other literal, historical people or that he is using a figure of speech. If it is a historical people, two possibilities have been proposed. One is the Assyrians (Clements)[13] and the other is the Medes (Kissane). In the first case the envoys would be being told in something of a sarcastic manner, "Don't talk to us about rebelling. Go talk to the Assyrians, the source of the problem. Tell them they will one day bring gifts to Yahweh [v. 7]. So we don't need an alliance with you."[14] A serious defect in this hypothesis is that the Assyrians are not named, which seems strange since there is no apparent reason why they should not be named. Furthermore, the nature of the message as just outlined has to be completely drawn from inference, which is asking a bit too much. Although the naming problem does remain for the Medes, the function of going to the Medes seems more clear. They are the destroyers and are being summoned to prepare to act as God's agents (13:17; 21:2).[15]

Yet, even this suggestion falters in view of the broad, general statement which the poem is making. The only thing approaching a message appears in v. 3, and all that it says is for the world to be alert to God's acts. This seems to support the figurative conception of the material. Swift envoys are called from the ends of the earth and sent to the mightiest people imaginable—a composite of all human greatness. But this mighty people is nothing before a God who works as inexorably as the heat and as imperceptibly as the mist. Ultimately, even this mighty people will bring its homage to God's dwelling (v. 4), in Zion (v. 7).

3 As has been mentioned, this verse makes it plain that the ultimate addressees of Isaiah's message are not merely a royal court somewhere. It is the whole human family which is called to witness the evidence of God's lordship. When the signals are given, then the world must be prepared to perceive the evidence which God grants us that he is indeed at work. Too often we do not see his hand in events because we are not expecting to see it. But having been alerted, we are able to perceive through faith the hand which moves the universe and the human heart.

13. Citing W. Jansen, *Mourning Cry and Woe Oracle,* BZAW 125 (New York: de Gruyter, 1972), p. 60.

14. For Assyrian claims illustrating its aptness to be described as this verse does, see *ARAB*, II:62, 63.

15. Note too that the benefactions of Cyrus, successor to the Medes, helped to rebuild the temple in Jerusalem (as per v. 7; cf. Ezra 1:7–11).

4 Isaiah now shares the word which has come to him. When the flag is raised and the trumpet sounds, what mighty acts will God perform? The answer will be disappointing to those who always expect God to do the stupendous and overwhelming. As in Elijah's "still small voice" (1 K. 19:12), the Lord asserts that his work will be quiet and unassuming, but nevertheless complete. God does not exist for those who expect to command him on their own behalf. He exists for the sake of his love and his saving purpose in the world. It is for these that he will act, and in his own way. But he will act.

From one point of view, v. 4 comes as a surprise. Swift messengers are summoned and sent to a mighty people. The world is called to hold itself in readiness. The suspense mounts. What cataclysm is going to be unleashed? The truth is that the quiet look of the Sovereign is of greater importance than the mightiest of the world's armies (Ps. 2:1–4; 33:13–17; 80:14; Lam. 5:1; Isa. 63:15). For to him to do nothing (*qwṭ*, "sit quietly") but merely look on is of greater significance than all the deliberations in all the world's chancelleries. But like the quiet heat which builds until it is almost unbearable by mid-afternoon, or the curtains of mist which drift up the valleys from the coast, God makes his presence known and felt.[16] As with the birth in Bethlehem, there is no pomp and fanfare, but the world is forever changed.

5 God will carefully watch the situation developing on the earth and then, like the farmer who prunes back his vines, God will cut off the luxuriant foliage and leave it. The image here refers to the practice of cutting off those tendrils and leaves which are not bearing fruit and would thus take sustenance from those that are. Like the farmer, God will not act too soon or too late. Once the fruit is formed and there is no doubt, God's pruning knife will go into action. The historical circumstance which comes most quickly to mind is that of Sennacherib's attack upon Judea. At the last moment, when the conclusion seemed foregone, God quietly put in his knife and the Assyrian tendrils lay on the ground, cut off. (Cf. Jesus' Parable of the Weeds [Matt. 13:24–30] for a similar thought.)

6 This verse picks up the thought of v. 5 with its cut-off tendrils,

16. A slightly different interpretation of the figures of heat and mist is that of Dillmann (cited by Gray). He suggests that the heat and the mist are necessary to the full development of the crops as portended in v. 5. The mist in the harvest is more than a heavy dew. It is a cloud of mist which hangs over the land when the cool breeze of the Mediterranean meets the hot air rising off the land. The moisture which it brings to the dry summer is of great importance not only physically but also psychologically (cf. D. Baly, *The Geography of the Bible*, rev. ed. [New York: Harper & Row, 1974], p. 60).

but moves to a more literal figure and pictures the corpses of the enemy strewn over the whole countryside (cf. Ezek. 39:11–16 for the same imagery). God has produced a victory no human army could achieve. The vultures and the wild animals have a year-round feast on the fallen. Undoubtedly this is an accurate prediction of this situation after Sennacherib's hasty departure. The burial of 185,000 corpses would have been a monumental task, leaving ample time for the carrion eaters to make their contribution.

7 The poem ends with a different kind of embassy in view than the one with which it began (Skinner). Instead of incitement to revolt by envoys from the Ethiopian king of Egypt, incitement for Judah to take its destiny into its own hand, Isaiah envisions a day when that mighty imaginary people who sum up all the world's power will come to Jerusalem bearing homage to her God, who is truly mightiest in the world (2:1–4). How often that has happened in the centuries since. How many of the monarchs of the world have come to what is really only a large town off the beaten track in the hills of Judea, there to bow the knee in memory of, and in honor to, a King who wears no crown.

the place of the name of the Lord of Hosts is often considered to be Deuteronomic and therefore too late for Isaiah of Jerusalem in 715 (Deut. 12:11). May it not also be that a verse such as this constitutes evidence against the hypothesis that Deuteronomic theology was unknown before 650 B.C.? In any case, the *name of the Lord* here is a significant theological concept. The name is a synonym for character or reputation. Why will the nations of the earth flow to Jerusalem? Because of the character of her God: righteous, but loving; all-powerful, but tender; judge, but deliverer, etc. We are all drawn to his place because there is truly none like him (40:25).

d. JUDGMENT ON EGYPT (19:1–20:6)

(1) Egypt has nothing to offer (19:1–24)

(a) Egypt's might confounded (19:1–15)

> 1 *The burden of Egypt:*
> *Behold, the Lord is riding on a swift cloud*
>   *and comes to Egypt;*
> *the idols of Egypt tremble[1] before him,*
> *and the heart of Egypt is dissolved before him.*

1. *nûaʿ*, "to quiver"; cf. 6:4, the doorposts in God's presence; 7:2, the house of David before the northern threat.

2 *I will spur Egypt against Egypt:*
   a man will fight with his brother,
   a man against his neighbor,
   city against city,
   kingdom against kingdom.[2]
3 *The spirit of Egypt will be emptied[3] from within,*
   and his counsel I will swallow up.
   They will inquire of the idols and mutterers,
   the mediums and the spiritualists.[4]
4 *I will shut up Egypt in the hand of a harsh lord;*[5]
   a strong king will rule over them,
       says the Lord of Hosts.
5 *The waters of the sea shall be dried up;*
   the river will be dried up and parched.
6 *The streams will stink;*[6]
   the rivers of Egypt will be low and dry.
   Reed and rush will be decayed,
7   *and the papyrus on the river, on the bank of the river.*[7]
   Every sown field along the river
   will be dried up, blown away, nothing.
8 *The fishermen will wail and mourn,*
       all who throw the hook into the Nile;
   those who spread the net on the face of the water
   will pine away.

2. LXX "province against province," probably an accurate reflection of the intent of the Hebrew.

3. One would expect *nabᵉqâ* (Niphal of *bqq*) to show doubling of the *qoph*. However, double *ayin* roots do not always follow this pattern (see Gen. 17:11; Judg. 5:5; Jer. 8:14; cf. Young). Skinner points to Jer. 19:7 where *bqq* has the sense "to make void."

4. See 8:19 for a discussion of the particular terms of spiritism.

5. "harsh" is singular while "lord" is plural. The latter is generally regarded as a plural of majesty (GKC, §§ 124l, 132k).

6. MT *wᵉheʾeznîḥû*, an anomalous form perhaps to be explained as a combination of Hebrew Hiphil and Aramaic Aphel of *zḥḥ*. 1QIsᵃ has no *aleph*, thus probably the normal *hiznîḥû*.

7. The opening phrase of v. 7 is problematic: AV "paper reeds by the brook," RV "meadows by the Nile," RSV "bare places by the Nile," NEB "lotus on the Nile," etc. The first word seems to mean "bare places" (*ʿārôt*, 13:7; 22:6, if from *ʿārâ*). "Meadows" is an attempt to make sense of this interpretation in the light of LXX, which has "the green plants." However, the LXX reading could also support another synonym for "reeds and rushes." That the Egyptian word for papyrus is *ʿrt* suggests that *ʿrt* here is an Egyptian loanword and that "papyrus" is the best reading. *BHS* proposes to drop "on the Nile" as repetitive (NEB instead drops "on the banks of the Nile").

9 *The workers with combed flax are ashamed,*
   the weavers of white cloth.[8]
10 *Its pillars will be crushed,*
   all the workers for hire[9] *sad of soul.*
11 *The princes of Zoan are nothing but*[10] *fools,*
   the wise men, counselors of Pharaoh—brutish[11] *counsel.*[12]
How can you say to Pharaoh,
   "I am a son of wise men,
   a son of ancient kings"?
12 *Where are your wise men?*
   Let them tell you and make known
what the Lord of Hosts plans
   concerning Egypt.
13 *The princes of Zoan have become fools;*
   the princes of Noph are deceived.
They have made Egypt go astray,
   the cornerstone of her tribes.
14 *The Lord has mixed into her midst*

8. That 1QIs[a] has *ḥwrw*, "they grow pale" (?), for MT *ḥwry*, "white stuff," is in the favor of those who have pointed out that the stich needs a verb (cf. Gray). However, LXX *býssos*, "linen," supports MT. There is also a question about the placement and form of *śᵉrîqôt*, "combed, combers" (?). According to the MT punctuation, it is the last word in the first phrase of the verse. This position would call for it to be an adjective modifying "flax" (masc. in form, but taking fem. modifiers). But the Targ. seems to take it with the second half of the verse, thus "combers and weavers therefrom." Several modern interpreters prefer this reading (cf. *BHS*, NEB; LXX agrees with MT).

9. LXX has "who make strong drink," evidently a confusion of *śeker*, "hire," with *śēkār*, "beer." (Note the same problem with 7:20, MT "hired," LXX "drunken"). This misunderstanding is possibly due to dialectal differences; note Akk. *šikāru*, "beer," and Arab. *śakira*, "to be drunk."

10. Understanding *ʾak* in a restrictive sense (RSV, NIV, etc.) and not an asseverative one (AV). Cf. Williams, *Syntax*, § 388.

11. *nibʿārâ* is a Niphal participle of *bʿr*, "to act like an animal" (Jer. 10:14, 21; 51:17).

12. The absence of a main verb in the second line of the verse is troublesome, and various proposals have been made to rectify the loss. Driver has suggested that *yôʿᵃṣê*, "counselors," should be repointed *yaʿᵃṣû*, "they counsel," yielding "The wise men of Pharaoh counsel stupid counsel" (*JTS* 38 [1937] 40). Dahood, noting that 1QIs[a] has *ḥkmyh*, "her wise men" (antecedent: Zoan), renders *yoʿᵃṣê* as a participle, "are counseling" (*Bib* 56 [1975] 420). The LXX has "their counsel shall be turned to stupid counsel." The Targ. appears to support Driver's hypothesis. But in the absence of compelling evidence for any one of these, it seems best to remain with the MT.

a spirit[13] *of distortion,*
and they have led Egypt astray in all its doings,
like a drunk going astray in his vomit.
15 *There will be nothing anyone can do for Egypt,*
whether head or tail, palm branch or reed.

Chapters 19–20 give us God's word against Egypt. As is evident from chs. 30 and 31, the leaders of Judah were tempted to rely more and more upon Egypt as the eighth century drew toward a close and as Assyria's threat loomed larger and larger. Isaiah's word was the same as it had been concerning Assyria earlier: whatever we trust in place of God will eventually turn on us and destroy us. Why trust Egypt, he asks, when Egypt has nothing to offer you that you do not already have (ch. 19)? Why trust Egypt when recent history shows she will betray you (ch. 20)? Why not trust the God who holds Egypt in the palm of his hand and to whom Egypt must one day turn?

In the two chapters three segments can be identified: 19:1–15 tells of Egypt's utter helplessness before God; 19:16–25 tells that Egypt will one day be a worshiper of God; 20:1–6 gives a vivid and concrete example of the lack of wisdom in trusting Egypt.

19:1–15 In this poem of three nearly equal strophes God successively exposes the weakness of all that would supposedly make Egypt great: her religion (vv. 1–4), her physical situation (vv. 5–10), her vaunted wisdom (vv. 11–15). None of these is ultimate, so what ground remains for committing Judah's national destiny to Egypt?

The occasion and authorship of this segment are matters of debate. Skinner says that similarities with known Isaianic passages prove it to be Isaiah's, while Kaiser says that these similarities coupled with "poor" poetry show that a later imitator of Isaiah wrote it. Similarly, attempts to date it by references to the "hard ruler" of v. 4 have extended from the Ethiopian Piankhy of 715 to Antiochus Epiphanes in 170. However, attempts to locate the poem in a specific historical context seem likely to be futile. Alexander is surely right when he says that the picture is metaphorical, as one would speak in a metaphorical way of Britain's demise by saying that her navy is sunk, her universities are empty, her throne abandoned, without any of those being literally true. Thus it seems impossible to prove or disprove Isaianic authorship from the internal evidence.

According to most commentators, 19:1–4 deals with fratricidal warfare taking place in Egypt with total political collapse preceding foreign conquest. Undoubtedly this theme is present. Yet, one wonders if this is

13. A "spirit" here refers to an attitude or way of approach. Cf. 29:10; 2 K. 19:7; Job 20:3.

the central theme or if it is in fact derivative. In the entire poem, the only references to Egypt's religion come in this strophe, in vv. 1 and 3. Is it not possible that the author is laying the blame for the internecine struggle at the foot of Egypt's lush polytheism? It is because she has no one god, like Yahweh, to unite her and because her gods are basically ineffectual and must scrabble for power, the prophet seems to be saying, that Egypt is doomed to disintegration and foreign domination.[14] Why should Judah be attracted to that?

1 *the Lord is riding on a swift cloud* expresses God's sovereignty over nature and suggests at the outset that the theme of this strophe is fundamentally a religious one. Similar expressions appear in Deut. 33:26; Ps. 18:11 (Eng. 10); 68:34 (Eng. 33); 104:3. The phrase is also used of Baal, the Canaanite storm-god, and may have been appropriated from that cult as being more fitting for the Creator of nature, rather than just one aspect of nature.[15]

Before the presence of the One who is God, Egypt's many-faceted idols are in fact nonentities.[16] They were shown to be this in the Exodus when the Lord had proven his complete superiority over them (Exod. 12:12), so their quivering before him is only to be expected. Before the revealed truth of one transcendent God who cannot be manipulated, but whose faithful love can be trusted to the end, the complex polytheisms of human religion pale into nothing. Well they might, for they offer neither hope nor help when life deals out its hard blows. The hearts of their worshipers dissolve before the onslaught, for there is nothing eternal to which they can attach themselves (cf. Luke 21:26).

2 *I will spur Egypt against Egypt* is a graphic way of expressing the inner discord which comes to a people who have no stay beyond themselves in this world. Throughout her history Egypt was especially prone to this kind of dissolution. After the six strong dynasties of the Old Kingdom (3000–2200 B.C.), there came a two-hundred-year period when each of the 42 nomes (city-states) became a country unto itself and general chaos reigned.[17] Then the Twelfth Dynasty united the land for about two hundred years (1990–1785 B.C.), but again chaos took over for two cen-

---

14. Cf. W. M. Smith, *Egypt in Biblical Prophecy* (Boston: Wilde, 1957), pp. 84, 85.

15. See, e.g., *UT,* 51:11, 18 (*ANET,* p. 132); 68:8, 29 (*ANET,* pp. 130, 131). Deut. 33:26, with its use of the term El, suggests that the epithet may have belonged to that high god, from whence it was borrowed both by Yahweh and Baal.

16. *ʾĕlîlîm,* "idols," lit. "nothings" (2:8, 18, 20; 10:10, 11; 19:3; 31:7).

17. See "A Dispute Over Suicide," esp. lines 105–129, where the writer contemplates suicide because the situation is so bad (*ANET,* pp. 405–407).

turies. So it went again and again. It may be that the concept of the king as god incarnate contributed to this tendency to fragment, because unless someone came forward with enough godlike qualities or antecedents, no one was fit to rule. But beyond that consideration, the fact that each nome had its own god certainly led to fratricide when there was no god-king to enforce national order. So Isaiah sees more of this kind of disaster ahead for Egypt. Her gods cannot hold her together because of the judgment of Israel's God.

3 When a people begin to lose their way, especially a normally complacent and self-confident people like the Egyptians, depression settles on them suddenly. They do not have much resilience. That attitude is what Isaiah describes here. They will be despondent, lacking in spirit. When that happens, spirit is easily replaced by spiritism. Egyptian religion, especially during the Middle Kingdom (1990–1785 B.C.) and the New Kingdom (1550–1221 B.C.), exhibited a number of universalistic and monolatrous trends. But after this time the ancient polytheisms and spiritist tendencies began to reassert themselves. That is the picture here. As the more intellectualized and conceptualized polytheisms break down under the stress of the times, the more magical, subliminal spiritism reasserts itself. This situation is not restricted to polytheistic lands. It can also happen to a land where a paganized, manipulative Yahwism is practiced (8:19–22). Only a robust, pure faith in the God of the Bible can stand the shocks which must eventually come to every person and nation.

4 The nation whose gods have deserted it is ripe for oppression. It lacks both the will and the raison d'être to resist the inner rot which eventuates in tyranny. While it is possible that Isaiah was predicting the rise of a particular tyrant in Egypt,[18] it is more likely, as Alexander and Kissane have suggested, that he is continuing to speak in a broadly figurative way and that the attempt to link the *harsh lord* to one particular individual would be bootless.

5–10 It is not an overstatement to say that without the Nile there would be no Egypt. Without the lifegiving flow of water out of central Africa the Sahara would simply extend unbroken to the shores of the Red Sea, for there is little or no rainfall east of the Sahara, making Egypt completely dependent upon irrigation water from the Nile. Very literally the desert begins where the irrigation canals end. Beyond this, the lack of any tributaries in its last one thousand miles makes the river very predictable. The annual flood, bringing new alluvium and washing the former

18. Throughout the midpart of the 7th century B.C., Assyria controlled the Nile Delta and dominated most of the rest of Egypt.

year's debris out to sea, could be expected to begin during the same week every year. Likewise, the receding of the floodwaters could be expected to start in the same week annually.[19] The predictability and abundance of this life resource contributed to the complacency and self-confidence of the Egyptian people, but it also created a tremendous dependency. If the Nile were ever shut off, this rich and seductive Egypt would cease to be.[20] This critical weakness is what Isaiah is emphasizing in this strophe: why depend upon a country whose only resource for life was not in its own hands, but in the hands of Israel's God?

5, 6 *the sea* probably refers to the appearance of the Nile in Lower Egypt when it is in flood.[21] The low hillocks all appear to be islands and the water reaches to the horizon (18:2; Job 14:11).

the streams probably denote the canals, and *the rivers of Egypt* the branches of the Nile in the Delta. Normally *Egypt* is *miṣrayim,* a dual noun form apparently reflecting the Egyptian description of their country as "two lands": the river valley (Upper Egypt) and the Delta (Lower Egypt). In "the rivers of Egypt" the name appears to be singular, *māṣôr* (AV "defence"). This form is taken to mean Egypt proper, from the Israelite point of view (i.e., the Delta; cf. 37:25; 2 K. 19:24; Mic. 7:12).

Before God, the mighty Nile can be shut off, the canals made dry and stinking, the Delta dry as a desert (Prov. 8:29). Why commit yourself to a nation as vulnerable as that?

6–7 The immediate result of the river's drying up would be the desiccation of the lush plant life along its edges. Not only would the rushes and characteristic papyrus reed disappear, but the sown fields would be reduced to nothing in short order. (Note the powerful language expressing this: in Hebrew only three words, "dried, blown, nothing.") Throughout her history Egypt was able to export grain to the rest of the world (Paul traveled to Rome on a grain ship from Egypt, Acts 28:11), but if the Nile were cut off that export would promptly cease.

8 As the Nile and its streams dried up and the plant life died, so also would the marine life in the river itself die. It is apparent that one of

19. See J. Baines and J. Malek, *Atlas of Ancient Egypt* (New York, 1980), pp. 14–15.

20. Note that the first plague was upon the Nile (Exod. 7:17–21). Note also the similarity of language between that passage and this. Isaiah is probably patterning himself on the Exodus language.

21. Kissane notes that "river" is parallel to "the deep" in Ezek. 31:4 and suggests that *yam,* "the sea," may function in the same way here. In that case, "the sea" would not equal the Nile but would be the watery abyss surrounding the earth that feeds the Nile. God would stop it and thus the Nile.

the major industries of Egypt was fishing (cf. Num. 11:5; Ezek. 29:4), and this industry would of course cease at once if the river should ever stop flowing.[22]

9 Another industry representative of the total Egyptian life would be the production of linen from flax. Like the previous two, this process was completely dependent on water, both for growing the flax and for making the linen from the flax. As in the other areas, the author exhibits detailed knowledge of Egyptian life in his reference to combing or carding, which was necessary to break down the flax fibers to produce a thread. Thus his antipathy to Egypt was not a matter of mere uninformed prejudice. He knew the country well, but was convinced that all its productivity was no more than a gift from God.

10 If the present translation is correct, this is a generalizing statement that all of Egyptian society, from the high ("the pillars"; cf. Ps. 11:3) to the low ("workers for hire") will feel the impact of God's acts upon the Nile. However, the versions have widely varying translations of *šāṭōṯêhā*, "pillars." The LXX reading, "its weavers," seems to make the most sense in the context of the preceding verse. That Akk. *šatu* and Coptic *štit* mean "to weave" suggests that the LXX has preserved the original reading at this point. If this interpretation is correct, the verse is not a conclusion to vv. 5–9, but is rather continuing the thought of v. 9 (cf. NIV).

11–15 If Egypt had reason to boast of her rich religion and her great productivity, she also had reason to be proud of her ancient wisdom (cf. 1 K. 4:30). The Egyptian wisdom literature, probably growing out of the highly organized court life, is some of the earliest and best preserved known to us.[23] The same is true of their reflections on the nature and meaning of life. Yet the Israelite prophet has the audacity to say that this tradition for wisdom is of no more value than the other two areas. This is so, in Gray's words, because Yahweh is able to frustrate their plans, while they cannot discover his. In words similar to those addressed to the idols in chs. 41–43, Isaiah challenges the wise men to a contest. Can they show Pharaoh God's plan now (any more than their predecessors could during the Exodus)? The answer is a flat no. What reason is there then for Judah to trust in or to fear Egypt? Her gods are helpless, her productivity is contingent on Yahweh's grace, and her wise men are stupid. What could Egypt possibly offer?

22. For pictures of Egyptian fishing practices with both hook and net, see *ANEP*, p. 34.

23. R. N. Whybray, *Wisdom in Proverbs*, SBT 1/45 (London: SCM; Naperville: Allenson, 1965), pp. 15–17, 53–61.

11a *The princes of Zoan* refers to the officials in Tanis, which was the chief city of northern Egypt from the Middle Bronze Age onward. It was situated on the east side of the Delta region and would be the first large Egyptian city encountered by a Semite traveling toward the Nile Valley. At several points when the nation had broken in two, Tanis had become the capital city of Lower Egypt. Thus one would expect her officials to be possessed of unusual perspective and awareness. In fact, says Isaiah, they are completely foolish. These supposedly insightful people are giving Pharaoh counsel which would not become an animal (1:2, 3).

11b, 12 In language reminiscent of the later challenges to the gods (43:8; 44:6; 45:20), Isaiah speaks directly to the wise men and then to the Pharaoh himself.[24] To the wise men he asks in sarcasm how they even have the temerity to claim to be a part of the class of wise men. *son* here does not mean so much a physical descendant as it does a member of a guild. (Cf. "sons of the prophets" for a prophetic school, e.g., 2 K. 2:3, 15.) Their plans have failed so many times that the prophet marvels that they are still willing to claim to be the heirs of the ancient wisdom. In fact, they do not understand either the past (14:24–27; 37:26) or the present.

Turning to Pharaoh, the writer again uses language of a sort echoed by Paul many years later (1 Cor. 1:20). God is going to treat Egypt again as he did at the Exodus. How will the wise men—who do not look at events in the light of faith in God—explain that? In fact, which of the Egyptian wise men is able to tell Pharaoh what God's plan of attack will be? None of them is able to do so and the prophet wonders why Pharaoh even keeps them around.

13 The tragedy of Egypt's situation is that the very ones who should have led her correctly have led her astray. Here the officials of the other great city of Lower Egypt, Memphis,[25] are also called to shoulder the blame. These people were the very cornerstones of Egyptian society (Judg. 20:2; 1 Sam. 14:38; Zech. 10:4), but if the cornerstone itself has no foundation, it cannot support anything else. Wisdom which is limited to this world is as short-sighted and confused as a person lost in a dense forest. Unless there is an overall perspective from outside this world from which to analyze and evaluate human experience, then no course of action makes any ultimate sense. This is why the fear of the Lord is the beginning

---

24. Presumably the suffixes would be fem. if Egypt were being addressed.

25. "Memphis" is Greek for Egyp. *Mennofer*, which would have been Heb. *mᵉnōp*. This is sometimes rendered *mōp* (Hos. 9:6), and sometimes *nōp*, as here.

of wisdom (Prov. 1:7); it is also why there is no other foundation than Christ (1 Cor. 3:11; Eph. 2:20; 1 Pet. 2:6; Isa. 28:16). Without him as the unifying factor in all existence, existence is a tale "full of sound and fury, signifying nothing."

14, 15 This situation of confusion in Egypt is not accidental. It is the Lord who has confounded all the brilliance and wisdom of that culture, just as he confounded the language of a people set upon deifying themselves (Gen. 11:1–9). Having refused to know God as he is, having warped the relation of Creator and creation, they are now doomed to see all other relationships through a distorted lens. This is not an arbitrary judgment on God's part, but it is from him in that it is a part of his plan of cause and effect that a false premise will affect the outcome of all premises dependent upon it (Rom. 1:18–32).

The metaphor of proud Egypt wandering unsteadily back and forth through the vomit of her drunkenness is a biting one, but it had been increasingly so from about 1200 B.C. onward. When the New Kingdom ended, there were no more periods of greatness for the Nile Valley culture. It first broke in two along the ancient lines of valley and delta. Then it was dominated by a whole series of foreign conquerors of whom the Ethiopians in Isaiah's time were the latest, but not the last. It is small wonder that Isaiah, recalling the language of 9:13 (Eng. 14), sees the situation as hopeless. Egypt is like an ancient whore who does not know that her beauty is gone. In that light, it does not come as a surprise that Ezekiel's words a century later are even more severe than Isaiah's (Ezek. 29:6, 7). Both prophets were horrified even to think that Judah might compromise her faith in the Almighty, all-caring God for such a patently false hope as conniving, drunken Egypt.

(b) Egypt will come to Judah (19:16–25)

16 *In that day, the Egyptians will be like women. They will tremble with dread[1] before the upraised hand[2] of the Lord of Hosts, which he is raising over them.*

17 *The land of Judah will become a cause of staggering to the Egyptians; whenever anyone reminds them of her, they will be in dread[3] on account of the plan of the Lord of Hosts that he is planning against them.*

1. $w^e\underline{h}\bar{a}ra\underline{d}$ $\hat{u}p\bar{a}\underline{h}a\underline{d}$, "he will tremble and he will dread." Note the assonance. The two verbs together convey one thought (Williams, *Syntax*, § 224).
2. $t^e n\hat{u}pa\underline{t}$, "upraised," may be also translated with "swinging" or "waving over." It implies a threat (10:32; 11:15; 30:32).
3. The phrase is lit. "every one who makes her remembered unto him, he will fear." The "her" refers to Judah and the "he" of the final verb is Egypt.

18 *In that day there will be five cities in the land of Egypt speaking the language of Canaan[4] and taking an oath[5] to the Lord of Hosts. One will be called "City of the Sun."[6]*

19 *In that day there will be an altar in the midst of the land of Egypt and a pillar to the Lord at its border.*

20 *It will be for a sign and a witness to the Lord of Hosts in the land of Egypt. When they cry to the Lord on account of oppressors, then he will send to them a savior and defender, and he will deliver them.[7]*

21 *The Lord will be known to Egypt, and Egypt will know the Lord in that day. And they will offer sacrifices and offerings and they will vow a vow to the Lord and will perform it.[8]*

22 *The Lord will strike Egypt, striking and healing. They will turn to the Lord and he will hear their prayer and heal them.*

23 *In that day there will be a highway from Egypt to Assyria, and Assyria*

4. Although the adjective "Canaanite" is often used in a negative way in the Bible, it is clearly not negative here. Moreover, the description is linguistically correct, as Hebrew is but one dialect of that branch of Northwest Semitic which included Ugaritic, Phoenician, Edomite, and Moabite (and now perhaps Eblaite?), all of which may be called "Canaanite." (Cf. S. Moscati, et al., *Introduction to the Comparative Grammar of the Semitic Languages* [Wiesbaden: Harrassowitz, 1969]; *IDB*, II:553–560.)

5. *nišba' l-*, "to swear to," means to take an oath of allegiance, as opposed to merely swearing that something is true (*nišba' b-*, 45:23; 65:16).

6. 1QIs[a], 15 Hebrew mss., Symm., Targ., Vulg., Arab., *ḥeres*, "sun"; MT *ḥeres*, "destruction" (?). The normal term for "sun" is *šemeš*, but *ḥeres* is used in a poetic fashion (Job 9:7; Judg. 14:18); note Akk. and Ugar. *ḥrṣ*, "gold" (like the sun?).

7. The exact syntax of v. 20a is not clear. The connecting particle between the two clauses is *kî*, normally translated "because" or "for" (AV " . . . in the land of Egypt, *for* they shall cry . . ."). However, the way in which sign and witness are the effect of calling is obscure. This leads to a second option: understanding the *kî* as "when" (Williams, *Syntax*, § 445; cf. RSV) and introducing a conditional clause ("when they call . . . then he will send"). As Gray points out, however, the *waw* plus imperfect (*wᵉyišlaḥ*, "and he will send") is not normally used to introduce an apodosis. So he translates "when they cry . . . that he should . . . then he will intervene" (taking *wārāḫ* as *waw* plus perfect). But this is a very awkward construction and is not supported by the versions, which take *wārāḫ* as a participle. Rubenstein ("Conditional Clauses in Isaiah," *VT* 6 [1956] 72) suggests that *wᵉyišlaḥ* should be emended with 1QIs[a] to *wᵉšalaḥ* (*waw* plus perfect), which would solve the anomaly and retain the sense. This may be correct, but it is also possible that we do have one of the anomalous forms appearing here.

8. *šālēm*, "to pay," comes from the same verbal root as does the noun *šālôm*, "peace." The person who has *šālôm* has a well-being which comes from a sense of integration, of unity. The unpaid vow is incomplete; paying it completes it and puts it to rest.

373

> *will come to Egypt and Egypt to Assyria and Egypt will serve [God]*
> *with[9] Assyria.*
>
> 24 *In that day Israel will be a third[10] with Egypt and Assyria, a blessing*
> *in the midst of the land,*
> 25 *of which the Lord of Hosts swears, saying, "Blessed be my people*
> *Egypt, and the work of my hand Assyria, and my inheritance Israel."*

This second half of the chapter moves from poetry to prose and from judgment upon Egypt to the most sweeping promises of redemption. The section is marked by five repetitions of "in that day" (vv. 16, 18, 19, 23, 24) which make it plain that the prophet sees these events as occurring in the end times, or at least at the point where God takes decisive action in world events.[11] The five segments introduced by the phrase seem to show a progression of thought from an Egypt terrorized by the very thought of Judah's God to an Egypt joining with Assyria and Israel in glad worship of God.[12]

But we may ask how these verses function in the overall context of the chapter and of chs. 13–23. The larger unit seems to have two purposes in relation to chs. 7–12. The first is to show how foolish it is to trust the nations, since they are under the judgment of God. But the second is to particularize the general promise that God could and would restore Israel from bondage (11:11–16).

This section fits those purposes very well. Verses 1–15 have negated all the Egyptian attributes which might draw Judah to Egypt. Verses

9. The particle *'eṭ* may be used as a definite direct object indicator or as the preposition "with." Alexander gives a balanced discussion of the pros and cons of each reading here.

10. *šelîšîyâ*, "a third," had the idea of a third part among three.

11. Cf. 4:1, 2; 7:18–23; 10:20; 11:10; 17:4, 7; 24:21; 27:1, 2; 30:23; 31:7. This use of "in that day" has been taken in recent years as evidence of a postexilic date for this part of the chapter, since it is said to reflect an apocalyptic worldview. If this is so, it is strange that no occurrence appears in chs. 56–66, which have been identified by Paul Hanson (*The Dawn of Apocalyptic* [Philadelphia: Westminster, 1975]) as being an expression of the struggle of an apocalyptic kind of Judaism for recognition and power. As for the dates, recent opinions have ranged from ca. 710 B.C. (Erlandsson, Mauchline) to the second century B.C. (Kaiser), with everything in between covered (e.g., Clements, who dismisses the "extremes" without saying why, is in favor of a date in the early Persian period). In fact, all the dates are derived from prior conclusions as to the dates of certain literary formations and theological concepts, and none of those conclusions is clearly demonstrable, as the wide variety of dates assigned to this section shows.

12. Wildberger's comment that this final thought could not be from Isaiah because of Isaiah's antipathy to Egypt is not worthy of Wildberger. A person as great as Isaiah was surely not limited to one narrow perspective at all times.

16–25 are saying it is foolish for Judah to turn to Egypt when Egypt is one day going to turn to Judah's God. In short, Judah already has the only thing of a positive nature which Egypt will one day have. Furthermore, because the Lord will be Egypt's God, there will be no trouble at all in achieving the second Exodus. In a different way each of these five thoughts illustrates in an ascending order Egypt's coming allegiance to Yahweh. Thus, they present the positive side to the point being made negatively in the first half of the chapter.[13] As such, they bring the whole argument to a fitting climax in a vision of all nations living in harmony because of their common submission to God (2:2–4).

16, 17 This first statement is a transitional one, something the student of Isaiah comes to expect with regularity. In thought, with its emphasis upon destruction, it follows vv. 1–15, whereas in form it agrees with vv. 18–25. However, a stonger reason than mere form for including these verses with the latter half of the chapter is the identification of the cause for Egypt's terror. It is that God whose seat of rule is on the territory (*ᵃdāmâ*, "ground, soil") of Judah. Thus these verses make the theme of the section plain at the outset: Egypt will look to Judah, at first fearfully, but then more confidently, rather than the opposite being true.[14]

This fearful looking is another expression of what is a fundamental truth to Isaiah: repentance and healing come through retribution and judgment (v. 22; chs. 1–5; 6:10–13; 17:7–11; 42:18–43:7; 59:1–21). Those who have not experienced the results of their sin are very likely to deny that they have any sin. But those who are crushed will be looking for a Redeemer, and Isaiah promises exactly that. It is not that punishment somehow "pays" for the sin. No one can do that short of forfeiting forever any relationship with the holy God. Rather, the judgment alerts us to start looking for the way out, a way God wants to show all of us, even the complacent Egyptians among us.

The hand of God upraised against Egypt simply immobilizes them. They are no longer warriors standing up against long odds. They are women come upon suddenly, who know themselves to be defenseless, cowering in fear before the inevitable. Isaiah, with the faith of a believer, is confident that it is his God alone who is responsible for the blows which Egypt is going to experience in the coming years. And all those blows will be in keeping with God's plans (10:6; 14:24; 46:10).

---

13. Delitzsch says the first half of the chapter descends to a pit and the second half ascends from the pit.
14. As Young points out, without vv. 1–15 the reader would not know in what way Egypt was brought to such terror.

As Israel had been a source of horror to the Egyptians hundreds of years earlier (Exod. 10:7; 12:33), so now Judah will be also. And the reason will be the same in both cases. It is not because Israel then, nor Judah now, posed any military threat. Rather, it is because of the way in which Israel's God made, and would make, his power plain.

The question inevitably arises whether Isaiah expected literal fulfillment of these words. If so, has it occurred, or is it yet to be? Alexander's answer from 140 years ago still seems the most judicious.[15] He maintained that the prophet was speaking in a primarily metaphorical vein to establish the primacy of Judah over Egypt. This interpretation seems more and more likely as the section unfolds, for literal interpretations became more and more difficult to support. At the same time, to say that the metaphor has no bearing on reality would be fallacious. Who can doubt that God's ultimate purpose is to bring Egypt and all nations to himself? The problem arises when believers attempt to create iron-clad ways in which the metaphor *must* express the reality. (So Cocceius was quite certain that the reference was to the events of the Protestant Reformation!)[16]

18 In this verse the writer begins to speak of an Egyptian turn to God, presumably as a result of the outworking of God's plan upon them. How often persons whose comfortable world has come crashing down around them turn to God in desperation and find, almost to their surprise, that he had been waiting to receive them. So Isaiah pictures Egypt's turning to God.

there will be five cities has occasioned a number of differing interpretations, partly because the statement seems so odd. Five cities out of 30,000 is hardly a large percentage. Calvin suggested that the intention was proportional. Out of every six cities, five would turn to God (expressed metaphorically by their adopting the "lip" [i.e., language, analogous to our use of "tongue"] of Canaan, the Hebrew language), whereas one would not and it would be marked for destruction (following the MT reading). Apart from the textual problem with "destruction" (see below), it must still be said that this interpretation is not the plain meaning which would emerge from the text. It appears to be identifying one of the five cities in a special way, not a sixth one.

The same question—is it the plain meaning?—can be addressed

15. See also W. M. Smith, *Egypt in Biblical Prophecy* (Boston: Wilde, 1957), pp. 77–98.

16. While this kind of literalism is often thought to be the special domain of the theological conservative, it is not. Those who do not accept the validity of predictive prophecy are frequently at great pains to find literal events which gave rise to the supposed prediction. See on the five cities of v. 18 below.

to a second interpretation. It has been observed that five is sometimes used for several, so "five shall chase one hundred" (Lev. 26:8; cf. also Gen. 43:34; 1 Sam. 17:40; 2 K. 7:13; Isa. 30:17; 1 Cor. 14:19). Thus, it is suggested that "a small number" is intended. Several of the cited references are ambiguous, however, and those which are clear have some key in their context that makes the intent plain. No such key exists here. Nevertheless, a generally metaphorical interpretation would at least leave this possibility open.

Many modern commentators assume that the statement must have originated after the fact and so have searched for some historical event that could have given rise to this statement. The only event of this sort is scattered references to Jewish colonies in Egypt after the Exile (Jer. 44:1, Migdol, Tahpanhes, Memphis, Pathros; *ANET*, p. 491, Elephantine; Sibylline Oracles v:488–510, Leontopolis). Thus it is suggested that these colonies gave a redactor the idea for this "prediction," which was then put in Isaiah's mouth. Aside from the rather questionable argumentation involved in such an origin,[17] Kissane's observation that the section is not talking about Jewish colonists in Egypt, but a turning of Egypt to God, seems entirely apropos.

The interpretation proposed here is that Isaiah, seeking to convey the idea that Egypt must come to Judah's God, uses the figure of the five cities to convey the radical nature of the turn. To think of even one city adopting the language of the "sand-dwellers," the Semites, whom the Egyptians held in contempt,[18] would be astonishing. But for five to do so, and especially if one is the center of the worship of the Egyptian sun-god Re (see below), would be truly amazing. So Isaiah says that Egypt's turn to God will be so complete that some cities will go so far as to adopt even the language of Judah. Whether we ought to expect this event to come to pass in a literal way then becomes secondary to the major concern: will Egypt one day turn to God in a radical way? To that we may answer a resounding yes!

The *City of the Sun* presents a complex textual problem which cannot be divorced from one's conclusions concerning the provenance of

17. The proposed logic seems to follow this pattern: (1) The writer wishes to convince the reader of God's greatness. (2) A great God would be able to predict the future. (3) Therefore the writer seeks to make it appear that God predicted current events long ago, although he knows God did not. This is rather strange behavior for adherents of what is often referred to as the world's most ethically rigid religion.

18. Cf. "The Tale of Sinuhe," lines 16–17, 31, 197, 203, 293 (*ANET*, pp. 18–22); also Gen. 43:32.

the text. The MT has *heres,* which is usually translated "destruction." This makes little sense in a context of salvation unless one resorts to an expedient like Calvin's in which the named city is not one of the five. While the grammar would permit that interpretation, it is not the obvious sense of the passage. Delitzsch understood the city to be one of the five but the destruction to be of idols. This suggestion is attractive, but the text gives no clue that idols are intended.

The question about the correctness of "destruction" is intensified by the fact that about fifteen Hebrew manuscripts and 1QIs[a] have *heres,* "sun," instead of *heres,* "destruction." This reading is supported by Symmachus, the Targum, the Vulgate, and the Arabic version. The "city of the sun" would undoubtedly be Heliopolis, the biblical On, the seat of the worship of Re, the great Egyptian sun-god. On this reading Isaiah would be remarking that none other than Re's own city would one day go so far in its allegiance to Yahweh as to adopt the language of his country. This makes excellent sense and many modern versions and commentators have adopted it. The MT reading may be explained as a slip of the eye (*ḥ* and *h* are alike except for one small space) or as an alteration out of religious scruples (changing a reference to a pagan temple-city to a pejorative term, just as the personal name "man of Baal," LXX, is changed to "man of shame" by the MT in 2 Sam. 2:8; etc.).[19]

But there is another variant which complicates the matter still further. This is the LXX reading, *asedek,* almost certainly a transliteration of the Hebrew *haṣṣeḏeq,* "righteousness." That Jerusalem is called "the city of righteousness" in 1:26 has led some commentators to suggest that the author was claiming that one of the five cities would be an Egyptian "Jerusalem." Since there was a Jewish temple at Leontopolis in the late intertestamental period,[20] some have speculated that this temple gave rise to the statement originally, and that the priests in Jerusalem replaced "righteousness" with "destruction," which rapidly became meaningless and was altered to the more sensible "sun."[21] However, the development of the temple at Leontopolis is so late that there is not time for the whole process to have taken place and for the *heres* to have ended up already in 1QIs[a] by 100 B.C. It seems more likely that the LXX represents an alteration of the original by Egyptian Jews who wished to aggrandize their own situation. Assuming the original to have been "sun," "the sun of

19. So Skinner and Wildberger; JPSV leaves *heres* untranslated.
20. Josephus *Antiquities* xiii.2. Cf. A. Barucq, "Is. 19:18 et Leontopolis," *DBS* 5 (1952) 336–370.
21. So Gray, Kissane, Kaiser. This alternative is especially attractive to those who see the five cities as Jewish colonies.

righteousness" in Mal. 3:20 (Eng. 4:2) may have given impetus to the alteration.[22]

19–22 The third announcement is the longest and it goes further still in expressing the depth of the future relationship between God and Egypt. One cannot escape the impression that certain highly emotive terms, ones intimately connected with Hebrew religion, are consciously applied to Egypt here in an effort to show how completely Egypt will come to Israel's God.

19 First, that there will be found in Egypt an *altar* and a memorial *pillar* dedicated to Yahweh. Again, this terminology has provided comparisons to the situation at Leontopolis (but also at Elephantine where a Jewish temple existed ca. 410 B.C.).[23] However, the passage as a whole is not talking about Jewish behavior in Egypt but about Egyptian behavior. Nor is the writer saying that there will be *one* altar in the land and *one* memorial pillar on the border. This is another figure expressing the nature of the envisioned conversion. Young's suggestion that patriarchal religion is in view is helpful. When Abraham wished to express his gratitude and allegiance, he built an altar (Gen. 12:8), and when Jacob wished to formalize his acceptance of God's covenant-offer, he set up a pillar (Gen. 28:22).[24] So too Egypt will express gratitude to God and enter into covenant with him, not necessarily by building altars and pillars, but in ways appropriate to the day and time when the turning takes place.[25]

20 The turning of Egypt to God will be evidence that God has himself turned to Egypt. Thus the One who had smitten them becomes their deliverer. If the language of v. 19 had overtones of Genesis, the language here is reminiscent of Judges. Just as the Hebrew people, crushed under oppressors unleashed by the Hebrews' own sin, cried out for deliverance, so will Egypt. And just as God sent his champions in response to that cry, so he will do again. Young comments that Egypt would be experiencing persecution because of their turn to God. While it is true that persecution often follows witness, the point here seems to be that Egypt will experience God just as Israel did (cf. Judg. 3:9, 15; 6:7; 10:10).

---

22. Alexander, citing LeMoyne.

23. Cf. Elephantine Papyri (*ANET,* pp. 491–92).

24. Later in Israel's history the pillars, like the bronze serpent, became so thoroughly associated with pagan religion that they were banned (Deut. 16:22; 2 K. 17:10). But as a symbol of dedication to God it was still a useful literary figure.

25. The placing of the pillar on the border would be a way of saying that the trip to Egypt would no longer mean leaving the holy land and entering a profane one. The pillar would declare that Egypt was God's land too (Young).

21 Not only will the Egyptians worship God openly (vv. 18, 19), not only will they experience God's patience and mercy (v. 20), but they will come to that experiential knowledge of him that is the ultimate goal of all relationships with him (Jer. 9:23–25; Hos. 4:1; 13:4, 5; Phil. 3:10; Isa. 1:3; 43:10; 45:3; 60:16). The language here harks back to the Exodus, when Egypt came to know Yahweh through bitter defeat (Exod. 7:5; 9:28 [Eng. 29]; 14:4; etc.). Now the knowledge will come through the positive aspects of experience with him and will be expressed through the same means which Judah knows: ceremonial worship and obedience.[26] This verse must be placed alongside 1:11–15 to get a full picture of Isaiah's attitude toward ritual. When ritual is substituted for an ethically transformed life, it is devilish, but when ritual is an expression of that life, it is a beautiful thing, giving tangibility and force to what is intangible and diverse. As such, it helps persons to combine body and spirit into a unity. In the Psalms, the making and paying of vows is frequently an expression of gratitude (22:26 [Eng. 25]; 50:14; 56:13 [Eng. 12]; 61:9 [Eng. 8]; 65:2 [Eng. 1]; 66:13; 116:14, 18), but there is also the sense in which making the vow is a promise to do something when a prayer is answered and paying the vow is an admission that it has been answered (Deut. 23:21–23; 1 Sam. 1:11). Thus, Egypt is to be admitted to that select fellowship in which people are privileged to be able to commit their needs to God in faith and to have the marvelous experience of seeing him meet those needs.

22 The relation between Egypt and Yahweh will be like that of parent and child. The Lord's blows will be for healing, not destruction (Hos. 6:1). And Egypt may know his healing at any point, just as Israel may.

23–25 The fourth and fifth announcements climax the whole. In a remarkable statement Isaiah sees the ancient enmity between Assyria and Egypt dissolved. No more will Israel be merely a pawn between these warring powers. Now she will take her place beside them to fulfill the ancient promise: " . . . in you all the families of earth shall be blessed" (Gen. 12:3). Nor will God's blessing be for her alone. It will be impartially given out to all nations.[27]

23 A *highway* is a favorite metaphor in this book for the removal of alienation and separation (11:16; 33:8; 35:8; 40:3; 49:11; 62:10). In

26. It is interesting that the Targ. does not want to allow such knowledge to Egypt. It has God revealing his might and them worshiping in fear, but the reciprocal knowledge is conspicuously absent.

27. Cf. I. Wilson, "In That Day: From Text to Sermon on Is. 19:23–25," *Int* 21 (1967) 66–68; W. Vogels, "L'Egypte Mon Peuple—L'Universalisme d'Isa. 19:16-25," *Bib* 57 (1976) 494–514.

rough and hilly Israel, the force of such a figure is obvious. God's longing is for swift and open communication between himself and all peoples, but also among all peoples. His promise is that it will be so one day. In this respect Assyria and Egypt stand for all the warring nations of the earth. Isaiah's message to Judah is clear: do not make a highway to Egypt in order to escape Assyria. Your only hope—and Egypt's—is in your God, who can break down the barriers.

Egypt will serve [God] with Assyria is a contextual understanding because the clause could equally well be read "the Egyptians will serve Assyria," and in fact all the versions do read it in this way. But the context demands the alternate reading, the "serving" being understood as worship, a common meaning for "serve" (*'ābaḏ;* cf. 43:23, 24; 60:11, 12).

24, 25 Israel, Egypt, and Assyria are placed on a par. Among them Israel will exist for blessing, but all of them are at one before God. In a remarkable statement Isaiah applies terms previously restricted to Israel to both Egypt and Assyria. He calls Egypt *my people* (cf. 10:24; 43:6, 7; Hos. 1:10; 2:23; Jer. 11:4) and Assyria *the work of my hand* (cf. 60:21; 64:8; Ps. 119:73; 138:8). It is true that the favorite term *my inheritance* is reserved for Israel (cf. Deut. 32:9), but claims that this term gives a slightly special standing to Israel lack evidence. The point being made is that if Israel turns to the nations in trust she will be prostituting her ministry to them. Instead, she is to be the vehicle whereby those very nations can turn to her God and become partners with her in service to him and enjoying his blessings.[28]

(2) The folly of trusting Egypt (20:1–6)

1 *In the year when the Tartan came to Ashdod, when Sargon the king of Assyria sent him and he fought with Ashdod and conquered it—*

2 *at that time the Lord spoke by the hand of Isaiah, son of Amoz, having said,[1] "Go, take off the sackcloth from your loins and loose your*

---

28. This was too much for the Targ., which severely altered these statements. Kaiser, who develops an elaborate argument for the late date of this universalistic theology, is then forced to date the Targum's narrowness to after the defeat of Bar Kochba (A.D. 137). This is altogether too late. As seen in the Essene writings, a narrowly Judaic vision of salvation was current well before the time of Christ.

1. It must be admitted that *l'ēmôr,* translated here as "having said," does not normally take this translation, but usually means "saying." The irregular translation is given here to convey the sequence of statements to the modern reader, whereas the Hebrew writer merely treats them as a package (cf. Delitzsch, who says v. 2a refers to v. 3). Duhm believes the present verses to be an abbreviation of a longer first-person document.

sandals from your feet." And he had done this, going naked and barefoot.

3 *Then the Lord said, "Just as my servant Isaiah went naked and barefoot, for three years[2] it is a sign and portent against Egypt and against Ethiopia;*

4 *so shall the king of Assyria lead away the captive of Egypt and the exile of Ethiopia: boys and elders, naked and barefoot, with bare buttocks,[3] the nakedness of Egypt.*

5 *They will be shattered and ashamed of Ethiopia their expectation, and Egypt their beauty.*

6 *The inhabitant of this coast[4] will say in that day, "Behold, so is our expectation[5] to whom we fled for help to be delivered from the king of Assyria. How then can we escape?"*

This passage concludes Isaiah's oracle against Egypt. As such it forms a graphic summary of the prophet's opinion of trust in Egypt. Egypt herself was under judgment, and reliance on her was useless. As an example, he takes the city of Ashdod, the northernmost of the five great Philistine cities, which lay about thirty-three miles west of Jerusalem and about two or three miles inland. When the Ethiopian Shabako was able to consolidate Upper and Lower Egypt in 714, he immediately began to foment rebellion against Sargon, who had been very busy for the better part of a decade quashing revolts in Babylon and the northwest (Urartu). Perhaps Shabako felt safe in this situation. But events were to prove otherwise, for Sargon

2. Although most modern translations punctuate "for three years" to go with the preceding clause, the MT clearly places it with the following clause (as does LXX; Targ. is not clear). If the MT punctuation is correct, this is a three-year sign, not necessarily indicating the duration of the behavior, but rather the length of time to which the sign points. Hitzig felt that Isaiah only appeared naked once. Vitringa believed that three days was to be understood. Thus " . . . and barefoot *three days*, a three-year sign and. . . ." Neither of these options seems to have much to commend it. If the MT is right, we are simply not told how long Isaiah acted in this way.

3. *ḥaśûpay*, "bare," is an anomalous form, perhaps an old form of the plural construct (GKC, § 87g). See 2 Sam. 10:4 for a similar example of disgrace through involuntary exposure. Note also Ps. 137:7, where the word "raze" (RSV) is the same as "strip" *(ʿārâ)*.

4. The reference to "this coast" has been puzzling to commentators. The reference is primarily to Philistia, whose only hope was Egypt. It is not necessary to think that Isaiah included Judah in the coastal region (although far-off Assyria did). The point is that those who were trusting Egypt would be ashamed. Why should Judah join the party?

5. *nbṭ*, "to look upon," has the full range of meaning from merely glancing at to gazing upon. Here it carries the idea of "to look at with expectation of help" (8:22; 63:5). Isaiah says they look in the wrong direction.

was rapidly getting the upper hand over his adversaries and that was to be true as much in the west as it was elsewhere.

Most commentators agree that at least part of the passage authentically relates to 713–711. However, Clements and Kaiser have each dated the present form later: Clements in 705 and Kaiser in 587. Clements argues that the original account must have depicted Ashdod's fall, whereas the present text represents a reworking of the earlier story for its use against Egypt at some time when Judah was particularly tempted to trust Egypt— thus, 705. Kaiser sees the story as a prophetic legend and thus applies it to a much later time, just before the fall of Jerusalem in 587 when Egypt seemed the only hope against Nebuchadrezzar. Neither of the proposed dates is anything but conjecture, the original having been discarded. But it is not necessary to do so. Kaiser's assignment of the material as prophetic legend is entirely subjective and Clements's objection to the reference to Egypt in Isaiah's acts assumes that there was always a near one-to-one relationship between setting and prophetic word. The diversity and complexity of the prophetic writings should make it plain that prophecy was much more dynamic than that.

The leading city of the revolt was Ashdod, over which Sargon had set up a regent favorable to himself, a man named Ahimiti. Now, probably with the backing of Shabako, Ahimiti was deposed and another man, Yamani, was made king,[6] apparently in 713. Sargon claims that he led his personal bodyguard in this action, apparently not waiting for levies to be raised from subject countries, as was normal practice. However, the biblical statement that the *tartan* (Akk. *turtanu*, one of the three chief officers of the empire, 2 K. 18:17) led the fight is probably more strictly accurate, since kings were prone to claim full responsibility for all victories in annalistic reports.[7]

The reference to the bodyguard may well indicate a very sudden attack. At any rate, the Assyrians report a swift victory, with Yamani fleeing to Egypt for asylum and Ashdod falling in 711. The Egyptians, faced with an Assyrian army on their borders, lost all of their bluster about defying Assyria and meekly handed over a bound Yamani, undertaking to send him all the way to Assyria. Undoubtedly, this action created a chill

---

6. If the statement in Sargon's annals is correctly understood, Yamani means "Ionian." This perhaps represents a continuing relation between the Philistines and their old homeland, the Aegean region (*ARAB*, II:62).

7. Cf. H. Tadmor, "The Campaigns of Sargon II of Assur: A Chronological-Historical Study," *JCS* 12 (1958) 22–42, 77–100, for a full study of this campaign in relation to the rest of Sargon's career. On the likelihood that Sargon did not lead the attack, which occurred in 712 B.C., see Tadmor, op. cit., p. 79.

in the hearts of Egypt's loyal allies and served to confirm the jaundiced view of Egypt held by people like Isaiah.

It is against this backdrop that Isaiah, prompted by God, took his stand. He acted out the truth that Egypt was as much subject to defeat and capture as any other nation and that reliance on her was as foolish as it had been for Ashdod and Yamani.

1 Like 7:1, this verse introduces the historic setting and gives a full resumé of the outcome. Having introduced the subject of the attack, it carries the topic through and gives us the results even though those results occur after the events described in the succeeding verses.

2–4 The language here does not express the sequence of events very clearly. Evidently the Lord had spoken to Isaiah prior to the actual attack on and fall of Ashdod, since he had acted out his prophecy for at least fourteen months (parts of three years, v. 3).[8] However, the interpretation of the activity was not given until the end of its duration.[9] Thus it may be that the speaking *by the hand* of Isaiah (normally speech directed to others) was not the directions contained in v. 2 but the interpretation given in v. 3. In that case, the appropriate reading would be: "At that time the Lord spoke by the hand of Isaiah, son of Amoz—having said, 'Go. . . .' And he had done this. . . .—then the Lord said, etc."

The symbolic action here is the only one reported of Isaiah, but such activity was fairly frequent with Jeremiah and Ezekiel. Like the parables of Jesus, these actions were capable of being misconstrued by hardened hearts, but they certainly could not be overlooked. Here Isaiah was acting out the fate of captives. Although it was not always the case (some art objects picture captives clothed to a greater or lesser extent),[10] captives were frequently stripped naked when led into captivity.[11] As much as anything else, such treatment would have a demoralizing effect upon the prisoners themselves and also on subject peoples who were watching. Of course, it also had a practical effect of increasing the difficulty of escape, but the chief aim seems to be public disgrace, the demonstration that the

8. An activity beginning in the final month of one year and continuing through the following year and into the first month of the third year would be counted as having gone on for three years. Cf. Thiele, *Mysterious Numbers,* pp. 30–31.

9. Clements believes that the interpretation could not have been so delayed, suggesting that the original meaning, a word against Ashdod, was given when the activity began. But this view assumes a uniformity in prophetic behavior that the data do not support. (Note that Ezekiel's activity of Ezek. 3:24–5:17 was apparently interpreted after the fact [3:25–27].)

10. *ANEP,* nos. 326, 366.

11. *ANEP,* nos. 333, 358, 365. (Cf. Isa. 42:2, 3; 2 Chr. 28:15; Amos 2:16.)

thing in which the captive had trusted for help had been unable to save his name and reputation (see on 1:29; 2:9).[12]

It is not clear whether Isaiah appeared in public completely nude. The word *'ārôm* can mean that (Gen. 2:25), but it also seems to be used in situations where only partial nudity is intended (58:7; 1 Sam. 19:24; Mic. 1:8; cf. also John 21:7). Particularly in that society where the part was identified with the whole, partial nudity would have conveyed its point very effectively (cf. 2 Sam. 6:20). The practical as well as ethical problems with complete exposure suggest that such may have been the case here, although they do not rule out the other. Thus, the outer garment and the inner tunic would have been removed, leaving only the loin cloth.[13]

Sackcloth suggests two possibilities. Normally sackcloth was a sign of mourning (Gen. 37:34; 2 K. 6:30; etc.), a rough, hairy cloth the wearing of which was designed to illustrate the spiritual discomfort with a physical one. Thus, Isaiah may have still been in mourning for the destruction of the northern kingdom completed by Sargon in 720, or for the depredations the Assyrians were going to commit on Judah (8:5–8, 16–22). The other possibility is that sackcloth was the customary dress of prophets (Elijah, 2 K. 1:8; John, Matt. 3:4). Zech. 13:4 seems to give weight to the latter alternative.

In any case, this behavior would not have been easy to undertake. Should someone do such things in our society, it is not difficult to imagine the comments and reactions. In a culture which makes well-balanced behavior a fetish (except in regard to sporting events), the prophets would not be welcomed. We are ill at ease in the presence of fanatics, people who are wholly committed to an idea, a program, or even another person. Our ideal is coolness, a noncommittal reserve which prevents us from belonging to anything but ourselves or to attachments we have defined. In truth, this has always been humanity's ideal, and it is one the prophets reject heartily. For Isaiah, once he knew God's will, this sort of behavior was not aberrant at all. It was wholly in keeping with the passion of his life—to live in glad response to that Holy One who had changed Isaiah, unbidden, from a filthy wreck to a clean person.[14]

12. Cf. *TWOT*, I:97–98.

13. Cf. A. van den Born, "Das Nackt gehen des Isias (Isa. 20, 1ff.)," *SKZ* (1946) 247–48; S. Mowinckel, "Om Jesajas striskjortet og hans nakenhet (über Jesajas Grobleinenschurz und seine Nacktheit, Is 20)," *NorTT* 49 (1948) 91–96.

14. Note the term of approval which God gave to Isaiah: my servant. This would have come as an affirmation to the humiliated prophet. It also strikes a resonant chord with the vision of the servant portrayed in later chapters of the book.

a sign and portent is a particularly biblical concept (8:18; Deut. 13:1, 2; 28:46; 29:3; 34:11; Ps. 135:9; Jer. 32:20, 21; etc.). Study of the occurrences makes it plain that the act was not understood to be related in any causal way to the event, as though the act caused the event, but had an evidentiary function. So the signs in Egypt proved that the Hebrews' God was God. So also Jesus' resurrection was evidence of his identity as redeemer and savior (Matt. 12:40). Here then Isaiah's actions do not guarantee that Egypt will go into captivity. Instead, they are a part of the evidence that Egypt is not trustworthy and that Yahweh is.[15]

captive of Egypt . . . exile of Ethiopia. At first it seems odd that a revolt by Ashdod should provoke a prediction of Egyptian (and Ethiopian, since the Ethiopian dynasty ruled Egypt) captivity. Furthermore, such captivity did not occur until the reign of Esarhaddon in 671, some forty years later. However, further reflection shows that his emphasis was not strange. In fact, it dealt with the real issue. For Ashdod's fate was not the major issue with which Judah should concern herself. The real issue was the fate of Egypt, fomenter of the rebellion. So Isaiah concerns himself with the cause of the rebellion, not the symptom. Not only will Egypt's lackeys go into exile, he says, but so will Egypt herself. Mighty Egypt, rich in culture and glory, will be carried off in shame.

the nakedness of Egypt is almost universally said to be a gloss, but equally universally, without evidence or argumentation. It appears in all the oldest versions. Duhm's primary argument was that a good writer would not have used both "buttocks" and "nakedness" in the same line, but that is a judgment which is very hard to support when the writer in question is at least twenty-five hundred years prior to the analyst. For further references to nakedness as disgrace, see 3:17; Ezek. 16:37; 23:10, 29.

5, 6 As Ashdod had looked to Egypt and been betrayed, so will all the other nations of the Levant. Egypt's shame will be theirs. She had not been strong enough to save Ashdod. She had not even been strong enough to defy Assyria's demand for Yamani. All these events pointed to the harsh truth that whenever Assyria came for her, she would not be able to save herself.[16] Why then, asks Isaiah, would we want to trust Egypt? It can only end in shame as it did for Yamani. Why look to Egypt's fading beauty when we can look to the glory of God?

15. See Lindblom, *Prophecy,* pp. 53–54, 246.
16. Again, over-literalism is to be avoided. Isaiah is not saying when Egypt will go into captivity, or precisely what will precede or follow that event. He is only saying that Egypt *will* fail and that, for that reason, it is foolish to put any trust in her.

e. JUDGMENT ON BABYLON AND HER ALLIES (21:1–22:25)

(1) Babylon (21:1–10)

1 *Burden of the desert of the sea:*
Like stormwinds from the Negeb[1]
   it comes passing[2] *on from the desert,*
from a land of terror.
2 *A severe vision has been told to me:*
the treacherous acts treacherously,
   the destroyer destroys.[3]
Go up, Elam;
   besiege, Media.
I will stop[4] *all her groaning.*[5]
3 *Therefore, my loins are filled with anguish;*
   pains have seized me like the pains of childbirth.
I am doubled up from hearing,
   dismayed from seeing.
4 *My heart went astray;*
   shuddering fell upon me.
The twilight I desired
   put me to trembling.
5 *Arranging tables,*
   spreading rugs,[6]

1. The reference to the Negeb, the region south of Judah, seems to argue against this statement having been made in 540, to people who had been living in Babylon nearly all their lives.

2. For the use of a masc. verb with a fem. subject see GKC, § 145.

3. Many commentators wish to follow the Syr. in making the second participle passive in each case. Thus, "the treacherous is treated treacherously and the spoiler is spoiled." This makes good sense (cf. 33:1), but the MT makes sense also, so no change is necessary.

4. Driver, *JTS* 38 (1937) 40, proposes to alter "I will stop" to "Stop" (fem. sing. imperative) and read "let all fatigue stop." This kind of reading is urged by some because the MT makes God's intervention too sudden. But as Wildberger points out, the sudden action of God is entirely consistent with the OT view (29:5, 6; Jer. 51:8; Mal. 3:1).

5. *'anhātâ* may be understood as having a double fem. ending (the root is *'nh*), or as having a fem. suffix, but without *mappiq* because of the following *he* (GKC, § 91e).

6. The versions understand *ṣāpōh haṣṣāpît* as "to set a watch." Hitzig's suggestion that another root is intended to mean "arranging rugs" seems to fit the context better. See also J. Reider, "Etymological Studies in Biblical Hebrew," *VT* 2 (1952) 116, who suggests "abundance of goods" on the basis of Arab. *ṣafa,* "to abound."

> *eating, drinking—*
> *arise, princes,*
> *anoint your shields!*
> 6 *For[7] thus said the Sovereign to me,*
> *"Go, post a watchman.*
> *Whatever he sees, he shall report.*
> 7 *When he sees chariotry,*
> *horsemen in pairs,*
> *riders on donkeys,*
> *riders on camels,*
> *then[8] let him pay attention,*
> *full attention."*
> 8 *The watcher[9] cried out,*
> *"On my watchtower, O Sovereign,*
> *I stand all day, every day.*
> *At my post*
> *I stand all night long.*
> 9 *Behold, this[10] is coming:*
> *chariotry of a man, horsemen in pairs."*
> *And he answers and says,*
> *"Fallen, fallen is Babylon!*
> *All the images of her gods*
> *are broken to the ground."*
> 10 *My threshed and winnowed one,*
> *child of the threshing floor,*
> *that which I heard from the Lord of Hosts, God of Israel,*
> *I have declared unto you.*

The four oracles contained in chs. 21–22 share a certain visionary character. They depend on less rational, more atmospheric elements for their impact (at least through 22:14), and have in common a rather fearful

7. *kî*, "for," which opens the verse, suggests that the watchman's report is the reason for the cry to the Babylonians to rise and defend themselves. However, the report is that Babylon is fallen. Thus it is too late for defense. More likely, the entire first five verses are the effect.

8. The sequence "and seeing . . . *and* he shall pay attention" expresses the protasis and apodosis: "When . . . then . . ." (GKC, § 164b).

9. MT "a lion" (*'ryh*); so also Targ.; LXX "Uriah"; Syr., 1QIs[a], "the watcher" (*hr'h*). Many attempts have been made to make sense of the MT. A typical example is Alexander's "with a loud voice like a lion" (cf. Rev. 10:3, also noted by Gesenius), but the view of Lowth (1778) that *hārō'eh*, "the seer," was intended has gained increasing favor and now seems confirmed by its presence in 1QIs[a].

10. *zeh*, "this," may refer to the sign mentioned in v. 7, but more probably its function is simply to fill out the kind of periphrastic construction described here.

watching for calamity, an expectation of death, in the midst of partying and hilarity. These common literary features may be the main reason that these four pieces are placed together here, but it is also possible that a deeper unity is at work. This unity would lie in the fact that Judah was tempted to put her reliance in Babylon as well as in Egypt during the last years of the eighth century B.C. This would have been especially true prior to 710, when Sargon administered a stinging defeat to the Babylonian rebel Merodach-baladan and forced Babylon to submit to him. But Sargon did not destroy either Merodach's or Babylon's rebellious designs, and in the ensuing decade they continued to be a thorn in Assyria's side. During this time, as indicated by 39:1, Babylon must have been encouraging revolt among Assyria's other tributaries, offering moral support if nothing else. Since Assyria held a firm grip on the lines of communication in the north, Babylon's only contact with the small countries of the Mediterranean coast would have been via the Persian Gulf and the Red Sea or across the northern end of Arabia through the oases of Dumah and Temah (so 21:11–16). But such help as the Babylonians could offer was severely restricted by their defeat under Sennacherib in 702 and his final destruction of the city in 689. Ch. 22 seems to deal with Jerusalem in the general light of this data. In the face of impending doom, given Babylon's collapse and failure, surely Jerusalem should repent and turn to God. Instead, they look to their weapons, hold parties, and build tombs. All this in the "Valley of Vision!"

The oracle in 21:1–10 is among the more obscure in the collection, both as to its historical provenance and as to its content. Verse 9 makes it appear that the entire address is to Babylon, but that is by no means clear, so that Penna and Kissane see vv. 1–5 as speaking about Judah.[11] The strange title only compounds the difficulty. Also, it is not clear what destruction of Babylon is being spoken of. The reference to Elam and Media (v. 2) seems to point to the Persian overthrow in 539 B.C., as does v. 5 with its apparent allusion to Belshazzar's feast (Dan. 5). As a result, given the rise of the Deutero-Isaiah hypothesis, many commentators assigned the oracle a date of about 540 (e.g., Delitzsch). Toward the end of the nineteenth century, however, such influential commentators as G. A. Smith and T. K. Cheyne[12] reverted to the idea of Isaianic authorship on the grounds that the reference was to one of the defeats in 710, 702, or

11. Kissane and Penna relate vv. 1–5 to Judah and the impending destruction under Assyria. To be sure, this relation explains the prophet's extreme grief, but it does not sufficiently explain the references to Elam and Media. The suggestion that they were tributary troops of the Assyrians is not adequate.

12. So also Boutflower, *The Book of Isaiah, I–XXXIX*, p. 148, all apparently following Kleinert.

689. More recently the move is back toward the 540 date or even later.[13] The most recent treatment of the chapter concludes that both points of view are correct.[14] A. A. Macintosh refers to the material as a palimpsest, by which he means that there was a sixth-century rewriting of an eighth-century document. This point of view seems to represent the most accurate observation of the data, for materials reflecting data from both centuries seem to be present (see below for further discussion). However, one wonders if, granting the possibility of prediction, an eighth-century origin could not include both materials. From the Judeans' point of view, between 715 and 700 it was important to say that Babylon could offer no lasting help to them at that time. That Babylon would fall to Cyrus in 539 would be of little significance. At the same time any historically accurate picture of Babylon's fate with regard to Judah and with regard to God's sovereignty over the nations would have had to reckon with the truth that Babylon's ultimate defeat was yet to come (39:5–7). Thus the vision seems to combine the pictures of both the near and the far situations in order to give a complete statement.

It is often said on the basis of v. 10 that the function of the segment is to encourage Judah. However, this is not at all clear. Obermann and Scott believe the verse applies to Babylon.[15] Moreover, even if the verse does speak to Judah, any comfort in it is strictly by implication. It is equally possible that the prophet is regretting that he has to announce to his people that they can expect no help from Babylon to escape the coming attacks by Assyria. If chs. 19–20 and 22 are taken into account as the context of this chapter, it seems even more certain that the function is not comfort, but warning—the continuing warning that the nations of this earth are under the judgment of God and are neither to be trusted nor feared as to our ultimate conditions and destiny.

1 *Burden of the desert of the sea* is enigmatic at best. Currently most scholars hold "of the sea" to be a textual corruption (it is missing from LXX) and take the origin of "desert" to be drawn from the succeeding statement "it comes passing on from the desert."[16] If the title is

13. So Kaiser, Clements, Wildberger.

14. A. A. Macintosh, *Isaiah XXI: A Palimpsest* (Cambridge: Cambridge University, 1980).

15. Obermann, "Yahweh's Victory over the Babylonian Pantheon; The Archetype of Is. 21:1–10," *JBL* 48 (1929) 322–24; Scott, *IB*.

16. So, e.g., Wildberger. The suggested origins of "of the sea" are numerous. 1QIs[a] has *dbr ym* instead of *mdbr ym* (MT), prompting Scott to argue that the original was *dᵉbārîm*, "words," which then got wrongly divided into the nonsensical "word of the sea," which in turn gave rise to "desert of the sea."

correct, it may be a reference to the fact that southern Mesopotamia was called "the Sealand" and may be an ironic statement mocking a country which is really a desert in terms of its capacity to help others (cf. Jer. 50:38; 51:13, 36).

Like stormwinds from the Negeb immediately thrusts the reader into the cognitive difficulties of the vision. For we are not told what comes. Gray inserted "roaring," while Driver and Scott altered the title to get a subject: "stormwind" and "words," respectively. Although this kind of elliptical writing seems out of place elsewhere in the book, it seems to fit this passage very well. The writer is not attempting to affect the reader cognitively but emotionally.[17] Thus the images are jumbled and incomplete. But they are entirely effective in conveying the impression of sudden, breathless doom. The translation here suggests that the vision itself may be what swept over the prophet like a storm. However, this translation also probably makes the statement more rational than intended. "It" comes, the more portentous because it is undefined.

Especially in the winter, as weather systems move to the north of Israel, strong windstorms come from the east and the southeast out of the wilderness (Job 1:19; Jer. 4:11; 13:24; Hos. 13:15; Zech. 9:14). These storms come with terrifying suddenness and force. So this experience strikes the prophet.

2 *A severe vision* speaks of the nature of the events which the prophet foresees. Merely because he prophesies doom and bloodshed does not mean that he delights in these. The same sensitivity which made the prophets aware of what God was saying to them also made them empathize with the human tragedies which their messages portended (cf. 1 K. 14:6).[18]

The thing which grips the prophet is the perverseness of warfare. He is not seeing courage, self-sacrifice, and commitment but rather treachery and greed as the works of a lifetime, patiently built up and cared for, are destroyed in a violent moment by all that is ugly in humanity.

(Given 1QIs[a]'s carelessness, it seems more likely that the *m* was accidentally dropped from an original *mdbr.*) Driver (*JSS* 13 [1968] 46–47) proposed that *ym* here meant "stormy weather," as in Akkadian, and that it was not part of the title originally but the subject of the verb *bā'*, "it came." Another suggestion is that it was inserted by a later writer who wished to distinguish this desert of Babylon from the desert of Arabia dealt with in v. 13 (Clements). Yet another alternative is that the word is a fragment of some missing word (Gray).

17. So Scott wrote of the passage as revealing the subjective experience of the prophet ("Inside of a Prophet's Mind," *VT* 2 [1952] 278–282).

18. A. Heschel, "The Divine Pathos, the Basic Category of the Prophetic Theology," *Judaism* 2 (1953) 61–67; *The Prophets* (New York: Harper & Row, 1962), pp. 221–278 (repr. in 2 vols., 1969; see vol. II:1–58).

Go up, Elam; besiege, Media is the command to Babylon's enemies to attack her. It is impossible to ascertain whether Elam and Media are the "treacherous" just referred to or whether Babylon is. Nor is it necessary to do so. As noted above, logical sequences are not as important here as is effect. Elam, in what is today southern Iran along the east coast of the Persian Gulf, formed a major part of the Persian homeland, and it was the Persians with the Medes, who lived in what is today north-central Iran, who brought down Babylon in 539. Thus, this statement is an apt prediction of what lay ahead. But would it have had any meaning in the late 700s? Those who accept the late date normally point out that Elam and the Medes were allies of Babylon in the 700s and that this command could not have been understood then. But that does not follow. First, as pointed out with reference to ch. 19, it is not necessary that there be some historical situation to which the prophetic word corresponds. The prophet may well be painting a general picture in which components are used in nonhistorical ways. Thus, if this passage was written before 689, the prophet could have been understood to be using peoples who were well-known marauders as figures in his picture of destruction.[19] It is also possible that Isaiah, with his well-known hostility toward alliances, could have been using irony here, calling on Babylon's "friends" to turn traitor against her and sack her.

I will stop all her groaning is another enigmatic statement. Generally it is taken to refer to groaning or complaining under Babylonian oppression when she became a world empire after 605. This is probably the ultimate meaning. One wonders if in the context of the late eighth century the groaning was understood to be Babylon's against the Assyrian empire. If so, God plans to put a stop to it, although not in quite the way Babylon hoped.

3,4 The violence of the vision which has come to the prophet is almost more than he can bear. He expresses this dismay in physical terms: abdominal cramps wrack him like birth-pains; he is doubled up and disoriented; his heart palpitates; he is seized with uncontrollable shuddering. One may ask why this should be. After all, Babylon was no true friend of Judah in 700, and she was an oppressor in 540. Kaiser suggests that such language was a rhetorical device used by prophets to underline the severity of their pronouncements (15:5; 16:9, 11; Ezek. 21:6, 7; Dan. 10:2, 3). Over against this view is Scott's opinion that these words betray the depth of the prophet's ecstatic involvement in the experience.[20] Without

---

19. It is to be wondered how many Judeans would have known about the alliance, or even where Media and Elam were located.

20. Scott, *VT* 2 (1952) 278–282.

endorsing all of Scott's opinions about prophetic ecstasy, it still seems that his point of view corresponds better with the sense of disorganized immediacy which the oracle projects. But in either case the problem is not solved, especially for the exilic date. No other prophet of the Exile manifests such a concern for Babylon. Most manifest positive satisfaction over Babylon's downfall. The earlier date would present less difficulty in that Babylon's collapse means certain failure for Judah. But it also needs to be said, as on v. 2 above, that the prophet's deep humanity is revealed in this kind of response. With terrific intensity the prophet is aware of individual persons bleeding and suffering, of families ripped apart and destroyed, of hope shattered. The prophet who does not feel some empathy for the personal horrors which destruction of his enemies will entail is not reflecting accurately the character of the God for whom he speaks.

The difference in tone between this oracle and the one contained in chs. 13 and 14 is probably to be explained by the fact that in the latter Babylon is used to represent or to typify human sin. No empathy is possible with a figure of speech. Here, however, a flesh-and-blood kingdom is being spoken of and a different response is elicited.

From hearing . . . from seeing are capable of two different interpretations, and commentators are about equally divided between them. One possibility is that the "from" *(min)* is privative,[21] meaning that the author is so overcome that he can see and hear no more. The other possibility is the causal: because of what he has heard and seen he experiences this pain.[22] Either one makes good sense. Perhaps the privative is best in that the rest of the verse does not deal with causes.

As is true of so much of the rest of the oracle, the reason why the prophet longed for twilight is not clear. Perhaps he hoped for rest at the end of the day. Alternatively, this may have been the time when he normally received visions.[23] At any rate, his hope was dashed: he was unable to rest or his vision was fearful rather than hopeful. Whatever the reason may have been, the hearers get the point. If they could see what the prophet has seen, they too would be seized with trembling instead of relief.

5 This verse accords very well with the report of Belshazzar's fall as contained in Dan. 5. At the moment when the king and his nobles are feasting in unconcern, the enemy troops are surrounding the city. Suddenly, in the midst of the feast, the call to arms is sounded, but it is already too late. This is always the story of judgment. One of sin's func-

21. Williams, *Syntax,* § 321.
22. Ibid., § 319.
23. This alternative rests upon a more mechanical view of prophecy than seems justified by the biblical data. Cf. Lindblom, *Prophecy,* pp. 94–95.

tions is to deaden moral sensitivities until the possibility of retribution becomes unthinkable. So it was at Sodom (Gen. 19:14), and so it will be at the last day (Mark 13:35, 36). While the prophet is convulsed with horror at what is about to take place, those on whom the horror will fall are destroying the very faculties which might have warned them.

The verbs here are infinitives, which give a sense of immediacy and activity. By contrast, the final imperatives are abrupt and cutting. All the busy activities of the feast are over—forever. Probably the shields were oiled to make the leather covering more flexible and less susceptible to cracking or being punctured in battle,[24] but several other possibilities have been mentioned, including making enemy blows slide off and making the edges of the leather softer against the user's body.

6–9 The scene now changes back from Babylon to Judah. In his vision, the prophet is charged to post a watchman who must watch the eastern horizon for the signs of Babylon's fall. Virtually all commentators are agreed that the watchman is Isaiah himself (Hab. 2:1; cf. also vv. 11, 12; 52:8). This identification has given rise to a rather elaborate theory of a dual consciousness in the prophet, whereby he is both watchman and listener to the watchman's message.[25] As Kaiser and others have pointed out, however, this is a visionary experience, not an ordinary day-to-day event. Thus, what is described in a vision ought not to be used to construct a theory of prophetic psychology.

This concept of the signs of the times is picked up by Jesus in his discourse on the last days. These signs are evidences of God's workings in history, bringing all things to final consummation. Not only will there be cataclysms in nature (Matt. 24:7, 29), but also in human society (Matt. 24:6) and in the Church (Matt. 24:9–12). The person who sees these signs can interpret the message. As surely as Babylon has fallen, Christ is coming.

6 God is here referred to as *the Sovereign* (as in v. 8). In the affairs of the world, he is Isaiah's Sovereign, but also Babylon's, indeed, the Sovereign of all time. He sends a watchman to his post and Babylon to its doom. Under this sovereignty, the watchman has no choice but to report what he sees, even if that should be painful and unpleasant. In fact, that is just why he is posted, not for his own sake, to discover interesting intelligence, but to pass on information for the sake of his people.

7 The watchman is given something to watch for: a procession of warriors riding in pairs on horses, donkeys, and camels. Although Kissane

24. Delitzsch cites Virgil (*Aeneid* vii.26).
25. Apparently originated by Ewald, but developed by G. Hölscher, *Die Profeten* (Leipzig: Hinrichs, 1914). Cf. also Lindblom, *Prophets*, pp. 129–131.

believes this to be only a caravan, virtually all other students of the passage agree that it is a military cavalcade (as the predominantly military usage of *reḵeḇ*, "chariotry, riders," would indicate; cf. 43:17; Jer. 46:9). Having said this, however, one finds it difficult to arrive at a precise picture of the scene, because of the wide range of meanings for the two key words *reḵeḇ* and *pārāšîm*, "horsemen." *rkb* has to do with riding and *prš* has to do with horses, but within those general fields there are many possibilities.[26]

If the present reading is correct,[27] it may refer to the Persian army, which Xenophon said advanced by twos and specially utilized donkeys and camels to unsettle the enemy.[28] Again the visionary nature of the experience must be stressed. The Persian army, if that is what it is, did not appear outside Jerusalem. Rather, in his vision the prophet sees Babylon's attackers. Interestingly enough, the watcher is not told the meaning of the vision at this point. He is only told to pay very careful attention when the sign does appear.

8, 9 In these verses the watchmen speaks, first telling of his perseverance, with perhaps a trace of impatience (*all day* long and *all night*), and second, announcing the appearance of the sign and its meaning for Babylon and her gods. Kaiser suggests plausibly that v. 8 functions to heighten the suspense between vv. 7 and 9. Certainly if the passage dates to 700 the wait was a very long one until the final signs of Babylon's doom appeared. Likewise the Church waits, and has waited, for the announcement of Babylon's doom (Rev. 18:2). And what of the watchmen in the meantime? Will they have the same testimony as Isaiah, or will they be like the ten foolish virgins (Matt. 25:1–13)?

But however long the wait, eventually the light dawns. There is an abruptness about *hinnēh zeh* that *Behold, this* does not convey. "Here it is!" captures some of the feeling. When an event has been anticipated for a long time, its actual arrival is almost surprising. One has gotten so used to the anticipation that its passing into reality comes unexpectedly. So here the moment comes when the sign appears.

That the sign is not exactly the same as it was described in v. 7 causes a problem. Two solutions have been proposed: (1) the prophet actually saw two processions, the first being a military one on its way to

---

26. RSV "When he sees riders, horsemen in pairs, riders on asses, riders on camels." NIV "When he sees chariots with teams of horses, riders on donkeys, or riders on camels." NEB "He sees chariots, two-horsed chariots, riders on asses, riders on camels. He will see mounted men, horsemen in pairs—riders on asses, riders on camels."

27. In opposition to "horsemen in pairs" see K. Galling, *ZTK* 53 (1956) 129–131.

28. *Cyropaedia* i.6, 10; iv.3–5; vi.1, 28; vii.4, 17.

destroy Babylon and the second merely a messenger coming to announce Babylon's fall; (2) the two signs are in fact identical, but only enough is described the second time to recall the fuller description in v. 7. The latter solution seems the more natural, requiring fewer suppositions to support it than does the former. However, the reference to *chariotry of a man* in v. 9 is troublesome. The NIV translates "a man in a chariot," but if that were intended, surely a clearer way of saying that could have been found. Probably Galling is right that it is a manned chariot,[29] but it is unlikely that the one at the beginning of v. 7 was unmanned. Perhaps v. 9 only gives a fuller description of the chariot mentioned in v. 7.

he answers is indefinite as to the identity of the speaker. There are at least three possibilities: God, a messenger, the watchman. The difficulty with the watchman is that he has not previously learned the meaning of the sign. Otherwise, this would be the most natural interpretation. Given that problem, one is left with the other alternatives. God seems the least likely since nothing else in the context indicates him. The messenger depends on the interpretation of "chariot of a man" and is thus questionable. Thus we come back to the watchman, and in fact, in an oracle where logical connection is not important, it presents very little difficulty to suppose that the watchman intuits the meaning of the sign at the critical moment. Overall, this interpretation seems to present fewest problems.

Fallen, fallen is Babylon strikes the ear with a sonorous kind of finality. The repetition of the verb adds to the impact of the statement. The mighty city, glory of mankind, is gone (cf. Rev. 18:2). The connection with idols corresponds to other statements in the prophecy that idolatry is a manifestation of the human thirst for glory, of which Babylon is the chief symbol (2:6–22; 13:10, where the heavenly bodies are deities; 17:7–9; 27:9; 46:1–13).[30] Idolatry is the attempt to project human values and understandings upon the stars. Modern humanism is simply ancient idolatry in a three-piece suit or a pair of designer jeans. But the city of human pride cannot stand, as the Londons and Dresdens and Hiroshimas of our own century ought to tell us, and when they fall, our human pretensions must go with them. But the marvel of humanity is our capacity to resurrect the old pride from the ruins and refurbish it again.

29. Galling (*ZTK* 53 [1956] 129–131) argued that *rekeb ʾîš* was used here in distinction from *rekeb ḥᵃmôr*, "chariot (?) of a donkey," in v. 7. But if that were so, the former should mean "chariot pulled by a man."

30. Clements's assertion that the oracle must be exilic because the Hebrews learned about Babylonian idols at the time of the Exile assumes much too high a degree of isolation for the Hebrews. They knew about the worldwide spread of idolatry.

10   As noted above, this verse can be taken in two ways, either as a word of encouragement or as a word of regret. Which way it is taken depends upon one's conclusions concerning the date of the passage. Those who take it to be from the sixth century see it as encouragement to the exiles: their oppressor is about to fall. Those who take the oracle as dating to the eighth century generally see in it the note of regret: although you hoped for relief from Assyria, Babylon will not be able to give any. That the verse can be taken in both ways is perhaps an indication of the twofold reference of the oracle.[31]

threshed and winnowed refers to the crushing and trampling used to separate grain from the stalks and husks. Animals were driven over the cut grain, sometimes pulling a sled or a heavy cart (28:27, 28; 41:15, 16; Amos 1:3; Mic. 4:13). The grain and chaff, having been thus separated, were tossed into the air on a windy day with the result that the chaff was blown away, while the heavier grain fell back to earth. So Isaiah envisions his people: trampled under the threshing sledge, tossed into the winds, falling back to earth. But there is a word of hope in all of this judgment. The whole process goes forward at the word of Israel's God. History is not out of control, nor in the hand of some demon who wishes to destroy Israel. The shocks that had come and were yet to come could be endured so long as Israel could yet believe that it was God who was bringing her through the fire.

(2) Dumah (21:11–12)

11 *Burden of Dumah:*[1]
   One calls[2] *to me from Seir,*
   "Guard, what is left of[3] *the night?*
   Guard, what is left of the night?"

---

31. Scott *(IB)* and Obermann *(JBL* 48 [1929] 322–24) hold that the verse applies to Babylon, but the reference to them as "my people" does not seem appropriate in this context.

1. Cf. Delitzsch and Wildberger. Usually commentators have followed the LXX (Idumea) and the reference to Seir and have taken Dumah to be a wordplay on Edom, or have taken the meaning of Heb. *dûmâ,* "stillness," to be a description of the content of the oracle. Neither of these does justice to the fact that all the other oracles are titled by place names. The LXX reading (Idumea) may be explained by the fact that in late Maccabean times when the LXX was translated, the Arabian significance had been forgotten. (Note that the LXX of v. 13 contains no reference to Arabia.)

2. The indefinite participle "One calls" lends a distant, ghostly quality to the call.

3. Lit. "what from the night." "From" *(min)* is being used in a privative sense; see Williams, *Syntax,* § 321.

12 *The guard says,*
   "Morning comes and also night.
   If you would seek, then seek.
   Return, come."

Like its predecessor, this brief oracle bristles with difficulties. These difficulties center around the persons to whom it is addressed and the interpretation of the message itself. As noted above on ch. 21, this commentary accepts the theory that the three oracles of the chapter are related and that vv. 11–17 deal with the Arabian allies of Babylon.[4] On this account Dumah refers to the oasis in northern Arabia known today as Dûmet ej-Jendel. This oasis stood at the intersection of the east-west trade route between the Persian Gulf and Petra and the incense route running northward from the Red Sea to Palmyra. It is about three hundred miles southwest of Jerusalem. The fate of Dumah would be of great interest to the people of Edom (Seir; cf. Gen. 32:3; 33:14; etc.), because were it to fall to the enemy, their eastern trade connections would be cut off. Furthermore, as noted above, if a rebellious Babylon wished to influence western Asia against Assyria, the route across the desert would take on increased importance, both to Babylon and to those who looked to Babylon for support.[5] On the other hand, if the oracle relates to Edom alone, it is difficult to understand why it is in this context or what its significance is.

Like the oracle to Babylon, this oracle could apply to both the eighth and the sixth centuries. In the late eighth century, both Sargon and Sennacherib led campaigns into northern Arabia, Sennacherib's taking him all the way to Dumah.[6] Likewise, in the sixth century the last Babylonian king, Nabonidus, moved his capital to Tema (v. 14), and made a concerted effort to bring the Arabian tribes under his control. So Isaiah's words could be directed to his contemporaries and yet have larger applicability in the future when God's trustworthiness and lordship of history would be subjected to an even more severe test.[7]

11 *Guard*, while similar in connotation to the "watchman" of 21:6 and undoubtedly also referring to the prophet, is not the same word.

---

4. See also Clements.

5. For the connection between Edom and Arabia, see D. J. Wiseman, ed., *Peoples of Old Testament Times*, p. 230.

6. *ARAB*, II:358; *ANET*, p. 291. Mauchline also notes that Sargon's attack on Babylon in 710 may have had repercussions among the Arabs.

7. Macintosh, *Palimpsest*, p. 79, believes that the absence of any anti-Edomite sentiment argues against the material having been first written in the sixth century.

This person is the night patrol whose function is to "keep" the city.[8] But from his position on the wall, he is able to see the first graying on the horizon and announce the end of a long night. The people of Edom are depicted as recognizing that the Israelite prophet was the person, among all others, to see the future course of events and give them some word about that course. This is the same note sounded again and again in the second half of the book: Israel's God is superior to all others because, being sole creator of the world, he alone can explain his purposes for the future (41:21–29; 42:5–9; 44:6–8; etc.).

what is left of the night is the cry of one who is ill or sleepless for whom the night seems interminable. The repetition of the phrase underscores the questioners' sense of this interminability. The minutes creep by. So also for those whose destiny hangs in the balance, being fought out on another battlefield. They ask Judah's guard if he can see whether the night is almost over for them, whether light is about to dawn.

12 The guard's answer is enigmatic at best and is capable of at least three interpretations. He may be saying that while morning is coming, another night will follow. Or he may be saying that morning for some will be night for others.[9] Or yet again, he may be saying that while morning will come, it is still dark. Each of these positions has strong advocates and the grammar does not rule out any. In any case, the seer cannot predict unequivocal hope. He can see some hope, but there is also impending doom. His invitation for them to inquire again suggests the last interpretation: although morning is surely coming, it is still night and too early to tell what the day portends for them. This would fit an eighth-century date, when the near and far events were yet intermingled in the prophet's vision.[10]

Return, come are two blunt imperatives made more abrupt by the lack of a conjunction. As early as the Targum the frequent theological overtones of "return" entered the interpretation with the translation "repent." Frequently since then commentators have seen in this abrupt speech a call for Edom to repent and then come back to the prophet for a more hopeful report on the future.[11] However, the context gives no clue that this

8. See 62:6; Ps. 127:1; 130:6; Cant. 5:7.
9. Targ. paraphrases "the righteous will be rewarded and the wicked punished."
10. The verbs "seek" and "come" are not the usual Hebrew words but are Aramaic. This fact has often been used as evidence for an exilic origin. However, Procksch argues that the language here reflects the Edomite dialect, which was "Aramaized" much earlier than Hebrew.
11. Cf. Delitzsch and Young.

is the intended meaning, and it seems likely that the two verbs are merely used to express a single idea, "come back yet again."[12]

(3) Arabia (21:13–17)

13 *Burden on Arabia:*
    In the wilderness in Arabia you spend the night.
O caravans of the Dedanites,
14 *bring water to meet the thirsty.*
    Inhabitants of the land of Tema,
    come before the refugee with his bread.
15 *For they have fled before the sword,*
    from before the drawn sword;[1]
from the bent bow,[2]
    from the weight of battle.[3]
16 *For thus says the Lord to me, "Within a year,*[4] *like the years of a hired man, all the glory of Kedar will be finished.*
17 *And the remnant of the number of the bow of the mighty men of the sons of Kedar will be few, for the Lord God of Israel has spoken."*

These verses address another group of Babylon's allies and, in my view, establish the likelihood that Dumah in the previous oracle is to be understood as one of these. Although the authenticity of the term "Arabia" is questionable for some,[5] the references to Tema, Dedan, and Kedar are clearly to Arabian places and, as such, secure the identity of the persons addressed.

Tema is about two hundred miles southeast of Dumah on the incense trade route, while Dedan is probably to be identified with modern al-Ula, which is another ninety miles southeast of Tema. Both these sites are located in the region known as Kedar (Akk. *mat kidri;* 42:11; 60:7; Gen. 25:13; Ps. 120:5; Cant. 1:5; Jer. 2:10; 49:28; Ezek. 27:21) in the northwestern part of the Arabian desert. Tema is of special interest because

12. See Williams, *Syntax,* § 225 (cf. 1 Sam. 3:5, 6). Cf. also Alexander.
1. *neṭûšâ,* "to let go," thus "unsheathed." BDB, p. 644, suggests *leṭûšâ,* "whetted."
2. Lit. "the stepped-on bow," referring to putting the bow against the foot in order to string it.
3. Cf. Judg. 20:34; 1 Sam. 31:3; 1 Chr. 10:3.
4. The absence of the numeral "one" has caused some commentators to speculate that the original numeral has fallen out, as apparently in 1 Sam. 13:1. 1QIs[a] supplies "three," but this is somewhat suspect in view of 16:14.
5. LXX lacks any reference to Arabia, including the "Burden" title. This probably reflects the choice that the whole segment, vv. 11–17, speaks of Edom, a choice which is insupportable. Alternatives are to emend *ʿarab* to *ʿereb,* "night" (Delitzsch), or to *ʿarābâ,* "wasteland" (Wildberger), but neither is necessary or compelling.

it became Nabonidus's capital upon his self-imposed exile from Babylon in 552.[6] Although the reasons for this move are not clear, it is at least possible that he was seeking to consolidate Arab support against what must have been the obviously growing strength of the Medes and Persians.[7] But Isaiah sees no success in an alliance with Babylon. All that Arabia will experience will be crowds of refugees fleeing from Babylon's successive defeats and the destructive blast of war kindling her own possessions.

13 *In the wilderness* translates Heb. *ya'ar*, "forest." However, there are no forests in Arabia, and unless the prophet is being sarcastic, which is not apparent from the context, probably the general connotation of "off the beaten path" is intended.[8] Apparently the caravans are being forced off the roads, either for protection or because of the crush of refugees.

Translators are divided as to whether the parallelism dictates that the caravans of Dedan, like the inhabitants of Tema, are to care for the needy, or whether the caravans are the needy to whom the people of Tema bring both food and water. If the first is correct, then the identity of the refugees is never spelled out, unless it be the people of Kedar as mentioned in vv. 16, 17 (so Kissane). However, this indefiniteness is entirely in keeping with the general lack of specificity in the chapter as a whole. The prophet says that trust in Babylon will result in flight. He states his message in the most vivid way he can, but without meaning to say exactly who, when, and how.

The second alternative is somewhat more consistent. The caravans of Dedan, southbound for home, but still north of Tema, have had to flee off the roads, away from the oases and are now exhausted and desperate. The residents of Tema are called out to help them. This picture could fit the Assyrian period when attacks came on Arabia from the north. But it would not fit the Babylonian defeat in 539.

In general, the first option seems to fit the grammar slightly better in that parallelism seems called for,[9] and its generality seems to agree with the larger context.

---

6. See *ANET*, p. 313.
7. Cf. K. Galling, "Jesaja 21 im Lichte der neuen Nabonidus texte," *Tradition und Situation*, ed. A. Weiser (Göttingen: Vandenhoeck & Ruprecht, 1963), pp. 49–51.
8. Cf. Arab. *wa'ara*, "rough, uneven ground."
9. So NEB, NIV, TEV. The problem with the Hebrew that leads to the AV, RSV, JPSV rendering is the presence of the indicative "you will/do lodge," where a relative clause "who lodge" is required for strict parallelism. Note the literal translation above and compare with NEB, etc.

14 *with his bread* evidently means "bread for the refugee."[10] In 539 any supporters of Nabonidus would have been pushed westward across the desert tracks toward Tema, from whom their only support might come. During the Assyrian period, each of a number of attacks into Arabia had displaced people and put them on the road: Tiglath-pileser III, 738; Sargon II, 715 (possibly 710 also); Sennacherib, 703, 689.

15 *before the sword* (lit. "from before swords"). The feminine plural is used to express the abstraction,[11] which is then followed by the particulars: *drawn sword, bent bow,* and *weight of battle.* So inner Arabia would become a haven for those fleeing from the warfare which would engulf the more fertile lands around the edges of the desert.

16, 17 But Arabia itself could not escape that warfare. Isaiah's word is that those who have trusted the nations will succumb with those nations. Within a year, figured as precisely as an indentured servant would calculate his time of service, all the glory *(kābôḏ)* of the Arabian merchants will also have collapsed under the weight *(kōḇēḏ)* of battle. *glory* expresses the acquisitions, both tangible and intangible, which give a lifetime significance and importance. It is the thirst for glory which fuels so much of human activity. But glory achieved apart from God is like so much tinder which goes up in flames at a moment's notice (1:31; 22:18). Ultimately, the only glory in the universe is God's; he is the only one who is truly significant. But his intent is to share that significance freely (24:23; 35:2; 60:9, 13; 66:11, 12, 18, 19).

The remnant . . . of Kedar is an unusually long construct chain as it is pointed in the MT. Possibly it is to be understood as two clauses related appositionally: "The remnant of the number of the bow, the mighty men of the sons of Kedar, will be few" ("number of the bow" being corps of bowmen). In any case the long, sonorous statement of Kedar's military prowess is abruptly cut short by the single brief word. So also Kedar's glory.

But what is the guarantee of all this? *For the Lord God of Israel has spoken.* The audacity of such a statement is lost on us today. What does Israel's God have to do with Babylon or Edom or Arabia? They have their own gods to whom their destiny is committed. Yet the Israelite prophet dares to say that it is *his* God alone who holds the nations in his hand. Dare we believe this today? Is it true that the word of Yahweh alone shapes the course of the nations? Or was that just nationalistic bombast which we,

---

10. 1QIs[a] lacks the suffix, probably because it did not recognize "refugee" as the antecedent and sought to simplify.

11. GKC, § 122q.

a more enlightened people, may dismiss? In fact, we may not dismiss it, for only in God's sovereignty is there any hope for a race of human beings that seems determined to destroy itself.

(4) Jerusalem (22:1–25)

(a) The valley of vision (22:1–14)

1 Burden of the valley of vision:
What is it to you now,
  that you go up, all of you, to the rooftops?
2 A roaring city, full of noise,
  an exultant town.
Your pierced were not pierced with the sword,
  not dead in battle.
3 All your chiefs have fled together;
  without[1] a bow they have been tied up.
All your found ones[2] have been bound together;
  afar they had fled.[3]
4 Therefore I said, "Look away from me.
  Let me weep bitterly.
Do not hurry to comfort me
  over the destruction of the daughter of my people."[4]
5 For the Sovereign, the Lord of Hosts,
  has had a day of upheaval and trampling
  and confusion in the valley of vision.

1. Lit. "from a bow." Here the "from" is taken to be privative, meaning either that they had not fired a shot before being taken captive, or that no shot was fired at them before they surrendered. Probably the latter in the light of v. 2. Cf. 2 K. 25:3–7 for the story of Zedekiah's flight.

2. Another problem is presented by "found ones," which the LXX translates as "mighty ones" (Heb. 'ammîṣîm instead of MT nimṣā'îm, so BHS). On the surface, "mighty ones" offers a better parallel to "chiefs" in v. 3a and may be correct. "Found ones" can refer to those who are captured, however, and that fits the general sense adequately.

3. The form of v. 3 has occasioned considerable comment, primarily because of the last stich. It presents two problems, the chief of which seems to be its faulty order. How can the captives flee after they have been captured? Thus Duhm proposed to reorder the phrases into an apparently more logical format. But as Kaiser points out, there is little warrant for such an approach. In fact, the verse seems to be in a chiastic structure where phrase one is paralleled by phrase four while phrase two is paralleled by phrase three. The present translation expresses this structure.

4. The phrase "daughter of my people" appears only here in Isaiah. Probably the people are being represented as a beloved daughter who has gone astray (cf. Jer. 8:12; Lam. 1:8–9; 2:13; Amos 5:2; Mic. 1:13; also see Isa. 47:1).

403

Lifting up the shout[5]
and crying out to the mountains.
6 *Elam lifted up the quiver*
with war chariots[6] and horsemen;
Kir[7] uncovered the shield.
7 *It came to pass that the choicest of your valleys*
was full of chariots;
Horsemen took their station at the gate;
8   *he removed the covering of Judah.*
You looked in that day
to the weapons in the House of the Forest.
9 *As for the breaches[8] in the City of David,*
you saw that they were many.
Then you gathered the water of the lower pool,
10   *and you listed the houses of Jerusalem.*
You tore down the houses to make the wall more defensible.
11   *and you made a reservoir between the two walls for the waters*
of the old pool.
But you did not look to its Maker;[9]

5. *me qarqar qir,* "lifting up the shout," has normally been translated as "tearing down walls," but the meaning of the verb is speculative since it occurs only here and the parallelism with the following stich is not good. Ewald proposed to take both *qir* and *šôa* (crying out) as proper names of Assyrian army contingents, and Guillaume translates *ḥezyôn,* "vision," as "opposite," giving "Kir occupies the valley opposite while Shoa is on the hilltop" (*JTS* 14 [1963] 383–85). More plausible is the suggestion of Weippert (*ZAW* 73 [1961] 97–99) and Driver (*JSS* 13 [1968] 47–48) that *qr* should be related to Ugar. *qr* and Arab. *qarqara,* "to make a sound," which yields excellent parallelism. Note that 1QIs[a] has *qdšw l hhr,* apparently reworking the consonants to try to correct a difficult passage. The meaning is very obscure.

6. Driver, *JTS* 38 (1937) 40, 41, finding "man" to be "impossible," alters *'ādām,* "man," to *'arām,* "Aram" (so NEB). "Chariot of a man" is no more impossible here than in ch. 21, and there is no mss. support for any such emendation.

7. Kir is presumably a far-off land like Elam (Amos 1:5; 9:7).

8. G. R. Driver (*JSS* 13 [1968] 48) argues that *be qî ê,* translated here and elsewhere as "breaches," should be translated as "pools" in keeping with v. 9b. This may be correct, but recognition of the structure makes such an alteration less necessary. (Note Amos 6:11, where "pools" will not do.) LXX takes the subject to be the enemies of Judah and translates this word as "secret things."

9. Note that the suffixes on "Maker" and "formed" are 3rd fem. sing., evidently referring to the city of Jerusalem. We can focus on human achievement as our ultimate value, or we can focus on the One who makes human achievement possible. The former passes away (40:6, 7; 1 John 2:17), but the latter endures forever (Isa. 40:8; Ps. 56:5 [Eng. 4]; 102:13 [Eng. 12]).

> *the One who formed*[10] *it long ago you did not see.*
> 12 *The Sovereign, the Lord of Hosts, called on that day*
> *for weeping and mourning,*
> *tearing out hair and putting on sackcloth.*
> 13 *But behold,*[11] *rejoicing and gladness,*
> *killing cattle and slaughtering sheep,*
> *eating meat and drinking wine,*[12]
> *"Eat and drink, for tomorrow we die."*[13]
> 14 *It was uncovered in my ears, the Lord of Hosts,*[14]
> *"If this iniquity is atoned for until you die,"*
> *says the Sovereign,*[15] *the Lord of Hosts.*

The presence of 22:1–25 at this point raises two prominent questions: (1) What is an oracle against Jerusalem doing in a collection of oracles against the nations; (2) Why is it put here in the collection? Since the passage itself does not answer these questions, we must attempt to answer them on other grounds. The first is perhaps the easier one, and the title may give us a clue. Surely the reference to "vision" is a sarcastic one, for the people described in this chapter are people whose paramount *lack* is vision. The jubilant people cannot see the inevitable destruction that waits them; the leaders cannot see that God the Sovereign Creator is a better defense than arms and fortifications; Shebna cannot see that courage and responsibility are a better memorial than bricks and mortar. In fact, then, the people of Israel are no better off than the Gentiles around them. Their

10. In chs. 43–46 *yṣr*, "to form, make," occurs 10 times, stressing that the One who made can redeem.

11. The opening *wᵉhinnēh*, "But behold," expresses the prophet's astonishment and dismay. Cf. 5:11–13 for a similar description of the situation.

12. The verbs in v. 13 are infinitives absolute, giving a sense of immediate and continuing activity. Driver uses the anomalous form *šātōt*, "drinking (wine)," to argue that all except the final two are in fact infinitives construct. But this seems unnecessary. Delitzsch plausibly explains the anomaly (normally *šātô*) as altered to provide assonance with *šāhōt* at the end of the previous line.

13. Although the MT has no verb of saying to introduce the quotation in the verse, the versions are agreed that one is intended. With the exception of the Targ., which places the verb at the end of the first phrase, all the rest follow LXX, which places it before the final "eating and drinking."

14. MT does not specify the correct reading of the first line, "It was uncovered in my ears, the Lord of Hosts." Cheyne wished to emend "my ears" to "ears of," arguing for an earlier alteration on theological grounds. But it is more plausible that "Lord" is in the accusative of specification, "(by) the Lord" (see Williams, *Syntax*, §§ 57, 58).

15. LXX lacks "Sovereign" and is followed by Gray, Kaiser, and others. But the Greek text would have translated MT *ᵃḏōnāy yhwh* (the Sovereign Lord) as *kýrios, kýrios* and probably dropped one through haplography.

perspective is the same as the world's and therefore they fall under the same judgment as the world.

As an explanation of the reason for placing the oracle at this point in the collection, three alternatives need exploring. The first would be that of Delitzsch, who says that the titles of all four oracles in chs. 21 and 22 are symbolic and that they have been grouped together. However, it is not at all clear that the oracles on Dumah and Arabia have symbolic titles, so this uncertainty undercuts the likelihood of this argument. A second possibility is that the oracles in chs. 14–23 have a rough chronological arrangement (chs. 17, 18 excepted) and that the events described here were the latest except for those involving Tyre.[16] This point of view seems to accord with the data, but one wonders if it probes deeply enough, for similarities with 21:1–10 include the titles (both seem to be sarcastic comments on each one's point of pride) but go beyond those. Other similarities would be the partying and lack of vision, the prophet's grief, the references to Elam, and the mention of "chariot of a man" and "horsemen." All these point in the direction of a more intentional connection between the oracles than the first two alternatives would suppose. Furthermore, and perhaps even more telling, there is the two-layered nature of both 21:1–10 and 22:1–14 (see above on 21:1–10). Both seem to function on one level for Isaiah's own time, yet point beyond that level to another dealing with later events (the fall of Babylon in 539; the fall of Jerusalem in 587).[17] All of these factors suggest that Jerusalem is being associated with Babylon here in a conscious way. It is not possible to be dogmatic about the purpose of that association, but surely the realization that Babylon was to be Jerusalem's ultimate enemy must have played a part in this association.[18]

The two sections of the chapter seem to function in a way similar to that of chs. 19 and 20, where the second portion (here vv. 15–25) forms a concrete illustration of what has been talked about in a more

16. Cf. H. L. Ginsberg, *JAOS* 88 (1968) 47. Ginsberg assigns the date of 712, but the same argument would be even more apropos of the common date of 701.

17. This two-layered aspect was already noted by Vitringa and Calvin. More recently cf. Clements and Vermeylen. Cf. also Clements, "The Prophecies of Isaiah and the Fall of Jerusalem in 587 B.C.," *VT* 30 (1980) 421–436.

18. While Clements and Vermeylen would not agree with conservative scholars that this connection is the result of predictive prophecy (they would see it as the work of an editor who believed Isaiah had been predicting such events in his original comments and who now supplied fuller remarks), nonetheless conservatives may agree with the content of their observations, namely, that materials relating to both eras are present here.

general way in the first. Here Shebna, supposedly a man of vision and leadership, is caught up in the building of his own tomb while great matters of state are left untended. Because he has failed in his stewardship, judgment is hastening down upon him. So it will be for Jerusalem and Judea, which also have failed in their stewardship of God's vision.

The historical setting of vv. 1–14 has been the cause of a great deal of scholarly interchange. Coupled with this problem is the question of the internal structure of the segment. The variety of opinions still being published is an indication of the complexity of the issue. Perhaps a consensus would see the following divisions: vv. 1–4; 5–8a; 8b–11; 12–14. However, there would be no consensus as to the time reference. In general terms, the prophet appears to be referring to a past[19] event of judgment where the destruction was not total. Unfortunately the experience did not provoke repentance and trust, but revelry and a blind dependence on armaments. In response to this reaction, Isaiah foresees a new and more devastating judgment ahead. However, the identity of this event is not at all clear.

The majority of writers take it to be the deliverance from Sennacherib in 701 B.C. Many of the particulars of that occasion would fit. Hezekiah does seem to have prepared his water system for the event (vv. 9, 11); there was a general destruction of the land (vv. 5–8a); there seems to have been a flight on the part of mercenary troops.[20] Furthermore, if Isaiah had been expecting a general revival after the deliverance from Sennacherib and it did not come, this would account for his extreme bitterness (vv. 4, 14).[21] Finally, the connection with Babylon here may express the same note as ch. 39: to follow Babylon instead of God is the way of destruction.

However, one or two elements suggest that some other event is in focus. Ultimately, Hezekiah did trust God for deliverance from Sennacherib.[22] There is no indication in this chapter that a siege had been undertaken; the enemy army is not surrounding the city.[23] The reference to

---

19. While the perfect tenses which appear in vv. 6–8 may be "prophetic" perfects which refer to the future, the converted imperfect *wayyᵉhî*, "and it came to pass," opening v. 5, must be taken as a past tense.

20. See Sennacherib's annals, *ANET*, p. 288.

21. So Skinner.

22. It is strange that nearly all commentators assume that Sennacherib's statement concerning why he left Jerusalem is trustworthy and that Isaiah's statement is not. Thus they discount the evidence of Hezekiah's trust in ch. 37.

23. Cf. Ginsberg, who argues that vv. 7 and 8a refer to Azekah, the "covering" of Jerusalem in the gateway, the valley of Elah (*JAOS* 88 [1968] 48–49).

flight and captivity in vv. 2b and 3 actually fits the times of Jehoiachin (2 K. 24:10–17) or Zedekiah (2 K. 25:4–7) better than they do Hezekiah's. Finally, Eliakim, not Shebna, was steward in 701 (2 K. 18:37). Thus it may be that the event referred to had occurred during Sargon's attack on Ashdod in 711.[24] On balance, this latter position seems more likely. The Assyrian army took Azekah, which certainly must have looked ominous to the Judeans, but then left. What a cause for rejoicing and revelry: "Isaiah was wrong. Babylon was right. We need not fear Assyria." Isaiah responds that that kind of blindness will lead to a destruction which would be more complete than anything they could imagine (and as it would turn out, at the hands of the very Babylon to which they were then tempted to turn for help against Assyria, should she return).

Classically vv. 1–4 have been taken as prophecy (Calvin, Vitringa), and a few modern scholars do also,[25] although most take this passage as reflective of a past event, as noted above. If the former is correct then Isaiah is looking beyond the present mindless rejoicing to a time when the city will be in ruins.[26] This thought is so horrifying that he refuses to join in the merrymaking. The correspondence noted above between vv. 2c–3 and 2 K. 25:4–7 would be in favor of this position. Isaiah is saying that the people have allowed the immediate present to blind their eyes to the long-range realities (39:8).

If the second position is correct, Isaiah is saying that the people are ignoring present realities. They are dancing and singing when in fact their leaders have deserted them and the land lies in ruins. Isaiah is desolated over the destruction, but even more so over the blindness. Somewhat against this interpretation would be the fact that while this could only apply to 701, that was a time when there was some legitimate cause for rejoicing in their deliverance (37:22, 23). This seems to point to a prophetic utterance referring to the destruction in 586 although prompted by the unspecified event in 711.[27]

24. So Ginsberg. Scott believes the passage looks back to 711 from the time of the preparation for revolt in 705. Childs argues plausibly that it is impossible to identify the event (*Assyrian Crisis,* p. 26).

25. See Delitzsch, Gray, Kissane, Ginsberg. Duhm saw vv. 2–8a as predictive.

26. Note the similarity to 21:5.

27. It is possible that no historical experience was the catalyst for these verses, but that they are part of the same vision as ch. 21. Thus it is in his vision that the prophet sees the people thronging to the housetops to receive the news of Babylon's fall. This event, of course, must portend their own fall, but instead of turning to God they look to their defenses and indulge in fatalistic orgies, much as Berliners did in the fateful winter of 1945.

1 *valley of vision,* as noted above, seems to be similar to the reference to Babylon as the "desert of the sea." Although it is possible that the term *valley* was being used descriptively, since the Hinnom, Kidron, and Tyropoean valleys all meet at the foot of the hill on which David's City stood, this possibility seems unlikely. Again and again, Jerusalem is referred to as Mount Zion. But here Isaiah says Jerusalem is not a mountain from which a long view is possible, but a valley from which nothing can be seen.[28]

What is it to you now is an expression of reproach, as seen in Judg. 18:23. The sense is "What's with you?" assuming, like the slang, that the activity in question is unwarranted. The prophet cannot understand why the people are thronging to the housetops when they should be in their closets in repentance and prayer. As noted above, several reasons may be imagined for their congregating on the roofs. They could be watching the retreating enemy, or they could be looking for the messengers bearing news of Babylon's defeat, or they could be partying on the flat roofs, the natural place for such activities in a city where ground-level space was at a premium and where cooler breezes could only be felt by getting above the closely packed buildings.[29] In any case they are not aware of the implications of their situation, a tendency the Bible warns us against. As believers in the sovereignty of God, we are to have our eyes open to discern his purposes at any moment (Mark 13:23; 1 Thess. 5:3, 4).

2, 3 The noise of the city is a roar as the whole population enters into the proceedings. Again these verses envision the close-packed Near Eastern city where the sound of several thousand inhabitants laughing, talking, and shouting melds into one continuous roar. But the prophet sees another view of the city, its walls broken down, the streets littered with bodies of those starved in the siege, *not dead in battle,* its leaders having been captured not in heroic defense of the city but in flight to save themselves. (This is the kind of leadership which Isaiah holds up to ridicule again and again; cf. 1:23; 3:2, 3; 5:13; 7:2; 28:7, 14; 29:15.) This is the city in which there is no vision, where the inhabitants cannot see that a selfish, pleasure-seeking society must finally pull its house down around it as it loses its capacity for self-sacrificial service and its capacity for commitment to those values of the spirit without which no human society can long exist (30:10; Prov. 29:18).

28. Cf. Young. Scott suggests that the reference is to the Hinnom Valley in which pagan rites were carried on in an attempt to divine the future (Jer. 7:31–34).

29. It is even possible that they were engaging in divination as did Kret of Ugarit upon his roof (*gg,* as here, KRT, line 80; *UT,* p. 250; *ANET,* p. 142).

4 Isaiah cannot take part in the revelry, which he regards as foolish in the light of what he knows, and indeed, what the revelers know (v. 14). He wants to be as deeply touched as possible when he thinks of his city. How rare such compassion is. Most human beings would react just as the rest of the Jerusalemites did. We do not want to experience pain and difficulty, especially if it is someone else's. But not Isaiah. Like Paul, he wants to enter into the suffering of his people because his Lord has done so (cf. Phil. 3:10). This is the key to compassion: identification with One who has suffered with us and for us.

5–8a Here the prophet begins to recall the recent situation.[30] He recounts Jerusalem's total helplessness before the oppressors who were operating under the command of the Sovereign. He seems to be saying that if this was the case there is no cause for rejoicing. The same thing could and will happen again, especially because the people have not learned anything from this experience.

5 Over against the present tumult within the city, Isaiah recalls another tumult: the uproar which had attended the apparently imminent destruction of Jerusalem. Instead of a quiet reliance upon God (30:15), there had been a frantic rushing to and fro until the shouts had echoed off the surrounding mountains. The prophet seems amazed at how quickly the merrymaking has succeeded the terror. Yet how easily this happens; utter despair is replaced by a kind of feverish hilarity. The nation which has found the ability to rest in God in a crisis will not go to pieces when the crisis passes.

6 Although Sennacherib claimed to have defeated the Elamite army on his first campaign against Babylon,[31] it is unlikely, even if the report is accurate, that Elamite troops formed any significant part of the Assyrian army which came against Jerusalem. Thus we have two possibilities: that Elam and Kir did form a significant part of Nebuchadnezzar's army which destroyed Jerusalem in 586 B.C., or that Elam is being used in a more figurative sense in line with the references in 21:2. The latter

---

30. Normally the day of the Lord was seen as a future event, but here it is a past event from which certain implications ought to be drawn for the future. Cf. J. A. Everson, "Days of Yahweh," *JBL* 93 (1974) 329–337. As noted above, the converted imperfect at the beginning of v. 7 seems to require that the rest of the perfect verbs be taken in the past tense. Commentators are not agreed on this point, however. Delitzsch takes the segment to refer to the future and Skinner inclines in that direction. (1QIs[a] agrees, making the opening verb a converted perfect and thus a future. But the rest of the converted imperfects remain as in MT.) Vermeylen (and Clements) believe it to be from the time of Jerusalem's destruction.

31. See *ARAB*, II:234.

seems to be more inclusive. Thus the prophet is saying that those enemies who will destroy Babylon are the very ones who have threatened Jerusalem. As Babylon goes, so must go those who have trusted in her. The duplication of the phrase "chariot of a man" (lit.) from ch. 21 seems to support such an understanding.

7   Although Ginsberg's assertion that vv. 5–14 reflect on Sargon's defeat of the Ashdod coalition in 711 B.C. seems to fit the data generally well, his attempt to demonstrate his claims from this verse seem forced.[32] Verses 5–8a appear to be a general statement that Jerusalem had tottered on the brink of destruction. To make Elah the choicest valley and Azekah the "gate" is to become too particular, especially since there is no indication in the context that such specificity is intended. It seems less strained to continue the general thrust. In this light it may be said that the best valleys were the broadest and that these were naturally the ones which would become thoroughfares for enemy attack. Here horsemen would be stationed to prevent any sallying out from within and also to press the attack should the gate be breached. So with chariots rumbling up the valleys, with horsemen taking up station at the gates, it had been obvious that Jerusalem was defenseless (v. 8a). She was completely exposed and could be picked off at the enemy's pleasure. The realization of such helplessness can be bane or blessing. The helpless one may grow frantic and plunge into a frenzy of useless activity. Or he may be finally moved to quit all his efforts and make that quiet release of himself into the hands of the One who had been holding him all along. At this point Judah could not do this. Later she could and did (37:14–20).

8b–14   The prophet now moves to his indictment. Verses 1–4 set the stage, contrasting the blindness of the people with his own prophetic vision. Verses 5–8a recount God's earlier threat to the city. Now these verses tell of the response to that threat and of the effects of that response.[33] In a word, the effect is disaster, for at the very moment when a people of vision would be looking at God and their relationship to him, these people are checking their defenses and preparing "Night before Destruction" parties. If Babylon is broken and can be of no help, then there is nothing to be done except to prepare for the worst. The tragedy was that there was something to be done—commit themselves and their situation to God—but they would not do it. Isaiah takes this unwillingness as the final evi-

---

32. See Ginsberg, op. cit.

33. Westermann takes vv. 8b–14 as a separate unit of the "Judgment to the Nations" type (*Prophetic Speech*, pp. 170–72). But Childs argues cogently that vv. 1–14 form a single unit on an invective-threat pattern (*Assyrian Crisis*, p. 26).

dence of the hopelessness of their condition. By their refusal to trust God in preparing for the worst, they have insured that the worst will come, but not through Assyria; in fact, it will be through their would-be ally, Babylon (cf. 6:9–12; 39:5–7).[34]

8b–11 Faced with the threat of imminent attack, the king of Judah, almost certainly Hezekiah, makes a choice as to his first priority. That priority is physical preparation. He looks to his armaments (v. 8b), to his walls (vv. 9a, 10), and to his water supply (vv. 9b, 11). Such preparations were prudent and Isaiah does not condemn them. What he does condemn is the order of priorities. Before looking to the physical (v. 8b), he should have looked at the spiritual (v. 11b); before paying attention to what is made, he should have paid attention to the Maker.[35] This sort of reversed priority is as common today as it was in Hezekiah's day. How easily we talk of the ultimate reality of spiritual values when we are comfortable and at ease. Yet, when difficulty comes our actions give the lie to our earlier easy words. If it is true that God is the Sovereign of the universe, then our first task in a moment of crisis is to be sure that all is clear between him and ourselves. Then other preparations, if necessary, can follow.

8b *The House of the Forest* was part of the temple complex built by Solomon (1 K. 7:2–6). It apparently received its name because of its profusion of cedar columns and wood work. It was the storehouse for weapons (Isa. 39:2) as well as for other precious items (1 K. 10:17; 2 Chr. 9:20).

9–11a These lines in their present order may offer an alternation between the two physical elements necessary to survive a siege successfully: sturdy walls (vv. 9a, 10a) and a reliable supply of water (vv. 9b, 11a). As noted above, however, v. 9a seems to go with v. 8b.[36] In that case vv. 9b–11a form the middle elements of the chiasm: water, one line; walls, two lines; water, one line. The exact identities of the pools men-

---

34. A passage such as this points up the fact that the book of Isaiah does not preach the "inviolability of Jerusalem." It does preach that a Jerusalem which will trust in the Lord need not fall, but it does not say that Jerusalem will never fall.

35. In the light of the fact that the same verbs are used in vv. 8b and 9a as in v. 11 (*nbṭ*, "look to," and *r'h*, "see"), the structure of the segment seems to be chiastic: vv. 8b, 9a, defenses (A); v. 9b, water (B); v. 10, walls (C, C); v. 11a, water (B); v. 11b, Lord (A). Cf. J. A. Emerton, "Notes on the Text and Translation of Isa. xxii 8–11 and lxv 5," *VT* 30 (1980) 437–446; and Vermeylen. Understanding the structure in this way renders Duhm's reworking of vv. 9, 10 unnecessary.

36. Observation of the Hebrew word order seems to support this analysis: verb of seeing—weapons—place; breaches—place—verb of seeing.

tioned in vv. 9b and 11a are unknown. Conjectures based upon presently existing pools abound. This much is known: at some point in his reign Hezekiah had a tunnel dug under the old city of Jerusalem south of the temple mount. This tunnel connected the spring of Gihon in the Kidron Valley on the east side of the city to the pool now known as the Pool of Siloam on the west side.[37] Its purpose was undoubtedly to bring the abundant flow of water from that spring inside the city walls, thus denying water to any besieging army and securing it for the inhabitants of the city. In that light one plausible interpretation is this: the Old, or Upper, Pool was the one which had been built earlier at Gihon to capture the water of the spring (7:3; 36:2; 2 K. 18:17). The Lower Pool was one which had been constructed by Ahaz at the foot of the Tyropoean Valley and was incorporated by Hezekiah in the larger construction related to the reservoir between the walls—the Pool of Siloam.[38]

10 *you listed the houses* probably refers to a survey of all the buildings inside the walls, noting which could be demolished to provide rubble for filling the interior of casemate walls and for repairing any broken places (2 Chr. 32:5). There may also have been some demolition to provide fire breaks and access to the wall for easy movement of reserve troops to any point of emergency (cf. Jer. 33:4).

11 *Maker* is another expression of the Isaianic theology of creation. It is this understanding which provides the foundation for much of Isaiah's approach to existence. The gods are rejected because they are a part of existence; they did not bring things into being, therefore they have no plan for life, and no effective purpose in their handling of affairs. By contrast, the One who made all things does have such a plan and the person who does not take him into account is being very foolish (37:26; 40:21, 28; 41:21–29). The same issues emerge today: any scheme of beginnings that does not allow for a personal Maker cannot have any concept of purpose in existence nor can it long maintain a coherent system

37. See 2 Chr. 32:3, 4; *ANET*, p. 321.
38. So Young, citing L.-H. Vincent and M.-A. Steve, *Jerusalem de L'Ancien Testament* (Paris: Gabalda, 1954), I:295. "Between the walls" is taken by most to mean that the pool lay in the acute angle formed where the new wall coming down off the western hill joined the earlier wall of David's City that extended up the Tyropoean Valley (2 Chr. 32:5?). However, Dahood suggests that the reference may be to a now unknown reservoir built into a casemate wall (*Bib* 42 [1961] 414–15). K. Kenyon believes that the original reservoir was actually outside the walls but was an underground cistern with hidden access. If so, it seems odd that the long tunnel was dug. Surely the cistern could have been dug on the east side of the city (*Royal Cities of the Old Testament* [London: Barrie & Jenkins, 1971], pp. 139–140).

of ethics. Human beings will do what they please, or they will submit their wills to some other human being, neither of which offers any ultimate purpose for life.

12–14 Not only had Judah offended the Sovereign by depending on her defenses instead of on him (vv. 8b–11), but she had also responded to his call for repentance with parties whose intended purpose was to put out of mind the terrible events which might soon engulf them. Instead of allowing the situation to prompt them to look at possible causes, they only let the grim effects unhinge their moral restraints. In the Lord's eyes this is the final mark of apostasy.

12 Obviously, the Isaiah who attacked useless cults in ch. 1 did not expect that acts of repentance alone would have restored Judah to favor with God. Rather, he is expressing the thought which is found throughout the OT: if cult which is not expressive of a real change of heart is disgusting, a supposed change of heart which is not expressed in appropriate physical behavior is cheap and superficial (Ps. 51:17–21 [Eng. 15–19]; Joel 2:12–17; Amos 8:10; Mal. 1:8–11; Isa. 32:11–13; cf. Acts 5:1–11).

13 Instead of a deep grief over a long series of offenses against a holy God (such as even Nineveh had been able to produce, Jon. 3:6–9), Jerusalem responds with an outburst of hilarity and self-indulgence. To put this experience in modern terms we may imagine the situation in our own country in the wake of a nuclear attack. Those who remain alive, expecting to die in a further attack or of radiation poisoning, could turn to God in repentance and faith or they could engage in one last orgy of looting, indulgence, and passion. Which course we would choose would say volumes about the true nature of our commitments (cf. Lam. 3:40–42).

killing cattle and slaughtering sheep probably connotes two things. The first is excess. It is likely that the normal diet did not contain a great deal of meat, both because of storage problems and because animals were too valuable for other purposes than food. The second is ironic. If there were really going to be a siege, then every food product would be needed. Here the population, perhaps thinking they could not keep the animals alive anyway, is devouring that precious food in a party atmosphere.

for tomorrow we die expresses the ultimate rationale for a life of acquisition and indulgence. If indeed there is nothing beyond the grave, then self-sacrifice, commitment, and self-denying discipline are foolish (28:15, 18; 1 Cor. 15:32). On the other hand, if there is life after death, it behooves us to do everything possible to discover the nature and conditions of that life and to be sure that we have met those conditions (Mark 10:17–22).

14 This chapter has depicted a people who are the fulfillment of

414

6:9, 10. In contrast to Isaiah, who had acknowledged his sinful condition and had experienced gracious cleansing, this people has become increasingly blind, deaf, and fat-hearted at every new revelation of God. The result is that their sin cannot, and will not, be covered or atoned for. So then the promise of 6:11–13 can also be expected to be fulfilled. A people who will not recognize their sin will never exercise that faith in God's provision which makes a right relationship to him possible (27:9; 2 Chr. 7:14; Rom. 5:1, 2). And since the Judeans are thus out from under God's covering (v. 8a), their enemies will eventually destroy them.

If this iniquity . . . expresses the standard oath form of the OT. As is typical, only the second half of the oath is preserved (14:24; Deut. 1:34; Jer. 22:6; etc.).[39] Probably the imprecation was something like "The Lord do so to me, if . . . ," and this may have fallen out of use early so no incongruency was felt in putting the oath in the mouth of the Lord. But the important point here is the seriousness of the oath. It is the Sovereign whom the Judeans and we treat so lightly. It is he who holds our mortal and immortal destinies, yet we act as if he were a doddering grandfather to whom no attention need be paid. He is not short-tempered and arbitrary; we do not need to live in terror of him. But he is Almighty, and failure to pay reverent and serious attention to him can only be considered foolish.

(b) Shebna the steward (22:15–25)

15 Thus says the Sovereign, the Lord of Hosts, "Come, go[1] to this steward, to Shebna,[2] who is over the house.

16 'What have you here and whom have you here, that you have hewn out a grave for yourself here? He[3] hews out his grave on the height! He cuts out a dwelling for himself in the rock!

17 Behold, the Lord is hurling a hurling, mighty man, and seizing a seizing;[4]

18 he will surely wind you into a winding like a ball into a broad land;

---

39. GCK, § 149.

1. The command to Isaiah is lit. "Go, come to," but the imperative of *hālaḵ*, "go," is used in an auxiliary way with other imperatives much as English "come" is used (BDB, p. 234; 2 K. 5:5; Isa. 26:20; Ezek. 3:4, 11; Judg. 19:11, 13; etc.).

2. R. Martin-Achard notes that the full name may have been Shebanijah, as Ezra is short for Azariah, etc. (*TZ* 24 [1968] 246).

3. On the shift from 2nd to 3rd person, cf. GKC, § 144p.

4. The verbs here are participles, expressing both immediacy and certainty. The LXX and Targ. have divergent readings from the MT, but they do not agree with each other. Each appears to be trying to make sense of a difficult text in its own way.

*there you will die and there will be your glorious chariots,[5] shame of
the house of your lord!*

19 *I[6] will thrust you from your place; from your position he will throw
you down.'*

20 *It will come to pass in that day that I will call my servant Eliakim,
son of Hilkiah,*

21 *and I will clothe him with your robe, and your sash I will fasten on
him, and your rule I will put in his hand, and he will become a father
to the inhabitant of Jerusalem and to the house of Judah.*

22 *I will place the key of the house of David on his shoulder: he will
open and none shall close; he will close and none shall open.*

23 *I will drive him like a peg into a firm place and he will become a
glorious throne for the house of his father.*

24 *They will hang on him all the glory of the house of his father, the
offspring and the offshoot, all the little vessels, from basins to jugs."*

25 *"In that day," says the Lord of Hosts, "the peg driven into a firm
place will let go. It will be hewn off and fall and the burden which
was upon it will be cut off, for the Lord has spoken."*

As mentioned above on ch. 22, this segment serves to particularize the
statements made concerning the nation in vv. 1–14. Just as the nation had
blinded itself in the face of death, choosing revelry instead of repentance,
so this individual Judean, a high-office holder, has betrayed his office by
attempting to memorialize himself in a lofty tomb. When he should be
acting in the interests of his people, formulating far-seeing policies which
will take all the factors, including God's word, into account, he is instead
looking only to the immediate future and only as it bears on him. As a
result, says Isaiah with biting words, God will toss him aside like a filthy
rag and give his office to another, who will truly act as a father to the
people, who will be trustworthy and dependable. But even that man will
not be able to save the nation single-handedly; ultimately the accumulated
weight will pull him down in keeping with v. 14. The sin of the nation,
its blindness, is such that one sighted man will be inadequate to turn it
from its blundering path.

Commentators are generally agreed that vv. 15–19 form the first
paragraph, although some follow Duhm in isolating v. 19 because it places
removal from office after exile and death. As Kissane bitingly observes,

5. Condamin (followed by Kissane) proposed to read "tomb" for "chariot." That would make a better parallel, but "chariot" is supported by all the
versions.

6. The shift in pronouns seems to be rather typical of prophetic speech.
The prophet varies in the degree of identification that he feels with God. Cf.
Lindblom, *Prophecy*, pp. 108–122.

that objection is irrelevant to a passage whose address is emotional and not cognitive. With v. 20 the description of Eliakim begins, but it is not clear where it starts to turn negative. Most scholars place this change at v. 24 on the basis that both vv. 24 and 25 are prose. However, there is every reason to believe that v. 23 is prose as well (RSV makes the entire passage prose), so a stronger argument than that is needed. That v. 25 begins with "On that day" suggests that v. 25 stands by itself as a negative pronouncement (so Delitzsch, Wright, NIV), although v. 24 certainly prepares the way for it. Recent historical criticism of the segment becomes more and more bizarre with Shebna being excised completely (Clements), vv. 20–23 being addressed to the king in Josiah's day (Vermeylen), and vv. 24, 25 referring to an unknown nepotist in the time of the Ptolemies (Kaiser). With all respect for the intense study and reflection which these opinions represent, they are still astonishing, requiring a greater credulity to accept than does the text as it stands.[7]

The historical setting of the pronouncement could be anywhere from 711 (the earliest date for vv. 1–14) to just before 701. The *terminus ad quem* seems to be given by the statement in 36:3, which has Eliakim "over the house" and Shebna as "secretary." In other words, the demotion of Shebna and the elevation of Eliakim forecast by Isaiah had taken place by that time.[8] It may be that the change in officials represented a change in official policy. Shebna may have advocated alliance with Egypt (and Babylon?) as in 28:14, 15 and 30:1–5, and Eliakim may have opposed this position, taking a stance more like Isaiah's. However, the passage here does not give any grounds for such a supposition. Shebna is deposed for seeking to memorialize himself in a grandiose way while failing to carry out the obligations of his office. He plans only for his own death and not for the ongoing life of the nation.

15 Contrary to most commentators, it is plain from the opening that this pronouncement is not to be understood separately from 22:1–14. It is not a separate oracle but is a part of the total content of this chapter. Thus the attempts to rework the verse to get the name and title first are

7. For a less skeptical analysis of the text, cf. R. Martin-Achard, "L'oracle contra Shebna et le pouvoir des clefs, Es. 22, 15–25," *TZ* 24 (1968) 241–254. Commentators are not agreed as to whether vv. 15–23 are in poetry or prose; most consider vv. 24–25 to be prose. Since there is only intermittent parallelism, as here, it seems best to cast them as prose, while recognizing that the diction is exalted.

8. K. Fullerton's novel view that this denunciation took place after 701 when Shebna had supposedly displaced Eliakim has not gained any adherents (*AJT* 9 [1905] 621–642).

unnecessary.[9] The exact repetition of the description of God from v. 14 reinforces the connection between the two segments. The Sovereign of the universe, the Master of the hosts of heaven, has something to say to one who styles himself as a somebody in the small circles of Judah, just as he did to the revelers on the rooftops. The One who sees everything is speaking to those who seem to see nothing.

this steward. The demonstrative expresses a contemptuous note (cf. 7:4; 8:6). The exact meaning of "steward" (*sōḵēn*) is not clear since it occurs only here in Hebrew. However, the appearance of cognates in other Semitic languages indicates that this was a very high official in the government, perhaps second only to the king.[10] If this is correct, then it is possibly synonymous with the title "the one who is over the house," the latter being the local Judean title for the office of *sōḵēn*. At any rate, it is clear that the "one over the house"[11] did function as prime minister in Judah, so it seems evident that God is tracing the rot among his people to the very highest levels. This is entirely in keeping with the outlook of the whole book. The tendency to adulate the mighty and to make superhumans of them will only serve to magnify their folly.[12] To the prophet only God and his Messiah are worthy of adulation. All others are merely human and must be looked upon as such.

Shebna is given without any father's name,[13] whereas Eliakim is always named with his father. This, plus the unusual form of the name,

9. So Gray and others, following Duhm. Such reworkings must of necessity issue in an unwarranted skepticism about the identity of the person to whom the address was made. So Clements argues that the original title is lost and the name of Shebna is a late insertion.

10. The fem. form of the word appears in 1 K. 1:2, 4 and has been translated "nurse," but in view of this occurrence and the cognate usages it may be best to translate "deputy"; cf. M. J. Mulder, *VT* 22 (1972) 43–54. In the Amarna Letters *zukinu* is a gloss on a term identifying the governor of the territory of Asshur as well as governors of conquered land; cf. R. de Vaux, *Ancient Israel*, tr. J. McHugh (New York: McGraw-Hill, 1961), p. 131. At Ugarit the term seems to identify the chief officer under the king (Gordon, *UT*, no. 1754), and it has a similar usage in Phoenician (Donner and Röllig, *KAI*, nos. 1, 31, 203).

11. This term appears first as applied to Ahishar in Solomon's court (1 K. 4:6), then to Arza under Ela (1 K. 16:9), Obadiah under Ahab (1 K. 18:3), and to Jotham, son of Uzziah, upon Uzziah's contracting leprosy (2 K. 15:5). Cf. also H. J. Katzenstein, "The Royal Steward," *IEJ* 10 (1960) 149–154. It is interesting that the prime minister under the Merovingian kings carried the same title, "master of the palace."

12. Cf. 1:23; 3:1–9; 5:22, 23; 7:13; 10:1–4; 14:4–21; 28:7, 8; etc.

13. Note that Ahishar (1 K. 4:6) and Obadiah (1 K. 18:3) do not have their fathers identified either.

has prompted many commentators to conclude that Shebna was a commoner and perhaps a foreigner with no right to such a prominent burial spot. However, this explanation hardly accounts for the bitterness of the denunciation unless the real heart of Isaiah's anger was Shebna's political policies, in which case the attack on the tomb-building was only a pretext. It seems better to take it, as above, that Isaiah is denouncing the tomb-building as a misplaced and self-serving priority.

16 It is likely that the tomb was being built on the hillside across the Kidron east of David's City where the village of Silwan is now located. A number of fine rock-cut tombs exist there, including the one attributed to Solomon's wife, the daughter of Pharaoh. In fact, it is possible that Shebna's particular tomb has been discovered in that area. Clermont-Ganneau gave the first report of the find in 1871, and in 1953 N. Avigad published a translation of the inscription, identifying the tomb as belonging to "[   ] yahu, who is over the house."[14] While this suggestion is very tantalizing, it must be borne in mind that names ending in -yah(u) were exceedingly common in biblical times and that there may have been several stewards who bore this kind of name.

What have you here and whom . . . are construed by some as evidence that Isaiah is questioning a commoner's right to a great tomb among the nobility. On this reading the prophet is asking what ancestors Shebna has there in the necropolis. It is also possible that he is merely using a challenging form of address to ask what the prime minister is doing there and who sent him there when he should be tending to the critical condition of the nation.[15] Note the recurrence of *here,* forcefully stressing the prophet's belief that Shebna should be elsewhere.

He hews . . . he cuts seem to be in the third person for emphasis.[16] These words may have been addressed to a surrounding crowd or simply to the elements, calling on them to look at the outrageous behavior (cf. 1:2). Probably Shebna had come out from the city in a handsomely equipped chariot (v. 18) to survey the work on his memorial. He may have been feeling particularly expansive and pleased with himself. If so, these biting words must have been especially humiliating. This kind of experience was typical of the prophets: when they were least wanted, in moments of fear or pride or self-sufficiency, that was the moment they appeared (7:3, 4;

14. Avigad, "Epitaph of a Royal Steward," *IEJ* 3 (1953) 137–152. He argues on the basis of epigraphy for a date ca. 700 B.C. and guardedly favors reading the name as Shebanyahu.

15. Cf. Judg. 18:3; 1 K. 19:9; Isa. 3:15; 22:1; 52:5.

16. The verbs are participles with the *hireq compagnis* for added passion and dignity; cf. GKC, § 90m.

1 Sam. 13:10; 1 K. 13:1–6; 18:16–17). But this is typical of God. One cannot escape from him. He will find us, and most especially at the time we wish to avoid him (Ps. 139:7–12). The issue, then, is not to seek to avoid him, but to seek to be with him at every moment (Ps. 139:23, 24).

17, 18 The language of these two verses is very difficult, but the sense seems clear enough. Instead of being buried in a lovely memorial in Judah, fit for a great man, Shebna will be tossed away like a filthy rag to die unheralded in a foreign land. It is not possible to tell whether Isaiah intended this as a literal prediction or was merely speaking hyperbolically. Either seems possible, and nothing is known of the circumstances of Shebna's death.

G. R. Driver proposes to read "hurl" in the sense of "shake out" and emend *geber*, "mighty man," to *beged*, "garment."[17] However, Jer. 22:26 expresses the same idea as here and the sense can only be to throw into a foreign land. Furthermore, although *geber* seems rough, it is an appropriate contrast to the Lord, as in Job 4:17; 10:5; 22:2. Who is a mighty man in comparison to God? All his pomp and glory are nothing but filthy rags.

He will surely wind you into a winding is three words in Hebrew, all three of which have the root *snp*. God will take the rag that is Shebna and twist it up into an insignificant wad.[18] "Let him who stands take heed lest he fall" (1 Cor. 10:12).

like a ball into a broad land seems to lack a verb in the MT, and both the LXX and the Targum supply one ("hurl" and "send," respectively). When vv. 17 and 18 are taken together, however, the sense may be as follows: "He will hurl you, having seized you and wadded you up like a ball, into a broad land." The *broad land* (lit. "broad of two hands"; Gen. 34:21; Judg. 18:10) would seem to apply most naturally to Assyria with its broad plains.

there you will die. Not *here* in dignity and honor (v. 16), but *there* in disgrace and ignominy (cf. Jer. 22:26). In many different ways the Bible tells us that true honor and glory come to us as gifts from God. That which we grasp for ourselves, like the manna kept overnight (Exod. 16:20), will only decay and grow foul.

there your chariots will be may indicate that Shebna had some special responsibility for the chariotry (so Clements). But equally likely Isaiah may have been pointing to the matched team and lovely chariot in which

17. Driver, *JSS* 13 (1968) 48–49, following Ginsberg, *JBL* 69 (1950) 55–56. Cf. NEB.
18. Clements suggests there may be an allusion to winding sheets here.

the steward had driven out from the city. One day it will belong to the Assyrians, says the prophet. So it is with all our acquisitions. We cannot keep them. If they outlast us, they will belong to others. Why will we not labor for those intangible values which will endure with us and in us forever? Why burn ourselves out to find some scraps of enjoyment before death overtakes us? Why not live as though we could never die? And indeed, we cannot! (Cf. Matt. 19:16–30; Luke 12:13–21.) In fact, says Isaiah, the quest for our own glory is most likely to disgrace us, so that Shebna, by his misplaced priorities, is actually a shame to his king and not an honor (cf. 23:9).

19 Whatever the ultimate results of Shebna's pride might be, the immediate results were clear: he would lose his position "over the house," a prediction which 36:3, 22 seem to indicate was fulfilled. That he was only demoted to "secretary," a still-prestigious role, may indicate that some sort of compromise had been necessary in order to get Eliakim into the top post. If policies of alliance versus nonalliance were at stake, then Hezekiah may have been unable or unwilling to cut completely loose from the previous policy. In any case, this is one more evidence of the remarkable ability of the bureaucrats to retain their hold on government. The titles may change, but the faces remain the same.

In vv. 20–24 the focus now shifts to Eliakim, Shebna's successor, and Shebna is further condemned by unfavorable comparison with that man. All the powers and prerequisites which Shebna had most likely delighted in would be given to another and Shebna could grind his teeth in frustrated envy. But Eliakim would be marked by dependability and faithfulness, characteristics conspicuously absent from Shebna's description.[19]

20 *my servant* is of course a title of great significance in the book as a whole. It is applied first to Isaiah in 20:3, then to Israel in chs. 40–55, as well as to the unnamed Suffering Servant, and finally, it is applied again to Israel in chs. 65 and 66. Although the term obviously involves obligation, even more it expresses privilege. Those who belong to God, who

---

19. The exalted nature of the description here and its similarity with some of the language of ch. 9 has prompted some students of the passage to conclude that Eliakim is either not original or is used to represent someone else. So E. Jenni, "Die Politischen Voraussagen der Propheten," *Abhandlungen zur Theologie des Alten und Neuen Testaments* 29 (1956) 42–44 (cited by Martin-Achard, *TZ* 24 [1968] 241), sees the reference as being to an eschatological figure, while Vermeylen believes Josiah was the original referent and Clements believes it refers to the royal house in Josianic times. Given the extravagance of the language against Shebna, however, one should not be surprised by equally extravagant language in favor of Eliakim.

are instruments in his hand,[20] are those who experience the fruits of his love and grace.

21, 22 Eliakim will wear the badges of honor and carry out the functions assigned to him (cf. Gen. 41:41–44). Evidently the prime minister at least, and perhaps other high officials, wore special uniforms. The terms used here for *robe* and *sash* appear elsewhere only for garb worn by the priests.[21] This does not mean necessarily that the court officers had usurped the prerogatives of the priests, but rather that there were standard terms for ceremonial clothing.

he will become a father expresses the attitude which a true governor should take toward his people (9:5 [Eng. 6]). This does not mean superiority or paternalism, but genuine care and self-sacrificing love. Thus his people will know that his rule is performed out of genuine care for them and not a self-serving pride. Again and again the prophets lay the ultimate blame for Israel's perdition at the foot of vain, silly leaders whom the people alternately adulate and despise, but who do not have the people's interests at heart. It was out of this experience that the longing for the Messiah came. Surely somewhere God would have a ruler who would rule justly. Eliakim would give a glimmer of that kind of rule, but as v. 25 makes plain, that hope must look beyond mere humanity.

the key of the house of David may have been a literal key of considerable size slung from the shoulder (so Skinner). But equally likely the reference here is symbolic. The authority to admit people to or exclude them from the king's presence is vested in, or put on the shoulder of (9:5 [Eng. 6]), the one "who is over the house." Obviously, this authority constituted tremendous power and required great character if it was not to be abused (cf. Gen. 39:6, 8). By the same token, the one to whom such power was given could know the depth of the king's trust in him. This was what Jesus was showing to his disciples in Matt. 16:19. Similar words are applied to Christ himself in Rev. 3:7.

23, 24 Eliakim will be like a peg set firmly in the wall, able to bear a prodigious weight without apparent strain. Those who do not see any historical or literary connection between these two verses suggest that the *peg* in v. 23 is a tent peg, which is the normal use of *yāṯēḏ* (cf. Judg. 4:22; Zech. 10:4). As noted above, however, there is no compelling reason for separating the two verses, and in that case the usage in v. 24 defines the one in v. 23 (cf. Ezek. 15:3).

In the second half of v. 23, Isaiah changes the metaphor but keeps

20. Cf. chs. 36, 37, where the "servants" of the Assyrian king are taken to be identified completely with their king.
21. See Exod. 28:4, 39, 40; 29:5, 8; 39:27–29; 40:14; Lev. 8:7, 13.

the same meaning. Rather than disgracing his lord, as Shebna did, Eliakim will be the vehicle through which his people will be honored, a seat upon which the family will be lifted up.[22] They can rest upon him with confidence.

24 As noted above in the introduction to vv. 15–25, many commentators take v. 24 with v. 25, giving as their reason that both verses are in prose. However, it is not at all clear that vv. 15–23 are not prose as well, so this argument is not conclusive. That v. 25 begins with "In that day," which is frequently taken to mark the beginning of a new section, is at least as strong an argument for seeing a division between the verses. In fact, the decision where to place v. 24 will depend largely on how one interprets the verse. If the prophet is speaking contemptuously[23] of a family which destroys its one notable member by overloading him with their ne'er-do-wells and incompetents, then v. 24 goes with v. 25. On the other hand, if it is describing a man who is so dependable that even the insignificant, not just the influential, can entrust themselves to him, then it goes with vv. 20–23.[24] Without denying the possibility of the former interpretation, the latter seems most consistent with the purpose of the passage, which is to show the kind of person Eliakim is. In that light, we are invited to measure ourselves against him and ask ourselves whether even juglets can depend on us, or whether we, like Shebna, will be too busy building memorials to ourselves.

25 Commentators have had difficulty with this verse because it seems to reverse field so abruptly. How can Eliakim, who has been so roundly praised, be the one who fails and is cut off? For it is surely Eliakim to whom reference is being made.[25] However, reflection shows that a word on Eliakim's fall is not at all unlikely in this setting. Over and over Isaiah had to say that any word of present deliverance was only temporary and that any word of future hope was beyond the fire.[26] Thus it is not surprising that the prophet should hasten to add that despite his faithfulness and the

22. There is some possibility that the "father's house" is not Eliakim's family, but in fact the royal house. The contrast with v. 18 suggests this possibility, as does 9:5 (Eng. 6). If this is so, then v. 24 does not speak of nepotism, as many posit, but of the impossible tasks assigned a faithful man by a careless royalty. Note that in Egypt Isis, the mother-goddess, was characterized as the throne on which the king sat.

23. It is said that offspring (masc.) and offshoots (fem.) are used contemptuously (Skinner; Mauchline; Driver, *JSS* 13 [1968] 49), but study of the occurrences does not support this view (34:1; 42:5; 44:3; 48:19).

24. So JPSV.

25. The attempt to force consistency on the passage by making this segment refer to Shebna cannot garner any support from the passage itself.

26. See ch. 5 at the end of chs. 2–4; chs. 11, 12 after ch. 10; ch. 39 after chs. 36–38, etc.

lofty things said about him, Eliakim was merely human and that if the nation reposed all its hopes in him, those hopes would certainly be dashed. The nation's only hope was in God and in that kind of repentance which would enable whole-hearted commitment. But Judah would be unable to do so, as v. 14 clearly envisioned. As a result, too much was demanded of too few Eliakims and they all fell. Modern nations have done the same. We adulate a Wilson or a Chamberlain as demi-gods and then, when they fail, as they must, we spit on them. *Sic transit gloriam.* Like Judah, we refuse to trust God and instead deify human leaders in the hope that they can save us. Inevitably, we must be disappointed, as Judah was. Our only hope is in God.

f. JUDGMENT ON TYRE (23:1–18)

1 *The burden of Tyre:*
Wail, ships of Tarshish,
    for there is neither home nor harbor.
From the land of Kittim[1]
    it is revealed to them.
2 *Mourn, inhabitants of the coast,*
    merchants of Sidon;
your messengers have gone over the sea.[2]
3 *On the great waters*[3] *the grain of Shihor,*[4]
    the harvest of the Nile, was brought to her.
She became merchandise of nations.
4 *Be ashamed, O Sidon, for Yam has spoken,*
    the Mighty One of the Sea, saying,
"I have not labored; I have not delivered;
    I have not reared young men, nor raised virgins."

    1. There are at least three textual obscurities here. The first two revolve around *mibbayit mibbô'*. "Spoiled from house" is a strange expression which may mean that the city is spoiled to the point that it is without a single house (privative *min*, Williams, *Syntax*, § 320), but that does not fit "from coming" or the idea of ships at all well. So it is taken here as "home" to which the ships would return. NEB depends on altering the two words to *māḇîṭ*, "harbour," and *māḇō'*, "entry port." The third problem involves the final phrase. Should it be read "from entering from the land of Kittim" (*BHK*, etc.), or according to the MT "from entering, from the land of Kittim. . . ." Unless one alters the sense of *niglâ* like NEB (from "uncovered" to "swept away"), MT seems best. That the Niphal of *gālâ* is "uncover" everywhere except Isa. 38:12 seems to favor this view.
    2. So 1QIs[a]. MT has "those who have gone over the sea have filled you." LXX lacks both "messenger" and "has filled."
    3. Ezek. 27:26 has Tyre, as a ship, being wrecked on the "mighty waters."
    4. "Shihor" (RSV Nile) appears as a synonym for Egypt in Jer. 2:18.

5 *Upon a report to Egypt,*[5]
   they will howl at the report of Tyre.
6 *Pass over to Tarshish,*
   howl, inhabitants of the coast.
7 *Has this happened to you, exultant one,*[6]
   whose antiquity[7] *is taken from ancient days,*
   whose feet have taken her to far-off places to sojourn?
8 *Who has purposed this against Tyre,*
   the giver of crowns,
   Whose merchants are princes,
   whose traders are the honored of earth?
9 *The Lord of Hosts has purposed it,*
   to profane the haughtiness[8] *of all beauty,*
   to bring down the honored of earth.
10 *Pass over your land like the Nile, daughter of Tarshish,*
   there is no waistband anymore.
11 *His hand he stretched out over the sea,*
   and made the kingdoms quiver.
   He commanded concerning Canaan[9]
   to destroy her strongholds.[10]
12 *And he said, "You shall not exult again,*
   O crushed virgin daughter of Sidon.
   Arise, go over to Cyprus;
   even there you will not find rest.
13 *Behold the land of the Chaldeans,*

5. Note the absence of a verb here. This gives a sense of abruptness and immediacy. Note also the predominance of sibilants: *ka'ªšer šēma' lᵉmiṣrāyim*.

6. AV "Is this your joyous *city*" (RSV is similar). However, Young seems correct in pointing out that the absence of the article supports the vocative here (note that 1QIsª adds the article).

7. W. Watson, *VT* 26 (1976) 371–74, has suggested that *qadmāṯāh*, "her antiquity," be read "her tribute." The Targ. would support this reading, but given the Targ.'s tendency to inventiveness in difficult passages, caution is indicated.

8. Driver, *JSS* 13 (1968) 49, suggests that *ṣᵉḇî* here means "nobles" (Proto-Semitic *dby*). This translation makes an excellent parallel with the following line and enhances the parallelism of vv. 8 and 9. 1QIsª has "all haughtiness" instead of "all beauty." Clements proposes to read "to humble every proud one, bring greatness into contempt—the honored of the earth." But Driver's suggestion seems to yield a smoother reading.

9. Note the use of "Canaan" for Phoenicia. The term may mean "traders" as in v. 8, but the broader use seems more appropriate here.

10. MT has *mā'uzneyhā*, which is generally taken to be for *mā'uzzeyhā*, "her strongholds." The nasalization of the double *z* occurs regularly in Aramaic but infrequently in Hebrew (GKC, § 200). 1QIsª lacks the *n*, probably signifying that they read *z* with *dagesh forte*. Driver, *JSS* 13 (1968) 49, however, wishes to see the *n* as a consonant and relates the word to Arab. *'azana*, "to distribute," and reads "mart."

this is the people which is not.
Asshur destined it for the desert-beasts.
They erected its siege-towers.
They stripped its palaces.
He made it a heap.[11]

14 *Wait, ships of Tarshish,*
for your refuge is destroyed."

15 *It shall be in that day that Tyre will be forgotten*[12] *for seventy years*
like the days of a king.[13] *At the end of seventy years it will be to Tyre*
as the song of the prostitute:

16 *Take the harp,*
circle the city,
forgotten harlot.

Play well,[14]

multiply songs,
that you may be remembered.

17 *And it shall be at the end of seventy years the Lord will visit Tyre and*
she will return to her hire, and she will prostitute herself with all the
kingdoms of the earth on the face of the earth.

18 *And it will be that her income and her hire will be holy to the Lord.*
They will not be stored up; they shall not be hoarded, but her income

11. This verse is frequently referred to as a *crux interpretum*. But this is only so if one rules out prediction and the Masoretic punctuation. Generally, modern interpreters take the verse to be a late gloss explaining that Babylon, not Assyria, fulfilled this prediction (so RSV ". . . Chaldeans. This is the people; it was not Assyria . . ."). However, this violates the MT punctuation and is not supported by any of the ancient versions. Duhm, followed by Marti and Kaiser, alters the entire verse to read "Behold, the land of Kittim, he has destroyed, laid in ruins." However, this kind of tour de force is unwarranted. The verse makes good sense as it stands if one's preconceptions about what the Bible can or cannot say are dispensed with. The phrase "this is the people which is not" relates well to a Babylon which was wont to say "I am" (47:8, 10); so also the idea that Babylon would become the haunt of desert beasts (13:21).

12. *niškahat*, "forgotten," appears to be a perfect "tense" with the older feminine ending "-*at*" still intact. Cf. *'āzlat*, from *'zl*, Deut. 32:36; cf. GKC, § 44f.

13. Another interpretation (Delitzsch, Cheyne) sees the reference to "a king" as a way of saying that just as there is normally no change in a king's decrees during his lifetime, so there will be no change in the decree concerning Tyre. This seems to stretch possibilities too far. Kaiser emends *'ahad*, "one," to *'ahar*, "another," and suggests that this is a late glossator's way of referring to a successor of Alexander who had first breached Tyre's island fortress. LXX reads "as is the time of a king, as is the time of a man."

14. Note that the fourth line is lit. "do good in playing," with "playing" functioning in an adverbial way.

426

shall belong to those who dwell before the Lord, for food to satiation and for choice clothing.

With this pronouncement Isaiah concludes his judgments upon the nations. It is a fitting conclusion. As Babylon, the great city at the eastern edge of the world, opened the section, so Tyre, the great city at the western edge, closes it. Just as Babylon was described in general, universalistic terms, so is Tyre. Just as it was difficult to pin down the precise historical events to which ch. 13 may have been referring, so also it is with this chapter. So much similar are the two chapters that the book of Revelation uses the language here applied to Tyre to describe the great world-city Babylon (Rev. 18:11–24). All these factors lead to the conclusion that Tyre here, like Babylon at the beginning, is being used in a representative way.[15]

If that is so, what does Tyre represent? Observation of the chapter must make it plain that the central focus is upon mercantile wealth. Tyre, southernmost of the Phoenician cities, was, at least until the fifth century B.C., when Sidon began to replace her, the dominant city of that region. Like all the Phoenician cities, with the Lebanon Mountains at their backs and the Mediterranean Sea at their feet, Tyre faced westward. The Phoenicians colonized and developed wherever possible around the whole Mediterranean basin, with two results: they became the preeminent seafarers of the region, and, like Spain and then England more than two millennia later, they became fabulously wealthy.[16] Babylon's greatness lay in her glory, the list of her achievements and accomplishments, her sophistication and culture. Tyre did not have all of that, but she did have her wealth and her vast maritime contacts. So between the two of them, Babylon and Tyre summed up from east to west all that the world of that day—and this—thought was significant. Isaiah's response was: "Do not trust the nations of this world. They are not preeminent. They do not hold your destiny in their hands. They, like you, are under the judgment of God—your God." When seen in this way, chs. 13–23 seem to be saying that since the glory of the nations (chs. 13, 14) equals nothing, and since the scheming of the nations (chs. 14–18) equals nothing, and since the wisdom of the nations (chs. 19–20) equals nothing, and since the vision of *this* nation (chs. 21, 22) equals nothing, and since the wealth of the nations (ch. 23) equals

---

15. Cf. Delitzsch and Young for similar positions.

16. As seafarers, they circumnavigated Africa in 608 B.C. under the patronage of Pharaoh Neco of Egypt. Their colony Carthage survived long enough to duel Rome in the titanic struggle from which Rome barely emerged victorious. Cf. D. J. Wiseman, ed., *People of Old Testament Times*, pp. 159–286. Note also the brief sketch of Tyre's history in Erlandsson, *Burden*, pp. 100–101.

nothing, don't trust the nations! The same is true today. If we believe that a system of alliances can save us, we have failed to learn the lessons of Isaiah and of history. God alone is our refuge and strength (Ps. 46:2 [Eng. 1]).

Because of the general nature of the prophecy, it is very difficult to determine whether Isaiah had some specific event in mind. Tyre came under attack five different times from Isaiah's time to 332 B.C.[17] Only the last of these, Alexander's, was entirely successful, because of the unique structure of the city. It was composed of the main city on the shore and a citadel on the larger of two islands just offshore. If the main city fell, the inhabitants merely withdrew to the citadel and outwaited the besieging army. Alexander succeeded by dismantling the onshore city and using its materials to build a causeway over which his siege machines could be drawn to break through the citadel wall. The inhabitants paid dearly for trying the great conqueror's patience. It is said that he crucified two thousand of the leaders and sold thirty thousand into slavery.[18] Whether Isaiah had this event or some earlier one in mind is not clear.[19] At any rate, Tyre never regained her ancient status and is today a small town of about six thousand inhabitants. Isaiah knew whereof he spoke.

The pronouncement is divided into two main segments: vv. 1–14, the overthrow of Tyre; vv. 15–18, the restoration of Tyre. The latter segment, like the prophecy concerning Egypt, has Tyre owning the sovereignty of Israel's God. (See below for a discussion of the possible historical connections.) The first segment is frequently divided into three stanzas: vv. 1–5, 6–9, and 10–14. However, this division separates the statement of God's part in the overthrow in vv. 8 and 9 from that of vv. 11 and 12. For this reason it seems better to follow the structure of NEB: vv. 1–7, Tyre's fall; vv. 8–14, God's hand in Tyre's fall.

1–7 This segment seems to follow the progress of the report of Tyre's fall. It begins with the homeward-bound Tyrian ships (v. 1), then to the Phoenician homeland (vv. 2–4), then to Egypt (v. 5), and finally to the end of the world (v. 6) before a concluding word to Tyre herself.

1 *The burden of Tyre* is considered by many modern commentators

17. Sennacherib (705–701), favored by Erlandsson and Rudolph; Esarhaddon (679–671), Wildberger, Vermeylen, and Clements; Nebuchadnezzar (585–573); Artaxerxes III Ochus in 343, Duhm, Marti, and Kaiser; Alexander (332), Procksch, Fohrer, J. Lindblom, "Der Ausspruch über Tyrus in Jes. 23," *ASTI* 4 (1965) 56–73.

18. Young, p. 144; *IDB*, IV:723.

19. See below on vv. 15–18.

to˙ be an addition.[20] As Young points out, however, the city addressed in
v. 1 is not identified apart from the title phrase and the verse becomes
meaningless without that identification.

ships of Tarshish refers to large trading ships able to travel on the
open sea (1 K. 10:22; 22:48; Ps. 48:8 [Eng. 7]; Isa. 2:16; 60:9; Ezek.
27:25; Jon. 1:3).[21] It appears likely that the general name of these ships
came from their original service, just as "East India man" came to describe
a large cargo ship originally developed for the trade between Europe and
the Far East. *Tarshish* refers most likely to Tartessus on the Guadalquivir
in Spain. Phoenician colonies in this area are reported to have existed as
early as the twelfth century B.C.[22] So these are long-range ships returning
homeward after a perhaps arduous voyage, their crews looking forward to
rest and leave in the home port.

But at some point, either upon making an intermediate stop in
Cyprus or upon meeting a ship outbound from Cyprus, they receive the
news that Tyre is destroyed and there is no home port to which they can
return. *Kittim* refers to Cyprus and the city Kition. In the Table of Nations,
Kittim, Elishah (another name applied to Cyprus or perhaps Crete in
ancient literature), and Tarshish are all said to be descendants of Javan,
or Greek Ionia (Gen. 10:4). This reference is almost certainly to the
Mycenean population of at least the northeastern portions of the Mediterranean Sea.

2 Here the scene changes from the sea to the Phoenician countryside. *coast* is literally "island" and may refer to the Tyrian citadel, but
the term is used in a general sense elsewhere in the book (e.g., 24:15)
and so caution is advised. Duhm, followed by Kaiser and others, wished
to make Sidon the original subject of the oracle, since it is mentioned here
and in v. 4 before any other city (assuming the title to be secondary). As
Young has shown, the title cannot be separated from v. 1, so Tyre is
mentioned first. More than that, mention of Sidon is not out of place in
an oracle addressed to Tyre. For Tyre's fate is not hers alone, but that of
all Phoenicia, just as Jerusalem's fate is Judah's. Sidon here represents all

20. Some because they believe all the titles in chs. 13–23 are secondary
(Wildberger), others because they believe the original oracle was to Sidon (Kaiser,
Vermeylen, following Duhm).

21. See *ANEP,* no. 106; cf. also D. J. Wiseman, ed., *Peoples of Old
Testament Times,* p. 276. Cf. Ezek. 27 for a picture of Tyre as one of her ships.

22. See *Peoples of Old Testament Times,* p. 280. Albright, *BASOR* 83 (1941)
14–16, argued that the name came from the Semitic (Akkadian) root *ršš,* "to
melt," and that the ships were originally ore carriers.

Phoenicia in her response to Tyre's overthrow (cf. Josh. 13:4, 6; Judg. 3:3).

mourn assumes that F. Delitzsch was correct in his suggestion that the root is not *dāmam*, "to be silent," but *dāmam*, "to mourn," first attested in Akkadian, but now also known to be West Semitic by its appearance in Ugaritic.[23] This rendering makes a much better parallel to "wail" in v. 1 and seems to fit the lament setting better, although silence in grief is not impossible, as Lam. 2:10 and Job 2:13 show.

your messengers reads *ml'kyk* after 1QIs[a] instead of MT *ml'wk*, "have filled you."[24] This reading seems to make better sense since the MT reading would have a plural verb following a singular subject. Also, the idea of commercial travelers fanning out across the sea from Phoenicia fits the facts very well.

3 It is apparent that then, as in more recent times, the transporters became the brokers. So the Phoenicians took the abundant grain of Egypt aboard their ships not merely as carriers but also as buyers and sellers. As a result, Tyre, like Beirut until the recent disastrous war, was the financial and commercial capital of that part of the world, and those whose livelihood depended upon Tyre's continued health could watch the accumulated labor of a lifetime destroyed in a day.

Commentators are agreed that "mart of the nations" (AV) is not justified. The verse is saying that Tyre herself is the commerce of the nations. People are not so much buying Tyre's wares as they are buying and selling Tyre herself. She has become so much involved in trade that she has become the trade. How easily that happens, and when it does, we are easily destroyed, for one has only to destroy that with which we have become identified and we are lost.

4 *Yam . . . the Mighty One of the Sea* has been handled in many different ways. Typically, it has been translated in some way similar to RSV, "The sea . . . the stronghold of the sea," with commentators frequently striking out one or even both phrases as a gloss.[25] Some assume

---

23. See M. Dahood, "Textual Problems in Isaiah," *CBQ* 22 (1960) 200–201.

24. Note that Duhm made a similar suggestion many years before the Dead Sea Scrolls were discovered. Cf. n. 2 above. It must be said that "filling you," apart from the disagreement of pronouns, could parallel "brought to her" (v. 3). The poetic structure of vv. 2 and 3 is difficult so that TEV and NEB simply rework them into one thought (following Duhm and Skinner).

25. Kaiser strikes out both phrases because the sea is male and only a woman could make such a statement! To force such agreement on poetry is to ask too much.

Tyre is speaking, while others assume the sea is the speaker. The present interpretation rests upon the recognition that the initial occurrence of *yam* has no article, suggesting that the term is being used as a proper noun, namely, the Canaanite god of the sea. And although *māʿôz* does mean "refuge" elsewhere in the OT, the root *ʿzz* means "to be strong," and a noun form meaning "mighty one" is entirely possible.[26] If this interpretation is correct, then Sidon, who has been dependent upon Tyre,[27] is told that his trust is misplaced because Yam, Tyre's father, is lamenting his loss, declaring that he is now bereft of children. The cry is that of parents, but especially mothers, whose children precede them in death. All the anguish of birth, all the struggle of raising the child, seems to have been in vain.[28]

5 From the Phoenician countryside the poet moves his focus to Egypt, to whom the news of Tyre's fall will come as a terrible shock for two reasons. Perhaps first would be the inevitable collapse of commerce. For all of her history Egypt had had a commercial alliance with the Phoenician cities, especially Byblos, which lay north of Tyre. The bulk of this trade was by sea. As soon as Tyre fell, all sea connections north of her would be cut off and Egypt's commerce would dry up. But also, the Egyptians could not help but realize that with Tyre neutralized, they must be next on the list of Assyria's victims.

6, 7 Now the word spreads around the Mediterranean, with the lament being carried as far as Tarshish itself. A part of the lament is the incredulous question, "Could this have actually happened to *Tyre*?" Three aspects of Tyre's existence made it hard to accept her destruction: her vitality, her antiquity, and her colonizing energy. As v. 3 suggests, Tyre must have been an exciting and cosmopolitan city, perhaps like Brazil's modern Rio de Janeiro. Can all that bustle and excitement really have been stifled? Furthermore, it seemed as though Tyre had been there forever. It had been a force to reckon with as long as anyone could remember.[29] Now it was gone. Likewise, the restless energy which had carried the Tyrians

26. Note that the Ugaritic cognate *ʿz* is applied to Yam in III AB,A:17 (*UT,* 68:17; *ANET,* p. 131). Cf. GKC, § 85g.

27. Cheyne reports that Tyrian coins bore the legend "Tyre, mother of the Sidonians."

28. The book of Isaiah refers frequently to the theme of childbirth and barrenness (7:14; 8:3; 9:5 [Eng. 6]; 26:16–18; 29:23; 37:3; 44:3–5; 45:10–11; 47:8; 49:21; 54:1–3; 66:9).

29. Herodotus (ii.44) reports that the temple of Tyre was 2300 years old in his day. The Ugaritic Kret Epic reports that Kret made a special visit to the Tyrian Ashtoreth on his way to reclaim his wife. This suggests a venerable shrine already by 1350 B.C. (*ANET,* p. 145).

everywhere, not merely to trade but also to establish colonies (*lāgûr*, "to sojourn"), has been drained away to be lost. So it is with all of us. We cannot accustom ourselves to the passing of the old and familiar, the settled. In the midst of ceaseless change, we keep fastening ourselves to forms, telling ourselves that they do not change. But they do; all things do. Only God endures, and the only wise course is that of Abraham, who sat very lightly on the forms of this world and looked steadily toward the eternal city (Heb. 11:9, 10; cf. also 1 John 2:15–17).

8–14 In this part of the lament the question which was implicit in the first segment (vv. 1–7) becomes explicit. Who could be responsible for the fall of so ancient and influential a city as Tyre? The prophet answers with complete confidence: Yahweh of Israel. He, the god of a small country whose size is exceeded by many counties in the United States, is in fact God of the whole world, including mighty Tyre, and he will call her to account for her pride. The instrument of his choice is the same one he used against Jerusalem, Babylon, and Egypt: Assyria. Moreover, the offense is the same one: the belief that humanity in itself can care for its needs.

8, 9 Tyre's fall is not merely an accident of history. Nor is it merely the result of Assyria's overwhelming need to dominate. For Isaiah, there is one great consciousness: it is God's consistent purposes which are being worked out in human affairs. It is true that the pagan deities are reported as having an interest in history and as influencing the outcome of historical events. But what is unique to Israel is the dawning consciousness that human history is the only arena through which God can be definitely known and that he has a greater purpose in that history than mere self-aggrandizement. In fact, he means to share his character with as much of humanity as will receive what he offers (2:1–5; 58:6–12).[30] So Tyre's destruction is not in order that Israel might rule, as the pagan view would suggest (36:13–20). Rather, God's purpose is to show the foolishness of human pride (2:11; 37:26).

the giver of crowns, along with the following two phrases, effectively depicts Tyre's impressive rank.[31] Then, as now, merchant travelers

30. This is why chs. 40–55 make such a point of God's creative power in achieving his purposes. For the pagan, only victory could be consistent with the deity's purpose being realized (42:1–9; 43:14–21; etc.). Cf. B. Albrektsôn, *History and the Gods*, ConBOT 1 (Lund: Gleerup, 1967).

31. This phrase is also taken by many to refer to Tyre's numerous colonies which became kingdoms in their own right somewhat like the British Commonwealth. However, others take it to refer to Tyre herself. So Lindblom, *ASTI* 4 (1965) 66, "who wears crowns"; NEB "city of battlements (crown)." So also Vulg.

were not people of great social status. They tended to be very common people. But their status varied greatly depending on the status of the country (and now, the company) they represented. In Tyre's case, her representatives acted like crowned heads of state. When they arrived in an area they came with all the presence of great noblemen. Why? They were conscious of the sophistication, culture, and power which stood behind them and they reflected its glory.

to profane the haughtiness expresses the reason why Tyre will fall. God is attempting to show the transitory nature of human glory and the foolishness of dependence upon such glory (2:11, 17; 4:2; 5:15, 16; 13:19; 14:12–20; 28:1–6; 60:15). It is not that God is opposed to humanity's being lifted up (60:7, 9, 13, 15; Ps. 8:6 [Eng. 5]). What he opposes is that pride which seeks to make itself independent of him. And he opposes it not merely because it denies his own preeminence, but more importantly, because it is in fact false (40:6–8), and so long as it exists, it prevents men and women from finding their true glory in God through Christ (Phil. 3:7–11; Col. 1:21, 22).

10 This verse is filled with difficulties with the result that the meaning is largely unclear. Three possibilities have been put forward. The oldest is the idea that with Tyre fallen, her colonies, represented by Tarshish, are set free from her constraint. A second interpretation would see Tarshish turning back from Tyre because she can no longer offer support or defense. The third rests upon an emendation prompted by the LXX (presupposing *'ibdî,* "till," rather than *'ibrî,* "pass over").[32] According to this point of view, Tyre is encouraged to turn to farming since the ships of Tarshish no longer can come. The second seems to fit the context of the poem best without undertaking the massive emendation required to follow the LXX. However, *like the Nile* is difficult to understand in any case. It perhaps fits the first suggestion best, with the idea of the flood of peoples escaping Tyre's grip. But even there the idea seems strained. Furthermore, if *waistband* (lit. "loincloth") is correct, its removal does not normally mean removal of restraint but defenselessness (Job 12:21). The possibility remains that "your land" refers to Tyre and that the daughter cities are being invited to plunder the mother. This alternative seems to require the least sleight of hand with the text.[33]

---

32. LXX "Till your own land, for the ships of Tarshish no longer come to you." This rendering has the appearance of a paraphrase.

33. Scott reads *'br* as "sail away from," which is attractive but not an attested meaning (cf. 1 Sam. 14:23; Jer. 5:22; etc., where the meaning is "to go beyond" but it is "to *go over* and beyond"). He also emends *mēzaḥ,* "waistband," to *mnḥ,* "harbor." Clements wishes to emend this word to *māḥōz,* "harbor, market."

11 It is at the Lord's command that Tyre falls. He is the one who has put the nations in upheaval. Again, we have Isaiah's statement of faith that behind the apparent chaos of history, God is at work. If empires march, it is only because he has raised them up and calls them forth (5:26; 9:10 [Eng. 11]; 10:6; 14:26; 41:2; etc.). The sea, which has seemed to be the Phoenicians' province, in fact belongs to God. He, not Tyre, controls the nations around it. It is this same view of history which makes it possible for Isaiah to declare that God will restore his people from apparently hopeless exile. It is he who disposes, not the nations of humanity (11:10–12; 48:14–16).

Procksch, followed by Gray and Clements, transposes the two halves of the verse. But there really is no sufficient reason to do this. All the versions read with the MT. The movement is from the general statement to the particular.

12 Since God has given the word for destruction, the Phoenicians' excitement (v. 7) is over. The young girl, fresh and untouched, laughing and dancing, is now beaten down and crushed.[34] Although the consummation of these things was to be years in the future, they were already done in the prophet's mind. When Isaiah looked at Tyre, he did not see a rich, exciting city to be envied by her country cousins. Instead, he saw a used-up old woman picking over her ruins. It is this long perspective which believers need to have as they look at the world. What now seems attractive cannot remain so if it flies in the face of the spiritual structure of the universe.

Nor will there be any escape for the Phoenicians. They may go to Cyprus as Lulli, king of Sidon, did to escape Sennacherib,[35] but it would do no good. Assyria's rapacity was not going to stop at the coast, and even if it had, the hand of God could reach farther than any Assyrian kings' (57:19–21).

13 If the Phoenicians believed they could escape, they were invited to contemplate their opposite number on the east, Babylon. Assyria, God's instrument, had, speaking metaphorically, almost exterminated Babylon. They had built siege towers against her wall. In the lower parts of these towers battering rams smashed at the wall, while above, soldiers shot arrows down into the city and let down ramps over which they could rush to attack the defenders.[36] As a result the Assyrians had conquered the city,

34. Cf. 47:1 where Babylon is addressed in the same way. In contrast is 37:22, where the virgin daughter of Jerusalem will not be crushed by Assyria. The use of Sidon here again underlines that Tyre's fate is the fate of all Phoenicia.

35. See *ANET*, p. 288.

36. Cf. *ANEP*, pp. 128–29 for several different types of siege machines.

stripping its palaces and reducing it to a ruin. While Sargon's attack in 710 may be the one referred to, it seems more likely that Sennacherib's much more thorough overthrow of the city in 689 is the one in view.[37] In any case, the prophet's argument is that if Babylon cannot escape, neither can Tyre, no matter where they flee.

14 The poetic section of the oracle ends on the same note on which it began. The ships of Tarshish are called upon to join the lament, for they have no place to which they can go for harbor. The implication of all of this is plain. Since the Lord has done all this, why should Judah seek refuge in Tyre? He is the only refuge. He rules the nations; he is our hope (Ps. 91:1, 2).

15–18 As in the pronouncement against Egypt (ch. 19), the prophet adds a further word to the announcement of destruction. It is a word of restoration and of submission to the Lord. Thus the word is clear: Judeans, do not envy Tyre for her great wealth. Ultimately, all that she possesses will come to our God and be enjoyed by his people (2:2, 3; 45:14; 49:22; 60:9–11). In this way these verses make a fitting summation to the message of chs. 13–23. Judah need not, indeed must not, prostitute herself to the nations. Rather, she should be true to her husband, the King of the nations, and in so doing she will find the nations coming to her.

15 As Judah was to be captive for seventy years, so too Tyre will lie in waste until a time will come when she will once again ply her trade. The *seventy years* need not be a reference to Jeremiah (cf. Jer. 29:10). In fact, both Jeremiah and this passage may reflect an idiom of the day in which seventy years would stand for fullness or completeness (so too Daniel's seventy weeks of years, Dan. 9:24).[38] Thus, the prophet is saying again that Tyre's fate is in the hands of the God of Israel.

like the days of a king is an enigmatic phrase which is open to several interpretations. Perhaps the least problematic is to see it as a figurative qualification of seventy, as "hireling" was used to qualify three years (16:14) and one year (21:16). Those were brief, incomplete times; this is a long time, a time of perfection. This understanding relieves us of saying that "seventy" was conceived of as an ideal royal reign or of making some other speculative equation.

the song of the prostitute is apparently the title of the poem which follows in v. 16. The poem was probably part of the popular parlance, and

37. Cf. Erlandsson, *Burden,* pp. 89–91.
38. Note that the Judean captivity did not take exactly 70 years, even if it is calculated as beginning in 605 B.C. Thus we are dealing with an ideal number there as well. Wildberger refers to an inscription of Esarhaddon in which Marduk is said to have condemned Babylon to 70 years of destruction.

like a modern preacher's reference to the songs of the day, would make the prophet's message the more vivid and comprehensible to the hearers.

16 The poem is composed of two couplets, each having three lines containing two words. Thus there is a lilting, ditty-like atmosphere to it. In a mild way it appears to deride the prostitute who, perhaps through age, is no longer popular, and challenges her to make music throughout the city in an attempt to build up a new clientele.[39] If the song was not created by the prophet, then it may well have supplied him with the image of Tyre as the forgotten prostitute (v. 15).

17 In a figurative way Tyre's music will have its effect, because after the period of forgottenness, she will attain something of her former eminence as a trading city of the world. The time frame here is as various as the commentators' assumptions. Erlandsson, who sees the destruction as having occurred before 700, points out that Tyre was indeed eclipsed during much of the seventh century B.C.[40] Others (e.g., Delitzsch), who see the destruction as occurring under Nebuchadnezzar, observe that Tyre did not regain prominence until the coming of Persia. From yet another perspective (e.g., Kaiser), it was only under the Ptolemies that Tyre regained her autonomy. This diversity tells us that no definitive explanation has yet been given and that the modern Christian should focus on the theological intent of the assertions rather than upon the supposed fulfillment.

the Lord will visit Tyre makes it plain that Tyre's restoration will be God's doing. The same language is used of Israel (Gen. 50:24, 25; Exod. 3:16–17; Ruth 1:6; Zech. 10:3) and speaks of his delivering grace which is applied on a universal scale. If Tyre is ever to regain her place, it will only be through God's grace.

she will prostitute herself seems to be strange language if God has delivered her from destruction. The LXX and Targum seem to feel this problem as well since they read (respectively) "be a port of merchandise" and "satisfy herself with merchandise." However, two observations may be made. Isaiah is continuing his metaphor in which he has compared trade to prostitution. This is a frequent comparison in the prophets, especially as applied to Israel, where such trade frequently involved dependency through alliances. Thus the full negative meaning of the term may not be intended here. But it is also true that God's grace does not guarantee positive response. Many persons have experienced God's hand of judgment and promised to

---

39. The reference to music is an indication that like Japan's Geisha girls, the prostitute in the ancient Near East was expected to be an entertainer with more than merely sexual skills.

40. *Burden,* p. 102.

436

do differently, but when deliverance came, they very quickly reverted to the old ways. This may be being said of Tyre.

on the face of the earth appears redundant and it is lacking in the LXX. However, scholars from as diverse points of view on textual reliability as Kaiser and Young agree that it may well be a means for stressing the universality of the trade involved.

18 *her hire will be holy* seems to fly directly in the face of Deut. 23:18, which states that a prostitute's hire may not be given as an offering. However, it is necessary to remember again that prostitution is a figure here and that there is nothing intrinsically immoral about trade or business.

As Young points out, Tyre now stands in relation to Jerusalem as her colonies once stood to Tyre. The wealth flows to the mother city. It is set apart now for God's use and he chooses to give it to his own, his royal priesthood (Exod. 19:5, 6; 1 Pet. 2:9; cf. Ps. 84:5 [Eng. 4]). So it is to God that his people should look, not to the nations, for ultimately they must look to him as well. Moreover, all the wealth which they have amassed with such difficulty and effort must eventually be his to redistribute as he pleases. If the glory of the nations (chs. 13 and 14) is nothing; if the scheming of the nations (chs. 14–18) is nothing; if the wisdom of the nations (chs. 19–20) is nothing; if the vision of the nation (chs. 21, 22) is nothing; if the wealth of the nations (ch. 23) is nothing, then the question is: why trust the nations? The answer is clear: There is no reason to do so.

2. GOD'S TRIUMPH OVER THE NATIONS (24:1–27:13)

a. THE STRONG CITY LAID WASTE (24:1–25:12)

(1) The earth is crushed (24:1–23)

1 *Behold, the Lord is about to empty the earth*
    and devastate it.[1]
He will mar its face
    and scatter its inhabitants.
2 *It shall be like people, like priest;*
    like servant, like his lord;
    like handmaid, like her lady;
    like buyer, like seller;

1. We are introduced here to the wordplays which are typical of this segment. *bqq*, "to empty," is followed by *blq*, "to devastate." Whether Driver is correct in arguing that both come from an original biconsonantal root *bq*, "to crack," is not clear (*JTS* 38 [1937] 41, 42).

like borrower, like lender;
like debtor, like the one who gives credit to him.
3 *The earth is surely emptied;*
it is surely spoiled.[2]
4 *The earth mourns and withers;*[3]
the world wastes away and withers;[4]
the highest of the people[5] *of earth waste away.*
5 *The earth is polluted beneath its inhabitants,*
for they have transgressed the law.
They have abandoned the statutes
and broken the eternal covenant.
6 *Therefore, a curse devours the earth*[6]
and its inhabitants are become guilty.[7]
Therefore, the inhabitants of the earth are burned[8]
and the remnant of humanity is small.
7 *The new wine mourns;*
the vine withers;
all the merry-hearted groan.[9]
8 *The mirth of the tambourines ceases;*
the roar of merry-makers dies away;
the mirth of the lyre[10] *ceases.*

2. "Spoil" may also have been chosen because of its assonance with "empty" *(bzz, bqq)*. The line is then *hibbôq tibbôq hāʾāreṣ hibbôz tibbôz*. Delitzsch comments that the Niphal imperfects are apparently vocalized with an *o* (instead of *a*) to increase the assonance further.

3. *ʾmll*, "wither, languish," means to lose fertility (1 Sam. 2:5; Jer. 15:9; Isa. 16:8; 24:7; Joel 1:12; cf. also 19:8; 33:9).

4. LXX lacks the first verb of the pair in the first two lines, giving ". . . wither . . . wither, . . . waste away." To Western ears, this seems superior. Whether it would have to Eastern ones is an open question.

5. *mᵉrôm ʿam*, "the highest of people," is an unusual phrase and two emendations have been proposed. One changes *ʿam* to *ʿim*, "with," reading "height (heavens) with earth" (RSV). But as Gray points out, there is no contextual warrant for reading "heavens" here. The other emendation would have *mᵉrômê hāʾāreṣ*, "high places of earth," which fits very well. (Cf. LXX "high ones.")

6. Note the repeated sounds: *ʿal-kēn ʾālâ ʾāḵlâ ʾereṣ*.

7. 1QIsᵃ has *yšmw*, probably from *šmm*, "to spoil." This reading is supported by Targ., but "guilty" seems to follow better on v. 5.

8. The imagery of curse is frequently a flame: 9:18 (Eng. 19); 10:16–19; 29:6; 30:27–28; 33:11–14. Cf. also Rev. 18:8–10, 16–19.

9. *ʾnḥ*, "to groan, sigh," was called a late word by BDB, but as Young noted, its Ugaritic cognate already appears in 1350 B.C. (2 Aqht I:18).

10. Cf. 30:32; Amos 6:5 for "tambourine" and "lyre."

9 *They do not drink wine with song;*
    the beer is bitter to those who drink it.
10 *The city of chaos[11] is broken down;*
    every house is closed to entry.
11 *There is an outcry over wine in the streets.*
    All joy is darkened;
    all earth's merriment banished.
12 *There remains for the city desolation;[12]*
    the gate is beaten[13] to ruins.
13 *Thus it shall be in the midst of the earth,*
    in the midst of the peoples:
as when an olive tree is beaten,
    as gleanings when the grape harvest is over.
14 *They lift up their voice, they cry aloud;*
    the majesty of the Lord they shout in the west.
15 *Therefore in the east glorify the Lord;*
    in the islands of the sea, the name of the Lord, the God of
    Israel.
16 *From the ends of the earth we hear[14] songs,*
    but I say, "Leanness[15] is mine, leanness is mine!
    Woe is me!
The treacherous commit treachery;
    with treachery the treacherous commit treachery!"
17 *Terror and pit and snare,*
    they are upon you, inhabitant of earth.

11. *tôhû,* "chaos," is a favorite word of Isaiah's, occurring 11 times in this book and only 9 in the rest of the OT. It is probably used to express the conviction that only God is the guarantor of order, not the idols. (Prevention of chaos is a major theme in mythic literature.)

12. As Young points out, the fact that the verb is masculine, while "desolation" is feminine, suggests that "desolation" is in fact an accusative of state (cf. GKC, § 118q).

13. As in Akkadian, when the final radical of a Hebrew verb should be doubled but cannot because of a vowelless ending, the preceding radical is doubled; thus *yukkaṭ* from *kāṭaṭ.*

14. The plural "we hear" seems to prepare the way for the coming "I say."

15. Targ. reads "mystery" instead of "leanness," and Gray asserts that MT intends "mystery," since "leanness" would be *rezî* or *rāzôn* (10:16), not *rāzî* as here. However, as Young shows, the connection with *lî* explains the vocalization here. Furthermore, "leanness" appears to be in contrast to *ṣebî,* "glory," in v. 16a. If "mystery" were correct it would convey the idea that the prophet is grieved because he knows the awful course of events through which the world and God's people must go before the end.

18 *It shall be that the one who flees the sound of terror*
    will fall into the pit,
  and the one comes up from the midst of the pit
    will be captured in the snare.
  For the windows of the height will be opened;
    and the foundations of the earth will shake.
19 *The earth will surely be broken;*
    earth will surely be broken;
      earth will surely be shaken to pieces.[16]
20 *The earth will wobble like a drunk,*
    sway like a hut.
  Its transgressions will be heavy upon it
    and it will fall, not to rise again.
21 *It shall be in that day that the Lord will punish*
    the host of the height in the height
    and the kings of the earth on the earth.
22 *They will be gathered together into a pit,*[17]
    and shut up in a dungeon.
        After many days they will be sentenced.
23 *The Silver One will be embarrassed,*
    and the Hot One ashamed;
  for the Lord of Hosts will reign on Mount Zion
    and in Jerusalem and before its elders in glory.[18]

Chapters 24–27 have often been called the Apocalypse of Isaiah, because their focus is upon the worldwide triumph of God. But there is now general agreement that the material is not truly apocalyptic, however that may be defined, but more correctly eschatological.[19] The interest is not in triumph outside time but within time. Nor is the imagery of the arcane, numerological sort usually associated with apocalyptic. Rather, the prophet is moving from the particular statements of chs. 13–23 to a broader, more generalized statement of God's lordship of the earth. There is an emerging

16. The LXX seems to move the point of the verse division and rework the final phrase of MT v. 19 as the opening of its v. 20, but the same ideas are present. Targ. changes the order of the words, or more likely, only uses generally similar vocabulary.

17. MT has ". . . together *prisoners* into a pit." However, none of the ancient versions (LXX, Targ., or 1QIs[a]) has "prisoners."

18. LXX makes *kāḇôḏ*, "glory," a verb: "he shall be glorified." However, it is also possible to take the noun as an adverbial accusative: "gloriously, in glory" (cf. NIV).

19. So, for instance, G. W. Anderson, "Isaiah XXIV-XXVII Reconsidered," *VTSup* 9 (1963) 123; G. Fohrer, "Der Aufbau der Apocalypse des Jesajabuches," *CBQ* 24 (1963) 34, 45. Cf. also Kissane, Scott.

consensus that these chapters cannot be understood independently but must be understood in context with chs. 13–23, as indeed those chapters must be understood in context with these.[20] This view is in contrast to an earlier position which tended to see chs. 24–27 as a self-contained entity which could be lifted out of the book without creating much dislocation of the ideas. But Delitzsch is certainly correct in his choice of the figure of a finale to describe the section. It sums up the great themes of the preceding segment and puts them in the most glorious settings. Like a finale, the chapters can be read by themselves, but their greatest contribution is made within the total piece.

EXCURSUS

There is a great variety of opinion on the date and authorship of these chapters, ranging all the way from Isaiah himself to Deutero-Isaiah to someone in the early second century.[21] Part of this divergency is due to the complete lack of datable historical allusions in the segment. Numerous attempts have been made to identify the overthrown city, reaching from Nineveh in 609 to Babylon at various times to Samaria in 107 B.C.,[22] but none of these has gained currency, and most contemporary writers agree that no specific city was intended but that the "city" symbolized the world. Ultimately, it is the theology, especially the references to resurrection (25:8; 26:19), that have caused many to opt for a date later than the seventh century.[23] However, the attempt to date materials on the basis of theology is extremely tenuous and often betrays a distinctly circular flavor.[24] Linguistic studies have likewise yielded very ambiguous results.

Recent studies have tended to follow form-critical and redaction-critical lines, emphasizing the stages in the development of the segments.[25] This approach, by its very method, denies the literary unity of the chapters, but it does provide for the thematic

20. See Young, Delitzsch, Wildberger, Clements, Vermeylen, etc.

21. On the first option, see Engnell, "Jesaja," quoted by H. Ringgren, "Style and Structure in the Isaiah Apocalypse," *ASTI* 9 (1973) 112. On the second, see Delitzsch, Anderson. On the third, see Kaiser.

22. See Duhm. This position was rendered untenable by the discovery of 1QIs[a] at Qumran and its date earlier than 107.

23. So Gray, Delitzsch, etc.

24. Note M. Dahood's evidence that resurrection may be more a part of OT thought than had previously been believed (*Psalms,* AB [New York: Doubleday, 1970], III: xli-lii). Cf. R. J. Coggins, "The Problem of Isa. 24–27," *ExpTim* 90 (1978–1979) 328–333, for a very incisive critique of the various "certainties" concerning the segment.

25. So Wildberger, Vermeylen, Kaiser, etc.

unity in that each succeeding stratum was shaped by the previous one. Parts of chs. 24 and 26 are generally placed in the first stratum, with the eschatological hymns coming in the second and/or third stratum, and most of ch. 24 coming in the final phase. However, this broad outline covers the extent of the agreement. The writers vary widely in their placement of certain paragraphs. Furthermore, there are still scholars like Ringgren and Lindblom who assert that the four chapters are a literary unity, the author having combined different forms into a cantata on God's triumph.[26]

Nor is the above diversity all. In the past ten years two students of F. M. Cross, Paul Hanson and William Millar, have argued that these chapters, as well as chs. 56–66, arose in Judah during the century following the return from exile and sprang from the conflict between those who wished to reestablish the conventional religion and those who had a more eschatological vision.[27] On the basis of complex sociological and linguistic grids, these scholars have reorganized the materials into their supposed original forms. In addition, Millar, whose primary interest was chs. 24–27, sought to see in them the recurrence of the four themes of the Canaanite cosmic warrior motif: threat-war-victory-peace. Unless one is prepared to grant a very large number of assumptions, Hanson's and Millar's case remains only interesting.[28]

In the light of the above, it cannot be said that there is anything but the broadest outline of a critical consensus on this segment. Even more significantly, none of the studies takes seriously the present form of the materials or makes anything but the most general attempt to see relations among the ideas as they now meet the reader. Yet it is precisely in its present form that this segment and the book as a whole have their power. This failure must stand as one of the modern critical movement's most serious defects. It is not necessary to say that Isaiah wrote every word of these chapters in precisely this order to explain their power and glory. But to suggest that the document may be best understood by first positing a group of unknown persons who made additions to a central idea from time to time, and by then trying to decide what each person contributed, is to do a disservice to all who wish to

26. J. Lindblom, *Die Jesaja Apokalypse, Jes 24–27* (Lund: Gleerup, 1938); Ringgren, *ASTI* 9 (1937) 107.

27. P. Hanson, *The Dawn of Apocalyptic* (Philadelphia: Fortress, 1975); W. Millar, *Isaiah 24–27 and the Origin of Apocalyptic,* HSM 11 (Missoula: Scholars, 1976). Cf. also O. Plöger, *Theocracy and Eschatology,* tr. S. Rudman (Richmond: John Knox, 1968).

28. See J. Oswalt, "Recent Studies in the OT Eschatology and Apocalyptic," *JETS* 24 (1981) 289–302, for a more detailed response.

understand the meaning and significance of the document as well as to the document itself.

As mentioned above, the overriding theme of the segment is the triumph of God, not only *over* his enemies but *for* his people. In chs. 13–23 the nations came to the attention first; here it is God. The prophet wants to make it plain that God is sovereign actor on the stage of history. It is not he who reacts to the nations, but the nations who respond to him. Thus Israel's hope is not in the nations of humanity. They will wither away in a moment under God's blast. Rather, her hope is in the Lord, who is the master of the nations. This theme is developed by means of a recurrence of contrast. There is the contrast between the City of Man and the City of God. The one is cast down, forsaken, destroyed. The other is a place of security, abundance, and life. There is also a contrast in song. In the city of chaos the drunken revelry which was once there is now silent. In its place there comes from the ends of the earth the song of Judah, a song about a God who is strong enough to save the helpless and compassionate enough to redeem the sinful.

Broadly speaking, one may divide the segment into two subsegments, chs. 24–25 and chs. 26–27. In the first subsegment, the major focus is upon the city of this world, its overthrow (ch. 24) and the response to its overthrow (ch. 25). The second subsegment centers upon God's efforts on behalf of his people. One of the major elements here is the admission of helplessness on the part of the people (26:7–18). Coupled with this is the conviction that God is able and willing to manifest his power among the nations and to deliver his people from them. In this way 27:12 and 13 climax chs. 13–27 and remind the reader of the promises of ch. 11, which the succeeding chapters serve to substantiate.

Chapter 24 functions as a transition between chs. 13–23 and 25–27. It does so by generalizing the particular treatments of chs. 13–23. Here all the nations of the world are gathered up into a single whole. No longer is it Babylon or Damascus or Tyre being confronted by God; now it is the earth itself (repeated 17 times) which stands before the bar of judgment. The chapter also functions transitionally by focusing attention on God, as chs. 25–27 do. He is the one who determines the fate of the nations by their relation to his law (24:1, 3, 5, 14, 21). The elements of the chapter seem to be: vv. 1–6, the desolation of earth; vv. 7–13, the end of revelry; vv. 14–16, joy over God, grief over earth; vv. 17–20, hopeless flight; vv. 21–23, the Lord's reign.

Verses 1–6 paint the central picture of worldwide destruction. The earth is under a curse because its people have broken God's laws. No one,

443

from the highest to the lowest, will escape the devastation; thus in the end only a remnant will remain. The language is similar to that often applied to Judah, so that some commentators, such as Kissane and Scott, hold that ʾereṣ here should be translated "the land" (of Judah) rather than "the earth." However, in addition to the parallel with tēḇēl, "world," in v. 4, the entirely universalistic tenor of the language argues for a reference to the whole earth. This being so, the application of the Judahistic terminology is an indication that the prophet sees God's treatment of, and expectations for, Judah and Israel as being the model for his treatment of the whole world (cf. Rom. 1–3).

1 *Behold, the Lord is about to* expresses the prophet's sense of immediacy through the use of *hinnēh* plus the participle (cf. 3:1; 17:1; 19:1; 30:27). Perhaps the now archaic "on the point of" captures some of the sense. Whether or not the events *will* happen in the next moment, they *could* happen. This kind of expectancy is difficult to maintain, yet it is an integral part of the biblical expectation. Only a God whose control of history is so complete that he could bring it all to a close in the next moment is worth worshiping (Mal. 3:1; Matt. 24:45–51; 2 Pet. 3:3–10). The teeming, scheming nations are not ultimate reality; God is. Thus he is the one on whom we should focus.

Although the inhabitants have sinned, the *earth* too will experience the results. In mighty convulsions similar to the Flood, the face of the earth will be devastated and changed, the population so reduced that the world will seem empty. It is not easy to know how literally these words will be fulfilled, but in these days of threatened ecological and nuclear catastrophe, it is not at all difficult to imagine a very literal fulfillment, and one which will indeed be the result of human greed and covetousness.

2 In this verse a lengthy series of comparisons is made, the point of which is to show that rank, wealth, and power are of no special significance in God's sight (1 Sam. 16:7). This point is directly in keeping with one of the central themes of the book: human pride and God cannot coexist. So the priest, the lord or lady, the wealthy person will fare no better in the world's last hour than will those who have nothing. The only issue will be righteousness in God's sight (Phil. 3:9).

Several commentators argue that the lack of reference to a king is evidence for a postexilic date. However, Hos. 4:9, which is frequently referred to as the inspiration for this verse, makes no mention of a king either and Hosea is surely preexilic (cf. Skinner and Cheyne).

3 The totality of the destruction envisioned is underlined through the use of infinitives absolute to emphasize the main verbs. Here, along with emptying out as in v. 1, there is plundering. This suggests again that the world's end will not be merely natural. Warfare, oppression, and greed will also bear their part. At the same time, it must be asserted that the writer is more concerned with images than with logic. He wants his hearers to picture the teeming, abundant earth as an abandoned heap when God finishes with it. Precisely how it becomes that way does not seem to be a major concern of his.

For the prophet, all of this is sure for one reason and one reason only—God has spoken. Although this is a frequent phrase in Isaiah, its importance cannot be overemphasized. He believed in a God who could communicate his truth and his will clearly. He not only believed he *could*, but that he *had*.[29] Thus the prophet could make completely dogmatic statements which rested on one support—God had spoken. Where the Church is anemic and helpless today, is it not because we no longer have the convictions of the prophets?

4–6 In these verses the prophet develops his images of desolation further, and in so doing explains more fully the causes of the desolation. Here the picture is of a drought where the earth is parched dry and the people are in mourning. It seems likely that the overtones of the fertility cult are in view here with its perpetual question, "How can we get rain?" As in Elijah's day, a nation or a world which attempts to manipulate its environment to supply its needs will only ensure that its needs will not be met (1 K. 17:1). One of the features of the fertility cult was mourning for the dead vegetation-god (1 K. 18:26, 28, 29; Ezek. 8:14; Zech. 12:11). It was thought that the failure of rain was an indication that Death had somehow conquered Life. But the biblical view will have none of a cosmic struggle between Life and Death. If there is a desolation in the earth, it is God's doing just as much as if there is abundance. The struggle is in the hearts of human beings and it is over the issue of pride or trust. The pride which says "I'll do it myself" receives drought from his hand. The trust which says "I'll commit myself to him" receives abundance.

4 Again, the language of the verse seems carefully structured with an abundance of labials, *aleph*s, and (fem.) *he*s. The repetition of *wither* and *waste away* also contributes to the assonance involved. One has only to study accounts of recent droughts to be reminded forcibly how very nonindependent we human beings are. This is true spiritually as well as physically. It is perhaps in this sense, and in line with v. 2, that the final phrase fits in. In that universal drought, even the high and the mighty of earth will be affected. No one's independence will be left untouched.

29. Cf. 1:2, 20; 16:13, 14; 21:17; 22:25; 25:8; 37:22; 39:8; 40:25; 46:11; 48:15, 16; 58:14.

5 *The earth is polluted* has a very modern ring to it. Sin has a way of making things unclean. This is not to say that bodily functions which produce environmental pollution are sinful. However, to refuse to clean up after oneself is. Such behavior assumes that convenience for oneself is all that matters, and that attitude is of the essence of sin. Those kinds of pollution are obvious to us, but there are other ways in which sin pollutes our environment. Hatred pollutes, as does dishonesty. Both of these, as surely as too many phosphates or too much sewage, create a setting in which human life cannot continue. This is so because there are spiritual laws which are just as ironclad as the physical ones. And like the physical laws, we do not break them, we only break ourselves upon them. Thus love, joy, patience, etc. (Gal. 5:22–23) are not desiderata, they are necessities if human life is to endure.

Isaiah is thus using law here just as Paul uses it in Rom. 1–3. It is not so much the revealed law of the Jews, although the principles are the same. Rather, it is the fundamental principles of human behavior that are as accessible, and as incumbent, as the elementary principles of physics. Whether or not persons recognize these principles, living in any other way than in accord with them must ultimately destroy us, as the history of numberless fallen civilizations ought to teach us. Thus while the *eternal covenant* may have specific reference to the Noachic covenant in Gen. 9:1–17 with its prohibition of bloodshed,[30] its broader reference is to the implicit covenant between Creator and creature, in which the Creator promises abundant life in return for the creature's living according to the norms laid down at Creation.

6 A part of the ancient Near Eastern covenants was the section on blessings and curses: blessings for keeping the covenant and curses for breaking it (cf. Deut. 27–28). So the writer here, having asserted that the inhabitants of earth have failed to keep the covenant, moves to a logical "therefore, a curse consumes the earth." This is not an arbitrary punishment on God's part any more than diphtheria or typhus is a punishment for polluting one's drinking water. It is a natural consesequence (Gen. 3:17). So is guilt, the internal response to failure. Guilt is in the world because the people of the world habitually break God's covenant. This is a part of the explanation for neurotic guilt. Though no specific personal failure can be pinpointed, yet we feel guilty. Why? It will not do to lay the blame on faulty parenting or poor environment. Where did *they* come

---

30. Cf. also Gen. 4:10; Num. 35:33; Deut. 21:1–9; Job 16:18; Ps. 106:38. But as Kissane points out, it is not merely bloodshed which defiles the earth, so also does worship of the creature; cf. Jer. 3:1, 2, 9; 16:18; Ezek. 36:17, 18.

from? And why does guilt persist in the face of a determined attack upon it as a negative emotion? Nothing can remove the overall sense of human failure except God himself (Ps. 34:23 [Eng. 22]; Isa. 4:2–4; 53:12; Zech. 3:9; 13:1; 2 Cor. 5:18–21). But if the people will not receive his pardon, either insisting they have no guilt or believing they can expiate it themselves, then there is no alternative but that they bear the consequences themselves. So the earth is parched dry like a desert and the people are reduced to a handful. Illustrations of this effect of sin on the world and its population are on every hand. The disastrous effects of the Thirty Years War crippled Europe for a century, and more recently, World War I took the lives of almost two-and-a-half million people. Our sin pollutes our environment to the point that it cannot maintain but begins to destroy life (13:11, 12).

7–13 These verses are unified by the recurring mention of wine and harvest (7, 8, 9, 11, 13). Traditionally, the grape harvest was a time of joy and hilarity. When the grapes were in, the last of the back-breaking work of summer was ended and there was time for a little merriment, helped along by the new wine, before the fall plowing and planting had to begin. However, if the harvest had been poor, then harvest time would be conspicuous for the absence of the usual hilarity (cf. Joel 1). Isaiah draws on that picture here. Probably the imagery of drought in vv. 4–6 underlies the thought. At least, v. 6 uses the same language as v. 4. Thus in place of a happy, abundant, self-sufficient world, the prophet shows us a world where merriment has ceased. So it must always be wherever joy is dependent upon alcohol and material blessings. The laughter always has a forced quality about it, for who knows how quickly it will end? By contrast, chs. 25–27 will speak of songs which do not need alcohol or record harvests to give them their lilt. Their joy springs from deeper dependency: trust in a God whose grace does not fail.

7 *new wine* was technically the unfermented juice from newly crushed grapes. It sometimes parallels "wine."[31] Here, however, it is paralleled with *vine* and this suggests that it may be referring to the grapes themselves. Thus the vines and grapes together have a sad and withered look about them. There will be no juice from these! Instead of ribald jokes and raucous laughter, there are only sighs and groans. The idiom "good of heart" to connote drunkenness (cf. Est. 1:10) suggests that *merry-hearted* here implies the same things.

8 This verse conveys the picture of a great modern city during what should be Mardi Gras, or Carnival, or Oktoberfest. But in place of

_____
31. See Mic. 6:15; cf. Hos. 4:11; see also in Ugaritic, 2 Aqht VI:7.

the teeming crowds and the music and the dancing, all is silent. Note the verbs: "Ceases . . . dies away . . . ceases." When the judgments of God come upon the earth all our contrived festivals melt away. Those who have depended upon their own sources of joy will have none. (Cf. 13:20–22; 22:1–4; 32:12–14.)

9 What drinking there is is without any gladness. Its only purpose is forgetfulness, and the experience is a bitter one. So it must always be when a thing is no longer for itself but for the effect it brings.

10–12 The focus now shifts from the drinking to the city in which the partying had taken place. Instead of a brightly lighted, rollicking metropolis, there are only silent ruins. In place of the rivers of wine, there is thirst. Earth City is desolate. One need only think of the vast deserted cities of Angkor Wat in Cambodia or Machu Picchu in Peru for visual images of what the prophet is portraying on a worldwide scale. He does not indicate the immediate cause of the desolation. Perhaps the first thought would be of a military activity. No mention of that is made, however, and such other causes as plague or famine are equally possible.[32] In any case, it is important to recognize that the writer is not so much working out a logical statement as he is creating an impression—an impression of a gray, mirthless, depopulated, and ruined world.[33] Attempts to reorganize or criticize elements of the picture on other grounds can only do disservice to it and nullify its impact.

10 *The city of chaos* may describe conditions before or after divine judgment. On the one hand, it may express the idea that the city of Man[34] had always been a place of disorder and confusion, a place of revolt against

32. Gesenius, believing v. 10 to describe results of a military conquest, took v. 11 to be intrusive (from Joel 1), because inhabitants of a conquered city would have greater things to worry about than absence of wine. Kissane also places v. 11 after v. 9. He does not explain how, if that was the original order, v. 11 got into its present place. Kaiser sees depopulation through drought as the cause.

33. Cf. the world of Charn in C. S. Lewis, *The Magician's Nephew* (New York: Macmillan, 1955).

34. As mentioned above, this study concludes that no specific city is intended. The welter of identifications put forward seems to support this view. W. Millar (*Origin*, pp. 20–117) and P. Hanson (*Dawn*, p. 314) have most recently argued in support of Jerusalem, but this argument is dependent upon the theory that a group of dissident visionaries during the postexilic period saw Jerusalem as defiled by the "hierocratic" party in control (derived from Plöger, *Theocracy*, pp. 111–12). However, the present form of the text argues conclusively that this city represents the world (ch. 24 is the finale to chs. 13–23) and is not merely a product of Jewish infighting (as Plöger notes, p. 56).

divine order (v. 5; Gen. 1:2).[35] Certainly a city in festival presents such a picture. Now it is quiet desolation. On the other hand, it is also possible that the city has become chaotic in destruction; it has been reduced to chaos, a jumble of ruins incapable of supporting life (34:11; cf. also Deut. 32:10; Ps. 107:40). But perhaps both ideas were intended. As Delitzsch says, "As destruction of the harmony of the divine order was its essence, destruction of its existence and precipitation back into the chaos of the primeval beginnings will be its end."

every house is closed may be interpreted in two ways, both of which fit the context. It may be that rubble from the nearly abandoned city blocks access to most of the houses, or it may be that the few remaining inhabitants, without an army or defenses, have shut themselves in. In either case, the picture is clear. Instead of a gay city, alive with banners, its streets full of laughing crowds going from house to house for free drinks, all is empty and tumbled down, doors tightly locked.

11 An outcry for wine is not out of place in this context. It refers to the now disappeared alcoholic gaiety.[36] Where there was an abundance of wine, there is now none and those who have developed a dependency are in desperate trouble.

All joy is darkened fits the picture very well in its evocation of the shift from bright, flashing color to dull grayness. Both the LXX and the Targum, however, seem to point to the root ʿbr, "pass away," as being the original instead of "to be dark," ʿrb.

12 All that remains of the city is desolation. Even the gates through which the crowds once thronged are fallen into rubble.

13 *Thus it shall be* signals a concluding statement to this part of the poem. Up until this point prophetic perfects have been in use, indicating the finality of the judgment to come. Now the imperfects appear to mark the fact that these events still lie in the future. In that day, the fate earlier predicted for Israel (17:6) will befall all the peoples. The world will look like an olive orchard or a vineyard after the harvest. As only a few stray clusters or a handful of small olives remain, so it will be for the world. Out of all its fullness, only bits and pieces remain. This is the destiny of a people or a world which will refuse to acknowledge that the earth is full of God's glory, not ours.

14–16 This enigmatic passage has elicited reams of comment but

---

35. The use of "chaos" to describe idols would seem to support this interpretation. There is the city of God and the city of chaos (cf. 1 Sam. 12:21; Isa. 41:29).

36. Kaiser says that the outcry will be provoked by memory of former times.

very little certainty. That this uncertainty extends very far back in the past is evidenced by the diversity of the LXX and Targum from the MT and from each other. It seems clear that the readings of these later versions are the results of attempts to explain what they saw as a somewhat incomprehensible text. While their confusion is comforting in that we know we are not alone, it is not very helpful. Here we can only make general suggestions as to the way the verses may function in this context and leave detailed questions until later.

Possibly vv. 14–16a are the response of the oppressed to the news of the destruction of the "city of chaos," the world power (cf. 14:4b–8). The worldwide nature of this singing seems to support this hypothesis. These persons recognize that the Lord is responsible for their deliverance and give him the glory due his name (cf. 9:1–4 [Eng. 2–5]; 12:4–6). But the prophet cannot join in the gladness yet. His vision is still filled with the sight of the world's evil which must come to a violent end. If this is the correct understanding, then his response is similar to that in ch. 1 where he refused to join in what was there a false merriment. Here it is genuine worship, and while he knows it is coming, he also knows that wave upon wave of human treachery must precede that day (cf. also 15:5; 16:9, 11; 22:4, and the comment at those places). If this understanding is correct, then the segment appears here as a momentary break in the clouds. As the drunken music of the world-city fades away, the reader is given a momentary glimpse of another kind of singing, which began before the world's birth and will continue forever when the world is but a memory.

14 *They lift up their voice* raises the question of the identity of the subjects, especially since *they* is emphasized in Hebrew. Those who take v. 13 as a part of this segment (e.g., Young and Scott) tend to take the subjects as the remnant mentioned in that verse.[37] But it is equally probable that no definite subjects are intended, the fact of the singing being more important than the identity of the singers. In any case, the emphasis on "they" seems to be in contrast to the "I" of v. 16.

the majesty of the Lord. The word used is gā'ôn, which the prophet roundly condemns in humanity (13:11, 19; 14:11; 16:6; 23:9; 28:1, 3). The reason he condemns it is because of its inappropriateness. Only God is truly exalted, and until the nations of the world recognize that, they are condemned to humiliate themselves before his majesty (2:10, 19, 21). But when they do recognize the truth through his judgments, he intends to share his majesty with them (60:15).

37. Gray, Skinner, Kaiser, Wildberger, etc., take the singers to be Jews. Kissane, Young, and Clements look for a larger representation.

in the west (lit. "from the [Mediterranean] sea") may indicate Israel, the homeland of the Jews, and that the singers invite the rest of the
world to join them. But more likely it is the opening line of a statement
of the universality of the song.[38] It extends from west to east and to the
islands of the sea (42:4, 10; 51:5; 59:18, 19; Ps. 96:1–13; 97:1, 6; 98:2–4).

15 *in the east* (lit. "in the lights") has been taken to mean "lands
of light" and thus the east, but it is a unique usage and thus open to
question.[39] If the interpretation is correct, the peoples of one end of the
world are being called on to join those of the other until the song resounds
to the very limits, the islands. The content of the song will be the glory
of the character *(name)* of Israel's God. It is not his label or his title which
is so marvelous, but who he is as Creator, Judge, Redeemer, and Lord.
As such he is worth praising forever (Rev. 4:8–5:13).

16 The description of the geographic extent of the celebration
reaches its climax in the phrase *the ends* (the wing) *of the earth*. Elsewhere
the term is plural (11:12; Ezek. 7:2; Job 37:3) when used in this way, but
the sense is the same: the outer edge, the hem of the world (cf. Phil.
2:9–11).

The Righteous One is taken here to refer to God on the basis of the
context; in the two previous verses it is the Lord's glory being hymned.
At the same time, Delitzsch's arguments that it must be Israel cannot be
dismissed lightly. These arguments are that *ṣebî*, "glory, beauty," is elsewhere God's gift to his people (4:2; 28:5), not an attribute of his, and that
while the people are called "the righteous" (3:10), God is not without
some additional qualifier. However, while it would certainly be consistent
for the nations to sing of what God had done for his people (60:2, 3; 62:2),
both of these are arguments from silence, and apart from other evidence,
should not outweigh the context.[40]

But I say, "Leanness is mine. . . ." This translation accepts that
there is a contrast intended between what *they* say in vv. 14–16a and what
the prophet says in v. 16b. Gray is correct in saying that we should normally expect *wa'ānî*, "but I," to precede the verb in such an antithesis,
but it is hardly possible to make an ironclad rule on the subject.[41] Unless

---

38. Gray thinks that the Diaspora from West and East are singing and that
the prophet, a Palestinian, is more cautious.

39. Cheyne suggests emendation to *bā'îyîm*, "island" (cf. *BHS*), and then
sees an ascending rhythm with the following line. LXX omits the phrase completely
and Targ. paraphrases "when light comes to the righteous."

40. So also RSV, NIV, Clements.

41. Cf. 1 K. 3:11, *weša'altā*, "but you asked." It may be that the contrast
in subject is not as important to the writer as the contrast in contents.

451

some contrast is intended, the presence of *hēmmâ,* "they," in v. 14 is inexplicable. Furthermore, if *rāzî* does mean "leanness" here, there seems to be a contrast with *ṣᵉbî,* "abundance," in the previous line.

In response to the songs of praise which he saw occurring in the future, the prophet says,[42] "But what of events until then?" This experience is similar to that of Daniel in his alarm over the portent of his visions (Dan. 7:28; 8:27), for he saw not merely the ultimate victory, but all that would lead up to it. So instead of glory and abundance he experiences leanness and woe.

The treacherous. Utilizing the Hebrew language's propensity for cognate accusatives through its root structure, the prophet drives home the ugliness of what he sees. The five words after "Woe is me" all come from the same root, *bgd,* which contains the idea of plunder through deceit. The plosive quality of the consonants lends a hammering sound which reinforces the idea of the statement. Before the gavel falls for the last time, how much treachery, how much brutal plunder must take place? In this sense, as in so many others, the Jewish people have represented the rest of us. How often they were to be plundered: by Greeks, Romans, Byzantines, Arabs, Spaniards, Russians, Germans. Nor have they suffered alone. They have indeed represented millions of others. Glimpsing a bit of that, who would not cry, "Woe is me"?[43]

17–23 In this final segment of the poem, the writer reverts to a description of the judgment which will come upon the earth before the Lord's glory hinted in vv. 14 and 15 will be fully seen. The segment divides naturally into two parts: vv. 17–20 and 21–23. In the first part all the emphasis is upon the cataclysms to be suffered on the earth. The diversity of images suggests again that the prophet is not so much interested in a logical and literal picture as he is in creating an impression of a stable, predictable world gone completely awry, to the horror of those whose only stability is in this world. The second part expands the picture to the whole cosmos. The earth's problem is rebellion (v. 20), and so the Lord against whom the rebellion is directed comes to judge. His action is directed against the mightiest of all creation with the result that they are cast into the depths (2:12–17; 5:14–16; 14:4b–21). In the end only God will reign. Again, one may wonder how literally the prophet intended to be taken, or was he using poetic language to make a theological point? If the latter is

---

42. Note the perfect verb, which takes one out of the vision back to the past narrative. Isaiah tells us what his response was when he first saw the vision. (Cf. Rev. 1:10; 4:1; 5:4; etc.)

43. Young aptly cites Rom. 9:2, 3 as an example of such empathy.

so, as I suspect it is, some of the lengthy technical discussions of the meaning of the "host of heaven" (see below on v. 22) may be beside the point. The issue is that no great nation or people is ultimate in creation. Only God is. This is the message of chs. 13–23, and it is all brought to a fine point in these three verses.

Virtually all commentators believe that vv. 21–23 were not written by the author of vv. 17–20 (Duhm believed they were originally with 25:6–8). However, there is now a growing awareness that they form a very apt conclusion to the previous verses. Millar comments that v. 20 makes a very lame conclusion while Kaiser believes that vv. 21–23 never had an independent existence, but were written as a conclusion by a redactor.[44]

17–18b Again, with pounding assonance,[45] Isaiah drives home the fate of those whose trust is in the earth. There is no reliability in earth, or at least in earth's inhabitants; only treachery (v. 16). As a result, it is terror which awaits such persons, the terror of knowing that life is a series of traps from which there is no final escape. This is a frequent theme in Scripture.[46] It is so because the writers are agreed that only commitment to a living, almighty, purposeful, transcendent God can make any sense out of life. Any other commitment is to falsehood and, as such, must lead to dead ends. What can be more terrible than breathing a sigh of relief that one has escaped one pitfall, and at that moment discovering one is in a worse situation? Yet, that awaits all who will not flee to the only refuge— God (Ps. 56:9–12 [Eng. 8–11]; 91:1–6; Isa. 33:18; 54:14).

18c–20 Here in a series of images the strong, dependable earth is shown weighed down, broken apart, tottering, and finally collapsed. The earth will not be able to endure the totality of the treachery perpetrated upon its surface—treachery toward one another and treachery toward God (24:5, 6).

The opening image is drawn from Gen. 7:11, where the windows of heaven opened to release a terrific weight of water upon the earth to wash it clean of its transgression. Here, the use of "height" *(mārôm)*[47] for heaven suggests that the poet's primary purpose is not to predict another flood, but in conjunction with "foundation" (underneath), to talk about destruction of normalcy both above and below, that is, on every side. Again, over-literalness is not warranted, as though the weight of water somehow shook the foundations.

44. The opening line of v. 17 is *pahad wāpahat wāpāh.*
45. Millar, *Origin*, p. 35 n. 2. Cf. Wildberger, Clements.
46. 2 Sam. 22:6; par. Ps. 18:6 (Eng. 5); Pss. 64:6 (Eng. 5); 106:36; 124:6, 7; Jer. 48:43, 44; Lam. 3:47; Amos 5:19; Job 18:5–11; 22:10.
47. See also 32:15; 33:5; 57:15; 58:4.

19 Once again the impact of language is used to its fullest. In three couplets of three words each, repetition of sound, word, and idea is used to make the thought triply emphatic.[48] This world is not the place where ultimate trust should be reposed. The writer of the book of Revelation makes a similar point using similar imagery in 6:12–15, etc.

20 Two more images of insecurity are used here: the drunkard (29:9; Ps. 107:27) and the hut (1:8). Like the drunkard staggering from lamppost to lamppost, or the temporary lean-to of twigs and leaves being whipped by a high wind, the earth's end is clear: collapse. Whatever one may believe about the earth's origins, no one believes that this planet has an infinite duration. It is running down sooner or later, much sooner if humanity handles the nuclear weapon in the same way it has handled every other weapon it has developed. Thus, the question for every human being is whether there is something or Someone infinite to whom we can leap when this branch upon which we are resting falls, as it must one day. Who would lean on a drunk, or trust a lean-to for protection from a winter gale?

21 *in that day* is used once again to express the prophet's conviction that all history will come to a point—a point where the just will be rewarded and the wicked punished.[49] He does not expect merely a turning of the wheel until all comes right again.[50] In fact, it is questionable whether the Hebrew understanding of promise-fulfillment even permitted the believer to entertain the idea of return to the old.[51] Instead, he looks to a time yet to be when all the divergent lines of experience will be gathered up in one hand—the Lord's. In that day he will come as the commander to inspect his troops and make all things right.[52] Those who had raised themselves up against him in foolish rebellion will be brought down in ignominy.

the host of the height is an expression used both for the stars (Jer. 33:22; Neh. 9:6) and for the pagan pantheon, since the gods were frequently identified with the stars (e.g., 2 Chr. 33:5). In late OT and intertestamental times the pantheon, as the hosts of heaven, was integrated into Hebrew thought as being rebellious angels who came to constitute the

---

48. Lit. "broken is broken the earth, split is split the earth, shaken is shaken the earth."

49. Cf. 4:2; 11:10; 17:7; 19:23; 25:9; 26:1; etc.

50. Contra M. Eliade, *Myth and Reality* (New York: Harper & Row, 1963), pp. 64–66.

51. Cf. von Rad, *Old Testament Theology*, II:108–109. Cf. also Isa. 48:6–8.

52. Thus *pāqaḏ* may mean "visit, appoint, reprove, strengthen," because it refers to the coming of the commanding officer.

spiritual powers at war with God and with his people.[53] It was also understood that certain angels were designated as patrons of nations.[54] Whether
the writer had any or all of these in mind is not clear. The use of *height*
for heavens suggests that this terminology is primarily used to convey
God's implacable enmity against all which raises itself against him, whether
a star in heaven or a king on earth (cf. 34:4, 5). While a more involved
symbolic structure of the sort mentioned above is certainly possible, nothing in the context demands it, and much in the context suggests that the
imagery was chosen primarily for its impact.[55]

22 All who have exalted themselves against God can expect to
be brought down, just as all who refuse to act according to natural law
can expect to bear the consequences. The chosen course has certain natural
results. So these great ones of creation go to the pit and the dungeon
(14:17). This picture, like that of the host of heaven, was developed in
much more detail in later times (2 Pet. 2:4; Rev. 9:2, 11; 11:7; 17:8). The
final phrase seems to suggest a temporary imprisonment until final judgment can be rendered.[56] Perhaps the picture is of a rebellion being put
down, with rebels being thrown into prison as the conflict proceeds, to be
held there until the king is finally in control and has the time to make a
reasoned judgment.[57]

23 When the Lord's full glory is seen, the brightest things the
world knows—the sun and the moon—will hang their heads in shame
(60:19; Joel 3:15; Zech. 14:7; Rev. 21:23; 22:5). The picturesque qualities
of the statement are enhanced by the personalized terms *the Silver One* for
the moon and *the Hot One* for the sun. That the sun and the moon were
important deities in the ancient Near East would add to the evocative
power of the terms as well. Nothing can stand beside God in his regal
splendor, no natural object and no combination of human concepts loaded
onto that object. God alone is king. The recurrence of emphasis upon
God's kingship (30:33; 32:1; 33:17, 22; 41:21; 43:15; 44:6; 52:7) should
come as no surprise in the writings of one whose initiation as a prophet

53. So 1 Enoch 6–10; Matt. 24:29; Rom. 8:38; Eph. 3:10; Col. 1:13, 16;
Rev. 12:4, 9. Interestingly enough, the Targ. has "the mighty host which dwells
in the stronghold," apparently avoiding any reference to a heavenly host.

54. See Deut. 32:8; Dan. 10:13.

55. Both Gray and Kaiser offer full discussions of the symbolic possibilities.

56. Kissane refers to the *Enuma Elish*, where the monsters are imprisoned
before execution, but the similarity is only of the most general sort.

57. This may be part of the development which gave rise to Jude 6 and
the sequence in Rev. 19:20–20:15.

THE BOOK OF ISAIAH

involved a visionary recognition of the absolute sovereignty and majesty of the Almighty (6:5).

In the last day the elders of Judah and Jerusalem will no longer be the objects of God's wrath (1:23; 3:14; 9:14 [Eng. 15]). Now they take part in his coronation (cf. also Mal. 3:3, 4). Finally, the ancient dream will have come true: God alone will be Israel's King. The picture in Revelation complements this one nicely (Rev. 4:4, 9–11). The elders worship God, casting down the crowns he had bestowed, giving him the glory.[58] In this context, it is not surprising that the figure of the Messiah does not appear, for the Messiah's kingship is God's and vice versa. In the consummation of all things God *is* the Messiah.[59] This is again spelled out in Rev. 4 and 5. The King and the Lamb are one. This is all the true glory of God: the Creator is Redeemer and his kingship is made possible by his condescension, without which there would be no kingdom to rule. The Christian knows that Isa. 24:24 is not possible without Isa. 53.

(2) God's feast (25:1–12)

1 *O Lord, you are my God,*
 I will exalt you;
  I will praise your name,
 for you have done wonderful things,[1]
  things planned long ago,[2] *in perfect faithfulness.*
2 *For you have made the city into a heap,*[3]

---

58. Note the correspondence to the manifestation of God to the elders on Mount Sinai (Exod. 24:9, 11). That experience was an earnest of the one being described here and in the Revelation.

59. It is not, as Gray argues, that God's kingship supersedes the Messiah's. God's kingship includes the Messiah's.

1. Modern versification tends to take *pele'*, "wonder(s)," as an adjective of *ʿēṣôt*, "plans." Cf. *BHS*. However, the MT puts "things planned long ago" in apposition to "wonderful things," as here.

2. For *mᵉrāḥōq*, "from afar," as a time reference, see 2 Sam. 7:9; 2 K. 19:25 (par. Isa. 37:26).

3. In the first line of the verse, MT reads lit. "for you have made *from* a town to a heap." This reading is not impossible but it is very strange and it is not supported by the versions. Suggestions for emendation have been multiplied but none has carried the day. The two most widely adhered to are: (1) that *mēʿîr* is a mistake for *hāʿîr*, "the city," in the light of the *mēʿîr* at the end of the verse; (2) that originally the *m* was at the end of the word as a plural: *ʿārîm* (cf. LXX, *BHS*, NEB). But both of these are difficult. It is simpler to take the *m* as an enclitic which was originally attached to the preceding verb, as is now known from Ugaritic (so H. D. Hummel, "Enclitic mem in Early Northwest Semitic, Especially Hebrew," *JBL* 76 [1954] 164). For a full review of the alternatives, see J. A. Emerton, "A Textual Problem in Isaiah 25:2," *ZAW* 89 (1977). He proposes (pp. 72–73) to read *mēʿîr* in "the citadel of strangers *from a city*" as a Hophal of *ʿrr*, "to destroy,"

the fortified town into a ruin,
the citadel of strangers⁴ from being a city.
It will not be built forever.
3 *Therefore a strong people will glorify you;*
a town⁵ of ruthless nations will fear you.
4 *For you are a stronghold to the poor,*
a stronghold for the needy in distress,
a refuge from the flood,
a shade from parching heat.
Though the breath of the ruthless
is like a flood against a wall,⁶
5 *like parching heat in the desert,*
you allay the roar of strangers.
As parching heat in the shadow of a cloud,
the song of the ruthless is put down.
6 *The Lord of Hosts will prepare on this mountain*
a feast of fatness⁷ for all peoples,
a feast of lees,
fatness full of marrow,⁸
rich wine well refined.
7 *And he will swallow up on this mountain*
the face of the covering,⁹

---

mūʿar. The meaning would be "the citadel of strangers is destroyed" (cf. 23:13 and Kissane).

Note that the present translation assumes that the verb *śîm,* "put, place, make," in this line governs the next two lines as well: "you have made the city . . . the fortified town . . . the citadel. . . ."

4. For MT *zārîm,* "strangers," LXX has *asebós,* "wicked, ungodly." This variant has prompted the plausible suggestion that the original was *zēḏîm,* "presumptuous" *(BHS).* Since Hebrew *r* and *d* are easily confused, it is possible to see how the variant could have arisen. However, the term "stranger" is used for oppression in Isaiah (1:7; 29:5), so dogmatism in either direction seems unwise.

5. "Town" seems a bit strange here and Clements suggests its omission. However, the versions include it. Perhaps its function is to connect with v. 2 and ch. 24.

6. Lit. "like a flood of a wall," a strange expression. Most modern commentators choose to emend *qîr,* "wall," to *qôr,* "winter" (cf. Gen. 8:22). This makes excellent sense and may be correct. However, Targ. supports MT (LXX completely alters the verse) and the MT can yield sense, esp. in the light of Matt. 7:24–27. Cf. Isa. 28:17.

7. "Fatness" is in the plural, indicating its superlative nature; GKC, § 124e.

8. The form of "marrow," *mᵉmuḥāyîm,* is uncommon. Delitzsch believes it was selected for its more musical quality in this context of feasting and rejoicing.

9. Lit. "the face of the shroud," an enigmatic phrase. It apparently refers to the outer surface or appearance of the shroud as the onlooker sees it. Skinner calls this a genitive of apposition.

Another problem is the MT's repetition, *hallôṭ hallôṭ,* "the covering, the

> the covering upon all the peoples,
>> the web woven over all the nations.[10]
>
> 8 He will swallow up Death forever;
>> the Sovereign Lord will wipe away tears from all faces.
> The reproach of his people
>> he will take away from upon the earth.
> For the Lord has spoken.
>
> 9 And it will be said[11] in that day,
>> "Behold, this is our God;
> we waited for him and he delivered us.
>> This is the Lord;
> we waited for him.[12]
>> Let us sing and rejoice in his salvation."
>
> 10 For the hand of the Lord will rest on this mountain.
>> And Moab will be trodden down in his place[13]
>> as straw is trodden down in the water of a dunghill.[14]
>
> 11 He[15] will spread out his hands in its midst
>> as the swimmer spreads his hands to swim.
> He will bring down his pride
>> in spite of the struggles of his hands.
>
> 12 The fortifications, the secure heights of your walls,

---

covering." As early as Kimchi the suggestion was made that the second be read as a passive participle, *hallûṭ*, thus "the covering which covers." The versions neither support nor deny this suggestion. The MT rendering may be for emphasis.

10. It is apparent that LXX does not understand v. 7 and has supplied an alternate. Targ. is paraphrasing MT but so as to bring it in line with the Targ. revision of v. 6.

11. *weʾāmar* (lit. "and he said"). The versions do not agree. 1QIs^a: "*you* will say." LXX: "*they* will say." Targ.: "*one* will say." Probably the Targ. is closest, with the indefinite 3rd person standing for the passive "it will be said."

12. LXX omits "This is the Lord: we waited for him," but this seems to be a classic case of haplography through homoioteleuton.

13. "in his place," *taḥtô*, may be translated "under him," but the identity of "him" is not clear. While it might refer to God, it could also refer to Moab. For this latter meaning see 46:7; 1 Sam. 14:9; 2 Sam. 2:23; 7:10; Hab. 3:16.

14. "dunghill," *madmēnâ*, may well be used as a derisive wordplay upon the name of the Moabite town Madmen (Jer. 48:2). It also rhymes with *maṭbēn*, "straw." The Ketib has *beme*, "in the waters of," while the Qere has merely "in," *bemô*. While some writers argue that the dung*hill* cannot logically hold water (the kind of argument which may have given rise to the Qere in the first place), if "dunghill" refers to the "barnyard," as is probable, then a barnyard does definitely hold water into which straw does get trodden down (so Skinner, Mauchline, Delitzsch, and Young).

15. Kissane supplies "the destroyer," *ûpēraś šōḏēḏ yāḏāyw*, at the beginning of v. 11 (cf. 33:1) and thinks that the verse refers to Assyria. However, he is alone in this novel interpretation.

he will bring down, he will lay low.[16]
He will level [them] to the ground,
   even to the dust.

Chapter 25 forms the response to the announcement of the destruction of Earth-City. As such, it is in three parts. The first, vv. 1–5, is a song of thanksgiving for God's faithfulness in caring for and delivering his people. It is as though this song is presented as part of the festivities mentioned in 24:23 (see above) and resumed in the second part of this chapter, vv. 6–8. In this second part, the announcement of the feast is accompanied by the triumphant word, as in v. 1, that God's purpose in the destruction of the earth is the redemption of the earth from the pall of death which has always hung over it. Verses 9–12 return to the theme of joy among God's people because he has delivered them from their enemies, here typified in Moab.

1–5 Like ch. 12, which follows the similar announcements of destruction of enemies in chs. 10 and 11, this song breathes with an intensely personal air. God's goodness has been vindicated as well as his power, and the writer is expressing for himself and for his people the feelings of attachment for God that this recognition has created. Young rightly expresses caution concerning the vantage point of the prophet. Older commentaries perhaps too easily put him in the future looking back. But when Kaiser dismisses that as "a fiction" and says that the prophet is speaking prophetically, one wonders if there is any practical difference in the resulting interpretation. In any case, the writer believes that God's mighty acts of judgment and deliverance will result in an outpouring of praise on the part of God's people and a humble recognition of his power on the part of those who had so fiercely exulted over God's people.[17] As many writers have observed, the singer here was a person steeped in the Scriptures. Numerous similarities to the Psalms and Prophets can be shown, yet they do not seem to be mechanical citations. They are the writer's own, but his categories are thoroughly biblical.

Both Duhm and Cheyne believed that the songs in chs. 24–27 were intrusive literary pieces which were drawn from other settings and inserted

16. The multiplication of verbs expressing the idea of bringing down seems excessive. Thus *BHS* may be correct in advising the deletion of *hišpîl*, "he will lay low" (the LXX actually omits both the last two verbs). However, the author may have been wishing to make emphatically clear the destructions of the defenses in which human beings so easily trust. Note also 26:5, where the same verbs appear in the same sequence.

17. Note esp. the causal statements in vv. 1, 2, 3, 4, 5: *kî, kî, 'al-kēn, kî, kî.*

459

into this one. Recent study, following the lead of Rudolph, Lindblom, and Fohrer, has increasingly abandoned that view. While not returning to the position that all four chapters were written by the same person and in this order, there has been the growing conviction that the hymns were specifically composed with the surrounding setting in mind (so, e.g., Clements, Kaiser, Wildberger). The present hymn is a case in point. The congruencies with ch. 24 are too direct for the piece to have been merely inserted. Some of these are the reference to the city and to the song, both of which are prominent in ch. 24. If this is a step in the right direction, and I believe it is, then we must ask the question which the critics too frequently omit: What is the function of the piece here between 24:23 and 25:6–8? Surely it is to say again that the response to God's acts is as much a part of the process of redemption as are the acts themselves. He may display his power and have himself crowned king as often as he wishes, but that is *not* what he wants. The appropriate effect for those causes is people responding to him in love and joy. That is what he wants and that must be why this song is precisely here.

1 *You are my God.* This intensely personal affirmation sets the tone for the whole song. In place of the raucous drinking songs whose purpose was forgetfulness and the loosening of inhibitions with the result that the worst side of humanity was revealed, this is a song of heightened awareness and true freedom in commitment.[18] The singer says, "I *want* a being like you for my God. I want to belong to one as powerful and faithful as you." But he also says, "You have shown me that you do truly belong to me, because you have not abandoned me to the oppressor, you have kept faith with me when I was so afraid you had forgotten me. You *are* my God." The personal note here is a helpful reminder that although God did deal with his people as a group, every individual in that group counted because God related to the group as to an individual. Thus instead of the person being lost in the group, the group became a person and the importance of persons was safeguarded.

for you have done wonderful things. The biblical faith is rooted in the concept of a God who is not captive to the normal. He is able to do the remarkable things, and does, in order to save his people.[19] Modern religion has stripped God of his miraculous powers and, using process parlance, has deified the physico-psycho-social system while continuing to call itself Christianity, and thus has drifted far from its biblical roots.

---

18. Cf. Ps. 30:3 (Eng. 2); 31:15 (Eng. 14); 40:6 (Eng. 5); 118:28; 145:1.
19. See Exod. 15:11; Ps. 40:6 (Eng. 5); 77:12, 15 (Eng. 11, 14); 78:12; 88:11, 13 (Eng. 10, 12); 89:6 (Eng. 5).

That kind of god neither excites nor deserves the kind of ecstatic praise recorded here. Wonders are not part of its makeup.

things planned long ago expresses a thought which is especially Isaianic. God's wonders, his amazing acts, are not "off-the-cuff." They are part of the divine purpose in the universe. The idols have no plans, which is to be expected since the wind and rain from which the idols come have none. People make plans feverishly, but all too often they come to nothing. But Isaiah knows a God who, at the right moment, does something which from one point of view is utterly new, but from another is consistent with plans formed before the universe began. This is the only being into whose hands it makes sense to entrust oneself from Isaiah's point of view. No other plan is worth anything.[20]

2 This verse explains what God's plans were that have now been executed. They were to humble all the works of human pride and oppression, here typified as the walled *city* and the *fortified town*. The usage here is the same as in ch. 24, in that no specific city is intended. This city is all those arrogant bastions of power that have crushed the righteous through all of time. But the prophet says that their power will not avail them in the end (9:3, 4 [Eng. 4, 5]). God will triumph, and it has been planned so from the beginning.

3 What will be the result of God's judgment? The *therefore* opening this verse makes it plain that the result is specified here. As elsewhere (17:7–9; 19:19, 20; 23:18), the prophet makes it plain that recognition of God will be the effect.[21] Why should destruction be necessary to cause such honor? Perhaps it is because we human beings do not recognize anything but power. Then, too, until all is lost we tend not to focus upon anything but ourselves. When the situation is hopeless, then we are likely to look to God and recognize him as the only remaining help.

4, 5 These verses continue the causal connection by expanding upon the reason for honoring God. He is to be honored not merely because he destroys the citadels of the proud, but also because he does so for the sake of the oppressed.[22] In so doing, he becomes a refuge for them. All of this indicates that God's reason for attacking pride is not merely that it is false in view of his own incomparability (40:6–26), but also because

20. See also 1:26; 3:3; 5:9; 7:5; 8:10; 9:5 (Eng. 6); 11:2; 14:24, 26, 27; 16:3; 19:3, 11, 12, 17; 23:8, 9; 28:29; 29:15; 30:11; 32:7, 8; 36:5; 40:13; 41:28; 44:26; 45:21; 46:10, 11; 47:13.

21. Cf. also Ps. 31:9 (Eng. 8); 40:4 (Eng. 3); 47:8, 9 (Eng. 7, 8); 67:5, 6, 8 (Eng. 4, 5, 7); 86:9; 96:7–10.

22. Probably the "poor" and the "needy" are seen as esp. referring to the people of Israel. Cf. 14:30; 25:4; 41:17.

of what it does to other human beings. Human pride and human well-being are incompatible and God is committed to human well-being.

The theme of God as a *refuge* is a favorite one in Scripture, especially in the hymnic literature.[23] This is again an expression of the sense of the personal involvement of God with his people. These writers are not conceiving of a life force or a deistic first principle. But neither are they thinking of an amulet or a personal idol. The genius of Hebrew religion is its capacity to weld together an almighty, transcendent Creator with an imminent, personal Father. Neither one of these alone will do, but no other religion has been successful in holding the two together. Without both of them, "God is our refuge and strength" (Ps. 46:2 [Eng. 1]) is a mockery.

Isaiah uses two extremes of weather typical of the Near East to symbolize the difficulties from which God desires to defend us. They are the thunderstorm and the unremitting heat. In either the sudden intensity of the cloudburst or the steady, enervating heat, life is threatened. Unless one has a stronghold against the flood (cf. Matt. 7:24–27) or a shade from the heat, there is no hope. Life is like that, with the mighty and the powerful breathing out destruction on those not strong enough to fight back. For those people the faith itself, an ability to trust in a Sovereign who cares about them, is a source of strength. But even more, his intervention on their behalf makes him a refuge. The mighty of earth may be great, but God is greater (51:12, 13).

The verse division between 4 and 5 is incorrect, coming as it does between parallel terms, "flood" and "heat." The present translation follows the suggestion of Kissane to translate *kî rûaḥ* as *though the breath* instead of "for the breath." If this rendering is correct, then the new thought starts at this point and the verse division should occur there.

As parching heat in the shadow of a cloud shows how quickly and silently God can overcome the mighty. Just as a cloud slipping between the earth and the sun produces moments of blessed coolness, so God interposes himself in hopeless situations so that life can go on.[24]

6–8 The focus of attention returns here to the banquet, the atmosphere having been heightened by the hymn of praise in vv. 1–5.[25] The

---

23. See Deut. 33:27; 2 Sam. 22:3, 33; Neh. 8:10; Ps. 14:6; 27:1; 28:8; 31:5 (Eng. 4); 37:39; 43:2; 46:2, 8, 12 (Eng. 1, 7, 11); 48:4 (Eng. 3); 52:9 (Eng. 7); 57:2 (Eng. 1); 62:8, 9 (Eng. 7, 8); 71:7; 91:2, 9; 94:22; 142:5, 6 (Eng. 4, 5); Isa. 4:6; 17:7; 27:5; Jer. 16:19.

24. See also 4:6; 30:2, 3; 32:2; 49:2; 51:16. Cf. also Ps. 17:8; 36:8 (Eng. 7); 57:2 (Eng. 1); 63:8 (Eng. 7); 91:1; 121:5, 6.

25. Cf. Delitzsch.

inaugural banquet seems to have been customary in the Near East when a king was crowned.[26] It was a time when the king bestowed favors and sought to establish a favorable tone for his reign. That seems to be the picture here. The subjects come from all over the world (2:2) to the mountain of the Lord (24:23; 2:2, 3; 4:5; 11:9; 65:25). There they receive the gifts which only God can bestow: the destruction of death and the removal of the sorrow which accompanies it. This is the key to the richness of the feast—it is the food and drink of life (John 4:13–14; 6:35, 58; 7:37–38).

6 *on this mountain . . . for all peoples* combines particularity with universality. It was comforting to the Jew to believe that one day his faith would be vindicated. On this not-too-significant hilltop, their God would manifest his glory and show that his people had been right to trust him (v. 8c). But that manifestation was not merely so the Jew could be vindicated. It was also so that the world could be delivered (Rev. 22:2). That took some of the cause of Jewish pride away.[27] But at the same time the universal deliverance could not occur without the particular manifestation. This is the genius of the revelation. Because God dealt with a certain people in certain ways, there is hope for all humanity. For it is God's acts which save us, not merely a generalized teaching about deity which could have been given apart from the Jewish people and Jerusalem.

a feast of fatness. To a people who did not have to worry about cholesterol, the fat portions of the meat were the best (Ps. 36:9 [Eng. 8]; 63:6 [Eng. 5]). Thus it is not surprising that these were the portions of the sacrifices reserved for God (Lev. 3:3; 4:8, 9). But here God is giving

26. See 1 Sam. 11:15; 1 K. 1:9, 19, 25; cf. also 2 Sam. 6:18; 1 K. 8:62–65. Scott, J. Gray ("Kingship of God in Prophets and Psalms," *VT* 11 [1961] 23), W. Millar *(Origins),* and others make a good deal of supposed Caananite mythological antecedents to this account. (Cf. Baal and Anat II AB 6:39–59; V AB A [*ANET*, pp. 134–146].) However, study of the myths and comparison with the biblical text show only the most minimal similarities. Millar reconstructs the Baal and Anat poems in a way which seems to give a flowing account of the relation of feast to victory (pp. 71–81). However, study of the texts themselves shows that relation to be tenuous since the connections among the texts are the subject of considerable scholarly disagreement. Furthermore, humanity is never involved in the mythological feasts whereas it is central here. There terminology of swallowing up Death (Canaanite *Mot*) may derive from a common literary substratum, but there is no reference to a feast in connection with Baal's victory over *Mot* (whom he does not swallow [I AB 6:12–50]). All of this argues that the biblical account is not derived from the Canaanite one.

27. Perhaps it is for this reason that the Targ. makes this verse a statement of judgment: "The Lord of Hosts will make for all the peoples on this mountain a feast and a festival. They shall consider it for honor but it shall be shame for them, even plagues which they cannot escape, plagues wherein they shall perish."

the rich food to his people, as the host (Ps. 24:6).[28] This is always the principle of sacrifice. God asks that we give to him in order that he may give to us. (Cf. the thank offering and the feasting associated with it, Lev. 7:11–18).

a feast of lees refers to wine which has been allowed to strengthen by leaving the dregs in the wine after the fermentation process. The wine, strained before drinking, was clear and strong, i.e., good wine. *šᵉmārîm*, "lees," was probably used here also because of its assonance with *šᵉmānîm*, "fatness."

7, 8 But the people who come to the great feast come with veils over their faces. Although some commentators believe this refers to the veil of ignorance which prevents the Gentiles from understanding and accepting God's revelation (2 Cor. 3:15),[29] most are agreed, in the light of v. 8, that the reference is to the shroud of death. Before human beings can experience the joy of God's great feast, something must be done about the universal curse. At the end of every pathway the Grim Reaper awaits us all, and that cold hand blights every human happiness. But God will *swallow*—not merely remove, but envelop in such a way as to destroy— that shroud. Moreover, he will do it on Mount Zion, the prophet says. For the Christian, what other meaning can this have than the death and resurrection of Jesus Christ? In him, death has been defeated once and for all, for all the peoples of the earth (Rom. 6:14; 1 Cor. 15:12–57;[30] 1 Thess. 4:14; Rev. 1:17, 18; 21:4). This is the ultimate deliverance. We may be delivered from want and from oppression, but until we are delivered from death, and the sin which issues in death, all these other deliverances are a mockery; death is the final conqueror.

Many modern commentators, following Duhm, take v. 8a to be an interpolation, but there is no unanimity. Wildberger argues for its originality in vv. 6–8, and W. Millar sees it as essential to the strophic structure.[31] Kissane's attempt to save the phrase for Isaiah by denying that it refers to immortality flies in the face of the plain meaning of the passage.

The Sovereign Lord will wipe away tears from all faces is a fine example of the power of imagery. The text could say that God will take away the sorrow associated with death, for that is obviously the meaning.

---

28. The feast theme is picked up in the NT: Matt. 8:11; Luke 13:29; 14:15; 22:16; Rev. 19:9.

29. So Delitzsch. Cf. also Kissane.

30. Paul's "Death is swallowed up in victory" (1 Cor. 15:54) is evidently dependent upon the Aramaic of v. 8a, where *nṣḥ* can mean both "victory" and "forever."

31. Millar, *Origins,* pp. 41–42.

But how much more expressive is the picture of the Master of the Universe tenderly wiping the tearstained faces as a mother might her child's. He is touched by that which rends our hearts, and his purpose, begun in Christ, is to put an end to it all. Once again, this demonstrates God's sovereignty over the nations. They cannot conquer death, but God can. Not only will he conquer death for himself and his own people, but for all people. This is sovereignty.

The reproach of his people he will take away is the result of God's conquest of death and his offer of the feast of life. Not only did their sin and disobedience bring them shame in the eyes of the nations, but so also did their stubborn faith in God and their refusal to violate their laws.[32] But in that day, as the nations turn toward Zion, all the shame, failure, and loss will be made up for. In fact, it will be known that the salvation of the world exists only through God's people. If one is to relate this text to the eschatological teaching of the NT, it may, with caution, be connected to the final ingathering of the Jews forecasted in Rom. 11:11–27.

9–12 This third section of ch. 25 returns to song, and again one can imagine that the writer intends for the reader to envision this song as a part of the festivities around God's throne. The theme turns once more from the salvation of the nations to the prior judgment, with Moab symbolizing the rest of the nations. Some commentators regret this return, arguing that the picture of universal salvation in vv. 6–8 is more noble. However, this movement is entirely consistent with the canonical shape of the book as well as of the complete Bible. God does wish to deliver all the peoples of the world. But this does not mean all will respond to his invitation. For those who refuse to do so, the grim final word is judgment. No one ought to be lulled into apathetic unconcern because of God's offer of limitless love. Any nation or person must either run with God or run into him. There is no other way. Those who are tempted to ignore vv. 6–8 because of God's soft heart will learn to regret that decision.[33]

9 Delitzsch is probably correct when he sees the reference to removing the reproach from God's people (v. 8) as the immediate stimulus for this song. Although it had seemed impossibly long at the time, eventually the "waiting" will have been shown to be worth it all, and the song will burst forth (Rev. 6:9–11; 7:9–12). This connection with v. 8 may also explain the use of Moab to symbolize the nations, just as Malachi was to

32. For the reproach, cf. Deut. 38:37; Josh. 5:9; Jer. 6:10; Ezek. 5:14, 15; Luke 6:22; Heb. 11:26; 1 Pet. 4:14.
33. Note how 2:6–4:1 follows 2:1–5. So also ch. 5 follows ch. 4 and ch. 39 follows chs. 36–38. Cf. also 66:22–24 as the conclusion to the book. Cf. Mal. 3:24 (Eng. 4:6); Rev. 22:14, 15.

use Edom later (Mal. 1:2–5). It was particularly these neighboring nations which had taunted Judah for her apparently ineffectual trust in Yahweh.[34] They had reproached Judah, but in the last day, the reproach would be all theirs (Ezek. 36:6–7).[35]

Again, as in v. 1, the personal element is strong. God has shown himself faithful to his people and the response is seen in a deep sense of affinity. Ultimately, this is what the whole Exodus had been about: "You will be my people, and I will be your God" (Exod. 29:45, 46, etc.). But somehow that vision had gotten lost in the intervening years, so that Ezekiel and Isaiah had to look for it to be reinstated by the deliverance from the Exile (Ezek. 36:28). And perhaps Isaiah is saying here that it will not be completely realized until the final deliverance.

we waited for him expresses a fundamental element of the OT, and the Isaianic, concept of trust.[36] It is the kind of confident expectation that is willing to put the times in God's hands and to believe in spite of a long interval. This kind of trust has forsaken that manipulation which seeks instant gratification, and it has demonstrated the reality of its commitment to God by refusing to make him vindicate himself according to a human timetable. When such confident expectation is satisfied, the result is, as here, jubilation, for the one who waits has proven the sovereignty of God. That jubilation springs from the certainty that God can save. What a relief and a delight that is, for without a sovereign deliverer, we are merely pawns of a cruel chance.

10 The same hand which will rest on Zion in blessing will strike Moab down. This is not the result of favoritism or arbitrary pique on God's behalf. It is the result of two different attitudes. Those who commit themselves to God in patient trust will experience his hand of blessing, shading them from the oppressive heat of the sun (49:2; Ezra 8:22, 31), but those who exalt themselves against God in their own self-sufficiency must sooner or later be crushed under that hand (vv. 11, 12; cf. also 16:6; Jer. 48:29; Zeph. 2:10).

The imagery here is very strong, so strong that some interpreters believe it must spring from a virulent hatred of Moab that is inconsistent with the kind of compassion expressed in chs. 15 and 16. However, this

34. See Num. 22:11; 1 Sam. 12:9; Ps. 60:12 (Eng. 10); Jer. 48:26, 27; Ezek. 25:8.

35. This connection with v. 8 argues against the widely held position that vv. 10b–11 were originally separate from vv. 9–10a. Both segments can be seen as springing from the same stimulus.

36. Cf. 26:8; 33:2; 40:31; Gen. 49:18; Ps. 25:3, 5; 37:9; 39:8 (Eng. 7); 130:5, 6.

view does not take adequate account of the use of language among the Semites. Strong, florid language was as typical of Jesus (see his rebukes of the Pharisees, Matt. 23:13–36) as it is of the modern Iranians. Yet Jesus' compassion was boundless, and when the springs of emotion opposite to anger are touched in an Arab there is no more compassionate person. Thus it is entirely consistent for these words and the words of chs. 15 and 16 to have been spoken by the same person. Furthermore, the use of these words does not denote an implacable, mindless sort of hatred. The writer is mustering all his verbal skills, unencumbered by the sensitivities of the modern urbanized taste, to say that just as God's deliverance must come to those who trust him, so also his judgment *cannot* be escaped by those who flaunt him.

11 It is not clear whether this verse is intended to continue the imagery of v. 10. Some commentators understand that Moab is simply lying spread-eagled on the ground with the conqueror's foot planted in the middle of his back.[37] In part, this uncertainty is because of the supposed impossibility of swimming in a manure pile. However, *in its midst* does not have any referent unless it does refer to the preceding verse, and if the reading "water of" is correct, then there is no incongruity at all, for a barnyard can become very much like quicksand in the winter and spring. So Moab sinks further in its own pride the more frantically it seeks to save itself.[38]

in spite of the struggles of his hands is somewhat obscure owing to the uncertainty of the meaning of ʿ*orbôt*, here translated "struggles."[39] If Driver's suggestion adopted here is correct, then this verse along with v. 10 seems to show a unified theme. If the more common reading is correct, then perhaps Moab's treachery toward Judah is intended.

12 The change of person (3rd to 2nd) in this verse seems to shift the focus from Moab back to a more generalized picture to the universal city which Moab had particularized for a moment (25:2; 26:5; 27:10).

---

37. So, e.g., Gray, following R. H. Kennett, *Ancient Hebrew Social Life and Custom as Indicated in Law, Narrative, and Metaphor* (London: Oxford, 1933).

38. For a similar evaluation of pride as manure, see Mal. 2:3; Phil. 3:8.

39. AV "spoils," RSV "cleverness," CBAT "tricks," NIV "cleverness," all from ʾ*rb*, "to lie in wait for." But cf. Driver, *JTS* 38 (1937) 42, 43, who suggests that the basic meaning is something oblique or on the other side. Thus he sees the reference as being to the oblique motions or struggles of the drowning man. For ʿ*im* with the meaning "in spite of" see Neh. 5:18. NEB takes the undefined 3rd masc. sing. subject to be Moab (not God) and reads "he will sink his pride *with* every stroke of his hands." The reference to God is preferred in the light of v. 12.

That mighty world-city with its apparently unshakable walls with be shivered to dust.[40] All its towering pride will be brought down to a dunghill.

b. THE LORD'S DAY (26:1–27:13)

(1) Judah's song (26:1–27:1)

(a) Hymn of thanksgiving (26:1–6)

> 1 *In that day this song will be sung*
> *in the land of Judah,*
> *"We have a strong city;*
> *He has made[1] salvation[2] its walls and ramparts.[3]*
> 2 *Open the gates, that the righteous nation,*
> *the one which keeps faithfulness,[4] may enter.*
> 3 *As for the steadfast mind,[5]*
> *you will keep it in perfect peace,[6]*
> *for in you it trusts.*

40. See 2:15. Cf. Gilgamesh 1:305–310 (*ANET*, p. 97) where all of Gilgamesh's frustrated search for immortality ends in a boast of the greatness of Uruk's walls.

1. The verb, "(He) has made," is without an expressed subject. Evidently, the main point is not who has made salvation the defense, but that it is.

2. Irwin, *CBQ* 41 (1979) 244, redivides the verse to place *yešûʿâ* with the first clause and reads "a city our mighty savior provides with walls and ramparts," but this syntax seems very strange.

3. The precise meaning of *ḥēl*, "ramparts," is not clear. It appears to refer to an outer structure beyond the main wall (cf. 2 Sam. 20:15), perhaps even the smooth incline, or glacis, leading up to the base of the wall. (Cf. Y. Yadin, *The Art of Warfare in Biblical Lands* [New York: McGraw-Hill, 1963], I:178–79.)

4. Irwin, *CBQ* 41 (1979) 259, understands both "righteous" and "keeper of the faithful" to be divine titles. This is possible but it breaks the accord with the entry formula.

5. *yēṣer*, "mind," comes from the root idea "to form." Thus as a noun it frequently refers to that which is formed (Isa. 29:16; Ps. 103:14; Hab. 2:18), often thoughts, purposes, or intentions (cf. Gen. 6:5; 8:21; Deut. 31:21; 1 Chr. 28:9; 29:18). As reflected in the present translation, the Hebrew seems to place "the steadfast mind" in an emphatic position in an independent clause at the beginning of the sentence.

6. *šālôm šālôm*, "peaceful peace," "complete peace." Duhm recommends dropping the second as a dittography. However, the evidence of the duplication appears in the Targ., the Vulg., and the Hexapla. (Also in 1QIs[a]. See J. Carmignac, "Six passages d'Isaïe éclairés par Qumran," in *Bibel und Qumran*, Festschrift H. Bardtke, ed. S. Wagner [Berlin: Evangelische Haupt-Bibelgesellschaft, 1968], pp. 42, 43.) For examples of similar kinds of formations, see 24:16; 27:5; 57:19; Jer. 6:14; 8:11. It is also possible that the second *šālôm* begins the next clause; see Irwin, *CBQ* 41 (1979) 259.

4 *Trust in the Lord forever,*
    even in Yah, the Lord, the Rock eternal.
5 *For he will bring down the inhabitant of the heights,*
    the fortified city, he will lay it low.
  He will lay it low[7] to the ground;
    he will level it to the dust.
6 *Feet will trample it—*
    the feet of the lowly,
    the feet[8] of the poor.

Chapters 26–27 continue the thought of chs. 24 and 25. (Note the recurrence of the song of joy, 26:1, 19; 27:2, because of God's victory over the city of oppression, 26:5; 27:10; cf. also 27:13.) However, the focus is changed somewhat. Whereas chs. 24 and 25 focus on the victory and the feast which follows, chs. 26 and 27 reflect in a somewhat more solemn vein upon the meaning of this victory for Judah. This is only a relative change in emphasis, however, for the general theme of God's sovereignty remains of central importance as does the atmosphere of hope stemming from that conviction. The thematic development seems to proceed in this fashion: (1) 26:1–6: a song of thanksgiving in which Judah encourages herself to keep faith with God who has kept faith with her; (2) 26:7–15: a reflection on the truth that the wicked can understand nothing except the rod of judgment upraised on behalf of God's people; (3) 26:16–19: a lament recognizing that God's people are helpless in themselves; (4) 26:29–27:1: the promise that God will indeed act; and (5) 27:2–12: God's passion for his vineyard.

There has been an almost incredible variety of opinions concerning the literary integrity of ch. 26.[9] It is difficult to find two scholars in

7. The repetition of *yašpîlāh* after *yašpîlennâ* has been called an error in the MT in that it is missing in 1QIs[a], LXX, and Syr. (cf. *BHS*). However, the omission in the versions may be by haplography and as a result of failing to recognize an anadiplosis. As the MT points the text, the second verb is redundant. But if the first verb is construed with the preceding clause, the difficulty disappears. In view of the anadiplosis in vv. 3 and 4 (see n. 13 below) it seems likely that this is the explanation here.

8. The precarious nature of criticism on the basis of style is illustrated by the diverse reactions of Kaiser and Clements to the threefold repetition of *regel*, "foot," in v. 6. Kaiser remarks that its presence is a mark of good poetry, whereas Clements believes the first should be removed because it yields "smoother sense." Without taking either to be necessarily incorrect, one can still see that such judgments are highly subjective.

9. Duhm (with Gray and Marti) argued that vv. 1–19 were a unit, largely on the basis of meter. Lindblom (followed by Ringgren) took vv. 1–14 as separate from vv. 15–19 and vv. 20–21. Wildberger (along with Procksch, Fohrer, and

agreement upon what constituted the original unit. Given this lack of agreement, both upon conclusions and upon methods for reaching conclusions, there can be no other base of interpretation than the present shape of the text.

Taken in this light, the chapter moves from contemplation of the glorious future and the kind of steadfast trust necessary to participate in that future (vv. 1–6) to a sober view of the present in which the people are not delivered (vv. 7–19). Nevertheless, in this sober view there is the repeated affirmation that God can and will keep his word. This train of thought is then met by the promise that God will punish the sinful earth and triumph over it for his people's sake (26:20–27:1). This movement from future to present to future has the function of assuring the reader that the promises are not merely rosy daydreams which ignore the contradictory present. In fact, these promises are made more convincing because they are made in the full light of the present. The book of Revelation served a similar purpose in NT times. It assured the people that God was aware of the present but was not defeated by it, and it called them to continued steadfast trust (cf. Rev. 2:10, 11, etc.). We are called to the same kind of confidence today. We do not deny the present, nor do we know of any power to help ourselves. But we know a God whose strength is as limitless as his love and whose purposes remain steadfast: to bless all those who will commit themselves to him.

1–6 Although this song does not manifest the features which form critics have identified as being typical of the classic hymn of praise (the call to praise, the thematic sentence, etc.),[10] it is still obviously in praise of God. In place of the city of chaos towering over the oppressed in grim splendor (24:10; 25:2; 26:5), God has another city, one whose walls are salvation, whose gates are open to all who will enter, whose might is not in arrogance but in humble commitment (65:17–25; Rev. 21:9–27). As always, God destroys the false, only to raise up the true. It may be that the specific stimulus for this song is the overthrow of Moab reported in 25:10–12, but particularly if Moab is used symbolically there

---

Clements) separates vv. 1–6 from vv. 7–21, and Wildberger makes vv. 7–21 part of the "original stratum." He quotes favorably Skinner's comment on the evidence that the entire chapter has undergone a careful literary crafting. Scott also points out that while differences among segments may be found, these are no more than appear in many of the Psalms. W. H. Irwin's careful study ("Syntax and Style in Isaiah 26," *CBQ* 14 [1979] 240–261) supports Skinner's (and Scott's) point and argues for literary unity.

10. Cf. K. Koch, *The Growth of the Biblical Tradition*, tr. S. M. Cupitt (New York: Scribners, 1969), pp. 159–170.

of the world-city, it seems more likely that the praise is offered for the positive side of all that is negatively represented in ch. 25.[11]

1 *He has made salvation its walls and ramparts.* This statement may be understood in one of two ways. First, it may be that in the ideal city ie walls and ramparts will be God's salvation. That is, walls of stone and earth can hardly save us from that which most threatens our existence. The only true defense is the deliverance which comes from God. The second possibility is that God has set the walls of the city for salvation. Skinner prefers this in the light of the mention of gates in v. 2. He believes that a city of spiritual walls and physical gates makes no sense. However, in poetry such literalism is uncalled for. Cheyne seems right in calling this a "happy inconsistency." In fact, the gates need not be literal either. The point is that access to God's city is free for those to whom righteousness and faithfulness are paramount.

2 *Open the gates* seems very reminiscent of such Pilgrim Psalms as 118:19, 20; 15:1–5; and 24:3–10, where the mark of acceptability is not cultic purity but that sort of ethical righteousness (1:26; 32:16, 17; 33:13–16; Hos. 2:18–20; 6:6; Amos 5:21–24) which is the result of the faithful keeping of the covenant (Deut. 6:25). Again, over-literalism is not in order.[12] We need think neither that the city is not yet inhabited (Young) nor that the gatekeepers are angels (Jerome). The point is simply that none can live in this city for whom God's character is not the passion of their lives (Rev. 21:6–8), and this entry formula is a way of expressing this truth. The prophet envisions a day when the adulterous spirit of his people will be changed to faithfulness and loyalty (4:3–4; 32:14–16).

The Christian will want to add the insight which is not foreign to the OT (witness 32:14; Jer. 31:33; Ezek. 36:26, 27) but which comes to its most explicit statement in the NT: no merely human righteousness can stand in the blaze of God's holiness (Rom. 3:20–26; Phil. 3:9; Gal. 3:10–14; cf. also Isa. 57:12; 64:6). What the Christian knows, the OT prophets knew: to expect to impress God with my righteousness is simply to indulge in another species of pride. The only genuinely "right" person is the one who admits that no good thing dwells in him (Rom. 7:18) but trusts God's promise of deliverance and cleansing. This trust and the thirst for God-likeness which flows from that trust are the true righteousness (Phil. 3:12–16).

---

11. The idea that vv. 1–6 were written in the light of ch. 25, either originally or secondarily, is now held by most scholars. Plöger, *Theocracy*, p. 69, is a notable exception.

12. See the comment on 19:18–24.

3 To experience the security of God's city one thing is required: a fixed disposition of trust. This is the opposite of James's "double-minded man" (Jas. 1:6–8) or Jesus' servant of two masters (Matt. 6:24). This person has cast himself upon God without any reservation. To trust one's ability partly and God partly is the surest prescription for insecurity and anxiety (8:11–22; 57:19–21). That person will never know the wholeness *(šālôm)* which having all his or her commitments in one place may mean. This is not to say that we denigrate or deny God-given abilities. But it is to say that we refuse to believe the lie that we are independent and have in ourselves the keys to ultimate success in life. The person who refuses the blandishments of such an idea and steadfastly looks to God can know an inner oneness which makes possible a confident outlook on the darkest scene. For our mortality, short-sightedness, and weakness, we receive in exchange God's immortality, omniscience, and omnipotence. That is security.

4 *Trust in the Lord forever* is the logical result of the assertion in v. 3.[13] If it is true that trust in God results in a steadfast mind which is kept in peace, then all persons should be urged to trust in him, and that is exactly what the singers in this passage do. As in 12:2, this trust is conceived of as a result of salvation. "In that day," the day to come, they will trust him. At the same time, of course, the writer is speaking prophetically and urging people in the present to trust now in the light of the certainty of the promises.

This issue of trust is the key to the entire segment beginning at 7:1 and concluding at 39:8. Will Judah commit her security to the nations or to God? Nothing further can be accomplished on her behalf until that question is definitely answered. So throughout the segment the issue is stated and restated with the same conclusion appearing again and again: only God is strong enough, only God is concerned enough with Judah's best interests, to be entrusted with her security (14:30; 30:12, 15; 31:1; 32:9, 10, 11, 17; 36:4, 5, 6, 7, 9, 15; 37:10; cf. also 42:17; 47:8, 10; 50:10; 59:4).

even in Yah, the Lord has been the source of some controversy on two counts: the use of the preposition b^e on *Yah*, and the likelihood of the duplication of the divine name. The first problem is solved by realizing that the *kî* which opens the second clause is not to be translated "for," thus demanding an independent clause, but rather as an emphatic particle,

---

13. Note the anadiplosis wherein the same word, here *bāṭaḥ*, "trust," is used to close one clause and open the next. See n. 7 above for another possible example and v. 7 below. On *bāṭaḥ* see *TDOT*, II:88–94; *TWOT*, I:101–102.

as here, which allows the clause to be dependent on the main verb.[14] As for the repetition of the divine name, note that such a repetition appears also in 12:2, which is a similar song of trust. This suggests that the repetition was a conventional device in settings such as this one and should not be deleted.[15]

the Rock is a favorite OT description of the Lord.[16] It describes a rocky crag upon which a harassed person could climb, sheltering himself in one of its crannies and there being able to beat off all attackers. In a world of uncertainty, the confidence that such a personality is at the center of all being is a priceless possession. That confidence is only enhanced by the recognition that this Rock is the Eternal One.

5, 6 In language reminiscent of 25:12, the writer gives the reason for trusting Yahweh.[17] He has brought the proud oppressive city down to the dust.[18] This means two things about trust: it would be foolish to repose trust in the city of Man; it is worth waiting for God to perform his wonders. But it also means that the hearers should beware that they are not inhabitants of that proud city. For just as the city of God is a spiritual condition, so is the city of Man. Thus, in words reminiscent of the Beatitudes (Matt. 5:1–12), Isaiah says it is better to be among the poor and the lowly who will triumph than to be among the mighty who will be triumphed over. This is contrary to all human wisdom, but it is the true wisdom (Jas. 3:13–18; 5:1–11).

(b) Psalm of dependence (26:7–19)

7 *The way*[1] *of the righteous is straight;*

14. If the clause is independent, the *beth* must be *bēṯ essentiae* (Skinner). Dahood takes it to be an "emphasizing particle" *(Or* 34 [1965] 87). On emphatic *kî,* cf. Williams, *Syntax,* § 449; and W. Irwin, *CBQ* 41 (1979) 248–49.

15. Contra *BHS,* which follows LXX. It is easier to explain the LXX omission (by haplography) than the MT insertion. 1QIs^a agrees with MT.

16. Deut. 32:4; 1 Sam. 2:2; 2 Sam. 22:2, 32; Ps. 19:15 (Eng. 14); 61:3 (Eng. 2); Isa. 30:29. Cf. also Exod. 33:21, 22; 1 Cor. 10:4. The LXX, apparently being over-scrupulous about identifying God with an inanimate object, never translates the metaphor literally.

17. This recurrence must argue that the passages were written in the knowledge of each other, perhaps not at the same time, but surely not independently.

18. Hanson's suggestion that this is actually a reference to Jerusalem on the part of the disestablished followers of II Isaiah does not seem plausible in the light of the present context. It is the nations which are in focus here. Cf. Edom in Obad. 3.

1. As J. Jensen comments, it is significant that *'ōraḥ,* "path," appears 8 times in Isaiah (2:3; 3:12; 26:7, 8; 30:11; 33:8; 40:14 and 41:3) and nowhere else in the prophetic corpus. This is a strong argument for at least the literary unity of

O Straight One,[2] the track of the righteous you make level.
8 *Moreover, in the way of your judgments*
we wait[3] for you, O Lord.
For your name and for your memory
the soul[4] longs.
9 *My soul desires you in the night;*
yes, my spirit within me seeks you early.
For[5] as your judgments are on the earth
the inhabitants of the earth learn righteousness.
10 *Shown favor,[6] the wicked does not learn righteousness.*
In an upright land he does wickedly
and does not see the majesty of the Lord.
11 *O Lord, your hand is lifted,*
but they do not see.
Let them see the jealousy of the people[7]

---

the book. It also attests to Isaiah's attempt to see wisdom as stemming from God alone (*The Use of torâ by Isaiah*, CBQMS 3 [Washington, D.C.: Catholic Biblical Association, 1973], pp. 3–5).

2. Note the anadiplosis in which the first clause ends with the abstract noun $m^e \check{s}ar\hat{i}m$, "straight," and the second clause begins with the same root, $y\bar{a}\check{s}\bar{a}r$, "straight one."

3. Virtually all the versions, including 1QIs[a], omit the 2nd masc. sing. suffix from "we wait," and the MT may be secondary. As vv. 8b and 9 make clear, however, the sense remains the same. It is for the Lord that we wait.

4. MT lacks a suffix on "soul," yielding "desire of soul"; but cf. LXX "our soul longed for." However, the author may have intended the more general and abstract connotation of the MT. Cf. v. 11 with its "jealousy of people."

5. $ka^{\,\partial a}\check{s}er$, lit. "according to which," has occasioned a great deal of comment because of its supposed unsuitability here. Most of the comment has centered around attempts to emend it to a verb, since the clause now lacks one (cf. Targ. "when your judgments are established"); Irwin, *CBQ* 41 (1979) 245–46, seeing a chiasm in vv. 9b–10a, looks for a parallel to $y^{e\,\mathcal{c}}aww\bar{e}l$, "he does wickedly," and proposes ʾšr, "to direct aright." Clements appears to follow Driver (*JTS* 38 [1937] 43) who asserts that the form is an infinitive of a verb meaning "to be strong, prevail." S. Talmon, "DSIa as a Witness to Ancient Exegesis of the Book of Isaiah," *ASTI* 1 (1962) 67–68, proposes to take it as a noun, $\partial\bar{o}\check{s}er$, $\partial e\check{s}er$, "happiness" (cf. LXX "light" [$\partial a\check{s}\bar{o}r$?]). In view of this variety, without denying the problem of the MT, it must be said that there is no more convincing alternative.

6. $yuḥān$, "shown favor," may be either a hophal imperfect with a virtually doubled ḥet or perhaps a remnant of an original Qal passive formation. Driver dismisses this meaning and posits a root ḥwn, meaning "was humbled" (*JTS* 38 [1937] 43); cf. NEB. But the MT yields perfectly good sense.

7. $qin\partial at\,\mathcal{c}am$, "jealousy of people," appears very strange because of its lack of definition. This has prompted some commentators to recommend its deletion (so, e.g., Gray). Clements, on the other hand, wishes to delete the previous verbs as marginal glosses. However, the versions give evidence that both elements were present in their originals. Three meanings are possible for the text as it stands: (1) objective genitive, God's jealousy for his people; (2) subjective genitive, the people's zeal against their enemies; (3) subjective genitive, the jealousy of the

and be ashamed.

Moreover, the fire of your enemies devours them.

12 *O Lord, you will bring about*[8] *peace for us;*

for, indeed, all our works you have done for us.[9]

13 *O Lord, our God, lords*[10] *other than*[11] *you have lorded it over us,*

but your name[12] *alone*[13] *have we recommended.*[14]

14 *They are dead, they shall not live;*

shades,[15] *they will not arise.*

Indeed, you have punished and you have destroyed them;

you have made every memory of them to perish.

15 *You have added to the nation,*[16] *O Lord;*

you have added to the nation[17] *and you are honored.*

You have extended all the borders of the land.

---

people (of earth) against Israel. The context favors the first meaning (cf. Wildberger). But if that is correct, why is the phrase not so defined, at least by pronouns? Delitzsch suggests plausibly that an abstraction is intended. If this is correct, then the sense would be: Let them see what a (divine) passion for humanity looks like.

8. *špt*, "to set," appears only here and in 2 K. 4:38; Ps. 22:16 (Eng. 15); Ezek. 24:3. BDB (p. 1046a) takes it as a denominal verb from "pot"; 1QIs[a] has *špṭ*, but that is a much easier reading than MT and therefore suspect.

9. Although most commentators agree on the interpretation of this statement, alternate interpretations have been proposed. Ringgren, following Lindblom, has "required all our misdeeds" (*ASTI* 9 [1973] 110; cf. also JPSV). Clements prefers "you have wrought a reward [emending *gam kol* to *gᵉmûl*] of our work for us." Young understands "our works" to mean "works on our behalf." But in fact, all these alternatives are forced to read something into the text that is not explicitly present. It is better to take the plain sense. (Cf. also Ps. 90:16, 17.)

10. *baʿal* suggests "owner" even more than "lord."

11. Elsewhere *zûlay*, "apart from," is preceded by a negative or appears in a question. But the sense seems clear enough.

12. The first part of v. 13 is somewhat difficult and LXX varies considerably from the MT: "Take us for your own; we know no other; we name your name." However, this smacks of a paraphrase, especially since the Targ. follows the MT rather closely.

13. In the final clause, *bᵉkā lᵉbaḏᵉkā*, "in you alone," would be more normal than the present reversed order (cf. Ps. 51:6 [Eng. 4]; Prov. 5:17; cf. *BHS*).

14. *nazkîr*, Hiphil of *zkr*, "remember," meaning "to commemorate, praise"; cf. v. 8.

15. For *rᵉpā'îm* as "shades, ghosts," cf. the sepulchral inscription of Eshmunazar, *ANET*, p. 662: "May they not have a resting place with the shades *[rᵉpā'îm].*"

16. For *gôy*, "nation," as a reference to Israel, see 10:6; Deut. 4:6; Ps. 33:12; Jer. 7:28.

17. Some mss. delete the repeated "you have added to the nation" and Clements argues that the repetition is a dittography. However, Millar, *Origin*, p. 52, calls the repetition good poetry and compares the verse to 24:8. Both LXX and Targ., although their general translations differ widely from the MT, point to the existence of the repetition in the mss. from which they were translating.

16 *O Lord, in distress they were constrained by you;*
   in straits, they were humbled by your discipline upon them.[18]
17 *Like a pregnant woman about to bear—*
   she writhes, she cries out in her pains—
   so were we because of you, O Lord.
18 *We have conceived, we have writhed,*
   but it is as though[19] *we brought forth wind.*
   Deliverance we have not brought on the earth,
   and the inhabitants of the world do not fall.
19 *Your dead shall live, my corpses shall rise.*
   Awake and shout for joy, dwellers in the dust!
   For the dew of light[20] *is your*[21] *dew,*
   and the earth will let fall[22] *the shades.*[23]

The poem now moves from thanksgiving to an expression of dependence. The writer declares that it is only as God manifests his power on the earth that the peoples will learn the level paths of righteousness. Foreshadowing

18. Not MT. See below.

19. Almost all commentators wish to delete the "as though," *k^emô* (cf. *BHS*). However, Irwin observes that vv. 17–18a show an aba pattern with *k^emô*, main clause, *kēn*, main clause, *k^emô*, which argues against the deletion (*CBQ* 41 [1979] 247). The LXX reading is so different that it can hardly be used as evidence against the MT.

20. On the basis of 2 K. 4:39, where *'ōrōt* is to be translated "herbs," the AV translates "herbs" here. This is possible; cf. Job 29:19 where dew on branches is a figure for abundance of life. However, the Latin tradition translates "light" for *'ōrâ* in Ps. 139:12 and Est. 8:16. The plural here would indicate greatness or extent. (Cheyne points to that light which existed before the sun [Gen. 1:3–15].) This gives a much broader connotation to the idea: the dew of First Light (cf. Ps. 110:3). As noted below, "light" now seems to be supported by the Ugaritic materials, if the identifications are correct.

21. "Your" dew may refer either to God or to the dwellers in the dust. 1QIs^a makes the imperatives "wake" and "shout" imperfects. If that were correct, "your" could only refer to God.

22. Note esp. in the latter its contrast with the jaws of death. This may explain the use of *nāpal* here. Again many commentators take it to be a reference to birth (see on v. 18), but the figure of earth as mother is strange in this context. Earth has swallowed up the dead. It is hardly the positive figure implied by birth and motherhood (cf. Num. 16:30, 32, 34; Ps. 106:17; Prov. 1:12). More appropriate would be the figure of the devourer forced *to drop, let fall,* its prey from its mouth (v. 21; Jer. 51:34, 44; Job 29:17; Rev. 20:13).

23. Dahood, *Psalms,* AB, I:222–23, proposes to read *'ōrōt,* "light," as *'ûrōt,* "fields," and *tappîl* as *tabbîl,* "to be parched," resulting in "your dew is the dew of the (Elysian) fields, but the land of the Shades will be parched." The RSV "on the land of the shades let it fall" is argued against by the pointing *'āreṣ,* which is normal when "earth" is functioning as subject.

the lament in v. 18, he affirms that it is only in God's grace that deliverance and understanding can come. The Jewish people can only wait for him.

Attempts to cast vv. 7–21 in a lament form are not successful.[24] For example, Scott must say that the typical opening cry of complaint and appeal is lost. Kaiser observes that the 3/2 meter is missing and points out that the base function is didactic. The same is true for claims that it was a wisdom psalm. Elements of lament and wisdom are here, but neither of the precise forms is dominant.

7 As is typical of the entire piece, this verse builds on the preceding thought. The image of the feet of the poor and needy naturally leads to a discussion of the road on which they walk. In a land where roadways went up and down with gruelling regularity, the most delightful thought was of a road which was level and straight. It was that way because of the character of the One who formed it (40:3–5). Because he is not crooked or twisted, the way on which his people were called to walk was not either.[25] This is not to say that this way is easy or that its outcome is always obvious. But it is to say that it is not devious or deceptive, with the hidden pitfalls which await the godless. Its demands are clear in advance and its final destination sure. Such a way may not be filled with illicit pleasures,[26] but it will offer excitement in plenty for those with the courage to take God at his word.

8 This verse makes it plain that the way is not an end in itself. Righteousness itself guarantees nothing (Ezek. 30:13). The goal of the way is God. But no one dare enter into the self-deception that by choosing a certain way they may bring themselves to God. We walk on the way that we do so that God may meet us there in his way and in his timing. "In the path . . . we wait."

we wait is the biblical expression of confident hope. It expresses the believer's expectation that God will demonstrate his faithfulness at the most appropriate moment.[27] Waiting is very difficult for most people, for it is an admission that there is nothing we can do at the moment to achieve our ends. Yet that admission is the first requirement for spiritual blessing. Until we have admitted that we cannot save ourselves, God cannot save

24. Cf. B. Anderson, *Out of the Depths*, rev. ed. (Philadelphia: Westminster, 1982), pp. 75–82, for a discussion of the characteristics of the form.

25. Cf. Ps. 1:6; Prov. 3:6; 4:26; 5:6, 21; 11:5; 15:19, on the way of the righteous.

26. Can it be only accidental that the word "straight" has come to have a contemptuous connotation in American colloquial speech?

27. Cf. Ps. 25:3; 37:9; 69:7 (Eng. 6); Isa. 25:9; 33:2; 40:31; 49:23; 51:5; 59:19; 60:9; Hos. 12:6; Mic. 7:7; see comment on 25:9.

us. So this waiting becomes a spiritual statement wherein we say, above all to ourselves, that we are not the key to our problems and that we are confident that God is the key.

It is significant that the stress here is not so much upon waiting for God's salvation as it is upon God himself. To be sure, Isaiah is looking toward God's mighty acts of judgment and deliverance, but he does not fall into the fallacy of separating Deliverer and deliverance. There is only hope for Israel because of who God is. Thus, his *name* and his *memory* are references to his character as it is has been manifested formerly.[28] Above all, then, the prophet cries out for God as a Person, a Person of consistency, life, and hope. It is not different today. The human soul longs for fellowship with its Creator. In that fellowship are deliverance and empowerment, but these are only by-products of the central reality, the relationship (cf. 1 John 1:1–4).

9a The first half of the verse continues the thought of the previous one. Note that v. 8 ends with *npš*, "soul," and that v. 9a opens with the same word, yet another case of anadiplosis. There is also here one of the phenomena of Hebrew poetic diction, nearer definition, whereby an adverbial idea is conveyed by a second subject, often occurring, as here, before the verb.[29] The parallelism of the two parts of the line suggests that some word for "morning" or "day" should appear in the second part to balance "night" in the first (cf. Ps. 30:6 [Eng. 5]; 92:3 [Eng. 2]; Isa. 17:14). Three suggestions have been made: (1) *bᵉqirbî*, "within me," is an error for original *babbōqer*, "in the morning" (cf. *BHS*, but lacking support in the versions); (2) the meaning of *ʾᵃšaḥᵃrekā* contains the idea of "to rise early" and so in itself balances "night" (Young); (3) in Arabic *qrb* has a verbal meaning of "to travel all night in order to arrive at dawn." Thus *bᵉqirbî* must mean something like "at my waking moment."[30] This last alternative is ingenious and attractive, but the pitfalls of Hebrew-Arabic lexicography are so many that great caution is advisable. The translation here follows Young as the alternative requiring the least heroic measures to render appropriate poetic sense.

9b–11 *For as your judgments* . . . introduces a shift in emphasis which continues through v. 11. A further explanation is given as to why

28. Cf. Ps. 20:2 (Eng. 1); 30:5 (Eng. 4); Isa. 30:27; 50:10 (also Matt. 6:9), for references to "name." For "remember" see Deut. 4:9; 8:2; Ps. 63:7 (Eng. 6); 77:12 (Eng. 11); 78:35; 119:52; Isa. 46:9; 63:11; 64:5. See also B. Childs, *Memory and Tradition in Israel*, SBT 1/37 (London: SCM; Naperville: Allenson, 1962), esp. pp. 31–44.

29. Lit. "my soul—I long for you . . . my spirit . . . I will seek you."

30. Driver, *JSS* 13 (1968) 50.

the author is looking to God so earnestly. It is not merely that God's people may be delivered from oppression, but that the wicked may learn righteousness. He is convinced that only divine retribution for their sins will ever bring the wicked to recognize the folly of their way (cf. Ps. 78:34). So long as their way is easy and prosperous, there is no reason for them to turn to the way of the righteous (v. 8). The Jewish people have not been able to teach the folly of wickedness, he says. Only God can do this through his hand of judgment.

judgments conveys not only the negative connotation usually applied to it, but also the more positive aspect of "government." This aspect is recognized in the book of Judges, where the heroes are neither judicial figures nor merely avenging angels. Rather, they are those who establish God's order and God's ways in Israel and with relation to the surrounding countries.[31] So here, when God's governance is recognized in the world, when the laws of cause and effect, of justice, are seen to operate, then the inhabitants of the world will learn righteousness. This suggests that *ka'ašer*, "according as" (see n. 5 above), may be used to express a proportionate effect: to the degree that God's judgments are recognized, the world learns righteousness.

10 Plöger argues that a distinction is intended between *the inhabitants of the earth* (v. 9) and *the wicked* and that the wicked are in fact the opposing party in the Jewish apocalyptic community.[32] While it is true that the Qumran community appears to have used such language for its opponents,[33] automatic extension to this passage is unwarranted for two reasons. First, "the wicked" are parallel with "the nations of the earth" elsewhere (cf. Ps. 9:18 [Eng. 17]). Second, the parallelism exhibited by vv. 9b and 10ab suggests that both terms refer to the same group. Verse 9b tells of a class of people who learn righteousness under one set of circumstances, and v. 10ab says they do not learn it under another set of circumstances. It is the circumstances which have changed, not the people. The two terms are then synonyms.[34]

Shown favor expresses one of the oddities of human behavior. We tend to interpret grace as weakness and to take advantage of it. It has been shown again and again, as recently as 1938, that aggressors see conciliation as an opportunity for further aggrandizement. So here Isaiah says that the

31. Von Rad, *Old Testament Theology,* I:242; II:149; Lindblom, *Prophecy in Ancient Israel,* p. 312.
32. Plöger, *Theocracy,* p. 65. Cf. also Gray, following Duhm.
33. See, e.g., the Damascus Rule, VIII. Cf. G. Vermes, *The Dead Sea Scrolls in English* (Harmondsworth: Penguin, 1969), pp. 105, 107.
34. Cf. Irwin, *CBQ* 41 (1979) 245–46.

wicked can live in the very midst of righteousness but not learn its lessons so long as their sins remain unpunished. God's majesty can be all about them, yet their own undisturbed pride ("pride" and "majesty" come from the same root, g 'h) prevents them from seeing that majesty.[35] Only when that pride receives its just reward are they able to see the truth (Deut. 8:3, 12–14).

11 In typical Isaianic manner, this verse picks up the final thought of the previous one as well as beginning with that verse's final word, the divine name. The author is troubled by this situation in which the wicked are not responding. They do not see the hand which he sees. His solution is for them to see God's concern for his people. That is the positive side. Let them look with envy at the faithfulness of Israel's God. The negative side is the destruction that will fall on the wicked as God wrests his people from their hands. These words have been precious to oppressed believers across tens of centuries. One day they will come to their final fulfillment and need be said no more (Rev. 21:4). That time is envisioned in 26:1–5, and here the prophet calls for it to come quickly.

your hand is lifted is an expression of God's authority and imminent judgment (cf. Gen. 17:11; 2 Sam. 24:16; Ps. 89:18 [Eng. 17]). By contrast, to say that a king had dropped his hands was to describe him as helpless (2 Sam. 4:1; 17:2; Jer. 50:43).

be ashamed expresses the result of seeing God's passion for his people. When the wicked see how the One in whom Israel has trusted is jealous for Israel, then they will recognize how foolish were all the things in which they trusted—most of all, their own pride.

the fire of your enemies is evidently an objective genitive meaning the fire reserved for your enemies (cf. NIV). The parallelism of "jealousy" and "fire" supports the authenticity of "jealousy" here (Ps. 70:6 [Eng. 5]; Zeph. 1:18).

12–15 In these verses the mood swings back from the petition for God to act to an expression of confidence in God. The general theme remains one of dependency. In herself Israel can do nothing, but God can do all things, and in the light of what he has done in the past, he will make all things well.

12 Although Judah's immediate future is dark, Isaiah is certain of the ultimate outcome. God's upraised hand will set up wholeness and well-being for his people. This is the result of the way of righteousness just as much as destruction is the result of the way of wickedness (Ps. 1).

35. Note 24:16 where the prospective insert sees the time when as a result of judgment that majesty will be praised.

But more than that, this will be the result because of what God has done in the past. The prophet recognizes that all Israel's accomplishments have come from God. That being so, he is confident of God's purposes toward them. He has not brought them so far to trap them or deceive them in the end. (Cf. Phil. 1:6; 2:12, 13.)

13–15 However, a glance at Israelite history might cause one to question such an assertion. Many times foreign overlords had dominated Israel, and the prophet knows by inspiration that worse is yet to come.[36] Does this not discredit the idea of God's lordship of Israel and his capacity to establish peace for them (cf. 63:19)? Isaiah's answer is twofold. First, Israel has never adopted the foreign "lords." "Our God" has always been the Lord. Israel has not believed that might makes right so that they felt the Lord had been defeated by some new overlord's god. God has enabled them not to forget him but to continue to remember.

His second answer is the continued existence of the nation long after the overlords are dead and forgotten. Again and again throughout its history Israel has been ground under the heel of some tyrant bent upon annihilating it, only to emerge and survive to dance on his grave. The present century is no different. Without minimizing the horror or the unanswered questions of the Holocaust, we may still observe that Israel has triumphed in the end. And if most Israelis assert that they did it without God's help, it only shows how far they have drifted from a correct understanding of their existence.

14 As in ch. 14, the prophet sees death as the mocker of human pride and the source of at least temporary relief from pride's oppression. The overlords are gone and nothing of them remains, not even a memory.[37] This verse should not be taken as proof against the doctrine of a general resurrection. That is not the question being addressed. The point is that mortal flesh has no hope of supplanting immortal God.[38]

Indeed, you have punished them approximates the connection of the two parts of the verse with *lāḵēn*, normally translated "therefore." How-

36. Kissane limits the reference to the times of the judges. But that seems to narrow the scope of the statement too much in a context which anticipates final deliverance.

37. Verse 13 ends with God's name being remembered. Here the overlord's memory has perished. The God whom they thought to have proven impotent still lives when they are forgotten.

38. So also other statements which depict the hopelessness of death (38:18; Ps. 6:6 [Eng. 5]; 30:10 [Eng. 9]; 115:17) must be placed alongside expectations to praise God forever: Ps. 23:6; 30:13 (Eng. 12); 48:15 (Eng. 14); etc. For both ideas see Ps. 49:11–16 (Eng. 10–15). The psalmist expects not to remain in Sheol.

ever, there is no causal connection here; the second sentence contains only a further development of what is implicit in the first.[39]

15 This verse supplies the conclusion to the preceding thought.[40] Far from being wiped out by those who have lorded it over her, Israel has increased while those oppressors have vanished from the earth. The verbs are in the perfect form so that it is legitimate to translate them with the past tense (so virtually all translations; Kaiser adopts the future tense), but it seems unlikely that past time is intended. Kissane's proposal (following Dillmann) that it refers to the Davidic and Solomonic kingdoms is plausible, but as with his reference of "overlords" to the time of the judges (n. 10 above) it seems to leave out too much succeeding history. Rather, it seems more likely that the prophet speaks from the point of view of the final restoration and that these are to be taken as prophetic perfects (cf. 33:17). This understanding does not rule out the awareness of God's grace in past events, but it does not limit the reference to those now-distant points. It is also an expression of prophetic certitude. He has said that God will (imperfect) establish peace for them (v. 12) and now he sees that as an accomplished fact. The idea of a land broadened out to accept an increased number of people is a theme which is frequent in the book both explicitly and implicitly.[41] Just as few offspring meant ultimate extinction, so many offspring meant increased power and significance in the world. The fertility cults sought this end through manipulation of the life forces. God promised his people the same results if only they would walk in his ways.

16–19 Here Isaiah turns back again to the present, as in vv. 7–11. As Delitzsch points out, this oscillation between the present and the future is typical of this section (chs. 24–27). But it is also typical of the life of faith. However strong the conviction of God's ultimate triumph, there come those moments when the believer is brought face to face with the contradictions which the present sets over against that conviction. And perhaps the most painful of all those contradictions is the recurring, humiliating evidence of one's own inability to do the work of salvation. Certainly the writer is here speaking for his people, but equally certainly for himself. Clarity of insight is not proof against questions. In fact, the

---

39. Cf. BDB, p. 487a.

40. Ringgren, following Lindblom, takes v. 15 to be the opening of the lament, but this hardly seems possible. To assume as he does that the verse is the protasis for an apodosis beginning in v. 16 is not supported by the grammar (*ASTI* 9 [1973] 111).

41. See 9:2 (Eng. 3); 49:19–21; 54:2, 3; cf. also Mic. 7:11, where *rḥq*, "make broad," is also used.

very clarity may make the questions the more disturbing (cf. John the Baptist's second thoughts about Jesus, Luke 7:18–23).

The passage continues the train of thought begun in v. 7. This thought has to do with the total dependency of humanity upon God. Here that dependency is set out in its strongest terms. We cannot save ourselves or anyone else. We labor and struggle, but nothing comes to birth. We are not able to demonstrate God's power to the wicked. The final proof of our helplessness is death, which stalks every person with the same quiet, relentless tread. To some who loudly proclaim human potential, this is a counsel of despair. But it should not be so. For just as v. 19 ends the segment on a note of triumph, so the recognition of human helplessness paves the way for the receiving of God's power. So the gloom here is not a hopeless one, but productive. It illustrates what the entire first thirty-nine chapters of the book are about: trust in human potential must bring disaster (8:16–22; 24:1–23; 30:1–5; 39:5–7), but an awareness of human weakness which results in trust in God will bring life forevermore (9:1–6 [Eng. 2–7]; 12:1–6; 25:1–9; 30:18; 32:14–20; 35:1–10; 37:3–7). This message of divine ability for our human inability comes to its climax in the NT teaching of life in the Spirit (cf. Gal. 5:16–26; Eph. 5:18–23).

16 The meaning of this verse is very obscure. The MT is not clear and the versions vary from it considerably, as does 1QIs[a].[42] Scholars

---

42. The MT reads: "O Lord, in straits they visited you, they poured out a charm (whispered incantation), your discipline (is) to them." The second part of the verse is obviously difficult, but the first part is questionable as well, since this is the only place *pqd*, "to visit (appoint, muster, judge, reward)," is used with humanity as the subject instead of God. LXX has "O Lord, in straits I remembered you, in slight affliction your discipline was upon us." "Affliction" in the second line suggests the emendation of *laḥaš*, "charm (whisper?)," to *laḥaṣ*, as suggested by Cheyne (followed by Gray and Scott). More recently, Irwin points out that no emendation may be necessary since final *ṣ* and *š* seem to have been interchangeable in certain words (Heb. *ḥrṣ/ḥrš*, Ugar. *maḥaṣ/maḥaš*) (*CBQ* 41 [1979] 251–52). Targ. has "O Lord, in distress they remembered your fear *[pḥd?]*, in their troubles they taught secretly the instruction of your law." This seems to take *laḥaš* as "teach secretly" and has *mûsār* as "instruction," not "discipline." But most significantly it requires that *ṣāqûn* be taken as coming from *ṣûq I*, "to constrain, press," and not from *ṣûq II*, "to pour." This is much more likely since *ṣrr/ṣûr*, "distress," frequently appears in parallel with *ṣûq I* (Deut. 28:53, 55, 57; Isa. 8:22; 30:6; Jer. 19:9; Zeph. 1:15; Prov. 1:27; Job 15:24). 1QIs[a] adds a further insight when it treats both *laḥaš* and *mûsār* as plurals *(lḥšw msryk)*. This could suggest that "instruction" is the subject of the verb, or that the verb is a Qal passive with an indefinite "they" as subject. Driver's suggestion that *laḥaš* be taken as in Akkadian, to mean "bowed down" (*JTS* 38 [1937] 43), seems to give the final clue. Verse 16b would then read as above, "(in) straits they were humbled (by) your discipline

have rushed into the gap with a considerable array of suggestions, emendations, etc. But the very variety of the possibilities makes one very cautious about endorsing any one with vigor. A new reading is proposed here which, if correct, may solve some of the linguistic problems. It clarifies the explicit sense of the verse, but does not differ from the general sense adopted by most interpreters. That sense is that the hard experiences of Israel's history are seen as chastisements from God for her sin. Far from driving her away from God, they have driven her to him. This interpretation corresponds to v. 17c: Israel's griefs are ultimately to be ascribed to God (41:23, 24; 45:7; Amos 3:6). This understanding, which skips lightly over intermediate causes to get at ultimate causes, surely grows from two convictions: monotheism (nothing happens apart from God) and gracious purpose (it is only the hand which has stricken that can heal). If some cause other than God has brought disaster upon us against his will, then he is helpless to deliver us, as he was helpless to prevent its coming in the first place. Undoubtedly this is a simplistic view, but it is also very logical.

17–18 In these two verses the figure of a woman in labor is used to convey Israel's situation.[43] The various judgments of God have made the people twist and groan.[44] But the one thing which helps a woman through her labor is the expectation that the pain will end in joy—the birth of the child. Not so in this case, says Isaiah. After all the grief and struggle, what has Israel produced? Nothing. It is as though they had given birth to wind. It is frequently suggested that this mood would have been typical of the postexilic returnees, and it certainly was (cf. Mal. 3:14, 15), but it did not first appear then, as indicated by Hezekiah's statement in 37:3. That verse suggests that the events of 710–701 could have also

---

upon them" or "(in) straits your discipline humbled them" (taking *l* on *lāmô* as an accusative indicator). This points the way to solving the problem of the anomolous *pqd* in the first stich. Irwin suggests it be taken as a Pual verb with a dative suffix (*CBQ* 41 [1979] 251–52). In the Pual it usually has the meaning of being deposited some place or imprisoned (cf. Isa. 38:10). That sense fits very well here. (On the dative suffix, see M. Bogaert, "Les Suffixes verbaux non accusatifs dans le sémitique nord-occidental et particulierement en hébreu," *Bib* 45 [1964] 220–247.) The preposition *b* governing *sar* would also extend to *ṣāqûn* (perhaps to be repointed to *ṣᵉqôn;* cf. *BHS*). On the "double-duty preposition" see GKC, § 119hh and Isa. 28:6; 40:19; 48:14. The resulting reading produces excellent parallel sense with a minimum of emendation.

43. Cf. also 13:8; 21:3; 42:14; Hos. 9:14; Mic. 4:10.

44. Note the style of v. 17 where the absence of conjunctions gives an abrupt jerking feeling appropriate to the content.

provided the impetus for the writing of this chapter as well as chs. 24, 25, and 27.

Verse 18b explains what would have made Israel's anguish worthwhile: bringing deliverance into the world. This theme seems to hark back to vv. 9–11, where the judgments of God are to be seen in the earth. The precise meaning of the deliverance is obscured by the ambiguity of *fall* in the last clause. The context suggests this might have to do with giving birth, as in Aramaic (though not elsewhere in Hebrew).[45] If so, then the deliverance is of the widest sort, for the writer expects that his people should have helped the whole world to a sort of rebirth. At the same time, vv. 9–11, and the use of the verb elsewhere, suggest that it means to fall in battle. If so, and I lean in this direction, then Isaiah says that the people have not been able to deliver themselves from oppression in all its forms and demonstrate God's power to the world by striking down the oppressive world power. As the following verse makes plain, the implication is that instead of new life resulting from the struggle, only death has resulted (59:10). This raises the underlying question of the lament: it is fine to believe that God will one day be crowned on Mount Zion and invite all his saints to feast with him in the presence of their enemies, but what about all those saints who have lived and struggled and died in the meantime with no apparent result?

Verse 19 is the answer to that implicit question. It flashes into the prophet's mind as the inspired response to his own musings. As such, it, along with 25:8, represents the highest conception of resurrection in the OT.[46] It asserts that the dead will be revived with shouts of joy to partake in the festivities of God's final triumph. This conviction was to become

45. To "drop" a baby would be appropriate terminology in a society where women gave birth in a kneeling or squatting position. Farmers speak of a cow "dropping" a calf. In Hebrew, the noun *nepel* (from *npl*, "to fall") is used of an abortion or a miscarriage. See also on v. 19.

46. Dan. 12:2 teaches the same truth, while Hos. 6:2 and Ezek. 37:1–14 speak more of a national restoration to life. An evolutionary scheme for the development of Hebrew religion is frequently imposed upon the OT, and passages like this, supposedly representing the peak of the development, are dated very late. Others, attempting to make the passage at least early postexilic, are forced to say that it does not actually refer to personal resurrection (Kissane, Clements, Wildberger, Fohrer, G. W. Anderson, *VTSup* 9 [1963] 126). The problem lies in the evolutionary scheme. The same process was used to date the Psalms: those with "high" theology were necessarily late. But recent studies in their style and diction show considerable similarities with Ugaritic poetry of 1350 B.C. Cf. Dahood, *Psalms*, 3 vols., AB (New York: Doubleday, 1965–1970). This suggests that the development of a theology, particularly a revealed one, ought not to be forced onto the procrustean bed of an over-neat, unilinear theory.

the anchor point of the Christian faith, in the light of Christ's resurrection. Without denying the reality or the goodness of this world (unlike some medieval theology), the NT continually calls persons not to live as though this world is the end. Again and again the appeal is to endure hardship, contradictions, and unanswered questions because of what is laid up for us beyond death (e.g., Rom. 8:18–25; 1 Cor. 15:20–28; Heb. 12:1–2; Rev. 2:7, 10, 11, 17, 26–29; 14:13; etc.).

The task of determining the speaker throughout the verse is not easy, particularly in view of the change in persons in the first line (*your* dead . . . *my* corpses). Presumably these words could have been said by God, the people, or the prophet. The people are the easiest to dismiss in the light of v. 20, where they are directly addressed. It appears that v. 19, like v. 20, is intended as a consolation to the people and an encouragement to their faith. The other two choices are more difficult to decide between. If God is the speaker, then he answers the questions and speaks the imperative to the "dwellers in the dust." This is attractive and logically correct, since, as Young says, only God can command the dead to rise. At the same time, there is no indication of a change of speaker from the previous verses where God was being addressed. Thus, it seems that the prophet remains the speaker. In that case *"your* dead" could refer to God or to the people. If it is to God, it is reminiscent of Ps. 116:15, "Precious in the sight of the Lord is the death of his saints" (cf. also Ps. 97:10; Rev. 14:13). The dead are not abandoned, they still belong to God.[47] This interpretation would be consistent with the MT *"my* corpses" (collective) in which the reference would be to the prophet speaking as a member of the nation.[48] If the people are addressed in *"your* dead," however, then *"my* corpses" makes no sense and needs to be emended to "their."[49]

Awake and shout for joy introduces a note of jubilation and excitement. The previous line talked *about* the dead. Now they are spoken *to*. The change is from theory to fact. If the prophet was speaking for the people to God, he now speaks to the dead in the light of God-given faith. Surely this confidence in God's resurrection power is the logical conclusion of the key points of OT faith: God is life; God is dependable; God's ways bring blessing. If life lived in and for God does not result in blessing, there are only two alternatives: (1) the faith was mistaken and misplaced, or

---

47. One must also consider the possibility that *-kâ* is a dative suffix in the light of vv. 16, 17. This would yield "the dead because of you."

48. Note the chiasm: "shall live your dead, my corpses shall rise."

49. So Targ., *BHS,* and most modern translations. LXX reworks to drop the suffixes altogether. The previous alternatives seem better. It is hard to see how *nᵉḇēlāṯêhem* could have been mistaken for *nᵉḇēlāṯî.* The shorter, harder reading is preferred. Cf. 1QIsᵃ.

(2) the outworking of God's faithfulness is not completed in this life (1 Cor. 15:19). God's faithfulness had been demonstrated often enough in the short run that the second alternative seemed inescapable. The resurrection of Christ confirms that this alternative is not merely wishful thinking, but indeed the capstone of our belief. For Isaiah, who still lived in the hope of Christ, these jubilant commands are a stirring expression of confidence in his God, made all the more stirring against the backdrop of the questions in vv. 16–18.

dwellers in the dust depicts the common understanding of the underworld in the ancient Near East. Not only was it *in* the dust in the sense of being underground, it was also a gray, dusty place (Job 21:26; Ps. 22:16 [Eng. 15]).[50] The conditions of the tomb prevailed everywhere. But death cannot conquer life. For the somber stillness of the grave there is jubilant singing. For the dry, crumbling dust of eternal night, there is the fresh dew of morning (cf. Job 14:7–12). The most the pagans could hope for was to be an unknown part of the vast cycle of life, but the biblical faith proclaims that individuals are important to God and live forever in his memory (Ps. 1:5, 6; Isa. 49:16; Mal. 3:16; Phil. 4:3; Rev. 3:5).

The equation of rain and dew in the OT points to the great importance of *dew* in Canaan during some parts of the year.[51] This importance seems to have given rise to a mythological figure who is one of Baal's maidens: Tly (Dewy?) daughter of Rbb.[52] That she is always accompanied by Pdry daughter of 'Ar (Light?) and 'Arsy (Earth?) daughter of Y'bdr is very suggestive for this passage since both 'ôr(ōt) and 'āreṣ appear here. It seems possible that, as in 27:1, Isaiah is using some of the literary stock

50. The following excerpt from the Akkadian "Descent of Ishtar to the Nether World" illustrates this point of view:
Yea, the daughter of Sin set [her] mind
To the dark house, the abode of Irkal[la],
To the house which none leave who have entered it,
To the road from which there is no way back,
To the house wherein the entrants are bereft of li[ght],
Where dust is their fare and clay their food,
(Where) they see no light, residing in darkness,
(Where) they are clothed like birds, with wings for garments,
(And where) over door and bolt is spread dust.
(lines 3–11; *ANET*, p. 107)
The similarity of lines 4 and 5 to Isa. 26:14 is clear, and this common understanding makes the affirmations of v. 19 the more startling. The descriptions in lines 6–11 would fit the conditions of a tomb and may have derived from that source. The underworld would be seen as one vast tomb.
51. See Gen. 2:5, 6; 27:28, 39; 2 Sam. 1:21; 1 K. 17:1; Zech. 8:12.
52. Cf. *UT*, 51:I:18; IV:56; VI:11; '*nt*, I:24; III:4; pl. vi:IV:4; V:50; *ANET*, p. 131.

of Canaan to make a much more profound statement than Canaan ever could. God's dew will rest upon the dead as he will force earth to give them up to life in his presence forever.[53]

(c) Oracle of salvation (26:20–27:1)

> 20 *Go,*[1] *my people, enter your rooms,*
> *and shut your door behind you.*
> *Hide for a little while*
> *until the indignation has passed by.*
> 21 *For behold, the Lord is coming forth from his place*
> *to punish*[2] *the iniquity of the inhabitants of earth.*
> *The earth will uncover her bloodshed;*[3]
> *she will no longer cover up her murdered.*
> 27:1 *In that day the Lord will punish*
> *with his hard, great, fierce sword*
> *Leviathan the slithering serpent,*
> *Leviathan the twisted serpent;*
> *he will kill the monster which is in the sea.*

These verses are an oracle of salvation in response to the lament and its immediate reply in 26:16–19. The resurrection is not yet; it is still necessary to exercise that confident waiting (26:8), but the outcome is sure. The dead who have suffered at the hands of the city of chaos (24:10; 25:2; 27:10) will be restored to life and their blood avenged. All this is summed up in a concrete way typical of Isaiah by reference to the well-known picture of the defeat of the chaos monster. All that which threatens the divine order (26:7, 8) will be forever destroyed. The verses express the conclusion to the theme of dependency.

20 *Go, my people, enter your rooms* is an expression of that compassion of God which has always made possible an escape from his wrath for those who would avail themselves of it. So Noah escaped the flood, Lot escaped Sodom, and the Hebrew people escaped the death of the firstborn. God does not want any to perish (Matt. 18:14; 2 Pet. 3:9), and anyone who will may find the refuge of his grace. *my people* was a term of special endearment, because it expressed the particular election-love of

---

53. For the life-giving properties of dew, cf. Ps. 133:3 and Prov. 19:12.

1. "Go," *lēk*, has no special significance here. It functions as an auxiliary with "enter," rather like "now" in English: "come on, now."

2. *BHS* recommends deleting *ʿālāyw*, "upon him," on the basis of LXX. However, this is not justified. LXX differs in more points than this, and *pqd* frequently takes its object with *ʿal;* cf. 27:1.

3. Note the plural of "blood," denoting "bloodshed" (cf. Ps. 51:16 [Eng. 14]).

God for Israel (Hos. 1:10, 11). It comes here as a response to the protests that Israel had not bowed down to the foreign overlords. The people have said "We are yours," and God here affirms that truth from his side.

Delitzsch calls special attention to the attitude of prayerful dependence as seen in Ps. 27:5 and 31:21 (Eng. 20) (cf. also 91:4). Israel cannot save herself, but neither need she merely subside into apathy. Instead, protected within the inner chamber while the storm of God's wrath howls outside, she may commit herself to him in the solitude of petition and intercession.[4] The indignation here does not seem to be directed against Israel, as in 10:25, but against Israel's oppressors (30:27; Dan. 11:36; Zeph. 3:8).

21 *the Lord is coming forth* is expressed by a particle of imminence, "he is just about to." This posture of anticipation is typical of the faith of Israel and the Church and is necessary for a correct perception of existence. We live immersed in time and the succession of days often makes the future appear hopelessly far away. But perceptions change. The child for whom the wait from December 1 to 25 was endless becomes the man who looks with astonishment at ten years which seem to have passed in a moment. The Lord *is* about to come, and it is his counting of days which must color ours and not vice versa. With his perspective we will not lose hope, nor let our eyes slip from the supreme objective—Christ-likeness—to the day-to-day round.

to punish is expressed by the verb *pqd*, which conveys the idea of personal visitation. In the end the master will return to set all things right and to balance all accounts. Then the servants to whom the house has been left in trust will receive their just deserts (Mark 13:34, 35; Luke 12:35–48). Again, the personal revelation and intervention of God in the end of all things is the logical conclusion of biblical faith. Of course, there is imagery involved, but interpretation which uses the appeal to imagery to deny the reality being imaged is false interpretation. The Eternal *will* intervene in time.

The result of that intervention is here expressed especially in terms of those unjustly killed. The earth which had received their blood now gives a full accounting,[5] and all the murdered are brought to life. This is in keeping with 26:14. The tables are now fully turned: the killers and the killed are alive forevermore.[6]

---

4. Delitzsch suggests that the feminine form of *hᵉḇî* may be used to stress the element of dependence.

5. Cf. Gen. 4:10; 37:26; Lev. 17:13; Job 16:18; Ps. 9:13 (Eng. 12); Ezek. 24:7–8; Rev. 6:10.

6. As the NT makes plain, the killers are not annihilated but rather "die" forever (Rev. 2:11; 20:6, 14; 21:8).

27:1 This appears to be a case of misplaced chapter division, although commentators are not fully agreed on this point. There seem to be three positions: the one taken here, that 27:1 concludes the larger segments beginning at 26:1; that 26:20 begins a new segment which continues through 27:13; that 27:1 is an independent piece, as indicated by *bayyôm hahû'*, "in that day."[7] The first two positions agree that 27:1 is intended to be taken with 26:20, 21. This seems correct as indicated by the recurrence of *pqd* and the general picture of judgment being concretized. That 26:20–27:1 form the conclusion to the promises begun in 26:1 is argued by the continuation of the idea of dependency and the divine intervention and vindication.

Ever since the discovery of the Babylonian creation epic with its account of Marduk killing the sea monster Tiamat,[8] it has been clear that there was some reflection of a similar account in this and several other biblical references.[9] The initial enthusiasm to make these a direct borrowing of Babylonian ideas could not be sustained, especially after the finds at Ugarit turned up an account of the defeat of Lotan, a sea monster, much nearer home. A similar story has appeared in Hittite literature,[10] so it now seems clear that the myth of the struggle between a high god and a sea/chaos monster was widespread in the ancient Near East and that the biblical writers did not at some point adopt terminology which was formerly unknown to them.[11] That being so, why did they use this terminology at certain points? This is not the place for a lengthy discussion, but suffice it to say that they were not adopting a mythological worldview.[12] The biblical understanding of existence is simply not compatible with such a view.[13] What they were doing was appropriating well-known emotive lan-

7. So, e.g., Plöger, *Theocracy*, p. 71.
8. Cf. *ANET*, pp. 66–68.
9. Cf. Job 3:8; 7:12; Ps. 74:14; 104:26; Isa. 59:1; etc.
10. *ANET*, pp. 125–26; *ANEP*, no. 670.
11. Some representative literature on this subject includes O. Kaiser, *Die Mythische Bedeutung des Meeres*, BZAW 78 (Berlin: de Gruyter, 1962), pp. 74–76; C. H. Gordon, "Leviathan, Symbol of Evil," *Biblical Motifs*, ed. A. Altmann (Cambridge, MA: 1966), pp. 1–9; M. Wakeman, *God's Battle with the Monster* (Leiden: Brill, 1973); A. Heidel, *The Babylonian Genesis* (Chicago: University of Chicago, 1951).
12. For an enlarged discussion see J. Oswalt, "The Myth of the Dragon and Old Testament Faith," *EQ* 49 (1977) 163–172.
13. Recent books whose purpose has been to refute views such as those of G. E. Wright, which are held to be simplistic, are still forced to admit that there is something about biblical faith which sets it off from that of its neighbors. So, e.g., B. Albrektson, *History and the Gods*, ConBOT 1 (Lund: Gleerup, 1966), p. 115; H. W. F. Saggs, *The Encounter with the Divine in Mesopotamia and Israel* (London: Athlone, 1978), pp. 92, 186–87.

guage into which they could put new meaning. So in Ps. 74 it was at the Red Sea, *within* history, that chaos was defeated, while here it is at the end. But the original myth had this event occurring *before* history so that it could be constitutive of continued order. The Hebrews did not need an extraspatial, extratemporal myth for that. They knew a God who was in absolute control. So the language of myth could be bent to new purposes, as here, where Isaiah, in need of strong imagery to cap his vision of God's victory over sin, oppression, and death, seizes on the Leviathan story and makes it say something much more profound than it had ever said before.[14]

Prior to the discovery of the Ugaritic materials a good deal of energy was expended attempting to determine what the three occurrences in this verse (Leviathan, Leviathan, monster . . . in the sea) portended. Most commonly it was believed that they referred to Assyria, Babylonia, and Egypt.[15] However, the way in which Leviathan is identified in the Ugaritic texts now makes it appear that this threefold form was simply a poetic convention in the Canaanite area. Note the similarities: "If you smite Lotan the serpent slant/[16] Destroy the serpent tortuous/[17] Shalyat of the seven heads. . . ."[18]

This verse is saying the same thing then as 24:21–23, although in different words. God is the sole sovereign of the universe, and while evil and destruction now seem to threaten the principles of justice upon which his order is founded, they will not prevail. God will triumph and those who have kept faith with him through dark days will triumph with him. But the true monster which must be destroyed, the one before which God's people find themselves helpless, is not some primordial chaos; it is the monster of moral evil. That, too, God will destroy, and his people may await that day with joy.

(2) The Lord delivers Judah (27:2–13)

(a) The Lord's vineyard (27:2–6)
2 *In that day—a vineyard of wine—sing of it.*

---

14. The book of Job does a similar thing when it makes the terrible Leviathan only a plaything of God (ch. 41).

15. Cf. the Targ., where Egypt, Assyria, and an unspecified nation are expressly stated.

16. *brḥ*, same as Hebrew, here translated "slithering." Albright, *BASOR* 83 (1941) 39, 40, suggests "primordial."

17. *ʿqltn*, same as Hebrew, here translated "twisted."

18. *UT*, p. 178 (67:1:1–3, 27–30; *ANET*, p. 138). Ringgren, *ASTI* 9 (1973) 114, points out that this close similarity favors an earlier date rather than a later one. But Löwenstamm argues against any direct connection (*Eretz-Israel* 9 [1969] 96–101, 136).

3 *I, the Lord, am its keeper;*
    each moment[1] I water it.
Lest someone should harm it,
    I guard it[2] night and day.
4 *I have no wrath.[3]*
    O that there were[4] thorns,[5] briers.
In war I would march against it;
    I would burn them all together.
5 *Unless[6] they lay hold of my stronghold,*
    making peace with me;
    let them make peace with me.[7]
6 *In the coming days,[8] Jacob will take root,[9]*
    Israel will blossom and bud
    and fill the surface of the ground with fruit.

The prophet closes this segment (chs. 24–27) with a collection of materials which both summarizes and illustrates God's sovereignty with respect to

1. The plural *lirgā'îm* used distributively (Delitzsch).
2. *'eṣṣºrennâ,* "I (will) guard it," shows a *hateph qameṣ* where a vocal shewa would be more common (cf. Ps. 119:33). The *hateph* vowel is a partial reduction of the imperfect theme vowel *o* before a heavy accent (cf. Num. 23:25; 35:20; Isa. 62:2; Hos. 10:10; etc.). Cf. GKC, § 60a.
3. Some interpreters find this concept incongruous here and so propose emendations. The LXX has "wall" at approximately this point, which would be Heb. *ḥômâ* instead of *ḥēmâ,* "wrath." However, the general sense of the LXX is quite different and the context here would seem to call for the *presence,* not the *absence,* of a wall. Millar (p. 56 n. 3) reports that Frank Cross has suggested *ḥmr,* "wine," instead of *ḥēmâ.* But this assumes that the vineyard is still producing no wine, an assumption which the context does not support. (Cf. also NEB.)
4. Lit. "who will give me," as an optative expression, cf. GKC, §§ 151a, b.
5. *BHS* suggests adding the conjunction before "briers," as does 1QIs[a]. However, Delitzsch says the asyndesis is a mark of passion. Adding the conjunction creates an easier (and therefore less likely) reading.
6. *'ô,* "or," when followed by the jussive yields the sense of "unless"; lit. "or let them take hold."
7. Young's suggestion that the verb *yaʿaśeh* be taken as a circumstantial is followed here. This makes the repetition of the phrase easier to understand. The fact that the word order is different in the two phrases argues against dittography. Both LXX and Targ. contain similar duplications.
8. MT has *habbā'îm,* "the coming ones." *BHS* suggests *bā' hayyôm wº,* "the day comes and. . . ." Possibly *hayyāmîm bā'îm,* "the days are coming," was omitted by homoioteleuton (cf. Gray). Young has "them that come from Jacob."
9. 1QIs[a] has *yšryš* (Hiphil imperfect) for MT *yašrēš,* "take root" (Hiphil short form imperfect). The other occurrence of this verb in the Hiphil imperfect also shows the *ṣere* (Ps. 80:10 [Eng. 9], a parallel passage). *BHS* suggests an original Piel.

Israel and to the nations. These are vv. 2–6, the Lord's vineyard; vv. 7–11, destruction of the Lord's enemies; vv. 12–13, return from the nations. The connection among these elements is rather loose, the major relationship being that all three tie into the materials of chs. 24–26. So vv. 2–6 and 7, 8 relate to the fears expressed in ch. 26. Verses 9–11 relate to ch. 24; 25:10–12; 26:5, 6. Verses 12 and 13 reflect 25:1–9. All three segments also share the same positive outlook. The result of God's sovereignty will be redemption.

Whether consciously or unconsciously, vv. 2–6 stand over against the picture of the vineyard in 5:1–7. There the vineyard had revealed a fundamentally perverse nature with the result that the farmer had abandoned it to the wild. Here, as there, the vineyard is Israel and the farmer is God. But this picture is on the other side of judgment and depicts a time when the only divine wrath remaining is for those who would threaten Israel's existence. God has not forsaken her utterly. His care for her has never ceased and now flows unimpeded. While the scene is probably eschatological in its fulfillment, it nonetheless expresses a fundamental truth for all times: God's wrath never supersedes his care. Behind the wrath the care continues unabated. It requires only repentance and change to experience it again.

2 From the outset, the correctness of the present text is in question.[10] The abruptness of this verse causes many commentators to suggest that a word or a phrase is lost, perhaps at least yō'mēr, "he will say." This may be the case, but it is not necessary in order to extract sense from the statement. Of considerably more moment is the discussion over ḥmr, "wine."[11] Many manuscripts have ḥmd, "pleasant," in agreement with the Targum, perhaps LXX, and Amos 5:11 (cf. also Isa. 32:12). However, 1QIsᵃ supports the MT and the sense accords very well with ch. 5, where the vineyard's failure to produce wine was its defect. Here, by contrast,

10. The LXX is very different throughout the passage and the Targ. varies considerably in vv. 4–6. P. Lohmann suggests that the Greek translator's Hebrew text may have been so fragmentary that only a few words could be made out. Taking these, the translator wove them into the city motif so common in the previous chapters ("Die selbstandigen lyrischen Abschnitte in Jes. 24:27," ZAW 37 [1917/1918] 37–38, 40–49, cited in Millar, Origin, p. 56). Whether this suggestion be correct or not, it seems some such heroic expedient is necessary to explain the several verbal agreements with MT and yet the wide variance in meaning.

11. Note that BHS diverges from Leningradensis here by reading ḥmd instead of ḥmr. Because of the similarity between the letters d and r in Hebrew and the suitability of either term, the variant was probably unintentional. Kissane reads "a garden enclosed" (Cant. 4:12; 5:12), altering 'annû-lāh to 'enḥālâ.

this is a productive vineyard, a vineyard of *wine* (cf. *kerem zāyiṯ*, Judg. 15:5). It is difficult to ascertain whether the following lines were intended to be the song (see on v. 3). But in any case, the repetition of "song" is worthy of note. Not only do the redeemed sing of God's triumph over the ruthless and their songs (24:9; 25:5; 26:1, 19) but God also sings of his beloved.

3 With the subject first, *I, the Lord, am its keeper* emphasizes who Israel's keeper is. It is not some lesser being, some hireling, but the Lord himself who watches over his own (John 10:11–13). That the Lord continues to speak here in a descriptive way makes it appear that the song is not being continued. In contrast to ch. 5, where the rain and the dew no longer fall on the vineyard, here God waters it moment by moment. The need and the supply are perfectly matched. Furthermore, instead of abandoning Israel to her enemies, God will be her watchman day and night (cf. Ps. 121:4–5; Isa. 5:2; Matt. 21:33).

Lest someone should harm it has been the subject of several suggested emendations, one of the more novel of which was to read *ʿāleyhā*, "upon her," as *ʿālehā*, "her leaf" (Lev. 26:36). This also presupposes that *yipqōḏ* be repointed *yippāqēḏ*. However, since *pqd* frequently takes its object with *ʿal* (cf. 26:21), there seems no reason to change the MT reading. Num. 16:29 would support Niphal, but the traditional translation would remain the same.

4 *I have no wrath* (lit. "wrath there is none to me") expresses in prospect the reality which will be explained more fully in chs. 40ff. God's wrath is propitiated and he is able to look at his people with nothing but fatherly affection. In that day the energy which had once been poured out upon the worthless vineyard will be turned to protecting the vineyard from its enemies. This is the good news of the gospel: God is not angry any more. He has found a way to satisfy his justice (Rom. 3:21–26; 5:8–11).

O that there were thorns, briers. Again, the contrast with ch. 5 is pointed. There the wall is thrown down and the thorns and briers invited in. Here the Lord wishes they were present so he could defend his vineyard from their encroachment. So, many a young suitor has almost wished someone would attack his beloved so that he could defend her. This is the tone here. God's ardor for his bride is still the same and will be on the last day (Eph. 5:25–27; 2 Cor. 11:2).

It has been argued at least since the time of Duhm that these "enemies" were the Samaritans. More recently, Hanson, following Plöger's lead, has argued that they represented an opposing sect within Judaism itself. Both of these arguments suffer from the same defects. There is nothing in the text which suggests that anyone in particular is represented.

Furthermore, these suggestions are the result of hypotheses resting upon hypotheses concerning the date and locus of the text. Of necessity, then, such conclusions must be highly tentative. Other hypotheses yield quite different results.[12]

5 *Unless they lay hold* follows on the statement of God's actions against Israel's enemies in v. 4. God will march against them and destroy them unless they seek refuge in him. Again, God is not committed to a relentless destruction of his enemies. He is more than willing to be reconciled to them. In fact, he will supply the refuge from his own just wrath.[13] The language here is reminiscent of 1 K. 1:50, where Adonijah "laid hold" of the horns of the altar for refuge from Solomon.

6 Since God will be Israel's keeper in the last day, supplying her needs and neutralizing her enemies, she will spread out to cover the whole earth (cf. also 37:31; Hos. 14:5–7). In the light of NT teaching, *Israel* here must include all the children of Abraham, Jew and Gentile alike, those who walk by faith (Rom. 11:22–27; Phil. 2:9–11). On the basis of this verse, as well as vv. 2 and 3 and the general context, it seems very unlikely that NEB is correct in taking vv. 4 and 5 as negatives addressed against Israel.[14] The entire segment (vv. 2–6) is positive as a response to the oracle of salvation in 26:20–27:1.

(b) Cleansing versus destruction (27:7–11)

> 7 *Has he struck him as he struck his striker,*
> *or has he slain like the slaying of his slain ones?*[1]
> 8 *By exact measure you contend with her in sending her away;*
> *he has removed*[2] *with his harsh wind*
> *in the day of the east wind.*

12. So NEB, reading "no wine," makes Israel the enemy.
13. There is no secure stronghold except God. Cf. 17:9, 10; 23:4, 14; 25:4; 30:2, 3.
14. Cf. also Millar, p. 57.
1. Except for the particle *'im*, "or," only two roots are used in the verse. In the first clause it is the root *nkh* from which the three words are derived. In the second, it is *hrg*. The sense of the verse is clear but the exact syntax is difficult. As it stands now, a literal rendering would be: "It is like the smiting of his smiter, he has smitten him, or like the killing of his killed ones, he was slain [Pual]." In the second phrase, "his killed ones" refers to the enemy's slain. An active participle would parallel the first phrase better, and 1QIs[a] appears to give this in *hwrgm*, although a Pual may be intended.
2. This verb lacks an object in MT. A fairly minor change would be to make the final *h* of *hōgâ*, "he removed," consonantal instead of *mater lectionis* (*hāgāh*, "he removed *her*"). So *BHS;* see Driver, *JTS* 38 (1937) 44.

9 *Therefore, in this the iniquity of Jacob is atoned for,*
and (in) this is all the fruit of turning away his sin:
When he makes all altar stones like smashed chalk,
no Asherahs or incense altars[3] will stand.
10 *For a fortified city is left desolate,*
a habitation deserted and abandoned like the wilderness.
There a calf[4] feeds,
there it lies down and strips its branches.
11 *In dryness, its branches are broken;*
women come and make fires with it.
For this is not a people of understanding.
Therefore its Maker will not have compassion on it;
its Shaper will not be gracious to it.

This segment is difficult both textually and interpretatively.[5] The often unaccountable changes in tense, person, and gender all contribute to the difficulty, as do rare vocabulary and intricate phrasings. Thus it is not surprising that many commentators treat it as a composite of two or more unrelated pieces. One of the major questions relating to the unity of the segment has to do with the identification of the city in vv. 10–11. Delitzsch, with many others, takes it to be Jerusalem.[6] This would seem to accord well with v. 11b (cf. 1:3; 42:18–19). Taking this point of view, Delitzsch is able to produce a very unified interpretation: God will, through a carefully controlled judgment, bring Israel to the point where they can be restored to their land. However, the focus of the chapter is upon the defeat of Israel's enemies, so this has caused many to look for the "enemy within"—Samaria.[7] The references to Asherahs and incense altars are reminiscent of 17:8, which is frequently taken to refer to Ephraim (but see above on those verses). But Duhm's proposal was tied to the destruction of Samaria by John Hyrcanus in 108 B.C., an impossibility now in light of the earlier date of the Qumran Isaiah scrolls. Contemporary revivals of this identification are based upon the theory that apocalyptic grew up in

3. On Asherahs and incense altars, see 17:8; also Lev. 26:30; Ezek. 6:6; 2 Chr. 14:4; 34:4, 7.

4. The use of "calf" rather than cattle or flocks is suggestive here. Note that it is used as a diminutive to mock bull worship elsewhere (Exod. 32:4; 1 K. 12:28; etc.). Perhaps the prophet is saying that because the people of the world worship "calves," real calves will graze on their cities.

5. Millar, *Origins,* p. 58, simply omits it as too questionable for analysis.

6. See Duhm, Rudolph, Fohrer, Fischer, Skinner, Young, et al.

7. This seems to be following Duhm's lead from other passages in chs. 24–27, although he does not take that position here. So Marti, Clements, Wildberger, Vermeylen, Plöger, pp. 74–75.

part out of the internecine struggles within Judaism—a theory lent credence by the Qumran materials, but very difficult to establish for an earlier
period. Furthermore, it is difficult to arrive at a single subject for the
passage. This has resulted in a tendency to split the passage into two
sections, vv. 7–9 and vv. 10–11.

A third alternative takes the city here to be the same as in 24:10–12;
25:2–3; 26:5, that is, the symbol of world might arrayed against God.[8]
This view has the advantage of being consistent with the entire section and
it also maintains the thrust of ch. 27 in depicting God's victory over Israel's
enemies. It does mean that v. 11b must be applied to the world at large
(cf. 44:18; Ps. 9:14–16 [Eng. 15–17]; 74:18–23; 86:9). If this interpretation is correct, the flow of thought is as follows: Israel *may* take root
(v. 6) because the blow which fell upon her was not fatal, whereas that
which will fall upon her enemies will be. The chastisement of Jacob sought
purification and so was tempered. That of her enemies will be without
compassion (cf. Jer. 10:24–25). The result will be that these nations will
no longer be able to hold captive a purified Israel (vv. 12–13; cf. 11:10–16;
35:8–10).[9] On balance this third alternative seems most likely, but the
possibility that Jerusalem is intended cannot be ruled out.

7 If Israel feels unfairly treated by God and wonders how the
prophecy of v. 6 could ever come true, she is invited to compare herself
to her enemies, there to discover that they have ultimately suffered worse
than she. That this has happened is evident if one looks at Nineveh and
Babylon today. The horrible slaughters which have taken place in and
around Jerusalem have been multiplied in those places. God's instruments
of judgment are not exempt from judgment themselves, and if they are
unrighteous, their punishment is the more severe (10:5–19; 33:1; 47:5–9).

8 *By exact measure* occurs only here and is a subject of debate.[10]
If this rendering is correct, then the sense is that God has carefully measured out the judgment of the Exile so that it will not destroy the people

8. See Dillmann, Procksch, Alexander, Feldmann, Gray, Kissane, Kaiser,
etc.

9. Note that chs. 34 and 35 use this same alternation: restoration of the
purified following the logical result of the nations' pride.

10. With the exception of the LXX, all the versions have some form of
"measure." In this light, the usual explanation of $b^e sa'ss^e'â$ is that it is a contraction
of $bis'â s^e'â$, "by measure, measure." LXX has "fighting and reproaching he will
send them forth." Given the general looseness of the LXX in difficult passages in
this section, one is not justified in following it against the other versions (contra
NIV).

but bring them to purification. The punishment is precisely fitted to the crime.

in sending her away is regarded by *BHS* (see also Clements) as a possible explanatory gloss on the preceding difficult word. However, if this is the case it must have entered the text very early, because all the versional evidence attests its presence. The sudden appearance of the feminine is somewhat troublesome since masculine suffixes appear in the previous verse and since Israel and Jacob are masculine. Duhm, Cheyne, Marti, Skinner, etc., take this verse to have been an original gloss on v. 10 ("city" being fem.) that somehow got displaced here. While the content of v. 8 would fit v. 10 well enough, it is very difficult to imagine how v. 8 could have gotten into its present place if that was its origin. A suggestion which demands less reconstruction of the text[11] is based on the recognition that *šlḥ*, "send away," sometimes has to do with divorce (Deut. 22:19; Isa. 50:1; etc.).[12] That being so, it seems possible that the changed image demanded the changed gender.

in the day of the east wind. Despite the promise that God's contention with his people would be of a more measured sort than that meted out upon her destroyers, there is no denying her punishment would be severe. Like the searing wind roaring out of the east, her fate would come upon her and sweep her away.[13]

9 This verse tells why Israel's punishment was not on the same order as that of her enemies. Hers was for the purpose of discipline and purification (54:6–8; Heb. 12:11). Though it would be wrong to build a whole theology of atonement upon this one verse, there are some interesting pointers here. First, there is a sense in which repentance and works of righteousness cover past sin. When the idol altars are smashed, the former works are no longer remembered against us. But it is also true that a new Israel could be born from the ashes on the altar (40:1–2). Individuals thus cannot atone for themselves. Here is where God's grace in Christ comes into play. He has suffered and we must repent, and in the two together our iniquity is covered.

(in) this is all the fruit is a difficult phrase to interpret exactly.[14] But it appears to be a parallel thought to the previous one (atoning for iniquity

11. Cf. NEB.
12. So Young, etc.
13. On the destructive nature of the east wind, see Gen. 41:6; Job 27:21; Ps. 48:8 (Eng. 7); Jer. 18:17; Ezek. 27:26; Hos. 13:15.
14. NEB omits. Cf. *BHS*. The "(in)" represents the preposition of the previous phrase doing double duty. Cf. Williams, *Syntax*, § 238.

and turning away sin are parallel ideas). This being so, the fruit must be both cause and result of the sin's removal.[15] On the one hand, smashing the idols is necessary if forgiveness is to be received; on the other hand, the announcement of forgiveness supplies the motivation to do the smashing (44:1–5; 57:17–19; 59:15b–20; Col. 3:1–17). As Gray says, he is glad that such a significant doctrine is not dependent upon this one obscure verse, but given the appearance of that truth in other parts of Scripture, it does not appear to be misinterpretation to apply it here.

10, 11 If it is correct to take the city here as the symbol of Judah's oppressors (see above on vv. 7–11), then the thought continues the idea of redemption.[16] When Israel's idols are broken down, then God's hand will be revealed against her enemies, who are in fact more idolatrous than she (45:20; 46:1–2; 47:5–9). The result will be complete desolation (13:19–22; 34:8–17), as that once mighty city becomes a pasture field (v. 10), or a once-spreading tree whose limbs are now stripped and dead (vv. 10b, 11a; cf. Ezek. 31; Dan. 4:13–26). For the OT writers, the true mark of human stupidity is idolatry, which is the result of our attempt to usurp the place of God (44:18–19; 45:20; 47:10–11; Ps. 53:2, 5 [Eng. 1, 4]; 82:5; cf. also Rom. 1:19–23). Since the idol makers have falsified the identity of the One who made them, he cannot show them his grace. But to the extent that the Israelites retained an awareness of God's sole creatorship and Lordship of the world (26:13), there is a spark of understanding that God's grace will be able to blow into a flame (Ezra 9:6–15).

(c) Restoration (27:12–13)

> 12 *It shall be in that day that the Lord will flail from the flowing streams[1] of the Euphrates to the wadi of Egypt, and you will be gathered one by one, O sons of Israel.*
>
> 13 *It will come to pass in that day that a great trumpet will be blown and the dead of the land of Assyria will come, and the exiles in the land of Egypt, and they will worship the Lord on the holy mountain in Jerusalem.*

15. So Cheyne.

16. *kî,* "for," at the beginning of v. 10, shows a causal relationship with the previous verse. There are two possibilities depending on which alternative one takes: (Jerusalem) the idols are broken *because* the city is desolated; (world) redemption is possible *because* the enemy city is destroyed.

1. The word "flowing streams" is spelled exactly the same as "ears of grain" (*šibbōleṭ*). It must be the former here because if it were "from the ears of the Euphrates unto the . . .," the "from" is misplaced. At the same time, one cannot help but feel that the poet would be very conscious of the fillip which this semi-pun gives to the thought.

These verses provide a fitting climax to chs. 24–27 with their emphasis upon God's sovereignty over the nations and his intention to restore his people from the nations. In this respect this is the second of three such passages. The others are 11:12–16 and 35:1–10. Each of these occurs at the end of a major segment. This fact suggests something about the structure of the book. As pointed out in the comments on ch. 11, chs. 7–12 make the point that if you trust in the nations, the nations will destroy you. Nonetheless, God will not leave his people in destruction; he intends to deliver them from the nations. But this raises the immediate question: *Can he deliver them from the nations?* Chs. 13–27 answer that question with a resounding affirmative. They do so first in a particularizing way, showing that all nations, including Israel, are under God's judgment (chs. 13–23). Then chs. 24–27 make the same point in a more generalized way, asserting that God is the main actor in the drama of human history. These things being so, God can deliver his people, and the promise is reaffirmed in these two closing verses.

12 God promises that there will be a great harvest at the end of time and that each one of his righteous ones will be gathered in.[2] The term used is not the normal one for "thresh" (so RSV, NIV), but is *ḥbṭ*, "to beat off." When used of grain, it seems to speak of using a flail on small amounts of material (Judg. 6:11, Gideon in the wine press; Ruth 2:17, Ruth with what she had gleaned). The term seems to fit better with harvesting of olives, where sticks are used to shake the ripe olives from the trees (Deut. 24:20; cf. also Isa. 17:6). The mention of gathering *one by one* could refer to the people as only a few scattered heads of grain (thus explaining the flailing), but again it seems to accord better with picking up olives. The sequence of beating first, then gathering also suggests olives. In any case, the picture of God gathering each of the scattered ones individually is a very tender one (cf. 49:14–16).

The region from the Euphrates to the Wadi el-Arish (about 50 miles southwest of Gaza) is the ideal homeland of Israel (Gen. 15:18; Exod. 23:31; Deut. 1:7; Josh. 1:4). Those who take the two verses as being separate from one another (because of v. 13 repeating "in that day") argue that the reference is to those who have died in the land.[3] However, Young, believing that the two verses are synonymous, argues cogently that the

2. Note the similar theme in the hymn "Come, Ye Thankful People, Come."

3. So also Delitzsch, who would not separate the verses. Modern commentators' use of "in that day" to separate elements seems overdone since it lacks any means of verification. That it sometimes does serve to separate is clear enough. That it *always* does is another matter.

reference is to the direction from which the returnees will be gathered—across the Euphrates from Assyria and across the Wadi el-Arish from Egypt.

13 *a great trumpet,* like the raising of an ensign, is a sign of the final ingathering. It is not necessarily any more literal than the ensign; it is merely an evocative figure.[4] But literal or figurative there will come a moment in the end of time when God will call his own to him. The term *dead* surely suggests that the resurrection is intended here. This would be in keeping with 25:8; 26:14, 19. But the parallel with "exiles in . . . Egypt" suggests that the reference ought not to be restricted in that way.[5] This seems to be confirmed by the fact that *'ābad* is used to convey "lost" in Jer. 50:6 and Ezek. 34:4–6, 12–16. The statement, then, seems to refer more broadly to restoration with all that that means. One of the things it means is that the return is not merely a physical one. This prophecy can hardly be fulfilled merely by there being Jews living in Jerusalem. Rather, God's people will be fully restored when they worship him on the holy mountain (2:2–4; 24:23; 25:6, 10). Perhaps this must await the final consummation (65:17–25; 66:22–23; Rev. 21:2–3), but it is a day devoutly to be hoped for.

3. THE FOLLY OF TRUSTING THE NATIONS (28:1–33:24)

a. WOE TO THE DRUNKEN RULERS (28:1–29:24)

(1) Ephraim (28:1–13)

1 *Woe to the proud garland of the drunkards of Ephraim,*
   the fading[1] blossom, his glorious beauty,

4. Cf. Exod. 19:16, 19; 2 Sam. 6:15; Ps. 47:6 (Eng. 5); 81:4 (Eng. 3); Isa. 18:3; Joel 2:15; Zech. 9:14. Cf. also Matt. 24:31; 1 Cor. 15:52; 1 Thess. 4:16; Rev. 10:7; 11:15.
5. Dahood suggests that *bammiṣrāyim* be read as "from Egypt," a plausible reading in the light of the parallel "from Assyria" ("Three Biblical Texts," *JNSL* 2 [1972] 20). The same suggestion was made earlier by F. C. Fensham, "The Preposition *b* in Isaiah 27:13," *EvQ* 29 (1957) 157–58.
1. Driver reinterprets the entire passage (28:1–22) in order to make it solely a diatribe against drunkenness; see " 'Another Little Drink'—Isaiah 28:1–22," in *Words and Meanings,* ed. P. R. Ackroyd and B. Lindars, Festschrift D. W. Thomas (Cambridge: Cambridge University, 1968), pp. 47–67. Here he takes *nbl* to mean "young shoot" (not "fading") and deletes references to the valley. For a general critique see G. Rice, "Isa. 28:1–22 and the New English Bible," *JRT* 30 (1973/1974) 13–17. Cf. also J. Barr's comments about this kind of approach in *Comparative Philology and the Text of the Old Testament* (Oxford: Oxford University, 1968), esp. pp. 116–121.

which is on the head of the lush valley—
[on the head] of those smitten by wine.

2 *Behold, the Sovereign has one who is strong and fierce,*
like a hailstorm, a destroying tempest,
like a cloudburst, mighty and overflowing,
he will make it lie on the earth with his hand.[2]

3 *The proud garland of the drunkards of Ephraim*
will be trampled[3] underfoot.

4 *The fading blossom, his glorious beauty,*
which is on the head of the lush valley,
will be like an early fig[4]
which, when someone sees it,[5] he gulps it down as soon as he
lays his hand on it.

5 *In that day[6] the Lord of Hosts will be a garland of beauty,*
a lovely coronet to the remnant of his people,

6 *A spirit of judgment to[7] the one who sits in judgment,*
strength to those who turn back war at the gate.

7 *And also these stagger with wine;*
with beer they wander about:
priests and prophets stagger with beer,
they are swallowed up by wine,[8]
they wander about from beer.

2. "hand" here can be understood as an abstraction: "power," or in a more literal way as a giant knocking things down with his fist. The use of "foot" in v. 3 suggests the literal imagery.

3. As the MT has it *terāmasnâ* is a Niphal 3rd fem. plural. Probably "crown . . . of the drunkards" is understood as a collective (cf. Exod. 1:10; Judg. 7:21; 1 Sam. 12:21).

4. MT appears to have "its [fem.] fig," which Delitzsch takes as referring to the valley. However, all other commentators agree that the *mappiq* does not necessarily signify that the *he* must be a possessive pronoun.

5. Lit. "the seer sees it," which seems awkward, and some emend *yir'eh*, "he sees," to *yēʾerê*, "he plucks." (So Clements, following Driver.) The MT is not impossible, however.

6. Those who see "in that day" as an eschatological tagline are inclined to treat these two verses as being of a later date than 1–4, added by someone who wished to give a positive note to the previous negative statements. However, there is as good a reason to take it as Isaianic, for the contrasting of polar opposites is a distinctive feature of the book (cf. chs. 1–5; 8:9–9:6 [Eng. 9:7]; 24:10–16, etc.), and if this does not stem from the prophet himself, it is difficult to understand where this stylistic feature had its origin.

7. It seems possible that the "to" on "the one who sits" functions as a double duty prefix and also applies to "the one who turns back" (so Schoors and Young). Driver denies this and says "to" must be inserted (*Words and Meanings*, p. 50).

8. Lit. "swallowed from wine" (*min* of means; Williams, *Syntax*, § 320).

They stagger in a vision;[9]
   they reel in[10] *a decision.*
8 *Indeed, the tables are covered with filthy vomit;*
   there is no place.[11]
9 *"Whom shall he teach knowledge;*
   whom shall he make to understand a message?
Those weaned from milk?[12]
   Those removed from the breast?
10 *For it is command upon command,*
   command upon command,
standard upon standard,
   standard upon standard,
a little there,
   a little there."
11 *Indeed, with mocking lip and foreign tongue*
   he will speak to this people,
12 *to whom*[13] *he said,*
   "This is rest, give rest to the faint,
this is repose,"
   but they would not.[14]
13 *So the word of the Lord will be to them*
   command upon command,
      command upon command,
   standard upon standard,

9. Note that *rō'eh* may denote the thing seen, as here, as well as the one who sees. The verbs here are perfects, which perhaps indicate habitual action.

10. "decision" lacks "in." Perhaps an accusative of specification.

11. The present translation follows the punctuation of the MT (cf. AV). Most modern translations (RSV, NEB, NIV, CBAT) separate "filth" from "vomit" and put it in the final phrase, "filth without place." However, the MT serves to bring the long repetitive lines of vv. 7–8a to a very sudden and abrupt close. That abruptness may have been intentional.

12. The form of "weanlings from milk" is unusual in that the preposition seems to follow a noun in construct (GKC, § 130a). Hummel, *JBL* 76 (1957) 98, suggests that the *m* was actually an enclitic inserted between the two words in construct.

13. *'ᵃšer*, with which the line opens, may be interpreted in several ways. Normally, it would be the relative pronoun "which." As such, it could be subjective ("God *who* spoke to them") or objective ("the people *to whom* he spoke"). The context seems to favor the latter. But Kissane points out that it could also mean "whereas" and cites 7:16. Delitzsch also adds Judg. 9:17; Jer. 16:3; 48:8; Ps. 144:12.

14. "not willing" shows a final *aleph* which is not part of the normal form (*'ābû'*). *hālᵉkû'*, "they went" (Josh. 10:24), exhibits a similar anomaly. Since there is no morphological explanation, it was probably only a matter of pronunciation.

standard upon standard,
a little there,
a little there,
so that they will go and stumble back,
and be crushed, and ensnared, and captured.

In chs. 28–33 Isaiah continues his treatment, begun in ch. 7, of the foolishness of trusting the nations instead of the Lord. He returns to a particularizing mode to do so. That is, he deals with the specific political situation in Judah, rather than with the worldwide picture. The same approach was seen in chs. 13–27 where particular situations were addressed (chs. 13–23) before a general truth was drawn (chs. 24–27). There the purpose was to show God's lordship over the nations. Here the focus is upon Judah's choice to trust him or not. The time seems to be somewhat later than in chs. 7–12. Now the threat which Isaiah had predicted there has come to pass. The Assyria with which Ahaz had allied himself is first finishing up with Samaria (28:1–13) and then turning its unwanted attentions on Judah (29:7–8). The flood which Isaiah had foretold (8:6, 8) is about to burst full force against the southern kingdom.

In the intervening years between Samaria's fall (721 B.C.) and Sennacherib's attack on Jerusalem (701 B.C.), it appears that Judah's foreign-policy makers turned more and more toward alliance with Egypt (30:3; 31:1). To Isaiah, this alliance was just as stupid as the earlier one with Assyria had been. Egypt might not someday seek to devour Judah, but any help she could give was distinctly unreliable (30:3–7; 31:3; cf. 20:1–6). To the prophet, the thought that someone would commit himself to fickle Egypt instead of to God who had proven himself again and again was simply incredible (30:15–33). It was a course of action which could only be proposed by a cynical, faithless leadership drunk on its own power and privilege (28:7–8; 29:15–16; 30:1; cf. also 1:23; 7:13; 9:14–16; 19:11–15), blind to the necessarily destructive results of such a course. Thus, this section is marked by the repetition of the funeral cries of "Woe!" (28:1; 29:1, 15; 30:1; 31:1; 33:1).[15] If Judah persists in this way there is only a funeral ahead for her as there is for Ephraim. Yet, she need not persist; there is an alternative. She may turn from blind, drunk politicians to the King whose character had been impressed upon Isaiah from the day of his calling (29:17–24; 30:18–33).

15. Cf. E. Gerstenberger, "The Woe Oracles of the Prophets," *JBL* 81 (1962) 249–263, for the suggestion that the "woe" form was originally a wisdom form parallel to the beatitude and adapted by the prophets.

The structure of the segment appears to be tripartite.[16] First, chs. 28 and 29 paint the picture for us: foolish leaders, a multitude of enemies, the false counsel that something must be done at once, humanly speaking, for there is no hope in God. Second, chs. 30 and 31 depict the proposed solution: dependence on Egypt and the folly of that solution. Chs. 32 and 33 then give the true solution: the revelation of the King and his presence in their midst.

Many commentators argue that ch. 33 should be separated from chs. 28–32 and joined with 34 and 35. However, the main reason for this is the supposed apocalyptic flavor to the language of ch. 33. But this is hardly conclusive. As noted above on chs. 24–27, the definition of apocalyptic is notoriously slippery. Surely every time a prophet speaks of salvation in expansive terms does not qualify as apocalyptic. On other grounds, there is good reason to connect this chapter with 28–32 and separate it from 34–35. First of all, 34 and 35 form a unit in themselves on the principle of contrast: 34 speaks of the desert which will result from trusting the nations, and 35 of the garden which will result from trusting God. As such they offer the conclusion to 13–33 in the broadest terms. Ch. 33 is not doing the same things. Above all, the concepts are those of 28–32: "woe" (33:1; 28:1, etc.); "wait" (33:2; 30:18); the king (33:17, 22; 32:1); foreign speech (33:19; 28:11); "apocalyptic" versions of salvation (33:3–6, 13–16; 29:17–24; 30:19–33). All of these argue forcefully that ch. 33 is in fact a conclusion to the themes of 28–32. As such it provides a much more convincing close to the segment than ch. 32 alone could do. If there are those who wish to say that the chapter was written at a later date for inclusion here, that may be. But it will not do to use "large" language to deny structural integrity.

As noted above, 28:1–29:24 are alive with scorn as the prophet depicts the situation in Judah and among its leaders. He begins by denouncing the leaders of the northern kingdom and predicting their doom (28:1–3), which was probably beginning to become apparent to even the most unperceptive. But then he destroys any Judean smugness which might have been arising by coming to his main point: the Judean leaders are just like their counterparts in Samaria and thus may expect the same fate. The shared characteristics are: indulgence manifested in drunkenness, lack of understanding, and the need to be taught as little children (cf. Hos. 7:5; Amos 4:1; 6:4–6). But the leaders in Jerusalem are accused of something

---

16. Skinner proposes that there may be no structure but just a diverse collection of "woes" which happen to concern some of the same events. This seems to settle for too little.

more severe than those in Samaria: a cynical mocking spirit which believes nothing and trusts no one. So also Ezekiel was to say that Judah's sin was worse than Samaria's (23:11–12). To whom much is given, much is required.

The position taken here is that all of 28:1–13 refers to Ephraim.[17] However, it is not possible to be dogmatic in this assertion. Although Jerusalem is not mentioned until v. 14, and this is a chief reason for referring the previous verses to the North, it must still be admitted that the address might shift to Judah as early as v. 7, a position many commentators take. However, the statement that "*also*" the prophet and priests are drunken suggests that it is the prophets and priests of the North being referred to. If this interpretation is correct, then the thought of the segment is causal: because the leaders of Samaria are drunken and senseless, the people are not able to understand the elemental truths of life. Therefore, God must teach them through the hard school of experience.

1 As the MT has it, this verse has a double meaning. On the one hand, it speaks of garlands of flowers worn on the heads of drunken partygoers. They had looked so attractive at first, but as the night wears on, neither flowers nor wearers look attractive any more. But there is another garland, one set at the head of a fertile valley. This must refer to Samaria, whose walls crowned a lovely hill in the middle of a rich valley leading out toward the coast.[18] Like the faded garland, Samaria's time of loveliness is gone. The Assyrians are at the gates and it is only a matter of time until the end.

Virtually all commentators take the references to Samaria (and the absence of any mention of Damascus) as evidence that this oracle was delivered first sometime between the fall of Damascus in 732 and the fall of Samaria in 721.[19] But its major function in the present setting seems to be for purposes of comparison. The major address is to Jerusalem, and Samaria is included to show the fate of Jerusalem. Thus, Ackroyd sees it here as an example of the reuse of older materials in a later setting (705–700).[20] This is entirely possible; however, it is also possible that the pronouncements against Jerusalem in chs. 28 and 29 were delivered at the same time as the denunciation of Samaria.

the head of the lush valley . . . of those smitten by wine has been

17. See also Wright.

18. For pictures of Samaria's setting see L. Grollenberg, *Atlas of the Bible* (London/New York: Nelson, 1976), pp. 78–79.

19. Kaiser is conspicuously alone in saying that it refers to the Samaria of Hellenistic times.

20. *ASTI* 1 (1962) 14–15.

troublesome for a long time and several solutions have been proposed. An ancient proposal is that *gy'*, "valley," was originally *g'y*, "proud," thus giving "on the heads of the proud fat ones, those overcome by wine."[21] Another alternative is to delete the first phrase as a gloss drawn from v. 4.[22] If one elects to remain with the MT, then *šᵉmānîm* appears to be an absolute governing a genitive, something which is highly unusual in the Semitic system.[23] H. D. Hummel proposes that the original was the plural construct *šᵉmānê* plus an enclitic *m*.[24] Another alternative would be the one elected here: that "head" is the governing noun for two construct phrases, each expressing one aspect of the double meaning: (1) "head of the lush valley," (2) "head of those overcome by wine."[25] This would give the double entendre mentioned above: both the drunkards and the rich valley wear faded garlands.

2 One of the characteristics of the Hebrew people seems to have been their ability to ignore the signs of the times (cf. ch. 22). They apparently adopted the view that they would not worry about tomorrow until it came and in the meantime would eat, drink, and play themselves into forgetfulness.[26] Thus Isaiah was not alone when he sought, as here, to get people to take corrective action by depicting the horrors about to fall on them (Jer. 25:32-38; Ezek. 24:6-14; Amos 3:9-15). Like Jonah, these prophets knew that their words need not come true if the people would repent and change (John 4:1-2). But they also knew that unheeding continuance would be the guarantee of the certainty of the visions they foresaw. So here Isaiah draws upon all his verbal powers to try to alert his people to their danger. The one who is coming (Assyria) is incredibly powerful and violent. He will burst upon them like a hailstorm, stripping the plants of their leaves, and the following downpour washing away even the ravaged stalks.[27] Everything will be flattened under the oppressor's hand.

21. Cf. JPSV. This reading is also supported by 1QIs[a].
22. So *BHS*, Kissane, etc.
23. Delitzsch lists the following as other examples of this phenomenon: 32:13; 63:11; Deut. 5:8; Josh. 8:11. Young adds Ezek. 6:11; 45:16; 46:19; 2 Chr. 15:8. Cf. also *UT*, 13:101.
24. H. D. Hummel, "Enclitic *mem* . . . ," *JBL* 76 (1957) 98.
25. For a single *nomen regens* governing two phrases, cf. GKC, § 128a, where he cites Gen. 14:19; Num. 20:5; 31:54; 1 Sam. 23:7; 2 Sam. 19:6; Isa. 22:5; Ps. 5:8 (Eng. 7); 8:4 (Eng. 3).
26. Clements suggests that the revelry here may have been over the breaking of the vassal relation with Assyria, the act which precipitated the final attack by Assyria (2 K. 17:4-6).
27. See also 8:7; 17:12; Ps. 18:14-16 (Eng. 13-15).

3, 4 After the storm has swept over the party nothing will be left but a few bedraggled garlands trampled in the mud. Again, the double imagery is present, for Samaria is also intended, as v. 4 makes plain. (There would be little reason to emphasize devouring a garland, but much reason to speak of devouring a city.) The city will be eaten up on sight, like an early fig. These fruits, appearing in June well before the main harvest in September and October, were large and sweet. Thus they were usually eaten at once (Hos. 9:10; Mic. 7:1; Nah. 3:12; Jer. 24:2). Samaria will be like that, says the prophet. And although the actual siege took three years, it was but an instant in the long span of time. All the pride of Ephraim, which had been so long in building, would be toppled very quickly unless the drunkards who were her leaders very quickly came to their senses.

5, 6 Isaiah here depicts what could have been, if the right crown had been put in place. Nevertheless, despite the present failure, God will achieve his ultimate purpose. This approach is similar to that of 4:2–6, where the true appears after the false has been done away with. When all the false garlands have been trampled in the mud, then the real one can appear. Indulgence must lose its appeal as more and more exotic forms are sought; the glories of the world's Samarias become so quickly tarnished by greed and oppression, but God remains. His beauty will not fade nor can he be defeated. The issue for us is whether we will remain. In every age there is a remnant[28] which is a part of that great final one. They are characterized by the ability to see through the tinsel of life, beyond the trappings of appearances, to those truths which are eternal, which will prevail.

But in what sense will God be the crown of his people? He will be the true king as depicted in 11:1–9. Instead of the drunken, craven rulers Israel and Judah had come to expect, he will bring a new spirit to the throne. In this sense these two verses are a prelude to the direction in which the larger section will develop. Chs. 28–31 depict the folly of the human leadership, but there is also a minor theme of God's faithfulness (29:17–24; 30:18–33). But finally this minor theme breaks through in chs. 32 and 33 to become the climax of the movement. God is our king!

The use of the term *spirit* here is instructive as regards the other occurrences in the book (50 times), for it implies both a changed atmo-

28. The appearance of "remnant" here is a further indication of Isaianic authorship (see above), for this is esp. characteristic of Isaiah's teaching (7:3; 10:19, 20, 21, 22; 11:11, 16; 14:22; 15:9; 16:14; 17:3; 21:17; 37:31, 32; 46:3). Cf. G. Hasel, *The Remnant*, pp. 301–309.

sphere and a new empowerment. Especially from the descriptions in Jeremiah, it is clear that the kings frequently lacked the nerve to stand up to the vested interests of injustice or to inspire those who faced the enemy (Jer. 38:5; 39:4; Isa. 19:3, 4, 14; 29:10, 24). Where God and his character are lifted up, there is a whole new spirit about the enterprise (4:4; 11:2, 3; 30:1; 37:7; 54:6; 57:15; 65:14): we may dare to be just, because he is just (Deut. 17:8–12; 2 Chr. 19:5–8); we may fight with courage because God's side will prevail, whether in our life or in our death. But there is also a meaning other than simply a changed atmosphere. There is divine empowerment. Ultimately, the human spirit is not able to do what it must. There must be an infusion of the divine spirit if life is to replace death, if victory is to come rather than defeat (32:14; 44:3, 5; 59:21; 61:1).

7–13 This segment continues the thought of vv. 1–6 by making the accusations more specific. Not only are the rulers drunken and foolish, but the religious leaders, the priests and the prophets, upon whom the nation depends for divine guidance, are in the same condition. Most commentators consider that the focus has shifted here from Ephraim to Judah, apparently because vv. 9 and 10 are taken to have come from Isaiah's own experience. However, there is no unambiguous indication of such a shift, while the "also these" of v. 7 seems to indicate an additional group rather than a different one.[29] Even if vv. 9 and 10 arose out of Isaiah's experience, it is entirely possible for him to have made a broader application of it. But it is also possible that he is reporting a generalized experience which all the prophets underwent in one way or another.[30] The debauched leaders mock the prophet's apparent repetitive simplicity, but he turns their own words back upon them to depict their fate. The atmosphere of the segment is grimly realistic. There is no more hardened nor cynical person in the world than a religious leader who has seared his conscience. For them, tender appeals which would move anyone else become sources of amusement. They have learned how to debunk everything and to believe nothing (Heb. 10:26–31), all the while speaking loftily of matters of the spirit (Jas. 3:13–18).

Those who take this segment to refer to Judah are forced to see at least v. 7a as a transitional line introduced to link the two originally unrelated statements. Some regard this as the work of the prophet; others as that of a much later redactor. Neither is necessary if vv. 1–13 are under-

29. The appearance of vv. 5 and 6 between the two indictments would be for the purpose of concluding the treatment of "garlands" false and true before moving on.
30. Jer. 14:14; 20:1–6; 23:9–40; 26:8–24; Hos. 4:1–6; Amos 5:10; 7:10–17; Mic. 2:6; 3:5–8; Mal. 1:6–7; 2:1–9; Ezek. 20:49.

stood as a unit. Kaiser, with others, takes vv. 12, 13 also to be the work
of redactors who feel it necessary to show why the disaster of 587 took
place. However, as Westermann shows, the entire segment, vv. 7–13,
takes the form of an oracle of judgment: 7–10 give the reason for judgment; 11, 12 include the messenger form; 13 is the announcement of
judgment.[31] This analysis constitutes a strong argument for the integrity
of the passage as it now stands.

7–8 A sense of horror is in the prophet's voice as he relates the
fact that the rot has reached even to the religious leadership. From the
beginning of Hebrew history the importance of these leaders had been
recognized and unusual steps had been taken to protect them from temptation (Lev. 10:8–10; 21:7–9; etc.). If the spring is defiled, how can good
water come from it? Yet that kind of defilement had happened soon enough
(1 Sam. 2:12–17, 22).

Some take it that the debauchery described here is in conjunction
with the worship. While this certainly may have been so, and v. 7d might
be urged in support of that idea, it is not defiled worship that is being
attacked so much as it is the overall blindness and stupidity which the
unrestrained indulgence produced.[32] The repetitive language (stagger-wine,
wander-beer, stagger-beer, swallowed up-wine, wander-beer, stagger-reel)
seems to imitate the stumblings and gigglings of the drunk.

swallowed up by wine introduces an ironic twist in the midst of the
repetition. The self-indulgent always imagine they can control their pas-
sions: it is they who swallow the wine. But it is a law of human nature
that unrestrained passion soon rules the person in its unrelenting demand
for greater satisfaction. Wine has now swallowed its drinkers.

They stagger in a vision, they reel in a decision expresses the fact
that their drunkenness was pervading even their official functions. These
functions were of critical importance in the last days before Samaria's fall.
The seers could show the people the horrifying future with the faint hope
of provoking them to repentance, or they could satisfy their own lusts and
tell the people pleasant lies they wished to hear (30:10; 2 Sam. 15:27;
2 Chr. 16:7, 10; Amos 7:12–13; Mic. 3:7). The priests could make the
difficult judgments which would alienate many but might perhaps restore
to the nation a sense of right and wrong, or they could make those decisions which would placate the poor and gratify the rich (Deut. 17:8–13;

31. Westermann, *Basic Forms of Prophetic Speech*, pp. 170–77.
32. G. Pfeifer, "Entwohnung und Entwohnungsfest im AT: der Schlüssel
zu Jes. 28, 7–13?" *ZAW* 84 (1972) 341–47, proposes that the occasion for the
revelry may have been a feast for the weaning of a child (thus v. 9; cf. Gen. 21:8).

19:17; Ezek. 44:24; Hos. 4:4–6). The lying vision and the self-serving decision are always easier in an alcoholic fog, but the hangover cannot be escaped in any case.[33]

8 This verse reaches the heights of realism and puts the writer's disgust in the strongest terms. The *tables* may have had to do with the cult, but not necessarily so. The same term could equally well describe mats around which party-goers sat. Perhaps these tables had been nicely decorated at the beginning of the evening. Not any more! Now self-indulgence has fully shown its ultimate end in degradation. These who should lead the nation in commitment to God's ways wallow in their own filth and think it amusing. The final two words, *be̯lî māqôm (there is no place)*, seem to utilize ellipsis to cap the tone of disgust. It is as though Isaiah had said, "There was not one clean spot in the place!" The abrupt phrase says it more bitingly.

9 It was bad enough that the religious leaders of Northern Israel were involved in such behavior, but even worse was their attitude about the behavior. They were not repentant or concerned. Instead, they justified themselves and mocked the prophets who sought to correct them. This is almost the necessary result of refusing to receive correction. We must very soon come to believe ourselves right and those who point out our errors as being in the wrong (5:18–23). So here, the drunkards lash out at the prophet, telling him that they are old enough to know what they are doing and that they do not need somebody to keep harping on their sins. Of course, the irony is that a drunk is more childish than a child.[34] At least the milk an infant draws from its mother's breast will make it more mature and not less so, unlike the alcohol they are drinking. How odd that the more correction we need, the less we think we need it.

Those weaned from milk with its parallel phrase expressed the thought that the prophet was treating them like toddlers in attempting to teach them righteousness. Normally, children in the Near East are weaned between the ages of three and five years, the time when the most rudimentary truths are being taught them. Thus any attempt to remind these people of the

---

33. Driver believes that the charge of debauchery has nothing to do with the functions of the prophets and priests and so reinterprets "vision" and "decision" to "tippling" and "frenzy" (*Words and Meanings,* pp. 52–53). However, the whole context of chs. 28–31 has to do with leaders who are either too stupid or too depraved to distinguish between wise and foolish counsel. Thus the traditional understanding seems best here.

34. So-called adult books and movies also portray behavior which is reminiscent of children exposing themselves to one another.

elements of right and wrong was construed as demeaning, treating them like weanlings.[35]

10 This verse has occasioned many suggestions but little agreement.[36] The sense is clear enough: the drunkards accuse the prophets of the simple, repetitive instruction used in teaching children. But the meaning of the words is a matter of controversy. The traditional rendering is in less and less favor, but it still has much to commend it as the simplest and most straightforward. The word *ṣaw* is taken, as in Hos. 5:11, as a shortened form of "commandment" (cf. *miṣwâ*). The shortening perhaps reflects the lighthearted, mocking tone. The weighty commands of God are nothing to take very seriously. "Line," *qaw,* represents a measuring line, which along with a plumb line was used to determine whether a building could be repaired or must be destroyed (2 K. 21:13; Isa. 28:17; 34:11; Lam. 2:8; cf. also Amos 7:7–9). The crooked never wishes to be compared with the straight, which seems to the twisted mind so simple and uninteresting but is, in fact, so damning.

11–13 The prophet now turns the mockers' words back upon themselves as he pronounces the word of judgment. God's words to them were in fact simple and gentle. But since they refused to hear them, they will indeed hear the harsh repetitive words, but from the lips of Assyrian taskmasters. Since they would not learn the simple truths of life from God's spokesmen, they will learn them at the end of whip and prod (8:6–8; Deut. 32:29; Matt. 23:37–39).

11 *Indeed* is the sense of the *kî* which opens the verse. It repeats the opening word of the mockers' speech but gives it another twist. Isaiah says that what they said in mockery will in fact come upon them.

foreign tongue undoubtedly refers to the language of the oppressors (Deut. 28:49; Jer. 5:15). Although Assyrian was a Semitic language, its vocabulary and grammar were different enough from Hebrew that it would

35. If Pfeifer's suggestion (see n. 32 above) is correct, then the occasion of the festival might have prompted this particular response.

36. Among the other alternatives proposed are: (1) meaningless words used in mockery (such as in English "blah, blah, blah") (Cheyne, Duhm); (2) meaningless words used to teach children to walk (Marti, Lindblom, *Prophecy,* p. 201); (3) drunken babbling (Driver, *Words and Meanings,* pp. 53–55; NEB); (4) as puns on *qî*ʾ, "vomit," and *ṣōʾâ*, "filth" (Skinner); (5) as portions of a rubric used to teach the alphabet (*q* follows *ṣ* in Hebrew) (first proposed by Houbigant, *Bibl Hebr* IV [1753] 73–74; Procksch; Fohrer; W. W. Hallo, "Isaiah 28:9–13 and the Ugaritic Abecdaries," *JBL* 77 [1958] 324–38); (6) actual Akkadian, to be read as "Go out, let him go out. . . ! Wait, let him wait. . . ! Servant, listen . . ." (A. Van Selms, "Isaiah 28:9–13: An attempt to give a new interpretation," *ZAW* 85 [1973] 332–39). Note that the Targ., both here and on v. 13, merely uses MT as a starting point from which to give a homily unrelated to the MT.

not be intelligible to an Israelite without study. Paul uses this passage in an illustrative way in 1 Cor. 14:21 in speaking about the phenomenon of glossolalia, but this passage has nothing to do with glossolalia per se.[37]

this people is frequently used in a bitter way by the prophet, and seems so here (8:6, 11, 12; 9:15 [Eng. 16]; 29:13, 14). It emphasized the sense of distance between them and God.

12 Actually, God's words had been simple and straightforward. He had made it plain to his people that they could rest in him, but that there was no rest in defensive alliances or military hardware (30:15; 31:1–3). Ultimately, the only security is in the conviction that God cares for us and will bring all the strands of the life committed to him to a joyous climax (Ps. 56:9–12 [Eng. 8–11]; Rom. 8:31–39). But something within the human heart wants to find its security in its own devices over which it has final control. So they would not listen.

Kaiser, with others, takes vv. 12 and 13 to be redactional additions to the previous verses, because they are written in the light of judgment. So, it is suggested, a later writer wished to validate God's word by making it appear that the promises had been made in advance. But if this is the case, then biblical faith is invalid, for the writers had no better proof of their faith than to resort to deception. Then the lofty proofs for God's superiority over the idols in the second part of the book ("the idols can do nothing, but God can, because he told us in advance of these events," 44:7; 48:3–5) are only so many empty words. Surely, the logical conclusion of such a position is that a faith which must resort to subterfuge to prove itself is unworthy of anything but antiquarian interest.

13 Since they would not listen to the gentle words of God, but mocked them, the people of Samaria were doomed to learn the effects of sin at the hands of a much harder teacher—experience.

so that they will go and stumble reiterates the truth which many modern child psychologists have discovered: in order for maturity to be reached, the child must be allowed to suffer the consequences of its actions. For the parent to intervene constantly and to nullify the results is to give the child a wholly misshapen understanding of life. So these events come upon God's people in order that they may fall and thus learn.

The piling up of synonyms is characteristic of Isaiah; cf. 29:6; 30:30; and especially 8:15, which contains many of the same terms in a similar setting.

37. Paul's point is that God only uses an extraordinary means of speaking to people when they refuse to listen to ordinary means. This point is borne out by Isaiah. See O. P. Robertson, "Tongues: Sign of Covenantal Curse and Blessing," *WTJ* 38 (1975) 43–53, for another interpretation.

(2) Jerusalem (28:14–29:24)

(a) Covenant with death (28:14–22)

14 *Therefore, hear the word of the Lord, you scoffers,*
rulers[1] of this people, who are in Jerusalem.
15 *Because you say, "We have made a covenant with death*
and an agreement[2] with Sheol.
The overflowing scourge,[3] when it sweeps past,[4]
will not come to us,
for we have made a lie our refuge,
and in falsehood we have hidden ourselves."
16 *Therefore, thus says the Sovereign Lord,*
"Behold, I am laying[5] in Zion a stone,[6]
a stone of testing, a precious cornerstone,
a sure foundation;
17 *I will make of justice a line[7]*
and of righteousness a plumb line;
hail will sweep away the refuge of lies,[8]
and water will overflow the hiding place.

1. Fohrer and Kaiser render *mōšlê* as "proverb-makers" (*mšl* II), but the larger context points to "rulers" (*mšl* I) as do the versions.

2. The term *hōzeh* here and in v. 18 (*ḥāzût*) is problematic. Normal Hebrew usage would call for these to be translated "seer" and "vision," neither of which fits the context. LXX has "agreement" and "hope" while the Targ. has "peace" (*šlm*). The emendation to *ḥsd* (Köhler, *ZAW* 48 [1930] 227–28) seems unwarranted, but the difficulty remains. It seems likely that a second root with the same consonants is involved. Delitzsch adduces "split" or "divide" with the sense of "decision" but Driver's reference to Arab. *ḥadâ*, "to be over against, correspond to," makes even better sense (*JTS* 38 [1937] 44; see also *Words and Meanings*, pp. 57–58).

3. 1QIs^a supports the Qere: *šōṭ*. Since "overflowing scourge" is in an emphatic position, the temporal *kî* does not stand first.

4. MT has Ketib *ʿbr* and Qere *yaʿᵃbōr*. The Qere is normally favored because of the parallel with v. 18 and because the imperfect makes better sense than a perfect. However, an infinitive absolute is also possible.

5. "I am laying" is pointed as an imperfect, *yissaḏ*. Normally the translation would be "I will lay." LXX and Targ. seem to be translating a participle form and 1QIs^a has *mysd*, presumably a Piel participle. Perhaps the original was a Qal participle *yōsēḏ* (cf. *BHS*).

6. Note that the Targ. translates "stone" with "kings." This receives some support from the development of the segment, which moves toward the revelation of the King.

7. *yāḥîš* appears to be a Hiphil of *ḥîš*, "to hurry." LXX reads "ashamed," which probably assumes *bôš* as the reading. Driver, *Words and Meanings*, p. 60, notes an Akk. *ḥâšu*, "to shake, be agitated," and this may be the sense in which *ḥîš* is used here. Note Targ. "not be agitated in distress."

8. Both LXX and Targ. disagree with MT and with each other over the reading of "hail will sweep away the refuge. . . ." But the parallelism with the second stich seems to argue in favor of the MT reading.

18 *Your covenant with death will be wiped out,*[9]
    and your agreement with Sheol will not stand.
  As for the overflowing scourge, when it sweeps over you,
    you will become a trampling place for it.
19 *Each time it passes through it will take you;*
      surely morning by morning it will pass through,
        by day[10] *and by night."*[11]
20 *For the bed is too short to stretch out on,*
    and the covering too narrow to wrap up in.[12]
21 *Surely the Lord will arise, as on Mount Perazim;*
      as in the valley of Gibeon he will rouse himself—
  to do his work, his strange work,
      to perform his deeds, his alien deeds.
22 *So now, do not scoff, lest your bonds be tightened;*
      for a final decree I have heard
  from the Sovereign, the Lord of Hosts,
      upon all the earth.

The focus now shifts to Jerusalem, as indicated by the "therefore" in 28:14. If a terrible fate has befallen Samaria, this is no time for rejoicing, says Isaiah. For the rulers of Jerusalem (28:14–22; 29:15–17) are as senseless as those of Samaria, and the priests and prophets are as drunken and blind (29:1, 9–14). Therefore, Jerusalem's fate will be as severe as Samaria's. But as in the former word (28:5, 6), there is a note of hope here too. God will fight against Jerusalem's enemies (29:5–8), and one day there will be a renewal of the spirit of God's people (29:17–24). Thus the segment is marked by the typically Isaianic interchange of judgment and hope. The foolish alliance with Egypt is not necessary because even in spite of that sin God will find a way to redeem. How much more he would

9. Since *kpr* normally means "cover up" and not "annul" as here, there have been numerous suggestions for emendation. The most popular of these has been *tpr*, a feminine imperfect of *prr*, "to break" or "frustrate." This is urged on the grounds of its occurrences with "covenant" in Isaiah (24:5; 33:8) and because its feminine gender accords with the feminine gender of covenant. However, as Driver notes, "Arabic, Akkadian and Syriac all know *kpr* with a meaning of 'wipe away' while a verb occurring first in a sentence need not agree in gender with a following subject" (*Words and Meanings*, p. 61).
10. Driver is incorrect when he says LXX lacks "day."
11. Many commentators take the whole verse or part of it to be a gloss, because of the repeated statement of a simple message. However, the versions are unanimous in their support, showing only minor differences. Thus, if it is a gloss, it is a very old one.
12. MT has "as it is gathered," but 1QIs[a] has "in [or from] being gathered," which is attractive. Neither the LXX nor the Targ. seems to have understood the meaning of the saying here. Both offer divergent interpretations.

be able to redeem if trusted now, and not only after the hard blows of experience.

The segment 28:14–22 is directed to those foolish leaders of Jerusalem whose plans are based upon the cynical and faithless projections of the future.[13] But Isaiah tells them that cynicism cannot provide a secure foundation against the shocks of life (v. 19). Only faith can do that (v. 16). So all their carefully laid plans, just like those of Samaria, will come to nothing. To their probable remarks that God does not act in history (cf. 5:18–23), he answers that God *does* work, either for us as in the past, or against us, as he will in their case (vv. 21, 22).

Kaiser points out that vv. 14–15 form a prophecy of reproach, and vv. 16–22 a prophecy of warning. However, he does not consider parts of vv. 16 and 17, nor any of vv. 19–22, to be original. Wildberger agrees that v. 19 may be a gloss, but sees no real reason for questioning the authenticity of the rest. In fact, vv. 20–22 may be viewed as a necessary development of the concept of a message of pure terror: God's power turned against his own.

14 *Therefore* is used in a somewhat elliptical way, but the sense is: if these things have befallen the drunkards of Ephraim, you scoffers in Jerusalem ought to take note.[14]

scoffers is the strongest negative term which the OT uses to describe the wicked. It is the diametric opposite of "faithful" (cf. Ps. 1:1, 2). Not only does this person choose the wrong way, but he mocks the right way. He is not merely misled, he delights to mislead others. So he is the very opposite of the wise man, who understands the order of things correctly (Prov. 15:12; 21:24; 22:10; 29:8; Hos. 7:5).[15] When such persons are in places of authority, as here, their impact is all the more serious. Faith is never easy for human beings and when the highest authorities model the opposite, it is not surprising if faith becomes increasingly rare among the people (1:21–23; 3:4, 5, 12–15; 5:22, 23; Jer. 21:11–14; 22:1–5; Hos. 4:1–6).

15 *We have made a covenant with death* may be interpreted in two ways. It may be a literal quotation and may indicate that the princes have engaged in sorcery and have entered into an agreement with the gods of the underworld: Death *(Mot)* and Plague *(Reshef)*. In return for protection

13. Note that the king and the house of David are not mentioned here (contra 7:1–13). This is typical of the oracles delivered during Hezekiah's reign.
14. This would be a particularly powerful point if the prophecies of Samaria's fall in vv. 11–13 were now seen to have been fulfilled.
15. *TWOT*, no. 1113a.

from these deities the worshiper agrees to do certain things.[16] But another possibility is that the prophet is engaging in sarcasm. The rulers may not have meant to, but in fact by their cynical refusal to trust God they have rejected life and chosen death. In view of the references to reliance upon Egypt in this segment, it may be that the reference is to that treaty which the rulers expect to protect them from Assyria. In either case, the references to *lie* and *falsehood* would be an instance of this note of irony. Obviously the princes would not have believed that their covenant was with "lie" and "falsehood." But Isaiah puts words in their mouths to show the true import of what they have done. Neither the gods of Egypt nor the gods of Canaan could protect their adherents (to this extent Isaiah agrees with the Rabshaqeh, 36:18, 19), and Egypt's protestations of undying friendship were simply untrue.

The overflowing scourge is somewhat of a mixed metaphor. The context makes it plain that a flood is intended, but the noun normally refers to a whip. Perhaps the stinging effect of wind-driven rain in a cloudburst or the stripping power of hail (v. 17) suggested the confluence of the images.[17] In any case, the point is clear: Isaiah does not believe lies can save anyone from the coming flood.

16 *Therefore* here does not merely restate the causal impact of the one in v. 14. Here it is because of the rulers' boast that they have secured themselves against trouble that the word of the Lord comes to them. And it comes to them as the word of the Sovereign of the universe. Whoever they may have been dealing with before, they are now facing the absolute monarch.

As in 8:14, the message here is a double-edged one. God is establishing a structure in Zion which will be a source of comfort and encouragement to those who will trust him but a bar of judgment for those who refuse to do so. The imagery of laying the foundation for a building is

16. Note Ps. 23:4 and 91:6, which may refer to these deities. Cf. *ANET*, p. 140, for the Ugaritic account of Mot devouring Baal, and Anat's attempt to force him to restore Baal. Cf. Albright, *Yahweh and the Gods of Canaan* (New York: Doubleday, 1968), pp. 139–140. Kaiser takes this point of view; see also Skinner, who points out that a treaty with Egypt would have involved Isis and Osiris, both related to the underworld. Cf. also 8:19, which speaks of consulting with the dead.

17. Note that the Koran (89:13) uses the same imagery: "Your lord pours over them the scourge of punishment." For biblical references to "the waters" and death, see Job 38:16, 17; Ps. 124:3–4; Jon. 2:2–9. On the work of the storm-god as an "overflowing flood," see the Code of Hammurapi, §§ 45, 48 (*ANET*, p. 168); also H. Gese, "Der Strömende Geissel des Hadad und Jes. 28:15 und 18," *Archäologie und Altes Testaments*, Festschrift K. Galling, ed. A. Kuschke and E. Kutsch (Tübingen: Mohr/Siebeck, 1970), pp. 127–134.

used to make the point. If the foundations are cheap stones, shoddily laid, it is not possible for the building to survive the shocks which will come to it (Matt. 7:24–27). That is what these rulers have done. They have rested the nation's survival upon the promises of the idolatrous rulers of Egypt, the negotiations perhaps engaged in secretly to avoid the wrath of such persons as Isaiah. By contrast, God is also laying a foundation whose very nature should be such as to condemn the false trusts which are filling Jerusalem (cf. v. 17).

The NT makes it plain that the ultimate foundation for trust in God is the character of God as revealed in Jesus. In his life and work all that the Bible has said about the trustworthiness of God comes to its fulfillment (Rom. 9:33; 10:11; 1 Pet. 2:4–6; 1 Tim. 1:16). Nor is there any incongruity between those assertions and the sense of this verse. The question being dealt with here is the basis for life's choices: the machinations of people or the trustworthiness of God. At the same time, it may be asked whether Isaiah had his primary focus upon the Messiah here (as he clearly does in chs. 9 and 11) or whether his initial intent is more general. If it is more general, as it seems, the possibilities for the identification of the stone are numerous. Some of them are listed by Kaiser. They are: the law (Eichhorn), the temple (Ewald), Yahweh's saving work (Feldmann), Yahweh's relation to this people (Duhm), the archetypal Davidic monarch (Delitzsch), true believers (Eichrodt), Zion (Childs), the remnant (Donner), Yahweh's promise (König), and faith itself (Kaiser, along with Marti, Fohrer, and Wildberger). To these may be added Yahweh himself (Cheyne). Although the law and the temple (as well as Zion) seem rather strained, each of the other positions has points in its favor. Perhaps no one identification is correct. The cornerstone may be the whole complex of ideas relating to the Lord's revelation of his faithfulness and the call to reciprocate with the same kind of faithfulness toward him. That entire message would one day be summed up in Jesus Christ. The issue remains the same today as then: upon what shall we build our lives, human schemes or divine trustworthiness?

a stone of testing may be a loanword from Egyptian, as first pointed out by Sethe, who noted that *bhn-w* was a particularly hard stone against which others could be measured.[18]

a precious cornerstone. Kohler disagrees with the rendering of *yiqrat*

---

18. K. Sethe, "Die Bau- und Denkmalstein der älten Ägypter und ihre Namen," *Sitzungsberichte der preussischen Akademie der Wissenschaften* (1933) 846–912. See also L. Köhler, "Zwei Factwörter der Bausprache in Jesaja 28, 16," *TZ* 3 (1947) 391–92; cf. T. Lambdin, "Egyptian Loan Words in the Old Testament," *JAOS* 73 (1953) 148.

as "precious," taking the root to be *qrh*, "to meet." Thus he translates "the corner where one foundation meets the other."[19] This rendering has the virtue of explaining the repetition of *mwsd* in the MT, but it is not supported by any of the versions.[20]

the one who trusts . . . may have been understood to be the inscription on the cornerstone, although there is nothing in the text which requires such an interpretation.[21] In any case, the sense is clear: for the person who puts his or her trust in God, there can be a serenity and a calm deliberateness which is not possible otherwise (26:3, 4; 30:15–17). To refuse to entrust my ways to God is to open myself to a hectic and feverish existence in which I rush here and there trying with decreasing success to control the disparate parts of my life. To commit my ways to him may not increase my success but it will grant peace through the realization that my times are in *his* hands.

17 As God erects his building upon the cornerstone of his own faithfulness, he will make justice and righteousness the standards for measurement. As a result, that building will stand. But every other structure will fall. It is so in life. Integrity is its own defense. But whenever a twisting of the truth begins, more must follow until the structure of lies is so heavy and complex that it falls of its own weight.

18 In the hour when the oppressor sweeps over the nation all her secret agreements and covenants will prove useless. The irony of a people who have a covenant with a God of life putting their trust in a covenant with death surfaces again. As a result of *that* overturning by the people, their relationship to God is also overturned. Their defender has become the marshaller of troops against them (5:26). They will end up beaten flat like a grainfield over which a flood has run.

19 Nor is Isaiah willing to leave the foolish rulers the small comfort that when they have endured the enemy flood, it will be over. Instead, he says, the flood will come again and again, taking the country over and over. This can be seen to be a correct assessment of Assyrian military doctrine. The Assyrian annals report numerous returns to the same areas, each return being accompanied by vast slaughter and pillage. The steady hammer blows of such an attack spread out over years, whether calculat-

19. Op. cit., pp. 390–91.

20. The second *mwsd* is pointed by MT as a Hophal participle, thus "a founded foundation." However, the versions (except for Vulg.) ignore the repetition. It may be that the two words are merely alternate spellings of the noun.

21. For examples of more lengthy building inscriptions, see *ANET*, pp. 499–501.

edly so, or as a result of political exigencies elsewhere, could be expected to reduce a people to shivering terror, as the prophet noted here.

20 This verse probably reflects a then popular proverb which is used here to cap the destruction of the foolishness of the alliances made. They cannot do what they claim. The bed is not big enough to contain them, nor the blanket wide enough to cover them. So promises are easy to make but difficult to keep.

21, 22 These two verses conclude the segment in a powerful way. The opening *kî,* "for," expresses the idea of summation, or "to put it simply." Their shaky covenants will collapse because, as of old, God will take the field. Very possibly false prophets were invoking the old stories as proof that God would side with his people come what may. Isaiah recalls the stories, too. As he broke out upon the Philistines at Mount Perazim ("flood," 2 Sam. 5:20; 1 Chr. 14:11) and stuck down the Canaanites fleeing from Gibeon ("hail," Josh. 10:11), so he would fight against his enemies again. But who are God's enemies? Those who do not obey him (Ps. 139:19–24). Thus God will work, he will perform his deeds, but they will be strange and foreign because they will be against his people, not for them. God never belongs to anyone, and if he cannot find those who will serve him in one place, he will find them in another (Mal. 1:11; Rev. 2:5).

The scoffers are already in bondage because of their mockery of God, and unless they stop at once, they will have forged their chains so tightly that nothing can break them. The sin from which there is no return is not merely refusing to listen to God, but making fun of the very means by which he addresses us (Heb. 10:26–31; 1 John 5:16–17). Ultimately such a person cannot even recognize the truth when it confronts him.[22] Destruction is decreed for the land, but people within the land may still find God, if they can hear his call and repent of their folly.

(b) The laws of nature (28:23–29)

> 23 *Give ear and listen to my voice;*
> *pay attention and listen to my speech.*
> 24 *Does the plowman plow every day*[1] *to sow;*[2]
> *does he continue to open and harrow his ground?*

---

22. So the Black Dwarves in C. S. Lewis's *The Last Battle* insist they are being forced to eat garbage when in fact they are being fed the finest banquet.

1. Lit. "all the day," but the sense is clearly "day after day."

2. Because "to sow" seems to be somewhat awkward in the first line and is not paralleled in the second, many commentators (cf. *BHS*) wish to delete it. However, the versions support its originality. Kissane's emendation to "for a moment" is ingenious, but groundless.

25 *Does he not, when he has leveled its face,*
    scatter black cummin and sow ordinary cummin,
  put wheat in rows, barley in its place,[3]
    and spelt at its borders?
26 *He will instruct him according to right principle;*
    his God will teach him.
27 *For black cummin is not threshed with a sledge,*
    nor is the cartwheel driven around[4] *upon ordinary cummin,*
  but with a staff black cummin is beaten off,
    ordinary cummin with a stick.
28 *Bread is ground, but not to nothing.*
  It will surely be threshed,[5]
  the wheels of his cart will rumble (over it),
    but his horses will not crush it.
29 *This too has gone forth from the Lord,*
    wonderful in counsel, great in wisdom.

After the furious denunciations of vv. 14–22, these verses, with their quiet pastoral allusions, come as something of a shock. Furthermore, because the writer gives no interpretation (contra 5:7), it is not certain what was the intended function of the segment. Broadly speaking, the prophet is pointing to a simple peasant who farms according to certain principles which he has learned from God. Thus he knows when to plow and when to sow. He knows what needs to be sown where (vv. 24–25) and how to adapt his threshing techniques to the different plants so as not to destroy the grain (vv. 27–28). How does he know these things? God, the great teacher and counselor, has shown him (26:29).

But what does this mean in this context? Several possibilities offer themselves: (1) The segment offers a note of hope (as chs. 5, 6). Despite their sin, God will not continue to plow his people under forever, nor will

3. Because "in rows" and "in its place" are missing from the Greek tradition as well as other ancient versions, some read as follows: "he places wheat and barley and spelt at its borders." This is at least as awkward as the MT, however. LXX reads, "he will scatter black cummin and ordinary cummin and again wheat and barley and spelt at your borders." The sower appears to be God and the verse taken as a promise. S. C. Thexton says that the emphasis upon purpose demands that the words be retained; however, he emends *śôrâ* to *śûmâ* to give a parallel meaning to *nismān*, "marked out, determined" (*VT* 2 [1952] 81–83).

4. 1QIs^a has *yswb* for MT *yûssāb*, "be made to go around." It is tempting to view 1QIs^a as having preserved an ancient Qal passive which had been revocalized to a Hophal by MT times.

5. Cf. Targ.; also Thexton, *VT* 2 (1952) 83. *'ādôš* appears to be a case of the prosthetic *aleph* appearing on a middle weak infinitive absolute (cf. 1QIs^a *ḥdš*). Cf. GKC, § 19m.

he drive his threshing sledge over them until they are crushed.[6] (2) God is not locked into merely one mode of activity. Those foolish leaders who said that the old God was inadequate for a new age did not even understand nature.[7] (3) God is the true counselor and his counsel is simple, straightforward, and productive (v. 12). What the leaders are proposing is as stupid as a farmer plowing all year, or trying to thresh tiny cummin seeds with an oxcart. Even an uneducated peasant, taught by God, knows better than that (cf. 1:2, 3).[8] Although all of these are possible, the last seems to fit the context best in its stress upon the importance of God's counsel, its simple wisdom, and its implied contrast of stupid counselors with wise peasants.

23 *Give ear . . .* appears to be a conventionalized form of address used in wisdom literature.[9] As such, it is a call to consider and learn (1:2). Thus Isaiah would have been appealing to a form which would have been very familiar to the royal counselors among whom the wisdom forms are now held to have been transmitted.[10] He thus turns their own tools back upon them.

24 The prophet opens with a rhetorical question which aims to get the hearers on the speaker's side. Of course, no plowman keeps on plowing every day. He does not keep on plowing and harrowing as if these were ends in themselves. Rather, because his aim is to sow, he will one day quit plowing. The plow in the ancient Near East seems to have been a metal-pointed stick pulled by an ox or a team of oxen. This device broke up the ground to a depth of three inches or so. It was then necessary to drag a harrow, a couple of logs with pieces of metal sticking out of them, over the plowed ground to level and smooth the seed-bed (v. 25a).[11] A

6. See esp. Delitzsch, but also Young. Fohrer's comments (followed by Kaiser) that the parable cannot refer to God because God is the peasant's teacher treat the segment not as parable but as allegory, which it is not. Clements takes the same meaning but in so doing denies it to Isaiah.

7. See Wildberger; see also S. Amsler and O. Mury, "Yahweh et la sagesse du paysan. Quelques remarques sur Esaie 28:23–29," *RHPR* 53 (1973) 1–5. Cf. Skinner and Scott.

8. See Cheyne (with Ewald, W. R. Smith, Wellhausen).

9. Gen. 4:23; Judg. 5:3; Job 33:1; 34:2; Ps. 49:5 (Eng. 4); Prov. 4:1; 7:24; Jer. 13:15; Hos. 5:1.

10. See J. Jansen, *The Use of torâ by Isaiah*, p. 122. Kaiser notes that the hearer is named in most instances where this form appears and concludes that this segment therefore never appeared in oral form. But note Jer. 13:15, where the identity of the hearers has been made known, as here, in the previous statements.

11. Cf. E. W. Heaton, *Everyday Life in Old Testament Times* (New York: 1956), pp. 99–100. M. S. Miller, et al., *Harper's Encyclopedia of Bible Life,* 3rd rev. ed. (New York: Harper & Row, 1978), pp. 174–77.

farmer knows this elemental fact of his profession. Surely it is not asking too much of the royal counselors to know as much about their business.

25 The farmer also knows how to plant each seed according to its own character. The very fine black cummin is scattered on the ground, whereas the larger seeds are sown in marked rows and plots. Finally, spelt is planted at the borders, perhaps partly as a viewblock, to prevent penurious neighbors from temptation to steal, but perhaps also to mark off one person's plot from another's.

26 *according to right principle* is a classic example of the fact that *mišpāṭ* means more than legal judgment or justice.[12] It is in fact the creation order, both physically and spiritually. There are principles in both realms upon which life depends and which, if followed, will lead to life. God has cried out to his people to live according to *mišpāṭ* in matters of the Spirit, but they cannot see why they should (1:21; 5:7; Mic. 6:8; Amos 5:24). Somehow, we do not have that problem with physical principles, so Isaiah reverts to that realm to show his people, and us, the importance and the simplicity of God's ways.

27, 28 From plowing and planting, Isaiah turns to the techniques of threshing. The same techniques cannot be used on small grains as are used on the larger ones. With wheat and barley, an animal might be tethered to a center post and then driven around and around on the pile of cut grain. Sometimes the animal might also pull a heavy cart or a wooden sled with bits of stone or metal embedded in the bottom of the timbers (Deut. 25:4; Isa. 41:15; Mic. 4:13). These methods separated the kernels from the husks.[13] But the smaller grains could easily be crushed and lost with that sort of threshing. Instead, a stick, or flail, had to be used (Judg. 6:11; Ruth 2:17).

28 *Bread is ground* has provoked controversy as to whether it is a rhetorical question expecting a "no" answer (so AV, RSV). The present translation (with NIV), on the basis of the absence of any interrogative indicator, takes the sentence to be indicative followed by an adversative *kî*, "but." Thus the sense is similar to v. 24. Yes, the wheat is threshed, but only until it is separated from the chaff, for the threshing itself is only a means, not an end.

his horses. It is protested that horses were too valuable to use in such menial work as threshing. Therefore, various emendations have been

---

12. *TWOT*, II:948–49.

13. Heaton, *Everyday Life*, pp. 100–103; Miller, *Harper's Encyclopedia*, pp. 180–81.

suggested.[14] Duhm suggests *p^erāśô w^elō'*, "it is broken, but not . . ." (cf. *BHS*), while Scott offers *pārāw,* "his bullocks." Scott's is the more attractive, but it must also be allowed that the poet may have used "horses" for some poetic reason not now evident to us. One possibility is that he wished to draw a parallel between threshing and destruction by an enemy army (17:4–6; cf. also 27:12; 41:15, 16).

29 *This too has gone forth* may mean that God has taught the farmer the principles of threshing as well as those of plowing and planting (vv. 24–26). But the exalted tone of this verse suggests that more than this is intended. This is the conclusion to the argument begun in v. 14. If the Almighty God has given both physical and spiritual counsel, and if the farmer accepts the physical as a matter of course and finds life, what are Jerusalem's leaders doing scoffing at his spiritual counsel? Only those who are drunk or blind could miss the implications, says the prophet (cf. 29:9–11).

(c) The city of God (29:1–14)

(i) Ariel (29:1–8)

1 *Woe to Ariel, Ariel, city where*[1] *David camped.*
> *Add year to year, let the festivals go through the cycle.*
2 *But I will besiege Ariel*
> *and she will become mourning and lament;*
> *she will become like Ariel to me.*
3 *I will encamp in a circle*[2] *against you;*
> *I will enclose you with towers;*
> *I will erect against you siege-works.*
4 *Having fallen,*[3] *you will speak from the earth;*
> *and from the dust your speech will be bowed low.*
> *Your voice will be like a ghost from the earth*
> *and from the dust your speech will chirp.*

14. Neither Targ. nor LXX supports MT, but they also do not support each other: (LXX) "neither shall the voice of my bitterness cast you down"; (Targ.) "separates the grain and casts the chaff to the wind."

1. The LXX reads "the city *against which* David camped" and some commentators prefer this, in the light of v. 3. However, the sense of pride of being David's dwelling seems most natural. In this case, v. 3 expresses a contrast. Note the virtual genitive "the place of David camped."

2. *kāḏûr,* "as a circle." LXX "like David" (reading *dwd* for *dwr;* Hebrew *r* and *d* are easily mistaken). Some commentators prefer David on the basis of v. 1, but see n. 1. Driver notes Assyrian *kîma dûri,* "like an encircling wall," and argues for the MT (*JSS* 13 [1968] 51).

3. Note that the opening *waw* functions as a circumstantial indicator: "and you fell" = "you having fallen."

5 *The crowds of your strangers*[4] *will be like fine dust,*
    and the crowd of the ruthless like driven chaff.
   It shall be in a fleeting instant
6   *you will be visited*[5] *by the Lord of Hosts*
   with thunder and earthquake and a great noise,
    windstorm and tempest and devouring flame of fire.
7 *It will be like a dream, a vision of the night,*
    the crowd of all the nations,
        those fighting against Ariel,
    all who make war with her
        and her stronghold,[6] *who oppress her.*
8 *It will be as when a famished person dreams,*
    and behold, he is eating;
   but at the end, his soul is empty.
   Or as when a thirsty person dreams,
    and behold, he is drinking;
    but at the end, behold, he is fainting
    and his soul is frantic.
   Thus will be the crowd of all the nations,
    those fighting against Mount Zion.

This third part of the denunciation of Jerusalem provides the formal parallel to 28:1–6, where Ephraim is denounced. There the charge was a sort of frantic partying. Here too a festive air pervades, but in special connection with the cult (v. 2). Jerusalem prided herself on her pure worship as opposed to idolatrous Samaria, but in fact, pure cult does not replace a

4. *zārāyik̲,* "your aliens," is proposed by many commentators to be an error for *zdyk,* "your insolent ones" (Clements, Skinner, Kissane, etc.; so also 1QIs[a]). However, the emendation is not necessary since *zr* carries with it the idea of hostility (1:7; 25:2, 5; Ps. 54:5 [Eng. 3]). At the same time, *zd* appears as a synonym of *ʿārîṣ,* "ruthless," in 13:11, so no dogmatic assertion can be made.

5. In view of the fact that the passive of *pqd,* "visit" (v. 6), is everywhere else in Scripture used negatively (to be punished, judged), some students of the book argue that v. 5ab is out of place and should come between vv. 6 and 7. Thus v. 6 would remain as a part of the judgment upon Jerusalem. However, as Kaiser points out, v. 6 does not follow v. 4 well, nor does it fit in smoothly at any point in vv. 1–4. In view of these facts it seems to be better to take *pqd* as positive here (as it often is in the active) and to accept the MT order, as do the versions. (Kaiser cites Sir. 49:13 as a positive use of passive *pqd.*) *BHS* suggests making *tippāqēd* 2nd feminine in agreement with the preceding verses. However, most commentators agree that the passive is neuter here.

6. For MT *mᵉṣōḏāṯāh,* "her strongholds," 1QIs[a] has *mṣrth* (cf. also Kissane), "her towers." However, the reversal goes in the opposite direction in v. 3, so that it appears that the two words are synonymous.

pure heart, and the very source of her pride contributed to her downfall.[7] But in that God would be responsible for her downfall, he would also be able to restore her, and as throughout the entire book, the word of judgment is very shortly followed by the word of redemption. To some scholars, this seems inconsistent, and there is a growing movement to deny these deliverance passages to Isaiah and to give them to a redactor in the time of Josiah.[8] However, the promise of redemption closely coupled with a threat of judgment need not be inconsistent in the light of the apparent nature of the prophet's opposition. It appears that the leadership was urging an alliance with Egypt precisely because they doubted God's capacity to save them (cf. 5:18, 19; 7:12; 30:2; 31:1; etc.). Isaiah's response would then be twofold: God is in fact so powerful that to refuse to trust him is to experience destruction from his hand (Assyria is not mentioned), *after which* destruction he is *still* able to save. Thus, if God's ability to save was in question, the simple threat of judgment would not have been a very powerful argument.[9]

1 *Woe to Ariel* expresses Isaiah's warning to Jerusalem for tending to rely upon its cult to save it, while refusing to rely upon God. That Jerusalem is intended is made plain by the references to David and to the festivals. However, the precise meaning of *Ariel* is still in dispute. There are essentially three alternatives: (1) a variant upon *urusalima,* "city of Salem" (Jerusalem), to *uruel,* "city of El" (Kissane). But the shift from *uru-* to *ari-* is not easily explained linguistically. (2) "Lion of God" as supported by references to Judah as a lion (Gen. 49:9), and the lion throne (1 K. 10:19, 20), as well as references to the devouring lion (Isa. 31:4; cf. also 2 Sam. 23:20; 1 Chr. 11:22). However, nothing in the immediate context lends any support to this rendering (Cheyne, Delitzsch). (3) "altar, hearth" (Ezek. 43:15, and probably the Mesha inscription, line 12). This interpretation of the word has gained considerable popularity in recent years because it agrees with "festivals" in v. 1, as well as explaining the sense of the final clause in v. 2. Jerusalem prides itself as being God's altar-hearth, the very heart of the only cult that pleases him. But, in fact, God is not pleased at all.

---

7. Cf. 1:10–17; 56:3–8; 58:4–7; 65:2–5; 66:17.

8. Cf. Clements, following leads of Barth and Vermeylen. Cf. also Clements's recent book, *Isaiah and the Deliverance of Jerusalem,* JSOTSup 13 (Sheffield: JSOT, 1980).

9. Furthermore, if there were no passages in the original Isaiah promising deliverance, there would be no rationale for attaching the supposed redactions to authentic Isaianic passages. But if such promises did exist, they obviate the need to posit a redactor.

The *city where David camped* expresses another part of Jerusalem's pride: her association with David, the ideal man of God. But again, association guarantees nothing. The nature of the house of David in Isaiah's time underscored that. For every Uzziah, there was an Ahaz, for every Hezekiah a Manasseh. Thus, even parentage cannot guarantee personal righteousness.

Add year to year seems to be a sarcastic invitation by the prophet to go right on with the useless round of rituals, which, like the pagan rituals built around nature's cycle, go nowhere. But although they continue to do them, they will not avert the disaster which lies ahead. They may please the worshiper; they do not please God (Hos. 8:11–14; Amos 4:4, 5).

2 God's response to the "altar-hearth" is to place it under siege! Whenever God's people become familiar with him and believe they have him under control, they are in desperate danger. He is the Maker, not we, and his power cannot be used by those who are not God (29:16). As noted above, there is no mention of Assyria here. Isaiah wants to make it plain that God is no mere spectator in the theater of history. God will be laying siege to Jerusalem when Assyria stands at the gate. While this leaves unanswered many of the questions of sovereignty versus free will, or of God's place in the practice of moral evil, it does emphasize and re-emphasize the point which is as easily forgotten today as then: all things are under God's superintendence.

She will become mourning and lament in place of light-hearted religious festivity. The impact of God's acts is underscored by the use of *hāyâ*. The city will not merely do these things, she will *become* them. Then indeed she will be Ariel, an altar-hearth, when the nation itself becomes the sacrifice. If we treat lightly the sacrifices God has made available (and in the Christian era, The Sacrifice) then we ourselves become the sacrifice. If we will not accept God's substitution, we must carry the burden of our own sin (Heb. 10:26, 27; Rom. 8:11–13).

3 *I will encamp . . . against you.* David may have camped within Jerusalem, but God will camp against her. As the besieging Assyrians encircle the city, walling it in so none can enter or leave, it will in fact be God in the form of the Assyrians. This kind of assertion could not help but have been shocking and apparently irreligious; but in fact, it was the conviction that God was in all things which made the Jews able to survive as a people through the centuries.

towers . . . siege-works. The Assyrian reliefs depict the many ingenious devices which the Assyrians developed in order to break into walled cities. Among these were great wheeled towers which included a battering ram on the bottom and spaces for attackers on the top. These were pushed up against the city walls on ramps of earth and wood.[10]

4 This verse may be composed of two figures, or only one. In the second part of the verse, death is clearly talked about as the formerly loud, boasting voices are reduced to the chirpings and twitterings of the dead.[11] Many commentators take the first part as the imagery of the captive who lies face down on the ground, with the tyrant's foot on his neck.[12] This may be, but the use of *earth* and *dust* here, as in the second part, suggests that both may be speaking of death. So God has the power of life and death. It is he whom the Judeans should pay attention to, not the Assyrians (cf. Luke 12:4).

5–8 Here the tone shifts from judgment to redemption. The prophet wants his hearers to know that not only can God save them now, he can also save them after they will have experienced the consequences of their refusal to trust him. How foolish to trust Egypt in view of such powerful grace. What now seems so horrifying and insurmountable is in fact of no more substance than a dream. But human beings have a very hard time getting above the immediate and getting perspective upon their lives. This is where the divine word assumes critical importance. When we see issues from God's point of view, we are much less likely to rush into foolish attempts to extricate ourselves (30:15–18; 33:2; 40:28–31).

5 The weighty, powerful enemies are in fact no more substantial than powder (dust beaten even finer) or wind-driven chaff. Because of our fear of humanity, God becomes less and less significant for us. But it is God who is real, whose presence in quiet glance (18:4) or terrifying storm (as here) reduces the human factor to its appropriate place (Ps. 56:4, 11).

6 God will *visit* his people as they cry out to him for mercy.[13] But this visiting is not merely to pay a call upon them. God comes to his people to right their wrongs. If they are wrong, his coming means punishment (24:21), but if they are now in a condition of being wronged, he comes to deliver.

As the besieging of Jerusalem was an expression of God's sovereignty, so also is his deliverance. He comes as the Lord of Hosts, the God

---

10. See *ANEP*, pp. 128–29; *Harper's Encyclopedia*, pp. 314, 320. Cf. Deut. 20:20; 2 K. 25:1–4; Ezek. 4:2; 21:22.

11. Cf. 8:19, where the mediums chirp like the dead. The people who consulted the dead (28:15) will then be dead themselves. Cf. M. Dahood, *Bib* 40 (1959) 165, for 'ereṣ, "underworld."

12. See Gen. 18:2 and 19:1 for šāḥâ, "be low in the dust."

13. Cf. Ruth 1:6; 1 Sam. 2:21; Ps. 8:5 (Eng. 4); 106:4; Jer. 15:15; 29:10; *TWOT*, II:731–32.

of armies, disposing of the troops of heaven and of earth as he will. He also comes as Lord of nature, with the forces of that realm responding to his presence in a sympathetic way. The language here is the classic language of theophany (Exod. 19:16–19; 1 K. 19:11–13; Ezek. 20:47–48), expressing through imagery the conviction that God can intervene in power in our world.[14] But unlike the pagan religions which identified the gods with natural forces, the Hebrews saw these manifestations only as accompaniments, not as essence (1 K. 19:13).

7, 8 Against the backdrop of God's terrifying reality, the nations and their might will seem but a dream. At the time, a dream can seem frighteningly real. What a relief it is to wake up and discover it is not so. It must have seemed that way when Sennacherib was suddenly gone from outside the city, leaving only his decimated camp behind (37:36, 37). Weeks later some of the inhabitants probably awakened to a dull sense of dread at having to face another day of the Assyrian threat, only to realize with a flash of delight that it was all over. So it will be on that last morning when we awake to the knowledge that once and for all we are truly awake, forevermore with him.

8 It is possible that the dreamer here is the attacker, in that satisfaction is dreamed of but not actually attained. On the other hand, it may be simply a further illustration of the unreality of a dream. This latter interpretation seems the more likely, since there would be no reason to shift the focus away from the Judeans.

(ii) Blindness of rote religion (29:9–14)

9 *Astonish yourselves*[1] *and be astonished;*
   blind yourselves and be blind.
Be drunk, but not with wine;
   stagger,[2] *but not with beer.*
10 *For the Lord has poured out upon you a spirit of deep sleep;*
   he has blinded your eyes—the prophets,
   he has covered your heads—the seers.[3]

---

14. Cf. J. Jeremias, *Theophanie. Die Geschichte einer alttestamentliche Gattung*, WMANT 10 (Neukirchen: Neukirchener-Vluyn, 1965), p. 71.

1. Reading *hittamm^e hû (tmh)* for MT *hitmahm^e hû (mhh)*, "restrain yourselves." Verse 9b argues that the two verbs in the first stich should be cognates. Cf. Hab. 1:5; *BHS*.

2. MT has indicatives.

3. Ever since Koppe (the editor of Lowth's commentary) and Eichhorn, it has been customary to regard "prophets" and "seers" as glosses which were, unfortunately, incorrect. As Delitzsch notices, the sentence structure is awkward and looks somewhat suspicious. However, if these are late eschatological inser-

11 *The vision of all this will be to you like the words of a sealed book*
   which, if it is given to one who knows how to read saying, "Read
   this," he will say, "I cannot, for it is sealed."
12 *And if the book is given to[4] someone who does not know how to read*
   saying, "Read this," he will say, "I do not know how to read."
13 *The sovereign says,*
   "In that this people draws near me with its mouth[5]
       and honors me with its lips
   while its heart is far from me—
       their fear of me is[6] a commandment taught by men.
14 *Therefore, behold I am going to do wonders*
       again with this people—wonder on wonder.
   This wisdom of its wise men will perish,
       and the discernment of its discerning will be hidden.

The thought here is parallel to 28:7–13. Why will it be necessary for God
to bring his people down to destruction before the salvation promised in
28:5–6 and 29:5–8 can be experienced? The answer is the same in each
case: those who should be gifted with discernment, who should be able
to perceive the mysterious workings of God in history, are so stupid that
they cannot understand God's ways even when they are presented to them
in plain script. As a result, the ordinary people are led astray by spurious
wisdom and the nation is sunk in degradation. The result is that God will
once again, as in Egypt, have to do something shocking to show himself.
But here, as in 28:21, the first shock will be destructive, so that new
growth can come up.

Here, following the lead of 29:1, the drunkenness seems not so
much literal (as opposed to 28:7, 8) as figurative. The leadership are so
drugged by the soporific of cult that they cannot recognize the disastrous

---

tions, the failure to mention the priests is unaccountable, as they became increasingly the focus of radical anger in the intertestamental era. Furthermore, if they
are glosses, they are not necessarily incorrect. They fit in perfectly with 28:7, 8
and with the whole segment from 28:1–29:14: it is the blind leaders who are
leading the nation astray. Thus it is to be argued that, while these may be additions
to the original, they are not 5 or 6 centuries later and they do not do violence to
the original intent.

4. "to" is *ʿal,* "upon" or "against," in MT. 1QIs[a] has *ʾel,* "unto." 1QIs[a]
is to be preferred unless the evidence of Aramaic is taken to show that *ʿal* can be
understood as "unto" along with the other meaning.

5. MT punctuates differently: " . . . this people draws near me; with its
mouth and with its lips it honors me." Parallelism favors the present reading.

6. LXX takes *wattᵉhî* as *wᵉtōhû,* "their fear of me *is empty*"; cf. Matt.
15:8–9. This is attractive, but MT is the harder reading. At any rate, the Pharisees
manifested the same problem as did the Judaizers (Col. 2:11–3:5).

state of their relationship to God. This is always the word to the orthodox: while God takes no pleasure in the debauched, neither does he delight in those who make their religion a substitute for a life-changing relationship with him (Ps. 51:18, 19 [Eng. 16, 17]; Mic. 6:6–8). This is not to say that God does not care for ceremony, but only that the ceremony he approves is not an end in itself (Deut. 10:12–16; Ps. 84:2–13 [Eng. 1–12]; Col. 3:12–17).

Virtually all modern commentators treat the segment as three separate pieces: vv. 9–10 and 13–14 as originals, with vv. 11–12 as a gloss on 9–10. However, this does not do justice to the unity of thought indicated here. If the portions ever had a separate existence, they have now been put together in such a way as to become meaningless apart from each other.

9 It is apparent that what the prophet has said about Judah's present and future has come as something of a wonder to Judah's rulers. Talk of trusting God instead of Egypt, of victory through defeat, leaves these men shaking their heads. They are not spiritual men, but are wise in the way of the world. To them, such talk is simply foolish (1 Cor. 2:14). The words accompanying Isaiah's call continue to come true. The more he speaks the truth, the less intelligible it becomes to his hearers (6:9, 10). So here in an agony of frustration he cries out to them, "Alright, go ahead and be blind; be insensible, like a drunk. But your problem does not come from alcohol, like the Samaritans'; your problem comes from God, whom you have offended so deeply that he no longer enables you to hear."[7] Characteristically for a Hebrew prophet, it is God who gives enabling grace, and if a people stubbornly misconstrue his words, then that enabling grace is withdrawn.[8] There can be no more frightening motivation to listen to God than this, the thought that if you refuse to hear today, one day you might no longer be able to hear (Acts 28:26–28; Rom. 1:24, 26, 28; Heb. 4:1–11).

10 Interestingly enough it is not the priests who are chiefly to blame for the blindness of the people. Surely they bore their share in suggesting that careful performance of the ceremonies was all that God wanted. But the ones really to blame were those who could have received

7. Cf. 1 Sam. 26:12; Job 4:13.
8. Young cites Penna with disapproval when Penna says Semites characteristically omit secondary causes. Young seems to wish to support double predestination. However, Calvin, whom he quotes approvingly, does not speak of a people who, despite their best efforts, are unable to hear. Instead he talks of God depriving of light those who "by a wicked and depraved hatred of truth of (their) own accord wish for darkness."

a corrective word from God as Amos did (5:21–24)—the prophets and the seers—but did not. So long as a nation has prophets in sufficient number and with sufficient integrity, the religious functionaries can have their perceptions continually purified. But if those upon whom the nation depends for a word from God lose contact with God, that nation is lost like an airliner in a fog with dead radios.

11, 12 These verses give a prose illustration of what has just been said. The wise men and the seers are compared to those who know how to read and write: the scribes upon whom the illiterate had to depend in order to carry on the business of life. But the scribe could not open a sealed scroll. Only the sealer or his designate could perform that task (Rev. 5:1–5). What Isaiah has seen ("the vision of the all" = "the vision of all this") is such a sealed scroll to these people.[9] They have the technical skills to understand God's word, but they lack the spiritual insight which would enable them to see the plain meaning. So, of course, the situation is hopeless for the common person. He cannot even read, let alone open and read. The Church today is in a perilously similar situation. The pews are full of people who look to someone who can "read," but for all too many who can do so, the document is still sealed.

13, 14 These verses take the form of a brief oracle of judgment[10] and sum up the nature of the problem (v. 13) and the solution (v. 14). The charge is one of hypocritical religion. Because the prophets have not been faithful to declare God's word, "this people" has lapsed into the manipulative style of religion typical of paganism.[11] This concern that Israel's religion be one involving the very seat of the personality, *the heart,* is typical of the Bible.[12] Thus the "fear of the Lord" is a way of life which involves an accurate understanding of who God is and a corresponding ordering of one's affairs. To speak of reducing this to a set of "do's" and "don't's" is to move one's faith from the center to the periphery of life. No longer does living with a mighty, dynamic, and free Being demand one's whole attention. Now it can be relegated to the level of the automatic and unthinking. In the same way, when "drawing near" to God becomes

9. Clements asserts that "all this" is the promise of eschatological deliverance known by the postexilic glossator. However, that assertion rests upon the prior conclusion that the material is a postexilic gloss. There is nothing about "all this" which is either postexilic or eschatological.

10. Westermann, *Basic Forms,* pp. 94–95.

11. For other examples of "this people" used in a negative way, cf. 6:10; 8:6; 28:11.

12. See Exod. 35:5; Deut. 10:16; 1 Sam. 10:9; 1 K. 3:9; 1 Chr. 28:9; Ps. 66:18; Isa. 6:10; 51:7; 57:15; Joel 2:13. Cf. *THAT,* I:861–67; *TWOT,* I:466–67.

anything less than awesome and a little eerie, we have evidently forgotten Sinai and replaced interest in the Giver with interest in the gift.[13]

14 Two themes of this book in both its parts are God's capacity to work wonders and his refusal to fit into prearranged, programmed categories.[14] Yet so often this is precisely what the function of religion is: to bring the ineffable within our sphere, to reduce it to our terms, to make God subject to us. Whenever that happens God breaks out, as he has done in St. Francis, the Pietists, the Reformation, the Wesleyan revival, and most recently, in the charismatic movement. However, despite his capacity for novelty, he is not self-contradictory. The new wonders are of a different order from the old, but they are not essentially different from the old. Thus, just as the deliverance from Egypt was a wonder,[15] so also will be deliverance from Babylon, especially when preceded by a fall of Jerusalem which was theoretically impossible for God to permit. Likewise, as it was a wonder for God to incarnate himself in the sons of Jacob, it would be an even greater wonder when he incarnated himself in the Son of Man. It is precisely this old/new continuum which is so difficult for conventional wisdom to handle. Wisdom's role is to make the present and future manageable by studying the results of past actions and synthesizing these into patterns for effective living. There is nothing wrong with this except as it becomes the servant of a wholly worldly desire to control all things for one's own benefit. It is this wisdom which God's passion for newness keeps knocking askew. The true wisdom, asserts the NT, recognizes that the meaning of life is to be open to God, to give him freedom with us, and to live in radical trust of him (1 Cor. 2:1–13; Jas. 1:5–8; 3:13–18).

(3) Those who hide counsel (29:15–24)

15 Woe to those who go deep from the Lord
    to hide counsel;
whose deeds are in a dark place and say,
    "Who sees us or knows us?"
16 Ah, your perversity![1]
    Should the potter be considered like the clay?

---

13. See Exod. 24:2; Num. 8:19; Jer. 30:21; Ezek. 44:13.

14. See 9:5 (Eng. 6); 20:3; 25:1; 28:29; 42:9, 10; 43:19; 48:6; 62:2; 65:17; 66:22.

15. See Exod. 3:20; 15:11; Ps. 78:11; etc.

1. Lit. "your overturning." LXX omits; Targ. "Do you see to overturn your work." 1QIs[a] *hpk mkm*, "things are overturned by you."(?) Cf. GKC, § 147c.

Should the workmanship say[2] to its maker,
"You did not make me"?
Or the design say of its designer,
"He does not understand"?

17 *Is it not but a little while till Lebanon becomes a field,*
and the field a forest?

18 *In that day the deaf will hear the words of a book,*
and out of deep darkness the eyes of the blind will see.

19 *The downtrodden will rejoice in the Lord once again,*
and the poorest of mankind[3] will exult in the Holy One of
Israel.

20 *For the ruthless will cease,*
and the scoffer come to an end,
and all who watch to do evil will be cut off;

21 *those who make a man a sinner with a word,*
who lay a trap for[4] the one who seeks justice in the gate,
and put the righteous down with empty lies.[5]

22 *Therefore, thus says the Lord, the redeemer of Abraham, to the house*
of Jacob,
No longer will Jacob be ashamed;
no longer will his face be pale.

23 *For when he sees it, his children,*
the work of my hands, in the midst,
they will sanctify my name.
They will sanctify the Holy One of Jacob,
and will hold the God of Israel in awe.

24 *Those who err in spirit will know understanding,*
and murmurers will learn knowledge.

With this segment the opening indictment of Judah's leaders comes to a

2. 1QIs[a] has *ḥmr*, "clay," for MT *ʾāmar*, "he says," thus reading "a shape of *clay* to its shaper." This reading is possibly better than MT, but both LXX and Targ. support MT.

3. "the poor of mankind" is probably an expression of the superlative "the poorest of all" (cf. GKC, § 133e). Dahood makes the plausible suggestion that *ʾāḏām* here be understood as a masculine form of *ʾaḏāmâ*, "land," as also in Prov. 30:14b; Jer. 32:20; Zech. 13:5 (*Proverbs and Northwest Semitic Philology* [Rome: Pontifical Biblical Institute, 1973], p. 58; also *Bib* 44 [1963] 272). The parallel with "meek" supports Clements's suggestion that "meek" here does not mean nonassertive as much as helpless or oppressed.

4. BDB lists *yᵉqōšûn*, "to lay a trap for," as a 3rd plural imperfect of an otherwise unknown root *qûš*. However, Young sees it as a perfect of the more common *yqš*. 26:16 shows a similar nunation on a perfect.

5. *tōhû*, "chaos, emptiness, formlessness," but also that which is antithetic to the creation order (Gen. 1:1; Isa. 34:11; 40:23; 44:9).

close. It follows the same pattern as noted previously: denunciation of their foolish plans, which are based on the premise that God cannot save, and reaffirmation of God's intention and ability *to* save after their folly will have precipitated disaster (cf. 28:1–6; 29:1–8, 9–14). Here the affirmation is much the longer part of the segment, perhaps because of its place in conclusion to the two-chapter opening section. The thrust of the affirmation is that God, in his care, will shortly free the weak and the helpless from the oppression of their rapacious leaders. In response to that freedom, the people will glorify God as the only true God.

Although Delitzsch could still speak of vv. 23, 24 as "an incontestably genuine prophecy of Isaiah," it has become almost universal since Duhm to take vv. 17–24 as postexilic, if not later. The chief reasons for this are theological, for it is argued that the glowing predictions of salvation to come are not to be found in preexilic prophecy. Apart from the fact that this point of view begs the question (cf. Mic. 4), it must also be asked why redactors felt encouraged to add these passages to Isaiah if the original form of the prophecy was so uniformly negative. Why not to Amos or Micah or Jeremiah? For that theory to be accepted, the original form of the book will have had to have contained the Judgment/Hope motif in more than a germinal way. Of course, if that is granted, then the whole theory of redactions which subtly altered the impact of the book becomes questionable. Of even more serious import, however, are the theological questions which this point of view raises. The supposed redactors, by putting their words and points of view into the mouth of the older prophet, are making a theological statement which is patently untrue. They are saying "If we repent, there is hope for us, *because* it was foretold by Isaiah." But, if the causal link is in fact false, their opinions are without force. The redactors then have falsified their evidence to win a case. Can this be the source of some of the world's great theology? Finally, there is a literary question. As the text stands now, it has an internal logic: your plans are stupid and corrupt because you will not believe the simplicity of God's promises. If in fact the prophet had no promises of redemption, what is it the rulers were rejecting? If it be said he had promises, but not these, we are faced once again with redactors whose ethics are decidedly questionable, for they have excised the original promises and replaced them with their own.

Verses 15–16 contain the third of the woes declared in chs. 29–33. The first was to the drunkards of Ephraim (28:1), and the second to David's city (29:1). This one now sums up the former two and the theme which emerged in the treatment of them: how foolish for the pot to think it knows more than the potter. That way can only bring woe, for God is the Maker and every other premise must rest on that one (Ps. 100:3). It is apparent that some sort of secret political plan had been made without consultation with people or prophet, and thus, in Isaiah's view, without consultation with God. Probably this is in reference to the decision to break the vassal-covenant with Assyria and to rely on help from Egypt (2 K. 18:7b).[6] Clearly, God has no brief for Assyria as he could have none for Babylon when he would lead Jeremiah to counsel against that revolt (Jer. 27:8–11). What he did contest was the idea that a nation calling itself God's people should endeavor to insure its own freedom and security through a system of secret compacts with other nations without reliance on God. The language of v. 15 is striking in this respect. The translation above is literal: "they go deep from the Lord to hide counsel" (cf. RSV "hide deep from the Lord their counsel"). This evokes the picture of a little group of officials huddled around a table in some basement room of the chancery, as if God could not see them there! (Cf. Ps. 64:3–7 [Eng. 2–6]; 94:7; 139:7–12.) But since Adam and Eve human beings have been trying to hide from God, our own blindness deluding us into believing that he is more blind. Thus, the implied statement that God does not understand is the fullest evidence that *we* do not understand. If our minds were not darkened by our own sinful determination to have our way at all costs, we would be able to understand that the Master Designer has a way for us and that the deepest joy is to find that way and cooperate with it.[7]

16 *Ah, your perversity* sums up the intensity of the prophet's feelings. They have turned things upside down. They tell God what to do rather than seeking to discern what he means to do. They, *they*, tell him that *he* lacks understanding.

For Isaiah, the doctrine of creation is fundamental. As the Maker of the world, God has the right to determine its direction, and moreover, he does have a direction in mind for it. This is not so for the pagan gods. Although those religions can speak of beginnings, their polytheism and their heavy involvements with the social and natural status quo prevent them from speaking of noncontingent, purposive creation. It is this which Isaiah has in mind in the numerous attacks on the idols in chs. 40–48 (41:21–24; 42:8–9; 43:8–9; 44:7–8; etc.). The gods do not know the origin of things and they do not know the end. For the pagan mind, beginnings are only theoretical and endings are all but unthinkable. The

6. Kissane thinks the reference may be to Ahaz's reliance on Assyria (ch. 7), but that seems unlikely in view of chs. 30 and 31 with their continued reference to Egypt.

7. See Ps. 1:6; 37:34; 119:59; Prov. 14:12; Isa. 30:21; 35:8.

continuance of the present is all it knows. Nor is this emphasis upon creation limited to chs. 40–48. It appears here in ch. 29 and also in 17:7, 8 (contrast between Maker and gods made with hands) and 37:16 (God, unlike the gods, made the earth; cf. 6:3).

It is the forgetting of God's right as Maker that leads to ethical relativism. After all, if he is but Bergson's "élan vitale" or Tillich's "ground of all being," then he has only the most generalized will for my behavior and it becomes impossible to speak of overturning anything. There are no explicit standards to overturn. One must do what one feels. On the other hand, the Maker can say, "that is good, and that is bad," because he has a known design which he is seeking to work out. Whether or not "the Force" even knows that I exist, my existence is of no importance to it. The Maker, says Isaiah, does know and cares passionately. Those who say he does not know and care confuse the clay with the Potter, and that is the fundamental error of all strictly human philosophies: they cannot admit of a transcendent God.[8] God is either a part of the system or he does not exist.

17–21 In these verses the writer promises in language echoed elsewhere in the book that the battle is not necessarily to the strong nor the race to the swift. In fact, God promises some overturning of his own. The leaders have taken counsel as if God did not exist, with the result that the ordinary people must bear the brunt of the disaster which those misguided policies will bring about. Nevertheless, God will change all that. The blind will see, the helpless will be empowered, and those who have made a living of injustice will disappear. If all the odds seem to be weighted in favor of the corrupt and the violent, that is the fault of the oddsmakers, for God is on the side of the powerless who trust in him.[9] Nor are we doomed merely to wait for some apocalyptic cataclysm to see this happen. While the Mafia slaughter each other and the rich live in mistrustful loneliness, those who love God and have very little live productive and beneficial lives because they are committed to God's ways. Ultimately the problem is to define successful living. The world's wisdom says power and comfort are success. God's wisdom says love and inner abundance are success. Is that foolishness? If so, God's foolishness is wiser than man's wisdom (1 Cor. 1:25).

Kaiser makes this segment Hellenistic because he says that the

8. For other references to the earth in God's hands, see 10:15; 45:9; Job 10:9; 33:6; Jer. 18:6.
9. Note that Jesus makes the same point in the Beatitudes (Matt. 5:1–12). Cf. also Isa. 11:4.

three groups—the scoffers, the blind, and the righteous— correspond to the divisions which such devout groups as the Essenes saw in Judaism. However, this interpretation fails to recognize that the scoffers and the blind are all through chs. 28 and 29, not all of which are Hellenistic. Is it not also possible that the Hellenistic groups got their language from Isaiah?

17 Although some question remains as to the exact meaning of this verse, it appears to support the interpretation just given, that is, of a coming reversal in the positions of the noble and the common. In several places in the book the forest of Lebanon is used as a symbol for the mighty (2:13; 10:34; 33:9; 35:2; 60:13), and the cutting down of the forest a symbol of humiliation (2:13; 10:34; 37:24). Therefore, it seems likely that the same imagery is in force here: the forest will become a plowed field, whereas the fields will grow up in such a luxurious tangle as to be called a forest. So the mighty of Judah and of the world will fall, but God's common people will flourish. (Blessed are the meek, for they shall inherit the earth, Matt. 5:5.)[10]

18 This verse may have both a general and a specific meaning in this context. In the general sense, the most downtrodden members of a society are likely to be handicapped, as typified by the deaf and the blind. Thus their hearing and seeing express what God will do for the lowly among his people when his kingship is established on the earth (32:3; 35:5). But there is a more specific sense in which these statements apply here; for the result of Isaiah's message, as God had foretold in his commissioning (6:10), had been to make the people more spiritually insensitive than they had been before he delivered the message.

So his preaching was a closed book to his own generation (8:16–18; 29:9–12). But God here promises that the day will come when the blind will see and the deaf will hear. No longer will the words of promise fall on hard, dry ground. Rather, they will find lodging in a receptive soil where they can spring up to that luxurious growth spoken of in v. 17.

19 This verse carries on the thought of v. 18, using the language of the helpless and oppressed. But a further thought is added, one which will reappear in v. 23. This is the idea that the coming deliverance will result in new praise to God, who will be seen as the Holy One (see below on v. 23). Not only will they praise him, but they will also rejoice in him. Thus there will be laughter and rejoicing in his presence and over his

10. An alternate interpretation sees the verse as a promise of blessing in an agricultural setting: even Lebanon will be available for cultivation. Cf. 32:15, where such is intended with "desert" replacing "Lebanon."

presence. There will be delight in his gifts and in his acts of deliverance. All the pent-up feelings of the years of doubt, fear, and anxiety will be released. This happened annually in the feasts. It also happened in the return from exile and supremely in Christ's coming as culminated in Pentecost. Yet we wait for another day when all these foretastes will be rolled into one, when we will rejoice in him forevermore (Rev. 22:1–5).

20–21 Verses 18–19 talked of the coming bliss of the helpless. These two verses speak of the destruction of the mighty who helped oppress the helpless. Thus we see the outworking of the reversal imaged in v. 17. Verse 20 lists three classes of the mighty and v. 21 expands on the third class. Synonymous verbs are used of all three: "cease," "come to an end," and "cut off." The point of the statements is not to teach annihilation of the wicked (as opposed to eternal punishment), but to say that these kinds of people will not flourish; their line will not be long on the earth, nor will they produce anything lasting (cf. Ps. 1; 92:6; 101:7, 8; 109:6–14 contra Ps. 72 in praise of the righteous king).

the ruthless are the oppressors who heartlessly squeeze the weak to extract what they can from them (13:11; 25:3, 4, 5; 29:5; 49:25).

the scoffer is the one who mocks the normal standards of truth, honor, and decency and delights to serve himself at the cost of others (28:15; cf. also Prov. 1:22; 13:1; etc.).

all who watch to do evil are especially defined by v. 22 as those in political and judicial authority who are ever on the alert for ways to use their power to prey on the innocent (cf. esp. Jer. 5:6, where the verb is applied to the leopard watching its prey). This predation is described in three ways. First, he uses false testimony to make an innocent man appear guilty (elsewhere the verb means "to cause to sin," but here the context makes it clear that the sense is "to cause him to be a sinner" [in the official sense!]). Second, when someone comes before the elders sitting in the city gate to plead a case, this person is there to trip up the supplicant in legal niceties (cf. Exod. 23:6; Amos 5:12; Mal. 3:5). Third, they use clouds of empty platitudes and verbosity to confuse the issue so that the genuinely righteous person is made to appear otherwise ("put down").

22–24 These verses offer the summation not only of vv. 15–21, but also of chs. 28 and 29. Evoking the patriarchs of the past and pointing to the children of the future, he looks to a time when the true holiness of God will be in the forefront of everyone's mind because he will have manifested his sole lordship through the deliverance of his people (cf. Ezek. 36:22–23).

22 *Therefore* is not merely causal here in the sense that it neatly states the effects of previously stated causes. Rather, it introduces a summation. It might be paraphrased loosely as "in the light of all that has been said, then, I wish to say." So to the scoffers he insists that God will deliver and that *he* will be recognized for the deliverance, not they and their flawed schemes; to the poor he says that he sees a day when they will be leading the praises of God, not the stuffy priesthood of the temple.

the redeemer of Abraham has been a troublesome phrase to commentators, both because of the awkward grammatical structure within which it stands and because of its unclear reference. The sentence reads literally, "Thus says the Lord to the house of Jacob, who redeemed Abraham, 'No longer. . . .'" The most natural construction would make Jacob the redeemer of Abraham, an obvious impossibility.[11] Lowenthal proposed reading, "The God of the house of Jacob" (reading *'el,* "God," instead of *'el,* "unto"). This suggestion is attractive and has been followed by many modern commentators. As Kaiser has pointed out, however, there is no warrant among the versions for such an emendation. So it seems best to retain the MT with its apparent awkwardness.

The theological problem is occasioned by the fact that nothing in the canonical literature speaks of any "redemption" of Abraham. An apocryphal legend tells of his being rescued from idolators in Ur, and particularly those scholars who see the segment as late take this as a possible basis for the statement here.[12] At the same time, it is clear that in the most general sense God did redeem Abraham, in that he called him to himself and delivered him from the death of sin, and that deliverance may be all that is intended here. The main point, as stated above, seems to be evocative ("hitherto has the Lord helped"), and we can trust him to continue that help.

No longer . . . ashamed reiterates one of the themes of Isaiah and of the Bible in general: Jacob will finally put its trust in God and not in other places. Those other places have let the nation down and it has been disgraced.[13] But there will come a day when God will demonstrate his power through them, or even in spite of them, and they will be exultant.

23 *his children* has been treated primarily in one of two ways, either as a gloss explaining "it" and referring to the works of God's hands (Ewald), or as an example of nearer definition: "When he, that is, his

---

11. LXX has resolved the problem by reading " . . . Jacob, which he separated from Abraham. . . ." But this reading looks simply like an attempt to solve the problem, not a witness to a better text. Kissane goes even further than Lowenthal and offers "the God of Abraham who redeemed the house of Jacob."

12. It is interesting that Abraham is rarely mentioned in the prophets (Mic. 7:20; Jer. 33:26; Ezek. 33:24; Isa. 41:8; 51:2; 63:16).

13. One of those places would be the one to which they were presently turning: Egypt (30:3).

children, see . . . *they* will praise. . . ." The latter has the advantage of explaining the shift from singular to plural in the sentence, but such a shift is common enough in the prophets not to need this kind of justification for its existence. As for the former, it must be admitted that the phrase does appear somewhat obtrusive in the sentence, but as with so many of what criticism has designated as glosses, it must be very old, if it is a gloss, for it appears in all the versions. Whatever its source, it fits the Isaianic setting well, for the image of child-bearing and of progeny is a prominent one in the book.[14] The point here would be that instead of being disgraced by its barrenness, the house of Jacob would be wonderfully fruitful, a condition provoking admiration on all sides.

The response of Jacob will be to sanctify the name of the Holy One. As indicated by Ezek. 36:19–26, to defile God's name is to make him appear less than God. Thus, to sanctify his name is to declare to oneself and the world that he is truly God. Indeed, he is the only one who can justly lay claim to the epithet "holy." For all the other deities are merely projections of creation. He alone is truly "Other," not only in existence but in character as well. One might think of such perfection as a source of terror, but because it is a perfection of love, though it is awe-ful, it is not terrifying (in the sense that terror is a response to the vicious and the arbitrary). In fact, his otherness, his holiness, is the source of our hope. For we have proven in this century, if not before, that the universe cannot save itself. We must have Someone from beyond who is holy enough to save us. So those who have experienced the depths of his grace have no desire to bring him down to their level. They wish to tell the world of his holiness. For them the opening lines of the Lord's Prayer come easily, especially the second: "Hallowed (sanctified) be thy name" (cf. Matt. 6:9).

24 The order of events is significant here: deliverance is followed by praise, which results in understanding (cf. Ps. 51:12–19 [Eng. 10–17] for the same order). To *know understanding* and *learn knowledge* is to come to an experiential grasp of truth. The erring and the murmurers would have understanding first and by it save themselves. But it will not work in that way. God saves through grace alone. Understanding comes from meditation on his work. (So the giving of the Torah follows the Exodus.) This order was a stumbling block to the Jews of Isaiah's day and it remains so to the nominal church as well as to the world today. But the truth remains: people come to know God through the demonstration of his holiness in the lives of other people.

14. See 26:16–18; 37:3; 49:20–22; 54:1; 56:3–5; 60:49; 66:8, 9. Cf. also 14:21; 39:7; 45:11; 51:18; 54:13; 65:20.

b. WOE TO THOSE WHO TRUST IN EGYPT (30:1–31:9)

(1) Woe to the rebellious children (30:1–18)

(a) Egypt—"Rahab-do-nothing" (30:1–7)

1 Woe to stubborn children, says the Lord,
  making[1] plans, but not from me,
weaving a web, but not from my Spirit,
  so that[2] sin is added[3] to sin.
2 Those who set out to go down to Egypt
  but did not inquire for my word,[4]
taking refuge[5] in Pharaoh's stronghold,
  and sheltering in the shadow of Egypt.
3 But the stronghold of Pharaoh will become your shame,
  and the shelter in the shade of Egypt humiliation.
4 Although[6] his princes are in Zoan,
  and his messengers have reached Tahpanhes,
5 everyone will be put to shame[7]
  on account of a people not able to profit them,
neither helping nor profiting,
  but bringing to shame, even reproach.
6 A burden on the beasts of the Negeb:[8]
In a land of distress and straits,
  of lion and roaring[9] lion,

1. The verbs here are infinitives which are used to describe the nature of the rebellion (rebellion . . . by doing. . .). Cf. Williams, *Syntax*, § 195.

2. Unless sarcasm is intended, it is best to understand *lᵉmaʿan* as introducing result rather than purpose.

3. Note that the infinitive *sᵉpôṯ* is being treated analogously to the *Lamed He* verbs (cf. 29:1; Num. 32:14; Deut. 29:18).

4. Lit. "my mouth," very frequent in the Pentateuch. Cf. also Josh. 9:14. The term "to inquire," *šāʾal*, takes on an almost technical sense in this respect; so Judg. 1:1; 20:18, 23, 27; 1 Sam. 10:22; 23:2, 4.

5. MT is vocalized as *ʿōz*, "strength" (so Targ. and AV). However, this is apparently only a variant form of *ʿûz*, "to take refuge."

6. Thus the opening *kî* is a concessive, "although." So A. Kushke, *ZAW* 64 (1952) 195.

7. MT Ketib has *hbʾyš*, which would appear to be "make to stink." Qere has *hôḇîš*, "put to shame," which accords better with the context although the former could fit. The suggestion of *BHS* that a conflation of *kōl-habbāʾ hôḇîš* explains the MT is supported by the Targ.: "They are all going to their shame."

8. In *Ugaritic-Hebrew Philology*, BibOr 17 (Rome: Pontifical Biblical Institute, 1965), p. 66, Dahood compares *ngb*, "Negeb," to the Ugar. *ngb*, "to supply," and suggests the phrase is "beast of burden."

9. MT "lion and lion *from them*" (*mēhem*). We suggest *mēhēm* would be "moving noisily" (cf. *BHS*) or *nōhām*, "growling, roaring." Cf. 5:29, 30.

    a viper and fiery serpent.
  They carry their riches on a donkey's shoulder,
    their treasure on a camel's hump,
    for the sake of a people who will not profit[10] *them.*
7 *As for Egypt,*
    their help is completely empty.
  Therefore, I call this one,
  "Rahab who sits still." [11]

Chapters 30–31 move from the more general denunciation of chs. 29–30 to specific ones aimed at the alliance with Egypt. In the earlier section, it seems to have been the condition and attitude of the people which the prophet was addressing. Now he turns to speak of the results which are flowing from those attitudes—namely, the dependence upon the very power which once enslaved them.

The segment follows much the same pattern of development already seen: denunciation followed by promise. Ch. 30 lengthens the form while ch. 31 shortens it, but the pattern is the same in each. In ch. 30 the denunciation extends at least to v. 17 and perhaps to v. 18 (see below), but hope bursts forth in v. 19 and continues through to the end of the chapter. Just as the denunciation is more specific here than formerly, so is the promise, with deliverance from Assyria being expressly stated (v. 31). In ch. 31, the denunciation of the alliance appears in vv. 1–3 and the promise of Assyria's defeat follows in vv. 4–9. So the point continues to be: all your human conniving cannot save you. Your only resource is God, and the good news is that he wants to save you—indeed, he *will*, so why go to Egypt?

In 30:1–18 Isaiah explores at considerable length the foolishness of the decision to depend on Egypt for help in view of Egypt's character (vv. 1–7) and God's word (vv. 2, 8, 15). Only an ingrained obstinacy could make them refuse to hear God's good news (vv. 1, 2, 9–11, 15b), he concludes. So, since they refuse to wait upon the Lord, the Lord must wait upon them, until the time when their follies have left them helpless and they must turn to him as a last resort (v. 18). Verse 18 may be taken either as the conclusion to vv. 1–17, as here, or as the introduction to vv. 19–33, as in most other commentaries, but little difference in sense results. It seems to be one of those transitional phrases which are charac-

10. On the plural verb "they will not profit" with the singular collective, see GKC, §§ 145b, c.
11. MT *rḥb hm šbt*, "Rahab are they, sitting" (?). Emendation produces *rḥb hmšbt*, "Rahab the one who sits."

teristic of the book.[12] Reasons for considering it with vv. 1–17 will be given below.

In 30:1–7 Isaiah heaps his scorn upon the idea of Egypt offering Judah any substantive help. God will not let them be put to shame if they will trust him (29:22), but Egypt surely would shame them. As ch. 19 argued, Egypt has nothing which Judah does not have in her Lord, so what help can she give? (So also 31:1–3.)

There is some disagreement over the precise time-reference of the events here described. Skinner and Wildberger take the passage to refer to the revolt against Sargon in 714–711 (20:1–6), to which they also consider 18:1–6 to refer. This would be early in the days of the Saite Dynasty before the Ethiopian Shabako had unified Egypt under his control. However, little is known about those events and 18:1–6 is sufficiently ambiguous to be understood in several ways. Furthermore, it appears that Isaiah's words here show some dependence upon the description of Egypt's fickleness to the ruler of Ashdod in 20:1–6. In the light of these uncertainties, it seems best to date this account, with the majority of commentators, to 701, either shortly before or shortly after the Egyptian army's advance to Eltekeh and Sennacherib's defeat of it there.[13]

By this time Judah was *in extremis*. Whatever hopes Hezekiah may have had for the success of his revolt, and it was evidently carefully planned, as the Siloam tunnel indicates, those hopes were now dashed. All his allies had either capitulated or been defeated, his outer fortresses were now defeated, and the end was clearly at hand. If any human help was to be found, Egypt was the only possibility. That Hezekiah's name is not mentioned in Isaiah's denunciation of the Egyptian alliance may suggest that he was not its instigator but that it was forced on him by his advisers. But from whatever source, the decision had evidently been made, and in fact, vv. 2, 4, and 6 may indicate that envoys were already on their way to Egypt.

1 For Isaiah this decision could only stem from the basic rebelliousness of his people (1:2–4, 20, 23). God's word concerning alliances with Egypt was very clear: they were forbidden (Exod. 13:17; Deut. 17:16). Without doubt the chief reason for this prohibition was to negate as much as possible the heavy influence such an old and established pagan culture could have had (and did have, if we look at Jeroboam's bull cult) upon a struggling and culturally deprived people like the Hebrews. So they had not needed a new word from God; they only needed to obey the one they

---

12. So 1:9; 2:5; ch. 6; 8:23 (Eng. 9:1); 17:9; etc.
13. *ARAB*, II:120–21; *ANET*, pp. 287–88.

had. But the mind which is set on this world's ways cannot see the wisdom of God's ways. To it, rebellion is not rebellion but simply common sense.[14]

weaving a web interprets the noun as in 25:7 and takes the verb as from *skk*.[15] In this sense then it speaks of the alliance with Egypt. It is also possible that the verb is *nsk,* "to pour out." In this case the noun would mean "libation." But those who read in this way would also see an alliance in view, with the libation being a part of the ceremonies involved with sealing the covenant between the two nations. Again, this act would constitute rebellion against Yahweh, for it would involve recognition, if not worship, of the Egyptian gods.

so that sin is added to sin may be understood in at least two ways. First, it may mean that to the sin of bringing Assyria into the land of Canaan through Ahaz's alliance with her, they now add the sin of allying themselves with Egypt to get Assyria out! But it is also possible that it is the sin of concealment being added to the sin of alliance.[16] In any case, it is true that something about the human condition leads us not to confess sin but to compound it with more. It is also true, as with Jacob, that when we once set out to make ourselves secure in ourselves, sin against God and others comes naturally, for we have made ourselves gods and our ends then justify any means.

2 *inquire for my word,* along with the two similar phrases in v. 1, "not from me," "not from my Spirit," all speak of the biblical insistence upon a life guided by God's revelation. Undoubtedly here it is a direct prophetic word which is intended. The decision-makers had not consulted with the prophet before or after making their plans, most probably because they knew that God would contradict what they wanted to do (30:10, 11; cf. also King Ahab's words concerning the prophet Micaiah, 1 K. 22:8). Yet the whole basis of the life of faith is summed up in Jesus' words in the garden of Gethsemane, "Not my will, but thine be done" (Mark 14:36). Only someone who is absolutely convinced of God's good intentions toward him can say those words. All others are doomed to distrust God and to believe that their will is better than his, that they, the pot, know better than the Potter (29:16). Nor is his word something static and dead. It is his mouth and comes to us by his Spirit (cf. Num. 12:8). Thus his will and way are dynamic and personal, as he is. The written word stands

---

14. Clements believes the major reference here is to rebellion against Assyria. It may be granted that there is a double entendre in the term, but the context makes it plain that it is chiefly God who is being rebelled against.

15. So Delitzsch and Alexander following the Vulgate.

16. So Skinner.

fixed as a check upon our easily deceived minds, but unless its truth is applied to us personally by God's Spirit, that truth remains purely academic.

refuge and *shelter* are words which have a particular poignancy because of their frequent appearance in the Psalms with reference to God.[17] Thus the nature of Judah's rebellion is further underlined. It is not merely the making of a defensive alliance with a neighboring country which is so odious. It is the repudiation of a personal relationship of dependence upon and affection for their God. Probably the people would not have described it so. They probably expected to continue as God's people. But they had in fact exchanged the shadow of the Almighty (Ps. 91:1) for the shadow of one very small human being, the Pharaoh. For Jesus' words were true then as now, "No man can serve two masters" (Matt. 6:24).

3 But Egypt cannot afford the protection Judah seeks. Her time as a world power was long past. Shabako, the pharaoh at this time, was a Nubian, not an Egyptian. Egypt did not even have the cultural strength to produce her own leadership, let alone protect anyone else. In the event, the Egyptians were put to rout barely one hundred miles from their own border by an Assyrian army six hundred miles from home. So, Isaiah says, to lean upon the staff of Egypt is to be publicly disgraced, for that staff will collapse under you (cf. 36:6, the words of an Assyrian!). So they have rejected trust in God who would not have failed them and instead have committed themselves to Pharaoh, who most assuredly will.

4 It is not made plain by the text whose princes and messengers are intended, the Pharaoh's or Judah's. In either case, the verse seems to be saying that the failure of Egyptian support will come in spite of what might be seen as indications to the contrary. These indications might be either that the Nubians had firmly established their control over the Delta region from Zoan (Tanis) in the northeast to Tahpanhes (Heracleopolis) south of Memphis, or that the Judean emissaries had been received from one end of Lower Egypt to the other.

5 At any rate, says Isaiah, Egypt will not be able to do Judah good; she will only plunge her to deeper disgrace.

6–7 The pronouncement concerning the animals of the Negeb closes this segment in a graphic and concrete way, a stylistic device typical

---

17. "refuge," "shelter," Ps. 14:6; 46:2 (Eng. 1); 57:2 (Eng. 1); 62:8, 9 (Eng. 7, 8); 71:7; 91:2, 9; 94:22; 104:18; 142:6 (Eng. 5); "shadow," Ps. 17:8; 36:8 (Eng. 7); 57:2 (Eng. 1); 63:8 (Eng. 7); 121:5. Of special interest are Isa. 4:6 and 25:4, as well as 28:15, 17. For additional references to *ʿōz* (or *ʿūz*; see n. 5 above) as "take refuge" or "refuge," see Isa. 10:31; Jer. 4:6; 6:1; Ps. 31:3 (Eng. 2); 37:39; 52:9 (Eng. 7); 60:9 (Eng. 7); etc.

of the book (cf. 3:18–4:1; 5:1–7; 14:3–21; 20:1–6; etc.). The original unity of these verses with vv. 1–5 has been much debated. The debate has generally revolved around the title, which, like those of chs. 20–22, seems to be based on catchwords in the context. According to normal form-critical theory, a piece so entitled had a separate existence independent of its present context. However, the content of the two verses shows so many connections with vv. 1–5 that such independence seems unlikely. That being so, it is frequently concluded that the title is not original.[18] However, one wonders if that expedient is necessary. In view of the reference to the burdens borne by the animals (v. 6b), the prophet may have used the term *maśśā*, "burden," as a kind of double pun. Here was a "burden" concerning the "burden-bearers."

The language is rather extravagant, but it makes its point well. A caravan loaded with treasures struggles through wild terrain infested with lions and snakes, all to buy the help of an old dragon who is in fact helpless. All the cost in effort and wealth will come to nothing, says the prophet.

6 Some scholars comment that the coastal road through the Negeb cannot have been so severe, and that this is an indication that Sennacherib had already cut that road, forcing the envoys to cross the harsh Sinai Peninsula, retracing the road over which their forefathers had come. (Note the reference to fiery serpents, Num. 21:6; Deut. 8:15.) While this explanation may be true, it is also true that this is poetic language and overliteralism is to be avoided in such a case.[19] So the author may be using these figures of lions and snakes merely to talk about the great danger and risk involved in these overtures to Egypt.

As for Egypt, their help is completely empty is rough and abrupt in Hebrew.[20] But evidently this is exactly the impact the author wishes to

18. So Duhm proposed to emend *maśśā' bahᵃmôt* to *baššammôt*, "in the desert." But as Delitzsch rightly observed, removal of the title would not remove the sense of the change in literary style. His suggestion to read *bahᵃmôt hannegeb* as "hippopotamus of the south" is interesting but has received little support (cf. Job 40:15; etc.). K. D. Schunck adopted it (without reference to Delitzsch), but he wishes to make the whole (with v. 8) an oracle against Egypt, which may or may not be the case (*ZAW* 78 [1966] 48–56).

19. Note Esarhaddon's mention of two-headed serpents on the border of Egypt (*ARAB*, II:220). There may be an element of convention involved here as well.

20. Lit. "Egypt, vanity and emptiness they will help." There may be an implied question mark after the name: Egypt? The synonymous terms "vanity and emptiness" are here taken as a hendiadys.

make, as indicated by his final taunt. Somehow, he must help his people
to drop their age-old sense of inferiority before Egypt's opulent culture
and realize that whatever she might have been, she is now impotent.

Rahab who sits still presents a striking dissonance in ideas.[21] On
the one hand, Rahab is the sea monster of popular legend. She is the
ancient chaotic Matter against whom the gods struggled for survival, only
subduing her by dint of the last bit of effort. The Hebrews used that legend
as a literary allusion when they spoke of God overcoming Egypt to set
them free.[22] So is that who Egypt is? Some ancient Rahab with all the
destructive powers of chaos at her command? Hardly. She is more like a
fat old grandmother sitting sleepily in the sun. Why go to all that effort
to buy her help?

(b) You would not (30:8–18)

8 *Now go, write upon a tablet with them*[1]
    and inscribe it in a book.
that it might be for another day,
    for a witness[2] *forever.*
9 *for this is a rebellious people, false sons,*
    sons who would not hear the instruction of the Lord.
10 *Who say to the seers, "Do not see,"*
    and to the visionaries, "Do not envision straight things for us.
Speak smooth things to us, envision deceptions.
11 *Turn aside from the way, turn off the path;*[3]
    take the Holy One of Israel from before us."
12 *Therefore, thus says the Holy One of Israel,*
    "Because you have rejected this word
        and have trusted in oppression and crookedness
        and have leaned on it,
13 *therefore this iniquity will be to you*

---

21. See n. 11 above. If the MT is correct, Young's translation has merit
in that it contains some of the flavor of the first line: "Rahab are they? A sitting!"

22. See J. Oswalt, "The Myth of the Dragon and Old Testament Faith,"
EvQ 49 (1977) 163–172. For references to "Rahab" see 51:9; Job 9:13; 26:12;
Ps. 87:4; 89:11 (Eng. 10). See also K. D. Schunck, "Jes. 30, 6–8 und die Deutung
der Rahab im AT," *ZAW* 78 (1966) 48–56.

1. Cf. Deut. 31:21, 26. The meaning of *'ittām*, "with them," perhaps is
"in their presence." So this generation is a witness to the witness against them.

2. Reading *'ēd* with Targ. instead of MT *'ad*, "forever." (?)

3. *minnê*, "from (the path)," is apparently an unusual poetic form of *min*
(usually *minnî;* cf. BDB, p. 577d). The parallel use of "way" and "path" is another
common feature of wisdom; Jensen, *Tora*, pp. 93–94.

> *like a break[4] falling,*
> a bulge in a high wall,
>> *whose breaking comes with breathtaking suddenness.*
> 14 *Its breaking will be like the breaking of a potter's jug;*
>> *broken,[5] it will not be spared.*
> *Nor will there be found among its pieces a sherd*
>> *with which to rake[6] the fire from the hearth,*
>> *or to scoop up water from a reservoir.[7]*
> 15 *For thus says the Sovereign Lord,*
>> *the Holy One of Israel,*
> *"In returning and rest, you will be saved;*
>> *in quietness and in trust shall be your strength.*
> *But you would not."*
> 16 *You said, "No, we will flee on horses."*
>> *Therefore, you will flee.*
> *"On the swift we will ride."*
>> *Therefore, your pursuers will be swift.*
> 17 *One thousand at the challenge of one,*
>> *at the challenge of five,[8] you will flee,*

4. The idea of a break in a wall falling as the MT has it is difficult for some to visualize. So Skinner suggests a crack which starts at the top of the wall and descends (so also Young). However, this may be overly literalistic. The idea of a bulge falling is not difficult and "bulge" and "break" seem to be treated synonymously here. Thus the sense is that a bulge appears high on the wall, eventually breaks open, and the "break"—the broken portion of the bulge—falls to the ground.

5. The verb is 3rd masc. sing. perfect, "he broke it," but the subject is left undefined. Some take God as the subject, but that seems out of place in the imagery, so it is more likely that the indefinite 3rd person is to be treated as a passive, "it is broken."

6. Dahood suggests that *ḥāṭâ* (rake) here does not mean so much "to snatch up" fire (BDB) as "to remove" and refers to removing coals from a hearth. He cites Prov. 25:22 ("Two Pauline quotations from the Old Testament," *CBQ* 17 [1955] 22).

7. *geḇeʾ*, "cistern, reservoir" (?), has aroused interest because a sherd would be useless for getting water from a cistern, which was typically rather deep and somewhat bell-shaped. P. Reymond, "Un tesson pour 'ramasser' de l'eau á la mare (Isaie xxx,14)," *VT* 7 (1957) 203–207, suggested "pool," but C. de Geus, "The Importance of Archeological Research into the Palestinian Agricultural Terraces, with an Excursus on the Hebrew Word *gbl*," *PEQ* 107 (1975) 65–74, makes an even better case for "reservoir" or "storage tank."

8. The Hebrew here seems very awkward, so that it is hard to avoid the conclusion that something is amiss. Translators who accept the MT almost universally supply words in parentheses to get good sense. So Mauchline "at the challenge of five (a people as great as) you will flee," or Delitzsch "or at the challenge of five (at most)," etc. 1QIs[a] drops the second "challenge" whereas

> *until your remnant is like a pole on the top of a mountain,*
> *like an ensign on a hilltop.*
> 18 *Therefore, the Lord waits to be gracious to you*
> *and therefore he is exalted[9] to be compassionate to you.*
> *For the Lord is a God of justice;*
> *blessed are all who wait for him.*

In these verses the prophet turns from talking about the reliance upon Egypt (vv. 1–7) to the attitudes which prompted that alliance. Fundamentally, it is a refusal to trust God (v. 15), which is in fact what the entire division (chs. 7–39) is about. And having decided that Egypt is to be trusted more than God, they do not wish to hear anything which would call their choice into question. They had constructed a conceptual framework. Jesus encountered much the same response from the Pharisees. They were convinced that right standing before God was achieved through legalistic righteousness and they refused even to hear data which might call their conviction into question (Luke 6:6–11). But Isaiah says that if they will not hear the truth from his lips, then they will hear it from history. They can construct a false model of reality for only a limited time. Then reality will smash their model. They have refused to wait for the Lord's help and have rushed off to help themselves. So the Lord must wait for them, as he did for Jacob, until circumstances will have reduced them to helplessness. But the good news is that he waits to be gracious (v. 18). It seems so strange that it is only after we break ourselves on the results of our pride that we are able to see him where he has been all along, offering his grace to us. But the truth remains—if we will not wait for him, then he will wait until our circumstances force us to turn to him.[10]

8 The exact contents of what Isaiah was to write is a matter for debate. Some (e.g., Delitzsch, Kaiser), taking their clue from the verb *inscribe* as well as the mention of *tablet,* conclude that only the name Rahab from v. 7 was intended, it being chiseled in stone in a public place. At the opposite pole are those (e.g., Scott, Skinner) who believe that

---

LXX changes "you will flee" to "a myriad will flee." In each case, it appears that the translator is struggling with a difficult text rather than giving a witness to another original reading.

9. Driver argues that "exalts" is not a good parallel to "wait" and so adduces the Arabic root *rwm,* "to wait eagerly" (*JTS* 38 [1937] 44). Both LXX and Targ. agree with MT.

10. Childs (*Crisis,* pp. 35–38) sees vv. 8–17 as an invective threat along the classical lines of that form in Amos. Others such as Kaiser and Wildberger see it as composed of semi-independent units (so Wildberger: vv. 8–11, 12–14, 15–17).

major parts of the diatribe against Egypt in chs. 28–32 were to be written, probably in a scroll. The latter seems more likely in view of the poetic nature of the command. "Write on a tablet, inscribe in a book" must be understood in a broad way, and not have its parts pulled out for a narrowly literal interpretation, such as would be required if "tablet" and "inscribe" were emphasized to the exclusion of "write" and "book."

The purpose of the writing is of great importance to the interpretation. The written material was to stand as an eternal witness about days to come. Thus, as indicated also by 8:16, its chief value was not for the present deafened, hardened generation, but for generations yet to be born. They would see the record of God's promises, both of disaster and blessing, see how those were realized, and believe. This interpretation argues that a rather complete record would be needed so that future readers could understanding the meaning of the witness.[11]

9–11 These verses reiterate for us why such a witness was necessary: The people refused to hear what the prophet was saying to them. As noted above, if they were to listen to this strange man, they would have to alter their view of God and their way of responding to him. Unwilling to make such an alteration, they refused to listen to Isaiah.

this is a rebellious people is a remarkable statement in the context of the ancient Near East. Every other people caused its victories and its triumphs to be recorded. If we know anything untoward about a people, it has had to be pieced together from other sources, certainly not from their own national literature. But the Hebrews somehow realized that they did not make reality. Reality was resident in One who was outside of themselves and outside of what they would wish to be so. That Isaiah's bitter words about his people have been preserved is evidence not only of the supernatural preservation of the Word, but also that his view that the Transcendent One's opinions of us are more important than our own of ourselves did triumph among the Hebrew people.

false sons carries with it implications which are difficult to convey in the translation. The versions are unanimous in translating "lying." While this is a technically correct translation of *kḥš*, it is not so much that the sons tell lies as that they *are* lies. They are untrue to what a son should

---

11. As noted in the Introduction, these references (here as well as 6:9–13 and 8:16) perhaps give a basis for answering the question, "Why would a prophet of the 8th century address people living in the 6th?" He was not writing for his own generation, he was writing for the future so that the follies of his own time would not be fatal for the nation.

be, which is respectful and obedient. So it could also be said that they are "disappointing sons."

Joseph Jensen points out the many allusions to the wisdom teachings here.[12] The reference to sons (Prov. 2:1, etc.) is one of those allusions, as is the use of *tôrâ* or "instruction." In terms of conventional, political wisdom, the alliance with Egypt made some sense. After all, who else could offer any help against the Assyrian juggernaut? And since the wisdom teaching seemed to flourish in the court setting, the princes may very well have been using some of the sayings of the wise to enforce their plans. If that is the case, Isaiah is then attacking them head on. Their "wisdom" in fact prevents them from responding as true sons of God, whose most happy duty is not to categorize all existence into pragmatic epigrams but to be taught by their Father.

10 It is generally agreed that the words quoted here are not the actual words of the people, but as in 29:15, they represent their true feelings. No one wishes to receive condemnation or to be challenged to behavior which is difficult or costly. We would much rather hear counsel which encourages us to take the path of least resistance and encourages us to good opinions of ourselves. But in fact such counsel takes no account of our unholiness and God's holiness. It is as though bright light could be brought into a barn and not reveal dust, dirt, and manure. So the universal experience of the biblical prophets was to speak words which were full of demand for renunciation and commitment and to be rejected for their harshness, while others were all too willing to receive privilege and honor for saying what people wanted to hear.[13]

Having made up their minds as to the course of action they intended to take, the people were no longer interested in hearing counsel which did not confirm their decision. Having become bent, they hated the picture of straightness which Isaiah kept putting before them. This is not to say that they acknowledged their bentness, but that they did recognize a discrepancy between what they thought was acceptable and what he thought was acceptable and that they were tired of hearing his point of view.

But Isaiah insists that what they are actually trying to get him to do is to lead them astray. When they tell him to alter his message, they are asking him to confirm them and to take them farther away from the Holy One. In the words *take the Holy One of Israel from before us*, it is almost possible to see the wry grins of people who see Isaiah coming in

---

12. *The Use of tôrâ by Isaiah*, pp. 113–120.
13. Cf. 1 K. 22:8; Jer. 6:14; 14:13–16; 20:9–10; 28:8–9; Ezek. 13:10–12; Hos. 9:7–9; Amos 2:12; 7:12, 16; Mic. 2:6–11; 3:5, 11.

the distance, and say, "Oh no, we're in for another dose of 'the Holy One'" (cf. 5:19). Their eyes were blind to the vision which Isaiah had seen and had spent his life trying to convey. They could not catch a glimpse of God's transcendent perfection, nor of his glory which is imminent in every scrap of this earth. And since they could not see it, they wished Isaiah would stop seeing (v. 10) too, so that he could speak of smooth, affirming things and not of a God whose splendor demanded impossible things of them.[14]

12–14 The opening line is heavy with irony in the light of v. 11. Do they wish to hear no more of the Holy One of Israel? Then it is precisely for them that the Holy One has a word. They have blinded and deafened themselves so that they may continue on their mad way. Now there only remains to announce the results of such an attitude. Slowly those results will gather weight, but they will come in an instant like a collapsed wall or a shattered jug. Probably there were some who had been mocking Isaiah and telling him to be quiet since none of the doom he had been forecasting from the Holy One had yet come to pass (5:19). But instead of subsiding, he asserts his prophecy with all the force of imagery at his command.

12 *this word* is troublesome to some commentators because it has no clear antecedent in the previous verses. Some therefore take vv. 12–14 as a fragment of another oracle that has been pressed into service here, while Kissane wished to place vv. 15–17 between vv. 11 and 12. But neither of these expedients seems required. The "word" is the "instruction" of the Lord (through Isaiah) that was rejected in vv. 9, 10, and 11.

oppression and crookedness are somewhat ambiguous in their reference. On the surface they would seem to refer to social injustice. But that meaning seems out of place in this passage, which addresses political misdealing. Some commentators (Delitzsch, Skinner) refer the oppression to that of war taxation, but that is hardly obvious. Others (Kaiser, *BHK*) suggest that ʿōšeq, "oppression," should be emended to ʿiqqēš, "twistedness."[15] This suggestion is attractive but lacks clear support in the versions.[16] If the MT is correct, the intent may be to condemn the style of leadership that has resulted in these bad decisions, one which has relied upon the politics of coercion and deception.

---

14. Just as had been predicted at his call, Isaiah's message had had the effect of blinding and deafening his people because they refused to hear or see what contradicted their wishes (6:9–10).

15. Note Prov. 2:15, where ʿiqqēš parallels nālôz, as here.

16. LXX has "lying" for "oppression," but also "murmuring" for "crookedness."

13 *this iniquity* contrasts with "this word" in v. 12. As is frequently the case with "iniquity," it is difficult to distinguish between the act and the culpability attaching to the act.[17] In any case, the refusal to be instructed by God brings a person into estrangement from him, and that estrangement is an estrangement from life that must be corrected at once if disaster is not to occur. This impending disaster is described in two figures, both of which indicate suddenness and totality. The first is a wall which is beginning to topple.[18] The interval from the first cracks until the actual collapse may be a long time, but when the collapse comes it is terribly sudden and irreversible. So it will be with this refusal to rely on God. Years may pass, but one day the Assyrians will stand at the door with all Judah in ruins behind them.

14 When the wall collapses it will be shattered as suddenly and completely as a jug dropped on a rock. One minute the jug was whole and the next minute it is only pieces. So also with the toppling wall. What this indicates is clear: that judgment has not yet come is hardly grounds for saying it will not come. The NT picks up the same kind of warning about the final judgment (Matt. 24:36–44; Mark 13:32–37; 2 Pet. 3:3–10). The only prevention for such sudden destruction is to listen to the word of God and to gaze upon the Holy One, no matter how that conflicts with our preconceived notions for our security.

15–18 In these verses Isaiah speaks again of God's message, the Judeans' insistence upon their own devices, the disaster which will come of that, and the necessity which all this places upon God to wait until they are in a position to receive before he can be gracious to them. Until we are ready to exercise trust, until we are ready to wait for him, he must wait for us. As noted above, many would separate v. 18 from vv. 8–17. However, it forms an apt conclusion to this whole section on refusing to listen to God. For what that refusal does is not merely to bring judgment upon us, but also to block the grace which God wants to give us.

15 *For* indicates a causal link between vv. 15–17 and what precedes. Why will judgment come with suddenness? Because the Hebrew people have preferred flying off on horses to resting in God's care. The Holy One had extended his arms to them with a gentle word of strength (28:12), but they refused. They could have hidden beneath his wings like chicks, but they would not (Matt. 23:37). Why not? Because to admit that

17. Interestingly, LXX has "sin" and Targ. has "transgression," which would seem to indicate that they considered the act primary.

18. Both LXX and Targ. have references to the wall of a ruined or taken city, but MT has nothing to explain this reference.

we need God is to admit our limitation, and that admission the fallen human spirit hates.

In returning and rest is God's prescription for their situation. Their frantic preparations will ultimately do them no good. How much better to admit their helplessness and to experience God's care than to insist upon their ability to cope and to deprive themselves of that comfort.

returning is customarily regarded as having to do with repentance: turning from their self-reliance back to God. However, a number of scholars have suggested that "sitting" would be a more appropriate parallel to "rest" and propose to take the root as from *yšb* rather than *šwb*.[19] However, the line is very probably chiastic with "returning" paralleling "trust" and "rest" paralleling "quietness."[20] This parallelism suggests that Driver is probably correct and that while "returning" may not carry heavy theological freight here, it does speak of relinquishing one's own efforts.[21] This is the same message which Moses had given to the Hebrew people (Exod. 14:13) and Isaiah had given to Ahaz (7:3–9). In the former case, it was heard, but in the latter, as here, it was not. Perhaps it was heard there because there was literally nowhere else to turn.

16 Their response to God's offer would be incredible if it were not of such a common sort. God offers himself and they choose horses (cf. also 31:1)! Horses no longer had the revolutionary military significance which they had had when first introduced during the Middle Bronze Age, but they were still the "glamour" weapons of the armies. Cavalry and chariotry had the same appeal as armor and air forces do today.[22] Thus, especially to a country which is militarily weaker than its adversaries, obtaining the very latest in military hardware becomes almost an obsession (as can be seen in the Third World today). But just as horse and chariot could not save 2700 years ago, neither can the Main Battle Tank and the F–16 today (cf. 31:2–3).

19. At least as early as Calvin. See also M. Dahood, "Some Ambiguous Texts in Isaias," *CBQ* 20 (1958) 41–43. Driver, *JSS* 13 (1968) 51, proposes to remain with *šwb* but with the sense of "stay at home, be quiet."

20. Dahood notes this parallelism and so in support of the position in n. 19 above takes *biṭḥâ*, "trust," as equal to Ugar. *batiti*, "at ease." But this rests a proposal on a proposal, which seems a little much. Cf. *Proverbs and Northwest Semitic Philology*, p. 7 n. 1.

21. Driver, op. cit. Cf. also Skinner, who takes the terms as a hendiadys, "calm neutrality, restful trust." Kaiser and Clements also favor "returning."

22. It was for these kinds of reasons that the Israelites were forbidden to use horses in their battles, a prohibition Solomon first broke (Deut. 17:16; Josh. 11:6, 9; 2 Sam. 8:4; 1 K. 10:28, 29; 2 K. 18:24). On the strength of a horse, cf. Job 39:19–25; Ps. 147:10. On trusting in horses see Ps. 20:8 (Eng. 7); 33:17.

The writer uses both wordplay and assonance in this verse.[23] In each of the cola, he turns the meaning around. The sense of the first is: "We will get horses so we can flee, if necessary," and he responds, "Then you really will have to flee." The second says: "We will ride on the swift one (the horse)," and he says, "Your pursuers will be swifter." The point is that when we rely on our own strength and speed to see us through, we may be sure that one day we will meet someone swifter and stronger than we. What then?

17 When that happens a thousand will be routed by a handful and nothing will be left.[24] Our hope was in ourselves, and when that is proven false, collapse comes suddenly, as with a toppling wall or a dropped jug. Had our hope been in the Sovereign God, we would have had nothing to fear, for he transcends all the revelations of our finiteness. This was what Isaiah was saying, but only a later generation could hear him, perhaps in part because there was a flagstaff left in his day—destruction was not final. Later, when Jerusalem was in ruins, it was easier to understand a word which says our *only* hope is in God.

Without taking poetic speech too literally, one is tempted to see in the mention of the pole[25] on the hilltop a reference to the fact that Jerusalem would survive the coming onslaught, although alone. If that is correct, it certainly was not understood to be a great cause for rejoicing. Isaiah was speaking of humiliation and destruction, so that only scraps would remain.

18 *Therefore* introduces a statement which is admitted on all sides to be transitional. However, since the tone of the verse is positive,[26] it is usually taken with vv. 19–33, which are also positive.[27] But this creates problems in understanding the "therefore." Young is representative when he tries to make it only an introductory word for a new section. That seems very unlikely in view of *lāḵēn*'s typical dependency upon a previous statement of conditions. Furthermore, it is in poetic form as opposed to vv.

23. E.g., *ʿal-sûs nānûs ʿal-kēn tᵉnûsûn*, "we will flee on horses. Therefore, you will flee."

24. The idea of a few chasing many seems to have been proverbial in nature; cf. Lev. 26:17; Deut. 32:30; Josh. 23:10. Nor was it limited to Israelite literature, for it appears at least once in Egyptian writings of the same period (Piankhy, tr. S. A. Cook, cited by Cheyne).

25. For references to "pole" see 33:23; Ezek. 27:5, where it is used of the mast of a ship. Evidently, from its use here it had wider connotations, as did many Hebrew words.

26. Young takes it negatively in that God's justice must proceed his mercy.

27. G. A. Smith is an exception. Note that the Letteris text has a space between vv. 18 and 19, but none between vv. 17 and 18.

19ff., which are in prose. All of these factors suggest that the case is at least as strong for the verse to be read in the light of the foregoing as of the following. Thus, because Judah will not wait on the Lord (26:8) but insists on rushing off on horses, the Lord must wait to show his grace until they are in a position to receive it. So to the repeated cry of "How long, O Lord?" his answer is, "Whenever you are ready."

the Lord is a God of justice may be understood in two ways, both of them possessing some validity. First, Young suggests that God's grace must wait because he is a just God and his justice must be experienced before his grace can be. Second, Calvin suggests the meaning to be moderation and order. There is hope because God does not simply go into a rage and destroy whole peoples. The latter view seems to be supported by the structure of the verse, which has "blessed are all who wait for him" following on the statement of his justice. Because he can be appealed to, because he will hear the cries of those who endure persecution and hardship for his Name's sake, therefore they are and will be a happy people.

In some ways this verse sums up the message of the book: those who exalt themselves in an effort to meet their own needs are doomed to failure, because only God is exalted in this universe (2:12–17) and because only he can meet their needs (40:27–31). The key to life is found in letting him be God and in training ourselves to complete dependence upon him until we discover that he can supply our needs a hundred times better than we can.

(2) Judah's blessing, Assyria's destruction (30:19–33)

(a) Judah's blessing (30:19–26)

19 *For a people shall live[1] in Zion, even Jerusalem.*
   You will not weep any longer.
   He will surely be gracious to you at the sound of your cry.
   When he hears it, he will answer you.
20 *The Sovereign will give you bread—affliction, and water—adversity,*
   but your Teacher will not hide himself again;
   your eyes will see your Teacher.
21 *Your ears will hear a word behind you saying,*
   "This is the way, walk in it,
   whether to the right or to the left."

1. It has been typical since Lowth to translate *yēšēḇ,* "shall dwell," as *yôšēḇ,* "who dwells," and to make this first line vocative: "O people . . . who dwell." While the 2nd person pronouns of the rest of the verse lend some support to this proposal, the opening *kî,* "for," is very much against it. LXX supports MT, while Targ. supports the emendation.

22 *You will defile your silver-plated idols*
   and your gold-covered images.
   You will scatter them like² something unclean:³
   "Out," you will say to them.
23 *He will give rain on your seed*
   with which you planted the ground.
   Bread will be the produce of the ground
   and there will be vegetation and oil.
   In that day, your cattle will graze in a broad region.
24 *The oxen and the donkey which work the soil*
   will eat seasoned mash, winnowed with fork and shovel.
25 *And there will be on every high mountain and every up-thrust hill*
   channels, courses of water,
   in the day of great slaughter when the towers fall.
26 *The light of the "white" will be like the light of the "hot" ⁴*
   and the light of the "hot" will be seven times,
   like the light of seven days,⁵
   in the day when the Lord binds up the breaking of his people,
   and heals the blow of his stroke.

In vv. 19–33 the author relates again the certainty of God's salvation. Although Judah's failure to trust him would indeed result in destruction, that destruction would be followed by redemption and a corresponding destruction of Judah's enemies. As is characteristic of the book, these predictions of salvation are couched in highly figurative language.⁶ When the prophet considered the wonder and the extent of what God planned to do for his people, ordinary language broke down.⁷ At the same time, we

2. Again LXX has "scatter them like water" (cf. Exod. 32:20; 2 K. 23:12), but this seems to be a misreading of *kāmô*, "like," as *kāmê*, "like water." MT reads more naturally.

3. *dāwâ*, "unclean," refers to menstruation.

4. Note the poetic description of the moon as the "white" and the sun as the "hot" (cf. 24:23).

5. LXX omits "like the light of seven days," which may indicate that the phrase is a gloss. Delitzsch suggests that it refers to the earth's last eternal Sabbath, when all the days of the week are concentrated into one. Targ. has "343 times brighter" (7 x 7 x 7)!

6. Cf. 2:1–5; 4:2–6; 11:1–16; 25:6–8; 27:12, 13; 34:1–10; 49:9–13; 55:12, 13; 60:1–22; 65:17–25.

7. The almost universal tendency to explain this language as early apocalyptic, and thus non-Isaian, seems to me to deal too lightly with both the literary question: why is this language so pervasive in the book as a whole? and the theological one: can we take with any seriousness a concept (God may be trusted because he announces grace even in the midst of judgment) which must be rooted in historical fiction? It is not clear whether the passage is poetic prose (RSV, NIV) or somewhat prosaic poetry (*BHS*, NEB). Because of the parallelism, esp. in vv. 19–23, I have opted for the latter.

may expect that the figures do indeed express a literal reality, although dogmatism over what that reality may be is not justified. But we may look forward with happy expectancy to a reality beside which even these glorious figures will fade into insignificance.

The segment is divided into two parts, vv. 19–26 and 27–33. The first of these relates the train of effects in Judah which will result from God's judgment and grace. The second depicts a festival of praise at which the participants watch their champion destroy their enemies on their behalf. Once more the implied question is: Why would you go to Egypt for help when it is only God who can save you? Furthermore, why would you distrust God, thereby bringing upon yourselves the very disaster you fear, when God's grace is so real that even after your disobedience he will save you?

19–26 As mentioned in the previous paragraph, this segment relates the effects which will stem from the manifestation of God's grace in the midst of judgment. First, the Judeans will perceive him (vv. 19–21); second, they will abandon the idolatry with which they had attempted to supply their own needs (v. 22); third, God will then supply the very things which the idols professed to supply but could not (vv. 23–26). The importance of both judgment and grace in this setting must not be overlooked. It is judgment which shatters the false values and makes one attentive. It is grace which motivates the broken to believe and obey. Neither is ultimately effective without the other.

19 *For a people shall live in Zion* speaks immediately of God's grace. The other great cities would be abandoned, heaps of rubble, homes for jackals (13:19–22; 34:10–17). God's judgment would have rested upon them and they would be gone. So they are. For us who live in the shadow of the mushroom cloud, it is not difficult to think of New York or London completely desolate. But for Isaiah's hearers, the thought of mighty Babylon or Nineveh empty and fallen to dust must have been ludicrous. On the other hand, to claim that this hill-country capital of Jerusalem would continue to be inhabited when the others were gone was simply preposterous. Yet Isaiah was right and his detractors were wrong. God's judgment did fall upon Jerusalem, but that judgment was tempered by grace.

You will not weep any longer is a consequence of Jerusalem being inhabited. What was empty will become full; what was barren will become fruitful. The reason for weeping will be taken away (25:8; 61:2–5; Ps. 30:6 [Eng. 5]; 126:1–6; Rev. 7:17).

He will surely be gracious speaks of a time when the sin which had separated them from God will be atoned for and no longer able to divide them from him (59:1, 2; Ezek. 36:33–38). The Father will be able to respond as he wants to. This reconciliation was achieved in prospect in the return, but in its fullness only in Jesus (Luke 23:45; Col. 1:21, 22).

20 *bread—affliction, and water—adversity* are appositional phrases and not genitives, as they are so often treated.[8] "Bread, that is, affliction" seems to be the sense. But the function of the phrase is not clear. Some suggest that the appositional words are late glosses which in fact misunderstood the positive nature of the passage. Thus we should only read " . . . gives you bread and water," namely, all the basic needs.[9] However, if the *waw* preceding "will not hide" is taken as an adversative, no emendation is called for. Yes, God will give them over to siege conditions, *but* as a result of that, he will no longer hide himself from them. This last statement assumes that God is the teacher intended, but there is no proof of that assumption. The word *môreykā*, "your teacher," may be either singular or plural[10] and commentators are divided as to which is intended (although the verb is clearly singular). Generally those who believe God cannot be intended adopt the plural and say the reference is to prophets, who had gone underground to avoid persecution. But the case for taking the teacher to be God is equally strong. It is clear from the previous chapters that he had tried to teach them (28:9–13; 29:11, 12; 30:15), but that their own obstinacy had blinded and deafened them to the truth. Now because of judgment, their eyes and ears will be opened to what it is he has been trying to say (26:9).[11]

21 *a word behind you* conveys both the nearness of the Teacher and the sensitivity of the pupil. Instead of the stubborn animal which has to be dragged or beaten into going in the proper direction, here is a person whose teacher is just at his shoulder and little more than a word of guidance from time to time is necessary for him to stay on the right path. This is the ideal of the Spirit-filled life, where the contact between us and him is so intimate that only a whisper is sufficient to move us in his way (Gal. 5:16–25). The opposite of this ideal is seen in 28:11 and 30:11, where stubbornness ultimately leads to a denial that God's way is right, with horrifying results.

whether to the right or to the left seems to be an antinomy which

8. 1QIs^a does have the genitive *mê* for the absolute *māyîm* of MT.

9. So Kaiser following Marti. Kissane moves all of v. 20a to the end of v. 17. Targ. paraphrases as "riches of the enemy" and "spoils of the oppressor," but LXX follows MT.

10. GKC, § 93ss.

11. The emphasis upon teaching and way, as well as idolatry, suggests a reliance upon some of the themes of Deuteronomy. Cf. L. Laberge, "Isa. 30:19–26: A Deuteronomic Text?" *Eet* 2 (1971) 35–54.

covers all the actions of life. The precise sense is a little obscure because of the *kî* which precedes each direction.[12] However, the use seems to be conditional, as translated here.[13]

22   With their eyes opened as a result both of judgment and of grace, the people will see the foolishness of idolatry. As compared with what God is, the idols are helpless stupidity (41:23, 24). Evidently it was customary, particularly with larger pieces where the expense would become exorbitant, to plate some less precious material, such as wood (Jer. 10:3, 4) or bronze,[14] with gold or silver (Deut. 7:25; Hos. 8:4). Thus the idol would be of worth materially as well as, supposedly, spiritually. This would make it all the more difficult to destroy it. Although people of the West in the twentieth century have taken off the faces of the gods of love, security, potency, and power, we still surround them with trappings of great material value. Thus it is no easier for us to desert our sources of support than it was for the people of Israel.

defile is explained by many commentators as abandoning. However, elsewhere it means a specific act of deconsecration, even to the point of destruction (cf. esp. 2 K. 23:4–14; also Exod. 32:20; Ezek. 7:19–24; Deut. 7:25). In this respect the connection of cleanness with the holy is significant. Instead of calling these things "holy" (i.e., partaking of the character of the divine) and giving them reverence, you declare them as specifically opposed to holiness—unclean. Sometimes those things most unclean are those which most easily masquerade as holy.

23–26   Most commentators assume a significant break between these verses and the previous ones.[15] But this is surely not the case. The idols were worshiped precisely because it was believed that they could supply abundance in all ways, but especially in agriculture. But the prophets, especially the preexilic ones, pointed out that abundance came from God and to look to an idol for what God provided was, in fact, to deprive oneself of abundance (1 K. 17:1; 18:1, 45; Hos. 2:8, 9, 21–23; 9:2; 14:8; Amos 4:7–9; 9:13–15).[16] The same point is being made here. It is only after the Israelites cease their dependence upon idols—their own devices— that they will experience what they had tried to get from the idols. There is a spiritual principle here. God is the source of all blessing, but that

---

12. Lit. "for you will go to the right; for you will go to the left."
13. Williams, *Syntax*, § 446.
14. *ANEP*, nos. 481, 483, 484, 497.
15. Note the space in NIV.
16. This is surely not a thought which would have had any significance to Jews of A.D. 167 (contra Kaiser).

blessing can be received only after an abandonment of one's own efforts and a complete commitment to God.

The mention of a spiritual principle provides a clue to the interpretation. The passage must not be restricted to either a wholly literal or a wholly symbolic meaning. The former would suggest that the OT restricts blessing to the material and physical, that it knows nothing of spiritual blessing. This is not the case. Spiritual values are always in focus along with material ones.[17] The latter would succumb to the false dichotomy between fact and value and suggest that God's realm is only the spiritual. In fact, the whole earth is the Lord's, and is full of his glory (cf. 6:3). Thus, the language here speaks of the effects in nature that redemption will bring, but it speaks of more than that, as the supernaturally heightened figures indicate.[18] Springs do not break out on mountaintops, nor could any living thing endure a sun seven times brighter than at present. Thus Isaiah makes it plain he is speaking of something more than mere physical blessing. He is speaking of a time when all that is good about human life will be made incredibly better, and that includes love, integrity, faithfulness, justice, righteousness, etc.[19]

24 The work animals are singled out as special beneficiaries of God's blessing. Grain will be so abundant after the harvest that even the oxen and the donkeys will eat mixtures *(belîl)* of the food grains (those which are winnowed), seasoned *(hāmîs)* with salt. Not only does this diet testify to abundance, but it also testifies to owners whose hearts have been enough softened by God's care of them as to be concerned for their animals.

25 This verse has two themes: the supply of water and the collapse of the towers. The relation of the two is not coincidental. Throughout the book, but especially in the first part, dryness and barrenness are associated with human pride. Likewise, water and fruitfulness are associated with trust in God and dependence upon him.[20] Thus it is that when the towers of Judah's pride are smashed (2:12–17; 32:14, 15; 57:15), she may expect a new era of unbelievable fruitfulness. This has already happened

17. A particular example of this is seen in 32:15–20. Cf. von Rad, *Old Testament Theology,* I:375–76, although he would generally support the idea that "blessing" was physical (see, e.g., II:286).

18. It is obviously true that literature of the late intertestamental period uses such imagery. But the conclusion that such imagery is therefore limited to that time does not follow. Function may have more to do with language than does date.

19. See 35:5–10; 44:3–5; 60:19–22; 65:17–66:2.

20. See 1:30; 3:1; 12:3; 15:6; 19:5; 32:2, 20; 33:16; 35:6, 7; 41:17, 18; 43:19, 20; 44:3, 4; 48:21; 49:10; 54:1; 55:1, 10; 58:11; 64:10; 65:10; 66:14.

in the Church. Little Judah, crushed under a whole succession of empires culminating in Rome, became the seedbed from which biblical faith was to grow to encompass the world. Nor is the end yet. For one day Judah herself will be gathered in (Rom. 11:12, 24). The dramatic and miraculous nature of God's salvation is depicted by springs and watercourses on the very tops of the hills, the places least likely to be well watered.[21]

26 There are two themes associated here: light and healing. The association is a natural one, just as darkness and disease are naturally taken together. Instead of the darkness of despair, uncertainty, and sin, and the misery of the pains resulting from running into God in the darkness, there will be perfect clarity and the tender ministry of the Father bandaging our wounds and bruises (60:19–22).[22] As noted above, it seems a mistake to take these promises over literally, as they would then be a curse and not a blessing. At the same time, redemption of nature must not be omitted in the light of the Bible's holistic world view (Rom. 8:19–21).

(b) Assyria's destruction (30:27–33)

> 27 *Behold, the name of the Lord comes from afar,*
> > *his anger burning, the burden heavy.*
> *His lips are full of wrath,*
> > *and his tongue is like a devouring fire.*
> 28 *His breath*[1] *is like an overflowing torrent,*
> > *it divides at the neck,*
> *sifting nations with a sieve of nothingness,*
> > *a halter*[2] *of error on the jaws of peoples.*
> 29 *You will have song*
> > *like a night of sanctifying a feast;*
> *joy of heart*
> > *like going with a flute to come to the hill of the Lord, the Rock of Israel.*

21. Clements makes the significant point that the agricultural deities were worshiped on the high places. Here, it is God alone who gives the water.

22. For healing cf. Isa. 1:6; Ezek. 34:16; Hos. 6:1; Mal. 3:20 (Eng. 4:2).

1. On *rûaḥ*, "spirit," as "breath," cf. 11:4, "the breath (spirit) of his mouth."

2. Driver cites Arab. *mtʿ* as "stout" or "twisted" and proposes "bridle of stout rope" (*JTS* 37 [1938] 144). The MT would seem to read "His breath is like an overflowing . . . (like) a halter of error. . . ." While this reading is not impossible, it seems somewhat strange. So Kaiser (following Delitzsch) proposes to insert *ûlᵉśîm*, "and to put," before "a halter." Perhaps this word might have been lost through haplography with the *š* of *šāwˀ*. Kissane sees *šāwˀ* as a corruption of *śîm*. LXX replaces "halter" with "shall lay hold of" while Targ. agrees with MT.

30 *The Lord will make the splendor of his voice heard,*
   and will show the falling of his arm,
   with storming anger and devouring flames of fire;
   windstorm, rainstorm, and hailstones.
31 *Indeed, at the voice of the Lord Assyria will be shattered;*
   he will smite[3] with the staff.
32 *Every blow of the appointed staff,*
   which the Lord will lay upon him,
   will be with timbrels and harps,
   with warrings waving, he makes war on them.[4]
33 *For a place of burning is prepared from of old,*
   even it, for the king it is established.
   He has made it deep and wide;
   its pyre of fire and much wood.
   The breath of the Lord is like a torrent of brimstone kindling it.

The writer now follows the promise of Judah's redemption with the promise of Assyria's destruction. Judah will not be the only one to feel the Lord's terrible anger. In fact, she will not feel it on anything like the scale which her enemies will. If Assyria had come in upon Judah like a torrent (8:5–8), God would sweep over the Assyrians. It is not the Egyptians who would deliver God's people, but God himself. This was the message Isaiah sought to impress upon the Judeans, but with little apparent success. They were too enamored of their own means of self-defense to hear a message which invited them to stand still and see God at work on their behalf. Yet this is the message of the Bible from Exodus to Chronicles (Exod. 14:13, 14; 2 Chr. 20:17). The flesh says with Frederick the Great, "God is on the side of the strongest battalions," but the spirit says, "Stand still and see your salvation" (1 Cor. 2:14).

According to Eichrodt, the setting is that of a covenant feast which is sealed by the sacrifice of God's enemies.[5] But this view seems to con-

---

3. Many commentators follow Symm. and the Vulg. in reading "he is smitten" *(yukkâ)* instead of "he will smite" *(yakkeh)* with MT. Undeniably the former is the smoother reading. However, both LXX and Targ. seem to be struggling with the MT reading.

4. Ketib, "on her."

5. W. Eichrodt, "Prophet and Covenant: The Exegesis of Isaiah," in *Proclamation and Presence: Old Testament Essays in Honor of G. H. Davies*, ed. J. I. Durham and J. R. Porter (London: SCM, 1970; repr. Macon: Mercer University, 1983), pp. 181–82. Cf. also A. Guillaume, "Isaiah's Oracle Against Assyria (30, 27–33) in the Light of Archaeology," *BSOAS* 17 (1956) 413–15; L. Sabotka, "Is. 30:27–33: Ein Übersetzungsvorschlag," *BZ* 12 (1968) 241–45; C. Schedl, "Gedanken zu einen 'Übersetzungsvorschlag,' Is. 30:27–33," *BZ* 13 (1969) 242–43.

clude too much, for v. 29 (on which see below) says the people's joy will be *like* that of a feast, and the precise import of v. 32 is very difficult to ascertain. Likewise, v. 33 speaks of the destruction of the king on a funeral pyre, but the association with a sacrifice to Moloch (Yahweh) is very tenuous (see below on this verse). It may be said, however, that God's deliverance of his people will be an occasion for worship and praise on their part (25:1; Ps. 105:2; 118:21–23).

Positions on the date of this segment range from Isaianic (Wildberger) to Hellenistic (Kaiser). This variety bears out Skinner's observation that matters of language and style are inconclusive (Kaiser argues that quotations and allusions to other parts of the book are all from "non-Isaianic" portions). This means that questions of content become all-important. Childs argues that an earlier theophany of judgment has been supplemented with promises characteristic of postexilic times.[6] Clements would attribute some of these promises to his Josianic redactor.[7] Most see vv. 29 and 32 as intrusive. As the segment stands now it seems to show a 3 + 3 + 1 structure: attack, rejoicing—27–29; attack, rejoicing—30–32; funeral pyre—33.

27, 28 In language reminiscent of other theophanies of judgment (Ps. 18:8–16 [Eng. 7–15]; 50:3; Nah. 1:3b–8; Hab. 3:3–15), God is depicted as coming from a great distance on the wings of a storm. With whirlwind, cloudburst, and pelting hail he destroys his enemies. Those who crouch in the dry wadis for protection are swept away in an instant by the walls of water which come rushing down on them. Assyria herself had been described in such terms earlier for the sake of those who had believed that they could somehow engineer safety from her onrush. But now God asserts his sovereignty again by showing that Assyria would not be acting independently but would be equally liable to God's judgment.

the name of the Lord is especially indicative of God's revealed character, both as sovereign and as redeemer.[8] Thus it is appropriate that this manifestation of him should begin on this note. For God's character, i.e., his name, which has been slandered by leaders and people alike in their

6. Childs, *Crisis*, pp. 48–49.
7. Following H. Barth, *Die Jesaja-Worte in der Josiazeit*.
8. See 12:4; 29:23; 59:19; Ps. 54:5 (Eng. 3); 124:8; etc. Kaiser suggests that the use of the name as a hypostasis of God is an evidence of a very late date. As he admits, however, the basis for the doctrine is at least Deuteronomic, which on his dating would put it at least to 650. In fact, the concept must be pushed back at least to the founding of the temple. If Deuteronomy is as late as 650, it is only putting into print doctrines held since David and Solomon.

trust of Egypt, will be manifested in his deliverance of them from the very forces which had sent them to Egypt for help.

comes from afar may have been conventional to this sort of theophany (Judg. 5:4; Hab. 3:3), but it may also result from two other sources: it is possible to stand on a hill and watch a storm build up far in the west until, with a roll of wind-driven cloud, it bursts over you; it may also have been addressed to those "deists" of that day who considered that God was too far away to be of any practical help. To them Isaiah responds that God may be far away, but that he can break in upon us at any moment.

the burden heavy has caused considerable discussion. Most modern translations take it to refer to a dense cloud of smoke accompanying the fire of his anger[9] (cf. Judg. 20:38, 40, but note that "cloud" is specified there). The alternative is to take it as here (with NEB and JPSV) as referring to the heavy burden of punishment which God will impose upon the Assyrians.

His lips . . . wrath . . . his tongue . . . fire . . . his breath . . . torrent speak of the understanding of the word of God in the OT.[10] While it is undoubtedly true that the imagery of thunder and lightning plays a part here, it is also clear that the OT writers considered that the decree of the God who speaks was ultimately the power which held all things together and which could plunge all things into dissolution.[11]

an overflowing torrent speaks of the wadis, or gulches, which are normally dry but can be brimming in a matter of minutes as a result of a cloudburst in the hills. So God's judgment will be as sudden and as complete (cf. Nah. 1:8).

it divides at the neck is a curious phrase, and Kissane suggests that "divides" (*ḥāṣâ*) is a corruption of "reaches" (*māṣā᾽*, Job 11:7; cf. Isa. 8:8). Another suggestion is that the waters divide a man in half (Delitzsch). But another possibility is that the waters divide or go around at the neck. In any case, the life-threatening effect of turbulent waters neck-deep is clear. In a moment a person would be swept off his feet and tossed to his death. As Kaiser suggests, this may explain the apparently abrupt shift in metaphors here: just as the flood would toss its victims to and fro, so the grain is tossed about in the sieve and so also the unbroken horse is jerked

9. So RSV, CBAT, NIV, TEV, but not NEB.

10. Skinner considers that the immoderate language is not that of Isaiah but of a disciple. Such an expedient seems unnecessary. Our views of refinement and taste can hardly have been theirs. Furthermore, the use of conventionalized language must be taken into account.

11. Cf. 11:4; 30:30; 34:16; 45:23; cf. also Lindblom, *Prophecy,* pp. 114–17. So Rev. 19:15.

about by the bridle (Ps. 32:9). Furthermore, each figure leads to destruction: the flood to drowning, the sieve to dividing the good grain from the useless chaff, the bridle which leads an unbreakable horse to its death.

29 The result of God's raging against the enemies outside will be rejoicing inside (cf. 9:1, 2 [Eng. 2, 3]). This joy at God's judgment is also reflected in Ps. 96. Nor is it odd that it should be compared to a time of feasting, for the biblical feasts were preeminently times of rejoicing over God's acts of deliverance in history.[12] Some commentators think it odd that Isaiah could have depicted a people still under judgment. But this is only a problem if one denies the possibility of predictive prophecy. If that possibility is admitted, then the thought of this section would be quite natural to Isaiah. The line of thinking is: you have abandoned God's ways because you thought he could not help; that abandonment will bring destruction upon you; but despite his bringing the Assyrians upon you, God has not abandoned you, and the proof of his power and his love is that you will one day be able to rejoice in his work on your behalf.

Since the joy is only compared to that of a *feast,* it is not of great importance to try to pinpoint whether the writer had one particular feast in mind. Passover, which begins at night, seems especially appropriate because of its connection with deliverance. However, this is traditionally a more pensive feast than Tabernacles. Calvin observes that since the new day began at sundown all the feasts technically began in the evening.

30, 31 The recapitulation of the theme begins with a return to the language of storm and flood. God's *voice* is emphasized even more explicitly here. Thunder as the voice of God is known in ancient Near Eastern literature and appears several times in the Bible.[13] But it is clear that the intent is more than literal here. God's anger is *like* the storm and his voice is *like* the thunder, but they are not identical (1 K. 19:11, 12). God transcends the natural phenomena, and his judgment is upon moral grounds and not merely physical and natural ones.

Note here, as in chs. 24–27, that it is God in sovereign isolation who redeems his people. Isaiah is saying in every way possible that humanity's only hope is in abandoning every other hope, including our own

12. Kaiser relates this reference to the New Year's feast, but the very existence of such a major feast is questionable, since there is no clear biblical evidence for it. Those who propose it (cf. S. Mowinckel, *He That Cometh,* tr. G. W. Anderson [New York: Abingdon, 1954], pp. 40–43) see it as a form of the a-historical New Year festival which existed in Mesopotamia.

13. See Ps. 18:14 (Eng. 13); 29:3–9; 77:19–21 (Eng. 18–20). The conventional figure of the storm-god as an Egyptian warrior with an upraised mace may be the image in the writer's mind. Cf. *ANEP,* nos. 481, 484, 490, 494, 496.

abilities, and casting ourselves upon God alone. Assyria had claimed to hold the scepter of the world, but God held that scepter and would shortly strike down the impostor—first outside Jerusalem's gates and then more completely a hundred years later at the hands of the Medo-Babylonian alliance.

32 Although certain elements of this verse are matters of considerable controversy, the general sense is quite clear. God's acts of judgment will be cause for an outpouring of joy, in part because it is his acts alone which will deliver. Israel will be but a joyous spectator to those acts. The reference to tambourines and harps is reminiscent of Chronicles' report of Jehoshaphat's defeat of the Edomites (2 Chr. 20:13–30, esp. 28). Israel need only praise God in confidence to receive the benefits of his power.

the appointed staff (lit. "the founded staff") admits of two possible explanations. The first is that adopted here, and proposed at least as early as Alexander. The staff is one whose purpose and destiny have been decreed (*mûsādâ* is a divine decree, as in Ezek. 4:1). So Isaiah emphasizes again that despite Assyria's pomp and power, she is in God's hands and the instrument of her destruction is already appointed. The alternative involves a slight emendation: exchanging *d* for *r*, letters which are easily confused in the Hebrew block script. The result is *mûsārô*, "his chastisement" (as in Prov. 22:15; so Procksch and almost all modern translations).[14]

with warrings waving, he makes war is very obscure. As it stands it perhaps refers to a warrior wading into battle and brandishing his sword or his staff overhead. However, this is by no means obvious and several alternatives have been proposed. Especially significant to many of these is the observation that *tᵉnûpâ*, "waving," occurs largely in cultic settings.[15] This observation has led to the suggestion that Assyria will be treated as an offering and that the words translated "warrings" and "he makes war" are either written or interpreted wrongly.[16] No scholarly consensus has emerged, however, so it seems best to stay with the MT.

33 This verse can either support, or mitigate against, the idea that v. 32 refers to a sacrifice. The present interpretation takes the latter position. As noted in the introduction to this segment, the verse is taken

---

14. Note, however, that God is not merely disciplining Assyria, but destroying her.

15. See Exod. 29:27; Lev. 7:34; Num. 8:11; 18:18; but cf. Isa. 19:16, where the setting is God's punishment.

16. So *BHS* proposes *bimḥōlôt*, "with dancing," instead of *bᵉmilḥᵃmôt*, "with warring." Driver made two suggestions, neither of which seems to take account of the other: (1) *lḥm* here is a kind of war dance or game (*JTS* 38 [1937] 45); (2) *lḥm* has to do with "harmony" and so refers to musical instruments (*JSS* 13 [1968] 51).

not as a direct concomitant of v. 32, but as a climax to the preceding six verses. In this light, it is not so much a sacrifice being pictured as it is a warrior's funeral pyre burning in the Hinnom Valley below Jerusalem. The assumption that a sacrifice is in view rests upon the observation that human victims were burned to death in worship of the god Moloch in this valley (2 K. 23:10; Jer. 19:6). On this basis, some would emend "for the king" *(lammelek)* to "for Molech" *(lāmôlek)*, but there is no textual evidence for such an emendation.[17] Without denying the allusive power of the reference to this place, it must still be said that nothing in the text calls for the sacrificial understanding. Rather, the author says that Assyria's funeral pyre, like the Lord's rod, has stood ready from ancient days. All it wants is the Lord's breath to kindle it into flame (cf. 31:9). So again Isaiah is counseling his people that they need not go to Egypt out of fear of Assyria. What they should do is to move even closer to the only One in the universe who truly holds Assyria's destiny in his hand.

(3) Woe to those who reject God's help (31:1–9)

(a) Helpless Egypt (31:1–3)

> 1 Woe to those who go down to Egypt for help;
>   upon horses they lean.
> They trust in chariots because they are many,
>   and upon horsemen because they are vast,
> and do not look to the Holy One of Israel,
>   nor seek[1] the Lord.
> 2 Yet he too is wise and will bring about[2] evil;
>   not turning aside his words.
> He will arise against the house of the wicked,
>   and against the help of the workers of iniquity.
> 3 But Egypt is a man and not God,
>   and their horses are flesh, not spirit.
> When the Lord extends his hand,
>   then the helper will stumble,
>   and the one helped will fall;
>   all them will come to an end together.

17. Furthermore, the necessary associating of Yahweh and Moloch strains credibility too far. On this subject, see J. G. Fevrier, "Essai de reconstitution du sacrifice *molek*," *JA* 248 (1960) 167–187.

1. *dāraš*, "to seek," indicates the formal placing of an inquiry before the Lord with an answer expected through mechanical means (lots, Urim and Thummim, etc.) or prophetic oracle. Cf. Gen. 25:22; 1 K. 22:8; 2 K. 3:11; 22:13, 18, etc.

2. 1QIs[a] has *wyby'*, which would appear to be an imperfect with *waw* conjunctive. Cf. GKC, § 111w, on the converted imperfect as prophetic perfect.

Chapter 31 duplicates, in shorter form, the structure and content of ch. 30. It begins by exposing the folly of dependence upon Egypt (vv. 1–3). Not only will Egypt not be able to help, but going to her necessarily involves rejection of God. Thus Judah has not merely chosen a poorer option; she has, in fact, rejected the true in order to choose the false (cf. 30:1–18).

The second emphasis (as in 30:19–33) is that the Lord will fight for Jerusalem and will destroy Assyria (vv. 4–9). Thus, with a recurrence of causal statements the prophet attempts to draw his people back to God. Negatively, he abolishes the false hope, and positively, he depicts the grace of God in such a way as to attract the people to God.[3]

It is especially the exclusion of dependence upon God which makes the Egyptian alliance so despicable to Isaiah. As Calvin sagely observes, a believer may use many intermediate means to benefit or defend himself or herself that do not conflict with a prior dependence upon God. But some means, by their very nature, involve abandonment of trust in him. Theft would be a simple example, and adultery another. Trust in Egypt is one of these, in part because it was a denial of the efficacy of the Exodus. As a result, Judah would be flying in God's face and would experience the terrible consequences of his reality.

1 The emphasis upon *horses* here suggests the likely reason why Egypt's help seemed especially desirable. Ever since the introduction of the horse into the Near East in the Middle Bronze Age (ca. 1800 B.C.), warfare in that part of the world had been revolutionized, first through chariotry,[4] and by this time through the beginnings of cavalry. The horse's speed, stamina, and maneuverability gave an army a mobility and a shock effect many times its numerical size. As a result equine forces came to have great prestige even in small, hilly countries like Judah where their effectiveness was greatly limited, much as Third World countries today insist on having the most sophisticated weaponry. The weapon is apparently felt to have an almost magical effect, apart from its actual utility in

3. It is almost universally held today that this twofold structure is secondary. Supposedly, Isaiah ben Amoz only preached judgment and the hope is added anywhere from 100 to 400 years later in the light of the (legendary) deliverance of Jerusalem from Sennacherib. But such a development is inexplicable unless there was a clear note of hope already in Isaiah's preaching. Furthermore, the theological problem is severe. If it is true that the positive nature of biblical hope is a secondary result of legends misunderstood as events, then biblical faith is self-delusion. Cf. Childs, *Crisis;* R. E. Clements, *Isaiah and the Deliverance of Jerusalem.*

4. Because of its flatness, Egypt was especially suited to, and noted for, chariotry. Cf. Homer *Iliad* ix.383.

a given situation. So the Rabshaqeh commented sarcastically that the Judeans would not know what to do with horses if they had them (36:8, 9).

But the destiny of a country does not rest upon either horses or missiles, and when any people feel that special weapons can relieve them of dependence upon God, they are on the road to destruction. This is not to say that weapons and faith in God are mutually exclusive in a fallen world, but it is to say that commitment to God's ways, with whatever that may mean for weapons in a given situation, is primary.

This kind of commitment was clearly lacking in Judah. They had not sought God's leadership, nor were they really putting any hope in him. They plainly believed, as does most existentialist Christianity, that God either cannot, or does not, intervene in history.

2 *Yet he too is wise* seems to be a jibe at the royal counselors who were supposed to be so wise, yet had counseled this kind of dependence upon Egypt (5:21; 19:11–15; 28:14, 15; 30:1, 2). These wise men were acting as if God knew nothing, as if the Creator of the universe did not understand enough to guide his creatures correctly. In modern speech Isaiah might have said, "You know, God knows a little something, too."

will bring about evil is somewhat difficult, both grammatically and theologically. The grammatical question relates to the time of the verb. In form it is a converted Hiphil imperfect (cf. Gen. 2:19). Thus the normal sense would be past tense. However, many commentators treat it as analogous to the "prophetic perfect" and so make it a prediction. If this analysis is correct, then the meaning is that God knows enough to frustrate all the plans of the wise and to bring the results of their folly upon them.

The theological question relates to the meaning of *evil* here. Unlike the English word "evil," Hebrew *ra*ʿ can mean both moral evil and what we would call misfortune. The Bible never attributes moral evil to God, but it does attribute to him those turns of events considered to be bad or unfortunate.[5] That is surely the case here (so RSV and NIV "disaster," NEB "trouble"). One of the charges being leveled against the gods was that they were impotent, unable to do anything fortunate *or* unfortunate. They could neither reward their adherents nor punish rebels (5:18, 19; 26:9–11; 41:21–24; 43:11–13). Isaiah insists that God is not bound by fate or chance, but is fully able to act and will do so in the present situation. Egypt's help will be useless if God has decided to bring trouble to Jerusalem (cf. 42:24 and 45:7).

not turning aside his words does not mean God will not change his approach to us if we change. He will, as the book of Jonah indicates, and

5. See *TWOT*, II:854–56.

as Jonah knew he would (Jon. 3:10; 4:1–2). What it does mean is that no avenue other than repentance can deflect God's pronouncements concerning us. He is as implacable as time itself *unless* we change, and all the Egypts in the world cannot alter what he says.

house of the wicked . . . help of the workers of iniquity probably refers to the nation of Judah.[6] If so, it is a strong denunciation. It does not matter what a people's birthright is, nor what its history may have been. Neither does it matter what their strength is, nor who they have as allies. If they refuse to trust in God and to conform their lives to his character, they are workers of iniquity and they will discover that God, far from being their possession, is against them to destroy them. The modern church would do well to wonder whether such a denunciation could be leveled against it.

3 This verse continues the contrast between Egypt and God by asserting that flesh is hardly equal to spirit. This is clearly true, but we human beings have continued difficulty acting upon it, because we tend to value tangible things more than intangible ones. So the Scriptures remind us in various ways that flesh can neither help us nor harm us in the face of God (Ps. 56:5, 12 [Eng. 4, 11]; 146:3; Hos. 11:9; Luke 12:4, 5; Rom. 8:35–39). Skinner makes the interesting point that while the pagans could have accepted the idea that deity is spirit, what the biblical revelation adds is that the divine Spirit has one consistent moral purpose against which all are judged.

(b) Mighty God (31:4–9)

> 4 *For thus says the Lord to me,*
>   *"Like a lion, even a young lion, growling over its prey,*
>   *when[1] a full group of shepherds is called against it*
>   *does not tremble at their voices,*
>   *nor slink away at their shouting,*
>   *so the Lord of hosts will descend to fight[2] upon Mount Zion,*
>   *upon its hill."*
> 5 *Like flying birds,*
>   *so the Lord of hosts defends Jerusalem.*
>   *Defending, he will deliver;*
>   *passing over, he will rescue.*

6. Thus the sense would be "He will arise against Judah and against Egypt which is helping Judah." Alternatively, the sense would be "He will arise against Egypt and against the help which iniquitous Egypt provides."

1. *ʾᵃšer* here introduces a dependent clause, perhaps concessive; cf. 7:15; 28:12 (so Kissane).

2. Note the wordplay between *ṣᵉbāʾ ôṭ*, "hosts," and *ṣābāʾ*, "fight." The use of "Lord of hosts" in the two verses indicates his total sovereignty.

6 *Turn*[3] *to the One from whom they have deepened turning away, O*
sons of Israel.
7 *For in that day each one will reject his idols of silver and his idols*
of gold which your hands made for you sinfully.[4]
8 *Then Assyria will fall by a more than human sword,*
and a superhuman sword will devour him.
He will be in flight before the sword,
and his choice men will be slave laborers.
9 *His rock will pass away because of fear;*
his princes will tremble because of the ensign.[5]
The oracle of the Lord whose flame is in Zion,
and whose furnace is in Jerusalem.

As in 30:19–33, Isaiah now turns from denunciation of the false hope to proclamation of the true hope. If God is implacable toward a sinful Judah, he is also implacable in the defense of a repentant Judah. Thus again the motivation to trust is both negative—Egypt cannot help—and positive—God will help even though we have sinned in refusing to trust him. This announcement of hope before the fact is typical of this book and, indeed, of the gospel.[6] God does not wait until we have repented to act in mercy. Rather, his mercy becomes the impetus to repent. Thus we are invited to repent as a result of attraction rather than because of avoidance.

While the segment is clearly a unity in thought, the fact that vv. 6–7 are prose while all the rest is poetic raises questions about the segment's literary unity. It seems possible that vv. 4–5 and vv. 8–9 were originally separate and that the prose section is used to join them. Attempts to determine when this happened are futile because of the extreme subjectivity of such efforts.

4, 5 In their present setting these two verses present two pictures of God's persistence in the face of enemies. The first is a picture of fierce

3. The disagreement in person between the imperative and the verb has prompted *BHS* to propose making the imperative a 3rd person verb. However, this proposal is without ms. support. All the versions, including 1QIs[a], retain the imperative. The variants occur with the finite verb. Targ. has 2nd person (as do most modern translations). LXX paraphrases "you that have counseled the deep counsel." If MT is correct, Young's interpretation, "against whom men have deeply revolted," seems the best. It is not merely Israel that *has turned away*, but all humanity. At least Israel can turn back if it will.

4. "sinfully" is syntactically awkward. LXX omits it and *BHS* counsels the same. However, it can be construed here as a second accusative of "made" functioning adverbially. If it is not original, it is hard to imagine how it got inserted here.

5. *nēs*, "ensign," is a favorite word of Isaiah's: 5:26; 11:10, 12; 13:2; 18:3; 30:17; 31:9; 33:23; 49:22; 62:10.

6. Cf. 1:18, 19; 40:1–5; 63:1–6; Rom. 5:8; 1 John 4:9–10.

strength while the second is a picture of passionate attachment. God is both.

4 There is disagreement over the intent of this verse. The majority of modern commentators, including several of a theologically conservative position (Delitzsch, Young, etc.), conclude that the sense is negative for two reasons. It does not make sense for Judah to be the lion's prey if the imagery is intended to convey God's love for Judah; and elsewhere *ṣābā' 'al* means to "fight against." Thus it is said that the verse conveys the same thing as vv. 2 and 3: Egypt (the shepherds) will not be able to protect Judah from God. However, the present context calls this view into question since v. 5, which is clearly positive, follows directly on v. 4 with no break and no evidence of any intended contrast.[7] In that light the two arguments mentioned above may be looked at more closely. First, there is no reason to take the figure allegorically, with each element having a specific symbolism. Rather, the main point is that a lion cannot be frightened away and neither can God.[8] To press the figure more closely is an unwarranted use of the imagery. Furthermore, while it is true that when *'al* occurs after *ṣābā'* it means "against," there are only a total of four such occurrences, so this evidence is hardly decisive. That *'al* can mean both "upon" and "against" with other verbs for "fight" seems to leave that possibility open here. Since these two arguments are not conclusive and since the present context calls for the positive interpretation, we conclude that this interpretation is most likely.[9] The Lion of Judah cannot be frightened off by a pack of people shouting and beating on pans.

5 This verse varies the figure by comparing God to a mother bird which flies back and forth over her nest when a predator is near, both to distract the enemy and, if necessary, to offer herself as a victim to save her little ones. As noted above, this verse presents another side of God's relationship to Judah. Not only is he strong and determined, he is also personally attached to his people and will *defend* (or shield, as this is the verb from which that noun is derived) them, if need be, with himself.[10]

passing over is parallel to "defending," and this suggests that the meaning is "protect," even "hover over." This meaning applies very well

---

7. Clements, who believes the original intent of v. 4 was negative, takes note of this and says that v. 5 was added later to change the sense of v. 4.

8. So Calvin and most other older commentators.

9. So also Kaiser.

10. The Christian cannot help but see this motif brought to its final fulfillment in Christ, who interposed himself between us and the just results of our sins.

to Exod. 12.[11] Although *BHS* suggests that all four verbs should be made infinitives, the MT pattern of perfects following infinitives is also attested in Gen. 26:13; 1 Sam. 2:26; Jer. 23:14.[12]

6, 7   As noted above (n. 2), these verses are in prose and seem to serve as a bridge between vv. 4–5 and 8–9. They express the result of the announcement of salvation and prepare for the fuller explication of the nature of that salvation. The results are twofold, as Kissane notes. First there is conversion, which is followed by renunciation. The theological pattern here is very consistent with the rest of the book. Sin, which is typically idolatrous (man making God in his image), results in judgment. That judgment not only calls the efficacy of the idols into question, but it also provides the backdrop against which God can disclose his unconditional love. That love prompts a turning back to God and a concomitant rejection of idolatry.

they have deepened turning away is a graphic phrase. Not only have people turned aside from following God, they have intentionally deepened that turning away. This situation is reminiscent of the action of the royal counselors in hiding away so that they could make their plans without reference to God.

7   When both the idols' helplessness and God's grace are revealed, the idols do not have a chance.[13] Though they are made of valuable metals, they are valueless. Not even their material worth means anything to their former worshipers. They now know that these objects are an abomination to God. As Calvin says, "True conversion does not ask the price." The converse is also true: so long as a person is still asking whether he can afford a possible turning to God, that cost will always be too high.

Mauchline shrewdly observes that this is not the first time that the Israelites had abandoned their idols, nor would it be the last.[14] This is a testimony to the fundamentally idolatrous nature of humanity. It is very difficult for us to admit to an intangible deity who cannot be manipulated but requires prior commitment on every point.

8, 9   These verses now put the seal upon God's promises. Mighty Assyria will be devastated by an other-than-human means with the result that she will flee in panic. It is hard to believe that this refers to anything

11. See T. F. Glasson, "The 'Passover,' a misnomer: the meaning of the verb *pāsaḥ*," *JTS* 10 (1959) 79–84.

12. In each of these cases the infinitive is *hlk*. The perfect seems to express the result of the ongoing process described by the infinitive.

13. Cf. also 2:8, 20; 17:8; 30:22.

14. See Gen. 35:2; Josh. 24:2, 23; Judg. 10:16; 1 Sam. 7:3; etc.

other than Sennacherib's loss of his army in Judah to the death angel.[15] At the same time it may be admitted that the language is poetic and need not be forced to literal equivalency. Thus it is not necessary to seek for a particular time when Assyrian soldiers became forced laborers. It is enough to say that the Assyrian army was no match for God.

8 *Then Assyria will fall* takes the opening *waw* as resumptive, expressing an apodosis flowing from vv. 6–7.[16] When Judah turns to God and destroys her idols, then Assyria will feel the hand of God's wrath. So God's grace is announced prior to repentance, but the repentance becomes a condition to experiencing the full outworking of that grace.

a superhuman sword makes the point that it is God, not man, who delivers. This truth surfaces again and again in Scripture. It appears in the conception of Isaac, when human power was long gone. It appears at the crossing of the Red Sea and again at Jericho. It is there in the Gideon story and in the rout of the Philistines in Samuel's day. Jehoshaphat experienced it in his fight with the Edomites, etc.[17] It is this truth which is at the heart of Paul's contrast of flesh and spirit (Gal. 5:16–26). When people believe they can save themselves, they effectively dethrone God in their lives and doom themselves (Phil. 3:7), for it is only as the king of our lives that he can help us.

9 *His rock* has raised many questions of identification. Proposals have included the god Ashur, the city of Nineveh, and King Sennacherib. The parallelism with *princes* suggests that *rock* should be treated as the subject of the clause and not (as in AV) as the object: "He will pass over his stronghold." However, that rendering seems to do more justice to the

---

15. Those who cannot accept prediction see this prophecy as written after the fact. Those who believe the account to be only legendary see it as having been written after the legend had gained currency. Apparently they do not recognize the devastating impact such a position has upon the worth of the Isaianic theology. To accept this point of view is to say that although there may be judgment in history, there is no grace, except what is made up.

16. So Calvin; cf. Williams, *Syntax,* § 440.

17. Kaiser says that this kind of statement must have come from a very late period when the Jews no longer themselves were able to play a part in their history. Therefore they had to posit an a-historical salvation. But, as we have shown, this theme runs through the Bible. The question is not historical salvation by man versus a-historical salvation by God. Rather, it is salvation in history by man or salvation in history by God. Dependence upon divine acts is not flight from history, but the external confirmation of an inward faith. If every time such evidence is adduced it is discounted, faith becomes a wholly inward thing and is, in every sense, a delusion.

impersonality of "rock." Perhaps the sense is "all his confidence will pass away."[18]

because of the ensign may denote either fleeing from their own ensign or being helpless at the sight of the enemy battle flags. The latter seems to fit the general sense of the verse best. When God raises his ensign against the powers of this world, not even the mightiest can stand against him.

whose flame is in Zion suggests that Jerusalem is the hearth upon which the flame of God burns. That flame denotes both God's sanctity and his destructive power (cf. the story of Nadab and Abihu, Lev. 10:1–5). Because Jerusalem is that hearth, those who touch it bring themselves under threat of destruction. However, the mistake which Jews and Christians alike have made over the years is confusing the source and the agent and assuming that what God used was therefore inviolate in spite of its own character. But again and again God has shown the fallacy of such confusion. God transcends all created things, and while he condescends to give certain places and persons special significance, he is never to be merely identified with those. Thus the answer to the question "Is Jerusalem inviolable?" is always no. But does God hover over Jerusalem with special concern and does he invest her with special significance? Yes!

c. BEHOLD THE KING (32:1–33:24)

(1) True leaders (32:1–8)

1 *Behold,*[1] *according to righteousness a king will reign,*
   and princes[2] *according to justice will rule.*
2 *A man*[3] *will be like a shelter from the wind,*
   and a hiding place from the storm,
like a stream of water in a dry place,
   like the shadow of a great rock in a land of exhaustion.

18. Driver cites Arabic examples where "hill" or "rock" can also mean "ruler" or "leader" (*JSS* 13 [1968] 52).
1. Kaiser, appealing to GKC, § 159w, opens the verse with "when" while Kissane adopts "if," but both suggestions seem prompted by literary-critical concerns and not by the text itself.
2. "princes" has a *lamed* prefixed to it, which may be translated "and as for." But none of the versions has such a reading and almost all commentators see it as an unintentional addition because of the other *lamed*'s in the verse.
3. The verse opens with "A man will be like. . . ." It is not clear whether this is to be taken as a distributive referring to "princes" (each of them will be), or a general term (the leaders will be). The general usage perhaps fits the setting better.

THE BOOK OF ISAIAH

3 *Then the eyes of those who see will not be blurred,*[4]
   and the ears of those who hear will be attentive;
4 *The heart of the impetuous will understand knowledge,*
   and the tongue of the inarticulate will be quick to speak
   dazzlingly.
5 *No longer will the fool be called a noble,*
   nor will the knave be said to be a gentleman.
6 *For a fool speaks foolishness*
   and his heart works iniquity[5]
   in order to practice ungodliness
   and to speak falsely about the Lord;
   to make the soul of the hungry empty
   and to deny a drink to the thirsty.
7 *As for the knave,*[6] *his devices*[7] *are evil;*
   he counsels false plans
   to destroy the poor with false words
   when the needy speak justly.
8 *But the noble counsels nobility,*
   and upon noble things he stands.

Chapters 32 and 33 represent an alternative to the situation described in chs. 30–31. There false counsel depicted reliance upon Egypt as Judah's hope. Crooked and venial rulers made their plans in secret and sought ways to foist those plans on a public which would not have acquiesced in them if they had known their true import. Here God, the God who will have delivered them from Assyria, is depicted as the true source of righteous rule. Although human kings may rule on his behalf (32:1–4), it is his Spirit which must energize them if they are to rule rightly (34:14, 15), and ultimately he alone is king (33:5–6, 22). Thus, as noted above (see at ch. 28), the larger segment (chs. 28–33) continues the contrast begun in ch. 7, which is a contrast between the results of trusting human resources and those of trusting in God. Trusting human resources leads to injustice,

4. *tišᵉeynâ* appears to be from *šāᶜaᶜ*, to "smear over," rather than *šāᶜâ*, "to see."

5. LXX translates "his heart *does* iniquity" with *noései*, prompting the suggestion that MT *ᶜāśâ*, "do," is an error for *ḥāšaḇ*, "to design, think" *(BHK)*. 1QIsᵃ reads *ḥwšb*. However, Orlinsky, *JBL* 69 (1950) 152–55, points out that LXX always translates *ḥšḇ* with *logízomai*.

6. *kēlay*, "knave," occurs only here, so its meaning is primarily derived from its position as a synonym of "fool." However, it is possible that its root is *nkl*, "to scheme, connive."

7. "Devices" is lit. "vessels, tools." It is probably used here for its assonance with "knave" *(kēlay kēlāyw)*.

blindness, corruption, and destruction. But trust in God leads to justice, clarity, integrity, and life. The thought in the two chapters moves through four stages. The first describes the nature of true leadership and the effects stemming from it (32:1–8). The second explains what is the fundamental ingredient for that kind of leadership to exist: God's Spirit (32:9–20). The third makes this necessity of divine intervention even more explicit, stating that Judah is helpless without him (33:1–16). Finally, in a more emotive segment, the author imagines the day when Yahweh rules over a serene and quiet land delivered from all her enemies (33:17–24).

The first segment, 32:1–8, utilizes the language of the wisdom tradition to talk about sense and nonsense. Throughout the section from ch. 28 onward the folly of stupid leaders has been castigated. Now, in the light of the promised divine destruction of Assyria (31:4–9), a result the human leadership could not produce, the author talks of the results which might be expected from good leaders. As signaled from the very outset of the book, Isaiah considers it as a given that life lived within the confines of the "natural" spiritual order will produce life and health, whereas life which flies in the face of God's order can only produce disorder and disaster. The results of the true leadership will be security (v. 2), insight and understanding (vv. 3–4), and judgment according to character (vv. 5–8).

A major question is whether the segment was intended as a messianic prophecy. The most significant argument raised against that point of view is that the language is not nearly so idealized as it is in such undoubtedly messianic passages as 8:23–9:6 (Eng. 9:1–7) and 11:1–9. Those who raise this argument urge that the references are to ordinary human beings. This point of view is supported by the references to "princes," who do not appear in the other messianic passages, where the focus is exclusively on the Messiah.

These arguments are not to be dismissed lightly, but at least two things may be said in favor of the messianic intent. First, while the idealization is not as great as in the other passages, there surely is idealization, so much so that it does not seem possible to say ordinary human beings are being discussed. Especially important in this regard are the references to seeing and hearing, since the absence of these was the ultimate mark of God's displeasure with the land (6:10). Second, the references to princes may be dictated by the context, in which corrupt officials have played such a part (cf. 28:14; 29:14; 30:4; 31:9). Thus, in talking of the ideal future, it may have been necessary to present good princes as a contrast with the bad ones. Thus, at the least, it seems that a quality of government is being discussed that could only be expected in its fullness under the rule of the Messiah.[8]

There is very little agreement concerning the authorship and date of the segment. Probably the majority of recent authors deny Isaian authorship (so Clements, Kaiser, Wildberger), but their reasons for doing so, and the dates they assign, vary widely. Whatever else may be said, Kaiser's observation that the connections with other parts of the book point to the segment's having been designed for inclusion at this point seems correct. Could not Isaiah have done this as well as a later redactor?

1 *Behold, according to righteousness* serves to underline the contrast with the preceding. However the leaders described in the previous chapters may have functioned, it was not, as far as Isaiah was concerned, according to the right path established by Yahweh. Indeed, they had been at pains to conceal their path from him (29:15, 16; 30:1, 2, etc.). Yet his willingness to discover right and to do it was understood to be the mark of a good king.[9] Thus Isaiah looks to a day when the king will be divinely enabled to do what thinking people had known from the beginning a true king should do. The coming of the Messiah became necessary because human beings could conceive of a kind of kingship which no human being could live up to. Where did such a concept come from except from the mind of God through revelation?

2 In the coming era, leaders will no longer be predators from whom the people will need to seek relief (29:20, 21). Rather, the leaders themselves will be sources of protection and support, as they ought to be. As Scott notes, the picturesque qualities of the Hebrew language come to the fore in this verse with its four vivid similes. The good leader breasts the storm for his people and enables them to carry on because of what he provides for them. Nowhere is this better typified than in Jesus the Good Shepherd who gives his life for the sheep (John 10:11), the Servant who did not come to be ministered to, but to minister unto (Matt. 20:28).[10]

3, 4 Not only will the true leaders provide security for their people, they will also make possible that spiritual transformation in which the

8. Cheyne suggests very plausibly that Isaiah may have still been hoping that Hezekiah would prove to be the Messiah.

9. See Prov. 16:10; 20:8, 26, 28; 29:4, 14; 31:4.

10. As is frequently the case in this book, these figures of speech posed interpretative problems for the writers of the Targ. and the LXX. Their results vary greatly from the MT, with the Targ. relating them to the righteous and the LXX going even further afield.

former blindness, deafness, and stammering[11] are taken away. Given the larger context with its references to the blindness and dullness of the leaders themselves (28:7, 8; 29:9, 10, 14; 30:1, 2; 31:1), it seems logical to assume that the writer expects the first manifestations of this transformation to appear in the leaders, after which it will spread to the people (29:18–19, 24). As noted above, here there seems to be a clear reversal of the situation described in 6:10, where blindness, deafness, and dullness were the predicted results of the prophet's preaching. Spiritual clarity and perception always follow from submission to God's ways. Refusal to submit is the surest prescription for an ultimate inability to discern any difference between good and evil (5:18–23; Prov. 4:14–19; John 7:17). Thus it is appropriate that here spiritual clarity is a result of faithful leaders who themselves submit to God and to whom their people thus have no difficulty submitting.

5 This verse provides a transition from the previous thought to the following one. One result of that clarity which comes from walking in God's ways is the ability to evaluate persons on the basis of character. Verses 6–8 describe at length what sets the fool off from the true nobleman.

A fortuitous assonance brought into play here between *fool (nbl)* and *noble (ndb)* highlights the idea of confusing one for the other. But the tendency is not merely a Hebrew one. In every society those who have managed to gain power are treated as great, deserving persons regardless of their true character, because the underlings are afraid of the power.[12] In the ideal setting which Isaiah envisions, the genuine qualities of the leaders will make it impossible to mistake a fool, no matter how rich and powerful he might be.

6, 7 *fool* is one of the strongest negative words in the OT because it depicts the person who has consciously rejected the ways of God, which are the road to life, and has chosen the ways of death. His folly is the more disastrous because its short-term results may make God's way appear wrong.[13] As that folly is depicted here, it involves a pattern of life which in its expression as well as in its principles is concertedly opposed to God. As a result, the helpless are oppressed. This is the connection seen elsewhere in Isaiah (ch. 14; etc.) as well as in the OT. If God cannot be relied

11. While it is tempting to relate the stammerer ("inarticulate") here to those in 28:11–13, closer examination shows, as Delitzsch argues, that two different groups are being talked about.

12. Calvin points out that in bad government the covetous are honored because possessions are everything.

13. On *nbl*, "fool," see *THAT*, II:26–31; *TWOT*, II:547.

upon to supply my needs, and if supply of my needs as I understand them is paramount, then those weaker than I had better take care.

8 Whatever else may be said of this way, it is not "noble." Just like the English "noble," Hebrew *ndb* may refer to social standing, but its root meaning refers to character, someone who is generous and large-hearted, someone who knows that an all-wise God supplies his needs and therefore can afford to be generous to those less well off than he.

(2) Deserted or fruitful (32:9–20)

9 *Complacent women,*
    arise, hear my voice.
Confident daughters,
    listen to my speech.
10 *Days upon a year*
    you trusting ones will be agitated;
the grape harvest will fail,
    the harvest will not[1] *come.*
11 *Tremble, complacent ones;*
    be agitated, secure ones.
Strip yourselves and go naked,[2]
    a loin cloth at your waist.
12 *Upon the breasts, moaning,*
    for the pleasant fields,
    for the fruitful vine,
13 *for the land of my people,*
    grown up with thorns and briars,
even for all the houses of rejoicing,
    the city of wealth.
14 *For the palace is forsaken,*
    the noisy city abandoned.
The "Hill" and the "Tower"[3]

1. *bᵉlî* is rare with the finite verb ("it will *not* come"). 1QIsᵃ has *bal*, which would be more common. Perhaps MT arose through dittography *(bly ybw')*.
2. The imperatives in v. 11 are anomalous. They appear to be in the fem. sing. (except for the first, *ḥirᵉḏû*, which is masc. plur.). GKC, § 48i, calls them Aramaizing forms of the 2nd fem. plur. (recommending that *ḥirᵉḏû* be emended), but Delitzsch says there is no warrant for this and takes them to be emphatic masc. sing. This suggestion requires the least emendation and accords (in gender) with the troublesome *sōpᵉḏîm* in v. 12 (see below). If the masculine is intended, it perhaps indicates that the mourning will be general and not restricted to women.
3. *baḥan* as a noun is unknown outside of this context. Since it occurs with *ʿōpel,* "hill," and since the verb means "try," "(watch-) tower" seems appropriate (LXX "villages").

will become[4] caves,
a delight of wild donkeys,
 pasturage for flocks.
15 *Until the Spirit from on high[5]*
 is poured out upon us.
Then the desert will become as a fertile field,
 and the fertile field will be considered a forest.
16 *Then justice will dwell in the desert*
 and righteousness will inhabit the fertile field.
17 *And the work of righteousness will be peace,*
 and the effect of righteousness will be quietness and security
 forever.
18 *Then my people will dwell in a peaceful habitation,*
 in secure dwellings and undisturbed resting places.[6]
19 *There will be hail[7] when the forest falls,*
 and the city will be laid utterly low.
20 *Blessed are you: sowing on all the waters,*
 sending out the ox and ass.

The prophet here uses direct address to make two points clear: the renewal promised in vv. 1–8 will not come without disaster, but it *will* come and that through the agency of the divine energy, God's spirit. These points are typical of the message of the book: humanity brings destruction upon itself; but there is hope for us through the sovereign grace of God. This similarity of thought has convinced many of the authenticity of this segment; but others, remaining unconvinced, remark upon the redactor's careful adaptation of Isaianic themes.[8]

Two segments can be observed within the passage. The first is covered in vv. 9–14. It is negative, utilizing agricultural imagery to predict

4. The rather odd use of *ba'ad*, "about, on behalf of," suggests that the comparison is not a matter of actually becoming caves. Driver suggests "what is next to," thus "no better than" (*JSS* 13 [1965] 52). Cf. also Prov. 6:26; Job 2:4.

5. "on high" is God's dwelling, so 24:21; 33:5; 38:14; 57:15; etc.

6. Note the contrast between the "flower" of v. 14 and the one here. Note further that v. 18 uses the same terms as vv. 9 and 10.

7. Since this would be the only place where "hail" is used as a verb, it has been widely accepted that *bārad*, "hail," is an error for *yārad*, "it will go down" (so RSV). NEB follows Driver's extensive reinterpretation (*JSS* 13 [1968] 52–53). Both LXX and Targ. read "hail." Note the article of S. Bar-Hon in *Beth Maacah* 7 (1962) 94–96, which I have not seen.

8. So Vermeylen takes it to be authentic, but Clements makes vv. 9–14 exilic and 15–20 Josianic; Wildberger makes it early postexilic and Kaiser late postexilic. One cannot help but observe that critical methodology is still highly imprecise for such a wide divergence of opinion to exist.

a land desolate and forsaken (cf. 5:5, 6; 16:8–10; 24:4–9; 34:13–15).[9] The second is positive, in fact diametrically opposite to the foregoing, predicting a day when the land will be inhabited and abundant, because of God's empowerment. While some deny the original unity of the passage, it is difficult to gainsay the chiastic structure involved: false security, disaster, restoration, true security. At the least one would have to say that whichever paragraph came later, it was specifically designed to complement the earlier one. This being so, arguments for the priority of one paragraph or the other rest more and more upon the a prioris of the arguers.[10]

In the book's present form, then, vv. 9–20 stand between 32:1–8, which introduce the true kingdom, and 33:1–24, which bring the ideas to full development. The segment is something of a parenthetical statement underlining those two foundational ideas upon which the kingdom rests.

9–14 The prophet speaks directly to a group of women who, from the context, are apparently taking part in the harvest festival. It is impossible to tell whether the prophecy was spoken to a particular group of women, or whether the author is simply using a general class to give concreteness to his message. Both seem equally possible. Perhaps the generality of the doom predicted slightly favors the latter.

G. A. Smith, to a great extent, and other commentators less so, suggest that women are addressed because they are especially prone to complacency and short-sightedness. That suggestion seems to be unwarranted. The whole nation of Israel, males and females alike, were prone to these defects apparently because they believed that they had God within their control (e.g., Jer. 7:1–12). In this case, for reasons not now clear, the women were particular examples of the problem (so also Amos 6:1). It may be that Isaiah, having failed to alert the men to the tragedy they were precipitating, turns to the women to try to get them to influence their husbands. At any rate, he warns them that the new day he has spoken of in vv. 1–8 is no warrant for a placid, business-as-usual approach to life (cf. 2:1–5 followed by 2:6–4:1).

9 While there is nothing inherently wrong with ease and security

9. Skinner and others suggest that this segment must have come from Isaiah's early ministry when he was preaching unconditional disaster. However, throughout his entire ministry he castigated reliance on anything other than God. Egypt, Babylon, and Baal were all one to him.

10. So for instance Clements argues that vv. 9–14 were inserted by a later writer who wished to separate vv. 1–5 (6–8 are not original according to him) from 15–20 since 15–20 had not been fulfilled in Josiah. As is apparent, there is nothing in the passage to support such speculation.

(as shown by their appearance in vv. 17 and 18), they are bad when they are based on false premises (so Amos 6:1; Zech. 1:15; Ps. 123:4). Throughout the Scriptures, the recurring question is, where is your trust? And the corollary to that is: if it is in anything other than God, you are in trouble. So, if I am at ease because I think I can manipulate God, or because the harvests have been so good, that is a false security which I had better be prepared to lose.

Isaiah had been attempting to warn the people of this problem, so the sight of a woman totally absorbed in her finery (3:16–4:1) or mindlessly fulfilled in a good harvest must have been especially maddening to him.

10 *Days upon a year* is somewhat obscure. Older interpreters generally understood it to refer to a long time of trouble. More recent scholars, however, have concluded that it refers to the length of time until the trouble occurs. In any case "year" seems to define the number of "days" involved. This makes sense in the light of the harvest imagery. "You may rejoice now, but what about next year when the harvest fails?" How easy it is to put one's confidence in circumstances, assuming that everything will go on unchanged. Trust in God rises above circumstances. To be sure, such persons feel the pain and uncertainty of suddenly altered circumstances, but they are not shattered and adrift (2 Cor. 4:16–18).

We are not told what the cause of the crop failure will be. In this setting it is tempting to think that it will be the invading Assyrian army. The failure to mention Assyria may be because the message was first given at another time (see n. 9 above), or it may be simply for the sake of keeping the agricultural figure intact.

11–14 The prophet calls the women to begin to mourn for the land about which they now feel so confident. If it is correct that they were engaged in a harvest feast, these words would have been most unwelcome. Particularly in our moments of happiness, we do not like to be reminded that death stares all of us in the face. But it does, and we must not allow present happiness to leave us unprepared to meet it.

It appears that it was typical for women in the ancient Near East to bare their breasts in mourning and to put sackcloth about their waists.[11] This custom explains the reference here. There is no indication that complete nakedness was intended.

---

11. For pictorial evidence, see *ANEP,* nos. 459, 636, 638. Note the material about the waists of the women in no. 459. C. Gordon's suggestion that this is a challenge to belt-wrestling as attested at Nuzi does not seem to be warranted in the context of mourning ("Methods of Biblical Archaeology: An Illustration [on Isa. 32,11 and a Nuzu Text]," *Crozier Quarterly* 27 [1950] 309–312).

Upon the breasts, moaning presents serious difficulties, all of which center upon the verb *(sōp⁽ᵉ⁾dîm)*. The versions unanimously translate it with "smite," but the Hebrew usage does not seem to include this meaning, only "wail" or "moan" being attested. Furthermore, the form is a masculine plural participle, which seems very strange with "breasts." Several suggestions have been put forward, but none has been so satisfactory as to gain a consensus.[12] The general sense is clear. The present confidence and security are only transitory. They will shortly be replaced by other emotions entirely (cf. 22:1, 2), when all the temporal sources of joy are removed.

13 *the land of my people* makes it expressly plain that just because the Israelites might be called the people of God, they do not have some sort of mechanical claim over him. The good land, a source of joy and abundance, could grow up in thorns and briars as quickly as any other if its people were out of harmony with God (cf. 1:7; 5:6; 7:23). Elsewhere *šāmîr*, "briars," occurs with *šayit*, "thorns," but here it is with *qôṣ*, which is the term used in Gen. 3:18 with respect to the curse on the land. It is tempting to see a conscious allusion here.

14 The climax of the mourning is reached in this verse. Why the mourning? Because the city of God will be empty. Perhaps most significantly in this section, the *palace* will be empty. No, the kingdom Isaiah is envisioning will not be brought in by the people simply going about as they have been. That course of action will result in no king. The craven, scheming leaders described in chs. 28–31 are not going to bring about a new day. They will bring disaster. The high and the mighty will become low. This probably explains the reference to caves. Commentators have long puzzled over how the references to "Hill" (Heb. *'ōpel*), the spur of the hill upon which the temple rests, and to the "Tower" could be about caves. Furthermore, how could flocks pasture in caves?[13] But this is to take the passage too literally. As in ch. 2, the point is that the supposedly high (and it is to be wondered if "the hill" and "the tower" were elite

---

12. If the verb could be emended to fem. (sing. or plur.), "wailing on the breasts" could certainly include "wailing (while beating) on the breasts." Mauchline and Clements assert that 1QIsᵃ has this correction. However, that is not true. *spwdnh* does appear (somewhat unaccountably) in v. 11, but the form in v. 12 is *swpdm*, exactly as in MT. Calvin suggested that "breasts" are to be understood as figurative for the land and introductory of the rest of vv. 12 and 13: "For the breasts, moaning." Yet another suggestion is that "breasts" *(š⁽ᵉ⁾dê)* is a mistake for "fields" *(ś⁽ᵉ⁾dê)* (cf. *BHK;* Clements). Perhaps "on the breasts" is merely elliptical, setting the stage, as it were, while "wailing" is to be related to the succeeding terms.

13. Duhm suggested *ma'⁽ᵃ⁾rōt*, "bare places," instead of MT *m⁽ᵉ⁾ārōt*, "caves."

sections of the city; cf. Skinner) will be cast down, become its opposite number, before the Lord comes in power to save his people.

In vv. 15–20 there is now a shift from the prophecy of warning (vv. 9–14) to a prophecy of salvation.[14] The promised kingdom will come. There will be peace and security. But it will come only through divine initiative and empowerment after the bankruptcy of human effort has been made plain. The reader will notice a change of emphasis from vv. 9–14. There the emphasis was wholly material. Here that imagery is maintained, but there is a spiritual note added which suggests that the ultimate mark of God's blessing is not good crops or secure states but righteous lives and just dealings. The world's definition of security and that of the believer in God are always different. The security of the believer is in a God who transcends this world. Thus, its vagaries and uncertainties, while surely having an effect on him or her, cannot ultimately destroy the security. But furthermore, it is only when the two parties know that there is One higher than either of them to whom they can entrust their rights that the two of them can live together in harmony. Thus Isaiah, having demonstrated the tenuousness of security based on this world, here shows both the source and the means of security which lasts. All this is directly in line with the central question of chs. 7–39: in whom (or in what) do you trust?[15]

15 In the OT there is a developing understanding of the *Spirit* of God. In many cases the term is used impersonally, analogously to the human spirit. Thus it is used as an hypostasis for the immanent, empowering, energizing activity of God (cf. Ps. 104:29–30). However, perhaps because of his filling of individuals, the identity of the Spirit becomes more and more explicit. In any case, the outpouring of the Spirit became a central facet of the OT hope.[16] If God's people were ever to share his character, an outcome devoutly to be hoped for, then it would have to come about through an infusion of God's Spirit into human beings.[17] This development relates fundamentally to a crisis of Lordship. God cannot fill where he does not rule. Thus, it is no accident that this statement occurs

14. Duhm, followed by Scott, would make this an independent oracle and alter the opening ʿaḏ, "until," to ʿōḏ, "yet," as in 29:17. However, the essential continuity of thought with vv. 9–14 argues against this emendation.

15. The numerous similarities to the second half of the book (cf. 44:3; 45:8; 54:13; 60:17, 21; 61:11) are utilized in different ways by critics depending on their presuppositions, but at the least they show that the book cannot be interpreted in discrete sections. It is a whole.

16. See J. Oswalt, "John Wesley and the OT Concept of the Holy Spirit," *Religion in Life* 48 (1979) 283–292.

17. Along with this passage, see 44:3; Jer. 31:33; Ezek. 36:26–27; Joel 3:1–2 (Eng. 2:28–29).

in this context of divine kingship. So long as human beings usurp ultimate rule of their lives, there is impotence, unrighteousness, and dependence upon the very forces which would destroy us. It is only when we come to the end of ourselves and acknowledge God's right to rule our lives that we can experience the divine empowerment for righteousness.

the desert will become as a fertile field is the same as in 29:17 except that "desert" is substituted for "Lebanon." The figure is of abundance. What was formerly useless for crops will become fertile, while what was fertile will become a veritable jungle. When the creative energy of God is let loose the results are always astonishing.

16 The true abundance will be in matters of the spirit. From the prophet's perspective, Judah's national life has been a desert. Righteousness and justice have withered away as people have abandoned God's ways to pursue their own advantage and comfort. This abandonment has led to oppression of the poor and the establishment of a very questionable foreign policy. In effect, Judah has cut herself off from the source of her life. But in the days to come, when she is once again in touch with that source, God's righteousness will be hers in abundance.

17, 18 It is this abundant righteousness which will produce true peace. As Young points out, this is a distinctively Isaianic concept and appears in both parts of the book (9:5 [Eng. 6]; 59:8–9). The mechanics of this relation are made more clear by the NT. The person who has received the grace of God's forgiveness is at peace with God. Knowing himself to be at peace with the Sovereign of the universe, it is no longer necessary to project his own turmoil upon those around him (Phil. 3:12–17). Furthermore, the person for whom God's character has become central will be less likely to oppress others in a frantic attempt to supply his or her own needs. This ought to produce qualitative changes in a genuinely Christian society. That it has often not done so is a testimony to the depths of the human problem. At the same time, the potential for the impact of these understandings has been demonstrated in lives and communities around the world.

19 This verse breaks in abruptly. It may be understood in one of three ways. (1) It is a promise of the destruction of Assyria (cf. 10:33; 30:31). (2) It speaks of the destruction of Israelite pride which must accompany the restoration of righteousness (1:29–31; 2:13; 29:2–4).[18] (3) It is, coupled with v. 20, a promise that despite shocks and upheavals around about, God will spare his people (cf. NIV; see also Ps. 91:5–6). While the third alternative is attractive, nothing in the grammar supports a con-

---

18. Delitzsch combines both, taking the city to represent Jerusalem and the forest Assyria.

cessive relationship between the two verses. On balance, the second alternative seems most likely, especially in view of v. 14. The promise of Assyrian destruction would certainly fit the tone of the segment, but there is nothing in the immediate context to point to such an understanding.

20 However v. 19 is to be understood, this verse closes the segment with a figure of unremitting blessing which stems from nearness to sources. Those who plant their crops on the banks of streams have no fear of crop failure. In fact, they can even let their livestock loose to crop the first growth, so abundant will the plants be. So it will be for God's people when they learn that the source of spiritual abundance is in God.

An unanswered question remains. Has this prediction been fulfilled? Or is it only figurative? One possibility is that it was fulfilled in the restoration; another would be that it was fulfilled at Pentecost. Yet the sensitive heart cries out, "Is that all we can expect of such glorious promises?"[19] Perhaps it may be said that they are potentially fulfilled at Pentecost and await complete fulfillment at the final day.

(3) The King redeems Zion (33:1–24)

(a) Woe to the destroyer (33:1–6)

1 *Woe, destroyer who has not been destroyed;*
      Betrayer whom they have not betrayed.
   When you have finished destroying,
      you will be destroyed;
   when you have completed betraying,
      they will betray you.
2 *O Lord, be gracious to us;*
      for you we wait.
   Be our[1] *strength in the morning;*
      yes, our salvation in the time of distress.
3 *From the roaring voice, peoples flee;*
      because of your exaltation, nations scatter.
4 *Your plunder is gathered as locusts*[2] *gather;*
      as locusts leap, so is it leapt upon.

---

19. So R. P. Carroll speaks of the Isaianic prophecies as consisting mostly of bombast (*When Prophecy Failed* [New York: Seabury, 1979], pp. 151–52).

1. MT has $z^e r \bar{o}\,\dot{a}$, "their strength." 1QIs[a] also has final *m*. However, this may be an enclitic *m* which was later misunderstood. The 1st person designation would be derived from the following "our salvation." Cf. Dahood, "Some Ambiguous Texts in Isaias," *CBQ* 20 (1958) 41–49. LXX does not have the phrase; other versions have "our" (see *BHS*).

2. AV has "caterpillar" for the first word, *ḥāsîl*. The term means merely a type of destructive insect. Cf. 1 K. 8:37; 2 Chr. 6:28; Ps. 78:46.

5 *Exalted is the Lord, for he dwells on high.*
   He fills Zion with justice and righteousness.
6 *He will be the foundation of your times,*
   an abundance of deliverance, wisdom, and knowledge.
   The fear of the Lord, it is his treasure.

Chapter 33 continues from ch. 32 the contrast to the outlook of chs. 28–31. Dependence upon Egypt for relief from Assyria (which dependence must end in disaster) is replaced by reliance upon the Lord, with correspondingly different results. G. A. Smith finds the most logical historical context for this chapter as being between the time when the tribute was paid to Sennacherib (2 K. 18:13–16) and when the final attack upon Jerusalem was begun. The leaders of Judah have tried every other avenue to extricate themselves from Assyria's grip. But each has been fruitless. Egypt has been defeated; Sennacherib has refused to be bought off; he has taken the tribute, but still remains, preparing for battle. In this moment, Smith suggests, Hezekiah leads his people to repentance and Isaiah gives God's response, which is recorded here.[3] This explanation is very attractive and may be correct. However, the text does not make the historical setting explicit. It is thus the logical connection which is most important here.[4] That setting is in contrast with the former way of thinking. When the Lord is merely a talisman and human reasoning prevails, destruction follows. When the Lord is not only called king but treated as one, the result is the very deliverance sought by the former methods.

3. Cf. J. Barton Payne, "The Effect of Sennacherib's Anticipated Destruction in Isaianic Prophecy," *WTJ* 34 (1971) 22–38, for a similar point of view.

4. Today commentators generally reject either a historical or a logical connection with chs. 28–32. The tendency has become to treat it with chs. 34 and 35 as an apocalyptic conclusion to the revised edition of Isaiah's speeches in chs. 1–32. As for the date of the chapter the widest kind of disagreement exists, extending from exilic (Barth, Clements) to Persian (Wildberger) to Maccabean (Duhm, Kaiser, Scott). Yet the problem exists here, as in many other passages denied to Isaiah on theological or stylistic grounds: how shall we explain the obvious connections with "authentic Isaianic prophecy" (whatever that is held to be)? To my mind, the now-current theory of a continuous writing and redaction process over 550 years asks too much. It asks less to believe in an inspired author who brought subtlety and complexity of thought to his work. In any case, the *theological import* of the present structure of the book is paramount for us.

Chapter 33 stands off from chs. 34–35 because those two are united by contrast; the general contrasts between the results of trusting the nations and trusting God. Ch. 33 talks about the benefits of having a divine ruler, instead of human ones (cf. chs. 28–31). It is difficult to explain the meaning of ch. 33 if it is isolated from chs. 28–32, for its content directly assumes the content of those chapters.

The structure of the chapter is not absolutely clear. Gunkel argued that it was a unit of a type called "prophetic liturgy."[5] This characterization reflects the fact that a good deal of language similar to that of the Psalms appears here (see below). More recent writers have modified this position, many seeing vv. 1–6 as separate from vv. 7–24.[6] Delitzsch had already taken a similar position in the last century when he described vv. 1–6 as an introduction to the rest of the chapter. This analysis seems to be accurate in that these verses summarize the content of what follows: God will arise, destroy the destroyer, and transform Zion.

Within vv. 7–24, there appear to be two subdivisions: vv. 7–16 and 17–24. The first can be seen as containing a lament (vv. 7–9) and an oracle of response (vv. 10–16). The second contains a description of the effects of God's kingly rule. The picture is in direct contrast to that painted of Judah and Jerusalem in chs. 28–31.

Verses 1–6 are marked by the opening "woe." In contrast to those which have appeared in the segment to this point (28:1; 29:1, 15; 30:1; 31:1), this "woe" is not addressed to Judah, and one must ask why the radical change. Surely the answer is to be found in the differing foci of trust. In the other occurrences the trust was in human rulers whose counsel was that God could not be depended upon to take an active part in human affairs. According to them the nation could not "wait for" God, but should take steps to ensure its own security, specifically by making an alliance with Egypt. In short, the policy was identical to that of Ahaz: trust the nations, do not trust God. That way could only end in a cry of lament for God's people; the destroyer would be upon them.

But if the people would look to their true ruler, they would discover that he had been waiting all along to deliver them (30:18). Then the "woe" would be for those who had put their hands upon God's people. Then, when Zion's God would be truly lifted up, the oppressors would flee and Jerusalem would be the city envisioned in 1:16–17 (v. 21).

The destroyer is not identified in the passage, and the identity assigned by commentators is usually determined by their conclusions on the historical setting of the chapter. Much depends on the determinations concerning the language. If such passages as vv. 5 and 6 are taken to be eschatological, then the destroyer is not a historical nation. It is personified evil. On the other hand, such verses as 18 and 19 suggest that a real historical situation is in view and that the figurative language is symbolic.

---

5. "Jesaja 32, eine prophetische Liturgie," *ZAW* 42 (1924) 177–208. Cf. also Mowinckel, *Psalmenstudien* (Kristiania: Dybwad, 1922), II:235–38.

6. So Clements, Scott, Kaiser, etc.

If that is true, then the literary context gives the key (30:31; 31:8) and tells us that the destroyer is Assyria. It is not strange that Isaiah could promise deliverance from Assyria when he had already promised destruction at the hands of that nation. In its present form the book is quite consistent: trust the nations, destruction; trust God, deliverance.[7]

In this setting, then, G. A. Smith's suggestion makes good sense: this message is in response to a wave of repentance which began when it became clear that Sennacherib did intend to attack the city despite the payment of tribute.[8]

1 *destroyer . . . betrayer,* as noted above, most likely refer to Assyria. As the royal annals demonstrate, Assyria took great pride in her capacity to destroy anyone who had the temerity to stand against her. By the same token, she had no qualms about breaking agreements which were not to her advantage, all the while punishing with great severity any who broke agreements with her.[9]

It is not hard to imagine how the smaller peoples under Assyria's heel ground their teeth and longed for a day when she would get her own back. Here Isaiah declares, as in 10:12–19, 24–25; 14:24–27; 30:30–33; and 31:8–9, that that day is not far distant when destruction and treachery will come back upon Assyria with interest.

When you have finished destroying reiterates one of the themes of ch. 14: human power is never absolute. However overwhelming an Assyria or Babylon or Rome or Germany or Russia or United States may be in its day, there will come another day when that power will wane. The wise nation will spend its power in such a way that when the inevitable comes, its successors will be inclined to be generous toward it.

2 *for you we wait* expresses a dramatic turnabout from the attitudes expressed in chs. 29–30. There God pleaded with his people to put their trust in him, but they refused to do so (30:15; 31:6). Instead, they rushed off to Egypt, certain that if they did not act quickly in their own behalf, all hope was lost. God's word was that if they chose that avenue, their ultimate deliverance was only put off that much longer, for they must eventually turn to him (30:18–19; 32:14–15). Here that eventuality has come to pass.

The statement may be understood either as a historical record or

7. The bifurcation between the messages of destruction and deliverance is solely the result of critical dissection of the book.

8. At the same time, it must be said again that the arrangement of materials in chs. 28–33 is more logical than chronological.

9. Cf. *ARAB*, II:127, 129, 135, 136, 141, 145, etc. It may be that "betray" is used here because Sennacherib accepted Hezekiah's tribute (2 K. 18:13–16) but still did not withdraw from Jerusalem.

as a theological conclusion. If it is a historical record, as Smith suggests, it refers to the chastened attitude of the people (as typified by Hezekiah, 37:14–20) when they realized that only the Lord stood between them and Sennacherib. If this is accurate, then the turning to God was only partial, as the future would demonstrate. But it would have been enough to show the correctness of Isaiah's message that God alone could be trusted.

On the other hand, it may be that the appearance of these ideas here is not so much dependent upon an actual turn of events as it is a reflection of a theological conclusion. That is, the point is being made that whenever people will recognize God's kingship and turn to him in faith, restoration and reconstruction will follow. This analysis corresponds with the general development of the segment: chs. 28, 29, the folly of the leaders; chs. 30, 31, the results of following the leaders; chs. 32, 33, the results of following God. Thus while there may have been a turning to God at this time, the occurrence of this passage at this point is probably not wholly dependent on such an event.[10]

Be our strength (lit. "arm") *in the morning* refers to the mighty man who at the time of attack, typically the morning, bares his arm in the defense of his people.[11] Thus it is parallel to "be our salvation in the time of distress."

3 *roaring voice* may refer to thunder, which the ancients often thought of as the voice of God.[12] He only needs to speak and the whole situation will be dramatically altered.

your exaltation is a *crux interpretum* in that the parallelism would seem to demand a synonym for "roaring" whereas *rmm* only means "to be high." To be sure, the "arising" of God is frequently associated with discomfiture of his enemies (as here in 33:10), but this is with the verb *qûm*, "arise."[13] Thus several alternatives have been proposed.[14]

In any case, the point is clear: why trust the nations in place of God, when it will take only a simple manifestation of his power to scatter them like chaff.

4 When God has driven off the nations, their spoil will be left

---

10. Cf. Ps. 25:3, 5, 21; 27:14; 37:9, 34; 39:8 (Eng. 7); 52:11 (Eng. 9); 69:7 (Eng. 6).

11. Cf. 51:9; 52:10; 53:1; 63:5.

12. See 30:30; 1 Sam. 2:10; 7:10; Job 37:4, 5; 40:9; Ps. 18:14 (Eng. 13); 29:3; 77:19 (Eng. 18); 104:7. Cf. also Dan. 10:6; Rev. 1:10; *UT,* 51:7:29–40; *ANET,* p. 135.

13. See Num. 10:35; Ps. 68:2 (Eng. 1).

14. For example, see *BHS, rimmāṯīkā,* "your cry"; Driver, *JTS* 2 (1951) 268, *dmm,* "rumbling," from Akkadian (so also 1QIs^a); surely one must also consider some derivative from *rᶜm,* "to thunder."

behind, where it will be stripped as locusts strip a grainfield (cf. 2 K. 7:3–16 for such an event). The Hebrew does not make it clear whether the spoil will be gathered "as one gathers up (dead) locusts" or "as locusts gather it." As Delitzsch points out, the context favors the latter.

5–6 This summarizing introduction (vv. 1–6) closes on the note of God's exaltation. He is the only one who is truly lifted up—not the Judean officials, not Egypt, and not Assyria. Whatever their pomp and circumstance, these are only men. If there is to be stability, deliverance, and true understanding, it will have to come from One who is not himself contingent on the passing world (cf. 1 John 2:17). No one else can even say what is just or right, let alone establish it. But the person who is willing to admit that his or her destiny is in another's hand (the practical meaning of "the fear of the Lord") can experience all these, for he or she is then in touch with the Source of all that is.

(b) The Lord is our King (33:7–24)

    (i) Now I will arise (33:7–16)

> 7 *Behold, their heroes cry out on the outside;*
> > *the envoys of peace weep bitterly.*
> 8 *The highways are desolate;*
> > *the wayfarer has stopped.*
> *Covenant is broken;*
> *Witnesses*[1] *are despised;*
> > *humanity is not taken into account.*
> 9 *The land pines away; it mourns.*
> > *Lebanon is ashamed; it decays.*
> *Sharon is like the desert,*
> > *while Bashan and Carmel shake off their leaves.*
> 10 *"Now I will arise," says*[2] *the Lord.*
> > *"Now I will be exalted;*[3]
> > *now I will be lifted up.*
> 11 *You conceive chaff;*
> > *you give birth to stubble.*
> *Your breath is a fire which will consume you.*
> 12 *The peoples will be a burning of lime;*
> > *cut-down thornbushes, they will be set on fire.*

1. Reading *ʿēdim* with 1QIs[a]; MT has *ʿārim*, "cities."
2. Young points out that the use of the vowel *patah* in *yōʾmar*, "says," is rather characteristic of Isaiah, occurring in 1:11, 18; 33:10; 40:1, 25; 41:21; 66:9.
3. *ʾērōmām* appears to be a shortened form of the Hithpael (GKC, § 54c). 1QIs[a] has retained the *taw* preformative.

13 *Hear,*[4] *O distant ones, what I have done.*
   Know my might, you who are near."
14 *The sinners in Zion are terrified;*
   trembling seizes the godless.
   "Who among us[5] *can sojourn in devouring fire;*
   who among us can sojourn in eternal burning?"
15 *He who walks uprightly*
   and speaks aright;
   who rejects gain from extortion
   and shakes his hands from seizing a bribe;
   who shuts his ears from hearing murder
   and closes his eyes from seeing evil.
16 *He will dwell in the high places;*
   the fortress of the crags will be his refuge.
   His bread will be given;
   his water dependable.

The writer, having introduced the subject in brief form in vv. 1–6, now proceeds to expand on it. Two subdivisions appear. First is vv. 7–16, which deals with the need (vv. 7–9) and God's promise to deliver (vv. 10–16). The second is vv. 17–24, which may again be divided in two: the results of God's deliverance (vv. 17–23) and a somewhat enigmatic, but still graphic, conclusion (vv. 23–24). As in vv. 1–6, the emphasis is upon the results of the recognition that God alone can save.

Verses 7–9 depict a situation where all hope is lost. The heroes cannot help, nor can the diplomats. The destroyer will not abide by his agreements (cf. 33:1) but comes on for destruction. Thus everyone mourns, even the land itself.

Although the text makes no specific allusion to its historical context, it is certainly most logical to associate it with that time when Sennacherib had accepted the tribute he had demanded for leaving Jerusalem unmolested and then proceeded straight ahead with plans to destroy the city. In a moment like that, when the ambassadors came back empty-handed from Sennacherib's camp at Lachish, bemoaning the Assyrians' treachery, it would have become soberingly clear that there was nothing more human effort could do. That is the sort of moment for which God waits, and for which he *must* wait. It is not until we have exhausted our

---

4. LXX and 1QIs[a] have future tenses rather than the MT imperatives in this line and the next. The future tenses would accord slightly better with the following verses.

5. Both Delitzsch and Young see *lānû*, lit. "to, for us," in this line and the next as an ethical dative, "who, for our sake, can dwell." But this interpretation seems to introduce an unnatural emphasis into what is an otherwise straightforward question.

efforts that we are finally able to recognize the hand of God at work and to stop claiming for ourselves what is rightfully his.

7 *Behold* introduces the setting which begins the new segment after the introduction.[6]

heroes is probably the best translation of '*r*'*lm,* but the meaning is still tenuous. The most frequent derivation is from "lion of God"; thus it is applied in this context to the valiant ones or heroes.[7] But another alternative is to refer it to Ariel, the apparent name for Jerusalem in 29:1, and to see it as a catch phrase for the inhabitants of Jerusalem.[8] This understanding may be correct, but the contrast with *envoys* seems less striking.

For a similar (or the same?) instance of diplomats in despair, see 36:22.

8 As Smith and Young both note, *highway* is a favorite word of Isaiah's.[9] When he speaks of deliverance, it is a frequent figure, depicting the ease with which God's people would come, unmolested, to him. Here, however (as in Judg. 5:6), the highways are deserted. Without a condition of peace, the heavily laden caravans would not dare set out. The "traverser of the way"[10] will cease his journeying because he does not know when he will be plundered.

The uncertainty would only be increased when it became known that Assyria had not kept the terms of her treaty with Judah. The rules of war are fragile indeed, but they give some semblance of order to a situation in which all the seeds of chaos are sown. If those basic rules are not kept, nothing but brutality remains.[11]

Witnesses is an emendation proposed by Duhm and now confirmed

6. Kissane points out a similar movement in such Psalms as 44, 80, 89.
7. Note 31:9. S. Schwantes, taking '*r*'*l* to be a proper name, concludes that this expression here refers to a royal bodyguard, which took its name from a famous warrior ("A Historical Approach to the '*r*'*lm* of Isa. 33," *AUSS* 3 [1965] 158–66). Cf. the Moabite Stone, line 12.
8. So Scott and Kissane, for example. In either case, the question remains as to whether a simple plural -*îm* is intended instead of MT -*ām*, "their." The versions are of little help because all vary widely (LXX has "fear," *yr*'[?], while Targ. has "see," *r*'*h*).
9. See 7:3; 11:16; 19:23; 40:3; 49:11; 59:7; 62:10. Cf. also 35:8.
10. Note how similar the English compound "way-farer" is to the Hebrew.
11. Undoubtedly Sennacherib justified his action on the ground that Hezekiah had first broken his covenant of vassalage. If indeed Sennacherib accepted the tribute and returned home (cf. B. Childs, *Crisis*; R. E. Clements, *Isaiah and the Deliverance of Jerusalem*), such a passage as this becomes almost unintelligible. Furthermore, it is asking too much to expect that Sennacherib would let the leader of the revolt buy his way out. See below on chs. 36 and 37 as well as in the section on historical background in the Introduction.

by 1QIs[a]. While MT "cities" is not impossible, the idea of despising or rejecting the witnesses to the covenant is a much more likely parallel to breaking the covenant.[12] The consonants of the two words are the same except for the letters *r* and *d*, which are easily interchanged in the Hebrew block script.

9 This verse expresses the solidarity of people and land as conceived of in the OT. Just as the people were downcast and disgraced, so was the land (cf. 24:4, 7). It is unclear whether the language is solely figurative or whether there is an element of literal truth. A traditional understanding has been that the attack took place in the fall (shaking off [leaves]), but this view is unconfirmed. There may also be the element of plundering by the enemy army. The general north to south movement of the place names may lend some support to this interpretation. However, the figurative usage still seems most meaningful. The four regions mentioned are those which were the most fruitful. Now they are barren. The interplay between fruitfulness and barrenness and the question of whence they come is a great favorite of Isaiah's. For him the answer is plain: barrenness is a result of self-reliance; fruitfulness is the result of reliance on God. Here, then, we have one more figurative expression of that truth.

10–16 As noted above, the second part of vv. 7–16 deals with God's response to the need and, in turn, the people's response to that. When God is manifested in his glory, the concern for ethical righteousness will suddenly come to the fore. It was so in Isaiah's experience (6:5), and he knew it would be true in his people's experience too. God's power and his character are inseparable. Those who have no deep concern for ethical righteousness have only a dim view of God.

10 *Now* appears three times in this short verse, before each verbal phrase. If the believer is called to abandon his or her own haste in patient waiting on the Lord, it is with the certainty that there always comes a divine "Now!" One part of the importance of waiting is so that we will be sensitive to recognize God's moment when it does come (cf. Simeon's prayer, Luke 2:25–32). Those who are consumed by their own plans are always taken unaware by God's work.

Nor is it surprising that God's "now" follows the hopeless setting depicted in vv. 7–9. Human failure is divine opportunity.

The language here is reminiscent of 33:5. When God's majesty is

12. While the disregarding of humanity is a logical concomitant of breaking a covenant, D. Hillers has proposed that Akk. *unussu*, "land-tax," was the original meaning of *'nš*, not "humanity" in this case. Such a tax would be one of the stipulations imposed on the vassal ("A Hebrew Cognate of *unussu/unt* in Is. 33:8," *HTR* 64 [1971] 257–59).

fully seen, the world recognizes its own smallness and its need to come to terms with the Almighty. Interestingly, the final two verbs, *exalted* and *lifted up*, are the same ones which appear in 6:1 and 52:13. Clearly, for Isaiah the manifestation of God was inseparably linked to the conquest of God's enemies and the deliverance of his people.

11 Although the person addressed is not specified here, the context makes it clear that it is the destroyer.[13] All his mighty plans and contrivances have no more substance than chaff and stubble before the awful reality of the God of this, to Sennacherib, little hill-country capital. In fact, says Isaiah, the destroyer's own breath, raging to devour its prey, will be the torch to light his own funeral pyre (9:17 [Eng. 18]; 25:4; 30:27, 28). Again there is similarity to 33:1, where it is said that the destroyer will experience the very things it has meted out to others.[14] So the prophet asserts that there is justice in the world. If it comes too slowly for most of us, it still comes. Although what Sennacherib received outside Jerusalem's gates was only a taste of Assyria's ultimate destruction, it was a genuine taste and one which would be violently completed within a century (609 B.C.).

12 *peoples* is a term used throughout the book in reference to the nations around about Judah.[15] Thus they have been a focal point from ch. 7 to this point. Because of the threat of some of the "peoples," Judah has been tempted to trust other "peoples" rather than God. Now God says that all of these, threat and trust alike, are no more than tinder in his presence (cf. 33:3).

The metaphors used here emphasize the completeness of the destruction to come. So when a rock like limestone is burned it is reduced to dust (note Amos 2:1 for a similar usage); and despite the hazardous nature of thorns when they are alive, once they are cut and dried, fire can consume them almost completely in a very short time. So it would be with Assyria and later with Babylon.[16] For all their pomp and glory, each one's collapse came with great suddenness.

Verses 13–16 relate the impact of God's appearance upon the world but especially upon Judah. When they see God's might displayed upon Assyria, there will be terror among those Jews who have been little more believing than the Assyrians. Like their forefathers at the foot of Sinai,

13. Targ. makes this explicit.
14. This connection with 30:27, 28 as well as with 33:1 seems to make unnecessary the suggestion of Lowth and others that the consonants be redivided to correspond to LXX "(my) breath will devour like fire."
15. See 2:3; 8:9; 11:10; 17:12; 25:3, 6, 7, etc.
16. Cf. 27:10; 29:5; 30:27–33; 31:8–9.

they question whether anyone mortal can live in the presence of such intensity. Isaiah answers that mortality is not the issue, but ethical purity. For the ethically pure God will not be destruction but refuge.

13 Sooner or later everyone must hear of God's greatness. But is it necessary to speak of those who are nearer (for other than poetic reasons)? The following verse would indicate so, as does life. Familiarity does breed contempt. How frequently the passion and devotion of one who has only just heard of Christ puts to shame some of us who have known of him for years. So it was at least as necessary for Judeans to recognize his working as anyone else.

14 The result of such a recognition was, and will be, terror. This is not to say that all persons must be terrified into trusting God. But it is to say that unless people have come at some point to a recognition of God's absolute otherness from themselves, they are very likely to devalue his grace, and their commitment is likely to be minimal at best.

This is what had happened in Judah. They had come to take God for granted. They were *sinners*, no longer aiming solely at God's target; they were those who defiled the land by living in ways inconsistent with God's character (24:5).[17] As a result, when God's fire would be revealed against Assyria, they too would tremble, knowing themselves to be no more able to endure that fiery embrace than their enemies had been. Such a recognition is the beginning of hope for the believing community. It is not enough for the Assyrians to recognize God's greatness. It is much more important for Zion to recognize it. For if there is a fire in Zion (31:9), her inhabitants must be ready to dwell in that fire.

sojourn conveys the idea that the dweller is not the host but the guest. The environment, then, is not one's native place. But the stranger may dwell in a spot where he is protected and cared for. The issue is, what will it take to endure in an environment so hostile as endless fire?[18]

Those who contend that *eternal* does not suggest duration as much as quality are probably correct. This fire of God is not a passing thing, it is of his very essence. There is no hope that after awhile the flame will die down; he *is* flame—destructive to what we human beings now are.

Verse 15 offers the answer to the question posed in v. 14. Although those who know the Bible will perhaps see it as familiar and predictable (Pss. 15 and 24 are very similar), it is in fact a rather strange answer.

17. Clements suggests that the situation described is postexilic when dissensions had arisen among various Jewish groups. But that is hardly necessary. As chs. 28 and 29 make plain, there were plenty of "sinners" in Zion in 701 B.C. from Isaiah's perspective.

18. On God as fire see Deut. 4:24; 9:3; Heb. 12:29.

What kind of change must a human being undergo to live with God? It is not a change of essence but a change of character. That is, what finally separates us from God is not our essence (finite to infinite, etc.) but our character (unholy to holy). This is the truth which the Hebrews discovered at Sinai (Lev. 19:2, etc.) and which Isaiah also recognized in his personal Sinai (see comments on ch. 6). If we are to dwell with God as his guests, we must share his character.

The elements of that character are described in three couplets. The first describes the general style of life:[19] a manifestation in life and speech of what is right and straight. The second and third amplify this element, making it plain that no privatistic righteousness will do. Gain achieved through oppression and graft is forbidden, as is conspiracy in any act which will harm or murder someone. (Closing the eyes and ears does not mean ignoring social evil, but refusing to be a part of such conspiracies.) Like all the prophets, Isaiah abhors a religion which suggests that cultic acts alone obviate any necessity for a radical change in our behavior toward others (1:10–17; 58:5–7; cf. Jer. 7:10; Ezek. 23:37–39; Hos. 4:1–4; Amos 5:21–24; Mal. 3:5; etc.).

But is this to say that it is possible by living a righteous life to merit union with God? No, for that would be to confuse the product with the method, a confusion into which Judaism was to fall. Rom. 7 is the cry of such a good Jew. To see the goodness of God's character was one thing, but to achieve it by one's own efforts was quite another. Entry into fellowship with God is only possible as a result of God's grace, a fact which the OT teaches as well as the NT. But that truth has its own pitfalls, as Protestantism has frequently shown. The suggestion has been made that since fellowship is by grace, realized righteousness is not attainable. A passage such as this one gives the lie to that position. The goal is always the same, conformity to the character of God. The revelation of God's grace in Christ has not changed the goal. But it has shown us we were going about reaching the goal in the wrong way.

16 The person who has made God's character the goal of his or her life dwells with God in the high places. What this means in practice is that circumstances no longer hold ultimate sway over that person.[20] Now God has integrated their personality (he gives šālôm, "peace, wholeness") in such a way that serenity is possible in trying circumstances.

19. The plurals perhaps indicate a more abstract and general point of view for this couplet.
20. To dwell on high, or in the house of the Lord (Ps. 23:6; 27:4) perhaps has a reference to the temple, but to restrict their meaning to the temple would make them superficial and trite.

Furthermore, this person has a source of supply of every need in God. Bread and water symbolize the most basic needs of human life. Many people today, as well as in Isaiah's day, need something more basic than food and drink. They are starving spiritually because they have been attempting to meet their own needs without realizing that God has provided refuge and sustenance for everyone who will appropriate his grace.[21]

(ii) The King in his beauty (33:17–24)

17 *A King in his beauty your eyes will see;*
     you will look on a land of distances.
18 *Your heart will meditate on the terror:*
     "Where is the scribe?
Where is the weigher?
     Where is the one who counted towers?"
19 *A fierce[1] people you will no longer see,*
     a people deep of lips—unintelligible,[2]
     a mocking tongue not understood.
20 *Look upon Zion, city of our appointments.*
     Your eyes will see Jerusalem,
untroubled habitation,
     a tent not moved;
     its stakes not pulled out forever,
          and none of its cords cut loose.
21 *Instead, the Lord will be mighty for us there;*
     a place of rivers and broad streams.[3]
No oared[4] ship will travel it,
     nor any mighty ship sail on it.
22 *For the Lord is our judge;*
     the Lord is our lawgiver.
The Lord is our king;
     he will save us.
23 *Your cords are forsaken;*

21. Note the emphasis upon security in God: 4:6; 26:1; 31:5; 32:17–18; 54:13–14.

1. MT *nôʿāz* is a hapax legomenon from *yʿz*, apparently meaning "arrogant" or "barbarous." Rashi proposed *lôʿēz*, "unintelligible," which occurs only in Ps. 114:1 (cf. *BHS*).

2. "unintelligible" is lit. "from hearing," Heb. *miššeʿmōaʿ*; the *min* here is taken as a privative, "away from." See GKC, §§ 119v-y.

3. There is no conjunction between "streams" and "rivers," perhaps because the two are so nearly synonymous.

4. *šayiṭ* occurs only here, but is apparently a derivative of *šûṭ*, meaning "oar." A "ship of oars" would be a rowed warship. Note the "mighty" ship. If God is mighty nothing else mighty poses a threat.

your mast is not firm;
your ensign[5] is not spread out.
Then spoil in abundance will be divided;
the lame will carry off spoil.
24 *No inhabitants will say, "I am sick."*
Those who live in it will have sin forgiven.

Verses 17–24 detail the results which flow from an admission of help-lessness and a turning to God. No longer will there be dependence upon a false and craven leadership. Then the true king will be revealed and honored as such. In that relation there will be the security which was sought in so many other ways. Ultimately, this is the question every person must face: who is king? Is it humanity, and in particular, me? If so, the result can only be a deep insecurity, for none of us is ultimate. But if we have discovered an ultimate One who is truly for us, then we may be secure, no matter what happens. That is the picture here.

The picture seems to mingle the historical and the eschatological as well as the physical and the spiritual. On the one hand, the deliverance from Sennacherib seems to be in view (vv. 18–19), yet the picture in vv. 20–22 is not merely of a historical deliverance. By the same token, "king" in v. 17 could refer to Hezekiah, yet the overall setting makes it plain we are talking of no merely human king. Furthermore, as v. 24b makes explicit, the true benefits of God's kingdom are spiritual. In the merely physical world there is no permanence; all things tend to decay. But in a world of the spirit where sin is truly forgiven (lit. lifted away), there is not merely stability, but growth from glory to glory (2 Cor. 3:18).

17 *A King in his beauty* does not refer to any particular human monarch. Several factors make this plain. Chief of these is the statement in v. 22 that the Lord is king. To equate someone such as Hezekiah, who is merely human, with God flies in the face of Isaiah's whole stance. He has shown again and again the folly of putting fallible mortal leaders in the place of God. For him now to reverse that stance is not likely (cf. chs. 38–39). Furthermore, the absence of a definite article on "king" suggests that an ideal is being spoken of, as in Ps. 45 where the Messiah is in view. This view is reinforced by the description of the royal realm as a *land of distances*.[6] This is hardly Hezekiah's constricted domain, even spoken of

5. Kissane even doubts that a ship is intended since everywhere else in the book *nēs* refers to "flag" and not "sail." However, the idea of "battle flag" is not impossible on a ship, or as Delitzsch suggests, a figure may have appeared on the sail itself. LXX and Targ. both have "sail."

6. Kissane suggests the reference is to the full extent of the territory promised the Davidides. See also 26:15; Gen. 13:14, 15; Ps. 72:8; Mic. 5:4; Zech. 9:10.

hyperbolically. Rather, the prophet is using the coming deliverance from Sennacherib to speak of a day when true and final deliverance will have come.[7]

18, 19 In that coming day, God's people will look back meditatively on the terror they had known. Typically, when we are in a particularly trying situation time seems to stand still, especially if there seems to be no way out. But time does pass and suddenly we find ourselves looking back with surprise on what seemed endless. So it will be for the Judeans, says the prophet. The scribes and weighers who would have weighed and recorded the tribute will be gone along with those who toted up the number of towers (perhaps for helping to determine the amount of tribute).[8] No more is their strange-sounding, unintelligible speech to be heard as they chatter to one another, delighting in the humiliation of those forced to pay tribute.[9] What had seemed so permanent at the time will be gone, and its passing will be a source of wonder.

20–22 Instead of seeing the Assyrian overlords, the Judeans will see Jerusalem secure and protected, because of her relation to her true king.

city of our appointments refers to Jerusalem as the appointed meeting place with God. Ultimately this is the city's significance. That it is David's royal city is not important. That it is a temple city is not the issue. What matters is that here God can meet human beings face to face.[10] When that function was blurred or lost, Jerusalem would become simply one more city.[11]

a tent not moved seems at first a very odd figure for permanence. Perhaps there were two factors in the prophet's choice of images. One might have been the idea of the tabernacle in the wilderness. The tabernacle was the place where God was, the place where he could be met. During the wandering of the Hebrew people the tabernacle—and in one sense,

7. Note that while Calvin believes the king referred to is Hezekiah, he sees him being described as a figure of Christ. For a brief treatment of further arguments in favor of the messianic interpretation, see Young.

8. The idea of counting towers is not mentioned elsewhere in Scripture, so other alternatives have been proposed: "treasure chests" (Driver, *JSS* 13 [1968] 53); "captives" (Kissane); "tax-gatherers" (Duhm). But there is nothing intrinsically implausible about the idea of counting towers, either as part of the treaty or as a part of reconnoitering for the coming siege.

9. Cf. 28:11; 36:11; Jer. 5:15; Ezek. 3:5.

10. The tabernacle was the "tent of meeting." Young remarks appositely that Isaiah was not against assemblies, but only vain assemblies (1:14).

11. Nowhere does Isaiah suggest that Jerusalem would be inviolate regardless of her spiritual condition.

God—was continually moving with the people. Now God would no longer move. He would come in the last days to a permanent rest.

The other aspect of the tent imagery is also in the disparity of something designed for mobility never moving. The traveler has truly come home when it can be said that he will never strike his tent again. So here the wanderers will have found that fertile valley where they can put up their tents on a permanent basis. In this life we are all in tents, and happy is the person who realizes that. But one day the tents will be pegged down forever (Heb. 11:9–10).[12]

21 *Instead* picks up from the negatives of v. 20. The sense is "we will not move; instead, God will defend us." Is Assyria mighty (*'addîr;* cf. 10:34)? God is mightier still, as was to be proven in the case of Sennacherib.

Where God is, there is security. Jerusalem had no great rivers to contribute to its defense such as Babylon or Nineveh had. Better to have God. With him one has all the benefits of a great river with none of its liabilities. For while a river makes crossing from side to side difficult, it also provides an excellent highway for a concerted naval attack. Not so with God. For he is not a thing, but a person, and a person whose power is exceeded only by his faithfulness.[13]

22 This confidence in God is expressed in three appellations given to him. The opening *kî,* "for," expresses the causal relation between the divine character and the effects cited in the previous verses. Because God is Israel's *judge* (in the sense of the book of Judges), he will be her champion and defender. Because he is her *lawgiver,* he will be more than fair in his dealings with her. Because he is her *king* by covenant, he will deliver her. This is the climactic moment in the entire segment (chs. 28–33). Throughout, the issue has been: can we trust God to save us? Here, however, the alternative is expressed for the people by the prophet: "Yes, he is our king and he alone will save us."

The significance of this verse goes beyond its being merely a climax to chs. 28–33, however. As noted above, one of the major issues in chs. 7–35 is whether the Hebrew people will allow God to be their king or whether they will deny that kingship in trusting the surrounding nations for their security. In many ways the single recurring theme of chs. 13–33 is God's sovereignty over the nations of mankind. Thus this statement comes as a capstone to that whole movement.

12. With God, a tabernacle is better than a fortress (Calvin).

13. Those who attempt to make too tight a connection between the images here must run into difficulties. Is God a place? Do ships run on God? On the other hand, it is wrong to ask poetry to conform to the same canons of logic as does prose. Poetry functions first on emotive levels.

Most modern commentators consider v. 23a to be intrusive, having come from some oracle like that against Tyre in ch. 23 and inserted here because of the references to ships in v. 21. Without denying the difficulty in interpreting the statement, it still seems to ask too much to believe that a redactor not only took a verse out of a meaningful context and put it in a meaningless one, but also that he put it in the wrong place (after v. 22 rather than v. 21) when he did it.

If the statement is original in this place, there are two alternative interpretations. The older one holds that it refers to Assyria: she is a ship in disarray about to be plundered by God's people. This view has in its favor that it keeps a continuity with the previous picture of victorious Israel. On the other hand, there are at least two points against this understanding: (1) there is no clue in the setting of any shift in the reference of the second person pronouns from Judah to Assyria; (2) the pronoun is feminine, in accord with "Judah" or "land," but not Assyria (always masc. "people").

The other alternative is to take Judah as the subject. This has the opposite disadvantage to the former: Judah, having been pictured as victorious, is now pictured in disarray. However, the appearance of *'āz* in v. 23b suggests a now/then contrast. If that is so, then v. 23a becomes more understandable: as in ch. 4, so here he is saying that his promises for the future do not spring from a denial of the present serious conditions. "Make no mistake," he says, "our glorious future, our triumph over our enemies, is not because we are some mighty ship such as I mentioned just now (v. 21). We are a drifting hulk. Our hope is in a king who heals disease and forgives sin."

If this understanding is correct, then the two verses function as a graphic (as opposed to an ideological) conclusion to the segment. This is the same technique that appears in 3:16–4:1 and elsewhere. This interpretation does not automatically explain away all difficulties. But it does offer a viable possibility.

The closing emphasis upon the forgiveness of iniquity is reminiscent of 4:3–4 and is of considerable importance. It makes the point that Judah's need is deeper than the need for deliverance from oppression. Ultimately, says Isaiah, our problem is a broken relation with God because of sin.[14] That being so, mere defeat of enemies and restoration to the land

---

14. As in ch. 53, forgiveness of sin and healing from disease are related. This is not to say that all disease can be related to specific sins committed by the ill person. But neither can we say no relation exists between the two. Disease is in the world because of sin.

605

will not do. The final goal is a forgiven people living a life in keeping with
God's character.

4. TRUSTING GOD OR THE NATIONS: RESULTS (34:1–35:10)

a. THE DESERT (34:1–17)

(1) Judgment on the nations (34:1–4)

1 *Draw near, O nations, to hear;*
  listen, you peoples.[1]
Let the earth hear and its fullness;
  the world and all that springs from it.
2 *For the Lord's wrath is upon all their host.*
  He has devoted them, giving them over to slaughter.[2]
3 *Their slain will be cast out,*
  and their corpses will send up their stench;
the mountains will be dissolved with blood.
4 *All the host of heaven will rot,*[3]
  and the heavens will be rolled up like a scroll;
all their host will fall as a leaf falls from a vine
  or as green figs[4] *from a fig tree.*

Chapters 34–35 present a striking contrast between a productive land
turned into a desert (ch. 34) and a desert turning into a garden (ch. 35).
As such they bring to a close the collection of teachings concerning the
nations and God's sovereignty over them (chs. 13–35). When all is said
and done, the prophet says, the issues are clear and rather simple. Arrogant, self-important humanity cannot stand before God. In our attempts
to be independent of him and to build the kingdom of Man on earth, we
have sinned, and the word is the same for all: "The soul that sins shall
die" (Ezek. 18:4, 20). In a real sense, to sin is to forfeit one's life into the
hands of God as a sacrifice (34:6, 7).

1. The *lamed* on "peoples" is used to specify the subject of the imperative
(GKC, § 119s; Williams, *Syntax*, § 273).
2. Note the succession of final *m*'s (in the Hebrew) throughout this verse
and the next.
3. There is some question about the text of this first phrase since LXX
lacks it entirely and 1QIs[a] has "The valleys will be split and all the host of heaven
carried away(?)" (cf. Mic. 1:4). On the other hand it has been suggested that "host
of heaven" be replaced by "hills" to give a better parallel to mountains in v. 3
(Skinner, Kaiser, *BHS*).
4. Driver (*JSS* 13 [1968] 54) points out that *nōbelet* means "unripe figs"
in Mishnaic Hebrew. This meaning fits the context better than "a falling" (AV).

On the other hand, those who reject the blandishments of this earth with its temptations to make their own way, those who choose to wait for God, to put themselves in his hands, though that be in a desert, will discover a highway which leads to a glory not their own. Rather, it is something which is freely shared by the One to whom glory belongs. To align oneself with the nations of the earth is to choose a desert; to trust in God is to choose a garden.

At least since the time of Ewald, some have said that ch. 34 was dependent upon Jeremiah (see esp. Jer. 46:10; 49:7–16; 50:35–38; 51:43). Furthermore, a scholar as essentially conservative as Delitzsch recognized that the language of the two chapters showed more affinity with chs. 40–66 than with 1–39. Finally, C. C. Torrey proposed that the two chapters had originally formed the introduction to chs. 40–66.[5] While this view has not gained absolute acceptance, it still has currency (cf. Wildberger). Others suggest even later dates.[6] The fact that 1QIs[a] shows a gap between chs. 33 and 34 has occasioned the suggestion that the final redaction of Isaiah appeared in two volumes, roughly parallel in structure, and that chs. 34 and 35 form the introduction to the second volume in a way similar to the way chs. 1–5 introduce the first volume.[7] However, as E. J. Young pointed out, a case may be made for the dependence of Jeremiah upon Isaiah.[8] If this were to be correct, then the demonstrations of affinity between the language of chs. 34 and 35 and that of 40–66 would have far-reaching effects, indeed. One of the major arguments against a pre-587 date for ch. 34—the reference to Edom—will be dealt with below. In any case, the chapters go with chs. 13–33 on structural grounds. In a way similar to chs. 24–27, they drive home the wisdom of trusting God and the folly of trusting the nations. In this they form the climax to the entire segment. See further the section on structure in the Introduction.[9]

The powerful poem in 34:1–17 depicts the effects of God's wrath upon the nations. In vv. 1–4 the universal nature of the judgment is pictured. Not even the heavens themselves will escape. Then vv. 5–8 particularize the statement by applying it to Edom, much as was done with Moab in 25:10–12. The language here is of sacrifice, reminding the reader

---

5. C. C. Torrey, *The Second Isaiah* (New York: Scribner's, 1928).

6. J. Morgenstern, *HUCA* 37 (1966) 1–28; Kaiser.

7. See esp. W. Brownlee, *The Meaning of the Qumran Scrolls for the Bible* (Oxford: Oxford University, 1964).

8. Young, "Isaiah 34 and Its Position in the Prophecy," *WTJ* 37 (1964) 93–114.

9. See J. Muilenburg, "The Literary Character of Isa. 34," *JBL* 59 (1940) 339–365, for a detailed analysis of the chapter.

that unless someone provides a sacrifice for our sins, we must ourselves become that sacrifice. Ultimately, as the NT makes plain, it is only God himself who can offer that sacrifice for all (Rom. 5:5–10; but cf. already Isa. 53).

Verses 9–17 continue the address to Edom as the typical nation, depicting the land as left utterly desolate, inhabited by nothing but desert wildlife. This is the end of all human grasping for abundance: death and desolation. If the language is severe and harsh here, it is because of the seriousness of sin. The rebellion of a whole world against God is not a matter for a tap on the wrist, nor are its natural effects negligible.

1 In a manner somewhat reminiscent of 1:2, the prophet calls for the whole world to gather round and hear its judgment pronounced. This is not, however, a call to be witnesses, but a call to be sentenced.[10] As already noted, this pronouncement to the nations looks back all the way to ch. 13, where the oracles of judgment began to be pronounced, but also to ch. 7, where Ahaz was challenged not to trust the nations. Where does servanthood begin? Does it begin in the assumption of the world that human pomp and power are the basis for all fulfillment? Again and again the answer has been no! All of that is under a curse. Servanthood begins in an abandonment of that assumption and the realization that God alone is to be trusted. Every other way must end in a desert.

the earth . . . and all that springs from it is reminiscent of 6:3, but even more so of Ps. 25:1, where it is plain that the "fullness" of the earth is its population. It seems likely that the same is the case here so that "all that springs from it" refers to humanity.

2 The pronouncement is one of divine wrath upon the nations. No cause is specified, but the statement of *ḥērem*, or devoting to destruction, would have been enough for any hearer, especially any Hebrew. This is the idea that no spoils of battle belonged to any human victor, but must belong totally to God. Typically this meant that the spoils must be completely destroyed to prevent any human misappropriation.[11] In the Hebrew setting at least two implications are significant: spoils are devoted to God to show that God alone has won a battle (Jericho); when a nation has deliberately blocked the flow of God's love to the world, it forfeits itself into God's hands (Amalek). We will belong to God, either voluntarily or involuntarily. Thus, the announcement of *ḥērem* here probably involves

10. In a somewhat similar way in 41:1 and 45:20 the nations are also summoned. There, however, it is to present their case. Here the case is already decided.

11. Cf. 11:15; Josh. 6:21; 1 Sam. 15:3. That the concept was not merely Hebrew is shown by its appearance on the Moabite Stone, lines 14–17. Cf. *THAT*, I:635–39; *TWOT*, I:324–25.

both of these implications: the ultimate offense of the nations is against God and he alone will be their conqueror; God's wrath is against them because of their refusal to accept his Lordship.

3 Added to the shame of defeat and slaughter is that of exposure of the dead. Not only for the ancient world but for the modern one as well, there is something especially horrifying and revolting about a rotting corpse. Perhaps it is the terrible indignity of something which was recently able to think and dream. Or perhaps it is too strong a reminder of our own imminent decay. At any rate, there is a strong instinct in us to dispose of the dead quickly. When we do not do so, it is either because of the necessity of too many bodies or as a specific act of contempt. Here again, as in 14:21 and 18:6, the attempt of the nations to gain some sort of dignity apart from God will ultimately have the very opposite effect.[12]

the mountains will be dissolved with blood is a figure which is impossible to explain literally. The general idea is that the rivers of blood which will flow down the hillsides will be like the rainwater which dissolves the soil into mud and carries it away. But it is the cosmic impact of judgment, as v. 4 makes even more clear, which is the point here. Whether mountains melt or stars rot is not so important as that the entire cosmos is under the hand of the one God to whom all owe allegiance.[13]

4 *the host of heaven* would refer not only to the physical stars but also to the pantheon of gods which the stars represented in the minds of the ancient hearers.[14] So, God would judge not only the nations but their heavenly patrons as well. He would lay low the nations and also their gigantic self-projections upon the universe. Once again, it is immaterial whether the literal stars will fall in the day of God's judgment; the point is that even the mysterious, unchanging stars, the seeming guarantors of the universe's perpetuity, are in the hands of the God of Jerusalem.[15]

(2) Judgment on Edom, type of the nations (34:5–17)

(a) Edom, a sacrifice (34:5–8)

5 When my sword is drunken[1] in the heavens,

---

12. Cf. also Joel 2:10; Amos 4:10; Ezek. 39:17; Rev. 19:17, 18.

13. By the same token, those who know God need not fear if the mountains do dissolve (Ps. 46:3, 4 [Eng. 2, 3]).

14. See 2 K. 17:16; 21:3, 5; 23:4, 5.

15. Cf. 51:6; Ps. 102:26–28 (Eng. 25–27); Matt. 24:29; Rev. 6:13, 14.

1. 1QIs[a] has *tr'h*, "will be seen," instead of *rwth*, "drunken." Driver (*JSS* 13 [1968] 55) thinks that MT is incredible. So it is if taken too literally, but cf. Deut. 32:41–43 for a similar figure. *BHS* emends "my sword" to "the sword of the Lord" and "my devoted people" to "his devoted people." But there is no real ms. support for these changes.

behold, upon Edom it shall fall,
upon my devoted people, for judgment.
6 *The sword of the Lord is full of blood,*
greased[2] with fat,
the blood of lambs and goats,
the fat kidneys of rams.
For the Lord has a sacrifice in Bozrah,
and a great slaughter in the land of Edom.
7 *The wild oxen[3] will go down with them,*
and bulls with rams.
Their land will be drunk with blood,
and their dust will be enriched with fat.
8 *For the Lord has a day of vengeance,*
a year of repayment for the controversy[4] of Zion.

After the general introduction in vv. 1–4, the prophet now moves to a concrete example of his topic.[5] This is why this passage is not included in the section of oracles against the nations (chs. 13–23): it is not speaking of Edom by itself, but of that nation and its fate as representative of all nations and their fates.[6]

Why should Edom be used in this way? The answer is that throughout the OT, from Genesis (25:23) to Malachi (1:2–3), Edom is treated as the antithesis to Israel. More so even than the Amalekites, Edom is noted for attempting to block what God was doing for the world in his self-revelation to Israel (Num. 20:14–21). Thus Edom was typical of those nations which insisted upon their own ways in opposition to those of God. Thus Isaiah says, "You can choose Edom's way or God's way, but these are the results."

Without doubt the Israelite antipathy for Edom was increased when the Edomites aided and abetted the Babylonian destruction of Jerusalem

2. *huddašnâ,* "greased," is apparently a passive Hithpael in which the *t* of the performative has assimilated to the *dalet* of the root. Cf. GKC, § 54h and Lev. 13:55, 56; Deut. 24:4.

3. *rᵉʾēmîm,* "wild oxen (?)," is not completely certain. Job 39:9 indicates that it is a wild animal, while Deut. 33:17 and Ps. 22:22 (Eng. 21) and 92:11 (Eng. 10) indicate it is horned.

4. *rîb,* "controversy," has occasioned a number of suggestions. Delitzsch takes it as a verb "to contend for," while Driver (*JSS* 13 [1968] 55) takes it as a noun but renders it "adversary." *BHS* (following Torrey) repoints to *rāb* ("champion"). There is no sufficient reason to change MT, however.

5. This use of example to drive home a general point is a frequent feature in the book (3:16–4:1; 5:1–7; 14:4–21; 20:1–6; 30:6–7).

6. So most commentators. See also M. Pope, "Is. 34 in Relation to Is. 35 and 40–66," *JBL* 71 (1952) 243.

in 587 B.C. (Obad. 11–14; Ezek. 35:1–15). This has caused most commentators to assume this poem was written after that date. Even Kissane, in order to retain Isaianic authorship, feels obliged to remove all the references to Edom. However, such heroics are unnecessary. For already in the 700s feeling against Edom ran very high (2 Chr. 21:8–10; 25:11; 28:17; Joel 4:19 [Eng. 3:19]; Amos 1:11–12).

Verses 5–8 depict one aspect of Edom's, and the world's, fate—a sacrifice to God. The language of these verses is unnerving because of its frankly gory tone. However, at least three things need to be kept in mind when interpreting the passage: (1) there were no rules of warfare and the writer was wishing that God would balance the scales, giving the nations what they had given Judah (v. 8); (2) Western tastes are not those of most of the world. Compared to some of the Ugaritic materials, the language is restrained, for there is no divine glee in indiscriminate slaughter;[7] (3) life is a gift, not a right, and its continuation is finally dependent upon an appropriate relation to a Being whose nature is to ours as fire is to stubble. Either some provision must be made for us all who have refused that appropriate relation or the result is destruction—not wreaked by a spiteful Master Ogre, but as the logical effect of our situation (see the comment on 30:6–7).

5 *When* reflects the temporal use of *kî* rather than the causal, which makes little sense here. "When" reflects the transition from the heavens in v. 4 to the earth in vv. 5–17.

drunken in the heavens is surely not expressive of a divine decree concerning Edom (Calvin, Young). This is especially true in the light of the fact that the verb connotes "filled up" or "satiated." The figure is that when the divine sword has done all it can do to the heavenly host, the pantheon of national gods, then it will fall on the nations themselves as represented by Edom.

devoted people, as in v. 2, refers to the fact that God has claimed them for himself alone. They refused to become devoted to him voluntarily, so now they will become so involuntarily. This is the issue which must face every human being: we do belong to God and we will belong to him; it is only up to us how we shall belong.

6, 7 The destruction of the nations is conceived of as a sacrifice.[8] Is this only a coincidental literary device, or is there a deeper connection? I think the latter is so. The OT makes it plain that sin is a matter of life

---

7. Note Anat's bloodlust in V AB B (*ANET,* p. 136).
8. For other references to slaughter as sacrifice, see 25:6; 30:32; Jer. 46:10; 51:40; Ezek. 39:17; Zeph. 1:7–9.

and death. Even the sin committed unaware must be atoned for by a sacrificial death (Lev. 4:1–12; etc.; cf. also Lev. 17:11; Ezek. 33:10–16). Thus in a real sense, all sin must end in a sacrifice, either of the sinner or of one in place of the sinner. It is this truth which Isa. 53 comprehends. The salvation which is proclaimed and promised in chs. 49–52 is only possible because Another has been sacrificed. The tragedy of an Edom, then, is that its sacrifice is unnecessary. If the nations of the world would learn the ways of God (2:1–4), they would learn that he has already offered the sacrifice whereby they could be forgiven.

Bozrah is probably to be identified with modern Buseirah, located about twenty miles southeast of the lower end of the Dead Sea. Its synonymous usage both here and in 63:1 suggests that it was the chief city in Edom (cf. also Gen. 36:33; Jer. 49:13, 22). The passage in ch. 63 is significant because of its stress, as here, that God alone must conquer the nations. One cannot help but feel that the defeat of Sennacherib was one evidence of this truth. The Edoms of this world eventually fall to God, whatever the degree of human instrumentality.

wild oxen . . . bulls with rams is probably a reference to the leaders of the nation who will fall with the common people. No one will be spared. The land will be like the earth around an altar: soaked with blood and enriched with fat. Like all the figures in this chapter, if these are interpreted over-literally, the point is missed. The point is not to try to find a time, or to envision one, when the people of Edom have been, or will be, slaughtered in an overwhelming manner. The point is that human pomp and pride which exalts itself against God does not lead to well-being, *shalom*, but to destruction where we shatter ourselves against his unalterable holiness.

8 But it is not merely the nations' rebellion against God that brings his wrath upon them. It is also that they have attacked his people. So it is not only his sovereignty which is called into question but also his capacity to keep his promises. Can he defend the helpless or must they abandon their hope in him and make whatever shift they can for themselves?

Isaiah's word here is the same as elsewhere: God will act, the enemies will be destroyed, and although his timetable is not ours, he does have one (12:1–6; 40:27–31; 62:1–5). The use of *day* and *year* expresses this idea of a definite time of action. In that day justice will be served in the controversy.

(b) Edom, a desolation (34:9–17)

> 9 *Her streams will be turned to pitch,*
> *and her dust to brimstone;*
> *her land will become burning pitch.*

10 *Night and day, it will not be quenched;*
   forever will its smoke ascend.
From generation to generation, it will be waste;
   for an eternity of eternities none will pass through it.
11 *The pelican and the hedgehog will possess it;*
   the owl and the raven will dwell in it.
He will stretch over it the line of chaos
   and the plummet of destruction.[1]
12 *Its nobles—there are none there to be called king;*
   all her princes are at an end.
13 *Its strongholds go up in thorns,*
   its fortresses in thistles and briers.
It will become a haunt of jackals,
   and an abode[2] *for ostriches.*[3]
14 *Howling beasts will meet jackals,*
   and the he-goat will call to his mate.
Moreover, the night-bird will rest there
   and will find a resting place for herself.
15 *There the owl nests and lays her eggs;*
   she hatches[4] *them and gathers her young in her shadow.*[5]
There, too, the vultures gather,
   each one with her mate.
16 *Seek from upon the book of the Lord and read.*
   Not one of these will be missing.
None will lack a mate.
For the mouth of the Lord,[6] *it commands,*
   and his Spirit, it gathers.

1. *tōhû,* "chaos," and *bōhû,* "destruction," appear in Gen. 1:2 as "without form and void."

2. *ḥāṣîr* means "green grass" everywhere else but perhaps 35:7 (where it is also parallel with *nᵉwēh,* "haunt"). LXX *aulē,* "court," usually translates *ḥāṣēr,* which also means "abode" (BDB).

3. Although the ancient versions are unanimous in translating *baṭ yaʿănâ* as "ostrich," there continues to be some question of the correctness of this translation. Some of the characteristics might be more appropriate to owls (cf. AV).

4. *mlṭ,* "to slip away," applies to laying of eggs.

5. BHS *bēṣeyhā* is a conjectural emendation from Duhm who proposed "heap up" in view of the acceptance of the translation "arrow-snake."

6. The MT has "For a mouth [or, my mouth], it has commanded." LXX has "For the Lord has commanded them"; Targ. "For by his *memra* (presence) they shall be gathered together"; Vulg. "my mouth"; 1QIs[a] "his mouth" (followed by RSV, NEB, JPSV, NIV). This diversity suggests that none of these preserves the original reading. The consonantal text of the reading proposed here would be *kypyyhwhhwʾ.* The succession of *ys* and *hs* would make accidental corruption very easy. Cf. *BHS;* Orlinsky, "Studies, VI," *HUCA* 25 (1954) 90.

17 *He is the one who casts the lot for them,*
and his hand apportions it by line.
They will possess it forever;
for all generations, they will dwell in it.

In the most forceful language he can muster, Isaiah pictures the future not only of the land of Edom but also of the whole world which believes it can find fulfillment apart from God. The people have become a sacrifice (vv. 5–8) and the land is reduced to a volcanic waste. For those of us who live in the nuclear age, these pictures are all too vivid. We have it in our power to reduce a beautiful world to a radioactive desert. Should that occur, it will not be because a vicious God decided to wreak punishment upon us, but because we have become so insistent upon dominating the world that, if we think we must reduce it to an ashheap to do so, we will. If there is any thought which emphasizes our human inability to take the place of God, it is this: the end result of the relentless quest for knowledge which first surfaced on the plains of Mesopotamia 6000 years ago is the capacity to destroy not only ourselves but our whole natural system as well.

9–10 In terms which are very reminiscent of those applied to Sodom and Gomorrah (Gen. 19:24–28; Deut. 29:23; Ps. 11:6; Jer. 49:18; Rev. 14:10, 11), the prophet pictures the land as a perpetual wasteland of burning pitch and brimstone. That Edom is never specified in this section of the poem, although it is implied,[7] strengthens the impression that the reference is broader than to a single nation.[8]

In v. 10, the primary emphasis is upon the perpetuity of the destruction. Each line begins with a stronger phrase denoting endlessness. Calvin notes aptly that the intensity of the language is used to produce an impression upon human hearts which are so hardened that plain language leaves them unmoved. With reference to the previous section, it may be noted that the fires on the altar of sacrifice in the temple were to be kept burning continually (Lev. 6:13).

Verses 11–15 depict the depopulated condition of the land in terms reminiscent of 13:21–22 and 14:23. Nor ought one to think of these as accidental congruencies. Chs. 13 and 14 speak of Babylon, the distant example of human pride. This chapter speaks of Edom as the near example. But in each case the glorious land becomes the home not of triumphant humanity but of unclean and mysterious desert animals. Again, as

---

7. The suffixes are all feminine, referring to 'ereṣ 'ĕḏōm.

8. In modern literature the destructive results of pride are seen in the kingdom of Charn in C. S. Lewis, *The Magician's Nephew* and in Sauron's land in J. R. R. Tolkien, *The Lord of the Rings.*

in the previous section, it will not do to take the figures too literally. Obviously a land of burning pitch and brimstone could hardly afford a home to animals of any kind. However, it is the points being made which are of significance, not the absolute, literal fulfillment of a poetic image. Here the point being made by both figures is entirely consistent: when humanity makes itself paramount in the world, it destroys both itself and its environment.

11 The exact identification of the birds and animals mentioned in this verse, with the exception of the raven, remains uncertain. The first has traditionally been identified as a *pelican*.[9] Since the pelican is a water bird, it seems odd that it would be associated with the desert, and for this reason "owl" has been suggested and appears in most modern versions.[10] However, the pelican's habit of nesting in solitary places may explain how it could appear here (cf. Zeph. 2:14; Ps. 102:7 [Eng. 6]).

hedgehog has come to replace "bittern" in several modern versions as a translation of *qippôḏ*.[11] However, there is no general agreement.

owl is the translation of *yanšôp*. If the name is intended to be onomatopoeic, as seems possible, a bird with an eerie cry is indicated (NEB "screech owl").[12]

the line of chaos and the plummet of destruction have an ironic tone about them. Normally the line and the plumb bob would be tools of construction, not of destruction. But here God has compared the crooked and deformed structures of the world to his own righteousness and has decreed demolition (1:21–24; 28:17; 2 K. 21:13; Lam. 2:8; Amos 7:7–9). Edom will return to the chaos from which she came, there to remain forever (Mal. 1:4–5).

Verses 12 and 13 speak of the downfall of the palaces and fortresses of the land. Gen. 36:20–43 seems to indicate that chieftainship and rule were a source of pride in Edom. If that is so, these verses report that all will be destroyed. The palaces through which courtiers hurried will be a meeting place for jackals, and the fortresses in which the warriors paraded will be nothing but brambles.

Its nobles and the following phrase have been a source of mystification to scholars. The grammar is odd and the sense is not clear. Procksch

---

9. Cf. V. Holmgren, *Bird Walk Through the Bible* (New York: Seabury, 1972), pp. 68–73, for a thorough discussion of the possible identifications. Cf. also G. R. Driver, "Birds in the OT," *PEQ* 87 (1955) 5–20.

10. Holmgren considers that the marabou, a stalking scavenger, would be more appropriate than an owl. *qā'aṭ* seems to be related to the verb *qā'â*, "regurgitate."

11. *qpd* means "roll up," and this would apply well to the hedgehog.

12. See Driver, op. cit., p. 15.

and Delitzsch gave currency to the idea that the Edomite nobles typically elected (proclaimed) their king.[13] However, there is no solid evidence in support of this idea. More recently the tendency has been to agree with those who would emend the text.[14] This alternative may be correct, but Dahood has made a suggestion (reflected in the present translation) which may make this expedient unnecessary.[15] He points out that *mᵉlûkâ* may be used as the concrete term "king" instead of the usual abstract "kingdom."[16] If this is so, and the third plural "they called" be taken as a virtual passive "be called," much of the difficulty disappears. In fact, if *nobles* is removed from the verse, *princes* loses any parallel term.

13 *Its strongholds* is an accusative of specification.[17] The literal rendering is "She [i.e., the land] goes up, her strongholds, thorns." The construction specifies that it is not merely that the land goes up in thorns, but in particular the busiest and most important places (cf. 32:14).

jackals and *ostriches* also appear together in Job 30:29 and Mic. 1:8, where their cries are compared to those of mourners, a figure certainly appropriate to this setting.

14 *he-goat* and *night-bird* are interpreted by some as demonic figures (RSV satyr, night-hag), and this meaning is possible.[18] However, since both the preceding and following verses speak of regular animals, it seems best to remain with that interpretation (as do NEB and NIV, but not JPSV).

15 *owl* is somewhat conjectural, but it is preferable to the alternative, "arrow-snake," which is dependent upon Bochart's report of an Arabic name *kiffaza* for this kind of snake.[19] Along with the tentativeness

13. Cf. G. B. Gray, "Critical Discussion," *ZAW* 31 (1911) 123–27.

14. LXX reads "Its nobles shall not be," while Targ. paraphrases "They who say, we are nobles." Skinner reads *hômāṭāh,* "her wall," and adds it to v. 11 (cf. *BHS*). Kissane and Driver (*JTS* 37 [1938] 46) also add the word to the previous verse, but Kissane reads "desolation" *(ḥārᵉbâ),* while Driver reads "circle" (from Akk. *ḥarru*) (NEB "frontiers"). Kaiser follows Duhm in suggesting that "nobles" may be the only word now remaining from a line that is lost.

15. See *Bib* 47 (1966) 419.

16. Cf. also 2 Sam. 12:26; Ps. 22:29 (Eng. 28); Jer. 10:7; Ezek. 16:13.

17. Williams, *Syntax,* §§ 57, 58.

18. *sāʿîr* is used as a name for an idol (goat-shaped?) in Lev. 17:7 and 2 Chr. 11:15, and *lîlît* is the name applied to a well-known female night demon in late Jewish tales (cf. Tobit 3:8; A. Rappoport, *Myth and Legend in Ancient Israel* [New York: KTAV, 1966], pp. 77–79). Driver, *PEQ* 91 (1959) 55–57, argues for the "goat-sucker" or "night jar."

19. Cf. Skinner.

of the identification, neither the hatching nor the keeping of the young under the mother's shadow applies to this snake.[20]

the vultures probably refers to the black kite, a particularly gregarious bird which eats both carrion and fresh meat.

Verses 16–17 form the conclusion not only to this section on the desert-dwellers but to the entire poem. It does so by making the part represent the whole. If it is true that God has decreed each species of bird that will inhabit the world city, it is also true that the destruction which must precede their inhabitance is also decreed. The writer's point is one: there is no question but that the conditions about which he has been talking will come to pass; God is sovereign of all things and the world which opposes him is irrevocably doomed.

the book of the Lord is problematic because it is not clear to what book the author is referring.[21] There are essentially four alternatives: (1) Isaiah is inviting later readers to compare this writing to the facts of their own day, confident that those facts will bear out the inspired nature of his prediction; (2) he is relating this prophecy to an earlier one and the reference is to 13:21–22; (3) v. 16a is a postexilic interpolation which seeks to prove the inspiration of the prophecy; (4) this is a literary allusion to a heavenly "Book of Destiny." Unfortunately, none of these is without difficulties.

The first alternative would be very attractive if there were anything in the text which indicated it was addressed to future readers. Unfortunately, there is nothing of the sort. Thus it must be assumed that the passage is addressed to readers of its own day.

The second alternative is also attractive in that both this chapter and ch. 13 seem to be addressing the world through a particular example: here Edom and there Babylon. But beyond this there is no connection between the two passages and there seems to be no logical reason to appeal to the former to authenticate the latter.

The third proposal springs from Kissane's attempt to retain a preexilic date for vv. 1–15. But if the reference is to the present text, then the preexilic writer is as likely to make such a statement as a postexilic writer would be. But the problem is the same: the text is not self-authenticating.

This leaves the fourth alternative. There does seem to have been a concept of a heavenly book of destiny among the Hebrews.[22] Thus the

---

20. Holmgren, op. cit., pp. 71–72, suggests the anhinga, a bird with a snaky neck.
21. LXX solves the problem by reading instead "by number they come."
22. See Ps. 40:8 (Eng. 7); 139:16; Mal. 3:16; Dan. 7:10; Rev. 20:12.

author is assuring the reader that all this is for certain; it is written in God's book. The major drawback is that the reader, or hearer, cannot inquire into that book, although he is invited to. The solution appears to be that the invitation is only a literary device. If this can be granted, this proposal seems to have the fewest difficulties.

None will lack is missing in 1QIs[a]. This omission would bring the phrase into line with the end of v. 15, where the phrase "a wife, her mate" also appears. But each verse makes good sense as it stands in the MT.

For the mouth of the Lord seems to be the original, though neither the MT nor any of the versions has transmitted it correctly. In any case it seems clear that the mouth is that of God. The parallel *his Spirit* (breath) serves to confirm this interpretation.[23] The Sovereign of the universe has commanded this desolation and he will bring it to pass. Just as he sovereignly apportioned Canaan to his people Israel, so he has apportioned the Edoms of this world to the birds of the desert. No nation or people is able to choose its destiny without regard its own behavior. Rather, by its behavior it earns a destiny in keeping with God's immutable character. So again Isaiah asks, "Why trust the nations? They are not masters of their own destiny. Rather, they belong to God who, like the landowner, can use a string to divide them into plots of his own choosing" (cf. Ps. 16:6; Mic. 2:5).

b. THE GARDEN (35:1–10)

1 *The desert and the dry land will rejoice;*[1]
  let the wilderness rejoice[2] *and blossom.*[3]
2 *Like the crocus it will surely blossom;*

23. In any case, it seems unlikely that "my voice" would refer to Isaiah (Young). At the same time Young is correct in pointing out that "the word" itself is not efficacious. The spirit of God must bring the word to reality (Ps. 33:6).

1. *y[e]śuśûm*, "they will rejoice," has an additional *m* at the end. Young tries to make it an object, but the result makes no sense. It seems much more likely that the *n* of an archaic *-ûn* ending has assimilated to the following *m* (Delitzsch). It may also be only a dittograph of that following *m*.

2. "let (it) rejoice," a jussive, occurs as the second member of the parallel phrase in both v. 1 and v. 2, where the first member has an indicative. Virtually all translations do nothing with the jussive force but treat it indicatively. It is interesting to observe that Targ. specifies that it is the returnees in the wilderness who will rejoice. If the chapter was written during postexilic times, it is odd that the author did not do the same thing. Does the generality point to preexilic authorship?

3. For vv. 1b and 2a MT has "Let the wilderness rejoice, and it will blossom like a crocus. It will surely blossom, etc." The present arrangement is followed by most versions (RSV, CBAT, NEB, NIV), because it seems to give a more satisfactory metric arrangement.

> let it rejoice even a rejoicing[4] and shouting aloud.
> The glory of Lebanon shall be given to it,
>   the honor of Carmel and Sharon.
> They will see the glory of the Lord,
>   the honor of our God.
> 3 Strengthen the drooping hands,
>   and steady the shaking knees;
> 4 say to those with racing hearts,
>   "Be strong, do not be afraid.
>   Behold, your God.
> With vengeance he comes, divine retribution;[5]
>   he comes that he might save you."[6]
> 5 Then the eyes of the blind will be opened,
>   and the ears of the deaf will be opened.
> 6 Then the lame will leap like a deer,
>   and the tongue of the dumb will shout aloud.
> For waters will break forth in the desert,
>   and streams in the wilderness.[7]
> 7 The parched ground will become a pool,
>   and the thirsty land springs of water.
> In the haunt of jackals its resting place,[8]
>   an abode[9] for reeds and rushes.

4. *gîlaṯ*, "rejoicing," seems to be a construct noun occurring before a conjunction, as in 33:6; 51:21; Ezek. 26:10.

5. The syntax of the sentence is troublesome in that it is not clear whether "vengeance" or "God" is the subject of *yāḇôʾ*, "he/it comes." However, *hûʾ yāḇôʾ* in the following line clearly refers to God and this makes it appear that the former does as well. In this case "vengeance" and "divine retribution" may be considered to be accusatives of specification. However, if Wernberg-Møller is correct, *yōšaʿᵃḵem* is a noun, and the two words are then subjects ("Two Different Passages in the OT [Ps. 12, 9 and Isa. 35, 4]," *ZAW* 69 [1957] 69–73).

6. *yōšaʿᵃḵem*, "let him save you," is another jussive (cf. 35:1, 2). Perhaps the sense here is captured by an English subjunctive.

7. 1QIs[a] adds *ylkw*, "they will go," after "streams in the wilderness," but that does not seem necessary, nor is it supported by the ancient versions.

8. *ribṣāh*, "its [fem.] resting place." Since a masc. plur. of animals may take fem. sing. suffixes, it is possible that "their resting place" is intended, meaning animals in general. *BHS* suggests reading the final *he* on *rbṣh* as a fem. noun ending (instead of a possessive suffix), thus yielding "a resting place." 1QIs[a] has no suffix on *rbṣ*.

9. *ḥaṣîr*, normally "grass," but translated as "abode" (of ostriches) in 34:13. The parallelism with *nᵉwê*, "haunt," is the same here as there and calls for the same translation, except that "grass" goes very well with "reeds and rushes." LXX appears to dodge the problem by substituting "a joy of birds" for "a haunt of jackals," while Targ. follows MT but has "grow" where *ḥaṣîr* would be. The 1QIs[a] reading suggested to Kissane the possibility of "a bed of grass."

8 *There shall be a highway*[10] *there;*
it will be called the Way of Holiness.
No one unclean shall pass over it.
It is for those who walk the way.[11]
No fools will stumble [upon it].
9 *There will be no lion there;*
no fierce animal will get up on it,
they will not be found there.
The redeemed will walk;
10 *the ransomed of the Lord will return.*
They will come to Zion with shouts,
eternal gladness on their heads.
Joy and gladness will overtake them;
sorrow and sighing will flee away.

In what Skinner calls "a brilliant contrast," this chapter stands over against ch. 34. There the luxuriant land of Edom was turned to a desert. Here the desert is changed into a garden. What desert is changed is not defined. Some take it to be Judah, while others understand it to refer to the Syrian desert across which the returning exiles would have to travel. But it is more likely that no particular place is intended. Rather, just as Edom in ch. 34 represented the nations in general, so here the desert represents the total world: physical, social, and spiritual, which, human arrogance having destroyed, God in his grace can make to bloom. Whereas trusting the nations results in a desert, trusting God results in a garden.

Several studies have demonstrated a considerable congruency between the ideas and phrasings of this chapter and those of chs. 40–66.[12] This similarity has led to a great deal of speculation concerning the origins of the chapter.[13] However those questions are answered, the issue of the

10. MT has "a highway and a way," but "and a way" is almost certainly a dittograph with the following. 1QIs[a] lacks the duplication.

11. MT punctuates the line to read "the unclean will not go upon it, but (and?) it is to them; this wayfarer and fools will not stumble." The present punctuation follows *BHS*. LXX has "there shall not be any unclean way there." Targ. has "the wayfarer will not cease." Neither of these seems to have a better claim to originality than MT.

12. See C. C. Torrey, *The Second Isaiah;* R. B. Y. Scott, "The Relation of Isaiah, Chapter 35, to Deutero-Isaiah," *AJSL* 52 (1935/1936) 178–191; A. T. Olmstead, "II Isaiah and Isaiah, Chapter 35," *AJSL* 53 (1936/1937) 251–53; J. D. Smart, *History and Theology in Second Isaiah* (London: Epworth, 1967), pp. 292–94; W. H. Brownlee, *The Meaning of the Qumran Scrolls for the Bible*, pp. 247–255.

13. The one broad agreement among nonconservative scholars today is that ch. 35 is not the work of "I Isaiah" or "Isaiah of Jerusalem." This is based upon the assumption that "I Isaiah" did not write chs. 40–66 and that, since ch. 35 shows numerous similarities with chs. 40–66, he did not write ch. 35 either. However, there is little agreement beyond that point. Torrey believed that chs. 34

author's intent remains. Was he speaking about a literal return from exile, a millennial kingdom, a spiritual condition to which these statements bear a typological reference, etc.? Two things may be said in response. First, as has been frequently noted to this point, it is improper to attempt to make poetry fit into a wholly cognitive mode. Poetry speaks to the affective side of the personality. This is not to say it is worth less than purely cognitive materials. It may well be worth more in its power to shape our thinking and to motivate us to action. But it is to say that any attempt to reduce the imagery to simple literal statements is an inappropriate method of interpretation.

Second, the poem may well be referring to all of the alternatives mentioned in the previous paragraph. Thus, it may indeed be talking about a return of exiles from Babylon, but that is not all. The language is too exalted for that. So also, it speaks of a time when fear, injustice, sickness, and accidental death are gone, yet the language is very much the language of this world. By the same token, it speaks of holiness, cleanness, and wisdom, yet the salvation is put in largely physical terms. One is thus reminded of 1 John 3:2, ". . . it does not appear what we shall be, but we know that when he appears, we shall be like him." So here, we cannot say with absolute certainty how all of this will work out in fact. But this we know: to walk with God is to walk in security, in blessing, in glory, and in joy. And if these are limited now, there will come a day when they will be as unlimited as he is.

The poem divides itself into three paragraphs. The first, vv. 1–4, is introductory in that it makes the promise of the desert's blossoming and offers encouragement to the faint-hearted. Verses 5–7 elaborate on the promise with the declaration of salvation. Two figures are used: the infirm

---

and 35 were written by "II Isaiah" as an introduction to his volume (cf. also Delitzsch). Duhm, on the other hand, believed that the apocalypticism of the two chapters called for a date as late as John Hyrcanus (so also Kaiser). Others, believing that chs. 34 and 35 show dependency upon chs. 40–66, rather than identity, regard them as having been written by a postexilic redactor who was under the influence of chs. 40–66 and wished to write a conclusion to "I Isaiah's" writings (so Wildberger, Clements, etc.). Undoubtedly, the numerous similarities with chs. 40–66 are noteworthy. But this is as one would expect, even if the book does come from a single source, for the theme of ch. 35 is salvation, which is also the theme of chs. 40–66. This was not the primary theme of chs. 1–39 (although it is certainly a significant element). There the theme was "Whom will you trust?" Ch. 35 effectively draws that teaching to a close (there are numerous similarities with chs. 7–33, as well as with chs. 40–66), and points to the hope ahead for those who will trust God. Thus the connections with chs. 40–66 could be seen as an argument for single authorship, unless one has already concluded that Isaiah of Jerusalem could not have written those chapters.

being healed, and water bursting forth in the desert. Verses 8–10 speak of the highway upon which the ransomed may come to God. Thus there is a focusing effect which moves from the general to the particular, the most particular promise being joyous fellowship with God in Zion.

1 With something of the same suddenness as in 8:22–23 (Eng. 9:1), the picture changes: in ch. 34 Edom has become a gloomy wilderness full of unclean animals. But suddenly the wilderness is a place of rejoicing, filled with blooming flowers.[14] One can only ask what has happened. The author keeps his readers in suspense until he gives a partial answer in v. 2 and then a fuller one in v. 4. The answer is God. He is the author of all joy. We human beings keep thinking we can produce joy on our own. But we never can. Joy is always a by-product of the presence of God in his world. When we, through our lack of trust, hold him at arm's length, the end result is desolation. It is only when we turn to him, recognizing the uselessness of all other help, that we can perceive his coming to us (v. 4) and find joy in becoming complete with him.

the crocus is the most widely accepted translation today of *ḥᵃbaṣ-ṣāleṭ*. However, this meaning is far from certain.[15] Evidently the author's intent is to call to mind one of the species of small flowers which turn the desert into a place of beauty almost instantly after any substantial rainfall.

2 Throughout the book the theme of glory is present.[16] God wants to share his glory with his creation, but any attempt by the creatures to produce their own glory will end in disaster. Thus it is appropriate in this segment (chs. 34 and 35), which sums up the two ways—God or the nations—that this theme should appear. If we will give God his glory, then he will give his to us.

As noted on 29:17; 32:15; and 33:9, Lebanon with its spreading cedars and Mount Carmel with the rich plain of Sharon at its foot were symbols of abundance. Now, Isaiah says, if you want to understand the abundance of God's promises, you will have to imagine a desert turning into one of those regions. That is the kind of thing God can do, especially with the human heart.

14. For other references to the desert, see 32:15–20; 41:18–19; 51:3; Ps. 107:33–38.

15. NEB "asphodel," TEV "flowers," Delitzsch "narcissus." Not a true rose in any case. Cf. *IDB*, II:744–45. For a photograph of the wilderness in bloom, see *Views of the Biblical World*, ed. B. Mazar (Jerusalem: International Publishing, 1960), III:62.

16. Thirty-seven occurrences in the book. Note esp. 3:8; 4:2, 5; 6:3; 10:3, 16; 11:10; 16:14; 17:3, 4: 22:23; 40:5; 42:12; 48:11; 60:1, 2, 13; 66:18, 19. See the comment on 6:3.

They will see does not have a clear antecedent. The LXX makes it clear by reading "my people" and the Targum does similarly with "the house of Israel." Delitzsch rather thinks that the reference is to the personified regions just named. If the "they" was not emphatic, it would be tempting to understand it as a virtual passive: "the Lord's glory will be seen." However, in view of the emphasis, Israel seems the most likely reference. God's people who will have long asked for him to show himself will see his glory.

3–4 *the drooping hands* is a figure for helplessness induced by fear. The English "throw up one's hands" has a somewhat similar connotation, although fear is not so prominent there.[17] *the shaking knees* and *racing heart* are similar figures. Confronted with mighty nations who use their power ruthlessly, what is one to do except bow one's head in terrified resignation?

But God's word, as in ch. 40 (esp. vv. 9–10, but cf. also 10:24–27), is a word of encouragement. God is greater than the nations and they cannot continue their oppressive ways with impunity. He will come to redress the balance and to execute vengeance upon the oppressor.[18] The people of Israel today would give no thanks to God, but the fact is, the national identity of Israel is a result of the Holocaust. There has been a remarkable rebalancing of power.

he comes is a powerful statement throughout Scripture, up to and including Mal. 3:1. To the heart which cries "He is too far away, I cannot reach him," the answer is, "You do not have to reach him; he comes to you." So God has been coming to us across the millennia: through the process of revelation, in the acts of his providence, in the first coming of Christ. And he will continue to come until that last day when we will be united with him forever.

As noted above, vv. 5–7 expand on vv. 1–4 by giving two figures of salvation: healing of infirmities and the breaking forth of water in the desert. Both the infirm and the desert were considered by the people of the Bible to be in the thrall of death, barren and worthless (2 Sam. 9:8; Jer. 2:6; John 9:2). Thus the thought that God can give abundant life to the lifeless is well expressed through these figures.[19]

That this prophecy was at least partly fulfilled in the ministry of

17. See 13:7 and the comment there.
18. Again, the connections go both forward and backward in the book. Cf. 43:4; 48:20; 49:24, 25; 62:11, but also 24:21–25:5 and 34:8.
19. Delitzsch argues that the healing is not a figure but is the outer side of a totality of redemption. This interpretation is certainly not impossible, but the use of water argues against it.

Jesus Christ may be seen in the way in which he appropriated these figures for himself (Luke 7:22; John 7:37). As Delitzsch well says, and as Jesus' ministry shows, the references to physical healing are not merely typological of spiritual healing. Rather, the physical healing is the outer side of a totality. Thus the part represents the whole (as "lips" in 6:5).

5 *Then* emphasizes the future aspect of the promise, but also serves to connect with statements of v. 4 and to show the impact of the promised salvation. It is perhaps significant that the figures used do not stress freedom from oppression as much as they do abundant life. To be sure, freedom from oppression is a part of the total promise (43:14; 48:20; etc.), but apart from a divinely given inner abundance, physical freedom can be a curse as well as a blessing. Liberation theology must couple inner abundance with outer freedom if it is to be truly biblical.

the blind and *the deaf* have been used frequently to speak of a spiritual condition as well as a physical one (6:10; 28:7; 29:9–10, 18; 30:20–21; 32:3–4).[20] So the prophet promises a day when true values are seen and true guidance is received. In short, in this context, they will cease to trust the nations and begin to trust God (cf. also 42:18–19).

6 *the lame will leap like a deer* has a particular fulfillment in Peter's healing of the lame man in the temple (Acts 3:8).

The theme of streams in the desert is a particular favorite of chs. 40–55, where the stress is upon the second "Exodus" and its similarities with the first.[21] Furthermore, in a land as dry as Israel, water is a special symbol of life and salvation.[22]

7 *The parched ground (šārāb)* was frequently translated as "mirage" in the latter part of the nineteenth century on the basis of an Arabic etymology. But while that translation will fit admirably here, it will not work in 49:10, the only other occurrence of *šārāb* in Biblical Hebrew. As a result, "mirage" has been dropped from all the modern translations. The connotation seems to be something burning, either ground, as here, or wind, as in 49:10.

the haunt of jackals seems to be another direct connection with ch. 34 (cf. v. 13; note also the similarity of 34:8 to 35:4). There the place will become a wilderness where jackals live; here the rocky crags which those animals normally inhabit have become a splashy meadow. The way

20. The Targ. makes this explicit here by reading "the eyes of the house of Israel which were as blind to the law .... and their ears which were as deaf in receiving the words of the prophets. . . ."
21. See Exod. 17:5–7; Ps. 78:15–16; Isa. 41:17, 18; 43:19–20; 44:3, 4; 48:21; 49:10; 51:3. Cf. also 32:15.
22. See 58:11; Ps. 1:3; 143:6; Jer. 2:13; 17:8. Cf. *TWOT*, I:501–503.

of man is to make the inhabited uninhabitable; the way of God is to take the barren and make it abundant.

Verses 8–10 give the climax of the poem using the particular image of the highway upon which the redeemed march to Zion. It is not clear whether this is construed as a highway from the countries of exile (cf. 11:12, 16) upon which the returnees can come to Jerusalem, or whether it is a festal way upon which holy pilgrims can go up to Zion. The very uncertainty suggests that it is probably both and more. Once again poetic imagery resists reduction to mere literalism. The point is that God's coming to his people (35:4) has its purpose in the people coming to him in holy lives for worship and fellowship (2:2–4; 4:2–6; 25:6–9; 66:18–23).

8 In a direct contrast with 34:10, this verse asserts that in God's country, as opposed to Man's, communication and travel are easy.[23] Sin divides, but true holiness unites.[24] This is not the spurious holiness which totes up its achievements (66:3–5), but that genuine Godlikeness which is the result of an experience of cleansing like Isaiah's (ch. 6). There the cleansing was received by Isaiah alone, but in the last days many from the entire nation will receive it. This is the very thing envisioned by ch. 6: when the nation can, in large part, experience what Isaiah experienced, the dilemma of chs. 1–5 will be solved—the nation will indeed serve the nations.

It is for those who walk the way seems the most likely translation of a difficult phrase. If this is the correct interpretation, it means that the way is holy because this is the character of those who walk there, not because of some intrinsic quality it has in itself.

No fools will stumble has been understood in two differing ways. On the one hand, it is taken that the highway will be so smooth that even a simpleton could walk there.[25] However, the word translated "fool" means not merely a simpleton but that morally perverse person who knowingly chooses the opposite to God's truth.[26] Thus the sense is the same as "no one unclean shall pass over it." Hence the arrangement is chiastic: the "unclean" will not walk on the way; it is a way possessed by the righteous, "fools" will not stumble on it.[27]

---

23. For other references to "highway," see 11:16; 19:23; 40:3; 43:19; 49:11; 62:10.

24. Cf. also 30:21 and 33:8.

25. So AV; also Young: "wayfarers, though fools, shall not stumble."

26. *ʾĕwîl;* cf. Job 5:3; Prov. 1:7, etc.

27. Calvin tries to find a middle way through the dilemma by suggesting that "fools" describes the condition of the people before they submitted to be led. This seems strained.

Verse 9 continues the contrast with ch. 34. There the wild animals took over what had been man's. Here, although the highway passes through lush watered regions where wildlife might be expected to abound, none of it will be of the ferocious sort. Our human attempts to care for ourselves only increase our insecurity, but to depend on God is to find a security none can harm.[28]

not be found there is taken by Duhm (cf. *BHS*) as a gloss on "no . . . get up on it." This interpretation may be possible if the MT is not punctuated correctly. As the MT has it, "they will not be found" is an appropriate antithetic parallel to "the redeemed."

redeemed is a very significant term in the second part of the book: *gāʾal* and its derivatives occur twenty-one times and *pāḏâ* twice. The occurrence of the concept here has been used as evidence that chs. 34 and 35 were written by Deutero-Isaiah. However, that is not necessarily the case. Redemption is not the central focus of chs. 1–39 but rather judgment. Thus it is not surprising that the terms only appear here and in 1:27 and 29:22 in the first half.[29] They do appear here because the judgment theme has been brought to a close and the promise is about to be developed.

10 This verse is quoted in 51:11 and sometimes taken to derive from that context. But observation will reveal that it fits better here where it functions as the climax and logical conclusion. The end of the Holy Way is Zion the Holy City. The result of supernatural protection and provision, but most of all, of redemption, is a gladness which will drive away all sadness forever. This is the apex of the eschatological vision: a day when the people of God can be set free from their own sins and the sins of others, when they can come home to their God and be fully restored to his image, when a lifelong struggle to avoid grief and pain will be ended in their being overwhelmed by gladness and joy.[30] This is the hope of biblical faith. To be sure, there are foretastes in this life, foreshadowings of what is to come. Furthermore, there is a sense in which it is true that virtue is its own reward. But if the faith is shorn of its eschatological promises, what remains is but a shell. If God is God at all, then we may believe all his promises (1 Cor. 15:19).

With this verse the segment encompassed by chs. 13–35 reaches

28. Cf. 11:6–9 and 65:25 for a similar set of images used to describe security in God. Lions seem to have been fairly common in Israel during biblical times. As such, they would have posed a constant source of anxiety to farmers and shepherds (Judg. 14:8; 1 Sam. 17:34; 1 K. 13:24–28; 20:36).

29. Both of these are *pāḏâ*, as 35:10, rather than *gāʾal*, as 35:9 and later.

30. Cf. Ps. 23:6: "Surely goodness and mercy *shall pursue* me all the days of my life."

its climactic conclusion. Chs. 7–12 posed a question: "Is God Sovereign of the nations?" Can God deliver from an Assyria? Or is he just one more of the gods, waiting to be gobbled up by a bigger god? In short, can God be trusted? Chs. 13–35 have sought to answer that question in four main sections: chs. 13–23; 24–27; 28–33; 34–35. In the first, God's lordship over each of the nations is asserted. In the second, it is shown that God is not merely the reactor to the nations, but is in fact the sovereign Actor on the world's stage. In the third, the superiority of God's counsel over that of the merely human leaders is shown. Finally, the last two chapters show the ultimate results of the two courses of action, with ch. 35 ending at exactly the same point as chs. 11–12, with the promise that God can, and will, redeem. He may be trusted. However, the issue remains: is this merely abstraction or can it become concrete reality? Ahaz had proved that the nations cannot be trusted. But what of God? Can his trustworthiness be demonstrated or only asserted? Must his promises for the distant future be clung to blindly or can an earnest of their reality be experienced now? This is what chs. 36–39 are about.

C. GOD OR ASSYRIA? TRUST (36:1–39:8)

1. THE ASSYRIAN THREAT (36:1–37:38)

a. THE RABSHAQEH'S CHALLENGE (36:1–37:7)

(1) The ultimatum (36:1–20)

1 *In the fourteenth year of King Hezekiah, Sennacherib, king of Assyria, went up against all the fortified cities of Judah and captured them.*

2 *Then the king of Assyria sent the Rabshaqeh[1] from Lachish to Jerusalem to King Hezekiah with an imposing army. He stood at the watercourse of the upper pool on the highway of the washer's field.*

3 *Eliakim, son of Hilkiah, who was over the house, and Shebna, the scribe, and Joah, son of Asaph, the reporter, went out to him.*

4 *The Rabshaqeh said to them, "Say to Hezekiah, 'Thus says the great king, king of Assyria: What is this trust in which you trust?*

1. The MT, recording only the third of the three officers mentioned in 2 Kings, is perhaps the result of a copyist's error when his eye skipped over the first two subjects of the verb. But Gray, *1 & 2 Kings*, OTL, rev. ed. (Philadelphia: Westminster, 1970), p. 677, suggests that the Isaiah text is the more original since only the Rabshaqeh speaks. See below.

5 *You[2] speak only a word of the lips, counsel and strength for war. Now upon what do you trust that you have rebelled against me?*

6 *Behold, you trust in this staff of a broken reed, in Egypt, which, if a man lean on it, it will go into his hand and pierce it. This is Pharaoh, king of Egypt, to all who trust in him.'*

7 *And if you say to me, 'In God we trust,' is it not he whose high places and altars Hezekiah turned aside, he who said, 'Behold, this altar you shall worship?'*

8 *Now make a bargain with my lord, the king of Assyria, and I will give you 2000 horses, if you are able to put riders for yourself upon them.*

9 *So how can you turn aside the face of[3] one governor,[4] of the least of my lord's servants, trusting in Egypt for chariots and horsemen?*

10 *Now, is it without the Lord that I have come up against this land to destroy it? The Lord said to me, 'Go up to this land and destroy it.'"[5]*

11 *Then Eliakim and Shebna and Joah said to the Rabshaqeh, "Speak to your servants in Aramaic, for we understand it. Do not speak to us in the Judean language in the ears of the people who are upon the wall."*

12 *Then the Rabshaqeh said, "Is it to your lord and to you[6] that my master sent me to speak these words? Does it not concern the men who sit on the wall, in that they will eat their dung and drink their urine with you?"*

13 *Then the Rabshaqeh stood and cried out in a loud voice in the Judean language, and he said, "Hear the words of the great king, the king of Assyria.*

14 *Thus says the King, 'Do not let Hezekiah deceive you, for he is not able to deliver you.*

2. MT "I," 1QIs[a] "You" (so also 2 K. 18:20).

3. Kissane and Young suggest that the meaning of "turn away the face of" is to refuse the request of and cite 1 K. 2:16, 17, 20; 2 Chr. 6:42; Ps. 132:10. Delitzsch, however, understands the phrase to mean "repel" and cites Isa. 28:6. Kissane and Young have the better part of the argument.

4. *BHS* (following Duhm) recommends the deletion of "governor" as a gloss on "servants." This deletion certainly does make for a smoother reading: " . . . the request of the least of the servants of my lord (himself?)." However, it is suspect for that very reason. The supposedly glossed reading of the MT is so much more difficult that it is hard to understand how anyone would alter an easy reading to this difficult one. Furthermore, the versions are unanimous in their support of "governor" (LXX alters the second phrase to "they are slaves who trust Egypt").

5. Note that LXX lacks the final sentence containing the claim of a direct command to God. Other versions support MT.

6. The use of the singular pronoun, "your leader," "you," perhaps indicates that the Rabshaqeh, with characteristic directness, has cut out the other two diplomats and is addressing only Eliakim.

15 *And do not let Hezekiah cause you to trust in the Lord, saying, "The Lord will surely deliver us; this city will not be given into the hand of the king of Assyria."'*

16 *Do not listen to Hezekiah. For thus says the king of Assyria, 'Make a blessing with me and come out⁷ to me, and each man shall eat from his vine and fig tree, and drink from his own well,*

17 *until I come and take you to a land like your land, a land of grain and wine, a land of bread and vineyards.'*

18 *[Beware,] lest Hezekiah seduce you saying, 'The Lord will deliver us.' Has any of the gods of the nations delivered his land from the hand of the king of Assyria?*

19 *Where are the gods of Hamath and Arpad? Where are the gods of Sepharvaim—that they delivered Samaria from my hand?*

20 *Which of all the gods of these lands delivered their land from my hand that the Lord should deliver Jerusalem from my hand?"*

Chapters 36–39 conclude the section relating to Assyria and the question of trust which that nation's presence on Judah's borders posed. They demonstrate that it is not necessary to revoke one's dependence on God and turn to human powers in order to survive. In this way they constitute a lived-out example of the truths taught in chs. 13–35. The nations of mankind are under God's hand; he is their ruler and those who trust in him need not, indeed, must not, bow down to those nations.

The section appears to be divided into three segments: chs. 36–37; 38; 39. In the first, Hezekiah, reduced to helplessness before Assyria, turns to God and finds relief. In the second, Hezekiah is again helpless, this time before illness. He again turns to God and is restored. In the third segment, Hezekiah has the opportunity to give glory to God in the presence of Babylon, but instead falls prey to the temptation to parade his own glory, with the result that the coming captivity to Babylon is announced.

The structure of the section raises a number of questions. Chief among these is: what are the functions of chs. 38 and 39? If, as will be argued at greater length below, the overall section is a reversal of chs. 7–12, exhibiting trust in the face of a military threat rather than untrust, it seems odd that these two incidents, which do not present Hezekiah in a very favorable light, should be included. Two alternatives present themselves. The first would consider the chapters separately, with ch. 38 presenting another example of trust in a hard situation, and ch. 39 a failure to trust. The second would see the two chapters as a unit. (Note that the recovery is said to provide the occasion for the visit of the Babylonian

---

7. In 1 Sam. 11:3 and Jer. 21:9 "come out" seems to be a technical term for surrender.

envoys, 39:1.) In this case, the stress would be upon Hezekiah's fallibility despite the trustworthiness of God.

Which of these alternatives is the more likely? The first is attractive in that it supports the general theme of God's trustworthiness and his ability to deliver in difficult circumstances. However, the lack of any relation to the theme of the nations, plus the generally doleful tone of the chapter (esp. the psalm, which does not appear in 2 Kings), calls this view into question.

The second alternative, which takes the two chapters together, minimizes the trust in ch. 38 and instead emphasizes Hezekiah's fallibility. It answers with a resounding no the question as to whether this Hezekiah, under whom the wonderful deliverance has occurred, is not the Messiah. Our trust is never to be in a human ruler, for every human being, no matter how often healed, is mortal. Moreover, every human ruler, no matter how many times he may have trusted God, is still prone to self-reliance when the pressure is withdrawn. Thus Hezekiah has shown (chs. 36–37) that Isaiah's teachings about trust are true. But he has also shown that it is in God that we trust and not in human perfectibility (chs. 38–39). In this way the section prepares for what follows. Will it still be possible to trust when Judah has no king and is in captivity to Babylon? Absolutely. First, this captivity is no surprise to God, and second, Judah's hope never was in a king, but in the God whom mortals, including kings, may call upon.

As mentioned in Excursus I below, chs. 36–37 deal with the Assyrian threat brought about by Ahaz's refusal to trust in God (ch. 7) and his son Hezekiah's response to that threat. As such, it represents a direct opposite to Ahaz's response. Thus the chapters function as a counterbalance to chs. 7–8. Hezekiah is a living demonstration of the truths taught in chs. 13–35, which truths Isaiah attempted to get Ahaz to act upon but could not.

Thus, this section is not placed here accidentally or haphazardly. It is located consciously to provide the climax to all which the prophet has said about the folly of trusting the nations. Several factors make it plain that a conscious contrast with Ahaz is intended. One of the most striking of these is that the place where the Rabshaqeh stood to blaspheme God (36:2) is the same place where Isaiah stood to urge Ahaz to trust God (7:3). It is because of Ahaz's refusal to trust in that place that the Rabshaqeh would stand there (8:5–8). Furthermore, it is not just any nation which threatens to engulf Hezekiah, but Assyria, the very nation Ahaz chose to trust in place of God. Thus we have two kings of Judah, father and son, both threatened with imminent destruction so far as they know, both recognizing the inadequacy of their own strength. But there the similarity ceases. Faced with a considerably less destructive threat, Ahaz chose to trust his worst enemy rather than God. He would not put God to the test. On the other hand, Hezekiah did put God on his mettle and God demonstrated that he was indeed master of the nations.

As noted above, the segment appears in two subsegments: 36:1–37:7, the Rabshaqeh's challenge, and 37:8–38, Sennacherib's letter. The last verses of the latter (37:36–38) contain the conclusion of the whole affair. (See Excursus I below for a discussion as to whether the two subsegments are merely variant reports of one event.) The two subsegments show a development in Hezekiah's level of commitment to God and an intensification of his determination to commit his own fate and his city's to God. To this God responds, through Isaiah, in a corresponding way. The first response is merely an oracle of deliverance. The second is a much more full-orbed expression of God's character and of hope for Judah.

1 *In the fourteenth year of King Hezekiah* poses a problem in that Sennacherib's attack cannot easily be dated prior to 701 B.C., which would be Hezekiah's twenty-fifth (or at best twenty-fourth) year, according to 2 K. 18:1, 9, 10. A widely accepted solution is to assume that the sickness alluded to in 38:1 occurred in the fourteenth year (712/11), but that its inclusion with the report of Sennacherib's attack caused some later scribe to believe the two events were contemporary and thus transfer the date to the first account, namely, the attack.[8] There is no evidence to support this theory, making it very tenuous. On the other hand, Edwin Thiele has argued that this dating (14th year) is the only correct one in Hezekiah's account, all others having succumbed to a twelve-year discrepancy which later scribes tried to smooth over.[9] This theory suffers, too, from its complexity. The simplest solution is that 14 is an error for an original 24. This change would involve only two letters and requires no reworking of other parts of the text.[10]

Sennacherib, king of Assyria, had been on his throne about four years by 701 B.C. Those four years had been largely taken up with attempts to put down revolts spurred by the death of his father, Sargon II, on the battlefield. When the east and south had been dealt with in an at least temporary fashion (Babylon was not to be finally subdued until 689),

8. Cf. Scott, Skinner, Delitzsch, etc.

9. E. R. Thiele, *Mysterious Numbers,* pp. 118–154.

10. See esp. Young. The difference would be between ʾarbaʿ ʿeśrēh and ʾarbaʿ ʿeśrîm. So also Clements. Cheyne proposed that the date in MT was correct, but that Sargon's attack on Ashdod in 713/11 was intended. This point of view has gained no support. For an account of Sennacherib's reign, cf. A. T. Olmstead, *History of Assyria* (Chicago: University of Chicago, repr. 1975), pp. 283–336.

the Assyrian emperor was ready to turn to the West. There Hezekiah, apparently prompted by promises of Egyptian aid, and perhaps also with Babylonian encouragement (if the sickness and recovery of ch. 38 were prior to 701), was spearheading the revolt of the small states west and south of Samaria, extending from Tyre in the north to Ashkelon in the south. According to Sennacherib's annals, the Assyrian army struck the coast at Sidon and from that point worked its way southward, devouring opponent after opponent until the Egyptian army finally made a stand at Eltekeh about twenty miles west of Jerusalem at the edge of the hill country. There Isaiah's prophecies concerning the foolishness of dependence upon Egypt (20:1–6; 30:1–5; 31:1–3) proved painfully true as the Egyptians were routed and the Assyrians continued on to Lachish, Judah's last hope for stemming the tide. If it be asked why Sennacherib did not move directly from Eltekeh to an attack upon Jerusalem, the answer is probably that he hoped to avoid a prolonged siege in the highlands of Judah that would tie down his army and leave them open to an attack on their rear if Egypt should recover. At Lachish, Egypt would still be before them and they could move quickly from the siege to battle positions if a new Egyptian threat appeared. This is in fact what they did according to 37:8. Once Lachish's fate was sure, Jerusalem would have no choice but to surrender, much as does the chess player who has lost his last rook.

2 It is likely that the siege of Lachish was drawing toward a successful close (from an Assyrian perspective) when Sennacherib judged that the right time had come to put pressure upon the isolated Hezekiah. He sent his three highest officials, the Tartan, the Rabsaris, and the Rabshaqeh, with a substantial force as a show of strength to demand Hezekiah's surrender (2 K. 18:17). All three officers bear Akkadian titles. As is shown from a number of royal inscriptions from this period, the *Tartan* (Akk. *turtanu*) was second to the king in command of the army (20:1). The precise function of the other two officers is less clear. The title *Rabsaris* is unattested in any Akkadian documents thus far. On the basis of Hebrew, its meaning would be chief eunuch, but the term "eunuch" seems to represent "officer" in the OT (as Potiphar, Gen. 39:1; so also 2 K. 25:19; for this title see Jer. 39:3, 13). *Rabshaqeh,* if from Akk. *šaqû,* "to drink," means "chief cupbearer." This person may have been the king's personal advisor (cf. Nehemiah's position, Neh. 1:11). If so, this would explain why it is this person who makes the representation and not the Tartan.

the watercourse of the upper pool, as mentioned above, is the place where Isaiah met Ahaz surveying his defenses. Now the representatives of the Assyrian horde which Isaiah foretold stand on the same spot. Because the one place where a large military force could assemble would be at the northwest corner of the city, there is some reason to think the washers' field was located there. However, the upper pool was apparently associated with the Gihon system at the south edge of the city (see above on 7:3). At any rate, given the preciousness of water in any siege, the decision of the Assyrians to make their threat at that point may have had a symbolic purpose as well.

3 Whether or not there were three Assyrian officers, three Judean officers were sent out to meet the enemy. None of these was a military man; they all came from the civilian side of the royal cabinet. It is interesting to note that this verse confirms one part of Isaiah's prophecy concerning Shebna and Eliakim (22:20–23), for Eliakim is now the prime minister, while Shebna has been demoted to the lower position of secretary. The third official, Joah, seems to have had the position of intermediary between king and people.[11]

If the order of the account in Kings is chronological, the appearance of the Assyrians outside the gates of Jerusalem must have been a rude shock. Hezekiah had thought he had bought the Assyrians off with tribute, but there they stood, with all the calm arrogance of those who have absolute power on their side. They *make* right; they are not subservient to it. Or so it seems. If ever Isaiah's preaching about the folly of human arrogance was faced with a direct challenge, this was it.

Estimates of the historical authenticity of the speech in vv. 4–20 vary widely. Some see it as a masterpiece of reporting, successfully capturing the atmosphere as well as the content of the event.[12] Others see it as a piece of historical fiction in which the writer has combined a number of contradictory ideas without concern for coherence or flow.[13] In fact, especially in an oral presentation, coherence of thought is not as important as impact. So the speaker drives home point after point, all the time betraying an intimate awareness of his hearers' situation and their likely responses. For every possible defense the people might raise he has a ready answer, making it apparent that his purpose is not rational argumentation but demoralization. This is supported by his insistence on speaking in the language of the common people. Thus, if this is fiction the writer has gone to great trouble to give it an air of authenticity, a practice for which there is no evidence in ancient literature.

11. Cf. T. N. D. Mettinger, *Solomonic State Officials*, ConBOT 5 (Lund: Gleerup, 1971), for a full treatment of the probable origins and functions of the three offices.
12. See Scott, Smith, Mauchline, also Eichrodt, but having been developed by redaction.
13. See Kaiser, Skinner, also Clements, but based on authentic sources.

The Rabshaqeh makes four points, not all of them complementary. First, he questions, in a way very similar to Isaiah's, what help Egypt can give (vv. 4–6, 8–9). This must have hit home especially hard after the Egyptian defeat at Eltekeh. Second, he argues that the Lord will not support Hezekiah, but has in fact called Assyria to attack Hezekiah because he has destroyed the altars and high places (vv. 7, 10). While this is almost ludicrous from a biblical perspective, it is completely logical coming from a convinced idolater and polytheist.

The Judean leaders, aware of the devastating impact of these remarks upon the listening populace, ask the Rabshaqeh to use the diplomatic language (v. 11), but he, sensing his advantage, refuses to do so and presses home his third and fourth points. Abandoning all pretense of subtle reasoning, he unveils the ultimate argument: brute force. In fact, God could not save Jerusalem if he wanted to. Assyria has conquered the domains of all the other gods and she will take this one too. But if the people will force surrender upon the recalcitrant Hezekiah, then the beneficent emperor will provide them with all the blessings their king and God cannot provide (cf. 8:21–22).

As noted above, this speech directly challenges all that Isaiah had said. God is *not* the sovereign; righteousness will *not* prevail; it is the nations of man with whom all must come to terms. As is made clear in ch. 37, both Hezekiah and Isaiah sensed the theological crisis which these taunts posed. If the Assyrian challenge was to stand unopposed, then all which had been said by the prophet and believed by many in Judah would be graphically shown to be worthless.[14] Thus in the fullest sense, as Smith points out, this is a war of words, between the word of the Assyrian monarch and the word of God (cf. v. 5). Which will prevail?

4 Without any diplomatic niceties, the Rabshaqeh moves directly to the attack. He bluntly bypasses the Judean emissaries and addresses himself to Hezekiah, whom he pointedly refuses to call king. Clearly, this is not a request but an ultimatum.

The reason for the refusal to give the title to Hezekiah is evidently that Hezekiah's kingship pales to nothing beside the splendor of *the great king, king of Assyria* (an abbreviated form of the classic Assyrian terminology, which lends authenticity to the narrative).[15] How could a "nobody" dare to stand up to one who contained in himself the splendor of all earthly

---

14. In fact, those who deny the historical veracity of the destruction of Sennacherib's army are forced to deny the authenticity of this speech as well. For if this speech was made, yet Sennacherib departed unscathed, Isaiah would have been unmasked as a false prophet who did not know what he was talking about.

15. *šar rabba*, "great king," is the favorite title by which the Assyrian kings introduced themselves in their royal annals.

authority? This incredulity is contained in the blunt opening question. Surely it would take some overwhelmingly secure confidence to enable a hill-country chieftain to rebel against Assyria! What is this confidence?

5 The Rabshaqeh's response is evident: mere words will not suffice when it comes to war, but that is really all you have. You have risked the wrath of Assyria with no support at all.

However, the precise meaning of the first sentence in the verse is not clear. The initial problem is with the first word, whether it is "I say" with the MT of Isaiah or "You say" with 1QIs[a] and the parallel in 2 Kings. Either makes sense and either could have arisen from the other by unintentional error.[16] The evidence of Qumran tips the scales slightly in favor of the 2 Kings form. Thus the Assyrian seems to say that whatever reasons Hezekiah gives, they are mere words. Representative alternatives are given by Cheyne: "Is a mere word counsel and strength for war?"; Delitzsch: "Your counsel and strength for war is empty talk"; Kissane: "the word of the lips (refusal of allegiance) is not strength and counsel for war." In any case, the Assyrian proceeds from this point to show why he believes that any argument which might be given to justify rebellion against Assyria is merely so much air.[17] His argument proceeds in a back-and-forth manner. In vv. 6 and 7 he presents the weakness of trusting either Egypt or the Lord, then in vv. 8 and 9 he returns to each in turn and expands on his previous points.

6 His first attack is against Egypt. Using words which are not so dissimilar from Isaiah's (19:14–16; 30:7; 31:3), he says that Egypt is a cracked staff which not only cannot help the one who leans upon it but presents a positive danger.[18] So it had been for the king of Ashdod, whom the Egyptians had handed over to the Assyrian (ch. 20). As their forefathers had once trusted Assyria, their worst enemy, to defeat Syria and Ephraim, so this generation trusted in Egypt, which had neither strength nor Judah's best interests at heart. Sometimes it is only our enemies who see the true folly of our behavior. As Calvin appropriately remarks, a people who will not receive the well-intentioned instruction of an Isaiah

---

16. 'āmartî (final y as vowel letter), "I say," versus 'āmartā (no final vowel letter), "you say." Thus in a consonantal text, the only difference in the forms would be the presence or absence of the final y.

17. The use of the term "rebel" reflects the fact that a covenant was in existence between Judah and Assyria. It is probable that this covenant was entered into at Damascus by Ahaz, as reported in 2 K. 16:10. The reference to the new altar in 2 K. 16:10–12 may well be an indication of the fact that a vassal had to recognize his overlord's gods. Cf. D. R. Hillers, *Covenant: the History of a Biblical Idea* (Baltimore: Johns Hopkins, 1969), pp. 43–45.

18. Cf. Ezek. 29:6, 7 for the same figure.

are forced to listen to the same instructions from the boastful lips of their enemies.

7 Before proceeding further with his attack on trust in Egypt, the Rabshaqeh apparently feels it necessary to demolish the hope of another group of hearers who might dismiss his remarks about Egypt by saying that they trust the Lord. To them his response shows the care with which the Assyrian foreign office kept track of events in vassal countries. Hezekiah's religious reforms would be a matter of no small import to the Assyrians. The gathering of all the priestly power into the royal city could only strengthen the hand of the rebellious Hezekiah. Furthermore, the exaltation of Yahweh would also involve a repudiation of the Assyrian pantheon who had witnessed the covenant between Judah and Assyria. Nonetheless, the destruction of the worship centers outside Jerusalem must have seemed like a colossal blunder to the idolatrous and polytheistic Assyrians. For them, the more places at which some form of the god was worshiped, the more manipulative power the ritual had. To limit the worship to one place could only lessen its power and infuriate the god. It is likely that the Assyrians also knew that substantial numbers of Israelites felt the same way (Hos. 2:5–10). Thus the Assyrian officer's confident assertion that God did not want to bless Judah probably touched the raw nerve of doubt which was already very near the surface of many a Judean consciousness (Jer. 44:18).

8, 9 Having put any alternate position in doubt, the challenger now returns to the Egyptian question. Here he laces his comments with irony born of absolute confidence. Little Judah had never had the wealth or the manpower to assemble a significant core of chariotry. Even less so could it mount the newest military innovation—cavalry.[19] The Assyrian knows this, and offers, tongue in cheek, to meet the Judeans halfway. The Assyrians are so powerful, they can afford to give Judah two thousand horses and still they will conquer the little Palestinian country. Judah could not even put trained riders on their own horses, so what good is it to ask for Egyptian help? The fact is, with or without Egypt's aid, Judah is not strong enough to defy the lowest of Sennacherib's underlings, let alone the great king himself.

10 But it is not merely Assyria's strength which will destroy Judah; it is her own God's will. It is not particularly surprising that the Rabshaqeh should say this. Other evidence from the ancient Near East shows that it was not unusual for a conqueror to claim that his conquest

19. Cf. Y. Yadin, *The Art of Warfare in Biblical Lands* (New York: McGraw-Hill, 1964), II:297–301.

was made possible because the god of the vanquished had joined the side of the conqueror.[20] But it is an open question whether the Assyrian office of propaganda was quite prepared for the impact which this rather perfunctory claim (see below on vv. 18–20) would have on the Judeans. We do not know whether the Assyrians were aware of Isaiah's claim that God would use the Assyrians to punish his people (8:7–8; 10:5–6). At any rate the Hebrews were aware, and the Rabshakeh's echoing of the prophet's words must have seemed to sound the last knell of doom.

It appears that the Rabshaqeh's final claim that the Assyrians were acting at God's command (v. 10) was so unsettling to the envoys that they requested the Assyrian officer to continue the parley in the diplomatic language of the day, Aramaic. But the Assyrian had not come to negotiate; he had come to destroy Jerusalem's will to resist. So with an instinct for the kill, he turned his appeal directly to the common people, who had no doubt ranged themselves on the walls to see the spectacle. His aim was to drive a wedge between them and Hezekiah, hoping that they would force surrender upon their stubborn king. However, one cannot help but wonder whether he committed a tactical error in the way he framed his appeal. Instead of continuing on in the vein which had so frightened the Judean envoys, namely, that God himself was responsible for the Assyrian attack, he abandoned that ploy and said, in an excess of confidence, what he really believed. That was that Assyria would defeat Judah because all the gods, of which Yahweh was but one more, were helpless before Assyria's might. Here is the ultimate blasphemy: God, whoever or whatever you are—*if* you are—human might and human glory will dictate to you the limits of your action or being. It is interesting to note that no mention of Assyria's gods is made. One cannot help but feel that this man, who might on another occasion give pious thanks to his god, has here, in the flush of his sense of utter domination of the helpless Jews, spoken his true faith. Perhaps this was a little too much even for those Jews who were tempted to feel that Hezekiah was somewhat too radical in his monotheism and his iconoclasm. At any rate, the evidence is that this *tour de force* failed to convince any substantial numbers of the people that surrender was their best hope.

What the Rabshaqeh did in his speech was to reveal the essential nature of the issue which is always before the human race: shall we commit ourselves to God or to human might and glory? Furthermore, he threw down the gauntlet to God: if God was to be known as God he would have

20. See *ANET,* pp. 277, 278, 283, 286, 289, 290, 291, 293, 301, 312–15, 462.

to reveal himself in events.[21] Sooner or later, all the silver-tongued, kid-gloved temptations to trust ourselves *along with God* or *in addition to God* will be revealed in all their ugly arrogance: there *is* no God but humanity. But that arrogant declamation becomes God's opportunity to demonstrate that he *is*! Unfortunately, it is usually only in our extremities that we give God this opportunity.

11, 12 *Aramaic* was the language of Syria that became the lingua franca under the Assyrians. It is not known why the Assyrians chose this language; it may be because Syria stood between Assyria and her western dominions and was thus intelligible to both sides.[22] But perhaps of more importance, Aramaic was alphabetic and thus easier to read and write than the syllabic cuneiform. Yet, it was still a Semitic language, like Assyrian and the West Semitic dialects of Palestine.

the Judean language refers to the Hebrew language as spoken in Judea.[23] This incident gives some indication of the thoroughness of the Assyrians. Although Judean was just one of the dialects of the region, at least one high officer was trained in that dialect should the need arise. Here the opportunity had presented itself and the Rabshaqeh was not about to stop using the language tool which he had at his disposal.

He denies that he has come on a merely diplomatic mission and asserts that his words have as much relevance to the common people as to the leaders, for all alike will experience the horrors of a siege. He says that his words are not merely "to" (*'el*) the leaders, but "upon, concerning" (*'al*) the people on the wall.

in that they will eat . . . and drink is a way of rendering simple infinitives, "to eat" and "to drink." Most commentators agree with Skinner, who understands them as infinitives of effect or result, the effect being understood to come to pass if they continue to sit on the wall and follow Hezekiah.

21. It is hard to understand how those who can assert that the theological function of this passage is to claim that God acts in history can then assert with equal force that God did not act in this event (cf. Clements). If they do so to demonstrate that biblical theology is self-discredited, that is one thing. But to speak of the worth of the theology while denying its evidence is very odd indeed.

22. Note that the Assyrian language appeared barbarous to the Hebrews, although it was as Semitic as Hebrew (28:11; 33:19).

23. Duhm considers that *yᵉhûḏît*, "Judean," is a postexilic term, but, as Kissane points out, it is not impossible that, Israel having fallen twenty years earlier, the language was beginning to be called Judean. Perhaps even more to the point, it may be that the envoys, talking to a foreigner, were simply using a functional designation, i.e., do not speak the language of this land, namely, Judah (cf. Neh. 13:24).

dung . . . urine are given more euphemistic readings by the Qere in each case, but there is every reason to believe that the Assyrian officer would have used the crudest, most shocking terms he knew in an attempt to brutalize and terrorize to a maximum extent.

13–17 The Rabshaqeh contrasts Hezekiah and Sennacherib. According to him, Hezekiah cannot prevent them from being destroyed if they resist, whereas submission to Sennacherib will result in plenty for all.

13, 14 The contrast is sharply delineated by the giving of the conventional titles (v. 4) to Sennacherib, while no title at all is given to Hezekiah. In other words, how dare this nobody range himself against *The King*? And how could anybody commit himself to this nobody and his god? For those who persisted in believing, faith was never more audacious than at that moment! But then, it is always audacious, or it is not faith.

15 *do not let Hezekiah cause you to trust in the Lord* is a critical statement, for it sums up what this entire section (chs. 7–39) is about. The question has been explored in scores of ways: Can God be trusted? Is he strong enough? Is he good enough? Is he faithful enough? If not him, then who or what should be trusted? The nations, humanity—what? The answer has come back in scores of ways: God *can* be trusted. Nothing else can be, but he can. The irony of this statement is that Sennacherib claims to be more trustworthy than God! God will let them down, but if they will but trust the Assyrian king and open their gates to him, all will be well (vv. 16–17). Now Isaiah's teaching would be put to the test.[24] The people were completely deprived of any hope but God. If there was any lingering doubt as to his lordship, this was the time to throw Hezekiah to the Assyrian wolves and make the best of a bad deal. Fortunately for us all, that was not the case. Apparently something of those oracles and sermons had struck more than one responsive chord, and the people elected to believe the word of God rather than that of the Assyrian.

16–17 The king of Assyria promises to let the people penned up

24. It is asserted by Clements and others that the belief in the "inviolability" of Jerusalem here is on the same order as that under Jeremiah a little more than a century later. In other words, it was a magical belief that God could not possibly desert his city, despite the warnings of Isaiah and others. However, there are no promises of deliverance in the book of Jeremiah, whereas there are such promises throughout Isaiah (10:12–34; 14:24–27; 31:8–9; 33:17–22). Furthermore, the call is not, as it is in Jeremiah, to repent or face destruction. Rather Isaiah's call is for Judah to stop trusting in falsity *for* deliverance, but to trust the Lord. Isaiah does not excoriate them for believing God will deliver them without repentance (as does Jeremiah), but for trying to find some other means of deliverance than God.

inside the city return to their own property for awhile before he deports them to an equally good land. A siege, as implied in v. 12, was a terrible experience. Thousands of people from outlying regions would have crowded into the rather small area contained within the city wall. Unless very careful plans had been laid and a great deal of money had been spent in advance (cf. 22:8–11), life swiftly became intolerable within the crowded confines. Starvation, disease, and violence would soon do their terrible work, and all the while the enemy would be pounding away at the walls outside. To people in those circumstances, the Assyrian offer to let people go back to their homes, to peace, privacy, and plenty, must have been like holding a cup of water before a man dying of thirst. Perhaps it was only a skepticism about Assyria's trustworthiness that saved Hezekiah from his people at that moment.[25]

Make a blessing is evidently an idiom for submission. Since covenant making ended with the pronouncement of blessings and curses for those who kept or broke the covenant, Young has suggested that the idiom refers to the making of a covenant. This is very plausible. More simply, it may refer to an act of obeisance as expressed in the command "Bless the Lord" (cf. Ps. 103:1, 2, 20, 21, 22).

17 *until I come* refers to the normal Assyrian policy of deporting the more influential people of a conquered territory to some distant place where their influence would be diluted and their patriotism nullified. In their place people believed to be docile would be brought in. Since this practice was well known, the Rabshaqeh apparently decided not to ignore it, but to try to put the best face on it and make it an asset. One cannot help but be impressed by such brassy confidence, all the while knowing that they who have the truth do not need brass.

18–20 In the contrast between Hezekiah and Sennacherib, appearing in vv. 13–17, a question is raised. Why can Hezekiah and his God not be trusted to deliver Judah from Assyria's hand? The answer is now given and the Rabshaqeh's true position is revealed. The Lord cannot deliver because he is not able to do so. He is merely one more of the gods whose dominions the Assyrians have so easily wrested from them. Therefore, since he is weaker than Assyria, it is foolish to trust him. This is one of the liabilities of merely human success: it leads one to challenge God. This is why Paul calls such gain loss (Phil. 3:7). The Assyrian

---

25. Probably the Judeans had heard enough about Assyrian treatment of other surrendered cities to turn a somewhat jaundiced eye upon these flowery promises.

accuses Hezekiah of seducing the people (v. 18); in fact, it is the Assyrian who has been seduced by his own power.

18 *[Beware,] lest Hezekiah seduce you* is elliptical in Hebrew, lacking the "beware," which must be added to bring out the sense in English.

19 *Hamath* was a major Syrian city located on the Orontes River about one hundred fifty miles north of Damascus and two hundred seventy-five miles northeast of Jerusalem. It is mentioned several times in the Bible, first in the Table of Nations (Gen. 10:18). It had been conquered by the Assyrians several times, but most recently by Sargon II, who had devastated it for rebellion.[26] *Arpad,* another of the Syrian or Aramean city-states, was situated about eighty-five miles north of Hamath, about midway between the Mediterranean and the Euphrates.[27] The site of *Sepharvaim* is presently unknown. The older suggestion that it referred to Sippar in southern Mesopotamia seems unlikely, in that its fall would have little significance for the Judeans. Some scholars believe it to have been located between Hamath and Damascus.[28] On the basis of 2 K. 17:24, 31, Aharoni takes it to be not a city but the region in which Hamath was located.[29] In any case, the point is clear. If the gods of these great places could not save their cities, how could the Lord save Jerusalem and Judah?

that they delivered Samaria is troublesome in that it seems to lack an appropriate antecedent. So in fact *BHS* proposes to insert "Where are the gods of the land of Samaria?" and cites 2 K. 18:34. But that passage is identical to this one on this point. Thus if textual corruption is at work here it is very ancient.[30] The following verse suggests that the sense is, "Which gods were able to save their own cities and thus save Samaria?" In any case it is interesting to note that the Assyrian Foreign Office apparently did not perceive Samaria to have worshiped the same God as Jerusalem did. Otherwise, it is impossible to imagine that the Rabshaqeh would have missed an opportunity to point out that the Lord had not been able to save Samaria, so why Jerusalem? The people of Northern Israel

26. *ARAB,* II:55; *ANET,* p. 285. Olmstead takes this to have happened early in Sargon's reign (*History of Assyria,* p. 207).

27. It is tempting to wonder if the original reference was to Arvad, not Arpad (so *ANET,* while *ARAB* reads Arpad). Arvad was located on the coast of the Mediterranean about fifty miles west-southwest of Hamath. It seems to have been a natural ally of Hamath, more so than Arpad.

28. Kissane, Skinner, etc. But this is based on an equation with Sibraim (Ezek. 47:16), which is possible but unproven.

29. *Macmillan Bible Atlas,* rev. ed. (New York: Macmillan, 1977), map 150.

30. Both LXX and Targ. seem to reflect MT, simply smoothing the reading to "were they able to deliver . . ." and "have they delivered . . ." respectively.

may have told themselves they were worshiping the Lord, but their neighbors knew better. So do our neighbors know what our true religion is.

20 As mentioned above, the whole speech comes to its point in this verse. Whatever the previous subtleties of argumentation, all the wraps are off here. Why should they surrender? Very simply, because Sennacherib is stronger than God. There is neither help nor hope for them in their faith. It is rare that the challenge is put to us so bluntly, but it comes to us in one form or another daily. We are tempted to think that God either cannot or will not help us and that we must either rely on, or at least bow to, human strength. Whom shall we trust? God or Man?

But Sennacherib made one fundamental mistake. The Lord is not one more of the earth's gods. He is not even the greatest of the earth's gods. He is *other* than this world, including its gods.[31] If he *is* one of the gods, if the biblical religion *is* just one more religion, Sennacherib's logic is irrefutable. But if the biblical claims are correct, then what Sennacherib may have done to other gods is totally irrelevant. He is here faced with a Being of a completely different order than any he has faced before. Against this One, his pride and his boasting are insupportable. Whether Jerusalem is to be delivered has nothing to do with Sennacherib's power. It has only to do with Jerusalem and whether she will cast herself upon her God in trust.

(2) Response to the challenge (36:21–37:7)

21 *They kept silent and did not answer him a word, for the commandment of the king had been, "Do not answer him."*

22 *So Eliakim, son of Hilkiah, who was over the house, went, along with Shebna the scribe and Joah, son of Asaph, the recorder, to Hezekiah with their garments torn. And they reported to him the words of the Rabshaqeh.*

37:1 *It came to pass when King Hezekiah heard, that he tore his garments, put on sackcloth, and went to the house of the Lord.*

2 *He sent Eliakim who was over the house and Shebna the scribe and the elders of the priests, clothed in sackcloth, to Isaiah, son of Amoz, the prophet.*

3 *They said to him, "Thus says Hezekiah, 'Today is a day of distress, of reproach and contempt. For children have come to the opening*[1] *of the womb, but there is no strength to deliver.*

---

31. See Deut. 32:37–39; 1 Chr. 16:26; Ps. 86:8; 96:5; 97:9; Isa. 2:8–11; 17:7–8; 40:18–26; 41:4; 42:8; 43:11–13; 44:6–8; Zeph. 2:11.

1. *mašbēr*, "place of parting" (Delitzsch "matrix"), thus "opening of the womb."

4 *Perhaps the Lord your God will hear the words of the Rabshaqeh whom the king of Assyria, his lord, sent to reproach the living God, and will rebuke him for the words which the Lord your God has heard. Now lift up a prayer on behalf of the remnant to be found [here].' "*

5 *So the servants of King Hezekiah came to Isaiah.*

6 *Isaiah said to them, "Thus you shall say to your lord, 'Thus says the Lord, "Do not be afraid of the words which you have heard, with which the lackeys of the king of Assyria have blasphemed me.*

7 *Behold, I am about to put a spirit in him, and he will hear a rumor and return to his land. And I will make him fall by the sword in his own land." ' "*

These nine verses describe a critical moment in Judah's history. What will she do at this time, stripped of all allies, face-to-face with the crushing realities of which the Rabshaqeh has spoken? Shall she admit his irrefutable logic and confess that God is simply one more national god, helpless before the Assyrian might? Or will she in fact be driven deeper into the Lord's embrace? Will she now admit the folly of her other trusts and, for the first time in a very long time, commit herself to God alone? Had she gone the first way, all succeeding human history would have been very much different. For Judah's unconquerable faith that God was unique was the necessary ground for the coming of Christ.

In fact, this challenge was what turned the tide. Somehow Judah lurched awake, realizing what Isaiah had been crying so long: Nothing else can be trusted, but God can!

Perhaps it was because Hezekiah had guessed in advance what kinds of demands the Assyrian would make that he had told his envoys to give no answer. Indeed, none would have been possible. They could only retire to their king in shock and dismay, unfolding for him the grim picture. It is here that the greatness of Hezekiah comes to the fore. He sees what is called for and does it. Repentance is the order of the day. Nor does he call the priests to him. Rather, it is he who must go to the Lord's house, to admit his and his nation's folly in their foolish dependence upon Egypt. But it is not only prayer which touches the heart in the hour of crisis. There must also be a word from God. So it is almost diffidently that the King has his envoys request Isaiah to intercede. No one involved could have been unaware of the irony in this situation. They had repudiated Isaiah for his hard words (30:8–11); would he now repudiate them, and leave them to wallow in the consequences of their own blindness?

But Isaiah would not repudiate them. To be sure, he did not intercede for them, but only because he had already heard a word from God.

The slur upon the divine name had been heard indeed, and Hezekiah need not fear. God would attend to the honor of his name. And in the process, trusting Judah would be delivered.

21–22 Even had Hezekiah not commanded silence, it is difficult to see what reply could have been given to the Assyrian officer. He had bluntly blasphemed God and had told them to capitulate or die. There is hardly any room for negotiation there. Furthermore, blasphemy of that order is by no means going to be corrected by words. Standing, as he was, with a long string of Assyrian victories at his back, a statement of Yahweh's incomparability, no matter how carefully worded, could scarcely be calculated to carry much weight with him. The envoys could only tear their robes in horror and anguish and turn away.[2] Calvin's comment is apropos: contending for truth can sometimes produce a strife which obscures the truth.

1 Hezekiah not only tears his garments at the dreadful report, but he also puts on *sackcloth,* the biblical sign of mourning but also of repentance and humiliation.[3] It is not clear how directly Hezekiah was implicated in the dependence upon Egypt (he is not named in any of the denunciations; cf. 28:14; 30:1; 31:1; 33:10, 11), but he could not have escaped some of the responsibility. In any case, he does not here evade the issue. He is the king; if the nation is under judgment from God, then it is he who must be the first to repent of his own sin. Furthermore, he knows that repentance which saves face by hiding away from public view is not worth the name. The repentance seen here is not concerned about human opinion but about divine opinion. We may be sure that when we cease to blame our troubles upon someone else and when we no longer care who knows our condition, help is not far away.

2 *Eliakim . . . Shebna . . . and the elders of the priests* were designated by Hezekiah to enlist Isaiah's help. This would have been the most influential delegation he could have mustered for this purpose. Eliakim and Shebna were the highest government officials, while the elders of the priests would have been the most senior religious leaders, whatever their chronological ages. As the Syrian king had realized about Elisha some 135 years earlier (2 K. 6:12), the prophet of the Lord was the most potent weapon an Israelite king could have.

The rank of the persons in the delegation and the fact that Hezekiah

---

2. For torn garments at supposed blasphemy, see Matt. 26:65, where Caiaphas reacts to Jesus.

3. Cf. 1 K. 20:31, 32; 21:27; Neh. 9:1; Dan. 9:3; Joel 1:13; Jon. 3:6; Matt. 11:21.

did not call Isaiah to come to him combine to suggest some concern on the king's part that the prophet might need to be handled with extreme care if he was not to refuse to help.[4] Hezekiah failed to realize that as a man under appointment, the prophet would respond at God's command and not for any other reason.

All the delegation were in sackcloth by this time. One wonders if Isaiah's and Shebna's eyes met for a moment as both remembered the time when Isaiah had denounced the then prime minister and prophesied his humiliation (22:15–19). So also Eliakim may have remembered Isaiah's words about too much weight being hung on a new peg (22:23–25). At any rate, the king's example had touched the entire government establishment at last. God was their only hope. Why had they not realized it sooner?

3–5 The opening words of Hezekiah's message to Isaiah are an abject admission of failure. Not only have his government's policies brought Judah into Assyria's contempt, as she lies helpless before the conqueror, they have also brought the country under reproach from God. All the foolishness of their attempts to strengthen themselves by cultivating outside help is now revealed for what Isaiah had always said it was—foolishness. Even more seriously, God himself has been brought into contempt. This is a principle of life: the believer who lives a slipshod life, refusing to trust God in any deep way, will bring reproach upon God in the eyes of the watching world. They will associate that believer's defeats with inability on God's part. So, many years after these events the Babylonians were to say of exiled Judah that their God could not deliver them (Ezek. 36:19). Of course this was not the case, but the watchers never make a distinction.

The metaphor of labor is a telling one. All too familiar to them was the breech birth, or some other complication, which caused the mother to be unable to deliver the child although she labored herself to exhaustion and death. Furthermore, once labor began there was no turning back; either the child was delivered or both mother and child died. Hezekiah sees himself in that predicament. Jerusalem *must* be delivered, but neither he nor his government nor his people has the strength to do it.[5]

This kind of admission of helplessness is frequently a necessity before divine help can be received. So long as we believe that we only need some assistance, we are still treating ourselves as lords of the situation, and that latent pride cuts us off from all that God would give us.

---

4. For similar deference of kings to prophets, cf. 2 K. 22:14; Jer. 37:3, but not so in 1 K. 22:9.

5. Note the emphatic position of "strength." It is strength which is lacking.

Only when we have admitted our complete bankruptcy are we able to receive what he has for us. This is what Hezekiah did.

4 It is this complete self-abnegation which explains the diffidence of Hezekiah's request. He realizes that he is in no position to demand anything from God. This is so both by reason of God's sovereignty and because of Hezekiah's creaturehood, but also because Hezekiah has not led the nation to trust God as he should have prior to this time. None of this is to deny the biblical witness that Hezekiah was a good king. Probably it was his tender heart which led him to this kind of repentance. (It is hard to see Ahaz doing anything like this.) But it is to say that even good men can be short-sighted.

Perhaps . . . God will hear. The issue here is not awareness but action. As the latter part of the verse indicates, the king has no doubt that God "heard" the Assyrian's blasphemous words. The issue is whether God will choose to take action against Assyria for this particular affront; will the Judge "hear" the case? Hezekiah prays that he will.

It is of great significance that both here and in the next incident Hezekiah's greatest concern is the honor of God. This is surely a testimony to the essential greatness of Hezekiah's heart. He is not first concerned with his or his nation's survival. He is chiefly concerned that their actions have provided the vehicle whereby God's name has been brought into contempt. Furthermore, he knows that if God's glory is made paramount, then the nation will survive. It was the putting of survival first which had brought them to this perilous state.

the living God (see also 37:17) is a phrase which expresses the Hebrew understanding of the difference between their God and the gods of their neighbors. Those gods were lifeless and helpless (46:5–7), but the Lord was *alive,* now and evermore. The thought that a follower of one of those could get away with defaming *God* was almost more than a devout Hebrew could stomach. (Note David's response to Goliath's taunts in 1 Sam. 17:26, 36.)[6]

your God is a source of some uncertainty to commentators. Some believe that it is only a witness to Isaiah's special calling as prophet (Calvin), but others (e.g., Delitzsch) believe it demonstrates a certain reticence on Hezekiah's part (cf. also Saul in 1 Sam. 15:30). The latter seems somewhat more likely. The king is aware that, from one perspective at least, had God been truly his, as he claimed, he would have been more careful of God's

6. Cf. also Deut. 5:26; Josh. 3:10; Ps. 42:3 (Eng. 2); 84:3 (Eng. 2); Jer. 5:2; 10:10; 23:36; Dan. 6:26; Matt. 16:16; 26:63.

honor. So here in shame he testifies that if God is to help them it will not be because he, the king, has some special claim upon God.

the remnant to be found probably refers to the inhabitants of Jerusalem, all that were left from Judea since the Assyrians had captured all the outlying garrisons and villages (36:1). (This is the reason for the insertion of *[here]* in the translation.) Since the word for "remnant" used here is different from that used in ch. 7, it is unlikely that any specific allusion to that prophecy was intended. Nevertheless, Isaiah's words had already begun to become true. Those who trusted in human strength were doomed to become but a shadow of themselves.

6–7 Isaiah manifests no hint of any satisfaction that his predictions have come true or that the leaders of Judah have had to admit their folly by coming meekly to him. On the other hand, he makes no great promises for Judah's recovery or deliverance. He first of all speaks a word to the king. It is the same word he had given to Ahaz: "Do not be afraid." In other words, the magnitude of the human threat is really not the issue. Whether it be the neighboring countries or the emperor of the world, God is greater, and that being so, we do not need to live in fear. So, although Hezekiah was concerned as to whether God would "hear" the blasphemy, God was concerned that Hezekiah had heard it and become frightened.

God's contempt for the Assyrian blasphemy is seen in the uses of "lads" or *lackeys* for the Rabshaqeh and the other officers. Human beings might be awed by their power and authority, but God was not particularly impressed. They were just errand boys for an overblown ego.

7 *I am about to put a spirit in him* reflects God's complete control of the situation. He is not troubled by Sennacherib, so that he must take hasty, world-shaking action. Things as ephemeral as a vague uneasiness or a distant rumor are all that is necessary to remove the emperor from before Jerusalem. For God, access to the psyche of humanity or the interrelationships of society is as nothing. The "spirit" mentioned here is neither the Holy Spirit nor an angelic spirit, but rather an attitude, disposition, or feeling.[7] God is going to predispose Sennacherib to leave.

There is, of course, no mention here of the coming destruction of the Assyrian army as reported in 37:36–37. This lack is taken by some commentators as evidence that the account in 37:36–37 is legendary. However, the account here is held by the same scholars to be legendary as well, so not much is proven by that argument. That one "legend" does not know of another is hardly conclusive as to the nature of either. Equally

7. For similar uses of "spirit" see 19:14; Num. 5:14; Hos. 4:12; Zech. 13:2; 2 Tim. 1:7.

647

likely, no mention was made of that event because the central issue here is not the deliverance of Jerusalem but what will become of Sennacherib for his blasphemy. For that reason divine control of Sennacherib's dispositions and his eventual death by treason were more significant.

b. THE KING'S CHALLENGE (37:8–35)

(1) The royal letter (37:8–13)

8 *Now the Rabshaqeh returned and found that the king of Assyria was fighting against Libnah, for he had heard that he had left Lachish.*

9 *Now he had heard concerning Tirhaqah, king of Ethiopia, saying, "He has gone forth to fight with you." He heard[1] and sent messengers to Hezekiah, saying,*

10 *"Thus you shall say to Hezekiah, king of Judah, saying, 'Do not let your god, in whom you trust, deceive you, saying, "Jerusalem will not be given into the hand of the king of Assyria."'*

11 *Behold, you have heard what the kings of Assyria did to all the lands to destroy[2] them—and will you be saved?*

12 *Did the gods of the nations which my fathers destroyed deliver Gozan and Haran, Rezeph and the people of Eden[3] who were in Telassar?*

13 *Where is the king of Hamath and the king of Arpad and the king of the city of Sepharvaim, Henah, and Ivvah?"*

Many commentators consider 37:8–35 (exclusive of vv. 8–9) to be a different account of the same original event as described in ch. 36. They base this conclusion upon two major arguments. First, it is said that the letter makes the same points as the Rabshaqeh did; and second, it is argued that if a personal embassy had failed it is hardly likely that Sennacherib would expect a letter to succeed. Neither of these is compelling. In the first place, if these are the best arguments the Assyrians can muster, there is no reason not to repeat them. Furthermore, there is a difference in the two presentations that will be noted below. Second, if Sennacherib was

---

1. 2 K. 19:9 has "he *turned* [*wyšb*] and sent messengers" (he sent messengers again?) instead of Isaiah's "he *heard* [*wyšmʿ*] and sent messengers." LXX and 1QIsᵃ have what appears to be a conflation: "He heard and turned and sent. . . ." Most modern commentators see the Kings reading as original, but no convincing evidence favors either reading.

2. "Destroy" is *ḥrm*, the technical term for devoting something to a deity by absolute destruction. It is usually associated with the Holy War concept (Josh. 6:18, etc.). Sennacherib may be asserting that the destruction which Assyria wrought upon her enemies was an act of devotion to their gods, or the term may have become watered down by this time to refer to destruction in general.

3. Eden does not refer to the Garden of Gen. 2 and 3 (Ezek. 28:13), but to the region of Bit-Adini on the Euphrates.

being faced with a threat from Egypt, as the text reports, then he needed the Rabshaqeh with him. However, he did not want Hezekiah to believe that he had had a reprieve; thus the letter comes to remind Hezekiah of the Rabshaqeh's words and to inform him that the present relief is only temporary. Beyond this evidence, there is most clearly a difference in the response of the prophet in the two accounts. As noted above in the general introduction, the response in 37:6–7 is a rather low-keyed statement that the Lord will act upon Sennacherib's blasphemy. But the response here is much more a full-blown oracle of deliverance. This passage seems, in turn, to be a response to a fuller commitment on the part of Hezekiah.

8 The clause *the Rabshaqeh returned* does not indicate why he returned. Two possibilities present themselves. On the one hand, receiving no answer from the inhabitants of Jerusalem, he may have returned to consult with his master and to receive instructions for the next step. Or he may have been ordered to return by Sennacherib in an attempt to consolidate his forces in view of the impending battle with the Egyptians (v. 9).

Libnah has not yet been definitely located. Previously it had been identified with Tell es-Safi, about twelve and one-half miles north of Lachish, but more recently Tell el-Bornat, six miles north, has been suggested.[4] Why the Assyrian monarch had moved there from Lachish is not clear. Perhaps Lachish had fallen and the Assyrians were now "mopping up" the outlying dependencies. Or perhaps Sennacherib was pulling back to the north to put Jerusalem on his flank rather than directly in his rear when he met the Egyptians.

9 *Tirhaqah, king of Ethiopia,* has been a source of considerable controversy. It is now clear that he did not become king of Egypt before 689 B.C. This fact has been used both to support the two-attack theory and to discredit the historical veracity of the account.[5] However, the majority of modern commentators admit the possibility that Tirhaqah is here identified by a position which he held later in his life.[6] Whether the two armies actually met is not clear. Assyrian records only mention the battle of Eltekeh, and they place that battle before the siege of Jerusalem. Of

4. See Y. Aharoni, *The Land of the Bible,* tr. A. F. Rainey, rev. ed. (Philadelphia: Westminster, 1979), p. 219; G. A. Turner, *Historical Geography of the Holy Land* (Grand Rapids: Baker, 1973), p. 180.

5. For the former, see J. Bright, *A History of Israel,* 3rd rev. ed. (Philadelphia: Westminster, 1981), pp. 298–309. For the latter, see G. Reisner, "Discoveries in Ethiopia," *HTR* 13 (1920) 38–40.

6. See K. A. Kitchen, *The Third Intermediate Period in Egypt* (London: 1973), pp. 154–172, 387–393.

course, if the Assyrians had suffered a setback at the hands of Egypt at this point, they would probably not have mentioned it.

He heard and sent messengers suggests two possible motives for Sennacherib's action. First, he may have been trying to force Jerusalem's capitulation before he faced the rumored Egyptian attack so as not to have enemies both behind and before him. Second, he may have wished to prevent Hezekiah from receiving any encouragement from the reported action. It is as though he says to the beleaguered Judean, "Everything is just as it was. There is no hope for you."

10 Unlike the Rabshaqeh's attack, which was upon Hezekiah, this one is upon God himself. In the Rabshaqeh's attack it was Hezekiah who was deceiving the people. Now it is God who deceives Hezekiah. Kissane suggests plausibly that the shift may have been due to the report of God's promise through Isaiah (37:7). Here too, since the purpose is not to discredit Hezekiah in the eyes of the people but to discredit God in the eyes of Hezekiah, Hezekiah is given the courtesy of the title "king," which was denied him in the earlier challenge. What Sennacherib does not realize is that petty courtesies will mean nothing to a man whose God is called a liar when that man has devoted his life to advancing the cause of the One he considers to be the only true God.

11 As Young points out, *Behold* is an indication that the Assyrian considers the facts which he is about to recite as indisputably well known.

Because Sennacherib does not know of a God who is master of history and can thus do unique things, he insists that the historical precedent is irrefutable. Judah is one more nation like all the rest which the Assyrians have destroyed. How can she alone be saved? Apart from the living God, his argumentation is sound. But that *apart from* is not a minor error; it is the one of earthshaking significance which human pride has been making since the dawn of time (Ps. 14:1–7; Luke 12:20).

12 Here Sennacherib sharpens his argument to make it plain that he considers the Lord to be merely one more of the gods whose lands his predecessors[7] had devastated in northern Mesopotamia. All the cities mentioned here lay between the Tigris and Euphrates, with Gozan being the farthest east on the Habur (2 K. 17:6) and Telassar (which name several sites bore) perhaps being in the region of Carchemish.

13 In this verse Sennacherib shifts the attack back from the theological issue to the matter of Hezekiah's own self-interest. The Mesopotamian cities had fallen in earlier generations, but the Syrian cities mentioned

---

7. "Fathers" is not a genetic term here since Sennacherib's father, Sargon II, had founded a new dynasty. It refers generally to predecessors.

here had fallen more recently. Terrible things had befallen kings whom Hezekiah may have known personally. They too may have trusted oracles from their gods and they had been flayed alive, impaled, mutilated, and killed. Theology is fine for discussion, but the real issue for every one of us is: will you stake your life on your faith? Sennacherib was depending on Hezekiah's being unwilling to do that. But he was wrong. Will the Sennacheribs of this world be wrong in our cases too? Unfortunately for most of us, the question is never as clear-cut as that. Instead, in a host of little battles where the outcome does not seem important, we succumb to the temptation to opt for the flesh, for self-preservation. The results are as disastrous for us as they would have been for Hezekiah here.

(2) Response to the challenge (37:14–35)

(a) Hezekiah's prayer (37:14–20)

14 *Hezekiah took the letter from the hand of the messengers and read it, and he went up to the house of the Lord, and Hezekiah spread it before the Lord.*

15 *And Hezekiah prayed to the Lord, saying,*

16 *"Lord of Hosts, God of Israel, who sits over the cherubim, you are*[1] *God, you alone, of all the kingdoms of the earth. You have made the heavens and the earth.*

17 *Incline your ear, O Lord, and hear; open your eyes, O Lord, and see. Hear all the words of Sennacherib which he sent to reproach the living God.*

18 *To be sure, O Lord, the kings of Assyria laid waste all the lands and their land,*[2]

19 *and put their gods in the fire—for they are not gods, but rather the work of human hands, wood and stone—so they destroyed them.*

20 *Now, O Lord our God, deliver us from his hand, that all the kingdoms of the earth may know that you are the Lord, you alone."*

---

1. *'attâ-hû'*, "you are he," is called an emphatic resumptive phrase by Delitzsch ("you, even you, are God"). GKC, §§ 141g, h, recognizes a combined emphasizing and copulative function. Similar expressions appear in 43:25; 51:12; 2 Sam. 7:28; Neh. 9:6; Ps. 44:5 (Eng. 4); Jer. 49:12.

2. The MT has "all the lands and their land," *hā'ᵃrāṣôṭ wᵉ'eṭ-'arṣām*, an unlikely sounding statement. 2 K. 19:17 has "the nations and their land," which may be supported by Targ. *(mᵉdînātā'*, "provinces"; but the normal Targ. translation of *gôyîm*, "nations," is *'ammayyā)*. 1QIsᵃ has "nations" but does not include "their land," while LXX reads "the whole world." This diversity suggests that while the MT may not be original, neither is any of the others necessarily a better witness to the original. The possibility of using "land" both as "people" and "territory" is clear enough (cf. Gen. 6:11, 12).

One of the principles of human manipulation which has been stressed in recent years is the value of a relaxation of stress followed by an immediate restoration of that stress. Prisoners who have successfully rebuffed all efforts to break their resistance have often been broken when some of their freedoms were restored, and friendly overtures were made by the captors only to have the harshest pressures abruptly restored. The captive relaxed and could not then restore the resistance. The same thing may have been true for Hezekiah. He had no doubt received news of the Egyptian approach; he had watched the Rabshaqeh depart; his hopes were raised and he breathed a sigh of relief. What an awful shock it must have been to see the Assyrian embassy back again with even more arrogant words. If ever Hezekiah was tempted to surrender, it must have been then. But at this critical moment he dared to do what his father Ahaz was never able to do: he dared to believe that the kingdoms of this world are the kingdoms of our Lord and of his Messiah (Rev. 11:15). Human pomp and glory and the gods made in that image are not the be-all and end-all, and he knew it well enough to know that he could not bow down to Assyria if it meant denying the sovereignty of the one true God. Unlike his father, Hezekiah would not let the fear of man prevent him from trusting God (Ps. 56:5, 12 [Eng. 4, 11]).

Prayers of monarchs in somewhat similar straits appear in extrabiblical sources. Two of these are the prayer of the Egyptian Sethos before the Assyrian threat, and the prayer of Ashurbanipal in the Elamite crisis.[3] In both cases the king perceives himself to be *in extremis* and cries out to his god, ultimately receiving assurances of help. The chief difference between those prayers and this one is that the latter contains no protestations of the king's righteousness or claims that he deserves to be helped. Can it be that this king knows that these are not the issues? The issue is whether the Lord alone is sovereign over the nations. It is this which Hezekiah has learned (the theme of chs. 7–35), and it is this upon which all his hope rests.

14 *the letter* is plural in Hebrew (*sᵉpārîm*, lit. "books") but Hezekiah is said to have read *it* (singular). The LXX takes "letter" as singular while the Targum leaves the plural "letters" and resolves the problem by having Hezekiah read "one of them." Probably there is no contradiction; the plural form may be normal for a singular item.[4]

he went up to the house of the Lord, as in the first instance (37:1),

---

3. On the former, see Herodotus ii.141. On the latter see *ARAB*, II:331–33.
4. Delitzsch points to Latin *litterae*, "letter" (plural form), while Cheyne suggests "leaves" or "pages" of "a letter."

indicates Hezekiah's essential orientation. Whereas Ahaz refused even to ask for a sign of God's help, Hezekiah knows that God is his only hope.

Hezekiah spread it before the Lord, as with the later Maccabees, who spread a copy of the defaced Law before the Lord (1 Macc. 3:48), is not an attempt to inform God of something he does not already know but an expression of shock and outrage. Hezekiah does not merely wish to tell God about the offending document; he places it before him in its entirety, as if to say, "Surely *this* cannot be left unanswered."

16 This verse is an invocation, proclaiming the basis upon which the following plea for deliverance is made. As noted above, that plea is not based on the righteousness of the petitioner or upon mitigating circumstances. Rather, it is based solely on the character and identity of God. Sennacherib is not to be defeated because the Judeans are so righteous. Indeed, they are not. Rather, it is because the Assyrian has called the name of God into question (Ezek. 36:20–32). If God is not sovereign, then trust in him is foolish. But if he is sovereign, we may trust him through whatever happens to us in life (Rom. 8:38–39).

Hezekiah identifies the Lord in two primary ways: as King and as Creator. It may be that he intends the former to proceed from the latter. In any case, it certainly does so proceed. If God made the heavens and the earth, then it is he who defines the earth and not vice versa. He is separate from the earth and nothing earthly can even be on a par with him, let alone claim superiority over him.[5] What we believe on this issue is of fundamental importance. Once surrender the belief in God as the Creator who stands apart from the world which he created by fiat, and biblical religion is untenable.

who sits over the cherubim is literally "sitter of the cherubim." This construction appears to be a species of epexegetical genitive defining the location of the sitting without specifically stating that God sits *on* the cherubim.[6] The same reluctance to be too explicit about God's sitting appears in the other places where the cherubim are mentioned in Scripture (Num. 7:89; 1 Sam. 4:4; 2 Sam. 6:2; Ps. 80:1 [Eng. 2]; etc.). The point seems to be that while God is especially and uniquely present in that space, he is not to be localized to the extent that he is conceived to sit *on* the

---

5. This is the starting point of the arguments against idols in chs. 41–48. Insofar as the idols are representations of elements within creation, they cannot have created themselves. Kaufmann (*The Religion of Israel*, pp. 146–47) argues that the Israelites betray a misunderstanding of paganism by employing such an argument, but this is not so. Idolatry is not accidental but essential to the view that deity is contained within the created system (Isa. 44:9–20, etc.).

6. Williams, *Syntax*, § 46.

cherubim.[7] Thus this concept delicately balances two truths: God is no idol, a force who exists for us; but, on the other hand, he is not absolutely removed from us. He is, in Isaiah's words, "God with us."

you are God, you alone, of all the kingdoms of the earth sums up all that chs. 13–35 were about. Hezekiah has learned the truth which his father Ahaz refused to consider. The nations of the earth are not ultimate, nor are they to be trusted. It is the God of Israel, the God who graciously manifests himself from above the cherubim, who rules the nations. It is not foolish to trust him, contrary to Sennacherib's assertions. In fact, it is the height of folly *not* to trust him, for he, as Maker, is the only God. In many ways, this confession that God alone rules the nations is the climax of the entire first part of the book.[8] God is the one in whom trust should reside, not in human glory, as typified in the nations. It is symptomatic of the understanding of this truth that nowhere in this prayer does Hezekiah boast of his or his nation's righteousness as a motive for God's deliverance.[9] The king knows too well that there is no hope for them in human achievements. Their only hope is in the undeserved grace of the Sovereign of the nations.

17 In contrast to the idols, which have eyes but cannot see and ears but cannot hear (43:8), Hezekiah appeals to the living God, who sees without eyes and hears without ears. The term *living God* appears largely in the context of the Israelite conflict with idols.[10] As such it expresses the conviction that the gods are indeed lifeless, for their only power is that derived from their makers. The living God is not dependent upon his creatures. They, in fact, derive their life from him. Thus, when God's true greatness is unfolded, his creatures can be delivered. If the creature is exalted, salvation is impossible.

18, 19 The audacity of Hezekiah's faith is made plain here. For

---

7. Cf. J. Oswalt, "What's In a Translation," *Asbury Seminarian* 26/2 (1972) 12–16.

8. Duhm, adhering to an evolutionary scheme for the development of Israelite religion, argued that the exclusively monotheistic tone of this prayer could not have existed before the Exile. But even taking the most narrow view of the authentic writings of so-called "Isaiah of Jerusalem," it must be plain that his message was identical to the content of Hezekiah's prayer: God alone is master of the nations. Furthermore, evolution has proven itself unable to explain Israelite monotheism. Israel's own explanation—revelation—demands less credulity. Cf. J. Oswalt, "A Case for Biblical Authority," *Asbury Seminarian*, 32/1 (1977) 4–14.

9. This is in contrast to Ashurbanipal's prayer for deliverance from the Elamites (*ARAB*, II:858–59).

10. See Deut. 5:26; Josh. 3:10; 1 Sam. 17:26, 36; Ps. 42:3 (Eng. 2); 84:3 (Eng. 2); Jer. 10:10; 23:36; Dan. 6:20, 26; Hos. 1:10.

him to assert that his God alone is alive would seem to fly in the face of the evidence. His country is small and weak, cowering before an Assyrian Colossus which stands astride the world. Nonetheless, the Judean king refuses to be deterred from what he knows to be true by evidence which is ultimately superficial. There is a word here for the modern age whose dictum too often is: if it works and if it feels good, it must be right. Had Jesus Christ believed that, there would be no cross and no Church today. What is right is not validated by winning in the short run (Dan. 3:16–17).

How shall Hezekiah refute the claims that Judah should not trust in her God because no other god had been able to deliver its nation? The answer was ready at hand: the Lord was a different order of being from all those other gods. In every way, this is an astonishing statement. Where could the Judeans have gotten such an idea? Why should one god be different from all the others? Is it because theirs was not represented by an idol? But lack of idolatry does not prove that the god is fundamentally different. Rather, all the evidence points to the fact that it was because the Hebrews conceived of their God differently that they were iconoclastic. Because God was other than this world, he could not be represented in the forms of this world.[11] The recognition of that otherness can only be explained as the Hebrews explained it: they received it by direct communication from beyond this world. Given that otherness, Sennacherib's arguments were worthless. Even if Judah were to fall, it would not be because Yahweh was simply one more of the gods.

20 In view of the king's evident dependence upon God, this would be the place to press that dependence as the motivation for God's deliverance. *Because* Hezekiah depends, God *must* deliver. In fact, that is not what Hezekiah did. His concern remained for God and his glory. What happened to Judah was not of ultimate importance; what happened to God's name mattered to all eternity. How rare this is. We can talk easily of the importance of God's being glorified until we are hurting. Then it is of chief importance that we be delivered, and how God is perceived in it all is of no consequence. Not so with Hezekiah; the chief motive for Judah's being delivered is that the world may know that God alone is God. How often the outcome of our lives and our praying might be different if we focused first upon God's glory and upon his reputation, believing that all would be well with us if his name was well served (Matt. 6:33). All too

11. The emphasis upon the iols being the product of human efforts appears in each of the places where idolatry is mentioned in the first part of the book (2:20; 17:8; 31:7). The idea also appears in the diatribes against idolatry in the second part, but it is less central (44:9–20; 46:6). For the particular phrase "of wood and stone," cf. Deut. 4:28; 28:36, 64; 29:17; Ezek. 20:32.

often our well-being is the end and God is only a means to that end. Here Hezekiah demonstrates the opposite: God is the end and deliverance is the means (cf. Phil. 1:20).

(b) Isaiah's pronouncement (37:21–35)

 (i) Assyria ruled by the Lord (37:21–29)

21 *Then Isaiah, son of Amoz, sent to Hezekiah, saying, "Thus says the* *Lord, the God of Israel: Because[1] you prayed to me concerning Sen-* *nacherib, king of Assyria,*
22 *this is the word which the Lord speaks against him,* '*She despises you, she mocks you—*   *the virgin daughter of Zion;* *behind you she shakes her head—*   *the daughter of Jerusalem.*
23 *Whom have you reproached and reviled?*   *Against whom have you lifted the voice* *and raised your eyes proudly?*   *Against the Holy One of Israel!*
24 *By your servants you have reproached the Lord.* *You have said, "With my many chariots* *I have ascended the heights of the mountains,*   *the recesses of Lebanon.* *I have cut down the tallest of its cedars,*   *the choicest of its pines.* *I have come to its most inaccessible heights,*   *and its densest forest.[2]*
25 *I have dug [wells]*

1. 2 K. 19:20 has "That which you prayed . . . I have heard." The parallel here in Isaiah lacks the verb, leaving an apparently incomplete relative clause. This has prompted some commentators (e.g., Delitzsch) to opt for the 2 Kings statement as the more original. However, the relative particle *ᵃšer* may also function as a causal element (Williams, *Syntax,* § 468; cf. Gen. 34:13; 1 Sam. 15:15). In this case the Isaiah passage may be considered more original because it makes sense but is the more difficult reading (so Skinner). NEB takes the former course, with most other English translations taking the latter (JPSV takes the relative as referring to God: " . . . God, to whom you have prayed . . .").

2. Lit. "forest of its garden-land," an attributive genitive (see GKC, §§ 128s–v), thus a forest as dense and lush as a garden. The construction is analogous to "mountain of my holiness," which means "my holy mountain." Cf. also 10:18; 29:17; 32:15. On the extensive cutting of cedars for Assyrian building projects, esp. by Sargon, see A. T. Olmstead, *History of Assyria,* pp. 272–74.

and drunk water.[3]
I have dried up with the sole of my foot
all the rivers of Egypt."'
26 Have you not heard from long ago?
I have done it.[4]
From ancient days I planned it.
Now I bring it to pass
that[5] you should cause fortified cities
to crash into heaps of ruins.[6]
27 Their inhabitants, short of hand,[7]
are shattered and ashamed.
They are like plants of the field,
green shoots;
grass of the roof,
dried up before the east wind.
28 But your rising up[8] and sitting down,
your going and coming, I know,

3. Lit. "I have dug and drunk water." NEB follows 1QIs[a] and 2 K. 19:24, both of which add *zārîm*, "strange, foreign," after "water."

4. Lit. "It I have done," the object coming first for emphasis (see GKC, § 142f).

5. Young analyzes the conjunction on *ûṯ*e*hî* as expressing purpose after the preceding perfect; thus "that."

6. The infinitive "to cause to crash" is followed by an accusative of product, "heaps of ruins," prior to the object "fortified cities."

7. The phrase "short of hand" is almost universally translated "powerless" or "helpless." But it seems possible that there is reference here to the ancient Near Eastern practice of cutting off the hands of dead and dying enemies as a sort of body count. See *ANEP*, nos. 340, 348.

8. For vv. 27c and 28a, MT has "grass of the roofs and terraced fields before it rises. And your sitting down. . . ." For "terraced fields," *š*e*dēmâ*, 2 K. 19:26 has *š*e*dēpâ*, "blighted (or blasted)." This reading is supported by the Targ. and 1QIs[a] and has been adopted by all the English translations since AV. For MT *qāmâ*, "it rises," Thenius was the first in modern times to suggest *q*e*dîm*, "east wind." This has now been confirmed by 1QIs[a]. Wellhausen (so Delitzsch) is credited with suggesting how the *qāmâ* came to replace *q*e*dîm*: by transposition from the beginning of v. 28 where the original would have been *qûm*e*kā w*e*šiḇ*e*kā*, "your rising up and your sitting down" (cf. Ps. 139:2). Once again this is confirmed by 1QIs[a]. It is not impossible that both the modern commentators and the ancient scribes created the same ways of smoothing out a hard (but original) passage. There are of course a limited number of plausible solutions which could be found. However, the odds against this happening three times in a row are very high indeed, so that the 1QIs[a] reading for the total complex seems likely to be a better witness to the original than is the MT. M. Burrows mistakes *d* for *r* when he dismisses the 1QIs[a] reading for *š*e*dēmâ* (*BASOR* 113 [1949] 28).

> *and your raging against me.*
> 29 *Because you rage against me,*[9]
> *and because your complacency*[10] *has reached my ears,*
> *I will put my hook*[11] *in your nose*
> *and my bit in your mouth*
> *and turn you back on the way*
> *by which you came."*

These verses report the words of reassurance which came from the Lord to Hezekiah through Isaiah. According to v. 21, they are in specific response to the king's prayer. As noted above (on 36:1), this is the second of the prayer-response structures here. In the first instance (36:1–7) Hezekiah's general repentance and his suggestion that Isaiah's God might choose to intervene were met with the rather cool statement that God will indeed take action for the sake of his own name. Here, however, Hezekiah has declared his own trust in God in a very complete way, and the divine response is commensurate with this declaration. In a much more vivid and emotional tone God declares that not only does he know of Assyria's boasting but that her achievements have only been possible because he has planned them (vv. 23–27). But now she has gone too far and God will prevent her from achieving her ultimate objective of this campaign—capture of Jerusalem (vv. 22, 28–35).[12] God's initial aim with all humanity is to evoke repentance and trust, and when we respond in these ways to him, we may be confident that he will respond to us in ways which are satisfyingly complete.

While some of the earlier followers of the theories of multiple authorship for the book (e.g., Smith, Cheyne) waxed eloquent about this passage as representative of the authentic preaching of Isaiah, the winds

9. Some suspect the opening clause, "Because you rage against me," to be a dittograph because it is an almost exact duplicate of the final clause of v. 28. Interestingly enough, LXX lacks the end of v. 28, while 1QIs[a] lacks the beginning of v. 29. In the absence of unambiguous manuscript evidence, it seems best to let MT stand (with the Targ.).

10. Targ. "tumult," which seems a better parallel with "raging." It has been suggested (cf. *BHS*) that the original was thus *šeʾônekā* instead of MT *šaʾanankā*. However, LXX seems to support MT, and there was a certain arrogant complacency in Sennacherib's pointed dismissal of Judah's God, so perhaps MT is best.

11. The precise significance of *ḥaḥ*, "hook," is unclear. Ezek. 29:4 seems to refer to a fishhook, but here, as elsewhere in Ezekiel (19:4; 38:4), something approximating the ring frequently put in a bull's nose to which a halter rope may be attached seems intended.

12. Like 14:4b–21, vv. 22–29 are a taunt song written using the form of the elegy, the 3/2 meter. Assyria's fall is not an occasion for sorrow but for mocking delight.

of opinion have now shifted to the degree that Wildberger, representing most modern commentators, can assert that there is no doubt that the materials do not stem from Isaiah, son of Amoz. These kinds of polar opposites, both put forward with equal certainty, do not create confidence in the methods or the results. As for the present position, there is now a consensus that vv. 21, 33–35 form the oldest unit with at least two interpolated segments (vv. 22–29, 30–32) having been added anywhere from Josianic to late postexilic times. However, the passage is now structured in a unitary way, moving from the opening statement of Jerusalem's triumph (v. 22) through Assyria's boasting (vv. 23–25) and the statement of God's control (vv. 26–29) and climaxing with the promises of Jerusalem's deliverance (vv. 30–35). Thus the division into earlier and later parts is hypothetical in the extreme. In fact, were it not for the inability of scholars to believe that Sennacherib really was defeated by God outside of Jerusalem, none of this reworking of the text would be necessary. As it is, it is quite difficult to imagine how the turning of a Judean surrender into a great divine victory has any theological value at all. Furthermore, the Bible does not elsewhere depict the buying off of defeat (as Hezekiah did) as a divine act (2 Chr. 16:7–10; 28:16–21). It is in fact treated as an act of un-faith. One is at a loss to understand why this one was fictionalized (or theologized) to make the result appear to come from great faith.

21 *Isaiah, son of Amoz* is one more attempt by the editor of the book, whether that be Isaiah himself or someone else, to let the reader know of the authenticity of the following statements (cf. 1:1; 13:1; 20:2). This conclusion cannot be easily gainsaid. Either the editor was correct, or he was innocently mistaken, or he is attempting to make a point he knows is incorrect. In any case he thought the precise identity of the speaker was quite important. If we now say it is unimportant, the burden of proof is upon us.

The answer to Hezekiah's prayer is depicted as coming at once, and the *waw* conjunctive, here translated *then*, shows that we are intended to link the response to the prayer. How fortunate Hezekiah was to have someone like Isaiah near him at this time, a person who was so much in touch with God that he could convey the comforting words at once while the work of God in history unfolded more slowly.

22 Sennacherib has spoken to Hezekiah concerning the Lord; Hezekiah has spoken to the Lord concerning Sennacherib; now the Lord speaks to Hezekiah concerning Sennacherib. It is always this last account which matters. God has the final word on our nature and destiny. We may say what we wish about him; others may say what they wish about us; but it is what God says about you and me which is of ultimate importance.

Sennacherib may style himself world ruler; he may terrify his small neighbors. But it is the God of one of the least of these who will close the book on who Sennacherib really is.

Because it is God who rules Sennacherib and not vice versa, Isaiah can look to a day when Jerusalem, now a prone maiden helpless before a swaggering rapist, will mock her would-be conqueror's impotence.[13] The word order of the phrases emphasizes this point. Who is it that will despise the Assyrian? Zion's virgin daughter, not some mighty hero. So as the oppressor slinks away, the intended victim will stick out her tongue at him and wag her head from side to side in derision (Ps. 22:8 [Eng. 7]; Jer. 18:16; Lam. 2:15). He could not do what he planned. And why not? Because Assyria has mocked the One who is the originator of all plans (cf. Jas. 4:13–16).

23–25 God has heard what Sennacherib has said (37:4). Both his belittling of God and his own boasting have been perfectly clear. If the Assyrians had done some background work on Judah before the attack (see on 36:4–10), background work had also been done on Assyria. Verses 24 and 25 read very much like portions of the Assyrian royal annals in which the kings boasted of their conquests. All those events are known to God and come as no surprise to him. Thus it is not little Judah against which Sennacherib has arrayed himself, but against the Holy One. Happy is that person who is so completely dependent upon God that those who attack him are actually attacking God (Gen. 12:3; Exod. 23:22).

23 Throughout the first part of the book the conflict between human self-sufficiency and the glory of God has recurred. Here it is again. To glorify human potential apart from its relation to God is to make humanity itself God. But that is not possible. For the Holy One occupies the throne already, as Isaiah well knew (6:3). The Holy is the One who is *other* than humanity and encounters it again and again, for good or for ill. We have no ultimate principle in ourselves, and to act as though we did is to guarantee that the encounter will bode ill, unless by its very cataclysmic nature it should bring us to our senses. So whether Sennacherib knows it or not, all his boasting, even that not directly against the

---

13. If Assyria merely went home because it was satisfied with Hezekiah's tribute and this account represents a fictionalized version of the events, it is necessary to believe the writers had lost complete touch with reality. For if that was the true nature of the case Jerusalem did the very opposite of mocking the Assyrians upon their departure.

Lord, *has* been against him, for God is truly ultimate and Sennacherib is not.[14]

24 *By your servants* is probably a way of saying that insult was added to injury. Not only did Sennacherib say these things, but he put them in the mouths of his lowest lackeys.

With my many chariots begins the section which has direct parallels with the royal annals (see Excursus II below). Chariots, like tanks or jet fighters today, were the most prestigious arm of the military, and even though they were useful only in flatland fighting, it was still a point of honor with the Assyrians to take them everywhere they went, even over the most difficult terrain.

All the language here is to be taken hyperbolically. The monarch is saying that nothing can stop him, neither high mountains in the north with their dense forests, nor the deserts of Sinai, nor the swamps of the Nile Delta in the south. This is not to say that he had actually done each of these, but that he could if he wished.[15]

Verses 26–29 report that Sennacherib is in for a rude shock. The very One whom he has accused of impotence before the Assyrian might is in fact the One who has decreed and directed the Assyrian conquest. Sennacherib is not the one who threatens to drive God from his throne. Rather, he is God's obedient servant, and the long string of victories which he cited as evidence of his superiority over any god are in fact all a part

---

14. At the beginning of the two statements, first in v. 24, "I have gone up . . ." and again in v. 26, "I dug wells . . ." the "I" is especially emphasized. This "I-problem" is at the heart of the human dilemma. Self-centered persons consume one another in their attempts at self-aggrandizement. The Christian message is that this dilemma can only be solved by displacing the all-consuming focus on "I" with a new focus on Christ. This teaching is most clearly seen in passages like Gal. 2:20; Phil. 1:15–20.

15. Since Sennacherib never reached the Delta of Egypt, some take these references as evidence of later interpolations. Others note the imperfect verbs and suggest he was boasting of what he intended to do. However, the verbs are almost certainly examples of the preterite in that the opening verbs of each sequence are perfect. However, this need not point to an interpolation if the whole statement is understood hyperbolically. Egypt had always been Assyria's ultimate goal, but the Egyptian Delta also served as an excellent representative of the kind of canal-laced land which others might find impassable, but which would pose no problem to a god-like Assyrian monarch. P. J. Calderone, "The Rivers of Maṣor," *Bib* 42 (1961) 423–432, makes the plausible suggestion that *māṣôr* is not Egypt at all, but *ṣûr*, "rock," to which an enclitic *mem* from the previous word has become attached. Thus the rivers would be mountain rivers, an obstacle which the Assyrians frequently boasted of conquering.

of the plan *of* God. But the tool has vaunted itself against the hand that swings it, and this attitude God will not abide (10:5–19). The Assyrians will be cut down just like the cedar forests they themselves boasted of decimating. At least two obvious lessons emerge here for the believer. (1) It is God who controls the sweep of history. He is not threatened by events. In fact, events are the arena in which he chooses to make himself known. It is the eye of faith which sees the hand of God in what seems to be catastrophe. (2) There is never room for human arrogance. All that we are and have are ultimately gifts from God.

26 *Have you not heard from long ago* expresses the conviction that God's ways have always been accessible to those who cared to look for them, whether Assyrian or Israelite. Paul held the same conviction (Rom. 1:19–20). This is not to deny the necessity of special revelation for salvation. But it is to say that the course of nature is more than enough to make it plain that we human beings are not ultimate in a world made in our image, and anyone who acts as though this were so is without excuse.

I have done it. The object is feminine in form, prompting Calvin to suggest that Jerusalem was intended. However, the general context points to "all of this," an abstract usage which the feminine ending would serve.[16] To paraphrase the verse: "Don't you understand? All these things to which you have been attaching your 'I,' *I* have done them!" The element of God's ancient plan and purpose is a special distinctive of the book as a whole.[17] It appears first in direct connection with Assyria, and one wonders whether it was this realization which then triggered the wider application in the book. It is hard to know how much the idea of the purpose of God in history had been a part of Israelite thinking prior to this time. If it had not been very common, then the revelation of God's plan in the movements of Assyria may have triggered the broader thoughts which appear later in the book where the idols are taunted for their purposelessness (chs. 43–45).

A further aspect of this whole matter relates to predictive prophecy. Prior to 732 B.C. Isaiah had predicted that the Assyrians would sweep over Judah to the neck (8:6–8). Now here they are. Whether or not the Assyrians had ever heard that they were a part of the plan of the God of Israel, the Judeans were certainly in a position to know the truth of that. So also in 550, the exiles would have been in a position to know that their

---

16. Williams, *Syntax*, § 24 (cf. also §§ 25, 26).
17. See 5:19; 10:5–6; 14:24–26; 19:12, 17; 23:8–9; 25:1; 28:29; 30:1; 43:7, 12; 44:7–8; 45:7, 9, 18.

God was God, if the whole matter had been predicted as part of the purpose of God many years prior to the fact.

27–29 Here the prophet begins by agreeing with the Assyrian as to the results of his conquests: people have been helpless before the onslaught; they have been disgraced for trusting in fortifications or deities which could not stand; they withered before the blast like grass with no roots.[18] But Sennacherib's mistake was in his estimation of the cause of these effects. He thought the cause was in himself, in his shrewd plans coupled with his awesome might. But, as v. 28 makes plain, that is not the case. Sennacherib is not ultimate but derivative from a higher Power. In language reminiscent of Ps. 139, the writer points out that no one is a first cause if there is Another who knows every thought and motion of ours. It is one thing not to be aware of this Being (although Isaiah questions whether that is possible), but it is another to belittle the very One from whom your life is derived, as Sennacherib has done through his servants.

Because of that belittling, God has no choice but to bring the Assyrian monarch to heel. The metaphors which Isaiah uses suggest just that. God will treat Sennacherib like a balky beast who must be made to do his master's bidding by means of bit and bridle. It is a vast come-down to go from self-made ruler of the world to stubborn mule, but the latter is a truer picture of the situation.

(ii) Jerusalem's deliverance (37:30–35)

30 *"And this is a sign to you: eating this year what grows by itself and in the second year what comes up from the roots, but in the third year sow and harvest and plant vineyards and eat fruit.*

31 *Those who escape from the house of Judah, the remnant, will again take root downward and produce fruit upward.*

32 *For from Jerusalem a remnant will go forth and an escaped one from Mount Zion. The zeal of the Lord of Hosts will do this.*

33 *Therefore, thus says the Lord concerning the king of Assyria: 'He will not come into this city and shall not shoot an arrow there, nor bring a shield before it, nor cast a siege-mound against it.*

34 *By the way on which he came he will return, and he will not come into this city,' says the Lord.*

35 *I will shield this city to deliver it, for my sake and for the sake of my servant David."*

---

18. On the flat, clay-covered roofs of ancient Near Eastern buildings a rain could make wind-borne grass seeds sprout in a short time. However, because there was no depth of soil, a dry period of any length could kill the grass just as quickly.

663

Having rebuked the would-be conqueror, God now makes the specific promise to deliver the city. As an indication that God is indeed at work in this, Isaiah makes a specific promise regarding the future when it will be possible to return to a normal agricultural life. But this sign of renewed fecundity also has significance as a symbol of Judah and Jerusalem, almost barren, but coming to fruitfulness again under the good hand of God.

Many modern commentators regard this section as being composed of two separate elements, the first covering vv. 30–32, while vv. 33–35 are taken with v. 21. The arguments for such a separation seem highly subjective, the claim being made that vv. 31–32 utilize the agricultural figure while vv. 33–35 do not refer to this. However, in a real way vv. 33–35 sum up the entire response (vv. 21–35). Verses 21–29 speak of Assyria's arrogance, while vv. 30–32 speak of Judah's fruitfulness. The upshot of those two ideas is that Assyria will not set foot in Jerusalem (vv. 33–35).

30 The sign here is not of the sort which comes before the event in order to create faith for the event, but rather after the fact to demonstrate that God was indeed at work. So Isaiah says in effect, when you see things developing over the next period of time just as I said they would, you will know that it was truly God who drove Sennacherib away.

The precise development of the sign is open to some conjecture, although the general outline is clear enough. It begins and ends with infinitives absolute of *'ākal*, "to eat," indicating to what the general experience relates. During the current year the only food is grain which came up from seed spilled in the field by accident.[1] During the next year only that which came up from the roots of the previous plants will be available. But in the third year life would return to normal with planting and harvesting. The general import of this saying is evidently that although the present state of siege had thoroughly disrupted the agricultural base of the economy, there would soon come a day when no trace of the Assyrian threat would remain. Young is probably correct in his suggestion that the imperatives "sow, harvest, plant, eat" are intended to convey the certainty of the prediction.

The problem arises with the duration of time involved. The indications are that the deliverance would come shortly and would be very complete. If so, why should it take three years for the effects to be felt? A number of solutions have been proposed, but two seem most feasible. On the one hand, the number "three" may have been conventional in Hebrew prophecy (cf. 16:14), so that specific calendar dates were not

1. Cf. Lev. 25:5, 11.

intended. However, this explanation would seem to undercut the prediction's value as a clear sign. Better seems to be the proposal of Delitzsch and others that while three actual calendar years are intended, only about fourteen to fifteen months would be covered. This view involves the suggestion that the prediction was made in the fall, as "this year" in which the accidental growth was being eaten was drawing to a close (32:10). The deliverance would not come in time for the fall planting to be done, meaning that only what came up from the roots of previous plants would be available during the next year. But by the following fall, when the third calendar year was beginning, normal life could resume, for the Assyrians would be gone. Overall, this seems to be the most satisfying solution.

The use of *sign* here continues the parallelism between this segment and the one referring to Ahaz (chs. 7–12). There too Isaiah offered to give a sign confirming Judah's deliverance from Syria and Ephraim. There, however, Ahaz refused to trust in God with the result that the sign he received was the much more far-reaching one of the Immanuel who would replace the corrupt Davidic dynasty and restore the people led astray by the Davidides (8:8; 9:6 [Eng. 7]; 11:10, 11). Here that judgment is deferred, because one of David's sons is willing to commit his way to God in his extremity (26:2–4).

31–32 In these verses the prophet extends the agricultural figure and applies it to Judah and Jerusalem. Like the spilled grain, the remnant of the people will bear fruit again; like the old root-stock, it will send up its shoots again; like the fields plowed and sown, God's people will spread over the land once more (4:2, 3; 10:20, 21; 11:1). God's ardor for them is in no way diminished, and whenever the faintest spark of trust appears in them, his breath is there to fan it into flame.

These figures also are reminiscent of chs. 7–12. There at the very outset, the figure of the remnant is prominent in Isaiah's son "A Remnant Shall Return" (7:3) and returns again in 10:20, 21 and 11:11, 16. Although Israel's sins may reduce her to a mere shadow of her former self, even that shadow is redolent of life because of God's unfailing grace.[2] Presumably the *remnant* here refers to those Judean people who still remain alive in Jerusalem after the Assyrian conquest of the rest of the country. The prophet promises that from this small seed the country will once again be replenished.

The zeal of the Lord of Hosts appears elsewhere at 9:6 (Eng. 7) where the establishment of the messianic kingdom is promised. As Young

---

2. See G. Hasel, *The Remnant*, rev. ed. (Berrien Springs: Andrews University, 1980).

aptly says, the temporary restoration promised here in ch. 37 is a sort of down payment upon that full and final restoration made possible through Christ. Were it not for God's passionate, yet wholly undeserved, attachment to his world, none of this would be possible. He would have long since abandoned us to our sins and transgressions (1:9).

As noted above, vv. 33–35 constitute the logical conclusion of the previous two points in the oracles: If Sennacherib's arrogant boasting against God is to be rebuffed, and if the remnant in Judah is once more to fill the land, then only one outcome is possible—Assyria will not be permitted to enter the city.

33 *will not shoot an arrow there* suggests that Herodotus's tradition (ii.141) that a plague befell the Assyrian army on the border of Egypt is generally correct and that the main body of the army never reached Jerusalem, or that if they did they were unable to begin preparations for the siege. So also the following.

cast (lit. "pour out") *a siege-mound*. Most ancient Near Eastern cities were built on hilltops, so that it was necessary for a besieging army to build ramps up which to push battering-rams, siege towers, etc. *cast* probably refers to the pouring out of earth from the baskets in which it was carried to the site (Hab. 1:10). Not only will the city be delivered, Isaiah says, it will not even be physically threatened.

34 By the same way that Sennacherib came, swaggering in his invincible might, he was to slink home, shorn of his army, only able to put the best face upon his failure by saying in his annals that he had shut up Hezekiah like a bird in a cage.[3] Why should this be? Because the Assyrian monarch had pitted himself against the one God who was not like all the other gods the Assyrians had vanquished. Sennacherib may say what he likes about the Lord, but it is what the Lord says about Sennacherib that really matters. So it is with each of us.

35 *for my sake* expresses again the awareness that Sennacherib had not finally threatened Jerusalem but God himself. Given the way in which the challenge was framed, one could only have interpreted Jerusalem's fall as evidence of the Lord's impotence. Many years later Ezekiel was to utter similar words for God (Ezek. 36:22). God had to deliver the exiles in order to vindicate his own godhood. The relation of repentance to deliverance is significant in both cases. The repentance and trust do not *cause* the deliverance; rather, the cause is God's faithfulness to his own

3. *ANET*, pp. 287–88.

character. However, without these human responses there is no deliverance. So it was in 587/86 that Jerusalem was allowed to fall in the absence of any real turning to God.[4]

for the sake of my servant David has two possible connotations. On the one hand, it may refer to the divine promise to David to perpetuate his line on the throne (2 Sam. 7:16).[5] However, it is evident that this loyalty to David did not mean an automatic commitment to any Davidide, no matter what his behavior. The scorn shown for the house of David in chs. 7–12 illustrates this point,[6] as does the abandonment of the monarchy after 586. Thus, it is also possible that Hezekiah is taken as the present representative of "my servant David" and it is for his sake that the Lord is acting.[7]

But yet another possibility presents itself in the recognition of the messianic promises (9:6 [Eng. 7]; 11:1; 55:3). If the true David were to sit upon the throne of Israel, then Israel must be enabled to survive whatever may befall her in the years ahead. Had Jerusalem succumbed at that point, might not the Judeans, like the Northern Israelites, simply have been absorbed into their new homes and disappeared as the covenant people? As it was, through this deliverance and through the subsequent prophetic ministries, there was sufficient commitment on the part of some for the faith to survive the Exile and to provide the basis for the messianic revelation in Christ.[8]

How happy that person, city, or nation which has God as its shield!

4. 43:25 and 48:9 express a similar thought. Here God is gracious because it is of his nature to forgive sin.

5. Cf. also 1 K. 11:13, 34; 15:4; 1 K. 8:19; Isa. 55:3.

6. See 7:2, 13. But note also the messianic promises of 9:6 (Eng. 7) and 11:1. This interest in David is one more connection between 7–12 and 36–39.

7. Note the favorable comparison of Hezekiah to David in 2 K. 18:3.

8. Some commentators point out that the prophecy in vv. 21–35 does not specify how the deliverance was to take place and use this as evidence that the miracle described in vv. 36–38 is in fact a fiction created in the following century to explain Sennacherib's unaccountable departure from Jerusalem. Two things need to be said about this view. First, critics cannot have it both ways. If the prophecy is too specific, then they take it to have occurred after the fact (so the reference to Cyrus in 45:1). Here when the prophecy is not specific enough, they say the fact did not occur. In fact, prophecy is only rarely precisely specific. It is only as clear as it needs to be to establish the issue at hand. The second point is that it is odd, if the prophecy in its present form is composed of several late interpolations, that it does not mention the miracle. That it does not appears to me to establish its priority to the fact when the prophet did not have specific information about the way in which God would deliver Jerusalem and send Sennacherib home.

667

How many things which we cannot bear he protects us from. When calamity comes, we often ask why we have been singled out. Rather, we ought to be thankful for all those calamities which might have befallen us, but did not because the Lord was our shield (Gen. 15:1; Ps. 13:4 [Eng. 3]; 28:7; 84:12 [Eng. 11]; etc.).

(c) The army of Assyria destroyed (37:36–38)

36 *The angel of the Lord went forth and struck 185,000 in the camp of Assyria. They arose early in the morning, and behold, all of them were dead corpses.*

37 *So Sennacherib, the king of Assyria, departed and went and returned and dwelt in Nineveh.*

38 *And it happened while he was worshiping in the house of Nisroch his god that Adram-melek and Sharezer, his sons, struck him with sword. But they fled to the land of Ararat, and Esarhaddon his son reigned after him.*

With a terrible suddenness, which is reinforced by the brevity and terseness of the account, the long interchange of chs. 36–37 is brought to a close. The mighty Assyrian emperor, stripped of his army, hurriedly departs for home, never to set foot in Judah again. As Napoleon discovered before Moscow and Hitler learned in Stalingrad, there are limits to even the most towering of human pretensions. But more than the two modern tyrants, the Bible makes it plain that Sennacherib confronted God himself and was defeated by God. It is the final irony of his life that it was in the temple of his god where he was praying (much as his intended victim Hezekiah had prayed twenty years earlier?) that he was murdered by his own sons.

36 This verse is the crux of the entire account, so it is not surprising that it has come under severe scrutiny by biblical scholars. Isaiah insists that the Assyrian monarch did not go home because he was satisfied with Hezekiah's surrender, or because his objectives in the West had been reached, or because of some crisis elsewhere in the empire. He went home, says the prophet, because of the upshot of two issues: Sennacherib had asserted that human glory was superior to God's, and Hezekiah had dared to trust God. Because of these God intervened in natural events and decimated a significant number of the Assyrian army.[1] Cut out this event

---

1. Clements insists very strongly that the writer intends to speak of a miraculous event and that it cannot be taken as "some shorthand way of referring to a natural disaster." But interestingly enough, he does this as a means of insisting that no such event took place.

as a historical fact, as all too many commentators wish to do, and the whole theological content of the passage falls to the ground. God did not deliver Hezekiah any more than he did Menahem (2 K. 15:19–20), and he did not punish Sennacherib any more than he did Tiglath-pileser III. The unknown redactors have built a lofty theological edifice, insisting either innocently or fraudulently that it was true because it was historically validated. If we now assert that the validation is false, then the theology is equally false.[2] Only if there was indeed a significant difference between the experience of Menahem and the experience of Hezekiah is there any satisfactory explanation for Isaiah's moving theology of God's sovereignty and his trustworthiness.

As noted above, Herodotus makes reference to a plague of mice which ate up the bowstrings, etc. of Sennacherib's army at Pelusium on the edge of the Delta in Egypt, precipitating them to flight.[3] Modern writers, noting that area's reputation for disease and the fact that mice are symbolic of pestilence, have conjectured that Herodotus was recounting an Egyptian legend which had sprung from an original account of the sudden onslaught of some such disease as bubonic plague.[4]

However Herodotus is to be interpreted, there is nothing in the biblical account which requires the Assyrian army to have been before Jerusalem when the Death Angel befell it.[5] In fact, as Smith points out, the references in 33:18 and Pss. 48 and 76 suggest that there was only a reconnaissance brigade guarding the city and that it quietly slipped away at the horrendous news concerning the main army.

As to the terrific losses involved, which Kaiser says are frankly impossible, Smith notes that the Third Crusade mounted over a million and a half men and that the losses of the First Crusade have been estimated at more than 300,000. Perhaps more to the point, H. W. F. Saggs, on the

2. Lest this argument be dismissed as a species of the "either-or" fallacy, it should be pointed out that the insistence of the original writers upon rooting their claims to theological authenticity on historical proof leaves us no other alternative. Had they not insisted that history offered such proof we could fall back upon subjective, existential authentication. But the biblical writers themselves have deprived us of such an alternative. Scott protests that it is no service to religion to refuse to recognize that the account is legend. But neither is it a service to a religion which roots itself in history to deny that history because it denies one's own view of the possible.

3. *History* ii.141.

4. See esp. Smith, who cites Gibbon and others on the pestilential climate of Pelusium.

5. Cf. Exod. 12:29 and 2 Sam. 24:15–16 for similar statements.

basis of Assyrian reports, concludes that the Assyrian "Grand Army" must have numbered in the hundreds of thousands.[6] Of course, none of this proves that the event took place as Isaiah reports it. But it does demonstrate that the account is not merely fantasy but is within the realm of possibility.[7]

37 Calling Sennacherib *king of Assyria* here serves to emphasize his impotence before God. Both he and the Rabshaqeh had repeatedly identified him as "the Great King, king of Assyria." But now this great king hurriedly departs for home, as the piled-up verbs *departed and went and returned and dwelt* suggest.[8] He has encountered the one who is truly King, and he knows it (cf. 6:5; 31:8, 9; 33:17).

38 This verse indicates that, in regard to Judah, Sennacherib did nothing significant again prior to his death. The topical treatment here could give the impression that his death took place shortly after his return from Jerusalem. In fact, he did not die for some twenty years, not until 681. However, there is nothing in the present statement to demand an immediate death, and the fact that the writer's report of the nature of the death coincides with the Assyrian account[9]—murder by his sons in his own temple—makes it plain that the author knows of the intervening period but is consciously telescoping events in order to show how God's promise concerning Sennacherib and Jerusalem was kept.[10]

The ancient adage "God's mills grind slowly, but they grind exceedingly fine" is applicable here. Sennacherib may have thought he was well away from Jerusalem, but he was not away from Jerusalem's God, against whom he had exalted himself. The years had passed and the devastating losses in the West had been replaced. Sennacherib had escaped. But had he? The irony of his death shows he did not. This man, who had

6. H. W. F. Saggs, *Everyday Life in Babylonia and Assyria* (London: Batsford, 1965), p. 115; *The Greatness That Was Babylon* (London: Athlone, 1962), p. 260.

7. We are not told, for instance, that the entire Assyrian army was turned into donkeys, or that Sennacherib was transported to China.

8. Skinner attributes the presence of the four verbs to conflation, but Cicero uses the same sort of sequence to describe a hasty departure in *Catinlinam* ii.

9. *ANET*, pp. 288–89. Cf. also Olmstead, *History*, pp. 337–39.

10. Since there is no evidence that Isaiah was still alive in 681, it has been argued by some that this verse is the work of a later hand. In itself this is not impossible, particularly since it is not written as prophecy but as narrative. So a disciple of Isaiah's, noting how God's promises had been kept, could have included this report as the theological conclusion to the account. At the same time it must be said that we have no reliable account of Isaiah's death and thus cannot be certain he did die prior to 681.

exalted himself to the heights, was as mortal as any other. Moreover, because his pretensions had been so high, his downfall was the more ignominious (cf. 14:4–20). When Hezekiah prayed to his God, he was delivered, both from enemies and from sickness. When Sennacherib prayed to his god,[11] not only was he not delivered, but his sons who, in God's economy, were expected to honor their father, slaughtered him. Like his father Sargon before him, Sennacherib was to prove that great pretensions are no security against final ignominy. In fact, according to Jesus, they are the surest way to reach that undesired goal (Luke 12:20).

2. THE HUMAN LIMITS OF TRUST (38:1–39:8)

a. HEZEKIAH'S ILLNESS (38:1–22)

(1) Prophecy and response (38:1–8)

1 *In those days Hezekiah was sick unto death and Isaiah the prophet, son of Amoz, went to him and said to him, "Thus says the Lord, 'Give charge to your household, for you are about to die; you will not live.'"*

2 *And Hezekiah turned his face to the wall[1] and prayed to the Lord.*

3 *He said, "Please, Lord, remember how I have walked before you in truth and with a whole heart, and have done good in your eyes." And Hezekiah wept greatly.*

4 *And the word of the Lord came to Isaiah, saying,*

5 *"Go and say to Hezekiah, 'Thus says the Lord, the God of David your father: I have heard your prayer; I have seen your tears; behold, I will add to your days fifteen years.*

6 *From the hand of the king of Assyria I will deliver you and this city and I will shield this city.*

7 *This is the sign to you from the Lord that the Lord will do this thing which he said:*

11. To date, no Assyrian god by the name of Nisroch is known. However, given the biblical record for accuracy in the reporting of obscure details of ancient life, it is reasonable to assume that archeology has simply failed to uncover the data as yet. The implication is that this was the private tutelary god of the king. Cf. E. Yamauchi, *The Stones and the Scriptures* (Philadelphia: Holman, 1972), pp. 146–166, for a discussion of the limitations of archeology. Note that Young and others see the name as a possible corruption of Marduk, perhaps in mockery.

1. Targ. has it as the wall of the sanctuary, but there is no reason to take it as other than the wall of his sickroom.

8 *Behold, I am going to make the shadow on the steps,[2] which went down on the steps of Ahaz by means of the sun,[3] go backward ten steps. The sun will go back the ten steps which it descended.'"*

As Young notes, chs. 38–39 serve to introduce chs. 40–66, which focus upon the Babylonian captivity. However, his explanation of their function does not go far enough. It is not enough to say that through the sickness of Hezekiah and the coming of the Babylonian envoys the future of Judah was revealed. Much more fundamental truths than this are being communicated here. In a real sense the king is depicted as the representative of the people in chs. 36–39 as a whole. In chs. 36–37 he represents the realization of all which chs. 7–35 are about. It is possible to turn to God in trust and find relief and deliverance. In that sense these chapters form an ideological pivot in the book. Chs. 40–66 can build upon the concept of God's trustworthiness as they delineate the other elements which are necessary to the life of servanthood.

But chs. 38 and 39 are also pivotal. For the question must be asked, "If Hezekiah is the ideal representative of the trusting people, why the captivity?" Or, "If God could deliver his people from Assyria, why not Babylon?" Or, "Is not Hezekiah the promised child of 7:14 and 9:5–6 (Eng. 6–7)? Is he not in fact the Messiah?" Chs. 38–39 answer these questions for us and in so doing point beyond Hezekiah and the Jerusalem of 700 B.C. Thus the relation of these chapters to chs. 36 and 37 may be logical rather than chronological (see below on v. 1).[4]

2. 1QIs[a] has "the steps of the upper chamber of Ahaz." Cf. S. Iwry, "The Qumran Isaiah and the End of the Dial of Ahaz," *BASOR* 147 (1977) 30–33. Iwry argues for the correctness of the Qumran reading (note LXX "steps of the *house* of Ahaz") and refers to 2 K. 23:12, where reference is made to the pagan altars associated with such an upper chamber. If this view is correct, it is tempting to relate the steps to some form of sun worship.

3. *baššemeš*, "in, with the sun," is not supported by the versions. Instead, they treat "sun" as articular: LXX "I will not turn the sun backward"; Targ. "which the sun has gone down." 1QIs[a] has *'eṭ-haššemeš*, which prompts Iwry (see n. 2 above) to reconstruct the verse as follows: "I am returning the shadow of the steps which the sun descended on the steps of the chamber of Ahaz your father. I am returning the sun backward ten steps. . . ." However, Driver (*JSS* 13 [1968] 55–56), noting the absence of "sun" in 2 K. 20:9, proposes to delete it here as a rather awkward gloss which the versions tried to make sense of. In view of this breadth of opinion, the present reading remains with the MT, taking "shadow" as absolute and "steps" as an adverbial accusative, while the preposition *b* on "sun" is understood as expressing agency (Williams, *Syntax*, § 245).

4. For a similar understanding of the theological significance of these chapters, see P. R. Ackroyd, "An Interpretation of the Babylonian Exile: A Study of 2 Kings 20, Isaiah 38–39," *SJT* 27 (1974) 329–352. Ackroyd sees Hezekiah representing the people as a whole, although in a more favorable way than does the present interpretation.

Chapter 38 presents Hezekiah in two lights: positive and negative. On the one hand, he is still the Hezekiah who can turn to God in submission and trust in a moment of dire necessity. But on the other hand, he is a Hezekiah who is distinctly mortal. In fact, the major thrust of the chapter, including the psalm (vv. 9–20), is upon the mortality of flesh. What is this saying? Two things, perhaps. Jerusalem, like Hezekiah, has been granted a reprieve (cf. v. 6), but it is only a temporary one. And it is conditional. The life of a man or of a city is solely in the hand of God. Furthermore, this Hezekiah is but a man. The promises which were made through Isaiah and recorded in the present chs. 7–12 had not been fulfilled in Hezekiah, and more revelation would be necessary in order to understand to whom they did refer. This man might be given fifteen years by God's grace, but he is only a man, not the Messiah.

Chapter 39 is wholly negative. Hezekiah, like Jerusalem, is all too easily diverted from his trust when the pressure is removed. All too easily God's people are seduced by this world's values and put their trust in human glory—wealth, arms, luxuries—when all along we live and prosper by God's good pleasure alone. Hezekiah demonstrates that trust must be a way of life and not merely a one-time affair. Furthermore, he demonstrates that the hope of humanity can never rest upon human perfectibility. If we are to be delivered from ourselves, the source of our hope does not lie in the Hezekiahs of this world. They are as mortal and fallible as the rest of us, whatever their good qualities may be. No, if there is hope for us, it must lie beyond us.

Thus chs. 36–39 make chs. 40–66 a necessity. Given that God may be trusted, what then? Given that salvation is not in Hezekiah, where is it? Given that one-time trust is not enough, how is a life of continuous trust possible? Given that the best of God's people fail, where is our hope? Like the rest of the OT, Isa. 1–39 points the way to possibilities beyond themselves. But by themselves they are an incomplete book.

The form of ch. 38, as it appears here, is somewhat enigmatic. Almost all commentators, whatever their critical persuasions, agree that 2 K. 20:1–11 preserves a better account of the story in that it is fuller and has a more logical sequence of events. It appears that the writer of the Isaiah account, abridging the original (perhaps to gain room for the psalm he wished to include?), inadvertently left out the reference to Isaiah's poultice and Hezekiah's request for a sign (2 K. 20:7–8). He then added these on at the end of the account.[5]

---

5. It is also possible that a later editor, knowing of the Kings account, felt that these details were important and added them at the end. If so, this was done very early, since both LXX and Targ. preserve the same form.

The psalm (vv. 9–20) is in the form of the individual lament.[6] Although it ends with the typical anticipation of deliverance, it is not a thanksgiving psalm. Thus it serves, as noted above, to emphasize the writer's mortality more than it does the wonder of his deliverance.[7] One cannot help but feel that the same truths are meant to apply to Judah and Jerusalem: delivered, yes, but most distinctly mortal.

1 *In those days* is a point of considerable debate owing to the controversy concerning Hezekiah's dates. If he began to reign in 716/15 and reigned for twenty-nine years (2 K. 18:2, 13), then this event (whereby fifteen years were added) would have occurred around 701, at the time of Sennacherib's invasion. In this case chs. 36–39 would be in approximate chronological order. (It is difficult to determine whether the illness came immediately before, during, or after the attack.) On the other hand, if Hezekiah began to reign in 727/26 (2 K. 18:1), his death would have occurred in 696 and his illness must be dated fifteen years earlier, about 711. In this case chs. 38 and 39 would be placed where they are for ideological reasons as noted above.

On balance the latter alternative seems slightly more likely. It appears that Hezekiah did begin to reign in 727/26, probably as co-regent with his father Ahaz.[8] Furthermore, the Babylonian rebel Merodach-baladan seems to have been out of the picture by 703. Beyond this, it is inconceivable that the Babylonian envoys would have come to congratulate Hezekiah solely on his recovery if he had recently experienced a great deliverance from Assyria. Furthermore, as Young and others point out, most of the temple treasures were stripped to pay the initial, abortive tribute to Sennacherib, leaving nothing to show the Babylonians if they came after that time.[9] Finally, the dates of the Babylonian revolutionary

6. S. Mowinckel, *The Psalms in Israel's Worship*, tr. D. R. Ap-Thomas (Nashville: Abingdon, 1962), II:1–15. Note esp. Pss. 6, 22, 28, 30, 32, 39, 41, 88.

7. There is nothing intrinsically impossible about Hezekiah's having been the author of the psalm. His literary interest is attested to by the ascription of Prov. 25–29 to his leadership.

8. But note Thiele's extensive argument against this position in *Mysterious Numbers*, pp. 128, 132–35. On the other hand, the attempt to place 36:1, with its 14th year dating, as the original opening of this chapter is groundless (cf. Duhm, etc.). For an older discussion of the implications of the later date, see B. R. Downer, "The Added Years of Hezekiah's Life," *BSac* 80 (1923) 249–271.

9. Kissane argues that Hezekiah could not have prayed his prayer of innocence after Isaiah had denounced his government's destructive Egyptian policy, but it is not clear that Hezekiah himself was the architect of that policy. It is interesting that Isaiah did not denounce Hezekiah at any point in the materials preserved in chs. 29–31.

Merodach-baladan (see below on 39:1) seem to confirm that the sickness did not occur after Sennacherib's attack, but before it.

If this is so, then we must ask why chs. 38 and 39 are placed out of chronological order, coming after chs. 36 and 37 instead of before them. Surely the answer is that it is for the theological reasons noted above. In fact, deliverance from the nations through trust in God and the establishment of the messianic kingdom through Hezekiah were not the last word for Judah at that time. Some of the guiding principles had now been demonstrated, but much more needed to take place before the meaning of servanthood could be realized in Judah's life. In that light it seems that the author or editor seized upon these prior events in Hezekiah's life to make these important points.

It is not clear what Hezekiah's sickness was, although v. 21 indicates that one of the symptoms was a boil. At any rate the king's life was manifestly ebbing away.

Give charge to your household is evidently a command that Hezekiah should make known his final will to his family. An example of what would have taken place may perhaps be seen in David's final instructions (1 K. 2:1–9), or in the actions of Ahithophel before he took his own life (2 Sam. 17:23).

you will not live must have sounded to Hezekiah like the final hammer blows on the nails of his coffin. They seem final and without apparent reprieve. Yet, as the following verses make plain, there was a reprieve. How can this be? It is evident that Hezekiah knew something of God's character that Moses also knew (Exod. 32:7–14): God is always ready to be entreated. He is unchanging in his intention to bless his creatures and is willing to change his word if people turn to him in intensity of faith (Jon. 4:2).[10] This does not mean that matters will always turn out as *we* wish. But it does mean that prayer can change the course of events, and that failure to pray is not necessarily a sign of submission to God's intractable will. Rather, it may be a sign of apathy and unwillingness to wrestle with God (note Jacob's refusal to let go of the man with whom he wrestled, Gen. 32:26).

2–3 The effect of Isaiah's words upon the king is apparent in his response: he turned his face to the wall and burst into tears. He was completely devastated and withdrew into himself. Ahab had had a similar reaction years earlier when his desire for Naboth's vineyard had seemed frustrated (1 K. 21:4). There are a number of reasons for such a reaction

10. Young quotes Vitringa as saying that although the pronouncement was conditional, the condition was not expressed, so that compliance with the condition would be entirely voluntary.

on Hezekiah's part, especially in a time prior to the evidence of Christ's resurrection as support for the hope of the resurrection of believers (note vv. 18–19). This life was certain and what lay beyond the grave was all too uncertain. Furthermore, he was a relatively young man, being only thirty-nine. Death was coming too soon. But even beyond that, it appears that he had no heir. Manasseh ascended the throne at age twelve (2 K. 21:1). Thus, he was not born until three years after this incident. No good Hebrew could view being cut off childless in midlife as anything but a most severe judgment from God.[11] This would be even more true for the scion of David, who would be contemplating the cessation of God's messianic promises in his own death. Perhaps to a godly man like Hezekiah this seeming injustice from his God was the cruelest blow of all.[12]

But Hezekiah's response is instructive. He does not withdraw completely, for he does not withdraw from God. Neither does he rage against God nor does he demand that God heal him in payment for "services rendered." Rather, he simply pours out the feelings of a wounded heart to a heavenly Father. No father's heart can be unaffected by such a cry. Nor was God's.

Hezekiah's plea focuses on his motivations. None of us, affected by the fallibility and the fallenness of our race, can ever hope to perform perfectly. And if our only hope before God lay in our performance, then we would be truly hopeless. But there is the glad potential for the intentions and motivations to be purified by God's Spirit. Had Hezekiah done everything correctly? Again, of course not. But he could live his life with one desire: to be absolutely faithful to God (Phil. 3:7–15; 1 Thess. 5:23). It is not necessary to live with divided loyalties between self and God, this world and God. It is God's purpose that his people be able to be true (faithful) to him and that their hearts might be one toward him. When that is so, then what we do, though broken and incomplete, like the blotted drawing of a child, is good in the parent's eyes. The good news of the gospel is that such a profession is not just for the Davidic monarch—it is for all people through Christ.

4 As 2 K. 20:4 indicates, Isaiah had not gotten out of the palace before the word of reprieve came to him. Another person might have been chagrined by the need to change a pronouncement so recently made with

11. See Gen. 15:2, 3; Lev. 20:20; 1 Sam. 1:10–11; Prov. 30:15–16; Isa. 53:8; 54:1; Jer. 22:30; Luke 1:7, 25.

12. Why would God permit this to come upon Hezekiah? Is it not possible that he wished to make it plain to all those who were adulating Hezekiah as the promised Messiah that this was not the case?

such certainty. But the prophet was a man under appointment. It was not his word but God's, and if God wished to change it, who was the prophet to quibble?[13]

5 *the God of David your father* evokes the faithfulness of God to his promise. Hezekiah's recovery is not merely because God has changed his mind but because of his willingness to keep faith with those to whom he has committed himself in the past (Deut. 4:37, 38). But it also evokes the memory of the impact of the faithful life. There is no limit to the effect of such a life. Although the sins of a person may affect the third or the fourth generation, the results of a person's faithfulness will reach to a thousand generations (Exod. 34:6, 7). But, as Calvin notes, there is also another evocation here, one which looks forward rather than backward. Ultimately it is only because of the divine David that God can change the word of condemnation into one of life. Best of all, that word is not to be a temporary reprieve but an eternal covenant (Isa. 55:3).

I have heard . . . I have seen speak of the living God who is able to be touched by our weaknesses. Unlike the idols, who have eyes and ears but can neither see nor hear, God both knows and intervenes in the life of his people (37:17; 41:23–24; 43:8).

fifteen years. Depending on the date of accession, Hezekiah lived until 696 or 685, so this event occurred around 710 or 700 (see above on v. 1).

6 Many commentators take this promise of deliverance from the king of Assyria as proof positive that this healing took place prior to Sennacherib's invasion. However, that conclusion does not necessarily follow. Just because Sennacherib had returned home in defeat did not mean that he would not be back the next year and the next and the next, making Hezekiah's added years ones of torment. But God promises that Hezekiah need not fear the Assyrians during his remaining life-span. Thus the verse as it stands does not solve the dating problem. In any case, Isaiah's prediction was correct. No king of Assyria ever captured Jerusalem.

7–8 Although the record here does not include it, 2 K. 20:8 reports that Hezekiah himself requested a confirmation sign (see v. 22). As Skinner notes, this action is diametrically opposite to Ahaz's refusal to accept a sign when one was offered. Hezekiah wished to trust God, Ahaz did not.

8 There is no certainty as to exactly what the *steps* mentioned

---

13. So also Nathan (2 Sam. 7:3–4); Jonah, however, did not respond with the same equanimity as Isaiah and Nathan (Jon. 4:2–3).

here involved. They may have been a part of a device consciously intended for measuring time, or they may have been an ordinary staircase on the exterior of the palace upon which the setting sun happened to cast a shadow. In the former case, the device was perhaps a stepped pyramid with a pillar on the top of it. Thus, in the morning the shadow of the pillar would retreat up the western steps and in the afternoon it would descend the eastern ones.

G. A. Smith paints a graphic picture of the dying king watching from his sickroom as the shadow inexorably descended the steps. How easily he could have associated his own ebbing strength with that lengthening shadow and contemplated the coming sunset with dread. Thus when the prophet offered to move the shadow forward ten steps, one can imagine the king reacting with alarm. Much better to move it backward, up the steps, as a sign of the divine reprieve (2 K. 20:9–10).

The means by which the sign was accomplished is left unstated. Since reversing the rotation of the earth carries with it so many other implications, it seems likely that some sort of refraction of light was involved. 2 Chr. 32:31 seems to imply that it was a local phenomenon.

(2) Hezekiah's psalm (38:9–20)

9 *A writing belonging to Hezekiah king of Judah when he was sick and became well.*

10 *I said, "In the quiet time of my days*
I must go into the gates of Sheol;
I am stripped¹ of the remainder of my years."

11 *I said, "I will not see the Lord,*
the Lord,² in the land of the living.

1. The present translation follows the punctuation of the MT. This creates some difficulty for the interpretation of *puqqaḏtî*, which would normally mean "appointed, visited, judged." The common thought is that it means here "I have been judged as to (deprived of) the remainder of my years." But this interpretation is somewhat strained, as Driver notes. He proposes that the term is an Aramaism meaning "be sought" and reads "within the gates of Sheol I shall be sought . . ." (*JTS* 38 [1937] 46–47). However, if this way of dividing the sentence is followed, then the normal Hebrew meaning is not difficult: "Into the gates of Sheol I have been assigned for the remainder of my years."

2. The repetition of the short form of the divine name "Yah, Yah" is commonly described as an error for the full consonantal form: *YHWH*. The versions are not very helpful on the point. 1QIsᵃ omits one of the Yahs, but that omission could be the result of haplography. The LXX has "look on the salvation of the

I will not gaze upon humanity again
    or the inhabitants of the world.[3]
12 *My span of life*[4] *is plucked up and folded away*
    like the tent of a shepherd.
I have rolled up[5] *my life like a weaver;*
    from the loom he has cut me off;
    from day unto night you have finished me.
13 *I cried out*[6] *until morning;*
    like a lion, thus he has shattered all my bones,
    from day unto night you have finished me.

Lord" in a fairly typical avoidance of anthropomorphism, while Targ., probably following MT, has "appear again before the Terrible One, the Lord. . . ." See Dahood's proposal below in n. 3.

3. The reading here assumes *ḥeled*, "the world." MT has apparently transposed the last two letters, resulting in *ḥedel*, "cessation." But "inhabitant of cessation" makes no sense as a parallel to "humanity." Thus it has become almost universal to emend *ḥedel* to *ḥeled*, "world." This simple transposition, which could have occurred in dictation, makes a good deal of sense. On the other hand, Dahood (*Bib* 52 [1971] 215–16) proposes to stay with the MT for the whole verse, and thus he reads:

I said, I shall not enjoy [cf. Job 20:17], O Yah,
    O Yah, the land of the living.
I shall behold the earth no more
    among the inhabitants of cessation.

This may be correct, but it has the appearance of something of a *tour de force*. The versions are not too helpful: Targ. has "land" while LXX lacks the entire clause. (Cf. *BHS*.) For support of the MT, as well as discussion of literary problems, see H. S. Nyberg, "Hiskias Danklied, Jes. 38, 9–20," *ASTI* 9 (1973) 85–97.

4. Lit. "my generation." Both LXX and Targ. construe the term in its literal sense but must supply additional words to do so. The English versions take it as "habitation" or "dwelling," apparently drawing from the Aramaic meaning as exemplified in Ps. 84:12 (Eng. 11). However, if the term is taken as referring to a duration of life and applied individually instead of in the usual collective way, the present effective parallel to "life" is achieved.

5. 1QIs[a] has *sprty*, "I numbered(?)," for MT *qippaḏtî*, "I rolled up." Driver proposed to read 1QIs[a] as "you cut off" (cf. Syr. *sappar*), and to emend the latter part of the verse to read "my life like a weaver, severing me from the thrum" (*JSS* 13 [1968] 56). But this is unnecessary. It is we who roll up our lives and it is the Lord who makes the decision when sufficiency has been reached.

6. MT has *šiwwîṯî* (from *šwh*), "I have composed myself" (cf. Ps. 131:2, but note the absence of *nepeš*, "self, soul," here). LXX lacks the verb, while Targ. renders "roared (like a lion)." *BHS* recommends *šiwwaʿtî*, "I cried out (for help)," on the basis of the Targ., but if so Targ. is a corruption in one direction, while MT is in another. 1QIs[a] has *špwty*, "laid bare (as bones)," but this appears to be only an attempt to make sense of the difficult MT. Note that the MT punctuation lends some support to the Targ., for it would naturally read, "I roared until morning like a lion." *šiwwaʿtî* is adopted here as the best alternative.

14 *Like a swallow or[7] a crane[8] thus I chirp;*
I moan like a dove.
My eyes grow weak looking up.
Oppression is mine. O Lord, be my surety.
15 *What shall I say,*
since he has said[9] it
and he himself has done it?
I will walk slowly[10] all my years
on account of the bitterness of my soul.
16 *My lord, on account of them they live*
and by all that is in them my spirit lives.
You give me health and make me live.
17 *Behold, for well-being my bitterness was bitter.[11]*
But you have held back[12] my soul from the pit of destruction.[13]
For you have put all my sins behind your back.
18 *For Sheol does not thank you;*
Death does not praise you.
Those who go down to the Pit do not hope in your faithfulness.
19 *The living, the living, he it is who praises you,*
as I do today;
a father makes known to sons
your faithfulness.
20 *The Lord [is at hand] to save me*

7. On the absence of the conjunction, cf. GKC, § 120h.

8. Both LXX and Targ. lack any reference to the crane, whose cry is something of a shrill croak. Skinner proposes that it is a conflation from Jer. 8:7. However, the contents of the two verses are so dissimilar that it is difficult to see what would motivate such an action.

9. Targ. has "What shall I say *and declare before him*" while 1QIs[a] appears to have *ʾômar*, "I say" (instead of "he said"), for the second verb. Delitzsch points to 2 Sam. 7:20 for a parallel: "What shall I say" (because he has spoken, v. 19).

10. As it occurs in Ps. 42:5 (Eng. 4), *ddh*, "to walk softly," refers to a festal procession. That may be the sense here, but there is a distinct absence of festal joy. Scott (following Ehrlich) recommends following the Syr. and reading *ndd kl šnty*, "all my sleep has fled" (so RSV, TEV, JPSV). Begrich, in support of his conclusion that the psalm is a psalm of thanks, emended the verse to read "I will give thanks [*ʾdk* for *ʾddh*] . . . for the healing of my soul [*mrpʾ npšy* for *mr npšy*]," *Psalm*, pp. 41–42). Unfortunately, there is no textual support for such an emendation.

11. 1QIs[a] has *mʾwdh*, "very(?)," in place of the second *mr*, "bitter," of MT. Presumably the translation would be "It was very bitter for me."

12. MT has *ḥāšaqtā*, "you loved," which is possible, but very unlikely. LXX has "delivered," which lends support to an original *ḥāśaḵ*, "hold back, spare" (so *BHS*). Cf. 1 Sam. 25:39; Job 33:18; Ps. 19:14 (Eng. 13); 78:50.

13. Everywhere else *bʿlî*, "destruction(?)," is an adverb of negation, "not, without." Driver suggests it is an Aramaism here, meaning "corruption, putrefaction" (*JTS* 38 [1937] 47).

and we will play my music[14]
all the days of our lives
in the house of the Lord.

This psalm poses some serious questions to contemporary students of psalmody, for it does not fit any of the commonly accepted forms. On first glance, especially in view of the title (v. 9), one would expect it to be a thanksgiving hymn. But except for vv. 19 and 20, neither the content nor the form clearly supports such an expectation. On the other hand, although the content and the meter (3/2) point toward a lament, the formal characteristics, such as the opening call to the Lord, are missing.[15] These factors should caution the scholar against forcing the material in one direction or another. They should also raise the question of the significance of the anomalous form: Why is it neither wholly lament nor wholly thanksgiving? What was the author attempting to convey?[16]

P. R. Ackroyd takes some note of this issue in his treatment of the canonical significance of these chapters.[17] He suggests that the king's misery, but eventual recovery, is intended to be seen as a type of the nation's near death in exile, but eventual restoration. While this interpretation is very suggestive, it does not pay enough attention to the preponderance of lament material in the psalm. Why the heavy emphasis upon mortality and loss? In my view the stress is not so much upon the restoration as it is upon the fallibility of king and people that, despite the present reprieve, must issue in coming destruction. Thus there is thanksgiving for the deliverance from death (and from Assyrian destruction), but that rejoicing is very much muted by the grim realization of death's reality.[18]

14. Translations vary on *nᵉginôtay*, here translated "my music" (cf. BDB). Since *nqn* is "to play a stringed instrument," some translate "stringed instruments" (cf. RSV, NIV, CBAT). The numerous appearances of the term in musical instructions would admit of either possibility (Ps. 4:1; 6:1; 54:1; 55:1; 67:1; 76:1 [all headings in Eng.]; Hab. 3:19). JPSV translates "music," noting that the ending is not the 1st person possessive pronoun, but a poetic ending (so also Hab. 3:19?).

15. For an extended study of this problem, cf. J. Begrich, *Der Psalm des Hiskia*, FRLANT 42 (Göttingen: Vandenhoeck & Ruprecht, 1926). He concludes that it is a thanksgiving psalm, e.g., p. 51.

16. As noted above on ch. 38, there is no sufficient reason to deny the psalm to Hezekiah. To be sure, the ascription "to Hezekiah" could mean other things besides authorship. However, given his concern for the temple music (2 Chr. 29:25), overskepticism is unwarranted.

17. See P. R. Ackroyd, "Interpretation of the Babylonian Exile: A Study of 2 Kings 20; Isaiah 38–39," *SJT* 27 (1974) 344–45.

18. The large number of similarities with Job is instructive at this point. Cf. Job 38:17 (v. 10); 4:21; 6:9 (v. 12); 17:3 (v. 14); 5:17, 18 (v. 17). The verbal similarities suggest there is also a similarity in outlook with a stress upon human impotence before divine sovereignty.

There are perhaps two important theological points being made here. One of these is the reiteration of human helplessness and divine trustworthiness. Even a king is helpless before the onslaught of death. Even the most powerful are laid low in its path. Why then should we put our trust in human mortality? On the other hand, God can and will snatch a person out of the very gates of death and restore him to life. He holds the keys of life and death and will use those to our benefit. Should not such a One be trusted?

The second point is more implicit than explicit. But it arises in answer to the question of why such an emphatic statement of Hezekiah's mortality and impotence should be placed here in the book. An answer which seems obvious is that there is a conscious attempt to make it plain that Hezekiah is not the promised Messiah. Despite his ability to trust God and to lead his nation back from the brink of destruction, he is not the Child of whom Isaiah has spoken. He has embodied the trust which is essential if the nation is to serve God, but he is *not* the One in whom that trust is to be reposed. Of that One a fuller revelation (chs. 40–66) still lies ahead.

Opinions on the structure of the psalm vary depending upon whether the obscure vv. 15 and 16 are read as thanksgiving. Generally speaking, however, it is agreed that vv. 10–14 state the condition and that vv. 15–20 reflect on God's response to that condition.

9 *A writing belonging to Hezekiah,* along with the rest of the verse, sounds very similar to the titles included for many of the Psalms. Since the authenticity of these titles is considered dubious by some scholars, some want to dismiss this one as well. However, there is no significant evidence to support such a course of action. In fact, as Kaiser points out, the anomalous form may be taken as evidence that the psalm was composed for this specific setting.

A writing does not appear in the heading of any other psalm and so it has been proposed that *miktāb,* "writing," be amended to *miktām,* a term used to identify Pss. 56–60.[19] The forms of the final *mem* and the *bet* are similar, so the confusion of one for the other is not difficult. Furthermore, there is some similarity between the content of this psalm and those. Thus, there is some possibility that the emendation is correct. On the other hand, there is nothing requiring the change, and as a result there is now some sentiment for keeping the MT reading.[20]

19. So Gesenius, followed by Duhm and many others. Young says that the psalm is a *miktām* in form.
20. So Clements. Targ. and 1QIs[a] support MT while LXX has the ambiguous "A Song. Prayer of Hezekiah."

10–14 The recurring theme in these verses is untimely death resulting in a sense of helplessness and gloom. The speaker could only look beyond himself for deliverance and none had seemed forthcoming. God had seemed silent and implacable.

10 The meaning of *In the quiet time* is highly uncertain. A number of possibilities have been put forward.[21] But most are agreed that something like NIV's "In the prime of my life" is intended. At the time when he least expects it, Hezekiah is confronted by the gaping maw of death.[22] Suddenly all the years upon which he had counted for more achievements and for the enjoyment of those achievements vanish away like a vapor. How easily we human beings consider the years of our lives an inviolate possession. But that is not true. We have only today and perhaps not all of it. We are distinctly dependent creatures, and if such experiences as Hezekiah's help us to face what that fact means for present living and eternal destiny, then they are very salutary experiences indeed.

11 As this verse stands, it expresses an interesting parallelism between divine and human fellowship. Hezekiah does not expect to find them in the netherworld. Ultimately this kind of fellowship is what life is about. We were made for God and for one another, and to be deprived of these is to be plunged into depression and despair (cf. 1 John 1:3; also Ps. 84:2–13 [Eng. 1–12]). For a discussion of the view of the netherworld which this verse presupposes, see below on v. 18.

12 Here the poet reverts to the abruptness of the apparent close of his life, using two graphic similes. The first is the shepherd's tent. It may have remained in one spot for some time while the grass lasted. In so doing, it would have given the illusion of some permanence, just as life does. But one day the grass gives out, and in a matter of hours nothing remains but a bit of trampled earth.

---

21. If "pause" or "quietness" is the correct root meaning, it may refer to the quiet middle years of life (Delitzsch) or to the sudden close of life (Kissane) or to the noonday pause (Cheyne). The somewhat similar plea found in Ps. 102:23–24 lends support to the idea of "midst." Something of the same idea comes from a different identification of the root. It is taken to come from *dāmâ*, "be like," and to mean "half" (Driver, *JTS* 38 [1937] 46; so also Scott and Clements). A radically different proposal was put forward by Dahood, and the same idea appears in Kaiser, but without reference to Dahood. Here the root is taken to be *dmm* II, "lament." In this case, the meaning would be "in my sorrow I must go" ("Textual Problems in Isaias," *CBQ* 22 [1960] 401).

22. For the idea of the underworld as having gates, see the Akkadian poem "The Descent of Ishtar" (*ANET*, pp. 107–108). The victim is required to pass through seven successive gates, being stripped of one more item at each until, having passed the seventh, she is completely naked. Cf. also Job 38:17; Ps. 9:14 [Eng. 13]; 108:19 [Eng. 18]; Matt. 16:18.

So also the weaver works on a piece of cloth on her loom day after day. Passersby become used to seeing that particular fabric on the structure. But one day the weaver decides the roll is big enough and with a few swift strokes cuts it loose and carries it away. Life is like that. Death removes in a moment what had seemed so permanent.[23] In the face of this truth there are two wrong alternatives. One is to say, "Eat, drink and be merry, for tomorrow we die" (22:13; Eccl. 8:15). But what is after death? Shall we mortgage eternity for a few heedless moments? The other alternative is to deny the reality of such an impermanent and transitory existence. This point of view would hold out that life is of no consequence and is better done away with. It would be characteristic of several of the eastern religions. The biblical position is that a good Creator made a world in which, though it is now corrupted, there are genuine values and real possibilities. However, those values and possibilities are not complete in themselves. They point to a reality which is deeper than mere flesh and material elements.

from day unto night you have finished me, appearing as it does at the end of both vv. 12 and 13 and having the change of pronoun (from "he" to "you"), may be a proverbial statement. It has at least two possible interpretations. On the one hand it may mean both day and night, i.e., continually, or it may mean between morning and evening, i.e., suddenly. Given the general context, the latter seems somewhat more likely (cf. also 40:6–8; Matt. 6:30).

13 The uncertainty as to the correct reading of the opening word of the verse (cf. n. 6 above) makes it difficult to give a final interpretation of the meaning of the verse. If the MT is correct ("I quieted myself"), then the sense is that the king calmly considered that his fate was at hand and without reprieve. However, that interpretation does not agree with the general atmosphere of the passage, which is hardly calm. The Targum's reading, "I roared like a lion," is rather more appropriate to the setting, but it is the Lord who is compared to a lion, not the king.[24] On balance the reading "I cried out (for help)" seems most appropriate. So the writer

23. Note the biblical use of the imagery of the pulling up of a tent peg to convey the ideas of permanence and impermanence (33:20; Job 4:21; Ps. 52:7 [Eng. 5]; 2 Cor. 5:1, 4; 2 Pet. 1:13, 14; cf. also Heb. 11:9, 10).
24. Note, however, that *nhm* (which the Targ. uses) can also be used for the groan of the sufferer: Ps. 38:10 (Eng. 9); Prov. 5:11; Ezek. 24:23. So an interesting wordplay is suggested: the sufferer groans like a lion, but the Lord crushes the bones like a lion. *š'g* has this same double possibility, and one wonders if this may have been the original from which the MT *šiwwîtî* sprang. Cf. esp. Ps. 38:9, 10 (Eng. 8, 9).

says he groaned for help through the night, but in the morning "the lion" was still cracking his bones between his powerful jaws (cf. Job 3:23–26). By nightfall there seemed no hope at all. The shadow had descended the steps and life had seemed to ebb away on each lower step (Isa. 38:8). Again, as in v. 12, the change in pronouns in the last clause suggests the possibility that it is a proverbial statement.

14 This verse continues to express the king's sense of helplessness: his cries are like the chirping[25] of a bird, or the moaning coo of a dove. He has looked up to God in seemingly futile petition for so long that his eyes grow weak. Nevertheless, he will not give up his plea; he knows that although God may be the one crushing his bones, so also God is the only one who cares enough to deliver him.

This is an important theological truth. Hezekiah looks to his "oppressor" for deliverance. This is the only direction which a true monotheism can take. The alternative is a dualism which pits "bad" gods against "good" ones. But in the biblical faith, nothing is beyond God's control. Without going to the lengths of Islam, which sees Allah as the immediate cause of every event, it is still possible to affirm that all which occurs is subject to God's veto. If not, it is vain to believe that he can alter the course of events after they happen. Hezekiah does not have this problem. He knows that God is willing and able to become the defense attorney against his own prosecution.

This truth comes to its full flower in the NT. There God the Son accepts our rightful judgment which God the Father has meted out. In Christ, Judge and Convict are one and the same, to our eternal benefit.[26]

It is tempting to say that vv. 15–20 change the tone of the psalm from lament to praise. This may be the case, but the interpretation (and in some cases the reading) of vv. 15 and 16 is so uncertain that it is not possible to make such an assertion with confidence.[27] By v. 17b the change has definitely occurred, however, and the psalm closes with the promises of continuous praise, a behavior which is not to be found in Sheol.

15 *he has said it,* if correct, speaks of the divine creative word.

---

25. The use of "chirp" here may be something of a pun since the same term is used of the speech of the dead (8:19; 29:4; cf. also 10:14).

26. See 2 Cor. 5:18–21; Eph. 2:14–16; Col. 1:20–22; Rom. 5:8–11. Begrich, *Der Psalm der Hiskia,* p. 38, identifies ʿošqâ, "oppression," and ʿārab, "be (my) surety," as legal terms.

27. The LXX lacks v. 15 altogether, while Targ. heavily alters the two verses in its paraphrase.

God has but to speak the word and the matter is done (Luke 7:6–10). Hezekiah knows that this matter is in God's hand and not in his own.

he himself has done it is clear in its confidence in God, but unclear as to its reference. If "it" refers to his healing, the king is asking the classic question of the Psalms, "How shall I respond to God's goodness?" (see, e.g., Ps. 116:12). On the other hand, it is possible that this is an utterance of resignation: "This affliction is from God and my words are useless" (cf., e.g., Ps. 39:10 [Eng. 9]; Luke 22:42). Both positions have scriptural warrant, and the context could be urged in support of either.

I will walk slowly has two possible interpretations. If the interpretation is positive, then Hezekiah seems to be saying that in his additional fifteen years he will not live in careless ease, taking his life for granted. Rather, this experience will cause him to live humbly and gratefully. He will not forget what he has endured. If a negative position is taken, then the statement must mean that for whatever time is left him, the victim will bow his head under the judgment which has befallen him. It is difficult to come to complete certainty concerning the two alternatives for understanding the verse. Neither is totally compelling. However, the final remark of the verse upon "bitterness of soul" seems to point in the direction of resignation under the divine hand of judgment.

16 The questions surrounding this verse are even more complex than those relating to the previous one. Both the LXX and the Targum differ markedly from the MT and from each other.[28] Furthermore, commentators are widely divided first of all over the authenticity of the text, but even more over the interpretation. This diversity suggests that further speculation could only add to the problem and that the best course of action here is to seek to understand the text as we have it.[29]

on account of them they live is enigmatic. Perhaps "them" refers to the words and acts of God (so Young). But Cheyne relates it to life's experiences, depending on the final clause of the previous verse. In any case, Hezekiah knows that it is God who is "Lord" of all that befalls him and that his life is in God's hands.

You give me health may be understood either as a plea or as an

---

28. LXX: "O Lord, yes, it was told you concerning it and you roused up my breath and I was comforted and came to life." Targ.: "My Lord, with regard to the dead you have declared that you would bring them back to life; but before them all you have caused my spirit to live and have preserved me alive and established me."

29. Skinner speaks rather approvingly of Duhm's emendations to the verse, but concludes dryly that they are "somewhat sweeping." Clements simply says the Hebrew is unintelligible.

affirmation. The verb is an imperfect so the action is not complete in any case. The following imperative, *make me live,* is perhaps an expression of confidence following the imperfect.[30] So the writer declares again that if he is to survive it must be God's doing. In keeping with the motif of this division of the book (chs. 7–39), the emphasis is upon God's sovereignty and trustworthiness.

17 The ambiguity of interpretation continues through the first clause here (lacking in LXX). Has Hezekiah found bitterness instead of well-being? Or is he saying that bitterness was for the sake of well-being? The commentators and translations are in general agreement that the latter is the case, although grammatical arguments for the one position as opposed to the other are not decisive.[31] If this majority reading is correct, it lends some support to the positive understanding of the final clause of v. 15. The bitterness has been turned to good purpose and Hezekiah will not forget it. Certainly many a believing person has been able to testify to the truth of such an observation. Why the calamity or adversity has come cannot be said, but God has used something seemingly wholly bad for good purposes (Rom. 8:28).

As Calvin remarked, and as Jesus demonstrated (Luke 5:17–26), forgiveness of sins and recovery from illness are two sides of God's saving power. Hezekiah apparently felt that had he died this untimely death it would have been in punishment for sin, perhaps the sin of pride. Now the fact that he is recovering is evidence that God has turned away from Hezekiah's sins and turned to Hezekiah. Whatever may have been Hezekiah's spiritual condition, the truth may be affirmed that a sense of unforgiven sin is a killer which often bars the way to physical and emotional healing. The corollary of this truth is that the confidence that our sins are buried in the sea of God's grace is frequently the key to healing in these areas (Ps. 103:3, 4).

18 This is a classic statement of the OT belief that the dead do not praise God.[32] There are at least three ways to understand this phenomenon, especially as it relates to the NT doctrine of resurrection: (1) it is speaking of those who die in sin; (2) it is only referring to the tomb and the corpses in the tomb; (3) it is a part of the process of progressive revelation whereby incomplete understandings were progressively replaced by better ones until the canon was complete. Each of these has some

30. Cf. GKC, § 110i.
31. In support of "instead of" cf. Calvin, Clements, NEB.
32. See also Job 10:21–22; Ps. 6:6 (Eng. 5); 30:10 (Eng. 9); 88:11–13 (Eng. 10–12); 115:17.

difficulties. With the first, it is hard to show any place in the OT where the righteous dead are spoken of differently than the unrighteous dead. There are no instances of the righteous dead praising God.[33] The difficulty of the second is that it seems to demand an excessively narrow interpretation of the expressions, not the one which would most naturally present itself. The third has the problem that progressive revelation generally expands the former teaching (as of the Messiah) rather than, as resurrection seems to do, contradicting the former. Perhaps the solution is to say that the fuller truth declares that some of the dead will praise God, although not all. An alternative is to say that the new truth teaches us that it is those who die the "second death" who will not praise him. On balance, the third alternative seems to have the fewest problems.

It may be wondered why God would have permitted this imperfect understanding to have existed for so long. The answer may be that he did not wish anything to distract his people from an understanding of the importance of this life and our response to him in it. Too often in the ancient world behavior here was seen to be of little significance because all activity was understood as part of the cycles of fate reflecting the actions of the gods. But this ancient view is not true, and it may be that the relative absence of mention of "the other realm" in the OT is for the purpose of highlighting the importance of this world in God's eyes.[34]

do not hope in your faithfulness underlines the chasm between B.C. and A.D.[35] Since the resurrection of Christ we know that it is precisely beyond the grave that we will praise God's faithfulness (lit. his truthfulness). God did speak the truth when he said that eternal life is in his Son (1 John 5:11–12) and when he said that our sin will never be counted against us (Heb. 10:17). Salvation was not in Hezekiah. Fifteen years or no, he *would* die and no longer be alive to praise God. But Jesus Christ is alive, and because he lives, all who put their trust in him, including the OT believers (1 Pet. 3:18–19), will live to praise him forever and ever (Rev. 5:9–14).

19 Thus it is indeed the living who will praise God and declare his faithfulness to their children. But the wonder of God's plan is that

33. It is true that there are instances where intimations of eternal bliss appear (e.g., Ps. 23:6; Isa. 26:19; etc.), nor can Job's longing for redemption in the hereafter be gainsaid (Job 19:25, 26). But these do not seem to represent developed, consciously held points of view.

34. Cf. "Dead, Abode of the," *IDB*, I:787–88; "Sheol," *ZPEB* V:395; N. J. Tromp, *Primitive Conceptions of Death and the Nether World in the Old Testament*, BibOr 21 (Rome: Pontifical Biblical Institute, 1969).

35. See esp. G. A. Smith on this theme.

living does not cease at the grave for his people. In fact, it enters a wonderful new dimension of life forevermore.

As Young notes, if it is correct that Hezekiah had no heir at this time (see on 38:3), then the opportunity to declare God's faithfulness to his children through the added years of life would have been a special blessing. Given Manasseh's apostasy, one can only wonder whether Hezekiah then missed the opportunity when it was given him.

20 *The Lord to save me* is a grammatical impossibility in Hebrew as well as English. But rather than resorting to emendation (cf. *BHS*), it is more appropriate to understand that the infinitive is being used to express the imminent future.[36] Thus the writer expresses his conviction that God has heard his cry and will deliver. This feature is typical of the lament form (e.g., Ps. 6:10 [Eng. 9]; 22:23–25 [Eng. 22–24]). While it is not impossible that these ejaculations were in response to some act of absolution by the priest at that point in the psalm, such observations hardly plumb the depths of the truth expressed here.[37] More to the point, these expressions of confidence in the midst of lament speak of an abiding conviction on the part of the Hebrew people concerning God's nature: however inscrutable his ways and fearsome his judgments, beneath all that beats a Father's heart which does hear the cries of his children and can be depended upon to deliver.

we will play my music (see n. 14 above) is another expression of confidence. Not only will the king hear music again (cf. Ps. 51:10 [Eng. 8]), he himself will make music. This is a mark of the redeemed. They can sing because they have been delivered. In the deepest sense, it is the free heart which sings (cf. Ps. 51:16 [Eng. 14]; 27:6; 30:12 [Eng. 11]; Isa. 12:2; 26:19; 65:14). The addition which the NT makes to this truth is that the heart may be free though the body is not (Acts 16:25), and until the heart is free, other freedoms must go sour (Rom. 1:28–32; cf. Col. 3:12–17 for the results of the free heart in community; note esp. v. 16).

all the days of our lives expresses the response of the heart which has truly encountered God's grace. Life is not long enough to give him the praise he is due. The pharisaical heart which is proud of its own achievements finds no reason to praise him (Luke 7:47). Its own pride blocks any recognition that it owes its very existence to him. But the person who has gazed into the depths of himself and has found nothing there and has then turned to see nothing but love in a Savior's eyes will never cease to marvel at the wonder of it. So Hezekiah knew for certain

---

36. Hence "[is at hand]"; see GKC, §§ 114 h–l.
37. S. Mowinckel, *The Psalms in Israel's Worship,* pp. 216–17.

he was a dead man, but suddenly, unaccountably, he was alive, and so long as he lived he would never get over his gratitude to God.

in the house of the Lord is also typical of this form. The house was of special value to the psalmists. Although God was present everywhere, it was there that his presence was especially real. And it was this sense of his presence which was the highest desire of the singers (cf. esp. Ps. 84). What good is a love song without the presence of the Lover? Moreover, it is apparent that the "Presence" is what the Hebrew and Christian religions are about from Eden through Sinai and Pentecost to the Throne. God can be known and experienced. Should we see how little of his presence we can experience and still survive? "Never," say the redeemed.

(3) Additional notes (38:21–22)

21 *Now Isaiah had said, "Let them take a cake of figs and rub it on the boil so that he might live."*
22 *And Hezekiah had said, "What is the sign that I shall go up to the house of God?"*

It is difficult to avoid the conclusion that these verses were not a part of the original Isaianic composition. They appear very much like an afterthought in their present position in the text in that they do not logically follow the preceding verses, nor do they serve any necessary function in this position. This feeling is only heightened when the parallel account in 2 K. 20 is consulted. There the information contained in these two verses is integrated into the narrative at the appropriate points and in ways which in fact strengthen the narrative. How then shall we explain the two accounts? Three alternatives present themselves: (1) Isaiah is original and Kings is dependent; (2) Kings is original and Isaiah is dependent; (3) both are dependent on a common original, but Isa. 37:20 and 21 have been added later to harmonize with the Kings account. I favor the third option because it has fewer problems than either of the first two. Although Isaiah is undoubtedly the harder reading, the Kings account is more than a merely smoothed-out handling of the Isaiah narrative. On the other hand, it will not do to say that the writer of the Isaiah account was copying the Kings version and accidentally left out a few details which he then added at the end upon discovering his errors. In fact, the Isaiah version seems to have been deliberately abbreviated at several points to make room for the psalm. In other words, the writer never intended to include the details now found in vv. 21 and 22, not feeling them essential to what he was attempting to say. However, a later copyist, knowing both versions and perhaps feeling that unintentional omissions had occurred, added the information from Kings at the end of the Isaiah account, not wishing to tamper with the now semi-fixed form by inserting them at more appropriate places within the narrative.[1]

As the account stands, these verses appear as explanatory notes, giving background to what has already been presented. Thus v. 21 explains that whatever the disease may have been, one of its symptoms was a boil. Furthermore, though it is not explicitly stated, we are led to believe that the miracle of healing was achieved through the application of a poultice of figs.[2] This is an important point in any theology of healing. All healing is of God. Sometimes he intervenes directly to produce health. At other times he works through intervening means, as here. But it is misleading to limit divine healing to those instances where no intervening means appears. If the poultice was instrumental in Hezekiah's healing, it was still divine providence which brought Isaiah to Hezekiah's bedside with the remedy at that moment.

The second note, which appears in v. 22, explains the giving of the sign in v. 7, as well as the reference to the house of God in v. 20. According to 2 K. 20:5, Isaiah had promised Hezekiah that he would be in the temple in three days' time praising God. Hezekiah requested confirmation of this promise, and God's response was the backward movement of the sun's shadow, suggesting both reprieve from the darkness of death and increased time for life.

Such a request for a sign could be understood as "tempting" or testing God in a negative sense (Deut. 6:16; Matt. 4:7): the person doubts God and demands proof. This kind of testing is forbidden (cf. Mal. 3:15; Matt. 12:39; John 6:30). But there is a positive sense in which such a request may be understood: the person who does believe and asks for confirmation (see above on 7:10; cf. Judg. 6:36–40; Mal. 3:10). God delights to show himself powerful to that person, as he did to Hezekiah.

b. BABYLONIAN SEDUCTION (39:1–8)

1 *At that time Merodach-baladan, son of Baladan, king of Babylon, having heard that Hezekiah was sick and recovered, sent letters and a gift.*

1. For a fuller treatment of this problem, see C. Jeremias, "Zu Jesaja 38.21f," *VT* 21 (1971) 104–111.

2. Grotius, evidently following a rabbinic writer, declared that figs were not good for boils. However, Pliny *Natural History* xix.34 indicates that they were. C. H. Gordon has translated a text from Ugarit (*UT,* 56:32, 33) which prescribes figs for certain horse ailments (*Ugaritic Literature* [Rome: 1949], p. 129), but boils are not among them. Delitzsch says they were a popular remedy used to hasten the bursting of the boil, but does not list his authority.

2 *And Hezekiah rejoiced*[1] *over them and showed them the treasure house:*[2] *the silver, the gold, the balsam, the precious oil, and all the house of the armory*[3] *and all which was found in his storehouses. There was nothing in his house or in all his kingdom which Hezekiah did not show them.*

3 *Now Isaiah the prophet came to king Hezekiah and he said to him, "What did these men say to you, and from whence did they come to you?" Hezekiah said, "They came to me from a distant land—from Babylon."*

4 *And he said, "What did they see in your house?" And Hezekiah said, "Everything in my house they saw; and there is nothing among my treasures I did not show them."*

5 *So Isaiah said, "Hear the word of the Lord of Hosts:*

6 *Behold, the days are coming when everything which is in your house, and which your fathers treasured up until this day, will be carried away to Babylon. Not a thing shall remain, says the Lord.*

7 *Some of your sons descended from you,*[4] *born of you, they will take and they will be eunuchs in the palace of the king of Babylon."*

8 *Then Hezekiah said to Isaiah, "Good is the word of the Lord which you have spoken." And he said, "For there will be peace and stability in my days."*

As noted above in the introduction to chs. 38 and 39, these two chapters serve as a counterpoint to the emphases of chs. 36 and 37. This is especially true of the present one. Instead of trusting God, there is every indication that Hezekiah is trusting the nations, as represented by Babylon. Beyond that, he is depending upon the accumulated wealth of Judah. It seems as if all the lessons of chs. 7–35, so brilliantly exampled in chs. 36 and 37, have been forgotten. In fact, there is good reason to believe that the events described in chs. 38 and 39 took place before those of chs. 36 and 37 (see above on 38:1 and below on 39:1). Therefore, we must

1. Virtually all commentators agree that Isaiah's "(he) rejoiced," *śmḥ*, is superior to "he listened," *šmʿ*, which appears in the parallel in 2 K. 20:13.

2. The meaning of *bêt nᵉḵōṯōh*, "treasure house," is derived from the Akk. *bit nakanti*, as suggested by F. Delitzsch.

3. "house of the armory" (cf. "house of the forest," 22:8) is lit. "house of the vessels." For "vessels" (or "equipment") as arms, see 1 Sam. 17:54; 21:6, 9 [Eng. 5, 8]; 31:9, 10; etc. However, Dahood believed it referred to a "wine cellar" in that all the other items shown were commodities (*Bib* 40 [1959] 162).

4. 1QIs^a has *mmʿykh*, "from your loins," in place of MT *mimmᵉḵā*, "from you." The 1QIs^a reading is more colorful and the MT reading might have arisen through a mistaken omission of the *ayin*. However, the ancient versions are unanimous in their support of the MT. Thus it seems likely that 1QIs^a is an expansion upon the MT.

ask why the author has reversed the chronological order. For surely Hezekiah did learn the lesson. He may not have trusted very well in 711 or 703 when these incidents took place, but he did trust in 701. So why has Isaiah transposed the accounts? It seems most likely that the reason is a theological one.[5] He is answering a fundamental question: if God could be trusted and would deliver from Assyria, why would there be defeat by Babylon? The answer is not that a certain king paraded his riches before a group of Babylonian envoys. It is in fact that trust must become a way of life and not merely a magic talisman to be rubbed at critical moments. Furthermore, the segment's ending on this note makes it plain that Judah's trust is not to be reposed in any human leader. He too is capable of failure. Israel's hope for righteousness and justice must be found in someone more than a Hezekiah. To be sure, Hezekiah has demonstrated the truth of the message of chs. 7–35: God is trustworthy. But he has also demonstrated why the book cannot close here. Servanthood will not be realized simply because God is proven trustworthy. The human problem, even for the Hezekiahs among us, is much deeper. Chs. 40–66, then, exist to go beyond chs. 1–39 in the solution to that problem. Chs. 1–39 provide the essential foundation but not the complete solution. Whatever may be said about the authorship of the book, it is a theological unit, and the arrangement of chs. 36–39 is one indication of that unitary nature.

1 *At that time* gives us no help in determining the calendrical date of these events. Fortunately, the Assyrian records give a good deal of information about Merodach-baladan that helps to establish a general time frame.[6] We are told that he held the throne of Babylon in defiance of Sargon from 721 until 710, when the latter finally ousted him. Then again in Sennacherib's reign, from about 705 to 703, he captured the Babylonian throne a second time. But even after his defeat in 703, he seems to have continued to foment revolt from bases in Elam across the Persian Gulf. As Delitzsch observes, this would permit any time from 721 to 701 for the Babylon embassy to Jerusalem. However, if Hezekiah died in 697/96 (29 years after his accession in 726/25), then the illness and recovery which gave the pretext for the visit would have occurred fifteen years earlier, in 712/11. This would have been a most opportune time for Merodach-bal-

---

5. Note that the account in 2 Kings follows this same order, where no such theological or historical motive presents itself. This suggests that the order of the materials was first set in Isaiah and then followed by the editors of Kings.

6. Akk. *Marduk-apal-iddina*, "Marduk has given a son." For a summary treatment of the life and exploits of Merodach-baladan, as we know them from the Assyrian annals, see C. Boutflower, *The Book of Isaiah, I-XXXIX* (London: SPCK, 1930), pp. 134–147.

adan to have sought to cement ties with the young West Semitic monarch, who seems to have been involved heavily in the anti-Assyrian coalition forming at that time in the West.[7]

son of Baladan suggests two possibilities: (1) the *Marduk-apalidina* referred to by Tiglath-pileser III in 731 is actually the father of the later usurper of the same name, or (2) the usurper had a son of the same name who is unmentioned in the annals. All things considered, the former possibility seems most likely.

By its very position at the end of the sentence, *having heard . . .* is made to appear as something of an afterthought to explain the visit.[8] Although the "miracle of the sundial" would surely have excited the Babylonian interest in astronomical phenomena (2 Chr. 32:31), it is highly unlikely that this alone accounts for the visit. It is much more likely that these events provided a pretext for an embassy whose primary purpose was political. The Babylonian monarch was undoubtedly eager to support rebellion wherever it occurred in the Assyrian empire, knowing that every additional revolt would lessen some of the pressure on himself.[9]

sent letters has raised some question since the verse does not mention the letter-bearers, while v. 2 does not mention the letters but deals with the ambassadors. Several attempts to correct this have been made,[10] but no change seems necessary. "Letters" stresses Merodach-baladan's personal involvement, while the sending of such letters implies the necessity of envoys to carry them.

2 *And Hezekiah rejoiced over them* is completely understandable from a human point of view. For little Judah to be favored by the attention of Babylon was an opportunity which did not come every day. Furthermore, whether in 712 or 703, Hezekiah would have been very glad to have the support of Babylon as he contemplated the impending arrival of the Assyrian army to put down either of the West Semitic revolts.

However, this kind of reliance upon, and delight in, human power and glory is exactly what the first half of the book is warning against. We dare not be seduced by these, for they lead only to a desert (ch. 34). Only

---

7. If the later accession date is taken (716/15), 703 would be the appropriate date.

8. On the circumstantial phrase with a finite verb, cf. Williams, *Syntax*, § 494.

9. So Josephus *Antiquities* x.2.2. However, the sending of condolences and congratulations relating to health matters was not uncommon, as indicated by the Amarna Tablets.

10. Duhm and others propose to emend to *sᵉrîsîm*, "eunuchs," in keeping with v. 7, while Driver (*JTS* 38 [1937] 47–48) and *BHS* suggest that the Akk. *šapīru*, "agent," was intended.

in trust in God is there abundance (ch. 35). This is not to say that Hezekiah had to turn the Babylonian envoys out in the street, but it is instructive to note how Jesus treated the blandishments of Nicodemus (John 3) and of the man called "the rich young ruler" (Mark 10). He was not at all flattered by their words; instead, he plunged directly past the flattery to their real reasons for coming.

showed them the treasure house . . . indicates that the visit was not merely a courtesy call, but was in fact related to diplomatic business. Here was a ready-made opportunity for Hezekiah to glorify God before the pagan Babylonians, to tell of his greatness and of his grace. Instead, he succumbed to the temptation to glorify himself and to prove to the Chaldeans that he was a worthy partner for any sort of coalition they might have in mind.[11] There is no indication that they were interested in such an alliance, however. Much more likely they simply wished to encourage someone whom they viewed as a petty kinglet without making any commitment on their part. An unsavory picture comes to mind of Hezekiah scuttling about showing off his tawdry wealth before the politely approving gaze of the Babylonians, who have in fact seen wealth many times the value of the Judean's little horde in their own homeland. Trust in God and his riches will deliver us from the need to make fools of ourselves in the presence of human glory.

3 As in other cases in the monarchy, the prophet arrived unbidden (2 Sam. 12:1; 1 K. 13:1; 18:16–17; etc.). Whatever an Israelite king's pretensions might be, he always had to operate with the knowledge that, at any point, a prophet who belonged to neither the royal nor the priestly establishments might stand up to rebuke him in the name of One who calls all human beings, king and commoner alike, to account. So Isaiah appears here. Whatever the Babylonians may have thought of Hezekiah's performance, the issue is, what did God think of it?

Isaiah's questions have an ominous simplicity about them. He makes no pronouncements but invites the king to judge himself with his own mouth. Interestingly, Hezekiah does not answer the question, "What did these men say to you?" Evidently Hezekiah knows enough of Isaiah's (and God's) position on foreign alliances to know that he can win no points by relating the conversation. His only hope is to make it appear that he was simply being hospitable to travelers from a famous and distant land.[12]

4 But Isaiah refuses to be taken in by that ploy. He does not

11. Moses succumbed to a similar temptation when he glorified himself instead of God at the rock in the wilderness (Num. 20:2–13). As with Hezekiah, this example of fallibility demonstrated that our hope is not in any human leader.
12. May not the emphasis on distance betray some reflection of Josh. 9, where it is permissible to make alliances with distant countries?

respond to it, but moves ahead to the more ominous question, "What did they see?" Now Hezekiah's answer seems to have something of a defiant ring. "Everything," he says, "I held *nothing* back!"[13] It is as though he knows he cannot win and has decided therefore to brazen it out. None of this is to deny the other biblical statements that Hezekiah was a generally good and godly king, but it is to point out that he was, in fact, not infallible. He was not the Messiah, and like the nation he represented, he needed to discover that trust is a way of life, not a magic talisman to be used only in crises.

5, 6 With deadly calm Isaiah announces that one day all those treasures would belong to Babylon. Mammon would go to Mammon. As pointed out above, we should not think that this one sin of Hezekiah's pride doomed Judah to Babylonian captivity.[14] Rather, this sin is illustrative of the kind of pride and refusal to trust that the entire nation would manifest and that would ultimately result in the captivity. Thus this act is not causal but typical.

It is for this reason that the subsequent Assyrian attack and the surrender of many of these same treasures to Assyria in tribute is not mentioned. In that incident trust would prevail and deliverance would result. Unfortunately, as Isaiah could see by inspiration, that attitude would be but temporary and, terrible irony, those now seducing Judah as friends would be her conquerors. In fact, Isaiah's message to Hezekiah is the same as it was to Ahaz, whose trust was in Assyria. "That which we trust in place of God will one day turn and destroy us."[15]

7 Not only will Hezekiah's treasure belong to the Babylonians but

---

13. In support of this interpretation, notice the emphatic position of *kol*, "everything," and of *lōʾ hāyâ ḏāḇār*, "there was not a thing."

14. That his sin was pride (as well as ingratitude) is supported by 2 Chr. 32:25: "his heart was lifted up."

15. Clements believes that this account was written between 598 and 586 B.C. to explain why Jerusalem had had to capitulate to Nebuchadnezzar (2 K. 24:10–17). According to him, this is why there is no mention of the temple being destroyed: it had not been destroyed at the time of the writing, but the treasures had been taken. This is, of course, an explicit denial of predictive prophecy, which is the cornerstone of the prophetic self-understanding. It is much less destructive to understand that Isaiah is merely using the simplest way to rebuke Hezekiah's pride: "You think you possess these things? In fact, the very people to whom you have shown them off will one day own them." Beyond this, Clements's theory contains the seeds of its own destruction. If the story of the Babylonian envoys had to be rewritten once to explain how Isaiah's supposedly inviolable Jerusalem could be forced to surrender to Babylon, how much more it should have been rewritten again a few years later when Jerusalem was utterly destroyed by the Babylonians.

so also will some of his descendants.[16] Moreover, they will not be merely captives but king's eunuchs, men who have been emasculated so that they no longer have thoughts of their own line and authority but are content to do their master's bidding. How the house of David will have fallen in that day, victim of decade after decade of the continued refusal to trust in God because of being blinded by human glory.

8 Commentators are divided over the proper interpretation of this verse. Does it portray Hezekiah in a favorable or an unfavorable light? The majority seem to take it as a positive statement. Calvin is perhaps typical here. He understands that Hezekiah is being submissive and repentant when he confesses that God's word is good. Furthermore, Calvin believes that it is a consciousness of God's ultimate grace that permits Hezekiah to receive this harsh word without railing. However, this position is called into serious question by the ensuing statement, "For there will be peace and stability in my days." While it may be that Hezekiah is humbly thankful for God's grace in not bringing the deserved punishment upon him immediately, it is hard to avoid the implication that the real reason for his saying that God's word is good is merely the very human relief that he is not going to be destroyed. Whether his descendants are to be consumed does not seem to affect him. Furthermore, his reaction was quite different when his own demise was imminent (38:3). All this leads me to believe that the picture here is essentially negative. Hezekiah is not the promised "child"; he is not infallible. Judah's hope rests in One who is yet to come. To be sure, Hezekiah was the demonstration that God can be trusted. But he is also the demonstration that our trust can no more be in good human beings than in bad ones. Our trust is in God alone.

The message of Isaiah does not reach its conclusion at the end of ch. 39. Too many questions remain unanswered. To be sure, the question "Whom shall we trust?" has been answered in an irrefutable way. Through two sets of historical incidents (chs. 7–12; 36–39), which bracket a didactic section (chs. 13–35), it is made plain that God alone is trustworthy. There is nothing else—especially not human glory—to which we can turn. However, all of this raises again the larger questions posed at the beginning of the book. How can a sinful, congenitally distrustful people, nay, race, become the servants of God? That he is trustworthy is eminently clear. But to get human beings to trust him is another matter entirely, as ch. 39

16. "sons" here can refer to grandchildren and great-grandchildren. It is not restricted to the first generation. If it is true that Hezekiah was still childless at this time (see above on 38:2–6), this prediction would have been all the more important.

brings into sharp focus. If trust in God is the basis for servanthood, what will motivate us to trust in him? Beyond this, what of God's holy character and human sinfulness? How shall these be reconciled? Are they ultimately irreconcilable? Must the conflict be ignored? Or is there some resolution to the problem? When all is said and done, while chs. 7–39 provide the groundwork for the solution to the problem raised in chs. 1–5, the problem still remains: how can sinful, rebellious Israel become holy, submissive Israel? Trust God? Yes, but how? Chs. 40–66 exist to provide the answer to that question.

Excursus I

There are a number of questions relating to the authenticity of these chapters.[1] The questions are provoked first of all by the similarities and differences between these chapters and their analogs in 2 K. 18–20. Second, while Sennacherib's annals refer to a campaign against Jerusalem and to Hezekiah's payment of a large tribute (2 K. 18:14–16), they make no mention of any loss of his army. Third, it is sometimes asserted that, being prose (except for Isaiah's pronouncement in 37:22–29 and Hezekiah's psalm in 38:10–20), they are a late addition to the original prophetic book, a sort of historical appendix. Fourth, the dates of Hezekiah as given in the passage do not coincide with other datings, both biblical and extrabiblical, for the period.

Perhaps the most common answer to these questions today is that there was no destruction of Sennacherib's army, but that the legend grew

1. The following are some of the more important books and articles on this issue: J. Buda, *De Origine Isaiae 36–39* (Bansha Bystrica: Machold, 1937); B. S. Childs, *Isaiah and the Assyrian Crisis*, SBT 2/3 (London: SCM; Naperville: Allenson, 1967); R. R. Deutsch, *Die Hiskiaerzahlungen: Eine formgeschichtliche Untersuchung der Texte Jes. 36–39 und 2 Reg. 18–20* (Basel: Basileia Verlag, 1969); K. Fullerton, "The Invasion of Sennacherib," *BSac* 63 (1906) 577–634; idem, "Isaiah's Attitude in the Sennacherib Campaign," *AJSL* 42 (1925/1926) 1–25; L. Honor, *Sennacherib's Invasion of Palestine* (repr. New York: AMS, 1966); W. A. Irwin, "The Attitude of Isaiah in the Crisis of 701," *JR* 16 (1936) 406–418; O. Kaiser, "Die Verkündigung des Propheten Jesaja im Jahre 701," *ZAW* 81 (1969) 304–315; H. M. Orlinsky, "The Kings–Isaiah Recensions of the Hezekiah Story," *JQR* 30 (1939) 33–49; J. B. Payne, "The Unity of Isaiah: Evidence from Chapters 36–39," *Bulletin of the Evangelical Theological Society* 6/2 (1963) 50–56; H. H. Rowley, "Hezekiah's Reform and Rebellion," *BJRL* 44 (1961/1962) 395–431; W. Rudolph, "Sanherib in Palastina," *PJB* 25 (1930) 59–80; W. Zimmerli, "Jesaja und Hiskia," *Wort und Geschichte*, Festschrift Karl Elliger, ed. H. Gese and H. R. Rüger, AOAT 18 (Neukirchen-Vluyn: Neukirchener, 1973), pp. 199–208; cf. also Young (II:540–569) for a very thorough treatment of the issues.

up to explain why the Assyrian emperor did not destroy Jerusalem when she lay helpless before him. According to this theory, the legend became incorporated into what is now the Kings account by the time of the Exile. Then, as the book of Isaiah was being put together, the redactor(s) excerpted those parts of Kings which had bearing on Isaiah.[2]

Apart from the obvious theological question—if the Hebrews needed to create evidence that God can be trusted, then one wonders why they trusted him in the first place and why their trust endured—there are several other questions which this point of view raises. Chief among these is why Sennacherib left Jerusalem untouched and Hezekiah undisturbed on his throne, when Jerusalem and Hezekiah were, according to the Assyrian annals, the ringleaders in the revolt. That is uncharacteristic of Assyria. Once a vassal revolted, the next step in Assyrian policy was to put a puppet on the throne.[3] Thus it seems unlikely that Sennacherib would have departed willingly. Nor is it surprising that having suffered some devastating reverse, he should make no mention of this in his annals, which were by nature self-congratulatory.

Another question which is raised by the above theory is why there are so many Isaianic features in the Kings account if it (rather than Isaiah) is primary. To be sure, there are certain features which are characteristic of Kings in the two accounts as well, but a theory which explains only one set of similarities will not do. So, the prominence of the personal element is uncharacteristic of Kings except in the Elijah/Elisha accounts, which many scholars believe to have been incorporated into Kings from another source. Likewise, the reference to the Holy One of Israel (37:23) is highly characteristic of Isaiah but not of Kings. Furthermore, if the language of Hezekiah's prayer is undoubtedly Deuteronomistic, the words of the oracle against Assyria are equally undoubtedly Isaianic. Thus any acceptable theory must account for both factors. Since Isaiah could know of Deuteronomy as well as the speech patterns of a king with whom he was close, it seems most likely that the passage stems from Isaiah, or those close to him, and was then incorporated into Kings (note that 2 Chr. 32:32 has the deeds of Hezekiah being written in the vision of Isaiah).[4] Beyond

---

2. See esp. Clements for a brief account of this position. For a more complete treatment, see his *Isaiah and the Deliverance of Jerusalem*.

3. Cf., e.g., *ARAB*, II:142, 207–208.

4. Delitzsch sees Kings as preserving a better version of an original which must have stemmed from Isaiah but which is now less perfectly preserved in Isaiah's book. Young argues forcefully that Isaiah is the better text, as Orlinsky also appears to have done in his incomplete "The Kings–Isaiah Recensions of the Hezekiah Story," *JQR* 30 (1939) 33–49. Wildberger also agrees that Kings is not the original

this, it is hard to explain why a late redactor would insert originals from Kings between the supposedly II Isaianic chs. 34 and 35 and 40–49 except as a rather crude transition to the treatment of Babylon.[5] On the other hand, particularly if the Kings editors had already drawn on prophetic sources for the Elijah/Elisha narratives, it is entirely understandable why those editors would have drawn on the Isaiah corpus for materials on Hezekiah.

Since 2 K. 18:1 makes it plain that Hezekiah began to rule in Hoshea of Israel's third year, which was six years before the fall of Samaria in 722/21 (2 K. 18:10), it is impossible for Hezekiah to have been in his fourteenth year during Sennacherib's attack in 701. Most of the commentators resolve this problem by suggesting the original reference was to the year of the illness (14+15=29) and that it somehow got transposed to Sennacherib's attack.[6] This is barely possible in the Isaiah account, where the royal datings do not directly precede as they do in Kings. It seems highly unlikely that such a thing could happen if the Kings version was original. But a more satisfying suggestion is that the original was "twenty-fourth year," which would only be different from "fourteenth" by two letters—ym vs. h. Here too, it is easier to see how the error could have crept into an Isaianic original than into a Kings original.

It is frequently asserted that the correct historical account of the event is recorded in 2 K. 18:14–16, since its account of the payment of tribute accords with Sennacherib's report.[7] It is furthermore said that the Rabshaqeh's threats and Sennacherib's letter make no sense since Hezekiah had already paid the tribute. Those who accept this line of reasoning either deny that there was a siege or adhere to some sort of double-attack theory. According to the latter, apparently first set forth by Winckler and most

---

from which Isaiah was drawn, pointing out that it is inferior on the basis of longer and easier readings. He proposes that neither text is dependent upon the other, but that both utilized common sources.

5. P. Ackroyd has pointed out that the chapters do not correspond in form or style to the historical appendix found in Jer. 52 ("Isa. i-xii: Presentation of a Prophet," *VTSup* 29 [1978] 201). On the other hand, if the chapters are part of a coherent plan, their presence at this point in the book makes sense.

6. On the other hand, E. R. Thiele has argued that the accession dates given for Hezekiah (as well as Pekah of Israel) are 12 years off and that the attack of Sennacherib in 701 did occur in Hezekiah's 14th year (*The Mysterious Numbers of the Hebrew Kings*, rev. ed. [Grand Rapids: Eerdmans, 1965], pp. 118–154).

7. Delitzsch points out that Hezekiah's name is spelled differently in 2 K. 18:14–16 (*ḥizqîyâ*) than it is elsewhere in the passage (*ḥizqîyāhû*). This difference suggests that the account of the tribute may have been excerpted from another source.

cogently expressed by John Bright,[8] Sennacherib did withdraw in 701, but returned some fourteen years later intending to capture the city. The two events are supposedly telescoped in the scriptural records. This telescoping might be possible if there were any extrabiblical evidence to support the theory. Unfortunately, there is none and in its absence the position can only be an interesting suggestion.

In fact, there is every reason for a siege to follow the giving of tribute. Why should the mightiest king in the world be troubled by convention? Why should he not take money to leave Jerusalem alone and, having taken the money, then refuse to perform the request? If Hezekiah wanted to shower Sennacherib with money, that was Hezekiah's business, but it surely would not have meant Sennacherib was honor-bound to go home. In fact, by his lights he would have been foolish to do so. Moreover, it is hard to believe that the man who memorialized himself for the taking of Lachish would not much rather have had himself depicted taking Jerusalem.[9] Surely he would not let a small matter of having accepted tribute money stand in the way of achieving complete devastation of the enemy. In fact, it is likely that he made such a production of having taken Lachish because he was deprived of the real prize—Jerusalem—by God.

A final problem relates to the nature of the events described in chs. 36–37. It is now commonly asserted that inner contradictions in the accounts make it impossible that the two chapters describe different events.[10] Rather, it is asserted, they give two different versions of the same event. Some of the problems are: the letter should logically precede the show of force; Hezekiah is even less likely to respond with the prospect of Tirhaqah's help; the contents of the letter and of the Rabshaqeh's message are nearly the same; the content of Isaiah's oracle is the same in both cases.

In response, it may be observed that history frequently is not logical. Thus, it is quite possible that Sennacherib wished to keep pressure on Hezekiah by means of a "follow-up" letter. This would be especially true if a new element had entered the picture. In those circumstances it would be normal to attempt to reinforce the points already made. In effect,

8. See J. Bright, *The History of Israel*, 3rd ed. (Philadelphia: Westminster, 1981), pp. 298–309; H. Winckler, *Alttestamentliche Untersuchungen* (Leipzig: 1892), pp. 26–49.

9. Monumental reliefs depicting Sennacherib receiving the capitulation of Lachish have been recovered at Nineveh; cf. *ANEP*, pp. 129–132. The fact that Sennacherib's annals make no mention of the attack on Lachish is used by some to argue that this must have occurred during the unreported second campaign.

10. For the most recent representations of this position, see Clements, Kaiser, and Wildberger.

Sennacherib says, Tirhaqah's advent changes nothing. For Hezekiah, the letter could then have constituted the breaking point. Hopes had been raised, but now the king is brought face to face with reality. He probably had a rather accurate estimate by this time of Tirhaqah's actual ability to help, and the letter's revelation that Sennacherib still intended to take Jerusalem would have been a dash of cold water.

There are two significant differences between the accounts. The more important of these differences is the level of Hezekiah's response. In the first instance he goes into mourning and requests Isaiah to pray. In the second instance the king betrays a much greater spiritual intensity as he humbles himself to pray. To this Isaiah responds with an oracle of equally heightened intensity. This greater intensity is the second difference. When separated as they are, the two oracles highlight the final denunciation of self-sufficient pride and the demonstration of the contrasting lordship of God. Thus it may justly be said that while the two accounts report aspects of one larger experience, there is still reason to see them as separate aspects.

Some may argue that Isaiah of Jerusalem, having preached doom upon the city both before (e.g., 32:9–14) and after (22:1–4 [but this dating is questionable; see the commentary above on ch. 22]) Sennacherib's attack, would hardly have preached deliverance during the attack.[11] But as Ackroyd notes, it is impossible to explain the consolation of chs. 40–66 if the original preaching of Isaiah was wholly condemnatory.[12] This is especially true if one accepts multiple authorship. Unless the basic document contained elements of hope, there is absolutely no reason why succeeding strata containing that motif would have been grafted to this original and not some other, more suitable one. In fact, Isaiah is the prophet who preached doom on all arrogance and self-sufficiency and hope for all who humbled themselves before God.

11. Cf. R. E. Clements, *Deliverance*, pp. 28–36; B. S. Childs, *Crisis*, pp. 63–68.
12. Ackroyd, op. cit.

Excursus II

The following is an extract from the royal annals of Sargon (724–705 B.C.) illustrating the kinds of claims which Isaiah summarized so effectively. Similar claims can be found in the annals of virtually all the Assyrian monarchs. The present text comes from a letter from Sargon to the god Ashur. The translation is mine. Cf. *ARAB*, II:142–44.

18 *I put the armies of Shamash and Marduk across the Lower Zab, whose passage is difficult, like a canal.*

19 *I entered through the passes of Kullar the high mountain of the land of Lulumi which they call Zamua.*

22 *In the province of Shubi I made an inspection of my troops. I saw the number of horses and chariots.*

24 *With the great help of Ashur, Shamash, Nabu, and Marduk, into the interior of the mountains I set rows of march for the third time.*

26 *I turned the yoke of the aegi which were going before me to Zikirte and Andia of Nirgal and Adad.*

28 *I passed through the midst of Nikipa and Upa, high mountains, which are covered with all kinds of trees, whose midst is chaos, whose passes are fearful, whose shade spreads over that region like a cedar forest so that the one who goes through them does not see the ray of Shamash.*

32 *I crossed over the Buya, a river between them, 26 times.*

33 *My army in its mass did not fear the high waters.*

34 *Simirria is a great mountain peak which sticks up like the point of a lance among the high-headed mountains, the dwelling of Belit-ili. Above, its twin heads support the sky. Beneath, its base is sunk into the midst of the underworld. Like the spine of a fish, there is no passage on one side to the other, and ascension of its front or back is very difficult. On its sides are abysses, mountain torrents wind about. When one has seen it with the eyes it sends fear (through him). Its way is no good for the ascent of chariots or the going of horses and (even) the passage for foot soldiers is very difficult.*

44 *With the opening of wisdom and the breath of knowledge which Ea and Belit-ili gave to me, they having opened my feet to cut down the land of the enemy, I caused my vanguard to carry mighty bronze pickaxes. They broke the border of the mountain in pieces like limestone and made good the way.*

50 *I placed engineer troops behind them and camels and pack donkeys climbed its peak like mountain goats.*

52 *I caused the mighty armies of Ashur to ascend its difficult heights easily. I set up my camp upon that mountain.*

54 *Sinahulzi and Biruatti, great mountains whose grass has a pleasant odor; Turtani, Sinabir, Ahshuru, and Suya, their seven mountains I passed over with difficulty.*

58 *I crossed over the Rappa and the Aratta rivers when their courses were at their height as though they were ditches.*

60 *I descended to Sirikiash the region of the land of the Manaites which is on the border of Karallu and Allabria.*

INDEXES

SUBJECTS

AUTHORS

Scriptures

(The Scriptures are indexed according to English verse divisions.)

OLD TESTAMENT

715

32:24	156	4:4	223	2:2	349
32:29	512	4:22	422	2:7	349
32:30	556	5:3	522	2:15	349
32:36	426	5:4	566	2:17	500, 523
32:37–39	642	5:5	364	3:4	179
32:41–43	609	5:6	596	3:7	179
33:17	610	5:17	169	3:8	179
33:26	367	6	244	4:1–6	333
33:27	462	6:7	379		
33:29	322	6:11	500, 523	*I Samuel*	
34:1	337	6:11–24	177	1:10–11	676
34:5	336	6:18	310	1:11	380
34:11	386	6:20	310	1:20	212
		6:25	353	2:2	473
Joshua		6:28	353	2:5	438
1:4	500	6:34	279	2:10	593
1:6–9	200	6:36–40	691	2:12–17	510
3:10	646, 654	7	244	2:21	528
5:8	258	7:4–8	225	2:22	510
5:9	465	7:21	502	2:26	575
6:18	648	7:25	272	2:34	205
6:21	608	8:21	142	3:11	251
6:23	310	8:26	142	4:4	653
6:25	312	9:15	342	4:21	212
7:15	255	9:17	503	6:6	129
7:19	181	10:10	379	6:18	310
8:11	507	10:16	575	7:3	575
9	695	11:22–26	336	7:10	593
9:14	542	11:29	279	10:3	357
10:11	520	13:3–5	211	10:9	532
10:24	503	13:22	177	10:10	279
11:6	555	13:24	212	10:22	542
11:9	555	13:25	279	11:3	629
12:2	348	14:6	279	11:15	463
13:4	430	14:8	626	12:9	466
13:6	430	14:18	373	12:21	449, 502
13:9	348	15:5	494	13:1	400
15:8	349	18:3	419	13:10	420
22:20	171	18:10	420	13:14	193
23:10	556	18:23	409	14:2	275
24:2	575	19:11	415	14:6–15	275
24:14–15	236	19:13	415	14:7	107
24:19	248	19:24	255	14:9	458
24:23	575	19:25	129	14:13	275
		20:2	371	14:23	433
Judges		20:18	542	14:38	371
1:1	542	20:23	542	14:47	336
1:36	341	20:27	542	15:3	608
3:3	430	20:34	400	15:15	646
3:7	111	20:38	566	15:26–30	209
3:9	379	20:40	566	15:30	646
3:12–30	336			16:7	444
3:15	379	*Ruth*		16:13	279
3:19	178	1:6	436, 528	17:26	646, 654
3:30	315	1:21	305	17:34	626

20:37	126	8:10	462	19:25		688
21:8–10	611	9:1	644	19:25–27		318
21:20	324	9:6	454, 651	19:26		82, 688
24:25	324	9:34	235	19:27		82
25:11	611	9:38	235	20:3		366
26:1–15	177	10:1	235	20:6		323
26:1–23	5	10:2	235	20:7		323
26:6–15	123	13	16	20:17		679
26:16–21	5	13:24	638	21:19		252
28:5–8	198			21:26		487
28:5–15	7	*Esther*		22:2		420
28:8–15	200	1:1	360	22:10		453
28:15	384	1:10	447	26:6		318
28:16–18	7	8:16	476	26:12		357, 548
28:16–21	659			27:21		498
28:17	198, 611	*Job*		29:3		242
28:18	198, 331	1:19	391	29:14		142
28:20–21	7	2:4	583	29:17		476
28:22–24	198	2:13	430	29:19		476
29:1–36	9	3:8	440	30:29		616
29:25	681	3:23–26	685	33:1		522
30:1–5	9	3:26	315	33:6		537
30:10–11	9	4:3	303	33:18		680
32:3	413	4:13	531	34:2		522
32:4	413	4:17	420	37:3		285, 451
32:5	413	4:21	681, 684	37:4		593
32:25	696	5:3	625	37:5		593
32:31	678, 694	5:17	681	38:3		228, 282
32:32	700	5:18	681	38:13		285
33:5	454	6:9	681	38:16		517
33:6	230	7:1–3	348	38:17	517, 681, 683
34:4	496	7:9	318	39:9		610
34:4–7	353	7:12	440	39:19–25		555
34:7	496	9:7	373	40:7		228
36:21	158	9:13	548	40:9		593
		9:21	136	40:15		547
Ezra		10:5	420	41		491
1:1–4	15	10:9	537			
1:7–11	361	10:21–22	687	*Psalms*		
2:1–2	15	11:7	202, 566	1		480, 539
2:64–65	15	11:8	202	1:1		516
3:1	15	12:18	282	1:2		516
4:17	16	12:21	433	1:3		111, 624
8:22	466	13:4	123	1:4		111
8:31	466	14:7–12	487	1:5		111, 487
9	16	14:8	284	1:6	477, 487, 536
9:6–15	499	14:11	369	2:1–4		362
		14:13–15	318	2:7		246
Nehemiah		15:24	483	2:11		289
1:11	632	16:18	446, 489	4:1		681
2:11–16	225	17:3	681	5:7		507
4:8	233	17:16	318	6		674
5:15	16	18:5–11	453	6:1		681
5:18	467	18:13	332	6:3		190
6:14	223	19:16	688	6:5	161, 318, 481, 687

6:1	32, 33, 41, 125, 234, 247, 598	7:9	38	8:13	34
6:1–3	35	7:10	691	8:14	240, 288, 517
6:1–5	55	7:10–17	220	8:15	288, 513
6:1–8:18	197	7:12	526	8:16	19, 195, 238, 551
6:1–9:6	114	7:13	279, 418, 504, 667	8:16–18	538
6:3	32, 33, 42, 295, 350, 537, 562, 608, 622, 660	7:13–25	195, 227	8:16–22	195, 385, 483
		7:14	195, 212, 220, 222, 226, 245, 247, 277, 431, 672	8:18	109, 195, 205, 245, 386
6:3–5	162	7:14–16	7	8:19	254, 364, 517, 528, 685
6:4	363	7:14–17	41	8:19–22	37, 368
6:5	33, 58, 87, 181, 255, 343, 456, 597, 624, 670	7:15	572	8:21–22	634
		7:16	503	8:22	382, 483
		7:17	194, 223, 226	9:1	83, 103, 194, 195, 242, 544, 622
6:5–7	40	7:18	169, 194, 226, 269, 292	9:1–6	277, 278
6:5–8	38	7:18–23	374	9:1–7	195, 201, 207, 579
6:6–7	41, 58, 179	7:18–25	278	9:2	119, 194, 567
6:6–8	55	7:20	194, 223, 226, 269, 292, 365	9:2–5	450
6:7	295			9:2–7	41, 113, 343, 483
6:8	58	7:20–23	243	9:3	329, 482, 567
6:9	225, 415, 531	7:21	269, 292	9:4	273, 317, 328, 461
6:9–10	553	7:23	269, 292, 586	9:4–7	288
6:9–12	412	8:1	243	9:5	276, 278, 461
6:9–13	55, 221, 288, 551	8:1–4	213, 245	9:6	32, 41, 167, 195, 271, 422, 423, 431, 461, 533, 588
6:10	415, 531, 532, 579, 581, 624	8:1–10	195, 227		
		8:3	195, 205, 213, 220, 431	9:6–7	672
6:10–13	375	8:3–10	201	9:7	250, 279, 665, 667
6:11	175	8:4	205, 214	9:8	250
6:11–13	278, 415	8:4–8	48	9:8–12	251
6:12	175	8:5–8	7, 385, 564, 630	9:8–21	167
6:13	111, 126, 175, 195, 199, 267, 269, 278, 295	8:6	188, 294, 418, 504, 513, 532	9:8–10:4	169, 194, 250, 261
7	578, 608, 647	8:6–8	175, 194, 356, 512, 662	9:9–10	60
7:1	30, 231, 241, 250, 270, 278, 330, 384, 472	8:7	31, 48, 132, 194, 507	9:10	126
		8:7–8	637	9:11	84, 434
7:1–2	83	8:8	195, 212, 220, 245, 267, 504, 566, 665	9:12	40, 167, 329
7:1–9	297			9:13–17	37
7:1–13	516	8:9	282, 598	9:14	372
7:1–17	137	8:9–10	38	9:14–16	504
7:1–8:22	261	8:9–9:7	502	9:15	456
7:1–9:7	194	8:10	191, 212, 213, 220, 461	9:16	188, 225, 513
7:2	7, 225, 363, 409, 667	8:11	241, 513	9:17	40, 167
		8:11–15	195	9:17–10:4	33
7:2–9	293	8:11–20	353	9:18	267, 598
7:3	4, 195, 200, 245, 413, 419, 508, 596, 633, 665, 667	8:11–22	472	9:18–25	119
		8:11–9:1	231	9:19	438
7:3–9	555	8:12	188, 225, 513	9:21	40, 158, 167
7:4	418, 419	8:12–13	33, 35	10	459
7:4–9	99	8:12–15	32, 194, 195, 275	10:1	311
7:5	461	8:12–9:1	292	10:1–4	167, 418
7:7	226, 228			10:3	622
7:8–9	48			10:4	40, 166, 167

Hebrew Words